The Mental Health Industry: A Cultural Phenomenon *by Peter A. Magaro, Robert Gripp, David McDowell, and Ivan W. Miller III*

Nonverbal Communication: The State of the Art *by Robert G. Harper, Arthur N. Weins, and Joseph D. Matarazzo*

Alcoholism and Treatment *by David J. Armor, J. Michael Polich, and Harriet B. Stambul*

A Biodevelopmental Approach to Clinical Child Psychology: Cognitive Controls and Cognitive Control Theory *by Sebastiano Santostefano*

Handbook of Infant Development *edited by Joy D. Osofsky*

Understanding the Rape Victim: A Synthesis of Research Findings *by Sedelle Katz and Mary Ann Mazur*

Childhood Pathology and Later Adjustment: The Question of Prediction *by Loretta K. Cass and Carolyn B. Thomas*

Intelligent Testing with the WISC-R *by Alan S. Kaufman*

Adaptation in Schizophrenia: The Theory of Segmental Set *by David Shakow*

Psychotherapy: An Eclectic Approach *by Sol L. Garfield*

Handbook of Minimal Brain Dysfunctions *edited by Herbert E. Rie and Ellen D. Rie*

Handbook of Behavioral Interventions: A Clinical Guide *edited by Alan Goldstein and Edna B. Foa*

Art Psychotherapy *by Harriet Wadeson*

Handbook of Adolescent Psychology *edited by Joseph Adelson*

Psychotherapy Supervision: Theory, Research and Practice *edited by Allen K. Hess*

Psychology and Psychiatry in Courts and Corrections: Controversy and Change *by Ellsworth A. Fersch, Jr.*

Restricted Environmental Stimulation: Research and Clinical Applications *by Peter Suedfeld*

Personal Construct Psychology: Psychotherapy and Personality *edited by Alvin W. Landfield and Larry M. Leitner*

Mothers, Grandmothers, and Daughters: Personality and Child Care in Three-Generation Families *by Bertram J. Cohler and Henry U. Grunebaum*

Further Explorations in Personality *edited by A.I. Rabin, Joel Aronoff, Andrew M. Barclay, and Robert A. Zucker*

Hypnosis and Relaxation: Modern Verification of an Old Equation *by William E. Edmonston, Jr.*

Handbook of Clinical Behavior Therapy *edited by Samuel M. Turner, Karen S. Calhoun, and Henry E. Adams*

Handbook of Clinical Neuropsychology *edited by Susan B. Filskov and Thomas J. Boll*

The Course of Alcoholism: Four Years After Treatment *by J. Michael Polich, David J. Armor, and Harriet B. Braiker*

Handbook of Innovative Psychotherapies *edited by Raymond J. Corsini*

The Role of the Father in Child Development (Second Edition) *edited by Michael E. Lamb*

Behavioral Medicine: Clinical Applications *by Susan S. Pinkerton, Howard Hughes, and W.W. Wenrich*

Handbook for the Practice of Pediatric Psychology *edited by June M. Tuma*

Change Through Interaction: Social Psychological Processes of Counseling and Psychotherapy *by Stanley R. Strong and Charles D. Claiborn*

Drugs and Behavior (Second Edition) *by Fred Leavitt*

Handbook of Research Methods in Clinical Psychology *edited by Philip C. Kendall and James N. Butcher*

A Social Psychology of Developing Adults *by Thomas O. Blank*

Women in the Middle Years: Current Knowledge and Directions for Research and Policy *edited by Janet Zollinger Giele*

Loneliness: A Sourcebook of Current Theory, Research and Therapy *edited by Letitia Anne Peplau and Daniel Perlman*

(*continued on back*)

Handbook of Comparative Treatments for Adult Disorders

Handbook of Comparative Treatments for Adult Disorders

Edited by

ALAN S. BELLACK
MICHEL HERSEN

WILEY

A WILEY-INTERSCIENCE PUBLICATION

JOHN WILEY & SONS

New York • Chichester • Brisbane • Toronto • Singapore

To cooler days together on the Chesapeake

Contributors

ROBERT E. BECKER, Ph.D., Department of Psychiatry, The Medical College of PA at EPPI, Philadelphia, Pennsylvania

ALAN S. BELLACK, Ph.D., Department of Psychiatry, The Medical College of PA at EPPI, Philadelphia, Pennsylvania

JULES R. BEMPORAD, M.D., Professor of Clinical Psychiatry, Cornell University Medical School, Cornell Medical Center, White Plains, New York

SCOTT BOHON, M.D., Assistant Professor of Psychiatry, Western Psychiatric Institute & Clinic, Pittsburgh, Pennsylvania

STEPHEN F. BUTLER, Ph.D., Department of Psychology, Vanderbilt University, Nashville, Tennessee

DANIEL J. BUYSSE, M.D., Assistant Professor of Psychiatry, University of Pittsburgh School of Medicine, Western Psychiatric Institute & Clinic, Pittsburgh, Pennsylvania

EDWARD M. CARROLL, Ph.D., Brentwood VA Medical Center, West Los Angeles, California

RICARDO CASTANEDA, M.D., Assistant Professor, Department of Psychiatry, New York University School of Medicine, New York, New York

JUNE CHIODO, Ph.D., Weight Management Program, Temple University Medical Practices, Ft. Washington, Pennsylvania

JONATHAN O. COLE, M.D., Harvard Medical School, Department of Psychiatry, McLean Hospital, Belmont, Massachusetts

MORRIS N. EAGLE, Ph.D., Psychology Department, York Unversity, Downsview, Ontario, Canada

MICHAEL FEINBERG, M.D., Hahnemann University, Philadelphia, Pennsylvania

EDNA FOA, Ph.D., Obsessive-Compulsive Disorder Clinic, Medical College of Pennsylvania at EPPI, Quarters Building, Philadelphia, Pennsylvania

DAVID W. FOY, Ph.D., Professor & Director of Clinical Training, Graduate School of Psychology, Fuller Theological Seminary, Pasadena, California

ARTHUR FREEMAN, Ph.D., University of Medicine & Dentistry of New Jersey, School of Osteopathic Medicine, Department of Psychiatry, Cherry Hill, New Jersey

MARC GALANTER, M.D., Department of Psychiatry, New York University School of Medicine, New York, New York

HARRY GWIRTSMAN, M.D., UCLA School of Medicine, Department of Psychiatry & Behavioral Sciences, Neuropsychiatric Institute, Los Angeles, California

RICHARD HEIMBERG, Ph.D., Center for Stress & Anxiety Disorders, Department of Psychology, University at Albany, State University of New York, Albany, New York

MICHEL HERSEN, Ph.D., Western Psychiatric Institute & Clinic, Department of Psychiatry, Pittsburgh, Pennsylvania

MARDI J. HOROWITZ, M.D., Professor of Psychiatry, Director, Center for Study of Neuroses, University of CA, San Francisco, California, Director, Program on Conscious and Unconscious Mental Processes, supported by the John D. and Catherine T. MacArthur Foundation

MICHAEL A. JENIKE, M.D., Associate Professor of Psychiatry, Harvard Medical School, Massachusetts General Hospital, Boston, Massachusetts

DAVID C. JIMERSON, M.D., Beth Israel Hospital, Department of Psychiatry, Boston, Massachusetts

WALTER H. KAYE, M.D., Western Psychiatric Institute & Clinic, Department of Psychiatry, Pittsburgh, Pennsylvania

CAROLA KIEVE, M.D., Perkasie, Pennsylvania

ANDREW P. LEVIN, M.D., Assistant Clinical Professor of Psychiatry, Columbia University, College of Physicians and Surgeons, New York State Psychiatric Institute, New York, New York

MICHAEL R. LIEBOWITZ, M.D., Associate Professor of Clinical Psychiatry, College of Physicians & Surgeons, Columbia University, Director, Anxiety Disorders Clinic, New York State Psychiatric Institute, New York, New York

MARSHA M. LINEHAN, Ph.D., Department of Psychology, University of Washington, Seattle, Washington

JÜRGEN MARGRAF, Ph.D., Fachbereich Psychologie, Phillipps-Universität, Marburg, West Germany

HOWARD MOSS, M.D., University of Pittsburgh School of Medicine, Western Psychiatric Institute & Clinic, Pittsburgh, Pennsylvania

R. SWAMI NATHAN, M.D., Associate Professor of Psychiatry, Western Psychiatric Institute & Clinic, University of Pittsburgh, School of Medicine, Pittsburgh, Pennsylvania

SHERYL S. OSATA, Ph.D., Postdoctoral Fellow, Neurophychiatric Institute, UCLA Medical School, Los Angeles, California

WILLIAM SHELLEY POLLACK, Ph.D., Harvard Medical School, McLean Hospital, Belmont, Massachussetts

RICHARD L. PYLE, M.D., Department of Psychiatry, University of Minnesota, Minneapolis, Minnesota

HEIDI S. RESNICK, Ph.D., Crime Victims Research and Treatment Center, Department of Psychiatry & Behavioral Sciences, Medical University of South Carolina, Charleston, South Carolina

JULES ROSEN, M.D., Assistant Professor of Psychiatry, Western Psychiatric Institute & Clinic, Pittsburgh, Pennsylvania

VIVIENNE ROWAN, St. Boniface General Hospital, Winnipeg, Manitoba, Canada

FRANKLIN SCHNEIER, M.D., New York State Psychiatric Institute, New York, New York

EDWARD SILBERMAN, M.D., Department of Psychiatry, The Medical College of Pennsylvania at EPPI, Philadelphia, Pennsylvania

GEORGE M. SIMPSON, M.D., Department of Psychiatry, The Medical College of Pennsylvania at EPPI, Philadelphia, Pennsylvania

LINDA C. SOBELL, Ph.D., Addiction Research Foundation, Toronto, Ontario, Canada

MARK B. SOBELL, Ph.D., Addiction Research Foundation, Toronto, Ontario, Canada

PAUL H. SOLOFF, M.D., Western Psychiatric Institute & Clinic, Pittsburgh, Pennsylvania

HANS H. STRUPP, Ph.D., Department of Psychology, Vanderbilt University, Nashville, Tennessee

ANTHONY TONEATTO, Ph.D., Addiction Research Foundation, Toronto, Ontario, Canada

RUSSELL G. VASILE, M.D., Assistant Professor of Psychiatry, Harvard Medical School, Director, Harvard In-Patient Psychiatric Service, New England Deaconess Hospital, Boston, Massachusetts

ELIZABETH J. WASSON, Department of Psychology, University of Washington, Seattle, Washington

THEODORE S. WELTZIN, M.D., Assistant Professor of Psychiatry, Western Psychiatric Institute & Clinic, Department of Psychiatry, University of Pittsburgh, Pittsburgh, Pennsylvania

KERRIN WHITE, M.D., Harvard Medical School, Department of Psychiatry, McLean Hospital, Belmont, Massachusetts

WILLIAM H. WILSON, M.D., Adjunct Assistant Professor of Psychiatry, Oregon Health Services University, Director, Training Unit, Dammasch State Hospital, Wilsonville, Oregon

JOHN T. WIXTED, Ph.D., Department of Psychology, University of California, San Diego, La Jolla, California

DAVID L. WOLITZKY, Ph.D., Research Center for Mental Health, New York University, New York, New York

Series Preface

This series of books is addressed to behavioral scientists interested in the nature of human personality. Its scope should prove pertinent to personality theorists and researchers, as well as to clinicians concerned with applying an understanding of personality processes to the amelioration of emotional difficulties in living. To this end, the series provides a scholarly integration of theoretical formulations, empirical data, and practical recommendations.

Six major aspects of studying and learning about human personality can be designated: personality theory, personality structure and dynamics, personality development, personality assessment, personality change, and personality adjustment. In exploring these aspects of personality, the books in the series discuss a number of distinct but related subject areas: the nature and implications of various theories of personality; personality characteristics that account for consistencies and variations in human behavior; the emergence of personality processes in children and adolescents; the use of interviewing and testing procedures to evaluate individual differences in personality; efforts to modify personality styles through psychotherapy, counseling, behavior therapy, and other methods of influence; and patterns of abnormal personality functioning that impair individual competence.

IRVING B. WEINER

University of South Florida
Tampa, Florida

Preface

The treatment of psychiatric disorders has undergone a dramatic change since the late 1960s. Before then, our field was saddled with an archaic and overgeneralized diagnostic system. More often than not, diagnoses were assigned on an ad hoc basis after an informal clinical interview. The resultant labels were apt to be unreliable and to provide little clear information in the way of etiology, course, or treatment needs. However, the consequences of this process were not as bad as one might imagine because treatment options were severely limited. Traditional psychoanalytic techniques predominated. Behavior therapy and biological psychiatry were nascent disciplines, and ego and cognitive psychology were still in formative stages of development. The critical diagnostic distinction was either psychotic or nonpsychotic. The latter were apt to receive a standard form of long-term analytic therapy or low-potency benzodiazepines, while psychotic patients were likely to receive low-potency neuroleptics.

The therapeutic environment has changed dramatically in the intervening decades. Behavior therapy has progressed through a series of developmental stages, from being an academic oddity, through being an unethical and dangerous or a clinically naive approach, to being a universal part of the treatment environment, crossing theoretical boundaries. Behavioral techniques have become the treatment of choice for a number of disorders.

Biological psychiatry has seen a similar development. Lithium, tricyclic antidepressants, high-potency neuroleptics, monamine oxidase inhibitors (MAOIs), and new-generation benzodiazepines have all proven to be useful parts of the therapeutic armamentarium. At the same time, there have been huge strides in the understanding of brain chemistry and how neurotransmitters affect behavior.

Developments in psychotherapy strategies have not been as dramatic, but they are no less significant. Greater emphasis is on the environment, on current functioning, on observable cognitive phenomena, and on the use of active strategies. In general, dynamic strategies are much more flexible and are more specifically targeted on the specific life situation of the patient. These therapeutic developments have been associated with increased understanding of the etiology of many disorders, as well as a substantially improved diagnostic system. It is now much more likely that treatment will be tailored to the needs (and diagnosis) of the individual patient.

Perhaps the one down side to the evolution of treatment has been an explosion in the volume of literature on psychopathology and treatment issues. Scores of new journals publish highly specialized material, and hundreds of relevant books appear each year. It is no longer possible to be thoroughly up to date in the literature on any one orientation or on any one disorder, let alone to maintain catholic reading habits. As a consequence, important new developments are frequently missed, and perspectives on alternative approaches are all too quickly outdated. It would probably be safe to say that most professionals maintain stereotyped views of alternative models, based substantially on the literature extant during the individual's postgraduate training.

The *Handbook of Comparative Treatments for Adult Disorders* was designed with the surfeit of literature in mind. The intent was to present an overview of the best current thinking and techniques, from two or more major different viewpoints, on each of the major adult disorders. It is our hope that this presentation would permit easy comparison for the student or professional. The contributors to this book, who are experts in the field, have been invited to describe how they think about their patients: how they conceptualize the respective disorders, how they design and implement treatment, and what they do when their favored approach does not work. To introduce each perspective, the first part of this book contains overviews of each of the major orientations. The remaining parts focus on individual disorders. In order to amplify the characterization of the treatment process, each of the chapters within each part contains a description of the treatment of a typical case. The contributing authors were explicitly requested *not* to write prototypical literature reviews arguing about which technique is better. To the contrary, the authors have attempted to communicate an understanding as to how and why they approach cases in a particular way.

The result is illuminating. While there are obvious differences among the approaches, there are also notable similarities. Even in cases where there is little overlap in strategy, the authors often see the same problems (e.g., the difficulty of treating patients with character pathology, or the limitations of current nosology). The commonalities *and* differences have been highlighted in the editorial commentaries that conclude all but the introductory section of the book. We have found the material to be most informative and thought provoking. We hope you will find it helpful as well.

We wish to thank a number of people, without whom this book could not have been completed. Herb Reich, our editor at Wiley, was a great source of encouragement in putting the project together, and he showed great patience in waiting for the final manuscript. As always, Mary Newell was essential in shepherding one of our projects along. Finally, special appreciation to Joan Gill, who joined Bellack's staff just in time to put all the pieces together, even though she was still learning what the pieces were.

ALAN S. BELLACK
MICHEL HERSEN

Philadelphia, Pennsylvania
Pittsburgh, Pennsylvania
January, 1990

Contents

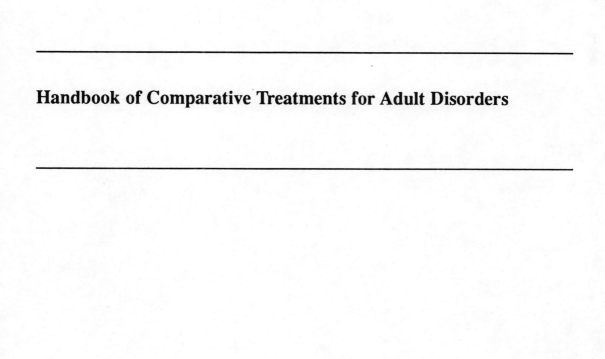

Handbook of Comparative Treatments for Adult Disorders

PART 1

Current Directions

CHAPTER 1

Psychotherapy

HANS H. STRUPP AND STEPHEN F. BUTLER

INTRODUCTION

Psychotherapy is often described as a "treatment," and because medical terminology (patient, therapist, diagnosis, etiology, etc.) has traditionally been used, the analogy of a physician ministering to a relatively passive patient readily springs to mind. In contrast, it is important to stress that in psychotherapy, the roles assumed by patient and therapist have only superficial resemblance to this medical model. Psychotherapy is more accurately defined as a *collaborative* endeavor, or a partnership, in which the patient is expected to play an active part almost from the beginning. This active role is essential if patients are to become more autonomous, more self-directing, and more responsible for their feelings, beliefs, and actions. To feel better about themselves, their relationships with others, and their behavior, patients must learn to make changes within themselves and in their environments that permit them to feel and act differently. The process of therapy is designed not to change patients but to help patients change themselves.

In this sense, psychotherapy is a learning process, and the role of the therapist is analogous to that of a teacher or mentor. Psychotherapy is based on the assumption that feelings, cognitions, attitudes, and behaviors are the product of a person's life experience; that is, they have been *learned*. If something has been learned, modification of the previous learning can occur. Where learning is impossible (for example, in conditions attributable to genetic or biochemical factors), psycho-

therapy has little to offer. Similarly, if the disturbance is solely due to factors in the person's social milieu (poverty, oppression, imprisonment), or if patients do not desire change on their own (e.g., they are referred by a court or school system), psychotherapists encounter great difficulties. Thus, psychotherapy works best (a) if patients desire change of their own accord and are motivated to work toward it, (b) if the environment in which they live tolerates the possibility of change, and (c) if the inner obstacles to learning (defenses and rigidities of character) are not insurmountable.

No single definition of psychotherapy has found universal acceptance. Depending on the therapist's theoretical orientation and other factors, psychotherapy is seen by some as a psychosocial treatment, by others as a special form of education, and by still others as a means of promoting personality growth and self-actualization, to cite but a few divergent views. Most therapists agree, however, that psychotherapy involves both a human relationship and a set of techniques for bringing about personality and behavior change.

Historically, psychotherapy has roots in ancient medicine, religion, faith healing, and hypnotism. In the 19th century psychotherapy emerged as a prominent treatment for so-called nervous and mental diseases, and its practice became a medical art, restricted to psychiatrists. Around the middle of the current century, other professions gained entry into the field, largely as a result of the growing demand for psychotherapeutic services. This broadened base of clinical and theoretical influence has led to modifications of the earlier disease-oriented treatment model. Today, the term *psychotherapy* is the generic term for psychological interventions designed to ameliorate emotional or behavioral problems of various kinds. Contemporary psychotherapy is characterized by a diversity of theoretical orientations (e.g., psychodynamic, client-centered, rational–emotive, cognitive–behavioral, Gestalt) and treatment modalities (individual, group, family, marital). Theories and techniques of behavior therapy, which have gained wide acceptance during the past few decades, are usually differentiated from psychotherapy, although behavioral interventions are clearly psychological.

In broadest terms, psychotherapy is concerned with personality and behavior *change*. The patient who seeks help for a psychological problem desires change—the patient wants to feel or act differently—and the psychotherapist agrees to assist the patient in achieving this goal. The major issues in psychotherapy relate to (1) *what* is to be changed, and (2) *how* change can be brought about. The first entails definition of the *problem* for which the patient is seeking help (depression, marital difficulties, shyness, nail biting, sexual dysfunctions, existential anxiety, etc.); the second pertains to the process and techniques by means of which change is effected (support, ventilation of feelings, interpretations, systematic desensitization, assertiveness training, etc.).

It is important to realize that, at this time, there remains considerable lack of consensus regarding both how to define problems in therapy and how to foster change. In a 1986 article, Messer highlighted major differences between behavioral and psychodynamic approaches to therapy in terms of how each would address important therapeutic choice points, including defining the problem (setting goals), deciding whether to promote action or explore mental content, determining whether to challenge or to understand irrational thoughts, ascertaining how to manage affect, and so forth.

Given the extraordinary complexity of the psychotherapeutic process, it is unlikely that any one perspective will emerge as clearly superior to all others. Indeed, any ultimate theory of psychotherapy will certainly encompass the clinical wisdom embodied in all important perspectives. Although the inclination toward a dynamic view is

evident in this chapter, the attempt has been to eschew theoretical rhetoric in favor of discussing the fundamental elements of the therapeutic encounter. In addition, conceptual and methodological concerns are examined; concerns which must be addressed if the field is to make appreciable scientific advances.

THE PATIENT: GENERAL CONSIDERATIONS

Perhaps the single most important characteristic of individuals who decide to consult a psychotherapist is that they are troubled. At times, they may be unaware of the cause of their suffering and unhappiness; more often, they have identified a set of circumstances they view as accounting for their disturbance. Typically, either they are dissatisfied with their lives and complain of troublesome feelings (anxiety, depression, etc.), or they see difficulties with some aspect of their behavior (phobia, impulsiveness, etc.). Usually, they have tried various means of combating their difficulties, without notable success. Not uncommonly, patients have previously consulted medical specialists who refer them to a psychotherapist because the physician senses either the involvement of emotional factors or the futility of other treatment approaches.

However the patient comes to therapy, the therapist is confronted with a unique set of problems and, most important, a unique individual. Not only do prospective patients differ in the kinds of problems for which they seek help, but also they show great variations in (a) the degree of subjective distress they experience, (b) the urgency with which they desire relief, and (c) the eagerness with which they accept help once it is offered.

Further, they differ in their expectations of what a helping professional might do to bring about relief. Virtually everyone has retained from childhood the hope of magical solutions to problems—a wish that tends to become intensified when a person experiences anxiety and distress. A magical solution involves the patient's wish to be relieved of distress simply by submitting to a powerful figure (in this case the doctor). For the uninitiated, such wishes contribute to unrealistically high expectations of what psychotherapy can do. Alternatively, people whose experience with authorities in the past has been profoundly disappointing may enter therapy with unrealistically low expectations. Such expectations occur not only among uneducated or unsophisticated patients, but also among those with broad educational and cultural backgrounds. At any rate, these expectations may have considerable bearing on a given patient's approach to psychotherapy and the evolving relationship with the therapist.

The patient typically wants to feel better or wants to act differently. Often, the patient wants to stop a pattern of behavior or wishes to shed inhibitions that prevent him or her from engaging in behavior considered to be desirable. In most instances, patients tend to complain of a lack of will power and they feel more or less helpless. At the same time, they tend to blame difficulties on the behavior of other persons in their lives, referring to themselves (explicitly or implicitly) as victims. Whatever the nature of the complaint, the patient generally measures the outcome of therapy by improvements in feelings and behavior.

From the therapist's standpoint, it is sometimes not possible to bring about the changes to which the patient aspires, or at least not in the manner the patient desires. In many cases, while patients ostensibly desire change of a certain kind, they are unwittingly committed to maintenance of the status quo and actively oppose any change. For example, patients may express a wish to become more assertive, yet on exploration, it becomes apparent that they are actually searching for a human relationship that allows them to be passive and dependent.

The task of therapy involves helping the patient identify and overcome the self-imposed obstacles to change. Such obstacles are present from the beginning of a therapy, so that the patient's problem is often not what it initially appears to be. Therefore, redefinitions of the problem and the goals of therapy may be indicated. As therapy proceeds, the patient and therapist (a) must work toward a mutual understanding of the problems and goals and (b) must neutralize the obstacles in order to develop a collaborative and constructive alliance. This is delicate and important work, and the achievement of this alliance alone often heralds increases in the patient's self-esteem and self-worth.

THE THERAPIST: GENERAL CONSIDERATIONS

The therapist attempts to be helpful to the patient or client. However, as a result of disagreements over both the purpose of psychotherapy and the way in which therapeutic change is to be brought about, there is little consensus concerning the precise role and function of the therapist. Some therapists view their primary task as providing patients with insight into their emotional conflicts; others seek to bring about a reorganization of the patient's cognitions and beliefs; still others work more directly toward behavior change in the hope that success experiences in one area will help patients gain greater self-confidence, which in turn may enable them to tackle other problems in living.

Most professionals agree that the therapist must acquire special skills, but for the aforementioned reasons, there is less agreement on the nature of these skills or how to perfect them. Consequently, training programs for psychotherapists differ markedly in content, breadth, and duration (Strupp, Butler, & Rosser, 1988). It has even been asserted that naturally helpful persons (indigenous helpers, nonprofessionals, and paraprofessionals) may be as helpful as professionally trained therapists, thus calling into question the necessity for training in specials skills or techniques.

Whatever the therapist's background or level of training, the therapist must necessarily (1) form some notions or hypotheses about the patient's problem or difficulty, and (2) decide what needs to be done to bring about an improvement in the patient's condition. Thus, therapists must first become diagnosticians before they engage in activities they consider therapeutic. The second requirement usually entails verbal (and nonverbal) communications, occurring in the context of a *relationship* that develops between patient and therapist.

In this therapeutic relationship, the patient (a) expresses fears, hopes, and expectations, and (b) views the therapist as a person who can provide relief from suffering. Some of the patient's expectations are realistic, but others, as already noted, are distorted, tinged with the hope of magic solutions.

Almost by definition, patients view themselves as persons in need of outside help. This places them, à priori, into a dependent position vis-à-vis the therapist. Thus, patients unwittingly tend to relate to the therapist as helpless children to a powerful parent (*transference*). This tendency of many patients to turn the therapeutic relationship into a quasi-parent–child relationship is of particular interest to psychodynamic therapists, who essentially define the therapist as a specialist in detecting and resolving transferences. Recently, the concept of transference has been expanded to include any maladaptive interpersonal behavior patterns that create difficulties in the patient's relationships with significant others and that also occur in the therapeutic relationship (e.g., Anchin & Kiesler, 1982; Butler & Binder, 1987; Gill, 1982; Strupp & Binder, 1984). While some may object to the term *transference*, there is increasing recognition of the importance of the therapeutic relationship by nonpsychodynamic theorists (e.g., behavior therapists: Wilson & Evans, 1977).

In any event, the therapist necessarily engages in a relationship with the patient and brings his or her personal influence to bear upon that relationship. Of course, both the patient's and therapist's personalities determine the character and quality of their interaction, but it is the therapist who defines the framework of the relationship and determines to a large extent how the relationship shall be used to achieve particular therapeutic ends. There is still a lively debate as to whether the therapist determines the outcome of therapy primarily by personal qualities or whether the outcome is more a function of the techniques employed by the therapist. It is likely that both sets of variables are interdependent and contribute significantly to the resulting therapeutic process and outcome (Butler & Strupp, 1986). Thus, whatever the role of technique (see next paragraph), it is clear that the *personal qualities* of the therapist must be an important factor in the equation (Beutler, Crago, & Arizmendi, 1986; Parloff, Waskow, & Wolfe, 1978).

Finally, it is important to examine how the professional therapist differs from other helpful persons. Above all, the therapist creates a professional rather than a personal relationship with the patient. While the patient may be lonely and in need of a friend, the therapist does not view the therapeutic task as fulfilling this need. Instead, the goal is to facilitate patients' interpersonal relationships with *others* and to help them cope more adaptively and effectively on their own. Consequently, the therapist seeks to avoid personal involvement with the patient, a stance frequently contrary to the patient's wishes.

This relative detachment allows the therapist to be more objective about the patient's difficulties. More important, the professional nature of this relationship enables the patient to communicate more freely by minimizing the potential for social consequences, such as shame, fear, anger, and retaliation from others, which, in other contexts, might accompany the overt expression of certain thoughts, fantasies, wishes, and so forth. As patients can learn to trust the therapist and the safety of the therapeutic situation, the experience of acceptance and understanding contributes to greater self-acceptance and diminishes the patient's sense of isolation or aloneness. Armed with enhanced confidence, patients can often begin to tackle other troublesome problems in life.

The professional therapist's stance of acceptance, respect, understanding, helpfulness, and warmth, combined with deliberate efforts not to criticize, pass judgment, or react emotionally to provocations, creates a framework and an atmosphere unmatched by any other human relationship. How to create such a relationship and to turn it to maximal therapeutic advantage is the challenge facing the modern psychotherapist.

DOMAINS OF INQUIRY

Psychotherapy and Research

Psychotherapy has always been a very *practical* undertaking, growing out of the clinician's desire to help a suffering human being in the most effective, economical, efficient, and humane way. The clinician's first question has always been, "Does a treatment help?" However, recognizing the importance of understanding *why* a treatment works, therapists have also devised theories of psychotherapy. Of course, a treatment or a set of therapeutic procedures may work when the theory is wrong; or the theory may be reasonable, but the techniques inefficient or ineffective. The point to be made is that individual practitioners have no sure way of answering these questions because they must necessarily rely on the clinical method—that is, naturalistic observation of a few cases. Furthermore, the history of science amply demonstrates that humanity's capacity for self-deception is so great that misconceptions (e.g., the geocentric view of the universe) may persist for centuries.

As modern psychotherapy gained momentum and its practitioners grew in number, questions were raised relating to the quality of the outcome, the nature of the problems to which it might be applied, the relative effectiveness of different techniques, the adequacy of the underlying theoretical formulations, the training and qualification of therapists, the possibility of harmful effects, and many other issues. From its slow beginnings in the 1940s, research in psychotherapy has grown impressively in size and quality. It is a product of contemporary behavioral science, and as such, it exemplifies the application of modern scientific methodology to the solution of important clinical and theoretical problems. We now take a closer look at some of these problems.

The Problem of Therapy Outcome

The single most important problem, overshadowing all others and placing them in perspective, is the issue of psychotherapeutic effectiveness. The question has usually been framed as, "Is psychotherapy effective?" Research efforts to address this question have been voluminous and sustained. In the years since Eysenck (1952) charged that psychotherapy produces no greater changes in emotionally disturbed individuals than naturally occurring life experiences, researchers and clinicians alike have felt compelled to answer the challenge.

Analyzing and synthesizing the data from 25 years of research on the efficacy of psychotherapy, Luborsky, Singer, and Luborsky (1975) concluded that most forms of psychotherapy produce changes in a substantial proportion of patients—changes that are often, but not always, greater than those achieved by control patients who did not receive therapy. Other reviewers (e.g., Lambert, Shapiro, & Bergin, 1986) have reached similar conclusions. In an ingenious analysis, Smith, Glass, and Miller (1980) demonstrated that across all types of therapy, patients, therapists, and outcome criteria, the average patient shows more improvement than 75% of untreated individuals. The preponderance of the evidence, it has become clear, does not support Eysenck's pessimistic conclusion.

Not all outcome studies are methodologically sound and clinically meaningful. Among the landmarks of outcome research are the investigations carried out at the University of Chicago Counseling Center with client-centered therapy (Rogers & Dymond, 1954); the Menninger Foundation Project (Kernberg et al., 1972); the Temple study, in which treatment results from behavior therapy and psychotherapy were studied under controlled conditions (Sloane, Staples, Cristol, Yorkston, & Whipple, 1975); the research by Paul (1967, 1969), DiLoreto (1971); and the NIMH Collaborative Depression Study, probably the single largest outcome study (Elkin, Parloff, Hadley, & Autry, 1985). The primary aims of some of these studies were to contrast variations in treatment and to investigate the impact of patient and therapist variables in determining outcomes. In each case, the results support the finding that patients improve as a result of therapy, yet no single therapy or set of techniques has proven uniquely superior (Lambert et al., 1986).

When considering psychotherapy outcome, researchers and therapists alike have difficulty adequately conceptualizing and defining the notion of outcome. This lack of clarity is problematic for both psychotherapy researchers and for those charged with policy decisions regarding psychotherapy (Strupp, 1986). For example, insurance companies and government agencies increasingly are demanding accountability for treatments they are asked to reimburse.

The problem of defining psychotherapy outcome touches on many facets of human life, and conceptions of mental health and illness cannot be considered apart from the problems of philosophy, ethics, religion, and public policy. Inescapably, we deal with human existence and the person's place in the world, and ultimately, any adequate conception of outcome must confront questions of *value* (Strupp & Hadley, 1977). Someone must make a judgment whether a person's concern with duty is a virtue or a symptom of compulsiveness; whether a decrement of 10 T-score points on the Depression Scale of the MMPI (Minnesota Multiphasic Personality Inventory) in the 90–100 range is a greater or a lesser improvement than a like change between 50 and 60; whether in one case we accept a patient's judgment that he or she feels better, whereas in another we set it aside, calling it "flight into health," "reaction formation," "delusional," and so forth. These decisions can only be made by reference to the values society assigns to feelings, attitudes, and actions. These values are inherent in conceptions of mental health and illness as well as in clinical judgments based on one of these models.

Freud (1916) already saw the outcome issue as a practical one, and this may well be the best way to treat it. When all is said and done, there may be commonsense agreement on what constitutes a mentally healthy, nonneurotic person. Knight (1941) postulated three major rubrics for considering therapeutic change, which still seem eminently reasonable: (1) disappearance of presenting symptoms; (2) real improvement in mental functioning; and (3) improved adjustment to reality.

Most therapists and researchers, while they may disagree on criteria and operations for assessing these changes, would concur that therapeutic success should be demonstrable in the person's (1) feeling state (well-being), (2) social functioning (performance), and (3) personality organization (structure). The first is clearly the individual's subjective perspective; the second is that of society, including prevailing standards of conduct and "normalcy"; the third is the perspective of mental health professionals, whose technical concepts (e.g., ego strength, impulse control) partake of information and standards derived from the preceding sources but are ostensibly scientific, objective, and value free.

As Strupp and Hadley (1977) have shown, few therapists or researchers have taken seriously the implications of this complex view of outcome. Therapists continue to assess treatment outcomes on the basis of global clinical impressions, whereas researchers persist in the assumption that quantitative indexes can be interpreted as if they were thermometer readings. In reality, values influence and suffuse every judgment of outcome.

Such outcome issues call into doubt the utility of the traditional, global question, Is psychotherapy effective? It has become increasingly apparent that psychotherapy is not a unitary process, nor is it applied to a unitary problem (Kiesler, 1966). Furthermore, therapists cannot be regarded as interchangeable units that deliver a standard treatment in uniform quantity or quality (see Beutler et al., 1986; Parloff et al., 1978). Patients, too, cannot be considered a uniform variable. Instead, they respond differentially to various forms of therapeutic influence, depending on personality, education, intelligence, nature of emotional difficulties, motivation, and other variables (Garfield, 1986). Finally, technique variables are thoroughly intertwined with the person of the therapist and cannot be considered in isolation (Butler & Strupp, 1986; Orlinsky & Howard, 1986).

Accordingly, the problem of therapeutic outcomes must be reformulated as a standard scientific question: What specific therapeutic activities of specific therapists produce specific changes in specific patients under specific conditions? This question implies the scientific imperative of improving descriptions and understanding of therapists' in-session actions, other therapist variables, patient variables, and the ways in which these interact. Progress along these lines, coupled with greater conceptual precision regarding outcome itself, will be essential if we are successfully to address the relationship between therapist actions and patient outcomes.

Patient Variables and the Problems of Diagnosis

Although it may not always be recognized, therapy outcomes depend to a significant extent on patient characteristics. When a therapist encounters a new patient, the first task is to define the nature of the problem in need of treatment or amelioration. As previously mentioned, therapists must be diagnosticians who attempt to identify a problem in order to take appropriate therapeutic steps. This requires not only an understanding of the diagnostic categories into which many patients fit, but also an appreciation of the vast array of *individual differences* among patients which may affect therapy. Deceptively simple, this problem is exceedingly fateful in its implications for therapy and research.

To illustrate, many therapists and researchers have come to realize that a phobia, a depression, or an anxiety state in one patient is not identical to a seemingly comparable problem in another. Accordingly, it may be hazardous to *categorize* or *type* patients on the basis of the presenting difficulty alone. Traditional diagnostic categories (e.g., *Diagnostic and Statistical Manual*, 3rd ed., rev.—DSM-III-R), while helpful (particularly with regard to the use of psychotropic medications), are limited in their utility for psychotherapeutic practice and research. Other systems of classification (e.g., in terms of defensive styles or ego functions), while sometimes useful, have shortcomings of their own.

The plain fact, long recognized by clinicians, is that patients differ on a host of dimensions—from intelligence, education, socioeconomic status, and age, to such variables as psychological-mindedness, motivation for psychotherapy, organization of defenses, and rigidity of character. The latter grouping of patient qualities are part of a relatively stable constellation of person characteristics usually thought of as "personality." In a very real sense, the psychotherapist confronts, not so much a diagnosed illness, but organized patient qualities or personality characteristics that help or hinder the therapeutic process.

Human personality is *organized*, and personality organization often forms an integral part of the therapeutic problem. For example, phobic patients tend to be generally shy, dependent, and anxious in many situations (Andrews, 1966). Genetic, social, temperamental, and environmental factors of various kinds all influence the patient's current disturbance. From the psychodynamic perspective, the patient's life history, particularly interpersonal relationships in early childhood, may be crucially important for understanding and treating the current problem. This reflects the recognition that the current problem must be understood in the *context* of this person's life (Butler & Strupp, 1986) and of the unique constellation of variables that constitute this person's personality. A growing interest in the study of the "Personality Disorders" (Axis II of the DSM-III-R) corresponds to an increasing awareness of this issue (cf. Frances, 1986).

As society has begun to recognize the importance of making psychotherapeutic services available to a broad spectrum of the population—not merely to its affluent members—the problem of defining and identifying those individuals most likely to benefit from particular forms of therapy has become increasingly pressing. A related issue involves the recognition that therapy must be tailored to individual patients, their problems, and their needs rather than the reverse (Goldstein & Stein, 1976).

The study of patient characteristics in relation to therapeutic change has for the most part focused on one basic issue: How do patient variables influence the course of psychotherapy? The ultimate goal is to answer the question, Which patient characteristics and problems are most amenable to which techniques conducted by which type of therapist in what kind of setting? Thus, rather than identifying patient characteristics associated with success across a broad band of different types of therapies, it is more important to devise reasonably specific therapies that will benefit particular kinds of patients. On the other hand, it may be the case that, as with other health care efforts, preexisting patient characteristics may seriously limit or preclude positive outcomes.

The Problem of Technique

Techniques are, of course, the core and raison d'être of modern psychotherapy and, as previously noted, are usually anchored in a theory of psychopathology or maladaptive learning. Psychoanalysis has stressed the interpretation of resistances and transference phenomena as the principal curative factor, contrasting these operations with the suggestions of early hypnotists. Behavior therapy, to cite another example, has developed its own armamentarium of techniques, such as systematic desensitization, modeling, aversive and operant conditioning, cognitive restructuring, and training in self-regulation and self-control. In general, the proponents of all systems of psychotherapy credit their successes to more or less *specific* operations, which are usually claimed to be uniquely effective. A corollary of this proposition is that a therapist is a professional who must receive systematic training in the application of the recommended techniques.

There has been a lack of evidence that one set of techniques is clearly superior to another, even under reasonably controlled conditions (e.g., Luborsky et al., 1975; Sloane et al., 1975). The commonly accepted finding that approximately two thirds of neurotic patients who enter outpatient psychotherapy of whatever description show noticeable improvement (Garfield, 1986; Lambert et al., 1986) likewise reinforces a skeptical attitude concerning the unique effectiveness of particular techniques. Finally, it often turns out that initial claims for a new technique cannot be sustained when the accumulating evidence is critically examined. For example, initial claims regarding the efficacy of systematic desensitization in the treatment of phobias appear not to hold up to long-term scrutiny (Marks, 1978).

An alternative hypothesis has been advanced (e.g., Frank, 1981), which asserts that psychotherapeutic change is predominantly a function of factors common to all therapeutic approaches. These factors are brought to bear on the human *relationship* between the patient and the healer. The proponents of this hypothesis hold that individuals, defined by themselves or others as patients, suffer from demoralization and a sense of hopelessness. Consequently, any benign human influence is likely to boost their morale, which in turn is registered as improvement. Primary ingredients of these common, *nonspecific* factors include understanding, respect, interest, encouragement, acceptance, forgiveness—in short, the kinds of human qualities that since time immemorial have been considered effective in buoying the human spirit.

Frank identifies another important common factor in all psychotherapies—that is, their tendency to operate in terms of a conceptual scheme and associated procedures that are thought to be beneficial. While the *contents* of the schemes and the procedures differ among therapies, they have common morale-building *functions*. They combat the patient's demoralization by providing an explanation, acceptable to both patient and therapist, for the patient's hitherto inexplicable feelings and behavior. This process serves to remove the mystery from the patient's suffering and eventually to supplant it with hope.

Frank's formulation implies that training in and enthusiasm for a special theory and method may increase the effectiveness of therapists, in contrast to nonprofessional helpers who may lack belief in a coherent system or rationale. This hypothesis also underscores the continuity between faith healers, shamans, and modern psychotherapists. While the latter may operate on the basis of sophisticated scientific theories (by contemporary standards), the function of these theories may intrinsically be no different from the most primitive rationale undergirding a faith healer's efforts. In both instances, techniques of whatever description are inseparable from the therapist's belief system, which in successful therapy is accepted and integrated by the patient. Of course, some patients more than others may be receptive to, and thus likely to benefit from, the therapist's manipulations.

Rogers (1956), from a different perspective, regarded a set of "facilitative conditions" (i.e., accurate empathy, genuineness, and unconditional positive regard) as necessary *and* sufficient conditions for beneficial therapeutic change. Thus, both Rogers and Frank deemphasize the effectiveness of therapeutic techniques per se and elevate relationship factors to a position of preeminence.

Although the hypothesis of nonspecific factors may be correct, it is still possible that *some* technical operations may be superior to others with particular patients, particular problems, and under particular circumstances (Strupp, 1973). Such claims are made, for example, by therapists who are interested in the treatment of sexual dysfunctions (cf. Kaplan, 1974) and by behavior therapists who have tackled a wide range of behavior disorders (Marks, 1978). As yet, many of these claims are untested.

In any event, it is clear that the problem has important ramifications for research and practice. For example, if further evidence can be adduced that techniques contribute less to good therapy outcomes than has been claimed, greater effort might be expended in selecting and training therapists who are able to provide the aforementioned nonspecific factors. We also need far more information about the kinds of therapeutic services that may be performed safely by individuals with relatively little formal training (paraprofessionals), as well as the limits set by their lack of comprehensive training.

Furthermore, there may be patients for whom the establishment of any sort of positively toned relationship may be extremely difficult (e.g., personality-disordered patients), and whose treatment should be relegated to professionals specially trained in techniques designed to help create and maintain a therapeutic relationship with such patients. We are currently engaged in developing a training program along these lines and investigating the potential utility of such training. Nevertheless, there may be definite limitations to what techniques, per se, can accomplish (Frank, 1974)—limits set by both patient characteristics and therapist qualities, including level of training.

While there have as yet been no major breakthroughs in our understanding of how psychotherapy works, recent developments in research methodologies may soon yield significant advances in this arena. Innovative methods of process analyses (e.g., Benjamin, 1982; Rice & Greenberg, 1984; Henry, Schacht, & Strupp, 1986; Silberschatz, Fretter, & Curtis, 1986) represent promising attempts to explore important patient–therapist interactions. Another major development has been the advent of so-called treatment manuals (e.g., Beck, Rush, Shaw, & Emery, 1979; Klerman, Rounsaville, Chevron, Neu, & Weissman, 1984; Luborsky, 1984; Strupp & Binder, 1984), which have begun to introduce greater specificity in defining the character of the interventions which comprise a particular approach. These relatively new scientific methods are sure to have an impact on the future of psychotherapy research and practice.

The Person of the Therapist

As previously suggested, psychotherapy prominently involves the interaction of two or more *persons*, and the therapeutic influence is by no means restricted to the formal techniques a therapist may use. The patient, like the therapist, reacts to the other as a total person; hence, both researchers and clinicians must become centrally concerned with the therapist as a human being. What has been said about enormous individual differences among patients applies, of course, with equal force to therapists. Indeed, it is difficult to fathom how, in early psychoanalysis, as well as in the later research studies, therapists could ever

have been treated as interchangeable units, presumably equal in skill and personal influence (Kiesler, 1966). Therapists, like patients, obviously differ on as many dimensions as one cares to mention—age, gender, cultural background, ethnic factors, level of professional experience, psychological sophistication, empathy, tact, social values, to name but a few. Any or all of these may have a significant bearing on the therapist's theoretical orientation, the therapist's techniques, and the manner in which the therapist interacts with and influences a given patient.

When considering the unique effects of each therapist as an individual, many therapist qualities elude definition. This elusiveness has posed serious obstacles to research in this area, though it is possible to specify human qualities a good therapist should possess (Holt & Luborsky, 1958), as well as those that may be harmful to patients (Bergin, 1966; Strupp, Hadley, & Gomes-Schwartz, 1977). Research and practical interest in identifying and describing therapist qualities that may be detrimental to patients is reminiscent of the ancient medical principle "above all, do no harm." It is clearly as important to know what a therapist should *not* do as it is to specify what the therapist *should* do.

Among the therapist variables that have been subjected to quantitative research are (a) the therapist's personal adjustment (often measured by standard personality tests like the MMPI); (b) the facilitative conditions already mentioned (warmth, empathy, genuineness, etc.); the therapist's type (e.g., therapists [called Type "A"] who subordinate technique to a truly collaborative relationship with the patient appear to be especially effective with schizophrenic patients); the therapist's cognitive style; the therapist's level of professional experience; the therapist's professional status (professionals versus nonprofessionals or paraprofessionals); gender; age; socioeconomic status; ethnicity; and the therapist's social and cultural values. Effects of personality conflicts, needs, and attitudes of the therapist toward the patient have also been investigated in a variety of studies (Beutler et al., 1986; Orlinsky & Howard, 1986; Parloff et al., 1978).

Furthermore, patient personality characteristics demonstrably influence the therapist's effectiveness, which suggests that patients should be selected more carefully to match the therapist's capabilities, or perhaps therapists should be more specifically trained to deal with different personalities. While therapists appear to be differentially effective with particular patients (Strupp 1980a, 1980b, 1980c, 1980d), it has proven difficult to isolate salient dimensions of the therapist's personality and to measure their impact. Indeed, it is becoming increasingly clear that *individual* therapist variables, except perhaps for glaring defects in the therapist's personality, are not likely to provide the answers sought by researchers and clinicians; instead, a combination of therapist attributes appears to form an integrated *gestalt*, to which the patient, other things being equal, responds positively, negatively, or neutrally.

Clinical wisdom suggest that the effective therapist must be able to instill trust, confidence, hope and conviction in the patient's personal strength and resilience. To have a therapeutic impact on the patient, the therapist's personality must have distinctive stimulus value or salience—therapists can never be impersonal technicians, nor can they apply therapeutic techniques in a vacuum. At times, therapists must be capable of encouraging patients to explore a particular feeling, belief, attitude, and so on; at other times, they must wait patiently for the patient to find his or her own solutions. They must be able to distinguish between the patient's neurotic and nonneurotic needs, and they must avoid getting entangled in the patient's neurotic maneuvers. Above all, they must make a careful assessment of how much help is needed, what kind of help is needed, and what obstacles prevent the patient from reaching a constructive solution.

The Therapeutic Alliance

Psychoanalytic theorists (e.g., Greenson, 1967; Langs, 1973; Menninger & Holtzman, 1973) have identified the relationship between patient and therapist as a major therapeutic force. As Freud developed the technique of psychoanalytic therapy, he recognized that the patient must become an active partner who collaborates with the therapist in his or her cure. Traditionally, psychoanalysts have postulated an "observing ego" (cf. Strupp &

Binder 1984, ; p. 39) which represents the reasonable and rational part of the patient's personality and is capable of forming an alliance with the therapist's efforts to analyze the irrational (transferential) aspects of the patient's personality. This alliance is the foundation for the necessary collaboration between therapist and patient which permits the analysis to proceed.

To the extent that factors within the patient or the therapist interfere with the establishment of a productive therapeutic alliance, therapeutic progress will be retarded or even vitiated. Premature termination or intractable dependency on the therapist are instances of such failures. It is also well known that patients who have relatively intact and strong egos have a better chance of succeeding in analytic therapy (Horwitz, 1974; Kernberg, 1976), and perhaps in other forms of therapy as well. Bordin (1974, 1979) has been a major proponent of intensified research efforts in this area.

While superficially resembling any good human relationship (of the kind discussed elsewhere in this chapter), the therapeutic alliance provides a unique starting point for the patient's growing *identification* with the therapist, a point stressed by the proponents of object relations theory (Fairbairn, 1952; Guntrip, 1971; Kernberg, 1976; Winnicott, 1965) who have spearheaded advances in psychoanalytic theory. According to these authors, the internalization of the therapist as a good object is crucial for significant psychotherapeutic change. Because the internalization of bad objects has made the patient "ill," therapy succeeds to the extent that the therapist can be internalized as a good object. However, because the patient tends to remain loyal to the early objects of childhood, defending them against modification, therapy inevitably becomes a struggle. From this perspective, patients' amenability to therapy (i.e., their ability to form a therapeutic alliance) is importantly influenced by their early relations with others. Work along these lines is judged exceedingly promising and is being pursued by a number of investigators (e.g., Frieswyk et al., 1986; Hartley & Strupp, 1983; Horowitz, Marmar, Weiss, DeWitt, & Rosenbaum, 1984; Horwitz, 1974; Luborsky et al., 1980; Morgan, Luborsky, Crits-Christoph, Curtis, & Solomon, 1982).

CODA: INTEGRATION BETWEEN RESEARCH AND PRACTICE

In the past, therapists have tended to regard researchers as unwelcome intruders who, disrupting the sanctity of the patient–therapist relationship and robbing a living human relationship of its excitement and vitality, produced findings of peripheral or trivial interest to the practitioner. To be sure, every scientific effort seeks to order, simplify, condense, and control. It is also true that practitioners, in their everyday dealings with patients, cannot directly profit from statistical trends obtained from research; they must deal with the inevitable idiosyncrasies of every patient–therapist interaction (Strupp, 1960).

The greater contribution of psychotherapy research may ultimately lie on a different plane. Researchers of the future, who must also be well-trained clinicians, will need to work more closely with practicing therapists on vital issues encountered in everyday clinical work, subjecting these issues to experimental analysis and test. The close collaboration of clinicians and researchers should be geared specifically toward yielding information that can be integrated readily into the clinical situation.

What is envisaged is a form of action research, originally proposed by Lewin (1947), in which research is brought to bear on a practical (clinical) problem; research findings are then promptly applied in the clinical setting; and their utility is again tested by means of research. The result is a continuous and productive feedback loop in which practice inspires research, and research provides information relevant to practice.

One example of such research might take place in a research clinic, where intensive analyses of the patient–therapist interactions could be made immediately after each therapeutic encounter. Information from these analyses would then be fed back to the therapist before the next session, in an effort to help the therapist make specified adjustments to the process expected to improve the quality of the patient–therapist interaction. The extent to which the therapist carried out the therapeutic plan, and the effectiveness of the interventions (in terms of improved process ratings) could be assessed in the following session.

Such an approach to psychotherapy research contrasts markedly with the usual research method, where a globally conceived therapy (e.g., cognitive behavior therapy, psychoanalytic therapy, interpersonal therapy) is evaluated vis-à-vis effectiveness at some outcome point that may be weeks or months away from a given intervention. From the standpoint of research, it seems more likely that the effects of a given therapist action will be detectable in the immediate therapeutic process (e.g., Does the patient become less self-criticizing, less hostile, more revealing, and less guarded?). The results of such research would be particularly informative to the clinician, whose task is to decide what to do or say *next*.[1]

Investigations into the utility of such research methods are currently being planned. Obviously, this type of approach has problems, not the least of which is the time-intensive nature of the undertaking; nor is it imagined that this would replace sustained research efforts along more traditional lines. However, this approach would be one means of bringing about a closer working alliance between therapists and researchers.

As responsible professionals, therapists must learn to think critically and scrutinize continually the quality of their professional activities and the therapeutic outcome. This has always been the hallmark of a mature profession (Peterson, 1976). As steps are taken in this direction, it is predictable that psychotherapy will become a better and more mature profession, meriting society's confidence and respect. Last, but not least, it will become a profession based on solid scientific knowledge.

REFERENCES

Anchin, J. C., & Kiesler, D. J. (1982). *Handbook of interpersonal psychotherapy*. New York: Pergamon.

Andrews, J. (1966). Psychotherapy of phobias. *Psychological Bulletin, 66*, 455–480.

[1]We would like to acknowledge the seminal contributions of Thomas Schacht and William Henry in the development of these ideas.

Beck, A. T., Rush, A. J., Shaw, B. I., & Emery, G. (1979). *Cognitive therapy of depression: A treatment manual.* New York: Guilford.

Benjamin, L. S. (1982). Use of structural analysis of social behavior to guide intervention in therapy. In J. C. Anchin & D. J. Kiesler (Eds.), *Handbook of interpersonal psychotherapy.* New York: Pergamon.

Bergin, A. E. (1966). Some implications of psychotherapy research for therapeutic practice. *Journal of Abnormal Psychology, 71,* 235–246.

Beutler, L. S., Crago, M., & Arizmendi, T. G. (1986). Therapist variables in psychotherapy process and outcome. In S. L. Garfield & A. E. Bergin (Eds.), *Handbook of psychotherapy and behavior change* (3rd ed.). New York: Wiley.

Bordin, E. S. (1974). *Research strategies in psychotherapy.* New York: Wiley.

Bordin, E. S. (1979). The generalizability of the psychoanalytic concept of the working alliance. *Psychotherapy: Theory, Research and Practice, 16,* 252–260.

Butler, S. F., & Binder, J. L. (1987). Cyclical psychodynamics and the triangle of insight: An integration. *Psychiatry, 50,* 218–231.

Butler, S. F., & Strupp, H. H. (1986). "Specific" and "nonspecific" factors in psychotherapy: A problematic paradigm for psychotherapy research. *Psychotherapy, 23,* 30–40.

DiLoreto, A. O. (1971). *Comparative psychotherapy: An experimental analysis.* Chicago: Aldine-Atherton.

Elkin, I., Parloff, M. B., Hadley, S. W., & Autry, J. H. (1985). NIMH treatment of depression collaborative research program: Background and research plan. *Archives of General Psychiatry, 43,* 305–316.

Eysenck, H. J. (1952). The effects of psychotherapy: An evaluation. *Journal of Consulting Psychology, 16,* 319–324.

Fairbairn, R. (1952). *Object relations theory of the personality.* New York: Basic.

Frances, A. J. (1986). Introduction to personality disorders. In A. M. Cooper, A. J. Frances, & M. H. Sacks (Eds.), *Psychiatry: Vol. 1. The personality disorders and neuroses* (pp. 171–189). New York: Basic.

Frank, J. D. (1974). Therapeutic components of psychotherapy: A 25-year progress report of research. *Journal of Consulting and Clinical Psychology, 47,* 310–316.

Frank, J. D. (1981). Therapeutic components shared by all psychotherapies. In J. H. Harvey & M. M. Parks (Eds.), *The Master Lecture Series: Vol. 1. Psycho-therapy research and behavior change.* Washington, DC: American Psychological Association.

Freud, S. (1916). Analytic therapy. In the *Standard edition of the complete psychological works of Sigmund Freud* 16: pp. 448–463). London: Hogarth.

Frieswyk, S. H., Allen, J. G., Colson, D. B., Coyne, L., Gabbard, G. O., Horwitz, L., & Newsom, G. (1986). Therapeutic alliance: Its place as a process and outcome variable in dynamic psychotherapy research. *Journal of Consulting and Clinical Psychology, 54,* 32–38.

Garfield, S. L. (1986). Research on client variables in psychotherapy. In S. L. Garfield & A. E. Bergin (Eds.), *Handbook of psychotherapy and behavior change* (3rd ed., pp. 213–256). New York: Wiley.

Gill, M. M. (1982). *Analysis of transference: Theory and technique.* New York: International Universities Press.

Goldstein, A. P., & Stein, N. (1976). *Prescriptive psychotherapies.* New York: Pergamon.

Greenson, R. (1967). *The technique and practice of psychoanalysis.* New York: International Universities Press.

Guntrip, H. (1971). *Psychoanalytic theory, therapy, and the self.* New York: Basic.

Hartley, D. E., & Strupp, H. H. (1983). The therapeutic alliance: Its relationship to outcome in brief psychotherapy. In J. Masling (Ed.), *Empirical studies of psychoanalytic theories* (Vol. 1, pp. 1–37). Hillsdale, NJ: Analytic Press.

Henry, W. P., Schacht, T. E., & Strupp, H. H. (1986). Structural analysis of social behavior: Application to a study of interpersonal process of differential therapeutic outcome. *Journal of Consulting and Clinical Psychology, 54,* 27–31.

Holt, R. R., & Luborsky, L. (1958). *Personality patterns of psychiatrists: A study in selection techniques* (Vol. 1). New York: Basic.

Horowitz, M. J., Marmar, C., Weiss, D. S., DeWitt, K. N., & Rosenbaum, R. (1984). Brief psychotherapy of bereavement reactions: The relationship of process to outcome. *Archives of General Psychiatry, 41,* 438–448.

Horwitz, L. (1974). *Clinical practice in psychotherapy.* New York: Jason Aronson.

Kaplan, H. S. (1974). *The new sex therapy: Active treatment of sexual dysfunctions.* New York: Brunner/Mazel.

Kernberg, O. F. (1976). Some methodological and strategic issues in psychotherapy research: Research implications of the Menninger Foundation's Psychotherapy Research Project. In R. L. Spitzer & D.

F. Klein (Eds.), *Evaluation of psychological therapies*. Baltimore: Johns Hopkins University Press.

Kernberg, O. F., Bernstein, E. D., Coyne, L., Appelbaum, A., Horwitz, J. L., & Voth, H. (1972). Psychotherapy and psychoanalysis: Final report of the Menninger Foundation's Psychotherapy Research Project. *Bulletin of the Menninger Clinic, 36,* 1–276.

Kiesler, D. J. (1966). Some myths of psychotherapy research and the search for a paradigm. *Psychological Bulletin, 65,* 110–136.

Klerman, G. L., Rounsaville, B., Chevron, E., Neu, C., & Weissman, M. M. (1984). *Interpersonal psychotherapy of depression (IPT)*. New York: Basic.

Knight, R. P. (1941). Evaluation of the results of psychoanalytic therapy. *American Journal of Psychiatry, 98,* 434–446.

Lambert, M. J., Shapiro, D. A., & Bergin, A. E. (1986). The effectiveness of psychotherapy. In S. L. Garfield & A. E. Bergin (Eds.), *Handbook of psychotherapy and behavior change* 3rd ed., (pp. 157–211). New York: Wiley.

Langs, R. (1973). *The technique of psychoanalytic psychotherapy*. New York: Jason Aronson.

Lewin, K. (1947). Frontiers in group dynamics: II. Channels of group life: Social planning and action research. *Human Relations, 1,* 143–153.

Luborsky, L. (1984). *Principles of psychoanalytic psychotherapy: A manual for supportive expressive treatment*. New York: Basic.

Luborsky, L., Mintz, J., Auerbach, A., Christoph, P., Bachrach, H., Todd, T., Johnson, M., Cohen, M., & O'Brien, C. P. (1980). Predicting the outcome of psychotherapy: Findings of the Penn Psychotherapy Project. *Archives of General Psychiatry, 37,* 471–481.

Luborsky, L., Singer, B., & Luborsky, L. (1975). Comparative studies of psychotherapies: Is it true that "Everybody has won and all must have prizes?" *Archives of General Psychiatry, 32,* 995–1008.

Marks, (1978). Behavioral psychotherapy of adult neurosis. In S. L. Garfield & A. E. Bergin (Eds.), *Handbook of psychotherapy and behavior change: An empirical analysis* (2nd ed., pp. 493–547). New York: Wiley.

Messer, S. B., (1986). Behavioral and psychoanalytic perspectives at therapeutic choice points. *American Psychologist, 41,* 1261–1272.

Menninger, K. A., & Holtzman, P. S. (1973). *Theory of psychoanalytic techniques* (2nd ed). New York: Basic.

Morgan, R., Luborsky, L., Crits-Christoph, P., Curtis, H., & Solomon, J. (1982). Predicting the outcomes of psychotherapy by the Penn Helping Alliance Rating Method. *Archives of General Psychiatry, 39,* 397–402.

Orlinsky, D. E., & Howard, K. I. (1986). Process and outcome in psychotherapy. In S. L. Garfield & A. E. Bergin (Eds.), *Handbook of psychotherapy and behavior change* (3rd ed., pp. 311–384). New York: Wiley.

Parloff, M. B., Waskow, I. E., & Wolfe, B. E. (1978). Research on therapist variables in relation to process and outcome. In S. L. Garfield & A. E. Bergin (Eds.), *Handbook of psychotherapy and behavior change* (2nd ed., pp. 233–282). New York: Wiley.

Paul, G. L. (1967). Strategy in outcome research in psychotherapy. *Journal of Consulting Psychology, 31,* 109–118.

Paul, G. L. (1969). Behavior modification research: Design and tactics. In C. M. Franks (Ed.), *Behavior therapy: Appraisal and status* (pp. 29–62). New York: McGraw-Hill.

Peterson, D. R. (1976). Is psychology a profession? *American Psychologist, 31,* 553–560.

Rice, L. N., & Greenberg, L. S. (Eds.) (1984). *Patterns of change*. New York: Guilford.

Rogers, C. R. (1956). The necessary and sufficient conditions of therapeutic personality change. *Journal of Consulting Psychology, 21,* 95–103.

Rogers, C. R., & Dymond, R. F. (1954). *Psychotherapy and personality change*. Chicago: University of Chicago Press.

Silberschatz, G., Fretter, P. B., & Curtis, J. T. (1986). How do interpretations influence the process of psychotherapy? *Journal of Consulting and Clinical Psychology, 54,* 646–652.

Sloane, R. B., Staples, F. R., Cristol, A. H., Yorkston, N. J., & Whipple, K. (1975). *Psychotherapy versus behavior therapy*. Cambridge: Harvard University Press.

Smith, M. L., Glass, G. V., & Miller, T. I. (1980). *The benefits of psychotherapy*. Baltimore: Johns Hopkins University Press.

Strupp, H. H. (1960). Some comments on the future of research in psychotherapy. *Behavioral Science, 5,* 60–71.

Strupp, H. H. (1973). On the basic ingredients of psychotherapy. *Journal of Consulting and Clinical Psychology, 41,* 1–8.

Strupp, H. H. (1980a). Success and failure in time-limited psychotherapy: A systematic comparison of two cases. (Comparison 1.) *Archives of General Psychiatry, 37,* 595–603.

Strupp, H. H. (1980b). Success and failure in time-limited psychotherapy: A systematic comparison of two cases. (Comparison 2.) *Archives of General Psychiatry, 37,* 708–716.

Strupp, H. H. (1980c). Success and failure in time-limited psychotherapy: With special reference to the performance of a lay counselor. (Comparison 3.) *Archives of General Psychiatry, 37,* 831–841.

Strupp, H. H. (1980d). Success and failure in time-limited psychotherapy: Further evidence. (Comparison 4.) *Archives of General Psychiatry, 37,* 947–954.

Strupp, H. H. (1986). Psychotherapy: Research, practice and public policy (How to avoid dead ends). *American Psychologist, 41,* 120–130.

Strupp, H. H., & Binder, J. L. (1984). *Psychotherapy in a new key: A guide to time-limited dynamic psychotherapy.* New York: Basic.

Strupp, H. H., Butler, S. F., & Rosser, C. L. (1988). Training in psychodynamic therapy. *Journal of Consulting and Clinical Psychology, 56,* 689–695.

Strupp, H. H., & Hadley, S. W. (1977). A tripartite model of mental health and therapeutic outcomes: With special reference to negative effects in psychotherapy. *American Psychologist, 32,* 187–196.

Strupp, H. H., Hadley, S. W., & Gomes-Schwartz, B. (1977). *Psychotherapy for better or worse: The problem of negative effects.* New York: Aronson.

Wilson, G. T., & Evans, I. M. (1977). The therapist–client relationship in behavior therapy. In A. S. Gurman & A. M. Razin (Eds.). *Effective psychotherapy: A handbook of research.* New York: Pergamon.

Winnicott, D. (1965). *The family and individual development.* New York: Basic.

CHAPTER 2

Behavior Therapy

JOHN T. WIXTED, ALAN S. BELLACK, AND MICHEL HERSEN

INTRODUCTION

Behavior therapy is a relatively new discipline, having substantially developed since the mid-1960s. Yet its roots extend back through recorded history. Many core behavioral techniques are part of the everyday wisdom of people attempting to rear children and change the behavior of others. Positive reinforcement and punishment are universal strategies for controlling the behavior of children and training animals: Desired behavior is rewarded, and undesired behavior is punished. For example, "Grandmother's rule" specifies that Suzy cannot go out to play until after her chores are done (i.e., play can be used as a reinforcement for appropriate behavior). Shaping is a well-established principle for teaching skills gradually. The child who is thrown from a horse is advised to get right back on, analogous to the strategy in exposure treatment of fears. Learning is often easiest to accomplish by first watching someone skilled (the basis of modeling treatments) and then practicing those skills (e.g., homework assignments and rehearsal). People with fears and worries have always been told to "think positively," "don't think about it," or "think about something pleasant"—elements of cognitive therapy for depression and anxiety.

Scientific Advancement of Behavior Therapy

These behavioral folk remedies have been developed over the centuries by trial and error, and most make intuitive sense. But it has only been in the 20th century that such procedures have been studied systematically and tied to scientific advances in our understanding of physiology, brain function, learning, and the rules governing behavior (Kazdin, 1978). Two lines of study have been particularly important in the development of a scientific behavior therapy. First, the Russian physiologists Sechenov, Pavlov, and Bechterev conducted a seminal series of studies of reflexes, which led to the development of classical conditioning in the first part of this century. At about the same time in the United States, the psychologist John B. Watson was advocating the rejection of mentalism and introspection as strategies for studying behavior in favor of a new, more objective approach: behaviorism. Together, these two lines of work highlighted the critical role of the environment in behavior and stimulated the scientific study of human behavior. There was marked progress in our understanding of conditioning and learning in the period between 1920 and 1950, including scattered demonstrations of how the principles could be applied both to understanding the development of psychopathology and to treating it.

It was not until the late 1950s and early 1960s, however, that contemporary behavior therapy emerged as a nascent discipline. During that period, the seminal works of B. F. Skinner, Joseph Wolpe, and Hans J. Eysenck combined to provide a beginning set of behavioral procedures and a theoretical framework with which to challenge

Preparation of this manuscript was supported in part by grants MH38636 and MH39998 from the National Institute of Mental Health.

existing models and develop new procedures. Skinner's work on operant conditioning was initially applied to severely handicapped children and adults, as reflected in the development of the token economy (Ayllon & Azrin, 1968). These operant techniques produced remarkable improvements in patients previously deemed unreachable. At the same time, Wolpe's systematic desensitization (Wolpe & Lazarus, 1966) revolutionized treatment of "neurotic" patients and led to the development of a host of procedures for reducing anxiety, depression, and other nonpsychotic disorders.

Eysenck made important theoretical contributions to the behavioral model, but his most important contribution may well have been his classic review papers on the outcome of verbal psychotherapy (Eysenck, 1952, 1965). It would be nice to argue that behavior therapy evolved solely due to the merits of its scientific base. However, dissatisfaction with existing techniques was probably just as much of a factor. There was a growing sense that the psychoanalytic approaches that were predominant at the time were not effective, yet there seemed to be no way to evaluate this assumption. The emphasis on poorly defined, inferential, unconscious processes precluded objective evaluation, in essence placing the analytical model above science. This was a source of considerable philosophical discontent, above and beyond questions of clinical efficacy. Eysenck's reviews purportedly demonstrated that verbal psychotherapy was not effective. While the scientific merits of his case may not have been overwhelming, they provided an empirical justification for rejecting the psychoanalytic approach and looking elsewhere. Behaviorism, with its emphasis on objective definition of concepts and empirical verification, was a very attractive alternative.

A New Orthodoxy

While dissatisfaction with traditional approaches served a critical role in stimulating the development of behavior therapy, it also resulted in a new orthodoxy: parsimony and operationalism above all else. It was assumed that all behavior could be explained by nonmediational conditioning concepts, and all inferences to cognitive and subjective phenomena were eschewed. Similarly, concepts such as *diagnosis, symptoms, mental illness,* and *biological* (e.g., genetic) *determinism* were rejected as invalid and/or useless overgeneralizations. As a result, the many successes of early behavior therapists were often vitiated by an overemphasis on analog research in lieu of real clinical trials, and the periodic reports of clinically naive interventions (e.g., teaching a schizophrenic to stop hallucinating by snapping a rubber band on his wrist whenever he heard voices).

The subsequent chapters in this book show that this situation has now changed dramatically. Diagnosis, cognition, and biology have become integral parts of behavioral treatments and conceptualizations. Analog studies with mildly distressed college student subjects have almost entirely disappeared in favor of sophisticated clinical trials. At the same time, behavior therapy is no longer a fringe discipline; it has proven itself to be so successful that it has become part of the mainstream. Many behavioral strategies are widely regarded as treatments of choice, including systematic desensitization for phobias, exposure for agoraphobia, exposure and response prevention for obsessive–compulsive disorder, cognitive therapy for depression, social skills training for schizophrenia, and operant programs (e.g., token economies) for severely disturbed children and mentally retarded citizens.

A Broader Focus

As the field of behaviorism has developed, it has broadened its focus, as well as become more sophisticated. New interventions have been developed for a much wider set of disorders, including the full gamut of DSM-III-R (*Diagnostic and Statistical Manual, 3rd ed., rev.*) categories. Behavior therapists are also using an ever-increasing array of techniques. Many of the new interventions fall under the behavioral rubric more because their developers identify themselves as behavioral than because they depend upon a specific set of procedures or principles. While behavior therapy was initially defined in substantial measure by its adherence to the principles of learning and conditioning, such is no longer the case (Franks & Barbrack, 1983; Krasner, 1984). Many current strategies (e.g., cognitive therapy, behavioral family therapy) have loose ties to learning theory at best.

Principles of Contemporary Behavior Therapy

Contemporary behavior therapy defies easy definition. It can better be conceptualized by a general group of guiding principles.

1. Emphasis on empiricism. In keeping with its origins, behavior therapy places a premium on empirical evaluation of assumptions, conceptual models, and clinical procedures. While strict operationalism is no longer viewed as a sine qua non, objectivity and measurability are still viewed as important guidelines. Inferential and mediational variables (e.g., attributions, affect states) are now widely accepted, but a premium is placed on defining such variables in a manner that permits them to be empirically evaluated.

2. Emphasis on assessment. In keeping with the value placed on empiricism and objectivity, assessment is viewed as an essential aspect of clinical intervention as well as of laboratory research. To the extent possible, assessment should address three issues: how, what, and where. Thus, assessment should entail ongoing observation (how) of behavior (what) in the natural environment (where). In general, a premium is placed on direct assessment (e.g., observation) in lieu of the more indirect, inferential approach characteristic of traditional psychological testing (e.g., projective techniques).

3. Idiographic focus. In keeping with the operant tradition espoused by Skinner, there is a continued emphasis on the individual case. While diagnosis has become an established aspect of behavioral assessment, nosological labels (i.e., medical classifications) are thought to represent overly general categories that mask individual differences. The idiographic emphasis is reflected in the extensive use of single-case research methodology for theory development, as well as for clinical practice (Barlow & Hersen, 1984).

4. Emphasis on the environment. Environmental factors are believed to play a vital role in shaping and maintaining behavior. Even when the cause of a disturbance is internal (e.g., biological), the environment may play a central role in the expression of undesired behavior. This is exemplified by the role of parental behavior (viz. expressed emotion) in relapse in schizophrenia (Hooley, 1985). Often, it is easier to modify behavior by altering the environment (e.g., changing parental communication, providing reinforcement for desired behavior) than by directing treatment at the identified patient. Even when the patient is the primary recipient of the intervention, it is often still useful (or necessary) to modify the environment as well.

5. Action orientation. Behavioral interventions place a premium on performance, as opposed to discussion. It is generally assumed that behavior can best be changed by practicing new responses (including cognitive responses) rather than by gaining insight or understanding. Therapy sessions often involve rehearsal of targeted behaviors and/or exposure to critical cues. In-session performance is supplemented by in vivo practice, in the form of homework. Behavior therapists are, therefore, very active teachers and directors. The therapeutic relationship is thought to be very important for facilitating change, but it is not in itself viewed as the essential vehicle of change.

6. Ahistorical focus. Behavior therapy places a premium on current functioning. Past behavior and history can provide important diagnostic cues and help in planning treatment. However, the critical factors involved in dysfunctional behavior are thought to be contemporary rather than historical. Behaviors are often maintained by quite different factors than were responsible for producing them in the first place, and it is the maintaining factors that must be addressed.

This brief overview is intended both to place contemporary behavior therapy into perspective and to highlight the primary tenets that guide the behavioral approach. Some of these issues are elaborated in the subsequent sections of this chapter by describing a sample of behavioral procedures. The reader is referred to the other behavioral chapters in this book for a more complete description of clinical operations and their underlying rationale.

ASSESSMENT

Behavioral assessment was designed to serve two basic functions: (1) to establish a baseline against which to objectively measure the effects of clinical intervention, and (2) to expose the environmental factors that may be associated with or controlling the behavior of interest. The focus was originally placed almost exclusively on the measurement of specific overt responses exhibited by the patient and by those with whom the patient interacted (i.e., *idiographic* techniques). As far as possible, these measurements were obtained through direct observation of behavior because that was the method assumed to be least vulnerable to contamination by subjective influences.

In recent years, however, these *idiographic* functions have been supplemented by more traditional *nomothetic* functions, which seek to measure broad traits or syndromes using techniques such as rating scales, self-report instruments, and diagnostic interviews (Cone, 1988). At present, the field is characterized by two categories of assessment techniques: those that seek to measure individual, molecular responses, and those that seek to measure broad constructs (Cone, 1978). Although these two approaches are sometimes contrasted as being theoretically incompatible, in practice, they operate in a complementary fashion, serving different needs for different therapists and patient populations (Bellack & Hersen, 1988). The range of procedures available to the practicing clinician that serve idiographic and/or nomothetic functions is large indeed and some of the more common ones are reviewed in the next two sections.

Direct Methods

Naturalistic Observation. Direct observation of a patient's behavior in his or her natural social environment is probably the method most closely identified with the field of behavioral assessment. It was one of the first techniques developed by behavior therapists, and it is well-suited to both the precise measurement of maladaptive behavior and the elucidation of its possible environmental determinants. By directly observing the behavior of a depressed patient, for example, the therapist may discover that depressive responses (e.g., crying,

remaining in bed) are most probable in the presence of certain sympathetic relatives. That information, which may never have been obtained by other means, yields obvious treatment implications.

The technique of naturalistic observation is simple in concept, but somewhat more difficult to apply. In order to conduct such an assessment, the behavior to be measured must be selected in advance and operationally defined. For example, a typical behavioral category used in the assessment of children is *noncompliance*, defined as the failure to initiate an appropriate motoric response within 5 seconds of an adult's command (Forehand & McMahon, 1981). Usually, multiple response categories are defined in this manner and observers are then provided with extensive training in the use of the coding system.

An especially detailed and comprehensive example of this approach to assessment is provided by the family interaction coding system (FICS) developed by Patterson and his colleagues (Patterson, Ray, Shaw, & Cobb, 1969). The FICS, which was designed to measure behavioral interactions in families with conduct-disordered children, consists of 29 behavioral codes, including common problem behaviors (e.g., noncompliance, crying) and positive and negative parental responses (e.g., approval, ignoring). Typically, a trained observer visits the home and targets each member of the family for 5 minutes of observation. During that time, the behavior of the targeted individual is coded, along with the behavior of anyone with whom he or she interacts. This analysis yields a detailed description of sequential interactions among family members, allowing the therapist to infer which actions on the part of a parent might be supporting deviant behavior on the part of the child.

Despite its obvious advantages, direct observation is clearly a time-consuming and expensive process. Even when trained observers are available, the procedure is often complicated by practical and ethical concerns. In the treatment of a sexual disorder, for example, this method of assessment is unlikely to be tolerated by most patients. In addition to these considerations, researchers have recently recognized that, even under the best of circumstances, observational methods are not, as once believed, immune to questions of validity (Hartmann, Roper, & Bradford, 1979). Originally, naturalistic observation was the preferred assessment method because it was, on the face of it, far more valid than alternative methods (such as self-report). However, an observational assessment necessarily records only a sample of behavior, which may or may not be representative of the subject's behavior in general. The validity of this approach, like any other assessment method, must therefore be empirically documented. Thus, while naturalistic observation continues to hold a place of importance, other procedures designed to measure behavior in more cost-effective ways have proliferated in recent years.

Self-monitoring.   Because of its practical utility, asking patients to record their own behavior between sessions has become a standard component of behavioral assessment. In the study and treatment of agoraphobia, for example, patients are routinely asked to record their daily activities (e.g., where they traveled, how long they stayed) and to rate the intensity of any fear or panic attacks they might have experienced (Arnow, Taylor, Agras, & Telch, 1985). Similarly, in the treatment of heterosocial anxiety and social phobia, therapists often request that patients maintain a daily record of social behavior in order to better monitor treatment progress (e.g., Heimberg, Madsen, Montgomery, & McNabb, 1980). The assumption underlying this procedure is that written records made at the time the targeted behaviors occur will be considerably more accurate than in-session recall of the events occurring over the previous week.

An important methodological concern often raised in the context of self-monitoring is the problem of reactivity. Basically, *reactivity* refers to the impact of the self-monitoring process on the measured behavior itself. An obese patient assigned the task of tracking food intake, for example, might start to eat less as soon as the measurements begin. Although such reactivity obviously complicates the acquisition of valid baseline measures, the direction of behavioral change is usually positive, and several studies have attested to the therapeutic effect of this form of assessment (Stunkard, 1982). Because of the reliability and validity problems inherent in this approach, how-

ever, self-monitoring is almost never used alone. Two additional cost-effective observational strategies, one designed to measure the avoidance behavior associated with fear (the Behavioral Approach Test) and the other designed to evaluate social deficits associated with a variety of psychiatric disorders (behavioral role play), are often used to supplement self-monitoring.

Behavioral Approach Test.   Developed in the early years of behavioral assessment, the Behavioral Approach Test remains a standard tool for measuring the severity of a phobia. Although it has been employed in various forms, this strategy basically involves a series of graded steps in which the patient and the feared object (e.g., a snake) are gradually moved closer together until the patient becomes uncomfortable. At that point, the test is terminated and the final distance between the patient and phobic object is recorded (e.g., Levis, 1969). The periodic use of this procedure provides an objective index of therapeutic gains, which should be reflected by a closer approach tolerance as treatment progresses.

Strategies similar to the Behavioral Approach Test have been employed with other anxiety patients, such as agoraphobics. The essential difference is that instead of increasing proximity to the feared object, the patient is instructed to proceed farther and farther away from a place of perceived "safety." For example, Michelson, Mavissakalian, and Marchione (1985) routinely ask their agoraphobic patients to walk down the street away from the treatment clinic until they begin to experience anxiety. The distance the patient is able to walk provides the therapist with an initial evaluation of the severity of the phobia and, as treatment progresses, an index of the effects of intervention.

Behavior Role Play.   With regard to the measurement of interpersonal behavior, a common alternative to naturalistic observation is role-play assessment, in which the patient and the therapist engage in a series of prearranged social interactions. In this way, the therapist can get some idea of the patient's performance in a range of social settings that would otherwise be impossible. In a typical test, a situation is described to the patient, and the therapist (playing the role of another person in the scene) issues a verbal prompt. The patient is instructed to respond to the prompt as realistically as possible, and the therapist may then extend the interaction for one or two more exchanges. These enactments can be videotaped and later scored for a variety of specific behavioral measures, including eye contact, voice quality, gestures, and so on, or the therapist may simply gauge the patient's performance on a global basis after each scene is completed.

Role-play assessment has become a preferred method of evaluating the social performance of patients involved in social skills and assertiveness training. A variety of standardized role-play tests have been devised for this purpose (e.g., St. Lawrence, 1987), beginning with the original Behavioral Assertiveness Test (Eisler, Hersen, Miller, & Blanchard, 1975; Eisler, Miller, & Hersen, 1973). Typically, these tests consist of a series of specific scenes covering a range of social domains in which assertive behavior might be appropriate (e.g., someone cutting into the front of a line, overcooked food presented by the waiter).

One concern that has been raised about standardized role-play assessment is the extent to which performance under those conditions mirrors the patient's behavior under more natural conditions (Bellack, 1979, 1983). Indeed, initial empirical tests of this question were rather discouraging, in that the concordance between role-play and in vivo performance was found to be minimal (e.g., Bellack, Hersen, & Turner, 1978). Improvements in the validity of this procedure have been obtained by using more extended role-play interactions and by personalizing role play scenes to some degree rather than relying exclusively on standardized formats (Bellack, 1983). Although additional work is needed to produce a truly sound procedure, role-play assessment often provides the practicing clinician with the only practical means of evaluating a patient's behavior across a range of social situations.

Indirect Methods

A variety of nonobservational measurement procedures have expanded the boundaries of behavioral assessment in recent years. These procedures, which include self-report instruments, therapist rating scales, and diagnostic interviews, did not originate from within the field of behavioral assessment and were once looked upon with great suspicion. They were often assumed to be inherently invalid because of their susceptibility to subjective influences, and because they tended to focus on nebulous traits or syndromes in preference to specific responses. However, as the need to document the reliability and validity of assessment procedures, observation based or otherwise, became clear, the field opened its doors to alternative procedures that were shown to possess adequate psychometric properties.

Self-Report Instruments.   Asking a patient to complete a questionnaire covering a wide range of symptoms can be an extraordinarily efficient means of gathering clinically relevant information. Indeed, some therapists mail a packet of such questionnaires to patients prior to the first session in order to expedite the assessment process (Chambless, 1985). Some of these instruments, such as the Hopkins Symptom Checklist (Derogatis, 1977), are designed to sample from a wide variety of disorders (e.g., anxiety, interpersonal sensitivity, depression, psychoticism), while others are targeted at specific psychiatric conditions. Many such instruments now exist specifically for measuring depression (Beck, Ward, Mendelson, Mock, & Erbaugh, 1961), eating disorders (Garner & Garfinkel, 1979), assertiveness (Wolpe & Lazarus, 1966), anxiety (Spielberger, Gorsuch, & Lushene, 1970), marital satisfaction (Locke & Wallace, 1959; Spanier, 1976), and obsessions and compulsions (Rachman & Hodgson, 1980), to name a few.

The popularity of self-report instruments derives from the fact that they can be completed quickly and efficiently by the patient prior to, during, and after a course of therapy, in order to gauge treatment effectiveness. Moreover, in most cases, they provide a quick overview of specific problem areas within a broader domain that may warrant special consideration. One of the most widely employed self-report instruments, the Beck Depression Inventory (BDI), illustrates some of the advantages of this approach to assessment. The BDI consists of 21 items covering a variety of cognitive, somatic, and behavioral symptoms of depression, each rated by the patient on a 4-point scale. Completion of this scale generally takes no more than about 15 minutes. The scale provides an overall depression rating, but it also apprises the clinician of the specific cognitive and behavioral dimensions of depression for an individual patient (e.g., the patient may obtain a low score for suicidal ideation and a high score for loss of interest in other people). Thus, when used in conjunction with other procedures, self-report measures may help to guide the focus of treatment intervention. Several studies have shown that the BDI possesses adequate psychometric properties in terms of test–retest reliability, correlation with other measures of depression, and sensitivity to change in level of depression as a function of treatment (Beck, 1972).

Therapist Rating Scales. In addition to self-report measures, therapist rating scales have recently attracted widespread interest. These instruments contain many of the advantages of self-report scales (e.g., cost-effectiveness, documented psychometric properties), but the information is acquired during a semistructured clinical interview rather than from paper-and-pencil tests. As with self-report measures, some of these scales are designed to sample from a broad range of psychopathology, such as the Brief Psychiatric Rating Scale (Overall & Gorham, 1962), while others provide a detailed analysis of a particular syndrome, such as the Hamilton Rating Scale for Depression (Hamilton, 1960). The Hamilton rating scale consists of 24 items covering a range of cognitive, behavioral, and somatic symptoms of depression each rated on a 4-point scale. The Brief Psychiatric Rating Scale is similar in structure, consisting of 18 items that address various aspects of thought disorder, hostility, anxiety–depression, and blunting. With both of these scales, the therapist begins with a specific category (e.g., somatic concern) and prompts the patient with a broad introductory question (e.g., "How has your physical health been lately?"). More detailed inquiries follow until the therapist has enough information to rate the severity of that symptom category. Because the completion of these scales is based on information obtained during an interview, they permit some degree of flexibility on the part of the therapist while they retain enough structure in the final rating system to achieve reliable evaluations.

Structured Interviews. Because DSM III and DSM-III-R diagnosis has become almost a prerequisite for the conduct of clinical outcome research, reliable methods for reaching a diagnostic decision have appeared on the scene. With earlier versions of the DSM, clinicians tended to conduct interviews in idiosyncratic ways, greatly contributing to the unreliability of psychiatric diagnosis. To combat this problem, several structured interviews were developed. These interviews consist of a series of detailed questions, each addressing some aspect of the DSM-III-R nosology. For a given diagnostic category, a structured interview would usually recommend a few broad questions (e.g., "Have you been sad or depressed lately?") and then suggest a series of more detailed inquiries to follow up a positive response. When the interview is completed, the patient's responses can be used to establish a diagnosis according to relatively clear rules and guidelines. Two of the more commonly employed structured interviews are the Schedule for the Assessment of Depression and Schizophrenia (SADS: Endicott & Spitzer, 1978) and the Diagnostic Interview Schedule (DIS: Robins, Helzer, Croughan, & Ratcliff, 1981). The psychometric properties of both of these interviews have been well-established (Endicott & Spitzer, 1978; Robins et al., 1981).

Several diagnostic interviews aimed at specific disorders or types of disorder have been developed in recent years. For example, the Anxiety Disorders Interview Schedule (DiNardo, O'Brien, Barlow, Waddel, & Blanchard, 1983) is an especially comprehensive and detailed interview designed to facilitate reliable diagnoses of DSM-III-R anxiety disorders. Similarly, a Structured Interview for DSM-III Personality Disorders (Stangl, Pfohl, Zimmerman, Bowers, & Corenthal, 1985) has been developed to increase the reliability of diagnosis of personality disorders, an area where diagnostic unreliability is especially problematic.

Summary of Assessment

As this brief review illustrates, the full range of assessment devices available to the clinician today is extensive. While the options can be bewildering, an advantage is that multiple measures can now be employed to obtain a more accurate and comprehensive picture of a patient's functioning. As described in the next section, the recent growth in the number and variety of behavioral assessment techniques has been paralleled by a corresponding increase in the range of therapeutic options available within the field of behavior therapy.

THERAPY

In spite of its ever-broadening scope, a number of important features continue to set behavior therapy apart from other, more traditional approaches to psychotherapy. First, the emphasis in behavior therapy is almost invariably placed upon changing *current* thoughts, feelings, or behavior. With a depressed patient, for example, the intervention might involve altering dysfunctional thoughts, changing the frequency of unrewarding activities, or learning more effective social skills. In each case, the object of change is some measurable facet of current functioning and not an unconscious fantasy or unresolved conflict stemming from traumatic events in childhood.

Second, most behavioral interventions require active participation on the part of the patient. In contrast to the passive posture patients often assume in verbal psychotherapies, behavior therapists almost always require patients to complete homework assignments between sessions. When teaching a patient new social skills, for example, a homework assignment might involve greeting a specified number of people and initiating a brief conversation with each of them prior to the next session. More traditional forms of psychotherapy often assume that consulting-room successes will automatically transfer to the patient's natural environment. This optimism is not shared in the behavioral literature; homework assignments designed to effect generalization are now extremely widespread (Shelton & Levy, 1979).

A final common thread among the various forms of behavior therapy concerns empirical validation. No therapy is presumed to be efficacious by virtue of the complexity or eloquence of its underlying theoretical assumptions. Virtually every method is actually tested for its ability to effect meaningful change in a patient's life. In what follows, some of the more common and effective procedures are reviewed.

Conditioning Approaches

Operant Conditioning Methods. One of the oldest and most straightforward techniques for effecting behavior change is based on the view that the frequency of a response will increase if it is followed by a reinforcing event and will decrease if followed by punishment. This basic perspective obviously has many practical applications. Indeed, interventions based on operant conditioning principles have been used to treat child behavior problems at home and in the classroom, to train self-care skills in psychiatric, autistic, and mentally retarded patients (Lovaas, 1981), and to reduce the frequency of undesirable behaviors in adult outpatients.

This approach to behavior change is perhaps most clearly exemplified by the token economy program introduced by Ayllon and Azrin (1968) to improve the self-care behavior of chronic psychiatric patients. In this program, patients could earn reinforcers (plastic tokens) for engaging in such behaviors as getting up on time, making their beds, combing their hair, and so on. These plastic tokens could later be exchanged for a variety of special privileges, including listening to records, going to the movies, and visiting the canteen. Although some of these psychiatric patients were extremely regressed and resistant to all earlier intervention efforts, the token economy program induced impressive changes in behavior.

In the years since Ayllon and Azrin introduced the token economy, their basic approach has been applied in diverse settings throughout the world. Although these programs typically emphasize the use of positive reinforcement made contingent on appropriate behavior, a number of successful applications of punishment made contingent on inappropriate behavior can also be identified. For example, a widely used technique for reducing inappropriate behavior in children, such as temper tantrums, is time-out, in which the child is removed from all reinforcing activities for a brief period of time (Forehand & McMahon, 1981).

Along this vein, in an effort to modify dependence on cigarettes, researchers have applied punishment techniques such as electric shock, aversive imaginal scenes, and "rapid smoking" (Lichtenstein & Danaher, 1976). Obviously, the use of punishment procedures may raise ethical and legal concerns, such as when electric shock is used to diminish an autistic child's self-injurious behavior. For such reasons, practitioners usually seek to exhaust alternative methods before resorting to the use of punishment.

Classical Conditioning.   Whereas operant conditioning methods are useful for altering the frequency of a motoric response, methods derived from classical conditioning are generally more applicable to maladaptive emotional reactions, especially fear. These approaches are loosely based on the assumption that adverse emotional responses, such as anger and fear, are learned when some originally neutral object is incidentally associated with an aversive experience. Because of that chance association, the neutral object acquires the ability to elicit the emotional state.

The first technique developed to reverse this conditioning process was developed by Wolpe (1958), and is termed *systematic desensitization.* This method is still widely used today, and its effectiveness in the treatment of simple phobias is no longer seriously questioned. The procedure is based on Wolpe's theory of reciprocal inhibition, according to which pairing of the feared object with the opposite of fear (i.e., relaxation) will eventually reverse the original conditioning process. Systematic desensitization involves the preparation of a series (or hierarchy) of descriptive scenes that vary in their ability to elicit anxiety. The therapist reads each scene, beginning with those that provoke minimal anxiety, until the patient is able to imagine them and remain completely relaxed through the use of muscular relaxation. After one scene is mastered, the next scene in the hierarchy is presented, and then the next, and so on until what was originally the most fear-eliciting scene can be imagined in a state of complete relaxation.

More recent research has shown that relaxation during the presentation of a phobic stimulus is not critical to treatment success (Marks, 1975). Instead, prolonged exposure (either in imagination or in vivo) to the phobic stimulus is now considered to be the essential variable. Indeed, exposure therapy has now become a primary treatment for a variety of anxiety disorders, especially obsessive–compulsive disorder and agoraphobia. Based on their review of the relevant literature, for example, Mathews, Gelder, and Johnston (1981) argue that agoraphobic anxiety can be effectively treated by requiring the patient to remain in a phobic situation (e.g., a supermarket) for up to 2 hours several times a week. Of primary impor-

tance is that the patient remain in that situation at least until subjective anxiety has peaked and is beginning to decline. While this procedure is initially distressing to patients, Mathews et al. have found it to be successful in the majority of cases.

The use of exposure therapy has recently been expanded to other domains, most notably, to the treatment of bulimia. Leitenberg, Gross, Peterson, and Rosen (1984) argued that eating food elicits anxiety and prompts the act of vomiting for a bulimic patient in the same way that contacting a contaminated object elicits anxiety and provokes a hand washing ritual for an obsessive–compulsive patient. To reduce this anxiety and eliminate vomiting, they exposed bulimic patients to the presumed phobic stimulus for long periods by instructing them to eat formerly forbidden food and then not permitting them to vomit. Their initial findings have been quite promising, though additional work is needed to substantiate this approach to the treatment of bulimia.

Cognitive–Behavioral Approaches

Social Learning.   Bandura (1969, 1977a, 1977b) introduced and refined a cognitive–behavioral approach to learning, termed "social learning theory," that represented a departure from the relatively restricted views of operant and classical conditioning. According to this account, a fundamental mechanism of learning both adaptive and maladaptive responses is vicarious rather than direct. That is, a child can learn to fear an object not only by directly experiencing some traumatic event associated with it, but also by witnessing someone else experiencing distress in the presence of that object or by otherwise acquiring *information* about some source of danger. An implication for treatment is that fears can be overcome simply by having the patient observe someone interact harmlessly with the feared object. This procedure represents one instance of a general therapeutic strategy termed "modeling."

Originally, the technique of modeling was applied only to the treatment of fear-related behavior. In a study of snake phobics, for example, Bandura, Blanchard, and Ritter (1969) showed that subjects exposed to a confederate interacting with a snake overcame their fear to a greater extent than subjects exposed to systematic desensitization. Eventually, the success of the technique led to broader application, and it is now used to teach self-care skills to mentally retarded and autistic children, and more effective ways to resist social pressures to substance abusers (Perry & Furukawa, 1980). Modeling has also become a standard component of social skills training, a widely used procedure that is reviewed in a subsequent section.

More recently, Bandura (1977a) has introduced the concept of *self-efficacy* to account for why procedures as diverse as systematic desensitization, exposure therapy, and modeling can successfully treat anxiety disorders. *Self-efficacy* basically refers to "the conviction that one can successfully execute the behavior required to produce the outcomes" (Bandura 1977a, p. 193). Thus, to the extent that any form of treatment convinces the patient that he or she can perform behaviors previously thought to be impossible (e.g., touching a snake), treatment will be successful. Techniques that exert a stronger impact on self-efficacy, such as modeling, will be more successful than treatments that have less of an impact on self-efficacy, such as systematic desensitization (Bandura, Adams, & Beyer, 1977). The construct of self-efficacy has been shown to predict behavior of a wide range of patients, including those under treatment for agoraphobia, depression, smoking, and unassertiveness.

Cognitive Therapy. Another view of learning, closely related to social learning theory, emphasizes the importance of the way in which people think about and interpret their experiences. If two people are exposed to identical circumstances, such as missing out on a promotion, one may interpret it as failure and become depressed, while the other might view it as a challenge to be confronted and eventually mastered. To the extent that such cognitive reactions determine emotional well-being, therapeutic interventions might be profitably aimed at altering beliefs, attitudes, assumptions, and/or self-talk. Since the early 1970s, a variety of cognitive procedures have been introduced for the treatment of depression and anxiety (Beck, 1972; Beck & Emergy, 1985; Ellis, 1962; Meichenbaum, 1974). Indeed, cognitive methods are often employed as one component of a compre-

hensive treatment package for almost every psychiatric disorder.

The efficacy of the cognitive approach has been most firmly established in the treatment of depression, using techniques developed by Beck and his colleagues (e.g., Rush, Beck, Kovacs, & Hollon, 1977). Their approach to therapy basically consists of a collaborative inquiry into the validity of patients' false beliefs about themselves, the world at large, or the future. For example, a patient who maintains the belief that he or she is a worthless individual may be encouraged to offer evidence in support of that view and then asked to consider possible alternative interpretations. In addition, the patient might be assigned the task of empirically testing the validity of a depressive belief. Eventually, the weight of evidence should serve to undermine the depressive attitude.

Interpersonal and Family Approaches

Social Skills Training. As early as the 1960s, behavior therapists began to recognize the connection between effective social behavior and mental health. In its initial incarnation, behavioral intervention for maladaptive social functioning was termed "assertiveness training" (Wolpe & Lazarus, 1966). This technique basically consists of training the patient to more effectively express positive or negative feelings both verbally and nonverbally. In the 1970s, this procedure was broadened to address a wider range of social behavior (e.g., conversational skills, job interview skills, heterosocial skills). The central assumption underlying *social skills training* is that individuals who lack social competence either failed to learn the appropriate skills or lost them due to a prolonged period of disuse (Bellack & Hersen, 1979). Because social behavior is viewed as a skill similar to any other (e.g., driving a car), direct training in the use of appropriate skills is an obvious solution.

Social skills training proceeds in a relatively straightforward manner, similar to that of assertiveness training. The deficient responses are first identified and then targeted for treatment one at a time. For example, a particular male patient might experience problems initiating a conversation with new female acquaintances because he cannot think of anything to say, he avoids eye contact, and he speaks in a very quiet voice. For each deficient response, the patient is offered clear instructions on how to perform the skill, after which the therapist demonstrates (models) its use. Thus, for example, the therapist might describe the difference between an open-ended versus a close-ended question and then provide several examples of the former. When the patient appears to understand the skill, some relevant social scenarios can be worked out (e.g., encountering a co-worker at lunch) and enacted in the form of a role play. Typically, the patient practices the new skill through role play until some degree of proficiency is attained in the therapeutic setting. At that point, the patient is instructed to practice the skill with friends, family members, or even strangers between sessions to solidify treatment gains.

This basic approach has been applied successfully to a wide range of problems including shyness (Twentyman & McFall, 1975), social anxiety (Curran, 1977), and depression (Hersen, Bellack, Himmelhoch, & Thase, 1984). In addition, social skills training has been shown to be an effective strategy for dealing with the profound social deficits associated with schizophrenia (Bellack, Turner, Hersen, & Luber, 1984; Morrison & Bellack, 1985).

Behavioral Family Therapy. Behavior therapists were initially somewhat slow to take into consideration the psychological impact of a patient's family environment. In recent years, this situation has changed rather dramatically. With regard to schizophrenia, for example, researchers have begun to establish a conclusive link between the patient's family environment and the probability of psychotic relapse. More specifically, patients living with families characterized by the exchange of critical comments, hostility, and intrusiveness have been shown to have a much higher probability of relapse than patients from families characterized by a more supportive emotional climate (Vaughn & Leff, 1976).

Recognition of the importance of family factors in the treatment of schizophrenia has led to the development of behavioral family therapies. This approach attempts to improve family interactions by directly teaching the family members more effective communication and problem-solving skills. The treatment is, in many respects, similar to social skills training, in that it entails instruction, modeling, role play, and in vivo practice of newly acquired problem-solving skills (Falloon, Boyd, McGill, Razani, Moss, & Gilderman, 1982; Vaughn, Snyder, Jones, Freeman, & Falloon, 1984). In addition, a strong emphasis is placed on psychoeducation, in which the patients and their families are taught about the course of the disorder, its signs and symptoms, factors related to the prevention of relapse, and medication strategies.

An increased emphasis on family systems issues (e.g., Minuchin, 1974) is evident in other areas of behavior therapy as well. The behavioral literature on marital therapy, for example, has experienced a transformation from its initial focus on behavioral contracting, in which couples reciprocally reinforced mutually agreed upon behaviors, to an emphasis on changing dysfunctional patterns of communication within the marital system (Jacobson & Margolin, 1979). In the treatment of agoraphobia, the inclusion of the spouse to deal with family systems issues is becoming increasingly common (Arnow et al., 1985; Cerny, Barlow, Craske, & Himadi, 1987). For example, Cerny et al. (1987) have encouraged spouses of agoraphobics to participate in therapy to preclude any attempts at interference and to forestall any unplanned detrimental effects on the marriage. Whether these efforts will ultimately prove to be as useful as those described previously for schizophrenia remains to be seen, but initial results suggest that attention to family issues may result in more durable treatment gains.

Combined Interventions

Multiple Behavioral Approaches.   As more and more therapeutic techniques are shown to be effective, an emerging trend is the use of multiple intervention strategies to treat various aspects of a single disorder. For example, in an effort to maximize treatment gains in the treatment of agoraphobia, clinicians commonly use a combination of exposure therapy, cognitive restructuring, and assertiveness training (Chambless, 1985; Marchione, Michelson, Greenwald, & Dancu, 1987). Similarly, in the treatment of obsessive–compulsive disorder, researchers are beginning to experiment with a combination of exposure and cognitive therapies (Grayson, Foa, & Steketee, 1985). One of the newest trends in this regard, however, is the integration of pharmacoherapy and behavior therapy.

Drugs and Behavior Therapy.   Because behavior therapy and pharmacotherapy have both been shown to be effective for a variety of psychiatric conditions, the possibility of maximizing treatment gains by combining the two approaches has stirred considerable interest recently (Agras, 1987; Hersen, 1986). In one study of behavior-therapy–pharmacotherapy interactions, Mavissakalian and Michelson (1986) examined the relative effectiveness of imipramine, exposure therapy, or a combination of the two in the treatment of chronic agoraphobia. Although the results were not clear-cut, the authors concluded that exposure therapy in conjunction with the prudent administration of imipramine was most likely to result in meaningful therapeutic change. With regard to depression, a number of studies have compared groups receiving cognitive therapy, antidepressants, or a combination of the two (e.g., Murphy, Simons, Wetzel, & Lustman, 1984; Rush et al., 1977; Simons, Murphy, Levine, & Wetzel, 1986). Thus far, the results are somewhat surprising in that the two approaches are most often found to be nonadditive and noninteractive. Additional research will be needed to clarify why some researchers are able to demonstrate additive effects (e.g., DiMascio, Weissman, Prusoff, Neu, Zwilling, & Klerman, 1979), while most are not.

Perhaps the most promising joint application of pharmacotherapy and behavior therapy is in the prevention of relapse in schizophrenia. The use of behavioral family therapy to address the social aspects of the disorder and low-dose neuroleptics to address the biological aspects of the disorder is currently regarded as the most effective strategy in the posthospitalization management of schizophrenia (e.g., Falloon et al., 1982). It seems likely that in the years ahead, the trend toward the conjoint application of drugs and behavior therapy will expand to include most areas of psychiatric illness.

CONTINUING PROBLEMS

Although the accomplishments of behavior therapy have been considerable, three difficult challenges still remain. First, perhaps the most important issue concerns the generalizability of treatment successes across subjects and across settings. The empirical demonstration of therapeutic gains with a highly select patient population, for example, does not guarantee that the methods will be effective in a less homogeneous outpatient population. Similarly, as already indicated, therapeutic gains in the consulting room cannot be assumed to automatically generalize to the patient's natural social environment. Second, the durability of treatment gains has also emerged as a troubling problem across a variety of disorders. All too often, dramatic treatment successes have been found to be transient. Third, the related issue of meaningfulness of therapeutic change has begun to receive increased attention. Successfully training a patient in the use of assertive skills, for example, does not necessarily assure that meaningful changes (in depression, anxiety, etc.) will follow.

Generalizability

Much of the early work in behavior therapy employed high functioning, minimally impaired college students (e.g., public-speaking phobics). Although the success rate was very high, the extent to which the findings would generalize to typical patients seen in most clinical settings was unclear. In recent years, the emphasis within behavior therapy has clearly been placed on studying treatment effectiveness in clinical rather than analog populations. For example, Hersen et al. (1984) tested the effectiveness of social skills training in the treatment of depression using female outpatients diagnosed as having major depressive disorder. This approach represents a considerable advance over the use of high-functioning college students who receive a moderate score on a depression questionnaire. Although clinical gains are much harder to achieve, the results are of much more use to the practicing clinician whose cases never seem to fit the mold of the ideal, textbook behavior-therapy patient.

In spite of this constructive development, however, effecting change in a patient's life outside of the consulting room (i.e., generalization across situations) remains a difficult problem. As already indicated, behavior therapists routinely rely on homework assignments to ensure that therapeutic successes transfer to the patient's natural social environment. Nevertheless, if a patient is not entirely compliant with therapeutic instructions (a common problem), generalization can be exceeding difficult. However, the increased use of family therapy in the behavioral literature may represent a step in the right direction. Because the therapist cannot be present at all times, family members can be trained as behavior change agents. Agras (1987) reviewed another innovative strategy in this regard: the use of "computer therapists" that can deliver treatment in the setting in which the patient functions rather than in the consulting room. It is too early to judge the ultimate value of such strategies, but the quest for effective tools of generalization represents a valuable addition to the field of behavior therapy.

Durability

Along with an increased understanding of the difficulties of treating clinical populations has come the recognition that the durability of treatment cannot be taken for granted. Empirical reports of 1-, 2-, and even 8-year follow-ups are increasingly common (e.g., Burns, Thorpe, & Cavallaro, 1986). Unfortunately, the results of these follow-up investigations are sometimes disappointing. Even in the most effective treatments for depression, for example, a fairly large number of patients can be expected to relapse within a year of treatment.

Such findings have stimulated a search for more effective maintenance strategies. In an effort to prevent a relapse of depression following cognitive therapy, for example, Baker and Wilson (1985) employed occasional "booster" sessions; unfortunately, they were to no avail. Alternatively, Marlatt and Gordon (1985) proposed that enhancing the patient's level of social support may serve to maintain treatment gains across a variety of disorders (cf. Brownell, Marlatt, Lichtenstein, & Wilson, 1986). In agreement with this idea, Lichtenstein, Glasgow, and Abrams (1986) reported that perceived social support on the part of the patient was an important determinant of durable treatment success in smoking cessation programs. Unfortunately, efforts to directly improve social support for patients who lack it has been relatively unsuccessful. Clearly, maintenance of treatment gains remains an important area of research for the future.

Social Validity

A final issue to be considered concerns the social validation of therapeutic gains (Kazdin, 1977). This issue is perhaps best illustrated by recent developments in assertiveness training, where social validation is of particular importance. In this form of treatment, patients are taught to use specific social responses (e.g., refusing unreasonable requests) that, in the absence of validational research, are of unknown utility in the natural social environment. Simply demonstrating that one approach imparts assertive skills more effectively than another is not enough. The responses must be shown to be useful and acceptable (i.e., socially valid) in the patient's social milieu.

To this end, untrained normal subjects are often used to evaluate the acceptability of particular assertive responses portrayed on videotape (Dow, 1985; Frisch & Froberg, 1987). On a more general level, if any therapeutic procedure is shown to be statistically more effective than a placebo control, the question of whether that change improves the patient's life in any meaningful way remains to be addressed. Thus, a treatment that is shown to be effective in alleviating depression may not be potent enough to restore adequate social and occupational functioning.

In this regard, the issue of *clinical significance* has recently emerged as a long overlooked parameter for gauging treatment success. For example, Jacobson, Follette, and Revenstrof (1984) have proposed that, in order to make research results of more use to practicing clinicians, authors should report both the statistical significance of treatment gains, as well as whether patients were likely to move from the dysfunctional range to the functional range. They proposed some quantitative methods for making that decision, but, as yet, a single method to deal with the problem of clinical significance has not found widespread acceptance (e.g., Christensen & Mendoza, 1986; Wampold & Jenson, 1986). Attention to this issue will perhaps represent a frontier of behavior therapy for some time to come.

CONCLUSION

As the field of behavior therapy has evolved, many have struggled with the question of how to maintain some measure of unity and conceptual cohesion. As its boundaries expand, the unique identity of behavior therapy seems to fade away. Although a concise definition of the defining principles of behavior therapy becomes more difficult every year, the field seems to be evolving in a healthy direction. Perhaps of central importance in this regard are the research efforts aimed at directly testing the many models and theories from which the multitude of behavior therapies have been derived.

Rachman and his colleagues, for example, have attempted to evaluate Mowrer's (1950) venerable two-factor theory of anxiety and avoidance in clinically meaningful ways (Rachman, Craske, Tallman, & Solyom, 1986). Their work has suggested that, in contrast to earlier expectations, escape from a phobic situation does not necessarily impede therapeutic progress in the treatment of agoraphobia.

As indicated earlier, Leitenberg et al. (1984) studied the viability of an anxiety model of bulimia nervosa by requiring bulimic subjects to consume large amounts of food and by preventing them from vomiting afterward. Their results generally supported the anxiety–conditioning model and suggested that response prevention is a useful technique in the treatment of bulimia.

Eventually, research directed at specifically testing these and other theories will undoubtedly select the most viable among them. Until that time, the field will be marked by an ongoing wave of therapeutic innovations.

REFERENCES

Agras, W. S. (1987). So where do we go from here? *Behavior Therapy, 18*, 203–217.

Arnow, B. A., Taylor, C. B., Agras, W. S. & Telch, M. J. (1985). Enhancing agoraphobic treatment outcome by changing couple communication patterns. *Behavior Therapy, 16*, 452–467.

Ayllon, T., & Azrin, N. H. (1968). *The token economy: A motivational system for therapy and rehabilitation.* New York: Appleton-Century-Crofts.

Baker, A. L., & Wilson, P. H. (1985). Cognitive behavior therapy for depression: the effects of booster sessions on relapse. *Behavior Therapy, 16*, 335–344.

Bandura, A. (1969). *Principles of behavior modification.* New York: Holt, Rinehart and Winston.

Bandura, A. (1977a). Self-efficacy: Toward a unifying theory of behavior change. *Psychological Review, 84*, 191–215.

Bandura, A. (1977b). *Social learning theory.* Englewood Cliffs, NJ: Prentice-Hall.

Bandura, A., Adams, N. E., & Beyer, J. (1977). Cognitive processes mediating behavioral change. *Journal of Personality and Social Psychology, 35*, 125–139.

Bandura, A., Blanchard, E. B., & Ritter, B. (1969). Relative efficacy of desensitization and modeling approaches for inducing behavioral, affective, and attitudinal changes. *Journal of Personality and Social Psychology, 13*, 173–199.

Barlow, D. H., & Hersen, M. (1984). *Single case experimental designs: Strategies for studying behavior change* (2nd ed.). New York: Pergamon.

Beck, A. T. (1972). *Depression: Causes and treatment.* Philadelphia: University of Pennsylvania Press.

Beck, A. T., & Emery, G. (1985). *Anxiety disorders and phobias: A cognitive perspective.* New York: Basic.

Beck, A. T., Ward, C. H., Mendelson, M., Mock, J. E., & Erbaugh, J. K. (1961). An inventory for measuring depression. *Archives of General Psychiatry, 4*, 561–571.

Bellack, A. S. (1979). A critical appraisal of strategies for assessing social skills. *Behavioral Assessment, 1*, 157–176.

Bellack, A. S. (1983). Recurrent problems in the behavioral assessment of social skills. *Behavior Research and Therapy, 21*, 29–41.

Bellack, A. S., & Hersen, M. (Eds.) (1979). *Research and practice in social skills training.* New York: Plenum.

Bellack, A. S., & Hersen, M. (1988). Future directions of behavioral assessment. In A. S. Bellack & M. Hersen (Eds.), *Behavioral assessment: A practical handbook* (pp. 610–615). New York: Pergamon.

Bellack, A. S., Hersen, M., & Turner, S. M. (1978). Role play tests for assessing social skill: Are they valid? *Behavior Therapy, 9*, 448–461.

Bellack, A. S., Turner, S. M., Hersen, M., & Luber, R. F. (1984). An examination of the efficacy of social skills training for chronic schizophrenic patients. *Hospital and Community Psychiatry, 35*, 1023–1028.

Brownell, K. D., Marlatt, G. A., Lichtenstein, E., & Wilson, G. P. (1986). Understanding and preventing relapse. *American Psychologist, 41*, 765–782.

Burns, L. E., Thorpe, G. L., & Cavallaro, L. A. (1986). Agoraphobia 8 years after behavioral treatment: A follow-up study with interview, self-report, and behavioral data. *Behavior Therapy, 17*, 580–591.

Cerny, J. A., Barlow, D. H., Craske, M. G., & Himadi, W. (1987). Couples treatment of agoraphobia: A two-year follow-up. *Behavior Therapy, 18,* 401–415.

Chambless, D. L. (1985). Agoraphobia, In M. Hersen & A. S. Bellack (Eds.), *Handbook of clinical behavior therapy with adults* (pp. 49–87). New York: Plenum.

Christensen, L., & Mendoza, J. L. (1986). Toward a standard definition of clinically significant change. *Behavior Therapy, 17,* 305–308.

Cone, J. D. (1978). The behavioral assessment grid (BAG): A conceptual framework and a taxonomy. *Behavior Therapy, 9,* 882–888.

Cone, J. D. (1988). Psychometric considerations and the multiple models of behavioral assessment. In A. S. Bellack & M. Hersen (Eds.), *Behavioral assessment: A practical handbook* (pp. 42–66). New York: Pergamon.

Curran, J. P. (1977). Social skill training as an approach to the treatment of heterosexual social anxiety. *Psychological Bulletin, 84,* 140–157.

Derogatis, L. R. (1977). *SCL-90 administration, scoring and procedures manual-I.* Johns Hopkins University Press.

DiMascio, A., Weissman, M. M., Prusoff, B. A., Neu, C., Zwilling, M., & Klerman, G. L. (1979). Differential symptom reduction by drugs and psychotherapy in acute depression. *Archives of General Psychiatry, 36,* 1450–1456.

DiNardo, P. A., O'Brien, G. T., Barlow, D. H., Waddell, M. T., & Blanchard, E. B. (1983). Reliability of DSM-III anxiety disorder categories using a new structured interview. *Archives of General Psychiatry, 40,* 1070–1074.

Dow, M. (1985). Peer validation and idiographic analysis of social skill deficits. *Behavior Therapy, 16,* 76–86.

Eisler, R. M., Hersen, M., Miller, P. M., & Blanchard, E. B. (1975). Situational determinants of assertive behavior. *Journal of Consulting and Clinical Psychology, 43,* 330–340.

Eisler, R. M., Miller, P., & Hersen, M. (1973). Components of assertive behavior. *Journal of Clinical Psychology, 29,* 295–299.

Ellis, A. (1962). *Reason and emotion in psychotherapy.* New York: Lyle Stewart.

Endicott, J., & Spitzer, R. (1978). A diagnostic interview: The Schedule for Affective Disorders and Schizophrenia. *Archives of General Psychiatry, 35,* 837–844.

Eysenck, H. J. (1952). The effects of psychotherapy: An evaluation. *Journal of Consulting Psychology, 16,* 319–324.

Eysenck, H. J. (1965). The effects of psychotherapy. *International Journal of Psychiatry, 1,* 99–144.

Falloon, I. R. H., Boyd, J. L., McGill, C. W., Razani, J., Moss, H. B., & Gilderman, A. M. (1982). Family management in the prevention of exacerbations of schizophrenia: A controlled study. *New England Journal of Medicine, 306,* 1437–1440.

Forehand, R. L., & McMahon, R. J. (1981). *Helping the noncompliant child: A clinician's guide to parent training.* New York: Guilford.

Franks, C. M., & Barbrack, C. R. (1983). Behavior therapy with adults: An integrative perspective. In M. Hersen, A. E. Kazdin, & A. S. Bellack (Eds.), *The clinical psychology handbook* (pp. 507–524.) New York: Pergamon.

Frisch, M. B., & Froberg, W. (1987). Social validation of assertion strategies for handling aggressive criticism: Evidence for consistency across situations. *Behavior Therapy, 18,* 181–191.

Garner, D. M., & Garfinkel, P. E. (1979). The Eating Attitudes Test: An index of the symptoms of anorexia nervosa. *Psychological Medicine, 9,* 273–279.

Grayson, J. B., Foa, E. B., & Steketee, G. (1985). Obsessive–compulsive disorder. In M. Hersen & A. S. Bellack (Eds.), *Handbook of clinical behavior therapy with adults* (pp. 133–162). New York: Plenum.

Hamilton, M. (1960). A rating scale for depression. *Journal of Neurology, Neurosurgery, and Psychiatry, 23,* 56–61.

Hartmann, D. P., Roper, B. L., & Bradford, D. C. (1979). Some relationships between behavioral and traditional assessment. *Journal of Behavioral Assessment, 1,* 3–19.

Heimberg, R. G., Madsen, C. H., Montgomery, D., & McNabb, C. E. (1980). Behavioral treatments for heterosocial problems: Effects on daily self-monitored and role-played interactions. *Behavior Modification, 4,* 147–172.

Hersen, M. (Ed.) (1986). *Pharmacological and behavioral treatment: An integrative approach.* New York: Wiley.

Hersen, M., Bellack, A. S., Himmelhoch, J. M., & Thase, M. E. (1984). Effects of social skills training, amitriptyline, and psychotherapy in unipolar depressed women. *Behavior Therapy, 15,* 21–40.

Hooley, J. (1985). Expressed emotion: A review of the critical literature. *Clinical Psychology Review, 5,* 119–140.

Jacobson, N. S., Follette, W. C., & Revenstorf, D.

(1984). Psychotherapy outcome research: Methods for reporting variability and evaluating clinical significance. *Behavior Therapy, 15,* 336–352.

Jacobson, N. S., & Margolin, G. (1979). *Marital therapy: Treatment strategies based on social learning and behavior exchange principles.* New York: Bruner/Mazel.

Kazdin, A. E. (1977). Assessing the clinical or applied importance of behavior change through social validation. *Behavior Modificiation, 1,* 427–451.

Kazdin, A. E. (1978). *History of behavior modification.* Baltimore: University Park Press.

Krasner, L. (1984). Behavior therapy. In R. J. Corsini (Ed.), *Encyclopedia of psychology* (Vol. 1, pp. 137–138). New York: Wiley.

Leitenberg, H., Gross, J., Peterson, J., & Rosen, S. C. (1984). Analysis of an anxiety model and the process of change during exposure plus response prevention treatment of bulimia nervosa. *Behavior Therapy, 15,* 3–20.

Levis, D. J. (1969). The phobic test apparatus: An objective measure of human avoidance behavior to small animals. *Behavior Research and Therapy, 7,* 309–315.

Lichtenstein, E., & Danaher, B. G. (1976). Modification of smoking behavior: A critical analysis of theory, research, and practice. In M. Hersen, R. M. Eisler, & P. M. Miller (Eds.), *Progress in behavior modification* (Vol. 3, pp. 79–132.) New York: Academic Press.

Lichtenstein, E., Glasgow, R. E., & Abrams, D. A. (1986). Social support in smoking cessation: In search of effective interventions. *Behavior Therapy, 17,* 607–619.

Locke, H. J., & Wallace, K. M. (1959). Short-term marital adjustment and prediction tests: Their reliability and validity. *Journal of Marriage and Family Living, 21,* 251–255.

Lovaas, O. I. (1981). *Teaching developmentally disabled children: The me book.* Baltimore, MD: University Park Press.

Marchione, K. E., Michelson, L., Greenwald, M., & Dancu, C. (1987). Cognitive behavioral treatment of agoraphobia. *Behaviour Research and Therapy, 25,* 319–328.

Marks, I. M. (1975). Behavioural treatments of phobic and obsessive–compulsive disorders: A critical appraisal. In M. Hersen, R. M. Eisler, & P. M. Miller (Eds.), *Progress in behavior modification* (Vol. 1, pp. 66–158). New York: Academic Press.

Marlatt, G. A., & Gordon, J. R. (Eds.) (1985). *Relapse prevention: Maintenance strategies in addictive behavior change.* New York: Guilford.

Mathews, A. M., Gelder, M. G., & Johnston, D. W. (1981). *Agoraphobia: Nature and treatment.* New York: Guilford.

Mavissakalian, M., & Michelson, L. (1986). Agoraphobia: Relative and combined effectiveness of therapist-assisted in vivo exposure and Imipramine. *Journal of Clinical Psychiatry, 47,* 117–122.

Meichenbaum, D. H. (1974). *Cognitive behavior modification.* Morristown, NJ: General Learning Press.

Michelson, L., Mavissakalian, M., & Marchione, K. (1985). Cognitive–behavioral treatment of agoraphobia: Clinical, behavioral, and psychophysiological outcome. *Journal of Consulting and Clinical Psychology, 53,* 913–925.

Minuchin, S. (1974). *Families and family therapy.* Cambridge, MA: Harvard University Press.

Morrison, R. L., & Bellack. A. S. (1985). Social skills training. In A. S. Bellack (Ed.), *Schizophrenia: Treatment, management, and rehabilitation* (pp. 247–279). Orlando, FL: Grune & Stratton.

Mowrer, O. H. (1950). *Learning theory and personality dynamics.* New York: Arnold Press.

Murphy, G. E., Simons, A. D., Wetzel, R. D., & Lustman, P. J. (1984). Cognitive therapy and pharmacotherapy: Singly and together in the treatment of depression. *Archives of General Psychiatry, 41,* 33–41.

Overall, J. E., & Gorham, D. R. (1962). The Brief Psychiatric Rating Scale. *Psychological Reports, 10,* 799–812.

Patterson, G. R., Ray, R. S., Shaw, D. A., & Cobb, J. A. (1969). *Manual for coding of interactions* (1969 rev.). New York: Microfiche.

Perry, M. A., & Furukawa (1980). Modeling methods. In F. H. Kanfer & A. P. Goldstein (Eds.), *Helping people change* (2nd ed., pp. 131–171). New York: Pergamon.

Rachman, S., Craske, M., Tallman, K., & Solyom, C. (1986). Does escape behavior strengthen agoraphobic avoidance? A replication. *Behavior Therapy, 17,* 366–384.

Rachman, S., & Hodgson, R. (1980). *Obsessions and compulsions.* Englewood Cliffs, NJ: Prentice-Hall.

Robins, L. N., Helzer, J. E., Croughan, J., & Ratcliff, K. S. (1981). National Institute of Mental Health Diagnostic Interview Schedule: Its history, characteristics, and validity. *Archives of General Psychiatry, 38,* 381–389.

Rush, A. J., Beck, A. T., Kovacs, M., & Hollon, S. D. (1977). Comparative efficacy of cognitive therapy and pharmacotherapy in the treatment of outpatient depressives. *Cognitive Therapy and Research, 1,* 17–37.

Shelton, J. L., & Levy, R. (1979). Instigation therapy: A survey of the reported use of assigned homework activities in contemporary behavior therapy literature. *Journal of Applied Behavior Analysis, 12,* 324.

Simons, A. D., Murphy, G. E., Levine, J. L., & Wetzel, R. D. (1986). Cognitive therapy and pharmacotherapy for depression: Sustained improvement over one year. *Archives of General Psychiatry, 43,* 43–48.

Spanier, G. B. (1976). Measuring dyadic adjustment: New scales for assessing the quality of marriage and similar dyads. *Journal of Marriage and the Family, 38,* 15–28.

Spielberger, C., Gorsuch, A., & Lushene, R. (1970). *The State–Trait Anxiety Inventory.* Palo Alto, CA: Consulting Psychologists Press.

Stangl, D., Pfohl, B., Zimmerman, M., Bowers, W., & Corenthal, C. (1985). A structured interview for the DSM-III personality disorders. *Archives of General Psychiatry, 42,* 591–596.

St. Lawrence, J. S. (1987). Assessment of assertion. In M. Hersen, R. M. Eisler, & P. M. Miller (Eds.), *Progress in behavior modification* (Vol. 1, pp. 152–190). Newbury Park, CA: Sage.

Stunkard, A. J. (1982). Obesity. In A. S. Bellack, M. Hersen, & A. E. Kazdin (Eds.), *International handbook of behavior modification and therapy* (pp. 535–573). New York: Plenum.

Twentyman, C. T., & McFall, R. M. (1975). Behavioral training of social skills in shy males. *Journal of Consulting and Clinical Psychology, 43,* 384–395.

Vaughn, C. E., & Leff, J. P. (1976). The influence of family and social factors on the course of psychiatric illness: A comparison of schizophrenic and depressed neurotic patients. *British Journal of Psychiatry, 129,* 125–137.

Vaughn, C. E., Snyder, K. S., Jones, S., Freeman, W. B., & Falloon, I. R. H. (1984). Family factors in schizophrenic relapse: Replication in California of British research on expressed emotion. *Archives of General Psychiatry, 41,* 1169–1177.

Wampold, B. E., & Jenson, W. R. (1986). Clinical significance revisited. *Behavior Therapy, 17,* 302–305.

Wolpe, J. (1958). *Psychotherapy by reciprocal inhibition.* Stanford, CA: Stanford University Press.

Wolpe, J., & Lazarus, A. A. (1966). *Behavior therapy techniques.* New York: Pergamon.

CHAPTER 3

Pharmacotherapy

WILLIAM H. WILSON AND GEORGE M. SIMPSON

INTRODUCTION

Psychopharmacology is a young science. Since time immemorial, people have used chemical substances to alter the way they think and feel. However, it has only been since the early 1950s that specific drugs have been used to treat specific mental illnesses (Ayd & Blackwell, 1970). The discovery that chlorpromazine could rapidly diminish the symptoms of schizophrenia was truly one of the major advances made by 20th century medicine. This finding, coupled with the discovery of lithium's efficacy in bipolar affective disorder (Cade, 1949), spurred research efforts to carefully describe and categorize the many separate entities that together comprise psychiatric disorder. The result has been a great refinement in systems of psychiatric diagnosis. This refinement has, in turn, allowed increased sophistication in developing specific treatment for specific disorders (Baldessarini, 1980; Carroll, Miller, Ross, & Simpson, 1980). The future promises even greater specificity as powerful new technologies such as positron emission tomography (PET) and magnetic resonance imaging (MRI) are used to further an understanding of the function of the central nervous system in mental illness.

There are abundant data supporting the therapeutic efficacy of various psychoactive drugs: neuroleptics for schizophrenia, heterocyclic and monoamine oxidase inhibitors (MAOI) antidepressants for depression, lithium for bipolar affective disorder, and anxiolytics for anxiety disorders. The indications for prescribing specific psychotropic agents are, in general, tied to current diagnostic criteria. For example, the diagnostic criteria for major affective disorder in the *Diagnostic and Statistical Manual* (3rd ed., rev.— DSM-III-R: American Psychiatric Association, 1987) not only describe a psychiatric syndrome but also define a group of patients who are quite likely to respond to heterocyclic antidepressants. This response to medications is independent of social and psychological precipitants or environmental reasons to be depressed, such as being passed over for a job promotion or losing a loved one. Thus, specific treatment can be based on a specific symptom cluster or diagnosis, which both illustrates the use of the right drug for the right patient and underscores the necessity of careful diagnosis as a guide to the use of medication and the prediction of treatment response.

With the use of specific drugs to treat specific disorders and an increased attention to underlying physiologic mechanisms, the use of drugs in psychiatry has come to resemble closely the use of drugs in other areas of medicine. The clinical use of psychopharmacological agents has followed a pattern all too typical of the way that medical advances are implemented. Initial optimism following introduction of chlorpromazine led to a period of overuse and an underestimation of the deleterious side effects of psychopharmacological agents. This has been followed by a more gradual delineation of the specific indications for the use of the various drugs and a more mature appreciation of the ways in which the drugs should be prescribed, monitored, and integrated with psychosocial treatment to achieve maximum therapeutic benefits.

In this chapter, we first review the general principles underlying the use of medications. We then briefly review the use of medications for the major diagnostic categories of mental illness.

GENERAL PRINCIPLES OF PSYCHOPHARMACOLOGY

Diagnosis

The importance of accurate diagnosis cannot be overly emphasized. A wide range of medical illnesses may be accompanied by psychological and behavioral symptoms (Jefferson & Marshall, 1981). It is essential that these disorders be properly diagnosed so that proper treatment can be administered. As noted in the preceding section, it is equally important that psychiatric disorders be carefully delineated from one another because drugs that are effective for one disorder may well be ineffective or harmful to a patient with another disorder.

Neuromechanisms

To understand the action of most psychopharmacological agents, one must be familiar with neurotransmitters and receptors (Axelrod, 1976; Cooper, Bloom, & Roth, 1982). Nerve cells communicate with each other at highly specialized junctions known as *synapses*. An electrical impulse traveling down the axon of the nerve cell causes the release of messenger molecules, known as *neurotransmitters*, into the synapse. The neurotransmitter molecules diffuse across the synaptic cleft, where they temporarily adhere to specific structures, known as *receptors*, on the membrane of another nerve cell. When neurotransmitters bind to receptors, the resting electrical charge of the neuron is altered, and the result is either the excitation or the inhibition of electrical discharge.

The balance of activity of neurotransmitters and receptors is central to the theories of the mode of action of psychotropic agents (Axelrod, 1976). Systems of neurotransmitters and their receptors have complex interconnections and regulatory mechanisms, so that altering one factor may result in compensatory adjustments in other components of the system. These adjustments are often impor-

tant in the action of psychotropic drugs. For example, the heterocyclic antidepressants increase the concentration of certain neurotransmitters (norepinephrine and serontonin), but it is probably the decreasing sensitivity of receptors ("down regulation" that occurs in response to increased levels of these neurotransmitters) that accounts for the therapeutic effects. Similarly, most antipsychotic drugs work by blocking receptors to the neurotransmitter dopamine. Receptor blockade occurs almost immediately after administration of the drug. The therapeutic response, however, occurs over a period of weeks, which parallels the time course of compensatory changes (Bunney, 1984).

A number of other neurotransmitters have been identified. Benzodiazepine antianxiety drugs increase the activity of gamma-aminobutyric acid (GABA) through a complex action involving the benzodiazepine receptor. Some drugs used to treat side effects of antipsychotic medicine function by blocking acetylcholine (ACH). The importance of numerous neurotransmitters remains to be determined.

Pharmacokinetics

Pharmacokinetics refers to the absorption, distribution, metabolism, and excretion of drugs. These factors determine the availability of a drug at its intended site of action. The study of pharmacokinetics has been advanced by recent techniques that allowed drugs to be measured in body fluids when present in ng/ml levels (i.e., 1 billionth of a gram per milliliter or less).

Absorption refers to the process by which a drug is made available for distribution in the body fluids. Absorption is affected by gastrointestinal pH and motility, and by the drug's solubility. It is important to know the characteristics of individual agents because they vary. When taken orally, diazepam (Valium®) is readily absorbed from the gastrointestinal (GI) tract and thus has a rapid onset of therapeutic effects. The onset of action of a similar drug, oxazepam (Serax®), is much slower because it is absorbed much more slowly by the GI tract. Parenteral administration usually achieves higher plasma levels than oral administration, but again, there is variability among the drugs. For example, chlordiazepoxide (Librium®) is readily absorbed through the GI tract but is poorly absorbed when given intramuscularly. Lorazepam (Ativan®), a drug very similar to chlordiazepoxide, is absorbed well intramuscularly, and thus, it would be a better choice when parenteral administration is indicated.

Distribution refers to the process by which a drug travels from the site of absorption to the various tissues throughout the body, including the drug's site of action. Many drugs do not readily transfer from the blood to the brain, giving rise to the concept of a blood–brain barrier. Distribution is also affected by the degree to which the drug binds to proteins in the plasma. The portion of a drug that is protein bound continues to circulate in the blood rather than entering other tissues, such as the central nervous system. The protein-bound drug is, therefore, inactive until it becomes unbound or free. Often as much as 95% of the drug in plasma is protein bound. Variations in protein binding among individuals are important factors in determining drug dose. For example, the elderly have fewer protein-binding sites than younger patients, and they therefore require lower doses of psychotropic drugs (Larny, 1980; Salzman, 1982).

The metabolism or breakdown of psychotropic agents occurs mainly in the liver and involves several enzyme systems. Drugs administered orally pass through the liver before they reach the systemic circulation. The breakdown during this initial passage through the liver (first-pass effect) can be significant for some drugs. For example, up to 80% of the dose may be converted to a combination of active or inactive metabolites. Variation in hepatic metabolism may account for individuals needing different dosages to reach similar blood levels.

The most important route of excretion for psychotropic drugs is the kidney. Drugs are excreted at varying rates. This rate is expressed as the *elimination half-life*—that is, the time required for half of the drug to be excreted from the body. If a drug is given on a frequent, regular schedule, a balance occurs between absorption and excretion so that no further change in the tissue drug level takes place. This equilibrium is reached in approximately 5 half-lives after starting the drug. Because of this, the elimination half-life has a bearing on how often drugs need to be administered and at what dose. For example, diazepam (Valium®) has a half-life in many patients of about 24 hours. A patient taking Valium® every day would have increasing blood levels for nearly a week. The injectable depot form of the antipsychotic drug fluphenazine decanoate (Prolixin®) has a much longer half-life. If the same dose of fluphenazine decanoate is administered every 2 weeks, plasma levels will continue to rise for 4 to 6 months. Thus, a patient might tolerate a given dose at the beginning of treatment with no side effects, but 4 months later have considerable side effects. The dose has not been changed, but the concentration in the brain has continued to rise. Some drugs have much shorter half-lives and must be given more frequently. Alprazolam, an antianxiety drug, must be given several times each day to maintain plasma levels.

For drugs such as lithium and carbamazepine, maintenance of plasma levels within a given range is essential to ensure efficacy while avoiding the serious toxicity that occurs at only slightly higher levels. To use measured plasma levels effectively, it is necessary to know at what point in the absorption and elimination cycle the levels were obtained. For example, to be meaningfully compared with reference values, lithium levels must be drawn approximately 12 hours after the last lithium dose. A measurement taken 1 hour after lithium administration would be spuriously high, and a level taken 16 hours later would be spuriously low.

Dose:Response Relationships

Obviously, in order for a drug to be effective, it must be given at the correct dosage. For some drugs, the efficacy increases as the dose is raised. For other drugs, however, efficacy either plateaus or, in fact, falls off after the dose is increased beyond a certain range (see Figure 3.1). The antianxiety drug diazepam (Valium®) is an example of a drug that has a linear dose:response relationship (i.e., the greater the dose, the greater the therapeutic effect). If a low dose of diazepam inhibits anxiety, a higher dose would lead to even less anxiety. Higher doses would also, however, lead to sedation and sleep.

Nortriptyline, a heterocyclic antidepressant, is

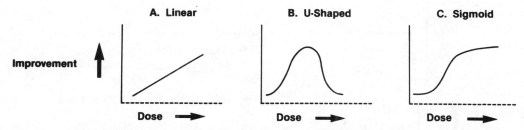

Figure 3.1. Dose:response relationships. Each drug has a characteristic dose:response relationship. (A) shows a linear relationship: the higher the dose, the more therapeutic the effect. Dose may be limited by side effects, which may also increase with the dose. (B) illustrates a "U-shaped" relationship: doses above and below an optimal range are ineffective. (C) shows a sigmoid relationship. Too low a dose is ineffective; raising the dose above a certain point does not increase efficacy.

an example of a drug that has a U-shaped dose:response curve; that is, efficacy increases with dose to a certain level and then falls off as the dose is increased further. The therapeutic range appears to be between 50 and 150 ng per ml, with decreased efficacy occurring on either side of this range (Simpson, Pi, & White, 1983).

The antipsychotic drugs (for example, haloperidol and chlorpromazine), have a sigmoid dose:response curve. There is little efficacy below a certain point. The efficacy then rises as the dose is increased to a certain point, after which, no further benefit accrues from further increases in dose. For most patients, maximum therapeutic gain is achieved with the administration of 400 to 800 mg of chlorpromazine per day or its equivalent. Increasing the dosage above this level results only in an increase in side effects, with no further therapeutic gains. Knowledge of dose:response characteristics of each drug are obviously important in determining the best dose of a drug for an individual patient. These relationships are too often neglected, and patients fail to respond to an effective medicine because they are receiving either too much or too little of it.

Time Course of Response

After defining the dosage, it is important to consider how long a drug must be given to achieve a therapeutic response. The time course of action among drugs is specific for each individual agent (see Figure 3.2). The antianxiety drug lorazepam (Ativan®) is one that works almost immediately. The drug is readily absorbed in the GI tract, is distributed to the brain, and has immediate effects to reduce anxiety.

These immediate effects are identical to its long-term antianxiety properties if it is taken continuously. The antidepressant drugs (e.g., imipramine, amitriptyline) have a very different time course. Typically, patients begin to show some signs of improvement after a week to 10 days of continuously taking the medication. However, true therapeutic response is not achieved until the drug has been taken continuously for 3 to 6 weeks. Thus, the implications are very different if a patient does not respond to lorazepam in the first day than if the patient does not respond to imipramine in the first day. Antipsychotic drugs such as haloperidol and chlorpromazine also require 3 to 6 weeks to reach maximum therapeutic benefit. Just as therapeutic efficacy is reduced if the proper dose is not used, efficacy is reduced if sufficient time is not allowed for a medication to be effective. Conversely, ineffective treatment should not be continued unduly.

Rational Therapeutics

A thorough grounding in the preceding basic principles allows a rational approach to pharmacotherapy that affords patients the greatest opportunity for relief of symptoms while minimizing the adverse effects. A specific drug (or combination of drugs) is used to treat specific aspects of a specific disorder. The drug is administered at a therapeutic dose for a sufficient period of time. Beneficial and adverse effects are carefully monitored. Adjustments are made as required to maximize therapeutic effects while minimizing discomfort and risk. Effective treatments are continued as long as they remain appropriate, whereas ineffective treatments are discontinued. Medication treatment is

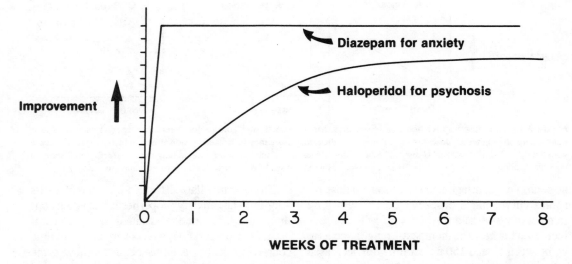

Figure 3.2.   Time course of response. Each drug has a characteristic time course of action that must be considered. Diazepam has a rapid onset of therapeutic activity after being ingested by patients with anxiety. The therapeutic effects of haloperidol in psychosis due to schizophrenia begin to appear within the first week, but full effects may not be evident for 6 to 8 weeks.

given in the context of a doctor–patient relationship that is recognized as an important element of the treatment plan.

This rational approach may seem self-evident and merely commonsensical, but it stands in sharp contrast to the irrational approach that is often reflected in the treatment records of psychiatric patients. All too commonly, patients are inadequately diagnosed and then receive too much or too little of idiosyncratically chosen combinations of psychotropic agents. Treatment is often judged to be ineffective and medication discontinued before sufficient time has passed for the drugs to have had therapeutic effects. Similarly, ineffective treatment is often continued despite the presence of clearly adverse side effects. Sometimes, combinations of similar drugs are given, based on the unfounded notion that the combination is more effective than the single agent. Such irrational and irresponsible practice has often been referred to by the term *polypharmacy*. The term is somewhat misleading, in that certain carefully chosen combinations of psychotropics are more effective than single agents in specific disorders; for example, antidepressants and antipsychotics are used together to treat psychotic depression. The term is, however, a useful reminder that each medication should be carefully selected because of a specific indication.

PHARMACOTHERAPY OF THE MAJOR CLASSES OF MENTAL DISORDERS

Psychotic Disorders

Introduction of antipsychotic medication in the 1950s revolutionized the treatment of psychoses in general and of schizophrenia in particular (see Table 3.1) (Davis, 1980; Simpson & May, 1984). The antipsychotic drugs continue to be the only treatment proven effective for schizophrenia, other than ECT. The reduction in symptoms and

TABLE 3.1.   Common Antipsychotic Agents[a]

Chemical name	Trade name	Equivalent dose (mg)
Chlorpromazine	Thorazine®	100
Thioridazine	Mellaril®	100
Mesoridazine	Serentil®	50
Loxapine	Loxitane®	15
Molindone	Moban®	10
Perphenazine	Trilafon®	10
Thiothixene	Navane®	5
Trifluoperazine	Stelazine®	5
Fluphenazine	Prolixin®[b]	2
Haloperidol	Haldol®[b]	2

[a]*All* of these drugs can induce tardive dyskinesia.
[b]Available long-acting injectable forms: Prolixin decanoate, Haldol decanoate.

improved social functioning afforded by these medications has allowed many chronically psychotic individuals to live in community settings rather than spending their lives within hospitals. These drugs are extremely effective in treating psychotic episodes of schizophrenia and as prophylaxis for further episodes. The antipsychotic drugs are not without problems, however, and must be used wisely to maximize therapeutic effects and minimize the significant side effects that these drugs induce (Simpson, Pi, & Sramek, 1981). Furthermore, the drugs are not a substitute for comprehensive psychosocial treatment programs, as most psychotic patients continue to have difficulty negotiating everyday life, even when adequately treated pharmacologically (Test & Stein, 1980).

The term *psychosis* refers to a profound loss in the ability to recognize everyday reality. In particular, it refers to the presence of faulty perceptions (*hallucinations*) and false, unshakable beliefs (*delusions*). Patients often have marked disorganization of their thoughts and speech (*loose associations, derailment*). Psychosis can be due to a great many different processes, all of which result in central nervous system dysfunction. Treatment depends on etiology. Recognized organic conditions that result in psychosis include intoxications, structural brain lesions (such as tumors), and metabolic abnormalities. Definitive treatment for these disorders is directed toward the organic pathology, while antipsychotic agents may be used to reduce the severity of the psychiatric symptoms.

Psychosis is a feature of a number of psychiatric disorders and treatment differs among these. For example, psychosis accompanying major depression in bipolar affective disorder is treated differently from the psychosis of schizophrenia. Yet another approach is indicated for brief reactive psychosis or for a patient with borderline personality disorder.

Antipsychotic medication is the mainstay of treatment for schizophrenia, both during acute exacerbations of psychosis and between episodes, for maintenance and prophylaxis. This is a severe, chronic psychotic disorder that affects about 1% of the population. Onset usually occurs in the early adult years. Diagnosis is based on the presence of chronic psychotic symptoms that cannot be attributed to recognizable organic causes or other major psychiatric disorders. Some psychosocial approaches have been shown to benefit schizophrenic patients, provided they are also receiving proper medication, but antipsychotic drugs are the only proven, primary treatment for this illness.

The antipsychotic drugs are members of several different chemical classes (phenothiazine, thioxanthene, dibenzoxazepine, dihydroindoline, butyrophenone). When given at equivalent doses, these drugs are most likely therapeutically equivalent. They differ, however, in the side effects that they induce. The therapeutic effects of all of these agents are probably due to blockade of dopamine receptors in the areas of the brain known as the mesolimbic and mesocortical tracts. Although the therapeutic activity of these agents is correlated with their ability to block dopamine receptors, the time course of action indicates that neurochemical events occurring subsequent to dopaminergic blockade are those accounting for the activity. Dopamine receptors are blocked almost immediately after the drugs are administered; however, therapeutic effects are seen over a period of about 6 weeks. Side effects are due to blockade of dopamine and other neurotransmitters elsewhere in the brain. Acute motor system side effects, such as parkinsonism (muscle stiffness, tremor, decreased spontaneous movement) and acute dystonias, are due to dopaminergic blockade in the basal ganglia. Approximately 20% of patients taking antipsychotics for extended periods of time develop abnormal movements, which may *not* disappear when the drug is discontinued. These movements, known as *tardive dyskinesia* (Jeste & Wyatt, 1982), are probably due to increased sensitivity of dopamine receptors in the basal ganglia, as a result of long-term dopaminergic blockade. Some researchers speculate that patients may develop psychiatric symptoms from similar mechanisms occurring in mesolimbic and mesocortical tracts (Chouinard & Jones, 1980). Blockade of acetylcholine receptors results in dry mouth, constipation, blurry vision, and other anticholinergic effects. Blockade of other receptors leads to sedation and orthostatic hypotension. The high-potency antipsychotic drugs, such as haloperidol, produce little in the way of anticholinergic effects and sedation, but they are very likely to cause motor abnormalities. The low-potency antipsychotics, such as chlorpromazine, are markedly anticholinergic, but they produce less in the way of acute motor symptoms. The differences in side effects are often the reason that one drug is preferred over another for a particular patient. All of the antipsychotic drugs may induce tardive dyskinesia.

Acute motor symptoms are effectively treated with anticholinergic agents, such as benztropine (Cogentin®) or by dose reduction (Wojcik, 1979). *Akathisia* (motor restlessness and a subjective feeling of having to move about) is often induced by the high-potency agents. Akathisia may respond to anticholinergic medication, but it is more likely to respond to beta blockers such as propranolol or benzodiazepines such as lorazepam. At present, there is no satisfactory treatment for tardive dyskinesia, so substantial efforts toward prevention are indicated (Pi & Simpson, 1986; Simpson, Pi, & Sramek, 1982).

The neuroleptic malignment syndrome (NMS) is a rare but potentially fatal side effect of these medications (Caroff, 1980). Some cases of NMS may result from idiosyncratic responses to the agents. Other reported cases of NMS are probably due to severe parkinsonian side effects complicated by medical illnesses (Levinson & Simpson, 1986).

Approximately 25% of schizophrenic patients show little to no response to antipsychotic medications even after careful adjustment of dose and blood level (Cooper, 1978; Pi & Simpson, 1981; Simpson, Pi, & Sramek, 1981; Simpson & Yadalam, 1985). Some of these patients may respond to the novel antipsychotic drug clozapine, which is available on an experimental basis in the United States (Small, Milstein, & Marhenke, 1987). Some of these patients may also benefit from the addition of other drugs, such as lithium, benzodiazepines, carbamazepine, or propranolol, combined with standard antipsychotic medicine (Donaldson, Gelenberg, & Baldessarini, 1983). Electroconvulsive therapy (ECT) is also useful at times (Taylor & Fleminger, 1980). The use of these agents is based largely on clinical experience, with little scientific evidence to guide their use.

A number of new antipsychotic agents are under development; some of these drugs hold out the promise of providing antipsychotic effects with a reduced level of acute and chronic side effects.

Affective Disorders

A number of distinct patterns of mood disturbance may respond to medication (Akiskal, 1986). Again, diagnosis is the key to predicting medication response. As with the psychotic disorders, many organic conditions may results in profound disturbances of affect (e.g., thyroid disease, use of medications such as reserpine). It is essential that these disorders be recognized and that appropriate treatment be directed to the organic problem.

Empirical research had given new insight into the concepts of reactive and endogenous affective disturbance. For many years, it was assumed that depressions that followed unfortunate life events, such as financial reversal or the loss of a spouse, were largely psychological events ("reactive" affective disturbance) and were best treated by psychotherapy. In contrast, depressions that seemingly came out of the blue were termed *endogenous*, thought to be caused by biological factors, and were treated with medication. However, studies show that it is not the reactive–endogenous distinction, but rather the type of symptom complex that predicts response to medication. Patients with major depression, as defined by DSM-III-R, are likely to respond to heterocyclic antidepressants whether or not there was a psychosocial precipitant of the depression. In fact, patients with major depression following a psychosocial precipitant are more likely to respond to heterocyclic antidepressants than are patients whose major depression came out of the blue.

Major affective disorder is subdivided into unipolar or bipolar types. In the *unipolar* disorder, major depression occurs without mania. *Major depression* consists of depressed mood or loss of interest in usual activities, coupled with vegetative symptoms such as decreased appetite, psychomotor retardation, difficulty falling asleep, frequent awakening during the night, and very early morning awakening. Depressions with this symptom complex usually respond to heterocyclic antidepressants (Pi & Simpson, 1985) or to ECT (see Table 3.2). Psychotic symptoms may be present, calling for the use of antipsychotic medication as well.

TABLE 3.2.   Agents for Affective Disorders

Class of agent (examples)	Principle indications
Heterocyclic antidepressant (HCA) (imipramine, amitriptyline)	Major depression accompanied by "vegetative symptoms": low energy, sleep continuity disturbance, very early morning awakening, loss of appetite
MAOIs	Major depression without vegetative signs
Lithium (lithium carbonate, lithium citrate)	Mania, prophylaxis of mania and depression in bipolar affective disorder
Electroconvulsive treatment (ECT)	Major depression, mania
Triazolobenzodiazepines (alprazolam)	Nonpsychiatric depression
Bright full-spectrum light	Seasonal affective disorder (SAD)

In *bipolar affective disorder*, major depression alternates with periods of mania. *Mania* is characterized by hyperactivity, rapid speech, grandiose ideas that may be delusional, decreased sleep, and euphoria or irritability. Most cases of mania respond to either lithium carbonate or ECT. Lithium effects occur over a period of 1–2 weeks. Benzodiazepines or antipsychotic drugs are also often used to reduce agitation until lithium effects are evident. Depressed bipolar patients are often treated with lithium and heterocyclic antidepressants. Lithium is useful as a prophylaxis against both manic and depressive episodes in patients with bipolar disorder.

Some severe depressions are not accompanied by the types of vegetative symptoms and diurnal variation noted in major depression. These depressions appear more likely to respond to MAOI antidepressant drugs. *Dysthymia* refers to chronic low-level depression, which may, at times, represent a milder form of major affective disorder or atypical depression, and which may respond to medication. In seasonal affective disorder (SAD), depression is limited to the winter months, when the period of daylight is short. Individuals with this disorder may respond to moving to more southern latitudes, where the photoperiod is longer or to treatment with intense bright full-spectrum light during the winter months (Rosenthal, Sack, Carpenter, Parry, Mendelson, & Wehr, 1985).

The heterocyclic antidepressants are a group of similar drugs that act by decreasing the reuptake of the neurotransmitters serotonin and norepinephrine (Sulser, 1983) (see Table 3.3). Response to these drugs appears over 4 to 6 weeks. The drugs differ somewhat in side effects; for example, amitriptyline (Elavil®) is more sedating than imipramine (Tofranil®). Both of these drugs are more

anticholinergic than nortriptyline. For most of the drugs, the therapeutic response increases as dose is increased, and the upper level of dose is determined by side effects. For nortriptyline, however, there seems to be a therapeutic window for blood levels: Best response is between 50 and 150 ng/ml (Burrows, Davies, and Scoggio, 1972). The MAOIs act by inhibiting the enzyme that normally degrades norepinephrine and serotonin, thereby increasing the availability of these neurotransmitters. Patients taking MAOIs must adhere to a low tyramine diet. Ingestion of foods such as aged cheese or other fermented products that are rich in this neurotransmitter precursor can result in dangerous elevation of blood pressure. A drawback to both the heterocyclics and the MAOIs is their toxicity in overdose. Thus, it may be necessary to limit the amount of medication made available to a very depressed patient, to avoid its use in a suicide attempt.

TABLE 3.3.   Common Antidepressant Drugs

Chemical name	Trade name
Heterocylcics	
Imipramine	Tofranil®, others
Amitriptyline	Elavil®, others
Nortriptyline	Aventyl®, Pamelor®
Trimipramine	Surmontil®
Desipramine	Norpramin®, Pertrofrane®
Doxepin	Sinequan®, Adapin®
Amoxapine	Ascendin®
Maprotaline	Ludiomil®
Trazodone	Desyrel®
MAOIs	
Isocarboxazid	Marplan®
Phenelzine	Nardil®
Tranylcypromine	Parnate®
Triazolobenzodiazepine	
Alprazolam	Xanax®

For major depression and mania, ECT is probably the fastest and most effective single treatment (Frankel, 1988). In ECT, an electric current is passed through a patient's brain, resulting in subsequent seizure activity. The mechanism of efficacy is unknown. Years ago, ECT was administered to awake patients, and it was a frightening, potentially dangerous treatment. The situation has changed. Currently, ECT is administered after a patient has been anesthetized and given a muscle relaxant. With use of the muscle relaxant, there are no muscle contractions during seizure activity. Thus, the seizure is limited to the nervous system. The principal risk of ECT for physically healthy patients is due to the anesthesia. Following ECT, patients usually have difficulty remembering events at about the time of treatment. There is little, if any, residual cognitive impairment from ECT, although some patients complain of mild memory loss.

The triazolobenzodiazepine, alprazolam, is helpful for some patients with depression (Fabre & McLendon, 1980). It is less efficacious than the heterocyclics in major depression, but it may be useful for some patients who cannot tolerate other medication. It is not clear whether alprazolam is truly a unique atypical benzodiazepine or if it is simply a very potent typical one.

Some patients with major affective disorders do not respond to the usual medicines. Carbamazepine, with or without lithium, is helpful to some patients with bipolar disorder (Bellenger, Post, & Bunney, 1980). Psychostimulants, thyroid hormone, combination of heterocyclics and MAOIs, and other more speculative treatments are sometimes employed with varying degrees of success.

Anxiety Disorders

The treatment of anxiety is also based on accurate diagnosis (Rosenbaum, 1982) (see Table 3.4). A number of recognized organic conditions can give rise to anxiety, and these must, of course, be ruled out or treated before other treatment for anxiety is considered. The benzodiazepines have become the usual treatment for generalized anxiety disorder (see Table 3.5). In this disorder, debilitating anxiety is experienced continuously for extended periods of time. The benzodiazepines are very effective in reducing such chronic anxiety for

TABLE 3.4.   Agents for Anxiety Disorders

Class of drug	Principle indications
Benzodiazepines	Generalized anxiety disorder
	Situational anxiety
MAOIs	Panic disorder
HCAs	Panic disorder
Beta blockers	Situational anxiety
Buspirone	Generalized anxiety disorder
Clomipramine	Obsessive–compulsive disorder

properly selected patients. When carefully diagnosed patients are treated under the ongoing supervision of a physician, there is little risk of such patients developing drug abuse (Petursson & Lader, 1981). The benzodiazepines are, however, frequently abused in less well-controlled circumstances. Addiction-prone individuals, such as alcoholics, polydrug abusers, and patients with borderline or antisocial personality, are at particular risk of developing patterns of benzodiazepine abuse or misuse. The risk of abuse is minimized by careful clinical supervision of their use and ongoing evaluation of their utility. The all-too-common practice of physicians prescribing large numbers of benzodiazepine tablets and then having minimal contact with the patient clearly promotes misuse and abuse (Dietch, 1983; Garvey & Tollefson, 1986).

In 1977, specific brain receptors for benzodiazepines were discovered (Mohler & Okada, 1978; Tallman, Paul, Skolnick, & Gallagher, 1980). These receptors are chemically linked to receptors for the neurotransmitter GABA and to a chloride channel. Benzodiazepines increase the inhibitory action of GABA. Animals that have differing

TABLE 3.5.   Benxodiazepines

Chemical name	Trade name
Diazepam	Valium®
Chlordiazepoxide	Librium®
Clorazepate	Tranxene®
Prazepam	Centrax®
Flurazepam	Dalmane®
Halazepam	Paxipam®
Alprazolam	Xanax®
Lorazepam	Ativan®
Oxazepam	Serax®
Temazepam	Restoril®
Triazolam	Halcion®
Clonazepam	Klonopin®

numbers of benzodiazepine receptors have been shown to behave differently in stressful situations. This finding suggests a possible genetic basis for anxiety as a trait. The presence of the benzodiazepine receptor suggests that the brain produces a substance that binds to the receptor and is involved in the regulation of anxiety (Paul, Marangos, Goodwin, & Skolnick, 1980). As yet, no such substance has been identified.

The onset of benzodiazepine action is rapid. Some benzodiazepines, such as diazepam (Valium®), are absorbed very rapidly, and antianxiety effects are recognizable within minutes of administration. Injectable forms of some agents are available, such as lorazepam (Ativan®). The half-life of benzodiazepines is variable. Some agents, such as diazepam and chlordiazepoxide (Librium®), have rather long half-lives and may be administered on a daily basis. Other benzodiazepines must be given several times during the day because of their short half-lives. Such short-acting agents include lorazepam and triazolam (Halcion®).

The most common side effect in benzodiazepines is sedation. Tolerance to sedation often develops within a period of days. Continuing sedation may call for a dose reduction. Memory disturbances can also occur (Ghoneim, Mewaldt, Berie, & Hinrichs, 1981). Benzodiazepines are rarely life-threatening when taken in overdose, except when combined with other drugs (including alcohol), which can lead to lethal respiratory depression (Greenblatt, Allen, Noel, & Shader, 1977). Benzodiazepines must be withdrawn gradually in order to prevent withdrawal syndromes, ranging from mild flulike illnesses to severe symptoms with seizures (Cole, Altesman, & Weingarten, 1980; Gelenberg, 1980).

A new, chemically unrelated drug, buspirone, has recently been introduced for the treatment of generalized anxiety disorder. Buspirone has an onset of action more like the antidepressant drugs, requiring at least a week of treatment before benefits are realized. Buspirone has no withdrawal syndrome and little to no abuse potential. It is not cross-reactive with the benzodiazepines, so benzodiazepine withdrawal could occur if buspirone were simply substituted for one of these drugs.

Panic disorder (Sheehan, 1982) is characterized by acute episodes of overwhelming anxiety, accompanied by autonomic symptoms such as rapid heart beat and sweating. Panic disorder may be so disturbing that patients fear going out of their homes and develop symptoms of agoraphobia. The MAOIs and heterocyclic antidepressants are the most effective treatment for panic disorder. The triazalobenzodiazepine alprazolam (Xanax®) has also been used successfully in some patients with panic disorder.

Some social situations, such as public speaking or taking examinations, can provoke intense symptoms of anxiety in otherwise normal people. These symptoms may markedly interfere with performance. In such instances, beta blockers such as propranolol may be useful (Cole et al., 1980). These drugs block the peripheral autonomic symptoms of anxiety such as sweating and rapid heartbeat.

In obsessive–compulsive disorder, patients perform repetitive and stereotypic actions (*compulsions*) to relieve anxiety, associated with repetitious unwanted thoughts (*obsessions*). Clomipramine, an antidepressant available on an experimental basis in this country, is often helpful (Thoren, Asberg, Bertilsson, Mellstrom, Sjoqvist, & Traskman, 1980), as are other drugs that effect serotonin uptake.

Personality Disorders

The personality disorders as defined in DSM-III-R are long-lasting maladaptive patterns of interpersonal behavior. The specific disorders have been delineated and validated to varying degrees. Patients with schizotypal personality disorder have symptoms similar to schizophrenia but of reduced severity. These patients may benefit from antipsychotic medication (Schulz, Schulz, & Wilson, 1988). Some patients with borderline personality disorder may have treatable affective disorders that respond to antidepressants or to lithium (Cowdry, 1987). Low-dose antipsychotic medication is also useful for some of these patients.

Organic Mental Disorders

Dementia refers to a marked decline in memory and other cognitive functions caused by global brain disease (Jenike, 1985). The two most common causes of dementia in the elderly are Alzheimer's disease and multi-infarct dementia. There are no specifically useful medications for dementia, although antipsychotics may be helpful in controlling agitation and disruptive behavior. Perhaps the most important contribution of psychopharmacology to dementia is in the treatment of conditions that clinically resemble dementia but that respond to treatment. Depression in the elderly may easily be confused with dementia, yet it very often responds to medication or ECT.

Psychiatric symptoms often accompany organic brain lesions caused by trauma, stroke, or developmental brain dysfunctions, such as is seen in mental retardation (Horvath, 1986). Lithium, carbamazepine, propranolol, and antipsychotics have all been used to treat the disruptive behavior that such individuals sometimes exhibit. Either ECT or the antidepressant may be useful in treating the depression that may follow from a stroke.

Eating Disorders

The pharmacological treatment of anorexia nervosa and bulimia nervosa is not well defined. Some patients do benefit from antidepressants or antipsychotic agents (Agras & Bachman, 1986).

Substance Abuse

Medications are used for four major functions in the treatment of substance abuse (Gorelick, 1983):

1. They are used in the process of detoxification. A drug is substituted for the abused agent and then the drug is slowly withdrawn. For example, chlordiazepoxide (Librium®) is often used in alcohol detoxification.

2. A prescribed drug may be substituted for similar abused substances in a maintenance program (e.g., methadone for heroin).

3. A drug may be given because it causes adverse effects when the abused drug is taken, and it therefore promotes abstinence. Disulfiram (Antibuse®) is prescribed daily for some abstinent alcoholics. Drinking alcohol while being treated with disulfiram produces very uncomfortable physical symptoms. Thus, an individual will think twice before taking a drink.

4. Psychotropic agents may be used to decrease the craving for an abused substance. For example, desipramine, a heterocyclic antidepressant, may decrease the craving for cocaine.

Medications in Context

The efficacy of medication in no way negates the need for psychosocial treatment approaches (Beck, Hollon, Young, Bedrosian, & Bendenz, 1985; Hogarty, 1984; Weissman, Jarrett, & Rush, 1987). What it does do, however, is make it imperative that psychosocial and pharmacological approaches be used together to formulate a plan for treatment that offers the greatest possible benefit for the least cost to the patient in terms of time, money, and suffering. Psychosocial treatments have the potential for enhancing the progress of psychiatric patients by teaching new skills for interpersonal coping and promoting more adaptive patterns of behavior (Bellack, Turner, Hersen, & Luber, 1984; Falloon, Boyd, McGill, 1984; Goldstein, Rodnick, & Evans, 1978). Psychosocial treatments can oftentimes enhance the effectiveness of medication, just as medications can contribute to progress in psychotherapy.

It is important to note that psychosocial treatments must be as carefully prescribed for a given patient as medications. Psychotherapeutic interventions carry their own risks and toxicities, just as medications do, and they should be matched carefully with the patient receiving them. For example, a confrontational group may be helpful for many patients with alcoholism, but it may lead to deterioration in an alcoholic–schizophrenic patient who finds the group too stressful.

A supportive relationship with a doctor or with a mental health team can be an essential part of psychopharmacological treatment. For example, the majority of patients with depression are treated not by psychiatrists but by family doctors. The stabilizing effects of moral support from a kind and knowledgeable general practitioner have gone largely unstudied but are probably quite substantial. Similar support can be given by a psychiatrist even when a patient is supposedly being seen only to obtain medication. Medication and support are often effectively used to screen patients for more time consuming and costly treatments in which the outcome is less predictable. For example, it would be reasonable to consider a 6-week trial of antidepressant medicine for a depressed patient before undertaking psychoanalysis to treat the depression. If the patient responds to medication, she or he is spared the need for years of costly treatment that would be of uncertain benefit.

SUMMARY

Substantial progress in psychopharmacology has been made since the late 1950s. The use of psychopharmacological agents is keyed to careful diagnosis of psychiatric disorders and is increasingly tied to an understanding of basic neuromechanisms. Concomitant use of properly selected and administered psychosocial treatments often are synergistic with drug treatment. When pharmacotherapy is clearly indicated, therapists who fail to prescribe or who intentionally deny patients drug treatment may be perceived as unethical or negligent. Thus, all mental health professionals, including nonphysicians, must be familiar with the uses of medication in psychiatric disorder.

REFERENCES

Agras, W. S., and Bachman, J. A. (1986). Anorexia nervosa and bulimia. In R. Michels (Ed.), *Psychiatry*. Philadelphia: Lippincott.

Akiskal, H. S. (1986). The clinical management of affective disorders. In R. Michaels (Ed.), *Psychiatry*. Philadelphia: Lippincott.

American Psychiatric Association. (1987). *Diagnostic and Statistical Manual of Mental Disorders* (3rd ed., rev.). Washington, DC: Author.

Axelrod, J. (1976). Neurotransmitters. In R. E. Thompson (Ed.), *Progress in psychology*, San Francisco: Freeman.

Ayd, F. J., & Blackwell, B. (1970) *Discoveries in biological psychiatry*. Philadelphia: Lippincott.

Baldessarini, R. J. (1980). Drugs and the treatment of psychiatric disorders. In A. G. Gilman, L. S. Goodman, A. Gilman (Eds.), *The pharmacological basis of therapeutics* (pp. 391–447). New York: Macmillan.

Beck, A. T., Hollon, S. D., Young, J. E., Bedrosian, R. C., & Bendenz, D. (1985). Treatment of depression with cognitive therapy and amitriptyline. *Archives of General Psychiatry, 42*, 142–148.

Bellack, A. S., Turner, S. M., Hersen, M., & Luber, R. F. (1984). An examination of the efficacy of social skills training for chronic schizophrenic patients. *Hospital and Community Psychiatry, 10*, 1023–1028.

Bellenger, J. C., Post, R. M., & Bunney, W. E. (1980). Carbamazepine in manic–depressive illness: A new treatment. *American Journal of Psychiatry, 137*, 782–790.

Bunney, B. S. (1984). Antipsychotic drug effects on the electrical activity of dopaminergic neurons. *Trends in Neuroscience, 7*, 212–215.

Burrows, G. D., Davies, B., & Scoggio, D. A. (1972). Plasma concentration of nortriptyline and clinical response in depressive illness. *Lancet, 2*, 619–623.

Cade, J. F. J. (1949). Lithium salts in the treatment of psychotic excitement. *Medical Journal of Australia, 36*, 349–352.

Caroff, S. N. (1980). The neuroleptic malignant syndrome. *Journal of Clinical Psychiatry, 41*, 79–83.

Carroll, R. S., Miller, A., Ross, B., & Simpson, G. M. (1980). Research as an impetus to improved treatment. *Archives of General Psychiatry, 37*, 377–380.

Chouinard, G., & Jones, B. D. (1980). Neuroleptic-induced supersensitivity psychosis: Clinical and pharmacologic characteristics. *American Journal of Psychiatry, 137*, 16–21.

Cole, J. O., Altesman, R. I., & Weingarten, C. H. (1980). Beta blocking drugs in psychiatry. In J. O. Cole (Ed.), *Psychopathology update* (pp. 43–68). Lexington, VA: Collamore Press.

Cooper, T. B. (1978). Plasma level monitoring of antipsychotic drugs. *Clinical Pharmacokinetics 3*, 14–38.

Cooper, J. R., Bloom, F. E., & Roth, R. H. (1982). *The biochemical basis of neuropharmacology*. New York: Oxford University Press.

Cowdry, R. W. (1987). Psychopharmacology of borderline personality disorder: A review. *Journal of Clinical Psychiatry, 48*, 15–22.

Davis, J. M. (1980). Antipsychotic drugs. In H. I. Kaplan, A. M. Freedman, & B. J. Sadock (Eds.), *Comprehsive textbook of psychiatry*, III. Baltimore: Williams & Wilkins.

Dietch, J. (1983). The nature and extent of benzodiazepine abuse: An overview of recent literature. *Hospital and Community Psychiatry, 34*, 1139–1145.

Donaldson, S. R., Gelenberg, A. J., & Baldessarini, R. J. (1983). The pharmacological treatment of schizophrenia: A progress report. *Schizophrenia Bulletin, 9*, 504–528.

Fabre, L. F., & McLendon, D. M. (1980). A double-blind study comparing the efficacy and safety of alprazolam with imipramine and placebo in primary depression. *Current Therapies in Research, 27*, 474–482.

Falloon, I. R. H., Boyd, J. L., McGill, C. W. (1984). Family care of schizophrenia: a problem solving approach to the treatment of mental illness. New York: Guilford Press.

Frankel, F. H. (1988). Electroconvulsive therapy. In M. A. Nicholi, Jr. (Ed.), *The new Harvard guide to modern psychiatry*. Cambridge, MA: Harvard University Press.

Garvey, M. J., & Tollefson, S. D. (1986). Prevalence of misuse of prescribed benzodiazepines in patients with primary anxiety disorder or major depression. *American Journal of Psychiatry, 143*, 1601–1603.

Gelenberg, A. J. (1980) Benzodiazepine withdrawal. *Massachusetts General Hospital Biological Therapies in Psychiatry Newsletter, 3*, 9–10.

Ghoneim, M. M., Mewaldt, S. P., Berie, J. L., & Hinrichs, J. V. (1981). Memory and performance effects of single and three-week administration of diazepam. *Psychopharmacology, 73*, 147–151.

Goldstein, M. J., Rodnick, E. H., & Evans, J. R. (1978). Drug and family therapy in the aftercare of acute schizophrenics. *Archives of General Psychiatry, 35*, 1169–1177.

Gorelick, D. A. (1983). Pharmacotherapy of alcohol and drug abuse. *Psychiatric Annals, 13*, 71–79.

Greenblatt, D. J., Allen, M. D., Noel, B. J., & Shader, R. I. (1977). Acute overdosages with benzodiazepine derivatives. *Clinical Pharmacology and Therapeutics, 21*, 497–514.

Hogarty, G. E. (1984). Depot neuroleptics: The relevance of psychosocial factors—a U.S. perspective. *Journal of Clinical Psychiatry, 45*, 36–42.

Horvath, T. B. (1986). Organic brain syndromes. In R. Michaels (Ed.), *Psychiatry*. Philadelphia: Lippincott.

Jefferson, J. W., & Marshall, J. R. (1981). *Neuropsychiatric features of medical disorders*. New York: Plenum.

Jenike, M. A. (1985). *Handbook of geriatric psychopharmacology*. Littleton, MA: PSG Publishing.

Jeste, D. V., & Wyatt, R. J. (1982). *Understanding and treating tardive dyskinesia*. New York: Guilford.

Larny, P. P. (1980). *Prescribing for the elderly*. Littleton, MA: PSG Publishing.

Levinson, D. F., & Simpson, G. M. (1986). Neuroleptic induced EPS with fever: Heterogeneity of the "neuroleptic malignant syndrome." *Archives of General Psychiatry, 43*, 839–848.

Mohler, H., & Okada, T. (1978). The benzodiazepine receptor in normal and pathological human brain. *British Journal of Psychiatry, 133*, 261–268.

Paul, S. M., Marangos, P. J., Goodwin, F. K., & Skolnick, P. (1980). Brain-specific benzodiazepine receptors and putative endogenous benzodiazepine-like compounds. *Biological Psychiatry, 15*, 407–428.

Petursson, H., & Lader, M. J. (1981). Benzodiazepine dependence. *British Journal of Addiction, 76*, 133–145.

Pi, E. H., & Simpson, G. M. (1981). The treatment of refractory schizophrenia: Pharmacotherapy and clinical implications of blood level measurement of neuroleptics. *International Pharmacopsychiatry, 16*, 154–161.

Pi, E. H., & Simpson, G. M. (1985). New antidepressants: A review. *Hospital Formulary, 20*, 580–588.

Pi, E. H., & Simpson, G. M. (1986). Prevention of tardive dyskinesia. In N. S. Shah & A. G. Donald (Eds.), *Movement disorders* (pp. 181–194). New York: Plenum.

Rosenbaum, J. F. (1982). The drug treatment of anxiety. *New England Journal of Medicine, 306*, 401–404.

Rosenthal, N. E., Sack, D. A., Carpenter, C. J., Parry, B. L., Mendelson, W. B., & Wehr, T. A. (1985). Antidepressant effects of light in seasonal affective disorder. *American Journal of Psychiatry, 142*, 163–170.

Salzman, C. (1982). A primer on geriatric psychopharmacology. *American Journal of Psychiatry, 139*, 67–74.

Schulz, S. C., Schulz, P., & Wilson, W. H. (1988). Drug treatment of schizotypal personality disorder. *Journal of Personality Disorders, 2*, 1–13.

Sheehan, D. V. (1982). Current perspectives in the treatment of panic and phobic disorders. *Drug Therapies, 12*, 173–193.

Simpson, G. M., & May, P. R. A. (1984). Treatment of schizophrenia. In H. I. Kaplan & B. J. Sadock (Eds.), *Comprehensive textbook of psychiatry, IV*, (pp. 713–723). Baltimore: Williams & Wilkins.

Simpson, G. M., Pi, E. H., & Sramek, J. J. (1981).

Adverse effects of antipsychotic agents. *Drugs, 21*, 138–151.

Simpson, G. M., Pi, E. H., & Sramek, J. J. (1982). Management of tardive dyskinesia: Current update. *Drugs, 23*, 381–383.

Simpson, G. M., Pi, E. H., & White, K. L. (1983). Plasma drug levels and clinical response to antidepressants. *Journal of Clinical Psychiatry, 44*, 27–34.

Simpson, G. M., & Yadalam, K. (1985). Blood levels of neuroleptics: State of the art. *Journal of Clinical Psychiatry, 46*, 22–28.

Small, J. G., Milstein, V., Marhenke, J. D., et al. (1987). Treatment outcome with clozapine in tardive dyskinesia, neuroleptic sensitivity, and treatment resistant psychosis. *Journal of Clinical Psychiatry, 48*, 263–267.

Sulser, F. (1983). Mode of action of antidepressant drugs. *Journal of Clinical Psychiatry, 44*, 14–20.

Tallman, J. F., Paul, S. M., Skolnick, P., & Gallagher, D. W. (1980). Receptors for the age of anxiety: Pharmacology of the benzodiazepines. *Science, 207*, 274–281.

Taylor, P., & Fleminger, J. J. (1980). ECT for Schizophrenia. *Lancet, 1*, 1380.

Test, M. A., & Stein, L. I. (1980). Alternatives to mental hospital treatment: III. *Archives of General Psychiatry, 37*, 409–412.

Thoren, P., Asberg, M., Bertilsson, L., Mellstrom, B., Sjoqvist, F., & Traskman, L. (1980). Clomipramine treatment of obsessive–compulsive disorder: II. Biochemical aspects. *Archives of General Psychiatry, 37*, 1289–1294.

Weissman, M. M., Jarrett, R. B., & Rush, J. A. (1987). Psychotherapy and its relevance to the pharmacotherapy of major depression: A decade later. In H. Y. Meltzer (Ed.), *Psychopharmacology: The third generation of progress* (pp. 1059–1070). New York: Raven Press.

Wojcik, J. D. (1979). Antiparkinson drug use. *Massachusetts General Hospital Biological Therapies Psychiatric Newsletter, 2*, 5–7.

PART 2

Depression

CHAPTER 4

Psychotherapy

JULES R. BEMPORAD AND RUSSELL G. VASILE

PSYCHOANALYTIC FORMULATIONS OF DEPRESSION

The earliest attempts to encompass depression from a psychodynamic point of view appear to have been direct applications of the then-prevailing psychoanalytic theory. In this manner, Abraham (1911) considered depression at first to be a blockage of libido and later (1916) to be a regression to pre-Oedipal modes of gratification and object relations.

It was not until the publication of *Mourning and Melancholia* in 1917 that Freud turned his attention to depressive states and formulated an original interpretation that was specific to these disorders. This work explained depression as resulting from anger directed inward toward a lost love object, which, by incorporation, had become part of the ego.

A decade later, Rado (1927) modified this basic formulation according to the general changes that had been introduced by the structural theory. In Rado's revision, the superego becomes the punishing agent, and the pre-Oedipal introjection is conceived of as a dual process, with the good aspects a part of the ego. These works are representative of the classical period of psychoanalytic thought, during which basic mental structures were proposed and then used to account for various clinical phenomena. During this formative and creative period of psychoanalytic thought, great emphasis was given to intrapsychic structures, processes, and conflicts, with theory becoming more complex and farther removed from the presenting clinical data.

DEPRESSION AS A BASIC AFFECT

A radically new way of conceptualizing depression arose in the 1950s and 1960s, which not only showed the influence of ego psychology but also reflected a disenchantment with both complicated and unprovable metapsychological theories; it also stemmed from the wish to propose simpler models that were conceptually closer to observable clinical manifestations. This newer view was initiated by Bibring (1953), who postulated that depression be considered a basic state of the ego, which cannot be reduced further, and which arises automatically when the individual is in a situation that forces the person to give up strongly held narcissistic aspirations. Because different frustrations or deprivations may cause different people to feel powerless in trying to attain needed narcissistic goals, depression could not be the universal manifestation of an oral fixation or of retroflected anger following object loss. Rather, the feeling of depression is seen as the emotional expression of the ego's helplessness in maintaining a desired sense of self. Bibring's innovative interpretations shifted the focus of study from the internal, intersystemic conflicts that were thought to produce depression intrapsychically to those situations that precipitated a sense of ego helplessness. Taking the experience of depression as a given, he also speculated on the type of person who would have difficulty overcoming or defending against lowered self-esteem following narcissistic frustration.

A decade after Bibring's postulation, Sandler and Joffee (1965) furthered this line of reasoning by suggesting that depression be considered a negative emotion, much like anxiety. Depression was said to arise whenever the individual experienced the loss of a former state of well-being. In the case of depression following the loss of a loved one, these authors postulated that it was not the loss of the object per se that provoked the dysphoria but rather the loss of the state of well-being that the object supplied. A consequence of considering depression to be a basic affect is that this emotional state is closely related to the body's normal physiological processes. Therefore, depression could be caused or alleviated, at times, by altering specific chemical reactions. Depression, as is discussed in the following text, may result either from psychological events that in turn alter basic neurochemical processes or, in some instances, from a direct intervention in those processes themselves.

Another significant contribution was Sandler and Joffee's delineation of two stages in the depressive sequence. The first type of depression immediately follows the loss of a state of well-being. This stage of depression was called a "psychobiological reaction" and was believed to be a ubiquitous, if not a normal, response. Most individuals would be able to overcome this initial dysphoria by finding new ways to obtain a state of well-being, and so their depressions are self-limited and, perhaps, even beneficial. However, some individuals cannot mobilize themselves to alter this condition of deprivation, and they go on to experience the second form of depression, which is the "clinical episode." The predisposition to clinical depression, therefore, resides in the particular individual's inability to find sources of well-being after a loss or frustration.

This two-stage sequence also proposes that depression be viewed as a process that culminates over time as the individual faces a future bereft of needed gratification. In this sense, clinical depression is more than a reactive dysphoria, which passes with time as the individual readjusts the internal narcissistic equilibrium. Clinical depression entails an alteration in one's sense of self and has definite clinical and psychodynamic features that go beyond the transient unhappiness secondary to the usual vicissitudes of life. Clinical depression may be seen as a way of organizing experience and as the reemergence of childhood

modes of thinking and relating toward oneself and others that are no longer appropriate to adult life.

In chronic depressions, it is postulated that external events reverberate with dimly conscious and threatening views of the self and others, confirming a negativistic world view, which now appears unalterable. These dreaded assumptions, believed to be based on childhood experiences, usually consist of the acceptance that one will never be loved, or that one does not deserve to be loved by one's needed others, or that one can never be a worthwhile human being, or that one will always suffer at the mercy of a world beyond one's control. When reality appears to prove, either in actuality or in distorted fantasy, the veracity of these assumptions, the individual automatically experiences a depressive affect appropriate to their content.

Bowlby (1980) has enumerated these underlying beliefs and the childhood experiences from which they are thought to derive. These experiences are not single events but long-term patterns of familial interaction that may occur singly or in combination. One pattern of interaction is the child's "bitter experience of never having attained a stable or secure relationship with the parents despite having made repeated efforts to do so, including having done his [or her] utmost to fulfill their demands and perhaps also unrealistic expectations they may have had of him [or her]" (p. 247). Another relates to the child having been "told repeatedly how unlovable, and/or how inadequate, and/or how incompetent he [or she] is" (p. 247). Last is the possibility that the child was "more likely than others to have experienced actual loss of a parent . . . with consequences to [herself or] himself that, however disagreeable they might have been, [she or] he was impotent to change" (p. 248).

Arieti and Bemporad (1978) have enumerated basic belief systems in depressives that are not dissimilar from those described by Bowlby. These authors have found a common theme in the lifestyle of the depressive to be a "bargain relationship," in which the individual forms an unspoken pact with the parent, agreeing to remain in a position of childish dependency in return for security and protection. Implicit in this bargain, is the notion that the individual will achieve in order to

bring honor or praise to the family but will not pursue independent avenues of gaining self-worth. Further assumptions are that no one but the parent could possibly love or care for the individual and that without the parent figure, the individual would be helpless in a hostile and overwhelming world. In this manner, the future depressive's abilities are perverted so that they bring no measure of worth in or of themselves, but they are used only in the frantic need to maintain a relationship with an allegedly needed other. These persons grow up believing they are somehow unable to face the challenges of life alone, that they are doomed to failure or isolation without the magical protection of the powerful parent figure, and that they are unworthy of genuine love or caring from others.

Most individuals prone to depression evolve intrapsychic defenses or particular modes of existence to protect themselves from the realization of these painful self-estimations. Some manipulate others to give them constant demonstrations of affection or care in order to reassure themselves that they are loved; others become overconscientious workers, to ensure the approval of surrogate parental figures while pursing wealth or power to compensate for a sense of inner inferiority and weakness. Still others must live according to unrealistic, scrupulous moral standards to confirm their worth. When these defensive maneuvers are removed by an external occurrence, such as the loss of a source of love, or of financial security, or the emergence of unremitting erotic longings, these individuals are forced to come to grips with their most dreaded beliefs about themselves, together with an overwhelming sense of despair. Depression is, thus, precipitated by an external event which, in the minds of predisposed individuals, reactivates an atavistic sense of lovelessness, powerlessness, and hopelessness of ever gaining a sense of adequacy and security.

Psychodynamic psychotherapy also aims at stripping away defensive operations that obscure underlying beliefs. However, in therapy, this goal is achieved in a gradual and supportive manner, and in the context of a trusted relationship. While the underlying beliefs emerge as negative self-evaluations, or while they are acted out in the patient–therapist transference, their validity can be examined, and their inapplicability to adult behavior can be recognized. Furthermore, the limitations that these beliefs imposed on the individual can be understood and can serve as a motivation for change.

DIAGNOSTIC ISSUES AND PROBLEMS

Suitability for psychodynamic psychotherapy rests on the capacity of the individual to mobilize sufficient observing ego processes (a) to maintain a therapeutic alliance, (b) to constructively use the transference neurosis to develop insight, and (c) to build on this insight to develop a corrective emotional experience. For psychodynamic psychotherapy to proceed, there must be a capacity to explore current relationships, including the real patient–therapist relationship in psychotherapy, the transference relationship, and past relationships, all of which exist in a dynamic equilibrium.

Any factors that might interfere with the cognitive and emotional capacities to engage in this process could potentially undermine any role for psychodynamic psychotherapy. Hence, careful attention to diagnostic issues and problems is vital in the initial assessment of the patient who seeks psychodynamic psychotherapy.

The tasks of assessing the depressed patient's suitability for psychotherapy involves a recognition of the differential diagnosis of mood disorders and their implications for treatment interventions. The primary versus secondary distinction refers to those depressions that occur independent of other conditions versus those depressions with an onset that is clearly associated with another medical or psychiatric condition.

While the majority of depressions are primary, it is critical for the psychotherapist to recognize the multiple etiologies of secondary depressive disorders, as their treatment is dependent on appropriate diagnosis. A variety of medications may be associated with psychiatric symptoms as an unwarranted side effect. Substance abuse may become manifest with depressive symptoms; for example, amphetamine or cocaine withdrawal may produce profound endogenous depressive symptoms. Alcoholism has been demonstrated to be strongly associated with affective illness and may exacerbate underlying disorders of mood. Failure to assess these conditions, which may be subtle or covert in their initial presentation, will undermine any psychotherapeutic initiatives.

Medical illnesses, including hypothyroidism and other endocrine disorders, anemia, cerebrovascular diseases, tumors, and other neurologic conditions, may be present along with symptoms of depression. For example, the differential diagnosis of dementia versus pseudodementia due to depression in the elderly may be particularly vexing and requires neuropsychological testing for clarification (McAllister, 1983).

Within the primary depressive disorders, the unipolar versus bipolar, or manic–depressive distinction, is paramount. Assessing severity and duration of depressive symptoms and the presence or absence of psychotic manifestations is vital to appropriate selection of a psychodynamic treatment program. Psychotic manifestations in depression may include delusions or hallucinations—including nihilistic content, such as the belief that one's intestines are cancerous—or they may take the form of command hallucinations, such as a voice telling a patient to jump from a window. Psychotic depression usually requires prompt somatic therapy treatment, either electroconvulsive therapy (ECT) or a combination neuroleptic–antidepressant medication, because response to psychotherapy alone would be expected to be poor (APA, 1978). It is therefore vital to ascertain the presence or absence of psychotic features. In the DSM-III and the DSM-III-R, melancholia is a subset of the primary depressions. Melancholia is defined by marked neurovegetative depressive features; this subcategory of depressed patients almost invariably requires somatic treatment for sufficient improvement prior to productively utilizing psychotherapy. Attention must be drawn to the presence or absence of suicidal ideation or intent. Particularly important are historical factors, including the past history of attempts and their degree of lethality (Brown, Sweeney, Kocsis, & Frances, 1984).

Studies exploring combined pharmacotherapy and psychotherapy of major depression have suggested that the patient's overall rate of improvement is likely to be facilitated by combined therapy, as opposed to either treatment modality alone. Neurovegetative symptoms of depression tend to improve most rapidly with somatic therapy, while measures of social adjustment tend to show greater amelioration with psychotherapy (Conte, Plutchik, Wild, & Karasu, 1986; DiMascio, Weissman, et al., 1979; Klerman & Schecter, 1982). In a combined psychotherapy and psychopharmacology treatment situation, the therapist should explore with the patient feelings regarding being placed on medication and should examine expectations concerning the potential benefits and limitations of the medications, administered in the context of overall psychotherapeutic treatment (Docherty, Marder, van Kammen, et al., 1977; Gutheil, 1982).

Of equal importance is the assessment of patients with borderline or narcissistic characters. The diagnosis of borderline personality disorder, as documented in DSM-III-R, includes identity confusion, inappropriate affect, rapid idealization or devaluation of significant others, emotional instability, and impulsive self-destructiveness, as well as feelings of emptiness and depression. The therapist must be able to assess and to diagnose borderline personality disorder and to develop a psychotherapy that is best suited to that disorder. The specific vulnerability of borderline patients in psychotherapy includes their capacity to develop a rapid, unmanageable transference to the therapist, which often involves marked oscillations between intensive overidealization and powerful devaluation and rage. This phenomenon is further exacerbated by an unstructured psychotherapy that searches for unconscious factors in the patient's distress, and this may lead to an unmanageable transference process (Adler, 1986).

For borderline or narcissistic patients, in general, a more highly structured psychotherapy is indicated. While there is debate in the literature as to what precise approach is psychodynamically best suited for the patients, there is little question that their vulnerability to affective disruption requires a modification of the psychodynamic technique, which would be appropriate for the healthier depressed patient. For example, dream interpretation, which might be well-suited for a neurotic depressed patient, would be inappropriate in the treatment of the borderline patient who is actively depressed and in a state of regression.

The narcissistic personality disorder patient, particularly in the context of the transference, does not experience the same vulnerability to psychotic disruption that is associated with the borderline patient. Several authors have viewed these patients as existing on a continuum with the borderline personality disorder, with a critical difference being the narcissistic patients' firmer grasp of a sense of self and their capacity to tolerate a certain psychological aloneness and self–other differentiation (Svrakic, 1985). Nonetheless, the psychotherapy of these patients is also fraught with potential complexities. Many of these patients cannot tolerate interpretations and require a kind of admiring, uncritical stance for long periods of time before feeling a capacity to self-critically explore their own contribution to becoming depressed.

The literature is replete with stratagems for coping with the narcissistic disordered patient, with emphasis placed on the importance of empathy and nurturing on the one hand, while on the other hand, certain authors feel that confrontation of the patient's inevitable hostile devaluing transference is required to achieve therapeutic results. These patients present feelings of emptiness, isolation, and conflicts around intimate relationships. They will also exhibit in fantasy a preoccupation with their own omnipotence, brilliance, and special qualities, and they expect a strong degree of admiration and uncritical approval on the part of the therapist.

A pattern of counterdependent devaluing hostility will become evident early in the psychotherapy of these patients. Their preoccupation with grandiose achievements conceals a profound sense of emptiness, unlovability, and defectiveness. As with the neurotically depressed patient, ultimately, the amelioration of their despair will involve important grief work around disappointed wishes, hopes, and aspirations, be they for love, for approval, or for accomplishment of deeply valued goals. But unlike the more typically neurotically depressed patient, a narcissistic patient's psychotherapy will be threatened with disruption early and often if the therapist is unaware of the extraordinary sensitivity to interpretations and self-observation that the narcissistic patient may experience as intensely hostile and unempathic.

While the borderline personality disorders and narcissistic personality disorders represent a significant psychodynamic challenge in the psychotherapy of depression, a challenge of a different nature arises in those patients who exhibit disorders more characteristically of an obsessive nature. These patients tend to cathect thinking, as opposed to feeling, which may become a significant impediment if one attempts to conduct psychodynamic psychotherapy. The patient may be temperamentally poorly suited for a psychodynamic relationship that involves exploration of feelings in the patient's current relationships in the world, as well as in the real and transferential relationship to the therapist. These patients may become impatient with subtle emotional concepts and shades of feelings and tend to find security in a more highly structured cognitive psychotherapy. The patient may prefer to feel a certainty of progress if progress can be quantified or described in some manifest, behavioral fashion. Elsewhere in this volume, approaches in cognitive and behavioral therapy are carefully explored. It suffices to say that in the evaluation of the patient for psychodynamic psychotherapy, the therapist must keep in mind the temperamental capacity of the patient to tolerate and emotionally invest in psychodynamic psychotherapy.

The issue of social rehabilitation and milieu and group therapies requires careful attention, particularly in the socially isolated and the elderly. The role of hospitalization in affording respite from overwhelming psychosocial stressors also requires consideration, although in general, suicidal ideation or behavior is the key indication for hospitalization (Ross, 1987).

Treatment options for the psychotherapy of the depressed patient involve assessments of the patient's underlying character traits, defenses, and overall ego functioning. Alternatives to insight-oriented psychodynamic psychotherapy prominently include interpersonal psychotherapy, a highly structured, educative here-and-now treatment approach, as well as cognitive and behavioral methodologies. Supportive short-term psychotherapy would appear best suited for adjustment disorders, depressed mood, bereavement disorders, and demoralization. Supportive psychotherapy (a) focuses on abreaction in the here and now, (b) is time limited, and (c) does not rely on the activation of transference or an exploration of unconscious determinants of illness.

The various forms and causes of depressive disorders underscore the importance of selecting appropriate treatment for each patient. Intensive psychodynamic psychotherapy, as described in the next section, is best suited for those patients who present chronic characteroligical depression in which psychopathology is a basic part of the individual's life-style, encompassing personal relationships, values, and modes of self-assessment.

TREATMENT STRATEGIES OF INTENSIVE PSYCHODYNAMIC PSYCHOTHERAPY

The aim of psychodynamic psychotherapy is to increase individuals' conscious knowledge of crucial aspects of their psychological makeup and functioning of which they were previously unaware or only dimly aware. It is assumed that although kept out of awareness, these aspects of the personality have a major effect on the experience and behavior of the individual. Once these unconscious aspects have been identified, integrated into the rest of the personality, and evaluated in terms of their validity, individuals can live their lives in a freer, more satisfying and constructive manner. Therefore, there are two major tasks in the therapeutic process: the first is to make the here-and-now experience between patient and therapist reveal those unconscious processes that still influence and direct the individual's current life, while the second is to help the patient understand how the present is different, in terms of autonomy and control, from those times in the distant past when the unconscious aspects were learned and subsequently repressed.

While most therapists would agree that atavistic parts of the self are inappropriately carried into the present, there is disagreement as to the actual conceptual nature of these archaic aspects. Originally, it was believed that memories laden with painful emotions were repressed but continued to exert their pathogenic effect. Later, forbidden instinctual desires or fantasies were thought to make up the content of the repressed aspects of the psyche. Both of these views are still held today, although, in recent decades, a growing body of literature has added a third component to the contents of the repressed. This more recent contribution suggests that archaic beliefs and assump-

tions of childhood often underlie the seemingly irrational behavior and emotional reactions of most individuals (Arieti & Bemporad, 1978; Beck, 1967; Bowlby, 1980). This more cognitive school asserts that individuals continue to live out their existence according to outmoded and maladaptive systems of belief that were formed in childhood and that continue to exist outside of awareness.

Because all individuals are assumed to harbor atavistic beliefs formulated in childhood, the nature, extent, and dread of these beliefs may determine the predisposition to psychopathology. Most, if not all, individuals will experience a period of dysphoria following a significant loss or disappointment. However, most will, in time reinstate avenues of obtaining meaning and worth from their activities. Similarly, sadness and loss of interest may follow deprivation or frustration, but individuals will continue to have relatively realistic appraisals of themselves or of others. However, if individuals have not altered a distorted childhood view of the self and, in fact, have defended against acknowledging these self-evaluations because of the psychic pain inherent in such awareness, then the abrupt discovery of this self-view would cause greater and longer-lasting dysphoria. Finally, many individuals create an interpersonal network based on these childhood beliefs, such as relationships based on excessive dependency or inhibition over pleasurable pursuits, which greatly hampers their ability to find ways of overcoming dysphoria.

STAGES OF THERAPY

For purposes of exposition, the therapeutic process can be separated into three stages, each with its own specific goals. However, it is to be understood that this division is artificial at best, because throughout therapy, new material may be uncovered, new transference distortions may appear, and new defensive resistances may emerge. Furthermore, everyday life does not stand still during the extensive period of therapy so that events outside the office often influence the course of treatment. With these provisos in mind, the usual progress of therapy with a depressed individual can be presented as consisting of three sequential stages.

Stage 1: Setting the Course of Therapy

The initial stage concerns the proper setting of the course of therapy, the handling of immediate transference reactions, and the relating of the precipitating event to the individual's particular personality style and unconscious beliefs. One of the most difficult steps in the therapy of depressives is the first one. These patients begin therapy in the midst of an episode; they feel overcome with painful dysphoria, they feel hopeless and helpless, and they desire only relief from the misery. It may be difficult for them to talk of anything other than their suffering, and asking them to reflect on their experience may only bring about more pain or seem a pointless exercise that will not ease their distress. At the same time, they may ask for reassurances that they will recover or that the therapist will take care of them, often proclaiming that the therapist is their last hope or that the therapist's extensive knowledge or skill enable the therapist to cure their disorder. This initial state of demandingness, actual misery, dependency, and often ingratiating behavior presents numerous difficulties for the therapist who desires to proceed with the uncovering process and to reveal those intrapsychic factors responsible for the illness.

Jacobson (1971, 1975) has described how depressed patients may overvalue the therapist and experience an initial improvement in their symptoms because they believe they have found a source of care and nurturance. There is the danger that the patient may become overly involved with obtaining gratification from the therapist and may try to obtain this gratification by devotion and excessive loyalty to the therapeutic process. When the expected care is not forthcoming, however, the patient may become incensed, may feel cheated, or may experience an exacerbation of symptoms.

During the initial sessions, the therapist must walk a fine line, being wary of becoming the center of patients' lives or their only hope of salvation while simultaneously extending a warm and encouraging stance that will facilitate trust and the mutual exploration of intrapsychic material. A further difficulty is breaking the repetitive litany of complaints and/or self-preoccupation with the symptoms of the disorder. New topics may be introduced by the therapist for exploration, and in those cases where the dysphoric mood or negative

signs so overwhelm patients' ability to participate in therapy, antidepressant medication is certainly indicated. These pharmacological agents are in no way contraindicated, and aside from the natural rule of easing any individual's pain, they help in making patients more accessible to the therapeutic process. Finally, patients are to be encouraged to be completely honest about their judgments and feelings about loved ones, colleagues, and the therapist. This openness is crucial because the depressive has frequently been raised in an atmosphere of secrecy and manipulativeness, where voiced criticism or hostility was certain to result in psychological abandonment or guilt-provoking responses.

Once therapy has begun on a more or less neutral course, the focus should turn to the inward search for those inner beliefs that were brought to light by the precipitating event and those defensive operations that served to keep those very beliefs at a safe distance. This connection is not consistently obvious at the outset and may become clarified only after a considerable period of therapy; however, the associations stemming from the context in which the depression occurred will lead the way to revealing the individual's mode of obtaining self-esteem and defending against feelings of unworthiness, guilt, and shame.

One depressed woman, for example, stated that she became symptomatic when she could no longer keep up with her work and felt herself to be a failure. This explanation was partially true but did not go far enough in describing her actual situation. Later it was revealed that she began to feel anxious and dysphoric when her boss, upon whom she depended for a sense of worth and who had transferentially become her psychological father, hired another female assistant. This threatened the patient's imagined special status with the boss, and she anticipated that he would favor the new employee, who was erroneously perceived as more able, attractive, and likeable than the patient. Much of this reaction was a recapitulation of the events surrounding the birth of a younger sibling when the patient was 5 years old. Just as in childhood, she attempted to win back the father's preferential regard by working harder and harder, in order to obtain praise and reassurance.

However, in contrast to her father, the boss

did not sufficiently recognize her increased effort, causing her to apply herself even harder so that her work did become too much for her. Therefore, she did become depressed as a result of being overwhelmed by her work; however, the initiative to do more and more was of her own choosing, and the basic reason for it was to become reinstated as the boss/father's favorite. Her failure to achieve this goal was identified as the real cause of her decompensation. Finally, she was not aware of her need for a father surrogate's approval in order to feel worthy and whole. Yet, lacking that approval, she sensed herself unlovable, inadequate, and at times wicked and vile, without really knowing why.

The first stage of therapy comprises resolving the (a) initial dependency and transference distortions, (b) understanding that the clinical episode results from aberrant premorbid personality functioning, and (c) beginning to connect the precipitating event with deep-seated belief systems.

Stage 2: Modifying Belief Systems

The second stage consists of the gradual identification of atavistic belief systems, their evaluation in terms of current possibilities, and their eventual modification. This is not an easy task, for while these basic beliefs result in the repetitive experience of dysphoria, they also serve to structure the psychic life of the depressive individuals and allow the persons a sense of security and emotional safety, albeit transient and precarious. The basic struggle revolves about the depressives relinquishing their excessive need for external sources of worth, which are adult transformations of their childhood interpersonal situations, and their daring to develop new, more appropriate and less precarious modes of feeling worthwhile. This process produces a great deal of anxiety in individuals, who believe that giving up the old values will leave them totally without structure or support and that they will be abandoned, criticized, or somehow damaged if they dare to assert their need for autonomous satisfaction.

For example, an executive was awarded an all-expenses paid vacation as the result of her outstanding work performance. As the time of her departure approached, she was haunted by incessant worries: (a) that in her absence her job would be given to someone else, (b) that her apartment would be burglarized, (c) that her parents would become sick and die. The irrationality of these fears is evidenced by the fact that her work forced her to travel at least once a month, which she was able to do without trepidation. It was only when she was to travel for her own pleasure rather than to comply with the needs of others that she developed her multiple fears.

As with the executive's, these irrational emotional reactions are traced back to childhood when they were indeed appropriate to the family system of beliefs. Gradually, the individual senses more and more clearly how these beliefs and how this structuring of experience were developed in order to avoid rejection, criticism, or guilt, and to ensure acceptance by needed adults. Concurrent with this process of reality testing, transference distortions manifest themselves as the patient unwittingly creates a new parental surrogate—complete with all the biases, restrictions, and manipulations—in the therapist. Usually, these distortions can be observed in the unwarranted behavior of the patient toward the therapist, although quite often, a dream is reported in which the therapist is confused with the original parent. When the therapist refuses to act out the expected parental role and instead identifies and examines the reactions the patient anticipates from the therapist, the therapist can make clear, in a vivid, living manner, the nature of the original relationship as it continues to affect the present. Of greatest importance is the realization of the concept of self that had been formed during crucial years of personality development. The patient comprehends, with some inescapable discomfort, that beneath the personal facade of a mature, responsible, and often successful adult, there remains a hated, helpless, and needy child who had never felt truly loved or appreciated, who lived in fear of criticism or abandonment, and who never dared to act on true deeply felt desires or ambitions.

As patients realize the atavistic nature of these attitudes, they begin the slow process of change, venturing to try new modes of relating to significant others, of obtaining worth, and of estimating themselves. These timorous forays are rewarded in the therapy by pointing out the sense of freedom and satisfaction that accompany these trial attempts and by pointing out that the terrible consequences that were anticipated have not transpired. More and more attempts are made and discussed in the therapeutic situation. Concurrently, the therapist begins to be seen as a concerned helper, with human limitations, rather than an omniscient and punitive parental image. Personal material, which had previously been avoided because of the fear of the reaction it might elicit, is now openly reported without the expectation of criticism and with the comfortable understanding that one need not be perfect in the eyes of others or oneself.

The middle stage of therapy generally comprises the identification of persistent childhood beliefs, the influence of those beliefs on current behavior and sense of self, the defensive maneuvers created to compensate for negative self-regard, and a decided effort to alter these old assumptions.

Stage 3: Consolidating and Integrating the New Beliefs

The final stage concerns the consolidation of a new sense of self, together with managing the reactions of others to this alteration. It is hoped that patients will exhibit a new integrity in their intimate relationships, free from the fear of being rejected or of needed reassurance. Humor, anger, and spontaneous enjoyment become a larger part of the individual's experience. A more relaxed view toward oneself, and a less critical evaluation of others, comes about as the childhood "shoulds" are modified. These changes not infrequently provoke dismay, and even anger, in significant others who had become accustomed to patients' prior ingratiating and overconscientious mode of being. Such reactions are seen in employers, parents, and colleagues, but most often in spouses of older depressives. While these individuals do not want patients to reexperience episodes of clinical depression, they are loathe to adjust to a new type of relationship. At this time, patients require an impartial confidant who will understand these obstacles objectively, and will share in patients' resolve to maintain those changes that were so arduously created.

INTERPERSONAL PSYCHOTHERAPY

This form of psychotherapy shares some basic concepts and techniques with more traditional psychodynamic treatment, although it differs markedly in important aspects. The basis for interpersonal psychotherapy (IPT) is the belief that depression is best understood in an interpersonal context, particularly in regard to existing social supports and the individual's social effectiveness. Meyer, Sullivan, and others have stressed the importance of the interpersonal and social milieu in the prevention of or vulnerability to mental illness. In 1978, Brown and Harris demonstrated the protective effect of strong social supports in the prevalence of depression in a large sample of British working-class women. Therefore, IPT aims to clarify the psychosocial context in which the depression had its onset and to alter the individual's social functioning to facilitate recovery and prevent further episodes.

These theoretical and practical tenets are much in agreement with psychodynamic therapy. The major difference resides in IPT's limiting its therapeutic endeavor to the conscious "here and now" and avoiding investigation of unconscious beliefs, transference manifestations, overall self-evaluations and handling of anger or guilt. The practitioners of IPT describe three components in depression: (1) the symptomatic clinical presentation, (2) the individual's social adjustment and interpersonal relationships, and (3) enduring personality traits resulting from childhood experience. IPT attempts to intervene only in the first few components, whereas traditional therapy, while not ignoring these, concentrates its efforts on the third component.

Despite this self-acknowledged limitation, IPT has been shown to be quite effective in clinical trials, although its benefits become apparent only after 6 to 8 months of therapy. Further advantages are that the technique can be described objectively in a treatment manual, that it is less time-intensive than traditional therapy and that, as a result of its communicability, it can be tested empirically. Evaluations at 1 year after termination of IPT have been favorable; however, longer-term studies of its effectiveness remain to be performed.

CASE ILLUSTRATION

A relatively typical individual with depression was Mr. A., a middle-aged executive who was seen after a brief psychiatric hospitalization, where he had been admitted in a state of agitation and despair. During his inpatient stay, he had been started on a tricyclic antidepressant and a benzodiazepine, with beneficial result. These medications had relieved his vegetative symptoms and some of his anxiety, but he still felt hopeless, finding each day a torment, and he was plagued with the idea that he was a failure and a disgrace to his family.

The acute episode had begun a few weeks after Mr. A. had decided on a major career change. For over the previous 10 years, he had worked for a large advertising agency in a major city; he had begun as a salesman, and, due to his great talent for selling the firm's product to clients, he had worked his way up to the director-ship of the sales division. Mr. A. had a knack for pleasing clients, he was full of entertaining stories and self-effacing humor, and he had a disarming manner that ingratiated himself and his firm to prospective customers. He displayed the same sort of upbeat and friendly attitude within the firm, where he was uniformly liked, and he seemed to have an encouraging word for all of the employees.

However, Mr. A. demonstrated an insatiable need for praise and reassurance from his superiors, and he would, at times, badger them with pointless questions or small talk banter in order to wrest from them an opinion that he was properly performing his job. His need to hear that he was doing well seemed independent of the sales figures from which the firm's principals actually derived evaluations. Another difficulty at work was that, although superficially friendly and caring, he had never developed a close relationship with any of his colleagues, preferring to spend his free time with or in search of, a superior.

His domestic situation revealed more serious problems. Mr. A. was often away on sales trips, during which he appeared to be unaware that he had a wife and children. Upon his return home, he would expect to be greeted with a great show of welcome and would become morose and withdrawn if any gift he brought back was not praised lavishly. At home, he subtly competed with his children for his wife's nurturance and attention, being easily offended if he felt she was neglecting him.

A further problem area related to a lifelong propensity toward excessive worry and self criticism and a lack of gratifying leisure activities. Mr. A. would replay situations in his mind, constantly seeking out instances in which he would have offended an important person or had not been sufficiently pleasant or friendly. He suffered greatly whenever he failed to conclude a sale, blaming himself and feeling depressed. At those times, he reacted to such setbacks as if he were a total failure as a person. He believed that the success of a business transaction depended solely on his being a likeable or lovable person, and he dismissed the importance of the quality of the product or other relevant factors. Most of his waking thoughts were filled with the impression he made on clients or superiors, and he derived little pleasure or meaning from anything else.

While Mr. A. described a chronic state of dysphoria, exacerbated by his believing that he failed to please his bosses, he had never suffered a major depressive episode until shortly after he made the decision to leave his job and go into business for himself. At that time, he experienced increasing anxiety and terrifying premonitions of failure. He sensed himself to be unable to work and to be doomed to failure. He was convinced that he was basically an inadequate and unlikable person whose prior success had been a sham, that if people really knew him, they would dislike him. These dreaded thoughts were accompanied by sleeplessness, anorexia, and a total lack of motivation. He refused to get out of bed and demanded infantile gratification from his wife. It was at this point that he was hospitalized.

During his inpatient treatment, he was started on medication and supportive therapy. He was discharged after a few weeks, with marked symptomatic improvement, but he was still plagued by self-doubts, feelings of futility, and a terrible sense of failure. He had not been able to follow through on his business venture and felt a mixture of relief and shame over his missed opportunity. Instead, he found employment at another advertising firm, where he was again placed in charge of sales.

Therapy began approximately 1 month after he was discharged from the hospital. He was on maintenance medication, had started back to work, and was attempting to resume his former life. He presented a mixture of glib, ingratiating statements together with a deep sense of self-hatred and despair. It was as if he had to keep up a pattern of small talk to avoid falling into a bottomless well of melancholia. Mr. A. was bewildered by his depressive episode and could not understand why such a terrible event had occurred in his life. He was frightened that he would become acutely depressed again, asking for reassurance that he was over the worst part of his disorder. On these occasions, it was suggested that he begin to look at what might have precipitated his clinical episode if he wished to avoid further decompensations. Mr. A. reacted to these suggestions with a sense of injury, feeling disappointed with the therapist's lack of positive assurance. However, he covered up these feelings with his usual facade of effusive good humor and small talk, which he believed would please the therapist. Mr. A. was confronted with those maneuvers as they occurred and encouraged to express his true feelings, however disagreeable.

In this manner, Mr. A. started to explore his relationships to imagined authority figures, his suppression of negative affects, and his particular vulnerabilities that so often resulted in dysphoric episodes. As he related his past, he recalled with sadness and bitterness that his father was full of criticism and that he could never wrench a word of praise from him. His childhood environment had been dominated by his father, who was an exacting patriarch, tyrannical in his rule over the family. The father made everyone else feel inadequate and frightened, seeming to undermine any sense of accomplishment. Good behavior, excellent grades, and community achievements were taken as a matter of course, as a proper means of carrying on some lofty family tradition. Failure to meet these high standards met with humiliation and guilt-inducing lectures. Mr. A's father also presented the extrafamilial world as a hostile and threatening jungle from which he protected his family through his superior talents and ability. Without him, the family could not cope and would be exploited by the alleged brutality of nonfamilial society.

Mr. A's mother concurred in these biased appraisals. She was remembered as an anxious, submissive woman who was terrified of upsetting her domineering husband. She also believed strongly in loyalty to the immediate family, using negative comparisons about neighbors as a means of inducing guilt if any of the children formed close relationships outside the extended family.

Mr. A. grew up believing that his sense of worth depended on getting praise or approval from his father, a feat that was never achieved. He always felt himself somehow unworthy and deficient for not living up to his father's standards, which he believed were fair and objective. He also believed that he would be doomed to failure in any pursuit without the support of a powerful father figure, sensing himself unequal to meet the challenges of the adult world. He had developed an ability to disarm the father and ward off his criticism by assuming a pleasant, self-effacing persona and committing to memory a host of entertaining stories that would divert the father's stern negativism. Although these were a successful defense against criticism, this facade never allowed him to experience or express his true feelings or true aspirations.

As Mr. A. reflected on his past, he became aware that he had always required the support and esteem of some father figure. Without this nurturing figure, he felt lost and helpless. This insight helped explain his decompensation, because forming his own company necessitated his giving up his dependent relationship with the boss, who had transferentially assumed the father role. This business venture also would have forced him to move away from his childhood family, whom he believed still magically protected him.

Mr. A. also became aware of how his superficial mode of interacting had been created as a means of placating the father and that it now had become generalized to almost all relationships, so that these were empty and ungratifying. This insight was achieved partially by interpretations of his behavior toward the therapist, who became yet another individual to "win over" and from whom to obtain assurance.

A few months after therapy had begun. Mr. A. reported a long series of dreams, all of which focused on his father. In some, the father was reprimanding him for some shortcoming or was punishing him for some misdeed, whereas in others, the father abandons the patient, causing great anxiety and sadness. These dreams helped to demonstrate and clarify Mr. A.'s excessive dependence on his father and, by relating the dreams to events in his working life, to his dependence on surrogate paternal figures.

Eventually, Mr. A. became aware of his overriding need to win approval from his father and from father substitutes (a) to feel worthy and whole, (b) to remain psychologically loyal to the family in order to continue being loved by his mother, and (c) to hide his true feelings so that others would find him likable. He also was able to conceptualize his enduring childhood sense of himself as helpless and unworthy if he was left alone or if he dared to gratify his own desires.

Once these childhood beliefs and the defensive maneuvers that had been constructed to fend off a dreaded view of the self were brought to consciousness, the slow process of change was initiated. This involved an extensive reevaluation of his relationships and of himself. As he ventured to try some more genuine assertion of himself, he would experience old fears, which in turn revived memories of how his autonomy had been eroded in childhood. For example, Mr. A. remembered his parents threatening to send him away from home if he disobeyed them; later, as a teenager, his budding interest in girls was ridiculed and shamed. He also recalled his mother threatening to abandon him if he did not demonstrate unswerving fidelity to her commands, as well as her using him as a go-between with her husband. These revelations helped him to understand the genesis of his current beliefs, defenses, and interpersonal maneuvers. He continued to make appropriate steps, in that he was more tolerant of setbacks and failures in himself and in others. He no longer felt he had to entertain or play up to others in order to be liked; he relied on his own judgment and enjoyed his achievements directly rather than for the praise they brought. He related to others more honestly, both in therapy and in his other relationships.

These changes brought about varying responses from those individuals with whom Mr. A. had close contact. His wife was delighted with lessened dependency on her, while at work, some of his colleagues were not as pleased with Mr. A.'s new honesty and straightforward manner. These reactions were discussed in therapy, which was now used as a source of support in the process of change. During this same period, Mr. A. began to pursue activities for their own sake rather than for how those activities would impress others. He took up golf more seriously and enjoyed his gradually increasing proficiency. He had played previously, but he had used the game to conclude business deals or to feel part of an idealized group.

These alterations gradually solidified, and the frequency of therapy was decreased to once every 2 weeks, until it was stopped by mutual agreement.

SUMMARY

In treating a depressed patient through the modality of psychodynamic psychotherapy, the clinician is choosing a specific treatment method predicated on assessments of the patient's underlying character structure, pattern of psychological conflict, and ego strengths. A capacity to grasp the impact of unconscious conflict and tolerate powerful affects as they emerge in the transference are important factors in selecting patients for this treatment modality. The clinician must be aware of possible biological factors contributing to depressive disorders and must recognize the role for appropriate medication management of depressive symptoms that may occur in conjunction with psychodynamic psychotherapy.

The authors contrasted psychodynamic psychotherapy with other psychotherapies that are used to treat depressive disorders. A case illustration was provided to underline principles of case selection for psychodynamic psychotherapy and to illuminate key therapeutic tactics as the treatment unfolded.

REFERENCES

Abraham, K. (1960). Notes on the psychoanalytic treatment of manic depressive insanity and allied conditions. In *Selected papers on psychoanalysis*. New York: Basic. (Original work published 1911).

Abraham, K. (1960). The first pregenital stage of libido. In *Selected papers on psychoanalysis*. New York: Basic Books. (Original work published 1916).

Adler, G. (1986). Psychotherapy of the narcissistic personality disorder. *American Journal of Psychiatry, 143,* 4.

Arieti, S., & Bemporad, J. (1978). *Severe and mild depression.* New York: Basic.

Beck, A. (1967) *Depression.* New York: Hoeber.

Bibring, E. (1953). The mechanism of depression. In P. Greenacre (Ed.), *Affective disorders.* New York: International.

Bowlby, J. (1980). *Loss.* New York: Basic.

Brown, G. W., & Harris, T. (1978). *Social origins of depression*. London: Tavistock.

Brown, R. P., Sweeney, E., Kocsis, J., & Frances, A. (1984). Involutional melancholia revisited. *American Journal of Psychiatry, 141*, 1.

Conte, H. R., Plutchik, R., Wild, K. V., & Karasu, T. B. (1986). Combined psychotherapy and pharmacotherapy for depression. *Archives of General Psychiatry, 43*, 471–479.

DiMascio, A., Weissman, M. M., Prusoff, B. A., et al. (1979). Differential symptom reduction by drugs and psychotherapy in acute depression. *Archives of General Psychiatry, 36*, 1450–1456.

Docherty, J. P., Marder, S. R., van Kammen, D. P., et al. (1977). Psychotherapy and pharmacotherapy: Conceptual issues. *American Journal of Psychiatry, 134*, 529–533.

Freud, S. (1960). Mourning and melancholia. In *Collected papers* (Vol. 4). New York: Basic. (Original work published in 1917.)

Gutheil, T. G. (1982).The psychology of psychopharmacology. *Bulletin of the Menninger Clinic, 46*, 321–330.

Jacobson, E. (1971). *Depression*. New York: International Universities Press.

Jacobson, E. (1975). The psychoanalytic treatment of depressed patients. In E. J. Anthony & T. Benedek (Eds.), *Depression and human existence*. Boston: Little Brown.

Klerman, G., & Schecter, G. (1982). Drugs and psychotherapy. In E. S. Paykel (Ed.), *Handbook of affective disorders*. New York: Guilford.

Klerman, G., Weissman, M. M., Rounsaville, B. J., & Chevron, E. S. (1984). *Interpersonal psychotherapy of depression*. New York: Basic.

McAllister, T. W. (1938). Overview: Pseudodementia. *American Journal of Psychiatry, 140*, 5.

The Medical Letter. (1984). Drugs that cause psychiatric symptoms. *26*.

Rado, S. (1956). The problem of melancholia. In *Collected papers* (Vol. 1). New York: Grune & Stratton. (Original work published in 1927.)

Ross, J. L. (1987). Principles of psychoanalytic hospital treatment. *Bulletin of the Menninger Clinic, 49*, 409–416.

Sandler, J., & Joffee, W. G. (1965). Notes on childhood depression. *International Journal of Psychoanalysis, 46*, 80–96.

Svrakic, D. M. (1985). Emotional features of narcissistic personality disorder. *American Journal of Psychiatry, 142*, 6.

American Psychiatric Association. (1978). *Task force on electroconvulsive therapy of the American Psychiatric Association: Electroconvulsive therapy* (Task Force Report No. 14).Washington, DC:.

CHAPTER 5

Cognitive Therapy

ARTHUR FREEMAN

CONCEPTUALIZATION OF DEPRESSION

The treatment of depression has a special place in any discussion of cognitive therapy (CT). Depression was, after all, the first area to which Beck applied CT (1967, 1976; Beck, Rush, Shaw, & Emery, 1979). It is also the clinical problem that has been most studied in terms of treatment efficacy (Blackburn, Bishop, Glen, Walley, & Christie, 1981; Kovacs, Rush, Beck, & Hollon, 1978, Murphy, Simons, Wetzel, & Lustman, 1984; Rush, Beck, Kovacs, & Hollon, 1977). Depression, often called "the common cold of emotional disorder," is both by itself and in combination with other disorders, the most common problem seen in clinical practice. The focus of this chapter is to offer the reader an overview of the cognitive model of depression and to discuss the various strategies and techniques developed for the CT treatment of depression. Finally, a case example is used to illustrate the assessment and treatment of depression.

Cognitive therapy is a short-term, active, directive, collaborative, psychoeducational, and dynamic model of psychotherapy. Cognitive therapy, developed by Beck (1967, 1976; Beck et al., 1979), is one of several cognitive-behavioral models of therapy. These include the works of Ellis (1962, 1973, 1977, 1985), Lazarus (1976, 1981), and Meichenbaum (1977). The major therapeutic focus in the cognitive-behavior models is helping patients to examine the manner in which they construe and understand the world (cognitions) and to experiment with ways of responding (behavioral). By learning to understand the idiosyncratic way in which they perceive the self, the world and their experience in it, and their prospects for the future, patients can be helped both to alter negative affect and to behave more adaptively. A cognitive focus in therapy is not new (Adler, 1927; Arieti, 1980; Bowlby, 1985; Frankl, 1985; Freud, 1892, Horney, 1936; Sullivan, 1953). Present-day cognitive therapy has developed as an amalgam of the dynamic therapies and the behavioral (Beck, 1970) and social learning therapies (Bandura, 1977a, 1977b, 1985). Arieti (1980) called cognition the "Cinderella of psychoanalysis and psychiatry. No other field of the psyche has been so consistently neglected by clinicians and theoreticians alike."

Cognitive therapy (CT) is a psychoeducational, or coping, model of therapy, as opposed to a mastery model of it. The major goal of CT is to increase patients' skills so that they can more effectively deal with the exigencies of life, and thereby experience greater control and self-efficacy in their lives. The directive nature of the model requires the therapist to be actively involved with the patient in the therapeutic collaboration. Through Socratic questioning, the therapist works to develop greater awareness in the patient. Further, the therapist can (a) offer hypotheses for consideration, (b) act as a resource person, or (c) directly point out areas of difficulty. By developing an understanding of the patient's problems, the therapist can begin to develop hypotheses about the patient's life issues, and thereby begin to develop a conceptualization of the patient within the cognitive-behavioral framework.

While best known for the outpatient treatment of depression, cognitive therapy may be the psychotherapeutic treatment of choice, along with appropriate pharmacotherapy, for depressed patients needing inpatient or day hospital treatment (Schrodt & Wright, 1987; Wright, 1989; Wright & Schrodt, 1987). A significant literature has emerged addressing the applications of CT with these patients (Bowers, 1989; Coche, 1987; Freeman & Greenwood, 1987; Greenwood, 1983; Grossman & Freet, 1987; Perris et al., 1987).

THE BASIC COGNITIVE THERAPY (CT) MODEL

The CT model posits three issues in the formation and maintenance of the common psychological disorders: the cognitive triad, cognitive distortions, and the schema (Beck, Rush, Shaw, & Emery, 1979).

The Cognitive Triad

The cognitive triad for depression (Beck et al., 1979) describes the patient's negative views of self, of world or experience, and of the future. Virtually all patient problems can be subsumed under one of these three areas. The therapist can start to focus and structure the therapy from the onset of treatment by paying special attention to the depressive features of the cognitive triad. Personal issues relating to the self, the world, and the future differ for each patient. Each constituent of the triad does not necessarily contribute equally to the depression. By assessing the degree of contribution of each of the three factors, the therapist can begin to develop a visual conceptualization of the patient's problem(s). This visualization can be used to help the patient better understand the problem focus of the therapy, which will be basic to the development of collaborative treatment strategies.

The triad can be pictured as an equilateral triangle. One can draw a perpendicular line from each of the three sides (Figure 5.1). The degree of importance of a particular factor is represented by the distance from the side of origin. The shorter the line (closer to the side), the greater the degree of importance of that factor for the individual. The

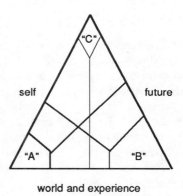

Figure 5.1. Graphic representation of the cognitive triad.

longer the line, the less important that particular factor appears to be. For example, for patient "A," the concerns are predominantly self and world and would be voiced by statements reflecting low self-esteem and negative views of world and experience. When questioned about hopelessness and suicidal potential, this patient might say, "Kill myself. Oh No! I'll just continue to live my poor, miserable life because I deserve to."

If the patient's concerns focus on world and future (patient "C"), the verbalizations would include those reflecting low self esteem and suicidal thoughts (e.g., "What good am I? I deserve to die. The world seems to get along pretty well; it's me that is at variance with the rest of the world").

Finally, if the patient's concerns involve a negative view of the work and the future (patient "B"), the patient's verbalizations might include a diatribe against the ills and evils of the world, and a multitude of reasons as to why the best course of action in dealing with the awful world is death. When asked about self-esteem or personal contributions to their difficulty, these kinds of patients often go on in great detail about how they have tried and not succeeded but are victimized because of the world's problems. They see themselves as the innocent victims. (This perceptual–response style is common among Axis II patients (Beck & Freeman, in press; Freeman & Leaf, 1989). By including the patient in the assessment and understanding of each of the triadic factors, the therapeutic collaboration can begin early in the therapy. Therapy can be directed at specific areas of concern rather than on vague, global, and amorphous treatment issues.

Cognitive Distortions

An individual can distort in a variety of ways. These distortions can be positive or negative. Patients who distort in a positive direction may be the "fools who rush in where angels fear to tread." Positive distorters may view life in an unrealistically positive way. They may take chances that most people would avoid (e.g., starting a new business, investing in a stock). If successful, positive distorters are vindicated. If unsuccessful, positive distorters may see their failure as a consequence of taking a low-yield chance. Positive distorters can, however, take chances that may lead to their being in situations of great danger (e.g., experiencing massive chest pains and not consulting a physician). The positive distortion in this case might be, "I'm too young/healthy for a heart attack."

The distortions become the initial focus of the therapy. The therapist works to help the patient recognize the distortions' content, degree of patient belief, style, and impact on the patient's life. The distortions become the thematic directional signs that point to the underlying cognitive schema. The following distortions are in no way a comprehensive list of all of the possible distortions the therapist might encounter. The distortions occur in many combinations and permutations. They are presented here in isolation for the sake of discussion. Typical distortions include:

1. *All-or-none thinking.* "I'm either a success or a failure." "The world is either black or white."

2. *Mind reading.* "They probably think that I'm incompetent." "I just know that he/she disapproves."

3. *Emotional reasoning.* "Because I feel inadequate, I am inadequate." "I believe that I must be funny to be liked, so that is a fact."

4. *Personalization.* "That comment wasn't just random, it must have been directed toward me." "Problems always emerge when I'm in a hurry."

5. *Overgeneralization.* "Everything I do turns out wrong." "It doesn't matter what my choices are, they always fall flat."

6. *Catastrophizing.* "If I go to the party, there will be terrible consequences." "I better not try because I might fail, and that would be awful."

7. *Should statements.* "I should visit my family every time they want me to." "They should be nicer to me."

8. *Control fallacies.* "If I'm not in complete control all the time, I will go out of control." "I must be able to control all of the contingencies in my life.

9. *Comparing.* "I am not as competent as my co-workers or supervisors." "Compared to others, there is clearly something flawed about me."

10. *Heaven's reward fallacy.* "If I do everything perfectly here, I will be rewarded later." "I have to muddle through this life; maybe things will be better later."

11. *Disqualifying the positive.* "This success experience was only a fluke." "The compliment I received was unwarranted."

12. *Perfectionism.* "I must do everything perfectly, or I will be criticized and a failure." "An adequate job is akin to a failure."

13. *Selective abstraction.* "The rest of the information doesn't matter. This is the salient point." "I must focus on the negative details while I ignore and filter out all the positive aspects of a situation."

14. *Externalization of self-worth.* "My worth is dependent upon what others think of me." "They think, therefore I am."

15. *Fallacy of change.* "You should change your behavior because I want you to." "They should act differently because I expect it."

16. *Fallacy of worrying.* "If I worry about it enough, it will be resolved." "One cannot be too concerned."

17. *Fallacy of ignoring.* "If I ignore it, maybe it will go away." "If I don't pay attention, I will not be held responsible."

18. *Fallacy of fairness.* "Life should be fair." "People should all be fair."

19. *Being right.* "I must prove that I am right, as being wrong is unthinkable." "To be wrong is to be a bad person."

20. *Fallacy of attachment.* "I can't live with-

out a man." "If I was in an intimate relationship, all of my problems would be solved."

While all of the preceding distortions are stated in the first person, they can also apply to expectations of others, including family and social, religious, or gender groups.

Schemas

An essential element of CT is understanding and making explicit the person's underlying rules/beliefs/schemas. Beck (1967, 1976) and Freeman (1986) have suggested that schemas generate the various cognitive distortions seen in patients. These *schemas* or basic rules of life begin to be established as a force in cognition and behavior from the earliest moments in life, and they are well fixed by the middle childhood years. They are the accumulation of the individual's learning and experience within the family group, the religious or ethnic group, the gender category, regional subgroups, and the broader society.

The schemas are very rarely isolated and separate, but like the distortions, they occur in complex combinations and permutations. The schemas become, in effect, how one defines oneself, both individually and as part of a group. The schemas can be active or dormant, with the more active schemas being the rules that govern day-to-day behavior. The dormant schemas are called into play to control behavior in times of stress. The schemas may be either compelling or noncompelling. The more compelling the particular schema, the more likely it is that the individual or family will respond to the schema.

The dynamic cognitive approach to therapy promotes self-disclosure of individual cognitions in order to increase understanding through enhanced knowledge and an understanding of thoughts, beliefs, and attitudes. Early schemas develop and are modified within the family group. Cognitive therapy with families can provide a context for observing these schemas in operation (Freeman & Zaken-Greenburg, 1988; Teichman, 1986).

The particular extent of a schema's effect on an individual's life depends on several factors: (a) How strongly held is the schema? (b) How essential does the individual perceive that schema to be

for personal safety, well-being, or existence? (c) Does the individual engage in any disputation of the particular schema when it is activated? (d) What was learned previously regarding the importance and essential nature of a particular schema? (e) How early was a particular schema internalized? and (f) How powerfully, and by whom, was the schema reinforced?

Schemas are in a constant state of change and evolution. From the child's earliest years, there is a need to alter old schemas and develop new schemas to meet the different and increasingly complex demands of the world. Infants' conceptions of reality are governed by their limited interaction with their world so that infants may initially perceive the world as their crib and the few caregivers that care for and comfort them. As infants develop the additional skills of mobility and interaction, they then perceive their world as significantly larger.

One way of conceptualizing the change process is to use the Piagetian concept of adaptation, with its two interrelated processes: assimilation and accommodation (Rosen, 1985, 1989). Environmental data and experience are only taken in by individuals as they can use these data in terms of their own subjective experiences. Their self-schemas then become self-selective, as individuals may ignore environmental stimuli that they were not able to integrate or synthesize. The assimilative and accommodative processes are interactive and stand in opposition to one another. Assimilation is an active and evolutionary process through which all existing perceptions and cognitive structures are applied to new functions, whereas accommodation requires that new cognitive structures be developed in order to serve old functions in new situations. Some individuals may persist in using old structures (assimilation), without fitting them to the new circumstances (accommodation) in which they are involved; instead, they use the old structures in toto, without measuring fit or appropriateness. They may further fail to accommodate, or build new structures for other situations.

A particular schema may engender a great deal of emotion and be emotionally bound by the individual's past experience, by the sheer weight of the time in which that schema has been held, or by the relative importance and meaning of the individuals from or with whom the schema were acquired.

A cognitive element of the schema pervades the individual's thoughts and images. The schemas are cognitive in that we can often, with the proper training, describe schemas in great detail, We can also deduce them from behavior or from automatic thoughts. Finally, a behavioral component of each schema involves the way the belief system governs the individual's responses to a particular stimulus or set of stimuli. In seeking to alter a particular schema that has endured for a long period of time, it would be necessary to help the individual to deal with the belief from as many different perspectives as possible. A purely cognitive strategy would leave the behavioral and affective perspectives untouched. The purely affective strategy is similarly limited, as is the strictly behavioral approach. In many cases, an individual's particular schemas are consensually validated. Significant others not only help to form the schemas, but also help to maintain the particular schemas, be they negative or positive. McGoldrick, Pearce, and Giordano (1982) emphasize that families view the world through their own cultural filters so that the particular belief systems may be familial or more broadly cultural. An example of a family schema based on the culture in which the family is immersed might be basic rules regarding sexual behavior; reaction to other racial, ethnic, or religious groups; or particular religious beliefs.

Patients often describe themselves as displaying particular characteristics "as far back as I can remember." Objective observation may support the patient's views that they have behaved a certain way as far back as early childhood. What then differentiates the child who develops a schema that is held with moderate strength and that is amenable to change later on and the individual who develops a core belief that is powerful and apparently immutable? Several possibilities exist: (a) In addition to the core belief, the individual maintains a powerful associated belief that cannot be changed; (b) the belief system is powerfully reinforced by parents or significant others; (c) while the dysfunctional belief system may not be especially reinforced, any attempt to believe the contrary may not be reinforced or may even be punished (e.g., children may be told, "You're no good," or the children might not be told that they lack worth, but any attempt to assert worth would

be ignored); (d) the parents or significant others may offer direct instruction contrary to developing a positive image (e.g., "It's not nice to brag" or "It's not nice to toot your own horn because people will think less of you").

GENERAL TREATMENT APPROACH

Cognitive therapy requires all of the usual characteristics of effective therapy, including rapport building, trust, empathy, active listening, and the maintenance of the therapeutic alliance. The presenting problems are investigated to get an overview of the problem(s). A full developmental, familial, social, occupational, educational, medical, and psychiatric history should be taken. These data are essential in helping to develop the problem list and the treatment conceptualization. The establishment of a discrete problem list helps both patient and therapist to have an idea of where the therapy is going, and how to know how the therapy is progressing. The content and the direction of the therapy are established early in the collaboration. Having established and agreed upon a problem list and a focus for therapy, the individual sessions are then structured through agenda setting and home work.

Many groups use agenda setting in meetings in order to help the participants have a direction for the meeting, add to the agenda, become more active in the meeting process, and generally allow for maximum success in the minimal time often allotted to the meeting. Rather than permitting the therapy session to meander, the therapist can work with the patient to set an agenda for the session, using the agenda to help focus the therapy work and make better use of time, energy, and available skills. Setting the agenda at the beginning of the session allows both patient and therapist to put issues of concern on the agenda for the day. We would make the point that the reason that individuals often become patients is that they have lost their ability to organize and solve problems. By setting an agenda, a problem-solving focus is modeled by the therapist. A typical agenda might include:

1. Review of Beck Depression Inventory

(BDI), Beck Anxiety Inventory (BAI) and other scales

2. A brief overview of the week's interactions/problems

3. Review of homework

4. Problem focus (e.g., specific areas of discussion)

5. Wrap-up, review of the session, and feedback to the therapist.

1. Review. The therapist reviews the BDI, BAI, and other scales filled out by the patient prior to the session. Specific issues or questions can be put on the agenda.

2. Overview of the week. The patient can be asked to tell the therapist about events of importance during the week, including the patient's response to the last therapy session.

3. Review of homework. The patient describes both problems in doing the homework and the results of the homework.

4. Problem focus. Particular problems are put on the agenda for work within the session. This might involve teaching a particular skill (social or assertiveness skills), or the questioning of particular dysfunctional thoughts.

5. Closure. The session can be halted 3–5 minutes prior to the end, and the patient can be asked to review the session and outline what the patient has gotten from the session. This gives the therapist an opportunity to help the patient to clarify the goals and accomplishments of the session. The homework for the next session can be emphasized and the session given a closure. Finally, the patient can be asked for his or her response to the session.

Cognitive therapy is a collaborative therapy. The therapist and patient work together as a team. The collaboration is not always 50:50; it may be 30:70, or 90:10, with the therapist providing most of the energy or work within the session or in the therapy more generally. The more severely depressed the patient, the less energy the patient may have available to use in the therapy. The therapeutic focus would be used to help patients both to make maximum use of their existing energy and to build greater reserves of energy.

ASSESSMENT METHODS

When depression is a primary problem, the BDI is among the most useful tools available to the therapist. The BDI (Beck, Ward, Mendelson, Mock, & Erbaugh, 1961), is a self-report measure that consists of 21 items designed to reflect the overall level of depression. Depressed individuals tend to negatively distort, thereby incorporating negative events and attributing those events to qualities lacking in themselves, simultaneously ignoring positive events and outcomes (Simon & Fleming, 1985). Depressed individuals may feel hopeless about positive changes, may attribute life problems to their own perceived shortcomings, and may frequently compare themselves negatively to other persons. Weekly administration of the BDI, prior to each session, can serve to provide objective data regarding therapeutic progress, and as an aid in helping to validate (or invalidate) assumptions about the self, the world, and the future. The BDI form is checked by the therapist at the beginning of each session. The score is charted to maintain a graph of mood fluctuations. When patients report diurnal mood fluctuations, the BDI can be used as a homework form. In this case, the patient is given a supply of the forms and is asked to fill them out at regular intervals each day. The therapist can then evaluate high and low points during the day.

In addition to its quantitative use, the BDI has great utility as a qualitative measure. By doing a weekly content analysis, the specific content of the depression can be elicited and then utilized in the agenda. For example, if a patient who is chronically a "1" on item 9 (suicide) endorses either a "0" or a "3," it would be incumbent on the therapist to elicit information about the reason(s) for the change.

Among the most difficult depressed patients to work with are those who present dysthymia (DSM-III-R, 300.40). This disorder may equate to a BDI score of 12 or 13. By definition, the dysthymic disorder is "characterized by a chronic mild depressive syndrome that has been present for many years. When dysthymia is of many years' duration, the mood disturbance cannot be distinguished from the person's 'usual' functioning" (DSM-III-R: American Psychiatric Association,

1987, p. 231). This patient often comes to therapy at the behest or the demand of a significant other. The patient may have a depression that meets criteria for recurrent major depression; however, the therapist discovers that even when the depression remits, there is still an underlying dysthymic personality style. While this might appear quite mild, compared to most depressed patients, the chronic nature of the depression makes it difficult to treat. The dysthymic patient seems to gain little pleasure from life without being severely depressively debilitated.

> For example, a 34-year-old attorney was referred for therapy by his wife. She threatened to leave him if he did not change his negative attitude. He was successful in his practice, married, and the father of two children. If he and his wife ate dinner in the best restaurant in their city, he would describe the meal as "tasty." Sex was "O.K." An evening at the ballet to see Mikhail Barishnikov dance elicited the comment that Barishnikov was "a fine dancer." He described his entire life (work, family, leisure) as "an underwhelming experience."

Patients who are more severely depressed may be far more powerfully motivated to change their depressive thoughts and behaviors. Further, when the more typical depressed patient changes from a BDI score of 32 to a score of 21, there is great change. The patient feels better, does more, and thinks differently. When the dysthymic goes from a BDI score of 13 to an 11, the change is hardly noticeable. Given the small changes, the initial low motivation for treatment is lowered even further.

When anxiety is a target symptom, the BAI is quite helpful. The BAI is a 21-item self-report symptom checklist designed to measure the severity of anxiety-related symptoms (Beck, Epstein, Brown, & Steer, 1985). The BAI was designed to complement the BDI. As with the BDI, the BAI is a useful weekly objective measure of the overall level of anxiety. As with the BDI, the BAI is diagnostic both quantitatively and qualitatively.

The Hopelessness Scale (HS) was developed as a measure of the negative view of the future and the intensity of that view (Beck, Weissman, Lester, & Trexler, 1974). The HS is frequently used in conjunction with the BDI as a measure of potential suicidal behavior. This measure may also be used as an index of change. As the patient (a) learns new ways of coping, (b) experiences greater self-efficacy, and (c) perceives internal and external change, the patient's level of hopelessness decreases.

The BDI, BAI, and HS basically measure dysfunctional thoughts and symptomatology that are generated by underlying assumptions and core beliefs. The Dysfunctional Attitude Scale (DAS) quantitatively measures the maladaptive underlying assumptions (Weissman, 1978). This scale provides measures of vulnerability, attraction–rejection, perfectionism, self-imposed imperatives, approval, dependence, autonomous attitudes, and cognitive philosophy. These measures allow the therapist to determine the individual's maladaptive assumptions, as well as how those assumptions overlap or discriminate and which of them are shared by the individual's family. These assumptions can then be challenged, upsetting both the homeostasis of the system and the personal beliefs, which open up the system for interventions leading to change.

An additional scale based on the cognitive model is the Sociotropy–Autonomy Scale (SAS) (Beck, Epstein, & Harrison, 1983), which was originally developed as a measure of relatively stable individual differences in motivational patterns in two major areas. These two areas refer to affiliation (*sociotropy*) and achievement (*autonomy*). It is hypothesized that these two personality styles may mediate a vulnerability to depression (Beck et al., 1983). An individual high in sociotropy is one who is invested in maintaining warm interpersonal relationships in order to satisfy strivings for "intimacy, sharing, empathy, understanding, approval, affection, protection, guidance and help" (Beck et al., 1983, pp. 1–2). Such individuals may be particularly vulnerable to interpersonal losses, separation, or rejection. Conversely, individuals high in autonomy may be more invested in themselves, in acquisition of personal power, and in control over their environment. A highly autonomous individual tends to be particularly vulnerable both to situations of failure in achieving desired outcomes and to situations in which freedom of action in thwarted or constrained.

DIAGNOSIS AND TREATMENT PLAN

There are several steps in establishing a treatment plan for the patient. The initial step involves the therapist developing a conceptualization of the problem(s). This conceptualization will, of necessity, be based on family and developmental histories, test data, interview material, and reports of previous therapists or other professionals. This conceptualization must meet several criteria. It must be (a) useful, (b) simple, (c) coherent, (d) explanatory of past behavior, and (e) capable of predicting future behavior.

Part of the conceptualization process is the compilation of a problem list. This list can then be prioritized in terms of identifying a sequence of problems to be treated in therapy. The reasons for choosing one problem ahead of another as the primary, secondary, or tertiary foci of the therapy depends on many factors. A particular problem may be the primary focus of therapy because of its debilitating effect on the individual. In another case, there may be no debilitating problems. The focus may be on the simplest problem, thereby giving the family practice in solving problems and some measure of success. In a third case, the choice of a primary focus might be on a *keystone problem*: that is, a problem for which the solution will cause a ripple effect for solving other problems. Having set out the treatment goals with the family, the therapist can begin to develop both the strategies and the interventions that will help effect the strategies.

The therapist must question what reinforces and maintains dysfunctional thinking and behavior. The major factor would appear to be the self-consonance of the belief system. If a particular belief is only partially believed by individuals, it is much easier for them to give it up because they are giving up a small piece of a belief system, as opposed to being asked to challenge what they see and regard as basic to their sense of self. The patients who exhibit chronic problems or symptoms of distorted belief patterns, including the chronic neurotic behaviors and character disorders, often see their symptoms as central to themselves. They readily verbalize, "This is who I/we are and this is the way I/we have always been." When asked to challenge or directly dispute their dysfunctional beliefs, they are being asked to challenge directly their very being. When individuals perceive the challenge to the self, they usually respond with anxiety. They are then placed in a conflict situation as to whether they would prefer to maintain their particular dysfunctional symptoms or to experience anxiety. Because they see themselves as being defined by the problem, they hesitate to give up the problem, as it would leave them nothing but an empty shell. We can see that any challenge to the self needs to be the result of a careful, guided discovery, based on collaboration, as opposed to a direct, confrontational, and disputational stance.

TREATMENT INTERVENTIONS

Several cognitive and behavioral techniques can be used by the therapist to help to question both the distortions and the schemas that underlie the distortions. These techniques can be taught to the patients to help them respond in more functional ways. A rule of thumb in treating severely depressed patients would be that the greater the severity of the depression, the more the therapist will use a larger proportion of behavioral interventions in relation to cognitive ones (Figure 5.2).

The precise mix of cognitive and behavioral techniques depends on the patient's skills, the patient's degree of depression, and the chosen treatment goals. Further, the use of pharmacotherapy may be essential with patients who are in a vegetative state. For severely depressed patients, the initial goals of treatment would be focused on having the patient perform self-help tasks. Graded

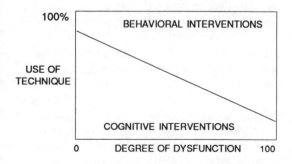

Figure 5.2. Relationship of degree of disturbance to proportion of cognitive and behavioral interventions required.

task assignments can be used with great success. Starting at the bottom of a hierarchy of difficulty, and moving through successively more difficult tasks, can help the patient achieve a greater sense of personal efficacy. This personal efficacy can then be used as evidence for the cognitive work in therapy.

COGNITIVE TECHNIQUES

1. Testing idiosyncratic meaning.   The therapist cannot assume that a term or statement used by a patient is completely understood by the therapist until the patient is asked for meaning and clarification. It is essential to question patients directly on the meanings of their verbalizations. While this may appear to be intrusive, it can be structured by the therapist to be less so, and it is essential as a way of making sure that the therapist is not merely in the right ballpark in understanding the patient's verbalizations, but is right on target. This also models for the patient the need for active listening skills, increased communication, and a means for checking out assumptions.

2. Questioning the evidence.   Individuals use certain evidence to maintain ideas and beliefs. It is essential to teach the individual to question the evidence that they are using to maintain and strengthen an idea or belief. Questioning the evidence also requires examining the source of data. The patient who is depressed often gives equal weight to all sources and all cues. For example, a spouse may appear to frown at the precise moment when the patient passes by the spouse. This may be used by the patient as evidence of being unloved and thus may as well kill themselves. Many patients have the ability to ignore major amounts of data and to focus on the few data that support their dysfunctional view. By having the patient question the evidence with family members or significant others, the patient can gain a fuller understanding of the available data. If the distorting evidence is strong, the therapist can help to structure alternative ways either of perceiving the data, or of changing behaviors so that the evidence is either modified or eliminated.

3. Retribution.   A common statement made by patients is, "It's all my fault." This is commonly heard in situations of relationship difficulty, separation, or divorce. While one cannot dismiss this out of hand, it is unlikely that a single person is totally responsible for everything going wrong within a relationship. Depressed patients often take responsibility for events and situations that are only minimally attributable to them. The therapist can help patients to distribute responsibility among all relevant parties. If the therapist takes a position of total support (e.g., "It wasn't your fault." "She isn't worth it." "You're better off without her." or "There are other fish in the ocean."), the therapist ends up sounding like friends and family whom the patient has already dismissed as being a cheering squad and as not understanding the patient's position. The therapist can, by taking a middle ground, help the patient to reattribute responsibility, neither taking all the blame nor unrealistically shifting all the blame to others.

4. Examining options and alternatives.   Many individuals see themselves as having lost all options. Perhaps the prime example of this lack of options appears in suicidal patients. They see their options and alternatives as so limited that among their few choices, death might be the easiest and simplest choice. This cognitive strategy involves working with the patient to generate additional options.

5. Decatastrophizing.   This is also called the "What if" technique. This involves helping the patient to evaluate whether they are overestimating the catastrophic nature of a situation. Questions that might be asked of the patient include, "What is the worst thing that can happen?" or, "If it does occur, what would be so terrible?" The therapist uses this technique to work against a "Chicken Little" style of thinking. If the patient sees an experience (or life itself) as a series of catastrophes and problems, the therapist can help the patient work toward reality testing. The patient can be helped to see the consequence of life actions as not being "all or none" and thereby as being less catastrophic. It is important that this technique be used with great gentleness and care so that the patient does not feel ridiculed or belittled by the therapist.

6. Fantasized consequences.   In this technique, individuals are asked to fantasize a situation and to describe their images and their attendant concerns. Patients often describe their concerns, and during the direct verbalization, they can see the irrationality of their ideas. If the fantasized consequences are unrealistic, the therapist can work with the patients to help them realistically assess the danger and develop appropriate coping strategies. This technique allows patients to bring into the consulting room various imagined events or situations, or interactions that have happened previously. By having the patient move the fantasy toward reality by being spoken, the images can become grist for the therapeutic mill. The fantasy, being colored by the same dysfunctional thinking that alters many of the patient's perceptions, may be overly negative. The explication and investigation of the style, format, and content of the fantasy can yield very good material for the therapy work, especially the fantasies that involve feedback from others.

7. Advantages and disadvantages. The advantages of maintaining a particular belief or behavior can help a patient to gain a more balanced perspective. By focusing on the advantages and disadvantages of a particular behavior or way of thinking, a broader perspective can be viewed. The depressed patient who has dichotomized life events may see only one side. By asking that they examine both the advantages and the disadvantages of both sides of an issue, they can see a broader perspective. This technique can be used to examine the advantages and disadvantages of acting a certain way (e.g., dressing in a particular manner), thinking a certain way (e.g., thinking of what others will think of them), or feeling a particular way (e.g., sad). While individuals may often claim that they cannot control their feelings, actions, and thoughts, it is precisely the development of this control that is the strength of CT.

8. Turning adversity to advantage. There are times that what seems to be a disaster can be used as an advantage. Losing one's job can be a disaster, but it may, in some cases, be the entry point or the stimulus to a new job or even a new career. Being given a deadline may be seen as oppressive and unfair, but it may also be used as a motivator. This CT technique asks patients to look for the silver lining in their clouds. Given that depressed indi-

viduals have taken a view that often leads to their finding a darkened shading to every silver cloud, focusing on a redeeming feature of the situation offers a balance that helps to put the experience into perspective. Looking for the kernel of positive in a negative situation can be very difficult for many patients. They simply may not see the positive. Some individuals may respond to the therapist's positive highlights with even greater negativity. They may accuse the therapist of being unrealistic, a Pollyanna, or a Mary Poppins. The therapist can then point out that if one view is unrealistically positive, the alternative offered by the patient is unrealistically negative.

9. Guided association or discovery. Through simple questions, such as "Then what?" "What would that mean?" "What would happen then?" the therapist can help the patient to explore the significance they attribute to events. This collaborative, therapist-guided technique stands in opposition to the technique of free association which is basic to the psychoanalytic process. The idea behind the free-association strategy is that the freely wandering mind will eventually meander to the hot areas of conflict and concern. The use of this *chained* or *guided association technique* involves the therapist working with the patient to connect ideas, thoughts, and images. The therapist provides the conjunctions for the patients' verbalizations. Statements such as "And then what?" "What evidence do we have that that is true?" and so forth allow the therapist to guide the patients along various therapeutic paths, depending on the therapist's conceptualization and therapeutic goals.

10. Use of exaggeration or paradox. By taking a patient's idea to its logical extreme, the therapist can often help to move the patient to a more central position vis-à-vis a particular belief. Care must be taken not to insult, ridicule, or embarrass the patient. Given a hypersensitivity to criticism and ridicule, some patients may experience the therapist who uses paradoxical strategies as making light of their problems. There seems to be room at the extreme for only one person. The patient may see things in their most extreme form. When the therapist takes a more extreme stance (e.g., focusing on the absolutes "never," "always," "no one," or "everyone"), the patient often may be forced to move from an extreme view to a position closer to center. This technique is risky, however; the patient may take the therapist's statement as reinforcement of their position of abject hopelessness. The therapist who chooses to use paradoxical or exaggeration techniques must have (a) a strong working relationship with the patient, (b) good timing, and (c) the good sense to know when to back away from the technique.

11. Scaling. For those patients who see things as all or none, the technique of *scaling*, or seeing things as existing on a continuum, can be very helpful. Scaling a feeling can force patients to gain distance and perspective. Because patients may be at a point of extreme thoughts and extreme behaviors, any movement toward a midpoint is helpful.

12. Externalization of voices. By having the therapist play the role of the dysfunctional voice, the patient can get practice in adaptively responding to it. The therapist can first model being adaptive to patients' verbalizations of their dysfunctional thoughts. After modeling the functional voice, the therapist can, via graded situations, become an increasingly difficult dysfunctional voice to which the patients must respond. Patients may hear the dysfunctional voices internally. When they externalize the voices, both patients and therapist are better able to deal with the voices/messages in a variety of ways. It would be hoped that the patient can recognize the dysfunctional nature of the therapist's verbalization of the dysfunctional voice. The therapist and patient can then hear the tone, content, and general context of the suicidal thoughts and can generate strategies for intervention.

13. Self-instruction. We all talk to ourselves. We give ourselves orders, directions, instructions, or information we need in order to solve problems. Meichenbaum (1977) has developed an extensive model for understanding self-instruction. According to Meichenbaum's model, the child moves from overt verbalization of instructions to subvocalization to nonverbalization. This same process can be developed in the adult. The patient can start with direct verbalization, which, with practice, will become part of the person's behavioral repertoire. Patients can be taught to offer direct self-instructions or in some cases counterinstructions.

In this technique, the therapist is not introducing anything new. Rather, the patients are being helped to utilize and strengthen a technique that we all use at various times.

14. Thought stopping. Dysfunctional thoughts often have a snowball effect for the individual. What may start as a small and insignificant problem can, if left to roll along, gather mass, speed, and momentum. Once on the roll, the thoughts have a force of their own, and they are very hard to stop. Thought stopping is best used when the thoughts first start, not once they have been rolling for a while. The patient can stop these thoughts by picturing a stop sign, hearing a bell, or envisioning a wall. Any of these can be helped to stop the progression and growth of the dysfunctional thoughts. A therapist hitting the desk sharply or ringing a small bell can serve to help the patient to stop the thoughts. The memory of that intervention can be used by the patient to assist their thought stopping. The therapist should recognize, however, that there is both a distractive and an aversive quality to this technique.

15. Distraction. This technique is especially helpful for patients with anxiety problems. Because it is almost impossible to maintain simultaneously, two thoughts at the same strength, anxiogenic thoughts generally preclude more adaptive thinking. Conversely, a focused thought distracts from the anxiogenic thoughts. By having patients focus on complex counting, addition, or subtraction (or on alphabetic sequences within a certain category, such as asparagus, beet, cabbage) they may be rather easily distracted from other thoughts. (One should take care that the person is not math or number phobic, in which case the counting may work to increase the anxiety and the alternative alphabetic task might be used.) Having the patient count to 200 by 13's is very effective (having the patient count by 2, 5, 10, or 11 is not as effective because these number sequences are overlearned). When out of doors, the patient might count cars, or people wearing the color red, or any other cognitively engaging set of objects.

Distraction or refocusing of attention may be also achieved by focusing on some aspect of the environment, engaging in mental exercise or imagery, or initiating physical activity. It is helpful if the distraction activity can also serve to challenge the patient's catastrophizing. For example, patients who are concerned about a loss of control can engage in physical activity that demonstrates they can take control. Patients who fear "losing their minds," can distract themselves with a mental distraction that provides evidence of being in control of their minds (Beck et al., 1979; Burns, 1980; Ellis & Harper, 1961; McMullin, 1987). While this technique is a short-term technique, it is very useful to allow patients the time to detach from the anxiety and to establish some degree of control over their thinking. Once some control is reestablished, patients can begin to use other cognitive techniques.

16. Direct disputation. While we do not advocate arguing with a patient, there are times when direct disputation is necessary. A major guideline for using disputation is the imminence of a suicide attempt. When it seems clear to the clinician that a patient is going to make an attempt, the therapist must directly and quickly work to challenge the patient's hopelessness. While it might appear to be the treatment technique of choice, the therapist risks becoming embroiled in a power struggle or argument with the patient. Disputation coming from outside the patient may, in fact, engender passive resistance and a passive-aggressive response that might include suicide. Disputation, argument, or debate are potentially dangerous tools. They must be used carefully, judiciously, and with skill. If the therapist becomes reduced to just one more harping contact, the patient may turn the therapist off completely.

17. Labeling of distortions. The fear of the unknown is a frequent issue for anxiety patients. The more that the therapist can do to identify the nature and content of the dysfunctional thinking, and to help label the types of distortions that patients use, the less frightening the entire process becomes.

18. Developing replacement imagery. Inasmuch as the anxiety is constantly being generated by imagery, patients can be helped to develop coping images. For example, rather than continuing with an image of failure, or recalling defeat or embarrassment, the therapist can practice with the patient new, more effective coping images. Once well-practiced, patients can do image substitution (Freeman, 1981).

BEHAVIORAL TECHNIQUES

The goals in using behavioral techniques within the context of cognitive therapy are manyfold. The first goal is to use direct behavioral strategies and techniques to test dysfunctional thoughts and behaviors. By having the patient *try* the feared or avoided behaviors, old ideas can be directly challenged. A second use of behavioral techniques is to practice new behaviors as homework. Certain behaviors can be practiced in the therapist's office and then practiced at home. Homework can include acting differently, practicing active listening, being verbally or physically affectionate, or doing things in a new way.

1. Activity scheduling. The activity schedule is, perhaps, the most widely applicable technique in the therapist's armamentarium. For patients who are feeling overwhelmed, the activity schedule can be used to plan more effective time use. The activity schedule illustrated in Figure 5.3 is both a retrospective tool to assess past time utilization and a prospective tool to help plan better time use.

2. Mastery and pleasure ratings. The activity schedule can also be used to assess and plan activities that offer patients a sense of both personal efficacy (mastery, 1–10) and personal pleasure (1–10). The greater the mastery and pleasure, the lower the rates of anxiety and depression. By discovering the low- or high-anxiety activities, plans can be made to increase the former and decrease the latter.

3. Social skills training. If reality testing is good, and patients actually lack specific skills, it is incumbent upon the therapist either to help them gain the skills or to make a referral for skills training. The skill acquisition may involve anything from teaching patients how to properly shake hands to practicing conversational skills.

4. Assertiveness training. As with the social skills training, assertiveness training may be an essential part of the therapy. Patients who are socially anxious can be helped to develop responsible assertive behavior skills (Jakubowski & Lange, 1978).

5. Bibliotherapy. Several excellent books can be assigned as readings for homework. These books

WEEKLY ACTIVITY SCHEDULE

NOTE: Grade activities M for Mastery and P for Pleasure 0–10

		M	T	W	Th	F	S	S
M O R N I N G	6–7							
	7–8							
	8–9							
	9–10							
	10–11							
	11–12							
A F T E R N O O N	12–1							
	1–2							
	2–3							
	3–4							
	4–5							
	5–6							

		M	T	W	Th	F	S	S
E V E N I N G	6–7							
	7–8							
	8–9							
	9–10							
	10–11							
	11–12							
	12–6							

REMARKS:

Figure 5.3.   Activity schedule for logging daily requirements.

can be used to socialize or educate patients to the basic CT model, to emphasize specific points made in the session, or to introduce new ideas for discussion at future sessions.

6. Graded task assignments (GTA). GTAs involve a shaping procedure of small sequential steps that lead to the desired goal. By setting out a task and then arranging the necessary steps in a hierarchy, patients can be helped to make reasonable progress with a minimum of stress. As patients attempt each step, the therapist can be available for support and guidance. For example, a GTA might be arranged for the patient who is having difficulty in social interaction areas:

Step 1. Walk down the street, and say hello to 20 people, and evaluate their response (minimal involvement).

Step 2. Stop 20 people to ask the time (greater involvement).

Step 3. Ask 20 people for travel directions (still greater involvement).

Step 4. Find a safe setting, such as school, and discuss the class with a classmate.

At each step, the therapist has the patient rate the likelihood of success, as well as the emotional and cognitive issues in the behaviors.

7. Behavioral rehearsal and role playing. The therapy session is the ideal place in which to practice many behaviors. The therapist can serve as teacher and guide, offering direct feedback on performance. The therapist can monitor the patient's performance, offer suggestions for improvement, and model new behaviors. In addition, anticipated and actual road blocks can be identified and worked on during the session. The patient can rehearse a behavior extensively before attempting the behavior in vivo.

8. In vivo exposure. There are times that the practice in the consulting room needs to be expanded. The therapist can go with patients into feared situations. The therapist can drive with a patient across a feared bridge, go to a feared shopping mall, or travel on a feared bus. The in vivo exposure can supplement the office-based practice and the patient-generated homework, as a laboratory experience.

9. Relaxation training. The anxious patient can profit from relaxation training inasmuch as the anxiety response and the quieting relaxation response are mutually exclusive. The relaxation training can be taught in the office and then practiced by the patient for homework. Ready-made relaxation tapes can be purchased, or the therapist may easily tailor a tape for a patient. The therapist-made tape can include the patient's name and can focus on particular symptoms. The tape can be then modified later, as needed.

CHALLENGING DYSFUNCTIONAL THINKING

One of the most powerful techniques in CT involves using the various cognitive techniques to challenge dysfunctional thinking. The CT model posits an interaction between the individual's thoughts and the individual's emotions. The model does *not* posit a direct, linear, causal relationship from thoughts to feelings. In fact, for some patients, the emotional response may actually precede the thought. For example, Patient A awakes in the morning and thinks, "Another lousy day. Nothing to do. It wouldn't make a difference what I did because I'm such a hopeless case." Patient A may begin to feel more and more depressed as a consequence of the dysfunctional thinking. Patient B, however, awakes and is overcome by feelings of depression. Patient B lays in bed and thinks, "Another lousy day. I've just gotten up and I'm already depressed. There is nothing I can do to ease my depression. I'm a hopeless case." Whether the therapist focuses on the preceding cognition or the subsequent attribution, the focus is cognitive.

The daily record of dysfunction thoughts (DTR) is an ideal form for this purpose. The goal is not to have the patient become expert at filling out forms, but to have them develop a model for solving problems. Whether the patients' problems are directly expressed as depression or are obscured as "masked depression," the therapeutic approach would be substantially the same. The clinician, attuned to the subtleties of the depressive syndrome, can easily identify the depressive synonyms, "blue," "down," "out of sorts," "sad," "hopeless," or "guilty," or "blahs." These descriptors are easily identified and questioned. Less easily identified are the many masks that depression can wear. These might include sleeping difficulty, eating problems, loss of appetite, loss of libido, or a loss of social drive, all with the feelings of sadness directly attributed to the patient's problems.

Kramlinger, Swanson, and Maruta (1983), Lesse (1974), and Ward and Bloom (1979) found that hypersensitivity to pain or the development of a chronic pain syndrome can be a concomitant of depression. Noll, Davis, and DeLeon-Jones (1985) suggest that a broad range of medical conditions may be related to the depressive syndrome (e.g., anxiety, phobias, panic attacks, school phobia, bulimia, and childhood enuresis; pp. 227–228). Another term that may be more appropriate is the term *secondary depression*, which may be used to describe patients who have a primary medical or psychiatric diagnosis but who also manifest the symptoms of depression secondary to the medical problems. Whether the depression is primary or secondary, cognitive therapy techniques can be used for the depression. In many cases, when the depression lifts, the associated problems are also lessened or ameliorated.

The process can begin with the thought, the emotion, or the situation. If the patient presents an emotion (e.g., "I'm very sad"), the therapist needs to inquire as to the situations that might engender the emotion and the attendant thoughts. If the patient presents a thought (e.g., "I'm a loser", the therapist needs to ascertain the feelings and the situation. Finally, the patient may present a situation (e.g., "My husband left me"). The therapist needs to determine the thoughts and the emotions. Statements such as, "I feel like a loser," need to be reframed as thoughts (i.e., "I think that I'm a loser") and the emotions that are a concomitant of the thought elicited.

Often, patients phrase their thoughts as questions (e.g., "Why does this always happen to me?" "Why can't I maintain a relationship?" or "Why doesn't my life turn out better?"). A heuristic view is that questions are generally functional. It is important to ask questions, and then to answer them (e.g., "Does this always happen to me?"

"Why do I have difficulty maintaining relationships?" or "What has caused my life to be less than I had hoped for?"). The dysfunctional thoughts are more generally declarative rather than interrogatory (e.g., "This always happens to me," "I can't maintain a relationship," and "My life is less than I had hoped for"). The several cognitive techniques can be used to question the patient's conclusions. For example:

> Dysfunctional thought—"I can't maintain a relationship"
> Sample adaptive responses—
> - What do you mean by "maintain a relationship"? (revealing an idiosyncratic meaning)
> - What evidence are you using that you cannot maintain a relationship? (seeking evidence)
> - Has it always been you who has caused the relationships to end? (encouraging reattribution)
> - Have you never maintained a relationship for any length of time? (revealing an exaggeration)
> - On a scale from 1 to 10, where would you place the quality of the relationship? (fostering scaling)

As can be seen, the use of these techniques is limited only by the creativity of the therapist. The techniques must be well learned so that the therapist can move quickly and easily among them.

HOMEWORK

Therapy, of necessity, should take place beyond the confines of the consulting room. It is important for the patient to understand that the extension of the therapy work to the nontherapy hours allows for greater therapeutic breadth. The homework can be either cognitive or behavioral. It might involve having the patient complete an activity schedule (an excellent homework for the first session), complete several DTRs, or try new behaviors. The homework should flow from the session material, rather than being tacked onto the end of the session simply because CT should include homework. The more meaningful and collaborative the homework, the greater the likelihood of patient compliance with the therapeutic regimen. The homework should be reviewed at the next session. If the homework is not part of the session agenda, the patient will quickly stop doing the homework.

For example, a 29-year-old female patient believed that her parents reinforced her depression. The homework experiment involved her calling her parents with her usual tales of woe (i.e., "Work is going poorly, I may get fired. There are no men in my life. Money is really tight and I can't pay my bills."). She was to assess their response. Her next call, 2 days later was to be more positive (i.e., "I was wrong about work, I may get a raise. I met this really great guy. I made an error in my bank account, I have more money than I thought."). She was then to assess their response to her more positive and more upbeat call. Her conclusion was that when she was depressed and down, they were willing to speak with her at great length. When she was more upbeat, the call was terminated rather quickly. In therapy, we were able to identify an interactional pattern that the message from her being, "I am helpless and needy." Her parents responded by being available and helpful. When she was not helpless and needy, her parents seemed to have no role to play in her life. This homework was the beginning of a renegotiation of her role with her parents.

TERMINATION

In CT termination begins in the first session. Because cure is not the goal of CT (more effective coping is the goal), the cognitive therapist does not plan for therapy to last indefinitely. As a skill-building model of psychotherapy, the therapist's goal is to assist patients in acquiring the skills to deal with the internal and external stressors. When the depression inventory, the patient report, the therapist observation, and the feedback from significant others confirm decreased depression, greater activity, and higher levels of adaptive abilities, the therapy can move toward termination. The termination is accomplished gradually,

to allow time for ongoing modifications, consolidation, and corrections. Sessions are tapered off from once weekly to biweekly. After that, sessions can continue on a monthly basis, with follow-up sessions at 3 and 6 months until therapy is ended. Patients can, of course, still call and set an appointment in the event of an emergency. Sometimes, patients will call simply to get some information, a reinforcement of a particular behavior, or to report a success. With the cognitive therapist in the role of a consultant/collaborator, this continued contact is appropriate and important.

Relapse prevention is an essential part of the therapy. Patients are made aware of the need for monitoring their moods. If they begin to feel more depressed, they can institute their previous learned skills. If they have any difficulty in doing this, an additional appointment can be scheduled for a booster session.

USE OF MEDICATION

For a number of patients, medication is an important part of the overall psychotherapy regimen. For the severely depressed patient with vegetative symptoms, medication may be essential in helping the patient reach a level where they can utilize the therapy. For bipolar or schizophrenic patients, medication is essential. In working with severely anxious patients, anxiolytic medication may be an important part of the therapeutic regimen. However, in the treatment of the more typical unipolar depressive patients, medication may not be indicated. In these cases, patients on medication may be withdrawn from medication over several weeks, with the consultation and agreement of a psychiatrist.

INDICATIONS FOR COGNITIVE THERAPY

Cognitive therapy is an effective treatment model for a broad range of patients and clinical problems. With the appropriate modifications, the basic model has been applied to families (Epstein, Dryden, & Schlesinger, 1988; Freeman, Epstein, & Simon, 1987; Freeman & Zaken-Greenburg,

1988; Teichman, 1987), to children (DiGiuseppe, 1987, 1989), to groups (Sank & Schaeffer, 1984; Wesler & Hanken-Wessler, 1989) to chronic psychiatric patients (Bowers, 1989; Greenwood, 1983), to substance abusers (Beck & Emery, 1980), to persons with eating disorders (Garner & Bemis, 1985; Edgette & Prout, 1989) to persons experiencing anxiety (Beck & Emery, 1985; Michelson & Ascher, 1987) and personality disorders (Beck & Freeman, in press; Freeman, 1988; Freeman & Leaf, 1989).

CASE EXAMPLE

In the following example, CT assessment, conceptualization, treatment strategies, and specific interventions are highlighted. The initial data are from the intake evaluation, and the treatment data are from the eighth session.

Sharon (a pseudonym) is a 33-year-old, married, white, Jewish, female. She was referred to the Center for Cognitive Therapy by her family physician. She described herself as depressed—so depressed, in fact, that during the past year she has, at times, been "paralyzed." She described her depression as affecting her work life, her marital life, and her social life. Paradoxically, she reports that she is not as depressed now as she used to be, but she thinks that she is not as functional as she has been in the past. She described her marital difficulty as being due, in part, to conflict between her career needs and her husband's life-style. She was fearful of making any changes in either her career or her marital status. She feared leaving her husband because she believed that she was unlovable and would never be able to live with anyone else.

Current life situation.   For the past 3 years, Sharon has been employed as vice president and assistant to the president of a small, prestigious company. She had begun to feel that her work had been unsatisfactory and that she was in danger of being fired, although she now has no evidence that her superior was thinking of firing her. She presently lives with her husband in a suburb of Philadelphia, and she works in Trenton, New Jersey—a situation that amounts to a 2-hour daily commute in each direction. She and her husband live in a large home near her husband's work. Previously, they had lived apart, with Sharon seeing her husband only on weekends to avoid the daily 140-mile round-trip commute. The other major conflict regarded her marriage and her wanting to stay married. She had been mar-

ried 7 years, but she and her husband had not had a sexual relationship for the preceding 3 years.

Developmental history.   Sharon was the second youngest of four children, having brothers 39 and 35 years old, and a sister 31. Her mother is an elementary school teacher and her father is a retired dentist. Both are active, her mother still working as a teacher. She described her childhood as relatively unhappy. She reported that her current episodes of depression dated from about age 12 years on. She was the butt of insults and teasing from her second oldest brother, who would constantly call her "rhinodermo," a reference to her being overweight and later having acne.

Social history.   Sharon described herself as unpopular both as a child and as an adolescent, having very poor social skills. She was seen as "brainy" and not very much involved in the social activities of her childhood and adolescent peers. She had no dates throughout her adolescence and first started dating in college. She met her husband when she was 24 years old; they dated for 2 years and then married. At the time of the interview, she reported having no friends outside of work. She did not know her neighbors or do anything socially with her friends at work.

School/occupational history.   She had always done well in school. She graduated high school with high honors, and was graduated from a small liberal arts college, where she was a member of Phi Beta Kappa, graduating summa cum laude. She continued her graduate work at Yale University, getting an M.A. and a Ph.D. in Sociology. She began working for her present employer in New Jersey after completing her graduate work. For the past 3 years, she has worked as assistant to the company president, with her administrative responsibility being (a) the implementation of equal opportunity and affirmative action programs at the company, and (b) the direction of marketing research.

Mental status.   Sharon was well groomed and neat. She was cooperative throughout the interview, and she tried to answer all questions. Her mood was depressed. She was sad and cried several times during the session. The therapist attempted to elicit a mirth response, and Sharon was able to smile and laugh. Her speech and thought were clear and appropriate, and there were no hallucinations or delusions. She was oriented in all spheres.

Major problem areas/cognitive distortions. She indicated that the major areas of difficulty, and her choice of targets for therapy were (a) depression, (b) marital difficulties, (c) sexual problems, (d) vocational difficulties.

Diagnosis. Axis I—dysthymic disorder; Axis II—r/o obsessive–compulsive disorder; Axis III—none; Axis IV—marital difficulty, job difficulty (moderate), Axis V—excellent functioning.

Results of testing. On intake, Sharon's BDI score was 42, placing her in the severely depressed range. She endorsed 10 of the 21 items at the highest level.

An assessment of her suicidal ideation indicated a score of 6, endorsing a weak wish to die, and her reasons for living and dying were about equal. Her general attitude toward the suicidal ideation was ambivalent; her reason for contemplating a suicide attempt was to escape and solve her problems through a cessation of the depression and difficulty she was presently experiencing. The major deterrent to her attempting suicide was her husband and the thought that, "It is going to get better."

On the Hamilton Anxiety Rating Scale for Depression, she described herself as a worrier who constantly anticipates the world with a fearful anticipation, with her general anxiety being severe (i.e., continuous and dominating her life). Feeling tense, fatiguing easily, and crying easily, were described as continuous and life-dominating experiences. She had difficulty with staying asleep, with sleep being generally unsatisfying, and with experiencing fatigue on waking. This, too, has been a continuous and life-dominating experience. She has had moderate difficulty in concentration and memory, a general loss of interest, a lack of pleasure and hobbies, and early waking, with a rather significant diurnal swing, with the anxiety being greater in the morning. She experienced some somatic difficulty (muscle twitching, mild sensory symptoms). She also had genitourinary symptoms of amenorrhea and loss of libido. She described no cardiovascular symptoms, respiratory symptoms, gastrointestinal symptoms, or phobic responses.

Treatment

Sharon was seen for a total of 28 sessions, from the initial interview to the termination interview, a period covering approximately 8 months. She was seen twice weekly for the first 2 weeks, and then approximately once weekly thereafter.

Formulation of the problem. The patient presented several discrete problems: (1) an overriding sense of hopelessness, with consequent suicidal ideation; (2) marital difficulty (i.e. relating to her husband and maintaining a marital relationship); (3) sexual difficulty (i.e., abstinence because of painful and uncomfortable sexual intercourse); (4) career difficulty—a sense of dissatisfaction with her present position in terms of whether she can effectively work and do the kind of job that she feels she needs to do; (5) lack of a social support network.

Conceptually, the patient was a perfectionist who utilized an all-or-none approach to problem solving. A major goal of treatment would be to have her alter this dichotomous thinking to allow herself to be more successful. Part of treatment would also necessitate an exploration of marital–sexual difficulties. Because of the suicidal ideation, a rather immediate set of interventions focused on her sense of hopelessness in order to make it less likely that she would commit suicide. The depression was the next therapy target, followed by the sexual difficulty and the vocational issues. This hierarchy was developed collaboratively between the therapist and Sharon.

Status of the problem. Sharon has maintained contact approximately once a year via a phone call since the termination of therapy. She had come in for four sessions as a booster and to receive additional coaching in the use of her cognitive-behavioral techniques. At termination and in 2 1/2 years of follow up, the patient has (1) changed her job so that she now works a job at higher pay, with equal prestige, only 4 miles from her home; (2) no longer been troubled with hopelessness and suicidality; (3) become more conscious of her health and physical appearance, has lost weight, has maintained the weight loss; (4) described her marital relationship now as excellent, with the patient and her husband maintaining an active and gratifying sexual relationship.

The following excerpts from Session 8 are used to illustrate typical interventions and patient–therapist interactions. An important part of the session focuses on Sharon's view of herself. The homework from the previous session and the DTRs she completed as homework are reproduced. At the previous session, Sharon had commented that "There are millions of things that I worry about." The therapist asked her if "a million" was an overestimate. Sharon's response was, "You know what I mean, there are so many things for me to worry about." Sharon's home-work involved making a list of problems around which she has many dysfunctional thoughts. She then prioritized the list in order of importance in her life. One immediate gain was that Sharon saw that her list was finite (25 items). She was then asked to look through the list for any themes. (The goal was to reduce the list into schematic categories.) By moving from "a million" to 25 to 5, Sharon experienced marked relief.

The following interactions illustrate tech-niques discussed in this chapter.

I.   Agenda setting

1 TH: Okay, where do you want to pick up? What do you have on tap for today?

1 PT: Well, first item would be the purpose of the videotaping, we can talk about that.

2 TH: Sure.

2 PT: What it will be used for and so forth. And then the topic that I wanted to discuss is body image, appearance, all related to self-esteem, being fat, feeling that I am fat and ugly. Clothes, buying clothes. When I categorized my problems, those came out as part of self-image.

3 TH: So, it relates to some of the homework you were working on?

3 PT: Right, and that's it for what I have.

4 TH: Okay, so we want to look at the home-work and to review how things have been going since the last session.

4 PT: Okay.

5 TH: Okay, what do we have? We have three things. The purpose of the videotaping, the whole thing of body image and how that relates to your homework, and there is some other homework, too. And just how things have been going since the last session.

5 PT: Why don't we do that one second since it is going to bring you up to date? Why don't we do the homework third and then get into the body image from there?

6 TH: Okay, and the videotaping first. So—one purpose of the videotaping is for me to monitor my performance. Secondly, with your permission, to have colleagues monitor what I do so that they can look at it and offer some critique and help me to be a better therapist. So that . . . is the prime purposes.

Certainly, since we're dealing with body image kinds of stuff, it will be useful for us to be able to look at it, and you can test out some of your ideas about you. I guess the body image is part of the homework.

6 PT: Yeah.

II.   Discussion of body image

8 TH: Okay, fine. About the videotaping—any thoughts that you are having?

8 PT: I just don't know. It would be interesting for me to see it.

9 TH: Sure, that's always available.

9 PT: Yeah, it will be interesting evidence for me. I'm always scared about seeing it because just that I hate hearing myself on audiotape. I hate seeing myself.

10 TH: What is going on? What you are think-ing?

10 PT: I'm ugly. I'm awkward.

11 TH: She says with a quiver in her voice.

11 PT: This really is no good. The tissues are too far away.

12 TH: We can remedy that. That's easy to rem-edy. Here you go. (Hands her tissues)

12 PT: My mannerisms are peculiar and annoy-ing and embarrassing. If I met me, I would think I was pretty unattractive, both physically and in behavior.

13 TH: So there is a thought that goes, "I'm ugly, awkward, and if I met me, I would be pretty upset."

13 PT: Well, just unimpressed.

14 TH: I would be unimpressed.

14 PT: Yeah.

15 TH: What might I say to myself?

15 PT: She's a loser. She's weird. Don't want to associate with her.

16 TH: She's weird, a loser, don't want to asso-ciate. So you have all of these—a whole stream of automatic thoughts that just kind of—not just a stream sounds more like a cascade.

16 PT: Right, a waterfall. (Sharon starts crying)

17 TH: A waterfall and it really does begin to fall, doesn't it?

17 PT: Yes, right.

18 TH: That is probably an apt image because as

you start thinking those things, you are feeling what?

18 PT: Uhm, sort of sorry for myself. Poor me, I'm so horrible.

19 TH: That is certainly sad.

19 PT: Yeah, very sad, yeah.

20 TH: Because even as I just ask you this, your voice begins to quiver again and what evidence do you have that all this is true? That you are ugly, awkward? Or that it is not true? What data do you have?

20 PT: Comparing myself to people that I consider extremely attractive and finding myself lacking.

21 TH: So if you look at that beautiful person, you're less?

21 PT: Yeah.

22 TH: Or if I look at that *perfect* person, I'm less? Is that what you are saying?

22 PT: Yeah.

23 TH: That they are somehow perfect and I am . . .

23 PT: Yeah. I always pick out, of course, the most attractive person and probably a person who spends 3 hours a day on grooming and appearance, clothes shopping, and I only compare myself to them. I don't compare myself to the run-of-the-mill—I have begun to try to contradict all this stuff and that's why I know that . . .

24 TH: I would like to hear some of that.

24 PT: Well, I have done very well this whole week. I'm a lot less depressed. I have done a couple of really tough dysfunctional thought analyses, which I feel I have made very good progress on, and I find myself thinking in those terms so that the thoughts come up again, and I find myself contradicting the negative thoughts, the automatic thoughts almost automatically, especially the ones I have written out. I have enjoyed what I have been doing this week. I didn't commute much this week, so that helped. But I don't think that was just that. It seems that it was more than that because there have been days when I haven't commuted, when I have stayed, and I have been depressed, too. I've laid in bed all day.

25 TH: So overall, you are saying that you had greater touch with just pleasure experiences.

25 PT: Yes.

26 TH: Felt more competent.

26 PT: Yes.

27 TH: Handled things much better.

27 PT: Yes.

28 TH: And less depressed.

28 PT: Yes, all of those.

29 TH: Phew!

29 PT: Yeah, it's a lot.

30 TH: Quite a lot, isn't it?

30 PT: And it does seem to be related to some of the dysfunctional thought analyses I did.

III. Discussion of homework

31 TH: Can you just briefly capsule one for me?

31 PT: Well, actually there are two that I gave you last time which I keep sort of coming back to.

32 TH: What two are those?

32 PT: 15 and 16. Number 15 and Number 16. I don't exactly remember what they were on, but I know they are very important. Ahh, 15 was when I canceled our therapy appointment right after the surgery because I felt a lot of pain, and I didn't feel motivated to do the homework. I felt really lousy about myself because of that. And 16 was when we decided I should work on more specific problems and I started out with low self-esteem, and that was the morning spent ruminating in bed and had 250 automatic thoughts in 3 hours. And then spent the whole afternoon doing the homework and contradicting that.

33 TH: And the result was what?

33 PT: The result was that although I didn't immediately stop being depressed, gradually that evening I felt less depressed, and then that weekend I felt even less depressed, and by Monday I felt pretty good, and then this whole next week from Monday to Monday.

34 TH: You are getting a sense of mastery.

34 PT: Yes.

35 TH: It has to be the exact size, color, fit?

35 PT: Right and if it isn't then, that means there is something wrong with me. It doesn't matter that a store doesn't have enough sizes, colors, . . .

36 TH: Maybe that is something you can work on.

36 PT: It is a good candidate for dysfunctional thought analysis.

37 TH: I think agree, it would be good to really look at yourself. With a mirror.

37 PT: Uh-huh. That's a good idea.

38 TH: To really sit down in front of mirror and just look at yourself and write down what you see and then deal with that, and I think it might be helpful to . . . -Hmm, do you have a full length mirror?

38 PT: Uh-huh.

39 TH: To do it nude. Do it dressed and do it nude and write down what you are feeling about your body and the thoughts that you have. And then sit down and knock the hell out of it. Not your body but your negative thoughts.

39 PT: Okay.

40 TH: Then challenge that. That it is there and to really almost to desensitize yourself to look in the mirror until you don't have to have that feeling anymore, because the feeling clearly stems from the thoughts. So that you then can remove that one more piece of anxiety about going clothes shopping. You can look in the mirror and . . .

40 PT: That's a good idea.

41 TH: So that is something you can work on. And then I think then deal with some of these issues of the ugly, awkward speech. I guess it is always too a matter of perspective. As you look towards the reserved, chiseled profile I wonder how many reserved chiseled types are looking for curly hair.

41PT: Now a days, a lot. They are all going and getting permanents.

42TH: I guess it's the perspective that they look and say, "Gee I wish I had naturally curly hair."

42 PT: Yeah, it is hilarious. We all want to be different than what we are. Society tells us we're not good enough the way we are, we've got to be different. Hairdressers—every hairdresser that a woman goes to tells her that she oughta do this, that and the other to her hair no matter what kind of hair she has. Just resisting that takes a lot of self-confidence.

43 TH: But, given what society says, it's what we say.

43 PT: Yeah, we internalize that and say it to ourselves, yeah.

IV. Summary and ending of the session

44 TH: Okay, let's see where we have been. We've talked about the videotaping, we've gotten through the homework, and you've brought me up since last session and spent a good part of the session on this issue of body image and talking about how you think about you and the clothing and covering yourself with either make-up or clothing that then you have to deal with in terms of, "Am I doing it for society or for me?" And that may be one way of dealing with that, maybe just the clothing. But to change how you look [on the] exterior because inside you are not so bad might go along with changing that image, and one piece of specific homework you'll be working on is doing some dysfunctional thoughts, specifically about your body image and your body and that will deal with several of the issues here of appearance, grooming, and body image. We've talked about the chocolate issue, and I think it will also evoke some of the issues here about money and spending it. If you buy clothes, it is going to cost you a bundle. No way around that.

44 PT: Yeah.

45 TH: It means, I think, going to spend money. That's what it is all about. And it depends [on] whether you then want to choose to try to go and buy as much as you can as cheaply as you can or buy what you are really talking [about] which may cost more. To get those fine, tailored pieces of a camel's hair coat, you can get a dacron-and-tissue-paper version, or the real one, which won't go out of style, so. Okay we're running close to the end of our time. Anything on the session, thoughts you have had. Anything about me today.

45 PT: Ummm. I don't think so.

46 TH: Anything I have said today that has upset you, annoyed you? Okay. Any closing comments? Okay. I will see you on Thursday.

46 PT: Okay, I'm having my 6 weeks evaluation just before the session.

47 TH: Okay.

The cognitive model of depression stresses the role played by the individual's perceptions, thoughts, images, beliefs, and other cognitive phenomena in the origins and maintenance of depression. Specifically, the central theme in the cognitions of depressed persons are a negative view of self, of the world and experience, and of the future. The negative view of the future, termed "hopelessness," is one of the prime factors in suicidal ideation. Cognitive distortions are the dysfunctional automatic thoughts and images that are depressogenic and are generated by the underlying belief systems or schema. These schema, often in place since early or middle childhood, may be cultural, religious, family-based, personal, or gender related. The schema are on continua, from active to dormant, and noncompelling to compelling. Active schema control behavior daily while dormant schema are evoked only when the individual is under stress. Noncompelling schema may be easily modified or surrendered, while compelling schema are viewed as part of the self, and are less easily modified. The goals of the therapy are to understand the distortions and to use them as directional signs that point to the underlying belief system.

Cognitive therapy of depression involves (a) the establishment of a collaborative working relationship with the patient; (b) assessment of the problem and collection of historical data; (c) development of a working conceptualization of the patient's problems; (d) socialization of the patient to the therapy model, explaining the interrelationship of the thoughts, feelings, and behavior; (e) identification of the dysfunctional thoughts and the schema; (f) use of cognitive and behavioral techniques to test the individual's thoughts and assumptions; (g) practice of adaptive cognitive and behavioral responses outside the therapy session (homework); (h) prevention of relapse.

Ongoing use of the BDI, the Scale of Suicidal Ideation, and the HS serve as important data collection tools. The therapy utilizes a broad range of cognitive and behavioral techniques. The proportion of cognitive to behavioral techniques may be estimated by the degree of dysfunction: The greater the dysfunction, the more behavioral techniques will be used.

The therapy is active, directive, structured, problem-focused, and collaborative. The emphasis on skill building serves to facilitate generalization and maintenance of gain. If necessary, pharmacotherapy is utilized conjointly with the therapy. The psychoeducational nature of CT works to provide the patient with the tools to cope effectively with the present depression and with any future depressive episodes.

REFERENCES

Adler, A. (1927). Understanding human nature. New York: Doubleday.

American Psychiatric Association. (1987). Diagnostic and statistical manual (3rd ed., rev.). Washington, DC: Author.

Arieti, S. (1980). Cognition in psychoanalysis. Journal of the American Academy of Psychoanalysis, 8, 3–23.

Bandura, A. (1977a). Self-efficacy: Towards a unifying theory of behavior change. Psychological Review, 84, 191–215.

Bandura, A. (1977b). Social learning theory. Englewood Cliffs, NJ: Prentice-Hall.

Bandura, A. (1985). Model of causality in social learning theory. In M. Mahoney & A. Freeman (Eds.). Cognition and psychotherapy (pp. 81–100). New York: Plenum.

Beck, A. T. (1967). Depression: Causes and treatment. Philadelphia: University of Pennsylvania Press.

Beck, A. T. (1970). Cognitive therapy: Nature and relation to behavior therapy. Behavioral Therapist, 1, 184–200.

Beck, A. T. (1976). Cognitive therapy and the emotional disorders. New York: International Universities Press.

Beck, A. T., & Emery, G. (1982). Cognitive therapy of substance abuse. Philadelphia: Center for Cognitive Therapy.

Beck, A. T., & Emery, G. (1985). Anxiety disorders and phobias: A cognitive perspective. New York: Basic Books.

Beck, A. T., Epstein, N., Brown, G., & Steer, R. A. (1985). An inventory for measuring clinical anxiety: Psychometric properties. Journal of Consulting and Clinical Psychology.

Beck, A. T., Epstein, N., & Harrison, R. (1983). Cognitions, attitudes and personality dimensions in depression. British Journal of Cognitive Psychotherapy, 1, 1–16.

Beck, A. T., & Freeman, A. (in press). Cognitive therapy of personality disorders. New York: Guilford.

Beck, A. T., Rush, A. J., Shaw, B. F., & Emery, G. (1979). Cognitive therapy of depression. New York: Guilford.

Beck, A. T., Ward, C. H., Mendelson, M., Mock, J. E., & Erbaugh, J. K. (1961). An inventory for measuring depression. Archives of General Psychiatry, 4, 561–571.

Beck, A. T., Weissman, S., Lester, D., & Trexler, L. (1974). The measurement of pessimism: The hopelessness scale. *Journal of Consulting and Clinical Psychology, 42*, 861–865.

Blackburn, I., Bishop, S., Glen, A. I. M., Walley, L. J., & Christie, J. E. (1981). The efficacy of cognitive therapy in depression: A treatment using cognitive therapy and pharmacotherapy, each alone and in combination. *British Journal of Psychiatry, 139*, 181–189.

Bowers, W. (1989). Cognitive therapy with inpatients. In A. Freeman, K. M. Simon, L. Beutler, & H. Arkowitz (Eds.), *Handbook of cognitive therapy*. New York: Plenum.

Bowlby, J. (1985). The role of childhood experience in cognitive disturbance. In M. Mahoney & A. Freeman (Eds.), *Cognition and psychotherapy* (pp. 181–200). New York: Plenum.

Burns, D. D. (1980). *Feeling good*. New York: Morrow.

Coche, E. (1987). Problem solving training: A cognitive group therapy modality. In A. Freeman & V. Greenwood, *Cognitive therapy: Applications in psychiatric and medical settings* (pp. 83–102). New York: Human Sciences Press.

DiGiuseppe, R. (1986). Cognitive therapy for childhood depression. In A. Freeman, N. Epstein, and K. M. Simon ((Eds.), *Depression in the family*. New York: Haworth Press

DiGiuseppe, R. (1989). Cognitive therapy with children. In A. Freeman, K. M. Simon, L. Beutler, and H. Arkowitz (Eds.), *Comprehensive handbook of cognitive therapy*. New York: Plenum Press.

Edgette, J. S., & Prout, M. F. Cognitive and behavioral approaches to the treatment of anorexia nervosa. In A. Freeman, K. M. Simon, L. Beutler, and H. Arkowitz (Eds.), *Comprehensive handbook of cognitive therapy*. New York: Plenum.

Ellis, A. (1962). *Reason and emotion in psychotherapy*. New York: Lyle Stuart.

Ellis, A. (1973). *Humanistic psychotherapy: The rational–emotive approach*. New York: Julian Press.

Ellis, A. (1977). The basic clinical theory of rational–emotive therapy. In A. Ellis & R. Grieger (Eds.), *Handbook of rational–emotive therapy* (pp. 81). New York: Springer.

Ellis, A. (1985). Expanding the ABC's of RET. In M. Mahoney & A. Freeman (Eds.), *Cognition and psychotherapy* (pp. 313–324). New York: Plenum.

Ellis, A., & Harper, R. (1961). *New guide to rational living*. New York: Crown.

Epstein, N., Schlesinger, S., & Dryden, W. (Eds.) (1988). *Cognitive behavioral treatment of families*. New York: Brunner/Mazel.

Frankl, V. (1985). Cognition and logotherapy. In M. Mahoney & A. Freeman (Eds.), *Cognition and psychotherapy* (pp. 259–276). New York: Plenum.

Freeman, A. (1980). Dreams and imagery. In G. Emery, S. D. Hollon, & R. C. Bedrosian (Eds.), *New directions in cognitive therapy*. New York: Guilford.

Freeman, A. (1986). Understanding personal, cultural, and family schema in psychotherapy. In A. Freeman, N. Epstein, & K. M. Simon (Eds.), *Depression in the family* (pp. 79–100). New York: Haworth.

Freeman, A., Epstein, N., & Simon, K. M. (1986). *Depression in the family*. New York: Haworth Press.

Freeman, A., & Greenwood, V. (1987). *Cognitive therapy: Applications in psychiatric and medical settings*. New York: Human Sciences Press.

Freeman, A., & Leaf, R. (1989). Cognitive therapy of personality disorders. In A. Freeman, K. M. Simon, L. Beutler, & H. Arkowitz (Eds.), *Handbook of cognitive therapy*. New York: Plenum.

Freeman, A., & Zaken-Greenburg, F. (1988). Cognitive family therapy. In C. Figley (Ed.), *Psychological stress*. New York: Brunner/Mazel.

Freud, S. (1892). Treatment by hypnosis. In S. Freud, *Collected works*. London: Hogarth.

Garner, D. M., & Bemis, K. M. (1985). *Cognitive therapy for anorexia nervosa*. In D. M. Garner & P. E. Garfinkel (Eds.), *Handbook for psychotherapy for anorexia nervosa and bulimia* (pp. 107–146). New York: Guilford.

Greenwood, V. (1983). Treating the chronic young adult patient. In A. Freeman (Ed.), *Cognitive therapy with couples and groups* (pp. 183–198). New York: Plenum.

Grossman, R., & Freet, B. (1987). A cognitive approach to group therapy with hospitalized adolescents. In A. Freeman & V. Greenwood, *Cognitive therapy: Applications in psychiatric and medical settings* (pp. 132–151). New York: Human Sciences Press.

Horney, K. (1936). *The neurotic personality*. New York: Norton.

Jakubowski, P., & Lange, A. J. (1978). *The assertive option*. Champaign, Il: Research Press.

Kovacs, M., Rush, A. J., Beck, A. T., & Hollon, S. D. (1978). A one year follow-up of depressed outpatients treated with cognitive therapy or pharmacotherapy.

Kramlinger, K. G., Swanson, D. W., & Maruta, I. (1983). Are patients with chronic pain depressed? *American Journal of Psychiatry, 140*, 747–749.

Lazarus, A. (Ed.). (1976). *Multimodal behavior therapy*, New York: Springer.

Lazarus, A. A. (1981). *The practice of multimodal therapy*. New York: McGraw-Hill.

Lesse, S. (1974). Atypical facial pain of psychogenic origin: A masked depression syndrome. In S. Lesse (Ed.), *Masked depression* (pp. 302–317). New York: Aronson.

McGoldrick, M., Pearce, J. K., & Giordano, J. (Eds.). (1982). *Ethnicity and family therapy*. New York: Guilford.

McMullin, R. (1987). *Handbook of cognitive therapy techniques*. New York: Norton.

Meichenbaum, D. (1977). *Cognitive-behavior modification*. New York: Plenum.

Michelson, L., & Ascher, L. M. (1987). *Anxiety and stress disorders: Cognitive-behavioral assessment and treatment*. New York: Guilford Press.

Murphy, G. E., Simons, A. D., Wetzel, R. D., & Lustman, P. J. (1984). Cognitive therapy versus tricyclic antidepressants in major depression. *Archives of General Psychiatry, 41*, 33–41.

Noll, K. M., Davis, J. M., & DeLeon-Jones, F. (1985). Medication and somatic therapies in the treatment of depression. In E. E. Beckham & W. R. Leber (Eds.), *Handbook of depression*. Homewood, Il: Dorsey.

Perris, C., Rodhe, K., Palm, A., Abelson, M., Hellgren, S., Lilja, C., & Soderman, H. (1987). Fully integrated in- and outpatient services in a psychiatric sector: Implementation of a new model for the care of psychiatric patients favoring continuity of care. In A. Freeman & V. Greenwood (Eds.), *Cognitive therapy: Applications in psychiatric and medical settings* (pp. 117–131). New York: Human Sciences Press.

Rosen, H. (1985). *Piagetian concepts of clinical relevance*. New York: Columbia University Press.

Rosen, H. (in press). Piagetian theory and cognitive therapy. In A. Freeman, K. M. Simon, L. Beutler, & H. Arkowitz (Eds.), *Handbook of cognitive therapy*. New York: Plenum.

Rush, A. J., Beck, A. T., Kovacs, M. & Hollon, S. (1977). Comparative efficacy of cognitive therapy and imipramine in the treatment of depressed outpatients. *Cognitive Therapy and Research, 1*, 17–37.

Sank, L. I., & Shaffer, C. S. (1984). *A therapist's manual for cognitive behavior therapy in groups*. New York: Plenum.

Schrodt, G. R., & Wright, J. H. (1987). Inpatient treatment of adolescents. In A. Freeman & V. Greenwood (Eds.), *Cognitive therapy: Applications in psychiatric and medical setting*. New York: Human Sciences Press.

Simon, K. M. & Fleming, B. M. (1985). Beck's cognitive therapy of depression: Treatment and outcome. In R. M. Turner & L. M. Ascher (Eds.), *Evaluation behavior therapy outcome*. New York: Springer.

Sullivan, H. S. (1953). *The interpersonal theory of psychiatry*. New York: Norton.

Teichman, Y. (1986). Family therapy of depression. In A. Freeman, N. Epstein, & K. M. Simon (Eds.), *Depression in the family* (pp. 9–40). New York: Haworth.

Ward, N. G., & Bloom, V. (1979). Treatment of patients with pain and depression. In *Somatic depression: Special insights for primary care physicians*. (Postgraduate Communications, Special report, March, 1979). New York: Pfizer Laboratories Division, Pfizer.

Weissman, A. N. (1978). *The Dysfunctional Attitude Survey: An inventory designed to assess the relationship between cognitive distortion and emotional disorder*. Dissertation submitted to the Graduate School of Education of the University of Pennsylvania.

Wright, J. (1987). Cognitive therapy and medication as combined treatment. In A. Freeman & V. Greenwood (Eds.), *Cognitive therapy: Applications in psychiatric and medical settings* (pp. 36–50). New York: Human Sciences Press.

Wright, J. (1989). Cognitive therapy and pharmacotherapy. In A. Freeman, K. M. Simon, L. Beutler, & H. Arkowitz (Eds.), *Handbook of cognitive therapy*. New York: Plenum.

CHAPTER 6

Social Skills Training

ROBERT E. BECKER

INTRODUCTION

Since the late 1970s, several carefully defined psychotherapies for the treatment of depression have been delineated. Many of these new treatments have undergone systematic evaluations of their effectiveness via controlled clinical trials, with results that show a good deal of effectiveness (Becker & Heimberg, 1985). This chapter focuses on only one of these treatments, namely *social skills training*. Other authors in this volume discuss alternative treatment approaches.

This chapter first conceptualizes major depressive disorder and dysthymic disorder from the perspective of social skills treatment. Next is a discussion of the diagnosis of depression as it pertains to social skills treatment. Following this discussion is a presentation of specific treatment strategies and procedures, along with a case illustration. Finally, there is a brief presentation of possible problems in treatment, with some suggested solutions, including alternative treatments.

CONCEPTUALIZATION OF DEPRESSION

Several authors have contributed to the conceptualization of depression currently employed in social skills approaches to treatment. Charles Ferster (1965, 1973, 1981) was the first behaviorally trained psychologist to propose a conceptualization of depression. His writings drew from the then-current body of knowledge about operant

behavior of animals. Ferster's initial assumptions about mood disturbance defined it as a low rate of behavior emitted by an individual, resulting from a disruption in environment, such that there was a significant decrease in response-contingent reinforcement or a significant increase in response-contingent punishment. (Readers who are not familiar with the definitions of reinforcement, punishment, and so on are referred to *Behavior Principles*, 1975, C. B. Ferster, S. Culbertson, and M. C. Boren, New Jersey: Prentice-Hall.) Such an arrangement of contingent events is labeled "extinction" in behavioral terminology. When extinction occurs, the behaviors no longer being reinforced occur at a lower and lower rate, further reducing the opportunities for positive reinforcement. If the rate of reinforcement drops low enough, then mood declines and depression can result. Ferster (1981) further refined this approach with the following four propositions:

1. Short-term mood swings (diagnostically, this would describe dysthymia, as well as sadness) and major depression lie on the same continuum.

2. Depression can result from large environmental changes that reduce response-contingent reinforcement (e.g., sudden illness and natural catastrophes).

3. Depression can result when the predominant control of behavior is based on the internal deprivation state of the person, as opposed to the responsivity to external

contingencies. When behavioral control is primarily internal, the depressed person relies on negative reinforcement to control others' behavior. For example, a depressed person would control others by complaints of not feeling well.

4. Development of adequate social and other behavior requires an interplay between the person and the environment. If the environment is unresponsive or highly controlling, then this natural interplay and development would be impaired, producing an inadequate skill level for autonomous behavior.

Lewinsohn and his colleagues (Lewinsohn, 1975; Lewinsohn, Youngren, & Grosscup, 1979) expanded the theoretical underpinnings of mood disturbances. In addition to the concept of *response-contingent reinforcement*, these writers added two other important ideas. First, mood disturbance is related to the failure to maintain a proportionate relationship between reinforcements and punishments, such that punishments remain a small, but stable proportion of reinforcements. If the proportion of punishments increases, either because reinforcements decrease or punishments increase, then mood is likely to become depressed. The amounts of reinforcements and punishments a person may receive is a function of how many of these are available in the person's environment and on the person's skillfulness in obtaining reinforcers and avoiding punishers. The second key idea is that most reinforcers and punishments are applied by other people in the environment— hence, the skill necessary to negotiate this environment is primarily interpersonal in nature. A depression prone person may be functioning well within a specific interpersonal–environmental niche, but if this niche is disturbed, the person is unable to reestablish the desired reinforcement–punishment proportion in another niche.

Hence, a person who has developed strong social interaction skills would show a mild mood disturbance to a powerful disruption of the environment, followed by correction of the reinforcement–punishment proportion and a return to normal mood. In contrast, a less socially skilled person would react with a mild disturbance, which deepens as the necessary corrective activities fail to occur. For example, a person experiencing a divorce may respond with initial upset and then put into motion plans and activities to make new friends as a basis for a new intimate relationship. In so doing, the new friendships and relationships would replace some or all of the reinforcements lost through the divorce. A less socially skilled person faced with the same circumstances would be either less able or unable to make and carry out such plans. Few new friendships would be made, and there would be little likelihood of finding a new intimate relationship. In this second case, depression of longer duration would ensue.

Two lines of investigation into the interpersonal functioning of depressed persons has been pursued. One line has examined interpersonal behavior of depressed persons within the context of intimate relationships, and the other when depressed persons are dealing with acquaintances.

Hinchliffe, Hooper, Roberts, and Vaughn (1975) investigated the communication patterns of depressed patients, both with their spouses and with a stranger. Comparison of communication styles between hospitalized depressed patients or surgical patients and their spouses showed major differences in both verbal and nonverbal behavior. Surgical patients displayed more gestures and used more tension-releasing and objective statements. This difference in interaction behavior between depressed and surgical patients was much less evident when the interaction partner was a stranger. Depressed patients interacting with a stranger showed much improved social behavior, much more like the surgical patients. This interaction pattern with the spouse also seems to vary with the course of the disorder. As the depressed patients' moods improved, their interaction pattern became more like the surgical patients.

Biglan, Hops, Sherman, Thoreson, Friedman, Arthur, and Osteen (1984) examined the problem-solving ability of depressed women and their husbands, as compared to 25 happily married couples in which neither partner was depressed. Couples that included a depressed woman displayed less self-disclosure, and the woman offered significantly fewer solutions to problems faced by the couple. Depressed wives tended to make self-derogating statements and to express physical and psychological discomfort, and thereby keep the discussion focused on these issues. In a similar study, Kahn, Coyne, and Margolin (1985) examined the interaction patterns of seven couples with a depressed husband and seven with a depressed wife and compared them to 14 couples in which both spouses were free from depression. Again, couples with a depressed spouse spent less time in problem solving and spent much more time focused on derogatory statements and physical and psychological complaints. The interactions appeared to be intense, with couples frequently shifting topics. After completion of the interaction being studied, the nondepressed spouse described themselves as sad and angry and their mate as hostile, competitive, mistrustful, disagreeable, and less nurturant and facilitative.

Kowalik and Gotlib (1987) studied the ability of a depressed spouse to accurately perceive her spouse's behavior and judge the impact of her own behavior on the spouse. Nine couples with one depressed spouse were compared to 10 couples with one psychiatrically impaired—but not depressed—spouse; 10 couples without any psychiatric history served as normal controls. Each member of the couple made ratings of the impact of each message over the course of a 20-minute conversation. Results showed that all three groups overestimated the amount of their spouses' agreement with their message, but the depressed group showed the smallest overestimate. Differences in the estimated impact of the message were also found. Depressed patients coded a much lower percentage of messages from their spouses as having a positive impact and a much higher percentage as possessing a negative impact, compared to both control groups.

Investigators focusing on the interaction of depressed persons with strangers have been concerned with the impression created in the stranger rather than on the specific behaviors of the patient. For example, Strack and Coyne (1983) studied the impact of an interaction with either a depressed female college student or a nondepressed female college student. After a 15-minute interaction, the subjects, who were not depressed, were asked to fill out a mood questionnaire and to specify their willingness to have future contact with their interaction partner. Results showed that the depressed person induced hostility, depression, and anxiety

in their interaction partners, as well as reducing the desire for future contact. This rejection of future contact was reciprocated by the depressed subjects—they also expressed less desire for future contact. In a similar vein, Boswell and Murray (1981) studied the impact of interacting with hospitalized depressives or schizophrenics, or hospital staff; 216 students listened to audiotaped interviews of these three groups and then made ratings on a mood adjective checklist and on an attraction questionnaire, and they then made interpersonal ratings. Results showed that both pathological groups—that is, both the depressed and the schizophrenic patients—created depressed mood and induced rejection, but only if the patient was male. Male schizophrenics induced the most rejection, while normal males produced the least. Females, regardless of pathology, induced the least rejection.

In a more behaviorally focused study, Libet and Lewinsohn (1973) compared the interpersonal behavior of eight depressed, eight normal, and four nonaffective psychiatric diagnosed subjects as they interacted in self-study groups. Trained observers blind to diagnosis took time-sampled observations. Results showed that depressed subjects initiated 50% fewer social interactions than normal subjects, responded less positively to social interaction initiated by others, and responded more slowly to others' social interaction attempts.

These studies, and several others not reviewed here, suggest that depressed persons are not as socially capable as nondepressed normals. In interactions with their spouses particularly, depressed persons initiate less conversation and suggest fewer solutions, while complaining about how they feel and carrying out behavior displays of their emotions. When others initiate social interaction, depressed patients seem to be slower to respond and to show fewer positive responses. Recall of their own past behavioral stream appears to be more accurate than normals, but immediate perception of the interaction partner's behavioral stream appears to be more negative. Summing these interaction propensities for a depressed person would appear to make social interaction much more demanding and less rewarding for the interaction partner. It may be exactly these two characteristics that induce the nondepressed interaction partner to have angry moods and the desire to lessen future contact. It is against this background of less skill, more negative perception of the behavioral stream of others, and the display of unpleasant behaviors that a social skills training program appears particularly well suited and to which we now turn.

DIAGNOSIS OF DEPRESSION WITH REFERENCE TO SOCIAL SKILL

For the clinician interested in a social skills treatment of depression, diagnosis would be a two-part process. First, the clinician needs to establish that depression is present and that other possibilities, such as an anxiety disorder, are not present. Second, an assessment of the social environment and interpersonal functioning of the patient is necessary. The first step is to arrive at a DSM-III-R diagnosis. In this process, it should be kept in mind that social skills training has been shown to be effective in the treatment of unipolar depressed women (Bellack, Hersen, & Himmelhoch, 1983; Hersen, Bellack, Himmelhoch, & Thase, 1984) and with men and women diagnosed with dysthymic disorder (Becker & Heimberg, 1987).

Assessment Tools

In our own work (Becker & Heimberg, 1987), we have found it useful to assess the full array of depressive symptoms included in the Schedule for Affective Disorders and Schizophrenia (SADS— Endicott & Spitzer, 1978). Aside from mood described as sad, blue, down, and so on, these symptoms are: (a) an increase or decrease in appetite; (b) weight gain or loss of 1 pound or more per week for several weeks or 10 or more pounds in a year when not dieting or on a special diet; (c) difficulty sleeping, with too little sleep or with oversleeping; (d) observable agitation; (e) observable slowed speech and thinking; (f) anhedonia; (g) self-reproach or guilt that may be delusional; (h) complaints of poor concentration; (i) complaints of indecisiveness; (j) recurrent thoughts of dying or an actual attempt of suicide; (k) tearfulness; (l) sad face; (m) pessimism; (n) brooding over past or current unpleasant events; (o) feelings of inadequacy; (p) resentfulness; (q) irritability; (r) demanding or clinging dependency; (s) self-pity; and

(t) excessive somatic concern. DSM-III-R delineates which of these symptoms must be present and for how long to make various depression diagnosis. One area in which we have disagreed with DSM-III-R is in the diagnosis of dysthymia. The current criteria exclude many of the last few symptoms mentioned, such as dependency, self pity, and pessimism. Our impression is that patients with dysthymia have a preponderance of symptoms such as these and have few somatic symptoms such as weight loss/gain, sleep disturbance, and agitation.

Several patient self-report rating scales may be helpful in quantifying the severity of depression. Scales that have been commonly used and that have psychometric data available include the Beck Depression Inventory (Beck, Ward, Mendelson, Mock, & Erbaugh, 1961), the Zung Self-Rating Depression Scale (Zung, 1974), the Inventory for Depressive Symptomatology (Rush, Giles, Schlesser, Fulton, Weissenburger, & Burns, 1985), the Depression Adjective Checklist (Lubin, 1981), and the Hopkins Symptom Checklist, which has a 35-, a 58-, and a 90-item form (Derogatis, Lipman, & Covi, 1973). Rating scales based on a structured or unstructured clinical interview may also be used. The following scales have been used extensively, and data about their psychometric properties has been obtained: the Raskin Global Severity of Depression Scale (Raskin, Schulterbrandt, Reating, & Rice, 1967), and the Hamilton Rating Scale of Depression (Hamilton, 1960), which now exists in several different lengths, ranging from the original 17 items through 21 and 24, to 27 items. The Global Assessment Scale (Endicott, Spitzer, Fleiss, & Cohen, 1976) is a 100-point rating scale designed to measure any impairments in the patient's ability to function as a result of any psychopathology, not just depression.

While these scales and interview schedules help to define the symptoms of depression and to estimate the severity of the episode, they do little to specify the interpersonal behaviors and skills that need to be understood prior to the application of a social skills treatment, and it is to this area that we now turn.

The social skill assessment procedures we have employed have been derived from the work of a number of investigators. These assessments are presented here, with a limited discussion of their various underpinnings and rationales. Such information is available to the interested reader in a 1988 paper (Becker & Heimberg, 1988) and in our book (Becker, Heimberg, & Bellack, 1987). A brief definition of various terms is presented before the various assessment techniques are discussed. The assessment package we have employed consists of a clinical interview, brief role-play assessments, extended role-play assessments, self-monitoring and self-report assessments, and self-monitoring homework assignments. As targets for treatment are discovered, they are organized into a hierarchy based on the subjective level of difficulty reported by the client.

Types of Interpersonal Performance Classes

1. *Positive assertion* includes behaviors that have a positive impact on the social interaction partner. Examples of behaviors that are commonly addressed in treatment are offering to do a favor for another, yielding to the other's request, displaying physical or verbal affection, treating others fairly, and display of respect for the other.

2. *Negative assertion* includes behaviors that have a negative impact on the social interaction partner. Common examples from this class include refusing a request from the other, not offering a favor, removal of resources given or lent to the other, requests for less future contact, requests for others to change some aspect of their behavior, and ignoring the other.

3. *Conversational skill* includes behaviors that allow the client to initiate, maintain, and end conversations. These skills emphasize exchange of information that does not have a positive or negative consequence for either member of the dyad.

Static Situational Factors in Social Behavior

1. Human characteristics
   a. Sex of the interaction partner
   b. Age of the partner (e.g., child versus adult)
   c. Superordinate versus subordinate social roles

d. Less ability versus greater ability (e.g., impaired intellectual ability, poor hearing, suffering from an impairing illness)
   e. Friends versus strangers
   f. Intimates versus strangers or friends

2. Setting characteristics
   a. Work
   b. Home
   c. Public places such as restaurants
   d. Within transportation systems (e.g., trains, planes, cars, buses)
   e. Within communications networks (e.g., telephones, computers)
   f. Recreational settings (e.g., pools, saunas, gymnasiums)

Dynamic Situational Factors in Social Behavior

1. Expressive–receptive shifts—Cues to indicate change from speaker to listener or vice versa.

2. Topic changes—Changes from one related line of conversation to another line

3. Clarifying the other person's communication—Restatements of other's message to clarify meaning

4. Persistence—Cues indicating that the other person is ambivalent, such as "Maybe, I'll think about it"

5. Detection of emotion of partner—Changes in voice volume, pitch, or speech rate; changes in facial expression, such as eye contact, flushing, widened eyes, muscle tone; changes in the intensity of gestures or speed of movement; abrupt speaker to listener shifts or topic changes

6. Provision of reinforcement or punishment from the partner—Offers of future reinforcements or punishments

7. Recall of past interactions—The history of past reinforcement and punishment providing information about the likelihood of particular behaviors as being well received or not

8. Unpredicted responses from others—Anger, affection, or indifference (e.g., insults or a romantic embrace)

Descriptions of Social Behavior

1. Molecular descriptions of social behavior focus on small discrete units of behavior, such as loudness, latency to respond, duration of response, smiling, speech disruptions, facial display of affect, and gaze. These behaviors have been shown in previous research to be related to social skill. If any of these assessments reveal lack of skill, then a skill deficit is presumed and this area becomes a legitimate target for later treatment.

2. Molar descriptions of social behavior consist of judgments of the overall social behavior on Likert type scales. These judgments may have anchor points that include some molecular aspects of the behavioral stream, but they usually include some judgment of the overall effectiveness of the entire performance.

The Clinical Interview

This assessment procedure can produce a wealth of information, yet at the same time, it is prone to error due to (a) the patient's reluctance to disclose information, (b) the patient's having a poor memory or being a poor self-observer, or (c) the interviewer's possession of less-than-adequate interviewing skill. The interview is designed to obtain the following:

1. Patients' histories of reinforcement and punishment from others

2. Patients' self-reported perceptions of the consequences of their social behavior and their understanding of the reinforcement–punishment behavior of significant others

3. Patients' reports of static and dynamic factors

4. An understanding of patients' current self-reinforcement–punishment rules and methods

5. Patients' self-perceived difficulties with the three performance classes: positive assertion, negative assertion, and casual conversation

6. Patients' moods and how they may covary with social events.

Once problematic situations are discovered, they are organized into a hierarchy, according to the patient's self-reported level of difficulty in carrying out the proper behavior. These situations also serve as scenarios for the extended role plays done later in treatment.

The interview behavior, in itself, is a natural sample of the patient's behavior. A well-trained interviewer will observe the patient during the interview, looking for problematic behaviors. This observational data may not corroborate the self-report data and may provide the clinician with hunches that can be verified with later role-play assessment.

Brief Role-Play Assessment

This assessment consists of 12 standardized simulations of interpersonal interaction. These scenarios are divided into three dichotomous categories: (1) scenes requiring positive or negative assertion; (2) scenes with a more familiar or less familiar partner; and (3) scenes with male or female partners. Each simulation consists of a narrative description of the setting (which sets some of the static factors and is read by the patient), followed by a brief response from a role-play assistant, then a response from the patient, a rejoinder from the assistant, and a final response from the patient. These same scenes are used with all patients, in order to sample from an array of factors that affect social behavior. In addition, two personalized scenes are structured individually for each patient. These scenes are ones that the patient sees as clearly pertinent to his or her mood and that constitute a current pressing interpersonal situation for the patient. The patient's behavior in these simulations is evaluated for molecular aspects, and problems identified become part of the hierarchy of targets for treatment.

Extended Role-Play Assessment

This assessment procedure is carried out individually with the clinician, using as a guide the data gathered from the clinical interview, the brief role plays, and the treatment hierarchy. A deliberate attempt should be made by the clinician to make the simulation as real as possible. We have even gone so far as to incorporate the limited use of props, as well as trying to improve the acting skill of the clinician. Setting the scene should be done carefully to include as many actual details as can be obtained. The clinician must both serve as the role-play partner and at the same time, be an observer of the patient's behavior to detect problems. Variations in some of the dynamic factors involved in social behavior can be portrayed, in order both to assess whether the patient notices them and, if the patient does notice them, to assess whether the patient changes his or her behavior accordingly. After observing the patient's usual behavior in the simulation of an actual event, the clinician may introduce variations into the situation, to test the durability of behavior under a wider range of circumstances. Cues regarding which variables to change are drawn from the previous lists of static and dynamic factors involved in social behavior, such as changes in the partner's emotion, topic changes, interruptions, talking in front of others, and so on. These variations can be used to test the clinical hunches that may have arisen as a result of discrepancies in the data gathered from the previous assessments. The clinician may have several hunches. For example, the clinician may suspect that "this person can do well with brief superficial social conversation, but extended conversation implying extended social contact produces a significant deterioration in behavior." If this were the case, extended role plays would be arranged to test this proposition.

A full session may be used to assess behavior in this fashion. The data gathered from these role plays can modify the hierarchy and may increase the number of problems that need to be addressed. The data about the patient's ability to detect changing dynamic cues will be important when this aspect of training is addressed later in treatment.

Self-Monitoring and Self-Report

Self-monitoring is used to gather information about the natural social behavior of the patient and to better understand the environment in which the patient functions. Log sheets and diaries can be used to collect data about discrete events. Clearly, labeled log sheets help gather information about the natural frequency of occurrence of positive and negative assertion, as well as about the amount of social contact and social conversation. These sheets can be used to find out the frequency of contact with certain persons, or the circumstances under which such contact usually occurs. Such records can be used to report patient behaviors such as sitting alone, not initiating conversations, and so on. This early data is invaluable later in treatment when homework is assigned to occur in certain settings and/or with certain people.

There are eight commonly used self-report inventories:

1. Wolpe–Lazarus Assertiveness Schedule (Wolpe & Lazarus, 1966)
2. Wolpe–Lazarus Assertiveness Schedule Revised (Hersen, Bellack, Turner, Williams, Harper, & Watts, 1979)
3. The Assertion Inventory (Gambrill & Richey, 1975)
4. The Adult Self-Expression Scale (Gay, Hollandsworth, & Galassi, 1975)
5. The College Self-Expression Scale (Galassi, DeLo, Galassi, & Bastien, 1974)
6. Rathus Assertiveness Schedule (Rathus, 1973)
7. Conflict Resolution Inventory (Mcfall & Lillesand, 1971)
8. Assertion Questionnaire (Callner & Ross, 1976)

The range of data about the psychometric properties of these various scales vary greatly. Norms for psychiatric patients are available for only two scales (Scales 2 and 6). Scales 5 and 7 specifically focus on college students, and norms exist only for this population. Scale 2 appears to have less than desirable test–retest reliability and does not appear to be treatment sensitive, while scales 6 and 7 have acceptable reliability and are treatment sensitive. The choice of a scale may depend on the age of the patient and the diagnosis. Most scales have been normed on college student samples, and only two scales have normative samples on patients with psychiatric diagnoses.

All of the various measures should allow the clinician both to formulate a plan of attack and to pinpoint problems the patient faces in his or her natural environment. Armed with this knowledge, the clinician can move on to considering the treatment.

SOCIAL SKILLS TRAINING PROCEDURES

Several techniques have been incorporated into social skills training procedures. In the interest of clarity for the novice, most descriptions of these techniques have classified the techniques into limited content areas. We follow this organization here as well. There are four major categories of social skills training, each designed to solve a particular problem for the patient. Movement among categories of social skills training is determined by the clinician's judgment of each patient's progress. Generally, more advanced kinds of skills appear later in treatment, but this may not always be true. One type of response may be trained through all four categories of training and when this has been achieved, the clinician may restart training at the beginning on another unrelated response. Sometimes, patients may apply skills learned for one response and generalize them to another, and sometimes they may not. To assist in the process of generalizing a newly learned skill to other responses, we usually continue role-play practices of the basic skill, but we vary the static and dynamic variables. However, it is always wise to reassess a basic skill when a shift to a new target for training has occurred. This extra practice will aid in strengthening the new response, which will have to compete with well-practiced old habits.

The four categories of social skills training and their purposes are as follows:

1. *Direct behavior training* is designed to teach the patient and to allow the practice of basic verbal and nonverbal skills, focusing on molecular aspects of complex behaviors and then gradually reassembling the complex behavior.

2. *Practice and generalization training* is designed to transplant and adapt the new skill into the patient's everyday environment.

3. *Social perception training* is designed to teach the patient to better recognize dynamic and static cues and to modify behavior according to changes in the environment.

4. *Self-evaluation and self-reinforcement training* is designed to change the information base and the evaluation criteria a patient uses as a basis for judgments about the quality of his or her behavior and to improve the quality and frequency of self-reinforcement.

Direct Behavior Training

Over the course of treating many patients with social skills training, we have developed several guidelines for treatment that yields good results. First, we always describe the course of treatment to the patient, along with a description of the usual response to treatment that can be expected. For example, we have found that for most patients, mood improves as they enter treatment, and this temporary improvement usually lasts about 4–5 weeks before a return to the usual depressed mood occurs. At this point, many patients and clinicians think about changing treatment. We have found that a change decision at this point is usually premature, and that 10 to 11 weeks of treatment constitutes a better trial. Number of sessions, length of sessions, failure to attend sessions, outside homework, as well as the typical content of a session are all discussed.

Next, we present the rationale for this type of treatment, illustrating several connections between depressed mood and interpersonal behavior. Having accomplished these tasks, the next focus is to introduce the patient to "role playing" with the aim of making the patient a good role player. During this task, the role play topics are usually bland and noncontroversial because we do not wish to interfere with the task of learning role plays by introducing both charged emotions and the fear of actually trying this new skill to solve a problem. Once the patient has become a good role-play partner, we then proceed to select the first target for training.

The four guidelines that follow have been quite helpful in improving the chances for a successful first training session:

1. Select a situation that is low on the client-created hierarchy. Clients often want to start with the most pressing problem first. This is usually unwise because highly emotionally charged areas will impede new learning and increase the likelihood of a poor treatment outcome.
2. Choose an initial response that is not too complicated and can serve to illustrate problem areas in the client's performance.
3. Choose a skill that is still relevant to the client.
4. Pick a set of skills that the client can eventually try in the natural environment.

Once the first target for training has been selected, then decisions must be made about which aspects of the patient's behavior should be trained first. We recommend that the initial focus be on molecular behavior and static situation variables; after these have been improved, the focus can shift to more complicated and molar behaviors and to dynamic situations. In addition, training should focus on just a few behaviors or situations at a time; as these improve, another two or three behaviors or situations can be addressed. All of the training that we have done has been guided by the following training sequence:

1. Give the patient specific instructions about what he or she should try to do.
2. Demonstrate the desired performance to the patient, and follow this demonstration with questions, to make certain that she or he has attended to the aspects of the performance that are being trained.
3. Ask the patient to carry out the role play he or she just witnessed.
4. Provide positive feedback to the patient about good aspects of the performance, and give new instructions and demonstrations for features of performance that still need to be improved.
5. Give praise for following instructions and for trying to carry out the role play, and give encouragement to continue with the next role play.

If the patient improves rapidly over the course of one session, and all of the basic molecular components have been trained, then more complex static and dynamic situations can be introduced in order to give more practice and broader application. As the session draws to a close, attention should shift to the homework assignment. During early sessions, we recommend that homework consist of data gathering via the diary and log sheets, in regard to particularly relevant natural behavior of the patient or others in the patient's world. Only after the clinician is certain that the patient has developed a high-quality response should homework consist of a real application of the new skill to one or more of the patient's problem areas. Patients sometimes become involved in a crisis and want to talk about the current pressing problem. (This issue is addressed in the "Problems Treatment" section following the case study.) Such pressure can derail a planned session and may lengthen the total time needed for successful treatment. The following session plan has been useful as an aid to keep us on course.

1. Review previous homework and incorporate this data into today's session (10 minutes).
2. Pick particular situations for role plays and carry out the following sequence (40 minutes).
   a. The therapist provides information about the components of the new performance being taught.
   b. The therapist demonstrates the new performance in a *reverse* role play in which the therapist plays the client and the client plays the other partner.
   c. The therapist checks to see that the client has attended to the relevant aspects of the demonstrated performance and understands what is expected of him or her.
   d. The client role-plays with the intent of imitating the demonstration just provided by the therapist.
   e. The therapist provides response-specific praise and feedback to the client and encourages the client to try some more role plays. The therapist provides praise for following instructions.

f. Several repetitions of the role plays are completed until the client appears to have improved to at least a minimally adequate level.

g. Similar situations are trained, or a different set of component behaviors receive attention.

3. Assign and explain the homework assignment and set the next meeting time (last 10 minutes)

Practice and Generalization Training

When the clinician has made a determination that the patient has attained enough skill and a strong enough response, then the clinician should consider a homework assignment that specifies an application of the new skills to one or more of the patient's problems. As the clinician observes the patient's performance, he or she should be aware of cues indicating both an improved performance and a strengthened response. The focus on the quality of various molecular components of a skill will aid in making a judgment of improved performance. Audio- or videotapes of earlier performances can be kept as a record against which judgments can be made. Cues that the clinician may use to judge the strength of the response include (a) a shorter latency to respond, (b) fewer patient-generated disruptions of the response, (c) the patient becoming more resilient to external disruptions of the new behavior, and (d) reductions in the patient's self-report of uneasiness with this new skill.

Assignment of homework is a test of the usefulness to the patient of the new skill, and the clinician can improve the chances for success with careful planning of the assignment, along with careful monitoring. In planning the assignment, the earlier homework sheets are invaluable sources of information about the rates of occurrence of a variety of events and typical response patterns of other persons. An assignment should target one or more events that have a high likelihood of occurring during the ensuing week. Moreover, because many of the static and dynamic circumstances involved with this event are known from the homework data, the clinician and patient can pick the timing and placement parameters that would be most likely to increase success. Further, the patient should be warned that the interaction partner may be surprised by the patient's new behavior and may not respond as he or she has in the past. Therefore, the patient should expect to be ready to respond to a wide range of possible performances. Finally, neither the patient nor the therapist should attempt to solve the most perplexing problems with this first attempt. Relatively minor problems should be addressed first.

Subsequent to this planning, some systematic method of monitoring the patient's homework performance should be devised. To avoid employing great technological sophistication, we have used audiotape recording and log sheets to record events. The combination of log sheets and tape recording can provide fairly accurate data about static and dynamic variables and the patient's actual behavior. The beginning of the next session should review the homework. Depending on the quality of the homework, the clinician may choose to retrain or to move on to the next targeted area.

Dynamic Cues and Social Perception Training

Interpersonal interaction is a constantly varying process. An unfolding interaction is affected (a) by the interaction history of the persons involved, (b) by the immediate events of the interaction, and (c) by what each of the interaction partners expect to happen in the future. The study of interpersonal interaction is an area of immense complexity that is only beginning to be understood. Because of this complexity and because the cues signaling some important event can be subtle, we have developed more training aids for this category of social skills training. The goals of this training are to increase patients' ability to recognize correctly many of the dynamic cues, as well as to adjust their own behavior to these shifting cues. Additionally, patients need to be aware of the norms of positive and negative reciprocity and to realize how these affect interpersonal interaction. Finally, patients should improve their ability to monitor their own behavior, in order to stop unproductive behavior before it unfolds and replace it with better alternatives.

Because of the added complexity in this area, we routinely supplement training through audiovisual aids, such as the use of videotaped demonstrations and feedback. During role-play practices, we have used flash cards to label the particular cue we are trying to teach, and we have often posted lists of cues the patient should attend to behind the interaction partner, within the patient's field of view.

Training is usually focused on the aforementioned eight areas of dynamic stimuli, and for these, we use the same training sequence described in direct behavior training except that the targets of training are one or more dynamic stimuli. Patient problems in this area can be broken into two classes. First, it may be that the patient never truly perceives the cues that are important. This may occur for any number of reasons, including (a) the patient is not attending to the stimuli; (b) the patient attends to them but judges the stimuli as irrelevant and discounts them; (c) the patient may attend to the stimuli but not see their connection to the problem; (d) the patient attends to the stimuli but has not learned finer gradations of the stimulus, along with a label for them, in order to further use the information. A second alternative is that the patient may attend to and register the stimuli but is unable to formulate a response to these cues.

Most often, we have presumed that problems exist in both areas; therefore, we first train the attentional part of the problem and then follow this with a variety of likely responses to these various nuances. Recognition training is carried out through the use of many role-play demonstrations, initially both exaggerating the cues and incorporating various training aids. As it becomes easier for the patient to recognize the various cues being taught, the exaggerations and aids are gradually dropped. After this, the patient should try to respond to some of the various cues in order for the clinician to determine whether functional skills already exist. If the skills exist (though the skills are limited) then the second phase of training follows, with the therapist carrying out the usual training sequence, but with several possible responses, depending on the cues picked up in the ongoing interaction. Once the patient understands these various responses and their purpose and can carry them out, then role plays are created that display a variety of the cues, and the patient tries to apply the new response to the situation as he or she recognizes it. During this phase, it may be necessary to reintroduce training aids because of

the likelihood of response deterioration as a result of the quantity and complexity of new behavior being trained.

Repeated practice is the rule until the therapist is assured that a reasonably strong series of high-quality responses have been achieved. Once a sufficient level of proficiency has been attained, then homework assignments can be considered, according to the planning and monitoring described earlier. Self-evaluation and self-reinforcement should be intertwined with the training process all along the way, as described in the next section.

Self-Evaluation and Self-Reinforcement Training

Parallel to the possible problems in perception of dynamic cues in others may be problems in perception of one's own behavior. This group of procedures are aimed at identifying and resolving such impediments. As with training in relation to the perception of others there are two segments to these procedures. First, patients may fail to attend to stimuli that are important or may attend to stimuli that are detrimental. Second, they may apply more stringent evaluation criteria than nondepressed persons would.

The first aspect of self-perception is subtly addressed throughout the training. At the very beginning, the therapist hands patients a data system to use in order to specify important stimuli. The focus on molecular portions of their own behaviors, followed by a focus on the static and dynamic cues of the environment, implies that these are the data that are important. Many depressed patients focus on the partner's behavior alone as the data against which to make an evaluation judgment. As training proceeds, patients have two sources of information to base evaluations upon: the partners' behaviors, and their own behavior. The next phase of training aims at replacing the patients' existing self-evaluation system. During the training, the therapist introduces a grading system for the patient's performance during role plays. An A-through-F, letter-grade system is employed; it differs from the patient's system in two respects. First, the system is relevant to the current skill level of the client, and higher grades are incremented *up* from this base; second, the grades are tied to improved performance in the patient's own behavior, not to success or failure in affecting the other person. The individually tailored grading usually meets with objections such as, "I have to be as good as or better than my competitor." This competitive approach grades them on a system designed for someone else, and in units distinct from the desired final goal; therefore, it can result in a poor fit for the patient and can show apparent failure even in the face of progress.

The new noncompetitive system is taught following a role play by the patient. The therapist may describe the A-to-F rating system, *with anchor points in gradations of improvement on the specific skill under treatment.* The patient then makes an evaluation based on the new grading system, after which the therapist announces his or her grade. Most often, the therapist's grade will exceed the patient's because the patient (a) has not included all of the various new and improved components, (b) has slipped into the old absolute grading system, or (c) has blended a competitive system designed for comparison with someone else into their own rating. Repeated practice of these evaluations are carried out over the entire course of training, to allow as many repetitions of the new evaluation procedures as possible. Finally, to further strengthen the new system, the therapist demonstrates appropriate self-reinforcements associated with each rating point and with gradual improvements in performance. After these are modeled, the patient is asked to try to carry out the same reward procedures. The reward training attempts to achieve two goals: One is to tie the rewards to the new evaluation system, and the other is to increase the rate of rewards overall because most depressed patients give themselves too few rewards.

While the introduction of changes in evaluation and reinforcement are subtle, they are powerful. At around Session 6 or 7, many patients complain of confusion related specifically to these shifting evaluation systems. Many will oscillate between the two at this stage and complain that they do not know where they are going, as well as being frightened of where this all might lead. This confusion subsides during later sessions, as the new system takes hold, and as the benefits of it continue

to accrue. Patients in later sessions usually comment either about slipping into their old style of self-evaluation in some unexpected circumstance, or about the difficulty they have in avoiding a return to the older style of self-evaluation.

CASE ILLUSTRATION

The descriptions provided so far imply a fairly steady course for a depressed patient. The following case illustration shows a steady and successful application of these procedures. Obviously, not all patients proceed this smoothly. Following the case illustration, some of the common problems in treatment are discussed.

Ms. SJ is a 43-year-old single woman with a masters degree in chemistry. She has worked as a laboratory assistant for a number of years. She came to the clinic complaining of (a) sad mood, (b) low energy, (c) trouble making decisions, (d) feeling worthless, (e) pessimism about her future, and (f) guilt about her unsuccessful past. She was involved in a 3-year intimate relationship, which has just ended. This event has rekindled symptoms of depression and a fear that this new episode would be as bad as a previous one 10 years earlier. Her Beck Depression Inventory score on admission was 21, the 27-item Hamilton Depression Scale score was 18, Global Assessment score was 65, and Wolpe–Lazarus score was 17. Clinical interview revealed that she worked in a solitary job and has done so for many years. She had been involved in a number of activities such as sailing, hiking, and traveling, but she had stopped most of these when this relationship began. She reports a few very close girlfriends who, she says, tell her that she tends to be aloof and difficult to know. The difficulties in the relationship focused on display of affection, and difficulty making joint plans and decisions. She described her childhood family as discouraging any display of affection or anger. When an argument did occur in her family, there would be weeks when no one would talk to or acknowledge the other person. She was very frightened that this would happen in her own intimate relationship if she became angry. As a result, she was very compliant, but she then felt very resentful.

Standardized role plays revealed difficulties with display of positive and negative assertion, as well as with conversation. She could not give a compliment to another person, particularly a male, and she could not touch a person. She felt that if she displayed this much interest in a male that it was a clear invitation to sexuality, and that she had been taught not to do this. In negative assertion situations, she could not state a contrary opinion. She would respond with a limited agreement and then would stop responding. She said that when this happened at home, she would be reclusive for several days. Conversation role plays revealed that she never started a conversation, never told anyone her name, never greeted others, and never touched others (including a hand shake).

Clinical role plays focused on both positive assertion and conversation skills. After evaluating all the information, conversation with acquaintances appeared to be the place to start. Her attendance at several club meetings could easily be increased and would serve as a fine homework testing ground. The first focus of clinical treatment was greeting people. Role plays focused on making eye contact with the other person, saying "Hello, I'm Sarah," and smiling. This behavior contrasted sharply with her current style of avoiding eye contact, not smiling, and only speaking if directly spoken to. Many role plays were carried out to train these skills. She continued to feel that this behavior was much too forward.

As she began to improve in this skill, touching the other person was added. Reverse role plays were first used, and her initial response to a touch on the hand was to become quite scared, to be silent, and to withdraw as fast as possible. Several practices were carried out in conjunction with a homework assignment. Her assignment was to observe other people in her clubs and to log each time one person touched another. After 1 week of observational data, she was astounded at how often people touched. Men shook hands, patted each other on the shoulders, hugged one another, poked each other in fun, and so on. Women hugged one another, patted each other on the shoulder, touched hands, and so on. Men and women hugged each other, touched hands, and patted or tapped each other on the shoulder.

Conversation role plays were repeated to include touching. After many repetitions, she became comfortable and began to enjoy the contact. Two further existing conversation behaviors were addressed before the first homework: First, she never wore a name tag because she believed that if someone really wanted to know her, they would find out her name. Second, she would always position herself to be out of the way in order not to impede other people. She

easily agreed to wearing a name tag, but she was still fearful of being in the way if she stood in a different location. Homework addressed this last problem. She attended her meetings with instructions (a) to introduce herself and say "Hello, I'm Sarah" to everyone, (b) to wear her name tag, (c) to locate herself in high-traffic areas, and (d) to smile with her greeting and with her departure. Previous role plays had shown that her conversation ability, once started, was adequate to keep her involved, and her ability to say good-bye was also adequate.

This homework assignment resulted in an astonishing response. People were friendly to her, included her in their conversations, and invited her into some of their activities. Not one person complained about the touching or about her being in the way. None of the men made any sexual overtures to her. This was such a success for her that she wondered why she had not done it before. These behaviors were practiced once more and then monitored. She continued these new behaviors, and they produced invitations to go sailing, to attend a special program in Florida, and to attend a meeting in Massachusetts as well. Her mood brightened considerably. She felt less alone, less like an outsider, and more worthwhile.

A second problem in this area was then addressed. She had exhibited this same aloof behavior with her old friends. She was given the task of trying out her new behavioral skills with them. Once again, she met with face-to-face success and very positive response. She still continued to be difficult to contact by telephone, however. Her friends rarely called her, and she took this to mean that they were not interested in her. She had changed her phone to an unlisted number and had not given this number out to many people; also, she had an answering machine respond to incoming calls, with a difficult-to-understand message in a male voice. She had done this to avoid sexually harassing phone calls. An alternative strategy was developed. She gave her new phone number to all her friends, told them that she would love to hear from them, and changed her answering machine message to her own voice and a clear statement. If she were to receive harassing phone calls, she was advised to notify the phone company, and if this failed, she would have her number changed again but would let her friends know the new number. This resulted in a substantial increase in phone contact, as well as her feeling that she now could call her friends and that this would not be intrusive.

Another focus of treatment was her approach

toward men in whom she had a romantic interest. Her usual strategy could be summarized by "watch and wait." A more proactive strategy was not considered because she thought that it would be intrusive and that it would be seen as sexually promiscuous. Role plays focused on the use of her new friendly behaviors with these men as well. These attempts failed because she feared that the behavior would be seen as a sexual invitation, which she would refuse and then an ugly argument would occur. Therefore, many role plays were carried out aimed at teaching her how to refuse a sexual overture, yet maintain the relationship. The important aspects of this refusal were to continue to be friendly because she did not want to destroy the beginning relationship nor did she want to put sexuality off forever. She was taught to make a friendly refusal but to offer to continue other contact. Many role plays were necessary until she felt comfortable with this new behavior.

Finally, a homework assignment seemed possible. She was going to attend a club dance, and she knew that a man she was attracted to would be there. Her task was to use her friendly behaviors with him, and if he was responsive, to invite him to dance. She carried this out and received a very positive response from this man. They spent a good deal of the time that evening dancing. She felt that she could handle pressure for sexuality if it should occur, and this confidence allowed her to take this more risky approach. She did receive an invitation for dinner from him and was now concerned about how to respond to such an invitation. She felt that if he had to drive a great distance to pick her up and if he paid for an expensive meal, then she had no right to refuse sexuality. Once again, friendly refusals were role played, as well as several scenarios in which she made a counter offer to drive and meet him at a more equally convenient location. A decision was made to offer to meet him, which was to be done as a homework. She called him and made this offer, which was readily accepted. The evening went well and another casual meeting was set to go hiking. The concern about pressure for sexuality had diminished considerably. As of this writing, this dating has continued, with an agreed-upon increase in intimacy.

This woman's mood had returned entirely to normal, but she did have a mild relapse when her employer told her that he could not continue her employment. She responded to this crisis with an active job search, after some mild self-doubts and concern that she was not worthwhile and could not get another job. Her previous response to such a crisis was a significant depression and social withdrawal. In fact, she decided on her own to apply her new skills to job interviews. Within 4 weeks, she had received two job offers, and these made her feel very good. She had another more attractive job possibility brought to her attention by one of her new friends. She chose to turn down these other offers and pursue this new possibility. She remarked that she would have never turned down these offers in the past; instead, she would have accepted one of them because she was convinced that no one else would be interested in her work skills.

PROBLEMS IN TREATMENT

In most applications of social skills training for depressed patients, our treatments have gone relatively smoothly. Not every patient will proceed smoothly however. Most of the difficulties in treatment have occurred within the first four sessions. These difficulties have run the gamut from suicidal patients to patients who are going on vacations for extended periods of time. In the interest of brevity, we present only common problems or those that imply serious risk. It should be apparent from the previous sections that social skills training is a structured, learning-oriented treatment. The heart of the approach is the new learning that takes place. Anything that interferes with this learning will interfere with treatment effectiveness. Common difficulties include the following:

1. Patient refusal to role play, thus eliminating practice, which is vital to treatment

2. Constant focus on patient crises, eliminating the structured approach and practice

3. Patients refusal to do homework, thereby minimizing the real practice and generalization opportunities needed to make permanent changes

4. Therapists moving too rapidly from one area to the next, thereby reducing needed practice, increasing the risk of patient failures, and reducing patient motivation

5. Patients under the influence of alcohol or

other drugs, thereby limiting their ability to learn

6. Highly constrained, unsupportive social world, which adds difficulty to the training but does not make training impossible

When we have encountered resistance to role plays, we have employed two lines of attack to change the patient's mind. First, we go back to train the general use of role plays without aiming at any problematic behavior, in the hopes that the resistance is based on anxiety and feeling silly and awkward. If that should fail, we would carry out a simulated role play with a very problematic situation and a very real portrayal in the hopes that the power of the emotions created in the patient will convince the patient of the power of the overall procedure. If this too fails, we would seriously consider abandoning social skills training as the form of treatment.

Another problem that arises on occasion is the emergence of a crisis in the life of the patient. This problem may lead to three detrimental outcomes: First, if the therapist ignores crises altogether, some important and potentially very serious situations could occur. Second, time spent solving a crisis is time taken away from social skills training, which could help the patient solve his or her own problem. Third, the patient may find it more useful to continually present the therapist with the next problem for a solution, resulting in the patient learning not to solve his or her own problems but to rely on the therapist. To handle this problem, we try to steer a middle course, making sure we hear about the current crisis, but then either working it into the skills training program or postponing it until later. Nonetheless, serious crises, such as risk of danger to life or property, produce immediate response and abandonment of social skills training until the crisis resolves.

Homework assignments tend to be a continual source of problems. There must be enough structure and clarity to guide the patient, and yet if there is too much work involved, the patient may become discouraged by the amount of effort that seems to be required. Well-conceived homework, which produces a desirable outcome for the patient, can go a long way in convincing the patient to continue.

Novice therapists tend to move through training at too quick a pace. They tend to be in a hurry to address the more pressing needs of the patient and prefer to move to these problems rapidly. Upon facing these problems, both the patient and the therapist realize that they are unprepared, which can result in the patient falling back to his or her old, ineffective solutions and the therapist falling back to other modes of psychotherapy. This problem is best avoided altogether by a slower pace and overpractice.

Finally, some patients will fail to respond even with a good effort and adherence to usual procedures. Once again, we caution about prematurely abandoning social skills training. Our data suggest that about 10 sessions should be tried before concluding that treatment is a failure. Exactly what to do with those patients who fail after a reasonable trial is another problem. Such patients have been tried on alternative treatments such as cognitive therapy and couples therapy, as well as pharmacotherapy.

In our work with the chronically depressed, the probability of failure on a second treatment appeared quite high. Patients who were nonresponders to social skills training often turned out to be nonresponders to other treatments, including pharmacotherapy. Given this state of affairs, one might consider adding another treatment on top of the failed one or trying the patient on a combination of two treatments simultaneously. While we have not specifically done so with our patients, our own data (Becker & Heimberg, 1987) does *not* show an enhanced effect when pharmacotherapy was combined with social skills training in the first attempt at treatment. It appears that patients who do not respond to the initial treatment will be a problem, but many patients do respond quite well to the initial treatment and do not have to face this problem. For the responders, another problem becomes important—namely, another episode of depression.

Clinicians and clinical researchers have recently become concerned with the recurrent nature of depression—that is, relapse. After the current episode responds to treatment, there continues to be a significant risk of reoccurrence (Gonzales, Lewinsohn, & Clarke, 1985; Keller, Lavori, Endicott, Coryell, & Klerman, 1983; Prien & Kupfer,

1986). For example, Keller et al. (1983) found recovery in about 85% of patients over the course of 2 years. Yet, 6 months after recovery, about 50% of patients had a relapse into either a major depression or dysthymia. Furthermore, patients whose history suggested both major depression and dysthymia tended to cycle into depression more frequently. These 1980s studies suggest that treatment not only should aim at recovery and symptom remission, but also should be concerned with reducing the risk of relapse. While few data are available about how to reduce the relapse risk, what few exist suggest that a minimum period of 8 consecutive weeks with *no* symptoms of depression provides some protection against relapse. Even infrequent occurrences of very mild symptoms of depression appeared to heighten the risk of later relapse. These data imply the need for a continuation of treatment to try to achieve the minimum 8 consecutive weeks of a symptom-free period. Even if this 8-week period can be achieved, the discontinuation of treatment appears to be associated with a higher risk of relapse in the subsequent month. On the other hand, patients who weather this 1-month higher-risk period appear to have a much lower risk of relapse.

CONCLUDING STATEMENT

Social skills training can be an effective treatment for depression, and many patients will respond positively to it. Clinicians may find this treatment strategy somewhat different from more traditional psychotherapy, and for those reasons, they may feel uncomfortable with it. Nonetheless, clinicians can learn to carry out this treatment successfully. We have trained several clinicians in the course of our investigations into the effectiveness of social skills training. Most of these clinicians were familiar with behavior therapy theory and many of the behavioral techniques. It appears that many of the techniques and at least part of the theory have become common training for many clinicians. For those clinicians who have had a smattering of behavioral training, this approach may seem more therapeutically confining. After seeing the power of the procedures, this concern about confinement seems to diminish. As this treatment is applied

more generally, other clinicians may discover some innovation to improve the application and to benefit both the field itself and many patients.

REFERENCES

Beck, A. T., Ward, C. H., Mendelson, M., Mock, J., & Erbaugh, J. (1961). An inventory for measuring depression. *Archives of General Psychiatry, 4,* 561–571.

Becker, R. E., & Heimberg, R. G. (1985). Social skills training approaches. In M. Hersen & A. S. Bellack (Eds.), *Handbook of clinical behavior therapy with adults.* New York: Plenum.

Becker, R. E., & Heimberg, R. G. (1987, November). *Dysthymia: Preliminary results of treatment with social skills training, crisis supportive psychotherapy, nortriptyline, and placebo.* Paper presented at the 21st annual meeting of the Association for the Advancement of Behavior Therapy, Boston, MA.

Becker, R. E., & Heimberg, R. G. (1988). Assessment of social skills. In A. S. Bellack & M. Hersen (Eds.), *Behavioral assessment: A practical handbook* (pp. 365–395). New York: Pergamon.

Becker, R. E., Heimberg, R. G., & Bellack, A. S. (1987). *Social skills training treatment for depression.* New York: Pergamon.

Bellack, A. S., Hersen, M., & Himmelhoch, J. M. (1983). A comparison of social skills training, pharmacotherapy and psychotherapy for depression. *Behaviour Research and Therapy, 21,* 101–107.

Biglan, A., Hops, H., Sherman, I., Thoreson, C., Friedman, L. S., Arthur, J., & Osteen, V. (1984, August). *Problem solving interactions of depressed women and their spouses.* Paper presented at the Annual Convention of the American Psychological Association.

Boswell, P. C., & Murray, E. J. (1981). Depression, schizophrenia, and social attraction. *Journal of Consulting and Clinical Psychology, 49,* 641–647.

Callner, D. A., & Ross, S. M. (1976). The reliability of three measures of assertion in a drug addiction population. *Behavior Therapy, 7,* 659–667.

Derogatis, L. R., Lipman, R. S., & Covi, L. (1973). SCL-90: An outpatient psychiatric rating scale—Preliminary report. *Psychopharmacology Bulletin, 9,* 18–27.

Endicott, J., & Spitzer, R. (1978). A diagnostic interview: The Schedule for Affective Disorders and

Schizophrenia. *Archives of General Psychiatry, 35,* 837–844.

Endicott, J. E., Spitzer, R. L., Fleiss, J. L., & Cohen, J. (1976). The Global Assessment Scale: A procedure for measuring overall severity of psychiatric disturbance. *Archives of General Psychiatry, 33,* 766–771.

Ferster, C. B. (1965). Classification of behavioral pathology. In L. Krasner & L. P. Ullmann (Eds.), *Research in behavior modification: New developments and implications* (pp. 6–26). New York: Holt, Rinehart and Winston.

Ferster, C. B. (1973). A functional analysis of depression. *American Psychologist, 10,* 857–863.

Ferster, C. B. (1981). A functional analysis of behavior therapy. In L. P. Rehm (Ed.), *Behavior therapy for depression.* New York: Academic.

Galassi, J. P., DeLo, J. S., Galassi, M. D., & Bastien, S. (1974). The College Self-expression Scale: A measure of assertiveness. *Behavior Therapy, 5,* 165–171.

Gambrill, E. D., & Richey, C. A. (1975). An assertion inventory for use in assessment and research. *Behavior Therapy, 6,* 550–561. New York: Academic.

Gay, M. L., Hollandsworth, J. G., & Galassi, J. P. (1975). An assertiveness inventory for adults. *Journal of Counseling Psychology, 22,* 340–344.

Gonzales, L. R., Lewinsohn, P. M., & Clarke, G. N. (1985). Longitudinal follow-up of unipolar depressives: An investigation of predictors of relapse. *Journal of Consulting and Clinical Psychology, 53,* 461–469.

Hamilton, M. (1960). A rating scale for depression. *Journal of Neurology, Neurosurgery, and Psychiatry, 23,* 56–62.

Hersen, M., Bellack, A. S., Himmelhoch, J. M., & Thase, M. E. (1984). Effects of social skills training, amitriptyline, and psychotherapy in unipolar depressed women. *Behavior Therapy, 15,* 21–40.

Hersen, M., Bellack, A. S., Turner, S. M., Williams, M. T., Harper, K., & Watts, J. G. (1979). Psychometric properties of the Wolpe–Lazarus Assertiveness Scale. *Behaviour Research and Therapy, 17,* 63–69.

Hinchliffe, M. A., Hopper, D., Roberts, F. J., & Vaughn, P. W. (1975). A study of the interaction between depressed patients and their spouses. *British Journal of Psychiatry, 126,* 164–172.

Kahn, J., Coyne, J. C., & Margolin, G. (1985). Depression and marital disagreement: The social construction of despair. *Journal of Social and Personal Relationships, 2,* 447–461.

Keller, M. B., Lavori, P. W., Endicott, J., Coryell, W., & Klerman, G. L. (1983). Double depression: A two

year follow-up. *American Journal of Psychiatry, 140,* 689–694.

Kowalik, D., & Gotlib, I. H. (1987). Depression and marital interaction: Concordance between intent and perception of communication. *Journal of Abnormal Psychology, 96,* 127–134.

Lewinsohn, P. M. (1975). The behavioral study and treatment of depression. In M. Hersen, R. M. Eisler, & P. M. Miller (Eds.), *Progress in behavior modification* (Vol. 1). New York: Academic.

Lewinsohn, P. M., Youngren, M. A., & Grosscup, S. (1979). Depression and reinforcement. In R. A. DePue (Ed.), *The psychobiology of depressive disorders.* New York: Academic.

Libet, J. M., & Lewinsohn, P. M. (1973). Concept of social skill with special reference to the behavior of depressed persons. *Journal of Consulting and Clinical Psychology, 40,* 304–312.

Lubin, B. (1981). *Manual for the Depression Adjective Checklist.* San Diego: Educational and Industrial Testing Service.

McFall, R. M., & Lillesand, D. B. (1971). Behavioral rehearsal with modeling and coaching in assertion training. *Journal of Abnormal Psychology, 77,* 313–323.

Prien, R. F., & Kupfer, D. J. (1986). Continuation drug therapy for major depressive episodes: How long should it be maintained? *American Journal of Psychiatry, 143,* 18–23.

Raskin, A., Schulterbrandt, J., Reatig, N., & Rice, C. (1967). Factors of psychopathology in interview, ward behavior, and self-report ratings of hospitalized depressives. *Journal of Consulting Psychology, 31,* 270–278.

Rathus, S. A. (1973). A 30 item schedule for assessing behavior. *Behavior Therapy, 4,* 398–406.

Rush, A. J., Giles, D. E., Schlesser, M. A., Fulton, C. L., Weissenburger, J., & Burns, C. (1985). The Inventory for Depressive Symptomatology: Preliminary findings. *Psychiatry Research, 18,* 65–87.

Strack, S., & Coyne, J. C. (1983). Social confirmation of dysphoria: Shared and private reactions to depression. *Journal of Personality and Social Psychology, 44,* 798–806.

Wolpe, J., & Lazarus, A. A. (1966). *Behavior therapy techniques: A guide to the treatment of neuroses.* Oxford, England: Pergamon.

Zung, W. K. K. (1974). The measurement of affects: Depression and anxiety. In P. Pichot & R. Oliver-Martin (Eds.), *Psychological measurements in psychopharmacology.* Basel, Switzerland: S. Karger, AG.

CHAPTER 7

Pharmacotherapy

CAROLA KIEVE AND MICHAEL FEINBERG

Affective disorders include a broad spectrum of illnesses classifiable according to the nature of the abnormal affect or mood (elevated or depressed) and the periodicity of the changes of mood. The nosology of affective disorders has been a subject of considerable controversy for more than 100 years; the issue is not trivial because response to treatment varies across diagnostic groups. We use the quasi-official DSM-III-R nomenclature, though it is not ideal, with exceptions as appropriate.

Major depression, as defined by DSM-III-R, is a broad, heterogeneous diagnostic category, with several subtypes, including both single episodes and recurrent illnesses. A *major depressive episode* is usually an acute episode of unipolar depression. Not all patients with major depressive disorder (MDD) have the same illness; nor do they all respond to the same treatment. More accurate diagnosis within the general category of major depression and more careful selection of appropriate treatment increase the probability of response.

OVERVIEW OF PHARMACOLOGIC TREATMENTS FOR DEPRESSION

It will be helpful to discuss (a) several of the drugs commonly used to treat depressed patients, (b) the hypotheses about their mechanisms of action, and (c) their side effects, before (d) dealing with their clinical use. The first clinically useful antidepressant drugs were the monoamine oxidase inhibitors (MAOIs). Some MAOIs are structurally similar to tuberculostatic drugs such as INH (isonicotinic acid hydrazide), and their antidepressant activity was discovered as a side effect of these drugs. The next major class of antidepressant drugs—the tricyclic antidepressants—is structurally similar to the phenothiazine group of antipsychotic drugs. Kuhn discovered the antidepressant action of imipramine in 1958, while searching for a better antipsychotic drug. Drugs from these two groups are still the standards in the pharmacological treatment of depression. Both classes of drugs can affect the transmission of impulses at noradrenergic and serotonergic synapses. In theory (and in the laboratory), synaptic transmission is enhanced; this led to the biogenic amine hypothesis of depression. The hypothesis, simply stated, is that depression is caused by a functional decrease in noradrenergic or serotonergic transmission at some critical part of the brain, and antidepressants act by causing a functional increase in transmission. (This is really two hypotheses, one involving norepinephrine, and the other, serotonin.) The hypothesis has had great heuristic value, but there is little or no evidence to support it as originally stated. Modified forms of the hypothesis are still being tested. Some newer antidepressant drugs may affect only noradrenergic or serotonergic transmission, but they are nonetheless clinically effective.

We discuss the use of imipramine in some detail; the other tricyclic antidepressants (TCAs) are variations on that theme. The most important rule in the clinical use of the TCAs is that the drug must be given at the right dose for a long enough period of time. There is no correlation across individuals between dose and plasma concentration of drug, even taking weight, age, and similar factors into account. The relationship between plasma concentration and clinical effect is best established for imipramine and nortriptyline (Task Force on the Use of Laboratory Tests in Psychiatry, 1985), and we therefore recommend these as drugs of first choice. Some patients will report improved sleep and appetite after a few doses of TCA, but they may not report significant clinical improvement until they have had a plasma drug level in the therapeutic range for 3 to 6 weeks. This delay in symptom relief often leads inexperienced clinicians to conclude that the treatment will not be effective. (It also presents a major problem for the biogenic amine hypothesis, because the drugs' effects on synaptic transmission begin with the first dose.) The usual dose of imipramine is 150–300 mg at bedtime; the effective plasma level is $\geq$ 200 ng/ml (imipramine plus desipramine). The usual dose of nortriptyline is 75–125 mg/day and the effective plasma level is 50–150 ng/ml. Both drugs are sedating and are slowly metabolized; they are therefore usually given in a single daily dose at bedtime. All of the tricyclics are anticholinergic; that is, they block the action of the neurotransmitter acetylcholine. This may be related to their main (antidepressant) effect. It is certainly related to many side effects, including dry mouth and constipation, difficulty urinating (particularly in older men), blurred near vision, and so on.

Monoamine oxidase inhibitors destroy the enzyme monoamine oxidase (MAO), which normally metabolizes norepinephrine and serotonin. These transmitters thus accumulate in the neurons that release them, thereby (according to the biogenic amine hypothesis) enhancing transmission and relieving depression. The destruction of MAO is certainly responsible for the best known and potentially most dangerous side effect of these drugs: extremely high blood pressure, particularly in the brain.

The hazardous increase in blood pressure occurs through a relatively simple mechanism. Many foods contain tyramine, a normal product of fermentation and digestion normally destroyed by MAO in the gut wall. When MAOIs have destroyed the enzyme, and the patient eats food high in tyramine, this increased tyramine enters the blood in relatively high concentration. It is actively taken up by neurons where it displaces bound norepinephrine. The surge of norepinephrine causes a large, rapid increase in blood pressure. Patients complain of a uniquely painful throbbing headache, and a few patients have died from rupture of a blood vessel in the brain. There are many lists of forbidden and permitted foods available; the classical culprits are cheddar cheese and Chianti. Many drugs can interact catastrophically with MAOI, and patients are best advised to take no medicine of any kind before consulting with the prescribing physician.

The MAOIs possess virtues that make them important and useful drugs despite their potential for harm. They do not bind to acetylcholine receptors, which makes them less likely to cause the aforementioned side effects. They tend to be stimulating, rather than sedating. Most important, they are effective for the vast majority of patients who respond to TCAs, and for other patients who do not (Liebowitz et al., 1988; Robinson, Nies, Ravaris, & Lamborn, 1973). The usual daily dose of phenelzine is about 1 mg/kg/day, with half the dose given at breakfast and half at midday. The other MAOI in common use is tranylcypromine; the dose is about 0.7 mg/kg/day, given on the same schedule. Some patients taking tranylcypromine complain of midafternoon drowsiness, which may be relieved by postponement of taking the last dose until about 3 p.m.

There are several newer classes of antidepressant drugs, some members of which are available in the United States. These include fluoxetine, which affects serotonergic transmission only; it does not bind to acetylcholine receptors. Like other inhibitors of serotonin reuptake, it can cause loss of appetite, perhaps as a direct result of (usually) mild nausea. The TCAs and MAOIs tend to increase appetite. Once the patient has regained any weight lost as a symptom of depression, he or she may object strongly to gaining additional weight. Fluoxetine is often mildly stimulating, possibly causing increased anxiety and insomnia. The usual dose is 20–40 mg/day, given early in the day. The half-life of fluoxetine is 2–3 days; its active metabolite, norfluoxetine, has a half-life of 7–9 days. This very long half-life becomes a factor when the drug must be discontinued for any reason. As with other antidepressants, treatment should continue for at least several weeks.

TREATMENT OF NONENDOGENOUS DEPRESSION (MAJOR DEPRESSION WITHOUT MELANCHOLIA)

This category of depression includes a broad spectrum of patients. At one end are those with mild, chronic depression who will benefit from psychotherapy; these patients may have a nonspecific response to antidepressants, some of which are excellent antianxiety agents. At the other extreme fall patients with endogenous depression who fail to meet criteria for melancholia, some of whom may be in the prodromal phase of a serious illness. (This presentation is not uncommon in patients with previous episodes.) These patients will have a specific response to antidepressant drugs, and they may have a nonspecific response to the supportive aspects of psychotherapy.

Diagnostic and treatment decisions may be difficult, especially when the patient's past history is unknown or unclear. We suggest one or two psychotherapy sessions to assess the patient's response; if the patient remains significantly depressed, an adequate trial of an antidepressant drug is indicated. This is likely to be effective within a few weeks, if at all. After this, it will be possible to reassess the need for psychotherapy.

TREATMENT OF ENDOGENOUS DEPRESSION (MELANCHOLIA)

Endogenous depression originally referred to an illness not caused by some exogenous agent, such as an infection. With time, *endogenous* has come to mean that the illness is not reactive and does not occur in response to a precipitant. This can lead to diagnostic confusion whenever an episode of depression follows a stressful event, suggesting an etiology and a treatment for the episode. Klein

(1974) suggested the term *endogenomorphic* to describe an illness with clinical features of endogenous depression, without regard to the presence or absence of precipitants. Although disagreement about nomenclature continues, DSM-III-R uses the term *melancholia.*

Klerman (1983) stated that about 60% of inpatients with major depression meet criteria for melancholia. The treatment of choice for major depression with melancholic features and without psychosis is TCA. Bielski and Friedel (1976) reviewed prospective, double-blind, placebo-controlled studies of amitriptyline and imipramine in depressed patients. They found that melancholic features (anorexia, weight loss, middle and late insomnia, and psychomotor disturbance) predicted a good response, whereas other features (neurotic, hypochondriacal, and hysterical traits; multiple prior episodes; delusions; and possibly also long duration of illness—more than 12 months) predicted a poor response. The bulk of the evidence suggests that the presence of melancholic features predicts a positive response to somatic treatment and a negative response to psychotherapy alone.

Major Depression with Psychotic Features

Psychotic depression can be viewed in several different ways. Some see it as a form of major depression; others see it as a clinical entity in its own right, and still others view it as a subtype of bipolar illness (Brotman, Falk, & Gelenberg, 1987). There is evidence to support each of these views; in any case, nonpsychotic and psychotic depressed patients differ clinically (Meltzer, Hyong, Carroll, & Russo, 1976; Schatzberg et al., 1983; Sweeney, Nelson, Bowers, Maas, & Heninger, 1978). These differences include serum and cerebrospinal fluid (CSF) levels of certain neurotransmitters and/or their metabolites, differences in postdexamethasone cortisol levels, in family history (of bipolar disorder), and in the probability of later developing manic symptoms (Coryell & Tsuang, 1985). Treatment choices vary somewhat, depending on how one thinks about the disorder.

Glassman and Roose (1981) found that psychotic depressed patients do not respond to TCAs alone and may become worse; they recommended using electroconvulsive therapy (ECT) or adding a neuroleptic to TCA treatment. The negative feeling among less well-informed mental health professionals and the general public about the use of ECT is largely unwarranted, as ECT has been shown to be quite safe (Task Force on Electroconvulsive Therapy, 1978) and is at least as effective as the TCA-neuroleptic combination. It may be particularly indicated in older or medically compromised patients and in cases where the risk of death from starvation, dehydration, or suicide is high (Fink, 1987).

In a 1985 prospective double-blind study, Spiker et al. showed that the combination of amitriptyline and perphenazine was superior to either drug alone in psychotic depression. Frangos, Tsitourides, Psilolignos, and Katsanou (1983) also suggested that the TCA-neuroleptic combination is the treatment of choice, as it leads to significant improvement in 80% of psychotically depressed patients. (Many of these patients can be safely tapered off the neuroleptic once there has been a full remission of psychotic symptoms.) In another study, Price, Conwell, and Nelson (1983) showed that patients who were refractory to the combination of TCA and neuroleptic responded when lithium was added. We recommend adding lithium if there is no response to a TCA, especially if there are bipolar relatives. Carbamazepine (Tegretol) may be an effective adjunct to the TCA-neuroleptic combination in patients who cannot tolerate lithium (Schaffer, Mungas, & Rockwell, 1985).

Bipolar Depression

Treatment of the Depressive Phase of Bipolar Depression

The diagnosis of bipolar disorder is made on the basis of a history of mania or hypomania. Bipolar patients may become hypomanic (and sometimes floridly manic) or begin to have frequent episodes ("rapid cycling") while taking antidepressants (Wehr, Sack, Rosenthal, & Cowdry, 1988). Hence, it is necessary to exercise caution in treating bipolar depressed patients with antidepres-

sants. On the other hand, bipolar depressed patients are more likely than the unipolar population to have an antidepressant response to lithium. Some researchers, having found that TCAs shorten the cycle length in bipolar patients, recommend avoiding them in favor of lithium alone or in combination with an MAOI (Dunner, 1979; Wehr, et al., 1988).

Bipolar depressed patients may be less severely ill than unipolar patients, and their symptoms may not warrant treatment other than with lithium, whether for treatment of the episode or for prophylaxis. (Structuring the patient's daily activities may be a useful adjunct to lithium in these cases.) If vegetative symptoms are severe, cautious use of TCAs may be warranted (in addition to lithium).

The treatment of *rapid cyclers* (patients with four or more episodes per year) deserves a word here. These patients often respond only partially to lithium treatment. Their interepisode interval increases, but they still have significant morbidity. The combination of lithium with carbamazepine or low-dose neuroleptic (Schou 1986b; Stromgren & Boller, 1985) may be more effective than lithium alone.

When initially diagnosing a patient with unipolar depression, it is important to keep in mind that up to one third of patients initially diagnosed with depression may later prove to be bipolar (Clayton, 1981). According to Dunner and Clayton (1987), 5% of first-episode depressives go on to switch to mania (Dunner, 1983), and therefore a patient should not be firmly diagnosed as unipolar until there has been a 6-month euthymic period after the first depressive episode. Perris (1966) suggested that patients should not be classified as unipolar until they had experienced three episodes of depression without mania or hypomania.

Treatment of the Manic Phase of Bipolar Disorder

Although lithium was first used to treat mania in 1949, it was not used in the United States until the 1960s (Schou, 1986b). Before that, antipsychotic medication was the treatment for acute mania (Dunner, 1983). Although lithium's efficacy in the treatment of acute mania is now widely and firmly established, antipsychotics are still useful and in many cases necessary.

There are three commonly used treatment strategies for the treatment of acute mania: (1) neuroleptics plus lithium, (2) neuroleptics alone, and (3) neuroleptics acutely, with the addition of lithium later on. Simpson (personal communication, 1988) prefers benzodiazepines (lorazepam) to neuroleptics for behavioral control, because of the risk of tardive dyskinesia that accompanies use of neuroleptics. It may take several days for lithium to have a therapeutic effect, perhaps because lithium levels in neurons equilibrate with those in plasma over several days. Therefore, it is common practice to combine lithium with an antipsychotic or sedating medication early in treatment. Ideally, the decision to use antipsychotic medication ought to be based on the presence of psychotic symptoms. However, because lithium is available for oral use only, its use can create problems with compliance. In addition, hospital stays are now considerably shorter than in the past, causing problems with patients who do not respond promptly. If one is faced with a manic patient who is either noncompliant with or nonresponsive to lithium, a decision must then be made whether to use either neuroleptics (depot neuroleptics may be considered with noncompliant patients) or carbamazepine.

Since the mid-1970s, there has been some controversy concerning the use of lithium plus neuroleptics. Cohen and Cohen (1974) reported serious neurotoxicity, although their flawed data weaken their conclusions (Ayd, 1975). Tardive dyskinesia has occurred in bipolar patients who have repeatedly been given potent neuroleptics for only brief periods (Levenson, 1985; Spring & Frankel, 1981).

In recent years, a host of other treatments for acute mania have come into experimental use. These include carbamazepine, clonidine (Zubenko, Cohen, Lipinski, & Jonas, 1984), clonazepam (Chouinard, 1987; Chouinard, Young, & Annable, 1983), lorazepam (Modell, Lenox, & Weiner, 1985), verapamil (Dubovsky, Franks, & Lifschitz, 1982; Dubovsky, Franks, & Schrier, 1985; Giannini, Houser, Loisette, Giannini, & Price, 1984), valproic acid (Puzynski & Kosiewicz, 1984), dextroamphetamine (Garvey, Huang, & Teubner-Rhodes, 1987), and L-tryptophan (Chambers & Naylor, 1978; Murphy et al., 1974; Prange, Wilson, Lynn, Altop, & Strikeleather, 1974).

OTHER DEPRESSIVE DISORDERS

Atypical Depression

Atypical depression refers to two groups of patients. In DSM-III-R, atypical patients are those who fail to meet criteria for a specific syndrome; in contrast, Quitkin, Rifkin, and Klein (1979) have defined a specific syndrome, which they call "atypical depression," and they have investigated the drug responses of patients with this syndrome (Liebowitz et al., 1984; 1988). We discuss only the group with atypical depression syndrome, defined as having reactivity of mood and two or more of the following symptoms: increased appetite or weight gain, oversleeping or spending more time in bed, severe fatigue creating a sensation of leaden paralysis or extreme heaviness of arms or legs, and rejection sensitivity as a trait throughout adulthood.

In 1959, West and Dally began treating these atypically depressed patients with MAOIs and found MAOIs to be effective for this group. Liebowitz et al. (1981; 1984; 1988) have shown that MAOIs are more effective than imipramine, which is more effective than placebo. MAOIs may therefore be a good first choice in patients who fit the atypically depressed profile.

Some have argued that atypical depression is not a well-defined syndrome and that this may account for the unpredictability of response to drug treatment regimens in these patients. If a trial of an MAOI at therapeutic doses for 6 weeks is ineffective, there are several ways to proceed. First, lithium may be added. If there is no response to therapeutic doses of lithium after 2 weeks, it is unlikely that lithium augmentation will be successful. It may be that psychotherapy is the appropriate treatment for patients who have not responded to MAOI plus lithium. The TCAs might be effective if the patient has not received an adequate trial. Patients should not start another antidepressant for 2 weeks after an MAOI has been discontinued.

Treatment of Dysthymic Disorder

Dysthymic disorder is a heterogeneous diagnostic entity, and definitive treatment recommendations are difficult. We can, however, make some general comments and suggestions. Dysthymia persisting after recovery from a major depressive episode warrants close observation and possible treatment (Keller, Lavori, Endicott, Coryell, & Klerman, 1983). The presence of either a family history of affective disorder or symptoms of melancholic–endogenous depression may predict a positive response to antidepressant agents (Weissman, Klerman, Prusoff, Sholomskas, & Padian, 1981). Therefore, when a patient meets DSM-III-R criteria for dysthymia and has either a positive family history or positive symptoms, a TCA or an MAOI may effect remission of symptoms and is worth trying. The presence of character pathology and/or a definite precipitating event should not necessarily preclude a trial of antidepressants.

Akiskal (1985) considers dysthymia to be synonymous with chronic depression. He has differentiated four subtypes of chronic depression and says that two of these may be responsive to pharmacological and psychosocial treatments. The first of these two, "subaffective primary depression," is characterized by an early onset and frequent, short-lived episodes of depression. Akiskal says that lithium and/or MAOIs, combined with social skills training, may be effective.

The second subtype, "late onset chronic depression," usually occurs in patients over age 40 years, in whom there has been no previous significant psychopathology. Typically, these patients fail to recover from major depressive episodes. Akiskal recommends heterocyclic antidepressants (HCAs) for this group, along with interpersonal cognitive therapy.

Treatment of Cyclothymia

Cyclothymia has been given a variety of names and has been thought of both as a type of personality disorder and as a subtype of bipolar disorder (Akiskal, Khani, & Scott-Strauss, 1979; Liebow-

itz & Klein, 1979). The current consensus (Depue et al., 1981; Dunner, Russek, & Fieve, 1982; Himmelhoch, Fuchs, May, Symons, & Neil, 1981; Kane et al., 1982) is that it is a variety of bipolar disorder. As such, lithium is often effective in controlling the emotional and behavioral lability of cyclothymic patients. In one open clinical trial (Kane et al., 1982), 60% of cyclothymics who met DSM-III criteria for the disorder and who were incapacitated due to the illness responded well to lithium, with a substantial decrease in mood swings (Jefferson, Greist, & Ackerman, 1983; Klerman, Endicott, Spitzer, & Hirschfeld, 1979; Peselow, Dunner, Fieve, & Lautin, 1982). However, other reports (Peselow, Dunner, Fieve, & Lautin, 1981) found lithium less effective in preventing depressive episodes in cyclothymic patients. Only a little over a quarter of patients on lithium prophylaxis remained free of depression after 1 year. There is evidence that the length of time between recurrences is lengthened with lithium prophylaxis and that the overall rate of recurrences at 2 years is reduced. This pattern of response is similar to that observed in rapid cyclers, and it may be that the two disorders are not distinct.

NONRESPONSE AND TREATMENT-RESISTANT DEPRESSION

Although nonresponse is not necessarily synonymous with treatment resistance, the two situations may be handled similarly, and we recommend the following suggestions. *Treatment-resistant depression* usually means inadequate or improper treatment. However, over 10% of patients do not improve acceptably after treatment with one or more medications, despite receiving maximum doses and having adequate blood levels for an adequate amount of time (4–6 weeks).

There are no clearly established guidelines about when or whether to switch drugs. In general, however, if a patient cannot tolerate one drug, he or she should be given a trial with a drug that has a different side-effect profile. If one or two heterocyclics are not effective, switching to an MAOI may be indicated. Not uncommonly, elderly patients have depression that is resistant to treatment both with TCAs and with ECT. Although MAOIs have not been widely used in elderly depressed patients, there is evidence that an MAOI may be effective when treatment with TCAs or other HCAs and/or ECT fails (Georgotas, Mann, & Friedman, 1981; Georgotas et al., 1983). Caution is appropriate, and a full medical history and physical exam are always warranted.

The combination of MAOI and TCA may be quite effective in some patients who do not respond to either agent alone, especially in those patients who are very anxious (Ananth & Luchins, 1977; Sethna, 1974; White & Simpson, 1981). Until recently, the combination of MAOIs and TCAs was deemed unsafe. However, the two can be given together if certain rules are kept in mind. Razani et al. (1983) recommend the following regimen: First allow a drug-free interval of 1 week, then begin both drugs within the same day at low dosage; gradually increase the doses of both drugs in parallel up to half the usual maximum daily dose of each drug. White and Simpson (1981) recommend that the TCA of choice might be amitriptyline, trimipramine, or doxepin, and there have been citations of dangers in the combination of MAOIs with selective serotonin reuptake inhibitors (Brotman, Falk, & Gelenberg, 1987).

Lithium may be added to an antidepressant when patients respond either only partly or not at all. (deMontigny, Cournoyer, Morisette, Langlois, & Caille, 1983; deMontigny, Grunberg, Mayer, & Deschenes, 1981; Heninger, Charney, & Sternberg, 1983; Louie & Meltzer, 1984; Meltzer, Lowry, Robertson, Goodnick, & Perline, 1984). There have been reports of dramatic, rapid improvement with the addition of lithium to TCAs and to MAOIs (Fein, Paz, Rao, & Lagrassa, 1988; Himmelhoch, Detre, Kupfer, Swartzburg, & Byck, 1972; Price, Charney, & Heninger, 1985) in patients who show little response to an antidepressant alone. There are also reports of lithium potentiating a neuroleptic–TCA combination in patients with psychotic depression (Price et al., 1983). The mechanism of this effect is not clear, but it may involve a synergistic effect on serotonergic transmission.

Prange and his co-workers (1969), as well as others (Schwarcz et al., 1984), have found that patients unresponsive to TCA alone improve when low-dose T_3 (25 to 50 ng/day) is added. However, success with this combination has not been universal (Garbutt, Mayo, Gillette, Little, &

Mason, 1986). There are also reports of success with various other combinations of TCAs, MAOIs, stimulants, tryptophan, and reserpine. However, these combinations have also been found ineffective or even dangerous, and we do not discuss them here.

LONG-TERM TREATMENT OF AFFECTIVE DISORDERS

Prien (1987) divided long-term treatment of affective disorders into three categories: (1) continuation of acute treatment, (2) preventive therapy, and (3) treatment of chronic illness. Treatment of an acute episode of depression should continue for 16 to 20 weeks after the patient has recovered in order to prevent relapse (Prien & Kupfer, 1986). At least 50% of patients who have an initial episode of major depression and over 80% of those who have been manic will have a recurrence (Panel, 1985). These relapses can be delayed and/or their severity decreased by continuing treatment with the same antidepressant or by preventive (prophylactic) treatment with lithium and/or carbamazepine (Prien, 1987; Schou, 1986b). Treatment of chronic affective disorders is discussed subsequently.

Lithium is effective in preventing or postponing future episodes in appropriate patients. In determining who should receive prophylactic treatment, one must consider the following: (a) the likelihood of recurrence in the near future, (b) the severity and abruptness of previous episodes, (c) the potential impact of a recurrence on the patient's life, (d) the patient's willingness to comply, (e) the presence of contraindications to treatment, and (f) the patient's response to prior treatments (Prien, 1987).

A patient should have had at least two well-defined episodes requiring psychiatric intervention within the past 5 years before prophylactic treatment is instituted. However, one should consider prophylactic treatment if a second episode would be threatening to life, family, or career. A possible final exception is the patient in whom a first manic episode occurs after age 30 years because the predicted time between episodes decreases with the age of the first episode (Zis, Grof, & Goodwin, 1979).

The NIMH Consensus Development Panel (1985) discussed the advantages of using TCAs for prophylaxis of unipolar depression. The evidence that lithium is effective is stronger than that supporting the use of TCAs, possibly because lithium has been studied more intensively. Although both lithium and TCAs are effective, it is often easier to continue the antidepressant used for acute treatment than to begin using a new drug—lithium.

Lithium is powerfully antimanic and is the treatment of choice for prophylaxis in bipolar patients. In fact, imipramine was associated with an increased incidence of manic relapses in bipolar patients (Prien, Klett, & Caffey, 1974; Prien et al., 1984). Some patients with an initial diagnosis of unipolar depression go on to have a manic or hypomanic episode later; lithium might prevent this (though it might also obscure the real diagnosis). Patients with a diagnosis of unipolar depression and a family history of mania are particularly likely to become (hypo)manic in the future, and lithium would be preferable to a TCA for prophylaxis. While the lithium–TCA combination may be better than either drug alone in the treatment of an acute episode of depression, there is no evidence that the combination is any more effective than either alone in preventing recurrences of unipolar depression (Prien et al., 1984). Both lithium and TCAs may pose risks for elderly patients (renal complications with lithium, and urinary retention, orthostatic hypotension, and cardiac arrhythmias with TCAs) and the benefit:risk ratio must be weighed in each case.

Patients Who Relapse Despite Prophylaxis

Some patients relapse despite adequate prophylactic treatment. In double-blind, placebo-controlled studies, between 0 and 55% of patients relapsed when treated with lithium (Davis, 1976), whereas 41% relapsed in a comparable study using imipramine (Prien et al., 1984). (*Prophylaxis failure* was defined as the occurrence of a major episode requiring either hospitalization or treatment with another drug.)

As with acute treatment, one must first be certain that the patient has adequate plasma levels of the drug(s) being used. Further, lithium may not be fully effective until the patient has been taking it for 6 months or more (Schou, 1986a). There are several strategies one can use to treat the patient who relapses while taking lithium and/or TCAs prophylactically. These include the use of carbamazepine alone (Fawcett & Kravitz, 1985; Okuma, 1983; Post, Uhde, Ballenger, & Squillace, 1983), carbamazepine plus lithium (Stromgren & Boller, 1985), lithium plus TCA, and less well-studied treatments, such as verapamil (Giannini et al., 1984; Gitlin & Weiss, 1984) or tryptophan (Beitman & Dunner, 1982).

How long do we continue preventive treatment? There is no evidence on which to base a firm guideline. Schou (1986a) says,

> There are patients who must continue with lithium for many years to remain free of relapses, but there are also those who need lithium only for a limited number of years. Patients with a unipolar course seem to have a better chance of stopping lithium with impunity after some years than patients with both manias and depressions. If a patient has been entirely free of relapses for 3–4 years, patient and physician may consider discontinuation of treatment under close supervision. In case of relapse, treatment is started again.

Although there are no data concerning the similar long-term use of HCAs and MAOIs, it seems reasonable to apply the foregoing guidelines to these drugs as well.

The Case of Ms. A

Ms. A was referred to Michael Feinberg (co-author of this chapter) when she was 35 years old. She had been depressed for several weeks and complained of feeling depressed and worthless, much as she had during a similar episode 14 years previously, beginning early in her second year of medical school. She had psychomotor retardation (slowed speech and movement) and diurnal variation of mood. She had lost interest in her job as business manager for a major clinical department at the medical center. She felt she was performing poorly and was in danger of being fired, despite her supervisor's assurances to the contrary. Her mother, a clinical psychologist, referred her for psychoanalysis. This treatment lasted several years, with considerable benefit. However, she dropped out of medical school during the episode, and she did not return. Ms. A also complained of marital problems; her husband was an engineer who had risen to vice president of a large company in that field. His job and his character made him unavailable to Ms. A and their 9-year-old son.

Ms. A seemed to be having her second episode of endogenous depression (major depressive disorder, recurrent, with melancholia). She initially responded well to imipramine, but she complained of a rash after about 2 weeks on the drug. The rash was typical for that seen in allergic reactions to drugs, and Ms. A began taking nortriptyline, a structurally dissimilar TCA. She soon developed a similar rash when taking nortriptyline and on a completely unrelated drug, maprotiline. The doctor prevailed on her to give up some of her favorite foods, and she began taking phenelzine. She responded well to this drug.

Ms. A spoke of feeling somewhat depressed every year, beginning in the fall. She regularly felt better every spring and blamed her symptoms on the long, gray northern winters. The physician believed that these were subclinical episodes of endogenous depression and that they would respond to maintenance treatment with lithium. Ms. A refused lithium but consented to maintenance treatment with an MAOI. As predicted, her usual winter "blahs" did not recur. As spring approached, she began to need much less sleep than usual and felt very well indeed. She told the doctor about this only because her husband complained of being awakened by her vacuuming the house at 3 a.m. Ms. A remained on the MAOI for several years without further problems. She ignored the dietary restrictions without ill effect until she tried an interesting new cheese from the gourmet deli. As she described it, "I was sitting there, reading and nibbling this cheese, when I felt as if the top of my head was coming off." Fortunately, there were no lasting effects of this reaction to a high-tyramine cheese.

Ms. A may be bipolar, even though she had only one episode of hypomania when taking an antidepressant. She almost certainly had yearly episodes of endogenous depression, the most common pattern of recurrence. Most of her episodes were not severe enough to cause her to seek treatment, although they did cause her significant distress and interfered with her enjoyment of life. She would probably have responded well to maintenance treatment with lithium without the risk of hypomania.

REFERENCES

Akiskal, H. S. (1985). The clinical management of affective disorders. In R. Michels, J. O. Cavenar, K. H. Brodie, A. M. Cooper, S. B. Guze, L. L. Judd, G. L. Klerman, & A. J. Solnit (Eds.), Psychiatry (Vol. 1, pp. 1–27). Philadelphia: Lippincott.

Akiskal, H. S., Khani, M. K., & Scott-Strauss, A. (1979). Cyclothymic temperamental disorders. Psychiatric Clinics of North America, 2, 527–554.

Ananth, J., & Luchins, D. (1977). A review of combined tricyclic and MAO therapy. Comprehensive Psychiatry, 18, 221–230.

Ayd, F. J. (1975). Lithium–haloperidol for mania: Is it safe or hazardous? International Drug Therapy Newsletter, 10, 29–36.

Beitman, B. D., & Dunner, D. L. (1982). L-Tryptophan in the maintenance treatment of Bipolar II manic–depressive illness. American Journal of Psychiatry, 139, 1498–1499.

Bielski, R. J., & Friedel, R. O. (1976). Prediction of tricyclic antidepressant response. Archives of General Psychiatry, 33, 1479–1489.

Brotman, A. W., Falk, W. E., & Gelenberg, A. J. (1987). Pharmacologic treatment of acute depressive subtypes. In H. Y. Meltzer (Ed.), Psychopharmacology: The third generation of progress (pp. 1031–1040). New York: Raven Press.

Chambers, C. A., & Naylor, G. J. (1978). A controlled trial of L-tryptophan in mania. British Journal of Psychiatry, 132, 555–559.

Chouinard, G. (1987). Clonazepam in acute and maintenance treatment of bipolar affective disorder. Journal of Clinical Psychiatry, 48(suppl), 29–36.

Chouinard, G., Young, S. N., & Annable, A. (1983). Antimanic effective of clonazepam. Biological Psychiatry, 18, 451–466.

Clayton, P. J. (1981). The epidemiology of bipolar affective disorder. Comprehensive Psychiatry, 22, 31–43.

Cohen, W. J., & Cohen, N. H. (1974). Lithium carbonate, haloperidol, and irreversible brain damage. Journal of the American Medical Association, 230, 1283–1287.

Coryell, W., & Tsuang, M. T. (1985). Major depression with mood-congruent or mood-incongruent features: Outcome after 40 years. American Journal of Psychiatry, 142, 479–482.

Davis, J. M. (1976). Overview: Maintenance therapy in psychiatry: II. Affective disorders. American Journal of Psychiatry, 133, 1–13.

deMontigny, C., Cournoyer, G., Morissette, R., Langlois, R., & Caille, G. (1983). Lithium carbonate addition in tricyclic antidepressant-resistant unipolar depression: Correlations with the neurobiologic actions of TCA drugs and lithium ion on the serotonin system. *Archives of General Psychiatry, 40,* 1327–1334.

deMontigny, C., Grunberg, F., Mayer, A., & Deschenes, J. P. (1981). Lithium induces rapid relief of depression in tricyclic antidepressant drug nonresponders. *British Journal of Psychiatry, 138,* 252–256.

Depue, R. A., Slater, J. F., Wolfstetter-Kausch, H., Klein, D., Gopelrud, E., & Farr, D. (1981). A behavioral paradigm for identifying persons at risk for bipolar depressive disorder: A conceptual framework and five validation studies. *Journal of Abnormal Psychology, 90,* 381–437.

Dubovsky, S. L., Franks, R. D., Lifschitz, M., & Coen, P. (1982). Effectiveness of verapamil in the treatment of a manic patient. *American Journal of Psychiatry, 139,* 502–504.

Dubovsky, S. L., Franks, R. D., & Schrier, D. (1985). Phenelzine-induced hypomania: Effect of verapamil. *Biological Psychiatry, 20,* 1009–1014.

Dunner, D. L. (1979). Rapid cycling bipolar manic–depressive illness. *Psychiatric Clinics of North America, 2,* 461–467.

Dunner, D. L. (1983). Drug treatment of the acute manic episode. In L. Grinspoon (Ed.), *Psychiatry update* (Vol. 2, pp. 293–303). Washington, DC: American Psychiatric Press.

Dunner, D. L., & Clayton, P. J. (1987). Drug treatment of bipolar disorder. In H. Y. (Ed.), *Psychopharmacology: The third generation of progress* (pp. 1077–1083). New York: Raven Press.

Dunner, D. L., Russek, F. D., & Fieve, R. R. (1982). Classification of bipolar affective disorder subtypes. *Comprehensive Psychiatry, 23,* 186–189.

Fawcett, J., & Kravitz, H. M. (1985). The long-term management of bipolar disorders with lithium, carbamazepine, and antidepressants. *Journal of Clinical Psychiatry, 46,* 58–60.

Fein, S., Paz, V., Rao, N., & Lagrassa, J. (1988). The combination of lithium carbonate and an MAO in refractory depressions. *American Journal of Psychiatry, 145,* 249–250.

Fink, M. (1987). Convulsive therapy in affective disorders: A decade of understanding and acceptance. In H. Y. Meltzer (Ed.), *Psychopharmacology: The third generation of progress* (pp. 1071–1076). New York: Raven Press.

Frangos, E., Tsitourides, A. S., Psilolignos, P., & Katsa-nou, N. (1983). Psychotic depressive disorder: A separate entity? *Journal of Affective Disorders, 5,* 259–265.

Garbutt, J. C., Mayo, J. P., Gillette, G. M., Little, K. Y., & Mason, G. A. (1986). Lithium potentiation of tricyclic antidepressants following lack of T^3 potentiation. *American Journal of Psychiatry, 143,* 1038–1039.

Garvey, M. J., Huang, S., & Teubner-Rhodes, D. (1987). Dextroamphetamine treatment of mania. *Journal of Clinical Psychiatry, 48,* 412–413.

Georgotas, A., Friedman, E., McCarthy, M., Mann, J., Krakowski, M., Siegel, R., & Ferris, S. (1983). Resistant geriatric depressions and therapeutic response to MAOI's. *Biological Psychiatry, 18,* 195–205.

Georgotas, A., Mann, J., & Friedman, E. (1981). Platelet MAO inhibition as a potential indicator of favorable response to MAOI's in geriatric depressions. *Biological Psychiatry, 16,* 997–1001.

Giannini, A. J., Houser, W. L., Loisette, R. H., Giannini, M. C., & Price, W. A. (1984). Antimanic effects of verapamil. *American Journal of Psychiatry, 141,* 1602–1603.

Gitlin, M. J., & Weiss, J. (1984). Verapamil as maintenance treatment in bipolar illness: A case report. *Journal of Clinical Psychiatry, 6,* 341–343.

Glassman, A. H., & Roose, S. P. (1981). Delusional depression: A distinct clinical entity? *Archives of General Psychiatry, 38,* 424–427.

Heninger, G. R., Charney, D. S., & Sternberg, D. E. (1983). Lithium carbonate augmentation of antidepressant treatment: An effective prescription for treatment-refractory depression. *Archives of General Psychiatry, 40,* 1335–1342.

Himmelhoch, J. M., Detre, T., Kupfer, D. J., Swartzburg, M., & Byck, R. (1972). Treatment of previously intractable depressions with tranylcypromine and lithium. *Journal of Nervous and Mental Disease, 155,* 216–220.

Himmelhoch, J. M., Fuchs, C. Z., May, S. J., Symons, B. J., & Neil, J. F. (1981). When a schizoaffective diagnosis has meaning. *Journal of Nervous and Mental Disease, 169,* 277–282.

Jefferson, J. W., Greist, J. H., & Ackerman, D. L. (1983). *Lithium encyclopedia for clinical practice.* Washington, DC: American Psychiatric Press.

Kane, J. M., Quitkin, F. M., Rifkin, A., Ramos-Lorenzi, J. R., Nayak, D. D., & Howard, A. (1982). Lithium carbonate and imipramine in the prophylaxis of unipolar and bipolar illness. *Archives of General Psychiatry, 39,* 1065–1069.

Keller, M. B., Lavori, P. W., Endicott, J., Coryell, W., & Klerman, G. L. (1983). "Double depression": Two year follow-up. *American Journal of Psychiatry, 140,* 689–694.

Klein, D. F. (1974). Endogenomorphic depression. *Archives of General Psychiatry, 31,* 447–454.

Klerman, G. L. (1983). The nosology and diagnosis of depressive disorders. In L. Grinspoon (Ed.), *Psychiatry update* (Vol. 2, pp. 356–382). Washington, DC: American Psychiatric Press.

Klerman, G. L., Endicott, J., Spitzer, R., & Hirschfeld, R. M. A. (1979). Neurotic depressions: A systematic analysis of multiple criteria and meanings. *American Journal of Psychiatry, 136,* 57–61.

Levenson, J. L. (1985). Neuroleptic malignant syndrome. *American Journal of Psychiatry, 142,* 1137–1145.

Liebowitz, M. R., & Klein, D. F. (1979). Hysteroid dysphoria. *Psychiatric Clinics of North America, 2,* 555–575.

Liebowitz, M. R., Quitkin, F. M., Stewart, J. W., McGrath, P. J., Harrison, W., Rabkin, J., Tricamo, E., Markowitz, J. S., & Klein, D. (1984). Phenelzine v[ersus] imipramine in atypical depression. *Archives of General Psychiatry, 41,* 669–677.

Liebowitz, M. R., Quitkin, F. M., Stewart, J. W., McGrath, P. J., Harrison, W., Schwartz, D., Rabkin, J., Tricamo, E., & Klein, D. (1981). Phenelzine and imipramine in atypical depression. *Psychopharmachology Bulletin, 17,* 159–161.

Liebowitz, M. R., Quitkin, F. M., Stewart, J. W., McGrath, P. J., Harrison, W. M., Markowitz, J. S., Rabkin, J. G., Tricamo, E., Goetz, D. M., & Klein, D. F. (1988). Antidepressant specificity in atypical depression. *Archives of General Psychiatry, 45,* 129–137.

Louie, A. K., & Meltzer, H. Y. (1984). Lithium potentiation of antidepressant treatment. *Journal of Clinical Psychopharmachology, 4,* 316–324.

Meltzer, H. Y., Hyong, W. C., Carroll, B. J., & Russo, P. (1976). Serum dopamine-ß-hydroxylase activity in the affective psychoses and schizophrenia. *Archives of General Psychiatry, 33,* 585–591.

Meltzer, H. Y., Lowry, M., Robertson, A., Goodnick, P., & Perline, R. (1984). Effect of 5-hydroxytryptophan on serum cortisol levels in major affective disorder: III. Effect of antidepressants and lithium carbonate. *Archives of General Psychiatry, 41,* 391–397.

Modell, J. G., Lenox, R. H., & Weiner, S. (1985). Inpatient clinical trial of lorazepam for the management of manic agitation. *Journal of Clinical Psychopharmachology, 5,* 109–113.

Murphy, D. L., Baker, M., Goodwin, F. K., Miller, H., Kotin, J., & Bunney, W. E. (1974). L-Tryptophan in affective disorders: Indoleamine changes and differential clinical effects. *Psychopharmacologia, 34,* 11–20.

Okuma, T. (1983). Therapeutic and prophylactic effects of carbamazepine in bipolar disorders. *Psychiatric Clinics of North America, 6,* 157–174.

Panel (1985). NIMH/NIH Consensus Development Conference statement. Mood disorders: pharmacologic prevention of recurrences. Consensus Development Panel. *American Journal of Psychiatry 142,* 469–476.

Perris, C. (1966). A study of bipolar (manic–depressive) and unipolar recurrent depressive psychoses. *Acta Psychiatrica Scandinavica, 42(Supp 194),* 1–189.

Peselow, E. D., Dunner, D. L., Fieve, R. R., & Lautin, A. (1981). Prophylactic effect of lithium against depression in cyclothymic patients: A life-table analysis. *Comprehensive Psychiatry, 22,* 257–264.

Peselow, E. D., Dunner, D. L., Fieve, R. R., & Lautin, A. (1982). Lithium prophylaxis of depression in unipolar, bipolar II and cyclothymic patients. *American Journal of Psychiatry, 139,* 747–752.

Post, R. M., Uhde, T. W., Ballenger, J. C., & Squillace, K. M. (1983). Prophylactic effect of carbamazepine in manic–depressive illness. *American Journal of Psychiatry, 140,* 1602–1604.

Prange, A. J., Wilson, I. C., Lynn, C. W., Altop, L. B., & Strikeleather, R. A. (1974). L-Tryptophan in mania: Contribution to a permissive hypothesis of affective disorders. *Archives of General Psychiatry, 30,* 56–62.

Prange, A. J., Wilson, I. C., Rabon, A. M., & et al. (1969). Enhancement of imipramine antidepressant activity by thyroid hormone. *American Journal of Psychiatry, 126,* 457–469.

Price, L. H., Charney, D. S., & Heninger, G. R. (1985). Efficacy of lithium-tranylcypromine treatment in refractory depression. *American Journal of Psychiatry, 142,* 619–623.

Price, L. H., Conwell, Y., & Nelson, C. J. (1983). Lithium augmentation of combined neuroleptic–tricyclic treatment in delusional depression. *American Journal of Psychiatry, 140,* 318–322.

Prien, R. F. (1987). Long-term treatment of affective disorders. In H. Y. Meltzer (Ed.), *Psychopharmacology: The third generation of progress* (pp. 1051–1058). New York: Raven Press.

Prien, R. F., & Kupfer, D. J. (1986). Continuation drug therapy for major depressive episodes: How long should it be maintained? *American Journal of Psychiatry, 143*, 18–23.

Prien, R. F., Klett, J. C., & Caffey, E. M. Jr. (1974). Lithium prophylaxis in recurrent affective illness. *American Journal of Psychiatry 131*, 198–203.

Prien, R. F., Kupfer, D. J., Mansky, P. A., Small, J. G., Tuason, V. B., Voss, C. B., & Johnson, W. E. (1984). Drug therapy in the prevention of recurrences in unipolar and bipolar affective disorders: Report of the NIMH collaborative study group comparing lithium carbonate and imipramine and a lithium–imipramine combination. *Archives of General Psychiatry, 41*, 1096–1104.

Puzynski, S., & Kosiewicz, L. (1984). Valproic acid amide in the treatment of affective and schizoaffective disorders. *Journal of Affective Disorders, 6*, 115–121.

Quitkin, F., Rifkin, A., & Klein D. F. (1979). Monoamine oxidase inhibitors. *Archives of General Psychiatry, 36*, 749–760.

Razani, J., White, K. L., White, J., Simpson, G., Sloane, R. B., Rebal, R., & Palmer, R. (1983). The safety and efficacy of combined amitriptyline and tranylcypromine antidepressant treatment: A controlled trial. *Archives of General Psychiatry, 40*, 657–661.

Robinson, D. S., Nies, A., Ravaris, C. L., & Lamborn, K. R. (1973). The monoamine oxidase inhibitor, phenelzine, in the treatment of depressive–anxiety states: A controlled clinical trial. *Archives of General Psychiatry, 29*, 407–413.

Schaffer, C. B., Mungas, D., & Rockwell, E. (1985). Successful treatment of psychotic depression with carbamazepine. *Journal of Clinical Psychopharmacology, 5*, 233–235.

Schatzberg, A. F., Rothschild, A. J., Stahl, J. B., Bond, T. C., Rosenbaum, A. H., Lofgren, S. B., Maclaughlin, R. A., Sullivan, M. A., & Cole, J. O. (1983). The dexamethasone suppression test: Identification of subtypes of depression. *American Journal of Psychiatry, 140*, 88–91.

Schou, M. (1986a). *Lithium treatment of manic–depressive illness* (3rd ed.). Basel: Karger.

Schou, M. (1986b). New developments in long-term preventive therapy. *Psychopathology, 19(suppl 2)*, 201–206.

Schwarcz, G., Halaris, A., Baxter, L., Escobar, J., Thompson, M., & Young, M. (1984). Normal thyroid function in desipramine nonresponders converted to responders by the addition of L-triodothyronine. *American Journal of Psychiatry, 141*, 1614–1616.

Sethna, E. R. (1974). A study of refractory cases of depressive illnesses and their response to combined antidepressant treatment. *British Journal of Psychiatry, 124*, 265–272.

Spiker, D. G., Weiss, J. C., Dealy, R. S., Griffin, S. J., Hanin, I., Neil, J. F., Perel, J. M., Rossi, A. J., & Soloff, P. H. (1985). The pharmacological treatment of delusional depression. *American Journal of Psychiatry, 142*, 430–436.

Spring, G., & Frankel, M. (1981). New data on lithium and haloperidol incompatibility. *American Journal of Psychiatry, 138*, 818–821.

Stancer, H. L., & Persad, E. (1982). Treatment of intractable rapid-cycling manic–depressive disorder with levothyroxine: Clinical observations. *Archives of General Psychiatry, 39*, 311–312.

Stromgren, L. S., & Boller, S. (1985). Carbamazepine in treatment and prophylaxis of manic–depressive disorder. *Psychiatric Developments, 4*, 349–367.

Sweeney, D., Nelson, C., Bowers, M., Maas, J., & Heninger, G. (1978). Delusional versus non-delusional depression: Neurochemical differences [letter]. *Lancet, ii*, 100–101.

Task Force on Electroconvulsive Therapy. (1978). *Electroconvulsive therapy*. Washington, DC: American Psychiatric Association.

Task Force on the Use of Laboratory Tests in Psychiatry. (1985). Tricyclic antidepressants—Blood level measurements and clinical outcome: An APA task force report. *American Journal of Psychiatry, 142*, 155–182.

Wehr, T. A., Sack, D. A., Rosenthal, N. E., & Cowdry, R. W. (1988). Rapid cycling affective disorder: Contributing factors and treatment responses in 51 patients. *American Journal of Psychiatry, 145*, 179–184.

Weissman, M. M., Klerman, G. L., Prusoff, B. A., Sholomskas, D., & Padian, N. (1981). Depressed outpatients: Results one year after treatment with drugs and/or interpersonal psychotherapy. *Archives of General Psychiatry, 38*, 51–55.

West, E. D., & Dally, P. J. (1959). Effect of iproniazid in depressive syndromes. *British Medical Journal, 1*, 1491–1494.

White, K., & Simpson, G. (1981). Combined MAOI–tricyclic antidepressant treatment: A reevaluation. *Journal of Clinical Psychopharmacology, 1*, 264–282.

Zis, A. P., Grof, P., & Goodwin, F. K. (1979). The natural course of affective disorders: Implications for lithium prophylaxis. In T. B. Cooper, S. Gershon, N. S. Kline, & M. Schou (Eds.), *Lithium: Controv-*

ersies and unresolved issues (pp. 381–398). Amsterdam: Excerpta Medica.

Zubenko, G. S., Cohen, B. M., Lipinski, J. F., & Jonas, J. M. (1984). Clonidine in the treatment of mania and mixed bipolar disorder. *American Journal of Psychiatry, 139*, 1617–1618.

Editorial Commentary: Depression

Affective disorders are among the most prevalent psychiatric dysfunctions, and have been widely acknowledged as a major public health problem. Consequently, there has been a tremendous volume of research on their etiology and treatment since the late 1970s, stimulated in no small part by the financial support of both the NIMH (National Institute of Mental Health) and pharmaceutical companies. In contrast to a number of other disorders examined in this volume, this research has led to the development of a number of new and effective treatments. There is evidence to support the use of several psychosocial interventions, as well as a number of pharmacological strategies. In recognition of the diversity and significance of these various approaches, we have opted to include four chapters in this section: social skills training (SST), cognitive-behavior therapy (CBT), psychodynamic therapy (including interpersonal psychotherapy—IPT), and pharmacotherapy. Each of these approaches has proven to be effective with at least some subsets of depressed patients in more than one well-controlled clinical trial.

The chapters in this section present exceptionally clear portraits of the clinical application of the various interventions. While it is evident that there are significant differences among the approaches, it is also apparent that there is considerable agreement on a number of strategic issues. The authors of all four chapters are in agreement about the value of medication with the more impaired patients. Mania, melancholia, and psychosis are uniformly viewed as indicators for pharmacotherapy and/or electroconvulsive therapy—ECT). Conversely, chronic mild depression (e.g., dysthymic disorder) is viewed as possibly more responsive to psychotherapy (including CBT and SST) than pharmacotherapy. There is also agreement that atypical patients, including those with character disorders, present unique problems for any approach. Kieve and Feinberg (Chapter 7) make the important distinction between atypical and treatment-resistant depression, arguing that the latter is often a reflection of inadequate or improper treatment.

Despite obvious conceptual differences, there is considerable strategic and tactical overlap among the psychosocial approaches. Bemporad and Vasile (Chapter 4), Freeman (Chapter 5), and Becker (Chapter 6) all emphasize the role of interpersonal factors in precipitating and/or maintaining depression. While SST is primarily and explicitly focused on enhancing social behavior as the vehicle of treatment, both CBT and psychodynamic therapy also pay considerable attention to the patient's social environment and interpersonal difficulties. IPT, in particular, is designed to modify social functioning, albeit without the specific behavioral training included in SST. While the precise techniques vary, all three approaches encourage the patient to practice new behaviors in social interactions at home and in the community.

All three approaches also place considerable emphasis on the role of maladaptive cognitions in the etiology and/or maintenance of the illness. Of course, this is the major focus of CBT. But, SST devotes considerable attention to cognitive phenomena in the context of social perception, including modification of inaccurate cognitive appraisals of others. Similarly, Bemporad and Vasile indicate that recent psychodynamic thinking emphasizes the role of faulty beliefs and assumptions about significant others (notably parents) in the etiology of depression, and that a major task of therapy is to point out and correct these cognitive errors. We have previously argued that the literature supports the conclusion that a number of different psychosocial interventions for depression (including IPT, SST, and CBT) are equally effective. Perhaps this result occurs because of the overlap in the various approaches.

Despite the existence of a number of effective strategies, one cannot be overly sanguine about our ability to treat depression. The chapters in this section raise a number of significant concerns. Kieve and Feinberg point out that depression is a recurrent disorder; more than 50% of unipolar patients and 80% of bipolars are likely to have at least one relapse. Yet, comparatively little is known about long-term maintenance strategies. Side effects and medical risks of the major medications make continued treatment a circumspect option for many patients. Psychotherapy would appear to be an attractive alternative to long-term pharmacotherapy. But, the long-term effects of psychotherapy, alone or in some combination with pharmacotherapy, are uncertain. It is hoped that ongoing clinical trials of maintenance strategies will shed some light on this issue over the next few years.

Bemporad and Vasile raise the important issue that many cases of depression are secondary to physical illnesses, including a number of endocrinological and hormonal disorders. Such cases often are misdiagnosed by both mental health professionals and primary care physicians. As pointed out in other sections of this volume, depression is also frequently associated with other psychiatric disorders, including obsessive–compulsive disorder, panic and agoraphobia, social phobia, and borderline personality. In some cases, the treatments are parallel, and differential diagnosis may not be absolutely critical (e.g., tricylic antidepressants for depression and panic disorder, CBT for depression and social phobia). However, fortuitous treatment based on inaccurate diagnosis is the exception rather than the rule. Even when the same medication may be appropriate for two different disorders, the required dosages, titration schedules, and so forth may be different. Categories such as atypical, treatment-resistant, double depression, and so on reflect the uncertain status of our understanding. Similarly, dual diagnosis or retrospective diagnosis based on treatment response is not satisfactory. The only way to resolve these problems and deliver the most effective treatment is to improve the diagnostic system and associated assessment instruments.

We know remarkably little about etiology considering the effectiveness of available treatments. Kieve and Feinberg indicate that the amine hypothesis is not supported by existing data, although a more refined version may ultimately be developed. While not discussed in the respective psychosocial chapters, there is little support for the models underlying any of the three approaches. It seems unlikely that further substantial progress in treatment will be made unless and until we learn more about etiology and translate that knowledge into a more valid and reliable diagnostic system.

PART 3

Panic and Agoraphobia

CHAPTER 8

Psychotherapy

DAVID L. WOLITZKY AND MORRIS N. EAGLE

Our aim in this chapter is to provide an account of the psychoanalytically oriented treatment of three DSM-III-R anxiety disorders—panic disorder with agoraphobia (300.21), panic disorder without agoraphobia (300.01), and agoraphobia without history of panic disorder (300.22). We proceed by presenting the psychoanalytic conceptualization of anxiety, its implications for diagnosis, and for the treatment of these disorders (American Psychiatric Association, 1987). We also include some case illustrations and comment briefly on alternative treatment approaches.

CONCEPTUALIZATION OF THE DISORDERS

According to traditional psychoanalytic theory (Meissner, 1985), anxiety is an aspect of virtually every psychiatric disorder. It can be (a) acute, quite intense, and unbound, as in panic disorder; (b) chronic, more moderate, and also unbound, as in generalized anxiety disorder; or (c) manifestly absent a good deal of the time, as in circumscribed phobic disorders, in which it is bound to specific objects or situations that often can be avoided.

The acute, intense form of anxiety is what Freud called "traumatic anxiety." It is a state of feeling overwhelmed with uncontrollable fear, terror, and a conviction of impending catastrophe or doom. The patient feels that his or her actual survival is at stake, and this great apprehension typically is accompanied by a variety of physical manifestations (e.g., dizziness, dyspnea, chest pain, tachycardia), which further intensify fears of loss of control, insanity, and or dying.

In its milder forms, anxiety is seen by Freud as a *signal* of the potential onset of traumatic anxiety. This signal, which is regarded as an ego affect, is the occasion for the automatic instigation of defenses aimed at reducing the anxiety.

Anxiety, in its signal or traumatic form, unlike fear, is not a response to a realistic, external danger, from which one could escape. The nature of the danger in anxiety is an internal one—in particular, an unconscious, instinctual wish that is assumed to be dangerous, especially if it reaches consciousness and is expressed through action.

There are typical danger situations associated with different phases of psychosexual development. In order, these are (1) loss of the love object, (2) loss of the object's love, (3) castration anxiety in males, and (4) superego anxiety or guilt. While each of these dangers predominates at different developmental phases, they each build on one another and typically have overlapping unconscious meanings.

These so-called danger situations converge on the common point that they can all lead to the traumatic situation of the excessive, overwhelming excitation of nongratified instinctual drives. The traumatic danger represented by the loss of the

We would like to thank Drs. Clive Robins and Judith Rabkin for their helpful comments on an earlier draft of this chapter.

love object, for example, is due to the threat that libidinal and aggressive wishes would not be able to be discharged, with the result that accumulated excitation would overwhelm and damage the nervous system and render the ego helpless.

Signal anxiety is a developmental achievement. Its presence presupposes the capacity for anticipation based on memories of traumatic situations and of experiences of gradations of anxiety. It is also based on the judgment that certain instinctual wishes are dangerous because they have led to or will meet with actual and/or fantasized disapproval and punishment. These judgments become internalized, creating intrapsychic conflict (most notably between the id and the superego). Ego deficits and ego regressions impair the effective operation of anxiety signals and make the patient more vulnerable to traumatic anxiety. These conditions make it more likely that ego defenses (of which repression is the prototype) will fail to contain the anxiety and that symptoms (e.g., phobias) will develop as a second line of defense. Symptoms are understood as expressing, often symbolically, both the forbidden wish and the attempt to defend against its awareness and expression, and they vary according to whether they show more manifest evidence of the wish or of the defense against the wish. It is recognized that there are individual differences (perhaps, in part, genetically based) in susceptibility to anxiety, capacity to tolerate it, and ways of defending against it. In traditional Freudian theory, all symptoms and defensive behavior are based on anxiety. Within the category of defensive behavior, we include not only the classic, mental mechanisms of repression, denial, projection, isolation of affect, and so on, but also behavioral patterns and attitudes (e.g., inability to make a commitment to a relationship, avoidance of certain situations or ideas).

It is not only defensive behavior that is instigated by anxiety. The development of character or personality style, of ego inhibitions, or interests, values, and so on are all regarded, in part, as expressing ways of coping with anxiety and as compromise means of achieving instinctual gratification within the context of a tolerable level of anxiety. In this formulation, anxiety is accorded a central, regulating role in all behavior. The distinction between so-called symptom neurosis and

character neurosis is seen as one of degree. Fluctuations in the level of symptomatic behaviors and in the intensity and pervasiveness in the expression of personality styles or traits are thought to reflect shifts in the dynamic equilibrium between strivings to gratify conflictual wishes and defensive efforts to prohibit their gratification. As Brenner (1982, p. 119) puts it, "The mind functions in such a way as to afford to drive derivatives the fullest degree of satisfaction compatible with a tolerable degree of anxiety and/or depressive affect." At the same time, it is recognized in psychoanalytic theory that personality growth, successful adaptation, creativity, and good reality-testing require the tolerance of anxiety.

Psychological symptoms reflect the sense of danger associated with the gratification of libidinal and/or aggressive wishes. The person (ego) judges that such gratification would bring catastrophic consequences. When agoraphobia is a prominent part of the symptom picture (as part of a panic disorder or as agoraphobia without a history of panic disorder), the anxiety associated with the drive gratification is displaced and projected onto leaving home, so that being housebound enables the patient to avoid the full-blown panic attacks. In either its free-floating or bound form, anxiety symptoms indicate the failure of repression and other defenses to keep the unconscious wishes sufficiently far from awareness and action and are a second line of defense against an awareness of the underlying conflicts.

Although we have summarized only Freud's last theory of anxiety, it needs to be stressed that it is no longer accurate to speak of *the* psychoanalytic theory of anxiety or phobias. There have been several influential psychodynamic theories of anxiety since Freud's formulations. In the interest of brevity, we do not present these theories here, but we refer the interested reader to a 1988 review (Eagle & Wolitzky, 1988). Two common features of these later theories are (1) the centrality of anxiety in explanations of personality development and psychopathology and (2) the rejection of Freud's emphasis on conflict-laden instinctual wishes as the trigger for anxiety. Theorists since Freud, particularly object relations theorists and self-psychologists following Kohut (1971, 1977, 1984), are inclined to view symptoms of anxiety less in terms of repressed, instinctual conflicts and more in terms of conflicts regarding (a) developmental challenges such as separation and individuation (Mahler, Pine, & Bergman, 1975), (b) both actual and internalized object relationships with others (Guntrip, 1968), and (c) one's sense of self-cohesion (Kohut, 1971, 1977, 1984). For example, Kohut (1971, 1977, 1984), whose views are embraced by many clinicians as a workable alternative to traditional Freudian theory, gives primary importance to the self as the supraordinate factor in personality functioning. In his view, the primary source of intense anxiety is the fear of fragmentation or loss of cohesion of one's self, not the feared consequences of drive gratification. The effect on drive gratification is viewed as the result of self-pathology, not its cause.

The classic Freudian interpretation of agoraphobia as expressing unconscious sexual fantasies has largely, but not entirely (e.g., Brenner, 1982), given way in later conceptualizations to an emphasis on separation anxiety and/or anxiety concerning self-cohesion as a key element in this and other anxiety disorders. Contemporary psychoanalytic ego-psychologists, who in many respects still adhere to traditional Freudian theory, also would place much less emphasis on sexual fantasies, not just those espousing an object relations or self-psychology framework. The point is that many psychoanalytic clinicians probably currently practice from a multimodel perspective (Silverman, 1986) in which drive theory, ego psychology, object relations theories, and self-psychology are all regarded as useful, potential guidelines for understanding the patient (Pine, 1985), even though their basic theoretical assumptions are incompatible. Which of these clinical perspectives or combinations of perspectives is given greater emphasis in the clinical understanding and interpretation of agoraphobic and panic disorder symptoms seems to depend, in part, on the therapist's preferred theoretical orientation and on the nature of the patient's productions.

Regardless of the issue of interpretive emphasis (and its unknown correlation with treatment outcome), all clinicians agree on the importance of a highly detailed inquiry into the specifics of a set of symptoms. For example, it is not sufficient to know that the patient has a barbershop phobia. One wants to know the circumstances surrounding its onset, the relative degree of fear of each element that ordinarily evokes fear in such a situation—the sense of being confined, the public nature of the situation, the possibility of mutilation, and so on. Such knowledge will enable the psychoanalytic clinician to help the patient understand the idiosyncratic meanings of the phobia. Having said that, it should be noted that a large part of the clinical and nonclinical evidence, at least in the case of agoraphobia, points to the central role of difficulties and conflicts in the area of separation–individuation and autonomy. Here is a case, we believe, in which the post-Freudian formulation of agoraphobia (e.g., Fairbairn, p. 43, 1952) in terms of conflicts between "the regressive lure of identification" (by which he means infantile dependence) and the "progressive urge toward separation" is more in accord with both the clinical and the research evidence than the early Freudian account that focuses on prostitution fantasies (see Eagle, 1979).

We should note that on the descriptive level, the psychodynamic conceptualization of agoraphobia is entirely compatible with some accounts that have emerged from a behavioral tradition. As an example of the latter, consider Mathews, Gelder, and Johnston's (1981) "integrated model" of agoraphobia. According to their model, the factors that would predispose one to agoraphobia include early family factors (e.g., overprotection, fostering of overdependency) and high trait anxiety (which, it should be noted, might well have a genetic component—for example, see Lader & Wing, 1966). At some particular time, increased nonspecific stress then leads to an acute anxiety attack while outdoors. Given the added factors of an individual's dependent and avoidant style, as well as a tendency to attribute the causes of anxiety to external situations, a probable outcome is the development of agoraphobic symptoms. Once the agoraphobic symptoms develop, the *maintaining* factors include secondary gain and the anticipatory fear of another anxiety or panic attack (see also, Beck & Emery, 1985).

Note that the foregoing model is entirely consistent with and indeed implicitly includes such psychodynamic factors as fostering of overdependency and defensive style (e.g., avoidance and externalization). Indeed, the description by Mathews et al. (1981) of the relationship between the initial outbreak of intense anxiety and the subsequent development of agoraphobia is remarkably similar to Fenichel's (1945) account in which "panic anxiety" in a particular situation is experienced and in which the phobia is maintained by a "secondary traumatic neurosis," the hallmark of which is "fear of anxiety" itself (see also Schur, 1971, who observes that this fear of anxiety is a key factor in perpetuating a phobia). Fenichel goes on to note that people who develop phobias are especially prone to anxiety and to a state of "heightened inner tension" (which is obviously parallel to Mathews et al.'s "high trait anxiety"). Fenichel's description is quite dramatic. He describes the state of phobia—the prone person—as "a powder keg in which the danger signal of the ego acts like a match" (Fenichel, 1945, p. 195).

One of the more important issues of interest in a psychodynamic perspective and relatively ignored in behavioral theory accounts of agoraphobia (including Mathews et al.'s 1981 account) is the role of *intrapsychic conflict*. According to the psychodynamic point of view, although there might be some fortuitous elements in generating the patient's initial outbreak of intense anxiety, key causal factors will have to do with intrapsychic conflict. Thus, an individual may have his or her major anxiety attack in the street and then come to avoid that situation. But, from a psychodynamic perspective, the street is not itself a fortuitous element in the whole story, but itself represents core conflictual issues—namely, those having to do with separation and symbiotic versus autonomous functioning.

Indeed, the multiple and sometimes shifting nature of the phobic situation (e.g., sitting in restaurants or theaters, being in cars or trains, being alone) suggests the essential irrelevance of the actual physical situation. Anything that can be symbolically equated with separation, being cut off from home, or the need for autonomous functioning can serve as the phobic stimulus. In short, although Fenichel describes the onset of the initial anxiety attack as analogous to "a match in a powder keg" (given the individual's chronic state of heightened tension), the stimulus that serves as the "match" in the case of agoraphobia must itself

have anxiety-inducing properties associated with particular psychological meanings.

Thus, it is not simply a matter of chance that the initial anxiety attack occurs in the street, but rather that the street, insofar as it represents such meanings as separation, aloneness, and so on, triggers core conflicts and thereby is an anxiety-eliciting stimulus. It is interesting to note that in some cases of agoraphobia, the initial anxiety occurs not simply when the patient is *in* the street, but when he or she is *crossing* a street, a bridge, a plaza, and so on. It is as if the act of crossing comes to symbolize, with great force, the transition and conflict between the symbiotic safety of home and the dangers associated with separation from home.

DIAGNOSTIC ISSUES AND PROBLEMS

According to the DSM-III-R (American Psychiatric Association, 1987), there are three categories in which the diagnosis of agoraphobia or panic disorder can be made: (1) "Agoraphobia without History of Panic Disorder" (300.22), (2) "Panic Disorder with Agoraphobia" (300.21), and, (3) "Panic Disorder without Agoraphobia" (300.01). The third diagnosis is made if the patient does not meet the criteria for the first two disorders.

Psychodynamically oriented clinicians treat many patients who do not strictly meet the DSM-III-R criteria for these or other disorders. In fact, the prototypical patient is apt simultaneously to approximate s*everal* of the DSM-III-R Axis I and Axis II categories but not fit formally into any of them. Given the complexity of etiological factors, the usual presence of multiple symptoms and character problems, the tendency to embark on the same general approach to treatment at least for problems within the neurotic range, and the uncertain relationship between diagnosis and response to treatment, the DSM-III-R classification is generally of limited utility to psychodynamically-oriented clinicians. Behaviorally-oriented clinicians also have misgivings about the DSM-III-R classifications of agoraphobia and panic disorder (Bowen & Kohout, 1979; Emmelkamp, 1988; Goldstein & Chambless, 1978; Hallam, 1978; Marks, 1970).

In the interest of brevity, we do not include a

more detailed discussion of diagnostic difficulties or problems with the DSM-III-R scheme. Suffice it to say that psychodynamically-oriented clinicians will want to assess the structure and functioning of the patient's overall personality in order to understand the psychological significance of the symptoms. This appraisal of the patient's level of adaptation (including reality-testing, adequacy of defenses, affect tolerance, etc.) will serve as a guide to treatment prognosis and planning (e.g., the relative balance of supportive versus uncovering treatment techniques).

TREATMENT STRATEGIES

In many respects, psychotherapy for panic disorder and for agoraphobia shares the same general principles of treatment that are relevant to the other syndromes among the so-called anxiety disorders, as well as to most of the other functional, nonpsychotic disorders in DSM-III-R. Before we can offer a meaningful discussion of treatment strategies, we need to present at least briefly the main principles of the overall theory of psychoanalytic psychotherapy.

Principles of Psychoanalytic Psychotherapy

The main features of the traditional psychoanalytic theory of psychotherapy can be summarized as follows:

1. The patient is suffering from pathological compromise formations (e.g., symptoms) based on repressed conflicts.
2. These conflicts become expressed in the context of the therapeutic relationship, particularly in the form of transference and resistance.
3. This process is facilitated when the treatment situation is unstructured and fosters the "free associations" that will allow the unconscious, unresolved conflicts to be expressed via dreams, memories, reactions to the therapist, and so on.
4. The analyst listens with free-floating attention and a neutral (i.e., nonbiased),

nonjudgmental attitude, which facilitates the "therapeutic alliance"—that is, the patient's desire to cooperate despite conflicting attitudes about wanting to recover.

5. These conditions promote the development of an analyzable transference.
6. The analyst's interpretations of the patient's unconscious conflicts and forms of resistance as manifest in the transference will yield insights into the nature and influence of the neurotic anxieties associated with these conflicts.
7. Through the repetitive, increasingly conscious, experiencing of long-standing conflicts, in the context of affectively vivid "here-and-now" transference reactions and their multiple meanings, the patient gradually works through his or her difficulties by shifting to more realistic, less anxious, more adaptive emotional and behavioral patterns inside and outside the treatment situation. Repeated insight into disavowed, split-off, disowned, anxiety-laden wishes, conflicts, and fantasies (in Freud's terminology, the id or drive derivatives) allows them to become more integrated into the ego, particularly when the insights are accompanied by behavioral changes that can show patients that their fears will not overcome them.
8. In addition to insight, there are other important ingredients of the therapeutic relationship which are considered to facilitate change. Clinicians who favor an object relations or self-psychology approach tend, relatively speaking, to de-emphasize insight in favor of the following factors: (1) The actual experience of a new, benign, relationship with a nonjudgmental parental figure helps reduce the harshness of the patient's superego. (2) The patient has an opportunity to form a new identification; the patient can form an identification with the analyst's approach (i.e., with the analytic attitude) and can introject and later identify with the analyst as a person. (3) The analyst and the analyst–patient relationship can provide a safe, supportive

base that can foster the patient's progressive urges toward greater autonomy and individuation (as against regressive longings to merge and cling to infantile dependence). (4) In Kohut's view (1984), the analyst serves a critical function by allowing the patient to use the analyst as a mirroring and idealized self-object to aid in the patient's efforts to regulate her or his own tension states. (5) The therapist's empathy, as experienced by the patient, is held to be a vital element in therapeutic change. This component is stressed particularly by Kohut (1984) and his followers, who regard feeling understood (and its positive implications for the experience of affirmed selfhood) as the ultimately curative factor, the factor that gives insight its impact.

While we can make conceptual distinctions among these several relationship factors and between these factors and insight, in actual practice, it is virtually impossible to accord these elements differential weightings in attempting to account for therapeutic change. To take one obvious example, the experience of an emotionally vivid insight conveyed through a well-timed interpretation usually will also simultaneously arouse a feeling of being profoundly understood. Thus, psychoanalytic insight is an experience that occurs in the context of a relationship.

Practice of Psychoanalytic Treatment of Panic Disorder and of Agoraphobia

Assessment

Based on the foregoing general principles of psychoanalytic psychotherapy, the therapist will begin with an assessment of the presenting symptoms and complaints, in the context of an evaluation of the patient's overall current functioning. This initial appraisal will include inquiries concerning the history, severity, duration, intensity, and precipitants of the patient's panic attacks and/or agoraphobic behavior. It will also focus on other problems the patient may be experiencing. As discussed earlier, panic disorder and/or agoraphobia rarely if ever occur as circumscribed, isolated symptoms in an otherwise nonneurotic, well-functioning individual.

In judging the prospective patient's suitability for dynamic psychotherapy we take account of the following factors: (a) positive motivation to change; (b) presence of an optimal degree of suffering and access to affective experience, adequate ego strength, psychological-mindedness, reality-testing, and tolerance of anxiety; (c) a reasonably decent history of satisfying object relations, and (d) a capacity to form a working alliance with the therapist. The final variable has been shown, in fact, to predict treatment outcome (Luborsky, 1984). Of course, this list of clinical criteria could make one question whether people who meet these criteria are in need of psychotherapy. In practice, the extent to which these criteria are met is a relative matter. There is now a cumulative body of research that indicates that better adjustment, mastery, ego strength, and so on are associated with better treatment outcomes (Luborsky, Crits-Christoph, Mintz, & Auerbach, 1988; see especially pp. 315–353 for a summary of these findings).

Approach to Treatment

The clinician's assessment of the degree of overall disturbance and the nature of the patient's current life situation will serve as a guide to the relative emphasis on a supportive versus an expressive approach. In general, "the greater the psychiatric severity, the more supportive and less expressive the therapy needs to be" (Luborsky, 1984, p. 56). That is, the more disturbed the patient and the more intractable or painful the symptom (whether agoraphobia or any other problem), the more likely the therapist will be to employ explicitly noninterpretive modes of intervention and/or to offer interpretations that border on advice or suggestion.

Given the state of the field of clinical practice, conceptualization and diagnosis of a disorder quite often do not clearly point to treatment strategy. This is less so in the case of agoraphobia and panic disorders. Here, conceptualization and diagnosis *do* suggest something about treatment strategies and approaches. Agoraphobic patients tend to be primarily women whose relationships to their often overprotective and controlling mothers reveal a pattern that has been variously referred to as "anxious attachment" (Bowlby, 1973), "painful ambivalence" (Buglass, Clarke, Henderson, Kreitman, & Presley, 1977), and "hostile dependency" (Quadrio, 1984).

Their core problem can be seen as one involving extreme difficulties along the developmental dimension of separation–individuation and autonomy. The agoraphobic symptom itself can be understood as rather graphically portraying this core issue: The desire to break away and achieve autonomy is enacted by actual or fantasied forays into the outside world, but due to experiencing too much anxiety and very strong dependency wishes, the patient does not successfully carry out this desire. As noted earlier, this entire pattern quite often gets repeated or even intensified in the marital relationship. What are the implications of this understanding of agoraphobia for treatment?

In our experience, it is useful to view the agoraphobic symptom as a rather dramatic and troubling expression of the unresolved developmental issue of growing up, separating, and leaving home (both physically and psychologically). We often communicate this point of view to the patient and suggest that psychotherapy can represent an opportunity to deal more fully with this set of unresolved issues (see the case illustration, later in this chapter). Generally, patients experience some relief at hearing this because although they may present the outbreak of the agoraphobic symptom as sudden, ego-alien, and bewildering, at some level, they often know that they have had difficulties with separation, individuation, and autonomy (of course, they do not refer to their difficulties in these terms) and that they have experienced milder symptoms linked to agoraphobia (e.g., varying degrees of school avoidance or discomfort, varying degrees of other expressions of separation anxiety) a good part of their lives. The initial relief comes from hearing a simple description of what, at some deep level, they knew all along to be the case.

Course of Treatment

On the basis of both our own experience and what we can glean from the literature, a number of common elements and a general pattern of treatment course in psychotherapy with agoraphobic patients can be discerned. Different patients show varying degrees of clear awareness of the possible psychological significance of their agoraphobic symptoms. Some patients can verbalize quite readily the links between their agoraphobic symptoms and earlier difficulties with leaving home or even between the symptom and an earlier enmeshed relationship, generally with the mother. Some of these highly verbal patients also acknowledge that, similar to their relationship with mother (or father), they feel trapped in their relationship with their husband (or wife). In general, the early phase of treatment is taken up with, to borrow Quadrio's (1984, p. 845) words, "deepening awareness of earlier levels of ambivalent dependency, of poor separation, and of passive-aggressive mechanisms." Much of this phase of treatment can be summed up by saying that the patient becomes aware that she or he has been living according to the "pathogenic belief" (Weiss & Sampson, 1986) that if "I leave my parent" (or spouse) and lead a separate, independent life "I will not survive." This is not, after all, such a great insight insofar as it is quite close to the actual experience of the agoraphobic symptom. Ideally, during this phase of treatment, the patient also becomes aware of the degree to which her or his current marital relationship (if, of course, she or he is married) duplicates her or his early hostile–dependent relationship with the parent. A similar pattern should emerge in the patient's relationship with the therapist, and later in this initial phase of treatment, appropriate transference interpretations will be made.

Additional Interventions

Exposure. Two interventions are often necessary with agoraphobic patients, which clearly depart from a strict psychoanalytic stance in the treatment: One is to encourage the patient to take steps to expose him- or herself to the phobic situation. Many patients who come for treatment have already made this attempt on their own in varying degrees. But insofar as they remain agoraphobic, these efforts need to be encouraged. As Mathews et al. (1981) suggest, however it comes about or however it is implemented, a critical therapeutic factor in the treatment of agoraphobia is increased exposure (without a companion) to the phobic situation while experiencing less than the traumatic anxiety anticipated. This appears to be a necessary step whatever one's therapeutic approach—behavioral or psychodynamic. *Whatever* makes increased exposure without traumatic anxiety possible and thereby reduces avoidance behavior will lead to symptomatic improvement.

The value of encouraging exposure to the phobic situation, something recognized by clinicians of all persuasions, would seem to have no place in the theory of psychoanalytic psychotherapy. However, as Freud notes, for those patients who completely avoid the phobic situation, exposure is important only insofar as it activates the anxiety and conflicts that underlie it so that these origins can be explored. The idea that exposure could contribute significantly to the amelioration of symptoms by means of extinction alone is not part of the psychodynamic view, even though it actually may turn out to be the case that it is so.

Spousal Involvement in Treatment. Another intervention often indicated, particularly when the patient shows little or no improvement, is to invite the patient's spouse to participate in varying degrees, in the treatment (of course, this is done only with the patient's agreement). The spouse may participate in only a few sessions or, when it is deemed advisable, in an ongoing conjoint therapy. There are clinicians who believe that conjoint therapy is generally advisable for agoraphobic patients. This is the case as the agoraphobic symptom serves to maintain a marital system in which the agoraphobic spouse reenacts in the marriage his or her early relationship of hostile dependency and early difficulties with separation and autonomy and in which the patient's spouse subtly encourages the agoraphobic spouse's dependency and helplessness because of personal inadequacies, extreme jealousy, (Hafner, 1979) denial of dependency, and fear of being abandoned (Quadrio, 1984). Indeed, there is evidence in one study that some patients' spouses were adversely affected when their agoraphobic mates showed symptomatic improvement (Hafner, 1976, 1984, 1986).

Themes of Treatment

To return to the context of individual therapy, we have already noted that during the earlier phase of treatment, many patients become aware of the pathogenic belief that "if I leave home and lead an independent life as a separate person, I will not survive." Only in a later phase of treatment does the patient begin to become aware of the more deeply buried pathogenic belief to the effect that "if I leave home and lead an independent life as a separate person, my parent will not survive." In other words, the patient becomes more aware of the degree to which what Modell (1984) has referred to as "survivor guilt" and "separation guilt" have dominated and continue to dominate much of the agoraphobic's life. Obviously, there are individual differences in regard to these themes. However, we have been impressed with the degree to which *some* variation of the theme is commonly seen in agoraphobia (see the case illustration).

Candidates for Psychoanalytic Treatment

It is our strong impression that the foregoing psychodynamic approach is most suitable for that subcategory of agoraphobic patients who are somewhat psychologically minded, who have a reasonably rich and differentiated inner life to which they have access, who have demonstrated a reasonable level of developmental achievements and psychological differentiation, and who are conflicted about their agoraphobic symptom. It is also our view that there is a subcategory of agoraphobic patients, particularly those who also experience panic and related symptoms apart from the usual agoraphobic situations, who do not fit the preceding description. These patients tend to be relatively undifferentiated, to show a somewhat primitive personality organization, to have a lifestyle in which the agoraphobic symptom does not seem to represent a major impediment to carrying out vital life goals (partly because of more limited life goals), and who (while distressed) do not seem especially conflicted about their agoraphobic symptoms. This latter category of patients is more likely to experience panic attacks or threats of panic attacks in an apparently random manner and somewhat independent of venturing outside the home. The seemingly random nature of the panic experiences is another factor that makes psychodynamic treatment more difficult. As far as treatment for this group of patients is concerned, it seems to us that behavior therapy (including group behavior therapy), primarily in vivo exposure, often combined with pharmacological treatment, are interventions likely to be far more appropriate than psychodynamic therapy of any kind.

Apparent Claustrophobic Symptoms

We want to bring up one important dynamic issue that we have not seen discussed much. The fact is that many agoraphobic patients also experience other symptoms, some of which appear to fall under the rubric of claustrophobic symptoms, the apparent opposite of agoraphobia. For example, it is not uncommon for agoraphobic patients to report that when going to movies or plays, they must sit right on the aisle. If they sit in the middle of the row, they feel "trapped" (see the case illustration). There are at least two ways in which one can interpret these claustrophobic symptoms, these feelings of being trapped. One way is to say that the usual "combination of agoraphobic with claustrophobic symptoms . . . nicely expresses the conflict [between wanting to break out and not being able to]—when she is in, she wants to get out; when she is out, she wants to get back in. Dependency and separation are the fundamental conflicts" (Quadrio, 1984, p. 82). This interpretation is consistent with Fairbairn's (1952) claim that agoraphobia is primarily an expression of conflict between the desires for infantile dependence and for separation and autonomous growth, "the regressive lure of identification and the progressive urge for separation."

According to the preceding view, the claustrophobic symptoms represent the patients' desire to get out once they are in—that is, the urge toward separation. An alternative to this view is that the seemingly claustrophobic symptoms represent an extension of the agoraphobic symptoms insofar as the apparently claustrophobic situations all have in common the fact that they are experienced as potential barriers to rush back home should the urgent need or impulse to do so arise. This view is consistent with many agoraphobic patients' subjective experience. Thus, the reported reason that the patient (M.C., discussed in the case illustration section) *had* to have an aisle seat is that she would be free to rush back home to safety should she panic and feel the need to reach a safe base. Sitting in the center of a row was symbolically experienced as being cut off or blocked from safety. In other words, it is not that the patient wants *out* in the sense of being free to separate, but rather that the patient *is* out (i.e., in the theater, train, elevator, or any other place away from home) and now wants a sure way of getting *back in* to the safety (even if it is a temporary safety) of home.

The preceding issue is not simply a theoretical one, of esoteric interest only. It is a question of the appropriate and correct interpretation to the patient, one that is in tune with the patient's experience and inner world. What Kohut (1984) refers to as "empathic resonance" is undoubtedly important for all patients, including agoraphobic patients. If the agoraphobic patient's experience of being trapped consists essentially in feeling cut off from the safety of home, it would not be especially therapeutic to interpret this experience as representing an urge toward separation. Often, at a deeper level, the fear of being trapped reflects the patient's anxiety surrounding the wish to fuse with another person.

We are not suggesting that in the so-called claustrophobic experience, agoraphobic patients do not experience intense conflicts between symbiotic dependence and separation. It is clear that they do. Indeed, the very act of venturing out and going, say, to a movie, but having to sit in a position that permits the feeling that they can get back home as soon as possible is already a compromise expressing that conflict. Agoraphobic patients' characteristic relationships of hostile dependence or anxious attachment with a parent and later with a spouse are probably the strongest and most important expressions of the conflict between symbiotic dependence and separation and autonomy. They often feel burdened and engulfed by the symbiotic dependence (and its elements of guilt and what Winnicott (1958) referred to as "impingement"), and they want *out* of this kind of relationship. However, the experience of separation anxiety and survivor guilt are strong forces propelling the patient back *into* the dependent relationship. The result of this *in–out* conflict (see Guntrip, 1968) is the characteristic relationship of hostile dependence, and it leads to episodes of separation attempts and fantasies, followed by regressive returns. Particularly in long-term psychodynamic treatment, the therapist should be sensitive to expressions of this pattern in the transference.

Conclusions

We now offer a few final global comments regarding treatment. Based on our own experiences and what we have learned from colleagues' experiences, we have become impressed with the special importance of early multimodal treatment (including pharmacological treatment) for people who have experienced their first or second panic attack. Whatever the reasons for the onset of panic attacks, the fact is that the experience of panic often quickly becomes associated with avoidant and other maladaptive feelings and behaviors, which, once developed and crystallized, become locked in and recalcitrant. The special importance of early treatment in these cases lies mainly in the need to prevent the reinforcement and crystallization of the avoidant (such as manifestations of agoraphobia) and other maladaptive behavior.

We want to note that our comments on treatment are based almost exclusively on case reports, our own clinical experiences, and the received wisdom of the psychodynamic approach. Although one should not ignore these sources and this sort of evidence, clearly they do not represent good substitutes for systematic, well-controlled, and clinically relevant therapeutic outcome and process studies. As for the availability of these kinds of studies, although some form of psychotherapy (which presumably contains some psychodynamic features) is often included in comparisons of the therapeutic effectiveness of different treatment modalities, we do not know of any study that systematically evaluates the relative effectiveness of long-term psychodynamic treatment of agoraphobia and panic disorders. This is obviously a serious gap in our knowledge.

Finally, and somewhat related to the foregoing, we want to emphasize the overriding importance of being informed about treatment approaches other than one's own and knowing when to make an appropriate referral to one of those other treatment approaches. There is an all-too-human tendency to assume implicitly the suitability of a treatment approach for just about any kind of patient if the approach is the one in which the clinician has been trained and is the one the clini-

cian believes to be most efficacious. The overwhelmingly strong likelihood is that this just is not the case. One good way of counteracting an excessively parochial or partisan attitude is by being both reasonably knowledgeable about alternative treatment approaches and reasonably aware of the literature dealing with the issue of which approach is most suitable for which set of problems.

In any case, there are few definitive answers to key questions in the area of treatment process and effectiveness. In presenting the psychodynamic approach to treatment of agoraphobia and panic disorder, we have not wanted to suggest that this approach is superior (or inferior) to all others. Rather, we have aimed to give the reader a clear conception of some of the basic assumptions and other ingredients of this approach. Armed with other background knowledge, he or she can then make independent judgments regarding the appropriateness and usefulness of psychodynamic treatment for particular cases of agoraphobia and panic disorders.

The Relative Balance of Supportive and Expressive (Interpretive) Therapeutic Techniques

We indicated earlier that encouraging the patient to expose him- or herself to the phobic situation often is a necessary step in the treatment of agoraphobia. It has become a basic feature of psychoanalysis and psychoanalytically oriented psychotherapy to keep suggestion to the minimum possible, on the grounds that substituting the therapist's authority for the parent's authority would limit the patient's growth and freedom to develop along lines most suited to his or her nature and goals. Thus, the radical feature of psychoanalytic treatment, and the aspect that differentiates it from other forms of therapy (such as those noted in the final sections of this chapter), is the seemingly paradoxical effort by the therapist to use the influence of parental authority to offer interpretations that often, at least implicitly, refer to the patient's excessive reliance on real and imagined internalized parental standards and prohibitions.

There are many cases in which the patient's level of disturbance, immediate symptoms, or current life circumstances do not permit a completely nondirective psychoanalytic approach. Freud (1919/1974, p. 168) was aware that the widespread application of analytic technique would "compel us to alloy the pure gold of analysis freely with the copper of direct suggestion." He also noted in the same paper that certain symptoms require a direct approach; the treatment of phobias (as opposed to hysteria) has "already made it necessary to go beyond our former limits." Freud (1919/1974, p. 165) stated that: "One can hardly master a phobia if one waits till the patient lets the analysis influence him [or her] to give it up. He [or she] will never in that case bring into the analysis the material indispensable for a convincing resolution of the phobia." Freud (1919/1974) thus viewed forced exposure as a necessary *first* step, to be followed by an exploration of the underlying conflicts. The question of the conditions under which it is necessary or desirable to attempt *directly* to alter a symptom is part of the larger issue of the place of deliberately supportive, noninterpretive interventions in psychoanalytically oriented psychotherapy. Ordinarily, the change hoped for by the psychoanalytic clinician is not that the patient engage in a specific behavior at the behest of the therapist. Rather, the therapist hopes to facilitate the patient's freedom to choose more readily among incompatible wishes as these wishes become less fraught with anxiety and peril. (See, in this connection, Schafer's excellent 1970 paper on the psychoanalytic visions of reality and its elaboration by Messer and Winokur in their 1980 discussion of the possibilities of integrating psychodynamic and behavioral approaches to treatment.)

In actual practice, the more disturbed the patient and the more intractable, painful, disabling, and life-threatening the symptom (whether agoraphobia or any other symptom), the more the therapist will be inclined to employ explicit and direct modes of intervention and to recommend or insist on adjunctive treatments (e.g., pharmacotherapy). For example, if the patient's agoraphobia has progressed to the point where he or she is unwilling to leave home alone, we take this as evidence that the ego has been unable to limit anxiety to an internal signal that could activate a less crippling defense. The patient's adaptive capacities are seriously compromised, and strong secondary gains

from the symptom have to be suspected. As suggested earlier, these patients often choose jealous, insecure, sexually inadequate husbands who collude with them in maintaining the symptoms. It is more likely, compared with simple phobias, that one will find both a history of significant difficulty negotiating the separation–individuation phase of development (Mahler, Pine, & Bergman, 1975) and evidence of borderline and narcissistic features. To the extent that these qualities are present, the therapist will depart more from a predominantly expressive approach (however, see Kernberg, 1975) and may include pharmacotherapy, marital therapy, or a multimodal approach in the treatment of agoraphobia.

Our discussion has focused on the psychotherapy of agoraphobia. The considerations and treatment strategies advanced herein apply as well to the psychotherapy of patients with panic disorder. The precipitants of the panic attacks, the particular symptoms that are prominent features of the attacks, and the patient's associations to these factors are explored in an effort to help the patient understand and resolve the underlying conflicts. The conflicts are likely to be more varied than in the case of agoraphobia. The extent to which the therapist relies on explicitly ego-supportive measures and on medication is a function of the frequency and severity of the attacks, the degree to which the patient experiences distress and impaired functioning between attacks, and the therapist's assessment of the patient's ego strength, characterological difficulties, and capacity to benefit from insight-oriented psychotherapy. This approach of course does not reflect a view that patients who are not likely to benefit from insight-oriented therapy are somehow "inferior."

CASE ILLUSTRATIONS

M.C. was a 28-year-old woman who had been married 2 1/2 years; 2 months before coming for treatment, she had given birth to a baby boy. The pregnancy had been a difficult one and had included toxemia. The patient's husband had taken a new job in a smaller city about 50 miles from the city in which the patient grew up and in which she and her husband and her parents now lived. The husband had rented a house in the smaller city and expected that after the baby was born, they

would all move to their new home. This anticipated move to the new city appeared to precipitate the outbreak of agoraphobic symptoms.
Because they had given up their apartment (in
anticipation of the move to the new house) and
because the patient felt quite anxious being
alone, she, her husband, and their new baby
moved into the patients' parents' house (which,
among other things, involved a 50-mile commute
each way for her husband).

When the patient appeared for treatment (she
was brought to treatment and driven back home
by her husband), she could not leave the house
without intense anxiety (she could barely manage going across the street for some minor grocery shopping). She also reported that she experienced a chronic, if manageable, level of anxiety
even while at home. The patient also reported that
she was quite anxious about her new baby, worried that he might succumb to crib death, and
concerned whether she could take good enough
care of him. M.C.'s extreme reluctance to move
to the new city presented a dilemma in which
symptomatic improvement meant moving to
what she experienced as this loathsome place,
whereas remaining agoraphobic protected her
from this fate.

Hence, whatever else was going on, it was
clear that the secondary gain derived from the
agoraphobic symptom would serve to maintain
that symptom and would constitute a powerful
and difficult obstacle to improvement. It seemed
that before therapy could proceed very far, this
no-win issue had to be confronted. The therapist
then saw the patient and her husband together for
two sessions in which he spelled out the aforementioned situation. The husband responded that
he was getting tired of the long commute and
would try to get a job in the city in which they
were now living. Fortunately, after a number of
joint sessions, the plan to move to the new city
was relinquished by both the patient and her
husband. Hence, the patient's agoraphobic
symptom could be dealt with relatively free of at
least one blatant and strong secondary-gain issue.

It should be noted that were the agoraphobic
symptom linked solely to the move to the new
city (which in its specificity, might make one
think of malingering or volitional manipulation),
it would presumably disappear, or at least become less pervasive and intense, once the plan to
move to the new city was relinquished. In fact,
this was not the case. Although M.C. felt relieved
and grateful about not having to move, her agoraphobic symptom continued at the same level.

At this point, let us briefly introduce some historical and familial material. Although never
manifestly agoraphobic, the patient did experience mild phobic symptoms in the past. She
reported, for example, that eating in a restaurant—other than a self-service fast food restaurant—was always a somewhat tense and anxious
experience, particularly during the interval between the time the waiter or waitress took her
order and the time the food arrived. Having given
her order, the patient felt that she had to remain in
the restaurant, at least until the food arrived, and
therefore felt trapped. M.C. had other experiences similar to her restaurant phobia. For example, whenever possible, she sat on the aisle
during a movie or theater performance because
sitting in the middle of the row also made her feel
trapped.

One additional item of information played a
very important role in the course of the treatment.
M.C.'s mother suffered from a kidney disease
requiring dialysis, and the patient reported that
ever since she was about 8 or 9 years of age, it was
her job to change the filters for her mother's
kidney dialysis machine. This task had become
habitual and was taken for granted, and, she
reported, she never thought much about it.

Therapy proceeded on a semi-weekly basis
and mild-to-moderate improvements occurred.
For example, after about 2 months of treatment,
M.C. became capable of driving to the sessions
unaccompanied by her husband. On weekends,
she, her husband, and their baby took short auto
trips. If these trips went beyond a particular
length of time and distance, M.C. would panic
and they would turn back. But they would make
another foray the next weekend.

From the beginning of treatment, the therapist
shared with M.C. his understanding of her agoraphobic symptom as expressing a developmental
issue, specifically as one involving separation
from parents (particularly, mother) and living
one's own independent life—in short, as a difficulty in growing up to become an independent
adult. She began to see her earlier preagorapho-
bic symptoms (i.e., anxiety in restaurants, having
to occupy an aisle seat in the theater) as more
subtle expressions of the same developmental
issue. As we discussed, it was as if the pervasive
feeling, "If I leave home, I will not survive," had
finally come to a head in the agoraphobic symptom.

The next phase of treatment was characterized by M.C. being able to make increasingly
longer and further trips (including solitary shop-

ping and family auto trips to the country on weekends). She related that when she became anxious during these trips, she would conjure up comments and interpretations the therapist had made in the therapy sessions and would repeat them to herself. This would serve to reduce her anxiety. In other words, during this time, much like a child who uses his or her favorite teddy bear or blanket to assuage anxiety, M.C. employed images, memories, and comments of the therapist as soothing transitional objects (Winnicott, 1958). Consistent with this idea, during this time, M.C. also reported dreams in which the therapist would appear and in which he was making a reassuring comment or interpretation.

Still later in the treatment, one was struck by the fact that M.C.'s dreams now included the therapist's words, but she was now saying them to herself. The therapist was no longer directly in the dreams. Then something occurred that truly constituted a turning point (Stone, 1982)—one of the very few dramatic ones that a therapist is likely to experience. It may be recalled that M.C. prepared the filters for her mother's kidney dialysis machine for many years. This hardly came up at all as a topic for discussion in the treatment. All the more surprising, then, that at the beginning of one session, M.C. announced that she had decided that she would no longer be responsible for this task and had so informed her mother, who appeared to accept this decision with equanimity. We should also note that the therapist made no comment or interpretation in response to M.C.'s announcement because he wanted to see what the patient herself would feel, think, and say after making this decision.

Then came a dramatic turn of events. At the next session, M.C. reported that her mother had gone to visit a relative who lived a few hundred miles away and had to return suddenly because she had not brought enough filters with her and thereby had literally endangered her life. While relating this incident, M.C. suddenly and emotionally exclaimed: "No wonder I had to move back home. This way I can oversee *both* my mother and M. (her new baby)." During the next and last phase of treatment, M.C. became more and more aware of the degree to which she had internalized her mother's implicit message, "If you leave me and live your own life, *I* (i.e., mother) will not survive." It was relatively easy to become aware of the feeling that "If I leave home *I* will not survive" because that feeling was very close to the actual experience of the agoraphobic symptom itself. But what was a revelation

was the awareness that she had been living according to what Weiss and Sampson (1986) call the "pathogenic belief" that "if I leave mother, *she* will not survive."

We referred to the preceding dialysis incident as a turning point, not only because it led to a powerful insight, but also because from that point on, M.C. made steady and rapid progress, eventually became virtually symptom free and, with her husband and baby, moved into their own apartment. One perhaps sobering note: Although from a reality point of view, the apartment was attractive and reasonably priced, the fact is that it was found by M.C.'s parents and just happened to be across the street from the parents' home. M.C. was certainly aware of the complex significance of this fact and tried to see certain realistic advantages to her parents' propinquity—such as the ready availability of baby sitters. Thus, in becoming symptom free, M.C. accepted the compromise of both moving into her own apartment and remaining physically close to her parents; this suggests, perhaps, the limited success of the treatment. However, at the last follow-up, 5 years after the termination of treatment, M.C. continued to be symptom free. She seemed reasonably content in her marriage and happy with her child. Because her little boy was now in school, she had taken a part-time job, which, she reported, was giving her a good deal of satisfaction.

In concluding this section, we note that in our clinical experience (which for the most part has been with private rather than with clinic patients) we have encountered many cases in which there are a number of mild variants of agoraphobic symptoms. These cases do not qualify for a formal diagnosis but perhaps can be characterized as a subclinical agoraphobia. The patient does not restrict travel, or need a companion in order to leave home, or experience intense anxiety on venturing out alone. However, there often is a clearly perceptible, mild discomfort (a low-level signal anxiety, if you will) associated with leaving home. This is the sort of feeling that can be largely unattended to and masked by a subtle feeling of safety and security on returning to the familiar environment of one's home. Of course, the boundary between the psychological state just described and the normal feeling of comfort associated with being at home often is not clear cut. Likewise, the boundary line between avoidance of leaving home and preference for being at home (i.e., between an ego inhibition and a personality style) can be fuzzy.

While it fails to meet the strict criteria for

agoraphobia without history of panic disorder, the aforementioned subtle avoidance behaviors are of strong interest to the psychoanalytic therapist in terms of their implications for such issues as self-esteem, sense of self, defenses against envy, separation anxiety, sexual and aggressive conflicts, degree of ego inhibition, identification with one's parents, perpetuation of maladaptive patterns, and the like.

Often, the patterns alluded to are not readily discernible on the basis of the limited information gathered during diagnostic interviews but emerge clearly during the course of psychotherapy. As a clinical illustration, we can cite the case of a divorced professional woman approaching her 40th birthday who was being seen twice a week in psychoanalytic psychotherapy. This woman lives in a large, metropolitan area and works about 2 miles from home. She has no difficulty in going to and from work or in attending work-related meetings elsewhere in the city. However, she reports an uneasiness in being far from home and away from her dog when she ventures out for social occasions (e.g., to meet a friend) or during her leisure time (e.g., to go shopping or to visit a museum). Only in these circumstances does she make reference to her "shtetl mentality" as a cultural reference to her immigrant parents who lived in a European Jewish ghetto. In one session, she mentioned that she had spent a little time with a woman friend and felt that she "had to get home." She was relieved that the woman did not suggest having dinner together, complained that she was tired of listening to this woman talk about her plans, and felt strongly that she wanted to be by herself. After leaving her friend, she forced herself to walk for awhile before getting on the subway to go home, feeling like a "tiny girl in a big city," and finally felt relaxed once she returned home. Her thoughts then turned to not wanting to get close to anyone for fear that it would be "too draining," that she could not set limits, and that it therefore was "easier to avoid contact with people." Subsequent associations included a recent phone conversation in which she "had to get off the phone," for fear that she would either say something hostile or appear incompetent. This eventually led both to childhood memories of feeling emotionally sapped and depleted by having to care for her chronically ill mother and her older, seriously ill sibling, and feeling criticized by her father for not wholeheartedly carrying out this burdensome responsibility assigned

to her by him, and then to ongoing issues and conflicts around deprivation, depletion, death wishes, envy, rivalry, and guilt.

There are two points to be highlighted in this case example. First, this patient's level of discomfort in being away from home varied, not with the distance from home, but with the *meanings* of the social situations in which she found herself. For instance, she could readily go on European vacations alone and without any anxiety. Although one often reads that the further from home the patient is the more anxious she is, with this patient, and with many others, our experience has been that it is not the distance from home that is critical in triggering agoraphobic symptoms, but the kinds of intrapsychic conflicts activated in particular situations. Second, for the psychoanalytic clinician it is these conflicts rather than the symptoms per se that are the main focus of therapeutic work.

PSYCHOTHERAPY FOR AGORAPHOBIA AND PANIC DISORDER: ALTERNATIVE TREATMENT OPTIONS

There are several alternative approaches to the treatment of agoraphobia and panic. We describe briefly a number of them.

1. Nonbehavioral psychotherapy. Quite apart from the specific context of agoraphobia and panic disorders, there are a number of different schools, techniques, and approaches of nonbehavioral psychotherapy. These include, for example, client-centered therapy, Jungian therapy, Gestalt therapy, and so on. Although there is little doubt that patients with agoraphobia and panic have been treated with all these different approaches, we know of no studies comparing their relative efficacy.

2. Conjoint and Family Therapy. There is a good deal of evidence that complex marital and family interactions and pathology are centrally implicated in the development and maintenance of agoraphobia (e.g., Kleiner & Marshall, 1985). Indeed, Quadrio (1984) states that agoraphobia is "a defense mechanism protecting the marital system or the marital dyad" (p. 81). Hence, the argument goes, effective treatment requires conjoint therapy (Barlow, O'Brien, & Last, 1984, report that including husbands facilitates treatment and improvement in work, social, and family functioning). Some family therapists go further and argue that effective treatment of agoraphobia requires, not simple conjoint, but family therapy. However, it should be kept in mind that some impassioned family therapists believe that family therapy is indicated for virtually all kinds of pathology. Unfortunately, there are mainly anecdotal reports and little systematic evidence to guide the clinician here.

As noted earlier, our own view is that even in individual psychodynamic psychotherapy, it is sometimes advisable to see the patient's spouse for a few sessions or to recommend conjoint therapy. However, we also believe that very often, individual psychotherapy alone is quite appropriate. Given the relatively wide consensus that agoraphobia centrally involves issues of separation–individuation and infantile dependence versus autonomy, it is often advisable to work only with the individual patient and his or her struggles in these areas. It is our belief that growth and improvement is not entirely a matter of effecting changes in the marital or family system. To imply to patients that it is seems to us to reinforce, in subtle ways, the very overenmeshment with family and overdependency that often characterizes agoraphobic patients. Consistent with our clinical view, Hafner's (1988) review of research on marital therapy for agoraphobia suggests that its usefulness is not yet clear.

3. Behavioral and Cognitive Therapy.

These techniques of various kinds represent an obvious alternative treatment strategy. Of the various behavioral approaches available (e.g., systematic desensitization, imaginal flooding, and in vivo exposure), there is some evidence that in vivo exposure is the most effective for treatment of agoraphobia. Comparisons of methods of in vivo exposure (group exposure, self-directed exposure, therapist-directed exposure, spouse-assisted exposure) suggest some effectiveness for each approach. Michelson, Mavissakalian, and Marchione (1985) compared graduated exposure, paradoxical intention, and progressive muscle relaxation in patients with agoraphobia and panic attacks. They found reductions in the frequency of panic attacks of 55%, 50%, and 60%, respectively. A 3-month

follow-up showed maintenance of these gains. Marshall and Segal (1986) conclude that graduated exposure with the spouse present, done in cohesive groups, combined with spouse-assisted home practice is best. However, follow-up data generally are not encouraging. For example, in one 4-year follow-up, less than 20% of patients were symptom-free (McPherson, Brougham, & McLaren, 1980). Also, Barlow (1981) reports a median dropout rate of 22%, and Barlow, O'Brien, and Last (1984) note a failure rate of about 30% among those patients who undertook in vivo exposure treatment.

Given the failure rate, dropout rate, and relapse rate of in vivo exposure, cognitive therapy strategies and pharmacotherapy have been used separately and in conjunction with in vivo exposure. The combination of in vivo exposure and imipramine (e.g., Telch, Agras, Taylor, Ruth, & Gallen, 1985) appears promising, whereas the addition of cognitive therapy appears to be equivocal (Emmelkamp, Kuipers, & Eggeraat, 1978; Emmelkamp & Mersch, 1982; Williams & Rappoport, 1983; Taylor & Arnow, 1988).

In a review of cognitive therapy, Clark and Beck (1988) state that "its contribution to the treatment of phobias is not well defined in current research" (p. 381), but they claim that the cognitive therapy procedures used were inadequate.

4. Group Treatments.

The various kinds of group treatment, including group psychotherapy and group exposure, have been employed in the treatment of agoraphobia and panic and obviously represent an economical alternative to individual treatment.

5. Pharmacological Treatments.

Particularly in the last number of years, pharmacological treatment for agoraphobia, panic, and generalized anxiety has become more common. Such treatment can be and has been combined with any of the aforementioned treatment approaches. There is also evidence that different drugs tend to be selectively effective for different diagnostic categories. Thus, imipramine and phenelzine have been reported to be especially effective for cases of panic disorder, including those associated with agoraphobia or lactate-induced panic (e.g., Sheehan, Ballenger, & Jacobson, 1980), while antianxiety benzodiazepines are held to be more effective for generalized anxiety (Ballenger, 1986).

A review (Taylor & Arnow, 1988) of nine studies using imipramine from 8 to 26 weeks at dosages from 122 mg up to 300 mg shows consistent evidence of reductions in the frequency and intensity of panic attacks, as well as diminished depression. However, the dropout rate in these studies ranged from 17% to 30%, and the relapse rate within the first 2 years following treatment can be as high as 30% (Kelly, Guirguis, Frommer, Mitchell-Heggs, & Sargant, 1970; Zitrin, Klein, Woerner, & Ross, 1983). According to Taylor and Arnow (1988) fewer than 50% of panic disorder patients showed a stable benefit from drug treatment if one combines relapse rate, dropouts, and patient intolerance. They therefore recommend an integrated approach that includes medication, education, relaxation techniques, changes in exercise and diet, paradoxical interventions, and cognitive therapy techniques (e.g., modification of self-statements).

Hyperventilation and CO_2 breathing also have been used to treat panic disorder (see Taylor & Arnow, 1988, for an account of this work, as well as for a useful discussion of the indications and contraindications for pharmacological treatments).

6. Multimodal Approach. This approach is often recommended for treatment of agoraphobia and panic, but the term itself is somewhat ambiguous. It can refer to different permutations and combinations of available treatment approaches. For example, the term *multimodal* can refer to (a) the combination of pharmacotherapy with individual behavioral therapy or individual psychotherapy, (b) pharmacotherapy with group therapies of various kinds, or (c) pharmacotherapy with conjoint or family therapy. *Multimodal* can also refer to different kinds of interventions entirely within the context of psychotherapy—for example, the combination of individual psychodynamic psychotherapy with conjoint therapy and even with some form of exposure therapy.

Whatever the particular combination of different techniques and interventions, the central point made by those who advocate a multimodal approach to the treatment of agoraphobia and panic is the need for flexibility in treating these frequently recalcitrant disorders. Remaining a purist and sticking to one approach, whether it is psychodynamic or behavioral or family oriented, may make the therapist feel comfortable. It may not, however, always be in the best interests of the patient. A syndrome such as agoraphobia is often pervasive and implicates many different aspects and levels of the patient's life—biochemical, intrapsychic, behavioral, marital, family, and social. Often, many of these different aspects must be addressed in order for treatment to be effective (e.g., Taylor & Arnow, 1988).

One practical problem involved in trying to implement a multimodal approach is the difficulty inherent in trying to coordinate different interventions and approaches. In some more limited and modest multimodal treatment, the therapist alone can carry out the different interventions. However, when a wide range of interventions are involved, each requiring different skills, training, and experience, it may be unrealistic (on occasion, even grandiose) for the therapist to believe that he or she is expert in all of them. On such occasions, issues of referral and coordination arise, which, if not handled appropriately, may confuse the patient and disrupt treatment.

7. Psychodynamic Behavior Therapy. Finally, we want to describe an alternative treatment strategy (Feather & Rhoads, 1972; Rhoads & Feather, 1974), which has been used mainly and only very rarely in the treatment of circumscribed phobias. We believe that this approach perhaps has been undeservedly neglected and that it may have potential for the treatment of agoraphobia and panic. Very briefly, the basic idea underlying psychodynamic behavior therapy is that the patient is desensitized, not to be overt phobic stimulus, but to the unconscious symbolic meaning of the stimulus—which is determined through prior careful clinical interviewing. In one paper, Feather and Rhoads (1972) describe the treatment of public speaking phobias, in which they attempt to desensitize patients, not to the phobic situation itself, but to the preconscious and unconscious *fantasies and meanings* associated with public speaking. For example, some patients have fantasies of urinating in their trousers or hurling obscenities at the audience, and it is these situations and fantasies, rather than public speaking itself, to which patients are desensitized.

It seems to us that this approach might be meaningfully extended in a number of ways. One also can employ behavioral techniques other than desensitization—for example, imaginal flooding. Also, one can vary the level of unconscious meanings to which the behavioral techniques of desensitization and flooding are applied. For example, if on the basis of clinical data for a particular patient, one has reason to believe that anxiety over public speaking is, at an unconscious level, related to Oedipal wishes and fears (e.g., fantasy of hurling obscenities at the audience is, in turn, linked to wishes to destroy father and fear of retaliation), one could apply the behavioral techniques to these Oedipal wishes and fears.

COMPARISONS OF DIFFERENT TREATMENT APPROACHES

The primary focus on this chapter has been the psychoanalytically oriented treatment of agoraphobia and panic disorder. We have briefly described alternative treatment approaches but have not commented on their relative efficacy or on the several different theoretical emphases within a psychodynamic framework.

Apart from an interest in brevity and our understanding that the main focus should be a clinical one, there is, to our knowledge, no body of research that indicates a clear superiority for a particular method of treatment among the three main therapeutic approaches—that is, psychodynamic, cognitive-behavioral, pharmacological—or for combinations of these approaches. In fact, there has been virtually no high-quality research that bears on the question of relative efficacy. The large-scale metanalytic studies of treatment outcome for a variety of disorders (Prioleau, Murdock, & Brody, 1983; Shapiro & Shapiro, 1982; Smith, Glass, & Miller, 1980) offer little confidence that we will soon have an answer to the question of treatment of choice for panic disorder and agoraphobia. Among the shortcomings of the treatment outcome research assessed in these meta-analytic reviews are (1) small number of sessions, (2) use of inexperienced therapists, (3) absence of treatment manuals against which conformity with the technique and the competence of the therapist are assessed, (4) tendency to exclude

complex cases and to use nonpatients, (5) failure to use multiple indexes of outcome and multiple perspectives (i.e., therapist, patient, and independent judges), and (6) the finding that effect size (i.e., mean of the treatment group minus mean of the control as comparison group, divided by the standard deviation of the control or comparison group) is a function of the theoretical allegiance of the investigators. Smith et al. (1980), for example, report a 0.29 mean difference in mean effect size in a comparison of the studies done by researchers who presumably were neutral (effect size = 0.66) with the studies conducted by those who had a prior belief in the superiority of the technique being assessed (effect size = 0.95).

With respect to the issue of type of patient studied, Hafner (1988) notes that simple, compared with complex, agoraphobia (Goldstein & Chambless, 1978; Hafner, 1977, 1982) is overrepresented in clinical research, often for good methodological reasons. The so-called complex cases are those in which other, significant psychopathology and marital conflict are part of the initial clinical picture. Bowen and Kohout (1979), for example, found that more than 90% of their agoraphobic patients also had a primary affective disorder. A treatment outcome study on the relative effectiveness of different types of therapy that excluded such subjects would yield results with limited generalizability. For example, in their study of agoraphobia, Zitrin, Klein, Woerner, and Ross (1983) excluded patients with "more than moderate" levels of depression. Although this may have been necessary and desirable from the standpoint of research methodology, it obviously poses problems of generalizability. Thus, the finding by Klein, Zitrin, Woerner, and Ross (1983) of no difference among agoraphobic patients in degree of symptomatic improvement when comparing behavior therapy and supportive therapy, even if replicated repeatedly, cannot be generalized to the more complex and apparently more typical cases of agoraphobia seen in clinical practice by psychoanalytically oriented therapists.

As Hafner (1988) reminds us, apparently only about half the agoraphobic patients referred for treatment in the context of a research project ever complete treatment, and a high percentage of those relapse. The other half either drop out (Mavissakalian & Michelson, 1982) or fail to meet the inclusion criteria of the research protocol (Jannoun, Munby, Catalan, & Gelder, 1980). It is probably patients from these two subgroups that come to the attention of psychodynamically oriented therapists. Therefore, it is not surprising that a reader of an earlier draft of this chapter, commenting on the differences between our treatment approach and that of a colleague who is a biologically oriented research psychiatrist, said that he and we "could be seeing different species!"

Suppose it could be shown decisively that, compared with psychodynamic therapy, pharmacotherapy and/or behavior therapy offered a greater and more rapid amelioration of the symptoms of agoraphobia and panic disorder. These methods would then become the treatment of choice for a symptom-focused approach to these disorders. They clearly have the advantage of economy. Thus, Marks (1987) believes that behavioral therapy is the treatment of choice for most phobic disorders and also reports that psychiatrists and nurses (it is not clear why he limits his comments to these professions) can learn the treatment methods of behavior therapy in a very brief period of time and that the application of this approach frequently requires the clinician to devote no more time than is typical in pharmacological or other routine psychiatric treatments.

However, unless it also could be shown that these methods had a positive feedback on the other DSM-III-R Axis I and Axis II diagnoses often associated with agoraphobia and panic disorder, we still would need to know which treatment approach or combination and sequence of approaches would be most beneficial, both short-term *and* in the long run, for patients with multiple diagnoses. Only when the necessary body of research has been done to answer this complex question will we be able to move beyond clinical experience in deciding the legitimate place of psychoanalytically oriented (supportive and insight) psychotherapy in the treatment of panic disorder and of agoraphobia.

CONCLUDING REMARKS

For a variety of historical, ideological, and philosophical reasons that we do not articulate here,

most psychodynamically oriented, compared with biologically oriented or cognitive-behaviorally oriented therapists come from a tradition in which formal research on the efficacy of treatment and the necessity for accountability are not highly valued. Even today, for example, most psychodynamically oriented therapists, view tape recording of sessions as an infringement that compromises the effectiveness of treatment. Clinical experience acquired through supervision and clinical lore are the main guidelines for treatment. Not surprisingly, the meta-analyses of therapy outcome (cf. Parloff, 1984) include so few comparisons that reflect the work of experienced psychodynamically oriented therapists that it is not yet possible to be guided by the research literature even if one were so inclined.

In light of these unfortunate limitations, as well as the absence of even informal follow-up reports from psychodynamically oriented clinicians, and given the somewhat positive but less than superlative results of medication and of behavioral, cognitive, and other approaches, what practical recommendations can we make for a psychoanalytically informed approach to the treatment of panic disorder and agoraphobia? First, initial treatment should be symptom-focused *to the extent* that the symptoms are disabling. When impairment is significant, some combination of pharmacological, supportive, cognitive, and in vivo exposure measures should be employed. These methods should be used in the context of a therapeutic atmosphere that promotes a good working alliance and a sense of safety, trust, and respect. These qualities will enhance the patient's experience of being in a helping relationship and should facilitate hope. This phase of providing symptomatic relief is regarded as *preliminary* to a psychotherapy that would combine supportive and insight-oriented features in a proportion that reflects the patient's motivation and capacity for self-understanding and tolerance for troublesome thoughts and feelings. To the degree that the patient can resolve the underlying core conflicts by making and internalizing needed behavioral and characterological changes (see Luborsky, Crits-Christoph, Mintz, & Auerbach, 1988), further symptomatic behavior and psychic pain are less likely to occur, given average expectable environmental conditions, or, as Freud (1937/1957, p. 321) put it, "it still of course remains an open question how much of this immunity is due to a benevolent fate which spares him [or her] too searching a test."

REFERENCES

American Psychiatric Association. (1987). *Diagnostic and statistical manual of mental disorders*, (3rd ed., rev.) (DSM-III-R). Washington, DC: Author.

Ballenger, J. C. (1986). Pharmacotherapy of the panic disorders. *Journal of Clinical Psychiatry, 47*, (Suppl.), 27–32.

Barlow, D. H. (1981). On the relation of clinical research to clinical practice: Current issues, new directions. *Journal of Consulting and Clinical Psychology, 49, 147–155.*

Barlow, D. H., O'Brien, G. T., & Last, C. G. (1984). Couples treatment of agoraphobia. *Behavior Therapy, 15*, 41–58.

Beck, A. T., & Emery, G. (1985). *Anxiety disorders and phobias*. New York: Basic Books.

Bowen, R. C., & Kohout, J. (1979). The relationship between agoraphobia and primary affective disorders. *Canadian Journal of Psychiatry, 24*, 317–322.

Bowlby, J. (1973). *Attachment and loss: Vol. 2. Separation*. New York: Basic Books.

Brenner, C. (1982). *The mind in conflict*. New York: International Universities Press.

Buglass, D., Clarke, J., Henderson, A. S., Kreitman, N., & Presley, A. S. (1977). A study of agoraphobic housewives. *Psychological Medicine, 7*, 73–86.

Clark, D. M., & Beck, A. T. (1988). Cognitive approaches. In C. G. Last & M. Hersen (Eds.), *Handbook of anxiety disorders* (pp. 362–385). New York: Pergamon.

Eagle, M. (1979). Psychoanalytic formulations of phobias. In L. Saretsky, G. D. Goldman, & D. S. Milman (Eds.), *Integrating ego psychology and object relations theory* (pp. 97–118). Dubuque, Iowa: Kendall/Hunt Publishing.

Eagle, M., & Wolitzky, D. L. (1988). Psychodynamics. In C. G. Last & M. Hersen (Eds.), *Handbook of anxiety disorders* (pp. 251–277). New York: Pergamon.

Emmelkamp, P. M. G. Phobic disorders. In C. G. Last & M. Hersen (Eds.), *Handbook of anxiety disorders*. New York: Pergamon.

Emmelkamp, P. M. G., Kiuipers, A. C., & Eggeraat, J. B. (1978). Cognitive modification versus prolonged exposure in vivo: A comparison with agoraphobics as subjects. *Behaviour Research and Therapy, 16*, 33–41.

Emmelkamp, P. M. G., & Mersch, P. (1982). Cognition and exposure in vivo in the treatment of agoraphobia: Short term and delayed effects. *Cognitive Therapy and Research, 6*, 77–78.

Fairbairn, W. R. D. (1952). *Psychoanalytic studies of the personality*. London: Tavistock; Routledge & Kegan Paul.

Feather, B. W., & Rhoads, J. M. (1972). Psychodynamic behavior therapy. *Archives of General Psychiatry, 26*, 496–511.

Fenichel, O. (1945). *The psychoanalytic theory of neurosis*. New York: Norton.

Freud, S. (1957). Analysis terminable and interminable. *Collected papers*. London: Hogarth. (Original published in 1937).

Freud, S. (1974). Lines of advance in psycho-analytic therapy. *Standard edition*. London: Hogarth. (Original published in 1919).

Goldstein, A. J., & Chambless, D. L. (1978). A reanalysis of agoraphobia. *Behavior Therapy, 9*, 47–59.

Guntrip, H. (1968). *Schizoid phenomena, object relations and the self*. New York: International Universities Press.

Hafner, R. J. (1976) Fresh symptom emergence after intensive behaviour therapy. *British Journal of Psychiatry, 129*, 378–383.

Hafner, R. J. (1977). The husbands of agoraphobic women and their influence on treatment outcome. *British Journal of Psychiatry, 131*, 289–294.

Hafner, R. J. (1979) Agoraphobic women married to abnormally jealous men. *British Journal of Medical Psychology, 52*, 99–104.

Hafner, R. J. (1982). The marital context of the agoraphobic syndrome. In D. L. Chambless & A. J. Goldstein (Eds.), *Agoraphobia: Multiple perspectives on theory and treatment*. New York: Wiley.

Hafner, R. J. (1984). The marital repercussions of behavior therapy for agoraphobia. *Psychotherapy, 21*, (4), 530–542.

Hafner, R. J. (1986). *Marriage and mental illness*. New York: Guilford.

Hafner, R. J. (1988). Marital and family therapy. In C. G. Last & M. Hersen (Eds.), *Handbook of anxiety disorders*. New York: Pergamon.

Hallam, R. S. (1978). Agoraphobia: A critical review of

the concept. *British Journal of Psychiatry, 133,* 314–319.

Jannoun, L., Murphy, M., Catalan, J., & Gelder, M. (1980). A home-based treatment programme for agoraphobia: Replication and controlled evaluation. *Behavior Therapy, 11,* 294–305.

Kelly, D., Guirguis, W., Frommer, E., Mitchell-Heggs, N., & Sargant, W. (1970). Treatment of phobic states with antidepressants: A retrospective study of 245 patients. *Journal of Psychiatry, 116,* 387–389.

Kernberg, O. (1975). *Borderline conditions and pathological narcissism.* New York: Aronson.

Klein, D. F., Zitrin, C. M., Woerner, M. G., & Ross, D. C. (1983). Treatment of phobias: II. Behavior therapy and supportive psychotherapy. Are there any specific ingredients? *Archives of General Psychiatry, 40,* 139–145.

Kleiner, L., & Marshall, W. L. (1985). Relationship difficulties and agoraphobia. *Clinical Psychology Review, 5,* 581–595.

Kohut, H. (1971). *The analysis of the self.* New York: International Universities Press.

Kohut, H. (1977). *The restoration of the self.* New York: International Universities Press.

Kohut, H. (1984). *How does analysis cure?* Chicago: University of Chicago Press.

Lader, M. H., & Wing, L. (1966). *Physiological measures, sedative drugs and morbid anxiety* (Maudsley Monograph No. 14). London: Oxford University Press.

Luborsky, L. (1984). *Principles of psychoanalytic psychotherapy: A manual for supportive–expressive treatment.* New York: Basic Books.

Luborsky, L., Crits-Cristoph, P., Mintz, J., & Auerbach, A. (1988). *Who will benefit from psychotherapy?* New York: Basic Books.

Mahler, M., Pine, F., & Bergman, A. (1975). *The psychological birth of the human infant: Symbiosis and individuation.* New York: Basic Books.

Marks, I. M. (1970). The classification of phobic disorders. *British Journal of Psychiatry, 116,* 377–386.

Marks, I. M. (1987). *Fears, phobias and rituals.* New York: Oxford University Press.

Marshall, W. L., & Segal, Z. (1986). Phobia and anxiety. In M. Hersen (Ed.), *Pharmacological and behavioral treatment: An integrative approach* (pp. 260–288). New York: Wiley.

Mathews, A. M., Gelder, M. G., & Johnston, D. W. (1981). *Agoraphobia: Nature and treatment.* London: Tavistock.

Mavissakalian, M., & Michelson, L. (1982). Agoraphobia: Behavioral and pharmacological treatments, preliminary outcome, and process findings. *Psychopharmacology Bulletin, 18,* 91–103.

McPherson, F. M., Brougham, L., & McLaren, S. (1980). Maintenance of improvement in agoraphobic patients treated by behavioral methods—A four-year follow-up. *Behaviour Research and Therapy, 18,* 150–152.

Meissner, W. W. (1985). Theories of personality and psychopathology: Classical psychoanalysis. In H. I. Kaplan & B. J. Sadock (Eds.), *Comprehensive textbook of psychiatry.* Baltimore: Williams & Wilkins.

Messer, S. B., & Winokur, M. (1980). Some limits to the integration of psychoanalytic and behavior therapy. *American Psychologist, 35,* 818–827.

Michelson, L., Mavissakalian, M., & Marchione, K. (1985). Cognitive and behavioral treatments of agoraphobia: Clinical, behavioral, and psychophysiological outcomes. *Journal of Consulting and Clinical Psychology, 53,* 913–925.

Modell, A. (1984). *Psychoanalysis in a new context.* New York: International Universities Press.

Parloff, M. (1984). Psychotherapy research and its incredible credibility crisis. *Clinical Psychology Review, 4,* 95–109.

Pine, F. (1985). *Developmental theory and clinical process.* New Haven: Yale University Press.

Prioleau, L., Murdock, M., & Brody, N. (1983). An analysis of psychotherapy versus placebo studies. *The Behavioral and Brain Sciences, 6,* 275–310.

Quadrio, C. (1984). The families of agoraphobic women. *Australian and New Zealand Journal of Psychiatry, 18,* 164–170.

Rhoads, J. M., & Feather, B. W. (1974). Application of psychodynamics to behavior therapy. *American Journal of Psychiatry, 131,* 17–20.

Schafer, R. (1970). The psychoanalytic vision of reality. *International Journal of Psychoanalysis, 51,* 279–297.

Schur, M. (1971). Metapsychological aspects of phobias in adults. In M. Kanzer (Ed.), *The unconscious today: Essays in honor of Max Schur.* New York: International Universities Press.

Shapiro, D. A., & Shapiro, D. (1982). Meta-analysis of comparative therapy outcome studies: A replication and refinement. *Psychological Bulletin, 92,* 581–604.

Sheehan, D. V., Ballenger, J., & Jacobsen, G. (1980). Treatment of endogenous anxiety with phobic, hysterical and hypochondriacal symptoms. *Archives of General Psychiatry, 37,* 51–59.

Silverman, D. (1986). A multi-model approach: Looking at clinical data from three theoretical perspectives. *Psychoanalytic Psychology, 3,* 121–132.

Smith, M. C., Glass, G. V., & Miller, J. I. (1980). *The benefits of psychotherapy.* Baltimore, MD: Johns Hopkins University Press.

Stone, M. (1982). Turning points in psychotherapy. In S. Slipp (Ed.), *Curative factors in dynamic psychotherapy* (pp. 259–279). New York: McGraw-Hill.

Taylor, C. B., & Arnow, B. (1988). *The nature and treatment of anxiety disorders.* New York: The Free Press.

Telch, M., Agras, W. S., Taylor, C. B., Roth, W. T., & Gallen, C. (1985). Combined pharmacological and behavioral treatment for agoraphobia. *Behaviour Research and Therapy, 23,* 325–335.

Weiss, J., & Sampson, H. (1986). *The psychoanalytic process.* New York: Guilford.

Williams, S. L., & Rappoport, A. (1983). Cognitive treatment in the natural environment for agoraphobics. *Behavior Therapy, 14,* 299–313.

Winnicott, D. W. (1958). Collected papers: *Through pediatrics to psychoanalysis.* New York: Basic Books.

Zitrin, C. M., Klein, D. F., Woerner, M. G., & Ross, D. C. (1983). Treatment of phobias: I. Comparison of imipramine hydrochloride and placebo. *Archives of General Psychiatry, 40,* 125–137.

CHAPTER 9

Behavior Therapy

JÜRGEN MARGRAF

INTRODUCTION

Phobos was a greek god with a special ability to frighten adversaries. His resemblance was painted on armor in order to scare enemies. His name thus became a synonym for fear and anxiety, as well as for flight. On the other hand, Pan, the Greek god of fertility, was generally a merry character in spite of his great ugliness. From time to time, however, he was ill-tempered and loved to chase travelers away by appearing suddenly. Sudden anxiety, as well as flight or avoidance behavior, are central characteristics of a group of anxiety disorders that today are called "panic disorder" and "agoraphobia." The oldest known description of an agoraphobic patient is usually attributed to Hippocrates. The term *agoraphobia*, however, was coined only in 1871 by Westphal, who used it to describe strong fear and avoidance of public places in three of his patients. Agoraphobia is often misunderstood as a specific fear of large, open spaces. The Greek term *agora*, however, refers not only to the market place but also to places of public assembly in general. Agoraphobics are usually afraid of numerous public places and crowds of people.

Anxiety attacks were already described by Freud (1947a/1895) as one cardinal feature of what he proposed to call "anxiety neurosis." Such attacks are frequent among agoraphobics but also occur in patients without phobic avoidance. Especially interesting for behavioral and biological researchers alike is that the patients often cannot tell exactly what caused their anxiety attacks. This so-called spontaneity has been given central importance in the definition of panic attacks in the DSM-III-R (American Psychiatric Association [APA], 1987). The DSM-III-R specifies that anxiety attacks are not caused by realistic danger or by specific phobic stimuli. Many patients report at least some instances in which their anxiety came "out of the blue." Recent research, however, suggests that internal cues may serve as triggers for anxiety in such patients. These are usually bodily sensations (e.g., palpitations, dyspnea, dizziness) that are associated with an immediately imminent bodily or mental catastrophe. Much more rare triggers are thoughts or images (e.g., "I am alone, there is no help").

Among the anxiety disorders that patients present for treatment, agoraphobia is by far the most important (Agras, Sylvester, & Oliveau, 1969; Marks, 1987b). In addition, panic patients seek professional help more often than patients with other psychological syndromes (Boyd, 1986). They cause unusually high health care costs because of both the great number of professionals consulted and the expensive diagnostic measures.

Preparation of this chapter was supported by German Research Foundation grant MA 1116/1-1.

CONCEPTUALIZATION OF THE DISORDERS

The Psychophysiological Model of Panic

Until a few years ago, most behavioral or psychological theorists focused on the avoidance behavior of agoraphobics and did not directly address the problem of panic attacks unrelated to external fear-arousing stimuli. The renewed emphasis on panic attacks was initiated by etiological models that attempted a simple biological explanation. Authors such as Klein (1980) or Sheehan (1982) proposed medical illness models of the disorder that assume panic to be a qualitatively distinct type of anxiety with a specific genetic vulnerability that has to be treated with specific pharmacological agents. However, medical illness approaches have not been well supported by empirical research (Margraf, Ehlers, & Roth, 1986a, 1986b; Margraf & Ehlers, in press). More recently, alternative models have been proposed that do receive increasing empirical support (Barlow, 1986; Beck, Emery, & Greenberg, 1985; Clark, 1986; Ehlers & Margraf, 1989; Goldstein & Chambless, 1978; Hallam, 1985; Ley, 1985; Margraf et al., 1986a, 1986b; Rapee, 1987; van den Hout, 1988). In spite of some differences, these models share enough of their central characteristics to be considered variants of the same theme. In the following, the term *psychophysiological models* is used because it emphasizes the interaction of psychological and physiological factors that most authors consider central to the etiology of panic attacks.

Psychophysiological models assume panic attacks to be *quantitatively* rather than *qualitatively* different from other types of anxiety on a number of dimensions. Some of the most important dimensions are (a) the nature of the triggering events (internal vs. external), (b) the nature and time course of the predominant symptoms (somatic vs. psychic, sudden vs. gradual), and (c) the feared consequences (immediate bodily–mental catastrophes vs. other more long-term negative events). Panic attacks are not seen as spontaneous in the sense of being unrelated to triggering stimuli. They are explained as the consequence of a positive feedback loop between bodily sensations or cognitive events and the person's reaction to them. A schematic representation of this model of panic, as proposed by Ehlers et al. (1988b, Ehlers & Margraf, 1989), is given in Figure 9.1.

The central part of the model in Figure 9.1 shows a positive feedback loop (illustrated by black arrows) leading to a panic attack. The positive feedback may start with any of the following elements:

- Physiological or cognitive changes occur as a consequence of various causes, such as physical effort, drug intake (e.g., caffeine), situational stressors (e.g., heat), or emotional responses (e.g., anxiety, anger).

- The person perceives these changes. Changes in body sensations may not accurately reflect actual physiological changes. For example, persons may feel that their heart has accelerated after going to bed because the change in body posture has increased their cardiac awareness.

- The bodily or cognitive changes are associated with immediate danger via mechanisms ranging from conditioning to catastrophic misinterpretations in conscious thoughts (Barlow, 1986; Clark, 1986; Goldstein & Chambless, 1978; Margraf et al., 1986a, 1986b; Ottaviani & Beck, 1987; van den Hout, 1988). The positive feedback loop may start at this point without prior bodily changes if situational variables are associated with immediate threat. For example, simple phobics may experience panic attacks when confronted with their phobic stimulus. In agoraphobics, however, the phobic situations are probably only indirectly associated with danger via their relation with body sensations (Foa & Kozak, 1986).

- The person responds to the perceived threat with anxiety, which in turn leads to physiological changes, body sensations, and/or cognitive symptoms (positive feedback).

- If these symptoms are again perceived and

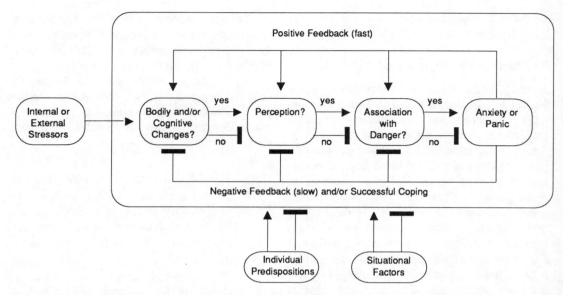

Figure 9.1. Schematic representation of the psychophysiological model of panic attacks, as proposed by Ehlers et al. (1988b).

associated with danger, further anxiety increases occur. This positive feedback may escalate in a panic attack. Note that positive feedback is a fast process. It is unclear at what point anxiety may be called panic because panic attacks are not an all-or-none phenomenon (Margraf, Taylor, Ehlers, Roth, & Agras, 1987).

- Simultaneously, negative feedback mechanisms (grey arrows) have an inhibitory influence on all components of the positive feedback loop. Negative feedback operates more slowly than positive feedback. Thus, a panic attack may develop rapidly, but anxiety will decrease with time. Examples for negative feedback processes are habituation, fatigue, self-limiting homeostatic mechanisms of hyperventilation, or cognitive reappraisal.

- Parallel to negative feedback, the perceived availability of coping strategies decreases anxiety. Again, coping attempts may influence any of the elements of the positive feedback loop.

A number of variables affect the probability of experiencing a panic attack. These factors are shown outside the central box in Figure 9.1:

- Internal or external stressors may increase the probability of physiological or cognitive events that may trigger the positive feedback loop.

- Individual predispositions (physiological and psychological) increase the likelihood of bodily sensations, their perception, and their association with immediate bodily–mental threat. Other predispositions, such as the patients' learning history (operant and modeling) with reports of somatic symptoms and emotional experiences, influence whether they report panic attacks and seek help for them.

- Situational factors have an impact on whether body sensations are perceived and associated with danger. In addition, situational variables can in themselves be associated with danger and thus directly trigger a panic attack.

Most patients worry about having another attack. This worry leads to tonically heightened anxiety and arousal, which in turn increase the probability of panicogenic body sensations and their catastrophic misinterpretation. Panic patients often are hypervigilant and repeatedly scan their bodies for any signs of danger. This leads to a greater probability of perceiving possible triggers for panic, similar to a self-fulfilling prophecy (Clark et al., 1988).

There is a rapidly growing body of research that supports the psychophysiological approach to panic attacks (reviewed in Clark et al., 1988; Ehlers & Margraf, 1989; Margraf et al., 1986a; van den Hout, 1988). Panic patients have much higher scores on questionnaires measuring fear of fear than do other clinical groups or normal controls (Chambless, Caputo, Bright, & Gallagher, 1984; Clark et al., 1988; Margraf & Ehlers 1987; Reiss, Peterson, Gursky, & McNally, 1986; van den Hout, 1988). In addition, structured interviews reveal that panic attacks usually begin with bodily sensations (Hibbert, 1984; Ley, 1985). False feedback of heart-rate increases induces anxiety and physiological arousal in panic patients but not in normal controls (Ehlers, Margraf, Roth, Taylor, & Birbaumer, 1988). Thus, only panic patients respond to perceived arousal in the direction of positive feedback predicted by the psychophysiological model.

Several authors emphasize the role of hyperventilation as either a trigger (acute hyperventilation) or a predisposition (chronic hyperventilation) for panic (e.g., Lum, 1981; Ley, 1985; Margraf et al., 1986a). Garssen, Van Veenendaal, and Bloemink (1983) found an overlap of about 60% between agoraphobia or panic disorder and hyperventilation syndrome. In another study, voluntary hyperventilation served to induce anxiety in the great majority of agoraphobic patients but not in normal controls (Bonn, Readhead, & Timmons, 1984). Almost all patients rated the effects of hyperventilation as similar to their naturally occurring panic attacks. Furthermore, panic patients have lower resting pCO_2 values than normal controls (Liebowitz et al., 1985; Salkovskis, Jones, & Clark, 1986a). In addition, there are now case reports that demonstrate hyperventilation in naturally occurring spontaneous panic attacks (Griez, Pols, & van den Hout, 1987; Hibbert, 1986; Salkovskis, Warwick, Clark & Wessels, 1986b).

The results of studies attempting to induce panic attacks experimentally using challenges such as lactate infusion, carbon-dioxide (CO_2) inhalation, or phobic exposure lend further support to the psychophysiological model (Ehlers et al., 1986; Margraf et al., 1986b). All of these challenges induce bodily sensations that are typical for the spectrum of panic attacks. According to the psychophysiological approach, these sensations act as triggers for anxiety. In addition, panic patients show higher anxiety and arousal in anticipation of panic induction challenges than controls (Ehlers, Margraf, & Roth, 1986, 1988a; Margraf et al., 1986b). By manipulating expectations, the responses of panic patients and normal controls to lactate infusion, CO_2 inhalation, or hyperventilation can be drastically increased or decreased (Margraf, Ehlers, & Roth, 1989; Rapee, Mattick, & Murrell, in press; van den Hout & Griez, 1982; van der Molen, van den Hout, Vroemen, Lousberg, & Griez 1986).

Cognitive-Behavioral Conceptualization of Agoraphobia

For a long time, the most influential approach to the etiology of agoraphobic behavior was Mowrer's two-factor theory (1947, 1960; see also Miller, 1951; Rescorla & Solomon, 1967; Solomon & Wynne, 1953). Mowrer assumed (1) that phobias result from the association of initially neutral stimuli with a central motivational state of fear via the experience of traumatic events (classical conditioning for first factor) and (2) that the subsequent avoidance of these stimuli is maintained by negative reinforcement through the reduction of this aversive state (operant conditioning for second factor). Although this theory is consistent with a large body of animal experiments, it is not sufficient as an explanation for clinical phobias (Goldstein & Chambless, 1978; Herrnstein, 1969; Marks, 1987b; Rachman, 1977; Seligman & Johnston, 1973; Thorpe & Burns, 1983). Agoraphobics usually cannot recall traumatic events other than a sudden anxiety attack at the onset of their disorder (Marks, 1987b). Several authors assume that the first anxiety attack acts as a traumatic stimulus in itself (Goldstein & Chambless, 1978; Hallam, 1985; Mathews, Gelder, & Johnston, 1981; cf. the critique by Marks, 1987b). Because all of these results are based on self-report, we have to consider that people cannot always attribute their behavior correctly to the relevant stimuli (Nisbett & Wilson, 1977).

Generalization to human phobias from animal research based on two-factor theory is dubious because there is no accepted animal model for agoraphobia (Marks, 1987b). Most attempts to condition phobias in humans failed (e.g., Bregman, 1934; English, 1929). Moreover, there is no equipotentiality of different stimuli to induce phobias. Phobic stimuli show a characteristic distribution that is stable across cultures and that does not correspond to the frequency of these stimuli in everyday life or to the probability of aversive (traumatic) experiences. Seligman (1971) therefore proposed that certain stimulus–response associations are learned more easily because of a biological preparedness. The distribution of clinical phobias and several but not all laboratory experiments support this notion (reviews in Marks, 1987b; McNally, 1987; Öhman, Dimberg, & Öst, 1984). It is conceivable that an association between anxiety responses and public places is biologically prepared. Mineka (1985) pointed out that certain internal cues, such as dizziness, can act as unconditioned triggers for anxiety reactions. In addition, learned anxiety responses to these stimuli may also be biologically prepared. Interoceptive conditioning in animal experiments has been highly resistant to extinction (Razran, 1961).

Several authors have proposed further additions or modifications of two-factor theory. Thorpe and Burns (1983) and Mineka and Tomarken (1988) review hypotheses of agoraphobia as operant behavior; special issues in classical conditioning such as the Garcia effect and incubation; vicarious learning; and cognitive biases. Marks (1987b) discusses the generalization of anxiety-provoking stimuli. In addition, agoraphobics do not just avoid certain situations—they actively approach other situations and people. Rachman (1984) has emphasized the role of such safety signals in the development and maintenance of agoraphobia.

In a reanalysis of earlier etiological models, Goldstein and Chambless (1978) proposed a distinction between simple and complex agoraphobia. In *simple agoraphobia*, the patients fear the phobic situations themselves, often due to traumatic experiences in those or similar situations. In the far more frequent *complex* form; however, they are primarily afraid of the anxiety response and its possible consequences. Lack of assertiveness, high trait anxiety, dependency, and the inability to attribute unpleasant emotions to their triggering events are considered predisposing factors. According to Goldstein and Chambless (1978), the actual onset of the disorder usually occurs in situations of interpersonal conflict (e.g., the wish to leave the parents' home). Anxiety attacks result if the conflict exists long enough or if additional negative life events occur. Because most patients do not relate their anxiety attacks to the triggering conflicts, they interpret them as signs of impending doom (undiagnosed illness, death, insanity). Through interoceptive conditioning, bodily sensations such as palpitations become learned stimuli for anxiety attacks. External situations are then associated via second-order conditioning. The patients' dependency and lack of assertiveness are further exacerbated by their fears, and they begin to avoid situations in which anxiety attacks may occur. Social reinforcement may then contribute to the maintenance of avoidance behavior.

Goldstein and Chambless's (1978) approach continues to have high heuristic value. It gave a good description of many clinical cases and for the first time systematically developed the role of internal cues as triggers for anxiety. As mentioned in the preceding paragraphs, this notion has received increasing empirical support. The main problem of the model is the difficulty in operationalizing its concept of conflict. Thorpe and Burns (1983) pointed out the danger of creating a circular definition because conflicts are first used to define complex agoraphobia and then to explain it. Furthermore, empirical support for the assumed dependent and unassertive premorbid personality is largely lacking. Clinical impressions about predisposing personality traits have not been confirmed empirically (Marks, 1987b). In the same vein, there is no consistent support for poor premorbid sexual adjustment, overprotective behavior of the mother, or instable family environment beyond the rates found in the general population (Tearnan, Telch, & Keefe, 1984). There is widespread agreement that the onset and exacerbations of agoraphobic symptoms are related to stressors such as illnesses, operations, marital problems, or financial problems (Marks, 1987b; Mathews et al., 1981). However, prospective studies about these factors are still lacking. Most family studies show an increased risk for anxiety disorders, depression, and alcoholism in first-degree relatives of agoraphobics. The risk was also higher in female relatives (Marks, 1987b). The relative contribution of genetic and environmental influences to these findings is not yet established because there are no existing adoption studies.

Mathews et al. (1981) formulated an integrated model of agoraphobia that in many aspects resembles that of Goldstein and Chambless (1978), but it does not use the concept of conflict. They consider possible vulnerability factors to be (a) the familial environment during childhood, (b) a high genetic loading for trait anxiety, and (c) nonspecific stress. Again, the most important factor for the development of the disorder is the first anxiety attack. This experience is assumed to activate a dependent, avoidant coping style that probably is acquired in childhood. An additional factor is seen in the causal attribution of the anxiety attack to external situations (e.g., crowds) or to other origins (e.g., being overworked). Avoidance behavior is then enhanced by variables such as fear of anxiety attacks or positive social reinforcement. The authors explicitly acknowledge that many of the postulated variables are speculative and require further empirical support. While the multitude of causal factors assumed by Mathews et al. (1981) seems appropriate to the complexity of the clinical phenomena, it also compromises the possibilities for experimental scrutiny.

The cognitive factors mentioned by Mathews et al. (1981) and Goldstein and Chambless (1978) are central to Beck's theory (Beck et al., 1985). Beck considers inadequate cognitive schemata that govern the perception and interpretation of the person's environment to be responsible for anxiety disorders. These patients are assumed to perceive themselves as especially vulnerable and are characterized by distorted appraisal of potential threat. Specific vulnerability factors for agoraphobia are latent fears of situations that are realistically dangerous to infants and small children (e.g., crowded shops). In addition, agoraphobics are considered overly sensitive to specific spatial configurations (e.g., too wide or too narrow). Under stress, patients have increasing difficulty both modulating their emotional responses to such situations and testing the reality content of their excessive fears (see also Hallam's 1985 concept of disinhibition of anxiety). Their own anxiety responses are interpreted as signs of dysfunction and loss of control (i.e., of being in danger). This is assumed to lead the patients to escape to a safe environment (usually home) and to seek help from a caregiver. Traumatic experiences may contribute to such a development. Anxiety attacks are considered to result from erroneous attribution of bodily sensations and catastrophizing thoughts or images. Beck et al. (1985) thus assume that agoraphobic fears are partly present before the first panic attack (see also Marks, 1987b). Numerous questionnaire results support the role of the cognitive distortions in the interpretation of threat cues (see Beck et al., 1985; McNally & Foa, 1987; Michelson, 1987). However, it is not yet clear whether these distortions are a cause or a consequence of agoraphobic behavior. Longitudinal studies are needed to resolve these questions.

At present, it is not possible to distinguish with certainty among the different complex models that have been proposed to account for agoraphobia. The empirical results are still too sparse or equivocal. It is clear, however, that agoraphobia is most likely multifactorially caused. A formulation is required that considers learning, cognitive mechanisms, and biological processes. Learning theory and cognitive approaches may be connected by noting that conditioning and modeling lead to the development of expectations about the probability of events (Reiss, 1980). In addition, unpredicted and uncontrolled negative stimuli are more aversive (Seligman, 1975). Early experiments used such stimuli to produce experimental neuroses (see Thorpe & Burns, 1983). This could lead to powerful learning experiences based on just a few unpredicted anxiety attacks. For many clinical cases, the renewed emphasis on panic attacks has proven useful. However, as the next section indicates, the connection between panic disorder and agoraphobia is more complex than is (a) currently assumed by many authors and (b) expressed in the classification of DSM-III-R.

DIAGNOSTIC ISSUES AND PROBLEMS

The Clinical Presentation of Panic and Agoraphobia

During anxiety attacks, the patients report a number of somatic symptoms, such as fast, strong, or irregular heart beat; dizziness or lightheadedness; dyspnea; nausea or abdominal distress; chest pain or discomfort; sweating; and trembling or shaking.

These symptoms are experienced as distressing and highly threatening (Barlow et al., 1985; Cameron, Thyer, Nesse, & Curtis, 1986; Margraf et al., 1987; Taylor et al., 1986). Central cognitive symptoms are (a) fear of losing control (e.g., doing something grossly inappropriate or going crazy), (b) fear of catastrophic consequences of anxiety symptoms (e.g., myocardial infarction or making a fool of oneself), and (c) derealization or depersonalization. Severe panic attacks often lead to escape or help-seeking behavior. The form of these behaviors depends on the situational context and the nature of the feared consequences. The patients may thus go to emergency rooms, stay close to a telephone, or simply go home.

The revision of the third edition of the *Diagnostic and Statistical Manual of Mental Disorders* (DSM-III-R: APA, 1987) operationalizes panic attacks via the number of symptoms (at least 4 of 13 predominantly somatic symptoms). In addition, the acute time course is emphasized: at least 4 of the symptoms have to occur within 10 minutes. Empirical studies show that the average duration of attacks is slightly less than 30 minutes (Margraf et al., 1987; Taylor et al., 1986). A central element in the definition of panic attacks in DSM-III-R is that at least some attacks need to occur *spontaneously* (i.e., the anxiety has to occur without realistic danger or phobic stimuli).

Systematic descriptive data on panic attacks are still rare. Most results have been obtained retrospectively using questionnaires or interviews (Anderson, Noyes, & Crowe, 1984; Barlow et al., 1985; Cameron et al., 1986; Turner, McCann, Beidel, & Mezzich, 1986). More informative are recent findings from studies using concurrent assessment of panic attacks in the natural environment via diaries and ambulatory psychophysiological moitoring (Baker & White, 1986; Freedman, Ianni, Ettedgui, & Puthezhath, 1985; Margraf et al., 1987; Shear et al., 1987; Taylor, Telch, & Harrick, 1983; Taylor et al., 1986). These studies show that clinical descriptions of panic attacks are misleading in many respects. Thus, only some panic attacks are accompanied by detectable changes in heart rate, although patients report palpitations in almost 70% of all attacks (Margraf et al., 1987). Attacks triggered by phobic situations were somewhat more severe than spontane-

ous attacks but were otherwise very similar. In retrospective accounts, patients describe their panic attacks as much more severe than when assessed concurrently by diary. The average attack showed only moderate severity (Margraf et al., 1987). Because the extreme anxiety denoted by the term *panic* usually does not occur, the older term *anxiety attack* seems more accurate than *panic attack*.

Phobias are fears that (a) are out of proportion to realistic danger, (b) cannot be reasoned away, (c) are largely beyond voluntary control, and (d) usually lead to avoidance behavior (Marks, 1987b). Some patients show no overt avoidance behavior but endure phobic situations despite intense anxiety. Agoraphobics typically avoid such significantly fearsome situations as driving, public transportation, elevators, department stores, supermarkets, or theaters. Important dimensions of agoraphobic situations are the distance from places or people considered to be safe and confinement of mobility (Marks, 1987b; Mathews et al., 1981; Thorpe & Burns, 1983). Some authors use the metaphor being trapped to describe typical agoraphobic situations (Beck et al., 1985; Goldstein & Chambless, 1978). The situations are often easier to endure when the patients are accompanied. This usually applies to significant others, such as spouses, but it can also include infants and pets in some cases. DSM-III-R defines *agoraphobia* (within panic disorder) as a fear of being in situations from which escape would be difficult or embarrassing or in which help would not be available in the event of a panic attack. For instance, the dentist is not feared because of potential pain but because leaving the dentists' chair because of a panic attack would be difficult. Patients who do not have panic attacks in the narrow sense fear such situations because of other distressing or embarrassing symptoms such as faintness or diarrhea ("agoraphobia without history of panic disorder" in DSM-III-R). Such patients fear driving on freeways because they might faint and not be able to stop or return fast enough rather than because of potential accidents.

In addition to external situations, internal cues are very important. Often these are bodily sensations that are associated with anxiety attacks. For example, one patient could not take a shower with the shower curtain closed because he would feel that he was choking. Many patients abandon physical exercise for similar reasons. Considering the importance of the fear of anxiety symptoms and their potential consequences, many authors (including Westphal in 1871) emphasize "fear of fear" as a central characteristic of panic and agoraphobia. For instance, Barlow and Waddell (1985) argue that the term *panphobia* would seem more appropriate for most clinical cases (see also Goldstein & Chambless, 1978, for a critique of the tendency to reduce agoraphobia to "fear of fear" see Marks, 1987b).

In addition, many patients develop safety signals (Gray, 1971; Mowrer, 1960; Rachman, 1984). These indicate to the patients that anxiety is not probable or would not have dangerous or unpleasant consequences. While such safety signals reduce anxiety, their absence may become a trigger for anxiety. Frequent examples are the bottle with tranquilizers in the purse, the therapist's phone number, or the presence of the spouse.

Nosology of Agoraphobia and Panic

The classification of anxiety disorders and their differentiation from other psychological disturbances is controversial. Currently used classificatory systems are based primarily on clinical experience and cross-sectional studies. There are numerous inconsistent results about the differentiation of anxiety and depression (Hallam, 1985; Stavrakaki & Vargo, 1986). Based on their large epidemiological study, Angst and his coworkers (Angst & Dobler-Mikola, 1985a, 1985b; Angst, Vollrath, Merinkangas, & Ernst, 1987) conclude that there is considerable overlap between anxiety disorders (especially with panic attacks) and depression. They consider a distinction between primary and secondary disorders as highly problematic because of the low reliability of the patients' reports. Thus, classifications that distinguish among discrete syndromes may not be generally valid, and it may be more appropriate to assume a continuum between anxiety and depressive disorders. This conclusion is supported by the rare studies that followed the course of these disorders longitudinally. Tyrer, Alexander,

Remington, and Riley (1987) and Angst et al. (1987) found great temporal variability of anxiety and depressive symptoms and a poor relationship between these symptoms and diagnostic classification.

The distinction between panic attacks and other types of anxiety introduced by DSM-III is also debatable. Panic attacks occur not only in patients with panic disorder or agoraphobia with panic attacks but also in major depression (Angst & Dobler-Mikola, 1985b; Barlow et al., 1985; Leckman, Weissman, Merinkangas, Pauls, & Prusoff, 1983) and in many organic illnesses (McCue & McCue, 1984). Phenomenologically indistinguishable attacks are also found both in other phobic patients when confronted with their phobic stimuli and in obsessive–compulsives (Barlow et al., 1985; Marks, 1987a). Studies of patients with generalized anxiety disorder and panic disorder usually yield very similar results with respect to personality variables, trait anxiety, social adjustment, and life events at the onset of the disorder (Anderson et al., 1984; Barlow et al., 1985; Cameron et al., 1986; Hibbert, 1984; Hoehn-Saric, 1981, 1982; Raskin, Peeke, Dickman, & Pinsker, 1982; Turner et al., 1986). So far, there is no convincing evidence for qualitative differences between panic and other types of anxiety.

Another area of controversy is whether agoraphobia should be considered a subtype of panic disorder, as is largely the case in DSM-III-R (cf. Tyrer, 1986). This notion will probably not be upheld in the upcoming 10th edition of the ICD (ICD-10; Marks, 1987a). Most agoraphobics that present for treatment also complain of panic attacks (Thyer & Himle, 1985). However, in community samples that are not self-selected, such as the National Institute of Mental Health (NIMH) Epidemiological Catchment Area Study, the Zurich Study, or the Munich Follow-up Study, the majority of agoraphobic subjects do not experience panic attacks. About half of all agoraphobics in these studies show so-called limited symptom attacks, but only 10 to 20% meet DSM-III criteria for panic disorder (Angst et al., in press; Weissman, Leaf, Blazer, Boyd, & Florio, 1986; Wittchen, 1986). The differences between epidemiological and clinical samples may simply be due to comorbidity. Patients with two disorders are more likely to seek treatment than those suffering from one.

Diagnostic Phase Before Treatment

In spite of the academic controversy surrounding the classification of anxiety and depressive disorders, a diagnosis of panic or agoraphobia has practical implications for treatment. Therefore, patients are routinely assessed in a diagnostic phase before therapy is initiated. During this phase, the problematic behaviors are described and differentiated from other possible disorders in several steps.

First, it has to be determined whether there are indications of psychotic disorders, major depression, other phobias, or obsessive–compulsive disorder. Panic and agoraphobia frequently lead to secondary depression. If anxiety problems occur only in phases of severe depression, however, it may be more appropriate to treat the depression first. Another frequent complication of panic attacks and agoraphobia are attempts to self-medicate with alcohol and other drugs (Bibb & Chambless, 1986). In some cases, this requires direct treatment. Abuse of street drugs other than at the onset of the disorder is rare. Many patients voluntarily decrease caffeine consumption. Structured clinical interviews, such as the Anxiety Disorders Interview Schedule (ADIS: DiNardo, O'Brien, Barlow, Waddell, & Blanchard, 1983) or the Structured Clinical Interview for DSM-III-R (SCID—Spitzer & Williams, 1986), are efficient and reliable tools at this stage of the diagnostic process.

Second, potential organic causes or complications must be clarified. The patients have usually had extensive medical workups before they seek psychological treatment. If this is not the case, the patient should undergo a physical examination, because numerous organic syndromes may be associated with panic attacks (McCue & McCue, 1984). Relevant differential diagnoses include cardiac diseases, temporal lobe epilepsy, pheochromocytoma, hypoglycemia, and thyroid dysfunction. However, the existence of a mitral valve prolapse syndrome usually does not preclude behavioral treatment (Margraf, Ehlers, & Roth, 1988).

Third, especially important for the personalized design of treatment, is a thorough behavioral analysis for each of the problem areas. Problems are described in terms of subjective, physiological, and behavioral responses. Preceding, modulating, and maintaining conditions are assessed. The help-seeking behavior and the patients' naive explanations for their problems and their (failed) coping strategies should be considered. During the clinical interview, an idiosyncratic anxiety and avoidance hierarchy is developed for each patient. The patients are asked to list difficult situations or sensations and to rank them in terms of associated anxiety and avoidance. Further information can be gained from clinical questionnaires, such as the Fear Questionnaire (FQ: Marks & Mathews, 1979) or the Mobility Inventory (MI), the Agoraphobic Cognitions Questionnaire (ACQ), and the Body Sensations Questionnaire (BSQ; Chambless et al., 1984; Chambless, Caputo, Jasin, Gracely, & Williams, 1985). In addition, general scales assessing trait anxiety, depression, alcoholism, and marital adjustment may be useful (see Corcoran & Fischer, 1987). If the patients complain of spontaneous panic attacks, specific hypotheses must be tested. These include possible connections to hyperventilation, interpersonal conflicts, specific activities, eating habits, or cognitions. For these purposes, self-monitoring via diaries is a useful addition to clinical interviews. Figure 9.2 shows an example of such a diary, based on the diaries used by Margraf et al. (1987).

Fourth, because panic patients often do not notice that they hyperventilate, it is helpful routinely to conduct a hyperventilation test. This test is a safe diagnostic tool if the patients are physically healthy. A standardized protocol can be described in six points (Margraf & Ehlers, 1986):

1. *Instruction.* The test is introduced as a diagnostic procedure. It is possible that the test will cause a panic attack. While this would be unpleasant, it would also have a positive side by clarifying a potential cause of the disorder. Patients are reminded that they can stop the test at any moment.

2. *Posture.* The patients sit upright with one hand on their chest and the other on their abdomen in order to be able to distinguish between thoracic and abdominal breathing.

3. *Hyperventilation.* The patients are paced

Name: ——————————————————   Date: ——————————————

Anxiety Attack Diary

Please enter every anxiety attack (continue on the back if necessary).

	Monday	Tuesday	Wednesday	Thursday	Friday	Saturday	Sunday
1. Attack:							
Begin:							
End:							
Anxiety (0–10):							
What happened before?							
Where were you (with whom)?							
What were you doing?							
Thoughts?							
Bodily sensations? What happened afterwards?							
2. Attack:							
Begin:							
End:							
Anxiety (0–10):							
What happened before?							
Where were you (with whom)?							
What were you doing?							
Thoughts?							
Bodily sensations? What happened afterwards?							

Please note at the end of each day:

Average anxiety level during day:							
Comments:							

Figure 9.2.   Diary for self-monitoring of anxiety attacks. This form is based on the diaries used by Margraf et al. (1987). In addition to the diary form, patients receive a list of symptoms. They are instructed to code symptoms by their list numbers on the diary. The symptoms and codings are (1) shortness of breath; (2) palpitations (heart racing, pounding, or skipping beats); (3) sweating; (4) choking or smothering sensations; (5) faintness; (6) dizziness, lightheadedness, or unsteady feelings; (7) chest pain or discomfort; (8) trembling or shaking; (9) fear of dying; (10) numbness or tingling sensations; (11) fear of going crazy or doing somehting uncontrolled; (12) hot or cold flashes; (13) nausea or abdominal distress; (14) feelings of unreality or being detached from parts of body or things around; (15) other (if other, specify).

at about 60 cycles per minute for 3 minutes. The therapist explains and demonstrates that this test can only be conducted with thoracic breathing through the open mouth. Patients are instructed to breathe out as deeply as possible with each signal given by the therapist (a metronome or prerecorded tape is recommended).

4. *Assessment.* At the end of hyperventilation, patients are given a fear thermometer and a symptom checklist, and they rate the similarity to naturally occurring panic attacks. The symptom checklist contains the relevant symptoms for hyperventilation and panic attacks, as well as five control items that are not usually associated with anxiety (see Figure 9.3). Persons that also check these symptoms may have a tendency to report somatic symptoms indiscriminately.

5. *Recovery.* If necessary (e.g., after strong responses), the patients are instructed to

Name: ———————————————————   *Date:* ———————————————————

Please indicate whether you experienced the following symptoms by circling the appropriate word.

1. Numbness or tingling sensations in parts of your body   yes   no

2. Sweating   yes   no

3. Dizziness, lightheadedness, or unsteady feelings   yes   no

4. Itchiness in parts of your body   yes   no

5. Fear of dying   yes   no

6. Feeling faint (you don't have to actually faint)   yes   no

7. Choking or smothering sensations   yes   no

8. Sore throat   yes   no

9. Trembling or shaking   yes   no

10. Feeling of unreality or being detached   yes   no

11. Shortness of breath   yes   no

12. Swollen tongue   yes   no

13. Palpitations (heart racing, pounding, or skipping beats)   yes   no

14. Chest pain, pressure, tightness, or discomfort   yes   no

15. Fear of losing control   yes   no

16. Burning ears   yes   no

17. Nausea or abdominal distress   yes   no

18. Hot or cold flashes   yes   no

19. Fear of going crazy   yes   no

20. Sweet taste in your mouth   yes   no

Figure 9.3.   Symptom checklist for hyperventilation test (Margraf & Ehlers, 1986). Items 4, 8, 12, 16 and 20 are control items not usually associated with anxiety. They serve to measure a tendency to report somatic symptoms indiscriminately.

recline and recover using a breathing rate of about 8–12 cycles per minute.

6. *Evaluation.* If the effects of hyperventilation are rated as similar to naturally occurring panic attacks, this serves as the starting point for therapy. The evaluation must take into account (a) that the presence of the therapist may greatly reassure some patients, and (b) that this may have altered the patient's response to the test. If no similarity is perceived, other methods for exposure treatment should be chosen (see next section).

TREATMENT STRATEGIES

For a long time, agoraphobia and panic were considered largely treatment refractory. Even today, many patients have experienced a series of failed attempts to resolve their problem. Since the late 1960s, the development and thorough testing of new successful behavioral treatments has changed this bleak outlook. The long-lasting benefits of these treatments have been documented in a number of research centers in Europe, North America, and Australia, with follow-up periods of up to 9 years. This makes the success of behavioral treatments for anxiety disorders "one of the better documented stories in mental health care" (Marks, 1987b, p. 496).

Because agoraphobia and panic are multifaceted disorders, the choice of the actual clinical approach depends partly on the individual symptomatology. The decision process can be represented schematically in a flowchart, as depicted in Figure 9.4 (modified from Margraf & Ehlers, 1986).

If there is significant phobic avoidance, and/or panic attacks are reliably triggered by external phobic stimuli, treatment should start with these features because they can be eliminated with a high probability. If there is no phobic avoidance, and panic attacks are triggered primarily by internal cues (e.g., bodily sensations such as palpitations or dizziness), then treatment should focus on these spontaneous panic attacks. Here, it is best to start with hyperventilation-based methods because they seem to offer the greatest chance of success. For the clarity of presentation, the treatment of agoraphobic behavior and panic attacks are described separately. In clinical practice, however, the two problems are often treated together.

Agoraphobic Avoidance Behavior and Panic Attacks with External Triggers

The basic principle in the behavioral treatment of agoraphobia—exposure to anxiety-provoking situations—has been known for a long time. One famous agoraphobic, the poet Johann Wolfgang Goethe, describes in his autobiographic work "On Poetry and Truth" how he cured himself by self-exposure in the late 18th century. He would climb to the highest tower of the Strassburg cathedral, and he visited hospitals, medical demonstrations, solitary places, nocturnal cemeteries, or noisy crowds in order to expose himself to his fears of heights, death, illness, or confinement until they disappeared. He reports being so successful that he could "vie with the carpenters in running over the freelying beams" and that "disgusting things" related to illness could not put him "out of countenance again" (all quotations from Goethe, 1970, p. 337; translation by the author).

In the same way, Oppenheim (1911), in his "Textbook of Nervous Diseases for Physicians and Students," recommended crossing the feared places together with the agoraphobic patients. Similarly, Freud stated that the analytic techniques developed in the treatment of hysteria were insufficient for the treatment of phobias. "One will hardly abolish any phobia by waiting until the sick person is moved by the analysis to abandon it." With severe agoraphobics, one "has success only if one can move them to go out into the street and fight with the anxiety" (both quotations from Freud, 1947b, p. 191; translation by the author).

Since the late 1960s, exposure-based treatments were systematically developed and tested experimentally. This confirmed that in vivo exposure is the method of choice. Attempts to treat agoraphobia with systematic desensitization have been less successful (Thorpe & Burns, 1983). For more extensive descriptions of the actual procedures and basic research, the reader is referred to Chambless and Goldstein (1980), Marks (1981,

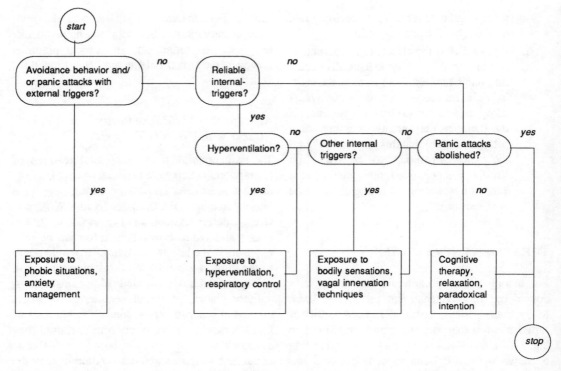

Figure 9.4. Flowchart of the decision process involved in planning treatment for panic and agoraphobia (modified from Margraf & Ehlers, 1986).

1987b), Mathews et al. (1981), and Barlow and Waddell (1985).

Before treatment, other areas of possible problematic behavior (e.g., alcoholism, depression) or organic syndromes (McCue & McCue, 1984) have to be clarified. In a behavioral analysis, anxiety-provoking situations and factors that intensify or reduce anxiety are determined. Using examples from the patients' history, a rationale for the development of the agoraphobia is then given, and the treatment plan is deduced from it. This enhances therapy effectiveness and acceptance, as well as generalization of success and relapse prevention (Barlow & Waddell, 1985; Margraf & Ehlers, 1986; Michelson, 1987). The rationale is based on the two-factor theory and the safety-signal hypothesis (see the preceding section). Thus, the therapist may speak of a vicious circle of anxiety and avoidance: Escape from anxiety-provoking situations is originally an understandable, natural response. In the long run, exaggerated avoidance (and the use of safety signals) leads to increased anticipatory anxiety, which in turn leads to more

avoidance. This vicious circle has to be broken by exposure treatment. The patients need to unlearn their fear of fear. Anxiety responses last only a limited time and diminish automatically. The patients should learn that they are able to endure even intense anxiety and that the feared catastrophic consequences of their anxiety will not occur. In order to achieve this, the patients have to enter the feared situations and get anxious. If they do not try to suppress anxiety but rather accept it and let it happen, anxiety will decrease (habituation). Figures depicting the time course of anxiety and arousal under the different conditions help the patients to grasp the central points of this rationale. Figure 9.5 shows the figures that we use (modified from Bartling, Fiegenbaum, & Krause, 1980).

The rationale has to be commensurate with the individual symptoms, behaviors, fears, and naive explanations of the patients. The ultimate goal of therapy is not zero anxiety, but a degree of fear and arousal that is situationally appropriate (e.g., being a completely fearless driver is not appropriate).

The situations for exposure are planned with

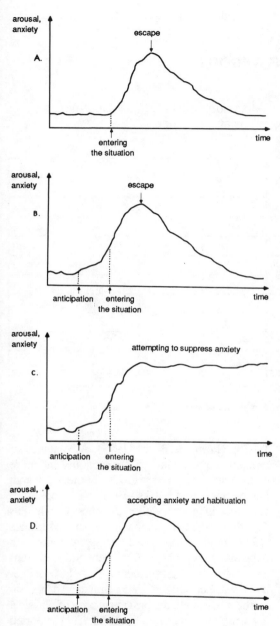

Figure 9.5. Diagrams depicting the course of anxiety and bodily arousal during exposure to anxiety-provoking stimuli under four different circumstances (modified from Bartling et al., 1980). (A) shows the effects of an escape response, (B) shows the additional anxiety caused by anticipation, and (C) shows the effects of attempts to suppress anxiety. (D) shows that anxiety and arousal will decrease (habituation) if the patients confront the situation with the goal of accepting anxiety.

the patients. Planning should be as concrete as possible, and there should be enough time for habituation to occur. Examples for exposure situations include using the elevator in a department store, standing in line at a checkout counter, driving to a deserted place and walking alone there, being enclosed in a small dark room (see Mathews et al., 1981, for a list of common situations). The patients are instructed to stay in each situation until anxiety has decreased by itself. They are not supposed to attempt to reduce anxiety or to distract themselves. The therapist should reinforce the patients for doing the exposure but not for lack of anxiety. In addition, self-reinforcement should be emphasized (Agras, Leitenberg, & Barlow, 1968; Leitenberg, Agras, Allen, Butz, & Edwards, 1975). The presence of the therapist should be faded out as soon as possible. The patients need to understand that they are supposed to learn skills that they can use on their own if anxiety occurs again. This contributes to relapse prevention. Each exposure practice should be recorded on a progress report form, because patients may tend to minimize their accomplishments retrospectively. In addition, it helps in planning and reviewing systematic homework assignments. Figure 9.6 shows an example of such a progress report.

While there is widespread agreement about the basic principles of exposure-based therapies, there are some differences between individual applications. Many treatment programs gradually expose patients, beginning with less difficult (less anxiety-provoking) situations and working toward more difficult ones. Patients thus practice step-by-step to increase their mobility (Barlow & Waddell, 1985; Mathews et al., 1981). This has the advantage that fewer patients reject treatment, and it may also lead to fewer dropouts. On the other hand, some follow-up studies now indicate better long-term outcomes for flooding approaches (Fiegenbaum, 1988; cf. O'Brien & Barlow, 1984). Basic research on animal models points in the same direction (e.g., Richardson, Riccio, & Ress, 1988; Solomon, Kamin, & Wynne, 1953). In flooding, treatment begins with situations that very probably will provoke intense anxiety. Several hours of exposure at a time (prolonged exposure) and on several consecutive days (massed practice) seems to yield the fastest and most certain success (Bartling et al., 1980; Fiegenbaum, 1988; Foa,

Name: _____ Date: _____ Problem area: _____

PROGRESS REPORT

Description of activities	When started/ ended?	Maximum anxiety (0–10)	Anxiety at end (0–10)	Comments

Figure 9.6. Progress report form on which all exposure practices should be recorded. This form is used for monitoring therapist-aided exposure and for homework assignments.

Jameson, Turner, & Payne, 1980; Marks, 1987b; Mathews & Shaw, 1973; Stern & Marks, 1973). The time needed for such massed flooding varies around a median of 10 days, depending on the duration of the individual sessions. In some cases (e.g., in the presence of significant cardiac illness), flooding should not be used for medical reasons.

Furthermore, individual treatment programs differ with respect to the amount of therapist-aided exposure. A large part of the exposure exercises can be performed by the patients either alone or with their spouses. Excellent descriptions of this approach are given by Mathews et al. (1981) and by Barlow and Waddell (1985). In 1987, Ghosh and Marks reported successful attempts to have patients treat themselves using written manuals without any therapist contact.

For a number of issues in the delivery of exposure, the empirical results are inconsistent. Thus, the question of group versus individual therapy has not yet been resolved (reviewed in Marks, 1987b; Thorpe & Burns, 1983). Advantages of group therapy include greater economy and more mutual support among group members. Hand, Lamontagne, and Marks (1974) observed better outcomes in groups with high cohesion, whereas Teasdale, Walsh, Lancashire, and Mathews (1977) could not replicate this result in groups with only moderate cohesion. A frequently encountered difficulty of group therapy is the heterogeneity of problems. Further, Rachman and his co-workers have called a basic principle of classical exposure treatment into question. They reported equal success when agoraphobic patients were allowed to leave the exposure situations as soon as they reached a predetermined high level of anxiety (DeSilva & Rachman, 1984; Rachman, Craske, Tallman, & Solyom, 1986). If other groups replicate this result, it might have theoretical as well as practical implications. Another unresolved issue is whether the efficacy of exposure treatments can be enhanced by additional treatment components.

This is discussed in the later section on alternative treatment options.

The long-term efficacy of exposure treatments for agoraphobia is clearly established by numerous studies with follow-ups of up to 9 years (Burns, Thorpe, & Gosling, 1983; Chambless & Goldstein, 1980; Emmelkamp & Kuipers, 1979; Fiegenbaum, 1988; Goldstein, 1982; Hand, Angenendt, Fischer, & Wilke, 1986; Hand et al., 1974; Lelliott, Marks, Monteiro, Tsakiris, & Noshirvani, 1987; Mathews, Teasdale, Munby, Johnston, & Shaw, 1977; McPherson, Brougham, & McLaren, 1980; Michelson, Mavissakalian, & Marchione, 1985; Munby & Johnston, 1980). The success rate (proportion of patients rated as "improved" or "much improved") averages 75–80% at the end of treatment. Follow-up results show that on the average, gains are maintained, and relapses are rare (Marks, 1987b). An especially high success rate has been reported for a program using a massed flooding approach: Of 104 patients, 78% were totally symptom free and another 19% "moderately" to "highly" improved 5 years after treatment (Fiegenbaum, 1988). The emergence of new symptoms ("symptom substitution") is no more frequent after successful exposure treatment than in the general population (Marks, 1987b; Mathews et al., 1981). The greatest problem of exposure therapy seems to be patients' acceptance. In some studies, up to 20 or 25% of the patients refused treatment or terminated it prematurely (Michelson, 1987; O'Brien & Barlow, 1984). Barlow and Waddell (1985) point out that treatment refusal seems to be less frequent during graded exposure (less than 5% in three studies). The search for predictors of outcome has so far been largely unsuccessful, which may partly be due to the lack of variance caused by high success rates (Chambless & Gracely, 1988; Emmelkamp & van der Hout, 1983; Fischer, Hand & Angenendt, 1988; Marks, 1987b; Mathews et al., 1981). Neither patient variables (sociodemographic, personality, or disorder) nor therapist characteristics show a consistent relationship to outcome. The effect of additional psychological disorders (e.g., alcoholism), however, cannot be estimated because published studies excluded such patients.

The active components of the different treatment programs have not yet been clarified sufficiently. The actual exposure to anxiety-provoking cues seems to be most promising as a specific factor. Marks (1978, 1987b) and Foa and Kozak (1986) have hypothesized that exposure is the common denominator of all successful treatments for anxiety. According to Marks (1987b), the active mechanism involved in exposure is still unknown. Foa and Kozak (1986) explain the efficacy of exposure by hypothesizing a modification of the semantic networks in which phobic stimuli and fear responses are centrally represented. A necessary condition for this modification to occur is an activation of this cognitive structure. This is hypothesized to occur during in vivo exposure. Physiological habituation during exposure (within the treatment session) is assumed to weaken the association between the stimulus (e.g., crowds) and the response (e.g., palpitations) elements of the network. This supposedly facilitates the integration of corrective information ("emotional processing," see Rachman, 1980) about the meaning of the feared elements of the network (e.g., palpitations did not lead to myocardial infarction and are therefore less dangerous than previously assumed). This in turn should lead to reduced physiological responses during the next exposure (habituation between treatment sessions). In addition, so-called nonspecific factors that are perhaps closer to process variables may also contribute to outcome. Relevant process variables are discussed by Howard and Orlinski (1986).

Panic Attacks Without Reliable External Triggers

Until recently, the direct treatment of panic attacks was not a focus of behavior therapy (Barlow & Waddell, 1985; Jacob & Rapport, 1984; Margraf & Ehlers, 1986; Margraf et al., 1986a). Only a few treatment studies on agoraphobia reported results on panic attacks. Jacob and Rapport (1984) found eight such studies. Six of these obtained a reduction in panic attacks as a consequence of treatment focusing on avoidance behavior. Measures of panic were insufficient in these early studies. However, most recent investigations have confirmed the earlier findings of a positive effect of exposure with anxiety-provoking situations on panic attack frequency and intensity in agoraphobics (Chambless, Goldstein, Gallagher, & Bright, 1986; Lelliott et al., 1987; Michelson, et al., 1985; Telch et al., 1985; cf. however, Arnow, Taylor, Agras, & Telch, 1985).

In the late 1980s, a number of authors have reported success in the direct treatment of panic attacks by using behavioral methods. Most programs combine exposure to internal cues (usually bodily sensations) with the teaching both of anxiety-management skills and of cognitive methods that aim at changing the appraisal of the symptoms of anxiety. These programs were primarily developed for patients with panic disorder without phobic avoidance behavior. However, they are a useful addition to the treatment of agoraphobics that also suffer from spontaneous panic attacks because relapses sometimes seem to follow the reoccurrence of one or more panic attacks (Gelder & Marks, 1966).

In a diagnostic phase, information is gathered about possible triggers for panic attacks and other factors that influence the probability of their occurrence (e.g., cognitions, hyperventilation, interpersonal events, eating habits). The patients are then given a rationale for the development of their attacks based on the aforementioned psychophysiological model. Spontaneous, as well as situational, panic attacks are explained as the result of a vicious circle involving the individually relevant bodily sensations (e.g., palpitations, dizziness), cognitions (e.g., "I am losing control"), and behaviors (e.g., hyperventilation). A schematic representation explaining the "vicious circle" is given in Figure 9.7. Depending on the individual symptoms, the appropriate techniques for exposure to anxiety symptoms and their management are deduced as the method to break the vicious circle (see Figure 9.1).

Respiration-based methods should be used if the hyperventilation test is positive (Clark, Salkovskis, & Chalkley, 1985; Salkovskis et al., 1986a). Habituation to feared bodily sensations can be achieved by exposure to the symptoms induced by hyperventilation. The patients repeatedly perform hyperventilation exercises similar to the hyperventilation test (not more than two per treatment session because of potential side effects, such as headache). They are instructed to pay attention to their bodily sensations, cognitions,

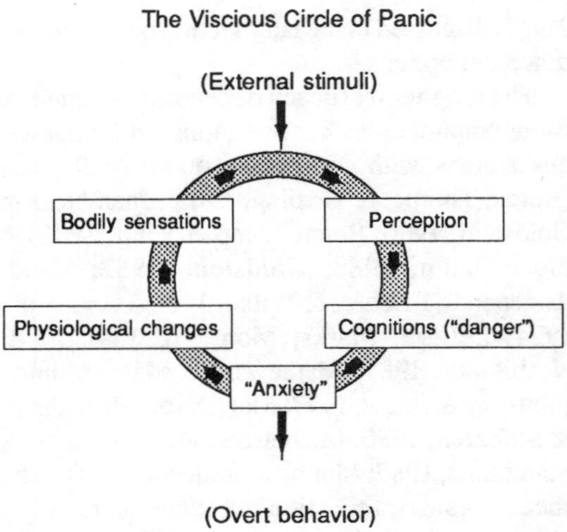

The Viscious Circle of Panic

Figure 9.7. Schematic representation of the vicious circle involved in panic. This diagram is used in explaining the treatment rationale for panic attacks.

and level of anxiety. After a few repetitions, the somatic symptoms are experienced as less dangerous, and anxiety decreases to appropriate levels. Homework assignments using hyperventilation should only be given after the patients have acquired some sense of control over the exercise. Anxiety-increasing thoughts (e.g., "I might faint") may be identified and replaced by more rational alternatives.

In addition, chronic hyperventilation can be treated by respiratory control approaches. In these, patients learn to use slow diaphragmatic breathing as a coping strategy that prevents or interrupts acute hyperventilation and the ensuing panicogenic symptoms. At first, the patients are lying on their bellies with their hands folded under their heads. In this position, abdominal breathing is automatic. The patients concentrate on the breathing movements of their abdomen and thus learn to perceive abdominal breathing. Subsequently, this is practiced while lying on the back, sitting, and eventually standing. Once the patients have mastered diaphragmatic breathing, they are instructed to imagine anxiety-inducing situations or sensations and to use correct breathing as a coping technique. Tape recordings may be useful for breathing exercises at home. A respiration rate of 8–12 cycles per minute has been favorable in most cases. An important caveat in this kind of breathing training is that the patients should not breathe too deeply (danger of hyperventilation).

Palpitations are the most frequent symptom of panic attacks, and consequently, many patients are afraid they may have a cardiac disease. Extreme cases of this fear have in the past been called "cardiac neurosis." Exposure to cardiac symptoms can be conducted by using physical exercises such as climbing stairs, knee-bending, or running. Even mild degrees of exercise lead to increases in heart rate and stroke volume that are much stronger than those that usually accompany panic attacks (Margraf et al., 1987; Taylor et al., 1986). In addition, most patients show low physical fitness, which makes them even more likely to experience palpitations subsequent to physical exertion (Taylor et al., 1987). A comparison of the symptoms accompanying physical exercise and panic attacks facilitates the reappraisal of sensations that are otherwise interpreted catastrophically. In addition, exposure to the patient's own electrocardiogram (EKG) is helpful in some cases.

There are numerous other methods to expose patients to their internal threat cues, depending on the individual symptoms of the patients. For example, Griez and van den Hout (1986) had patients breathe high concentrations of carbon dioxide (CO_2). This leads to symptoms similar to those of hyperventilation. Bonn, Harrison, and Rees (1973) used lactate infusion to produce anxiety symptoms. Other examples include rowing on a remote lake, riding on a roller coaster, or going to the sauna (Bartling et al., 1980).

Many patients fear symptoms or catastrophic consequences of their panic attacks that either cannot be produced voluntarily or cannot be controlled by the patients or therapist (e.g., going crazy, being stared at by strangers, getting in trouble with the boss). In these cases, exposure in sensu is usually a helpful complement to exposure in vivo. Flooding in imagination has been used successfully by Foa (e.g., Steketee & Foa, 1985) in obsessive–compulsives and by Chambless, Foa, Groves, and Goldstein (1982) in agoraphobics. During these exercises, the therapist attempts to induce a high level of anxiety and to encourage the patient to keep the image vivid until anxiety decreases.

In patients who are especially frightened by tachycardias, Sartory and Olajide (1988) have shown vagal innervation techniques to be clinically effective. Sartory and Olajide (1988) used three techniques. For all three techniques, patients are given a heart rate monitor that displays beat-by-beat heart rate. The therapist then instructs the patients about (a) assessment of heart rate, (b) the phenomenon of sinus arrhythmia and its relationship to breathing, and (c) the effects of vagal and sympathetic innervation on cardiac activity. Through stimulation of baroreceptors, vagal activity can be increased, which results in decreased heart rate and stroke volume.

In the first technique, patients have to press slightly on one eye during expiration. The second technique consists of massaging the carotid at about the level of the larynx. The third strategy, the Valsalva maneuver, involves increasing pressure in the chest by means of tensing abdominal and intracostal muscles after a deep inhalation. All techniques are modeled by the therapist and practiced, using the help of the heart rate monitor. As soon as patients have mastered vagal innervation techniques, they are instructed to use them to control panic attacks.

So far, there are fewer studies of the efficacy of behavioral treatment for patients who suffer primarily from panic attacks unrelated to external phobic stimuli than for agoraphobic patients. Many of these few studies are case studies or uncontrolled studies of small samples (Clark et al., 1985; Gitlin, Martin, Shear, Frances, Ball, & Josephson, 1985; Griez & van den Hout, 1983; Rapee, 1985; Salkovskis et al., 1986a; Shear, Ball, Josephson, & Gitlin, 1988; Waddell et al., 1984). In addition, some recent studies compared several treatment conditions (Barlow et al., 1984; Bonn et al., 1984; Griez & van den Hout, 1986; Klosko, Barlow, Tassinari, & Cerny, 1988; Öst, 1988; Sartory & Olajide, 1988). Patients in these studies generally met DSM-III-R criteria for panic disorder, sometimes also meeting criteria for agoraphobia with panic attacks. About 15 sessions was the most common duration of treatment, although there was considerable variation across studies. The most important outcome measures were the frequency and intensity of panic attacks, usually assessed by standardized diaries. The most frequently used treatment components, in addition to giving patients an extensive treatment rationale, were exposure to anxiety symptoms, cognitive techniques (see the following section on relapse prevention measures), and respiratory control.

In all studies, strong and stable improvement or complete remission was obtained for the majority of patients. Gains made by the end of treatment on the average were retained, or patients improved even further during follow-up. In the great majority of patients, panic attacks could be abolished completely. The direct treatment of panic attacks was superior to indirect approaches in the three studies that investigated this topic (Bonn et al., 1984; Griez & van den Hout, 1986; Sartory & Olajide, 1988). Although further controlled studies of larger samples should investigate the active ingredients of the different treatment programs, these results are encouraging in their consistency. They justify the clinical application and further research of the treatment methods presented here.

Special Measures to Prevent Relapse

Relapse prevention is of crucial importance in the treatment of panic and agoraphobia. Both disorders often show a fluctuating course, and periods with frequent attacks may alternate with periods of relatively few complaints. However, complete spontaneous remission is very rare once the disorder has persisted for a year or more (Marks, 1987b). The long-term outcome is unfavorable (Coryell, Noyes, & Clancy, 1982). In a large epidemiological study, over 90% of panic patients still met DSM-III diagnostic criteria at a 7-year follow-up (Wittchen, 1988). Schapira, Roth, Kerr, and Gurney (1972) and Coryell, Noyes, and Clancy (1983) observed significantly poorer long-term outcome in panic and agoraphobia than in major depression.

A number of strategies are used to prevent relapse:

1. First, the therapist must emphasize that treatment means learning skills for how to deal with anxiety and avoidance. These techniques will help the patients to confront situations that have not been practiced in therapy (generalization). In the same way, they will help patients to confront the reoccurrence of anxiety (relapse).

Thus, the patients are supposed to learn skills that they can use independently outside of the original treatment setting.

2. It is useful to predict to the patients that fluctuations of anxiety or relapses will occur. These should not be misinterpreted as catastrophes because relapses are not all-or-none phenomena (i.e., "one panic attack and the whole treatment was useless"). Fluctuations in anxiety and avoidance behavior relapses are explained on the basis of a diathesis–stress model. This is introduced to the patients as a motivation to reduce stressors and conflicts in their everyday environment.

3. Sometimes, other unresolved problems are associated with relapse (e.g., marital distress). If such a major problem becomes apparent toward the end of the treatment of the anxiety disorder, it should be addressed directly in additional treatment measures.

4. Homework assignments in as many different and realistic situations as possible contribute to generalization of treatment gains as well as to relapse prevention. Homework assignments should focus on situations that are relevant for the patients' everyday lives.

5. Especially toward the end of treatment, the therapist should enable the patients to make as many decisions and take as much responsibility in treatment planning as possible. The relevance of self-reinforcement should be emphasized. It is often necessary to teach patients adequate self-reinforcement through coaching and modeling.

6. Finally, additional treatment sessions after the end of the original therapy (booster sessions) aid in preventing relapse.

Case Illustration

Ms. P. sought help because of increased impairment due to agoraphobia and panic attacks. She was 31 years old, not married, and still living in her parents' home; she had been working as a secretary until her agoraphobia forced her to leave her job. Three years before coming to us, the patient had been hospitalized because of surgery due to a sports injury. The operation went well, and after 3 weeks she was released. While she was waiting at the bus stop on her way home she smoked a cigarette and had a cup of coffee. In the hospital, she had not had any coffee or cigarettes. All of a sudden, she felt her heart racing at a tremendous rate. Her hands got sweaty, and she felt that she was going to die right there. After about 20 minutes, the attack subsided and she had no trouble riding on the bus. The next day, she went to see her physician who, after a series of tests, told her that her health was perfectly okay (after all, she had been doing sports on a regular basis, playing on a basketball team). However, a few weeks later, she had another strong anxiety attack while shopping. She became very frightened of having another attack. Because she felt safe only in her home, she started to avoid going out. After a few weeks, even the thought of leaving home would trigger intense terror. She lost her job and her boyfriend, and her mother had to take turns doing the shopping for her. In return, she took care of the house. For 2 years, she did not leave the house once. Then her grandfather, whom she loved very much, implored her to join the family for his 80th birthday. After much initial fear, she had her boyfriend drive her to her grandparents' house. To her great surprise, she was not anxious during the party. After this event, she felt the courage to leave home again. Although she did not resume work and carefully avoided anything that, in her opinion, might trigger another anxiety attack, she started to go shopping again. However, when a friend fainted during a commonplace visit to a restaurant, she relapsed completely. Other than her family physician, she had never seen anyone for treatment of her anxiety problems. She had heard about our treatment program on the local radio.

After a brief telephone contact, she was sent a package of questionnaires and screening forms. Her scores on the MI (Chambless et al., 1985) were 3.6 for avoidance alone and 2.8 for avoidance accompanied. Scores on the ACQ and BSQ were 2.8 and 3.2, respectively (Chambless et al., 1984). The FQ (Marks & Mathews, 1979) revealed that she suffered not only from agoraphobia (FQ subscore: 31) but also from blood-injury phobia (FQ subscore: 21). Her FQ subscore for social phobia was only 12, which is somewhat lower than usual for agoraphobics. Slight depres-

sion was evidenced by a score of 15 points on the Beck Depression Inventory (Beck, Ward, Mendelson, Mock, & Erbaugh, 1961). In the clinical interview, she met DSM-III-R criteria for agoraphobia with panic attacks. When asked to describe a common panic attack, she gave the following account:

All of a sudden, I feel sensations in my body, my heart races, and I get nervous. I breathe too much and at the same time feel like I cannot get enough air. My hands are all sweaty. I feel like going to the bathroom, and then I get the shakes. Often, things around me don't appear the way they should, as if I were far away from them. Then I get afraid that I might lose control totally, that I might just slip away. I think I'm going to die, I can't breathe, I'm never going to make it. Sometimes I am afraid that I am going crazy. I have had to go to the emergency room because I have not been able to control it. If I am with someone I know, someone I trust, it goes away faster.

There was no indication of alcoholism or drug abuse, and she had switched to decaffeinated coffee. Smoking was down to about 10 cigarettes per day. Eating patterns were reported to be normal. A physical examination again revealed no signs of organic causation. There had been no additional life stress preceding the onset of the anxiety problems other than some minor trouble at work involving a new boss. About 4 months before her hospitalization, an uncle had died of a heart attack. Ms. P. described her childhood and family background as "average" and her relationship to her boyfriend as "fine." After the initial assessment session, she was instructed to keep a diary of all anxiety experiences for a week until the next appointment.

In the second session, the diary was reviewed, and an anxiety and avoidance hierarchy was constructed. The hierarchy is displayed in Table 9.1. In her diary, Ms. P. had reported two anxiety attacks. She insisted that she did not have more attacks because she successfully avoided anxiety-provoking situations. The two attacks that did occur came unexpectedly. Both attacks started with palpitations and a feeling of dyspnea. Her main treatment goals were "to get rid of anxiety and be able to move freely" and resume working. We then conducted a hyperventilation test and Ms. P. responded strongly to it. She terminated the hyperventilation after about 80 seconds and reported 8 out of 15 panic symptoms

TABLE 9.1.   Anxiety and Avoidance Hierarchy of Ms. P.

Situation or sensation	Anxiety rating[a] (0–10)	Avoidance rating[a] (0–10)
Racing heart and difficulty breathing	10	10
Using public transportation (train, bus, subway; unaccompanied)	10	10
Shopping at a crowded supermarket/department store (unaccompanied)	9	10
Being alone in small enclosed rooms	8	10
Eating in a crowded restaurant (unaccompanied)	8	10
Walking away from home (10 minutes, unaccompanied)	8	10
Driving on freeway (unaccompanied)	7	8
Driving on highway in unfamiliar places (unaccompanied)	6	8
Eating in an empty restaurant (unaccompanied)	6	8
Shopping in empty supermarket (unaccompanied)	6	8
Shopping in small local store (unaccompanied)	5	7
Being alone at home	3	3

[a]On the anxiety rating, 0 is labeled as "not at all," and 10 is labeled "extreme." The respective labels for the avoidance rating are "never" and "always."

but only one control item (sore throat). The effects of hyperventilation were rated as very similar to a naturally occurring panic attack. They were not rated as identical "because I knew what was going on" and that "you would not let me die here." Although she felt shaky after the test, she also reported being glad that we had discovered a possible cause of her symptoms.

We then gave her a rationale for the development of her symptoms that was based on the psychophysiological model of panic attacks. Her initial attack was explained as an anxiety response to palpitations induced by the first cigarette and coffee after a period of abstinence. Later anxiety attacks were explained as a consequence of her fear of fear and her hyperventilation. It was clear to the patient that her avoidance behavior followed from a fear of having anxiety attacks, although she indicated being somewhat scared by certain situations in themselves. From this rationale, we deduced a treatment plan emphasizing unlearning fear of fear. We proposed to carry out a massive flooding program, including exposure in vivo to agoraphobic situations and bodily symptoms of anxiety attacks, as well as exposure in sensu to the feared consequences of being anxious and having palpitations and dyspnea. We asked her not to agree to the treatment at once. Instead, she was instructed to go home and think about it carefully because treatment would be very demanding and would require full cooperation. She was told to call us back within a week

and to let us know whether she wanted to undergo the treatment.

After 5 days, she called and said that she was willing to participate if we could guarantee that she would not die from the anxiety suffered during flooding. We told her that we could not give her a guarantee but that we and other colleagues around the world had treated many patients with such methods and that we were not aware of any deaths as a consequence of treatment. We told her that the average heart rate increase during anxiety attacks was much smaller than that during physical exercise such as climbing stairs, which she regularly did in her home. She then decided to participate, and we scheduled an appointment for specific treatment planning. During that session, we agreed on the stimuli for exposure in vivo and on a 5-day period during which the intensive part of exposure was to be carried out. The procedures during exposure were explained carefully. The patient knew that she would not be allowed either to decide on the sequence of exposure targets or to avoid any of them. However, she was assured that only situations to which she had agreed in advance would occur, and that there would be no surprise situations. Exposure situations included all items from her anxiety–avoidance hierarchy and voluntary hyperventilation. It was made clear that the initial goal of exposure was to get anxious. Treatment would therefore start with a situation that would induce strong anxiety with a high degree of probability. In addition, Ms. P. was instructed to focus on her anxiety, accept it, and attempt to intensify it as much as possible. Her boyfriend was allowed to drive her to our office and pick her up again, but he could not be with her during exposure.

On the first day of her intensive exposure in vivo (Monday), Ms. P. arrived at 9 a.m. She was first confined in a small windowless room in another part of the building. This lasted 35 minutes. She did not know in advance how long she would have to stay there. To her surprise, she reported having experienced only very little anxiety during confinement (a "3" on the progress report). We told her in a concerned way that this was a problem because the goal of treatment was to get as anxious as possible in order to experience how even the worst anxiety does not lead to catastrophic consequences and decreases with time. The next step was to take a train to a nearby city (about 1 hour), with the therapist being in a compartment at the other end of the train. Her peak anxiety during this was 10. Although it decreased to 8 several times, it always went up again. The therapist praised her for confronting the situation and for completing the progress report. Ms. P. stated that "she felt scared to death but might as well go on with the treatment." She then had to travel on the subway on her own for 2 hours without interruption while the therapist stayed at the central station. When she reported back for lunch, she felt excited because her anxiety level had gone down from an initial 10 to a 6 and she had not been on a subway for years. Lunch was taken in a crowded self-service restaurant that involved standing in a long line. Nevertheless, she ate much more than she had thought possible because she felt exhausted.

After lunch, she traveled again on the subway for another 90 minutes until her anxiety level had gone down to 5. She was then sent into a crowded street with several large department stores and instructed to enter the biggest one, take the elevator to the top floor, stay on the top floor until her anxiety had gone down at least 2 points, and return via the emergency staircase. By this time, the rush hour traffic had started, and the store was full of people. Although her anxiety level again went up to 10, it took only a few minutes until it decreased. However, on her way down the stairs, she experienced another strong anxiety attack accompanied by pounding heartbeat and shortness of breath. She was still gasping for air ("I can't breathe") when she met the therapist at the

exit of the store. The therapist gave her a paradoxical instruction, telling her to exhale completely and to hold her breath as long as possible. After this was repeated twice, she felt no more dyspnea. The first day was ended by taking the train back home. The therapist instructed Ms. P. to focus on her anxiety during the train ride and to compare it to her experience in the morning. It turned out that her anxiety level never went higher than 7 and was at 5 most of the time. Upon arrival at the office, the progress report was reviewed and Ms. P. expressed amazement that she had been able to do all these exercises. The therapist praised her cooperation and told her that she had made great progress and well earned her rest. She was advised, however, that her anxiety would be worse again at the beginning of the second day but that the increase was a common phenomenon and would be overcome faster than on the first day.

The next day, Ms. P. said that she had slept "like a rock," as if she had been doing rigorous physical work all day long. Because she had been very cooperative, we decided that it was possible to send her out on her own. She was instructed to repeat the program of the first day and to call in every 2 hours to report on her progress and possible difficulties. The phone calls showed that she indeed experienced a return of anxiety back to initial levels while traveling on the subway but that it took only about 20 minutes to get back to the level at which she had ended on Monday. After less than 2 hours, her anxiety dropped as low as 3, and she felt that she would profit more from exposing herself to the department stores. The stores proved to be more difficult, but she still managed to stay in them until her anxiety decreased to 5. On the train on her way back, she felt "exhausted but relieved." When reviewing her progress report, we emphasized the differences between the first and the second day.

On Wednesday, Ms. P. was driven to a nearby forest and asked to walk away on a dirt road across a rather steep hill. Though the area was a popular spot for weekend hikes, it was deserted on this normal working day. The hike took about 2 1/2 hours. On the other side of the hill was a bus stop. Ms. P. was instructed to take the bus to a small town about 30 minutes away and eat there in an unfamiliar restaurant before taking a bus back to the office. She did so. For Thursday and Friday, the task was to take a train to a large city about 8 hours away, spend the night in a hotel, and come back on Friday afternoon to discuss progress. During the meeting on Friday afternoon, Ms. P. stated that she felt better than in years although she had slept very poorly in a noisy hotel near the central station. It was agreed that treatment should continue twice weekly, focusing on hyperventilation and imagery exercises. In addition, Ms. P. was given the assignment to practice every day one situation or activity that she had previously avoided. She was given free choice of situations to be practiced but was asked to record all activities on a progress report form.

The two sessions in the second week started with a review of homework assignments. Then a hyperventilation task (60 cycles for 3 minutes) was given. Ms. P. was instructed to concentrate on the bodily sensations arising from hyperventilation. While she terminated the first hyperventilation after roughly 2 minutes and reported strong anxiety, she was able to complete the second and all further ones. During the second hyperventilation, her peak anxiety level dropped to 6. In the second half of the sessions, a detailed script for an imagery exercise centering around her fear of losing control and going crazy was developed. Because she described herself as having a vivid fantasy, no imagery practice was given. Instead, the script was directly used for two sessions of exposure in sensu in the third treatment week. The actual imagery practice lasted about 15 minutes each time. The script involved a description of having an anxiety attack while standing in line in a crowded supermarket, losing control, crying loudly with all the other people watching her, and finally being taken away by two men in white uniforms while a neighbor was pointing at her saying "we knew it all along." Ms. P. felt quite anxious, initially rating 8, but the anxiety decreased rapidly down to 2.

Because Ms. P. reported that she still frequently experienced breathing difficulty, we introduced a training in diaphragmatic breathing in Week 3. Ms. P. was instructed to practice slow diaphragmatic breathing once a day for 20 minutes, using a prerecorded tape. After 1 week, she reported feeling comfortable with this technique. She was then told to imagine anxiety-inducing situations or sensations and to use correct breathing as a coping technique. In the meantime, the frequency of practicing self-exposure had decreased because she reported no longer feeling anxious beyond a level of 2 or 3. In the fifth week,

it was decided that Ms. P. was now able to continue treatment on her own. Her scores on the various questionnaires had decreased considerably (FQ-agoraphobia: 8, FQ-blood-injury phobia: 11, MI—avoidance alone 1.4, ACQ: 1.7, BSQ: 1.3). We scheduled a final appointment and asked Ms. P.'s boyfriend to join. During the session, possible changes in life-style resulting from the cure of Ms. P.'s agoraphobia were discussed. We addressed not only positive effects but also asked for possible negative consequences. Neither Ms. P. nor her boyfriend were concerned about adverse effects on their relationship. One of their immediate goals was to take a vacation in a southern, sunnier country (involving air travel of about 4.5 hours each way). After their return, Ms. P. should attempt to find a job as a secretary because she had liked working and the additional income would be very welcome. We emphasized that anxiety levels would continue to fluctuate and that it was possible that there would be reoccurrences of intense anxiety. In these cases, Ms. P. should immediately use the techniques she had learned in treatment and expose herself to any feared situations or sensations until anxiety decreased. A follow-up appointment was scheduled to occur 3 months later.

At follow-up, Ms. P. had made further gains. She had practiced additional activities that had not been addressed during treatment, such as driving on freeways and in unfamiliar places. Although she had not practiced diaphragmatic breathing on a regular basis, she had not experienced sudden unexplained palpitations or dyspnea. She had found a job with her old employer. However, she reported some trouble at work. Specifically, she did not know how to tell her boss that she was insecure about working with the word processor that had been newly installed. A role play was used to practice telling her boss that she needed additional training, as she had not worked with computers before.

ALTERNATIVE TREATMENT OPTIONS

The treatments described in the preceding case have meant great progress for many patients with these severe and disabling anxiety disorders. However, not all patients accept these treatments; some drop out before progress is achieved, and some do not profit from them. The search for ways to further enhance treatment success has motivated many clinicians and researchers to turn to other psychotherapeutic and pharmacological treatments as complements or alternatives to exposure-based methods.

Other Psychotherapeutic Interventions

It is not yet certain whether additional treatment components enhance the efficacy of exposure-based treatments. Both the explicit focus on giving a treatment rationale and the reappraisal of anxiety symptoms as not being dangerous are cognitive features common to all therapeutic approaches discussed here. Many therapists also modify their patients' self-instructions and identify anxiety-increasing cognitions (e.g., possible catastrophical consequences of panic attacks) in order to replace them with more rational alternatives (e.g., concentration on real aspects of the patients' current situation). While this is often done within an exposure-therapy framework, more specific cognitive techniques, for instance, those that rely on Beck's work (e.g., Beck et al., 1985), have also been applied. Cerny, Klosko, and Barlow (1984) and Clark et al. (1985) developed specific applications of Beck's approach for the treatment of panic patients. The patients are acquainted with a number of standard cognitive techniques, including identification and monitoring of dysfunctional thoughts, exploring alternatives, analyzing faulty logic, reattribution, decatastrophizing, discovering help factors, testing hypotheses, and self-instruction training. These techniques are not only applied with respect to background stress but are also specifically aimed at the appraisal of physiological triggers for panic. Treatments that use such techniques have been very successful (Barlow et al., 1984; Clark et al., 1985; Klosko et al., 1988; Waddell, Barlow, & O'Brien, 1984). However, they were always given in combination with exposure methods, relaxation, or other strategies. A review of published outcome studies leads Marks (1987b) to conclude that an additional independent effect of specific cognitive techniques (e.g., problem-solving training) has not yet been well supported.

Chambless and Goldstein (1980; Chambless et al., 1986) attempt to integrate elements from other therapeutic approaches in order to increase treatment efficacy, especially in agoraphobics with personality disorders. Arnow et al. (1985) found that couples communication or relaxation training further enhanced the results of successful exposure therapy in agoraphobics. Family systems therapists frequently predict that successful exposure treatment will adversely affect marital relationships. However, this appears to be the exception rather than the rule. For most couples, marital satisfaction increases after successful treatment of agoraphobia, although an initially bad marriage is related to poor treatment outcome in some cases (Cobb, Matthews, Childs-Clark, & Blowers, 1984; Himadi, Cerny, Barlow, Cohen, & O'Brien, 1986; Lelliott et al., 1987).

Behavior therapists use paradoxical intention, with similar goals to exposure methods (Ascher, 1981; Chambless & Goldstein, 1980). This method has been evaluated empirically in agoraphobics by Mavissakalian, Michelson, Greenwald, Kornblith, and Greenwald (1983) and by Michelson et al. (1985; Michelson, Mavissakalian, Marchione, Dancu, & Greenwald, 1986). In general, therapeutic progress comes more slowly with paradoxical intention than with the other aforementioned behavioral techniques, and it depends on an especially good therapeutic relationship (Michelson et al., 1985, 1986). In contrast to the approach of strategic family therapy, the patients are informed about the goals of paradoxical intention. It is presented as a way to break the vicious circle underlying panic attacks and avoidance behavior. The patients are instructed to attempt to produce anxiety voluntarily or, if this is not possible, to try to stay anxious as long as possible whenever anxiety occurs. In this way, anxiety is not experienced as totally undesirable and catastrophic, but rather as an actively wanted consequence of their own effort. For some patients, it is helpful to exaggerate their sensations and fears humorously, as suggested by Lazarus' (1971) "blow up" technique. Paradoxical instructions can also be used as coping strategies in dealing with specific symptoms or feared consequences during exposure to anxiety-provoking situations in agoraphobics (Chambless & Goldstein, 1980). However, because of the higher demands on the patients' sense of humor, their patience, and the therapeutic relationship, we suggest that paradoxical intention not be used as a routine treatment. In our view, it is especially appropriate in cases where reliable external or internal triggers for anxiety and avoidance behavior cannot be established.

Pharmacological Treatment

Most patients who come to treatment because of panic attacks or agoraphobia have experienced a series of unsuccessful chemotherapeutic attempts. In addition, medication abuse is a frequent complication. One might infer from this that pharmacological treatments are not effective for these conditions. More thorough questioning, however, usually reveals that the patients have not been treated with what is currently considered optimal drug treatment. Oftentimes, benzodiazepines are prescribed because they are considered safer than other drugs. The usual instruction is to take the drug intermittently ("only when needed") in order to reduce the danger of dependency. However, this approach is not favorable in the treatment of panic and agoraphobia for both pharmacological and learning theory reasons. The optimal drug treatment entails the prescription of high doses of tricyclic antidepressants (especially imipramine, 100 to 300 mg/day), monoamine oxidase inhibitors (e.g., phenelzine, 45–60 mg/day), or high potency benzodiazepines (e.g., alprazolam, 4–10 mg/day) (Ballenger, 1986). These drugs have to be given at consistently high doses for varying lengths of time before a good response is achieved (Ballenger, 1986; Marks, 1983; Telch, Tearnan, & Taylor, 1983).

We cannot address in depth here the difficult issue of whether behavioral treatments should be combined with pharmacological treatments. Some authors have observed short-term positive effects of combining exposure therapy with antidepressants (Mavissakalian, 1988; Mavissakalian & Michelson, 1986). Other authors have not found additional benefits (Marks, 1987b). There are a number of problems with the drug treatments. First, the long-term outcome of these therapies is not well known (Grunhaus, Gloger, & Weisturb, 1981; Marks, 1983, 1987b; Telch et al., 1983). Relapse rates after discontinuation may be high

(Ballenger, 1986; Fyer et al., 1987; Marks, 1983, 1987b; Pecknold & Swinson, 1986; Pohl, Berchou, & Rainey, 1982). Follow-up studies have usually involved patients treated with drugs plus some kind of psychological therapy. Two such studies found no difference between agoraphobics treated with behavior therapy plus imipramine or plus a placebo up to 2 years (Mavissakalian & Michelson, 1986) or up to 5 years (Lelliott et al., 1987) after treatment. Tyrer and Steinberg (1975) reported on a 1-year follow-up of 26 agoraphobics. Blind comparisons showed no significant differences between patients treated with phenelzine or with a placebo. Despite the intention to stop all drugs at the end of treatment, 10 of 13 phenelzine patients continued to take it, and 3 (23%) were still taking it at the 1-year follow-up because of a return of symptoms on stopping or reducing the drug.

Difficulties in discontinuing the drug are especially frequent when benzodiazepines are used (Fyer et al., 1987; Pecknold & Swinson, 1986). In a partial analysis of a large cross-national collaborative panic disorder study, Pecknold and Swinson (1986) found that only 57% of their alprazolam patients completed regular withdrawal. Among those who did, the proportion of patients with zero panic attacks dropped from roughly 60% at peak dose to about 40% 2 weeks after discontinuation of the drug. In contrast, among the 43% of the placebo-treated patients who completed withdrawal, the number of panic-free patients rose from about 40% to 50% 2 weeks after stopping the drug. Thus, placebo-treated patients did significantly worse only at peak drug dose, but significantly better at 2-week follow-up. While the mechanism of action of drug therapy remains unknown, the relatively high proportion of positive responses to placebo (e.g., Dager, Cowley, & Dunner, 1987; Mavissakalian, 1987; Pecknold & Swinson, 1986) points to a significant contribution of nonpharmacological effects. Based on (a) the lack of confirmation for long-term benefits of drug treatments, (b) the problems with discontinuation, and (c) the possible side effects of the drugs, it is suggested that patients first receive an adequate trial with behavior therapy alone. Only if this does not yield sufficient results should additional drug treatment be instituted.

REFERENCES

Agras, W. S., Leitenberg, H., & Barlow, D. H. (1968). Social reinforcement in the modification of agoraphobia. *Archives of General Psychiatry, 19,* 423–427.

Agras, W. S., Sylvester, D., & Oliveau, D. (1969). The epidemiology of common fears and phobias. *Comprehensive Psychiatry, 10,* 151–156.

American Psychiatric Association (Ed.). (1987). *Diagnostic and statistical manual of mental disorders,* (3rd ed., rev.) (DSM-III-R). Washington, DC: Author.

Anderson, D. J., Noyes, R., & Crowe, R. R. (1984). A comparison of panic disorder and generalized anxiety disorder. *American Journal of Psychiatry, 141,* 572–575.

Angst, J., & Dobler-Mikola, A. (1985a). The Zurich study: V. Anxiety and phobia in young adults. *European Archives of Psychiatry and Neurological Sciences, 235,* 171–178.

Angst, J., & Dobler-Mikola, A. (1985b). The Zurich study: VI. A continuum from depression to anxiety disorders? *European Archives of Psychiatry and Neurological Sciences, 235,* 179–186.

Angst, J., Vollrath, M., Merinkangas, K. R., & Ernst, C. (1987). Comorbidity of anxiety and depression in the Zurich cohort study of young adults. Paper presented at the Conference on Symptom Comorbidity in Anxiety and Depressive Disorders, Tuxedo, NY, September, 1987).

Arnow, B. A., Taylor, C. B., Agras, W. S., & Telch, M. J. (1985). Enhancing agoraphobia treatment outcome by changing couple communication patterns. *Behavior Therapy, 16,* 452–467.

Ascher, L. M. (1981). Employing paradoxical intention in the treatment of agoraphobia. *Behaviour Research and Therapy, 19,* 533–542.

Baker, W. B., & White, L. H. (1986). Episodic hypertension secondary to panic disorder. *Archives of Internal Medicine, 146,* 1129–1130.

Ballenger, J. C. (1986). Pharmacotherapy of the panic disorders. *Psychopharmacology Bulletin, Supplement 6, 47,* 27–32.

Barlow, D. H. (1986). Behavioral conception and treatment of panic. *Psychopharmacology Bulletin, 22,* 803–806.

Barlow, D. H., Cohen, A. S., Waddell, M. T., Vermilyea, B. B., Klosko, J. S., Blanchard, E. B., & DiNardo, P. A. (1984). Panic and generalized anxiety disorders: Nature and treatment. *Behavior Therapy, 15,* 431–449.

Barlow, D. H., Vermilyea, J., Blanchard, E. B., Vermilyea, B. B., DiNardo, P. A., & Cerny, J. A. (1985). The phenomenon of panic. *Journal of Abnormal Psychology, 94,* 320–328.

Barlow, D. H., & Waddell, M. T. (1985). Agoraphobia. In D. H. Barlow (Ed.), *Clinical handbook of psychological disorders.* New York: Guilford.

Bartling, G., Fiegenbaum, W., & Krause, R. (1980). *Reizüberflutung: Theorie und praxis.* Stuttgart: Kohlhammer.

Beck, A. T., Emery, G., & Greenberg, R. L. (1985). *Anxiety disorders and phobias—A cognitive perspective.* New York: Basic Books.

Beck, A. T., Ward, C. H., Mendelson, M., Mock, J., & Erbaugh, J. (1961). An inventory for measuring depression. *Archives of General Psychiatry, 4,* 561–571.

Bibb, J. L., & Chambless, D. L. (1986). Alcohol use and abuse among diagnosed agoraphobics. *Behaviour Research and Therapy, 24,* 49–58.

Bonn, J. A., Harrison, J., & Rees, W. (1973). Lactate-induced anxiety: Therapeutic application. *British Journal of Psychiatry, 119,* 468–470.

Bonn, J. A., Readhead, C. P. A., & Timmons, B. A. (1984). Enhanced adaptive behavioral response in agoraphobic patients pretreated with breathing retraining. *Lancet,* 665–669.

Boyd, J. H. (1986). Use of mental health services for treatment of panic disorder. *American Journal of Psychiatry, 143,* 1569–1574.

Bregman, E. (1934). An attempt to modify the emotional attitude of infants by the conditioned response technique. *Journal of Genetic Psychology, 95,* 169–198.

Burns, L. E., Thorpe, G. L., Cavallero, A., & Gosling, J. (1983, November). *Agoraphobia eight years after behavioral treatment: A follow-up study with interview, questionnaire and behavioral data.* Presented at the 17th Annual Meeting of the Association for the Advancement of Behavior Therapy/World Congress of Behavior Therapy, Washington, DC.

Cameron, O. G., Thyer, B. A., Nesse, R. M., & Curtis, G. C. (1986). Symptom profiles of patients with DSM-III anxiety disorders. *American Journal of Psychiatry, 143,* 1132–1137.

Cerny, J., Klosko, J. S., & Barlow, D. H. (1984). *Cognitive therapy manual.* Unpublished manuscript, Phobia and Anxiety Disorders Clinic, State University of New York at Albany.

Chambless, D. L., Caputo, G. C., Bright, P., & Gallagher, R. (1984). Assessment of fear of fear in agoraphobics: The Body Sensations Questionnaire and the Agoraphobic Cognitions Questionnaire. *Journal of Consulting and Clinical Psychology, 52,* 1090–1097.

Chambless, D. L., Caputo, G. C., Jasin, S. E., Gracely, E. J., & Williams, C. (1985). The mobility inventory for agoraphobia. *Behaviour Research and Therapy, 23,* 35–44.

Chambless, D. L., Foa, E. B., Groves, G. A., & Goldstein, A. J. (1982). Exposure and communication training in the treatment of agoraphobia. *Behaviour Research and Therapy, 20,* 219–231.

Chambless, D. L., & Goldstein, A. J. (1980). Agoraphobia. In A. J. Goldstein & E. B. Foa (Eds.), *Handbook of behavioral interventions: A clinical guide.* New York: Wiley.

Chambless, D. L., Goldstein, A. J., Gallagher, R., & Bright, P. (1986). Integrating behavior therapy and psychotherapy in the treatment of agoraphobia. *Psychotherapy, 23,* 150–159.

Chambless, D. L., & Gracely, E. J. (1988). Prediction of outcome following in vivo exposure treatment of agoraphobia. In I. Hand & H.-U. Wittchen (Eds.), *Treatments of panic and phobias.* Berlin: Springer.

Clark, D. M. (1986). A cognitive approach to panic. *Behaviour Research and Therapy, 24,* 461–470.

Clark, D. M., Salkovskis, P. M., & Chalkley, A. J. (1985). Respiratory control as a treatment for panic attacks. *Journal of Experimental Psychiatry and Behavior Therapy, 16,* 23–30.

Clark, D. M., Salkovskis, P. M., Gelder, M., Koehler, K., Martin, M., Anastasiades, P., Hackman, A., Middleton, H., & Jeavonne, A. (1988). Test of a cognitive theory of panic. In I. Hand & H.-U. Wittchen (Eds.), *Treatments of panic and phobias.* Berlin: Springer.

Cobb, J. P., Mathews, A. M., Childs-Clark, A., & Blowers, C. M. (1984). The spouse as cotherapist in the treatment of agoraphobia. *British Journal of Psychiatry, 144,* 282–287.

Corcoran, K., & Fischer, J. (1987). *Measures for clinical practice: A sourcebook.* New York: Free Press.

Coryell, W., Noyes, R., & Clancy, J. (1982). Excess mortality in panic disorder. *Archives of General Psychiatry, 39,* 701–703.

Coryell, W., Noyes, R., & Clancy, J. (1983). Panic disorder and primary unipolar depression. *Journal of Affective Disorders, 5,* 311–317.

Dager, S. R., Cowley, D. S., & Dunner, D. L. (1987). Biological markers in panic states: Lactate-induced panic and mitral valve prolapse. *Biological Psychiatry, 22,* 339–359.

de Silva, P., & Rachman, S. (1984). Does escape behavior strengthen agoraphobic avoidance? A preliminary study. *Behaviour Research and Therapy, 22,* 87–91.

DiNardo, P. A., O'Brien, G. T., Barlow, D. H., Waddell, M. T., & Blanchard, E. B. (1983). Reliability of DSM-III anxiety disorder categories using a new structured interview. *Archives of General Psychiatry, 40,* 1070–1074.

Ehlers, A., & Margraf, J. (1989). The psychophysiological model of panic. In P. M. G. Emmelkamp, W. Everaerd, F. Kraaymaat, & M. van Son (Eds.), *Anxiety disorders.* Amsterdam: Swets.

Ehlers, A., Margraf, J., & Roth, W. T. (1986). Experimental induction of panic attacks. In I. Hand & H.-U. Wittchen (Eds.), *Panic and phobias.* Berlin: Springer.

Ehlers, A., Margraf, J., & Roth, W. T. (1988a). Interaction of expectancy and physiological stressors in a laboratory model of panic. In D. Hellhammer, I. Florin, & H. Weiner (Eds.), *Neurobiological approaches to human disease.* Toronto: Huber.

Ehlers, A., Margraf, J., & Roth, W. T. (1988b). Selective information processing, interoception, and panic attacks. In I. Hand & H.-U. Wittchen (Eds.), *Treatments of panic and phobias.* Berlin: Springer.

Ehlers, A., Margraf, J., Roth, W. T., Taylor, C. B., & Birbaumer, N. (1988c). Anxiety induced by false heart rate feedback in patients with panic disorder. *Behaviour Research and Therapy, 26,* 1–11.

Emmelkamp, P. M. G., & Kuipers, A. C. M. (1979). Agoraphobia: A follow-up study four years after treatment. *British Journal of Psychiatry, 134,* 352–355.

Emmelkamp, P. M. G., & van der Hout, A. (1983). Failures in treating agoraphobia. In E. B. Foa & P. M. G. Emmelkamp (Eds.), *Failures in behavior therapy.* New York: Wiley.

English, H. B. (1929). Three cases of the "conditioned fear response." *Journal of Abnormal Psychology, 34,* 221–225.

Fiegenbaum, W. (1988). Longterm efficacy of graded and massed exposure in agoraphobics. In I. Hand & H.-U. Wittchen (Eds.), *Treatments of panic and phobias.* Berlin: Springer.

Fischer, M., Hand, I., & Angenendt, J. (1988). Failures in exposure treatment of agoraphobia: An exploratory analysis. In I. Hand & H.-U. Wittchen (Eds.), *Treatments of panic and phobias.* Berlin: Springer.

Foa, E. B., Jameson, J. S., Turner, R. M., & Payne, L. L.

(1980). Massed vs. spaced exposure sessions in the treatment of agoraphobia. *Behaviour Research and Therapy, 18*, 333–338.

Foa, E. B., & Kozak, M. (1986). Emotional processing of fear: Exposure to corrective information. *Psychological Bulletin, 99*, 20–35.

Freedman, R., Ianni, B., Ettedgui, E., & Puthezhath, N. (1985). Ambulatory monitoring of panic disorder. *Archives of General Psychiatry, 42*, 244–248.

Freud, S. (1947). Über die Berechtigung, von der Neurasthenie einen bestimmten Symptomenkomplex als "Angstneurose" abzutrennen. Neurologisches Zentralblatt, 2. In S. Freud, *Gesammelte Werke. Band I.* London: Imago. (Original work published in 1895.)

Freud, S. (1947b). Wege der psychoanalytischen Therapie. In S. Freud, *Gesammelte Werke. Band I.* London: Imago.

Fyer, A. J., Liebowitz, M. R., Gorman, J. M., Campeas, R., Levin, A., Davies, S. O., Goetz, D., & Klein, D. F. (1987). Discontinuation of alprazolam treatment in panic patients. *American Journal of Psychiatry, 144*, 304–308.

Garssen, B., Van Veenendaal, W., & Bloemink, R. (1983). Agoraphobia and the hyperventilation syndrome. *Behaviour Research and Therapy, 21*, 643–649.

Gelder, M. G., & Marks, I. (1966). Severe agoraphobia: A controlled prospective trial of behavior therapy. *British Journal of Psychiatry, 112*, 309–319.

Ghosh, A., & Marks, I. (1987). Self-directed exposure for agoraphobia: A controlled trial. *Behavior Therapy, 18*, 3–16.

Gitlin, B., Martin, J., Shear, M. K., Frances, A., Ball, G., & Josephson, S. (1985). Behavior therapy for panic disorder. *Journal of Nervous and Mental Disease, 173*, 742–743.

Goethe, J. W. (1970). Dichtung und Wahrheit. In J. W. Goethe, *Werke* (Vol. 5). Frankfurt: Insel Verlag. Original work published in 1811.

Goldstein, A. J. (1982). Agoraphobia: Treatment successes, treatment failures, and theoretical implications. In D. L. Chambless & A. J. Goldstein (Eds.), *Agoraphobia: Multiple perspectives on theory and treatment.* New York: Wiley.

Goldstein, A. J., & Chambless, D. L. (1978). A reanalysis of agoraphobia. *Behavior Therapy, 9*, 47–59.

Gray, J. A. (1971). *The psychology of fear and stress.* London: Weidenfeld and Nicholson.

Griez, E., Pols, H. J., & van den Hout, M. A. (1987). Acid–base balance in real life. *Journal of Affective Disorders, 12*, 263–266.

Griez, E., & van den Hout, M. A. (1983). Treatment of phobophobia by exposure to CO_2-induced anxiety symptoms. *Journal of Nervous and Mental Disease, 171*, 506–508.

Griez, E., & van den Hout, M. A. (1986). CO_2 inhalation in the treatment of panic attacks. *Behaviour Research and Therapy, 24*, 145–150.

Grunhaus, L., Gloger, S., & Weisturb, E. (1981). Panic attacks. A review of treatments and pathogenesis. *Journal of Nervous and Mental Disease, 169*, 608–613.

Hallam, R. S. (1985). *Anxiety: Psychological perspectives on panic and agoraphobia.* London: Academic.

Hand, I., Lamontagne, Y., & Marks, I. (1974). Group exposure (flooding) in vivo for agoraphobics. *British Journal of Psychiatry, 124*, 588–602.

Hand, I., Angenendt, J., Fischer, M., & Wilke, C. (1986). Exposure in vivo with panic management: Treatment rationale and longterm outcome. In I. Hand & H.-U. Wittchen (Eds.), *Panic and phobias.* Berlin: Springer.

Herrnstein, R. J. (1969). Method and theory in the study of avoidance. *Psychological Review, 76*, 49–69.

Hibbert, G. A. (1984). Ideational components of anxiety. *British Journal of Psychiatry, 144*, 618–624.

Hibbert, G. A. (1986). The diagnosis of hyperventilation using ambulatory carbon dioxide monitoring. In H. Lacey & J. Sturgeon (Eds.), *Proceedings of the 15th European Conference for Psychosomatic Research.* London: Libby.

Himadi, W. G., Cerny, J. A., Barlow, D. H., Cohen, S., & O'Brien, G. T. (1986). The relationship of marital adjustment to agoraphobia treatment outcome. *Behaviour Research and Therapy, 24*, 107–115.

Hoehn-Saric, R. (1981). Characteristics of chronic anxiety patients. In D. F. Klein & J. G. Rabkin (Eds.), *Anxiety: New research and changing concepts.* New York: Raven.

Hoehn-Saric, R. (1982). Comparison of generalized anxiety disorder with panic disorder patients. *Psychopharmacology Bulletin, 18*, 104–108.

Howard, K. I., & Orlinski, D. E. (1986). Process and outcome in psychotherapy. In S. L. Garfield & A. E. Bergin (Eds.), *Handbook of psychotherapy and behavior change—An empirical analysis* (3rd ed.). New York: Wiley.

Jacob, R., & Rapport, M. D. (1984). Panic disorder: Medical and psychological parameters. In S. M. Turner (Ed.), *Behavioral theories and treatment of anxiety.* New York: Plenum.

Klein, D. F. (1980). Anxiety reconceptualized. *Comprehensive Psychiatry, 21,* 411–427.

Klosko, J. S., Barlow, D. H., Tassinari, R. B., & Cerny, J. A. (1988). Comparison of alprazolam and cognitive behavior therapy in the treatment of panic disorder. A preliminary report. In I. Hand & H.-U. Wittchen (Eds.), *Treatments of panic and phobias.* Berlin: Springer.

Lazarus, A. A. (1971). *Behavior therapy and beyond.* New York: McGraw-Hill.

Leckman, J. F., Weissman, M. M., Merinkangas, K. R., Pauls, D. L., & Prusoff, B. A. (1983). Panic disorder and major depression. *Archives of General Psychiatry, 40,* 1055–1060.

Leitenberg, H., Agras, W. S., Allen, R., Butz, R., & Edwards, J. (1975). Feedback and therapist praise during treatment of phobia. *Journal of Consulting and Clinical Psychology, 43,* 396–404.

Lelliott, P. T., Marks, I. M., Monteiro, W. O., Tsakiris, F., & Noshirvani, H. (1987). Agoraphobia 5 years after imipramine and exposure. Outcome and predictors. *Journal of Nervous and Mental Disease, 175,* 599–605.

Ley, R. A. (1985). Agoraphobia, the panic attack, and the hyperventilation syndrome. *Behaviour Research and Therapy, 23,* 79–81.

Liebowitz, M. R., Gorman, J., Fyer, A., Levitt, M., Dillon, D., Levy, G., Appleby, I., Anderson, S., Palij, M., Davies, S., & Klein, D. F. (1985). Lactate provocation of panic attacks: II. Biochemical and physiological findings. *Archives of General Psychiatry, 42,* 709–719.

Lum, C. (1981). Hyperventilation and anxiety state. *Journal of the Royal Society of Medicine, 74,* 1–4.

Margraf, J., & Ehlers, A. (1986). Erkennung und Behandlung von akuten Angstanfällen. In J. C. Brengelmann & G. Bhringer (Eds.), *Therapieforschung für die praxis 6.* München: Röttger.

Margraf, J., & Ehlers, A. (1987, August). *Panic and agoraphobia profile.* Presented at the 17th Annual Meeting of the European Association for Behaviour Therapy, Amsterdam.

Margraf, J., & Ehlers, A. (in press). Biological models of agoraphobia and panic disorder: Theory and evidence. In M. Roth, M. D. Burrows, & R. Noyes (Eds.), *Handbook of anxiety* (Vol. 3). Amsterdam: Elsevier.

Margraf, J., Ehlers, A., & Roth, W. T. (1986a). Biological models of panic disorder and agoraphobia—A review. *Behaviour Research and Therapy, 24,* 553–567.

Margraf, J., Ehlers, A., & Roth, W. T. (1986b). Sodium lactate infusions and panic attacks: A review and critique. *Psychosomatic Medicine, 48,* 23–51.

Margraf, J., Ehlers, A., & Roth, W. T. (1988). Mitral valve prolapse and panic disorder: A review of their relationship. *Psychosomatic Medicine, 50,* 93–113.

Margraf, J., Ehlers, A., & Roth, W. T. (1989). Hyperventilation and expectancy as laboratory stressors. In D. Hellhammer, I. Florin, H. Weiner, & R. Murison (Eds.), *Frontiers of stress research.* Toronto: Huber.

Margraf, J., Taylor, C. B., Ehlers, A., Roth, W. T., & Agras, W. S. (1987). Panic attacks in the natural environment. *Journal of Nervous and Mental Disease, 175,* 558–565.

Marks, I. (1978). Behavioral psychotherapy of adult neurosis. In S. L. Garfield & A. E. Bergin (Eds.), *Handbook of psychotherapy and behavior change—An empirical analysis* (2nd ed.). New York: Wiley.

Marks, I. (1981). *The cure and care of the neuroses.* New York: Wiley.

Marks, I. (1983). Are there anticompulsive or antiphobic drugs? Review of evidence. *British Journal of Psychiatry, 143,* 338–347.

Marks, I. (1987a). Agoraphobia, panic disorder and related conditions in the DSM-III-R and ICD-10. *Journal of Psychopharmacology, 1,* 6–12.

Marks, I. (1987b). *Fears, phobias, and rituals: Panic, anxiety, and their disorders.* New York: Oxford University Press.

Marks, I., & Mathews, A. M. (1979). Brief standard self-rating for agoraphobics. *Behaviour Research and Therapy, 17,* 263–267.

Mathews, A. M., Gelder, M. G., & Johnston, D. W. (1981). *Agoraphobia: Nature and treatment.* New York: Guilford.

Mathews, A. M., & Shaw, P. M. (1973). Emotional arousal and persuasion effects in flooding. *Behaviour Research and Therapy, 11,* 587–598.

Mathews, A. M., Teasdale, J., Munby, M., Johnston, D. W., & Shaw, P. (1977). A home-based treatment program for agoraphobia. *Behavior Therapy, 8,* 915–924.

Mavissakalian, M. (1987). The placebo effect in agoraphobia. *Journal of Nervous and Mental Disease, 175,* 95–99.

Mavissakalian, M. (1988). The case for psychotropic medication in combination with exposure treatment. In I. Hand & H.-U. Wittchen (Eds.), *Treatments of panic and phobias.* Berlin: Springer.

Mavissakalian, M., & Michelson, L. (1986). Agoraphobia: Therapy-assisted in vivo exposure and imipramine. *Journal of Clinical Psychiatry, 47,* 117–122.

Mavissakalian, M., Michelson, L., Greenwald, D., Kornblith, S., & Greenwald, M. (1983). Cognitive-behavioral treatment of agoraphobia: Paradoxical intention vs. self-statement training. *Behaviour Research and Therapy, 21,* 75–86.

McCue, E. C., & McCue, P. A. (1984). Organic and hyperventilatory causes of anxiety-type symptoms. *Behavioural Psychotherapy, 12,* 308–317.

McNally, R. (1987). Preparedness and phobias: A review. *Psychological Bulletin, 101,* 283–303.

McNally, R., & Foa, E. B. (1987). Cognition and agoraphobia. *Cognitive Therapy and Research, 11,* 567–582.

McPherson, F. M., Brougham, I., & McLaren, S. (1980). Maintenance of improvement of agoraphobic patients treated by behavioural methods—Four year follow-up. *Behaviour Research and Therapy, 18,* 150–152.

Michelson, L. (1987). Cognitive behavioral assessment and treatment of agoraphobia. In L. Michelson & L. M. Ascher (Eds.), *Anxiety and stress disorders.* New York: Guilford.

Michelson, L., Mavissakalian, M., & Marchione, K. (1985). Cognitive and behavioral treatments of agoraphobia: Clinical, behavioral, and psychophysiological outcomes. *Journal of Consulting and Clinical Psychology, 53,* 913–925.

Michelson, L., Mavissakalian, M., Marchione, K., Dancu, C., & Greenwald, M. (1986). The role of self-directed in vivo exposure in cognitive, behavioral, and psychophysiological treatments of agoraphobia. *Behavior Therapy, 17,* 91–108.

Miller, N. E. (1951). Learnable drives and rewards. In S. S. Stevens (Ed.), *Handbook of experimental psychology.* Chichester: Wiley.

Mineka, S. (1985). Animal models of anxiety-based disorders: Their usefulness and limitations. In J. Maser & A. H. Tuma (Eds.), *Anxiety and the anxiety disorders.* Hillsdale, NJ: Erlbaum.

Mineka, S., & Tomarken, A. J. (1988). *The role of cognitive biases in the origins and maintenance of fear and anxiety disorders.* Manuscript submitted for publication.

Mowrer, O. H. (1947). On the dual nature of learning as a reinterpretation of "conditioning" and "problem-solving." *Harvard Educational Review,* 102–148.

Mowrer, O. H. (1960). *Learning theory and behavior.* New York: Wiley.

Munby, M., & Johnston, D. W. (1980). Agoraphobia: The long-term follow-up of behavioural treatment. *British Journal of Psychiatry, 137,* 418–427.

Nisbett, R. F., & Wilson, T. P. (1977). Telling more than we know: Verbal reports on mental processes. *Psychological Review, 84,* 231–279.

O'Brien, G. T., & Barlow, D. H. (1984). Agoraphobia. In S. M. Turner (Ed.), *Behavioral theories and treatment of anxiety.* New York: Plenum.

Öhman, A., Dimberg, U., & Öst, L. G. (1985). Animal and social phobias: Biological constraints on learned fear responses. In S. Reiss & R. Bootzin (Eds.), *Theoretical issues in behavior therapy.* New York: Academic.

Oppenheim, H. (1911). *Textbook of nervous diseases for physicians and students.* New York: Stechert.

Öst, L. G. (1988). Applied relaxation vs. progressive relaxation in the treatment of panic disorder. *Behaviour Research and Therapy, 26,* 13–22.

Ottaviani, R., & Beck, A. T. (1987). Cognitive aspects of panic disorder. *Journal of Anxiety Disorders, 1,* 15–28.

Pecknold, J. C., & Swinson, R. P. (1986). Taper withdrawal studies with alprazolam in patients with panic disorder and agoraphobia. *Psychopharmacology Bulletin, 22,* 173–176.

Pohl, R. P., Berchou, R., & Rainey, J. M. (1982). Tricyclic antidepressants and monoamine oxidase inhibitors in the treatment of agoraphobia. *Journal of Clinical Psychopharmacology, 2,* 399–407.

Rachman, S. (1977). The conditioning theory of fear acquisition: A critical examination. *Behaviour Research and Therapy, 15,* 375–387.

Rachman, S. (1980). Emotional processing. *Behaviour Research and Therapy, 18,* 51–60.

Rachman, S. (1984). Agoraphobia—A safety signal perspective. *Behaviour Research and Therapy, 22,* 59–70.

Rachman, S., Craske, M., Tallman, K., & Solyom, C. (1986). Does escape behavior strengthen agoraphobic avoidance? A replication. *Behavior Therapy, 17,* 366–384.

Rapee, R. M. (1985). A case of panic disorder treated with breathing retraining. *Journal of Behavior Therapy and Experimental Psychiatry, 16,* 63–65.

Rapee, R. M. (1987). The psychological treatment of panic attacks: Theoretical conceptualization and review of evidence. *Clinical Psychology Review, 7,* 427–438.

Rapee, R., Mattick, R., & Murrell, E. (1988). Cognitive mediation in the affective component of spontaneous panic attacks. *Journal of Experimental Psychiatry and Behavior Therapy.*

Raskin, M., Peeke, H. V. S., Dickman, W., & Pinsker, H. (1982). Panic and generalized anxiety disorder. *Archives of General Psychiatry, 39*, 687–689.

Razran, G. (1961). The observable unconscious and the inferable conscious in current Soviet psychophysiology: Interoceptive conditioning, semantic conditioning, and the orienting reflex. *Psychological Review, 68*, 81–147.

Reiss, S. (1980). Pavlovian conditioning and human fear: An expectancy model. *Behavior Therapy, 11*, 380–396.

Reiss, S., Peterson, R. A., Gursky, D. M., & McNally, R. J. (1986). Anxiety sensitivity, anxiety frequency, and the prediction of fearfulness. *Behaviour Research and Therapy, 24*, 1–8.

Rescorla, R. A., & Solomon, R. L. (1967). Two-process learning theory: Relationships between Pavlovian conditioning and instrumental learning. *Psychological Review, 74*, 151–182.

Richardson, R., Riccio, D. C., & Ress, J. (1988). Extinction of avoidance through response prevention: Enhancement by administration of epinephrine or ACTH. *Behaviour Research and Therapy, 26*, 23–32.

Salkovskis, P. M., Jones, D. R. O., & Clark, D. M. (1986a). Respiratory control in the treatment of panic attacks: Replication and extension with concurrent measurement of behaviour and pCO_2. *British Journal of Psychiatry, 148*, 526–532.

Salkovskis, P. M., Warwick, H. M. C., Clark, D. M., & Wessels, D. J. (1986b). A demonstration of acute hyperventilation during naturally occurring panic attacks. *Behaviour Research and Therapy, 24*, 91–94.

Sartory, G., & Olajide, D. (1988). Vagal innervation techniques in the treatment of panic disorder. *Behaviour Research and Therapy, 26*, 431–434.

Schapira, K., Roth, M., Kerr, T. A., & Gurney, C. (1972). The prognosis of affective disorders: The differentiation of anxiety states and depressive illnesses. *British Journal of Psychiatry, 121*, 175–181.

Seligman, M. E. P. (1971). Phobias and preparedness. *Behavior Therapy, 2*, 307–320.

Seligman, M. E. P. (1975). *Helplessness: On depression, development, and death.* San Francisco: Freeman.

Seligman, M. E. P., & Johnston, J. A. (1973). A cognitive theory of avoidance learning. In F. McGuigan & D. Lumsden (Eds.), *Contemporary approaches to conditioning and learning.* New York: Academic.

Shear, M. K., Ball, G. G., Josephson, S. C., & Gitlin, B. C. (1988). Behavioral therapy efficacy for panic. In I. Hand & H.-U. Wittchen (Eds.), *Treatments of panic and phobias.* Berlin: Springer.

Shear, M. K., Kligfield, P., Harshfield, G., Devereux, R. B., Polan, J. J., Mann, J. J., Pickering, T., & Frances, A. (1987). Ambulatory monitoring of blood pressure and heart rate in panic patients. *American Journal of Psychiatry, 144*, 633–637.

Sheehan, D. V. (1982). Panic attacks and phobias. *New England Journal of Medicine, 307*, 156–158.

Solomon, R. L., Kamin, L. J., & Wynne, L. C. (1953). Traumatic avoidance learning: The outcome of several extinction procedures with dogs. *Journal of Abnormal and Social Psychology, 48*, 291–302.

Solomon, R. L., & Wynne, L. C. (1953). Traumatic avoidance learning: Acquisition in normal dogs. *Psychological Monographs, 67*, Whole No. 354.

Spitzer, R. L., & Williams, J. (1986). *Structured clinical interview for DSM (SCID).* Unpublished manuscript, Biometrics Division, New York State Psychiatric Institute.

Stavrakaki, C., & Vargo, B. (1986). The relationship of anxiety and depression: A review of the literature. *British Journal of Psychiatry, 149*, 7–16.

Steketee, G., & Foa, E. B. (1985). Obsessive–compulsive disorder. In D. H. Barlow (Ed.), *Clinical handbook of psychological disorders.* New York: Guilford.

Stern, R., & Marks, I. (1973). Brief and prolonged flooding: A comparison in agoraphobic patients. *Archives of General Psychiatry, 28*, 270–276.

Taylor, C. B., King, R. J., Ehlers, A., Margraf, J., Clark, D., Roth, W. T., & Agras, W. S. (1987). Treadmill exercise test and ambulatory measures in patients with panic attacks. *American Journal of Cardiology, 60*, 48J–52J.

Taylor, C. B., King, R. J., Margraf, J., Ehlers, A., Telch, M. J., Roth, W. T., & Agras, W. S. (in press). Utilization of imipramine and exposure therapy for the treatment of panic and agoraphobia: Results from a community sample. *American Journal of Psychiatry.*

Taylor, C. B., Sheikh, J., Agras, W. S., Roth, W. T., Margraf, J., Ehlers, A., Maddock, R. J., & Gossard, D. (1986). Ambulatory heart rate changes in patients with panic attacks. *American Journal of Psychiatry, 143*, 478–482.

Taylor, C. B., Telch, M. J., & Havvik., D. (1983). Ambulatory heart rate changes during panic attacks. *Journal of Psychiatric Research, 17*, 261–266.

Tearnan, B. H., Telch, M. J., & Keefe, P. (1984). Etiology and onset of agoraphobia: A critical review. *Behaviour Research and Therapy, 21,* 505–517.

Teasdale, J. D., Walsh, P. A., Lancashire, M., & Mathews, A. M. (1977). Group exposure for agoraphobics: A replicaton study. *British Journal of Psychiatry, 130,* 186–193.

Telch, M. J., Agras, W. S., Taylor, C. B., Roth, W. T., & Gallen, C. C. (1985). Combined pharmacological and behavioral treatment for agoraphobia. *Behaviour Research and Therapy, 23,* 325–335.

Telch, M. J., Tearnan, B. H., & Taylor, C. B. (1983). Antidepressant medication in the treatment of agoraphobia: A critical review. *Behaviour Research and Therapy, 21,* 505–517.

Thorpe, G. L., & Burns, L. E. (1983). *The agoraphobic syndrome.* Chichester: Wiley.

Thyer, B. A., & Himle, J. (1985). Temporal relationship between panic attack onset and phobic avoidance in agoraphobia. *Behaviour Research and Therapy, 23,* 607–608.

Turner, S. M., McCann, B. S., Beidel, D. C., & Mezzich, J. E. (1986). DSM-III classification of the anxiety disorders: A psychometric study. *Journal of Abnormal Psychology, 95,* 168–172.

Tyrer, P. (1986). New rows of neuroses—Are they an illusion? *Integrative Psychiatry, 4,* 25–31.

Tyrer, P., Alexander, J., Remington, M., & Riley, P. (1987). Relationship between neurotic symptoms and neurotic diagnosis: A longitudinal study. *Journal of Affective Disorders, 13,* 13–21.

Tyrer, P., & Steinberg, D. (1975). Symptomatic treatment of agoraphobia and social phobias: A follow-up study. *British Journal of Psychiatry, 127,* 163–168.

van den Hout, M. A. (1988). The psychology of panic. In S. Rachman & J. Maser (Eds.), *Cognitive approaches to panic.* Hillsdale, NJ: Erlbaum.

van den Hout, M. A., & Griez, E. (1982). Cognitive factors in carbon dioxide therapy. *Journal of Psychosomatic Research, 26,* 219–224.

van der Molen, G. M., van den Hout, M. A., Vroemen, J., Lousberg, H., & Griez, E. (1986). Cognitive determinants of lactate-induced anxiety. *Behaviour Research and Therapy, 24,* 677–680.

Waddell, M. T., Barlow, D. H., & O'Brien, G. T. (1984). A preliminary investigation of cognitive and relaxation treatment of panic disorder: Effects on intense anxiety vs. "background" anxiety. *Behaviour Research and Therapy, 22,* 393–402.

Weissman, M. M., Leaf, P. J., Blazer, D. G., Boyd, J. H., & Florio, L. (1986). The relationship between panic disorder and agoraphobia: An epidemiologic perspective. *Psychopharmacology Bulletin, 22,* 787–791.

Westphal, C. (1871). Die Agoraphobie, eine neuropathische Erscheinung. *Archiv für Psychiatrie und Nervenkrankheiten, 3,* 138–161.

Wittchen, H. U. (1986). Epidemiology of panic attacks and panic disorder. In I. Hand & H.-U. Wittchen (Eds.), *Panic and phobias.* Berlin: Springer.

Wittchen, H. U. (1988). The natural course and outcome of anxiety disorders. What cases remit without treatment? In I. Hand & H.-U. Wittchen (Eds.), *Treatments of panic and phobias.* Berlin: Springer.

CHAPTER 10

Pharmacotherapy

EDWARD SILBERMAN

DIAGNOSTIC CONSIDERATIONS

Central to the medical–biological conception of panic disorder and agoraphobia is identification of the panic attack as a unique syndrome different from other forms of anxiety. The older *Diagnostic and Statistical Manual* (2nd ed. DSM-II) classification of anxiety disorders into "anxiety neurosis" and "phobic neurosis" depended not on the profile of symptoms accompanying subjective anxiety, but on the presence or absence of an external trigger in the form of either an object or a situation. Such a classification reflects the then-prevalent psychodynamic view that the symptoms of phobic and anxiety neuroses are merely surface manifestations of underlying internal conflicts and, thus, of little significance in themselves.

The current psychiatric conception of panic disorder and agoraphobia is based on the work of Klein and his co-workers, who described a group of patients "with sudden onset of subjectively inexplicable panic attacks, accompanied by hot and cold flashes, rapid breathing, palpitations, weakness, unsteadiness, and a feeling of impending death .... They were often lively, popular, and friendly when not anxious" (Klein & Fink, 1962). Such patients, in contrast to those with more diffuse and less intense "generalized anxiety" or "anticipatory anxiety," were unresponsive to phenothiazine tranquilizers, but they experienced symptom relief from imipramine or monoamine oxidase inhibitors (MAOIs). Klein suggested that the distinct response of panic attacks to antidepressants might reflect their etiology as a "disorder of

an innate [i.e., biological] separation anxiety mechanism" (Klein, 1964). Ironically, the descriptive distinction between panic and anticipatory anxiety was made quite clearly by Freud in his writings on the anxiety neuroses (Freud, 1962, 1963), but it was left to the psychopharmacologists to pursue the possible meaning of the differences.

In the currently prevalent psychiatric view, as developed by Klein and others, agoraphobia is not a separate disorder, but a secondary avoidant reaction to the fear of having a panic attack when in a public place where escape is not possible or help is not available. This formulation depends on the empirically testable proposition that panic attacks inevitably precede the onset of phobic avoidance in agoraphobic patients. While most clinical experience and some systematic research support this hypothesis, others, such as Marks (Marks et al., 1983), contend that agoraphobia itself is primary in substantial numbers of patients. Furthermore, DSM-III-R provides a category of agoraphobia without panic attacks. Thus, the extent to which agoraphobia exists independently of panic attacks remains unsettled in the current literature.

Proponents of the biological view of panic attacks have stressed the idea that such attacks are endogenous (Sheehan, Ballenger, & Jacobsen, 1980). *Endogenicity* implies that the root cause of the symptoms is a disturbance of physiology, rather than a learned response to external stimuli. Clinically, this has usually been translated such that *spontaneity* is the defining feature of true panic attacks, as opposed to phobic or anticipatory anxiety which would be linked to external triggers (Sheehan et al., 1980, Zitrin, Klein, Woerner, & Ross, 1983). While many panic disorder patients do report having attacks with no apparent external stimulus, the requirement of spontaneity is not logically necessary for a biological conception of the disorder (and is not used at all, for example, in attempting to delineate endogenous or biological forms of depression). The concept of spontaneity has also been hard to validate. Panic attacks are experienced very similarly by patients whether or not they are externally triggered (Barlow et al., 1985). Physiological concomitants have been found to be similar whether panic attacks are spontaneous, triggered by phobic stimuli, or stimulated physiologically by lactate infusion (Liebowitz et al., 1985; Taylor et al., 1986; Woods, Charney, McPherson, Gradman, & Heninger, 1987). Furthermore, it is hard to be certain when panics are truly spontaneous and when they arise in response to stimuli that are not noticed by the patient. Subtle alterations in bodily sensations, to which panic-prone patients might overreact, have been proposed as one possible type of covert stimulus for panic attacks (Barlow, 1986).

It may be more practical to view the possible physiological abnormality of panic attacks as a lowered threshold for intense anxiety reactions to either internal *or* external stimuli. It may be difficult to decide which anxiety attacks to call panics, and which to call phobic or anticipatory anxiety. Therefore, it is probably safest to view intense paroxysmal anxiety with accompanying autonomic, cardiac, respiratory, and gastrointestinal symptoms as composing a syndrome highly likely to respond to pharmacological treatments regardless of whether there are accompanying phobic or avoidant features.

BIOLOGICAL CONCEPTUALIZATION OF PANIC DISORDER

The current psychiatric conception of panic disorder as a primary neurophysiological disturbance is based on inference from a number of clinical observations. The evidence collected by Klein and co-workers that (a) the panic disorder responds to tricyclics, but not to tranquilizing medications, and (b) tricyclics are effective in treating panics,

but not simple phobias or generalized anxiety, suggests the possibility of specific underlying neurochemical abnormalities that are responsive to antidepressants (Klein, 1964; Klein & Fink, 1962; Zitrin et al., 1983). Added to these observations are reports showing that patients with panic disorder, and families of such patients, are at higher risk for depressive disorders than is the general population (Breier, Charney, & Heninger, 1986; Leckman, Merikanges, Pauls, Prusoff, & Weissman, 1983). This has led some workers to speculate that depression and panic disorder are part of a spectrum of biochemically mediated disorders that respond to antidepressant treatment.

A third line of evidence stems from the reports of Pitts and McClure (1967), since confirmed by many others, that intravenous sodium lactate infusions induce paniclike symptoms in 70% or more of panic disorder patients, but in less than 20% of controls. This finding can be interpreted as reflecting a specific biological vulnerability to lactate-induced panic attacks in panic disorder patients.

Biological theories have attempted (a) to localize panic disorder anatomically, (b) to associate it with dysregulation of the adrenergic neurotransmitter system, and (c) to explain it in terms of alterations in respiratory physiology. The role of the locus coeruleus (LC) in mediating anxiety has been the focus of research by Redmond and his colleagues. The LC is a pontine nucleus containing 70% of the brain's adrenergic neurons. These neurons—which have widespread projections to the cerebral cortex, limbic structures, the brain stem, the cerebellum, and the spinal cord—are hypothesized to be part of the neuronal system mediating arousal–alertness, as well as the accompanying affect of anxiety (Redmond, 1979). Redmond (1977) has shown that electrical or chemical stimulation of the LC in monkeys produces behaviors similar to those produced in response to danger under natural conditions. A connection to humans is made by the observation that drugs that suppress firing of the LC (including morphine, ethanol, benzodiazepines, tricyclic antidepressants, and clonidine) tend to have antianxiety effects. Conversely, yohimbine and piperoxan, which have been shown to increase LC firing, also tend to produce anxiety or panic in human subjects (Uhde, Boulenger, Vittone, & Post, 1984a).

These lines of evidence suggest that increased

firing of the LC may underlie the phenomena of panic disorder. The centrality of the LC as a mediator of panics is open to some question, however. Some investigators have questioned whether there is a one-to-one relationship between LC activity and anxiety, while others have suggested that the LC mediates reaction to all novel stimuli, rather than just to threatening ones (Aston-Jones, Foote, & Bloom, 1984; Mason & Fibiger, 1979).

A great variety of neuroactive substances have been found to alter activity of the LC. Among those that decrease firing are epinephrine, serotonin, and metenkephalin, while firing is increased in response to acetylcholine and substance P (Charney, Heninger, & Breier, 1984). To date, most attention has been paid to LC-mediated changes in noradrenergic function in relation to anxiety and panic. Increased LC firing has been correlated with increased levels of norepinephrine and its metabolic 3-methoxy-4-hydroxy-phenyle-thylene glycol (MHPG) in plasma and cerebrospinal fluid (CSF), suggesting that anxiety levels might be mediated by adrenergic neurotransmission (Redmond, 1979; Redmond & Huang, 1979). In support of this hypothesis is a variety of studies showing that people in high-stress situations (such as pilots landing on aircraft carriers or students taking examinations) show either increases in excretion of noradrenergic metabolites or increases in noradrenergically mediated autonomic activity (Jones, Bridges, & Leob, 1968; Rubin, Miller, Clarke, Poland, & Ransom, 1970).

Analogy to a variety of medical conditions suggests that the beta-adrenergic system in particular may play a role in panic attacks. A syndrome of "hyperdynamic beta-adrenergic circulatory state" has been described in which patients have paniclike reaction in response to isoproterenol, a beta-adrenergic agonist (Frohlich, Tarazi, & Duston, 1969). The attacks are prevented by treatment with the beta blocker propranolol (Easton & Sherman, 1976). Mitral valve prolapse, which has been associated with increased levels of plasma epinephrine and norepinephrine, has been found by many investigators to occur more frequently in panic-prone patients than in the general population (Gorman, Fyer, Gliklich, King, & Klein, 1981; Kantor, Zitrin, & Zeldis, 1980). Increased

numbers of beta-adrenergic receptors have also been found in both animals and humans with hyperthyroidism, a condition that produces symptoms that mimic anxiety (Motulsky & Insel, 1982). A further inference has been drawn from the finding that antidepressants tend to decrease the number of beta-adrenergic receptors with about the same time course as they take to reduce panic attacks (Charney et al., 1984).

A separate line of speculation has focused on dysfunction of respiratory control as a possible etiology for panic attacks. Carr and Sheehan (1984) point out that "air hunger" and hyperventilation are prominent features of panics. Starting from the susceptibility of patients to panic during lactate infusions, they suggest that the operative mechanism is increased central nervous system (CNS) sensitivity to elevations in hydrogen ion concentrations (that is, increased acidity) in medullary chemoreceptor zones. Thus, lactate-induced drops in pH in these zones might stimulate the respiratory drive, with concomitant subjective symptoms of panic. A similar mechanism would apply when acidosis is induced by breathing air with high carbon dioxide content, which has also been shown to produce panic attacks in patients, but not in controls.

Carr and Sheehan also propose that panics induced by hyperventilation of room air, which causes not acidosis but alkalosis, might result from reflex cerebral ischemia and acidosis occurring in response to the elevations in peripheral pH. An alternate view of the ventilatory control hypothesis is that CNS response to carbon dioxide concentration, rather than to hydrogen ion concentration (pH), is altered in panic disorder patients (Gorman et al., 1988). If the internal set point for carbon dioxide concentration were too low, the respiratory drive would be too easily triggered, with accompanying subjective symptoms of air hunger and anxiety. Although both versions of the theory would predict that panic disorder patients might be prone to chronic hyperventilation, which does seem to be the case (as elaborated herein later), neither explains what triggers the acute episodes of panic.

Despite the plausibility of current biological speculations about the origins of panic disorder, it has been surprisingly difficult to garner convincing evidence in favor of any theory. Indeed, some of the original premises on which the medical–biological models were based are now more questionable. It would now appear, for example, that panic disorder can be treated successfully with high-potency benzodiazepines, and possibly even with lower potency forms given in high enough doses, as well as with antidepressants (Rickels & Schweizer, 1986). Conversely, a 1986 study has suggested that generalized anxiety responds as well to antidepressants as to traditional anxiolytics, further blurring the pharmacological distinctions among the anxiety disorders (Kahn et al., 1986).

In their original discussion, Pitts and McClure (1967) proposed that the effects of lactate infusion are similar to those of endogenous production of lactate in people who experience paniclike symptoms after exercise. They also proposed that a lactate-mediated decrease in ionized calcium in peripheral tissues was crucial to the effect. Subsequently, other workers have pointed out that sodium lactate infusions increase tissue pH, whereas endogenous lactate production decreases it. Studies have also demonstrated that changes in lactate, pH, or calcium levels by themselves are not sufficient to induce panic attacks (Ackerman & Sachar, 1974). The physiological mechanism of lactate-induced panic attacks has been very hard to pin down, despite recent, careful, detailed studies of the effect. While patients who panic following lactate infusion tend to have increased baseline levels of anxiety and autonomic arousal, their biochemical and autonomic responses to lactate differ very little from those of nonpanicking controls (Gaffney, Fenton, Lane, & Lake, 1988; Liebowitz et al., 1985).

Challenge with air mixtures containing 5% or more carbon dioxide has been found to result in panic attacks in about 40% of panic disorder patients, but not in controls (Woods et al., 1986). As with lactate-induced panic attacks, studies have so far failed to uncover the physiological mechanism for this process. While some investigators have found exaggerated ventilatory responses to carbon dioxide, as predicted by theory, others have not (Gorman et al., 1988; Woods, Charney, Goodman, & Heninger, 1988). The only consistent respiratory abnormality reported in panic patients is that they are chronic hyperventilators. As with many physiological correlates of panic disorder, it is unclear whether hyperventilation is related to the cause of the disorder or is merely the result of chronic anxiety.

A major difficulty with physiological challenge models is that they are not very specific. In the years since the discovery of the lactate effect, similar responses have been demonstrated with caffeine, isoproterenol, and yohimbine, in addition to carbon dioxide (Charney et al., 1984; Charney, Heninger, & Jatlow, 1985; Easton & Sherman, 1976). Although these drugs produce similar subjective effects in susceptible patients, they vary widely in their physiologic effects and target organs. As one example, MHPG (a major metabolite of norepinephrine) has been found elevated during yohimbine-induced anxiety (Charney et al., 1984), but not following lactate or carbon dioxide infusions (Gaffney et al., 1988; Woods et al., 1988). Such diversity limits the usefulness of challenges in understanding panic disorder, and it suggests that these methods may do no more than produce bodily sensations that patients respond to with intense anxiety.

The role of the adrenergic–noradrenergic neurotransmitter system in panic disorder has also been surprisingly difficult to confirm. While some researchers have found elevations of epinephrine, norepinephrine, and their metabolites in patients at baseline or during panic attacks (Ballenger et al., 1984; Ko et al., 1983), the association between adrenergic variables and symptoms in naturally occurring panics has been variable and inconsistent. Lactate-induced panics are striking for their lack of associated adrenergic or hormonal changes (Gaffney et al., 1988). Furthermore, they are not prevented by pretreatment with the beta-adrenergic blocker propranolol (Gorman et al., 1983). Autonomic measures such as increased heart rate, reflecting increased beta-adrenergic activity, have been found to distinguish panic attacks from nonpanic high anxiety (Taylor et al., 1986). However, not all panic attacks are accompanied by elevated heart rate.

Evidence from pharmacological studies has been similarly equivocal. Drugs such as clonidine and propranolol, which have very direct adrenergic effects, have been less impressive therapeutically than tricyclic antidepressants and MAOIs. Similarly, although tricyclics are considerably more potent than alprazolam in reducing MHPG production, they are about equal in their therapeutic effect (Charney & Heninger, 1985). Results of trials with nonadrenergic antidepressants bupropion and trazodone have been mixed to date (Mavissakalian, Perel, Bowler, & Dealy, 1987; Sheehan, Davidson, Manshrek, & Fleet, 1983), while levels of desmethylimipramine, a purely adrenergic metabolite of imipramine, have not been found to predict degree of panic relief (Mavissakalian, Perel, & Michelson, 1984).

A variety of biological markers have been reported to distinguish panic disorder (PD) patients from controls. These reports, which await replication, include (a) low inorganic phosphate levels as a predictor of panic response to lactate (Gorman et al., 1986), (b) reduced thyroid-stimulating hormone (TSH) and prolactin responses to thyrotropin-releasing hormone (Roy-Byrne, Uhde, Rubinow, & Post, 1986), (c) low plasma serotonin levels (Evans et al., 1985), and (d) increase in right versus left parahippocampal blood flow, as measured by positron emission tomography (PET) scan (Reiman et al., 1986). Early reports of the dexamethasone test in PD patients described very low rates of nonsuppression (Curtis, Cameron, & Nesse, 1982; Lieberman et al., 1983). However, Coryell, Noyes, Crowe, and Chaudhry (1985), in a more recent study, point out that earlier work was based on samples of partially treated outpatients whose low rates of DST escape might reflect both treatment status and relative mildness of illness. These authors report comparable rates of DST nonsuppression (about 20%) in untreated outpatients with either PD or major depression.

In summary, a convincing biological etiology for PD has not yet been found. The null hypothesis for current biological findings is that physiological differences between PD patients and controls are the results of anxiety states rather than the causes, and that the variety of physiological methods for provoking panic attacks merely cause anxietylike bodily sensations, to which panic-prone patients overreact. The alternative psychological explanation views panic attacks as a learned response to interoceptive stimuli, to which

panic patients have extreme sensitivity. It is a commonplace clinical observation that panic patients are highly attuned to bodily sensations, a trait that often gives them a very low tolerance for side effects of psychotropic medications. Furthermore, some workers have reported that the major difference between PD patients and controls in response to lactate infusion is not the physiological effects produced, but the tendency of patients, but not controls, to respond to these effects with anxiety. It may be that only certain physical sensations can trigger panics, however, because hypoglycemia, cold pressor tests, hypocalcemia, and mental arithmetic have been reported to induce physiological changes without producing panic in susceptible subjects (Grunhaus, Gloger, Birmacher, Palmer, Ben-David, 1983; Kelly, Mitchell-Heggs, & Sherman, 1971; Uhde, Vittone, & Post, 1984b).

There is also evidence that both naturally occurring and physiologically provoked panic attacks can be moderated by cognitive factors such as plausible explanations of the patient's bodily sensations (Breier et al., 1986). While biological theories have given inadequate attention to such factors, it is equally true that a psychological model fails to explain why some people are supersensitive to minute changes in bodily function and others are not. A definitive theory of panic disorder would have to include a model of the biology of altered learning patterns that seem typical of the illness.

MEDICATIONS FOR PANIC–AGORAPHOBIA

In the medical model of panic–agoraphobia, drug therapy is the central aspect of the treatment plan. While drugs have clearly been shown to provide symptomatic relief and to improve general functioning in patients with the disorder, it is less clear which features of the illness are primarily affected by medication. The model proposed by Klein would predict primary, specific effects on spontaneous panic attacks, but this has not invariably been found. Along with medication prescription, it is also important to provide the patient with education about the illness, with support, and with a certain amount of instruction to face feared situations once the medication has had a chance to work. These nonpharmacological aspects of the treatment are often not systematically studied by psychopharmacologists, so that the minimum necessary directive-behavioral elements of the treatment, and the extent of their interaction with drug therapy, remain open to question.

The vast majority of the literature of PD and agoraphobia deals with three medications: the tricyclic antidepressant imipramine, the MAOI phenelzine, and the triazolobenzodiazepine alprazolam. Despite the research focus on these three particular drugs, there is little or no reason to believe that they are unique within their classes in therapeutic effects. Drugs that decrease noradrenergic transmission, such as clonidine and propranolol, may also play a role in treatment of PD and agoraphobia, although at present, it appears to be a more minor one. Choices for prescribing are generally made on the basis of practical considerations, such as the patient's ability to tolerate the side effects, rather than on differences in specificity or efficacy.

Imipramine

Imipramine is the drug most systematically studied for treatment of PD and agoraphobia. Of 10 studies in which imipramine has been compared to placebo under double-blind conditions, 7 have clearly demonstrated the drug's efficacy. In a more equivocal study by Telch and colleagues (Telch et al., 1985), imipramine plus intensive group exposure to phobic stimuli was superior to placebo plus exposure, but imipramine without exposure had little effect on panic or phobic anxiety. The most negative results have been reported by Marks et al. (1983) and by Evans, Kenardy, Schneider, and Hoey (1986), who found no significant antianxiety effect of imipramine alone; further, Marks et al. (1983) found no benefit of adding imipramine to exposure therapy.

Marks explains the negative result on the basis of low initial levels of depression in his patients. He contends that the benefits from imipramine reported by others are primarily antidepressant effects in panic–agoraphobic patients with concurrent depression. This explanation appears highly unlikely, however, because numerous other investigators who have addressed the question have found either no relationsip or negative correlations between degree of depression and medication effects on panic (Mavissakalian, 1987a; Nurnberg & Cocarco, 1982; Zitrin et al., 1983). Others have questioned Marks's negative interpretation of his data because, after 28 weeks of treatment, imipramine tended to be superior to placebo in 9 out of 10 of his anxiety measures. Thus, the overwhelming weight of the evidence shows that imipramine has true antianxiety and not merely antidepressant effects in panic–agoraphobic patients.

There is, however, more question about which symptoms are the primary targets of imipramine in these patients. In their clinical studies, Klein and colleagues have found clear antipanic effects of the drug. In 1987, Klein used a mathematical path analysis to further evaluate the causal chain in improvement of drug-treated agoraphobic patients (Klein, Ross, & Cohen, 1987). His results suggest that exposure therapy decreases avoidance, but not panic attacks, while drug therapy decreases avoidance by first reducing panics. This conclusion supports the clinical impression of many workers that alleviation of panic attacks precedes reduction in agoraphobia.

Not all studies have supported the specific antipanic effect of imipramine, however. Telch, Agras, Taylor, Roth, and Gallen (1985) found no specific antipanic effect at all, while Mavissakalian and co-workers reported a dose response for phobic and anticipatory anxiety but not for panic (Mavissakalian & Perel, 1985). Some workers have found a direct antiphobic response to imipramine that correlates with the drug's antidepressant, but not antipanic effects (McNair & Kahn, 1981).

Differences both in evaluation measures and in the context in which medications are given may account for some of the variance in reported antianxiety effects. The use of concurrent behavioral therapy or of supportive therapies (with poorly controlled behavioral and cognitive elements) is an important confound of many studies of imipramine. The efficacy of imipramine without concurrent behavioral therapies has been somewhat less convincingly demonstrated than the benefit of adding imipramine to such therapies. Of seven blind, placebo-controlled studies of imipramine alone, four have been positive, and three negative. A number of studies do suggest that imipramine is effective without concurrent formal behavioral therapy, however (Garakani, Zitrin, & Klein, 1984; Rizley, Kahn, McNair, & Frankenthaler, 1986; Sheehan et al., 1980). Klein and co-workers found no benefit of imipramine combined with formal exposure therapy over supportive therapy in which the patient is urged to face feared situations after the panic attacks have begun to abate (Klein, Zitrin, Woerner, & Ross, 1983). However, Telch et al. (1985) found that imipramine alone was not helpful when patients were told to continue avoidant behavior during the first 8 weeks of treatment. The weight of the evidence, therefore, suggests an interaction between medication and supportive aspects of treatment, whether delivered formally or informally.

The dose response and the time course of action of imipramine are somewhat less well understood for treatment of PD than for depression, but they seem to be generally similar. The average dose reported in controlled studies is about 160 mg daily, which is comparable to the usual minimum antidepressant dose in nongeriatric adults. Mavissakalian and Perel (1985) have reported that more patients respond at doses above than at doses below 150 mg daily, and Munjack et al. (1985) found a 20% response in those taking less than 50 mg, but a 67% in those taking more than 50 mg. However, Ballenger et al. (1984) reported better response in the 100–150 mg range than in the 200–250 mg range. One possible reason for these differences is that side effects might be more pronounced at the higher doses, and they therefore may begin to interfere with overall efficacy as doses are raised above optimal levels. Furthermore, some patients seem to get good therapeutic responses at very small doses—at times as low as 10 or 15 mg daily. One study of two such patients demonstrated that this is not necessarily due to unusually slow metabolism of the drug because blood levels in these cases were well below the established therapeutic level (Jobson, Linnoila, Gillan, & Sullivan, 1978). At present, there is no way of predicting who might respond at very low levels.

The relationship of response to blood levels has

not yet been well established. Mavissakalian et al. (1984) found a positive correlation between imipramine, but not desipramine, levels and response. The mean combined IMI + DMI levels in their study was 241 ng/ml. Marks et al. (1983) failed to find any relationship between plasma levels and outcome (mean combined level 220 ng/ml), while Ballenger et al. (1984) reported a trend toward better outcomes in those maintained in the 100–150 ng/ml than in the 200–250 ng/ml range. More studies are clearly needed to determine whether blood levels provide useful information in dealing with treatment-resistant cases.

It is difficult to make a general statement about overall response rate with imipramine, because rates depend on which symptoms are targeted and what degree of improvement is required to define a responder. The range of response rates in published reports is 60–80%, with a mean of about 78% substantially improved on medication. Most, though not all of these rates, have been measured in terms of efficacy of antipanic effects. By comparison, the range of reported placebo responses is 33%–72%, with a mean of 51%. Thus, a great many potentially medication-responsive patients may do equally well on placebo (Mavissakalian, 1987b).

Time of onset of antipanic action is similar to antidepressant action, generally being from 2 to 4 weeks. However, some authors have reported continued improvement as far as 5 or 6 months into treatment, so that maximum benefit may require a fairly lengthy trial (Zitrin et al., 1983). A major factor effecting time of onset is the difficulty in getting patients up to a therapeutic dose because of poorly tolerated side effects. In addition to the usual anticholinergic and hypotensive effects, panic patients appear to be especially prone to amphetaminelike effects of imipramine, including feelings of increased anxiety, energy, tension, restlessness, or shakiness, with or without concomitant palpitations, diaphoresis, tremulousness, and sleep disturbance. Difficulty tolerating such symptoms is undoubtedly a major factor in the rather high medication dropout rate, which in 12 studies averaged 27%, with a range of 18% to 43%. One must view this number in the perspective of the *placebo dropout* rate, which averages 20% or more in those studies reporting it (Evans et al., 1988; Marks et al., 1983; Mavissakalian &

Perel, 1985; Telch et al., 1985; Zitrin, Klein, & Woerner, 1980; Zitrin et al., 1983). Thus, it is the extreme somatic sensitivity of panic patients as much as the properties of the medication itself that makes pharmacological treatment difficult.

There is general agreement that substantial numbers of patients will relapse when taken off medication, but there are few systematic data about it in the literature. Zitrin et al. (1983) report a 27% relapse rate 6 months after the start of treatment; at 2 years, there was a relapse of 35% among patients treated with imipramine plus supportive therapy, and of 20% in those treated with the drug plus exposure therapy. The authors do not make clear what proportion of patients were off medication at the time of relapse. Clinical experience suggests that at least one third to one half of patients will relapse when medication is tapered. However, how this may vary with length of treatment and other parameters is not known.

At present, the literature offers few predictors of imipramine response. Long duration of illness, increased severity, prominent depressive symptoms, relative lack of panic attacks, and predominance of simple phobia have all been associated with poorer outcome (Mavissakalian & Michelson, 1986; Sheehan et al., 1980; Zitrin et al., 1980). Recently, personality pathology has been associated with poorer global outcome, but not with antipanic effects of medication (Reich, 1988).

Other Cyclic Antidepressants

Following imipramine, the best studied cyclic antidepressant is clomipramine, a highly serotonergic drug that has never been approved for nonexperimental use in the United States. Numerous uncontrolled studies and four controlled studies of the drug have been published, all of which have indicated its efficacy in anxiety-related conditions (Ballenger, 1986; Pohl, Berchou, & Rainey, 1982). However, almost all of these studies have dealt with mixed populations of patients, including those with simple and social phobias, and hypochondriacal and depressive anxiety, in addition to those with PD and agoraphobia. Relatively few have used direct measures of antipanic effects. A recent controlled study with a carefully selected population of agoraphobic patients has confirmed the efficacy of clomipramine both in ameliorating

panic attacks, phobic anxiety, and depressive symptoms and in improving social and work functioning (Johnston, Trayer, & Whitsett, 1988). Parameters of medication dosage and treatment response in this study were typical of other published clomipramine studies and similar to results generally obtained with imipramine: (a) The mean dose after 8 weeks was about 82 mg daily (with a maximum of 300 mg), (b) patients showed significant improvement after 2 to 4 weeks of treatment, and (c) 22% dropped out during the medication trial. Dry mouth, constipation, increased energy levels, and sweating were the most prominent side effects in this study. Patients were generally encouraged to face their feared situations after starting medication but were not given formal behavioral therapy.

There are scattered reports suggesting the efficacy of other cyclic antidepressants. One 6-week trial of zimelidine (150 mg) showed it to be comparably well tolerated, and significantly more effective than either imipramine or placebo (Evans et al., 1986). Two controlled studies of trazodone have produced mixed results. One reported little benefit and a 90% dropout rate after 4 weeks of treatment (Charney, Menkes, & Heninger, 1981), while the other reported both significant benefits when compared to placebo and a dropout of about 30% over a similar time period (Mavissakalian et al., 1987). Desipramine, amitriptyline, and nortriptyline have been reported effective anecdotally or in uncontrolled studies (Davidson, Linnoila, Raft, & Turnbull, 1981; Lidyard, 1987; Muskin & Fyer, 1981). Bupropion has been found ineffective in one controlled trial (Sheehan et al., 1983).

In summary, there is little reason at this point to believe that imipramine is unique in its benefits to panic–agoraphobic patients. Further controlled trials are necessary to determine the range and characteristics of response to other cyclic antidepressants.

Monoamine Oxidase Inhibitors

The antipanic effect of MAOIs has been less thoroughly studied than that of imipramine and other cyclic antidepressants. The literature contains six controlled studies (Lipsedge, Hajioff, Huggins, et al., 1973; Mountjoy, Roth, Garside, &

Leitch, 1977; Sheehan, et al., 1980; Solyom, Solyom, LaPierre, Pecknold, & Morton, 1981; Solyom et al., 1973; Tyrer, Candy, & Kelly, 1973) (five dealing with phenelzine) and a number of uncontrolled clinical trials of MAOIs in panic–agoraphobic patients. Interpretation of these reports is difficult because many of them have dealt with a mixture of anxiety disorders, used relatively small numbers of patients, and administered medications in modest doses. Furthermore, few of them used specific measures of antipanic response. Despite these shortcomings, all published reports have found some type of anxiolytic effect of MAOIs, with an average response rate of about 80%.

As with imipramine, target symptoms of phenelzine have covered a broad range and have not been limited to reduction of panic attacks. In the best MAOI study to date, Sheehan et al. (1980) reported (a) reduction in somatic, depressive, and obsessive symptoms, (b) reduction in phobic anxiety, and (c) improvement in work and social functioning, in addition to (d) reduction in frequency and severity of panic attacks. The authors state their impression that improvement in phobic avoidance tends to lag behind panic reduction by about 3 months. The Sheehan study also provides the only controlled comparison of phenelzine and imipramine, showing a nonsignificant trend toward superiority of the former drug on most measures of improvement.

Doses of phenelzine have been reported in the range of 30–90 mg daily, but most studies have not used more than 45 mg. The possibility that this might represent underdosage is supported by Tyrer et al. (1973), who found that raising the dose as high as 90 mg converted many of the initial nonresponders. It seems possible, therefore, that the extant literature somewhat underestimates the efficacy of MAOIs in panic–agoraphobic patients. There is, as yet, no published data on the relationship of platelet MAOI activity to therapeutic effect.

Time of improvement ranges from 3 to 8 weeks of treatment, with a mean of about 4 weeks. Only about 20% of patients failed to complete treatment across studies, suggesting that MAOIs may be somewhat better tolerated by panic–agoraphobic patients than cyclic antidepressants. Commonly reported side effects include dizziness, postural hypotension, dry mouth, blurred vision, edema, decreased libido or potency, weight gain, sweating, nausea, and headache. As with cyclic antidepressants, the initial period of treatment is the most difficult in terms of side effects, which generally diminish after 1 to 2 weeks.

Unlike the imipramine literature, most controlled studies of phenelzine have evaluated medication alone, without concurrent behavior therapy. Studies that have compared behavioral treatments to phenelzine have tended to find few qualitative or quantitative differences in response between the two (Lipsedge et al., 1973; Solyom et al., 1973). Combined drug and behavioral treatment was superior to either treatment alone in some, but not all, studies (Solyom et al., 1981); some degree of supportive psychotherapy accompanied medication prescription in most published reports, but such therapy was generally not controlled or carefully described. While there is some suggestion that MAOIs may work more quickly than behavioral treatment, estimates of relapse rates off medication range from 66 to 100% in those studies reporting it, which is considerably greater than that following behavioral treatment.

At present there is little guidance for predicting either which patients will respond to MAOIs or which drug within the class may be most effective. In addition to phenelzine, iproniazid has been found effective in a controlled trial (Lipsedge et al., 1973), and tranylcypromine and isocarboxazid have also been reported anecdotally to be effective (Kelly, Guirguis, Frommer, Mitchell-Heggs, & Sargant, 1970). Level of depression and of personality pathology and duration of illness have been associated with poorer outcome in some, but not all studies.

In summary, the present evidence suggests that MAOIs are as good as or better than cyclic antidepressants in their effect on panic–agoraphobia. As in treatment of depression, however, such medications are seldom drugs of first choice because of the necessity for a low-tyramine diet and the possibility of dangerous drug interactions.

Alprazolam and Other Benzodiazepines

Although Klein suggested in early reports that benzodiazepine-type anxiolytics were ineffective for panic attacks, interest in possible antipanic properties of these medications has revived considerably since the late 1970s. The major focus of attention has been on the triazolobenzodiazepine alprazolam, although this compound is probably not unique among benzodiazepines in its antipanic effects.

Of six controlled studies of alprazolam in panic disorder, all have shown the effectiveness of the drug, with a mean response rate of about 75% compared to a placebo response ranging from 31 to 63% (Ballenger et al., 1988; Charney et al., 1986; Dunner, Ishiki, Avery, Wilson, & Hyde, 1980; Rizley et al., 1986; Sheehan et al., 1984; Swinson, Pecknold, & Kuch, 1986). Although the numbers of patients treated was small in most studies, a recent large-scale study of alprazolam compared to placebo, using over 500 patients, reported very similar findings (Ballenger et al., 1988). Alprazolam has been found to reduce both spontaneous and situational panic attacks, as well as anticipatory anxiety. However, higher generalized anxiety predicted poorer response in one study (Liebowitz et al., 1986), and there is some indication that avoidant behaviors respond more poorly to the drug than anxiety symptoms themselves. Surprisingly, one study has found alprazolam superior to imipramine in mood improvement (Rizley et al., 1986). Most studies to date have not employed concurrent behavioral treatments, except to the extent that they are part of supportive–instructive medication management.

Daily doses of alprazolam have ranged from 1 to 10 mg, with a mean of 3.7 mg. Although carefully designed studies of dose response have not been done, some authors have suggested that 40% or more of patients may need 4 to 10 mg daily to obtain a good response. Alexander and Alexander (1986) obtained good antipanic effects at a mean dose of 2.2 mg, but they needed an average of 3.9 mg for substantial improvement of phobic avoidance.

Alprazolam appears to be both faster in onset and better tolerated than antidepressants. Virtually all reports have described a clinically significant response in 1 week or less, although continued improvement has been found after 6 or 7 weeks of treatment. Alprazolam is the only antipanic drug so far studied for which the placebo dropout rate (28% in three studies) exceeds the dropout on active drug (12% in six studies). By far the most

common side effect is sedation, which is reported in more than two thirds of patients taking the drug. Other common side effects include slurred speech, fatigue, and changes in cognitive ability, most often confusion and amnesia. Serious side effects such as delirium, combativeness, and hepatotoxicity appear to occur in no more than about 1% of patients (Noyes et al., 1988). Manic reactions also occasionally occur in panic patients with no known bipolar history, just as such reactions occur in some depressed patients (Pecknold & Fleury, 1986).

The most problematic features of alprazolam are the tendency for panic symptoms to break through, requiring escalating doses, and the risk of rebound–withdrawal syndromes when the dose is lowered. Liebowitz et al. (1986) found that 40% or more of patients in a 12-week study required an increase over their initial therapeutic dose, confirming the common clinical observation that patients frequently habituate to the effects of benzodiazepines.

Problems of dependency and abstinence syndromes with benzodiazepines have been recognized and described for many years. Withdrawal may entail such serious complications as grand mal seizures or confusional states. In the recent multicenter study of panic–agoraphobia, Pecknold, Swinson, Kuch, and Lewis (1988) monitored discontinuation effects prospectively. They distinguished among *relapse*, a return of reported symptoms that had been ameliorated or abolished by treatment; *rebound*, recurrence of such symptoms to a greater degree following discontinuation than occurred before treatment; and *withdrawal*, the appearance of new symptoms on discontinuation, which had not been present before treatment. The study design called for 8 weeks of active treatment, followed by a 4-week taperdown period, and 2 weeks of posttaper assessment.

Patients' medication was tapered at a maximum rate of 1 mg every 3 days, but many could tolerate reductions of no more than 1 mg weekly. At this rate of tapering, 35% of patients experienced rebound panic attacks (defined as at least twice the pretreatment panic frequency), and another 35% experienced withdrawal phenomena, confirming the findings of others that patients may experience difficulties even when medication is slowly tapered. The most prominent withdrawal

symptoms included confusion, clouded sensorium, muscular cramps or twitches, gastrointestinal discomfort, paresthesias, and altered sensory
perceptions. No patients had these symptoms to a
life-threatening or incapacitating degree. Not surprisingly, those with more severe withdrawal
symptoms also tended to have rebound panic attacks. Rebound and withdrawal phenomena generally abated over the course of the 2-week follow-
up. Of all patients, 90% were rated as globally
improved during the last week of active treatment;
only 39% were so judged 1 week after discontinuation, but after 2 weeks, the figure was back up to
73%. The authors recommend a tapering period of
8 weeks or longer, with weekly reductions of no
more than 0.5 mg, using four daily divided doses.
Because follow-up continued for only 2 weeks
after tapering, it is hard to assess the true relapse
rate, as opposed to transient worsening due to
withdrawal symptoms. The literature does not yet
provide the answer to this question.

Alprazolam is an atypical benzodiazepine in
that it contains a triazole ring not found in other
drugs of its class, and it has been reported to
possess antidepressant effects (Fawcett & Kravitz,
1982). Although one may question whether alprazolam's antipanic effects are due to its special
characteristics, recent studies of other benzodiazepines, including diazepam, lorazepam, and
clonazepam, suggest that this is not the case
(Rickels & Schweizer, 1986). Two controlled
studies have found diazepam significantly more
effective against panic–agoraphobia than placebo,
with success rates comparable to the higher range
of doses for generalized anxiety disorder (Noyes et
al., 1984; Taylor, Kenigsberg, & Robinson, 1982).
Dunner et al. (1986) compared diazepam (10–100
mg, mean 44 mg) to alprazolam (1–10 mg, mean
4 mg) in patients with generalized anxiety, agoraphobia, and panic attacks, and they found essentially no difference between the active drugs in
their effects on panic and generalized anxiety;
placebo decreased anticipatory anxiety, but not
panics. The major side effect of diazepam was
drowsiness, which tended to abate over the first 2
weeks.

Clonazepam, a high-potency benzodiazepine
with a half-life of 18–54 hours (as compared to
8–14 hours for alprazolam) has received consider-

able recent attention. Uncontrolled studies have
found improvement in panic attacks in 80% or
more of patients remaining on the drug (Fontaine,
1985; Spier, 1986). Mean doses in these studies
correspond to a potency of about twice that of
alprazolam, although doses of up to 10 mg daily
have been used. A potential advantage of clonazepam is that its longer half-life mitigates against
interdose rebound–withdrawal effects and attendant anticipatory anxiety. Herman, Rosenbaum,
and Brotman (1987) crossed 48 patients having
difficulties with interdose anxiety from alprazolam over to clonazepam. A mean dose of 2.95
mg alprazolam mapped onto 1.5 mg clonazepam,
which provided a superior therapeutic effect in
82% of the study patients. Most of the clonazepam
patients were able to use a twice-daily dosing
schedule, whereas they had required four or more
daily doses when taking alprazolam. The major
side effect of clonazepam is drowsiness, and current studies report a dropout rate of about 15%,
which is roughly comparable to that of alprazolam. The need to increase dosage over time may
be a problem with clonazepam, as it is with other
benzodiazepines. Pollack, Tesar, Rosenbaum, and
Spier (1986) found that 40% of patients treated
with clonazepam over the course of a year required
dose elevations.

In summary, the efficacy of alprazolam in
panic–agoraphobia has been clearly established,
and the efficacy of other benzodiazepine compounds is strongly suggested. Further controlled
studies will be needed to determine both the range
of effective drugs in this class and the parameters
for their use.

Antiadrenergic Drugs

Although the adrenergic theory of panic attacks
would predict an important place for adrenergic
antagonists in treatment, relatively little systematic work has been done with such medications,
and the results to date have been unimpressive.
The beta-adrenergic blocker propranolol has long
been recognized as diminishing some forms of
anxiety, but it has been very little studied in patients with well-defined PD. Heiser and De-
Francisco (1976) have suggested that propranolol
in doses of 30 to 60 mg daily may alleviate panics

of recent onset but may be less effective in more chronic panic patients. Munjack et al. (1985) compared propranolol in doses up to 160 mg daily with imipramine in doses up to 300 mg and found generally comparable effects on most measures of anxiety; after 6 weeks, 57% of imipramine patients and 43% of propranolol patients were panic free. Patients with greater severity of phobic ideation tended to do better on imipramine. Patients had difficulty tolerating the side effects of both drugs, with an overall dropout rate of about 40%. Those who could not tolerate more than 40 mg daily of propranolol had less therapeutic benefit.

A conflicting result was reported by Noyes et al. (1984), who gave propranolol in doses of 80–320 mg daily (mean 240 mg) and found no overall improvement in panic attacks after 2 weeks. A few patients who initially improved on the drug had escaped the effect by the end of the study. Similarly, Gorman et al. (1983) found that propranolol failed to block panic-inducing effects of lactate infusions. No studies have yet compared propranolol to placebo. Thus, the place, if any, of this medication in treatment of panic–agoraphobia is as yet unclear.

Clonidine is an alpha-2 adrenergic agonist that, at low to moderate doses, binds primarily to presynaptic receptors, thereby decreasing release of norepinephrine. It has been shown to markedly decrease firing of the LC. Two studies have suggested a limited effect of clonidine in panic patients. Liebowitz, Fyer, McGrath, and Klein (1981) found good antipanic response in 4 of 11 patients given 0.2–0.5 mg in divided doses. However, by the end of 8 weeks, all subjects tended to escape from the therapeutic effects. Hoehn-Saric, Merchant, Keyser, and Smith (1982) used comparable doses in a placebo-controlled study. They found that 75% had at least a mild antianxiety response, and almost 20% had an excellent response, although no specific measures of panic were included in the assessment. No tolerance to the beneficial effects was found over 6 weeks of observation. Typical side effects in both studies included dry mouth, blurred vision, tension, irritability, sleep disturbance, and sexual dysfunction.

At present, not enough is known about the benefits of propranolol or clonidine to recommend their routine use in treatment of panic–agoraphobia. At most, they may be considered adjunctive in treatment-resistant patients, or those unable to tolerate sufficient doses of other medications.

TREATMENT STRATEGIES

Successful treatment of panic–agoraphobia requires skillful management of the psychological context in which medications are given, as well as judicious prescription of the medications themselves. Treatment that includes adequate consideration of the following three elements will maximize the patient's comfort, sense of mastery and control, compliance with medication, and ultimate outcome of treatment: (1) patient education, (2) treatment planning, and (3) choice of medication.

Patient Education

Once a solid diagnosis of panic disorder with or without agoraphobia is made, it is very important to give the patient an accurate, simple model of his or her disease. Many patients with this condition are chronically demoralized, suspecting that some personal failing is responsible for their symptoms. Others may fear that something is seriously wrong with them physically. Patients often report spending much time in psychotherapy attempting to deal with possible underlying emotional issues, but getting no symptomatic relief. Family members may view the symptoms as attention-getting or dependent maneuvers that the patient can willfully control.

Explaining that biological, possibly genetic factors are thought to be necessary for developing the disease, and that it bears no specific relationship to any personality type or life situation can help to lift the patient's self-esteem and to alleviate blame and stigma within his or her family. The physician's description of the variety of the most commonly experienced panic symptoms and the circumstances under which they occur usually helps the patient to feel understood and to understand that his or her condition is not bizarre, unique, or life-threatening. For patients (probably a majority) in whom spontaneous panic attacks precede the onset of phobic avoidance, the "fear of becoming afraid" model of agoraphobia can have considerable explanatory power and can pave the way for acceptance of medications to eliminate panics. The most important and useful points in presenting the medical view of panic–agoraphobia are that panic attacks, whether or not associated with current stressors or feared situations, (a) have a life of their own, (b) do not necessarily remit with environmental changes, and (c) may need to be treated pharmacologically.

It is also important to keep in mind that personality traits and interpersonal stresses may affect the course of the illness. Studies have shown that while personality factors do not influence the antipanic response to medications, they do influence outcome in terms of overall level of functioning (Reich, 1988). It is therefore important to assess the degree to which family conflict or maladaptive patterns of behavior play a part in the patient's current life. Where these are prominent, their effects on the patient's ability to cope with her or his illness should be stressed, and adjunctive psychotherapy may be recommended.

Treatment Planning

Collaborative treatment planning, important in any form of psychiatric treatment, is essential to success with panic–agoraphobic patients because they feel a great need to be in control, and they are often both highly apprehensive about medications and hypersensitive to their effects. Patients should be told that the primary action of the medication is to block panic attacks, but that it will probably also help diminish general anxiety and improve overall sense of well-being. Patients with avoidant behaviors should be encouraged to begin to try to face their feared situations once medicaton has been stabilized and they notice a beneficial effect on panic attacks. They must be helped to understand the need to test for themselves their susceptibility to panicking in various situations.

The physician should also discuss the range of medication options, side effects of each type of medication, and the major points for and against each. The patient's reaction to the description of side effects is an important guide to choice of a starting regimen. The patient's history of toleration and effectiveness of prior treatments should also influence medication choice. Whichever

medication is chosen, the patient should receive a full description of likely side effects; the danger of frightening the patient away from treatment is not as great as that of losing him or her when unanticipated side effects are noticed. It is also important for the physician to be available by telephone between appointments so that the patient can check in about troublesome physical symptoms and receive reassurance or revised medication instructions. The knowledge that someone is available to help if needed exerts a powerful moderating effect on the symptoms of panic–agoraphobia, so that an appropriate degree of availability is in itself an important component of the physician's treatment regimen.

Choice of Medication

There is no universally best type of medication for treatment of panic–agoraphobia. Benzodiazepines are easily tolerated and fast acting, but they may need to be used in escalating doses and may have unpleasant or dangerous withdrawal effects. Cyclic antidepressants are generally free of these liabilities, but they are often poorly tolerated. Monoamine oxidase inhibitors may be the most potent antipanic agents currently available, but they necessitate a special diet and carry the risk of potentially dangerous medication interactions. Furthermore, there are presently no known patient variables that predict differential drug response. Thus, the patient's preferences about medication may be the best determinant of where to start.

When the patient has no past history of medication treatment and no strong predilections, it is reasonable to begin with low doses of a benzodiazepine, because these drugs are well tolerated and may ameliorate the early side effects of an antidepressant if it becomes necessary to add one. Furthermore, such a starting regimen capitalizes on the tendency of panic patients to be placebo responders. While we have no hard evidence that any benzodiazepine is more effective or better tolerated than any other in treatment of panic disorder, more is known about panic patients' response to alprazolam than to other benzodiazepines, so it is a reasonable drug of first choice. A starting level of 1 mg daily, given in three or four divided doses is conservative, and it can be evaluated for efficacy within several days. If the benefits at this level are partial or minimal, the dose can be raised to the 3–4 mg level at which many patients will respond.

Patients who fail to respond satisfactorily to benzodiazepines, or who require repeated elevation of dose to maintain a therapeutic effect, should be considered for an antidepressant trial. Imipramine is usually the drug of first choice, simply because there is so much published clinical experience with it; however, other cyclic antidepressants should not be excluded if their side effect profiles better fit the patient's needs. Most published studies have used a starting dose of 25 mg of imipramine, with increases of 25 mg every 2 to 3 days, but either higher or lower doses might be used, depending upon the patient's apprehensiveness about medication and past history of medication trials. Some patients are so sensitive to side effects, particularly the early feelings of shakiness and tension, that they may require months to arrive at a therapeutic dose. In such cases, reassurance, support, and gentle persistence are essential to a successful outcome. Dividing the dose may help to alleviate the side effects. Concomitant treatment with benzodiazepines may also be very helpful in moderating the stimulant effects of antidepressants, as well as patients' secondary anxiety responses to them. Many patients will ultimately do well on one medication alone, so that an attempt should be made slowly to taper benzodiazepines once an effective dose of antidepressant has been reached.

Monoamine oxidase inhibitors are available as third-line medications if others have been ineffective or poorly tolerated. Most published clinical experience has been with phenelzine. A starting dose of 15 mg may be increased to 45 mg daily in divided doses over the course of a week. The dose must be pushed up to 90 mg daily in some patients, to achieve maximum therapeutic benefit. Propranolol or clonidine may be added to other medications if therapeutic benefits are unsatisfactory, although they must be used cautiously, to avoid hypotensive difficulties when given with antidepressants. One might expect that propranolol and clonidine would be particularly effective in alleviating the somatic manifestations of anxiety, but this has not been found thus far in panic–agoraphobic patients. Dosing with these drugs must still be a matter of trial and error, but one could not

be sure of a negative result unless more than 200 mg propranolol or 0.3–0.5 mg clonidine had been used. Propranolol dose increases should be kept to 40 mg every 2 or 3 days, with frequent blood pressure checks, to avoid undue hypotension.

Despite the physician's best efforts, there remain cases in which the patient fails to respond adequately to medication or is unable to tolerate any combination of medications in sufficient doses for a therapeutic effect. For such patients, behavioral treatments are the major option, either alone, or in combination with medications. Combined treatment is most frequently needed when patients are unable to break avoidant patterns using only medication and supportive psychotherapy. In such cases, concurrent structured exposure treatments are likely to be more effective in reducing agoraphobic behaviors. Furthermore, although the literature is divided on the issue, some authors have found combined behavior and drug treatment to be more effective for anxiety and avoidant behaviors than either type of treatment alone (Telch et al., 1985). A relatively recent behavioral strategy aims at reducing panic symptoms directly, rather than the more traditional approach of focusing on avoidant behaviors. Treatment of this kind, which is based on desensitizing patients to the physical symptoms of their own panic attacks, may become increasingly available for patients unable or unwilling to use medication for panic reduction.

CASE EXAMPLES

Case 1. The patient is a 26-year-old married woman with one child. She has a long psychiatric history, going back to her teenage years, which were notable for school truancy and polysubstance abuse. Her family history includes a mother with several "nervous breakdowns" and a father who chronically uses antianxiety medication. The patient dates the onset of her anxiety disorder to her early teen years, when she began to have spontaneous panic attacks, characterized by intense fear, palpitations, and air hunger. She began avoiding public transportation and other public situations from which she could not exit easily (such as school) soon after the onset of panics. The drugs she abused were various but mostly restricted to alcohol, marijuana, and prescription medications such as barbiturates and diazepam. Although she did not finish high school, she successfully completed a GED (general education diploma) course when she was 19 years old, walking 3 miles each way to attend classes. She had a series of clinging relationships with one boyfriend after another, and she married when she was 20. At the time she presented herself for treatment, she had recently discovered that her husband was having an affair.

The patient had participated in behavioral therapy several times, for several months at a time. The therapy did not help her panic attacks, but it moderated her avoidant behavior to some extent. However, she always dropped out because of the difficulty getting to her appointments. She had been tried briefly on imipramine, which did help the panic attacks, but she stopped taking it because it made her feel "like a zombie" and made her very dizzy whenever she stood up; she therefore feared that the medication was making her sicker. At the time of presentation, she had stopped using most drugs, but she sedated herself with alcohol and with diazepam, which she got from physicians, friends, and relatives. The diazepam was used erratically, according to when she felt she needed it, in doses up to 70 mg daily.

The patient presented herself for treatment, brought by her husband, who complained of her dependency and her "hysterical" behavior. After going over her history, the diagnosis and nature of the disorder were reviewed with the patient and her husband. It was explained that the patient was probably not a primary substance abuser, but she had been attempting to self-medicate with what was available. The initial goals of treatment were (1) to get control of the panic attacks, which were occurring at the rate of several daily, and (2) to reduce and regularize the patient's use of diazepam. An antidepressant was chosen as the drug of first choice because the patient (a) was still having panic attacks on large doses of benzodiazepine, (b) had continuing difficulty using such medications appropriately, and (3) had a history of good antipanic response to imipramine. Desipramine was chosen as the starting medication because of its structural similarity to imipramine, with a more favorable side effect profile.

Because the patient was extremely apprehensive about starting another antidepressant, she was begun on only 10 mg daily and told to call in after 3 days to report the effect, or earlier if she had any questions or concerns. She was also asked to restrict her diazepam intake to 10 mg three times daily, to be taken regularly every day.

The patient called after the second dose of medication, saying that she was *more* anxious than before taking it. Following discussion, she was able to distinguish between the physical sense of tremulousness related to the medication and her usual symptoms of anxiety. She was able to agree to take the same dose until her next appointment the following week. At that time, she was tolerating the medication well enough to raise the dose to 10 mg twice daily. At this dose, she felt "freaked out" and very jumpy, but she was able to tolerate 15 mg per day.

By the end of the third month of treatment, the patient was taking 50 mg of desipramine and noticing some moderation of her panic attacks. She described feeling as if a panic attack were coming on, with fearfulness and palpitations, but she never developed hyperventilation or the full degree of severity. She was less successful in regulating her diazepam intake, often taking extra doses during stressful situations, such as fights with her husband.

During her appointments, the patient was helped to distinguish between panic anxiety, anticipatory anxiety, and somatic sensations associated with medication increase. She was counseled about the danger of rebound anxiety following high doses of benzodiazepines. She was encouraged to begin to venture into feared situations as her panic attacks moderated, but for some time, she continued to demand that her husband accompany her when she went outside her home. Several sessions were spent with the patient and her husband, reviewing the course of her illness and considering the ways in which it had interfered with her functioning in the marriage. With the advice of the physician, the couple agreed to a course of marital counseling to address issues of control and dependency in the relationship.

Over the next few months, the patient was able to become less avoidant and to begin to perform routine errands outside the house. Her dose of desipramine was gradually increased to 150 mg daily, first in divided doses, and then taken all at bedtime. At this dose, she was entirely free of panic attacks and able to stay on a steady dose of diazepam, 30 mg daily. As her concerns about panics diminished and her relationship with her husband improved, she agreed to withdraw from diazepam over a 1-month period. She was maintained on desipramine alone, with monthly psychiatric appointments, and no recurrence of panic attacks or return to inappropriate self-medication. She was able to perform her daily routine, both in and out of the house, without anxiety. She continued to insist on monthly psychiatric visits and continued to be somewhat dependent in her marriage, although less clinging and demanding.

Case 2. The patient is a 45-year-old married man with three children. He had grown up in a household with a highly irritable father who drank to excess and physically abused the children. The patient had had a series of severe depressive episodes starting in college and recurring every 5 to 7 years. These had been untreated, and remitted spontaneously after 2 to 3 months. He had had no episodes of mania or hypomania.

Two months after a depressive episode at age 34, he noted the onset of acute episodes of palpitations, tingling of the arms and legs, churning stomach, and intense fear that he was about to die of a heart attack. These attacks occurred as often as three or four times in some weeks, and the patient became constantly tense and apprehensive in anticipation of the next attack. Attacks seemed to be increased at times of high pressure on his job as a corporate executive, and though they could occur anywhere, they were especially likely when he was driving his car. After a physical evaluation revealed no medical problems, the patient pushed himself through his panic episodes by verbally reassuring himself; he did not curtail his usual activities. He noted increased irritability around the time of panic attacks, and on occasion found himself raising his fist to his wife or children.

Seeing his problem as "emotional" he entered insight-oriented weekly psychotherapy, where he examined his emotionally distant interpersonal style and its probable antecedents in early family life. After 18 months of therapy he noted closer relationships with his wife and children, but no effects on his panic attacks, anticipatory anxiety, or irritability. After seeing a magazine article describing panic disorder and its possible biological causes, his wife suggested he seek a psychopharmacological consultation. He expressed a willingness to try medication, but he continued to feel that he should be able to control his anxiety, and that some ill-understood aspect of his personality was responsible for it. He accepted the medical model, but he frequently checked with the psychiatrist about whether he might be able to control his symptoms by willpower or further self-awareness.

The patient was begun on 25 mg of imipramine daily, with a plan to increase by 25 mg every 3 days. However, at his 1-week follow-up visit, he noted that he had only one full panic attack since starting medication. The dose was held at 50 mg daily for 1 month, during which the patient reported no further panic attacks. However, he continued to have sensations of tension, stomach churning, and irritability, which occurred in an unpredictable waxing and waning pattern. An attempt to raise the imipramine further brought no added relief, but it produced an uncomfortable "spacy" feeling. The dose of imipramine was returned to 50 mg, and a regimen of lorazepam, 1 mg three times daily (t.i.d.) was begun. The patient reported dimished tension, but continued periods of irritability, difficulty controlling his temper, and churning stomach. Raising lorazepam to 2 mg t.i.d. produced lethargy, but it did not change the irritability or gastrointestinal symptoms. Propranolol 20 mg t.i.d. was started. Within 1 week, the patient reported markedly diminished GI symptoms, and his family no longer found him to be snappish and irritable. He continued to do well on the combination therapy, but periodic attempts to withdraw any of the medication brought a return of symptoms. Two years after the onset of pharmacotherapy, the patient again became severely depressed. Imipramine was raised to 250 mg daily, and the depression remitted within 3 weeks. Although the patient tolerated the higher dose during his depression, he quickly became uncomfortable on it when euthymic again, thereby requiring another lowering of the dose to 100 mg, with no recurrence of depression.

Case 3. The patient is a 40-year-old twice-divorced woman. She described a history of frequent low moods dating back to her early 20s. Typically, she would experience severe depression with lethargy and hypersomnia for several weeks following bad fights or breakups with her husbands or boyfriends; however, she had had two such depressive episodes that lasted for several months. One of the depressions had been treated with amitriptyline, which she stopped taking as soon as she began to feel slightly better because of severe dry mouth, blurred vision, and constipation. She was known as a "nervous" and "overly sensitive" person, and she felt that these traits had contributed to her difficulty forming a lasting relationship with a man.

She presented herself for consultation when, in the midst of a turbulent romantic involvement, she began to have periods of intense panic, with tingling of her face and hands, palpitations, and dizziness. These occurred at a rate of 5–10 times weekly. The nature of the problem and its treatment were discussed with the patient. Because of her susceptibility to depressions, it was decided to begin with an antidepressant trial, which might stabilize her mood as well as alleviate the panics. She was begun on 25 mg of imipramine, with semiweekly dose increases until a dose of 200 mg daily was reached, at which point the panics were completely blocked. She continued to be generally anxious, however, and to go through periods of intense dysphoria and lethargy following interpersonal disappointments.

After 3 months on imipramine, the patient began to complain of episodes of severe orthostatic hypotension. Because she was not comfortable with adding medications to counteract this problem, she was crossed over to nortriptyline, by adding 25 mg of nortriptyline and dropping 50 mg imipramine every 2 days until the patient was on 75 mg daily of nortriptyline alone. On this dose, her blood level was 45 mcg/L. Her dose was raised to 125 mg daily, with a blood level of 76 mcg/L, on which she did as well as she had on imipramine, with no orthostatic hypotension. She did complain of persistent dry mouth and blurred vision, however.

Over the next 6 months, an attempt was made to control the patient's generalized anxiety by adding alprazolam. However, because her levels of anxiety fluctuated considerably from day to day, requiring between 1 and 6 mg daily for adequate control, it was difficult to establish an appropriate standing dose. Large pro re nata (p.r.n.–as needed) dosing changes became problematic because of rebound anxiety and withdrawal effects. Furthermore, although the patient experienced no extended periods of severe depression, she continued to describe hyperreactive moods with frequent dysphoria and lethargy.

A trial on MAOIs was proposed as a possible way to control both the panic attacks and the depressions. Nortriptyline was stopped, while alprazolam was maintained at a level of 1 mg three times daily. The patient was given a 5-day washout period, during which she had two limited-symptom panic attacks, with some degree of fear and tingling of her hands and face. Phenelzine was started with a daily 15 mg dose, which was raised by 15 mg every 3 days, to a level of 45 mg daily. During the following 2 weeks, the patient reported three more limited-symptom attacks, requiring the dose of phenelzine to be raised to 30 mg twice daily. No further panic

symptoms occurred at this dose. The patient had reported initial sleep disturbance at the lower dose, which cleared after 1 week, but returned transiently when the dose was raised. At 60 mg daily, she also began to report severe dizziness when standing up, which was found to be accompanied by a 25 mm systolic blood pressure drop. The patient was put on a regimen of increased salt and fluid intake, which moderated the symptom to the point of being tolerable.

After 2 months on the combined phenelzine–alprazolam regimen, the patient noted marked diminution of her reactive mood swings, along with a general decrease in her level of anxiety. She noted that it was the first time in her life when she was not constantly expecting to become depressed or panicky. Alprazolam was slowly tapered over the next 2 months, with no return of panic or generalized anxiety. The patient noted a 10-pound weight gain, as well as slight dry mouth, but she was willing to tolerate these because of her general improvement. After 1 year of treatment, she reported continued absence of panics and improved mood stability. She felt calmer, more self-confident, and more satisfied with her personal relationships.

REFERENCES

Ackerman, S. H., & Sachar, E. J. (1974). The lactate theory of anxiety: A review and reevaluation. *Psychosomatic Medicine, 36*, 69–81.

Alexander, P. E., & Alexander, D. D. (1986). Alprazolam treatment for panic disorder. *Journal of Clinical Psychiatry, 47*, 301–304.

Aronson, T. A. (1987). A naturalistic study of imipramine in panic disorder and agoraphobia. *American Journal of Psychiatry, 144*, 1014–1019.

Aston-Jones, S. L., Foote, F. E., & Bloom, F. E. (1984). Anatomy and physiology of locus coeruleus neurons: Functional implications. In M. G. Ziegler & C. R. Lake (Eds.), *Norepinephrine: Frontiers of clinical neuroscience* (Vol. 2). Baltimore, MD: Williams & Wilkins.

Ballenger, J. C. (1986). Pharmacotherapy of panic disorder. *Journal of Clinical Psychiatry, 47* (6 suppl.), 27–32.

Ballenger, J. C., Burrows, G. D., DuPont, R. L., Lesser, I. M., Noyes, R., Pecknold, J. D., Rifkin, A., & Swinson, R. P. (1988). Alprazolam in panic disorder and agoraphobia: Results from a multicenter trial. I.

Efficacy in short-term treatment. *Archives of General Psychiatry, 45*, 413–422.

Ballenger, J. C., Peterson, G. A., Laraia, M., Hucek, A., Lake, C. R., Jimerson, D., Cox, D. J., Trockman, C., Shipe, J., & Wilkinson, C. (1984). A study of plasma catecholamines in agoraphobia and the relationship of serum tricyclic levels to treatment response. In J. C. Ballenger (Ed.), *Biology of agoraphobia*. Washington, DC: American Psychiatric Press.

Barlow, D. H. (1986). A psychological model of panic. In B. F. Shaw, F. Cushman, Z. V. Segal, & T. M. Vallis (Eds.), *Anxiety disorders: Theory, diagnosis, and treatment*. New York: Plenum.

Barlow, D. H., Vermilyea, J. A., Blanchard, E. B., Vermiliyea, B. B., DiNardo, P. A., & Cery, J. A. (1985). The phenomenon of panic. *Journal of Abnormal Psychology, 94*, 320–328.

Breier, A., Charney, D. S., & Heninger, E. R. (1986). Agoraphobia with panic attacks: Development, diagnostic stability, and course of illness. *Archives of General Psychiatry, 43*, 1029–1036.

Carr, D. B., & Sheehan, D. V. (1984). Panic anxiety: A new biological model. *Journal of Clinical Psychiatry, 45*, 323–330.

Charney, D. S., & Heninger, G. R. (1985). Noradrenergic function and the mechanism of action of antianxiety treatment: I. The effect of long-term alprazolam treatment. *Archives of General Psychiatry, 42*, 458–467.

Charney, D. S., Heninger, G. R., & Breier, A. (1984). Noradrenergic function in panic anxiety. Effects of yohimbine in healthy subjects and patients with agoraphobia and panic disorder. *Archives of General Psychiatry, 41*, 751–763.

Charney, D. S., Heninger, G. R., & Jatlow, P. I. (1985). Increased anxiogenic effects of caffeine in panic disorders. *Archives of General Psychiatry, 42*, 233–243.

Charney, D. S., Menkes, D. B., & Heninger, G. R. (1981). Receptor sensitivity and the mechanism of action of antidepressant treatment. *Archives of General Psychiatry, 38*, 1160–1180.

Charney, D. S., Woods, S. W., Goodman, W. K., Rifkin, G., Kinch, M., Aiken, B., Quadrino, L. M., & Heninger, G. R. (1988). Drug treatment of panic disorder: The comparative efficacy of imipramine, alprazolam, and triazolam. *Journal of Clinical Psychiatry, 47*, 580–586.

Coryell, W., Noyes, R., Crowe, R., & Chaudhry, D. (1985). Abnormal escape from dexamethasone suppression in agoraphobia with panic attacks. *Psychiatry Research, 15*, 301–311.

Curtis, G. C., Cameron, O. G., & Nesse, R. (1982). The dexamethasone suppression test in panic disorder and agoraphobia. *American Journal of Psychiatry, 139*, 1042–1046.

Davidson, J., Linnoila, M., Raft, D., & Turnbull, C. D. (1981). MAO inhibition and control of anxiety following amitriptyline therapy. *Acta Psychiatrica Scandinavica, 63*, 147–152.

Dunner, D. L., Ishiki, D., Avery, D. H., Wilson, L. G., & Hyde, T. S. (1986). Effect of alprazolam and diazepam on anxiety and panic attacks in panic disorder: A controlled study. *Journal of Clinical Psychiatry, 47*, 458–480.

Easton, J. D., & Sherman, D. G. (1976). Somatic anxiety attacks and propranolol. *Archives of Neurology, 33*, 689–691.

Evans, L., Kenardy, J., Schneider, P., & Hoey, H. (1986). Effect of a selective serotonin uptake inhibitor in agoraphobia with panic attacks. A double-blind comparison of zimelidine, imipramine, and placebo. *Acta Psychiatrica Scandinavica, 73*, 49–53.

Evans, L., Schneider, P., Ross-Lee, L., Wiltshire, G., Eadie, M., Kenardy, J., & Hoey, H. (1985). Plasma serotonin levels in agoraphobia (letter). *American Journal of Psychiatry, 142*, 267.

Fawcett, J., & Kravitz, H. M. (1982). Alprazolam: Pharmacokinetics, clinical efficacy, and mechanism of action. *Pharmacotherapy, 2*, 243–254.

Fontaine, R. (1985). Clonazepam for panic disorders and agitation. *Psychosomatics, 20* (12, suppl.), 13–18.

Freud, S. (1962). Obsessions and phobias: Their psychological mechanism and their etiology. In J. Strachey (Ed. and Trans.), *The standard edition of the complete psychological works of Sigmund Freud* (Vol. 3). London: Hogarth.

Freud, S. (1963). Introductory lectures on psychoanalysis: Lecture 25. Anxiety. In J. Strachey (Ed. and Trans.), *The standard edition of the complete psychological works of Sigmund Freud* (Vol. 16). London: Hogarth.

Frohlich, E. D., Tarazi, K. C., & Duston, H. P. (1969). Hyperdynamic beta-adrenergic circulatory state. *Archives of Internal Medicine, 123*, 1–7.

Gaffney, F. A., Fenton, B. J., Lane, L. D., & Lake, C. R. (1988). Hemodynamic, ventilatory, and biochemical responses of panic patients and normal controls with sodium lactate infusion and spontaneous panic attacks. *Archives of General Psychiatry, 45*, 53–60.

Garakani, H., Zitrin, C. M., & Klein, D. F. (1984).

Treatment of panic disorder with imipramine alone. *American Journal of Psychiatry, 141*, 446–448.

Gorman, J. M., Cohen, B. S., Liebowitz, M. R., Fyer, A. J., Ross, D., Davies, S., & Klein, D. F. (1986). Blood gas changes and hypophosphatemia in lactate-induced panic. *Archives of General Psychiatry, 43*, 1067–1071.

Gorman, J. M., Fyer, A. F., Gliklich, J., King, D., & Klein, D. F. (1981). Effect of imipramine on prolapsed mitral valves of patients with panic disorder. *American Journal of Psychiatry, 138*, 477–478.

Gorman, J. M., Fyer, M. R., Goetz, R., Askanazi, J., Liebowitz, M. R., Fyer, A. J., Kinney, J., & Klein, D. F. (1988). Ventilatory physiology of patients with panic disorder. *Archives of General Psychiatry, 45*, 31–39.

Gorman, J. M., Levy, G. F., Liebowitz, M. R., McGrath, P., Appleby, I. L., Dillon, D. J., Davies, S. O., & Klein, D. F. (1983). Effect of acute B-adrenergic blockade on lactate-induced panic. *Archives of General Psychiatry, 40*, 1079–1082.

Grunhaus, L., Gloger, S., Birmacher, B., Palmer, C., & Ben-David, M. (1983). Prolactin response to the cold pressor test in patients with panic attacks. *Psychiatry Research, 8*, 171–177.

Heiser, J. F., & DeFrancisco, D. (1976). The treatment of pathological panic states with propranolol. *American Journal of Psychiatry, 133*, 1384–1393.

Herman, J. B., Rosenbaum, J. F., & Brotman, A. W. (1987). The alprazolam to clonazepam switch for the treatment of panic disorder. *Journal of Clinical Psychopharmacology, 7*, 175–178.

Hoehn-Saric, R., Merchant, A. F., Keyser, M. L., & Smith, V. K. (1982). Effects of clonidine on anxiety disorders. *Archives of General Psychiatry, 38*, 1278–1282.

Jobson, K., Linnoila, M., Gillan, J., & Sullivan, J. L. (1978). A successful treatment of severe anxiety attacks with tricyclic antidepressants: A potential mechanism of action. *American Journal of Psychiatry, 135*, 863–864.

Johnston, D. G., Trayer, I. E., & Whitsett, S. F. (1988). Clomipramine treatment of agoraphobic women. An eight week controlled trial. *Archives of General Psychiatry, 45*, 453–459.

Jones, M. T., Bridges, O. K., & Leob, P. (1968). Relationship between the cardiovascular and sympathetic response to the psychological stress of an examination. *Clinical Science, 35*, 73–79.

Kahn, R. J., McNair, D. M., Lipman, R. S., Covi, L., Rickels, K., Downing, R., Fisher, S., & Frankenthaler, L. M. (1986). Imipramine and chlordiazepoxide in depressive and anxiety disorders: II. Efficacy in anxious outpatients. *Archives of General Psychiatry, 43*, 79–85.

Kantor, J. S., Zitrin, C. M., & Zeldis, S. M. (1980). Mitral valve prolapse syndrome in agoraphobic patients. *American Journal of Psychiatry, 137*, 467–469.

Kelly, D., Guirguis, W., Frommer, E., Mitchell-Heggs, N., & Sargant, W. (1970). Treatment of phobic states with antidepressants: A retrospective study of 246 patients. *British Journal of Psychiatry, 116*, 387–398.

Kelly, D., Mitchell-Heggs, N., & Sherman D. (1971). Anxiety and the effects of sodium lactate assessed clinically and physiologically. *British Journal of Psychiatry, 119*, 129–141.

Klein, D. F. (1964). Delineation of two drug-responsive anxiety syndromes. *Psychopharmacologia, 5*, 347–408.

Klein, D. F., & Fink, M. (1962). Behavioral reaction patterns with phenothiazines. *Archives of General Psychiatry, 7*, 444–454.

Klein, D. F., Ross, D. C., & Cohen, P. (1987). Panic and avoidance in agoraphobia. Application of path analysis to treatment studies. *Archives of General Psychiatry, 44*, 377–385.

Klein, D. F., Zitrin, C. M., Woerner, M. G., & Ross, D. C. (1983). Treatment of phobias. II. Behavior therapy and supportive psychotherapy: Are there any specific ingredients? *Archives of General Psychiatry, 40*, 139–145.

Ko, G. N., Elsworth, J. D., Roth, R. H., Rifkin, B. G., Leigh, H., & Redmond, D. E. (1983). Panic-induced elevation of plasma MHPG levels in phobic–anxious patients. *Archives of General Psychiatry, 40*, 425–430.

Leckman, J. F., Merikanges, K. R., Pauls, D. L., Prusoff, B. A., & Weissman, M. M. (1983). Anxiety disorders associated with episodes of depression: Family study data contradict DSM-III convention. *American Journal of Psychiatry, 140*, 880–882.

Lidyard, R. B. (1987). Desipramine in agoraphobia with panic attacks: An open, fixed-dose study. *Journal of Clinical Psychopharmacology, 7*, 258–260.

Lieberman, J. A., Brenner, R., Lesser, M., Coccane, E., Borenstein, M., & Kane, J. M. (1983). Dexamethasone suppression test in patients with panic disorder. *American Journal of Psychiatry, 140*, 917–919.

Liebowitz, M. R., Fyer, A. J., Gorman, J. M., Campeas, R., Levin, A., Davies, S., Goetz, D., & Klein, D. F. (1986). Alprazolam in the treatment of panic disorders. *Journal of Clinical Psychopharmacology, 6,* 13–20.

Liebowitz, M. R., Fyer, A. J., McGrath, P., & Klein, D. F. (1981). Clonidine treatment of panic disorder. *Psychopharmacology Bulletin, 17,* 122–123.

Liebowitz, M. R., Gorman, J. M., Fyer, A. J., Levitt, M., Dillon, D., Levy, G., Appleby, I. L., Anderson, S., Palij, M., Davies, S., & Klein, D. F. (1985). Lactate provocation of panic attacks: II. Biochemical and physiological findings. *Archives of General Psychiatry, 42,* 709–714.

Lipsedge, M. S., Hajioff, J., Huggins, P., Napier, L., Peerce, J., Pike, D. J., & Rich, M. (1973). The management of severe agoraphobia: A comparison of iproniazid and systematic desensitization. *Psychopharmacologia, 32,* 67–80.

Marks, I. M., Gray, S., Cohen, D., Hill, R., Mawson, D., Ramm, E., & Stern, R. (1983). Imipramine and brief therapist-aided exposure in agoraphobics having self-exposure homework. *Archives of General Psychiatry, 40,* 153–162.

Mason, F. T., & Fibiger, H. C. (1979). Anxiety: The locus coeruleus disconnection. *Life Science, 25,* 2141–2147.

Mavissakalian, M. (1987a). Initial depression and response to imipramine in agoraphobia. *Journal of Nervous and Mental Disease, 175,* 358–361.

Mavissakalian, M. (1987b). The placebo effect in agoraphobia. *Journal of Nervous and Mental Disease, 175,* 95–99.

Mavissakalian, M., & Michelson, L. (1986). Agoraphobia: Relative and combined effectiveness of therapist-assisted in vivo exposure and imipramine. *Journal of Clinical Psychiatry, 47,* 117–122.

Mavissakalian, M., & Perel, J. (1985). Imipramine in the treatment of agoraphobia: Dose–response relationship. *American Journal of Psychiatry, 142,* 1032–1036.

Mavissakalian, M., Perel, J., Bowler, K., & Dealy, R. (1987). Trazodone in the treatment of panic disorder and agoraphobia with panic attacks. *American Journal of Psychiatry, 144,* 785–787.

Mavissakalian, M., Perel, J., & Michelson, J. (1984). The relationship of plasma imipramine and N-desmethyl imipramine to improvement in agoraphobia. *Journal of Clinical Psychopharmacology, 4,* 36–40.

McNair, D. M., & Kahn, R. J. (1981). Imipramine compared with a benzodiazepine for agoraphobia. In D. M. Klein & J. Rabkin (Eds.), *Anxiety: New research and changing concepts.* New York: Raven Press.

Motulsky, H. J., & Insel, P. A. (1982). Adrenergic receptors in man: Direct identification, physiologic regulation, and clinical alterations. *New England Journal of Medicine, 307,* 18–29.

Mountjoy, C. Q., Roth, M., Garside, R. F., & Leitch, I. M. (1977). A clinical trial of phenelzine in anxiety depressive and phobic neuroses. *British Journal of Psychiatry, 131,* 486–492.

Munjack, D. J., Rebal, R., Shaner, R., Staples, F., Braun, R., & Leonard, M. (1985). Imipramine versus propranolol in the treatment of panic attacks: A pilot study. *Comprehensive Psychiatry, 26,* 80–89.

Muskin, P. R., & Fyer, A. J. (1981). Treatment of panic disorder. *Journal of Clinical Psychopharmacology, 1,* 81–90.

Noyes, R., Anderson, D. J., Clancy, J., Crowe, R. R., Slymen, D. J., Ghoneim, M. M., & Hinrichs, J. V. (1984). Diazepam and propranolol in panic disorder and agoraphobia. *Archives of General Psychiatry, 41,* 287–292.

Noyes, R. E., DuPont, R. L., Pecknold, J. C., Rifkin, A., Rubin, R. T., Swinson, R. P., Ballenger, J. C., & Burrows, G. D. (1988). Alprazolam in panic disorder and agoraphobia: Results from a multicenter trial: II. Patient acceptance, side effects, and safety. *Archives of General Psychiatry, 45,* 423–428.

Nurnberg, H. G., & Coccaro, E. F. (1982). Response of panic disorder and resistance of depression to imipramine. *American Journal of Psychiatry, 139,* 1060–1062.

Pecknold, J. C., & Fleury, D. (1986). Alprazolam-induced manic episode in two patients with panic disorder. *American Journal of Psychiatry, 143,* 652–653.

Pecknold, J. C., Swinson, R. P., Kuch, K., & Lewis, C. P. (1988). Alprazolam in panic disorder and agoraphobia: Results from a multicenter trial. III. Discontinuation effects. *Archives of General Psychiatry, 45,* 429–436.

Pitts, F., & McClure, J. N. (1967). Lactate metabolism in anxiety neurosis. *New England Journal of Medicine, 277,* 1329–1331.

Pohl, R., Berchou, R., & Rainey, J. M. (1982). Tricyclic antidepressants and monoamine oxidase inhibitors in the treatment of agoraphobia. *Journal of Clinical Psychopharmacology, 2,* 399–407.

Pollack, M. H., Tesar, G. E., Rosenbaum, J. F., & Spier, S. A. (1986). Clonazepam in the treatment of panic disorder and agoraphobia: A one-year follow-up. *Journal of Clinical Psychopharmacology, 6,* 302–304.

Redmond, D. E. (1977). Alterations in the function of

the locus coeruleus: A possible model for studies of anxiety. In I. Hannin & E. Usdin (Eds.), *Animal models in psychiatry and neurology*. New York: Pergamon.

Redmond, D. E. (1979). New and old evidence for the involvement of a brain norepinephrine system in anxiety. In W. E. Fann, A. D. Pokorny, & I. Karacan (Eds.), *Phenomenology and treatment of anxiety*. New York: Spectrum.

Redmond, D. E., & Huang, Y. M. (1979). Current concepts: II. New evidence for a locus coeruleus–norepinephrine connection with anxiety. *Life Science, 25*, 2149–2162.

Reich, J. H. (1988). DMS-III personality disorders and the outcome of treated panic disorder. *American Journal of Psychiatry, 145*, 1149–1152.

Reiman, E. M., Raichle, M. E., Robins, E., Butler, F. K., Herscovitch, P., Fox, P., & Perlmutter, J. (1986). The application of position emission tomography to the study of panic disorder. *American Journal of Psychiatry, 143*, 469–477.

Rickels, K. ,& Schweizer, E. E. (1986). Benzodiazepines for treatment of panic attacks: A new look. *Psychopharmacology Bulletin, 22*, 93–99.

Rizley, R., Kahn, R. J., McNair, D. M., & Frankenthaler, L. M. (1986). A comparison of alprozalam and imipramine in the treatment of agoraphobia and panic disorder. *Psychopharmacology Bulletin, 22*, 167–172.

Roy-Byrne, P., Uhde, T. W., Rubinow, D. R., & Post, R. M. (1986). Reduced TSH and prolactin response to TRH in patients with panic disorder. *American Journal of Psychiatry, 143*, 503–507.

Rubin, R. T., Miller, R. G., Clark, B. R., Poland, R. E., & Ransom, A. J. (1970). The stress of aircraft carrier landings: II. 3-methoxy-4-hydroxy-phenylethylene glycol excretion in naval aviators. *Psychosomatic Medicine, 32*, 589–597.

Sheehan, D. V., Ballenger, J., & Jacobsen, G. (1980). Treatment of endogenous anxiety with phobic, hysterical and hypochondriacal symptoms. *Archives of General Psychiatry, 37*, 51–59.

Sheehan, D. V., Coleman, J. H., Greenblatt, D. J., Jones, K. J., Levine, P. H., Orsulak, P. J., Peterson, M., Schildkraut, J. J., Uzogare, E., & Watkins, D. (1984). Some biochemical correlates of panic attacks with agoraphobia and their response to a new treatment. *Journal of Clinical Psychopharmacology, 4*, 66–75.

Sheehan, D. V., Davidson, J., Manshrek, T., & Fleet, J. (1983). Lack of efficacy of a new antidepressant (bupropion) in the treatment of panic disorder with phobias.

Solyom, C., Solyom, L., LaPierre, Y., Pecknold, J., & Morton, L. (1981). Phenelzine and exposure in the treatment of phobias. *Biological Psychiatry, 16*, 239–247.

Solyom, L., Heseltine, G. F. D., McClure, D. J., Solyom, C., Ledwidge, B., & Steinberg, G. (1973). Behavior therapy versus drug therapy in the treatment of neurosis. *Canadian Psychiatric Association Journal, 18*, 25–32.

Spier, S. A., Tesar, G. E., Rosenbaum, J. F., & Woods, S. W. (1982). Treatment of panic disorder and agoraphobia with clonazepam. *Journal of Clinical Psychiatry, 47*, 238–242.

Swinson, R. P., Pecknold, J. C., & Kuch, K. (1986). Psychopharmacological treatment of panic disorder and related states: A placebo controlled study of alprazolam. *Progress in Neuro-psychopharmacology and Biological Psychiatry, 11*, 105–113.

Taylor, C. B., Kenigsberg, M. L., & Robinson, J. M. (1982). A controlled comparison of relaxation and diazepam in panic disorder. *Journal of Clinical Psychiatry, 43*, 423–425.

Taylor, C. B., Sheikh, J., Agras, W. S., Roth, W. T., Margraf, J., Ehlers, A., Maddock, R. J., & Gossard, D. (1986). Ambulatory heart rate changes in patients with panic attacks. *American Journal of Psychiatry, 143*, 478–482.

Telch, M. J., Agras, W. S., Taylor, C. B., Roth, W. T., & Gallen, C. C. (1985). Combined pharmacological and behavioral treatment for agoraphobia. *Behavior Therapy and Research, 23*, 325–335.

Tyrer, P., Candy, J., & Kelly, D. (1973). A study of the clinical effects of phenelzine and placebo in the treatment of phobic anxiety. *Psychopharmacologia, 32*, 237–254.

Uhde, T. W., Boulenger, J. P., Vittone, B. J., & Post, R. M. (1984a). Historical and modern concepts of anxiety: A focus on adrenergic function. In J. Ballenger (Ed.), *Biology of agoraphobia*. Washington, DC: American Psychiatric Press.

Uhde, T. W., Vittone, B. J., & Post, R. M. (1984b). Glucose tolerance testing in panic disorder. *American Journal of Psychiatry, 141*, 1401–03.

Woods, S. W., Charney, D. S., Goodman, W. K., & Heninger, G. R. (1988). Carbon dioxide-induced anxiety: Behavioral, physiologic, and biochemical effects of carbon dioxide in patients with panic disorder and healthy subjects. *Archives of General Psychiatry, 45*, 43–52.

Woods, S. W., Charney, D. S., Lake, J., Goodman, W. K., Redmond, D. E., & Heninger, D. R. (1986). Carbon dioxide sensitivity in panic anxiety: Ventilatory and anxiogenic response to carbon dioxide in healthy subjects and panic anxiety patients before and after alprazolam treatment. *Archives of General Psychiatry, 43*, 900–909.

Woods, S. W., Charney, D. S., McPherson, C. A., Gradman, A. H., & Heninger, G. R. (1987). Situational panic attacks: Behavioral, physiologic, and biochemical characterization. *Archives of General Psychiatry, 44*, 365–375.

Zitrin, C. M., Klein, D. F., & Woerner, M. G. (1980). Treatment of agoraphobia with group exposure in vivo and imipramine. *Archives of General Psychiatry, 37*, 63–73.

Zitrin, C. M., Klein, D. F., Woerner, M. G., & Ross, D. C. (1983). Treatment of phobias: I. Comparison of imipramine hydrochloride and placebo. *Archives of General Psychiatry, 40*, 125–138.

Editorial Commentary: Panic and Agoraphobia

All three chapters in this section reflect the substantial changes that recently have occurred in the conceptualization of panic and agoraphobia. Previously, panic was viewed as little more than an intense form of the same excessive anxiety characteristic of all anxiety disorders. It was given little attention in either etiological models or treatment programs. In contrast, current views hold that panic is a significant phenomenon in its own right. It is still not clear if it is physiologically distinct from other forms of anxiety, but its severity and distinct quality apparently make it phenomenologically different. Agoraphobia had been viewed narrowly as a fear of open spaces, not unlike other specific phobias. Here too, recent findings document that it has a much more pervasive impact and can be better conceptualized as a fear of fear.

The sophistication and effectiveness of interventions for panic and agoraphobia have also progressed dramatically in the past 10 years. Since the late 1970s, Silberman has reviewed the extensive pharmacological literature, which documents the effectiveness of several classes of medication, including atypical benzodiazepines, tricyclic antidepressants, and MAOIs. Treatment dropouts and relapses after termination of medication remain notable problems. However, these problems are no worse than they are in treatment of many other disorders, while overall success rates appear to be notable.

As indicated by Margraf, behavior therapy has long been successful in treating agoraphobic avoidance. Systematic exposure appears to be the key ingredient, whether (a) in imagination or in vivo, (b) self-directed or therapist-directed, and (c) alone, in groups, or with the aid of a cooperative spouse. Conversely, it had been assumed that behavior therapy was not useful for treatment of panic, especially so-called spontaneous attacks. The inference was that such unprecipitated events were purely biological phenomena, and thus required pharmacological interventions. Apparently, neither of these assumptions is true. There are considerable data to suggest that spontaneous attacks may, in actuality, be stimulated by subtle autonomic feedback and associated expectations of some impending catastrophe. Several new behavioral treatment programs have been developed, which attempt to break this pattern by habituating the person to the proprioceptive feedback and teaching a more adaptive cognitive style. The preliminary results are at least as positive as those reported for pharmacotherapy.

Wolitzky and Eagle report that psychoanalytic models have also evolved as research has clarified the nature and relationship of panic and avoidance. The core analytic techniques have been supplemented by exposure in vivo, while either behavior therapy or pharmacotherapy are recommended for patients whose panic attacks are not closely tied to environmental stimuli (e.g., crowds, driving). Conversely, they contend that the key issues in most cases of agoraphobia are interpersonal conflicts, especially in regard to dependency and fear and guilt about separation from significant others.

A number of procedural and conceptual commonalities are apparent in the three chapters. First and foremost, all three approaches recognize the importance of exposure to the feared situation. Exposure represents the key aspect of behavioral interventions, but its precise role in pharmacotherapy and psychoanalytic therapy is less clear. Patients receiving the latter two approaches are urged to expose themselves once panic and anticipatory anxiety begin to subside. However, exposure is sometimes viewed simply as a facilitative strategy that speeds overall recovery rather than as an activity that is essential if recovery is to occur. Unfortunately, the existing literature does not resolve this issue. Further research is necessary in order to determine precisely how and when exposure should be conducted, both with and without associated medication. Similarly, additional work is needed to analyze the relative effects of medication and exposure on panic (when used separately) and on avoidance (when used in combination).

Both the psychoanalytic and behavioral approaches recognize the possible effects of personality problems, notably dependency and interpersonal conflicts. Agoraphobia is viewed, at least in part, as relating to conflicts over separation from significant others—parents or spouses. Both approaches recognize the potential value of including spouses in treatment, both to facilitate exposure and to resolve the possible conflicts over autonomy. As might be expected, these issues play a more central role in the analytic treatment than in the behavioral approaches.

Finally, all three chapters recognize the significant advance provided by DSM-III-R in categorization of patients, while simultaneously indicating that the current system does not provide enough information about treatment choices. A variety of pharmacological agents have proven to be effective in treatment despite dramatically different chemical structures and sites of action. Similarly, diverse behavioral strategies have yielded significant results. This diversity suggests some higher-order etiology that can be redressed in a variety of ways, or a very heterogeneous category that includes a number of different disorders with similar phenomenology. This is the most perplexing and pressing issue in the search for improved outcome and for a reduction in the number of nonresponders.

PART 4

Social Phobia

CHAPTER 11

Cognitive Behavior Therapy

RICHARD G. HEIMBERG

CONCEPTUALIZATION OF THE DISORDER

Social phobia was first described as a clinical syndrome by Marks (1970). However, it was not until the publication of the third edition of the *Diagnostic and Statistical Manual of Mental Disorder* (DSM-III, American Psychiatric Association, 1980) that social phobia received official recognition as an anxiety disorder. As a result, social phobia has received less research attention than other anxiety disorders and has been labeled the "neglected anxiety disorder" (Liebowitz, Gorman, Fyer, & Klein, 1985b).

According to the DSM-III-R (American Psychiatric Association, 1987, p. 241), the essential feature of social phobia is "a persistent fear of one or more situations . . . in which the person is exposed to possible scrutiny by others and fears that he or she may do something or act in a way that will be humiliating or embarrassing." Examples of social phobias listed in DSM-III-R include fears of speaking or performing in public, eating or drinking with others, writing in the presence of others, and using public restrooms. While DSM-III limited the diagnosis of social phobia to these specific social fears, DSM-III-R has broadened the definition to include a *generalized type* in which the individual fears most or all social situations.

Social fears are quite common in the general population, and many people define themselves as shy (Pilkonis & Zimbardo, 1979). Further, social fear of severity sufficient to warrant a diagnosis of social phobia is also common. Myers et al. (1984), in their report of the NIMH epidemiological cachement area studies, put the 6-month prevalence of social phobia at 0.9–1.7% for men and at 1.5–2.6% for women, placing the total number of individuals suffering from social phobia over 2 million. Pollard and Henderson (1988) also suggest that more than 20% of the general population may suffer social phobic anxiety, but only 2% will judge their impairment as severe enough to warrant treatment. Social phobics may constitute between 8 and 18% of patients seeking treatment at clinics specializing in the treatment of anxiety disorders (Barlow, 1985; Marks, 1970; Sanderson, Rapee, & Barlow, 1987). However, for several reasons, the observed prevalence of social phobia may be an underestimate (Heimberg & Barlow, 1988; Heimberg, Dodge, & Becker, 1987). First, individuals may avoid treatment because the idea of talking openly about themselves may elicit fears of scrutiny. Second, they may judge their problems to be unsolvable and themselves to be beyond help. In fact, recent data from our laboratory (Heimberg et al., 1989) suggest that social phobics do make these self-defeating attributions.

Third, social phobics may present themselves

The development of the procedures described in this chapter were supported by grant 38368 to the author from the National Institute of Mental Health (NIMH). I wish to acknowledge the substantial contributions of Robert E. Becker to that effort. Thanks also to Monroe A. Bruch and Debra A. Hope, who provided feedback on earlier drafts of this chapter.

for treatment of alcoholism or other substance abuse rather than of anxiety. Social phobia was reported to be the most common anxiety disorder in a sample of inpatient alcoholics (Chambless, Cherney, Caputo, & Rheinstein, 1987). In another study, 25% of men and 17% of women at an alcohol treatment facility experienced debilitating anxiety in social situations or could not handle these situations without the anxiety-reducing effects of alcohol (Mullaney & Trippett, 1979). Most patients reported that their anxiety predated their abuse of alcohol and that they used alcohol to self-medicate their fear. In yet another investigation (Smail, Stockwell, Canter, & Hodgson, 1984), 39% of alcoholics experienced clinically severe social anxiety during their last typical drinking period.

While DSM-III originally stated that social phobias do not appear to be severe or incapacitating, more recent data suggest otherwise. Turner, Beidel, Dancu, and Keys (1986) report that 71.4% of their social phobic patients avoid multiple situations, that 92.3% believe that their anxiety has interfered with their occupational functioning, and that 69.2% were unable to attend social events. Liebowitz et al. (1985b) provide a similar picture of impairment—inability to work, incomplete educational attainment, limited career advancement, and limited social functioning.

I now turn to an understanding of the phenomenon of social phobia. Butler (1985) and Emmelkamp (1982) have suggested that cognitive factors may be more central to the understanding of social phobia than is the case for other anxiety disorders, and several theoretical accounts have been advanced that emphasize the cognitive functioning of the social phobic individual and how that individual may respond to social-evaluative threat (Beck & Emery, 1985; Hartman, 1983; Schlenker & Leary, 1982; Trower & Turland, 1984). We refer the reader to Heimberg et al. (1987) for a review of these positions. We focus here on the model of social phobia recently advanced by Heimberg and Barlow (1988). The model, which emphasizes the differences between social phobics and socially functional persons when presented with demands for social performance, is presented in Figure 11.1.

Heimberg and Barlow's model focuses on the individual during a social interaction and does not address developmental, historical, or evolutionary antecedents of social phobia (see Ohman, Dimberg, & Ost, 1985, or Trower & Gilbert, 1989, for discussions of these topics). By focusing on the immediate social situation, the model may produce clues to points of intervention in the social phobic individual's experience. It suggests that the social phobic individual responds to performance demands with a series of negative cognitions. These cognitions serve to focus the individual's attention, to his or her detriment, away from the demands of the current situation. Rather than focusing on the social task (e.g., listening to the other person in a conversation and formulating a response or organizing one's thoughts to respond to a question), the individual may become concerned about whether he or she will become anxious, whether this anxiety will be perceived by others, or whether this perception will have negative social consequences. Any of these catastrophic cognitions will lead the individual to appraise the situation as one of significant personal threat and thus lead to the activation of the autonomic nervous system. As physiological symptoms of anxiety increase, the individual becomes increasingly efficient in his or her focus on the consequences of poor performance. By focusing so intensely on the threatening aspects of the situation (including one's own arousal), the individual may have become so distracted from the specific demands of the situation that performance indeed deteriorates. When exposed to a similar situation in the future, the individual will be increasingly likely to avoid the situation or to endure it only with intense discomfort. As suggested by Figure 11.1, the socially functional individual is unlikely to enter into this vicious cycle. Heimberg and Barlow (1988, pp. 30–31) describe this process in the following case example:

J, a 23-year-old male with an extreme fear of negative evaluation and rejection by women, found himself attracted to K, a woman with whom he worked but to whom he had never spoken. After several days of rumination, he approached her desk and attempted to initiate a conversation (demand for social performance). He became extremely self-conscious, and, as was his habit, began to fantasize the numerous ways in which the interaction might go awry. He

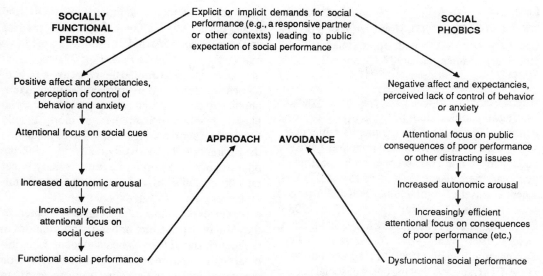

Figure 11.1. Model of social dysfunction in social phobia. From R. G. Heimberg & D. H. Barlow (1988). Psychosocial treatments for social phobia. *Psychosomatics, 29*, 31. Copyright 1988, The Academy of Psychosomatic Medicine. Used with permission.

began to think that he would not be able to talk, that she would not want to speak with him, that he was inadequate and that he would become uncontrollably nervous (focus on task-irrelevant thoughts). He became further concerned that she would reject him and that he would be humiliated and embarrassed in this rather public work setting (attentional focus on consequences of poor performance). Of course, he was unable to concentrate on making conversation and began to stumble over his words. His perception of his halting speech led him to focus even more intensely on all the bad things that could happen (further focus on consequences of poor performance). His anxiety continued to escalate (increased autonomic arousal). His physiological symptoms, which by now included tachycardia, palpitations, sweating, and dry mouth, caused him to focus more completely on his vulnerable state and added the concern that K would perceive his nervousness and wonder what was wrong with him (increasingly efficient focus on negative consequences of poor performance). Although she was, in fact, interested in getting to know him, he walked away from her desk while in midsentence (dysfunctional social performance) and avoided her for several months (avoidance).

I return to the case of J in a later section of this chapter. In the next section, I focus on two issues

of importance to the study of social phobia, the distinctiveness of the diagnostic category and the heterogeneity of patients who receive the diagnosis of social phobia.

DIAGNOSTIC ISSUES AND PROBLEMS

As with any new diagnostic category, it is important to determine the boundaries between the new category and other related diagnostic categories. In the case of social phobia, it is important to examine the similarities and differences between social phobia and two other categories of disorder: (1) other anxiety disorders, and (2) avoidant personality disorder.

Distinctiveness from Other Anxiety Disorders

Several studies have examined similarities and differences among social phobia, agoraphobia, panic disorder, and simple phobia. Herein, I examine studies of demographic characteristics, family background, specific symptom patterns, and response to biological challenge.

Gender. A number of studies have examined the gender composition of samples of anxiety disorder patients. The large majority of agoraphobic patients, for instance, are female (75%–Marks, 1980; 87%—Ost, 1987). However, social phobia occurs in both sexes with approximately equal frequency (Amies, Gelder, & Shaw, 1983; Ost, 1987).

Age. Social phobics also appear to be younger than agoraphobics, both in terms of age of onset and age of presentation for treatment (Amies et al., 1983). Age of onset for social phobia is typically described as late adolescence, with specific reports varying between the ages of 15 and 20 years, whereas onset of agoraphobia is usually placed between ages 24 and 28 (Amies et al., 1983; Liebowitz et al., 1985b; Marks, 1970; Marks & Gelder, 1966; Ost, 1987; Turner et al., 1986). Turner and Beidel (1989), in agreement with DSM-III-R, suggest that the onset of social phobic anxiety may be more accurately placed in late childhood or early adolescence. Their suggestion is consistent with the fact that children of this age may be exposed to an increasing number of social-evaluative situations as they enter junior high school and begin to show interest in dating behaviors (Buss, 1986). In a study comparing social phobic and agoraphobic patients' perceptions of their social experiences during adolescence (Bruch, Heimberg, Berger, & Collins, in press), adult social phobics reported greater self-consciousness while in junior high school and fewer dating partners from ages 12 to 21.

Age of presentation has been reported to range from ages 27 to 34 years for social phobics, compared to 32–37 for agoraphobics (Amies et al., 1983; Marks & Gelder, 1966; Ost, 1987). However, social phobics have been reported to suffer with their anxieties for a longer time before seeking treatment than agoraphobics (18 vs. 8 years—Ost, 1987).

Other Demographic Characteristics. Amies et al. (1983) also report that social phobics are less likely to be married but more likely to come from a higher socioeconomic class than agoraphobics at the time of presentation for treatment. Ost (1987) reports similar findings for marital status.

Family Background. In addition to perceptions of adolescent social experiences, Bruch et al. (in press) compared social phobics' and agoraphobics' report of their childhood family environment. Earlier studies comparing social phobics and agoraphobics (Arrindell, Emmelkamp, Monsma, & Brilman, 1983; Parker, 1979) suggested that social phobics recalled their parents to be both *less* caring and *more* overprotective than agoraphobics' parents. Bruch et al. reported that social phobics recalled their mothers as more socially fearful than agoraphobics. They also remembered their parents as being overly concerned with the opinions of others, as emphasizing solitary rather than group activities, and as sheltering their children from new social experiences. That these experiences may hinder the social development of the child or deprive him or her of opportunities to extinguish social fears appears evident. Longitudinal studies that are not subject to biased recall on the part of social phobic subjects are necessary to further delineate the impact of family environment on the development of social phobia.

That social phobics recall their mothers to be socially fearful raises the question of mode of transmission of social phobia. Is this disorder transmitted from parent to child via learning mechanisms, or is there a genetic component? Unfortunately, data on this important topic are sparse. Reich and Yates (1988) report a higher incidence of social phobia in the families of social phobic patients than among the families of panic patients, but as noted by Turner and Beidel (1989), their sample was very small. Turner and Beidel (1989) also report the results of an uncontrolled study in their laboratory in which 9 of 21 (43%) social phobic patients could identify at least one first-degree relative who experienced distress in social situations. Torgersen (1979, 1983) conducted two studies of monozygotic and dizygotic twins. The first study demonstrated a genetic component in the social fears of a mixed group of neurotic and normal twins. In the second study, all probands suffered from an anxiety disorder. While the concordance rate was substantially higher for monozygotic twins (34%) than for dizygotic twins (17%), no cotwin was diagnosed as having the same anxiety disorder as the proband. Among the four twin pairs with a social phobic proband, two cotwins received a diagnosis of generalized anxiety disorder while the other two received no anxiety disorder diagnosis. As suggested by Turner and Beidel (1989), these data may support the notion of an inherited constitutional vulnerability, but they do not appear to provide support for direct genetic transmission. Obviously, more research is needed.

Symptom Patterns.   Social phobics and agoraphobics also appear to differ in the specific pattern of anxiety symptoms they experience (Amies et al. 1983; Gorman & Gorman, 1987). Gorman and Gorman observe that social phobics experience a high incidence of palpitations, trembling, sweating, and blushing. In fact, Amies et al. reported that their sample of social phobics reported more muscle twitching and blushing than the agoraphobic comparison group. This is of central importance to the understanding of social phobia because these symptoms are potentially observable by others, and social phobics are notably concerned that their anxiety may be detected by others (McEwan & Devins, 1983). Social phobics were *less* likely than agoraphobics to experience dizziness/faintness, difficulty breathing, weakness of the limbs, fainting episodes or buzzing/ringing in the ears when exposed to their own specific phobic situations. On a more general level, social phobics complain of a greater number of fears than do those with simple phobia, but fewer than do agoraphobic patients (Cerny, Himadi, & Barlow, 1984).

Social phobics also appear to be more depressed than subjects in a normal comparison group, although their depression is not as great as that experienced by panic disorder or agoraphobic patients (Heimberg et al.,1989). Although less depressed than agoraphobics in our study, social phobics reported more suicide attempts in the study by Amies et al. (1983). They also were more likely to report habitual alcohol abuse. Turner et al. (1986) report that 46% of their sample used alcohol to feel more sociable at a party, and 50% used alcohol prior to attending social functions. As noted, social phobics are often observed in alcohol treatment settings, but their involvement with substances is not limited to alcohol. Sanderson et al. (1987) report that 17% of their sample regularly used anxiolytics while equal numbers used beta blockers and antidepressants. Turner et al. (1986) report that 52% of their sample used anxiolytics to relieve anxiety and 13.3% used anxiolytics prior to attending a social event.

Response to Biological Challenge.   A final area in which social phobics appear to differ from agoraphobics and panic patients is in the area of biological challenge. While the mechanisms remain controversial, it has been documented that agoraphobic and panic disorder patients will experience panic or panic-like symptoms in response to infusion of sodium lactate (Liebowitz et al., 1985c). When patients were challenged with 0.5 M. racemic sodium lactate (10 ml/kg of body weight) intravenously for 20 minutes, 4 of 9 agoraphobic patients and 10 of 20 panic disorder patients responded with panic symptoms. However, only 1 of 15 social phobic patients responded in this way (Liebowitz et al., 1985a).

Inhalation of various mixtures of carbon dioxide and oxygen has also been shown to produce panic-like symptoms in some panic disorder patients (Gorman et al., 1988). However, neither Gorman et al. (1988), using a 5% CO_2 mixture, nor Rapee, Mattick, and Murrell (1986), using 50% CO_2, were able to produce these symptoms in social phobic patients.

Distinctiveness from Avoidant Personality Disorder (APD)

Avoidant personality disorder is defined as a "pervasive pattern of social discomfort, fear of negative evaluation, and timidity, beginning by early adulthood and present in a variety of contexts" (DSM-III-R, p. 352). Obviously, APD may be very similar to social phobia. In fact, there is substantial overlap in the criteria for the two disorders, and both diagnoses may be given to the same person. What then are the distinctions between social phobia and APD? Greenberg and Stravynski (1983) and Marks (1985) suggest that the patient with APD is more broadly impaired and is, in addition to being anxious in social situations, also deficient in social skills. By implication, social phobics and APDs should respond to different intervention techniques: exposure for social phobics and social skills training for APDs (Greenberg & Stravynski, 1983). To date, however, only a single study (Turner et al., 1986) has attempted to compare social phobic and APD patients. Social phobics and APDs completed a number of questionnaires and took part in a series of role plays (same-sex interaction, opposite-sex interaction, impromptu speech). APDs scored significantly higher on the Social Avoidance and Distress Scale (Watson & Friend, 1969) and on the obsessive–compulsive, interpersonal sensitivity, depression, anxiety, and general symptom subscales of the Symptom Checklist-90-Revised (SCL-90-R—Derogatis, 1983). In addition, APDs demonstrated significantly poorer gaze and voice tone during the behavioral tests and were rated significantly less skillful during the opposite-sex interaction.

The findings of this study are indeed provocative, but their ultimate meaning is unclear. For instance, the finding of less skillful social performance by APD patients cannot be taken to mean that they are truly deficient in social skills because the competing hypothesis that more severe anxiety has led to more pervasive inhibition of social behavior cannot be ruled out. Differences on questionnaire measures can be taken as differences in degree as well as in kind. Thus, we are left with unanswered questions. Is APD simply a more severe variant of social phobia? Are APD and social phobia two related and overlapping but distinct disorders? Is there indeed a justification for the existence of both diagnostic categories? The answers are unknown and further complicated by the fact that social phobics do not comprise a highly homogeneous group.

Subtypes of Social Phobia

Social phobics are *not* all the same. While this may be self-evident, it is useful to determine the nature of social phobic subgroups and whether or not they differ in terms of symptoms, course, treatment response, and so on. DSM-III-R has recognized this stance with the specification of social phobia, generalized type. The generalized social phobic is fearful of most or all social situations. Other social phobic patients, who may fear specific situations in which they might be observed and evaluated (such as eating, drinking, or writing in public) are not grouped together in DSM-III-R, but for present purposes, they may be labeled *discrete*. It has been suggested that some discrete social phobics

(e.g., public-speaking phobics) feel less distress in social interaction (McNeil & Lewin, 1986) and may have less associated personality pathology than generalized social phobics (Spitzer & Williams, 1985). However, the boundary between social phobia and APD is now further complicated because most individuals who meet the criteria for generalized social phobia also meet the criteria for APD.

In order to examine the differences between generalized and discrete social phobics (as previously defined), Heimberg, Hope, Dodge, and Becker (in press-b) divided patients awaiting treatment for social phobia into two groups—35 generalized social phobics and 22 public-speaking phobics. Other types of discrete social phobics were not included because of insufficient cell sizes (*n*). The two groups were then compared on demographic characteristics and on self-report, behavioral, and physiological measures. A number of interesting differences emerged.

Generalized social phobics were younger when they presented for treatment, they had received less education than would be expected for their age, and they were less likely to be employed. Clinical interviewers, unaware of the nature of the study, also rated their phobias to have resulted in greater impairment in functioning.

On self-report measures, generalized social phobics reported greater social avoidance and distress, greater fear of negative evaluation, more generalized anxiety, and more depression (note the similarity to Turner et al.'s 1986 finding for APDs and social phobics). Of greater interest, however, was the response of the two groups to an individualized behavioral test. Patients role-played situations that were selected at interview to elicit a Subjective Units of Discomfort Scale (SUDS) rating of 75 or greater (0–100 scale). During that performance, they provided SUDS ratings every 60 seconds; heart rate was continuously monitored; and the performance was videotaped for later rating by a panel of judges.

Generalized social phobic and public-speaking phobic patients reported similar anxiety (SUDS) during their behavioral tests and gave similar ratings of how well they performed. In general, both groups were quite hard on themselves. However, judges' ratings on both dimensions significantly differed between generalized social phobics and public-speaking phobics. Public-speaking phobics were rated as less anxious and more skillful than generalized social phobics. Viewed from another perspective, judges validated the poor self-ratings of generalized social phobics but were considerably more positive about the public-speaking phobics. These findings would appear to suggest that public-speaking phobics are overly negative in their judgments about their own performance. While generalized social phobics appear more accurate, their poorer performances can be attributed either to skill deficits or to anxiety-based inhibition of performance.

Public-speaking and generalized social phobics exhibited very different patterns of cardiac arousal during their behavioral tests. Generalized social phobics showed only a minor increase in heart rate during the behavioral test (approximately 4 beats per minute—bpm). In contrast, public-speaking phobics showed a strong surge of cardiac arousal at the beginning of the behavioral test (approximately 20 bpm). While heart rate began to decline after the first minute, public-speaking phobics showed greater heart rate than generalized social phobics throughout the behavioral test.

To summarize, generalized social phobic and public-speaking phobic patients showed differing patterns of impairment. Generalized social phobics showed the greatest impairment in overall functioning. In terms of specific symptoms, generalized social phobics showed the greatest decrement on measures of behavior; public-speaking phobics showed the greatest decrement on measures of cognition and physiological functioning. In addition, preliminary data from our laboratory (Heimberg, 1986) suggest that both groups of social phobics improve with the cognitive-behavioral group treatment (described in the next section), but that public-speaking phobics may fare significantly better.

TREATMENT STRATEGIES

Several behavioral and cognitive-behavioral treatments for social phobia have been attempted in the late 1970s and 1980s. These have been reviewed in detail elsewhere (Heimberg, 1989; Heimberg & Barlow, 1988; Heimberg et al., 1987) and are discussed briefly in the closing section of this chapter. Here, I focus on the treatment protocol that has been developed and investigated in our laboratory over the past 6 years, a treatment that we have called "cognitive behavioral group therapy" (or "CBGT") for social phobia.

In its current form, CBGT is administered to groups of 5–6 social phobic patients in 12 weekly 2-hour sessions, typically by a mixed-gender team of cotherapists. It comprises several treatment components:

1. Developing a cognitive-behavioral explanation of social phobia and a rationale for the effectiveness of CBGT

2. Training patients in the skills of identification, analysis, and disputation of problematic cognitions through the use of structured exercises

3. Exposing patients to simulations of anxiety-provoking situations in the context of the treatment group

4. Using cognitive restructuring procedures, such as those mentioned in Step 2, to teach patients to control their maladaptive thinking before and during the exposure simulations

5. Using similar procedures to teach patients to engage in rational self-analysis rather than negative self-evaluation after completion of an exposure simulation

6. Assigning homework in which patients expose themselves to real anxiety-provoking events after they have confronted these events in exposure simulations

7. Teaching patients a self-administered cognitive restructuring routine so that they may engage in cognitive preparation for homework assignments and rational self-analysis after their completion.

Two studies of CBGT have been completed to date. An early version of CBGT was examined with seven social phobic patients in a series of controlled case studies (Heimberg, Becker, Goldfinger, & Vermilyea, 1985). After treatment, all patients demonstrated significant reductions in anxiety, as reflected in a series of behavioral, physiological, and subjective measures. These gains were maintained across a 6-month follow-up period for six of the seven patients. The current package has also been compared to a group treatment package based on education and group support (Heimberg et al., in press-a). The comparison package was developed in our laboratory to equal CBGT in credibility and in ability to generate positive expectations for treatment outcome, and it has been shown to compare favorably to CBGT, social skills training, and systematic desensitization on these dimensions (Kennedy & Heimberg, 1986). At each assessment point, patients completed a comprehensive assessment battery that included a rating by a clinical assessor on a nine-point scale of phobic severity (see Heimberg et al., in press-a, for the full details of the study). Patients were classified as improved if they showed a decrease in two or more points and their posttreatment (or follow-up) rating was less than four (i.e., subclinical severity). According to these criteria, 75% of CBGT patients were judged to be improved at the end of the 12-week treatment, compared to only 40% of patients in the comparison treatment. After a 6-month follow-up period, 81% of patients receiving CBGT and 47% of comparison patients were classified as improved. CBGT patients also showed superior reductions in anxiety during an individualized behavioral test and greater change on a measure of positive and negative self-statements during the behavioral test at the 6-month follow-up.

Early Sessions of CBGT

Portions of Session 1 are devoted to introductions and review of group rules (attendance, participation, confidentiality, etc.). Patients are then asked to speak briefly, with support from therapists, about their phobias and about what they hope to accomplish in treatment. All patients describe the situation that is their greatest concern, what happens to them when they think about "doing it," what happens to them when they actually "do it," what physiological symptoms they experience, and what they would like to do that their anxiety keeps them from doing. Therapists draw out simi-

larities among patients in the situations they fear; the cognitive, behavioral, and physiological symptoms they experience; and their overriding concern with negative evaluation and scrutiny. This activity appears to be an important one because, by their very nature, social phobics may be hesitant to talk with other people about their fears and may have come to the erroneous conclusion that they are the only ones who feel this way. In the next part of Session 1, therapists present a model of social phobia based on cognitive-behavioral principles. The model emphasizes that social anxiety is a learned phenomenon, and that cognitive, behavioral, and physiological components of anxiety reciprocally influence one another. The major treatment components of exposure simulations, cognitive restructuring, and homework assignments are then reviewed and their potential effectiveness discussed in terms of the cognitive-behavioral model of social phobia.

During Sessions 2 and 3, a didactic approach to the teaching of cognitive-behavioral concepts is adopted. A series of structured exercises (developed in our research program or adapted from the work of other cognitive-behavioral therapists—Burns, 1980; Moorey & Burns, 1983; Sank & Shaffer, 1984) is used to help patients accomplish several goals:

1. Reconceptualize their thoughts as hypotheses to be tested rather than facts to be accepted

2. Develop an awareness of the frequency with which they engage in maladaptive thinking

3. Develop skills for identifying distortions or logical errors in their own thinking

4. Develop an awareness of the connection between distorted thinking and social phobic anxiety

5. Develop skills for challenging and changing negative thinking patterns.

Exercises are selected to elicit only minimal anxiety and thus allow patients to devote their full powers of concentration to the learning of cognitive concepts. Activities in later sessions are facilitated if patients have a firm grasp on cognitive concepts *before* they are asked to apply them during exposure simulations. In the first exercise (adapted from Sank & Shaffer, 1984), one of the therapists presents a situation in which he or she has recently experienced difficulty and the automatic thoughts that occurred to him or her before, during, or after that situation. Group members are questioned about each thought: How would an objective observer view the situation? What is the evidence that the therapist's automatic thought is the only way to view the situation? Is there an alternative explanation? The two therapists then demonstrate the roles of automatic thought and rational response in a brief role play. Each automatic thought is presented and thoroughly rebutted, using the externalization-of-voices technique described by Moorey and Burns (1983).

In a second exercise, from the same source, patients are asked to generate their own automatic thoughts. Because they all share the experience of beginning a new treatment effort, the exercise asks them to list their thoughts about entering into treatment ("I won't be able to talk in front of others," "People will think there is something wrong with me," "Treatment will never work for me," etc.). These thoughts are then role-played and rebutted (as just described). Patients are given the homework assignment of keeping a log of automatic thoughts and anxious feelings in problematic situations (SUDS) during the week and to bring their logs to the next group session.

Using the automatic thoughts generated in the previous exercise and additional thoughts that were self-monitored between sessions, the third session begins by teaching patients the skills of logical analysis of their automatic thoughts. Thoughts provided by each patient are examined with the aid of a list of cognitive distortions compiled by Burns (1980). After a review of the categories of cognitive distortion (e.g., all-or-none thinking, disqualifying the positive, fortune telling, emotional reasoning, "should" statements), each patient attempts to categorize his or her own thoughts that had been volunteered previously. Similarities and differences among group members and propensities to engage in specific cognitive errors are highlighted, as is the covariation between specific cognitive distortions and patients' anxiety (from self-monitoring logs). In the final exercise, the therapists pose a situation that

might be anxiety provoking (e.g., being criticized by your boss) and a series of behavioral and physiological reactions that a person might experience in that situation. The group members generate a list of automatic thoughts that might lead a person to have these reactions. Using a list of questions developed by Sank and Shaffer (1984), they dispute each thought and develop a more rational response. Discussion highlights the probable shift in behavioral and physiological reactions that might accompany the rational response.

Exposure Simulation Sessions

Sessions 4–11 are devoted to the primary treatment techniques of simulated exposures, cognitive restructuring, and homework assignments. Butler (1985) has noted that in vivo exposure may be difficult to conduct with social phobic patients because of the uncontrolled and variable nature of social interaction. In contrast, the exposure simulations utilized in CBGT are schedulable, controllable, and easily molded to patients' specific needs. Each patient, in turn, selects a target situation for attention (based on a contract established during preliminary interviews and the current events in the patient's life). That situation is then simulated in the group, with the roles of other persons or audiences assumed by therapists, group members, or (occasionally) other research assistants. Staging of the simulation is directed by the therapists, but instructions are provided by the target patient to the other participants on how they should behave. Examples of exposure simulations utilized in our groups have included meeting someone for the first time at a party, joining in an ongoing conversation, making a telephone call to someone you like, speaking in a group, and presenting your opinion at a meeting at work.

The target patient is queried about his or her worst fears in the situation, and these fears are incorporated into simulated exposures. Thus, if a patient fears that he or she will be publicly ridiculed while speaking to a group, participants may be instructed to do so even if the objective probability of that outcome is small. During simulations, patients give periodic ratings of their anxiety on the 0–100 SUDS. These ratings are used in later cognitive restructuring discussions.

Prior to the initiation of a simulated exposure, a series of cognitive restructuring activities is conducted. First, the patient is asked to visualize the situation and describe the automatic thoughts that occur to him or her during the visualization or in anticipation of the simulation. Using the procedures presented in Sessions 2–3, the distortions in these thoughts are identified and rational responses to them constructed. These rebuttals are written on an easel in clear view of the patient, and the patient is encouraged to use them as appropriate during the upcoming simulation. (During a simulation, when a patient is asked to report his or her SUDS score, he or she may be asked to read the rational response aloud.) Also, the patient is asked to verbalize a specific goal for the simulation. The appropriateness of the goal and the standards that the patient has applied in choosing that goal are discussed, and the goal is modified accordingly.

After the conclusion of the simulation, attention is again devoted to the patient's cognitions. He or she is asked to evaluate whether or not the stated goal was accomplished and to report on any problematic cognitions that occurred and the degree to which the use of cognitive coping skills was effective. The patient's SUDS scores are reviewed, and an attempt is made to link changes in SUDS to the occurrence of automatic thoughts or the active use of rational responses. Further attention is devoted to automatic thoughts that were not effectively rebutted or thoughts that occurred during the simulation but were not anticipated by the patient. In addition, behavioral experiments are conducted to further test the validity of the patient's thinking. For instance, a patient who believed that her anxiety was visible to everyone and that she would be negatively evaluated because of it was directed to rate the visibility of her anxiety during an exposure on the SUDS scale while the other patients were asked to do the same. Her rating (90) was much higher than those provided by the other patients (20–40). These ratings were compared and the difference discussed.

The importance of exposing oneself to anxiety-provoking situations and utilizing cognitive coping skills in real life is stressed throughout treatment. Homework assignments are made throughout treatment to facilitate this process and are tied as closely as possible to simulated exposures.

Patients are asked to perform behaviors or place themselves in situations that were previously avoided or tolerated only with excessive anxiety. Before entering a situation, each patient conducts a cognitive self-analysis, similar in content to the aforementioned presimulation cognitive restructuring, to identify automatic thoughts that may have a high likelihood of occurrence in the target situation, and to prepare responses to them. Patients are then instructed (1) to enter the situation or to perform the behavior to the best of their ability, (2) to attempt to control anxiety with their cognitive coping techniques, and (3) to tolerate any anxiety that they might experience. Thereafter, they conduct what we call a "cognitive autopsy" of the situation, just as was done in the group after a simulation. Written instructions are provided to help patients remember this rather complicated chain of events, and homework assignments from the previous week are discussed at the beginning of each session.

During the final session, some time is devoted to review of homework and the conduct of simulated exposures. The remainder of the session is devoted to a discussion of what the patients had learned and how this learning might be applied in the future.

CASE ILLUSTRATION

We now return to the case of J, the 23-year-old male with a fear of negative evaluation and rejection in heterosexual interactions. In the preliminary interview, J contracted with the therapist to devote his treatment to confronting his anxiety in these situations, and a series of subgoals was outlined: (a) increasing the number of settings he frequented in which he might have the opportunity to meet women, (b) initiating conversations and engaging in small talk with women, (c) initiating second conversations with women he had previously approached, and (d) asking a woman to join him for a social activity. Treatment was not directed specifically at his interest in K.

In the early treatment sessions, J shared these goals with the group and began to identify the negative thinking patterns that inhibited his social behavior. He learned the skills of identifying, analyzing, and disputing distorted thoughts. Homework assignments included monitoring of automatic thoughts and anxiety (using the SUDS) and determining a list of potential social settings that would serve as a basis for exposure simulations and homework assignments. For the latter assignment, he decided that he would join a local health club, take a noncredit class at a local university, and attend some functions of a local singles organization. He was asked to obtain the necessary information and make the necessary applications, but no specific performance demands were made at this time.

In Session 4, J's first exposure simulation was devoted to attendance at the first class of the noncredit course. The exposure was designed so that J would act as if he were an early comer to the first class and that he would initiate a brief conversation with the first female class member who came to class and sat nearby. A female group member was chosen to play the role of the classmate and instructed to act in a receptive fashion but to let J initiate and carry the conversation. J was asked to "play a movie in his head" of the situation and to anticipate his thoughts about the interaction. As suggested by the earlier summary, he listed the following thoughts:

1. "I won't be able to talk."
2. "I'll be incredibly anxious."
3. "She'll see my anxiety and will think there is something wrong with me—like I'm mentally ill or something."
4. "She won't want to talk with me."

Cognitive restructuring prior to the exposure simulation focused on the first and third automatic thoughts. It was accepted without question that he would be quite anxious in this first exposure simulation. J was asked to identify the cognitive distortion(s) in the first automatic thought, using the Burns (1980) list, and he labeled it as a "fortune telling error" (predicting the outcome of an event without sufficient evidence). With the help of the group, he was able to develop a rational rebuttal that had some meaning for him—that he was quite able to make small talk with men at his job or with women for whom he felt no special attraction. The phrase "I have been able to talk just fine in other situations" was written on the easel. In regard to the third automatic thought, J was afraid that his anxiety would lead to a shaky voice, halting speech, and a visible tremor. It was pointed out to him that no group member had as yet observed such behav-

ior. He identified the cognitive distortions of emotional reasoning (if I feel nervous, I must be doing badly) and fortune telling (if I am nervous, she will see that I am, and she will inevitably draw a negative conclusion). A series of additional questions were advanced: If you become nervous, will it inevitably affect your behavior? If you were to do this 100 times, how many times would you become so nervous that it would show and you could not go on? Have there been times when you were as nervous as you expect to be but you did not shake? If you do show physical signs of anxiety, what is the probability that they will be detected? If they are detected, are there other possible conclusions that she may draw? From this series of questions, the rational rebuttals of "I may be nervous, but that doesn't mean it will show" and "If she does see my anxiety, it doesn't mean she'll think I'm mentally ill" were derived and placed on the easel.

Before the exposure simulation began, J was asked to publicly set a goal for evaluating his performance. The goal of talking fluently without anxiety, a typically perfectionistic goal offered by our patients, was rejected. The goal of "hanging in there" despite the anxiety and attending to the rational responses was substituted and grudgingly accepted by J. The exposure simulation lasted for about 10 minutes, during which time J was quite anxious but performed admirably. SUDS ratings were collected each minute by simply interrupting and asking J for a verbal report—90, 90, 100, 80, 60, 40, 75, 40, 35, 35. At each point, he was also asked to read the rational rebuttals before returning to the conversation.

After the exposure simulation, J was asked if he met his goal. He first said that he did not because he became quite anxious. A reassessment of his behavior showed this to be a clearly distorted view. He did not behave without anxiety (the rejected goal), but he did meet the goal of continuing the conversation until its conclusion was signaled by a therapist. SUDS ratings were reviewed, and the occurrence of automatic thoughts was examined. He was obviously anxious in the first few minutes and reported that the targeted automatic thoughts occurred frequently. With repetition of the rebuttals, he became less focused on the automatic thoughts, and there was a concomitant decrease in his anxiety. A prolonged slience in the seventh minute was followed by a surge of anxiety, but this was controlled by the use of the rational responses. J was able to see, on this one occasion, that none of his fears had come true. He was congratulated and praised by his fellow group members and then sat back for awhile as one of his peers began her exposure simulation.

J was given the assignment to initiate a conversation in the upcoming class meeting and to engage in his own cognitive restructuring session before and after doing so. He did, despite substantial anxiety, and he was rewarded with a warm, pleasant, but brief exchange. He was not the target of an exposure simulation in the next session, but he served as an audience member in the exposure simulation of a female patient with fears of speaking in public. After this session, he was given a similar homework assignment to initiate a conversation with a different woman in his class and to do the same thing one evening while at the health club. These also went well, although J put off the second part of the assignment until the night before group and caused himself considerable anticipatory anxiety.

In the interest of brevity, I do not provide a detailed presentation of the remainder of J's treatment, as it proceeded in roughly the same fashion. After the early success experiences, he had initiated several conversations, and he began to do so spontaneously. The next exposure simulation focused on initiating conversations with women he had previously spoken to and increasingly disclosing information about himself and his interests while collecting the same information from the woman. He was given a homework assignment to do so at least twice during each of the next 2 weeks, and he did so. Anxiety was notably high during the first week and declined during the second. In each case, J practiced his cognitive coping skills, as described here previously. While J noted that these skills rarely prevented the occurrence of anxiety, consistent use led to an increased sense that he would not be overwhelmed or unable to perform. He found himself increasingly able to focus on the woman rather than on himself and his anxious feelings. Before the end of treatment, J had requested dates with several women; he had some rejections, but he also had some rewarding outcomes. A 6-month follow-up showed that he was still actively dating. Although anxiety remained at a moderate level, he was generally able to control it with his cognitive coping skills. He reported an increase in anxiety when he began to enter more overtly sexual situations. With two individual booster sessions, he practiced the application of his cognitive skills to these situations, and he has reported no additional need for treatment after an additional 6 months has passed.

ALTERNATIVE TREATMENT OPTIONS

CBGT appears to be a promising treatment for social phobia. However, it is clear that not all patients benefit at all—or benefit as substantially as one would like. Recall the 19% of CBGT patients who were unimproved after a 6-month follow-up period (Heimberg et al., in press-a) and that J, a successfully treated patient, continued to report social anxiety and required booster treatment during his follow-up period. While other investigators have reported positive outcomes with cognitive-behavioral treatment strategies (Butler, Cullington, Munby, Amies, & Gelder, 1984; Emmelkamp, Mersch, Vissia, & van der Helm, 1985; Jerremalm, Jansson, & Ost, 1986; Kanter & Goldfried, 1979; Mattick & Peters, 1988; Mattick, Peters, & Clarke, 1989), there is clearly a need to examine other treatment procedures, either as adjuncts to cognitive-behavioral treatments or as alternatives. Furthermore, the evaluation of cognitive-behavioral treatments is far from complete. While Mattick and colleagues (Mattick & Peters, 1988; Mattick et al., 1989) have demonstrated that the cognitive procedures are an important component of treatment, significantly enhancing the effectiveness of exposure as a primary treatment, other investigators have not shown this to be the case. Studies by Biran, Augusto, and Wilson (1981) and Stravynski, Marks, and Yule (1982) have shown no benefit of the addition of cognitive restructuring procedures to exposure and to social skills training, respectively. My colleagues and I are currently evaluating the effectiveness of the cognitive component of CBGT in our laboratory.

The most investigated treatment for social phobia has been social skills training (SST), a set of procedures designed to teach effective social behaviors and typically consisting of (a) instructions for effective behavior, (b) modeling of effective responses by therapists, (c) behavioral rehearsal, (d) corrective feedback, (e) further rehearsal, and (f) social reinforcement. SST was examined in several studies conducted abroad before the formalization of criteria for social phobia in DSM-III. Description of patients in these studies suggests that they may be better described as socially inadequate than as social phobic. Many may also be appropriately diagnosed as APD, a group of patients that is believed to be more deficient in social skills than are social phobic patients (Greenberg & Stravynski, 1983; Marks, 1985; Turner et al., 1986), although as noted earlier, this remains controversial. Thus the applicability of some of these studies to social phobic samples is open to question.

Five studies of SST have been conducted (Falloon, Lloyd, & Harpin, 1981; Marzillier, Lambert, & Kellett, 1976; Ost, Jerremalm, & Johansson, 1981; Stravynski et al., 1982; Trower, Yardley, Bryant, & Shaw, 1978). Marzillier et al. (1976) compared SST to systematic desensitization and a waiting-list control. Both treatments led to patient improvements, and SST patients maintained their gains at a 6-month follow-up. However, treatment effects were not clearly superior to those achieved by control subjects. Trower et al. (1978) attempted a similar comparison but first subdivided their patients into socially inadequate and social phobic subgroups. Social phobic patients improved equally with both treatments, but gains were largely restricted to self-report measures, and there was little evidence of behavioral change.

Studies by Falloon et al. (1981) and Stravynski et al. (1982) provide a more optimistic picture of the effectiveness of SST, although both studies have a serious problem of experimental design. Neither includes a control condition that can lead to the attribution of change specifically to SST. Falloon compared SST to SST combined with propranolol, a beta blocker; SST led to significant changes that were not enhanced by propranolol. Stravynski et al. (1982) compared SST to SST combined with cognitive modification procedures. Both treatments led to substantial patient improvement, but the cognitive procedures did not increase the effectiveness of SST alone. Elsewhere, my colleagues and I have reviewed the method of administration of the cognitive procedures and questioned whether they were administered in a way that would restrict their effectiveness (Heimberg & Barlow, 1988; Heimberg et al., 1987). In addition, a follow-up study of the process of change in these patients (Stravynski, Grey, &

Elie, 1987) describes them as having APD rather than social phobia.

The most supportive study of SST in the treatment of social phobia was reported by Ost et al. (1981). These investigators divided their subjects into groups of "physiological reactors" and "behavioral reactors," based on heart rate and behavioral measurements taken during a simulated social interaction. *Behavioral reactors* demonstrated inadequate social behavior but a relative absence of cardiovascular arousal, while *physiological reactors* showed the reverse pattern. SST was compared to a treatment called "applied relaxation (AR)," which teaches patients to relax, altering the technique over time so that they may relax quickly and without the benefit of external aids; it provides the opportunity for patients to practice their relaxation skills during role plays and to do so in natural settings. Outcome was a function of treatment classification, with behavioral reactors doing better with SST and physiological reactors doing better with AR.

Also, AR appears to be a promising treatment for some social phobic patients. A follow-up study compared AR to self-instructional training (SIT), a cognitive-behavioral technique, and a waiting-list control (Jerremalm et al., 1986); AR was as effective as SIT and more effective than the waiting-list. This was the case whether patients had been classified as physiological reactors or as "cognitive reactors."

Again, I return to the question of exposure as a treatment for social phobia. Exposure is often called the treatment of choice for other anxiety disorders (Barlow & Beck, 1984), but only a few studies have examined exposure alone for the treatment of social phobia. At this point, it appears that exposure to naturally occurring social phobic events can be an effective treatment (Alstrom, Nordlund, Persson, Harding, & Ljungqvist, 1984; Biran et al., 1981; Butler et al., 1984; Emmelkamp et al., 1985; Mattick & Peters, 1988; Mattick et al., 1989). However, while Biran et al. and Alstrom et al. found exposure to be effective, and Biran et al. reported that the addition of cognitive restructuring did not add to the effectiveness of exposure, Emmelkamp et al. found exposure to be no more effective than SIT or rational–emotive therapy. Each of the other studies found that the addition of other procedures, either cognitive restructuring or anxiety management training, did enhance exposure effects.

What can be drawn from these studies for the clinician treating social phobia? First, it appears that exposure should be a component of treatment, but at present, it does not appear that exposure alone will yield the best results. I suggest that for most social phobic patients, who do appear to possess adequate social skills despite sometimes considerable behavioral disruption, that cognitive coping skills, such as those included in CBGT, become a central part of treatment. However, AR skills may have a very meaningful place in the treatment of social phobic patients who experience disruptive physiological arousal, and AR and CBGT procedures may be combined. SST may play an important role for patients with documented behavioral deficits (e.g., Ost et al.'s 1981 behavioral reactors), but it may be an unnecessary addition to the treatment of other social phobic patients. However, much work remains to be done to determine the best set of procedures for the treatment of social phobia.

REFERENCES

Alstrom, J. E., Nordlund, C. L., Persson, G., Harding, M., & Ljungqvist, C. (1984). Effects of four treatment methods on social phobic patients not suitable for insight-oriented psychotherapy. *Acta Psychiatrica Scandinavica, 70,* 97–110.

American Psychiatric Association. (1980). *Diagnostic and statistical manual of mental disorders* (3rd ed.). Washington, DC: Author.

American Psychiatric Association. (1987). *Diagnostic and statistical manual of mental disorders* (3rd ed., rev.). Washington, DC: Author.

Amies, P. L., Gelder, M. G., & Shaw, P. M. (1983). Social phobia: A comparative clinical study. *British Journal of Psychiatry, 142,* 174–179.

Arrindell, W. A., Emmelkamp, P. M. G., Monsma, A., & Brilman, E. (1983). The role of perceived parental rearing practices in the aetiology of phobic disorders: A controlled study. *British Journal of Psychiatry, 143,* 183–187.

Barlow, D. H. (1985). The dimensions of anxiety disorders. In A. H. Tuma & J. D. Maser (Eds.), *Anxiety and the anxiety disorders* (pp. 479–500). Hillsdale, NJ: Erlbaum.

Barlow, D. H., & Beck, J. G. (1984). The psychosocial treatment of anxiety disorders: Current status, future directions. In J. B. W. Williams & R. L. Spitzer (Eds.), *Psychotherapy research: Where are we and where should we go?* (pp. 29–66). New York: Guilford.

Beck, A. T., & Emery, G. (1985). *Anxiety disorders and phobias: A cognitive perspective.* New York: Basic Books.

Biran, M., Augusto, F., & Wilson, G. T. (1981). *In vivo* exposure vs. cognitive restructuring in the treatment of scriptophobia. *Behaviour Research and Therapy, 19,* 525–532.

Bruch, M. A., Heimberg, R. G., Berger, P., & Collins, T. M. (in press). Social phobia and perceptions of early parental and personal characteristics. *Anxiety Research: An International Journal.*

Burns, D. D. (1980). *Feeling good: The new mood therapy.* New York: William Morrow.

Buss, A. H. (1986). A theory of shyness. In W. H. Jones, J. M. Cheek, & S. R. Briggs (Eds.), *Shyness: Perspectives on research and treatment* (pp. 39–46). New York: Plenum.

Butler, G. (1985). Exposure as a treatment for social phobia: Some instructive difficulties. *Behaviour Research and Therapy, 23,* 651–657.

Butler, G., Cullington, A., Munby, M., Amies, P., & Gelder, M. (1984). Exposure and anxiety management in the treatment of social phobia. *Journal of Consulting and Clinical Psychology, 52,* 642–650.

Cerny, J. A., Himadi, W. G., & Barlow, D. H. (1984). Issues in diagnosing anxiety disorders. *Journal of Behavioral Assessment, 6,* 301–329.

Chambless, D. L., Cherney, J., Caputo, G. C., & Rheinstein, B. J. G. (1987). Anxiety disorders and alcoholism: A study with inpatient alcoholics. *Journal of Anxiety Disorders, 1,* 29–40.

Derogatis, L. R., (1983). *SCL-90-R: Administration, scoring, and procedure manual.* Baltimore, MD: Clinical Psychometric Research.

Emmelkamp, P. M. G. (1982). *Phobic and obsessive-compulsive disorders: Theory, research and practice.* New York: Plenum.

Emmelkamp, P. M. G., Mersch, P. P., Vissia, E., & van der Helm, M. (1985). Social phobia: A comparative evaluation of cognitive and behavioral interventions. *Behaviour Research and Therapy, 23,* 365–369.

Falloon, I. R. H., Lloyd, G. G., & Harpin, R. E. (1981). The treatment of social phobia: Real-life rehearsal with nonprofessional therapists. *Journal of Nervous and Mental Disease, 169,* 180–184.

Gorman, J. M., Fyer, M. R., Goetz, R., Askanazi, J., Liebowitz, M. R., Fyer, A. J., Kinney, J., & Klein, D. F. (1988). Ventilatory physiology of patients with panic disorder. *Archives of General Psychiatry, 45*, 31–39.

Gorman, J. M., & Gorman, L. K. (1987). Drug treatment of social phobia. *Journal of Affective Disorders, 13*, 183–192.

Greenberg, D., & Stravynski, A. (1983). Social phobia (letter). *British Journal of Psychiatry, 143*, 526.

Hartman, L. M. (1983). A metacognitive model of social anxiety: Implications for treatment. *Clinical Psychology Review, 3*, 435–456.

Heimberg, R. G. (1986, June). *Predicting the outcome of cognitive-behavioral treatment of social phobia.* Paper presented at the annual meeting of the Society for Psychotherapy Research, Wellesley, MA.

Heimberg, R. G. (1989). Cognitive and behavioral treatments for social phobia: A critical review. *Clinical Psychology Review, 9*, 107–128.

Heimberg, R. G., & Barlow, D. H. (1988). Psychosocial treatments for social phobia. *Psychosomatics, 29*, 27–37.

Heimberg, R. G., Becker, R. E., Goldfinger, K., & Vermilyea, J. A. (1985). Treatment of social phobia by exposure, cognitive restructuring, and homework assignments. *Journal of Nervous and Mental Disease, 173*, 236–245.

Heimberg, R. G., Dodge, C. S., & Becker, R. E. (1987). Social phobia. In L. Michelson & M. Ascher (Eds.), *Anxiety and stress disorders: Cognitive behavioral assessment and treatment* (pp. 280–309). New York: Guilford.

Heimberg, R. G., Dodge, C. S., Kennedy, C. R., Hope, D. A., Zollo, L., & Becker, R. E. (in press-a). Cognitive behavioral treatment of social phobia: Comparison to a credible placebo control. *Cognitive Therapy and Research.*

Heimberg, R. G., Hope, D. A., Dodge, C. S., & Becker, R. E. (in press-b). DSM-III-R subtypes of social phobia: Comparison of generalized social phobics and public speaking phobics. *Journal of Nervous and Mental Disease.*

Heimberg, R. G., Klosko, J. S., Dodge, C. S., Shadick, R., Becker, R. E., & Barlow, D. H. (1989). Anxiety disorders, depression, and attributional style: A further test of the specificity of depressive attributions. *Cognitive Therapy and Research, 13*, 21–36.

Jerremalm, A., Jansson, L., & Ost, L. G. (1986). Cognitive and physiological reactivity and the effects of different behavioral methods in the treatment of social phobia. *Behaviour Research and Therapy, 24*, 171–180.

Kanter, N. J., & Goldfried, M. R. (1979). Relative effectiveness of rational restructuring and self-control desensitization in the reduction of interpersonal anxiety. *Behavior Therapy, 10*, 472–490.

Kennedy, C. R., & Heimberg, R. G. (1986, November). *Treatment credibility and client outcome expectancy: An evaluation of five treatment rationales.* Paper presented at the annual meeting of the Association for the Advancement of Behavior Therapy, Chicago, IL.

Liebowitz, M. R., Fyer, A. J., Gorman, J. M., Dillon, D., Davies, S., Stein, J. M., Cohen, B. S., & Klein, D. F. (1985a). Specificity of lactate infusions in social phobia versus panic disorders. *American Journal of Psychiatry, 142*, 947–950.

Liebowitz, M. R., Gorman, J. M., Fyer, A. J., & Klein, D. F. (1985b). Social phobia: Review of a neglected anxiety disorder. *Archives of General Psychiatry, 42*, 729–736.

Liebowitz, M. R., Gorman, J. M., Fyer, A. J., Levitt, M., Dillon, D., Levy, G., Appleby, I. L., Anderson, S., Palij, M., Davies, S. O., & Klein, D. F. (1985c). Lactate provocation of panic attacks: II. Biochemical and physiological findings. *Archives of General Psychiatry, 42*, 709–719.

Marks, I. M. (1970). The classification of phobic disorders. *British Journal of Psychiatry, 116*, 377–386.

Marks, I. M. (1985). Behavioral treatment of social phobia. *Psychopharmacology Bulletin, 21*, 615–618.

Marks, I. M., & Gelder, M. C. (1966). Different ages of onset in varieties of phobia. *American Journal of Psychiatry, 123*, 218–221.

Marzillier, J. S., Lambert, C., & Kellett, J. (1976). A controlled evaluation of systematic desensitization and social skills training for socially inadequate psychiatric patients. *Behaviour Research and Therapy, 14*, 225–238.

Mattick, R. P., & Peters, L. (1988). Treatment of severe social phobia: Effects of guided exposure with and without cognitive restructuring. *Journal of Consulting and Clinical Psychology, 56*, 251–260.

Mattick, R. P., Peters, L., & Clarke, J. C. (1988). Exposure and cognitive restructuring for severe social phobia: A controlled study. *Behavior Therapy, 20*, 3–23.

McEwan, K. L., & Devins, G. M. (1983). Is increased arousal in social anxiety noticed by others? *Journal of Abnormal Psychology, 92*, 417–421.

McNeil, D. W., & Lewin, M. R. (1986, November). *Public speaking anxiety: A meaningful subtype of social phobia?* Paper presented at the annual meeting of the Association for Advancement of Behavior Therapy, Chicago, IL.

Moorey, S., & Burns, D. D. (1983). The apprenticeship model: Training in cognitive therapy by participation. In A. Freeman (Ed.), *Cognitive therapy with couples and groups* (pp. 303–321). New York: Plenum.

Mullaney, J. A., & Trippett, C. J. (1979). Alcohol dependence and phobias: Clinical description and relevance. *British Journal of Psychiatry, 135*, 563–573.

Myers, J. K., Weissman, M. M., Tischler, G. L., Holzer, C. E., III, Leaf, P. J., Orvaschel, H., Anthony, J. D., Boyd, J. H., Burke, J. D., Jr., Kramer, M., & Stoltzman, R. (1984). Six-month prevalence of psychiatric disorders in three communities. *Archives of General Psychiatry, 41*, 959–967.

Ohman, A., Dimberg, V., & Ost, L.-G. (1985). Animal and social phobias: Biological constraints on learned fear responses. In S. Reiss & R. Bootzin (Eds.), *Theoretical issues in behavior therapy* (pp. 123–175). New York: Academic.

Ost, L.-G. (1987). Age of onset in different phobias. *Journal of Abnormal Psychology, 96*, 223–229.

Ost, L.-G., Jerremalm, A., & Johansson, J. (1981). Individual response patterns and the effects of different behavioral methods in the treatment of social phobia. *Behaviour Research and Therapy, 19*, 1–16.

Parker, G. (1979). Reported parental characteristics of agoraphobics and social phobics. *British Journal of Psychiatry, 135*, 555–560.

Pilkonis, P. A., & Zimbardo, P. G. (1979). The personal and social dynamics of shyness. In C. E. Izard (Ed.), *Emotions in personality and psychopathology* (pp. 133–160). New York: Plenum.

Pollard, C. A., & Henderson, J. G. (1988). Four types of social phobia in a community sample. *Journal of Nervous and Mental Disease, 176*, 440–445.

Rapee, R., Mattick, R., & Murrell, E. (1986). Cognitive mediation in the affective component of spontaneous panic attacks. *Journal of Behavior Therapy and Experimental Psychiatry, 17*, 245–253.

Reich, J., & Yates, W. (1988). Family history of psychiatric disorders in social phobia. *Comprehensive Psychiatry, 29*, 72–75.

Sanderson, W. C., Rapee, R. M., & Barlow, D. H. (1987, November). *The DSM-III-R anxiety disorder categories: Descriptions and patterns of comorbidity.* Paper presented at the Annual Meeting of the Association for Advancement of Behavior Therapy, Boston, MA.

Sank, L. I., & Shaffer, C. S. (1984). A therapist's *manual for cognitive behavior therapy in groups.* New York: Plenum.

Schlenker, B. R., & Leary, M. R. (1982). Social anxiety and self-presentation: A conceptualization and model. *Psychological Bulletin, 92*, 641–669.

Smail, P., Stockwell, T., Canter, S., & Hodgson, R. (1984). Alcohol dependence and phobic anxiety states: I. A prevalence study. *British Journal of Psychiatry, 144*, 53–57.

Spitzer, R., & Williams, J. B. W. (1985). Proposed revisions in the DSM-III classification of anxiety disorders based on research and clinical experience. In A. H. Tuma & J. D. Maser (Eds.), *Anxiety and the anxiety disorders* (pp. 759–773). Hillsdale, NJ: Erlbaum.

Stravynski, A., Grey, S., & Elie, R. (1987). Outline of the therapeutic process in social skills training with socially dysfunctional patients. *Journal of Consulting and Clinical Psychology, 55*, 224–228.

Stravynski, A., Marks, I., & Yule, W. (1982). Social skills problems in neurotic outpatients: Social skills training with and without cognitive modification. *Archives of General Psychiatry, 39*, 1378–1385.

Torgersen, S. (1979). The nature and origin of common phobic fears. *British Journal of Psychiatry, 134*, 343–351.

Torgersen, S. (1983). Genetic factors in anxiety disorders. *Archives of General Psychiatry, 40*, 1085–1089.

Trower, P., & Gilbert, P. (1989). New theoretical conceptions of social anxiety and social phobia. *Clinical Psychology Review, 9*, 19–36.

Trower, P., & Turland, D. (1984). Social phobia. In S. Turner (Ed.), *Behavioral theories and treatment of anxiety.* New York: Plenum.

Trower, P., Yardley, K., Bryant, B., & Shaw, P. (1978). The treatment of social failure: A comparison of anxiety-reduction and skills acquisition procedures on two social problems. *Behavior Modification, 2*, 41–60.

Turner, S. M., & Beidel, D. C. (1989). Social phobia: Clinical syndrome, diagnosis, and comorbidity. *Clinical Psychology Review, 9*, 3–18.

Turner, S. M., Beidel, D. C., Dancu, C. V., & Keys, D. J. (1986). Psychopathology of social phobia and comparison to avoidant personality disorder. *Journal of Abnormal Psychology, 95*, 389–394.

Watson, D., & Friend, R. (1969). Measurement of social-evaluative anxiety. *Journal of Consulting and Clinical Psychology, 33*, 448–457.

CHAPTER 12

Pharmacotherapy

FRANKLIN R. SCHNEIER, ANDREW P. LEVIN, AND MICHAEL R. LIEBOWITZ

CONCEPTUALIZATION OF THE DISORDER

Introduction

A few years ago, a chapter with this title could have contained little more than speculation based on analogies from pharmacological treatment of related disorders and performance anxiety in nonclinical populations. American researchers and clinicians had largely ignored social phobia while focusing more attention on other anxiety disorders, such as panic disorder, agoraphobia, and simple phobia. Recently, however, research interest in the pharmacological treatment of social phobia has grown. The emerging data are relevant to both clinical diagnosis and treatment of this disorder.

Definition

Social phobia is characterized by recurrent attacks of significant anxiety, usually accompanied by symptoms of autonomic discharge, in one or more social situations. Patients typically experience fear of embarrassing themselves, and they then actively avoid the situations or endure them with dread, which leads to social and/or occupational impairment.

In its milder forms, social phobia may involve fear of a single situation, such as public speaking. For example, an otherwise well-adjusted research scientist may be unable to present her work at a symposium and finds her career therefore limited. At the other end of the social phobic spectrum,

social anxiety intrudes into virtually every aspect of life. Such situations as talking to colleagues or supervisors, asking someone for a date or attending a party may become intolerable, leaving the patient quite disabled socially and occupationally.

History

Janet (1903, 1909) introduced the term *social phobia* ("phobie du situations sociales") to describe patients who feared public speaking, performing at the piano, and writing while being observed. Before Janet, these behaviors were considered normal human traits, rather than symptoms of a psychiatric disorder. In 1926, Freud (1961) explicated his theory of anxiety, which grouped all phobias as psychological symptoms produced by ego defenses externalizing unacceptable instinctual drives. This grouping of all phobias, and its implicit etiological uniformity, was accepted by the American Psychiatric Association in 1952 in the first *Diagnostic and Statistical Manual of Mental Disorders* (DSM-I) and in 1968 in DSM-II.

Marks and Gelder (1966) divided phobias into agoraphobia, social phobia, and simple or specific phobias. They noted that social phobics tended to have a younger age of onset than agoraphobics, a finding supported by subsequent studies (Amies, Gelder, & Shaw, 1983; Marks, 1970). They established the modern definition of *social phobia*, which includes "fears of eating, drinking, shaking, blushing, speaking, writing or vomiting in the presence of other people," with the essential characteristic of fear of seeming ridiculous to others. This concept of social phobia, which includes patients with specific social fears as well as those with more generalized forms of social anxiety, has been adopted by DSM-III-R. On the other hand, DSM-III, without empirical basis, restricted social phobia to discrete performance anxiety and suggested that the generalized form should be labeled avoidant personality disorder (APD).

While DSM-III asserted that social phobics generally have only one specific social fear, DSM-III-R acknowledges that many social phobics have multiple fears or generalized social anxiety rather than a single fear or discrete performance anxiety. Even in DSM-III-R, however, the examples are still limited to specific social fears. Unlike DSM-III, DSM-III-R also recognizes that social phobia may overlap with APD, but it permits no other concurrent related diagnoses.

The current criteria thus exclude patients who develop social phobia as an apparent result of another disorder. A common example is the subgroup of patients with spontaneous panic attacks leading to panic disorder or agoraphobia, who then begin to avoid social or performance situations for fear of humiliation should they panic. These patients (*secondary* social phobics, as opposed to *primary* social phobics with no antecedent history of spontaneous panic attacks) are also motivated by fear of embarrassment to avoid situations, but the embarrassment would be related to having a panic attack in front of others. Panic may also co-occur in primary social phobics who later develop spontaneous panic attacks that appear unrelated to their social phobia.

Primary social phobics differ significantly from secondary social phobics, in that their severe anxiety is confined to social situations or the anticipation of such situations. Patients with social phobia secondary to panic disorder, however, also have panic attacks in a variety of nonsocial situations (e.g., subways, supermarkets, bridges, tunnels), and they tend to fear or avoid any situation where easy exit is difficult. Patients with primary panic disorder also tend to feel comforted by the presence of familiar figures, whereas primary social phobics feel more comfortable when alone. These preliminary observations regarding the

distinctions between primary and secondary social phobias should be validated by developmental, biological, treatment, family, and follow-up studies. There is also little empirical evidence for the automatic exclusion of patients whose social avoidance is due to Axis III conditions such as stuttering or trembling. In the absence of data, a flexible definition seems warranted that would allow social phobia to coexist and overlap with other Axis I, II, and III disorders if an embarrassment and humiliation fear is excessive.

Another issue in the definition of this disorder is the validity of subtypes within social phobia. DSM-III-R implies two subtypes: (1) The *discrete performance anxiety subtype* includes those individuals who have adequate social relationships but demonstrate marked anxieties either about public speaking or speaking in a group setting or in discrete acts such as using a pen, eating utensil, drinking cup, or urinal in front of others. (2) In contrast, individuals with *generalized social fears* suffer great anxiety when talking to strangers, acquaintances, colleagues, or bosses. They avoid work or seek jobs with limited interpersonal demands, remain with their family of origin or live alone, and avoid dating, marriage, or friendships. Many meet criteria for APD. They often also suffer from performance anxiety, similar to the discrete subtype.

These subtypes have received tentative validation from several evaluations, which have found differential responses to social stressors and to various treatments. In a double-blind controlled study in our clinic (Liebowitz et al., 1988), 42 generalized social phobics responded significantly better to phenelzine than to atenolol or placebo. A smaller group of patients with discrete performance anxiety showed a nonsignificant superior response to atenolol over phenelzine and placebo.

Heimberg (1986) found that public speaking phobics responded better than generalized social phobics to a treatment including simulated exposures, cognitive restructuring, and homework assignments. A more recent comparison of these groups found generalized social phobics (a) to appear more anxious and perform more poorly in an individualized behavioral test, (b) to differ in their responses to cognitive assessment tasks, and

(c) to differ in their patterns of heart rate acceleration during behavioral tests (Heimberg, unpublished data).

Epidemiology

Because social phobia tends to run a long, chronic course, studies of prevalence also approximate the incidence of the disorder. A recent epidemiological study of two urban populations found 6-month prevalences of social phobia ranging from 0.9 to 1.7% for men and 1.5% to 2.6% for women (Myers et al., 1984). However, these figures may overestimate the presence of primary social phobia by including subjects whose social anxiety was secondary to another disorder, such as agoraphobia.

Another community survey (Pollard & Henderson, 1988) measured the prevalence of four specific social fears—public speaking, writing in public, eating in public, and using public rest rooms. While the combined prevalence rates of these fears was quite high (greater than 20%), the prevalence fell to 2% when the additional criterion of impairment or distress from the fears was added. Many people with subsyndromal social phobia may be able to avoid their feared social situations without substantial negative consequences.

Preliminary data from other epidemiological studies (Fyer, personal communication, July 1, 1988) show significant (25–50%) overlap between social phobia and panic disorder. In another prevalence study, Bryant and Trower (1974) estimated that 3–10% of first-year students at a British college manifested typical social phobic symptoms. In studies of clinical samples, Marks (1970) found that 8% of a phobic population had social phobia, while 60% had agoraphobia. Other investigators, however, have noted that the ratio of social phobics to agoraphobics increased after the investigators' interest in social phobia became known (Amies et al., 1983). Among outpatients applying for treatment to an American anxiety and phobia center, 8 (13.3%) of 60 were found to be DSM-III social phobic, which equaled the proportion with panic disorder and was exceeded only by those with agoraphobia (DiNardo, O'Brien, Barlow, Waddell, & Blanchard, 1983). Unlike panic disorder patients, however, many social phobics do not think of themselves as having a disorder, viewing their condition instead as part of their personality makeup.

Morbidity

In terms of morbidity, social phobia seems to begin early (characteristically between ages 15 and 20 years) and to follow a chronic, unremitting course (Marks & Gelder, 1966). The physical manifestations of anxiety in performance or social situations tend to be quite similar, with tachycardia, pounding heart, trembling, and sweating. Resultant social and occupational impairment is often severe. In one unselected series of 11 patients meeting DSM-III social phobia criteria in our clinic, 2 were unable to work, 2 had dropped out of school, 4 had abused alcohol, 1 had abused tranquilizers, 6 were blocked from work advancement, and 5 avoided almost all social interaction outside their immediate family. Of the 11, 5 had either past or present secondary major depression.

In another series of social phobics, one third were found to have either a past or present history of depression (Munjack & Moss, 1981). Amies et al. (1983) found depressive symptoms in one half of social phobics in a large sample. They also found that 14% of their social phobics had a history of parasuicidal acts, far exceeding the 2% rate among agoraphobics.

Social phobia is also frequently complicated by alcoholism. Thyer et al. (1986) found a 36% prevalence of alcoholism among social phobic patients entering an anxiety disorder clinic, the highest prevalence of alcoholism among any DSM-III diagnostic group. Although another study found very little alcohol abuse in another anxiety clinic population (Barlow, DiNardo, Vermilyea, Vermilyea, & Blanchard, 1986), several studies of alcoholic populations support the association. Mullaney and Trippett (1979) reported a 23.5% prevalence of social phobia among alcohol program inpatients, with an additional 33% with social anxiety that was distressing but not disabling or leading to avoidance. A majority of these patients reported that the phobia predated the alcohol abuse. Other studies of alcohol program inpatients have found a 39% prevalence of social phobia during the last drinking period (Smail, Stockwell, Canter, & Hodgson, 1984), and an 8% and a 21% lifetime history of social phobia (Bowen, Cipywnyk, D'Arcy, & Keegan, 1984; Chambless, Cherney, Caputo, & Rheinstein, 1987, respectively). In the latter study, social phobia was again the most common of all anxiety disorders, and the anxiety disorder preceded alcohol abuse in 80% of patients.

Etiology

The etiology of social phobia is unclear, and several theories attempt to explain its development.

Biological Theories

One of the biological theories is based on the observation that social phobics experience heightened autonomic arousal, as manifested by symptoms of tachycardia, sweating, and trembling when feeling that they were under evaluation or scrutiny. Normal subjects also experience autonomic arousal under stressful conditions, and it has been shown that during stressful public speaking, plasma epinephrine levels briefly increase by two to three times baseline levels (Dimsdale & Moss, 1974). This has generated hypotheses that social phobia is due either to exaggerated catecholamine production in stressful conditions or to increased sensitivity to normal catecholamine elevation in response to stress.

This hypothesis has been supported by evidence that acute treatment with beta blockers alleviates performance anxiety in normal subjects (Desai, Taylor-Davies, & Barnett, 1983; Liden & Gottfries, 1974), but the efficacy of beta blockers in social phobia is in doubt (as discussed in the section on treatment). In a more direct test of the theory that social phobia is related to elevated epinephrine production or response, 11 patients meeting DSM-III criteria for social phobia were infused intravenously with epinephrine over 60 minutes. Although the mean plasma epinephrine level increased from 113 picograms per milliliter (pg/ml) to 928 pg/ml, only 1 of the 11 patients experienced observable anxiety. Increase in plasma epinephrine level alone appears insufficient to explain social anxiety (Papp et al., 1988).

In another study of catecholamine function (Levin et al., 1989), 23 DSM-III social phobics and 14 normal controls gave a speech before laboratory staff in a simulation of a situation provoking social anxiety. Heart rate and blood chemistry were directly monitored. Although social phobic patients reported significantly more subjective complaints and demonstrated more anxious behaviors than controls, there were no differences in heart rate or plasma epinephrine, norepinephrine, or cortisol. In addition, there was no correlation between subjective or behavioral responses.

To the degree that peripheral autonomic arousal contributes to performance anxiety, social phobics appear to suffer from an exaggerated awareness rather than an exaggerated amount of such activation. This would account for those patients whose symptoms do respond to peripheral beta blockade. Generalized social phobics, who do not appear to benefit from beta blockers, may suffer from biological differences in central nervous system (CNS) function. Evidence for CNS dysfunction in social phobia includes the successful treatment of social phobia with the monoamine oxidase inhibitors (MAOIs—as discussed in the treatment section), which presumably act by a central mechanism.

To date, no family studies of social phobia have been reported, so the genetic component of the disorder is unclear. Social anxiety, however, may have a heritable component. Torgersen (1979) compared social fears among 95 monozygotic and dizygotic twin pairs. The monozygotic twins were significantly more concordant for such social phobic features as discomfort when eating with strangers or when being watched working or writing, or trembling, suggesting a genetic contribution to social anxiety.

Cognitive-Behavioral Theories

Learning theory postulates that the symptoms of social phobia are a conditioned response acquired through association of the phobic object (the conditioned stimulus) with a noxious experience (the unconditioned stimulus). Avoidance of the phobic object prevents or reduces the conditioned anxiety, thereby reinforcing the avoidance. Conflicting data, however, has led to modification of this theory. Most social phobics do not recall a traumatic incident in which the phobic object was associated with an unpleasant unconditioned stimulus. Laboratory conditioned avoidance behavior in animals is easily extinguished, but social phobias are not extinguished easily by exposure to the feared situation or by rational explanations of the harmless nature of the situation.

Another model emphasizes cognitive dysfunction in social phobia (Heimberg & Barlow, 1988). In stressful situations, social phobics tend to focus their thoughts toward task-irrelevant stimuli, such as negative expectancies, perceived lack of control, and public consequences of poor performance, and away from the task at hand. This leads to a cycle of poor performance and worsening expectations for social situations. This theory suggests that exposure therapy should be coupled with social skills training and/or cognitive restructuring to enhance the individual's ability to focus on thoughts relevant to the social task.

Other Theories

Psychoanalytic theory, as developed by Freud (1926/1961), postulates that phobias represent the transformation of internal anxiety into external fear through displacement, and that the specific content of a phobia has symbolic meaning. This line of reasoning is theoretically applicable to social phobia, but it has not as yet been subject to systematic controlled investigation.

Nichols (1974) has catalogued a variety of psychological and somatic traits observed in a social phobic sample. These include (a) low self-evaluation, (b) an unrealistic tendency to experience others as critical or disapproving, (c) rigid concepts of appropriate social behavior, (d) a negative-fantasy-producing anticipatory anxiety, (e) an increased awareness and fear of scrutiny by others, (f) a fear of social situations from which it is difficult to leave unobtrusively, (g) an exaggerated awareness of minimal somatic symptoms such as blushing or feeling faint, (h) a tendency to overreact with greater anxiety to the somatic symptoms of anxiety, and (i) an exaggerated fear of others noticing that one is anxious. It is unclear, however, which among these or other factors are causal, which are consequential, and which are not even specifically related to social phobia. The

feature of hypersensitivity to rejection or criticism suggests an overlap of social phobia with atypical depression or hysteroid dysphoria, in which extreme rejection sensitivity is a cardinal feature (Liebowitz et al., 1984b).

Several controlled studies have evaluated developmental contributions to the genesis of social phobia by comparing how social phobics, agoraphobics, simple phobics, and normal controls retrospectively rate their parents' child-rearing practices and attitudes. As a group, social phobics tend to perceive their parents as having been *less* caring, *more* overprotective, *more* lacking in emotional warmth, and *more* rejecting as compared to normal controls (Arrindell, Emmelkamp, Monsma, & Brilman, 1983; Parker, 1979). There were no differences reported, however, among the phobic groups, so the specificity of these findings for social phobia is uncertain. In contrast, Amies et al. (1983) reported that in comparison to agoraphobics, significantly more social phobic patients reported that during adolescence, their fathers were dominant and they had an unsatisfactory relationship with their fathers. These retrospective, self-report studies suffer the limitation of inability to distinguish true differences in parenting behavior from differences in subjects' perceptions of parenting.

DIFFERENTIAL DIAGNOSIS

Avoidance of social situations can occur in many psychiatric disorders, including agoraphobia, panic disorder, simple phobias, substance abuse disorders, avoidant and paranoid personality disorders, schizophrenia, and paranoid disorder, and depressive disorder. Although the boundaries of social phobia remain to be defined through scientific study, a number of distinguishing characteristics can be useful theoretically and clinically for diagnosis and treatment selection.

Panic Disorder and Agoraphobia

Agoraphobics often share with social phobics similar anxiety attack symptoms, with resultant demoralization and functional impairment. However, agoraphobia is generally distinguished from social phobia by the presence of spontaneous panic attacks and the avoidance of nonsocial situations where it would be difficult to get help in the event of a panic attack such as closed spaces or being alone. Agoraphobics prefer to be with others and usually seek people out when having an anxiety attack, whereas social phobics actively avoid people to prevent an anxiety attack. When agoraphobics do avoid certain social situations, their fear of humiliation is not general but is instead limited to the circumstance of having a panic attack.

Demographic data also support the distinction between social phobia and agoraphobia. In Marks's (1970) series, social phobics were 50% male, had an average age of onset of 19 years, and sought treatment at a mean age of 27 years. Agoraphobics were less likely to be male (25%), had an older mean age of onset (24 years) and sought treatment at an older mean age (32 years). While these differences were not significant, they were confirmed in a study by Amies et al. (1983). Males comprised 60% of social phobic subjects, but only 14% of agoraphobic subjects. Social phobics were also referred at a younger age than agoraphobics— 30.7 years versus 37.2 years,—and they came from a higher socioeconomic class. Persson and Nordlund (1985) also reported that social phobics belonged to a higher socioeconomic class, had higher education and higher verbal intelligence, and had an earlier onset of illness, in a comparison of 31 social phobic and 73 agoraphobic subjects. Another recent comparison (Solyom, Ledwidge, & Solyom, 1986) agreed that social phobics were younger, more likely to be male, and better educated than agoraphobics.

Although the physical manifestations of anxiety show overlap between social phobics and agoraphobics, several investigators have also noted differences in these symptoms. Amies et al. (1983) found that social phobics reported more blushing and muscle twitching, and less limb weakness, breathing difficulty, dizziness or faintness, actual fainting, and buzzing or ringing in the ears. Cameron, Thyer, Nesse, and Curtis, (1986) compared symptom profiles by patient diagnosis among 316 patients with anxiety disorders (excluding posttraumatic stress disorder), including 37 with social phobia. He found that results on the

Acute Panic Inventory (API) differentiated social phobia from all other anxiety disorders. In comparison to panic disorder patients, social phobics scored significantly lower on most symptoms, including feeling faint, fear of dying, palpitations, breathing changes, dizziness, confusion, derealization, depersonalization, difficulty concentrating, and nausea. Social phobics scored higher only on sweating and on difficulty speaking. In another study (Munjack, Brown, & McDowell, 1987), social phobics had significantly fewer somatic symptoms than panic disorder patients, as measured by the Symptom Checklist—90—Revised (SCL-90-R). These differences in symptom profiles of panic disorder with agoraphobia versus social phobia may reflect differences in pathophysiology of these syndromes. Social phobics were also found to have significantly lower extroversion scores than agoraphobics and normal controls on the Eysenck Personality Inventory (EPI—Amies et al., 1983).

Biological challenge studies have also differentiated social phobia from panic disorder and agoraphobia. Sodium lactate infusion induces panic attacks in most panic disorder patients but in few normal controls (Liebowitz et al., 1984a); Pitts & McClure, 1967). Social phobics have a significantly lower rate of panic in response to sodium lactate than do agoraphobics (Liebowitz et al., 1985). When patients meeting DSM-III criteria for agoraphobia with panic attacks or social phobia were challenged with 0.5 M racemic sodium lactate (10 mL/kg of body weight) administered intravenously over 20 minutes, 4 (44%) of 9 agoraphobics panicked, in contrast to 1 (7%) of 15 social phobics ($p < .03$). Another biological method of provoking panic is the inhalation of carbon dioxide. The inhalation of 5% carbon dioxide for 20 minutes in a canopy system induced panic in 12 of 31 panic disorder patients, but in none of 8 social phobics ($p < .01$) (Gorman et al., 1988). Inhalation of higher concentrations of carbon dioxide have produced mixed results. While Rapee, Mattick, and Murrell (1986) found significantly less anxiety in social phobics than in panic patients in response to single inhalation of 50% carbon dioxide, the preliminary finding in our clinic is that 35% carbon dioxide provokes panic at a similar rate in both groups of patients. Another biological factor differentiating patients with these disorders—their response to medications—is discussed subsequently.

While the distinctions between agoraphobia and panic disorder versus social phobia justify the separation of these disorders, it is clear that their symptoms can also overlap. Solyom et al. (1986) reported that 55% of a sample of DSM-III agoraphobics suffered from clinically significant social phobias and 30% of DSM-III social phobics suffered from clinically significant agoraphobic symptoms. Family studies and long-term follow-up studies, currently lacking for social phobia, may help clarify its relationship to agoraphobia.

Simple Phobias

Several studies have substantiated the distinction between social phobia and the simple phobias, which include specific animal phobias (e.g., birds, cats, insects) and situational phobias (e.g., heights, darkness, thunderstorms). Marks (1970) noted that social phobics showed a later age of onset, higher overt anxiety levels, and higher Maudsley neuroticism scores than animal phobics. Solyom et al. (1986) confirmed the findings of a significantly later age of onset and higher Maudsley neuroticism scores for social phobics in comparison to simple phobics. They also found that social phobics had significantly lower Maudsley extroversion scores and were more likely to report occupational or school difficulties as precipitants for the onset of their illness. Simple phobics were significantly more likely to report fright, generally involving an incident with the phobic object, as precipitating their illness. Another comparison of social and simple phobics (Thyer, Parrish, Curtis, Nesse, & Cameron, 1985) found no difference in ages of onset for these disorders.

These disorders may also differ in their characteristic physiological parameters of anxiety. Lader, Gelder, and Marks (1967) found social phobics to have more spontaneous fluctuations in galvanic skin response (GSR) than animal phobics. Weerts and Lang (1978) reported that students fearful of spiders react with greater affect and greater change in heart rate to fear-relevant scenes than did students fearful of public speaking. Response to medication may also differentiate

social and simple phobias. Unfortunately, family history and long-term follow-up studies are not now available.

Personality Disorders

Avoidant personality disorder (APD), which is characterized in DSM-III-R by a chronic pattern of difficulty in relating comfortably to others, social withdrawal and a fear of rejection and humiliation, appears to overlap with social phobia, particularly the generalized type. However, APD is also defined by exaggeration of risks involved in novel activities, and it is unclear to what extent social phobics share this feature. Whereas DSM-III allowed the diagnosis of social phobia only in the absence of APD, the revised version permits the diagnoses to coexist. The validity of the current distinction between these diagnoses remains to be tested empirically. In a preliminary study, Turner, Beidel, Dancu, and Keys (1986) compared performance of 10 subjects with DSM-III social phobia and 8 subjects with DSM-III APD on behavioral, psychophysiological, and cognitive parameters. The APD group reported significantly more social avoidance and distress and scored significantly higher on the SCL-90-R interpersonal sensitivity subscale, anxiety subscale, obsessive–compulsive subscale, depression subscale and general symptom index. In a series of structured role-play social interactions, the social phobic group was rated as having significantly more appropriate gaze, higher ratings for voice tone, higher levels of social competence in simulated social interactions and in giving an impromptu speech. It is unclear to what extent these findings represent quantitative differences in severity of social phobic symptoms, as opposed to qualitative differences between these groups. Consonant with this uncertainty, many of the APD personalities here might also be labeled social phobic by DSM-III-R. Further studies are needed to clarify the extent to which social phobia, in its discrete and generalized forms, and APD differ and/or overlap.

In schizoid, schizotypal, and paranoid personality disorders, individuals may prefer to avoid social situations due to a mistrust of others or a lack of interest in forming relationships with others. In contrast, social phobics do not generally mistrust or dislike other people. Instead of lacking interest, they desire to make social contact, but they are blocked by fear that they will act inappropriately and cause their own embarrassment or humiliation.

Psychoses

Patients with psychotic disorders may be socially avoidant, but they are distinguished from social phobia by the presence of delusions and/or hallucinations that may support the avoidance. Panic anxiety or fears of humiliation leading to social avoidance are not diagnosed as social phobia when occurring in the context of schizophrenia, schizophreniform disorder, or brief reactive psychoses. This should be studied further, however, because both behavioral and drug therapies for social phobia may have some utility in socially avoidant schizophrenics on concurrent antipsychotic medications.

Obsessive–Compulsive Disorder

Individuals with obsessive–compulsive disorder will sometimes avoid social situations that are involved in their obsessional thoughts or compulsive rituals. For example, patients with contamination fears may avoid eating with others. They may also avoid social situations in order to conceal embarrassing rituals. In both cases, the avoidance is secondary to obsessive–compulsive symptomatology.

Depression

The social withdrawal commonly seen in depressive disorders is usually associated with a lack of interest or pleasure in the company of others rather than a fear of scrutiny. In contrast, social phobics generally express the wish to be able to interact appropriately with others. They believe they would find socialization pleasurable if they were able to be less anxious.

Often, however, the distinction between social phobia and depression is less clear. Depression is very common among social phobics, although the latter diagnosis can only be made if there is a history of social phobia in the absence of major depression. Interpersonal hypersensitivity is characteristic of both social phobics and many depressed patients, especially those with atypical depression. Some atypical depressives experience phasic social phobia while depressed and can subsequently become chronically avoidant.

Stage Fright

It is unclear whether normal social or performance anxieties differ qualitatively from social phobia or only differ in severity. A certain amount of social or performance anxiety is ubiquitous and may have evolutionary adaptive advantage by motivating preparation and rehearsal for important or novel interpersonal events. Repeated exposure, however, usually lessens such anxiety in normals, and it tends to attenuate over the course of any given performance or social encounter (Dimsdale & Moss, 1974). Social phobics, however, often report that their symptoms *increase* as initial somatic discomfort becomes a further distraction and embarrassment to the already anxious individuals, leading to further symptoms and, in turn, to more anxiety, in an escalating spiral. Systematic studies are needed to determine whether social phobics lack the ability to habituate in social or performance situations, and, if so, why they lack it.

Additionally, social anxiety in normal individuals is generally proportional to the realistic danger of the situation. For example, a job interview would provoke more anxiety than a conversation with a casual acquaintance. For social phobics, as with simple phobics, the anxiety symptoms are greatly out of proportion to the realistic threat of the situation.

TREATMENT STUDIES

Until recently, psychopharmacologists had not regarded social phobia as a discrete syndrome meriting independent study. They viewed the disorder instead as a more severe form of the normal human trait of social anxiety. Treatment of social phobia was examined indirectly by studying performance anxiety in nonclinical populations, and directly by studying mixed phobic groups, including subjects with simple phobias and agoraphobia, in addition to social phobics. Two independent lines of investigation have led to development of substantial treatment study data on two classes of medications: monoamine oxidase inhibitors (MAOIs) and beta-adrenergic blockers. Additionally, this chapter describes some research on tricyclic antidepressants, benzodiazepines, and other medications.

Monoamine Oxidase Inhibitors (MAOIs)

In the 1960s, several studies (Kline, 1967; Sargant, 1962) reported that MAOIs were effective treatment for patients with vaguely defined phobic anxiety states. Subsequent investigations have examined the efficacy of MAOIs in agoraphobics and social phobics, although the earlier of these studies made no effort to separate these two diagnostic groups.

Solyom et al. (1973) treated a mixed group of 50 agoraphobics, social phobics, and specific phobics for 3 months with one of the following: (a) phenelzine 45 mg/day with brief psychotherapy, (b) placebo with brief psychotherapy, (c) aversion relief (with electric shock), (d) systematic desensitization, or (e) flooding therapy. The MAOI phenelzine led to significant improvement in anxiety, phobia, and social maladjustment ratings, and it was consistently more effective than placebo and brief psychotherapy. That drug treatment group, however, had the highest relapse rate 2 years after discontinuation of treatment.

The same research group (Solyom, Solyom, La Pierre, Pecknold, & Morton, 1981) found weaker drug effects in a comparison of phenelzine and placebo, with or without exposure therapy, in a mixed group of 40 agoraphobic and social phobic patients. Although phenelzine was superior to placebo in reducing anxiety, in overall phobia ratings, phenelzine was not significantly different from placebo. The apparent lack of effect of the MAOI here may have been due to the low dose (45 mg/day) of phenelzine used, which could have been insufficient for many patients.

Kelly, Guirguis, Fromme, Mitchell-Heggs, and Sargant (1970) retrospectively studied 246 patients (including 50 children) with "mixed phobias," including agoraphobia, social phobias, and

simple phobias. The MAOIs isocarboxazid and phenelzine were found to result in significant improvement in phobias and social adjustment. Here, phenelzine was used in a more substantial dose of up to 60 mg/day, but the results are complicated by concurrent treatment with other psychotropic medications.

In another study of mixed agoraphobic and social phobic patients, Tyrer, Candy, and Kelly (1973) compared double-blind treatment with phenelzine, up to 90 mg/day over 8 weeks, versus placebo. The MAOI yielded superior results in improvement of secondary phobias and in overall outcome. They additionally noted that the response of phobic symptoms was unrelated to patients' levels of depression. This suggests that the antiphobic effect of MAOIs is independent of their well-established antidepressant activity.

Tyrer and Steinberg (1975) followed up 26 of the aforementioned social phobic and agoraphobic patients who had completed the preceding 2-month trial of phenelzine or placebo. Although those who had been given phenelzine generally maintained their initial improvement 1 year later, the group that had received placebo demonstrated gradual improvement during the follow-up period, so that at 1-year follow-up, the two groups were not significantly different. The specificity of the initial phenelzine and placebo treatment effects was confounded, however, by the addition of other treatments, including behavioral therapies, minor tranquilizers, supportive interviews, and tricyclic antidepressants.

Mountjoy, Roth, Garside, and Leitch (1977) treated 36 patients with anxiety neurosis and 22 with either agoraphobia or social phobia, using either phenelzine up to 75 mg/day or placebo for 4 weeks. All patients additionally received diazepam, 15 mg/day. Phobic patients treated with phenelzine showed superior improvement on the social phobia scale, suggesting a specific effect of MAOIs on social phobic symptoms.

While the foregoing studies suggest possible MAOI efficacy for social phobics, some are limited by lack of specified diagnostic criteria, low dosages of phenelzine, small sample sizes, and no specification as to whether patients also suffered spontaneous panic attacks or associated depressive features. Most importantly, none reported response among the social phobics separately from the sample as a whole. Because agoraphobic patients have been shown to benefit from MAOIs, these studies cannot prove that the social phobic patients benefited from MAOI therapy. Several recent studies have examined social phobics more specifically.

Liebowitz, Fyer, Gorman, Campeas, and Levin (1986) studied treatment of social phobic patients with phenelzine, following the observation that MAOI medication was superior to imipramine in specifically reducing interpersonal sensitivity in a group of atypical depressives (Liebowitz et al., 1984b). A group of social phobics was first given 1 week of placebo. Patients who did not respond were treated openly with phenelzine, 60–90 mg/day for 8 weeks. Of the 11 patients treated in this study, 7 showed marked improvement, while the remaining 4 experienced moderate improvement.

Another open trial (Versiani, Mundim, Nardi, & Liebowitz, 1988) examined the efficacy of a different MAOI in 32 patients meeting DSM-III criteria for social phobia. Patients were treated with tranylcypromine, 40–60 mg/day for 1 year, and concurrent benzodiazepines were used by 7 patients, generally for brief periods. Six of the patients had previously shown no improvement in social phobic symptoms on clomipramine, 175–250 mg/day for at least 3 months. Throughout this study, treating physicians were instructed to avoid influencing patients' behavior by minimizing rewards for improvement, such as not commenting on patients' reports of progress, even if remarkable.

Out of 29 patients who achieved a dose of 40 mg/day of tranylcypromine for at least 2 weeks, 18 (61.9%) were rated marked responders, 5 (17.2%) were moderate responders, and 6 (20.6%) were nonresponders. Responders and nonresponders did not differ in age, gender, age of onset of illness, duration of illness, or previous treatments. Three out of four patients with a history of alcohol abuse were nonresponders, suggesting that MAOIs may not be as helpful for the subgroup who abuse alcohol. All responders maintained their improvement throughout the 1-year study period, but after discontinuation of the medication, 19 of the 23 responders relapsed partially or fully over the following 6 months.

These positive results for MAOIs in social phobia are being replicated in a double-blind trial. In a preliminary report (Liebowitz et al., 1988) of a large-scale trial in progress, 59 patients meeting DSM-III criteria for social phobia received placebo for 1 week, and nonresponders were then randomized to double-blind treatment with phenelzine, atenolol (a beta blocker), or placebo. Patients who were at least minimally improved after 8 weeks were continued on the same medication, in a blind fashion, for another 8 weeks to test the durability of the response, and to see if minimally improved patients would make further gains. After 16 weeks of treatment, all medication was tapered in a double-blind fashion over 4 weeks, to see if continued medication is necessary to maintain clinical gains.

Subjects were prospectively divided into limited and generalized social phobia subtypes, which were separately randomized to the three treatments. As per DSM-III-R, the *limited subtype* consists of patients with fears of engaging in one to several discrete public acts, where the *generalized subtype* involves more global interpersonal difficulty, such as fears of speaking to colleagues or supervisors at work, seeing friends, having romantic relationships, being introduced to strangers, going to parties, and so on. Patients with generalized social anxiety tended to score high on ratings of discrete fears as well, while those with limited social phobia did not score high on generalized pervasive social anxiety. Ratings were also made to detect symptoms of atypical depression and APD.

Assessment instruments included the Clinical Global Impression Scale (CGI), Hamilton Anxiety Scale (HAM-A) and 21-item Hamilton Depression Rating Scale (HAM-D) and Covi Anxiety and Raskin Depression Scales. The Liebowitz Social Phobia Scale (Liebowitz, 1987), which contains 12 common types of discrete performance fears and 12 common manifestations of generalized social anxiety, was used to rate social anxiety and avoidance. Patients were also rated on the Panic and Social Phobic Disorders—Severity Rating Form (PSPD-S), and separately on a change version (PSPD-C). While the full study will include 90 patients, data have been analyzed for the first 59 patients entering the 8-week acute phase medication trial. Six responded to placebo in the initial single blind week, and 6 others dropped out during this phase. Of the remaining 47 patients randomized to the three comparison treatments, 41 completed the 8-week acute treatment phase. Six others dropped out during the first 3 weeks of randomized treatment (3 on phenelzine, 2 on atenolol, and 1 on placebo) and are considered dropouts.

There were no significant gender or age differences among the three treatment groups. Of the 41 completers, 25 were male, and the mean age of completers was 32.8. CGI severity ratings conformed that the patients in each group were "markedly ill." This was operationally defined as significant impairment in work and social activity, but not a gross impairment. A "markedly ill" patient could hold a reasonably decent job and have some social activities that were fairly comfortable, but he or she had limitations in both areas because of social anxiety. Mean HAM-D scores were less than 8 for each group, demonstrating minimal current depressive symptomatology. Patients meeting simultaneous major depression criteria had been excluded from the study.

After 8 weeks of treatment, the response rates were 64% (9 of 14) for phenelzine, 36% (4 of 11) for atenolol, and 31% (5 of 16) for placebo. Although these proportions do not differ significantly, significant phenelzine–placebo differences were noted for the CGI severity and change subscales and the PSPD-S overall severity subscale. Examination of PSPD subscales showed significant phenelzine superiority in improving functional impairment and anticipatory anxiety. (Atenolol findings are discussed in the next section.)

In summary, results from the first half of this placebo-controlled study suggest phenelzine efficacy in social phobia after 8 weeks of treatment, with specific improvement in anticipatory anxiety and functional impairment. Anticipatory anxiety is a measure of how much an individual fears social or performance encounters, and it reflects degree of self-confidence. Functional impairment measures the extent of social and vocational disability. Overall severity is a composite measure of these two features, plus actual intensity and frequency of social anxiety episodes and specific

phobic avoidance of social or performance situations. The data thus suggest moderate phenelzine efficacy on all components of social phobia.

Other trends in the ongoing study suggest that phenelzine is more effective for patients with generalized social phobia, rather than with limited specific social fears. This would support the report of Deltito and Perugi (1986), who noted improvement in a patient with generalized social phobia and avoidant personality treated with phenelzine. Prior to treatment, this patient could not speak in front of groups, avoided eating outside his home, visited only with members of his immediate family, and turned down promotions at work that would have increased social contacts. Benzodiazepines and 3 years of weekly psychodynamically oriented psychotherapy had not been helpful. On phenelzine, 45 mg/day, the patient's social phobia began to improve after 4 weeks, and it continued progressively better over the next 2 months. At this time, the patient was "now taking joy in encountering new people and new situations." Avoidance behavior, anticipatory anxiety, and anxiety in social encounters were all greatly reduced.

CASE ILLUSTRATIONS OF RESPONSE TO PHENELZINE

The following additional case summaries illustrate responses to phenelzine:

Case 1

A 19-year-old man, living with his parents and working part-time in a department store, presented himself to the clinic with a history of severe social anxiety since age 15. At that time, he began to feel self-conscious about his appearance—the way he talked, his speech, and his being overweight. He began to get nervous in situations where he might be observed, such as walking down a hallway. This feeling would be accompanied by dry mouth, tremor, light-headedness, palpitations, and the sense that his ears were clogged. Although he had been an "A" student, he began skipping school and arguing with his parents. The school psychologist began seeing him, and he also received imipramine, 70 mg/day for 4 months, without effect. He tried running away from home and was subsequently hospitalized for 9 months and treated with intensive psychotherapy, and he later tried behavior therapy, hypnotherapy, and alprazolam therapy, all without significant effect. On presentation at our clinic, he continued to be socially withdrawn and unable to date, and he was thinking of quitting his job.

The patient was diagnosed as having social phobia with generalized social fears and also APD, and he was started on phenelzine, which was increased over a few weeks to 90 mg/day. Within 4 weeks, he noted a decrease in his social anxiety and avoidance. The improvement continued over the course of several months, and he began socializing, attending parties, and making friends, free of physical anxiety symptoms and with only mild residual anticipatory anxiety. After being continued on medication for 6 months, he was tapered off the phenelzine, and he has been able to maintain his improvement off all medication for 2 years to date. He no longer meets criteria for social phobia or for APD.

Case 2

Another patient in our clinic was a 26-year-old male mechanic who had experienced social phobic symptoms since elementary school, when going to parties made him self-conscious and anxious. In 12th grade, when he had to give a speech in front of his class, he fled the room and never returned to school again. Casual social contact would cause him to feel self-conscious, twitch, sweat, and experience palpitations. He would often drink six beers on weekend nights to enable himself to socialize. Although he worked for his brother, he felt quite anxious around other employees at work, and he was frequently absent. He tried psychotherapy, but he left after 2 months, feeling it was not helpful.

The patient was diagnosed as having the generalized subtype of social phobia and was entered into a treatment protocol of atenolol, 100 mg/day for 8 weeks, but he did not improve. On phenelzine, 60 mg/day, he began to feel significantly better after 3 weeks, and his anxiety symptoms virtually disappeared. Unfortunately, he developed decreased libido, weight gain, and urinary hesitancy, and the phenelzine was discontinued. His social phobic symptoms then recurred, and after a brief trial of tranylcypromine, which made him feel unpleasantly "speedy," he resumed phenelzine. Despite recurrent anorgasmia unrelieved by cyproheptadine, he has chosen to continue the phenelzine, which allows him to feel much more comfortable in social situations and to work more effectively.

Beta-Adrenergic Blockers

The other major approach to drug treatment of social phobia developed from the observation that many of the physical symptoms experienced by social phobics appear to be manifestations of beta-adrenergic hyperactivity. These include palpitations, sweating, trembling, hyperventilating, and blushing. The James–Lange theory (James, 1907) postulates that such peripheral bodily changes define an emotion such as anxiety, rather than merely being symptomatic of it. Subsequently, a large literature developed, which suggests that beta blockers reduce all forms of anxiety (Cole, Altesman, & Weingarten, 1980). Unfortunately, most earlier studies made no diagnostic distinctions among subjects treated, and the relevance of their findings to social phobia is thus uncertain.

More useful are the studies of the effect of beta blockers on anxiety during observed performance by musicians and other nonpatient performers. "Stage fright" shares many features with the anxiety of social phobics with limited discrete fears, including both the symptoms of sweating, trembling, and palpitations, and the experience of being scrutinized. Because these studies involve volunteers rather than actual patient populations, they may be considered analogue studies.

A majority of controlled analogue studies have found beta blockers to be superior to placebo in reducing performance anxiety, and some suggest that the effect is greater in subjects who are most anxious. In studies of musician volunteers (Brantigan, Brantigan, & Joseph, 1982; James, Burgoyne, & Savage, 1983; James, Griffith, Pearson, & Newby, 1977; Liden & Gottfries, 1974; Neftel et al., 1982), single doses of beta blockers given immediately prior to a performance decreased anxiety more than placebo did. In similarly designed studies, propranolol was effective in decreasing anxiety during public speaking (Hartley, Ungapen, Davie, & Spencer, 1983) and before a stressful interview (Gottschalk, Stone, & Gleser, 1974) among volunteer subjects.

The performance anxiety experienced by students taking examinations has also been studied. Krishnan (1975) found that oxprenolol, 40 mg twice a day, resulted in better examination performance than diazepam, 2 mg twice a day, although both drugs reduced tension and anxiety.

Two other studies (Desai et al., 1983; Krope, Kohrs, Ott, Wagner, & Fichts, 1982), however, reported that beta blockers were no better than placebo in decreasing anxiety or increasing performance during testing.

Finally, a study of amateur bowlers (Siitonen & Janne, 1976) found no difference in performance between groups given a single dose of oxprenolol (40 mg) or placebo. A subgroup of bowlers with high heart rate (one third of the sample) did, however, benefit from the beta blocker. These findings demonstrate efficacy of a variety of beta-blocking drugs on reducing performance anxiety and sometimes improving performance in different stressful settings. Because they used normal volunteer subjects, they only indirectly address the question of beta blocker efficacy in social phobia. The majority of these studies involved administration of short-term doses prior to a performance situation, and they are thus most closely analogous to treatment of social phobics who experience only occasional and predictable anxiety episodes, such as anxiety limited to public speaking.

Only a few studies have examined the effectiveness of beta blockers directly in patients with social phobia. Falloon, Lloyd, and Harpin (1981) studied 16 social phobics who were receiving social skills training. These patients differed from those in the aforementioned beta blocker studies in that they met DSM-III criteria for social phobia, and they had a variety of social fears, rather than only limited performance anxiety. Patients were randomized to propranolol or placebo, and propranolol dose was adjusted to lower heart rate to 60 beats per minute. There were no significant differences in improvement between the six patients who received propranolol and the six patients who received placebo who completed the treatment. The results suggest that the beta blocker may be ineffective for patients with generalized social phobia. This study is limited, however, by its small sample size, lack of controls, lack of blind ratings for social skills training, and the inclusion of four patients with panic attacks. The presence of spontaneous panic attacks must be considered in assessing response to beta blockers in social phobia because beta blockers may not be effective in patients with panic disorder (Noyes et al., 1984).

Atenolol was an effective treatment in an open

trial (Gorman, Liebowitz, Fyer, Campeas, & Klein, 1985) with 10 patients meeting DSM-III criteria for social phobia. These social phobics' symptomatology ranged from limited specific social fears, such as fear of giving a public speech, to global fears of almost all social encounters. Feared situations provoked typical symptoms, including palpitations, sweating, trembling or shaking, difficulty breathing, blushing, confusion or depersonalization. Half of the patients reported a history of alcohol abuse, and 5 had histories of at least one depressive episode, although none were depressed or actively abusing alcohol at the time of the study.

Patients were treated with atenolol, 50–100 mg/day for 6 weeks. At completion of the study, 5 of the 10 patients had a "marked" response, defined by both patient and treating psychiatrist agreeing that almost all symptoms of social anxiety and phobias were relieved. Four of the 10 patients had a "moderate" response, meaning that the patient reported significant improvement in the ability to enter phobic situations, but some degree of anxiety and apprehension persisted. Only one patient had no response. Adverse effects were limited to two patients with complaints of fatigue and lowered energy, one episode of bradycardia below 50 beats per minute, requiring lowering the dose to 50 mg, and one "fainting spell," which led to discontinuation of the medication.

Atenolol differs from most beta blockers in having low lipophilicity, which may result in less diffusion across the blood–brain barrier. This property both results in fewer central nervous system (CNS) side effects than other beta blockers and tests the hypothesis that specifically reducing peripheral autonomic activity will relieve social phobia. If the cognitive component of social phobia is in fact a conditioned response to an overactive autonomic nervous system (ANS), then beta blockers would be expected to correct the underlying overactivity. Such relief of the peripheral symptoms might eventually allow the patients to become deconditioned and could thus lead to resolution of fear and avoidance.

The only double-blind controlled trial of a beta blocker in social phobia has so far failed to confirm its efficacy. In the preliminary report (Liebowitz et al., 1988) of this study, as discussed here previously for phenelzine, 59 patients have so far completed an 8-week randomized trial of atenolol, phenelzine, or placebo. Only 36% (4 of 11) of patients taking atenolol, 50–100 mg/day, were considered responders, not significantly different from the 31% (5 of 16) who responded to placebo. There were no significant atenolol–placebo differences in any ratings of symptom subscales.

The failure of the beta blocker atenolol to ameliorate social phobia in this most rigorous test to date is surprising in light of the substantial success of beta blockers in the open trial and in the foregoing analogue studies. Evidence that beta blockers may be no more effective than placebo in social phobia would support a qualitative distinction between the symptoms of social phobia and the performance anxiety experienced by normals. Alternatively, because the analogue study subjects most closely approximate the limited social phobia subtype, patients with this subtype of social phobia may be expected to respond better to beta blockers than would patients with generalized social phobia. In fact, patients with limited, discrete performance anxiety in this study show a trend toward superior response to atenolol over phenelzine. An assessment that pools social phobia subtypes would miss such a differential response among subgroups. Until more data are available to clarify this issue, the treatment of social phobia with beta blockers remains promising but uncertain.

Case Illustrations of Responses to Beta Blockers

The following are several case summaries of patients with social phobia who were treated with beta blockers:

Case 3

A 38-year-old man, employed as a manager in a government agency presented himself to the clinic with a 14-year history of fear of public speaking. When his job required him to meet with a group of three or more people he would get very anxious and develop palpitations and labored breathing, and he would start sweating. He passed up a promotion because it would have involved additional meetings and presentations. His anxiety spread to other situations in which he

was the center of attention, such as ordering wine at a restaurant or even playing a word game with his family. The symptoms were not helped by 3 years of psychotherapy, and the patient had taken to premedicating himself with Valium before going into a meeting at which he might be called on. He also had a past history of spontaneous panic attacks, but upon presentation to the clinic, he had not had one in 10 years.

The patient was diagnosed as having social phobia with discrete performance anxiety and was entered into a double-blind controlled study in which he received placebo for 8 weeks without effect. When he was switched, however, to open treatment with atenolol, 100 mg/day, he began to notice improvement within 2 weeks. Both the physical symptoms and the cognitive aspects of his anxiety attacks improved over the course of several weeks. He reported improved performance at work and the ability to speak before groups without fear. He continued, nonetheless, to experience mild anticipatory anxiety. Several months later, he was continuing on atenolol and had maintained his improvement.

Case 4

A 29-year-old single female musician presented herself to the clinic, with a history of severe social anxiety since early childhood. Whenever she met new people, she would become fearful and would try to avoid them. She would tremble, sweat, and speak in a quavering voice, and she would develop facial twitching and heart palpitations. Although she had been a shy and quiet child, she did have friends. She avoided speaking in class and did not go to parties until her late teens. Dating, however was tolerable for her because that involved relating to only one person at a time. Nevertheless, she was able to perform as a musician—her performance anxiety would attenuate once she began playing.

The patient had grown up in a chaotic home environment, and as a teenager, she was briefly involved in alcohol and heroin abuse. She had tried psychotherapy twice without substantial improvement of her anxiety.

She was diagnosed as having the generalized subtype of social phobia and was started on atenolol, up to 100 mg/day. Six weeks later, she began to notice a substantial decrease in the somatic symptoms, with much less anxiety in social situations and in anticipation of them. This improvement continued to progress for several months, although mild performance anxiety and avoidance of parties persisted. After 6 months, two attempts to discontinue the medication were abandoned when they led to increased anxiety symptoms, and the patient is currently continuing to take atenolol at a lower dose, to minimize the side effect of fatigue.

Tricyclic Antidepressants

The use of tricyclic antidepressants in social phobia has gone virtually unstudied, in contrast to treatment with MAOIs and beta blockers. The tricyclic antidepressant that has been most studied in social phobia is clomipramine, which has not yet been approved for use in the United States. Experience with the drug in clinical trials and in years of general clinical use in Europe and Canada suggest that its efficacy and side effect profile in depression are generally similar to other commercially available tricyclic antidepressants.

There have been several uncontrolled trials of clomipramine in social phobia. Gringras (1977) treated 14 social phobics with clomipramine as part of a larger study encompassing multiple phobic and obsessional disorders. Doses of 75 to 225 mg/day for 6 weeks led to decreases in general anxiety, situational anxiety, and avoidance behavior. Social phobics showed greater improvement than did agoraphobics or diffuse phobics in the study, but it is unclear whether these diagnostic groups had other additional diagnoses.

Positive results were also reported by Beaumont (1977), who used clomipramine, 150–200 mg/day for 12 weeks in a large mixed group of social phobics and agoraphobics in private practice. Here the significance of the improvement for the social phobic subgroup is unclear because the data were not analyzed separately by diagnosis. In a similar study examining pooled social and agoraphobics (Allsopp, Cooper, & Poole, 1984), clomipramine, 25–150 mg/day, was superior to diazepam, 10–30 mg/day, in improving situational anxiety and agoraphobic symptoms over 12 weeks. Social phobic symptoms were not analyzed separately.

Pecknold, McClure, Appletauer, Allan, and Wrzesinski (1982) treated 24 agoraphobics and 16 social phobics with clomipramine, up to 200 mg/day, plus L-tryptophan or placebo. There was no difference between L-tryptophan and placebo, but

patients in both groups showed improvement in mood, phobic symptoms, anxiety, and social avoidance. Drawbacks to this study include the pooling of data on agoraphobics and social phobics, the presence of panic attacks in 80% of the social phobics (which suggests a preponderance of secondary social phobia), and the lack of a control group without clomipramine.

Among tricyclic antidepressants commercially available in the United States, we are aware of only one report examining efficacy in social phobia. Benca, Matuzas, and Al-Sadir (1986) found imipramine to be effective in two patients with DSM-III social phobia and mitral valve prolapse. On 250 mg of imipramine, both patients initially reported a decrease in physical symptoms of anxiety within 4 weeks, followed by self-initiated programs of social exposure and decreasing anticipatory anxiety. The significance of mitral valve prolapse and its prevalence among social phobic patients is unclear.

Benzodiazepines

Benzodiazepines have also received little study as a treatment for social phobia. In studies of performance anxiety, Krishnan (1975) found that diazepam, 4 mg/day, reduced tension and anxiety as well as the beta blocker oxprenolol, in students taking examinations. However, while the students believed that diazepam had improved their performance, for most, in fact, their exam scores were higher after the beta blocker in this double-blind trial. A similar study (Desai et al., 1983) included 44 normal student volunteers, divided into high- and low-anxiety groups, who received diazepam 5 mg/day, oxprenolol 80 mg/day, or placebo in double-blind fashion. Diazepam improved performance more than placebo in the high-anxiety group, but there were no oxprenolol–placebo differences noted.

Silverstone (1973) treated three agoraphobic patients and three social phobic patients with successive month-long double-blind trials of lorazepam, 3 mg/day; diazepam, 15 mg/day; and placebo. Although lorazepam was significantly superior to placebo and diazepam in reducing phobic ratings among all six patients, only one of the three social phobics improved on lorazepam.

Two of the three social phobics improved on diazepam, and none showed much improvement on placebo. These findings are limited by the small sample and the lack of strict diagnostic criteria.

More recently, alprazolam, a benzodiazepine with well-documented efficacy in panic disorder, has been studied in social phobic populations. Lydiard, Laraia, Howell, and Ballenger (1988) treated four DSM-III social phobics with alprazolam. Three of the four had previously tried tricyclic antidepressants without success. At doses of 3–8 mg/day of alprazolam, each patient showed marked to complete improvement of social phobic symptoms. One patient who experienced some residual social anxiety and panic symptoms responded completely when phenelzine, 75 mg/day, was added.

In another open trial, Reich and Yates (1988) treated 14 patients meeting DSM-III criteria for social phobia with a flexible dose of alprazolam, up to 10 mg/day, for 8 weeks. At Week 8, 10 of the patients were rated as very much improved (the highest possible rating), and the remaining 4 were rated as much improved. Eleven patients had a 50% or greater reduction in symptoms from baseline. Measures of social phobic symptoms improved markedly during the first 2 weeks of treatment, whereas measures of disability tended to improve by Week 4 or later. The mean dosage at Week 8 was 2.9 mg/day of alprazolam. After medication was tapered off, following 8 weeks of treatment, symptom scores returned to near-baseline values.

These open trials suggest that alprazolam may be an effective treatment for social phobia. The findings should be confirmed, however, in double-blind placebo-controlled studies. An additional consideration in use of benzodiazepines is the possibility of significant abuse potential in this population with a documented propensity to abuse another CNS depressant, alcohol. The effective dosages in these pilot studies of social phobia are similar to dosage of alprazolam in studies of panic disorder. Preliminary evidence that discontinuation of alprazolam in social phobics leads to rapid relapse also parallels experience with this medication in panic disorder, but it clearly requires further study both with placebo controls and with longer periods of treatment.

Other Medications

We are aware of no systematic study of medications other than those preceding. A single case report (Goldstein, 1987) noted efficacy of the alpha-adrenergic agonist clonidine, 0.1 mg twice a day, in a patient with generalized social phobia who had not responded to alprazolam, phenelzine, or propranolol.

RECOMMENDATIONS FOR TREATMENT

Out of the recent rapid growth of research on pharmacotherapy of social phobia has developed a database to guide effective prescription. The field remains in a state of considerable flux, however, as double-blind, controlled studies of proposed therapies have only recently begun to yield results.

Certainly, the foundation for treatment selection lies in establishing the correct diagnosis. The symptoms of social phobia are often overlooked by the practitioner in search of more familiar diagnoses. When other diagnoses co-occur with social phobia, it is important to establish which disorder is temporally primary, to guide treatment of the underlying disorder. For example, social phobia that occurs as one of the sequelae of panic disorder may best respond to treatment with a tricyclic antidepressant or to alprazolam, drugs with uncertain efficacy in primary social phobia.

Likewise, the practitioner should actively try to elicit any history of those disorders that often complicate social phobia, such as alcohol and other drug abuse. Establishing which disorder began first may again help guide the focus of treatment, and a several-week period of abstinence may clarify whether social phobia exists independent of the substance abuse. Many patients with a dual diagnosis require detoxification and specific interventions to curb substance abuse before pharmacological treatment of social phobic can be pursued safely and effectively.

Psychotic disorders should be ruled out in social phobic patients, but nonpsychotic depression frequently complicates social phobia, and it may resolve with treatment of the underlying social phobia. The diagnosis of APD shows substantial overlap with the generalized subtype of social phobia as defined by DSM-III-R. There is no reason to believe that social phobics with concurrent APD will not respond to appropriate medication as well as other social phobics, despite the common assumption that personality disorders are not responsive to medication. In fact, preliminary data (Deltito & Perugi, 1986) and our experience suggest that patients with APD can respond dramatically to medication, particularly to MAOIs.

Once the diagnosis of social phobia is made, subclassification into the subtypes of either discrete performance anxiety or generalized social fears can be of further help in treatment selection. For the patient with discrete performance fears, such as isolated fear of public speaking, beta blockers are the treatment of choice. While there is no evidence for superior efficacy of any particular beta blocker, we prefer to use atenolol for several reasons: First, it has a relatively long half-life, permitting once-daily dosing. Second, it has only a fourfold interpatient plasma level variability, far lower than most beta blockers. Third, it is relatively cardioselective and is thus less likely to produce bronchoconstriction. Finally, because it is relatively hydrophilic and does not readily cross the blood–brain barrier, it may cause fewer adverse CNS effects. Contraindications include history of (a) asthma or allergies that cause wheezing, (b) bradycardia or congestive heart failure, and in some cases (c) diabetes mellitus.

Patients can be started on a dose of atenolol of 50 mg, given once per day. We instruct patients to take their own resting pulse daily and to withhold medication if heart rate drops below 50, although this method can be problematic in athletes with low resting heart rate. The only adverse effect we have regularly observed is fatigue, which is rarely severe enough to warrant lowering the dosage or discontinuing the beta blocker. In general, the dose of atenolol can be increased to 100 mg/day after 1 week. This dose is well tolerated by most patients, and higher doses are not recommended.

Once medication has been started, patients should be urged to expose themselves actively to feared situations as much as possible. This both tests the effectiveness of the medication and promotes unlearning of avoidance behavior. The ef-

fect of a beta blocker on social phobia is generally apparent within 2 weeks. Occasionally, severe avoidance prevents the patient from testing the effect of the medication. In such instances, longer trials of the drug, combined with a more formal behavioral program of gradated exposure homework, may be necessary.

The efficacy of beta blockers in generalized social phobia is much less certain. While a brief trial of these medications in this subtype is relatively safe and simple, we believe that MAOIs are currently the best-documented effective treatment for patients with generalized social fears. They also have demonstrated efficacy in social phobic populations as a whole. The necessary precautions and potential adverse effects for MAOI medications have been reviewed by Rabkin, Quitkin, McGrath, Harrison, and Tricamo (1985). Risk of the dangerous hypertensive reaction is low when proper dietary precautions are taken. Particular caution should be exercised in patients prone to self-medicate with substances such as with those alcoholic beverages that contain tyramine. Other possible side effects—such as orthostatic hypotension, insomnia, weight gain, edema, paresthesias, and anorgasmia—sometimes limit the use of MAOIs, but more often, they can be controlled with a variety of counteractive measures.

Phenelzine is the MAOI most studied in treatment of social phobia. It can usually be started at 30 mg/day and increased at a rate of 15 mg/day every 3 days to a maximum of 90 mg/day. Many patients will respond to a lower dose, but it is essential to attempt an adequate trial of 4–6 weeks at the maximal dose tolerated before judging the treatment to be ineffective. Improvement in symptoms often progresses further over a period of months. As with the beta blockers, patients must expose themselves to feared situations while on an MAOI, to maximize progress. Aside from phenelzine, the only other MAOI studied in social phobia, tranylcypromine, appears to be effective in doses ranging from 40 to 60 mg/day.

The role of other medications in social phobia has not been examined in controlled studies. Based on some successful open trials, however, alprazolam and tricyclic antidepressants should be considered as experimental treatment alternatives for patients who cannot tolerate or do not respond to beta blockers or MAOIs. The preliminary data suggest that alprazolam may be effective in doses of 3–8 mg/day, a range similar to that effective in panic disorder. The patient's risk of abuse of CNS depressants should be considered before starting alprazolam. Case reports of tricyclic antidepressants suggest that effective dosage and time to response may be similar to those in depression.

Additional work is needed to replicate the existing findings of drug treatment in social phobia and to further clarify predictors of response to particular medications. Although for some patients, medication alone may suffice in relieving social phobia and its attendant disabilities, many patients will benefit from various other therapeutic modalities. The specific indications for selection of one treatment approach over another, however, remain to be determined. It will also be important to explore whether combining modalities of treatment can have synergistic effects.

REFERENCES

Allsopp, L. F., Cooper, G. L., & Poole, P. H. (1984). Clomipramine and diazepam in the treatment of agoraphobia and social phobia in general practice. *Current Medical Research and Opinion, 9*, 64–70.

American Psychiatric Association. (1952). *Diagnostic and statistical manual of mental disorders* (DSM-I). Washington, DC: Author.

American Psychiatric Association. (1968). *Diagnostic and statistical manual of mental disorders* (2nd ed., DSM-II). Washington, DC: Author.

Amies, P. L., Gelder, M. G., & Shaw, P. M. (1983). Social phobia: A comparative clinical study. *British Journal of Psychiatry, 142*, 174–179.

Arrindell, W. A., Emmelkamp, P. M. G., Monsma, A., & Brilman, E. (1983). The role of perceived parental rearing practices in the aetiology of phobic disorders: A controlled study. *British Journal of Psychiatry, 143*, 183–187.

Barlow, D. H., DiNardo, P. A., Vermilyea, B. B., Vermilyea, J., & Blanchard, E. B. (1986). Co-morbidity and depression among the anxiety disorders: Issues in diagnosis and classification. *Journal of Nervous and Mental Disease, 174*, 63–72.

Beaumont, G. (1977). A large open multicenter trial of clomipramine (Anafranil) in the management of phobic disorders. *Journal of International Medical Research, 5*(Suppl. 5), 116–123.

Benca, R., Matuzas, W., & Al-Sadir, J. (1986). Social phobia, MVP, and response to imipramine. *Journal of Clinical Psychopharmacology, 6*, 50–51.

Bowen, R. C., Cipywnyk, D., D'Arcy, C., & Keegan, D. (1984). Alcoholism, anxiety disorders, and agoraphobia. *Alcoholism: Clinical and Experimental Research, 8*, 48–50.

Brantigan, C. O., Brantigan, T. A., & Joseph, N. (1982). Effect of beta blockade and beta stimulation on stage fright. *American Journal of Medicine, 72*, 88–94.

Bryant, B., & Trower, P. E. (1974). Social difficulty in a student sample. *British Journal of Educational Psychology, 44*, 13–21.

Cameron, P. G., Thyer, B. A., Nesse, R. M., & Curtis, G. C. (1986). Symptom profiles of patients with DSM-III anxiety disorders. *American Journal of Psychiatry, 143*, 1132–1137.

Chambless, D. L., Cherney, J., Caputo, G. C., & Rheinstein, B. J. G. (1987). Anxiety disorders and alcoholism: A study with inpatient alcoholics. *Journal of Anxiety Disorders, 1*, 29–40.

Cole, J. O., Altesman, R. I., & Weingarten, C. H. (1980). Beta-blocking drugs in psychiatry. In J. O. Cole (Ed.), *Psychopharmacology update* (pp. 43–68). Lexington, MA: Colamore Press.

Deltito, J. A., & Perugi, G. (1986). A case of social phobia with avoidant personality disorder treated with MAOI. *Comprehensive Psychiatry, 27*, 255–258.

Desai, N., Taylor-Davies, A., & Barnett, D. B. (1983). The effects of diazepam and oxprenolol on short term memory in individuals of high and low state anxiety. *British Journal of Clinical Pharmacology, 15*, 197–202.

Dimsdale, J. E., & Moss, J. (1974). Short-term catecholamine response to psychological stress. *Psychosomatic Medicine, 42*, 493–497.

DiNardo, P. A., O'Brien, G. T., Barlow, D. H., Waddell, M. T., & Blanchard, E. B. (1983). Reliability of DSM-III anxiety disorder categories using a new structured interview. *Archives of General Psychiatry, 40*, 1070–1074.

Falloon, I. R. H., Lloyd, G. G., & Harpin, R. E. (1981). The treatment of social phobia: Real-life rehearsal with non-professional therapists. *Journal of Nervous and Mental Disease, 169*, 180–184.

Freud, S. (1961). Inhibitions, symptoms and anxiety. In J. Strachey (Ed.), *The standard edition of the complete works of Sigmund Freud* (Vol. 20). London: Hogarth. (Original published in 1926)

Goldstein, S. (1987). Treatment of social phobia with clonidine. *Biological Psychiatry, 22*, 369–372.

Gorman, J. M., Liebowitz, M. R., Fyer, A. J., Campeas, R., & Klein, D. F. (1985). Treatment of social phobia with atenolol. *Journal of Clinical Psychopharmacology, 5*, 298–301.

Gorman, J. M., Fyer, M. R., Goetz, R., Askanazi, J., Liebowitz, M. R., Fyer, A. J., Kinney, J., & Klein, D. F. (1988). Ventilatory physiology of patients with panic disorder. *Archives of General Psychiatry, 45*, 31–39.

Gottschalk, L. A., Stone, W. N., & Gleser, C. G. (1974). Peripheral versus central mechanisms accounting for anti-anxiety effects of propranolol. *Psychosomatic Medicine, 37*, 47–56.

Gringras, M. (1977). An uncontrolled trial of clomipramine (Anafranil) in the treatment of phobic and obsessional states in general practice. *Journal of International Medical Research, 5*(Suppl. 5), 111–115.

Hartley, L. R., Ungapen, S., Davie, I., & Spencer, D. J. (1983). The effect of beta adrenergic blocking drugs on speakers' performance and memory. *British Journal of Psychiatry, 142*, 512–517.

Heimberg, R. G. (June, 1986). *Predicting the outcome of cognitive-behavioral treatment of social phobia.* Paper presented at the annual meeting of the Society for Psychotherapy Research, Wellesley, MA.

Heimberg, R. G., & Barlow, D. H. (1988). Psychosocial treatments for social phobia. *Psychosomatics, 29*, 27–37.

Heimberg, R. G., Hope, D. A., Dodge, C. S., & Becker, R. E. (in press). DSM-III-R subtypes of social phobia: Comparison of generalized social phobics and public speaking phobics. *Journal of Nervous and Mental Disease.*

James, I. M., Burgoyne, W., & Savage, I. T. (1983). Effect of pindolol on stress-related disturbances of musical performance: Preliminary communication. *Journal of the Royal Society of Medicine, 76*, 194–196.

James, I. M., Griffith, D. N. W., Pearson, R. M., & Newby, P. (1977). Effect of oxprenolol on stage-fright in musicians. *Lancet, 2*, 952–954.

James, W. (1907). *The principles of psychology* (Vol. 1 & 2). New York: Holt.

Janet, P. (1903). *Les obsessions et la psychasthenie.* Paris: F. Alcan.

Janet, P. (1909). *Les nevroses.* Paris: Flammarion.

Kelly, D., Guirguis, W., Frommer, E., Mitchell-Heggs, N., & Sargant, W. (1970). Treatment of phobic states with antidepressants: A retrospective study of 246 patients. *British Journal of Psychiatry, 116*, 387–398.

Kline, N. (1967). Drug treatment of phobic disorders. *American Journal of Psychiatry, 123*, 1447–1450.

Krishnan, G. (1975). Oxprenolol in the treatment of examination nerves. *Scottish Medical Journal, 20*, 288–289.

Krope, P., Kohrs, A., Ott, H., Wagner, W., & Fichte, K. (1982). Evaluating mepindolol in a test model of examination anxiety in students. *Pharmacopsychiatria, 15*, 41–47.

Lader, M., Gelder, M., & Marks, I. (1967). Palmar skinconductance measures as predictors of response to desensitization. *Journal of Psychosomatic Research, 11*, 283–290.

Levin, A. P., Sandberg, D., Stein, J., & Liebowitz, M. R. (May, 1989). *Public speaking in social phobic subtypes.* Paper presented at the annual meeting of the American Psychiatric Association, San Francisco, CA.

Liden, S., & Gottfries, C. G. (1974). Beta blocking agents in treatment of catecholamine-induced symptoms in musicians. *Lancet, 2*, 529.

Liebowitz, M. R. (1987). Social phobia. In D. F. Klein (Ed.), *Modern problems of pharmacopsychiatry: Anxiety.* Basel, Switzerland: Karger.

Liebowitz, M. R., Fyer, A. J., Gorman, J. M., Campeas, R., & Levin, A. (1986). Phenelzine in social phobia. *Journal of Clinical Psychopharmacology, 6*, 93–98.

Liebowitz, M. R., Fyer, A. J., Gorman, J. M., Dillon, D., Davies, S., Stein, J. M., Cohen, B., & Klein, D. F. (1985). Specificity of lactate infusions in social phobia vs. panic disorders. *American Journal of Psychiatry, 142*, 947–949.

Liebowitz, M. R., Gorman, J. M., Fyer, A. J., Campeas, R., Levin, A. P., Sandberg, D., Hollander, E., Papp, L., & Goetz, D. (1988). Pharmacotherapy of social phobia: A placebo controlled comparison of phenelzine and atenolol. *Journal of Clinical Psychiatry, 49*, 252–257.

Liebowitz, M. R., Gorman, J., Fyer, A., Levitt, M., Levy, G., Appleby, I., Dillon, D., Palij, M., Davies, S., & Klein, D. (1984a). Lactate provocation of panic attacks: I. Clinical and behavioral findings. *Archives of General Psychiatry, 41*, 764–770.

Liebowitz, M. R., Quitkin, F. M., Stewart, J. W., McGrath, P. J., Harrison, W., Rabkin, J., Tricamo, E., Markowitz, J. S., & Klein, D. K. (1984b). Phenelzine versus imipramine in atypical depression: A preliminary report. *Archives of General Psychiatry, 41*, 669–677.

Lydiard, R. B., Laraia, M. T., Howell, E. F., & Ballenger, J. C. (1988). Alprazolam in the treatment of social phobia. *Journal of Clinical Psychiatry, 49,* 17–19.

Marks, I. M. (1970). The classification of phobic disorders. *British Journal of Psychiatry, 116,* 377–386.

Marks, I. M., & Gelder, M. G. (1966). Different ages of onset in varieties of phobia. *American Journal of Psychiatry, 123,* 218–221.

Mountjoy, C. Q., Roth, M., Garside, R. F., & Leitch, I. M. (1977). A clinical trial of phenelzine in anxiety depressive and phobic neuroses. *British Journal of Psychiatry, 131,* 486–492.

Mullaney, J. A., &Trippett, C. J. (1979). Alcohol dependence and phobias: Clinical description and relevance. *British Journal of Psychiatry, 135,* 563–573.

Munjack, D. J., & Moss, H. B. (1981). Affective disorder and alcoholism in families of agoraphobics. *Archives of General Psychiatry, 38,* 869–871.

Munjack, D. J., Brown, R. A., & McDowell, D. E. (1987). Comparison of social anxiety in patients with social phobia and panic disorder. *Journal of Nervous and Mental Disease, 175,* 49–51.

Myers, J. K., Weissman, M. M., Tischler, G. L., Holzer, C. E., Leaf, P. J., Orvaschel, H., Anthony, J. C., Boyd, J. H., Burke, J. D., Kramer, M., & Stoltzman, R. (1984). Six-month prevalence of psychiatric disorders in three communities: 1980–1982. *Archives of General Psychiatry, 41,* 959–967.

Neftel, K. A., Adler, R. H., Kappell, L., Rossi, M., Dolder, M., Kaser, H. E., Bruggesser, H. H., & Vorkauf, H. (1982). Stage fright in musicians: A model illustrating the effect of beta blockers. *Psychosomatic Medicine, 44,* 461–469.

Nichols, K. A. (1974). Severe social anxiety. *British Journal of Medical Psychology, 47,* 301–306.

Noyes, R., Anderson, D. J., Clancy, J., Crowe, R. R., Slymen, D. J., Ghoneim, M. M., & Hinrichs, J. V. (1984). Diazepam and propranolol in panic disorder and agoraphobia. *Archives of General Psychiatry, 41,* 287–292.

Papp, L. A., Gorman, J. M., Liebowitz, M. R., Fyer, A. J., Cohen, B., & Klein, D. F. (1988). Epinephrine infusions in patients with social phobia. *American Journal of Psychiatry, 145,* 733–736.

Parker, G. (1979). Reported parental characteristics of agoraphobics and social phobics. *British Journal of Psychiatry, 135,* 555–560.

Pecknold, J. C., McClure, D. J., Appeltauer, L., Allan, T., & Wrzesinski, L. (1982). Does tryptophan potentiate clomipramine in the treatment of agoraphobic

and social phobic patients? *British Journal of Psychiatry, 140,* 484–490.

Persson, G., & Nordlund, C. L. (1985). Agoraphobics and social phobics: Differences in background factors, syndrome profiles and therapeutic response. *Acta Psychiatrica Scandinavica, 71,* 148–159.

Pollard, C. A., & Henderson, J. G. (1988). Four types of social phobia in a community sample. *Journal of Nervous and Mental Disease, 176,* 440–445.

Rabkin, J. G., Quitkin, F. M., McGrath, P., Harrison, W., & Tricamo, E. (1985). Adverse reactions to monoamine oxidase inhibitors: II. Treatment correlates and clinical management. *Journal of Clinical Psychopharmacology, 5,* 2–9.

Rapee, R., Mattick, R., & Murrell, E. (1986). Cognitive mediation in the affective component of spontaneous panic attacks. *Journal of Behavior Therapy and Experimental Psychiatry, 17,* 245–254.

Reich, J., & Yates, W. (1988). A pilot study of treatment of social phobia with alprazolam. *American Journal of Psychiatry, 145,* 590–594.

Sargant, W. (1962). The treatment of anxiety states and atypical depression by the monoamine inhibitor drugs. *Journal of Neuropsychiatry, 3*(Suppl. 1), 96–103.

Siitonen, L., & Janne, J. (1976). Effect of beta-blockade during bowling competitions. *Annals of Clinical Research, 8,* 393–398.

Silverstone, J. T. (1973). Lorazepam in phobic disorders: A pilot study. *Current Medical Research and Opinion, 1,* 272–275.

Smail, P., Stockwell, T., Canter, S., & Hodgson, R. (1984). Alcohol dependence and phobic anxiety states: I. A prevalence study. *British Journal of Psychiatry, 144,* 53–57.

Solyom, C., Solyom, L., LaPierre, Y., Pecknold, J., & Morton, L. (1981). Phenelzine and exposure in the treatment of phobias. *Biological Psychiatry, 16,* 239–247.

Solyom, L., Heseltine, G. F. D., McClure, D. J., Solyom, C., Ledwedge, B., & Steinberg, G. (1973). Behaviour therapy v. drug therapy in the treatment of phobic neurosis. *Canadian Journal of Psychiatry, 18,* 25–31.

Solyom, L., Ledwidge, B., & Solyom, C. (1986). Delineating social phobia. *British Journal of Psychiatry, 149,* 464–470.

Thyer, B. A., Parrish, R. T., Curtis, G. C., Nesse, R. M., & Cameron, O. G. (1985). Ages of onset of DSM-III anxiety disorders. *Comprehensive Psychiatry, 26,* 113–122.

Thyer, B. A., Parrish, R. T., Himle, J., Cameron, O. G., Curtis, G. C., & Nesse, R. M. (1986). Alcohol abuse among clinically anxious patients. *Behaviour Research and Therapy, 24*, 357–359.

Torgersen, S. (1979). The nature and origin of common phobic fears. *British Journal of Psychiatry, 134*, 343–351.

Turner, S. M., Beidel, D. C., Dancu, C. V., & Keys, D. J. (1986). Psychopathology of social phobia and comparison to avoidant personality disorder. *Journal of Abnormal Psychology, 95*, 389–394.

Tyrer, P., Candy, J., & Kelly, D. (1973). A study of the clinical effects of phenelzine and placebo in the treatment of phobic anxiety. *Psychopharmacology, 32*, 237–254.

Tyrer, P., & Steinberg, D. (1975). Symptomatic treatment of agoraphobia and social phobias: A follow-up study. *British Journal of Psychiatry, 127*, 163–168.

Versiani, M., Mundim, F. D., Nardi, A. E., & Liebowitz, M. R. (1988). Tranylcypromine in social phobia. *Journal of Clinical Psychopharmacology, 8*, 279–283.

Weerts, T. C., & Lang, P. J. (1978). Psychophysiology of fear imagery: Differences between focal phobia and social performance anxiety. *Journal of Consulting and Clinical Psychology, 46*, 1157–1159.

Editorial Commentary: Social Phobia

This section contains excellent and thought-provoking chapters on behavioral and pharmacological treatments for social phobia. It is the only section of the book that does not contain a chapter on verbal psychotherapy. After consultation with a number of colleagues who are expert on verbal psychotherapies, we concluded that there was not a sufficiently well-defined psychotherapeutic approach for social phobia to justify a separate chapter. That is not to say that psychotherapists do not treat patients who present interpersonal fears and a sense of social inadequacy. To the contrary, we believe that it reflects the historical place of social phobia in the literature. As indicated both by Schneier, Levin, and Liebowitz and by Heimberg, social phobia has not received much attention until the past few years. It was variously assumed to be clinically unimportant, infrequent, or a manifestation of other, more significant pathology. Consequently, it was not subject to careful scientific scrutiny, and it was treated with procedures developed for other dysfunctions (e.g., benzodiazepines, systematic desensitization).

It has now become apparent that social phobia is a common disorder that can cause substantial distress and disruption of daily functioning. It appears to have notable etiological and phenomenological differences from other anxiety disorders, which result in varied treatment needs. For example, monoamine oxidase inhibitors (MAOIs) seem to be more effective than either antidepressants (which have proven effective in treating panic disorder) or beta blockers (which are useful in reducing performance anxiety). Similarly, exposure and cognitive therapy alone do not appear to be as effective as a combination of the two. Unfortunately, both chapters emphasized the tentativeness of these conclusions. There simply have not been enough methodologically sound studies to allow for great confidence in treatment recommendations.

One factor that seems to have plagued the clinical trials has been inconsistency in diagnosis. Different studies have employed different populations of patients with some degree of social anxiety. This is especially true of the literature that antedates DSM-III-R. In many cases, it would seem to be impossible to compare trials conducted at different times or in different laboratories. As indicated, there seem to be distinct differences between social phobia and the more common performance anxieties (e.g., fear associated with musical performance). Two other nosological distinctions are less clear-cut. First, there seem to be notable differences between the specific social phobias, such as fear of public speaking or of urination in public rest rooms, and the generalized type, which is characterized by multiple social fears and avoidance. These two subgroups appear to have different responses to both pharmacological and behavioral interventions. It may be that the generalized type is etiologically different from the specific type; alternatively, it may simply be a more severe variation.

Similar confusion pertains to the distinction between social phobia and avoidant personality disorder (APD). It seems illogical to have two distinct nosological categories that exhibit the same phenomenology and respond to more or less the same treatments, especially in the absence of clear data on differences in etiology or course. It would seem to be critical to resolve these two diagnostic dilemmas if we are to conduct replicable treatment trials and develop effective interventions. Moreover, the entire issue of treatment for APD requires further study. Axis II disorders have characteristically been viewed as treatment resistant. It may be that effective treatments for this disorder will alter this conception; conversely, existence of an effective treatment may (tacitly or otherwise) remove the disorder from Axis II.

Neither Heimberg nor Schneier et al. discussed combined behavioral–pharmacological interventions. This is especially curious in light of the trends in treatment of other anxiety disorders, such as panic and agoraphobia, and obsessive–compulsive disorder. Further, Schneier et al. indicated that exposure to anxiety-provoking cues is an important adjunct to pharmacological treatment of generalized social phobia. Although they did not conceptualize exposure as a behavioral intervention, it is a characteristic component of behavioral treatments for anxiety. In fact, Heimberg also suggested that exposure was essential for the generalized social phobics. Given that (1) there is agreement on one of the necessary components of treatment for this subtype, and (2) the fact that they apparently are less responsive to either treatment alone, a controlled trial with a combined intervention would be a logical next step. In a similar vein, it would be interesting to test verbal psychotherapies developed specifically to deal with social phobia in order to examine their effectiveness, to determine whether they must also include guided exposure, and to study their interaction with other modalities. Overall, the current literature offers considerable promise for the development of effective treatments, but much more work is required.

PART 5

Obsessive–Compulsive Disorder

CHAPTER 13

Psychotherapy

MICHAEL A. JENIKE

CONCEPTUALIZATION OF THE DISORDERS

Obsessive thoughts and compulsive urges are part of everyday life. We return to check that we locked a door and shut off a stove, or we cannot stop thinking about that frightening event coming up next week. We refuse to eat with a fork that dropped on the floor, even though we know the chance of contamination is remote. These events are part of the normal feedback and control loop between our thoughts and our actions. It is only when these obsessive thoughts become so frequent or intense, or these compulsive rituals become so extensive that they interfere with an individual's function that the diagnosis of obsessive–compulsive disorder (OCD) is made.

OCD is categorized as an anxiety disorder because the central factor seems to be anxiety and discomfort that is either increased or decreased by the obsessions or the compulsive rituals. Although patients with OCD frequently present irrational or bizarre thoughts regarding their symptoms, they remain in touch with reality in all other areas of their lives; therefore, OCD is not a psychotic disorder.

DIAGNOSTIC ISSUES AND PROBLEMS

The currently accepted definition of OCD is given in the *Diagnostic and Statistical Manual of Mental Disorders* (3rd ed., rev.); (DSM-III-R, 1987). In order to be diagnosed with OCD, a patient must have obsessions and/or compulsions that are a significant source of distress to the individual or that interfere with social or role functioning.

Obsessions are defined as, "Recurrent, persistent ideas, thoughts, images, or impulses that are ego-dystonic, i.e., they are not experienced as voluntarily produced, but rather as thoughts that invade consciousness and are experienced as senseless or repugnant. Attempts are made to ignore or suppress them."

Compulsions are defined as, "Repetitive and seemingly purposeful behaviors that are performed according to certain rules or in a stereotyped fashion. The behavior is not an end in itself, but [it] is designed to produce or prevent some future event or situation. However, either the activity is not connected in a realistic way with what it is designed to produce or prevent or it may be clearly excessive. The act is performed with a sense of subjective compulsion coupled with desire to resist the compulsion (at least initially). The individual generally recognizes the senselessness of the behavior (this may not be true for young children) and does not derive pleasure from carrying out the activity, although it provides a release of tension."

Although traditional estimates of the prevalence of OCD in the general population were approximately 0.05%, recent studies have suggested a significantly higher lifetime prevalence of 2–3% (Myers et al., 1984; Robins et al., 1984); thus, OCD is not the rare psychiatric disorder it was once thought to be.

Obsessions and compulsions of OCD can be

severely incapacitating; not only is depression a frequent concomitant problem, but also the symptoms often spread to interfere with social and occupational functioning and involve the person's family. Occasionally, entire families are moved to new houses in an attempt to escape the patients' contamination fears and resultant cleaning rituals.

Obsessive–compulsive symptoms tend to fall into one of several major categories: checking rituals, cleaning rituals, obsessive thoughts, obsessional slowness, or mixed rituals. Checking and cleaning rituals form the overwhelming majority of compulsive rituals (53% and 48%, respectively) (Hodgson & Rachman, 1977). More than one type of symptom frequently occurs in a single patient.

Less common subtypes of OCD symptoms are (a) patients who engage in rituals that involve placing objects in a certain order; (b) patients with primary obsessional slowness, who become "stuck" for hours while performing everyday tasks such as dressing and are unable to finish these tasks. As clinics see larger numbers of OCD patients, relatively rare subtypes are being identified, such as patients with obsessions and compulsions primarily aimed at controlling an overwhelming fear of having a bowel movement or of being incontinent of urine in public (Jenike, Vitagliano, Rabinovitz, Goff, & Baer, 1987), or young women who have extensive face-picking rituals that can last for hours each day. Other disorders closely related to OCD are monosymptomatic hypochondriasis (Brotman & Jenike, 1984), dysmorphophobia (Jenike, 1985), and obsessive fear of AIDS (Jenike, 1987; Jenike & Pato, 1986); cancer, or some other illness (Jenike, 1986a).

TREATMENT STRATEGIES

Until recently, all patients with OCD were thought to be refractory to treatment. We now know that if patients receive appropriate therapy, usually consisting of behavior therapy (see Chapter 14), and psychotropic medication (see Chapter 15), the majority (but not all) will improve substantially, and occasionally completely, within a few months (Jenike, Baer, & Minichiello, 1986a).

Treatment Failures

Predictors of treatment failure for behavioral techniques have been evaluated in some detail and include noncompliance with treatment, concomitant severe depression (Foa, 1979), absence of rituals, fixed beliefs in rituals, presence of concomitant personality disorder (Jenike, Baer, Minichiello, Schwartz, & Carey, 1986b; Baer, Jenike, & Minichiello, 1987), and some types of compulsive rituals. Patients with schizotypal and possibly other severe personality disorders (Axis II in DSM-III-R) also do poorly with pharmacotherapy (Jenike, 1986b).

If a patient has only obsessive thoughts without rituals, behavior therapy is unlikely to succeed. In these cases, pharmacotherapy is the treatment of choice (Jenike, 1987).

As noted, patients meeting DSM-III-R criteria for both OCD and schizotypal personality disorder do not respond well to either behavior therapy or pharmacotherapy. The idea of concomitant schizotypal personality disorder as a poor prognostic indicator in OCD appears to have validity in light of the literature on treatment failure. This personality disorder encompasses several of the aforementioned poor predictive factors. Most noticeably, these patients have strongly held beliefs that their rituals are necessary to prevent some terrible event. Also, these patients have a difficult time complying with proscribed treatment and assigned record keeping. Rachman and Hodgson (1980) have similarly found that the presence of an abnormal personality disorder is a negative predictor of outcome in behavior therapy for OCD; and more recently, Solyom, DiNicola, Phil, Sookman, and Luchins, (1985) reported on a subcategory of patients with "obsessional psychosis" similar to the schizotypal subgroup, who also respond poorly to both behavior therapy and pharmacotherapy.

The Role of Psychotherapy

Traditional psychodynamic psychotherapy alone is not an effective treatment for patients with OCD; there are no reports in the modern psychiatric literature of patients who managed to stop ritualizing or discontinued obsessions when treated with this modality alone. Insel (1984) has noted that patients with this disorder frequently present symptoms seemingly laden with unconscious symbolism and dynamic meaning; yet psychodynamic treatments, particularly if they are loosely structured and nondirective, rarely reduce the symptoms. Many traditional psychotherapists find themselves becoming more directive with OCD patients and thus approach some of the techniques used by behavioral therapists.

Why then write a chapter on the use of psychotherapy in patients with OCD? Because some psychotherapeutic techniques are helpful adjuncts to more effective treatments and may enhance compliance. In addition, some OCD patients also suffer from the DSM-III-R Axis II diagnosis of compulsive personality disorder, which may be more responsive to traditional psychotherapy. In this chapter, I will explore some of the issues that arise in therapy with patients with OCD and also those with DSM-III-R compulsive personality disorder, and I outline specific recommendations for obsessional patients in order to maximize therapeutic interventions and compliance.

In treating many of these patients, there is a role for psychodynamic psychotherapy as an adjunct to behavioral and pharmacological techniques and, in fact, most behavioral therapists are aware of conflicts and unconscious drives and use this knowledge to their advantage in helping their patients. One must pay attention to the patients' individual styles and also to their environment.

Treatment of OCD Patients with Compulsive Personality Disorder

OCD patients also suffering from compulsive personality disorders may present a grim and cheerless demeanor to convey their characteristic air of austerity and serious-mindedness (Millon, 1981; Shapiro, 1965). Posture and movement reflect their underlying tightness, a tense control of emotions that are kept well in check. They may be viewed by others as industrious and efficient, though lacking in flexibility and spontaneity. Many consider them to be stubborn, to procrastinate, to appear indecisive, and to be easily upset by the unfamiliar or by deviations from routines to

which they have become accustomed. Content to have their "noses to the grindstone," many work diligently and patiently with activities that require being tidy and meticulous. They are especially concerned with matters of organization and efficiency, and they tend to be rigid and unbending about rules and procedures. These behaviors often lead others to see them as perfectionistic. They are polite and formal and may relate to others in terms of rank or status; they tend to be authoritarian. These patients can be very difficult to manage, and certain psychodynamic principles can be very effective in facilitating treatment.

Psychodynamic Psychotherapy

Psychodynamic therapy is the process in which an individual's behavior is examined in order to determine those characterological styles that impair interpersonal relationships, produce symptoms, and interfere with productive and rewarding activity. Behaviors that are not productive or satisfying are labeled "neurotic" or "maladaptive," and the therapist tries to understand their roots and to introduce new ways of adapting.

Salzman (1980, 1983) has outlined three premises of psychodynamic psychotherapy that must be mutually accepted by both patient and therapist in any productive relationship. First, behavior is derived from processes that can be defined and traced to motivational or adaptational sources. Some of these sources, however, are outside of one's immediate awareness.

Second, distorted maladaptive behavior is caused by anxiety, which transforms goal-directed conduct into activity designed to relieve or eliminate anxiety—referred to as "defenses." Thus, energy that could be channeled into productive and satisfying activities is spent alleviating anxiety. Freud and later theorists focused on the defenses of isolation, displacement, reaction formation, and undoing in the obsessional patient (Coursey, 1984).

Third, when these defenses are clarified, the resulting insight can be directed toward altering or abandoning the behavior, with notable changes in the characterological structure, productivity, and satisfaction of the individual. All such therapies require verbal interaction and some intellectual capacity and focus on the emotional elements of behavior, as well as on the relationship between therapist and patient. All involve issues of transference, countertransference, interpretation, and exhortation toward change (Salzman, 1983).

Cognitive Therapy

There has been some preliminary work on the use of cognitive approaches to obsessive–compulsive symptomatology (Hamilton & Alagna, 1984). Beck (1976) described various emotional disorders in terms of their characteristic thought content, primary rules, and other cognitive features. Cognitive therapy is generally directed at correcting faulty premises and beliefs or altering thinking habits via self-monitoring techniques, discussion, or the rehearsal of new thinking habits. Much later work has focused on cognitive approaches to affective illness, but others have applied similar techniques in combination with behavior techniques to OCD patients with little success (Emmelkamp, van de Helm, & van Zanten, 1980; Foa & Kozak, 1983). Despite this lack of success of preliminary studies, some of the principles that derive from this work can be of help to the therapist. One of the basic rules of the obsessive is that "danger is imminent," and they therefore tend to exaggerate risks (see Table 13.1). This would suggest that it may be important to reeducate obsessives to reappraise situations more realistically (Hamilton & Alagna, 1984). Obsessives show increased requirements for information before they take the risk of making a decision; encouragement of risk taking is a major part of any therapy, whether behavioral, cognitive, or psychodynamic, that is likely to be of help to the obsessive.

Rorschach Findings and Treatment Implications

In a study designed to look at the primary issues and defenses of patients with obsessive–compulsive disorder, Coursey (1984) administered the Rorschach Inkblot test to 15 patients. He found that, even though it is rare to have any explicit hostility on the Rorschach, OCD patients had explicitly aggressive responses on 60% of the protocols. If he included mild or symbolically hostile responses, 80% of the patients gave such responses. He noted that these typical responses contrasted markedly with the socially timid, inhibited, and fearful demeanor and behavior of these patients.

Except among children, oral-dependent responses (such as mouth, food, touching) and oral-aggressive responses are not common; yet among the OCD patients, two thirds gave mouth and food responses and over one third gave touching and holding responses. In addition, a third of the patients gave unusual genital and anal content for more than 10% of their responses.

Even though the OCD patients had been carefully screened to rule out schizophrenia, about 20% had some formal thinking impairment of a variety of types. Coursey felt that this was an indicator that impulsive primitive material is not always repressed and that, at least in some patients, it is readily and consciously available to the patient, and it sometimes even forms the basis of their obsessive thoughts. Moreover, this material was not due to prior psychotherapy experiences because few previously had much contact with therapy and fewer still with psychoanalytically oriented therapy.

In order to control and neutralize the primitive material that had erupted into consciousness, these OCD patients displayed a variety of responses. Some expressed the everyday reactions of embarrassment, guilt, and apologies while about half used classical defenses such as undoing and denial. These defense mechanisms were usually seen across responses, balancing the impulse with its opposite. For instance, one patient first saw "piercing mean eyes peering at me through the dark," then next saw "some type of face smiling, a cartoon figure." Interestingly, 20% of the subjects demonstrated denial that failed—first denying any response, then revealing a sexual or hostile one. The most widespread way that these patients controlled their affect was through language, mostly through the choice of emotionally flat, neutral words. About two thirds used this form of cold factual language, rather than emotionally hot words.

Coursey (1984) concluded that obsessive–compulsives are marked by the extent to which primitive material has invaded their consciousness and the equally powerful neutralizing strategies these patients have developed to handle these impulses. Unlike other neurotics (in whom the primitive drives never fully reach consciousness except in symbolic or symptomatic forms), and unlike the psychotic (in whom primary process is conscious but defenses have completely failed), most of the OCD patients represented a third possibility, in that primitive impulse material is conscious, and the defenses other than repression and denial have not failed. Rather, the defenses that do work are those that neutralize and contain the primary process material. Thus, the central characteristic of most of these patients is this highly charged impasse, a deadlock between the failure of repression and denial, and the success of the aforementioned neutralizing strategies and other containing defenses such as preoccupation with detail.

Coursey felt that his Rorschach data appeared to confirm the observations of Freud and others that hostile and sadistic impulses are a central component of this disorder. They are also in accord with a self-report descriptive study by Rachman and DeSilva (1978) of the obsessions of patients and normals, in which 70% of the obsessions in their patients focused on violence and physical aggression, 17% on deviant sexual impulses, another 9% on being out of control, and only 4% on neutral phrases.

The descriptive Rorschach material presented by Coursey also suggests that repression and denial are not very effective at preventing primary process material from becoming conscious. So, in contradiction to some Freudian theorists, there is no evidence in his material that there are "even more horrible" unconscious underlying impulses. Coursey feels that this is strong evidence that *the psychotherapeutic process may better focus on what is present than on what might be underlying.* This would entail working with the secondary features of the disorder—the anxiety, rituals, and so forth. In addition, it would be important to help patients deal with and accept the heightening impulses they experience.

TREATMENT TECHNIQUES

Some commonly encountered difficulties that arise in the psychotherapy of obsessional patients, as well as suggested psychotherapeutic techniques, are outlined in Table 13.1. As noted, when

obsessional patients are in a therapeutic relationship, issues of aggression, sexuality, and control invariably arise. In addition, such patients have a pervasive and persistent tendency to resist change and to try desperately to be in control of all situations. They tend to doubt and may be ambivalent about almost everything. They may be perfectionistic and feel that any unacceptable thought can produce disaster.

When attempting to deal with the obsessional patients' resistance to change, the therapist must be aware that such defenses against change are extremely strong and that they mitigate against exposure to the patients' deficits. Salzman (1983) has noted that obsessionals often steadfastly reject any new awareness that would require admissions that there are matters about which they are unaware. Thus, they frequently reject an observation as invalid, only to present it later as their own discovery. The therapist may have to tolerate this tactic early in treatment and not confront it aggressively until a strong therapeutic relationship has developed; such a relationship may take considerable time because these patients have a fear of trust and commitment.

As noted earlier, an issue that arises over and over in the therapy of these patients is the need for control. In fact, symptoms such as rituals, doubting, and striving for perfection can all be viewed as neurotic attempts to control one's inner and external worlds. Patients have the illusion that such mechanisms can make the world safe and secure. For example, the young male who must persistently think of his mother's vagina to keep her safe has the illusion that no harm can come to her as long as he persists in this disturbing thought. Somehow, by his own discomfort, he is able to sacrifice himself and keep a loved one safe and is thus in control. He is, therefore, opposed to taking any risks; that is, he refuses to try to give up his thoughts for fear of a catastrophic occurrence. Encouraging risk taking is an integral part of any therapy with obsessional patients.

Salzman (1983) has noted that obsessionals spend endless time in distracting avoidances and contentious disagreements, although they are intellectually astute and cognitively capable of clearer analysis. This is likely a mechanism to control the therapist. Another tactic is affective isolation with little acknowledgment of the importance of the therapist in the patient's life; this may

TABLE 13.1. Characteristics of Obsessional Patients and Therapeutic Strategies

Characteristic belief or tendency	Result	Treatment
Danger is imminent	Exaggerates risks	Encourage risk taking; help assess risks realistically
Gives excessive details	Confuses issues; never gets to the point	Keep treatment plan firmly in mind
Needs to be in control	Resists change	Explore benefits of not controlling; therapist can model less controlling behaviors; therapist and patient partners in therapy
Confuses past with details and qualifications	Unproductive therapy	Focus on "here and now"
Avoids expressions of feelings	Tends to be cognitive and cold	Encourage feelings, whether positive or negative
Persistent doubt	Reluctance to change	Encourage risk-taking
Feels superior to therapist	Devaluing and controlling	Therapist and patient partners in therapy
Equates thoughts and impulses with action	Enhances fears	Clarify distinction at every opportunity
Loses sight of normal behavior	Excessive washing and checking	Model and explain "normal" behavior
Excessive insecurity	Fears any action	Reassure repetitively that anxiety is natural
Aggressive or hostile impulses	Fears hurting others	Focus on what is present, rather than underlying impulses
Needs unlimited information before decisions	Procrastinates	Encourage risk-taking

Reprinted from: Jenike, M A., Baer, L., & Minichiello, W. E. (Eds.), *Obsessive-compulsive disorders: Theory and management.* PSG Publishing, Littleton, MA, 1986, p. 119.

continue until well into the therapy. Patients may be critical of the therapist's inability to alter symptoms, but they will resist steadfastly any attempts to do so. Forging a therapeutic relationship may form the bulk of the work in treating the obsessional patient. Any expression of feeling by the patient should be encouraged, whether positive or negative. The obsessional patient may become even more rigid and controlling or may become petty or derogatory when the appropriate response should be anger (e.g., when the therapist is unavoidably late for an appointment or raises therapy fees). Sharing feelings of dislike, distrust, or affection for the therapist is very difficult for these patients because of their fear of loss of control. They need to appear rational and calm. Affectionate reactions are tightly controlled and are felt to be undesirable, fearful, and in need of tight management. Such control over tender feelings constitutes the essence of the obsessional defense, and it not infrequently yields hostile reactions from family members and colleagues.

Obsessional patients are frequently unable to commit themselves on issues, and they will explore every aspect of each issue to assure that they are correct and in control. Pervasive doubt is most pronounced in the obsessional patients with checking behaviors. For example, they may check the faucet 50 times before going to bed or open and close their car door a dozen times to be sure it is locked. To be completely safe and certain about everything, patients maintain the illusion that they must never make an error or admit to any deficiency; thus, they will not risk making definite decisions or committing themselves to a point of view or course of action in case it turns out to be the wrong one (Salzman, 1980). When patients with frank checking forms of OCD are coerced into not checking, they are surprised that nothing happens.

Many obsessives equate words, impulses, or thoughts with action and feel that somehow particular thoughts may control the behavior of others. Salzman (1983) has labeled this "omnipotence of thought": words can magically undo unacceptable behavior or produce untold malevolence for which obsessives assume guilt. In order to be absolutely precise and clear and to be fair to all parties, obsessives typically introduce more and more qualifications and explanations to be sure that the issue at hand has been explained to its fullest. Rather than clarifying, this tends to confuse issues even more. Because of this tendency never to get to the point, such patients can be extremely boring to the therapist who is interested in feelings, insight, and change.

In traditional psychodynamic psychotherapy, inactivity on the part of the therapist is encouraged, and it is not uncommon for the therapist to listen to the patient for long periods of time without intervening. With the obsessive patient, this will usually be unproductive. As a general rule, the therapist will have to be much more active from the beginning of the therapy. It is important, however, not to overwhelm the patient and to give the patient the feeling that the therapist is running the therapy. Salzman (1983) notes that detailed communication designed to prevent omission or error must be interrupted to enable the therapist to understand the overall theme and not get caught in the confusing minutia. Failure to do so caused long and fruitless analyses in the early stages of the psychoanalytic treatment of the obsessive. For most therapists, interruption will be necessary for them to remain alert and awake during the therapy sessions. One of the most frequent countertransference reactions is drowsiness or inability to keep one's mind on the therapy; this should be a self-alerting sign that the patient is not on a productive track.

Salzman (1983) recommends that the therapist keep a treatment plan firmly in mind. This will allow the therapist some framework on which to decide which of the patient's random associations or innumerable details are of importance to the task at hand. For instance, the topic under discussion may be the patient's feelings that he contributed to his father's death when he visited him in the hospital and his ambivalent relationship with his father while he was alive. But he may start to discuss the location of the hospital, the food that was served, the level of nursing care, the types of fluids that were being administered, the level which his father's head was tilted, and so on. The

therapist can easily forget that the goal at this time is to help the patient to come to grasp with strong opposite feelings of love and anger toward his deceased father.

Salzman (1983) has outlined some of the specific goals that are often helpful in the treatment of these patients. First, it is necessary to discover and elucidate the basis for excessive feelings of insecurity that require absolutes to guarantee one's existence before any action is attempted. This requires the examination of each symptom and obsessional tactic to show how it ties into the overriding need to control. Rituals, phobias, and personality traits are explored in terms of their role in giving the patient the illusory feeling of absolute control.

Second, one must demonstrate by repeated interpretation and encouragement to action that such guarantees are not necessary and instead interfere with living. This involves motivating the individual to attempt novel and unfamiliar patterns of behavior through active assistance in stimulating new adventures. This can help patients to attempt counterphobic activity and overcome conditioned avoidance reactions to unexplored areas of functioning.

Third, it is necessary to get the patient to accept that anxiety is a natural part of living and a companion to all human endeavors. This means abandoning attempts at perfection and accepting limited goals, using the most creative resources available. Patients must learn to accept their human limitations.

One of the most frequent pitfalls to befall the therapist is discussing the past for long periods of time with the obsessive patient. Recollections of the patients' past are usually clouded by doubts that lead to ambivalence. Interpretations of past events are subject to endless bickering, qualifying, and uncertainty (Salzman, 1983). The safest tactic to take with the obsessive patient is to focus on the present situation and discuss current functioning, relationships, and issues; this is most likely to yield the greatest clarity and conviction and is also least open to persistent doubt and distortion.

Salzman notes that this focus on current issues will also maximize productive exploration of emotions. While past feelings can be described and experienced calmly, judiciously, and intellectually, the present hostilities and frustrations, especially as they involve ongoing relationships, are much more difficult to camouflage because they represent failures or deficiencies and expose much of the patient's feelings. It is important that the obsessive learns to recognize and express hostile and affectionate feelings. A tolerant and patient therapist can be of major assistance in this seemingly impossible task. If the patient is keeping her or his appointments, the therapist should assume that the patient is finding therapy helpful even though this is rarely acknowledged, especially early in such a relationship.

On the other hand, most of these patients suffer from a pervasive lack of self-esteem despite the fact that they may be very successful; and on the other hand, they often appear condescending and exude a sense of contempt for the abilities and sensibilities of others, including the therapist. Salzman notes that they secretly may feel superior to and contemptuous of the therapist and feel they are aware of all that is going on in the therapy. The obsessive patient will, however, appear to be pursuing the suggested course and will take delight in fooling the therapist and thereby feel in control of the therapy. Therapists need to be alert for such tactics and gently confront them when the opportunity presents itself. Obsessive patients will resist interpretations that suggest that they are not aware of something.

Before patients will change in therapy, it will be necessary for a firm therapeutic relationship to develop, and the patient will need to experience a desire to change. As an example, a female patient with severe handwashing compulsions had been refractory to all therapeutic interventions and was referred to a neurosurgeon for evaluation for "cingulotomy"; she became so frightened at this prospect that she actively engaged in previously ineffective behavior therapy and improved greatly over the next 3 months. The threat of surgery had brought the seriousness of her situation to the forefront. Any technique that strengthens the patients' awareness of their maladaptive patterns will assist them in making changes. Salzman feels that before any moves can be made to change behavior, individuals must have a strong conviction about the need to change and a trust in the understanding derived from collaboration with the

therapist. They must be encouraged to see how they will be benefited by the therapy instead of visualizing the disasters that will confront them when they feel helpless and not in total control of everything.

Not all patients will present themselves in the same way, and the effectiveness of the therapist will lie in his or her ability to detect recurring issues and to allow patients to see those issues in a new way. It is sometimes helpful for the therapist to define what is generally considered normal and to model normal behavior for the patient. Obsessive patients will keenly observe the therapist, and if they consider the therapist to be a successful person, they will try to copy certain actions. The therapist must be somewhat spontaneous in expressing some personal feelings and weaknesses, thus allowing the patient to recognize that human fallibility is not a cause for total rejection by others. Whenever possible, it is safest to assume the position that the therapist and the patient together are going to examine pertinent issues rather than the therapist assuming the role of expert who is going to assist a helpless patient.

Compulsive symptoms and styles are repeated without deviation in spite of the awareness that they are nonproductive and potentially destructive. Thus, much of the therapy must involve a repetitive review of issues that recur many times. When patients begin to change, anxiety may become very severe, and occasionally low doses of benzodiazepines may facilitate therapy. When anxiety becomes overwhelming, performance is adversely affected; moderate anxiety, however, facilitates performance. The therapist must induce some anxiety in order to produce change, but must be mindful of the pain of too much anxiety in the patient. The therapist must maintain anxiety at a level that will facilitate learning rather than impede it.

The focus must be on feelings rather than on cognitive exchanges, and it must concentrate on the here and now. Salzman (1983) summarizes the essence of the therapeutic process with these patients as follows: "Before patients will relinquish their extensive defense system, they must allow themselves to experience and accept failure, some loss of false pride and prestige, and possible humiliation."

CASE EXAMPLE

Mr. Johnson, a 44-year-old computer executive, presented for an evaluation to the Obsessive–Compulsive Disorders Clinic and Research Unit, at the suggestion of an orthopedic surgeon friend. Upon examination, Mr. Johnson was found to be suffering from long-standing obsessive–compulsive disorder, as well as a more recent major depression. There was no evidence of psychosis in the patient's history or on mental status examination.

Depressive symptoms consisted of early morning awakening, loss of appetite with a resultant 15-pound weight loss, fatigue, and great difficulty concentrating. He felt that depression resulted from his inability to control pronounced obsessive–compulsive symptoms. He denied that anyone in his family had suffered from depression, and he was medically well and was taking no medication. It was clear from his history that obsessive–compulsive symptoms predated the depression by at least 20 years.

His compulsions largely revolved around checking. He would often have to retrace the route that he takes to work for 30 to 45 minutes per day. It was not uncommon for him to take over an hour to drive 3 miles to and from his office. On an occasional "terrible" day, he may have spent over 5 hours checking the route that he had driven to his office to be sure that he had not caused an accident and "not know it." Even in the winter, he drove with both his front windows almost completely down with the radio off to be sure that he did not miss any screeching or crashing. Despite these precautions, he still "couldn't be certain" that he did not cause an accident, and he had to return over and over again until some internal feeling was satisfied.

In addition to the driving rituals, he performed a number of work-related checking procedures. Memos were read dozens of times and he would stare at checks that he had written to be sure that he had not written something obscene on them such as the number "69" or the word "homosexual." He also checked and rechecked the amount that he had written to be certain that there was no mistake. Similar rituals were performed at home.

One of the most distressing aspects of Mr. Johnson's disorder was the fact that he tried to get his wife and three sons to perform checking rituals as well. His wife was so frustrated by his apparently nonsensical incessant demands that she was thinking of taking the children and moving back to her parents' house in another state. He was "devastated" by this thought and felt that he "may not be able to go on living" if this were to happen. He wanted psychotherapy in an effort to "get my life under control."

While developing a therapeutic agreement with Mr. Johnson, it was clarified that psychodynamic psychotherapy would have to be done concomitantly with other treatments in order to maximize benefits. Specifically, his severe depression would require pharmacological intervention and the obsessive–compulsive symptoms mandated concomitant behavioral treatments that should begin as soon as he gets some relief from the depression. He agreed with this plan.

After about 5 weeks on therapeutic doses of a tricyclic antidepressant, his mood improved, and he began behavior therapy consisting of exposure and response prevention aimed at controlling his rituals. In psychotherapy, he initially discussed his compulsive symptoms at length, giving innumerable details and qualifications. Feelings were largely glossed over or avoided, and it became clear that he had difficulty grasping the big picture and tended to focus and dwell on seemingly minor details of almost any situation. He tended to procrastinate, but he would put in such long hours at work that his colleagues felt that he was reasonably productive. He was generally inflexible about routines and rules and spent considerable time discussing the shortcomings of others, including previous psychiatrists that he had manipulated. He tended to be polite and formal in his dealings with therapists. When his wife accompanied him to one appointment, she pointed out that he had generally been a good provider and that she admired his ability to work hard and to produce but that she had difficulty dealing with his rituals, especially when he wanted her and the children to check things repetitively. Mr. Johnson would even schedule time for "pleasure and fun" when he felt compelled to have a good time; he rarely spontaneously had a good time. The children generally viewed him as aloof and somewhat unemotional.

After about 4 months of weekly sessions, Mr. Johnson talked about his relationship with his father with some emotion. Prior to this time, he stated that his father "was dead and that was that." On one session, tears came to his eyes and he acknowledged that he missed his father very much. He talked about how he viewed his father as the most important person in his life and that, even though he felt that his father was probably proud of him, his father never acknowledged that. Mr. Johnson saw himself as doing all he could to impress his father and to get his approval, but that it never came. He had been a star athlete and had attended a top college, graduating with honors; his father did not even attend his graduation. He cried for himself as well as for the loss of his father. Later in the session, he verbalized rage toward his father and then covered it with guilty feelings and apologies.

In the next session, with great difficulty, we returned to the topic of his father's death, and he admitted that he had strong feelings that he had killed his father in a very real sense. His father had a slowly growing brain tumor that presented suddenly with neurological symptoms. He underwent emergency surgery and spent 3 weeks in the intensive care unit in a coma prior to dying suddenly during the night. Mr. Johnson visited him daily during this time.

The evening prior to his father's death, Mr. Johnson had commented to the nurse that his father's head seemed too high and that he might be uncomfortable. She then lowered the head of the bed. Mr. Johnson kissed his father and went home. Three hours later he received a call notifying him that his father had died and immediately thought that he had killed his father by getting the nurse to move the head of the bed. He felt that somehow (aspiration, moving head, etc.) this contributed to his father's dying and that his underlying hostility toward his father had caused him to kill his father.

Over the next months, when we tried to discuss this in psychotherapy, he would immediately start with innumerable details about the hospital, the angle of the bed, the stains on the sheets, the dress that the nurse was wearing, the intensity of the lights, the color of the intravenous fluids, the smell of the room, and so on. Each time the topic was shifted toward the ambivalent feelings toward his father, he would start with a smoke screen of details. Inevitably, he would induce boredom in the therapist, and it was most difficult to keep the game plan (explore ambivalent feelings toward his father) in mind. After months of counterpunching feelings for details, both therapist and patient felt that there was some sense of relief, and the patient was able to give up the expectation that somehow his father would return from the grave and give him the recognition that he so dearly craved. It appeared that coming to grips with this longing improved his

mood and allowed him to focus more clearly on the behavior therapy and his present relationships in his life—especially his children and wife. He started to attend his sons' baseball games and commented on how well they were doing in school. Despite being far from ideal, the family members all felt that the quality of their lives was greatly improved over the 18 months that he remained in therapy.

REFERENCES

American Psychiatric Association. (1987). *Diagnostic and statistical manual of mental disorders* (3rd ed., rev.). Washington, DC: Author.

Beck, A. J. (1976). *Cognitive therapy and the emotional disorders*. New York: International Universities Press.

Brotman, A. W., & Jenike, M. A. (1984). Monosymptomatic hypochondriasis treated with tricyclic antidepressants. *American Journal of Psychiatry, 141*, 1608–1609.

Coursey, R. D. (1984). The dynamics of obsessive–compulsive disorder. In T. R. Insel (Ed.), *New findings in obsessive–compulsive disorder* (pp. 104–121). Washington, DC: American Psychiatric Press.

Emmelkamp, P. M. G., van de Helm, H., & van Zanten, B. (1980). Contributions of self-instructional training to the effectiveness of exposure in vivo: A comparison with obsessive–compulsive patients. *Behaviour Research and Therapy, 18*, 61–66.

Foa, E. B. (1979). Failure in treating obsessive–compulsives. *Behaviour Research and Therapy, 17*, 169–176.

Foa, E. B., & Kozak, M. J. (September, 1983). *Treatment of anxiety disorders: Implications for psychopathology*. Paper presented at the National Institute of Mental Health Conference on Anxiety and Anxiety Disorders, Tuxedo, NY.

Hamilton, J. A., & Alagna, S. W. (1984). Obsessive–compulsive disorder: Cognitive approaches in context. In T. R. Insel (Ed.), *New findings in obsessive–compulsive disorder*. Washington, DC: American Psychiatric Press.

Hodgson, J., & Rachman, S. (1977). Obsessional compulsive complaints. *Behaviour Research and Therapy, 15*, 389–395.

Insel, T. R. (Ed.), (1984). *New findings in obsessive–compulsive disorder*. Washington, DC: American Psychiatric Press.

Jenike, M. A. (1984). A case report of successful treatment of dysmorphophobia with tranylcypromine. *American Journal of Psychiatry, 141*, 1463–1464.

Jenike, M. A. (1986a). Illnesses related to obsessive-compulsive disorder. In M. A. Jenike, L. Baer, & W. E. Minichiello (Eds.), *Obsessive–compulsive disorders: Theory and management*. Littleton, MA: PSG Publishing.

Jenike, M. A. (1986b). Predictors of treatment failure. In M. A. Jenike, L. Baer, & W. E. Minichiello (Eds.), *Obsessive–compulsive disorders: Theory and management*. Littleton, MA: PSG Publishing.

Jenike, M. A. (1986c). Psychotherapy of the obsessional patient. In M. A. Jenike, L. Baer, & W. E. Minichiello (Eds.), *Obsessive–compulsive disorders: Theory and management*. Littleton, MA: PSG Publishing.

Jenike, M. A. (1987). Coping with fear responses to AIDS. *Human Sexuality, 21*, 22–28.

Jenike, M. A., Armentano, M., & Baer, L. (1987a). Disabling obsessive thoughts responsive to antidepressants. *Journal of Clinical Psychopharmacology, 7*, 33–35.

Jenike, M. A., Baer, L., & Minichiello, W. E. (Eds.). (1986a). *Obsessive–compulsive disorders: Theory and management*. Littleton, MA: PSG Publishing.

Jenike, M. A., Baer, L., Minichiello, W. E., Schwartz, C. E., & Carey, R. J. (1986b). Coexistent obsessive-compulsive disorder and schizotypal personality disorder: A poor prognostic indicator. *Archives of General Psychiatry, 43*, 296.

Jenike, M. A., Baer, L., Minichiello, W. E., Schwartz, C. E., & Carey, R. J. (1986c). Concomitant obsessive-compulsive disorder and schzotypal personality disorder. *American Journal of Psychiatry, 143*, 530–533.

Jenike, M. A., & Pato, C. (1986). Disabling fear of AIDS responsive to imipramine. *Psychosomatics, 27*, 143–144.

Jenike, M. A., Vitagliano, H. L., Rabinovitz, J., Goff, D. C., & Baer, L. (1987b). Bowel obsessions: A variant of obsessive–compulsive disorder responsive to antidepressants. *American Journal of Psychiatry, 144*, 1347–1348.

Millon, T. (1981). *Disorders of personality—DSM III: Axis II*. New York: Wiley.

Minichiello, W. E., Baer, L., & Jenike, M. A. (1987). Schizotypal personality disorder: A poor prognostic indicator for behavior therapy in the treatment of obsessive–compulsive disorder. *Journal of Anxiety Disorders, 1*, 273–276.

Myers, J. K., Weissman, M. M., Tischler, G. L., Holzer, C. E., Leaf, P. J., Orvaschel, H., Anthony, J. C., Boyd, J. H., & Kramer, M. (1984). Six month prevalence of psychiatric disorders in three commitments. *Archives of General Psychiatry, 41*, 959–967.

Rachman, S., & DeSilva, P. (1978). Abnormal and normal obsessions. *Behaviour Research and Therapy, 16*, 233–248.

Rachman, S., & Hodgson, R. (1980). *Obsessions and compulsions*. Englewood Cliffs, NJ: Prentice-Hall.

Robins, L. N., Helzer, J. E., Weissman, M. M., Orvaschel, H., Gruenberg, E., Burke, J. D., Jr., & Regier, D. A. (1984). Lifetime prevalence of specific psychiatric disorders in three sites. *Archives of General Psychiatry, 41*, 949–958.

Salzman, L. (1968). *The obsessive personality*. New York: Science House.

Salzman, L. (1980). Psychotherapy of the obsessional. *Psychiatric Annals, 10*, 491–494.

Salzman, L. (1983). Psychoanalytic therapy of the obsessional patient. *Current Psychiatric Therapy, 9*, 53–59.

Shapiro, D. (1965). *Neurotic styles*. New York: Basic Books.

Solyom, L., DiNicola, V. F., Phil, M., Sookman, D., & Luchins, D. (1985). Is there an obsessive psychosis? Aetiological and prognostic factors of an atypical form of obsessive–compulsive neurosis. *Canadian Journal of Psychiatry, 30*, 372–380.

CHAPTER 14

Behavior Therapy

EDNA B. FOA AND VIVIENNE C. ROWAN

CONCEPTUALIZATION OF THE DISORDER

Definition

In DSM-III-R, the official diagnostic manual of the American Psychiatric Association (1987), obsessive–compulsive disorder (OCD) is listed among the anxiety disorders. Diagnostic requirements include the presence of either obsessions and/or compulsions. *Obsessions* are defined as recurrent, persistent thoughts, images, or impulses that are experienced as intrusive and senseless and are perceived as the product of one's own mind, rather than as imposed from without, as in thought insertion. Typically, the person tries to ignore and suppress the obsession or to neutralize it with another thought or action. Common obsessions are repetitive thoughts of harm, contamination, and doubt. The other class of symptoms, *compulsions*, are defined as repetitive, purposeful, stereotyped behavior that are performed in an attempt to neutralize or to prevent discomfort of an unrealistically feared harm. Usually, the person recognizes that the compulsion is excessive and irrational. Common compulsions are handwashing, counting, checking, and touching.

The DSM-III-R seems to follow the traditional modality-based distinction between obsessions and compulsions in which obsessions are *internal* (covert) events and compulsions are *overt* (external) behaviors. This distinction poses serious conceptual problems that become apparent when symptoms of individuals are examined. For ex-

ample, one patient felt contaminated by physical contact with chocolate, as well as by the thought of chocolate. She relieved the discomfort aroused by the former with washing (an overt compulsion), and that of the latter with the thought "sunlight" (a covert compulsion). Clearly, the thought "chocolate" differs from the thought "sunlight" although both are "internal" events. In another case, the number "3" produced anxiety whereas repeating the number "7" reduced it: here again, the two numbers differ in their functional relations to anxiety.

Based on these observations, Foa and Tillmanns (1980) proposed a definition that focuses on the functional relationship between OC symptoms and anxiety. Accordingly, *obsessions* are defined as thoughts, images, or actions that *generate* that anxiety. Consequently, *compulsions* can be conceptualized as either overt actions or covert (neutralizing) thoughts that usually *reduce* anxiety. As noted by Rachman (1976), these two types of responses are functionally equivalent. This conceptualization is consistent with the behavioral model of OCD (Dollard & Miller, 1950), as well as with empirical findings (Carr, 1971; Roper, Rachman, & Hodgson, 1973).

Classification

Modern attempts to identify subtypes of OCD have focused on the ritualistic activity (i.e., compulsions) rather than on the obsessions. Although many patients complain of more than one form of ritual, usually one predominates and determines how the individual will be categorized. Thus, patients are classified as washers, checkers, orderers, and so on.

Ritualistic washing is the most common compulsion. It is performed to decrease discomfort associated with contamination obsessions. For example, individuals who fear contact with AIDS germs clean themselves and their environment excessively, to prevent either becoming inflicted by AIDS or spreading it to others. Some washers do not fear that a specific disaster will befall if they refrain from ritualistic washing. Rather, the state of being contaminated itself generates intolerable discomfort. To decrease this aversive state, they feel compelled to engage in rituals.

The second common compulsion is repetitive *checking*, which one performs in order to prevent an anticipated catastrophe. The person who fears that a burglar will enter his or her home, take his or her valuables, and possibly harm his or her family, will repeatedly check doors and windows. Likewise, the individual who dreads that, while driving, he or she will run over another person and fail to notice it, will repeat his or her route over and over, searching for a possible victim. *Repeaters* are a subtype of checkers. They too are driven by the wish to circumvent disasters; however, they differ from checkers in that their rituals are unrelated logically to their feared consequences. For example, it is logical to repeatedly check door locks if one fears a burglary, but illogical to dress and redress to prevent the death of a loved one.

Other compulsions are ordering, counting, and hoarding. An additional category, obsessional slowness, was proposed by Rachman and Hodgson (1980) to account for persons whose daily activities (e.g., toileting) take many hours. However, unlike other OCs (washers, checkers, and orderers), individuals with obsessional slowness do not have distinct obsessions associated with their actions; perhaps their slowness can be explained as an effort to achieve perfection.

Behavioral Cognitive Theories

The most commonly adopted behavioral conceptualization of OCD is based on Mowrer's (1939) two-stage theory of the acquisition and maintenance of fear and avoidance. In the first stage, a neutral event becomes associated with a fear response by being paired with a stimulus that innately evokes anxiety (e.g., pain). In the second stage, escape and avoidance responses are developed in order to alleviate the fear evoked by the aversive stimulus. Because of extensive generalization and second-order conditioning, a panorama of situations come to elicit anxiety, and passive avoidance becomes ineffective. Active avoidance behavior, in the form of ritualistic actions, is then developed. There is no convincing evidence to support the hypothesis that obsessions are acquired via classical conditioning. This explanation for the maintenance of the ritualistic behavior, on the other hand, has gained empirical support (e.g., Carr, 1971; Hodgson & Rachman, 1972).

To account for the development of obsessions, several cognitive theories have been advanced. Carr (1974) proposed that OCs have abnormally high expectations of negative outcomes. They exaggerate normal concerns such as the welfare of loved ones, health, sex, religious issues, and work performance. Clearly, one of the distinguishing features of OCs is their erroneous belief systems. McFall and Wollersheim (1979) focused on some erroneous beliefs of OCD individuals. These included the notion that one's worthiness is based on being perfect in all endeavors at all times. or that the failure to attain perfection deserves punishment. The authors suggested that these types of erroneous beliefs lead to misperceptions of threat, which evoke anxiety. Because OCs tend to feel uncertain and to devalue their ability to cope with threats, they devise magical rituals to decrease discomfort, thereby gaining apparent control of their environment.

Conceptualizing anxiety disorders as manifestations of impairments in information processing, Foa and Kozak (1985) view these disorders as representing pathological memory structures. Fear is defined as an affective memory that includes information about feared stimuli, fear responses, and their meanings (Lang, 1979). They further proposed that pathological fears differ from normal fears. The former are characterized by the presence of erroneous estimates of threat, an unusually high negative valence for the threatening event, and excessive response elements (e.g., physiological, avoidance). In addition, pathological fear structures are distinguished by their resistance to modification. This persistence may reflect failure to access the fear structure, either because of successful avoidance (e.g., refraining from using elevators) or because the content of the fear structure precludes spontaneous confrontation with situations that evoke anxiety in everyday life (e.g., the city dweller who is snake phobic). Anxiety may also persist because of some impairment in the mechanism of change. Cognitive defenses, excessive arousal with failure to habituate, faulty premises, and erroneous rules of inference may all hinder the processing of information necessary for correcting the fear structure of the OC. According to Foa and Kozak, during successful treatment, information incompatible with the existing fear structures becomes available; when incorporated, this information corrects the specific psychopathology that underlies the disorder.

DIAGNOSTIC ISSUES AND PROBLEMS

Two major diagnostic issues in OCD, overvalued ideation and depression, are discussed in this section.

Overvalued Ideation

According to the DSM-III-R's definition, "the person recognizes that his or her compulsive behavior is excessive or unreasonable" (p. 245). However, OCD individuals differ with respect to how sensible they view their obsessions and compulsions to be; those with strong convictions of the validity of their obsessions are referred to as overvalued ideators (Foa, 1979). At the extreme, overvalued ideators may appear to be delusional. But, unlike schizophrenics in an acute psychotic state, overvalued ideators do not evidence a general disorganization in the form and/or content of their thought. In this respect, they resemble delusional paranoid-disordered individuals who, apart from an encapsulated delusion, do not evidence odd or bizarre thoughts. As noted in the DSM-III-R, "the overvalued ideator, after considerable discussion, usually can acknowledge that his/her belief may be unfounded. In contrast, a person with a true delusion usually has a fixed conviction that cannot be shaken" (p. 246). In addition, the

overvalued ideator, but not the delusional person, recognizes that his or her belief differs from that of others and, therefore, tries to cast it in rational terms that are shared by others.

An example of an overvalued ideator is a woman who functioned well as a mother, wife, hostess, and artist. She did not evidence disorganized thinking. Yet she held an extremely strong belief that, through direct or indirect contact with "leukemia germs," she would inflict the dreaded disease on her husband and children. To prevent this disaster, she washed excessively. When asked to assess the validity of her belief, this patient was absolutely certain that her failure to wash would result in her family catching leukemia. Following a lengthy discussion, this patient, like other overvalued ideators, was willing to entertain the possibility that her belief may be unfounded in general. Yet she held her view by claiming that her family was especially vulnerable and therefore needed extra protection.

It is not uncommon for schizophrenics to exhibit repetitive stereotyped behavior that resembles compulsive rituals. Nor is it uncommon for such behaviors to be displayed by the mentally retarded and the organically disordered (Turner, Beidel, & Swami Nathan, 1985). The presence of ritualistic behavior, however, is not a sufficient condition for a diagnosis of OCD. As noted earlier, what characterizes OCD is the functional relationship between obsessions and compulsions: Obsessions generate anxiety, and compulsions alleviate this anxiety. Many schizophrenics who manifest repetitive behavior do not report negative cognitions (thoughts, images, impulses) associated with it. Others associate ritualistic behavior with ego-syntonic delusions. The logical thinking (although based on irrational assumptions) exhibited by the OC individual is absent in the schizophrenic.

Insel and Akiskal (1986) describe two interesting clinical cases whose obsessions temporarily intensified and become more bizarre while under stress. However, within a brief period, these patients resumed their previous OC characteristics. A careful examination of these cases suggests that increased anxiety and/or major depression may have intensified the level of distress associated with the obsessions, rendering them similar to a delusional belief.

Depression

A strong associate between depression and OC symptoms has been noted by several authors (Beech, 1971; Foa, Steketee, & Milby, 1980; Lewis, 1935; Mellet, 1974; Rachman, 1976). Studies investigating the incidence of obsessive symptoms in samples of depressed patients reported high frequency of a joint occurrence between the two symptomatologies (17–35%). When the frequency of depression was studied in an OC population, a somewhat similar picture emerged. Solyom, Zamanzadeh, Ledwidge, and Kenny (1971) found that two thirds of a sample of 15 obsessives showed mild to moderate depression; only 2 were severely depressed. Following observations of 20 OCs, Mellet (1974) reported that 95% were "unusually prone to depressive reactions." In a study of 21 OCs (Foa & Goldstein, 1978), mild to moderate depression was evident with a mean depression rating of 4.8 on a 9-point scale. Only 3 patients in this sample were classified as severely depressed. In a recent study of 38 OCs, the mean score on the Beck Depression Inventory was 23, indicating a moderate to high level of depression (Foa, Steketee, Kozak, & Dugger, 1987).

Although the existence of a relationship between OC symptoms and depression is well established, its nature remains unclear. Does depression produce obsessive symptoms? Or do patients become depressed as a result of the discomfort and limitations imposed by the OC symptoms? Or are the two related through a third unidentified variable? If depression causes OC symptoms, then antidepressants would reduce such symptoms only if they also reduce depression. This hypothesis was investigated in several drug trials, primarily using clomipramine. Montgomery (1980) found clomipramine superior to placebo in decreasing obsessions. However, depression level was unaffected by the drug. These results support the view that obsessions and depression are independent pathologies. Likewise, Ananth, Pecknold, Van den Steen, and Engelsmann (1981) found that changes in OC symptoms following administration of clomipramine and of amytriptyline were not associated with changes in depression.

On the other hand, some support for the hypothesis that depression mediates reduction of OC symptoms via drugs gained some support by Marks, Stern, Mawson, Cobb, and McDonald (1980). Whereas an overall effect of clomipramine on reducing OC symptoms was observed, a post hoc analysis revealed that only the 10 most depressed OCs improved via the drug. This hypothesis was not confirmed in other drug studies with OCs. (For an extensive review, see Foa et al., 1987).

Support for the hypothesis that depression observed in these patients is caused by the OC symptoms was discussed in the Foa et al. (1987) study in which depressed and nondepressed patients received either imipramine or placebo. Imipramine reduced depression in the depressed group, but it did not reduce OC symptoms in either group. Following behavior therapy, a significant reduction in depression was noted for both groups, concomitant with a significant decrease in OC symptoms. This finding suggests that depression in OC patients is secondary to their OC symptoms, and it ameliorates with their reduction.

TREATMENT STRATEGIES

Obsessive–compulsive disorders have long been considered among the most intractable of the neurotic disorders. As recently as 1960, Breitner concluded that "most of us are agreed that the treatment of obsessional states is one of the most difficult tasks confronting the psychiatrist and many of us consider it hopeless" (p. 32). Traditional psychotherapeutic techniques have not proven effective in ameliorating OC symptomatology (Black, 1974). Only 20% of 90 inpatients had improved at a 13- to 20-year follow-up (Kringlen, 1965). Somewhat more favorable results were reported by Grimshaw (1965) with an outpatient sample; 40% evidenced symptom amelioration at a 1- to 14-year follow-up.

Remarkable improvement in the prognostic picture has emerged from the application of behavioral techniques, especially exposure and response prevention (Meyer, Levy, & Schnurer, 1974). This treatment consists of two basic components: (1) exposure to discomfort-evoking stimuli (i.e., having the patient confront the real-life feared situations), and (2) response prevention (i.e., blocking the compulsive behavior). Some investigators also used imaginal exposure (e.g., Boulougouris, Rabavilas, & Stefanis, 1977; Chambless, Foa, Groves, & Goldstein, 1982).

Variants of exposure and response prevention have been investigated in numerous studies. In marked contrast to the poor prognosis for OCD with traditional psychotherapy, the success rate using these two behavioral procedures are quite high: About 75% evidenced significant improvement in OC symptomatology (e.g., Emmelkamp & Kraanen, 1977; Marks, Hodgson, & Rachman, 1975). Slightly better results have been noted with a combination of imaginal and in vivo exposure (Foa & Goldstein, 1978; for an extensive review, see Foa, Steketee, & Ozarow, 1985.) At present, exposure and response prevention is the treatment of choice for OC ritualizers. However, a critical question is whether it is necessary to employ all three procedures for optimal treatment gains. To answer this question, effects of each treatment component were examined in several studies.

Because obsessions evoke anxiety, therapeutic procedures that reduce obsessional anxiety must be included in treatment. Prolonged exposure has been found to produce anxiety decrements in OCs (Foa & Chambless, 1978; Kozak, Foa, & Steketee, (1988). If rituals are maintained *only* because of their ability to reduce obsessional anxiety, then prolonged exposure alone should effectively ameliorate them, and response prevention should be superfluous. However, existing evidence indicates that prolonged exposure occasionally eliminated anxiety, yet the compulsive behavior persisted (Marks, Crowe, Drewe, Young, & Drewhurst, 1969; Walton & Mather, 1963). These results suggest that exposure and response prevention operate through separate mechanisms, both of which must be treated to successfully reduce OC symptoms.

In a series of studies, Foa and her colleagues investigated the short- and long-term effects of exposure and of response prevention. In one experiment (Foa, Steketee, Grayson, Turner, & Latimer, 1984), 32 OCs with washing rituals were treated with 15 sessions daily of either in vivo exposure only, response prevention only, or a combination. Immediately after treatment, deliberate exposure decreased anxiety to contaminants

more than did response prevention. The combined treatment yielded the best outcome. Ritualistic behavior, in turn, was ameliorated more by response prevention than by exposure; again the combined treatment was superior. This superiority was maintained at follow-up ranging from 3 months to 2 years (mean = 12 months).

Most studies employ in vivo exposure; few have used only imaginal exposure (Frankl, 1960; Stampfl, 1967). Some investigators found imaginal exposure (i.e., systematic desensitization) ineffective for OCD (Marks et al., 1969; Roper et al., 1973; Wolpe, 1964). With simple phobics, actual confrontation with feared situations is superior to exposure in fantasy (cf. Mathews, 1978). However, with agoraphobics and OCs, the superiority of in vivo exposure over imaginal flooding is questionable (for a review, see Foa & Kozak, 1985).

For many OCs, anxiety is generated both by tangible cues from their environment and by anticipation of harm (e.g., death, disease, brain damage). The latter can be presented only in fantasy. For example, the patient who fears becoming brain damaged from toxic substances can be exposed to this fear via only imaginal exposure. Obviously, in vivo exposure to such a disaster cannot be accomplished.

Foa and Kozak (1986) suggested that during treatment, matching the content of the exposure material to the patient's fear structure is important for decreasing anxiety symptoms. Accordingly, those who fear disastrous consequences and are exposed imaginally to them should improve more than those who do not confront such images. To study this issue, data from 49 OCs were analyzed (Steketee, Foa, & Grayson, 1982). Twenty-six patients (9 checkers, 17 washers) received imaginal exposure followed by in vivo exposure; the remaining subjects received in vivo exposure only. Both groups received response prevention instructions. On the basis of assessor's rated percentage of change scores of obsessions and compulsions, patients were divided into three groups: (1) "much improved" were those who showed treatment gains for 70% or more; (2) "improved" were those who evidenced treatment gains of 31% to 69%; and (3) "failures" were those who improved 30% or less.

These results suggest that the addition of imaginal exposure to in vivo exposure does not affect short-term treatment gains, but it facilitates the maintenance of such gains. Only 19% of patients who received imaginal exposure lost gains over time, in contrast to the 40% relapse rate among those who received exposure in vivo only.

In summary, the results of the preceding studies argue for the use of both deliberate in vivo exposure and response prevention in the treatment of OCs. They also suggest that imaginal exposure be added for those who manifest fears of future catastrophes. (For details of how to implement this treatment, see Steketee & Foa, 1985.)

CASE ILLUSTRATION

Steve, a 16-year-old patient, requested treatment for excessive handwashing triggered by contact with toxic substances such as glue, paint, and household cleaning products. He feared that any contact with such substances, either directly (e.g., personal touch) or indirectly (e.g., contact with another person who had touched the substance), would cause irreversible damage to his brain. Previous therapies as well as the negative results of a computerized axial tomography (CAT) scan failed to dispel his fears or to stop him from washing his hands. Steve's OC symptoms were also complicated by severe depression and intense social anxiety.

For 2 years prior to the commencement of behavioral treatment, Steve was living in a residential care facility for emotionally disturbed children. During his stay at that facility, he received psychoanalysis and group psychotherapy combined with various courses of pharmacological treatment. None were successful. Six weeks prior to behavior therapy, Steve returned home to his family, which consisted of his mother and his 8-year-old brother, Michael. Steve's family became increasingly distressed by his OC symptoms. His mother complained that he continuously changed clothes, refused to touch numerous things at home (e.g., household appliances, door knobs, light switches, faucets, furniture, dishes), and washed his hands extensively until they bled. Because of his intense fears, Steve frequently requested his mother and brother to perform ritualistic actions to decontaminate articles and to repeatedly assure him that his brain had not deteriorated. Steve's mother washed many loads of "contaminated clothing" daily, helped Steve with personal grooming and, at his request, repeatedly called physicians for reassuring information. Michael complained that Steve refused to play with him for fear that he had used glue at school. Michael was never permitted to come closer than a few feet of his brother and developed the habit of saying "No, I didn't touch you" before Steve's requests for reassurance escalated. As a form of reassurance, Steve often requested family members to smell various substances that he feared. He then would closely observe them for several hours, searching for signs of brain damage (e.g., loss of coordination, inability to answer difficult questions).

At the time Steve applied for treatment, he spent most of his time in his room worrying about the possibility of becoming brain damaged and devising strategies to protect himself. He was hypervigilant for sensations of dizziness and sinus congestion, which he interpreted as symptoms of brain damage. To prevent brain damage, Steve washed his hands repeatedly, and he used excessive amounts of paper towels and napkins to ensure no contact with contaminated articles.

Treatment consisted of imaginal and in vivo exposure, with the addition of response prevention (i.e., blocking the rituals). In the first session, Steve was asked to imagine the following scenario: his brother, Michael, after working with toxic glue, is touching several things in Steve's room. Because Michael is unsure of which articles he had touched and because Steve's mother refuses to provide the usual reassurance, Steven becomes extremely anxious and starts to feel dizzy. Imagining this scenario, his Subjective Units of Discomfort Scale (SUDS, ranging from 0 to 100) score rose to 100, and he remained highly anxious throughout the entire 45 minutes of imagery.

By the third session, it became clear that Steve's anxiety was not habituating. Because failure to habituate is infrequent and predicts poor response to treatment, it was important to examine which factors impeded habituation. It became clear that Steve was so fearful of having brain damage that, while imagining the scene, he began memorizing the therapist's verbal presentation in order to recount it in precise detail, thereby convincing himself that his brain functions were intact. To circumvent this problem, imaginal exposure was discontinued and was substituted with in vivo exposure. This consisted of bringing toxic substances (e.g., glue, paint) and contaminated items (e.g., books, board games) into the session and touching them for prolonged periods without washing. Homework assignments involved prolonged exposure to the items used in the session, as well as to additional objects at home, such as appliances, furnishings, doorknobs, and light switches. Exposure was combined with response prevention. By Session 8, when asked to monitor the degree of discomfort experienced while handling toxic products, Steve reported a SUDS level of 25. It was important to instruct Steve to differentiate among the various feared objects because his ratings reflected a combination of several fears.

Five days into treatment, Steve suddenly refused to complete homework assignments. Initially, he was reluctant to elaborate on his reasons of noncompliance, except to state that he had "no energy." However, he revealed to a male therapist that he felt physically and emotionally drained because of a wet dream (nocturnal ejaculation) that had occurred the night prior to that session; these dreams occurred about once a month. For Steve, having a wet dream meant that he could not complete homework until 24 hours later, when he "filled up." Because Steve felt completely immobilized whenever this occurred, he developed many checking rituals and avoidance behaviors to prevent himself from having a wet dream. For example, he frequently checked his penis and undershorts for evidence of semen. His avoidance strategies included wearing tight underwear and jeans to bed, sleeping on his right side, and jumping out of bed whenever he experienced a sexual thought.

An additional treatment strategy was immediately developed to reduce Steve's fear of having wet dreams. He agreed (a) to stop checking his penis and underwear, and (b) to gradually confront feared situations related to wet dreams. Accordingly, he was required to sleep without jeans, to write stories of a sexual nature, to wear loose underwear, to peruse *Playboy Magazine*, to watch X-rated home movies, to sleep nude, and to masturbate daily. Within 5 days, Steve completed the hierarchy and reported only minimal anxiety for all situations, with the exception of writing sexual stories. Steve attributed his distress about story writing to his belief that his brain had been damaged. Two possible explanations for the lack of habituation to story writing can be offered. First, Steve may have been afraid of being criticized about the quality of the stories. Thus, the fear of story writing might have been related to Steve's social anxiety rather than to his sexual fears. A second plausible explanation is

Steve's fear that inferior stories would reflect brain damage.

At the end of the 3-week treatment program, Steve no longer washed hands or feared having wet dreams, but he continued to fear being brain damaged. He complained about sensations of "fogginess," which were strongly associated with situations that "could cause" brain damage (e.g., riding the bus to and from therapy sessions was perceived dangerous because of gas fumes), and with social pressures and anticipated negative evaluation (e.g., riding the bus, writing essay exams). We devised a treatment strategy to treat both fears simultaneously. Treatment involved confrontation with these situations in imagery and in vivo.

ALTERNATIVE TREATMENT

A variety of drugs have been used in the treatment of OCD, but the most commonly used are the antidepressants, primarily tricyclics. Some degree of symptom reduction has been reported in case studies using antipsychotic and anxiolytic agents, as well as lithium. Whereas numerous case studies have been reported, only a few controlled investigations have been conducted. Of those studies, seven employed clomipramine, a tricyclic that has gained a reputation for its antiobsessional properties (e.g., Wyndowe, Solyom, & Ananth, 1975).

In a crossover design comparing 4 weeks of clomipramine with placebo, Montgomery (1980) found the former superior in reducing obsessions and general anxiety despite low dosage (75 mg). No effects were observed on ritualistic behavior. In another trial involving 40 patients, clomipramine was compared with placebo for 7 weeks (Marks et al., 1980). Effects of the active drug were observed on only three of eight measures of OC symptoms. A longer comparison (12 weeks) of clomipramine versus placebo evidenced a stronger effect of the drug on OC symptoms (Mavissakalian, Turner, Michelson, & Jacob, 1985).

Clomipramine has also been compared to other antidepressants. It produced greater reduction in OC symptoms then nortriptyline, though the effects of both drugs were modest (Thoren, Asberg, Cronholm, Jornestedt, & Traskman, 1980). Only clomipramine differed significantly from placebo. In a comparison of clomipramine and amitriptyline, Ananth et al. (1981) found that clomipramine, but not amitriptyline, produced significant improvement pre- to posttreatment. However, at each of the assessment periods, the drugs did not differ significantly. In a crossover design, Insel, Alterman, and Murphy (1982) compared clomipramine with the MAOI clorgyline and with placebo. After 6 weeks, clomipramine reduced OC symptoms, whereas clorgyline and placebo did not. A controlled comparison of clompramine with imipramine conducted by Volavka, Naziroglu, and Yaryura-Tobias (1985) indicated that both OC and depressive symptoms were improved with each of the drugs but more so with clomipramine. The finding that imipramine was effective in reducing OC symptoms is inconsistent with the finding of Foa et al. (1987), who reported statistical but not clinically significant improvement with this drug. Comparable improvement was also found in the placebo group. In summary, all of the foregoing comparisons evidenced a tendency for clomipramine to produce more improvement than other antidepressants, but the observed difference did not always reach statistical or clinical significance.

Recent preliminary work has generated considerable interest in two highly specific serotonergic reuptake blocking agents, fluvoxetine and fluvoxamine. In a single-blind crossover design, Turner, Jacob, Beidel, and Himmelhoch (1985) compared 10 weeks of fluoxetine with placebo in eight OCs. A statistically significant drug effect was found on the Hopkins Obsessive–Compulsive Scale, but not on the Maudsley Obsessional–Compulsive Inventory.

A study by Perse, Greist, Jefferson, Rosenfeld, and Dar (in press) used a double-blind crossover design to compare the effects of 8 weeks of fluvoxamine to 8 weeks of placebo in 16 OCs. Modest improvement was reported in 9 patients. Inspection of the means cast doubt whether this reduction is clinically significant. Using a double-blind procedure, Price, Goodman, Charney, and Heninger (1987) studied the effects of a 4-week trial of fluvoxamine and placebo on 10 OC patients. Whereas significant reductions on the Yale–Brown Obsessive–Compulsive Scale were

reported, no drug effect was found on the Maudsley Obsessive–Compulsive Inventory.

In summary, psychopharmacological studies seem to indicate that clomipramine is consistently superior to placebo in effecting change in OC symptoms, whereas other antidepressants are not. Preliminary work examining the more pure serotonin blockers, fluoxetine and fluvoxamine, do not indicate increased efficacy of these drugs over clomipramine.

It is important to note that when drugs produced changes in OC symptoms, the reduction was relatively small in comparison with the effects of behavioral treatment. Approximately 30% improvement has been reported with clomipramine (Insel, Murphy, Cohen, Alterman, Kilts, & Linnoila, 1982; Marks et al., 1980; Volavka et al., 1985). The only exception is a study by Mavissakalian et al. (1985), who found 50% improvement. Mean improvements from 60 to 70% were reported with behavior therapy (e.g., Foa & Goldstein, 1978). Even if the efficacy of drug and behavior therapy were equal, relapse rates on drug withdrawal is problematic. Indeed, Thoren et al. (1980) reported that "amelioration of obsessive–compulsive disorder with clomipramine is only maintained as long as the drug treatment continues" (p. 1285). Similar results were found by Zohar (June, 1987, personal communication). Furthermore, the gains achieved by the drug may often be at the expense of uncomfortable side effects. It appears, then, that behavior therapy (exposure plus response prevention), and not antidepressant agents, is currently the treatment of choice for OC ritualizers.

REFERENCES

American Psychiatric Association (1987). *Diagnostic and statistical manual of mental disorders* (3rd ed.). Washington, DC: Author.

Ananth, J., Pecknold, J. C., Van den Steen, N., & Englesmann, F. (1981). Double blind comparative study of clomipramine and amitriptyline in obsessive neurosis. *Progress in Neuropsychopharmacology, 5,* 257–262.

Beech, H. R. (1971). Ritualistic activity in obsessional patients. *Journal of Psychosomatic Research, 15,* 417–422.

Black, A. (1974). The natural history of obsessional neurosis. In H. R. Beech (Ed.), *Obsessional states.* London: Methuen.

Boulougouris, J. C., Rabavilas, A. D., & Stefanis, C. (1977). Psychophysiological responses in obsessive–compulsive patients. *Behaviour Research and Therapy, 15,* 221–230.

Breitner, C. (1960). Durg therapy in obsessional states and other psychiatric problems. *Diseases of the Nervous System, 31,* 354.

Carr, A. T. (1971). Compulsive neurosis: Two psychophysiological studies. *Bulletin of the British Psychological Society, 24,* 256–257.

Carr, A. T. (1974). Compulsive neurosis: A review of the literature. *Psychological Bulletin, 81,* 311–318.

Chambless, D. L., Foa, E. B., Groves, G. A., & Goldstein, A. J. (1982). Exposure and communications training in the treatment of agoraphobia. *Behaviour Research and Therapy, 20,* 219–231.

Dollard, J., & Miller, N. E. (1950). *Personality and psychotherapy: An analysis in terms of learning, thinking, and culture.* New York: McGraw-Hill.

Emmelkamp, P. M. G., & Kraanen, J. (1977). Therapist-controlled exposure *in vivo*: A comparison with obsessive–compulsive patients. *Behaviour Research and Therapy, 15,* 491–495.

Foa, E. B. (1979). Failure in treating obsessive–compulsives. *Behaviour Research and Therapy, 16,* 391–399.

Foa, E. B., & Chambless, D. L. (1978). Habituation of subjective anxiety during flooding in imagery. *Behaviour Research and Therapy, 16,* 391–399.

Foa, E. B., & Goldstein, A. (1978). Continuous exposure and complete response prevention of obsessive–compulsive neurosis. *Behaviour Therapy, 9,* 821–829.

Foa, E. B., & Kozak, M. J. (1985). Treatment of anxiety disorders: Implications for psychopathology. In A. H. Tuma & J. D. Maser (Eds.), *Anxiety and the anxiety disorders.* Hillsdale, NJ: Erlbaum.

Foa, E. B., & Kozak, M. J. (1986). Emotional processing of fear: Exposure to corrective information. *Psychological Bulletin, 99,* 20–35.

Foa, E. B., Steketee, G., Grayson, J. B., Turner, R. M., & Latimer, P. (1984). Deliberate exposure and blocking of obsessive–compulsive rituals: Immediate and long-term effects. *Behavior Therapy, 15,* 450–472.

Foa, E. B., Steketee, G. S., Kozak, M. J., & Dugger, D. (1987). Effects of imipramine on depression and on obsessive–compulsive symptoms. *Psychiatry Research, 23,* 8–11.

Foa, E. B., Steketee, G., & Milby, J. B. (1980). Differential effects of exposure and response prevention in obsessive–compulsive washers. *Journal of Consulting and Clinical Psychology, 48,* 71–79.

Foa, E. B., Steketee, G. S., & Ozarow, B. J. (1985). Behavior therapy with obsessive–compulsives: From theory to treatment. In M. Mavissakalian (Ed.), *Obsessive–compulsive disorders: Psychological and pharmacological treatments.* New York: Plenum.

Foa, E. B., & Tillmanns, A. (1980). The treatment of obsessive–compulsive neurosis. In A. Goldstein & E. B. Foa (Eds.), *Handbook of behavioral interventions: A clinical guide.* New York: Wiley.

Frankl, V. E. (1960). Paradoxical intention: A logotherapeutic technique. *American Journal of Psychotherapy, 14,* 520–525.

Grimshaw, L. (1965). The outcome of obsessional disorder, a follow-up study of 100 cases. *British Journal of Psychiatry, 111,* 1051–1056.

Hodgson, R. J., & Rachman, S. (1972). The effects of contamination and washing in obsessional patients. *Behaviour Research and Therapy, 10,* 111–117.

Insel, T. R., & Akiskal, H. (1986). Obsessive–compulsive disorder with psychotic features: A phenomenological analysis. *American Journal of Psychiatry, 12,* 1527–1533.

Insel, T. R., Alterman, I., & Murphy, D. L. (1982). Antiobsessional and antidepressant effects of clomipramine in the treatment of obsessive–compulsive disorder. *Psychopharmacology Bulletin, 18,* 115–117.

Insel, T. R., Murphy, D. L., Cohen, R. M., Alterman, I., Kilts, C., & Linnoila, M. (1982). Obsessive–compulsive disorder: A double blind trial of clomipramine and clorgyline. *Archives of General Psychiatry, 40,* 605–612.

Kozak, M. J., Foa, E. B., & Steketee, G. (in press). Process and outcome of exposure treatment with obsessive–compulsives: Psychophysiological indicators of emotional processing. *Behavior Therapy.*

Kringlen, E. (1965). Obsessional neurotics, a long term follow-up. *British Journal of Psychiatry, 111,* 709–722.

Lang, P. J. (1979). A bio-informational theory of emotional imagery. *Psychophysiology, 16,* 495–512.

Lewis, A. (1935). Problems of obsessional illness. *Proceedings of the Royal Society of Medicine, 29,* 325–336.

Marks, I. M., Crowe, E., Drewe, E., Young, J., & Drewhurst, W. G. (1969). Obsessive–compulsive neurosis in identical twins. *British Journal of Psychiatry, 15,* 991–998.

Marks, I. M., Hodgson, R., & Rachman, S. (1975). Treatment of chronic obsessive–compulsive neurosis by *in vivo* exposure. *British Journal of Psychiatry, 127,* 349–364.

Marks, I. M., Stern, R. S., Mawson, D., Cobb, J., & McDonald, R. (1980). Clomipramine and exposure for obsessive–compulsive rituals: I. *British Journal of Psychiatry, 136,* 1–25.

Mathews, A. M. (1978). Fear-reduction research and clinical phobias. *Psychological Bulletin, 85,* 390–404.

Mavissakalian, M., Turner, S. M., Michelson, L., & Jacob, R. (1985). Tricyclic antidepressants in obsessive–compulsive disorders: Antiobsessional or antidepressant agents? *American Journal of Psychiatry, 142,* 572–576.

McFall, M. E., & Wollersheim, J. P. (1979). Obsessive–compulsive neurosis: A cognitive behavioral formulation and approach to treatment. *Cognitive Therapy and Research, 3,* 333–348.

Mellet, P. G. (1974). The clinical problem. In H. R. Beech (Ed.), *Obsessional states.* London: Methuen.

Meyer, V., Levy, R., & Schnurer, A. (1974). A behavioral treatment of obsessive–compulsive disorders. In H. R. Beech (Ed.), *Obsessional states.* London: Methuen.

Montgomery, S. A. (1980). Clomipramine in obsessional neurosis: A placebo controlled trial. *Pharmaceutical Medicine, 1,* 189–192.

Mowrer, O. A. (1939). Stimulus–response analysis of anxiety and its role as a reinforcing agent. *Psychological Review, 46,* 553–565.

Perse, T. L., Greist, J. H., Jefferson, J. W., Rosenfeld, R., & Dar, R. (in press). Fluvoxamine treatment of obsessive–compulsive disorder. *American Journal of Psychiatry.*

Price, L. H., Goodman, W. K., Charney, D. S., & Heninger, G. R. (1987). Treatment of severe obsessive–compulsive disorder with fluvoxamine. *American Journal of Psychiatry, 144,* 1059–1061.

Rachman, S. (1976). The modification of obsessions: A new formulation. *Behaviour Research and Therapy, 14,* 437–443.

Rachman, S., & Hodgson, R. (1980). *Obsessions and compulsions.* Englewood Cliffs, NJ: Prentice-Hall.

Roper, G., Rachman, S., & Hodgson, R. (1973). An experiment on obsessional checking. *Behaviour Research and Therapy, 11,* 271–277.

Solyom, L., Zamanzadeh, D., Ledwidge, B., & Kenny, K. (1971). Aversion relief treatment of obsessive neurosis. In R. D. Rubin, J. P. Brady, & J. D. Henderson (Eds.), *Advances in behavior therapy.* New York: Academic.

Stampfl, T. G. (1967). Implosive therapy: The theory, the subhuman analogue, the strategy, and the technique—Part I: The theory. In S. G. Armitage (Ed.), *Behavior modification techniques in the treatment of emotional disorders.* Battle Creek, MI: V.A. Publications.

Steketee, G. S., & Foa, E. B. (1985). Behavioral treatment of obsessive–compulsive disorder: A guide for practice. In D. H. Barlow (Ed.), *Clinical handbook of psychological disorders: A step-by-step treatment manual.* New York: Guilford.

Steketee, G. S., Foa, E. B., & Grayson, J. B. (1982). Recent advances in the treatment of obsessive–compulsives. *Archives of General Psychiatry, 39,* 1365–1371.

Thoren, P., Asberg, M., Cronholm, B., Jornestedt, L., & Traskman, L. (1980). Clorimipramine treatment of obsessive–compulsive disorder. *Archives of General Psychiatry, 37,* 1281–1285.

Turner, S. M., Beidel, D. C., & Swami, Nathan, R. (1985). Biological factors in obsessive–compulsive disorders. *Psychological Bulletin, 97,* 430–450.

Turner, S. M., Jacob, R. G., Beidel, D. C., & Himmelhoch, J. (1985). Fluoxetine treatment of obsessive–compulsive disorder. *Journal of Clinical Psychopharmacology, 5,* 207–212.

Volavka, J., Naziroglu, F., & Yaryura-Tobias, J. A. (1985). Clomipramine and imipramine in obsessive–compulsive disorder. *Psychiatry Research, 14,* 85–93.

Walton, D., & Mather, M. D. (1963). The application of learning principle to the treatment of obsessive–compulsive states in the acute and chronic phases of illness. *Behaviour Research and Therapy, 1,* 163–174.

Wolpe, J. (1964). Behaviour therapy in complex neurotic states. *British Journal of Psychiatry, 110,* 28–34.

Wyndowe, J., Solyom, L., & Ananth, J. (1975). Anafranil in obsessive–compulsive neurosis. *Current Therapeutic Research, 18,* 611–617.

Pharmacotherapy

KERRIN WHITE AND JONATHAN O. COLE

CONCEPTUALIZATION OF THE DISORDER

Obsessive–compulsive disorder (OCD), as defined by the American Psychiatric Association (1980, 1987), means that the patient so diagnosed suffers from either obsessions or compulsions (or both) that cause significant distress or impairment. *Obsessions* are defined as recurrent and persistent ideas, thoughts, images, or impulses that are experienced by the patient as part of his or her own mind (i.e., not thought insertions), yet also as intrusive, unwanted, senseless, or repugnant, and which the patient attempts to ignore, suppress, or neutralize in some way. Though not a requirement of these diagnostic criteria, obsessions generally give rise to anxiety, which compulsions often reduce. *Compulsions* are defined as repetitive, seemingly purposeful or intentional behaviors that meet three criteria: (a) the behaviors are not pleasurable in themselves (i.e., unlike eating, drinking, or sexual intercourse); (2) they are designed to neutralize or prevent some feared event; yet (3) they are recognized by the patient as being excessive or unreasonable.

In the 1980s, there has been some change in diagnostic practice with respect to the relationship of OCD to other disorders. Previously, many patients with obsessions or compulsions would be excluded from a diagnosis of OCD by the concurrent presence of another diagnosis, such as schizophrenia, Tourette's syndrome, or major depression. Now, such patients may receive concurrent diagnoses of OCD. On the other hand, the additional diagnosis of OCD is not applied where the content of obsessions and compulsions is entirely related to another concurrent Axis I disorder. For example, a patient with an eating disorder who is obsessed with weight and food and has many eating and exercising rituals would not receive a diagnosis of OCD unless there were also significant obsessive–compulsive symptoms unrelated to the eating disorder, such as cleaning rituals.

Although the presence of either obsessions or compulsions alone is sufficient to make a diagnosis of the disorder, often both types of symptoms coexist and interrelate, in that the obsessive thoughts (for example, that one's hands are contaminated with dangerous germs) raise anxiety, which leads to and is reduced by the compulsive behavior (such as washing one's hands). This example represents one of the more common manifestations of OCD: obsessive concerns with dirt, germs, toxins, or other contaminants, coupled with compulsive cleaning.

There are other common forms of this disorder. A person who obsessively doubts that something important has been done in a satisfactory way—such as turning off the stove or locking the door—may compulsively check and recheck to make sure this is done properly. Another may feel a need for things to be arranged or done in a certain manner or order, sometimes requiring a kind of symmetry or a specific number of repetitions, often coupled with obsessive feelings that the arrangements or actions are otherwise just not right. As yet another example, hoarders cannot throw away—or go out of their way to collect—useless objects, even garbage and dustballs, which come to fill their homes, sometimes coupled with the obsessive concern that these things "might be needed," although no reasonable need is apparent.

Obsessive thoughts may occur without compulsive behaviors. One such manifestation may be the experience of violent impulses or images, usually in the absence of angry feelings or intent; such experiences can be horrifying to the patient. On the other hand, certain entirely mental phenomena, such as silent counting or praying, may have the anxiety-reducing characteristics of compulsions and therefore be described as "cognitive compulsions" rather than obsessions.

Compulsive behaviors generally occupy a considerable amount of time, and they thereby cause delays in getting other things done. There is also a well-recognized but apparently uncommon form of OCD in which the patient does many ordinary things, such as eating or dressing, in such a slow, careful way that these take inordinate amounts of time and preclude accomplishing much else.

Unfortunately, the usual practice of describing OCD in terms of the common groups of cleaners, checkers, hoarders, and so on fails to represent the wide range of idiosyncratic manifestations that OCD can assume and may hinder the clinician in recognizing some less typical forms. For example, one patient may slap herself when anxious; another prays to pictures that he recognizes as lacking any religious significance; another is obliged to drink all liquids through a straw lest her teeth be stained; another feels he has expressed himself incorrectly, so keeps repeating sentences; another becomes preoccupied with an inchoate idea about "feminine hygiene commercials"; another finds himself mentally rearranging letters in certain words whenever he reads them. This listing of variegated manifestations could go on and on. It suggests issues concerning the relationship of OCD to other disorders that have many similarities to OCD, though they are given different labels— such as kleptomania, trichotillomania (compulsive pulling out of own hair), monosymptomatic hypochondriasis, and body dysmorphic disorder (the excessive concern that a part of one's body might be deformed).

For a long time, OCD was thought to be quite a rare disorder, affecting as little as 0.05% of the population in general and less than 1% of individuals actually in psychiatric treatment (Coryell, 1981; Nemiah, 1980; Rasmussen & Tsuang, 1984). In contrast, recent research has shown it to affect 1–2% of the general population and to represent the fourth or fifth most common psychiatric disorder (Myers et al., 1984). How could the psychiatric community have so drastically underestimated its prevalence?

OCD patients are typically embarrassed by or ashamed of their symptoms, which often seem to reflect either a defect in self-control or an irrationality that the sufferers are still rational enough to appreciate as such. Sometimes, the content of OC symptoms (such as violent thoughts) are socially unacceptable. For such reasons, the OCD patient may attempt to conceal symptoms. Furthermore, because the typical case of OCD is not incapacitating, the patient is able to continue functioning at work, and there is rarely a dramatic event, such as a suicide attempt or an act of violence to draw outside attention to the patient, so such secretiveness may succeed in keeping the disorder unknown even to those close to the sufferer. With conventional psychotherapy and many drugs that are in common use seeming ineffective, it is only recently that the development of behavior therapy and specific antiobsessional drugs has drawn public attention to the likelihood of effective treatment that will draw into treatment patients who might otherwise be reluctant. Finally, relinquishing the hierarchical subordination of OCD to other diagnoses (particularly depression) and recognizing its potential manifestation in forms now labeled differently (e.g., as impulse control disorders) may lead to a still higher prevalence of OCD.

DIAGNOSTIC ISSUES AND PROBLEMS

Even in the research literature, there is frequently confusion between OCD and compulsive personality disorder (or compulsive personality traits), sometimes leaving uncertainty as to which type of patient was treated. The distinction is often made on the basis of OCD symptoms being ego-dystonic—experienced by the individual as being repugnant and resisted—versus compulsive traits being ego-syntonic. However, a listing of compulsive traits includes several (such as emotional coldness) that bear little resemblance to the symptoms of OCD. There may be greater than chance association of OCD with compulsive personality, but even this remains controversial, and OCD can clearly arise in patients without compulsive personalities (Insel, 1982; Lewis, 1936; Solyom, Ledwidge, & Solyom, 1986).

OCD is not generally thought of as a psychotic disorder, but patients with OCD may appear psychotic for various reasons. A small percentage of schizophrenics have obsessions and compulsions, which may coexist with their more typical delusions and hallucinations (Fenton & McGlashan, 1986; Stroebel, Szarek, & Glueck, 1984; Rasmussen & Tsuang, 1986). Patients with schizotypal personality disorder may also develop OCD (Jenike, Baer, Minichiello, Schwartz, & Carey, 1986) with associated features of psychotic character. The line between obsession and delusion may become unclear even in typical OCD when patients lose insight into and resistance against some of their symptoms, thereby developing what might be called "OCD with psychotic features" (Insel & Akiskal, 1986). Further, the presence of overvalued ideation may add to confusion about where obsessions leave off and delusions begin. Finally, some patients with particularly bizarre but typically ego-dystonic OCD symptoms may be misdiagnosed as psychotic; for example, intrusive thoughts characterized by the patient as "inner voices" may be misidentified as hallucinations, or the verbal perseveration sometimes seen with OCD may be mistaken for the formal thought disorder of schizophrenics.

OCD commonly coexists with depression (Insel, Gillin, Moore, Mendelson, Loewenstein, & Murphy, 1982; Rasmussen & Tsuang, 1986; Turner, Beidel, & Nathan, 1985) but also shows distinctive features of phenomenology, time course, epidemiology, family history, and specific treatment response. For example, OCD is typically chronic, though fluctuating in severity over time, whereas depression is more episodic; and sex distribution is even in OCD but weighted toward females in depression (Jenike, 1983; Rasmussen & Tsuang, 1984). Where depression predominates, OCD may be overlooked, or dis-

counted as merely secondary; on the other hand, many depressed patients may engage in ruminative thinking, characteristically a voluntary though excessive brooding on issues of real concern, which may be mislabeled as obsessions.

OCD is classified in DSM-III-R as an anxiety disorder, and anxiety commonly occurs in association with obsessions and plays a key role in the behavioral theory of compulsive behavior. Panic disorder and OCD may clearly coexist (Mellman & Uhde, 1987; Rasmussen & Tsuang, 1984, 1986). OCD patients may exhibit phobic avoidance of situations, such as "contaminated" places, which trigger their obsessive–compulsive symptoms. A subgroup of OCD patients may be described as "germ phobics," though the ubiquity of the feared stimuli creates a situation distinct from that of most phobics. Another subgroup with obsessions related to excretory functions (Jenike, Vitagliano, Rabinowitz, Goff, & Baer, 1987) may overlap with that of social phobics, who avoid using public bathrooms. Posttraumatic stress disorder, also characterized by prominent anxiety, may involve an apparent obsession with the traumatic event, which does not by itself add a second diagnosis of OCD. However, the exact relationship between OCD and other anxiety disorders remains to be elucidated, and many patients will require more than one diagnosis in this category.

Tourette's syndrome, previously a basis for excluding the diagnosis of OCD, appears commonly associated with OCD, both within individuals and within families (Bodkin & White, 1989; Cummings & Frankel, 1985; Pauls & Leckman, 1986; Pitman, Green, Jenike, & Mesulam, 1987; Rasmussen & Tsuang, 1984). Also, tics are distinguished from compulsions as being without volitional or intentional character, but the distinction may not always be so easily made.

In contradiction to current diagnostic practices, OCD may actually encompass disorders now diagnosed otherwise. There are many features of eating disorders that resemble OCD; although DSM-III-R explicitly separates the two, without such a specific diagnostic directive, many patients with eating disorders (especially anorexics, but even some bulimics who seem to gain no pleasure from their binge-eating) might be viewed as having a subtype of OCD. The same observation may apply to some impulse control disorders, such as kleptomania and trichotillomania. Certain individuals labeled as sexual deviates may repetitively engage in unacceptable behavior with sexual elements (such as masochistic self-abuse) without obtaining sexual gratification or even arousal, and they present a picture closer to OCD than to a sexual disorder. Certain somatoform disorders, particularly those often referred to as body dysmorphic disorder and monosymptomatic hypochondriasis, seem diagnosable as OCD even within the strictures of DSM-III-R; an obsession with fear of having AIDS is an especially current manifestation.

TREATMENT STRATEGIES

At this time, the most researched pharmacotherapeutic approach to OCD involves drugs we generally group as antidepressants. Table 15.1 lists 18 double-blind, reasonably well-controlled studies of antidepressants in OCD, along with the general sense of their results.

The majority of these studies involve clomipramine (CMI, Anafranil), a tricyclic antidepressant (TCA) available on the world market for two decades but only now becoming clinically available in the United States. All studies comparing CMI with placebo have shown an advantage for CMI in alleviating specific OC symptoms. In addition to the published and listed studies, a large, multicenter comparison of CMI and placebo involving about 600 patients has been completed, yielding clearly positive results. Similar large studies of fluvoxamine and sertraline are under way, and a multicenter study of fluoxetine in OCD is soon to begin; none of these are listed in Table 15.1.

Many of the listed studies have examined the antiobsessional effects of other antidepressants— imipramine (IMI), desipramine (DMI), amitriptyline (AMI), nortriptyline (NT), clorgyline, zimelidine, mianserin, and fluvoxamine. Of these, only IMI, DMI, and fluvoxamine have been subject to more than one controlled study in OCD. All seven studies with IMI or DMI have yielded disappointing results in comparing these drugs with CMI, zimelidine, or even placebo. Similarly negative are results of the single studies examining AMI and NT. However, most studies involving TCAs other than CMI have been small in size and do not add up to convincing proof of ineffectiveness. On the other hand, evidence for the effectiveness of CMI has been consistent, and several comparisons of CMI with other antidepressants have almost all found CMI superior.

If the implication is correct that CMI works better than other TCAs that are structurally quite similar to CMI, an important question is why? The answer most often advanced has been that CMI has greater potency in inhibiting specific neuronal reuptake of serotonin (versus other neurotransmitters such as norepinephrine and dopamine) than other TCAs, and that there is other evidence to suggest a defect in serotonergic function in OCD. This serotonin hypothesis of OCD remains a speculation, but it has generated interest in the antiobsessional potential of other, newer drugs that are not TCAs but that have potent and specific serotonin-reuptake-inhibiting properties. Such drugs include fluvoxamine, fluoxetine, and sertraline. So far, only fluvoxamine has been reported consistently effective in repeated controlled studies. Open trials of fluoxetine have been encouraging, but a single unpublished controlled study was disappointing. Preliminary results from an initial controlled study of sertraline are reported to show favorable trends. So at this time, one might say that the group of serotonin-reuptake-inhibitor antidepressants has shown the most promise and has certainly evoked the most research interest for the treatment of OCD. This assertion must, however, be viewed as tentative and possibly an artifact of the limited range of drugs that have been subjected to controlled research.

Nevertheless, until more research accumulates on other drugs, CMI must be regarded as the standard of pharmacotherapy for OCD, and the more specific serotonin reuptake inhibitors may be its likeliest successors, possibly preferable to CMI for their lower side-effect profiles. It is worthwhile to examine in greater detail the nature of CMI therapeutic effects and the issues that have been raised, as a model for assessing treatment with other drugs.

One issue is the fact that, as mentioned, many OCD patients are also depressed. Is it possible that

TABLE 15.1.   Controlled Studies of Antidepressants in the Treatment of Obsessive–Compulsive Disorder

Studies	N	Design
Marks et al. (1980)	40	2 x 2 factorial; CMI vs. PBO (random, double-blind) and exposure vs. relaxation
Montgomery (1980)	14	Double-blind crossover
Thoren et al. (1980)	24	Double-blind, 3 parallel treatement groups, randomized
Jaskari (1980)	27	Double-blind, 3 parallel treatment groups, randomized
Ananth et al. (1981)	17	Double-blind, 2 parallel treatment groups, randomized
Insel et al. (1983b)	13	Double-blind, randomized, crossover (PBO/CMI/CLG/PBO or PBO/CLG/CMI/PBO)
Mavissakalian and Michelson (1983)	8	Double-blind, 2 parallel treatment groups, randomized
Prasad (1984a)	6	Double-blind, 2 parallel treatment groups, randomized
Insel et al. (1985a)	13	Double-blind, parallel comparison (ZMD vs. DMI) then sequential (CMI)
Mavissakalian et al. (1985)	12	Double-blind, 2 parallel treatment groups, randomized
Volavka et al. (1985)	16	Double-blind, 2 parallel treatment
Flament et al. (1985b)	19	Double-blind, crossover, children only
Zohar and Insel (1987)	10	Double-blind, crossover
Foa et al. (1987)	37	Double-blind, 2 parallel treatment groups, balanced for high vs. low depression
Perse et al. (1987)	16	Double-blind, randomized, crossover
Cottraux et al. (1988)	44	Double-blind, randomized, 3 parallel treatment groups; AntiEXP + FVX, DXF + FVX, EXP + PBO
Goodman et al. (1988)	42	Double-blind, 2 parallel treatment groups, randomized
Leonard et al. (1988)	21	Double-blind crossover with single-blind PBO lead-in; adolescents

Drugs compared (average/maximum dose)[a]	Treatment (Tx) duration weeks	Effects on OC symptoms (Sx)	Effects on depression	OC–depression relationship
CMI (145–183 mg) PBO	36	CMI > PBO EXP > RLX	CMI > PBO EPX = RLX	CMI effective only with the more depressed patients
CMI (75 mg) PBO	4	CMI > PBO	CMI = PVO	Nondepresed patients only
CMI (150 mg) NT (150 mg) PBO	5	CMI > PBO NI = PBO	CMI > PBO NT = PBO	Few depressed, outcome unrelated
CMI (150 mg) MIAN (60 mg) PBO	4	No statistical analyses Ooverall, MIAN = CMI > PBO	No analysis available	
CMI (150 mg) AMI (197 mg)	4	CMI > AMI	CMI > AMI	OC/depression improvement unrelated
CMI (236 mg) CLG (30 mg) PBO	6 (CMI/CLG) 4 (PBO)	CMI > PBO CLG = PBO	CMI > PBO CLG = PBO	Depression unnecessary for OC sx improvement
CMI (170 mg) IMI (250 mg)	12	CMI = IMI	CMI = IMI	Responders were more depressed
IMI (?) ZMD (?)	4	ZMD > IMI	ZMD > IMI	No analysis
ZMD (280 mg) DMI (275 mg) CMI (258 mg)	5	CMI > ZMD = DMI	CMI > ZMD = DMI	No analysis
CMI (228 mg) PBO	12	CMI > PBO	CMI > PBO	OC–depression improvement separable
CMI (289 mg) IMI (270 mg)	12	CMI > IMI	CMI > IMI	No predictive value of pre-Tx depression
CMI (141 mg) PBO	5	CMI > PBO	CMI = PBO	No predictive value of pre-Tx depression
CMI (235 mg) DMI (290 mg)	6	CMI > DMI	CMI = DMI	No analysis
IMI (233 mg) PBO	6	IMI = PBO	IMI > PBO	Depressed patients on IMI did better only on "main fear"
FVX (300 mg) PBO	8	FVX > PBO	FVX > PBO	No predictive value of pre-Tx depression
FVX (300 mg) PBO	23	FVX > PBO	FVX > PBO	No predicitve value of pre-Tx depression
FVX (255 mg) PBO	6–8	FVX > PBO	FVX > PBO	No predictive value of pre-Tx depression
DMI (152 mg) DMI (158 mg) PBO	5	CMI > DMI	CMI > DMI	No analysis

[a]CMI = Clomipramine (Anafranil); IMI = imipramine; CLG = clorgyline; ZMD = zimelidine; FVX = fluvoxamine; NT = nortriptyline; AMI = amitriptyline; MIAN = mianserin; DMI = desipramine; PBO = placebo; EXP = exposure therapy; AntiEXP = antiexposure instructions; RLX = relaxation training; Tx = treatment; Sx = symptom.

improvement in these patients represents only a secondary consequence of antidepressant effects? This hypothesis has been promoted by Marks and associates (Marks, Stern, Mawson, Cobb, & McDonald, 1980), who found that, when they separated from the 40 OCD patients in their double-blind, placebo-controlled study of CMI the 10 least and the 10 most depressed, only the latter showed a significant drug–placebo advantage. However, their study involved an intervening period of behavior therapy, which may have complicated the drug effects. Many subsequent researchers have addressed the same issue in their studies, and with the exception of one small study (Mavissakalian & Michelson, 1983), most have failed to corroborate Marks's finding (Ananth, Pecknold, Van Den Steen, & Engelsmann, 1981; Cottraux, Nury, Mollard, Bouvard, & Sluys, 1988; Flament et al., 1985a, 1985b; Goodman et al., 1988; Insel et al., 1983b; Mavissakalian, Turner, Michelson, & Jacob, 1985; Montgomery, 1980; Perse, Greist, Jefferson, Rosenfeld, & Dar, 1987; Thoren, Asberg, Cronholm, Jornestedt, & Traskman, 1980; Volavka, Neziroglu, & Yaryura-Tobias, 1985).

Specifically, these studies have shown that antiobsessional efficacy of CMI does not depend on pretreatment levels of depression. Furthermore, it has been shown (Foa, Steketee, Kozak, & Dugger, 1987) that IMI, unlike CMI, has antidepressant effects in OCD patients without significant antiobsessional effects, providing further evidence that these two kinds of effects are separable.

Another issue is the extent of change to be expected with effective pharmacotherapy for OCD. Unlike the situation with affective disorders, OCD tends to respond only partially, typically with a 30–60% symptom reduction, and OCD patients tend to remain chronically symptomatic to some degree despite the best of treatment. Nevertheless, patients often experience this degree of improvement as quite significant. One distinguishing characteristic of OCD seems to be a relatively low rate of placebo response, typically on the order of 10%, which makes even limited active drug response easier to identify. There is also an impression that, in contrast to depressed patients, OCD patients may take longer to respond to drugs and may require higher dosages; this is not

well proven, and comparisons of CMI with placebo in OCD have yielded significant results with as little as 4 weeks of treatment and as little as 75 mg/day of CMI. But to demonstrate full effects (or lack of effect), clinical use of CMI and other serotonin reuptake inhibitors should probably allow at least 10 to 12 weeks and employ the maximum dosage tolerated (up to 250 mg/day, in the case of CMI).

Consistent with the chronicity typical of the natural course of OCD, there are frequent reports of relapse (which usually manifests as symptom increase rather than as recurrence) within a few weeks after discontinuation of effective pharmacotherapy (Flament et al., 1985a, 1985b; Insel et al., 1984; Leonard, Swedo, Rapoport, Coffey, & Cheslow, 1988; Marks et al., 1980; Pato, Zohar, Kadouch, Zohar, & Murphy, 1988; Thoren et al., 1980; Yaryura-Tobias, Neziroglu, & Bergman, 1976). Behavior therapy that accompanies pharmacotherapy may increase the extent of symptom reduction and enhance the persistence of improvement after treatment discontinuation. However, many patients may not be susceptible to this modality, especially (a) those who remain quite depressed, (b) those with only obsessions without associated compulsions, and (c) those who are reluctant to engage in the often stressful process of exposure to feared situations with prevention of the obsessional response.

Diagnoses present another issue in prognosis and drug choice. Early studies (e.g., Karabanow, 1977) sometimes mixed OCD with other disorders such as phobias, or they left it unclear whether a distinction had been made between OCD and compulsive personality traits. The latter distinction certainly should be made because it is clear that the two disorders often occur separately, and there is little evidence for beneficial drug effects on the personality disorder. Concurrent diagnoses of schizophrenia or schizotypal personality disorder seem also to substantially worsen the prognosis for pharmacotherapy of OCD (Fenton & McGlashan, 1986; Jenike et al., 1986; Stroebel, Szarek, & Glueck, 1984) and they may require other or additional treatment, such as neuroleptic medications or social skills training, so these patients should probably be considered separately as well.

It is noteworthy that childhood and adolescent

OCD, reported to be phenomenologically quite similar to adult OCD, has also been shown responsive to CMI and relatively unresponsive to DMI (Flament et al., 1985a, b; Leonard et al., 1988). Although so far unreported in any study, other serotonin reuptake inhibitors might be considered for this age group as well.

One question that remains unresolved is whether sufficient evidence for antiobsessional effectiveness of other TCAs besides CMI exists to warrant their clinical use for OCD. Because many OCD patients are depressed, and standard TCAs seem to work at least for their depression (Foa et al., 1987), many will receive such drugs, and individual treatment response histories may make clear whether such TCAs have had antiobsessional effects on given patients. Certainly, controlled studies fail to substantiate antiobsessional effects of any TCAs except CMI, but here the body of research is quite limited, with only three placebo-controlled studies of such TCAs (NT, IMI, DMI)—all negative. In various studies of these TCAs (Ananth et al., 1981; Foa et al., 1987; Leonard et al., 1988; Mavissakalian & Michelson, 1983; Prasad, 1984a; Thoren et al., 1980; Volavka et al., 1985), specific OC symptom improvement has ranged from 0% to 36% reduction from baseline levels.

Where there is insufficient data from controlled trials to judge the effectiveness of a given treatment, it is usual to look to the results of uncontrolled clinical experience for further evidence. Such a search of case reports on efficacy of TCAs other than CMI in OCD yields surprisingly few that are at all convincing. Some (Freed, Kerr, & Roth, 1972; Hussain & Ahad, 1970) lack essential details both about concomitant other treatments and about the nature of improvement reported, whether specifically in OC symptomatology or not. Some cases (Bartucci, Stewart, & Kemph, 1987; Gordon & Rasmussen, 1988; Jenike, Armentano, & Baer, 1987; Jenike et al., 1987; Pies, 1984) are atypical with respect to phenomenology or course, or they are questionable as to diagnosis. Only a few reports seem to document convincingly dramatic response of typical OCD to TCAs such as AMI (Snyder, 1980), IMI, or doxepin (Jenike et al., 1987). A series of 13 cases treated with doxepin (Ananth, Solyom, Solyom, & Sookin, 1975) described 9 (69%) as moderately improved, with OC symptoms decreased 36%. In retrospect, however, doxepin appeared to have meager effects when compared to a similar study by the same group of treatment with CMI (Ananth & Van Den Steen, 1977; Ananth, Solyom, Bryntwek, & Krishnappa, 1979). Outside of the English-speaking literature, other case report material exists (e.g., Gattuso & Coaciuri, 1964; Guyotat, Marin, Dubor, Bonhomme, & Rozier, 1960), but it is difficult to assess.

This negative appraisal of TCA effects in OCD does not apply to other, nontricyclic antidepressants with particularly strong effects upon serotonergic function. The best-established antiobsessional agents among these at present is fluvoxamine, a highly specific inhibitor of serotonin reuptake. Three double-blind comparisons with placebo (Cottraux et al., 1988; Goodman et al., 1988; Perse et al., 1987), and one partially blinded trial (Price, Goodman, Charney, Rasmussen, & Heninger, 1987) now support its efficacy in OCD. Comparisons with CMI have yet to be reported, but improvement in 43–81% of patients treated in various studies of fluvoxamine (with symptom reductions ranging from 23 to 69% on various OC scales) suggest that antiobsessional effects may be comparable to CMI. The advantage of fluvoxamine, if any, would seem to lie in its lower spectrum of side effects, particularly in the relative absence of anticholinergic and hypotensive effects, which are prevalent with CMI. Though available in some countries, this drug seems likely to remain investigational in the United States for several years, as does another serotonin reuptake inhibitor antidepressant, sertraline, which has been less studied in OCD but is also promising. At the time of writing, CMI remains an investigational drug in the U.S., though the pharmaceutical company has embarked on a program to make it available to practitioners willing to comply with the extensive paperwork and restrictions on other treatment required for its use; when it does become freely available on the American market, it will probably become the standard pharmacotherapy for OCD, although many patients may find its side effects difficult to tolerate.

A serotonin reuptake inhibitor neuropharmacologically similar (though chemically dissimilar) to fluvoxamine, which is already available in the U.S., is fluoxetine (Prozac). Unfortunately, this drug has received considerably less study than CMI or fluvoxamine for OCD. Two small, open clinical trials (Fontaine & Chouinard, 1986; Turner, Jacob, Beidel, & Himmelhoch, 1985) do suggest its effectiveness, but the only placebo-controlled study to date, still unpublished and methodologically flawed, was largely negative. One case report (White, Keck, & Lipinski, 1986) suggested that CMI, fluoxetine, and another serotonin reuptake inhibitor, citalopram, had similar effects on a single patient, who responded to all three with suppression of OC symptoms concurrent with manic reactions.

Further evidence that researchers may be on the right track with serotonin reuptake inhibitors may derive from favorable experience with zimelidine, no longer available due to its association with CNS hypersensitivity reactions. Two small open trials (Fontaine & Chouinard, 1985; Kahn, Westenberg, & Jolles, 1984) and one small double-blind comparison with IMI (Prasad, 1984a) were positive, though another double-blind comparison with DMI (Insel, Mueller, Alterman, Linnoila, & Murphy, 1985a) was not.

Fenfluramine (Pondimin), an anorectic agent with mixed serotonin releasing and reuptake-inhibiting effects, has been reported (Hollander & Liebowitz, 1988) to potentiate the antiobsessional effects of fluvoxamine when given on a daily basis (40 mg/day) in one case, though it proved ineffective as compared to placebo when administered as a single dose to seven OCD patients (Hollender, Fay, Cohen, Campeas, Gorman, & Liebowitz, 1988).

Finally, trazodone (or Desyrel) is often misidentified as a serotonin reuptake inhibitor; it is actually more likely to represent an antagonist of serotonin receptors (Schatzberg, Dessain, O'Neil, Katz, & Cole, 1987) and has been persuasively reported as effective in some open trials (Baxter, 1985; Kim, 1987; Lydiard, 1986; Prasad, 1984b, Prasad, 1985). There is, however, a negative report on its effectiveness in combination with L-tryptophan (Mattes, 1986). Mianserin, another serotonin receptor antagonist available in Europe but not the United States, has been reported as being both moderately effective in one open trial (Vaisanen, Ranta, Nummikko-Pelkonen, & Tienari, 1977) and comparable to CMI in an incomplete double-blind trial (Jaskari, 1980).

Yet another approach to manipulating serotonin systems, the serotonin precursor L-tryptophan, was reported to be somewhat effective in an unconvincing series of seven cases (Yaryura-Tobias & Bhavagan, 1977) and in a single case report (Rasmussen, 1984), but it proved disappointing when used in combination with trazodone (Mattes, 1986).

At this point, the likeliest pharmacotherapeutic strategy for treating OCD seems to involve the so-called serotonergic antidepressants, above all CMI, but also fluvoxamine. Trazodone may also be worth trying. Fluoxetine needs further study in OCD, but the ready availability of this serotonin reuptake inhibitor on the American market may give it extensive usage for this purpose even before supportive data from controlled research is available. In addition, though fluoxetine can cause its own troublesome side effects—particularly gastrointestinal distress and transient increases in anxiety or insomnia—it probably has side-effect advantages over CMI that will encourage its use even after CMI becomes freely available on the American market. For these reasons, the following case example involves the use of fluoxetine.

Case Illustration

A 35-year-old Catholic woman, a legal secretary now on maternity leave with her first baby, was referred from her psychotherapist with a chief complaint of "excessive handwashing, associated with fear of glass and other contaminants." Her husband, a manager of his own printing company, accompanied her and brought along their baby, whom he appeared to be in charge of.

Her obsessive–compulsive symptoms had started about 8 years earlier, when she developed a fear of having "done something terribly wrong which was nothing," but which she nevertheless refused to specify. She went to confession about this a few times, but she continued feeling guilty.

About a year later, the focus of her symptomatology changed. After breaking a glass pitcher, she feared that undetected slivers of glass had gotten on her hands and might then get into food that she prepared, endangering herself and others who might ingest them. Washing her hands made her feel less anxious, but every time she touched something that she might have touched prior to washing, and every time she picked up a glass with a nick on it, she felt contaminated again. She washed her hands to the point of rawness. She began avoiding certain surfaces, such as cabinets and files, which would leave her feeling contaminated on touching them. If she had to touch them, she would make a point of cleaning the area first, but then had to be careful to "do it right" when cleaning, so this became a big production. Furthermore, her husband insisted on using these areas, which she felt spread the contamination further.

Her husband noted that the nature of the contaminant of concern would change from time to time, focusing alternately on battery acid, herpes virus, insecticide, and so on—all generally associated with the fear that someone would ingest them.

For several years, she obtained counseling from various sources without benefit. Then 3 years prior, at the time of her marriage, she began cognitive therapy with a psychologist and pharmacotherapy with a psychiatrist, who prescribed NT up to 125 mg/day for several months. She felt this medication reduced her anxiety but not her compulsive behaviors. Trial of higher dosage (150 mg/day) resulted in the limiting side effects of dizziness and confusion. Subsequently stopping NT (but continuing in therapy) in order to get pregnant, she gradually relapsed into a state equivalent to that prior to treatment. Once she delivered, matters worsened, as she experienced heightened concern over danger to her baby.

She felt that her cognitive therapy—which involved writing down descriptions of her compulsive behaviors and anxiety levels and her level of belief in the reality of the dangers, then discussing with her therapist issues of rational and irrational thinking—had been helpful, but she could not specify in what ways. Her cognitive therapist told her to discourage her husband from cooperating with her symptoms, but she never relayed this message to him for fear he would do this even more than he already did without being told!

At the time of presentation for further pharmacotherapy, she denied feeling depressed, described her sleep and appetite as normal, and did not evidence psychomotor agitation or retardation. But she did admit to crying spells, feelings of helplessness and hopelessness in the face of her illness, guilt feelings about her illness, some loss of ability to experience pleasure, low energy, decreased libido, vague suicidal thoughts, and poor concentration, which she attributed to her obsessive thoughts.

At that time, fluoxetine had not yet been approved for widespread clinical use but was available under a humanitarian use protocol for the treatment of OCD. The patient had a lot of anxiety about the prospect of taking an "experimental" drug and required a month to make up her mind to do it. Her husband felt that they were near the end of their 3-year marriage if she did not get better soon, which may have been a factor in her decision to proceed.

She started on 20 mg of fluoxetine each morning and, within the first week, raised the dosage to 60 mg each morning, but she immediately reduced it again to 40 mg when she experienced side effects of increased nervousness, insomnia, nausea, and loss of appetite. She also complained of paresthesias, lightheadedness, and feeling even more depressed and unmotivated than usual. Because her anxiety seemed clearly worse, to the point that active consideration was given to hospitalization, she was also started on alprazolam, initially at 0.25 mg twice during the day and 0.5 mg at bedtime; this regimen helped dramatically, but it left her still anxious just before each scheduled dose, so it was increased to 0.5 mg three times during the day and 1.0 mg at bedtime, which worked quite well.

Within 6 weeks of starting on these medications, she found that her obsessive–compulsive symptoms had decreased. She gave two examples: after cracking a bowl, she wiped the floor, but she did not commence protracted cleaning; and she was able to let her baby ride in the back of her van, where previously she had felt there might be broken glass. Her husband also noted that after he broke a glass, she did not pester him endlessly about it as she usually did, though she did clean the area again, even after he had already done so. Also, he noted that she could now take 5-minute showers when pressed for time instead of her usual 20–25-minute showers, which had made them late for church in the past. At this point, she considered her OCD to have improved about 30% from pretreatment, though her husband thought the improvement a little less.

Meanwhile, the patient had heard about the behavioral techniques of in vivo exposure with response prevention, and she asked her cognitive therapist to undertake this with her at her home, but the therapist refused because of the distances involved. The patient then proposed that her mother could assist in conducting this and asked for literature to serve as a guide. When this was not forthcoming from her therapist, she terminated her cognitive therapy and undertook a form of behavior therapy on her own. Her mother assisted by directing her in person to do problematic behaviors—such as touching "contaminated" surfaces—without washing afterward.

After 2 months of combined pharmacotherapy with fluoxetine (now increased to 80 mg/day) and alprazolam (now reduced to 0.5 mg each morning and 1.0 mg each evening), the patient and her husband agreed that she had progressed further, to about 50% improvement from baseline. After 3 months, improvement had progressed to 70%; after 5 months, 80%. At this point, she began seeing a behavior therapist, and she also reduced her alprazolam dosage further. After 7 months, she noted that she could now easily do things that had once been difficult or impossible for her, such as the laundry or the preparation of baby bottles. She still felt she had difficulty handling real broken glass, but her husband noted that she handled with composure the breaking of a Christmas tree ornament above some presents. She appeared more excitable than usual, talking rapidly and sometimes getting words mixed up, which raised a suspicion of hypomania and resulted in reduction of fluoxetine dosage to 60 mg/day.

By the 10th month, this problem had resolved, and the patient considered her improvement to have reached 85%. Fluoxetine dosage was lowered to 40 mg/day and alprazolam to 1.0 mg at bedtime only. By the end of a year of treatment, the patient had on her own reduced further her doses of fluoxetine, now 20 mg/day, and alprazolam, now 0.5 mg at bedtime, with continued improvement to over 90% from baseline. Her husband agreed with this but noted that she still sometimes sought reassurances from him about such things as whether their son had touched a poisonous plant. She strongly desired another child and therefore requested a trial off all medication, which was approved by her psychiatrist. Two months later, continuing in behavior therapy, she felt that her improvement had "slipped" but only 5–10%, and that she would feel comfortable getting pregnant again if she stayed as well as this for a few more months.

This case has been described in detail not to demonstrate the effectiveness of fluoxetine, because it is possible that concomitant alprazolam and even the patient's self-administered exposure treatment may have played an important role in her improvement, but rather to dem-onstrate some typical features of such cases as seen in clinical practice, where it is usual for more than one therapeutic intervention to proceed concurrently.

This case was typical for its phenomenology—an anxiety-producing "contamination" obsession leading to compulsive handwashing, associated with a variable degree of depression—and for its course, one of years of chronicity (but persisting ability to function, at least at work) despite treatment with a TCA, psychotherapy, and cognitive therapy. Often, these patients become stuck in treatment that is not working; they fear to change it until external circumstances compel them, in this case the aggravating birth of her first child and her husband's threat of divorce.

The increase in anxiety early in treatment is also typical. Reassurance, dosage reduction of fluoxetine, and counteractive pharmacotherapy with a benzodiazepine are often effective in getting through this phase, only after which may antiobsessional effects become apparent. The long delay in improvement and slow progress are typical, as is the end result still short of complete remission even after 1 year of combined pharmacotherapy and behavior therapy. Nevertheless, the results were quite significant and gratifying to patient, husband, and therapist. Unfortunately, also typical is the increase in symptomatology subsequent to drug discontinuation; it is hoped that continued behavior therapy might help to stop this from becoming a full relapse.

ALTERNATIVE TREATMENT OPTIONS

In this chapter, pharmacotherapy with serotonergic antidepressants and behavior therapy involving in vivo exposure with response prevention have been advanced as the most promising treatments for OCD. Despite the status of the best-established antiobsessional drug, CMI, as a tricyclic antidepressant, the group of other TCAs seems to hold less promise, at least for reducing OC symptomatology.

Perhaps the most likely alternative to the serotonergic drug at this point is represented by the monoamine oxidase inhibitors (MAOIs), drugs commonly used as alternatives for the treatment of refractory depression. There are presently no controlled studies of standard MAOIs in the treatment of OCD. The sole study to date (Insel et al.,

1983; Jenike et al., 1987a) involved an atypical MAO$_A$ inhibitor, clorgyline. However, there are many positive case reports (Annesley, 1969; Isberg, 1981; Jain, Swinson, & Thomas, 1970; Jenike, 1981; Jenike et al., 1987a; Jenike, Surman, Cassem, Zusky, & Anderson, 1983; Rihmer, Szanto, Arato, Szabo, & Bagdy, 1982; Swinson, 1984), some of which are substantially more convincing than analogous reports of TCA effects in OCD. For example, Annesley (1969) described a severe, chronically hospitalized, symptomatically typical case that had proven unresponsive to electroconvulsive therapy (ECT), phenothiazines, TCAs, leukotomy, and behavior therapy, then responded rapidly and completely to phenelzine (60 mg/day) combined with chlordiazepoxide (50 mg/day), and thereafter remained in remission over at least 6 months' follow-up.

Jain et al. (1970) described a purely obsessional patient, ill for 12 years and hospitalized nine times, with unsatisfactory response to ECT, phenothiazines, benzodiazepines, TCAs, relaxation therapy, and leukotomy, who responded markedly within 2 weeks of starting phenelzine (45 mg/day) alone and was maintained symptom-free on this drug 4 months later. Isberg (1981) described a chronic case of OCD with panic attacks that responded only minimally to high doses of IMI, then completely to phenelzine (75 mg/day) and maintained this response 1 year later.

There are also case reports of response to tranylcypromine (Jenike, 1981; Swinson, 1984; Jenike et al., 1987a) and nialamide (Rihmer et al., 1982). The absence of controlled study on MAOIs in OCD is understandable in view of the fact that these drugs were nearly abandoned by the early 1970s, before pharmacotherapy of OCD became a subject of interest, and by the time interest in MAOIs was revived, MAOIs had lost commercial research appeal due to expiration of patents and liability concerns. Nevertheless, in the treatment of OCD, as of depression, MAOIs probably deserve an important place when the primary treatment has failed.

Because OCD is classified as an anxiety disorder, the use of antianxiety drugs such as benzodiazepines naturally suggests itself and is often employed. In fact, however, the ubiquity of these drugs in the unsuccessful treatment histories of many OCD patients argues against their effectiveness. Nonetheless, it is possible that anxious OCD patients successfully treated with benzodiazepines, perhaps prescribed by nonpsychiatric physicians, may never come to the attention of academic centers from which they would be likely to get reported. It is also possible that specific benzodiazepines, particularly the newer and less widely used ones, may offer special benefits for OCD patients.

There are some reports, including a few controlled studies, that are presented as showing antiobsessional effects of various benzodiazepines, but for the most part, closer inspection fails to sustain a positive impression. For example, Venkoba Rao (1964) conducted a placebo-controlled 6-week trial of diazepam in 16 patients identified as obsessive–compulsive according to idiosyncratic criteria emphasizing the presence of premorbid obsessive–compulsive personality, with cursory case descriptions—which raise rather than allay doubts about the diagnosis of OCD. Of the eight cases likeliest to represent true OCD, because of the presence of rituals, only two of four improved on diazepam versus one of four on placebo. Orvin (1967) reported a double-blind study in which 24 patients with obsessive–compulsive and phobic reactions were treated for variable durations (1 to 28 weeks, each trial terminated "when a medication had produced its apparent maximum effect"), with single or sequential trials of oxazepam, chlordiazepoxide, and placebo—a confusing design, which makes it difficult to interpret the surprising finding that oxazepam yielded criterion improvement in 68% of trials, versus 13% of chlordiazepoxide trials and 0% of placebo trials. Disparity in therapeutic dosage equivalency between oxazepam (30–60 mg/day) and chlordiazepoxide (30–40 mg/day) may have accounted for the differences in improvement rates, which were based on global assessments rather than any specific measures of OC symptoms, particularly problematic in a study such as this where diagnoses were mixed. A double-blind, 10-center study by Cassano and associates (Cassano, Castrogiovanni, Mauri, Rutigliano, Pirro, Cerrone, et al., 1981) compared 2 months of treatment with (a) CMI alone versus (b) CMI with diazepam versus (c) CMI with haloperidol, and they found that the diazepam–CMI group had a lower dropout rate than the CMI-only group, but it actually improved slightly less on OC measures.

Clinical reports of benzodiazepines in OCD are, for the most part, equally unconvincing. Breitner (1960) reported "good" response in six of seven obsessional patients treated with chlordiazepoxide (used as an investigational drug, before its availability for widespread clinical use), but case vignettes suggested confounding of chlordiazepoxide with other treatments (such as isocarboxazid and ECT) and also an atypical lack of chronicity in some cases. Bethune, Burrell, and Culpan (1964) similarly reported encouraging results with diazepam used for 140 patients with various anxiety disorders, including some with OCD, but they failed to tabulate the OCD cases separately and gave only one example, which might have been alternatively diagnosed as hypochondriasis. In this single case, the beneficial effects of diazepam on the patient's preoccupation with weather affecting her neck and back pain might have been attributable to muscular relaxation. Also lacking in important detail is the passing reference made by Hussain and Ahad (1970) to three OCD patients who improved on high doses of chlordiazepoxide or diazepam. Burrell, Culpan, Newton, Ogg, and Short (1974) reported good effects of bromazepam in 44 (70%) of 63 patients with "obsessive personality traits" and 23 (72%) of 32 with compulsive rituals. However, the four case examples of improvement that were provided include one with compulsive personality traits but no clear OC symptoms, one with phobias, one with spasmodic torticollis, and one with rather modest checking (once or twice) of doors and windows, raising serious question as to how many of their patients really deserved diagnoses of OCD. Buspirone, a nonbenzodiazepine antianxiety agent, appeared quite ineffective in an open 8-week trial with 14 OCD patients, none of whom improved (Jenike & Baer, 1988).

Three exceptions to the unconvincing impressions left by the aforementioned reports on antianxiety agents in OCD are clinical reports of antiobsessional effects with alprazolam (Tesar & Jenike, 1984; Tollefson, 1985) and clonazepam (Bodkin & White, 1989). Because these reports comprise only five cases, further clinical evidence is needed.

Although OCD is not generally considered a psychotic disorder, many OCD patients receive antipsychotic drugs for a variety of reasons—including misdiagnosis, psychotic features to the OCD itself, coexistence of OCD with other disorders (such as schizophrenia or Tourette's syndrome) requiring antipsychotic medication, and severe intractable anxiety refractory to the usual antianxiety drugs. One theory (Cummings & Frankel, 1985) links OCD, Tourette's syndrome, and schizophrenia as all manifestations of dopaminergic hyperactivity, treatable with dopamine-blocking agents.

Nevertheless, there is a conspicuous lack of evidence for antiobsessional efficacy of neuroleptics. Two old studies (Garmany, May, & Folkson, 1954; Trethowan & Scott, 1955) described use of chlorpromazine with mixed groups of neurotic patients, including some with obsessional features. They did not provide details, but they reported generally poor response of OC symptoms to this drug in contrast to better response of other symptoms, such as tension. Hussain and Ahad (1970) and Altschuler (1962) also described disappointing results with neuroleptics in OCD. Rivers-Bulkeley and Hollender (1982) described a good response to loxapine in a patient obsessed with what seems to have represented a delusion that he was being poisoned; he may have been schizophrenic. The only really typical case of OCD described in detail as responding to a neuroleptic (haloperidol at 15 mg/day) was reported by O'Regan (1970). The only controlled study involving a neuroleptic in OCD (Cassano et al., 1981) found the combination of CMI and haloperidol (5 mg/day) *less* effective on OC symptoms than CMI alone. In summary, the evidence for neuroleptic efficacy in OCD is so scanty that the risk of tardive dyskinesia and other side effects would suggest avoiding them entirely or limiting them to brief trial unless clear-cut improvement ensues.

A few cases have been reported in which lithium, either alone (Forssman & Walinder, 1969; Stern & Jenike, 1983; Van Putten & Sanders, 1975) or in combination with a TCA (Eisenberg & Asnis, 1985; Gordon & Rasmussen, 1988; Rasmussen, 1984) seemed to yield significant benefits in OCD. However, two early, small double-blind comparisons of lithium with placebo in OCD

(Geisler & Schou, 1970; Hesso & Thorell, 1970) yielded negative results. Nevertheless, use has been found for a few weeks of trial lithium "augmentation" of a preestablished treatment with a serotonergic antidepressant or an MAOI that has proven insufficiently effective; this use is appealing, due to its ease of administration and its parallel to the better-established practice of lithium augmentation for refractory depression (Heninger, Charney, & Sternberg, 1983).

Other drugs have received even less adequate research and clinical attention for the treatment of OCD. Psychostimulants such as dextroamphetamine (Insel et al., 1983a) and methylphenidate (Joffe & Swinson, 1987b) have been tried mostly as single doses, with limited benefits in a few patients. Yohimbine, an alpha-2-adrenergic antagonist that might be expected to have similar pro-adrenergic effects, proved ineffective in a brief controlled trial (Rasmussen, Goodman, Woods, Heninger, & Charney, 1987).

A contrasting alpha-2-adrenergic agonist, clonidine, was reported to show antiobsessional effects in two trials with a single patient (Knesevich, 1982) and in three cases where it was combined (and confounded) with CMI or flupenthixol (Lipsedge & Prothero, 1987). Cohen, Detlor, Young, and Shaywitz (1980) reported clonidine effective on OC symptoms in the context of Tourette's syndrome. Most encouraging to date is Hollender and associates' (1988) report of substantial (81%) acute reduction of OC symptoms in all of six chronic OCD patients given intravenous clonidine, though this effect may be transient.

A double-blind, placebo-controlled study (Insel & Pickar, 1983) of intravenous naloxone (an opiate antagonist) in two chronic OCD patients yielded a significant exacerbation of obsessional doubts. This seems to represent the only research attention to date paid to drugs affecting the endogenous opiate system in OCD.

The anticonvulsants have also received little study in OCD. Carbamazepine, a tricyclic drug with mood-stabilizing properties in bipolar disorder, has been reported (Jenike & Brotman, 1984; Joffe & Swinson, 1987a) in a total of 12 OCD patients; the overall results were unimpressive, although two patients apparently received partial benefits. Reference has been made (McElroy, Keck, & Pope, 1987; McElroy & Pope, 1988) to the ineffectiveness of another anticonvulsant, sodium valproate, in two cases of OCD. As previously mentioned, a single case (Bodkin & White, 1989) seems to have shown good antiobsessional effects from the benzodiazepine anticonvulsant clonazepam.

In summary, drugs that have been tried for the treatment of OCD include almost the full spectrum of psychopharmacological agents, but for the most part, the evidence for their effectiveness is very limited. If a serotonergic antidepressant has failed to help a patient, MAOIs seem the most promising alternative, although a brief trial of lithium augmentation with either the original serotonergic drug, the MAOI, or both seems reasonable. Benzodiazepines may often have been tried before the patient even sees a psychiatrist, and they should generally not be considered a major treatment for this disorder, though alprazolam or clonazepam might be distinguished from other benzodiazepines in this regard. Clonidine may deserve clinical trial, and it certainly deserves further research. Neuroleptics should be avoided in nonpsychotic OCD patients, or they should be given only brief trial unless clearly effective. The role of psychostimulants, anticonvulsants, and drugs affecting the endogenous opiate system will require further study before any clinical recommendations can be made.

A final reminder should be made that behavior therapy represents a nonpharmacological treatment of demonstrated efficacy at least equal to pharmacotherapy (Christensen, Hadzi-Pavlovic, Andrews, & Mattick, 1987), and it may readily be combined with pharmacotherapy, at least for OCD patients with compulsive rituals, a fair degree of motivation to change, and the ability to cooperate with the demands of the treatment. For others, pharmacotherapy may remain the mainstay.

REFERENCES

Altschuler, M. (1962). Massive doses of trifluoperazine in the treatment of compulsive rituals. *American Journal of Psychiatry, 119*, 367–368.

American Psychiatric Association. (1980). Diagnostic and statistical manual of mental disorders (3rd ed.). Washington, DC: Author.

American Psychiatric Association. (1987). Diagnostic

and statistical manual of mental disorders (3rd ed., rev.). Washington, DC: Author.

Ananth, J., Pecknold, J. C., Van Den Steen, M., & Engelsmann, F. (1981). Double-blind comparative study of clomipramine and amitriptyline in obsessive neurosis. *Progress in Neuro-Psychopharmacology, 5*, 257–262.

Ananth, J., Solyom, L., Bryntwek, S., & Krishnappa, V. (1979). Chlorimipramine therapy for neurosis. *American Journal of Psychiatry, 136*, 700–701.

Ananth, J., Solyom, L., Solyom, C., & Sookin, D. (1975). Doxepin in the treatment of obsessive compulsive neurosis. *Psychosomatics, 16*, 185–187.

Ananth, J., & Van den Steen, N. (1977). Systematic studies in the treatment of obsessive–compulsive neurosis with tricyclic anti-depressants. *Current Therapeutic Research, 21*, 495–500.

Annesley, P. T. (1969). Nardil response in a chronic obsessive compulsive (letter). *British Journal of Psychiatry, 115*, 748.

Bartucci, R. J., Stewart, J. T., & Kemph, J. P. (1987). Trimipramine in the treatment of obsessive–compulsive disorder (letter). *American Journal of Psychiatry, 144*, 964–965.

Baxter, L. R. (1985). Two cases of obsessive–compulsive disorder with depression responsive to trazodone. *Journal of Nervous and Mental Disease, 73*, 432–433.

Bethune, H. D., Burrell, R. H., & Culpan, R. H. (1964). A new compound in the treatment of severe anxiety states. Report on the use of diazepam. *New Zealand Medical Journal, 63*, 153–156.

Bodkin, A., & White, K. (in presss). Clonazepam in the treatment of obsessive compulsive disorder associated with panic disorder. *Journal of Clinical Psychiatry.*

Breitner, C. (1960). Drug therapy in obsessional states and other psychiatric problems. *Diseases of the Nervous System Supplement, 21*, 31–35.

Burrell, R. H., Culpan, R. H., Newton, K. J., Ogg, G. J., & Short, J. H. W. (1974). Use of bromazepam in obsessional, phobic and related states. *Current Medical Research and Opinion, 2*, 430–436.

Capstick, N. (1971). Chlorimipramine in obsessional states. *Psychosomatics, 12*, 332–335.

Carey, R. J., Baer, L., Jenike, M. A., Minichiello, W. E., Schwartz, C., & Regan, N. J. (1986). MMPI correlates to obsessive–compulsive disorder. *Journal of Clinical Psychiatry, 47*, 371–372.

Cassano, G. B., Castrogiovanni, P., Mauri, M., Rutigliano, G., Pirro, R., Cerone, G., et al. (1981). A mul-

ticenter controlled trial in phobic–obsessive psychoneurosis: The effect of chlorimipramine and of its combinations with haloperidol and diazepam. *Progress in Neuro-psychopharmacology, 5*, 129–138.

Christensen, H., Hadzi-Pavlovic, D., Andrews, G., & Mattick, R. (1987). Behavior therapy and tricyclic medication in the treatment of obsessive–compulsive disorder: A quantitative review. *Journal of Consulting and Clinical Psychology, 55*, 701–711.

Cohen, D. J., Detlor, J., Young, J. G., & Shaywitz, B. A. (1980). Clonidine ameliorates Gilles de la Tourette syndrome. *Archives of General Psychiatry, 37*, 1350–1357.

Collins, G. H. (1973). The use of parenteral and oral chlorimipramine (Anafranil) in the treatment of depressive states. *British Journal of Psychiatry, 122*, 189–190.

Coryell, W. (1981). Obsessive compulsive disorder and primary unipolar depression. *Journal of Nervous and Mental Disease, 169*, 220–224.

Cottraux, J., Nury, A. M., Mollard, E., Bouvard, M., & Sluys, M. (1988). Fluvoxamine and exposure in obsessive–compulsive disorders. Post-test evaluation of a controlled study. *Annual Series of the European Association for Behaviour Therapy.*

Cummings, J. L., & Frankel, M. (1985). Gilles de la Tourette syndrome and the neurologic basis of obsessions and compulsions. *Biological Psychiatry, 20*, 1117–1126.

Fenton, W. S., & McGlashan, T. H. (1986). The prognostic significance of obsessive compulsive symptoms in schizophrenia. *American Journal of Psychiatry, 143*, 437–441.

Flament, M. F., Rapoport, J. L., Berg, C. J., & Kitts, C. (1985a). A controlled trial of clomipramine in childhood obsessive compulsive disorder. *Psychopharmacology Bulletin, 21*, 149–152.

Flament, M. F., Rapoport, J. L., Berg, C., Sceery, W., Kilts, C., Mellstrom, B., & Linnoila, B. (1985a). Clomipramine treatment of childhood obsessive–compulsive disorder. A double-blind controlled study. *Archives of General Psychiatry, 42*, 977–983.

Foa, E. B., Steketee, G., Kozak, M. J., & Dugger, D. (1987). Effects of imipramine on depression and on obsessive–compulsive symptoms. *Psychiatry Research, 21*, 123–136.

Fontaine, R., & Chouinard, G. (1985). Antiobsessive effects of fluoxetine (letter). *American Journal of Psychiatry, 142*, 989.

Fontaine, R., & Chouinard, G. (1986). An open clinical trial of fluoxetine in the treatment of obsessive–

compulsive disorder. *Journal of Clinical Psychopharmacology, 6*, 98–101.

Fontaine, R., Chouinard, G., & Iny, L. (1985). An open clinical trial of zimelidine in the treatment of obsessive compulsive disorder. *Current Therapeutic Research, 37*, 326–332.

Forssman, H., & Walinder, J. (1969). Lithium treatment on atypical indication. *Acta Psychiatrica Scandinavia, 207*(Suppl), 34–40.

Freed, A., Kerr, T. A., & Roth, M. (1972). The treatment of obsessional neurosis (letter). *British Journal of Psychiatry, 120*, 590–591.

Garmany, G., May, A. R., & Folkson, A. (1954). The use and action of chlorpromazine in psychoneuroses. *British Medical Journal, 2*, 439–441.

Gattuso, R., & Coaciuri, V. (1964). L'imipramine nella terapia della nevrosi ossessiva. *Acta Neurologica* (Napoli), *19*, 424–431.

Geisler, A., & Schou, M. (1970). Lithium treatment of obsessive–compulsive neurosis: A double-blind therapeutic trial. *Nord. Psychkiatr. Tidsskrift, 23*, 493–495.

Goodman, W. K., Price, L. H., Rasmussen, S. A., Delgado, P. L., Heninger, G. R., & Charney, D. S. (1988). Efficacy of fluvoxamine in obsessive compulsive disorder: A double-blind comparison with placebo. *Archives of General Psychiatry, 46*, 36–44.

Gordon, A., & Rasmussen, S. A. (1988). Mood-related obsessive–compulsive symptoms in a patient with bipolar affective disorder. *Journal of Clinical Psychiatry, 49*, 27–28.

Guyotat, J., Marin, Dubor, Bonhomme, & Rozier, (1960). L'imipramine en dehors des etats depressits. *Le Journal de Medecine de Lyon, 41*, 367–375.

Heninger, G. R., Charney, D. S., & Sternberg, D. E. (1983). Lithium carbonate augmentation of antidepressant treatment. *Archives of General Psychiatry, 40*, 1335–1342.

Hesso, R., & Thorell, L.-H. (1970). Lithium and obsessive–compulsive neurosis: A double-blind crossover clinical therapeutic pilot trial. *Nord. Psykiatr. Tidsskirft, 23*, 496–499.

Hollender, E., Fay, M., Cohen, B., Campeas, R., Gorman, J. M., & Liebowitz, M. (1988). Serotonergic and noradrenergic sensitivity in obsessive–compulsive disorder: Behavioral findings. *American Journal of Psychiatry, 145*, 1015–1017.

Hollander, E., & Liebowitz, M. R. (1988). Augmentation of antiobsessional treatment with fenfluramine. *American Journal of Psychiatry, 145*, 1314–1315.

Hussain, M. Z., & Ahad, A. (1970). Treatment of obsessive–compulsive neurosis. *Canadian Medical Association Journal, 103*, 648–650.

Insel, T. R. (1982). Obsessive compulsive disorder: Five clinical questions and a suggested approach. *Comprehensive Psychiatry, 23*, 241–251.

Insel, T. R., & Akiskal, H. S. (1986). Obsessive compulsive disorder with psychotic features: A phenomenological analysts. *American Journal of Psychiatry, 143*, 1527–1533.

Insel, T. R., Gillin, C., Moore, A., Mendelson, W. B., Loewenstein, R. J., & Murphy, D. L. (1982). The sleep of patients with obsessive compulsive disorder. *Archives of General Psychiatry, 39*, 1372–1377.

Insel, T. R., Hamilton, J. A., Guttmacher, L. B., & Murphy, D. L. (1983a). D-amphetamine in obsessive–compulsive disorder. *Psychopharmacology, 80*, 231–235.

Insel, T. R., Mueller, E. A., Alterman, I., Linnoila, M., & Murphy, D L. (1985a). Obsessive–compulsive disorder and serotonin: Is there a connection? *Biological Psychiatry, 20*, 174–1188.

Insel, T. R., Murphy, D. L., Cohen, R. M., Alterman, I., Kilts, C., & Linnoila, M. (1983b). Obsessive–compulsive disorder: A double-blind trial of clomipramine and clorgyline. *Archives of General Psychiatry, 40*, 605–612.

Insel, T. R., & Pickar, D. (1983). Naloxone administration in obsessive–compulsive disorder: Report of two cases. *American Journal of Psychiatry, 140*, 1219–1220.

Isberg, R. S. (1981). A comparison of phenelzine and imipramine in an obsessive–compulsive patient. *American Journal of Psychiatry, 138*, 1250–1251.

Jain, V. K., Swinson, R. P., & Thomas, J. G. (1970). Phenelzine in obsessional neurosis (letter). *British Journal of Psychiatry, 117*, 237–238.

Jaskari, M. O. (1980). Observations on mianserin in the treatment of obsessive neuroses. *Current Medical Research and Opinion, 6*, 128–131.

Jenike, M. A. (1981). Rapid response of severe obsessive–compulsive disorder to tranylcypromine. *American Journal of Psychiatry, 138*, 1249–1250.

Jenike, M. A. (1983). Obsessive compulsive disorder. *Comprehensive Psychiatry, 24*, 99–115.

Jenike, M. A., Armentano, M. E., & Baer, L. (1987a). Disabling obsessive thoughts responsive to antidepressants. *Journal of Clinical Psychopharmacology, 7*, 33–35.

Jenike, M. A., & Baer, L. (1988). An open trial of

buspirone in obsessive–compulsive disorder. *American Journal of Psychiatry, 145*, 1285–1286.

Jenike, M. A., Baer, L., Minichiello, W. E., Schwartz, C. E., & Carey, R. J. (1986). Concomitant obsessive compulsive disorder and schizotypal personality disorder. *American Journal of Psychiatry, 143*, 530–532.

Jenike, M. A., & Brotman, A. W. (1984). The EEG in obsessive–compulsive disorder. *Journal of Clinical Psychiatry, 45*, 122–124.

Jenike, M. A., Surman, O. S., Cassem, N. H., Zusky, P., & Anderson, W. H. (1983). Monoamine oxidase inhibitors in obsessive–compulsive disorder. *Journal of Clinical Psychiatry, 44*, 131–132.

Jenike, M. A., Vitagliano, H. L., Rabinowitz, J., Goff, D. C., & Baer, L. (1987b). Bowel obsessions responsive to tricyclic antidepressants in four patients. *American Journal of Psychiatry, 144*, 1347–1348.

Joffe, R. T., & Swinson, R. P. (1987a). Carbamazepine in obsessive–compulsive disorder. *Biological Psychiatry, 22*, 1169–1171.

Joffe, R. T., & Swinson, R. P. (1987b). Methylphenidate in primary obsessive–compulsive disorder. *Journal of Clinical Psychopharmacology, 7*, 420–422.

Kahn, R. S., Westenberg, H. G. M., & Jolles, J. (1984). Zimelidine treatment of obsessive–compulsive disorder. *Acta Psychiatrica Scandinavia, 69*, 259–261.

Karabanow, O. (1977). Double-blind controlled study in phobias and obsessions. *Journal of International Medical Research, 5*, 42–48.

Kim, S. W. (1987). Trazodone in the treatment of obsessive–compulsive disorder. *Journal of Clinical Psychopharmacology, 7*, 278–279.

Knesevich, J. W. (1982). Successful treatment of obsessive–compulsive disorder with clonidine hydrochloride. *American Journal of Psychiatry, 139*, 364–365.

Leonard, H., Swedo, S., Rapoport, J. L., Coffey, M., & Cheslow, D. (1988). Treatment of childhood obsessive–compulsive disorder with clomipramine and desmethylimipramine: A double-blind cross-over comparison. *Psychopharmacology Bulletin, 24*, 93–95.

Lewis, A.. (1936). Problems of obsessional illness. *Proceedings of the Royal Society of Medicine, 29*, 325–336.

Lipsedge, M. S., & Prothero, W. (1987). Clonidine and clomipramine in obsessive–compulsive disorder (letter). *American Journal of Psychiatry, 144*, 965–966.

Lydiard, R. B. (1986). Obsessive–compulsive disorder successfully treated with trazodone. *Psychosomatics, 27*, 858–859.

Marks, I. M., Stern, R. S., Mawson, D., Cobb, J., & McDonald, R. (1980). Clomipramine and exposure for obsessive–compulsive rituals: I. *British Journal of Psychiatry, 136*, 1–25.

Mattes, J. A. (1986). A pilot study of combined trazodone and tryptophan in obsessive–compulsive disorder. *International Clinical Psychopharmacology, 1*, 170–173.

Mavissakalian, M., & Michelson, L. (1983). Tricyclic antidepressants in obsessive–compulsive disorder: Antiobsessional or antidepressant agents? *Journal of Nervous and Mental Disease, 171*, 301–306.

Mavissakalian, M., Turner, S. M., Michelson, L., & Jacob, R. (1985). Tricyclic antidepressants in obsessive–compulsive disorder: II. Antiobsessional or antidepressant agents? *American Journal of Psychiatry, 142*, 572–576.

McElroy, S. L., Keck, P. E., & Pope, H. G., Jr. (1987). Sodium valproate: Its use in primary psychiatric disorders. *Journal of Clinical Psychopharmacology, 7*, 16–24.

McElroy, S. L., & Pope, H. G., Jr. (Eds.). (1988). *Use of anticonvulsants in psychiatry: Recent advances.* Clifton, NJ: Oxford Health Care.

Mellman, T. A., & Uhde, T. W. (1987). Obsessive–compulsive symptoms in panic disorder. *American Journal of Psychiatry, 144*, 1573–1576.

Montgomery, S. A. (1980). Clomipramine in obsessional neurosis: A placebo-controlled trial. *Pharmaceutical Medicine, 1*, 189–192.

Myers, J. K., Weissman, M. M., Tischler, G. L., Holzer, C. E., Leaf, P. J., Gruaschel, H., Anthony, J. C., Boyd, J. H., Burke, J. D., Kramer, M., & Stoltzman, R. (1984). Six-month prevalence of psychiatric disorders in three communities. *Archives of General Psychiatry, 41*, 959–967.

Nemiah, J. C. (1980). Obsessive compulsive disorder. In A. M. Freedman & B. S. Sadock (Eds.), *Comprehensive textbook of psychiatry* (Vol. 3). Baltimore: Williams & Wilkins.

O'Regan, J. B. (1970). Treatment of obsessive–compulsive neurosis with haloperidol. *Canadian Medical Association Journal, 103*, 167–168.

Orvin, G. H. (1967). Treatment of the phobic obsessive–compulsive patient with oxazepam, an improved benzodiazepine compound. *Psychosomatics, 8*, 278–280.

Pato, M. T., Zohar-Kadouch, R., Zohar, J., & Murphy,

D. L. (1988). Return of symptoms after discontinuation of clomipramine in patients with obsessive compulsive disorder. *American Journal of Psychiatry, 145,* 1521–1525.

Pauls, D. K., & Leckman, J. (1986). The inheritance of Gilles de la Tourette's syndrome and associated behaviors. *New England Journal of Medicine, 315,* 993–997.

Perse, T. (1988). Obsessive–compulsive disorder: A treatment review. *Journal of Clinical Psychiatry, 49,* 48–55.

Perse, T. L., Greist, J. H., Jefferson, J. W., Rosenfeld, R., & Dar, R. (1987). Fluvoxamine treatment of obsessive–compulsive disorder. *American Journal of Psychiatry, 144,* 1543–1548.

Pies, R. (1984). Distinguishing obsessional from psychotic phenomena. *Journal of Clinical Psychopharmacology, 4,* 345–347.

Pitman, R. K., Green, R. C., Jenike, M. A., & Mesulam, M. M. (1987). Clinical comparison of Tourette's disorder and obsessive compulsive disorder. *American Journal of Psychiatry, 144,* 1166–1171.

Prasad, A. J. (1984a). A double-blind study of imipramine versus zimelidine in treatment of obsessive compulsive neurosis. *Pharmacopsychiatric, 17,* 61–62.

Prasad, A. J. (1984b). Obsessive–compulsive disorder and trazodone (letter). *American Journal of Psychiatry, 141,* 612–613.

Prasad, A. J. (1985). Efficacy of trazodone as an antiobsessional agent. *Pharmacology Biochemistry and Behavior, 22,* 347–348.

Price, L. H., Goodman, W. K., Charney, D. S., Rasmussen, S. A., & Heninger, G. R. (1987). Treatment of severe obsessive–compulsive disorder with fluvoxamine. *American Journal of Psychiatry, 144,* 1059–1061.

Rasmussen, S. A. (1984). Lithium and tryptophan augmentation in clomipramine-resistant obsessive–compulsive disorder. *American Journal of Psychiatry, 141,* 1283–1285.

Rasmussen, S. A., Goodman, W. K., Woods, S. W., Heninger, G. R., & Charney, D. S. (1987). Effects of yohimbine in obsessive compulsive disorder. *Psychopharmacology, 93,* 308–313.

Rasmussen, S. A., & Tsuang, M. T. (1984). The epidemiology of obsessive compulsive disorder. *Journal of Clinical Psychiatry, 45,* 450–457.

Rasmussen, S. A., & Tsuang, M. T. (1986). Epidemiology and clinical findings of significance to the design of neuropharmacological studies of obsessive

compulsive disorder. *Psychopharmacology Bulletin, 22,* 723–729.

Rihmer, Z., Szanto, K., Arato, M., Szabo, M., & Bagdy, G. (1982). Response of phobic disorders with obsessive symptoms to MAO inhibitors (letter). *American Journal of Psychiatry, 139,* 1374.

Rivers-Bulkeley, N., & Hollender, M. H. (1982). Successful treatment of obsessive–compulsive disorder with loxapine. *American Journal of Psychiatry, 139,* 1345–1346.

Schatzberg, A. F., Dessain, E., O'Neil, P., Katz, D. L., & Cole, J. O. (1987). Recent studies on selective serotonergic antidepressants: Trazodone, fluoxetine, and fluvoxamine. *Journal of Clinical Psychopharmacology, 7,* 44S–49S.

Snyder, S. (1980). Amitriptyline therapy of obsessive–compulsive neurosis. *Journal of Clinical Psychiatry, 41,* 286–289.

Solyom, L., Ledwidge, B., & Solyom, C. (1986). Obsessiveness and adjustment. *Comprehensive Psychiatry, 27,* 234–240.

Sommi, R. W., Crismon, M. L., & Bowden, C. L. (1987). Fluoxetine: A serotonin-specific, second-generation antidepressant. *Pharmacotherapy, 7,* 1–15.

Stern, T. A., & Jenike, M. A. (1983). Treatment of obsessive–compulsive disorder with lithium carbonate. *Psychosomatics, 24,* 671–673.

Stroebel, C. F., Szarek, B. L., & Glueck, B. C. (1984). Use of clomipramine in treatment of obsessive–compulsive symptomatology. *Journal of Clinical Psychopharmacology, 4,* 98–100.

Swinson, R. P. (1984). Response to tranylcypromine and thought stopping in obsessional disorder. *British Journal of Psychiatry, 144,* 425–427.

Tesar, G. E., & Jenike, M. A. (1984). Alprazolam as treatment for a case of obsessive–compulsive disorder. *American Journal of Psychiatry, 141,* 689–690.

Thoren, P., Asberg, M., Cronholm, B., Jornestedt, L., & Traskman, L. (1980). Clomipramine treatment of obsessive–compulsive disorder. I. A controlled clinical trial. *Archives of General Psychiatry, 37,* 1281–1285.

Tollefson, G. (1985). Alprazolam in the treatment of obsessive symptoms. *Journal of Clinical Psychopharmacology, 5,* 39–42.

Towbin, K. E., Leckman, J. F., & Cohen, D. J. (1987). Drug treatment of obsessive–compulsive disorder: A review of findings in the light of diagnostic and metric limitations. *Psychiatric Developments, 1*, 25–50.

Trethowan, W. H., & Scott, P. A. L. (1955). Chlorpromazine in obsessive–compulsive and allied disorders. *Lancet, 1*, 781–785.

Turner, S. M., Beidel, D. C., & Nathan, R. S. (1985). Biological factors in obsessive-compulsive disorders. *Psychopharmacology Bulletin, 97*, 430–450.

Turner, S. M., Jacob, R. G., Beidel, D. C., & Himmelhoch, J. (1985). Fluoxetine treatment of obsessive–compulsive disorder. *Journal of Clinical Psychopharmacology, 5*, 207–212.

Vaisanen, E., Ranta, P., Nummikko-Pelkonen, A., & Tienari, P. (1977). Mianserin hydrochloride (Org GB 94) in the treatment of obsessional states. *Journal of Internal Medicine Research, 5*, 280.

Van Putten, T., & Sanders, D. G. (1975). Lithium in treatment failures. *Journal of Nervous and Mental Disease, 161*, 255–264.

Venkoba Rao, A. (1964). A controlled trial with 'Valium' in obsessive compulsive state. *Journal of Indian Medical Association, 42*, 564–567.

Volavka, J., Neziroglu, F., & Yaryura-Tobias, J. A. (1985). Clomipramine and imipramine in obsessive–compulsive disorder. *Psychiatry Research, 14*, 83–91.

Warnecke, L. B. (1985). Intravenous chlorimipramine in the treatment of obsessional disorder in adolescence: Case report. *Journal of Clinical Psychiatry, 46*, 100–103.

White, K., Keck, P. E., & Lipinski, J. (1986). Serotonin-uptake inhibitors in obsessive–compulsive disorder: A case report. *Comprehensive Psychiatry, 27*, 211–214.

Yaryura-Tobias, J. A., & Bhagavan, H. N. (1977). Ltryptophan in obsessive–compulsive disorders. *American Journal of Psychiatry, 134*, 1298–1299.

Yaryura-Tobias, J. A., Neziroglu, F., & Bergman, L. (1976). Chlorimipramine, for obsessive–compulsive neurosis: An organic approach. *Current Therapeutic Research, 20*, 541–548.

Zohar, J., & Insel, T. R. (1987). Obsessive–compulsive disorder: Psychobiological approaches to diagnosis, treatment, and pathophysiology. *Biological Psychiatry, 22*, 667–687.

Editorial Commentary: Obsessive–Compulsive Disorder

Obsessive–compulsive disorder (OCD) presents one of the most perplexing pictures of any dysfunction discussed in this volume. It is associated with a considerable range of severity. At the mild end, it encompasses idiosyncratic rituals that appear as little more than curious eccentricities, such as rechecking doors and windows. At its extreme, the disorder can be incapacitating, requiring 8–10 hours to perform simple chores, such as washing hands. Many OCDs are misdiagnosed as psychotic because their obsessions appear to be delusional. OCD is often associated with depression, and it has occasionally been viewed as an affective disorder; but treatment outcome data do not support this assumption.

OCD also has a superficial relationship to a number of other disorders that have a ruminative or compulsive quality, including social phobia associated with fear of urinating or eating in public; kleptomania and compulsive gambling; eating disorders, including compulsive dieting, bulimia, and anorexia; extreme, monosymptomatic hypochondriacal fears (e.g., fear of getting cancer or AIDS); and tics, such as Tourette's syndrome and trichotillomania. It is unclear whether some (or all) of these dysfunctions represent subcategories of the core OCD disturbance or whether they simply represent phenomenologically similar conditions. This same question pertains to OCD patients with and without concomitant depression, as well as patients with delusion-like symptoms (overvalued ideators). A related uncertainty is the prevalence of the disorder. It had been thought to be relatively rare: less than 1% of the population. More recent studies make it one of the most widespread anxiety disorders, with a prevalence between 1 and 3%.

There are two primary etiological models for the disorder: biological and behavioral. The former hypothesizes a dysfunction in the serotonin system, which results in decreased availability of serotonin. The problem could be in decreased production, inefficient receptors, or excessive reuptake. The primary evidence for this hypothesis is the differential effectiveness of tricyclic antidepressants that inhibit reuptake, notably clomipramine. The behavioral model posits that obsessions are conditioned anxiety stimuli and that compulsions are maintained by their capacity to reduce anxiety. Foa and Rowan emphasize that the most useful definitions of obsessions and compulsions focus on their ability to increase and decrease anxiety, respectively, in contrast to the traditional distinctions between cognitive or overt behavioral events. The primary support for this position comes from laboratory work demonstrating predicted increases in anxiety when patients are exposed to their phobic object (e.g., dirt), followed by sharp decreases upon performance of the compulsive ritual (e.g., washing, reciting certain sequences of numbers). The behavioral hypothesis also receives indirect support from the effectiveness of behavioral treatment programs.

These two hypotheses have led to the development of the two predominant treatments for OCD: clomipramine and behavior therapy. White and Cole report that clomipramine has differential antiobsessional effects, in contrast to other antidepressants. However, the results seem to be more modest than those achieved with pharmacological treatment of other disorders (e.g., panic, depression). White and Coles conclude that OCD is a difficult disorder to treat, with lower placebo response rates, less symptom reduction, and higher rate of relapse. They note this to be especially the case if the primary symptoms are obsessions rather than compulsions, and if there is substantial depression. Writing from a different perspective, Jenike also suggests that OCD is one of the more difficult disorders to treat. He goes on to suggest that psychodynamic treatment is generally not effective for OCD, and he suggests the use of pharmacotherapy and/or behavior therapy. He advocates psychodynamic treatment for patients with obsessive–compulsive personality. There are few data on treatment of this group with any modality. It is assumed that they are a distinct entity from OCDs, but the overlap between the two disorders is not at all clear.

Foa and Rowan have a more sanguine view of the treatment prospects for OCD. They report success rates of up to 75% with an intensive treatment program consisting of exposure and response prevention. Curiously, White and Cole report lower response rates for pharmacotherapy but argue that OCD is a difficult disorder to treat. Foa and Rowan interpret the same data to mean that pharmacotherapy is not as effective as behavior therapy. Given the similarity of outcome on pharmacological and behavioral treatments for other disorders discussed in this book, this issue requires more careful consideration. It could be two views of the same phenomenon (i.e., Is the glass half full or half empty?). Or it could reflect a

different degree of efficacy. The prototypic argument that behavior therapists see less impaired patients than do pharmacologists does not seem to be the case with OCD; thus, another explanation for the discrepancy must be discerned.

There are some interesting parallels between behavioral and psychodynamic treatments. Jenike emphasizes that treatment for this disorder must be more direct than is often the case for psychodynamic treatment. He also highlights the importance of reeducation to reduce obsessive beliefs about unrealistic dangers (e.g., the risk of contamination from germs), especially when they take the form of overvalued ideation. He also argues that treatment must focus on current issues and behaviors, rather than on the more typical historical perspective. Finally, he suggests that treatment is more effective if therapists can help patients to maintain just a moderate amount of anxiety in their discussion of key issues. In sum, his treatment guidelines overlap with many aspects of behavior therapy, the obvious exception being intensive exposure and response prevention.

This brief discussion underscores the need for further research on this disorder. Current treatments are much more effective than might have been imagined 10 years ago, when OCD was viewed as almost completely refractory. Nevertheless, we need to learn much more about the appropriate classification of subcategories, about the interaction of treatments, about the maintenance of treatment gains (especially when the initial treatment only produced a partial response), and about the treatment of patients who cannot tolerate the side effects of pharmacotherapy or the discomfort associated with behavior therapy.

PART 6

Posttraumatic Stress Disorder

CHAPTER 16

Psychotherapy

MARDI J. HOROWITZ

CONCEPTUALIZATION OF THE DISORDER

Posttraumatic stress disorders are only one of the many types of stress response syndromes. Others include adjustment disorders, uncomplicated bereavement, and pathological grief reactions. All these diagnoses would fit within the larger category of stress response syndromes and could be treated in the ways discussed in this chapter.

Events that incite posttraumatic stress disorders are marked by their severity. Nonetheless, the preexisting personality of the patient always plays some role in how the event is experienced, interpreted, mastered, or defended against. In the main, stressful life experiences are injuries and losses, or at least the threat of such traumas. The most serious of these involve fear of death, a suddenness of perception, and perhaps the brutality of other people who seek to harm, or, in any event, not to save the self. Yet there are also traumas arising from subjugation of the self to rules that, at some time before or after, seem alien to personal values or even to human nature.

Populations

Experimental, field, and clinical studies of posttraumatic stress disorders indicate general response tendencies to such serious life events. While varying in resiliency, areas of personal vulnerability, and available support systems, populations exhibit a tendency to extremes of conscious experience. These extremes are characterized by both unusual episodes of intrusion and unusual episodes of avoidance or denial of the implications embedded in the stressful life experiences.

Phases of Reaction

Contrasting phases marked by either relatively more intrusive experiences or relatively more denial experiences tend to alternate following a stressful event. Phases of intrusion and denial may overlap, and, depending on the nature of the event, individuals may enter or move through one phase more quickly than another. Prototypically, however, an emotional outcry occurs first, followed by a period of relative denial, which in turn is followed by intrusive experiences. The person then gradually may work through the stressful life event, at last reaching a relative completion of response.

Normal and Abnormal

If any of these phases becomes excessively intense, or is blocked, pathological intensifications may develop. The discomfort of such pathological

This chapter is a product of empirical research and theory formation funded by the National Institutes of Health (National Heart, Lung, and Blood Institute: NHLBI); and Mental Health: (NIMH) from 1967 to 1984 and the Program on Conscious and Unconscious Mental Processes of the John D. and Catherine T. MacArthur Foundation (1983–1988). Important colleagues listed in part include, in alphabetical order, Nancy Kaltreider, Janice Krupnick, Charles Marmar, Alan Skolnikoff, Daniel Weiss, and Nancy Wilner.

intensifications is what leads the person to seek psychotherapy. Table 16.1 shows this concept of phases of response to serious life events.

Signs and Symptoms

The cardinal symptoms of posttraumatic stress disorder, as catalogued in DSM-III-R, are derived from the experience of intrusiveness. Table 16.2 shows the variety of intrusive signs and symptoms found in the posttraumatic stress disorder. A similar listing of symptoms and signs related to the denial and numbing experiences of these syndromes is found in Table 16.3.

Theory of Explanation

The psychodynamic theory of the formation of such symptoms as those listed in Tables 16.1–16.3 was first formulated by Josef Breuer and Sigmund Freud (1895) in the context of hysteria. Freud (1920) later devised a more advanced model in which the repetition compulsion was seen to supercede the libidinal drive and pleasure principle in mental functioning.

Contemporary psychodynamics has revised Freud's theory into a general systems model with a feedback loop. In this view of symptom forma-tion, the information from the traumatic event is stored and tends to be repeated in the conscious mind. Such repetition leads to painful levels of negative emotion because the event was an injury or loss, and the memory is still threatening to the individual. To avoid being overwhelmed with emotional responses upon recollection, the person might impose various degrees of defenses. Conscious inhibitions would be called *suppression*: unconscious inhibitions would be called *repression*. A variety of other types of defenses might also be used to modulate the degree of emotion experienced.

I have omitted Freud's theories about psychic energy because they are no longer an agreed-upon part of psychodynamic theory. However, modern psychodynamics still embraces the principle that memory of traumatic events is repeated and that a motive for such repetition is the need to master the information contained in such events. (For a recent summary and a revision of the theory of conscious and unconscious mental processes, see Horowitz, 1988.) This contemporary model seeks to explain the persistence of recurrent recollection of the stressful event, and the maladaptive distortions of character that may result from a failure to integrate such memories, as in instances of excessive and prolonged inhibitions.

TABLE 16.1.   Common Poststress Experiences and Their Pathological Intensification

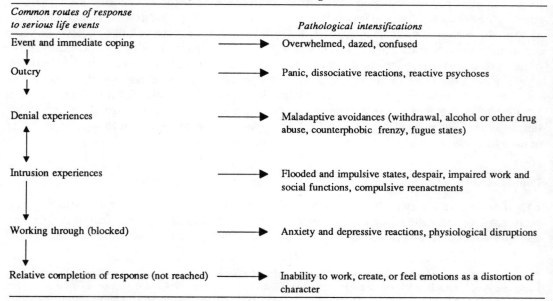

Common routes of response to serious life events	*Pathological intensifications*
Event and immediate coping	Overwhelmed, dazed, confused
Outcry	Panic, dissociative reactions, reactive psychoses
Denial experiences	Maladaptive avoidances (withdrawal, alcohol or other drug abuse, counterphobic frenzy, fugue states)
Intrusion experiences	Flooded and impulsive states, despair, impaired work and social functions, compulsive reenactments
Working through (blocked)	Anxiety and depressive reactions, physiological disruptions
Relative completion of response (not reached)	Inability to work, create, or feel emotions as a distortion of character

Source: M. Horowitz, 1986, *Stress Response Syndromes*, p. 27.

TABLE 16.2.   Symptoms and Signs Related to Intrusive Experience and Behavior

- Hypervigilance, including hypersensitivity to associated events
- Startle reactions
- Illusions or pseudohallucinations, including sensation of recurrence
- Intrusive–repetitive thoughts, images, emotions, and behaviors
- Overgeneralization of associations
- Inability to concentrate on other topics because of preoccupation with event-related themes
- Confusion or thought disruption when thinking about event-related themes
- Labile or explosive entry into intensely emotional and undermodulated states of mind
- Sleep and dream disturbances, including recurrent dreams
- Sensations or symptoms of flight or flight readiness (or of exhaustion from chronic arousal), including tremor, nausea, diarrhea, and sweating (adrenergic, noradrenergic, or histaminic arousals)
- Search for lost persons or situations, compulsive repetitions

Source: M. Horowitz, 1986, *Stress Response Syndromes*, p. 24.

A stressful life event is, by definition, out of accord with inner working models (Bowlby, 1969). It contains either too much or too little of some familiar situation, or, as is much more often the case, it presents an entirely new threat to the equilibrium of the person. The importance of these new perceptions means that they have high priority for retention in memory. This type of memory apparently tends to actively repeat in conscious experience unless a control maneuver is employed specifically to inhibit it.

An *active memory storage* exists, I hypothesize, that contains memories of traumatic events. It tends to repeat such memories as conscious representations until there is an accord between the information in the memory and the working models of the event. This need to bring inner mental models up to date with a changing reality can be called a *completion tendency*. Moreover, the repeated representation does not contain only perceptions of external facts; a mixture of external and internal sets of information are reorganized according to schemas and then experienced. Thus, the active memory collates awareness of the traumatic event with information about emotional responses and beliefs, and it may include errors in terms of what really happened.

Because the information in active memory is so unusual and also so important, it will be difficult to process. Many repetitions of processing may be necessary. This processing may proceed while the person is awake and while the person is asleep; dreams may be important memory and schema integrators in ways that we do not yet fully understand.

A complete working-through process (shown as a phase of response in Table 16.1) may require many repetitions and changes in inner schemas. As completion is approached, intrusion and denial will be experienced less. Until that time, however,

TABLE 16.3.   Symptoms and Signs Related to Denial or Numbing Experiences and Behavior

- Daze
- Selective inattention
- Inability to appreciate significance of stimuli
- Amnesia (complete or partial)
- Inability to visualize memories
- Disavowal of meanings of stimuli
- Constriction and inflexibility of thought
- Presence of fantasies to counteract reality
- A sense of numbness or unreality, including detachment and estrangement
- Overcontrolled states of mind, including behavioral avoidances
- Sleep disturbances (e.g., too little or too much)
- Tension–inhibition responses of the autonomic nervous system, with felt sensations such as bowel symptoms, fatigue, and headache
- Frantic overactivity to jam attention with stimuli
- Withdrawal from ordinary life activities

Source: M. Horowitz, 1986, *Stress Response Syndromes*, p. 26.

intrusive experiences may occur, as the pressure for repeated representation of the traumatic memories leads to interruption of other topics of thought.

Denial experiences occur as inner inhibitory control processes overtake the repetition tendency. Other effects of the control processes may include conscious experiences, such as feeling numb or being aware of avoiding certain topics that might arouse the intense negative emotions associated with traumatic events. Denial states are not necessarily to be evaluated or judged as pathological; they may be a period of adaptive self-restoration if not prolonged excessively.

In other words, the controls that modulate the degree of reaction have the purpose of maintaining emotional equilibrium within tolerable limits. The outcomes may be adaptive or maladaptive. Adaptive outcomes might be called *coping*. Maladaptive outcomes might be called *pathological levels of defense*, depending on how one wants to define the word *defense*. Failure of self-regulation, also called a failure of defense, is a third type of outcome, and it involves being so flooded with emotion that one cannot plan and take realistic action.

Theory of Therapeutic Action

The concept of defense is very important to psychodynamic case formulation because psychotherapists often work either *to increase* or *to decrease* the control processes of the patient. In people who have excessive inhibitions, the therapist first might seek to counteract these and help the person to gain access to the repressed memories. Subsequently, the patient can begin to deal with the emotions related to the traumatic experience and the emotional themes and person schemas that are activated through the associative processes.

In people who have maladaptive failures of control, the therapist may help the person to restructure his or her activities, thoughts and emotions to feel more in control. In persons using aberrant schemas and beliefs to organize their conscious views and preconscious or unconscious schemas about what happened, the therapist helps the patient to differentiate reality and fantasy, and

to work through preexisting, focally relevant neurotic or psychotic levels of conflict.

Very often the therapist is following a middle course, helping the patient to set aside extreme defenses, and to modulate consciously and effectively out-of-control trains of ideas, feelings, and behaviors using more moderate control processes. The *therapeutic relationship* helps the patient tolerate some of the painful experience and working through of memories. As tolerance increases, control processes become progressively less necessary; the person is able *both* to deliberately remember *and* to transiently forget the traumatic event.

DIAGNOSTIC ISSUES AND PROBLEMS

Preexisting character structure consists in part of the schemas of self and other that the subject might use to interpret a traumatic experience, together with the subject's habitual control processes. It also, in part, consists of the person's capacity for integrating dissimilar self schemas into supraordinate, containing forms. Other elements of this structure include (a) the habitual styles of schema management used to regulate emotional experience and states of mind, (b) the controls exercised on conscious representation, and (c) the individual's inhibition or facilitation of various intentions to act. My colleagues and I have dealt with this in detail elsewhere (Horowitz, 1986; Horowitz, Marmar, Krupnick, Wilner, Kaltreider, & Wallerstein, 1984), but a brief summary is made here.

Different character styles may be represented as prototypes. An individual will fit a given prototype only to a degree. Only people with a relatively rigid set of patterns will fit the prototype well, whereas others present a more mixed and less conforming picture.

Information-processing style may be seen while observing short-order patterns in the subject's flow of thought and emotion on a topic. The stressful life event is an apt topic for such observation because habitual defensive styles are sometimes thrown into bold relief by intense emotional themes. However, the schemas of self and other are more commonly seen in medium- or long-order patterns. Those patterns may be either observed directly in the patients' interpersonal behavior or inferred indirectly from their stories of how they have behaved with others over longer periods of time. The repetitive roles and actions assumed for self and other in these stories may be especially useful for the therapist.

A grasp of the formulation of personality patterns is important in helping a particular person work through the specific meaning of the traumatic event in terms of his or her own habitual style of responding to stressful events. In working through the meaning of the stressful event, the person may also benefit by reducing character rigidity or armor (Horowitz, 1988; Horowitz et al., 1984; Reich, 1949; Shapiro, 1965).

Some patterns in a prototype of a *histrionic personality style* are shown in Table 16.4. The characteristic "global deployment of attention" observed in this type often makes the experience of a traumatic event especially shocking. Their tendency to short-circuit a topic makes it important for the therapist to increase the time that these patients spend on the topic by offering comments about it. Their attention-seeking behaviors may lead others to think that they are using their status as victims of trauma to get something they want. Professionals may be misled into thinking that the person is being manipulative rather than experiencing a serious posttraumatic stress disorder. Therapists should be careful to avoid such errors.

The prototype of the *compulsive personality style* is shown in Table 16.5. The sharp focus on peripheral details may mislead professionals into thinking that such individuals do not have emotional intrusions when they are by themselves. Nevertheless, while the compulsive or obsessional typology is associated with marked low affect in conversations, when alone, such individuals with posttraumatic stress disorders may have episodes of searingly intense emotion. Such individuals exhibit a tendency to have power and control struggles with a psychotherapist, but this tendency usually does not surface while the person is in the intrusive phase of a stress response syndrome. Instead, it may arise when the person is sustained enough by the relationship with the therapist that the person can enter a denial phase of response. It is important at that point to recognize what is happening and to help the person maintain a focus on working through the stressful event. Otherwise, the patient may insist that the event is no longer an important focus.

The *narcissistic personality style*, too, has ways of coloring the signs and symptoms observed in a posttraumatic stress disorder, as well as characteristic effects on the resolution process. It is

---

TABLE 16.4. Patterns in the Histrionic Personality Style Prototype

Information-Processing Style
Short-order patterns—Observe in flow of thought and emotion on a topic
- Global deployment of attention
- Unclear or incomplete representations of ideas and feelings, possibly with lack of details or clear labels in communication; nonverbal communications not translated into words or conscious meanings
- Only partial or unidirectional associational lines
- Short circuit to apparent completion of problematic thoughts

Traits
Medium-order patterns—Observe in interviews
- Attention-seeking behaviors, possibly including demands for attention, and/or the use of charm, vivacity, sex appeal, childishness
- Fluid change in mood and emotion, possibly including breakthroughs of feeling
- Inconsistency of apparent attitudes

Interpersonal Relations
Long-order patterns—Observe in a patient's history
- Repetitive, impulsive, stereotyped interpersonal relationships often characterized by victim–aggressor, child–parent, and rescue or rape themes
- "Cardboard" fantasies and self–object attitudes
- Drifting but possibly dramatic lives with an existential sense that reality is not really real

Source: M. Horowitz, 1986, *Stress Response Syndromes*, p. 152.

TABLE 16.5.   Patterns in the Compulsive Personality Style Prototype

Information-Processing Style

Short-order patterns—Observe in flow of thought and emotion on a topic
- Sharp focus of attention on details
- Clear representation of ideas, meager representation of emotions
- Shifting organization and implications of ideas rather than following an associational line to conclusion as directed by original intent or intrinsic meanings
- Avoiding completion on decision or a given problem; instead, switching back and forth between attitudes

Traits

Medium-order patterns—Observe in interviews
- Doubt, worry, overly detailed productivity and/or procrastination
- Single-minded, unperturbable, intellectualizing
- Tense, deliberate, unenthusiastic
- Rigid, ritualistic

Interpersonal Relations

Long-order patterns—Observe in a patient's history
- Develops regimented, routine, and continuous interpersonal relationships low in vivacity, vividness, or pleasure; often frustrating to be with
- Prone to dominance–submission themes or power and control struggles
- Duty filling, hardworking, seeks or makes strain and pressure, does what one should do rather than what one decides to do
- Experiences self as remote from emotional connection with others although feels committed to operating with others because of role or principles

Source: M. Horowitz, 1986, *Stress Response Syndromes*, p. 164.

especially important to recognize that such patients may lie about aspects of their role in the traumatic event in order to create a safe space in the therapy in which they can tell the truth about it without the revulsion of shame they might otherwise experience. The self-centered behavior should not mislead clinical evaluators into thinking these people have not been traumatized or that they are unworthy of professional care. The focus on reviewing the meaning of the traumatic events to the patient's self may be especially difficult to maintain if the patient's priority is to recover a sense of cohesion in identity. The same division into short-, medium-, and long-order patterns is used in Table 16.6 as was used in Tables 16.4 and 16.5.

The particular control maneuver of the narcissistic typology, which is the sliding of evaluations and meanings in order to preserve a sense of strong self-concept, often works alongside the inhibitory and shifting controls used in the histrionic and compulsive personality styles. Indeed, it is possible to regard narcissistic controls as a distinct dimension in personality formulation. That is, the person may primarily tend to use either a histrionic or compulsive style, and within one style or the other have various degrees of narcissistic vulnerability.

TREATMENT STRATEGIES

The treatment strategy depends partly on both the formulation of the personality style and the nature of the individual's response to the event. Elapsed time after the event is also a factor. In general, the longer the patient waits before seeking help, the longer the treatment may take. This may seem paradoxical at first; however, the longer that therapy is deferred, the deeper the person may become embedded in some kind of pathological belief about the event. Such enduring schemas take more time to change.

Time-limited dynamic psychotherapy can lift a tendency to avoid an event, and sometimes a single session or two of crucial work starts the person on a normal working-through process. Consider the mourning process as an example. People seldom can complete the process of mourning for a loved one who has died in less than a year. In instances of pathological grief, the person may (a) suffer far longer than that, or (b) experience overwhelming

TABLE 16.6.   Patterns in the Narcissistic Personality Style Prototype

Information-Processing Style
Short-order patterns—Observe in thought and emotion on a topic
- Slides meanings of information that might damage self-concept; also uses denial, disavowal, and negation for this purpose
- Attention to sources of praise and criticism
- Shifts subject–object focus of meanings, externalizes bad attributes, internalizes good attributes
- Occasionally dissociates incompatible psychological attitudes into separate clusters

Traits
Medium-order patterns—Observe in interviews
- Self-centered
- Overestimates or underestimates self and others
- Self-enhancement in accomplishments real or fantasied, in garb or demeanor
- Avoids self-deflating situations
- Variable demeanors depending on state of self-esteem and context:
- Charm, "wooing-winning" quality, controlling efforts, or charisma
- Superiority, contemptuousness, coldness, or withdrawal
- Shame, panic, helplessness, hypochondriasis, depersonalization, or self-destructiveness
- Envy, rage, paranoia, or demands

Interpersonal Relations
Long-order patterns—Observe in patient's history
- Often impoverished interpersonally or oriented to power over others or controlling use of others as accessories (self–objects)
- Absence of "I–thou" feelings
- Social climbing or using others for positive reflection
- Avoidance of self-criticism by goading others to unfair criticism
- Discarding of persons no longer of use
- Pseudo twinning relationship

Source: M. Horowitz, 1986, *Stress Response Syndromes*, p. 179.

feelings during the year, or (c) in some instances avoid mourning altogether. Psychotherapy does not seek to eliminate the painful sadness and other feelings that occur, and it need not continue until the person has completed a normal mourning process. Its purpose, rather, is to help the person shift to the track of a normal mourning process from some type of pathological deflection or overintensification of it. Then a person can suffer the necessary pangs of grief without continuing therapy he or she has the intuition (and the intuition is warranted) that this is the optimal way of getting through it.

The choice between a brief or a time-unlimited dynamic psychotherapy depends on each individual case. A time-limited dynamic therapy is described here as a prototype for what may happen during the course of a dynamic psychotherapy (Horowitz, 1986). Table 16.7 gives a sample outline from our research studies; this example used a time-limited 12-session dynamic therapy for stress disorders.

Dynamic therapy that is focused on a traumatic event is both phase oriented and personality oriented. The phase orientation begins with an assessment of the patient's current degree of control over his or her tendency to repeat memories of and reactions to the traumatic event. The variety of goals for treatment are determined by the patient's prevailing state, as summarized in Table 16.8.

The nuances of psychotherapy technique may be based on a conceptualization of the patient's personality style. In order to get into this issue, it is important to examine the problem of establishing a focus. One aspect of the focus in a posttraumatic stress disorder is the event itself, of course. In addition, however, some kind of linkage exists between the experience of the event and some aspect of the self of the patient.

Early in treatment, the facts about the event and the nature of the response may suffice as a focus, if only because one cannot know in a few interviews all there is to know that is relevant about a patient. Thus, the focus may be something like

TABLE 16.7.   A Sample 12-Session Dynamic Therapy for Posttraumatic Stress Disorder

Session	Relationship issues	Patient activity	Therapist activity
1	Initial positive feeling for helper	Patient tells story of event	Preliminary focus is discussed
2	Lull as sense of pressure is reduced	Event is related to previous life	Takes psychiatric history. Gives patient realistic appraisal of syndrome
3	Patient testing therapist for various relationship possibilities	Patient adds associations to indicate expanded meaning of event	Focus is realigned; resistances to contemplating stress-related themes are interpreted
4	Therapeutic alliance deepened	Implications of event in the present are contemplated	Defenses and warded-off contents are interpreted; linking of latter to stress-event and responses
5		Themes that have been avoided are worked on	Active confrontation with feared topics and reengagement in feared activities are encouraged
6		The future is contemplated	Time of termination is discussed
7–11	Transference reactions are interpreted and linked to other configurations; acknowledgment of pending separation	The working-through of central conflicts and issues of termination, as related to the life event and reactions to it, is continued	Central conflicts, termination, unfinished issues, and recommendations all are clarified and interpreted
12	Saying good-bye	Work to be continued independently and plans for the future are discussed	Real gains and summary of future work for patient to do independently are acknowledged

Source: M. Horowitz, 1986, Stress Response Syndromes, p. 131.

TABLE 16.8.   Priorities of Treatment, by Phases of Patient's Responses

Patient's current state	Treatment goal
Under continuing impact of external stress event	• Terminate external event or remove patient from contiguity with it • Provide temporary relationship • Help with decisions, plans, or working through
Swings to intolerable levels: • Ideational–emotional attacks • Paralyzing denial and numbness	• Reduce amplitude of oscillations to swings of tolerable intensity of ideation and emotion • Continue emotional and ideational support
Frozen in overcontrol state of denial and numbness with or without intrusive repetitions	• Help patient selectively attend to limited reexperience of the events and implications; help patient remember for a time, put out of mind for a time, remember for a time, and so on • During periods of recollection, help patient organize and express experience; increase sense of safety in therapeutic relationship so patient can resume processing of the event
Able to experience and tolerate episodes of ideation and waves of emotion	• Help patient work through associations: the conceptual, emotional, object relations, and self-image implications of the stress event • Help patient relate this stress event to earlier threats, relationship models, self-concepts, and future plans
Able to work through ideas and emotions independently	• Work through loss of therapeutic relationship • Terminate treatment

Source: M. Horowitz, 1986, Stress Response Syndromes, p. 125.

"our purpose, if you agree, will be to understand the impact of this event upon you." That sounds straightforward and simple; nonetheless, establishing the link between the stressful life event and the patient's self-concept often surprises the patient. Indeed, it is often what the patient has been trying to ward off.

When a very simple focus, such as the link between the stress event and the self-concept of the subject, is employed initially, it can be realigned in midtherapy to deal with particular topics that are especially conflicted.

The kind of habitual defenses associated with different personality styles will affect not only the way that the focus is realigned, but also how the topic of the focus is processed over time. The goal of the treatment is to allow the person (a) to have *full access to associations* linked to the traumatic event, (b) to *differentiate reality from fantasy* about it, and (c) to reach a variety of appropriate

conclusions. Rendered graphically, the goal is to flow down the column shown at the left of Table 16.9. This series of control processes begins with putting associations together in a sequence, and it progresses to revising inner and enduring schemas while practicing new modes of behavior made necessary by the realities in the stressful event. The control processes in this column each relate to a variety of rows representing subdivisions into one of three categories: adaptive and maladaptive levels of regulation; and states of relative failure of regulation, efforts, or capacities. The therapist encourages the patient to use control processes at the adaptive level of regulation.

Each of the prototypical styles mentioned previously can be thought of as if it were a defect in following the normal working-through process. For each defect, a corresponding type of corrective is proposed that might be used in therapy. Tables 16.10, 16.11, and 16.12 illustrate prototypes for

TABLE 16.9.   Regulation of Sequences of Conscious Representations

Processes	Outcomes		
	Regulaton		
Types of control	Adaptive	Maladaptive	Dysregulation
Representing next ideas			
• Facilitaton of associations	Contemplation of implications	Rumination and doubting	
• Inhibition of associations	Dosing; selective inattention; careful choice of what is expressed; suppression	Denial; disavowal; repression; isolation; numbing; communicative reluctance; somatization; acting out	
Sequencing ideas			
• Seeking information	Understanding; learning new skills	Intellectualization	
• Switching concepts	Emotional balancing	Undoing; reaction formation; displacement	Intrusion of ideas; emotional flooding; indecision; paralysis of action
Sliding meanings and valuations	Humor, wisdom	Exaggeration; minimization; devaluation; reaction formation	
Arranging information into decision trees	Problem solving	Rationalization	
Revising working models	Learning; identifications; acceptance	Externalization; introjection	
Practicing new modes of thinking and acting	Replace previous automatic reactions with new ways of responding	Counterphobic behavioral patterns	

Source: M. Horowitz, 1988, *Introduction to Psychodynamics*, p. 202.

TABLE 16.10.   Some of the Maladaptive Features of the Histrionic Personality Style Prototype and How They Might Be Counteracted in Psychotherapy

Function	Style as maladaptive	Therapeutic counter
Perception	Global or selective inattention	Asking for details
Representation	Impressionistic rather than accurate	Abreaction and reconstruction
Translation of images and enactions into words	Limited	Encouraging talk Providing verbal labels
Associations	Limted by inhibitions Misinterpretations based on schematic stereotypes, deflected from reality to wishes and fears	Encouraging production Repetition Clarifications
Problem solving	Short circuit to rapid but often erroneous conclusions	Keeping subject open Interpretations
	Avoidance of topic when emotions are unbearable	Support

Source: M. Horowtiz, 1986, *Stress Response Syndromes*, p. 157.

such cases, which require a longer exposition than this chapter's coverage allows. Full discussions that provide the kind of detail necessary to make a psychodynamic view clear are available elsewhere (Horowitz et al., 1984).

CASE ILLUSTRATION

Flora was a 46-year-old woman who was driving when a severe accident occurred. While she was relatively uninjured, except for minor scratches and bruises, her 10-year-old daughter, who was riding beside her in the front seat, was flung into the windshield. Her otherwise beautiful face was severely scarred as a result of the injuries sustained. The daughter had been wearing a seatbelt, but apparently it did not function during the crash.

Flora handled the emergency and the follow-up surgical care of her daughter with careful and intelligent consistency. While she was emotionally upset and had periods of weeping, she was able to manage family affairs with the support of her husband. She was quite an intelligent and competent woman, and this greatly helped her daughter in the immediate phase of recovery. There were several plastic surgery procedures, and then there was to be a long period of recovery.

Eight months after the accident, Flora began to have intrusive images of her daughter's raw and torn face, nightmares in which blood appeared and she awoke with terror, she was preoccupied with anger at the car manufacturer, and with related symptoms. The suit against the automobile manufacturer was a lengthy legal process, and it had not yet come to any kind of action.

TABLE 16.11.   Some of the Maladaptive Features of the Compulsive Personality Style Prototype and How They Might Be Counteracted in Psychotherapy

Function	Style as maladaptive	Therapeutic counteraction
Perception	Detailed and factual	Asking for overall impressions and statements about emotional experiences
Representation	Isolation of ideas from emotions	Linkage of emotional meanings to ideational meanings
Translation of images and enactions into words	Missing emotional meaning in a rapid transition to partial word meanings	Focus of attention on images and felt reactions to them
Associations	Shifting sets of meanings back and forth	Holding operations Interpretations of defense and of warded-off meanings
Problem solving	Endless rumination without reaching decisions	Interpretations of reasons for warding off clear decisions

Source: M. Horowtiz, 1986, *Stress Response Syndromes*, p. 172.

TABLE 16.12. Some of the Maladaptive Features of the Narcissistic Personality Style Prototype and How They Might Be Counteracted in Psychotherapy

Function	Style as maladaptive	Therapeutic counteraction
Perception	Focus on praise and blame	Avoiding being provoked into either praising or blaming but realistically supportive
	Denial of information about wounding	Use of tactful timing and wording to counteract denials by selective confrontation
Representation	Dislocation of bad traits from self to other	Repeated review in order to clarify who is who in terms of the sequence of acts and intentions in a recalled interpersonal transaction
Translation of images into words	Sliding of meanings	Consistent definition of meanings; encourages decisions as to most relevant meanings and how much to weight them
Associations	Overbalances when finding routes to self-enhancement	Holding to other meanings: cautiously deflates grandiose beliefs
Problem solving	Distortion of reality to maintain self-esteem	Indication of distortion while (tactfully) encouraging and supporting fidelity to reality
	Obtaining of illusory gratification	Support of patient's self-esteem during period of surrender of illusory gratification (helped by the real interest of the therapist, by identification with the therapist, and by identification with the therapist as a noncorrupt person); discovery of and gradual discouragement from unrealistic gratifications from therapy
	Forgiving of self too easily	Aid of development of appropriate sense of responsibility

Source: M. Horowitz, 1986, Stress Response Syndromes, p. 186.

The opening phase of treatment consisted of taking a careful history both of the stress event and of Flora's subsequent reactions to it. This included exploration of the nature of her reactions to physicians and surgeons, to lawyers, to her daughter, to her husband, and to her other children. This extended to a history of how Flora had done before the accident, including general psychiatric history. To summarize this, she was an intelligent and competent woman who struggled against some passive–aggressive tendencies in her personality, and who was prone to some periods of anxiety and depression, but these did not merit a psychiatric diagnostic classification. Thus, her diagnosis was posttraumatic stress disorder, with more of a passive–aggressive style than a passive–aggressive personality disorder.

Flora was seen once a week, with a focus on understanding conscious and unconscious reactions to the accident and to its other cascading events (such as litigation) in such a way that she would aim to have relief of her symptoms and also work through her responses to the traumatic events. In 3 or 4 hours, Flora gave the aforementioned information, and she explored in particular a topic having to do with her feelings of guilt that she was driving an inexpensive car that was about 8 years old, which might have contributed to the accident. The other driver was the one clearly negligent; nonetheless, she felt guilty that she had involved her daughter in what would be a permanent loss of beauty. An aspect of this topic was to feel angry at her husband, who was the principal wage earner in the household, for being too stingy to spend more money for a newer car, and for not being competent enough to make enough money that they could have a larger automobile.

Her husband had been very supportive in the aftermath of the accident. Nonetheless, she had strong but warded-off feelings of hostility toward the husband around his not having symptoms, and she even felt some anger and hostility that the daughter, Clara, was back in school and adapting fairly well to her situation. Flora felt isolated in terms of having symptoms, and she worried secondarily that she was "going crazy" because she was having such intrusive and out-of-control symptoms at such a late date. Discussion of the nature of these symptoms in relation to common findings, and expectations of time needed for recovery, was very reassuring to Flora, as was having someone to tell of the warded-off hostile themes. Her symptoms rapidly subsided in this 1-month early period of treatment.

The first month was followed by a middle phase of four weekly hour-long psychotherapy sessions during which Flora found herself with little to discuss. She brought up other current issues, such as an argument with a neighbor. The therapist was aware that there were ideas and feelings that had not yet been brought up around the theme of hostility toward her husband and, especially, toward her daughter. He commented on her displacement of hostility from Clara to the neighbor, saying it was difficult for Flora to acknowledge that she suppressed anger toward her daughter because her daughter was the one who had primarily suffered from the accident. Flora disavowed any anger at Clara but then had an uncontrolled temper outburst when Clara indicated no interest in the progress of the litigation against the automobile manufacturer. Flora screamed at her that she (Flora) always had to do everything for her (Clara) and that no one ever helped Flora.

The description of this episode led to a linkage of ideas around the accident to ideas Flora had toward her own mother. Flora's mother had taken very good care of her up until the age of approximately 4 years old. At that time, Flora's brother was born, and her mother began to scold Flora whenever Flora wanted attention. Flora felt betrayed and alone, and for years carried a resentment toward her mother and her sibling.

Flora then had a dream in which Clara was bitterly accusing her of being a negligent mother. Instead of waking with terror, as she had during the dreams of blood that preceded treatment, Flora awoke racked with sobs. She was extremely grateful to her husband, who woke up with her and spent more than an hour tenderly consoling her. It seemed very important to Flora that the husband was not only comforting but "sorry for her." The therapist suggested that perhaps Flora's mother had never said she was sorry for neglecting her and that perhaps Flora had never said she was sorry to Clara.

Flora then became preoccupied with the idea of telling her daughter how sorry she was that the accident had happened. She realized that she had never expressed this in words. She felt strangely anxious at doing this. Given plenty of time in therapy to explore gradually what she expected to happen, it slowly became clear that she expected that Clara would explode viciously at her, would withdraw love from her, and would have the same kind of bitter resentment that Flora felt she had harbored for so long against her own mother.

With further exploration of this theme, Flora was able to have a very intimate conversation with Clara about how sorry she was about the accident. Mother and daughter cried, clasped each other, rocked each other, and both felt that an intimacy that had been disrupted by the accident was now restored.

During the middle, quieter phase of the brief therapy, Flora had treated the therapist as if he could no longer be of help to her. She considered him helpful in the early phase; but in the middle phase, she saw his relative silence as a desire to turn his attention to a new patient, one more needy than she was. The therapist interpreted this transference theme to Flora. This concern that the therapist wanted to go on to "more serious business" by terminating the brief therapy then led to work on another topic in the closing phase of the treatment.

The third phase of treatment addressed Flora's feeling that she had had her own traumatic event in the accident. Because she was not injured, she believed all attention (including her own) had to go to Clara. She now complained more bitterly about the automobile manufacturer and was asked by the therapist if she did not want some human sympathy and not just compensation. Flora was very startled by this remark and became very contemplative about it. In that hour, she reviewed how much sympathy she had indeed had from Clara and her husband, as well as from her other children and her friends, but how she had walled it off. After that hour, she told people how grateful she was for the support that she had received, and she told them that because she was caught up in the stress, she had not sufficiently acknowledged this. They reacted to this statement with renewed expressions of support and love for her. This feeling of support in her surrounding relationships made it relatively easy for Flora to accept the termination of the 3 ½ months of weekly psychotherapy.

ALTERNATIVE TREATMENT OPTIONS

Within a single case, one might use a variety of treatment strategies. I see psychodynamic formulation as an overarching envelope. One always considers the effects of the strategy on the overall picture, including issues of transference and expectation. For example, if the patient has a phobic avoidance of a situation that it would be adaptive to confront, but which is associated with traumatic anxiety, the therapist would encourage in vivo exposure (much as I think the behavior therapy chapter would recommend in the part on anxiety disorders). The effects of suggestion (in terms of offering a series of steps to the patient), or of praise, reinforcement, or support would always be weighed in relation to (a) the character style of the patient, (b) the degree of regression sustained due to the stress event, (c) the phase of response in working through the event, and (d) the nature of any transference phenomena present.

Similarly, biological treatments, including psychopharmacological agents, have to be considered. The use of antianxiety agents may be helpful to people who have overwhelming anxiety; however, some memory impairment may be a consequence of use of certain of these agents. Excessive or prolonged use can lead not only to psychological addiction, but might also conceivably slow down a working-through process. In my own experience, I have preferred to use very small doses and single doses of antianxiety agents rather than to use medication routinely every 6 hours or so.

Some people may have a major depressive disorder precipitated by the traumatic life event, and the use of antidepressants has to be considered in such disorders. While the person is in a severely depressed mood, it may be difficult or impossible to process all the extended meanings of a traumatic event. Medication may cause lifting of the severe vegetative signs, which in turn may be followed by marked progress in the psychological dimensions of recovery.

As for cognitive therapy, my own approach to psychodynamics is a mixture of psychodynamic and cognitive methods, and it is described in more detail elsewhere (Horowitz, 1987, 1988).

Family therapy may also be very important, not only for families who have been jointly exposed to serious life events such as earthquakes or floods, but also for families needing help to integrate a person who has had an unusual experience that differs substantially from the experiences of other family members.

REFERENCES

Bowlby, J. (1969). *Attachment and loss*: Vol. 1. Attachment. New York: Basic Books.

Breuer, J., & Freud, S. (1957–1974). Studies on hysteria. In *The standard edition of the complete psychological works of Sigmund Freud* (Vol. 2). London: Hogarth. (Original published in 1895).

Freud, S. (1920). Beyond the pleasure principle. In *The standard edition* (Vol. 18). London: Hogarth.

Horowitz, M. J. (1986). *Stress response syndromes*. Northvale, New Jersey: Aronson.

Horowitz, M. J. (1987). *States of mind* (2nd ed.). New York: Plenum.

Horowitz, M. J. (1988). *Introduction to psychodynamics*. New York: Basic Books.

Horowitz, M. J., Marmar, C., Krupnick, J., Wilner, N., Kaltreider, N., & Wallerstein, R. (1984). *Personality styles and brief psychotherapy*. New York: Basic Books.

Reich, W. (1949). *Character analysis*. New York: Farrar, Straus & Giroux.

Shapiro, D. (1965). *Neurotic styles*. New York: Basic Books.

CHAPTER 17

Behavior Therapy

DAVID W. FOY, HEIDI S. RESNICK, EDWARD M. CARROLL, AND SHERYL S. OSATO

CONCEPTUALIZATION OF THE DISORDER

This chapter on behavior therapy for posttraumatic stress disorder (PTSD) is intended to provide a practical overview of behavioral methods that are either in current use or potentially useful for problems associated with the experience of psychological trauma. The orientation of our work necessarily reflects the tenuous nature of early clinical work with a disorder that has only recently been included in current psychiatric nosology. At present, no controlled, group comparison studies have been reported.

A myriad of unresolved issues are apparent when the emerging field of traumatic stress study is considered. Several especially challenging issues bear mentioning. First, it is often unclear as to what is meant operationally by the term *posttraumatic stress*. The timing of the posttrauma reaction makes a difference as to whether the immediate psychological reactions to catastrophe are seen as normal crisis reactions or whether the same persistent reaction patterns are seen as PTSD symptoms several months later. Criteria recently published in the revision of the *Diagnostic and Statistical Manual of Mental Disorders* (3rd ed. rev.; DSM-III-R, American Psychiatric Association, 1987) now specify a symptom duration of 1 month for PTSD diagnosis.

Second, specific diagnostic criteria for the disorder are still evolving. It remains for future research to determine what kinds of adverse events, at which intensity levels constitute extreme stressors likely to elicit PTSD reactions in predictable numbers of exposed individuals.

A third unresolved issue concerns the extent to which psychological reaction patterns are alike when comparing different trauma types. Cross-trauma comparison studies with adequate methodology are virtually nonexistent. Thus, we are on shaky scientific ground if we attempt to generalize findings directly from one type of trauma to another. A similar issue concerns the identification of person variables or individual characteristics that may contribute to either resilience or vulnerability to PTSD. Finally, while behavioral techniques have been used successfully for other kinds of anxiety disorders (e.g., simple phobia and agoraphobia), the extent to which these techniques are applicable to PTSD, only recently categorized as an anxiety disorder, remains to be empirically determined.

Despite these and many other unresolved challenges to understanding PTSD, scientific progress has been made since the late 1970s. Conceptually, there are several useful models now available to guide research and treatment efforts. Preliminary assessment and treatment procedures have been published so that standardization in methodology across studies is now possible. Epidemiological findings, along with observations in clinical samples, have established "partial PTSD" as a meaningful category among populations of trauma-exposed persons. Just as we have learned to conceptualize trauma exposure as a continuous variable, the number of PTSD criterion symptoms exhibited is now often seen as a continuum.

Given the infant status of our scientific understanding of PTSD, it would be pretentious to suggest that behavioral techniques, or treatments derived from any other theoretical orientation, are known to be effective for this disorder. Rather, the preliminary nature of our current knowledge is emphasized and appropriate caution is urged in the clinical use of the techniques described herein.

Similar psychological reactions have been observed in rape victims and in combat-traumatized veterans. These patterns include emotional numbing, intrusive cognitions, avoidance behavior, and increased physiological responsivity to trauma-related stimuli. Thus, similar formulations have been proposed to account for the development of PTSD symptoms following sexual assault or combat-related trauma. Behavioral conceptualizations of PTSD have focused on Mowrer's two-factor theory (a classically conditioned emotional response, and subsequent avoidance responses motivated by fear, and reinforced by fear reduction) as central to the origin and persistence of symptoms of PTSD (Fairbank & Brown, 1987).

This model has been implicated by Keane, Zimering, and Caddell (1985), and by Kilpatrick, Veronen, and Resick (1979) in the development of PTSD associated with combat exposure and sexual assault, respectively. Although this model was proposed in the sexual assault literature prior to introduction of DSM-III (American Psychiatric Association, 1980) criteria for PTSD, Kilpatrick, Veronen, and Best (1985) noted that the most frequently observed symptoms in rape victims, including fear and anxiety, intrusive cognitions, avoidance behavior, and sleep disturbance, are consistent with the diagnostic criteria. In addition, Kilpatrick, Saunders, Veronen, Best, and Von (1987) found that 57% of rape victims in a community sample met lifetime diagnostic criteria for PTSD.

Sexual assault and some combat experiences are often perceived by victims as life threatening. As Kilpatrick, Veronen, and Resick (1979) described it, "Most victims view rape as a life-threatening event in that they are threatened or overwhelmed by force or threat of force." (p. 135). In the learning theory model, this type of experience is viewed as an *unlearned* or unconditioned stimulus (UCS), which elicits an automatic or unconditioned response (UCR) of extreme anxiety, including physiological, behavioral, and cognitive components. By the mechanism of classical conditioning, other stimuli present in the situation can become *learned* or conditioned stimuli (CSs) capable of eliciting a conditioned response (CR) of anxiety, due to the original association with the UCS. These previously neutral stimuli, such as the sights and sounds of combat, or characteristics of the setting in which a sexual assault has taken place, then maintain the capacity to elicit a conditioned emotional response in the absence of the original UCS (combat or sexual stimuli). Kilpatrick et al. have proposed that via instrumental learning, or negative reinforcement, resistance to extinction of the anxiety response (CR), despite the absence of the UCS, is due to continued avoidance of the trauma-associated cues (CSs), which is followed and reinforced by fear reduction.

Other learning principles postulated as factors in the maintenance of anxiety and distress include stimulus generalization and higher-order conditioning. By the process of stimulus generalization, new stimuli that are similar to the CSs that elicit anxiety may also acquire this capacity. An example of this, cited by Keane et al. (1985), is the arousal and avoidance behavior that may be observed in some combat veterans with PTSD upon hearing sounds that resemble gunfire, such as a car backfiring. For victims of sexual assault, men with physical characteristics similar to those of the assailant may elicit a fear response (Kilpatrick et al., 1985). Higher-order conditioning is a process whereby currently neutral stimuli that are paired or associated with CSs, such as cognitions about the event, may acquire an independent capacity to elicit fear. Through these processes, a great variety of stimuli in the environment may elicit anxiety and motivate further restriction of activity for trauma victims. Kilpatrick et al. (1985) suggested that this restriction may also contribute to associated symptoms of depression in some victims.

Some evidence in support of a learning theory model of PTSD etiology in the combat-related literature is the observation that veterans with PTSD display significantly higher levels of physiological arousal and behavioral avoidance in response to combat-related stimuli, such as slides or tapes of combat sights or sounds, than combat veterans without PTSD (Blanchard, Kolb, Pall-meyer, & Gerardi, 1982; Malloy, Fairbank, & Keane, 1983). As Foy, Carroll, and Donahoe (1987a) noted, the observation that veterans with PTSD did not differ from veterans without PTSD on measures of responding to control stimuli in these studies indicated that differences between groups were not due to a generally higher level of arousal in the PTSD group, but to specific responses to combat-related stimuli.

Some data obtained in studies of symptomatology of rape victims also support the learning theory model. Kilpatrick et al. (1979) found that the kinds of fears reported discriminated between rape victims and nonvictims across four different time intervals. Results indicated that items that discriminated between groups were predominantly rape-related cues, such as weapons, or cues signaling vulnerability to assault, such as darkness or a dimly lit street. The authors concluded that these findings support a learning theory model of fear acquisition. Kilpatrick et al. also noted their previous finding that indexes of generalized psychological distress had decreased by 3 months postassault, while measures specific to anxiety and phobic anxiety remained elevated in rape victims. They suggested that this finding was consistent with persistent anxiety over time as a function of avoidance to assault-related cues.

Additional evidence in support of a learning theory model stems from the finding in the combat trauma literature that degree of combat exposure was the strongest predictor of PTSD symptom intensity observed in multiple regression analyses conducted with data from clinical populations (Foy et al., 1987a), as well as from a non-help-seeking population (Foy & Card, 1987). In these studies, combat exposure levels were rated on the basis of a Combat Exposure Scale (Lund, Foy, Sipprelle, & Strachan, 1984), a scale with Guttman Scalogram properties that includes seven war-related events (such as being wounded and being responsible for civilian deaths). The observation that exposure to more traumatic events (e.g., witnessing death versus merely firing a weapon or being fired on) was associated with increased symptom severity is consistent with the central role attributed to the UCS in the behavioral model.

In the rape literature, findings related to characteristics of the assault are mixed. Steketee and Foa

(1987) reviewed this literature and noted that the results of three studies indicated a positive relationship between severity or brutality of the assault and later psychological problems, while results of two other studies indicated positive adaptation positively associated with degree of threat. A limitation of this review is that no studies assessed for PTSD specifically. However, it was suggested that the context of rape may have complex effects on adjustment, such that degree of force, or perceived threat, may be associated with less self-blame, but it may also be associated with increased fear in the situation. It may also be the case that, in contrast to the aforementioned combat-related literature, the range of gradation of trauma factors may be limited in situations of rape, such that all victims experience a relatively high degree of threat. A more appropriate comparison group might be victims of attempted rape. In fact, Kilpatrick et al. (1987), in their community survey, found that only 15.7% of victims of attempted rape versus 57.1% of victims of completed rape met lifetime criteria for PTSD. This finding may be seen as consistent with a learning theory model.

Despite supporting evidence for the learning theory model, the factor of individual differences in response to trauma needs to be addressed thoroughly. In both the sexual assault and the combat trauma literature, the importance of examining potential mediating factors that may contribute to differential adaptation following trauma has been acknowledged (Fairbank & Brown, 1987; Foa & Steketee, 1987; Foy, Resnick, Sipprelle, & Carroll, 1987c; Keane et al, 1985; Kilpatrick et al., 1985). These factors include coping skills, prior psychiatric history, family history of psychopathology, social support, and history of other life stressors. One goal of future research might be to observe the range of adaptation in response to specific levels or gradations of trauma exposure as a function of these mediating factors. For example, Foy et al. (1987) proposed the strategy of examining the rates of PTSD in combat veterans as a function of both relatively higher or lower combat exposure, as well as presence or absence of family history of psychopathology.

In addition to the necessity of addressing the foregoing mediating factors, Fairbank and Brown (1987) noted that a learning theory model may need to address more adequately the possible influence of cognitive mediating factors (such as the meaning of the event) on psychological adaptation. A recently proposed model of PTSD development outlined by Foa, Olasov, Rothbaum, and Steketee (in press) addresses this issue. This model, which is compatible with a learning theory model, is based on the premise that PTSD symptoms (including intrusive cognitions and avoidance behavior elements) are the result of inadequate emotional processing of the traumatic event. Foa and Kozak (1986) described this model in detail, using literature relevant to a variety of anxiety disorders. Possible mechanisms by which exposure-based therapy could be effective in promoting emotional processing (fear reduction) and associated symptom reduction were proposed.

Specifically, Foa and Kozak (1986) proposed that the fear memory is represented as a cognitive network structure with three major components: (1) information related to the stimulus situation; (2) information about cognitive, behavioral, and physiological components of the response; and (3) the meaning related to these first two components, as well as their association. They suggested that the fear structures of anxiety-disorder patients are characterized as containing pathological elements, such as excessive physiological arousal, extreme negative valence associated with the stimulus, and dysfunctional perceptions of danger or threat. The authors proposed that this structure, once activated, functions as a "program to escape or avoid danger."

Implications for behavioral treatment flow from this conceptual model. Based on data from the anxiety treatment literature, Foa and Kozak (1986) concluded that two main elements of treatment appear to be necessary for the modification of pathological elements of the fear structure or emotional processing: Activation of the fear structure is cited as the first component, and integration of new information that is incompatible with the current fear structure is the second component. As discussed by Foa and Kozak, activation of the fear structure can be accomplished through in vivo or imaginal exposure. The choice of method may depend on the mode that (a) is most compatible with the fear structure, and (b) will thereby elicit it. For example, the authors suggested that in vivo exposure may be sufficient for eliciting the fear structure for simple phobics, while Fairbank and Brown (1987) suggested that imaginal exposure may be most effective with combat veterans be-

cause it allows them to present their own most personal fear-related situations.

Foa and Kozak (1986) observed that the elements of exposure associated with successful treatment outcome included not only initial activation, but also habituation both within and across sessions. They suggested that these processes allow for integration of several kinds of information that is incompatible with the fear structure, such as distinction between physiological responses and stimulus elements, indicating that anxiety does not persist indefinitely; knowledge that avoidance is not the only means to terminate arousal; modification of views regarding the experience of anxiety itself as dangerous; and appraisal of danger or threat from a longer-term perspective. Some factors in the exposure therapy situation identified as necessary for either within- or across-session habituation were attention, optimal level of arousal, and adequate duration of exposure.

DIAGNOSTIC ISSUES AND PROBLEMS

The PTSD diagnostic category has been the object of considerable controversy since it was first introduced in DSM-III (American Psychiatric Association, 1980). Much of this concern has been focused on two issues relating to the validity of the diagnostic category. First, the construct validity of the disorder as a unique, homogeneous clinical entity has been questioned. Second, the degree to which PTSD can be reliably distinguished from other clinical disorders has generated discussion and debate in the literature. Although the diagnosis of PTSD is intended to characterize the predictable emotional, cognitive, and behavioral sequelae that may follow exposure to many types of catastrophic events, the literature on combat-related PTSD among Vietnam veterans has contained the preponderance of concern about diagnosis. Accordingly, the following overview of diagnostic issues uses the body of work on combat-related PTSD.

Validity of the PTSD Diagnosis

Specific psychiatric syndromes were first described in association with the combat-related problems found among veterans of the two world wars. In contrast to the more narrowly defined concept of "shell shock" generated during World War I, Grinker and Spiegel (1945) provided detailed case histories of World War II veterans, which described a wide variety of psychological problems following combat. These investigators presented a symptom picture that included anxiety attacks, depression, suicidal and homicidal ideation, sleep difficulties, and combat-related nightmares.

While these and other case studies of combat veterans provided a rich body of descriptive data on the sequelae of trauma exposure, it was the relatively better controlled research in which Vietnam combat veterans were contrasted to peer comparison groups that provided much of the basis for the current diagnostic category of PTSD. For example, early reports by Figley (1978), Wilson (1978), and Egendorf, Kadushin, Laufer, Rothbart, and Sloan (1981) made significant empirical contributions supporting the notion that Vietnam combat exposure was related to a characteristic pattern of clinical symptoms and psychosocial dysfunction. A sizable amount of subsequent research has generally supported the construct validity of a trauma-related clinical syndrome that significantly overlaps the diagnostic criteria presented in the DSM-III (e.g., Atkinson, Sparr, Sheff, White, & Fitzsimmons, 1984; Carroll, Rueger, Foy, & Donahoe, 1985; Penk, Robinowitz, Roberts, Patterson, Dolan, & Atkins, 1981). In addition, the symptoms associated with combat trauma are similar to those found in victims of other trauma such as human-error disasters (Wilkinson, 1983), natural disasters (Logue, Melick, & Hansen, 1981), and rape (Kilpatrick et al., 1987). Although current research on the validity of the PTSD diagnostic category is incomplete and particularly lacking in longitudinal examinations of the disorder, it does provide encouraging empirical support for the viability of a unique disorder predictably related to the experience of extreme trauma.

Differential Diagnosis

A second diagnostic issue concerns whether or not PTSD is a diagnostic entity clearly distinct from other diagnostic categories. This issue is somewhat more controversial and, unfortunately, much

less well researched. Much of the controlled research using Vietnam veterans has used a design in which PTSD-positive psychiatric veterans are compared with diagnostically heterogeneous groups of PTSD-negative psychiatric veterans. This approach has left the issue of discriminant validity largely unaddressed in the empirical literature. Thus, the degree to which PTSD can be distinguished from other specific, homogeneous clinical syndromes has yet to be determined adequately.

One area of diagnostic discrimination that has received some research attention has been whether posttraumatic symptomatology reflects longstanding characterological vulnerabilities or results primarily from the acute impact of a traumatic stressor. The preponderance of research evidence since the issue was first formulated by Figley (1978) has supported the view that severe trauma is sufficient to cause posttraumatic symptomatology (e.g., Foy, Sipprelle, Rueger, & Carroll, 1984). That is, symptoms of PTSD can result even among very well adjusted persons who are exposed to catastrophic events. Thus, an Axis I diagnosis of PTSD can be distinguished from long-term, Axis II designations.

Affective disorders and other anxiety disorders also should be distinguished from PTSD. The clinical presentation of PTSD, as well as current diagnostic criteria, shows considerable overlap with criteria for depression, generalized anxiety disorders, panic attack, and phobic disorders. Clearly, more research will be necessary to demonstrate that PTSD can be reliably discriminated from these disorders. In particular, research designed to directly contrast diagnostically homogeneous groups with groups of PTSD subjects would be beneficial.

One other problem of differential diagnosis merits mention. A growing number of cases of malingering and factitious PTSD have appeared in the literature (Pary, Tobias, & Lippman, 1987; Sparr & Pankrantz, 1983). Unfortunately, the considerable media attention given to the problems of Vietnam veterans in recent years may have increased the ease by which PTSD symptoms can be faked. Thus, the PTSD diagnostic workup should include consideration of potential influence presented by monetary or other secondary gains. The next section discusses assessment methods that can help address this problem.

Comprehensive Assessment of PTSD

The foregoing discussion underscores the need for a comprehensive approach to the assessment and diagnosis of PTSD. Both the identification of symptoms that meet the criteria for a PTSD diagnosis and the exploration of competing or coexisting disorders require a varied, multimodal approach to assessment. Although time, assessment conditions, and resources may limit a comprehensive evaluation, the following five methods are recommended: (1) structured clinical interview aimed at identifying current symptomatology; (2) determination of pretrauma history and functioning; (3) psychometric assessment; (4) collection of behavioral and physiological response data; and (5) review of archival information.

The most useful way to begin a PTSD assessment is to verify actual exposure to a catastrophic stressor. Although this may be easily accomplished in many circumstances through referral sources and objective accounts or evidence, simple self-report of exposure should be cross-validated if at all possible. As noted, there is growing evidence of convincing combat-related PTSD presentations that are found to be factitious or faked, upon closer investigation. Considerable professional time and effort can be saved by an initial cross-validation of the individual's exposure to trauma and careful assessment of the severity of the trauma. For example, an examination of veterans' discharge papers and "C-file" can establish whether the veteran was in Vietnam and can provide a preliminary validation of combat experience (Carroll et al., 1985).

The combination of a diagnostic clinical interview and psychometric testing is central to establishing the salience of PTSD symptoms in the current clinical picture and in identifying coexistent disorder(s). It is often necessary to supplement the more general interview with one of a number of interviews aimed specifically at determining the severity of PTSD symptomatology (e.g., Foy et al., 1984). While the choice of specific instruments is a matter of training, familiarity, and preference, the need to assess a range of diagnostic possibilities is an often-neglected undertaking (Sierles, Chen, McFarland, & Taylor, 1983).

A number of psychometric measures are available that can assist in establishing a firm PTSD diagnosis. For example, Foy et al. (1984), and Keane, Wolfe, and Taylor (1987) have developed symptom rating scales based on DSM-III criteria for PTSD. Among the more traditional psychological tests, the Minnesota Multiphasic Personality Inventory (MMPI) has not surprisingly received the most research attention. A number of existing studies indicate that the MMPI may have diagnostic and discriminative merit in terms of PTSD (Foy et al., 1984; Keane, Malloy, & Fairbank, 1984; Penk et al., 1981). However, the utility of the MMPI as a primary diagnostic tool in PTSD is limited by its incomplete empirical base. Preliminary studies suffer from limitations in subject selection, heterogeneous comparison groups, and a lack of cross-validations studies, necessitating caution when using the MMPI as an aid in assessing PTSD. However, the MMPI does show promise, and it benefits from more research attention than other traditional testing instruments.

An evaluation of pretrauma psychosocial functioning also is a necessary component of a thorough PTSD assessment. The prior level of adjustment and the possibility of preexisting psychopathology can be assessed by victims' self-report, reports from significant others, and archival information. While such information will not rule out or confirm a PTSD diagnosis, it does provide a historical context that will assist the determination of Axis II personality features, support network resources, and other treatment-relevant information.

A final component of a PTSD evaluation is careful behavioral and physiological assessment. Formal objective methods are available in which trauma-related stimuli are presented systematically, and behavioral avoidance, physiological reactivity, and subjective distress are measured (Malloy et al., 1983). While such procedures may be burdensome for clinical settings, their use for both diagnostic and treatment purposes is strongly recommended. Because a critical element in behavioral treatment is the careful evaluation of changes in target behaviors, comprehensive assessment procedures both within and across treatment phases are needed. The case study presented later in this chapter provides an example of the use of these assessment procedures.

TREATMENT STRATEGIES

Behaviorally based treatments for victims of trauma can be categorized according to the primary goal of the intervention strategy. *Exposure* strategies are used to reduce intrusive memories, flashbacks, and nightmares about the original traumatic event(s) by repeated reexposure of the victim to cues associated with the feared situation. Through habituation and ultimate extinction of negative arousal associated with the original trauma(s), the positive symptoms (i.e., symptoms that are noticed due to their *presence*, not due to their *absence*) of PTSD (i.e., intrusive thoughts, nightmares, and exaggerated startle response) may be reduced.

Systematic desensitization, flooding, and implosive therapy are examples of exposure strategies. Imaginal reexposure is a format used when it is impractical or impossible to recreate the actual original traumatic situation(s). Treatment of victims whose traumatic experiences are remote, through time or distance factors, such as adult incest and combat-related PTSD, is often accomplished through imaginal presentation of the feared memories.

Actual presentation of the feared object (in vivo) or return to the original feared situation (in vitro) are alternate formats that may be used when the treatment situation permits. For example, in vivo exposure might be used for transportation accident survivors, while an in vitro format could be selected for victims of physical or sexual assault. Although literature on exposure therapy for simple phobias suggests that actual exposure is superior to an imaginal format (Foa & Kozak, 1986), results from controlled comparison studies for PTSD are not yet available.

Procedurally, there is some consistency across clinical reports of exposure therapy for PTSD, in that 10–15 reexposure trials are used to achieve reduction of conditioned negative arousal (Foy et al., 1987). Treatment sessions range from 60 to 120 minutes in length and are usually scheduled on a weekly or twice-weekly basis. Relaxation procedures may be used before and after exposure trials. Some clinical reports describe a therapist-directed exposure procedure (e.g., Keane & Kaloupek, 1982), while others (e.g., the case reported in this chapter) feature a client self-exposure style.

Cognitive restructuring or trauma-processing strategies deal with the meaning assigned to the traumatic experience(s) by the victim and elaborations on the meanings of the original event(s) that adversely affect the individual's current life assumptions. Janoff-Bulman (1985) has identified basic life assumptions that are often radically changed following a traumatic experience. These include (1) self-invulnerability; (2) life equitability and fairness; and (3) positive self-esteem through life experiences. These assumptions are adaptive prior to trauma experience. However, trauma exposure may render these assumptions inaccurate in light of the experience. Thus, victimization often involves a polarization of these life assumptions from pretrauma naiveté to perceptions of extreme vulnerability, an overwhelming sense of life's unfairness, and self-blame.

Trauma processing, or cognitive restructuring as applied to victimization, involves systematic therapeutic examination of the individual's life assumptions. Pretrauma, impact, and posttraumatic time frames are used to track critical changes made in life assumptions that may reflect overgeneralization of fear from the traumatic event(s). The therapist's role is to guide the client's self-exploration of meanings assigned to the traumatic experience(s) and assist in challenging misinterpretations and overgeneralizations that may perpetuate victimization.

A third behavioral strategy for dealing with problems associated with victimization is a *skills training* approach. Early clinical reports (e.g., Fairbank, Gross, & Keane, 1983; Kilpatrick & Veronen, 1983) incorporated relaxation training into treatment of trauma victims. Teaching relaxation skills to reduce unpleasant levels of autonomic arousal represents an additional coping strategy or skill that clients can then use under a variety of conditions.

Training in other kinds of coping skills may also be indicated in individual victim's cases. Anger management, problem solving, and assertion represent other kinds of specific skills for which structured behavioral training methods are available.

An important area in which skills training is indicated involves family or dyadic functioning. Communication skills training can be employed to treat predictable problems in intimate relationships following victimization. In particular, victims' self-disclosure skills and spouses' active listening skills can be targeted to counteract the frequent tendency in victim dyads to avoid discussion of intense negative feelings associated with the traumatic experience (Carroll et al., 1985).

As Table 17.1 indicates, reports of behavioral treatment in recent literature reflect a combined approach to treating victimization problems.

Mixing strategies to include exposure and skills training or cognitive restructuring techniques appears to typify current behavioral treatments. Thus, it is not surprising that the case illustration that follows exemplifies this approach.

CASE ILLUSTRATION

The present case study uses multimodal assessment (Malloy et al., 1983) in the treatment of a Vietnam veteran with combat-related PTSD. Imaginal flooding was used in conjunction with cognitive-restructuring procedures to treat high levels of target PTSD symptoms. Cognitive restructuring was included in an effort to improve interpersonal relations by increasing interest in

TABLE 17.1. Studies Showing Various Behavioral Treatments of Trauma Victims

Trauma type	Study	Treatment procedure	Target symptoms
Combat	Fairbank, Gross, & Keane (1983)	a. Implosive therapy b. Relaxation training	PTSD symptoms, depression
	Black & Keane (1982)	a. Implosive therapy b. In vivo flooding	PTSD symtpoms, driving phobia
Incest	Rychtarik, Silverman, Van Landingham, & Prue (1984)	Implosive therapy	Incest-related anxiety responses
Rape	Kilpatrick & Veronen (1983)	Brief behavioral intervention package (BBIP): a. Relaxation training b. Thought stopping c. Guided self-dialogue d. "Reentry" strategies	Rape-related fear, anxiety, & depression
	Veronen & Kilpatrick (1983)	Stress inoculation training (SIT): a. Relaxation training b. Diaphragmatic breathing c. Role-playing d. Covert modeling e. Thought stopping f. Guided self-dialogue	Rape-related fears & avoidance
	Turner & Frank (1981)	Cognitive therapy	Aggression, fear, & low self-esteem
	Turner & Frank (19181)	Systematic desensitization	Rape-related fears
	Wolff (1977)	Systematic desensitization	Rape-related fears
Transportation accidents	McCaffrey & Fairbank (1985)	Broad-spectrum behavioral treatment package (BSBTP): a. Relaxation training b. Implosive therapy c. Self-directed in vivo exposure	PTSD symtoms related to helicopter, car crashes
War-related bombing/ terrorism (children)	Saigh (1986)	a. Imaginal flooding b. Relaxation	PTSD symptoms avoidance

usual activities and by diminishing difficulties in establishing and maintaining trust.

Mr. M. was a 35-year-old Caucasian, non-service-connected Vietnam veteran, referred for behavioral assessment and treatment of possible PTSD at a Los Angeles area Veterans Administration medical center. His preliminary social history was significant in that he reported being sexually abused by his father at age 12 years. Additionally, he reported that his mother had a history of hospitalization for depression.

Mr. M. served in the U.S. Marine Corps, with training as a rifleman. He reported intense combat exposure, which was supported by his official military records. Specifically, Mr. M. was wounded during heavy combat involvement in the battle of Hue City during the Tet Offensive in February, 1968. His tour of Vietnam was terminated prematurely by his medical evacuation to the United States. On the basis of these combat experiences, he scored six on the seven-point Guttman scale used to assess combat exposure (Lund et al., 1984).

After Mr. M's discharge from military service, he was employed in a succession of short-term, entry-level jobs. Mr. M. had been married prior to Vietnam service, but he was divorced by his wife shortly after returning from Vietnam. At the time of current treatment, he had been in a cohabitation relationship for more than a year. Mr. M. had a history of one prior 2-week psychiatric hospitalization immediately following his divorce. He reported that he was experiencing severe depression and an increase in Vietnam-related nightmares and memories at that time.

The precipitant to Mr. M.'s current hospitalization was a crisis in his cohabitation relationship during which he threatened to kill another man who showed interest in his girlfriend. Upon admission, Mr. M. met full DSM-III criteria for PTSD, having symptoms of reexperiencing combat-related trauma, reduced involvement with the external world, sleep disturbance, and survivor guilt.

Crisis Intervention and Pharmacological Treatment

During the crisis in which Mr. M. was being overwhelmed by jealousy and homicidal ideation, he was involuntarily admitted to a locked crisis-intervention unit. Mr. M. was prescribed 200 mg of Sinequan, and 1.5 mg of Xanax, both taken daily, and 500 mg of chloral hydrate for sleep. Upon stabilization, he was transferred within the hospital to an open general psychiatric unit for further evaluation and treatment. After discharge from inpatient status, he was maintained on 150 mg of Sinequan, and the Xanax and chloral hydrate prescriptions were discontinued.

Behavioral Assessment and Treatment

Initially, multimodal assessment procedures, including physiological, self-report, and behavioral components, were administered. These measures included a PTSD intensity score derived from the PTSD Symptom Checklist (Foy et al., 1984); psychophysiological data (i.e., heart rate—beats per minute [BPM]—response), and Subjective Units of Discomfort Scale (SUDS) ratings in response to standard videotaped combat scenes (Malloy et al., 1983). Detailed step-by-step description of these procedures for pretreatment assessment and flooding treatment are available (Foy, Donahoe, Carroll, Gallers, & Reno, 1987b).

Figure 17.1 depicts the course of behavioral assessment and treatment administered over 47 inpatient days. Data points for the flooding and the cognitive treatment phases represent means over two treatment sessions. Thus, Mr. M. was treated with 14 flooding and 6 cognitive-restructuring therapy sessions.

The brief course of cognitive restructuring focused on identifying and changing dysfunctional life assumptions derived from the experience of severe combat trauma. The conceptual framework described earlier in this chapter was used. Initially, premilitary experiences and related assumptions were explored. In this client's case, early life stressors (e.g., childhood sexual assault and mother's mental illness) had already posed obstacles to development of interpersonal trust and positive self-esteem.

Next, reasons for joining the Marine Corps were explored, in light of Mr. M.'s previous family stresses. His reactions to combat, especially the traumatic events, and his subsequent changes in attitude and world view were explored. Finally, relationships between attitudes developed under extreme life threat and his current behavior patterns were processed. Implications of a survivor versus a victim role for life assumptions and adaptive behavior were emphasized. The advantages of being a survivor were underscored, including more positive self-esteem and greater control over personal activities in life.

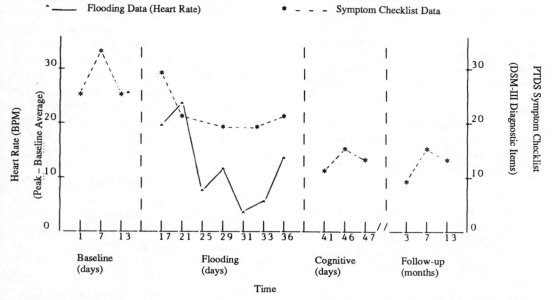

FIGURE 17.1. Changes in heart rate and PTSD symptom scores in a combat trauma subject, both within and across treatment phases.

Treatment Results

Pretreatment levels of reported PTSD symptoms, mean SUDS ratings, and mean heart rate (HR) response for standard combat scenes are depicted in Figures 17.1 and 17.2. Additionally, Figure

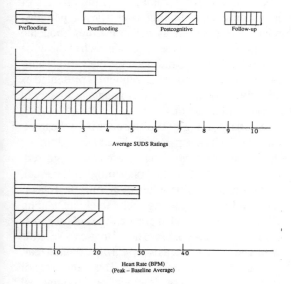

FIGURE 17.2. Standard psychophysiological assessment measures (Malloy, et al., 1983) before and after flooding and cognitive treatment.

17.1 shows HR changes over flooding treatment sessions for Mr. M.'s personal combat trauma.

The most striking change from pretreatment to posttreatment assessment was obtained in HR response to standard combat scenes. Mean change scores were computed by subtracting the mean BPM obtained on neutral scenes from the highest mean scores from the combat scenes. This change score was 30 BPM at pretreatment, 21.5 BPM after the flooding sessions, 22.0 BPM after the cognitive treatment, and 8 BPM at the 1-year follow-up.

Reductions were also observed in the PTSD symptoms. These scores showed a 10-point decrease from pretreatment to posttreatment, with this decrease in symptomatology being maintained at the 1-year follow-up. The most significant reductions at the 1-year follow-up were noted in the following specific symptoms: numbing of emotion, loss of interest in usual activities, early morning awakening, difficulty falling asleep, and excessive jumpiness.

The MMPI was used sequentially to assess potential changes in severity of general psychopathology. At pretreatment, t of 10 clinical scale scores were elevated beyond the normal range (T score, 70). Immediately after treatment, no scales were elevated, while at a 13-month follow-up, two scales were slightly elevated, with T scores in the 70–75 range.

Reductions in PTSD-related measures also occurred within the treatment phase of the study. Data on HR and SUDS, in Figure 17.1, show decreases across sessions during flooding. Data points were calculated by taking the peak heart rate average per session and subtracting the baseline averages from this figure, thus obtaining an average difference score for each session. This HR data showed a peak difference score of 24 in Session 3, which then declined to a score of 4 in Session 9. Consistent with these data were gradual decreases in SUDS ratings from 9 to 3 over the course of flooding treatment.

Discussion

Our combined behavioral treatment approach, used in conjunction with ongoing pharmacotherapy, was followed by reduced PTSD-related symptoms in this individual. Further, these reductions were maintained 1 year after the treatment.

Positive gains also were made in psychosocial functioning during the 1-year posttreatment interval. Mr. M. successfully completed a technical training course for electricians. Subsequently, he has been employed in the same job and has been promoted. He has also maintained his cohabitation relationship and has made progress in remediating some of its previous difficulties.

Bimonthly follow-up visits seemed to be important for maintaining treatment gains by providing an opportunity to monitor progress and to address new problems in a timely fashion. Indeed, these problem-solving sessions served as boosters, thereby underscoring the importance of providing planned aftercare.

ALTERNATIVE TREATMENT OPTIONS

As described earlier in this chapter, behavioral methods for PTSD can be categorized as exposure-based, cognitive restructuring, or skills training. Our case illustration presented a combination treatment approach, including exposure and cognitive methods. Therefore, the alternative treatment we now consider represents a skills training approach.

Comprehensive coping skills training is featured in a program referred to as stress inoculation training (SIT), tailored after Meichenbaum's stress inoculation procedures. The program was developed as part of the Sexual Assault Research Project at the Medical University of South Carolina, to treat anxiety-related symptoms of rape victims (Veronen & Kilpatrick, 1983). As previously noted, Veronen and Kilpatrick proposed a learning theory model of PTSD and rape-related fear and anxiety. Accordingly, component skills in SIT were developed to teach victims ways to manage such fear and anxiety. Victims are taught to use these skills to manage rape-related fear, as well as anxiety related to a variety of other situations.

Veronen and Kilpatrick (1983) applied SIT with rape victims experiencing persistent symptoms of anxiety beyond 3 months postassault. This latter requirement was based on their finding that generalized symptoms of psychological distress diminished by that point for most victims. The SIT program contains an initial educational phase and then instructions in sets of coping skills that specifically address anxiety-related symptoms in the physiological, cognitive, and behavioral response channels.

In the first two sessions, clients are presented with the learning theory model of fear acquisition related to rape trauma, as well as an explanation of Lang's (1968) model of anxiety expressed in the physiological, cognitive, and behavioral channels. Clients are active participants in the process of identifying fear-eliciting cues (target phobias) related to the assault, as well as learning about the specific responses experienced in each of the three channels. Then, the rationale for the various coping skills is outlined, and treatment is presented as an active way for the victim to manage anxiety in a variety of situations.

Similar to Lang's (1968) proposal for the treatment of anxiety, separate skills are applied for the three channels in which anxiety may be expressed. First, in relation to the physiological channel, Jacobsonian tension–relaxation muscle relaxation, and deep-breathing techniques are taught. Clients are instructed to practice all skills at home. Additionally, they are instructed to use these skills with a nontarget fear, as well as a rape-related fear, such as staying alone at night. The techniques of role playing and covert modeling, or imaginal progression through an anxiety-producing situation, are applied to reduce behavioral avoidance.

Finally, to address cognitive expressions of fear, the techniques of thought stopping and guided self-dialogue are taught. The latter includes self-assessment of irrational or dysfunctional cognitions and identification and use of more adaptive cognitions to cope with a stressor. As can be seen from this description, SIT also includes an element of exposure in the assignments, for application of skills with target fears.

Veronen and Kilpatrick (1983) noted in their report that six clients who had completed SIT improved on measures of anxiety and mood. A subsequent single case report that included physiological, behavioral, and cognitive assessment measures also yielded positive results (Kilpatrick & Amick, 1985). In addition, a recent comparison study conducted by Resick, Jordan, Girelli, Hutter, and Marhoefer-Dvorak (1987) found that SIT was associated with significant improvement in anxiety-related symptoms when compared to a waiting-list control group. However, SIT results were not significantly different from assertion training or from supportive–educational psychotherapy conditions.

FUTURE DIRECTIONS

Several recent reviews of literature on behavioral treatments for trauma victims produced convergent conclusions (Fairbank & Brown, 1987; Foa et al., in press; Foy et al., 1987). First, no single treatment emerged as clearly being most effective, although almost all published reports include some element of reexposure to original traumatic cues. Second, major methodological limitations characterize the existing literature, including lack of comparison groups and nonrandom group assignment. A third conclusion is that few published studies clearly include a theoretical rationale relating treatment strategy to target symptoms.

Currently, a controlled comparison study of SIT, exposure therapy, supportive counseling, and a no-treatment control is being conducted with sexual assault victims who are at least 3 months postassault and meet criteria for PTSD (Foa et al., in press). In this study, the exposure therapy is described as including in vivo exposure to feared situations, as well as imaginal exposure to sub-

jects' rape experiences. A modification of SIT, excluding homework related to in vivo exposure to feared situations, is being used.

The rationale for the exposure condition is based on the model of emotional processing, in which exposure activates the fear structure, and consequent habituation allows for the integration of information that is incompatible with the fear structure. The authors also suggested that although SIT does not include direct exposure to the trauma situation, this treatment may also alter the fear structure. That is, relaxation training may promote dissociation between physiological arousal and stimuli that previously elicited fear, while cognitive techniques may alter assessments of threat to a variety of stimuli. Preliminary results were reported by Foa et al. (in press) for six subjects who completed SIT. The results indicated that symptom improvement was maintained at 3-month follow-up on measures of PTSD, anxiety, and depression.

In general, the aforementioned study is commendable for the rigorous methodology employed, the clear rationale relating symptoms and treatment, as well as the inclusion of an assessment of PTSD symptoms. The results of this study may yield important information regarding the relative efficacy of two different treatment strategies that represent prominent behavioral alternatives for the treatment of PTSD.

REFERENCES

American Psychiatric Association. (1980). *Diagnostic and statistical manual of mental disorders* (3rd ed.). Washington, DC: Author.

American Psychiatric Association. (1987). *Diagnostic and statistical manual of mental disorders* (3rd ed. rev.). Washington, DC: Author.

Atkinson, R. M., Sparr, L. F., Sheff, A. G., White, R. A., & Fitzsimmons, J. T. (1984). The diagnosis of posttraumatic stress disorder in Vietnam veterans: Preliminary findings. *American Journal of Psychiatry, 141*, 694–696.

Black, J. L., & Keane, T. M. (1982). Implosive therapy in the treatment of combat related fears in a World War II veteran. *Journal of Behavior Therapy and Experimental Psychiatry, 13*, 163–165.

Blanchard, E. B., Kolb, L. C., Pallmeyer, T. P., & Gerardi, R. (1982). The development of a psychophysiological assessment procedure for posttraumatic stress disorder in Vietnam veterans. *Psychiatric Quarterly, 4,* 220–229.

Carroll, E. M., Rueger, D. B., Foy, D. W., & Donahoe, C. P. (1985). Vietnam combat veterans with posttraumatic stress disorder: Analysis of marital and cohabiting adjustment. *Journal of Abnormal Psychology, 94,* 329–337.

Egendorf, A., Kadushin, C., Laufer, R. S., Rothbart, G., & Sloan, L. (1981). *Legacies of Vietnam: Comparative adjustment of veterans and their peers* (Publication No. V101134P–630). Washington, DC: Government Printing Office.

Fairbank, J. A., & Brown, T. A. (1987). Current behavioral approaches to the treatment of posttraumatic stress disorder. *The Behavior Therapist, 3,* 57–64.

Fairbank, J. A., Gross, R. T., & Keane, T. M. (1983). Treatment of posttraumatic stress disorder: Evaluation of outcome with a behavioral code. *Behavior Modification, 7,* 557–568.

Figley, C. R. (1978). *Stress disorders among Vietnam veterans: Theory, research, and treatment.* New York: Brunner/Mazel.

Foa, E. B., & Kozak, M. J. (1986). Emotional processing of fear: Exposure to corrective information. *Psychological Bulletin, 99,* 20–35.

Foa, E. B., Olasov, B., Rothbaum, B., & Steketee, G. S. (in press). Treatment of rape victims. *NIMH Monograph Series, "State of the art in sexual assault research."*

Foy, D. W., & Card, J. J. (1987). Combat-related posttraumatic stress disorder etiology: Replicated findings in a national sample of Vietnam-era men. *Journal of Clinical Psychology, 43,* 28–31.

Foy, D. W., Carroll, E. M., & Donahoe, C. P. (1987a). Etiological factors in the development of PTSD in clinical samples of Vietnam combat veterans. *Journal of Clinical Psychology, 43,* 17–27.

Foy, D. W., Donahoe, C. P., Carroll, E. M., Gallers, J., & Reno, R. (1987b). Posttraumatic stress disorder. In L. Michelson & M. Ascher (Eds.), *Cognitive-behavioral assessment and treatment of anxiety disorders.* New York: Guilford.

Foy, D. W., Resnick, H. S., Sipprelle, R. C., & Carroll, E. M. (1987c). Premilitary, military, and postmilitary factors in the development of combat-related posttraumatic stress disorders. *The Behavior Therapist, 10,* 3–9.

Foy, D. W., Sipprelle, R. C., Rueger, D. B., & Carroll, E. M. (1984). Etiology of posttraumatic stress disorder in Vietnam veterans: Analysis of premilitary, military, and combat exposure influences. *Journal of Consulting and Clinical Psychology, 52,* 79–87.

Grinker, R. R., & Spiegel, J. P. (1945). *Men under stress.* Philadelphia: Blackinston.

Janoff-Bulman, R. (1985). The aftermath of victimization: Rebuilding shattered assumptions. In C. R. Figley (Ed.), *Trauma and its wake.* New York: Brunner/Mazel.

Keane, T. M., & Kaloupek, D. G. (1982). Imaginal flooding in the treatment of a posttraumatic stress disorder. *Journal of Consulting and Clinical Psychology, 50,* 138–140.

Keane, T. M., Malloy, P. F., & Fairbank, J. A. (1984). Empirical development of an MMPI subscale for the assessment of combat-related posttraumatic stress disorder. *Journal of Consulting and Clinical Psychology, 52,* 888–891.

Keane, T. M., Wolfe, J., & Taylor, K. L. (1987). Posttraumatic stress disorder: Evidence for diagnostic validity and methods of psychological assessment. *Journal of Clinical Psychology, 43,* 32–43.

Keane, T. M., Zimering, R. T., & Caddell, J. M. (1985). A behavioral formulation of posttraumatic stress disorder in Vietnam veterans. *The Behavior Therapist, 8,* 9–12.

Kilpatrick, D. G., & Amick, A. E. (1985). Rape trauma. In M. Hersen & C. G. Last (Eds.), *Behavior therapy casebook.* New York: Springer.

Kilpatrick, D. G., Saunders, B. E., Veronen, L. J., Best, C. L., & Von, J. M. (1987). Criminal victimization: Lifetime prevalence, reporting to police, and psychological impact. *Crime and Delinquency, 33,* 479–489.

Kilpatrick, D. G., & Veronen, L. J. (1983). Treatment for rape-related problems: Crisis intervention is not enough. In L. H. Cohen, W. L. Claiborn, & G. A. Specter (Eds.), *Crisis intervention* (pp. 165–185). New York: Human Sciences Press.

Kilpatrick, D. G., Veronen, L. J., & Best, C. L. (1985). Factors predicting psychological distress among rape victims. In C. R. Figley (Ed.), *Trauma and its wake.* New York: Brunner/Mazel.

Kilpatrick, D. G., Veronen, L. J., & Resick, P. A. (1979). Assessment of the aftermath of rape: Changing patterns of fear. *Journal of Behavioral Assessment, 1,* 133–148.

Lang, P. J. (1968). Fear reduction and fear behavior: Problems in treating a construct. *Research in Psychotherapy, 3,* 90–102.

Logue, J. N., Melick, M. E., & Hansen, H. (1981). Research issues and directions in the epidemiology of health effects of disasters. *Epidemiologic Reviews, 3,* 140–162.

Lund, M., Foy, D. W., Sipprelle, R. C., & Strachan, A. (1984). The combat exposure scale: A systematic assessment of trauma in the Vietnam war. *Journal of Clinical Psychology, 40,* 1323–1328.

Malloy, P. F., Fairbank, J. A., & Keane, T. M. (1983). Validation of a multimethod assessment of posttraumatic stress disorder in Vietnam veterans. *Journal of Consulting and Clinical Psychology, 51,* 488–494.

McCaffrey, R. J., & Fairbank, J. A. (1985). Posttraumatic stress disorder associated with transportation accidents: Two case studies. *Behavior Therapy, 16,* 406–416.

Pary, R., Tobias, C., & Lippman, S. (1987). Recognizing shammed and genuine posttraumatic stress disorder. *VA Practitioner,* July, 37–43.

Penk, W. E., Robinowitz, R., Roberts, W. R., Patterson, E. T., Dolan, M. P., & Atkins, H. G. (1981). Adjustment differences among male substance abusers varying in degree of combat experience in Vietnam. *Journal of Consulting and Clinical Psychology, 49,* 426–437.

Resick, P. A., Jordan, D. G., Girelli, S. A., Hutter, C. K., & Marhoefer-Dvorak, S. (1987). *A comparative outcome study of group therapy for sexual assault victims.* Unpublished manuscript, University of Missouri—St. Louis.

Rychtarik, R. G., Silverman, W. K., Van Landingham, W. P., & Prue, D. M. (1984). Treatment of an incest victim with implosive therapy: A case study. *Behavior Therapy, 15,* 410–420.

Saigh, P. A. (1986). In vitro flooding in the treatment of a 6-yr-old boy's post-traumatic stress disorder. *Behaviour Research and Therapy, 24,* 685–688.

Sierles, F. S., Chen, J., McFarland, R. E., & Taylor, M. A. (1983). Posttraumatic stress disorder and concurrent psychiatric illness: A preliminary report. *American Journal of Psychiatry, 140,* 1177–1179.

Sparr, L. S., & Pankratz, L. D. (1983). Factitious posttraumatic stress disorder. *American Journal of Psychiatry, 140,* 1015–1019.

Steketee, G., & Foa, E. B. (1987). Rape victims: Posttraumatic stress responses and their treatment: A review of the literature. *Journal of Anxiety Disorders, 1,* 69–86.

Turner, S. M., & Frank, E. (1981). Behavior therapy in the treatment of rape victims. In L. Michelson, M. Hersen, & S. M. Turner (Eds.), *Future perspectives in behavior therapy* (pp. 269–291). New York: Plenum.

Veronen, L. J., & Kilpatrick, D. G. (1983). Stress management for rape victims. In D. Meichenbaum & M. E. Jaremko (Eds.), *Stress reduction and prevention* (pp. 341–374). New York: Plenum.

Wilkinson, C. B. (1983). Aftermath of a disaster: The collapse of the Hyatt Regency Hotel skywalk. *American Journal of Psychiatry, 140,* 1134–1139.

Wilson, J. P. (1978). *Identity, ideology, and crisis: The Vietnam veteran in transition* (Part 2). Washington, DC: Disabled American Veterans Association.

Wolff, R. (1977). Systematic desensitization and negative practice to alter the aftereffects of a rape attempt. *Journal of Behavior Therapy and Experimental Psychiatry, 8,* 423–425.

CHAPTER 18

Pharmacotherapy

JULES ROSEN AND SCOTT BOHON

CONCEPTUALIZATION OF THE DISORDER

Posttraumatic stress disorder (PTSD) can be conceptualized in both psychological and neurobiological terms. Effective treatment of this disabling and enigmatic disorder requires considerable skill and flexibility. The clinician should consider various psychological as well as pharmacological interventions. This chapter reviews the available literature on the pharmacological treatment of PTSD. In addition, we discuss three of the biological theories of traumatic stress that are relevant to a rational conceptualization of drug therapy.

PTSD as a Physioneurosis

Kardiner and Spiegel (1947), in their work with veterans of both world wars, proposed that traumatic war neurosis is a "physioneurosis" in which the central nervous system (CNS) is unable to modulate the body's physiological response to stress. Recent studies have confirmed that the physiological response to combat sounds and imagery is exaggerated in subjects with PTSD (Blanchard, Kolb, Gerandi, Ryan, & Pallmeyer, 1986; Malloy, Fairbanks, & Keane, 1983; Pitman, Orr, Forgue, deJong, & Claiborn, 1987), and physiological reactivity has been included in the DSM-III-R (American Psychiatric Association, 1987) criteria of the disorder.

Van der Kolk, Greenberg, Boyd, and Krystal (1985), in their discussion of the neurobiology of trauma, suggest that some symptoms of PTSD are reminiscent of the animal paradigm of inescapable shock, in which repeated shock results in neurochemical changes. Animals exposed to inescapable shock have decreased activity in the locus coeruleus, which, as the primary center of norepinephrine in the brain, plays a critical role in regulating the physiological response to stress (Weiss, Glazer, Pohorecky, Brick, & Miller, 1975). Van der Kolk et al. propose that norepinephrine depletion resulting from emotional trauma causes a destabilization of the noradrenergic system. Furthermore, they postulate that different subsets of symptoms of PTSD may result from specific neurochemical processes (e.g. negative symptoms from noradrenergic depletion and positive symptoms from postsynaptic supersensitivity) (see Table 18.1). There is evidence that both tricyclic antidepressant (TCA) (Sulser, Vetulani & Mobley, 1982) and monoamine oxidase inhibitor (MAOI) (McDaniel, 1986) administration results in downregulation of norepinephrine receptors and stabilization of the noradrenergic system.

Impulsivity and Serotonin

The DSM-III-R includes "irritability or outbursts of anger" and "hypervigilance" as part of the diagnostic profile of PTSD. The neurotransmitter serotonin has been associated with aggressive and impulsive behavior. There is an inverse relationship between aggressiveness and the cerebrospinal fluid (CSF) measurement of the serotonin metabolite 5-hydroxyindoleacetic acid (5-HIAA) (Brown, Goodwin, Ballenger, Goyer, & Major, 1979), which would indicate less serotonergic

TABLE 18.1.   Positive and Negative Symptoms

Positive symptoms	Negative symptoms
Startle responses	Constriction of affect
Explosive outbursts	Decline in occupational functioning
Nightmares	Feeling of estrangement or detachment
Intrusive recollections	

activity in aggressive individuals. Although CSF 5-HIAA has never been studied in subjects with PTSD, the association between aggression and decreased levels of this metabolite appears constant across a spectrum of diagnostic groups (Brown et al., 1982). Serotonin synthesis is stimulated by lithium carbonate (Perez-Cruet, Tagliamonte, Tagliamonte, & Gessa, 1971)—interestingly, lithium carbonate has been shown to reduce symptoms of aggression and impulsivity in a variety of psychiatric disorders (Sheard & Marini, 1980), including PTSD (Kitchner & Greenstein, 1985). All MAOIs and some TCAs enhance serotonergic activity as well.

The "Kindling Theory"

The concept of kindling has been proposed as a basis for some PTSD symptoms. *Kindling* refers to the process of applying small repetitive, subclinical electrical impulses to the limbic system of the brain (Goddard, McIntyre, & Leech, 1969). Eventually, epileptic seizures occur as a result of enhanced brain sensitivity to the stimuli. When the electrical impulses are discontinued, the system does not return to normal; instead, it remains in a state of enhanced responsiveness to a variety of epileptogenic agents. Post and Kopanda (1975) demonstrated that electrical impulses are not essential to this process, and kindling can result from a variety of pharmacological stimuli. Furthermore, kindling may result in behavioral sensitization, in which there is an enhancement of drug-induced behavior rather than seizure. Drugs such as lidocaine, cocaine, and amphetamine have been used in animal studies of behavioral sensitization.

Antelman, Eichler, Black, and Kocan (1980) demonstrated that stress alone has similar kindling properties in laboratory animals. Repetitive intermittent stressful stimuli may result in behavioral sensitization to future stressful stimuli, as well as in cross-sensitization to the kindling effect of

amphetamine. Although these laboratory-induced stressors are very different from the stressors that result in PTSD, van der Kolk et al. (1985) theorized that the stress of a traumatic event, followed by repetitive, intermittent reminders of the event, in the form of dreams, flashbacks, or environmentally induced memories could result in kindling that sensitizes the brain to subsequent stressful stimuli. If this occurs, relatively innocuous stimuli, such as smells or heightened emotional states, could result in disproportionate symptoms of anxiety or aggression. Flashbacks or nightmares might also be triggered. Carbamazepine (Post & Uhde, 1985) is thought to inhibit the kindling process and has been used to alleviate some PTSD symptoms.

In summary, several biological models of PTSD support a rationale for pharmacological treatment trials. These models, though theoretical, may help the clinician initiate drug treatment based on specific presenting symptoms.

DIAGNOSTIC ISSUES AND PROBLEMS

Obviously, accurate diagnosis of PTSD must be made prior to the initiation of any therapy. The frequent presence of concomitant Axis I disorders, as well as premorbid character pathology, can adversely affect the diagnostic process. Illnesses having considerable symptom overlap with PTSD include major depression, generalized anxiety, obsessive–compulsive disorder, somatization disorder, and panic disorder (Horowitz, Wilner, Kaltreider, & Alvarez, 1980; Mellman & Davis, 1985). Sierles, Chen, McFarland, & Taylor (1983) report that Vietnam veterans with PTSD commonly have substance abuse disorders as well. As veterans with combat-related PTSD may qualify for a service-connected disability and monetary compensation, malingerers, as well as patients with factitious illness, have been known to present this disorder (Sparr & Pankratz, 1983). Another problem in diagnosing PTSD is the *priming effect* (LaGuardia, Smith, Francois, & Bachman, 1983)—that is, when subjects were questioned about past traumatization, the questioning itself served as a reminder of the trauma and resulted in the reporting of more symptoms than the patient actually experienced on a day-to-day basis.

Although symptom overlap and dual diagnoses may at times lead to overdiagnosis of PTSD, underdiagnosing is also a problem. Rosen, Fields, Hand, Falcetti, and van Kammen (1989) studied the incidence of previously undiagnosed PTSD in World War II veterans with another Axis I diagnosis. They found that 25% of these patients met DSM-III criteria for the disorder, highlighting the point that PTSD occurs in individuals of all ages and is not, as it is sometimes perceived, limited to veterans of the Vietnam war. Individuals exposed to extreme trauma of many types can develop all of the symptoms of the disorder.

Several factors influence the presentation and intensity of PTSD, such as (a) the nature of the primary trauma, (b) time elapsed since the traumatic event(s), (c) age of the victim when traumatized, (d) social support systems, (e) premorbid personality, and (f) individual emotional and biological makeup of the subject. For example, a World War II veteran who had not had symptoms for four decades might develop flashbacks, insomnia, and combat nightmares later in life when faced with the death of friends and colleagues. The presentation of delayed-onset PTSD in the elderly is often not as conspicuous as in the well-publicized disturbances of Vietnam veterans. During standard clinical evaluations, many clinicians do not consider PTSD a diagnostic possibility. A thorough history of traumatic life events is often missed, which leads to underdiagnosis.

Besides the difficulties of diagnosis, treatment response is difficult to quantify. Other than sleep disturbance and physiological reactivity, the symptoms of PTSD are subjective in nature and cannot be measured readily. In several recent studies, scales such as the Impact of Events Scale (Horowitz, Wilner, & Alvarez, 1979) or a DSM-III symptom checklist (Lerer et al., 1987) have been used to monitor symptom change in PTSD. Unfortunately, reliability and validity of scales across studies has not yet been established.

Essential to the diagnosis is a traumatic event that would cause symptoms of distress in most people. Combat stress has been both categorized and quantified (Lund, Foy, Sipprelle, & Strachan, 1984); however, there is no systematic way to compare the severity of stress of two unrelated events. For instance, is the stress of combat in the Vietnam War equivalent to the stress experienced by Israeli soldiers in the 1973 war? Or is the traumatic event of rape more or less stressful that losing one's home in a tornado? Furthermore, it is probable that a given stressor would be more or less traumatic depending on the individual experiencing it. Quantification of the impact of trauma is not crucial for the clinician who is treating a patient with PTSD; however, it is important in research of treatment outcome.

Other than physiological reactivity, there are no biological tests that have *clinical* utility in the diagnosis or monitoring of treatment response in PTSD. Kudler, Davidson, Meador, Lipper, and Ely (1987) reported that the dexamethasone suppression test was not helpful in diagnosing PTSD.

In summary, PTSD is likely to be either under- or overdiagnosed in most clinical settings. Of the following research reports of treatment outcome, few used rigorous diagnostic criteria.

TREATMENT STRATEGIES

Given the variability in methodology used in the studies reviewed herein, definitive conclusions on drug treatment outcome in PTSD are not currently possible. Although only one study used double-blind methods, there is considerable evidence in the literature that can guide the clinician in reducing some of the distressing symptoms of PTSD. The available findings are described according to a *symptom-oriented* profile. Table 18.2 presents an overview by which target symptoms may be matched with specific pharmacological agents. It must be emphasized that, in a clinical setting, each case of PTSD requires individual tailoring of pharmacotherapy and often requires considerable pharmacological flexibility.

Drugs that Reduce Hyperarousal

The concept of noradrenergic dysregulation was discussed earlier in this chapter. Somewhat recent evidence suggests that both TCA (Sulser et al., 1982) and MAOI (McDaniel, 1986) administration result in downregulation of receptor-mediated noradrenergic supersensitivity.

The most frequent complaints in patients with PTSD are sleep disorders and nightmares (Birkhimer, DeVane, & Muniz, 1985); however,

TABLE 18.2.   Drug Choice Based on Symptomatic
Presentation

Drug	Symptoms
Tricyclic antidepressants	dysphoria, sleep disturbance, nightmares
MAOIs	Depression, nightmares, panic symptoms
Neuroleptics	Dissociative symptoms, psychotic symptoms
Lithium	Loss of control, impulsiveness
Carbamazepine	Flashbacks, nightmares, intrusive recollections
Propranolol	Explosiveness, nightmares
Clonidine	Explosiveness, nightmares
Benzodiazepines	Chronic anxiety

studies of sleep architecture have not revealed a consistently abnormal pattern (Lavie, Hefez, Halpern, & Enoch, 1979; van der Kolk, Blitz, Burr, Sherry, & Hartmann, 1984). Improved sleep has been reported during treatment with both TCAs and MAOIs.

In addition to reduced insomnia, tricyclics and MAOIs decrease frequency of nightmares. This may be due to their rapid-eye-movement (REM) sleep-suppressant effects (Cohen et al., 1982; Dunleavy, Brezinova, Oswald, Maclean, & Tinker, 1972); however, the localization of trauma dreams within sleep architecture is not established, and nightmares have been reported in both Stage 2 and REM sleep (Schlossberg & Benjamin, 1978; van der Kolk et al., 1984).

Clinical Studies of Tricyclics

Burstein (1984) used imipramine in an open study of 10 patients with PTSD in which intrusive symptoms (e.g., nightmares and flashbacks) were reduced, and sleep improved dramatically. The subjects in this study were victims of civilian trauma (i.e., motor vehicle accidents), rather than the more commonly studied combat veteran. Of interest, none of the patients in this study had a prior psychiatric history, and 5 of the 10 had trials of benzodiazepines without therapeutic success.

Falcon, Ryan, Chamberlain, and Curtis (1985) did a retrospective chart review of the efficacy of amitriptyline ($n = 10$), desipramine ($n = 4$), imipramine ($n = 2$), and doxepin ($n = 1$) in the treatment of veterans with PTSD. The dosage ranged from 100 to 250 mg per day. They found that their patients experienced considerable im-

provement in intrusive symptoms (nightmares, flashbacks, and startle response) and in panic attacks. At least 10 of their patients had concurrent DSM-III diagnoses (panic disorder in 3, generalized anxiety disorder in 2, and substance abuse in 5). There was no stated advantage of one tricyclic over another in this study.

Toland, Goetz, Slawsky, and van Kammen (1987) compared desipramine to carbamazepine in an open clinical study. Patients on desipramine ($n = 7$) experienced improvement of anxiety and depressive symptoms, as well as diminished nightmares and flashbacks. The average desipramine blood level was 236 ng/ml, which is within the presumed therapeutic range for the treatment of depression with this drug. The group treated with carbamazepine did not improve in this study.

TCAs and Adjunctive Chemotherapy

Thompson (1977) and Burstein (1986) reported on the effectiveness of the combination of TCAs and neuroleptics in open trials of patients with PTSD. Both studies reported varying degrees of success, but neither attempted to differentiate the clinical effect of the TCA from the neuroleptic.

Monoamine Oxidase Inhibitors (MAOIs)

Hogben and Cornfield (1981) reported that 5 patients with PTSD improved on 45–75 mg/day of phenelzine in an open clinical trial. Nightmares and flashbacks were reduced in all subjects. Over the 1 to 18-month duration of the study, some improvement in outbursts and somatic complaints were also noted. Shen and Park (1983) described similar improvement in one patient on phenelzine and a second on tranylcypromine.

Davidson, Walker, and Kilts (1987) reported a beneficial effect of 45–60 mg of phenelzine per day in 8 of 11 Vietnam and World War II veterans with PTSD. This prospective open study monitored percentage of inhibition of platelet MAO activity. Platelet MAO activity inhibition of 80% or more is required to effectively treat depressive disorders with phenelzine (Davidson, McLeod, & White, 1978); however, guidelines pertaining to platelet MAO activity have not been established for treating PTSD. Interestingly, in this study, responders had a platelet MAOI value of at least 81% at Week 6, whereas the three nonresponders had levels of 31%, 48%, and 80%. Flashbacks, intrusive recollections, and constricted affect were the symptoms that were most responsive to treatment. Sleep disturbances improved in some patients; however, four subjects reported exacerbation of preexisting sleep disorder.

Contrary to these positive case reports, a recent study of Israeli combat veterans ($n = 25$) (Lerer et al., 1987) reported limited benefit of 30–90 mg/day of phenelzine. In this prospective outpatient study, statistically significant improvement was observed on 7 of the 12 items of their PTSD scale derived from DSM-III criteria. However, the authors comment that many of these patients did not have a *clinically* significant resolution of PTSD, except for the symptom of sleep disturbance. Of note, two of four patients with an additional diagnosis of panic disorder experienced improvement of panic as well as of PTSD symptoms.

Imipramine Versus MAOI Versus Placebo

There is only one reported prospective double-blind study of the pharmacological treatment of PTSD (Frank, Kosten, Giller, & Dan, 1987). Veterans with PTSD ($N = 31$) were randomly assigned to 8-week trial of placebo ($n = 10$), imipramine ($n = 11$), or phenelzine ($n = 10$). The three groups did not differ demographically or in baseline assessments, including combat experience. Significant improvement of PTSD and anxiety scales were noted in both treatment groups, when compared to placebo. Phenelzine was somewhat more effective than imipramine in reducing PTSD symptoms. Of particular interest, there was no significant difference in depressive symptoms between the placebo and either treatment group.

The TCAs and MAOIs are commonly used as a first-line approach to the amelioration of PTSD symptoms. Although dysphoria is commonly present in patients with PTSD, it appears that these medications are of benefit to patients with PTSD in the absence of affective illness. At this time, there are no data supporting the use of one TCA over another, and the choice should be made based on minimizing undesirable side effects. Similarly, there are no documented therapeutic advantages of any particular MAOI in reducing symptoms of PTSD. Of note, one study of MAOIs (Rabkin et al., 1984) reported a markedly higher incidence of sexual dysfunction with phenelzine compared to tranylcypromine, especially in male patients. In our experience, sexual dysfunction is often part of the PTSD symptom constellation and should be assessed at baseline and monitored during the course of pharmacological intervention.

Propranolol and Clonidine

Rage and violent behavior are frequently part of the symptom profile of PTSD. Recent evidence suggests that patients with PTSD may have elevated levels of urinary catecholamines (Kosten, Mason, Giller, Ostroff, & Harkness, 1987). Propranolol, a drug that blocks the effect of catecholamines on noradrenergic beta receptors, has been shown to reduce symptoms of rage and violence in a variety of diagnostic groups (Yudofsky, Williams, & Gorman, 1981). Kolb, Burris, and Griffith (1984) reported on the use of propranolol in reducing PTSD symptoms. In this open study, Vietnam veterans were given 120–160 mg/day of propranolol over a 6-month period. Of the 12 subjects in this clinical trial, 11 reported improvement of symptoms of explosiveness, nightmares, sleep disturbance, and intrusive thoughts on a self-assessment scale.

Clonidine, an alpha-2 noradrenergic agonist, stimulates the presynaptic receptor that inhibits release of the catecholamine norepinephrine. In an open clinical trial, Kolb et al. (1984) administered clonidine to subjects with PTSD. The total daily dose of clonidine was 0.2–0.4 mg, and the duration of the study was 6 months. Improvement was self-reported in eight of nine patients. The profile of symptom change was similar to that reported by the subjects who received propranolol. Although the results of both of these studies are encouraging, further exploration of these agents in studies using a placebo-controlled design is warranted.

Drugs that Affect Impulsive and Explosive Behavior

As impulsiveness and explosive behavior are often part of the symptom constellation of PTSD, there is a conceptual basis for the use of lithium in this disorder. It is not known if the therapeutic action of lithium in PTSD is due to its effect of correcting a serotonergic deficiency as has been postulated in other disorders of impulsiveness and aggression. Kitchner and Greenstein (1985) reported that low-dose lithium (0.2–0.4 [milliequivalents] meg/liter) improved PTSD symptoms in an open trial of 5 veterans. Rage, irritability, nightmares, and intrusive thoughts, as well as the chronic pain of headaches or back injuries, were eased during lithium therapy. Van der Kolk (1983) also found lithium to be helpful in the clinical management of 14 of 22 patients with PTSD who felt chronically out of control and on the verge of exploding. In cases where aggression and rage are prominent, lithium carbonate may be a first-line drug.

Drugs that Affect Kindling Phenomena and Flashbacks

The role of kindling phenomena possibly resulting in behavioral changes and flashbacks was explored by Lipper et al. (1986). In a 5-week open trial of carbamazepine (*n* = 10), significant improvement was observed in 7 PTSD patients. The total daily dose was adjusted to maintain serum levels within standard anticonvulsant therapeutic range (5.0–10.0 µg/ml). Baseline data and corresponding values after 5 weeks of drug treatment were compared. Symptoms of intrusive recollections and recurrent dreams were particularly improved. In addition, flashbacks and getting upset at reminders of stressors were also significantly reduced in intensity and frequency. The authors suggest that an antikindling effect of carbamazepine may be responsible for selective amelioration of intrusive symptoms.

On the other hand, Toland et al. (1987) found that carbamazepine treatment was *not* effective in an open study comparing desipramine to carbamazepine in patients with PTSD. The carbamazepine level was within the usual therapeutic range and the duration of study was 4 weeks.

Additional work is needed to determine the role of kindling in symptoms of PTSD and the usefulness of carbamazepine or other anticonvulsants in treating this disorder.

Other Pharmacotherapeutic Agents

Antipsychotic Agents

There have been no prospective studies that specifically explore the role of antipsychotic agents alone in PTSD. In a clinical setting, they are often used in individuals suffering from dissociative reactions, agitation, rage, and paranoid-like avoidance symptoms. A retrospective chart review (Birkhimer et al., 1985) revealed that 13 of 15 PTSD patients had received neuroleptics and calculated that the average number of different neuroleptics tried per patient was 2.47 (range 1–7). Walker, in a 1982 review, suggested short-term use of low-dose, high-potency neuroleptics to control flashbacks and severe agitation. Bleich, Siegel, Garb, and Lerer (1986) reviewed the charts of Israeli veterans with PTSD. Of patients on neuroleptics (*n* = 8), 37% had a good to moderate response compared to 50% on TCAs (*n* = 28). Those who responded favorably to neuroleptics tended to have more symptoms of explosiveness and hypervigilance compared to the TCA responders. None was psychotic. It is unclear from the available literature how efficacious antipsychotic agents are in this disorder, and the risk of tardive dyskinesia must be considered and discussed with the patient prior to using these agents.

Benzodiazepines

Benzodiazepines may have an important role in the pharmacological armamentarium used to treat PTSD, but they warrant special caution. There are no controlled treatment trials of this class of drug, and there is small—albeit real—risk of disinhibition of aggressiveness (DiMascio, Shader, & Giller, 1970; Lion, Azcarate, & Koepke, 1975).

Although relatively few people who are prescribed benzodiazepines actually develop drug dependence (Mellinger, Balter, & Uhlenhuth, 1984), cautious use of these agents is warranted, especially in patients who have a history of alcohol or other drug dependence (Jaffe, Ciraulo, Nies, Dixon, & Monroe, 1983). Vietnam veterans with PTSD, in particular, may be at higher risk to develop benzodiazepine dependence. As Sierles et al. (1983) found, 65% of these patients also had a diagnosis of substance abuse.

The risks, benefits, and efficacy of benzodiazepine treatment in PTSD have not been established.

Case Illustration

Presenting Complaints

Mr. A is a 70-year-old white male, referred by the neurology service to the geropsychiatry unit for evaluation of visual hallucinations, blackouts, and headaches of 1-year duration. The hallucinations were described as a recurrent visual image of a dried-up riverbed that would be superimposed on his visual field while looking over a landscape scene. The image would appear periodically and would last several seconds. He was always aware that he was experiencing a hallucination, and would remain oriented and have complete awareness of the real world. The patient identified the image as being derived from a particular combat event he experienced in Italy during World War II.

Blackouts occurred on three occasions, always while driving and never witnessed. They lasted less that 1 minute, and there was no evidence of ictal phenomena, such as incontinence or postblackout confusion. The patient denied concomitant alcohol abuse. Although he had voluntarily quit driving, he expressed a ruminative worry that he might "kill a kid" with his car.

The headaches occurred several times per week and would last several hours. They "felt like a band" around his head. There were no accompanying sensory changes or history of migraine.

In addition, he complained of prolonged episodes of dysphoria, of both sleep onset and sleep continuity disturbances, of combat-related nightmares, of nervousness, of increased irritability, and of difficulty concentrating. He denied anhedonia, appetite disturbance, or weight loss. There were no delusions or auditory hallucinations.

Significantly, the onset of symptoms coincided with his mother's death from a prolonged terminal illness.

Past Psychiatric History

Past psychiatric history was significant for a 2-week hospitalization in 1944 for "battle fatigue," after which he returned to combat. He was unable to specify the symptoms he had at that time, and records were not available. In addition, he had a long history of alcohol abuse, drinking 6 to 8 beers per day. While drinking, he was occasionally physically abusive toward his wife.

Social History

The patient had been married for 42 years. He had an excellent work record in a steel mill until his retirement. Since retirement 3 years prior to admission, he had been drinking more heavily, and there had been a reduction in his usual hobbies and activities. He described himself as a "workaholic," and his wife described him as "always busy."

Military and Postmilitary History

The patient enlisted in the army in 1941 and experienced extensive combat duty in North Africa and Europe. He was wounded three times and was removed from the front for 2 weeks for the aforementioned "battle fatigue." Two particularly stressful combat events were (1) after being wounded with shrapnel behind enemy lines, the patient hid for 3 days, alone, in a dry riverbed until he was rescued by American troops, and (2) during the invasion of Germany, Mr. A shot and killed a sniper who turned out to be a "12-year-old boy dressed in a soldier's uniform."

Following discharge from the service, the patient had significant sleep disturbance, frequent nightmares, and increased startle response. He had avoided reminders of the war and never talked to his family about his combat experiences. He immersed himself in work; indeed, vacations or unstructured leisure activities were avoided.

Although the sleep disturbance, startle response, and nightmares decreased in frequency and intensity over the 5 years following the war, Mr. A was frequently troubled with frightening recollections of combat and guilty ruminations of shooting the young boy.

Treatment Course

Initially, Mr. A was treated with diazepam by his family physician. He experienced transient improvement, but despite a daily dose that was slowly increased to 40 mg, his headaches and visual hallucinations persisted. After 1 year, he was referred to a neurologist. The diazepam was stopped, and a thorough neurological evaluation (which included computerized axial tomography (CAT) and electroencephalograph (EEG) with nasopharangeal leads) was negative. Ophthalmological examination was normal. The patient was referred to psychiatry for further evaluation.

A thorough diagnostic evaluation on an inpatient unit was initiated. The patient was neither psychotic nor suffering from major depression. Mr. A showed no significant abnormalities on neuropsychiatric evaluation, and there was no evidence supporting a diagnosis of an organic mental disorder. Diagnoses of PTSD—chronic, delayed, and of alcohol abuse were made.

A treatment plan of supportive psychotherapy and pharmacotherapy was instituted while he was an inpatient and continued when he was an outpatient. With his therapist, the patient was able to talk for the first time about his wartime experiences, as well as his alcohol abuse and physical abusiveness. His wife, who knew nothing of his war trauma, participated in the treatment. The psychotherapy helped the patient clarify several pivotal issues. The recurrent visual hallucinations of a river bed (probably dissociative episodes similar to flashbacks) were related to his combat experiences when wounded behind enemy lines. The blackouts and ruminative thought of killing a child while driving appeared to be related to the guilt he experienced when he killed the young boy dressed in a German uniform. (During this time, the patient did not drive and did not experience any further blackouts). Furthermore, he was able to discuss the guilt he experienced surrounding his mother's death, due to his inability to visit her during the last several weeks of her life. He described his efforts to cope with his mother's illness as similar to his avoidance of combat memories, and the grief and pain reminded him of his response to fallen comrades in the war.

After 2 weeks of alcohol abstinence, his sleep disturbance, visual disturbances, and mood disturbance persisted, and a trial of imipramine was initiated. Initial target symptoms were the sleep-continuity disturbance, the intrusive thoughts, the nervousness, and the dysphoria. Despite continued alcohol abstinence and therapeutic blood levels for 8 weeks, Mr. A did not experience relief of symptoms. The TCA was stopped, and a trial of an MAOI, phenelzine, was initiated. After 2 weeks at a dose of 60 mg per day, the patient reported improved sleep and felt less depressed and anxious.

As he continued in psychotherapy, he realized that his workaholism prior to retirement was an important adaptive pattern that protected him from intrusive thoughts and feelings of guilt. As he felt better on the MAOI, he was motivated to seek and acquire volunteer employment in an automotive repair shop.

Although he still has his "bad" days, his anxiety and depression are much improved, and he no longer experiences disrupted sleep or nightmares. He has no further visual hallucinations or blackouts and only occasionally complains of mild headaches. He remains alcohol free and is compliant with the phenelzine and its dietary restrictions. Both the patient and his wife continue in bimonthly supportive therapy.

Summary

This case illustrates several important points:

1. PTSD should be considered in the differential diagnosis in patients with symptoms of anxiety regardless of age.

2. The patient is not always aware that the presenting complaint is related to a prior significant traumatic event.

3. Comorbidity, in this case alcohol dependence, must be recognized and treated.

4. Benzodiazepines offered temporary relief, but this particular patient developed tolerance and subsequent loss of therapeutic benefit.

5. When imipramine and psychotherapy were ineffective, other interventions were initiated.

6. Phenelzine and psychotherapy were effective. The MAOI appeared to ease the sleep disturbance. In addition, intrusive thoughts, anxiety, and depression were diminished. There have been no further blackouts or visual hallucinations. Psychotherapy aided the patient with his marital problems and helped him decide to reenter the workforce. Pharmacotherapy and psychotherapy both contributed to the overall improvement of this patient's quality of life.

ALTERNATIVE TREATMENT OPTIONS

Pharmacotherapy has been shown to play a role in the treatment of PTSD. As 84% of the Vietnam veterans with PTSD have another significant psychiatric diagnosis (Sierles et al., 1983), a thorough diagnostic evaluation is an essential first step in designing a pharmacological treatment plan. There are no data detailing the effect of successful PTSD treatment on comorbid symptoms or vice versa. In our experience, however, resolution of an episode of major depression or reduction of psychosis in a patient with schizophrenia can reduce symptoms of concomitant PTSD.

With respect to substance abuse, the clinician must resist the simplistic rationalization that the substance abuse is the patient's attempt at self-treatment. Historically, such an approach has been used in patients with coexistent alcoholism and depression; however, we now know that people with alcohol dependence and symptoms of major depression often experience complete resolution of depressive symptoms after 2 weeks of abstinence (Dackis, Gold, Pottash, & Sweeney, 1986).

Although no data are available regarding the interaction of PTSD symptoms and substance abuse, a 2-week period of abstinence prior to prescribing medications in subjects with PTSD is a safe and rational approach.

In a patient with PTSD as the primary diagnosis, in whom pharmacological intervention is desired, a logical, symptom-directed approach should ensue. Our general approach is to start pharmacotherapy with a TCA or an MAOI, especially in patients with prominent complaints of sleep disturbance and nightmares. In those patients whose symptoms clearly tend toward aggressiveness and impulsiveness, lithium is an appropriate medication, either alone or in conjunction with an MAOI or a TCA. Carbamazepine and lithium should be considered in patients with complaints of intrusive thoughts and flashbacks. Clonidine and propranolol have specialized roles in subjects with increased physiological reactivity and associated loss of control or rage. Unfortunately, the literature does not provide well-defined scientific data to guide pharmacological options more precisely. The preceding guidelines are meant to provide a rational starting point for the clinician, but the optimal pharmacological intervention for a given patient may require a series of clinical drug trials with adequate dosage and duration.

Future research in this area should compare the efficacy of different medications and combinations of drugs under double-blind, placebo-controlled conditions. Standardized diagnostic and severity rating scales must be used, and patients with additional diagnoses, especially substance abuse, must be considered separately from the patient with a pure PTSD.

REFERENCES

American Psychiatric Association. (1987). *Diagnostic and statistical manual of mental disorders* (3rd ed., rev.). Washington, DC: Author.

Antelman, S. M., Eichler, A. J., Black, C. A., & Kocan, D. (1980). Interchangeability of stress and amphetamine in sensitization. *Science, 207*, 329–331.

Birkhimer, L. J., DeVane, C. L., & Muniz, C. E. (1985). Posttraumatic stress disorder: Characteristics and pharmacological response in the veteran population. *Comprehensive Psychiatry, 26*, 304–310.

Blanchard, E. B., Kolb, L. C., Gerandi, R. J., Ryan, P., & Pallmeyer, T. P. (1986). Cardiac response to relevant stimuli as an adjunctive tool for diagnosis post-traumatic stress disorder in Vietnam veterans. *Behavior Therapy, 17*, 592–606.

Bleich, A., Siegel, B., Garb, R., & Lerer, B. (1986). Post-traumatic stress disorder following combat exposure: Clinical features and psychopharmacological treatment. *British Journal of Psychiatry, 149*, 365–369.

Brown, G. L., Ebert, M. H., Goyer, P. F., Jimerson, D. C., Klein, W. J., Bunney, W. E., & Goodwin, F. K. (1982). Aggression, suicide and serotonin: Relationship to CSF amine metabolites. *American Journal of Psychiatry, 139*, 741–746.

Brown, G. L., Goodwin, F. K., Ballenger, J. C., Goyer, P. F., & Major, L. F. (1979). Aggression in humans correlates with cerebrospinal fluid amine metabolites. *Psychiatry Research, 1*, 131–139.

Burstein, A. (1984). Treatment of post-traumatic stress disorder with imipramine. *Psychosomatics, 25*, 681–687.

Burstein, A. (1986). Treatment length in post-traumatic stress disorder. *Psychosomatics, 27*, 632–637.

Cohen, R. M., Pickar, D., Garnett, D., Lipper, S., Gillin, J. C., & Murphy, D. L. (1982). REM sleep suppression induced by selective monoamine oxidase inhibitors. *Psychopharmacology, 78*, 137–140.

Dackis, C. A., Gold, M. S., Pottash, A. L. C., & Sweeney, B. R. (1986). Evaluating depression in alcoholics. *Psychiatry Research, 17*, 105–109.

Davidson, J., McLeod, M., & White, H. (1978). Inhibition of platelet monoamine oxidase in depressed subjects treated with phenelzine. *American Journal of Psychiatry, 135*, 470–472.

Davidson, J., Walker, J. I., & Kilts, C. (1987). A pilot study of phenelzine in posttraumatic stress disorder. *British Journal of Psychiatry, 50*, 252–255.

DiMascio, A., Shader, R. I., & Giller, D. R. (1970). Behavioral toxicity, Part IV: Emotional (mood) states. In A. DiMascio & R. I. Shader (Eds.), *Psychotropic drug effects*, Baltimore, MD: Williams & Wilkins.

Dunleavy, D. L. F., Brezinova, V., Oswald, I., Maclean, A. W., & Tinker, M. (1972). Changes during weeks in effects of tricyclic drugs in the human sleeping brain. *British Journal of Psychiatry, 120*, 663–672.

Falcon, S., Ryan, C., Chamberlain, K., & Curtis, G. (1985). Tricyclics: Possible treatment for posttraumatic stress disorder. *Journal of Clinical Psychiatry, 46*, 385–389.

Frank, J. B., Kosten, T. R., Giller, E. L., & Dan, E. (1987). A randomized clinical trial of phenelzine and imipramine for post-traumatic stress disorder. Submitted for publication.

Goddard, G. V., McIntyre, D. C., & Leech, C. K. (1969). A permanent change in brain functioning resulting from daily electrical stimulation. *Experimental Neurology, 25*, 295–330.

Hogben, G. L., & Cornfield, R. B. (1981). Treatment of traumatic war neurosis with phenelzine. *Archives of General Psychiatry, 38*, 440–445.

Horowitz, M. J., Wilner, N., & Alvarez, W. (1979). Impact of Events Scale: A measure of subjective stress. *Psychosomatic Medicine, 41*, 209–218.

Horowitz, M. J., Wilner, N., Kaltreider, N., & Alvarez, W. (1980). Signs and symptoms of posttraumatic stress disorder. *Archives of General Psychiatry, 37*, 85–92.

Jaffe, J. H., Ciraulo, D. A., Nies, A., Dixon, R. B., & Monroe, L. L. (1983). Abuse potential of halazepam and of diazepam in patients recently treated for acute alcohol withdrawal. *Clinical Pharmacology and Therapeutics, 34*, 623–630.

Kardiner, A., & Spiegel, H. (1947). *War stress and neurotic illness.* New York: Paul B. Hoeber.

Kitchner, I., Greenstein, R. (1985). Low dose lithium carbonate in the treatment of post traumatic stress disorder: Brief communication. *Military Medicine, 150*, 378–381.

Kolb, L. C., Burris, B. C., & Griffith, S. (1984). Propranolol and clonidine in the treatment of post traumatic stress disorders of war. In B. A. van der Kolk (Ed.), *Post traumatic stress disorder: Psychological and biological sequelae,* (pp. 98–105). Washington, DC: American Psychiatric Press.

Kosten, T. R., Mason, J. W., Giller, E., Ostroff, R. B., & Harkness, L. (1987). Sustained urinary norepinephrine and epinephrine elevation in post traumatic stress disorder. *Psychoneuroendocrinology, 12*, 13–20.

Kudler, H., Davidson, J., Meador, D., Lipper, S., & Ely, T. (1987). The DST and posttraumatic stress disorder. *American Journal of Psychiatry, 144*, 1068–1070.

LaGuardia, R. L., Smith, G., Francois, R., & Bachman, L. (1983). Incidence of delayed stress disorder among Vietnam era veterans: The effect of priming on response set. *American Journal of Orthopsychiatry, 53*, 18–26.

Lavie, P., Hefez, A., Halpern, G., & Enoch, D. (1979). Long-term effects of traumatic war-related events of sleep. *American Journal of Psychiatry, 136*, 175–178.

Lerer, B., Bleich, A., Kotler, M., Garb, R., Hertzberg, M., & Levin, B. (1987). Posttraumatic stress disor-

der in Israeli combat veterans. *Archives of General Psychiatry, 44*, 976–981.

Lion, J. R., Azcarate, C. L., & Koepke, H. H. (1975). "Paradoxical rage reactions" during psychotropic medication. *Diseases of the Nervous System, 36*, 557–558.

Lipper, S., Davidson, J. R., Grady, T. A., Edinger, J. D., Hammett, E. B., Mahorney, S. L., & Cavenar, J. O. (1986). Preliminary study of carbamazepine in posttraumatic stress disorder. *Psychosomatics, 27*, 849–854.

Lund, M., Foy D., Sipprelle, C., & Strachan, A. (1984). The combat exposure scale: A systematic assessment of trauma in the Vietnam War, *Journal of Clinical Psychology, 40*, 1323–1328.

Malloy, P. F., Fairbanks, J. A., & Keane, T. M. (1983). Validation of a multimethod assessment of post traumatic stress disorder in Vietnam veterans. *Journal of Consulting and Clinical Psychology, 51*, 488–494.

McDaniel, K. D. (1986). Clinical pharmacology of monoamine oxidase inhibitors. *Clinical Neuropharmacology, 9*, 201–234.

Mellinger, G. D., Balter, M. B., & Uhlenhuth, E. H. (1984). Prevalence and correlates of long-term regular use of anxiolytics. *Journal of American Medical Association, 251*, 375–379.

Mellman, T. A., & Glenn, C. D. (1985). Combat-related flashbacks in posttraumatic stress disorder: Phenomenology and similarity to panic attacks. *Journal of Clinical Psychiatry, 46*, 379–382.

Perez-Cruet, J., Tagliamonte, A., Tagliamonte, P., & Gessa, G. L. (1971). Stimulation of serotonin synthesis by lithium. *Journal of Pharmacology and Experimental Therapeutics, 178*, 325–330.

Pitman, R. K., Orr, S. P., Forgue, D. F., de Jong, J. B., Claiborn, J. M. (1987). Psychophysiologic assessment of posttraumatic stress disorder imagery in Viet Nam combat veterans. *Archives of General Psychiatry, 44*, 970–975.

Post, R. M., & Kopanda, R. T. (1975). Progressive behavioral changes during lidocaine administration: Relationship to kindling. *Life Science, 17*, 943–950.

Post, R. M., & Uhde, T. W. (1985). Carbamazepine in bipolar illness. *Psychopharmacology Bulletin, 21*, 10–17.

Rabkin, J. G., Quitkin, F. M., Harrison, W., McGrath, P., Harrison, W., & Tricamo, E. (1984). Adverse reactions to monoamine oxidase inhibitors: Part II. Treatment correlates and clinical management. *Journal of Clinical Psychopharmacology, 5*, 2–9.

Rosen, J., Fields, R. B., Hand, A. M., Falcetti, G., & van Kammen, D. P. (in press). Concurrent posttraumatic stress disorder in psychogeriatric patients. *Journal of Geriatric Psychiatry and Neurology.*

Schlossberg, A., & Benjamin, M. (1978). Sleep patterns in three acute combat fatigue cases. *Journal of Clinical Psychiatry, 39,* 546–548.

Sheard, M. N., & Marini, J. L. (1980). The effect of lithium on impulsive aggressive behavior in man. *American Journal of Psychiatry, 137,* 782–790.

Shen, W. W., & Park, S. (1983). The use of monoamine oxidase inhibitors in the treatment of traumatic war neurosis: Case report. *Military Medicine, 148,* 430–431.

Sierles, F. S., Chen, J., McFarland, R. E., & Taylor, M. A. (1983). Posttraumatic stress disorder and concurrent psychiatric illness: A preliminary report. *American Journal of Psychiatry, 140,* 1177–1179.

Sparr, L., & Pankratz, L. D. (1983). Factitious post traumatic stress disorder. *American Journal Psychiatry, 140,* 1016–1019.

Sulser, F., Vetulani, J., & Mobley, P. L. (1982). Mode of action of antidepressant drugs. *Biochemical Pharmacology, 27,* 257–261.

Thompson, G. N. (1977). Post-traumatic psychoneurosis: Evaluation of drug therapy. *Diseases of the Nervous System, 38,* 617–619.

Toland, A. M., Goetz, K. L., Slawsky, R. C., & van Kammen, D. P. (1987). *Comparative therapeutic efficacy of desipramine and carbamazepine in posttraumatic stress disorder.* Presentation at the annual meeting of the American Psychological Association, New York.

van der Kolk, B. A. (1983). Psychopharmacological issues in posttraumatic stress disorder. *Hospital and Community Psychiatry, 34,* 683–691.

van der Kolk, B. A., Blitz, R., Burr, W., Sherry, S., & Hartmann, E. (1984). Nightmares and trauma: A comparison of nightmares after combat with lifelong nightmares in veterans. *American Journal of Psychiatry, 141,* 187–190.

van der Kolk, B. A., Greenberg, M. S., Boyd, H., & Krystal, J. (1985). Inescapable shock, neurotransmitters and addiction to trauma: Towards a psychobiology of post traumatic stress. *Biological Psychiatry, 20,* 314–325.

Walker, J. I. (1982). Chemotherapy of traumatic war stress. *Military Medicine, 147,* 1029–1033.

Weiss, J. M., Glazer, H. I., Pohorecky, L. A., Brick, J., & Miller, N. E. (1975). Effects of chronic exposure to stressors on avoidance–escape behavior and on brain norepinephrine. *Psychosomatic Medicine, 37,* 522–531.

Yudofsky, S., Williams, D., & Gorman, J. (1981). Propranolol in the treatment of rage and violent behavior in patients with chronic brain syndromes. *American Journal of Psychiatry, 138,* 218–220.

Editorial Commentary: Posttraumatic Stress Disorder

In accordance with DSM-III-R, the cardinal feature of posttraumatic stress disorder (PTSD) is the development of characteristic symptoms following a psychologically distressing event that is outside the range of usual human experience. "The stressor producing this syndrome would be markedly distressing to almost anyone, and is usually experienced with intense fear, terror, and helplessness" (p. 247). Excluded from making the diagnosis, then, would be marital conflict, business losses, chronic illness, and simple bereavement. However, on the other hand, severely traumatic, physically threatening, or life-threatening events, such as threat to one's children, seeing another individual maimed or killed in an accident or fire, rape, being a prisoner of war, combat experiences in war, or the horror of cataclysmic events (e.g., floods, tornadoes, earthquakes), definitely are considered as contributors to the diagnosis. The reaction to such events (immediate or delayed) is marked by a reliving of the experience in the form of intrusive thoughts or dreams, avoidance of stimuli associated with the original trauma, persistent symptoms of increased arousal not present before the trauma, and diminished responsiveness or psychic numbness to the world.

Although posttraumatic stress disorder first appeared formally in the psychiatric nomenclature in DSM-III, its forebears had been referred to as "shell shock" and "traumatic war neurosis." However, it is with DSM-III and DSM-III-R that the range of disorders subsumed under this rubric has increased beyond those traumas only associated with war.

Despite some of the commonalities across the analytic, behavioral, and biological approaches to conceptualizations of PTSD, there obviously are some marked distinctions in focus and, of course, in treatment. The analytic view, presented as a feedback loop (Horowitz), posits that the traumatic event is stored in the conscious mind and undergoes repetition. Because repetition results in painful affects, the memory still poses a threat to the individual. Such pain elicits varying degrees of defense, ranging from conscious inhibition (suppression) to unconscious inhibition (repression). According to Horowitz, "the active memory collates awareness of the traumatic event with information about emotional responses and beliefs, and may include errors in terms of what really happened."

The learning model (Foy, Resnick, Carroll, & Osato) is based on Mowrer's two-factor theory, in which the original trauma results in a classically conditioned emotional response, with subsequent avoidance of all stimuli associated with the trauma, motivated by fear and maintained via fear reduction. Thus, in the case of rape as the traumatic event, the unconditioned stimulus yields an unconditioned response of extreme fear (including psychological, cognitive, and physiological aspects). Through classical conditioning, associated stimuli with the rape (e.g., place and time of day) become conditioned stimuli and are able to evoke either a full or a partial conditioned response of fear.

In both the analytic and the behavioral conceptions of PTSD, learning (albeit different in each case) is implicated as the underlying mechanism, with subsequent avoidance as the maintaining factor. By contrast, the biological interpretation is more molecular and presumes enhanced brain reactivity to stimuli (as a consequence of the original trauma) that fails to return to its pretrauma levels. Known as the "kindling theory," it follows that repetitions or reminders of the event, in the form of dreams or flashbacks, further sensitize the brain to associated innocuous stimuli. In the animal literature, where models of trauma induction have been tested, certain pharmacological agents have been shown to reduce such heightened levels of brain activity—hence, the use of drugs (e.g., tricyclics, monoamine oxidase inhibitors, beta blockers, phenothiazenes, and benzodiazepenes) with human PTSD victims (Rosen & Bohon).

With respect to treatment, Horowitz describes a time-limited dynamic therapy of 12 sessions that is devoted to helping the patient with a "normal working through process." By contrast, Foy et al. review the use of more direct behavioral exposure treatments, such as systematic desensitization, flooding, and implosion. The goal here, of course, is to decondition stimuli associated with the original trauma. Another strategy of value appears to be stress inoculation training, which underscores the importance of teaching PTSD patients (e.g., rape victims) to manage rape-related fear and other anxieties.

In considering alternative treatment options, it is clear that none of the existing treatment strategies has clear hegemony over the other. Thus, Horowitz recommends the concurrent use of drugs and psychotherapy, with a carefully titrated pharmacological regime, consistent with the patient's symptomatic presentation. Although Foy et al. and Rosen and Bohon do not suggest a two-pronged behavioral–pharmacological approach, as does Horowitz with psychotherapy and drugs, related work in other anxiety-based disorders would suggest its inherent value.

Unfortunately, the status of research in PTSD is still in its early stages. Although various psychotherapeutic approaches show promise, the controlled trials showing the superiority of one or the other technique are lacking, as are the double-blind, drug–placebo trials with respect to pharmacotherapy. So far, most of the pharmacological interventions have been carried out in the form of open trials. At present, some of the needed controlled research is underway in several clinical-research centers, but the evidence is not yet accumulated. In the future, evaluation of the relative efficacy of various combined drug–psychotherapy approaches should yield important information. Furthermore, the matching of specific individual or combined techniques with the patient's particular trauma and associated symptomatic presentation will help to refine the treatment process.

PART 7

Anorexia and Bulimia

CHAPTER 19

Psychotherapy

RICHARD L. PYLE

CONCEPTUALIZATION OF THE DISORDER

Concerns with weight and food restriction have become so pervasive among young females today that they are considered normative (Rodin, Silberstein, & Striegel-Moore, 1983). Food restriction, often used to enhance thinness, has been shown to be associated with increased desire to binge-eat (Wardle, 1980). It is understandable, then, that 60–70% of college females report having engaged in binge-eating (that is, the consumption of very large amounts of food in a short period of time). A significant number also report purging behaviors, such as self-induced vomiting and laxative abuse to rid the body of unwanted food. A majority of female college students report a fear of becoming fat. These data suggest that eating problems are very common among college-age women (Halmi, Falk, & Schwartz, 1981; Hawkins & Clement, 1982; Pyle, Mitchell, Eckert, Halvorson, Neuman, & Goff, 1983).

These disordered eating habits and attitudes, when severe, can be associated with the development of the serious eating disorder syndromes anorexia nervosa and bulimia nervosa (DSM-III-R: American Psychiatric Association, 1987). These syndromes constitute a major problem among women between the ages of 18 and 25 (Crisp, Palmer, & Kalucy, 1976; Pyle, Mitchell, & Eckert, 1981; Pyle et al., 1983; Theander, 1970) and are associated with adverse emotional, vocational, social, financial, and physical conse-

quences (Hatsukami, Owen, Pyle, & Mitchell, 1982; Johnson & Larson, 1982; Mitchell, 1983; Mitchell, Hatsukami, Eckert, & Pyle, 1985a; Weiss & Ebert, 1983).

Anorexia Nervosa

The essential features of anorexia nervosa are "refusal to maintain body weight over a minimal normal weight for age and height; intense fear of gaining weight or becoming fat, even though underweight; a distorted body image; and amenorrhea (in females). (The term *anorexia* is a misnomer since loss of appetite is rare.) The disturbance in body image is manifested by the way in which the person's body weight, size, or shape is experienced. People with this disorder say that they feel fat, or that parts of their body are fat, when they are obviously underweight or even emaciated. They are preoccupied with their body size and usually dissatisfied with some feature of their physical appearance. The weight loss is usually accomplished by a reduction in total food intake, often with extensive exercising. Frequently there is also self-induced vomiting or use of laxatives or diuretics. The person usually comes to professional attention when weight loss (or failure to gain expected weight) is marked. By the time the person is profoundly underweight, there are other signs, such as hypothermia, bradycardia, hypotension, edema, lanugo (neonatal-downlike hair), and a variety of metabolic changes. In most cases amenorrhea follows weight loss, but it is not unusual for amenorrhea to appear before noticeable weight loss has occurred" (American Psychiatric Association, 1987).

People with anorexia nervosa tend to limit themselves to a narrow selection of low-calorie foods. In addition, they may hoard, conceal, crumble, or throw away food. Most people with this disorder steadfastly deny or minimize the severity of their illness and are uninterested in, or resistant to, therapy. Many of the adolescents have delayed psychosexual development, and adults may have a markedly decreased interest in sex. Compulsive behavior, such as hand washing, may also be present during the illness (American Psychiatric Association, 1987).

Bulimia Nervosa

The essential features of bulimia nervosa are "recurrent episodes of binge-eating (rapid consumption of a large amount of food in a discrete period of time); a feeling of lack of control over eating behavior during the eating binges; self-induced vomiting, use of laxatives or diuretics, strict dieting or fasting, or vigorous exercise in order to prevent weight gain; and persistent over-concern with body shape and weight" (American Psychiatric Association, 1987).

The food consumed during a binge is often high calorie and easily ingested, with a texture that facilitates rapid eating. The food is usually eaten surreptitiously. A binge is usually terminated by abdominal discomfort or induced vomiting, which decreases the physical pain of abdominal distenssion, allowing either continued eating or termination of the binge. In some cases, vomiting itself may be desired, so that the person either will binge in order to vomit or will vomit after eating a small amount of food. Although eating binges may be pleasurable, disparaging self-criticism and a depressed mood often follow.

People with bulimia nervosa invariably exhibit great concern about their weight and make repeated attempts to control it by dieting, vomiting, or using cathartics or diuretics. These people often feel that their life is dominated by conflicts about eating (American Psychiatric Association, 1987).

Many patients with eating disorders do not meet DSM-III-R diagnostic criteria. They may resemble patients with bulimia nervosa who no longer binge-eat (common in chronic cases) or patients with anorexia nervosa who do not meet weight criteria or who deny one or more of the diagnostic criteria in order to conceal their illness.

Epidemiology of Both Disorders

Early studies indicated that 8–19% of college women may develop symptoms that meet operationalized diagnostic criteria for the eating disorder bulimia (Halmi et al., 1981; Pyle et al., 1983). More severe forms of bulimia—that is, with at least weekly binge-eating and self-induced vomiting or laxative abuse—are reported by up to 3% of college women (Pyle, Halvorson, Neuman, & Mitchell, 1986). The frequency of anorexia nervosa is lower, with approximately 0.5% in the highest risk group of females ages 12 to 18 years in boarding schools (higher socioeconomic standing) meeting daignostic criteria (Crisp et al., 1976). There is indication from studies in both Europe and the United States that anorexia nervosa and the more severe forms of bulimia with weekly binge-eating and self-induced vomiting are increasing in frequency (Jones, Fox, Babigan, & Hutton, 1980; Pyle et al., 1986; Theander, 1970). Less than 5% of patients in treatment for eating disorders are males. There are no reported frequencies for males with anorexia nervosa, but less than 1 of 300 meet the criteria for DSM-III bulimia with weekly binge-eating and self-induced vomiting in surveys of college students (Pyle et al., 1983).

The prognosis for the successful recovery of most patients treated in outpatient programs for uncomplicated bulimia nervosa can be quite good. However, even in the best treatment facilities, the prognosis for anorexia nervosa is guarded. In addition, the long-term outcome for anorexia nervosa treatment still leaves much to be desired, particularly with respect to social adjustment and chronic medical complications. Mortality studies indicate that as many as 20% of women with anorexia nervosa may die from the illness (American Psychiatric Association, 1987).

One of the problems in designing treatment programs for eating disorders is the lack of prospective studies to identify the risk factors for these disorders (Pyle, 1986). However, the available research has suggested some obvious and some probable risk factors. The risk factors that have been defined by existing epidemiological studies are gender, age, and socioeconomic status. These disorders are primarily confined to females with a median age of onset of about 18 years for bulimia nervosa and somewhat younger for anorexia nervosa. Higher socioeconomic status is considered to be a risk factor for anorexia nervosa but not for bulimia. Many authors have suggested that psychosocial pressure for thinness, and more recently for physical fitness and to exercise, contribute to the apparent increase in incidence of eating disorders (Garner, Garfinkel, Schwartz, & Thompson, 1980).

Several antecedents, sufficiently documented by existing studies, may be considered probable risk factors for eating disorders. Eating disorders may be more frequent among individuals with a higher familial prevalence of depression and/or chemical dependency (Hudson, Pope, Jonas, & Yurgelun-Todd, 1983; Pyle et al., 1981; Strober, Salkin, Burroughs, & Morrell, 1982). Increased stress, perceived stress, or personal loss have been reported antecedent to the development of eating disorders in retrospective studies, but they have not been studied systematically (Pyle et al., 1981; Strober, 1984). An association between the onset of bulimia and strict dieting and the presence of depression and alcohol abuse have all been reported, and they may be viewed as risk factors as well (Mitchell et al., 1985a; Pyle et al., 1981). Sudden weight gain or loss have also been reported as antecedent to eating disorders (Fairburn, 1983).

Other characteristics associated with eating disorders have been suggested as either consequences or potential risk factors, including social isolation, impaired social adjustment, and low self-esteem (Hatsukami et al., 1982; Weiss & Ebert, 1983). Loss of control (impulsivity) has been described in bulimics and bulimic anorexics (Garner, Garfinkel, & O'Shaughnessy, 1985; Hatsukami et al., 1982). In addition, issues regarding body image, exercise, and maturity fears have all been implicated with anorexia nervosa as consequences or risk factors (Bruch, 1978; Garner & Garfinkel, 1980). Prospective studies may provide valuable data regarding the status of these charac-teristics as either risk factors for or consequences of eating disorders.

DIAGNOSTIC ISSUES AND PROBLEMS

Engaging the Patient in Therapy

To engage the patient in therapy is often difficult. In summarizing this problem in anorexia nervosa, Hsu (1986) recommended that, "the clinician establish a treatment alliance by openly acknowledging the significance of the anorexic patient's striving for thinness and control, while . . . stressing the negative and possibly dangerous effects of her [or his] endeavor, such as resultant depression, malnutrition, fatigue, insomnia, restlessness, social isolation, and constant preoccupation with food and exercising." He further points out that the clinician should explain the effects of starvation and outline the course and outcome of the illness while emphasizing the benefits of treatment with the assurance that the treatment will not destroy her (or his) specialness or control. In addition, because the cooperation of the family may determine whether or not the patient enters treatment, joint meetings with the patient and the family to discuss the illness and the treatment are considered to be essential. Literature for the patient and the family to read may also be of value (Garfinkel & Garner, 1982). Hsu (1986) also points out that few data exist on the percentage of patients who refuse treatment and their eventual outcome, noting that in Crisp's series, 30% of the patients declined the offer of treatment, and their outcome appeared to be poor (Hsu, Crisp, & Harding, 1979). Because anorexic patients and their families tend to deny the illness, particularly its severity, negative reactions are often noted in treatment staff, who view patients with anorexia nervosa as being willfully resistant to treatment, leaving them with a feeling of extreme exasperation (Brotman, Stern, & Herzog, 1984).

Patients with bulimia nervosa may leave therapists with the same feeling, for although they may be more motivated to seek treatment, they have difficulty tolerating therapeutic interventions that do not produce immediate relief of symptoms or that do not have sufficient structure and definition to reduce their feelings of being out of control (Pyle & Mitchell, 1985).

When Is Inpatient Care Indicated?

All clinicians offering psychotherapy for eating disorders, especially anorexia nervosa, need to consider the timing of inpatient admission. The use of inpatient admission as a contingency for failure to maintain weight in outpatient therapy for anorexia nervosa, has been made much more difficult in the United States, with admission criteria set up on the basis of insurance company standards. For many years, it was considered that a patient who weighed less than 70% of average or "ideal" weight would require admission for weight restoration (Hsu, 1986). At present, hospitalization is indicated for (1) weight loss of greater than 30% over 3 months; (2) severe metabolic disturbance such as pulse lower than 40 per minute or temperature lower than 36°C, systolic blood pressure less than 70 mm of mercury and serum potassium under 2.5 moles/liter despite oral potassium replacement; (3) severe depression or suicide risk; and (4) severe bingeing and purging (with a risk of aspiration) (Herzog & Copeland, 1985).

Another relevant issue is that of involuntary hospitalization for the patient who absolutely refuses treatment in spite of obvious need. Because adult patients with anorexia nervosa seem capable of making judgments about treatment, requests for involuntary treatment may often be refused by the same courts who might not hesitate to commit patients for chemical dependency treatment. Consequently, families will require support to develop new contingencies, which may include withdrawal of emotional or physical support until the family member enters treatment.

The role of hospitalization for bulimia nervosa is unclear because the reported treatment studies involving treatment success have been outpatient studies. Inpatient admission may be indicated for those patients with more severe loss of control over their eating and more severe character pathology, including borderline, histrionic, and dependent personality features. Until these mitigating factors are more closely studied and confirmed through controlled studies, the lack of positive treatment results reported to date would suggest against inpatient care.

The Management of Bulimic Behaviors

There are several controversies regarding the management of bulimic behaviors: the intensive versus nonintensive approach (the former designed to provide sufficient support for interruption of the daily habitual binge–purging process, and the latter allowing patients to proceed more at their own pace); the abstinence versus nonabstinence model; and contracting for either cessation or reduction of the bulimic behaviors prior to treatment. All of these controversies require further study. None of the major treatment centers currently uses an abstinence model, which has been criticized for playing into the dichotomous thinking of patients with bulimia nervosa, with the risk of precipitating a major relapse should brief lapses of bulimic behavior occur (Bemis, 1985). While there are no data to support this theoretical position, this position has also been applied to the rapid interruption of bulimic behavior versus a more gradual interruption. The University of Minnesota eating disorders program has always advocated the rapid interruption as part of an intensive outpatient group format (Mitchell, Hatsukami, Goff, Pyle, Eckert, & Davis, 1985b; Pyle & Mitchell, 1985). Lacey (1983) has required his patients to contract to follow specific treatment prescriptions, a practice that has been criticized by some clinicians who feel that this may cause some patients to forgo treatment (Johnson & Connors, 1987).

The time of confronting interpersonal, environmental, or psychological precipitants that maintain disordered eating has been open to discussion, with Garner (1986) feeling that this should be done early, while others would wait until the habitual daily behavior is reduced so that environmental and psychological cues can be more easily determined before confronting the precipitants for binge–purge behavior (Fairburn, 1981; Pyle & Mitchell, 1985).

Depression

Significant depression has been associated with both anorexia nervosa and bulimia nervosa (Cantwell, Sturzenberger, Borroughs, Salkin, & Green, 1977; Hudson, Laffer, & Pope, 1982). Most researchers now believe such depression to be secondary to the syndromes. In fact, depression ratings are reduced for those patients with bulimia nervosa who have positive treatment outcome (Garner, Olmstead, Davis, Rockert, Goldbloom, & Eagle, 1988). Nevertheless, a subgroup of patients (a) have had episodes of major depression prior to the onset of their eating disorder, (b) have symptoms of major depression with vegetative signs during the disorder, or (c) have mood disturbances following normalization of eating behaviors. A trial on antidepressant medication may be indicated for these patients, even though the therapist does not elect to use antidepressant therapy as a primary treatment for the eating disorder.

Special Populations

Lacey (1984) noted two diverse groups of patients who came to the eating disorders clinic. He defined 8% of them as secondary bulimia in association with physical illness, such as epilepsy or diabetes. Of Lacey's clinic population, 18% were diagnosed as having personality disorders and were noted to have many features of loss of control disorders, including chemical dependency. Lacey associated this group with poor treatment outcome. Levin and Hyler (1986) noted that 25% of a group of bulimic patients that they studied met the diagnostic criteria for borderline personality and that 54% met the criteria for either borderline or histrionic personality or mixed personality disorder with histrionic or borderline features. Diagnoses of personality disorder, diabetes, and chemical abuse may all prove to be associated with poor treatment outcome for bulimia nervosa. To date, there are no controlled treatment studies that would provide guidance for the therapy of these patient subgroups.

Weight Issues

Weight Restoration and Psychotherapy

Hsu (1986) pointed out the importance of psychotherapeutic intervention in weight restoration, including individual and family therapy, so that the patient does not feel that eating and weight gain are the only goals of treatment. He believes (a) that a carefully planned, structured inpatient program implemented consistently by a competent treatment team is effective in a vast majority of cases in restoring weight, (b) that coercive treatments, overrestrictive measures, and pharmacotherapy are usually unnecessary; and (c) that such measures, if used at all, should be used only in refractory cases or when definite clinical indications are present. Other clinicians have also emphasized the importance of introducing psychotherapy, noting that behavioral therapy alone is only good for providing short-term weight gain (Garfinkel & Garner, 1982) and that behavior modification techniques may be "potentially dangerous methods," as they may completely remove control from a patient who is struggling to maintain some control (Bruch, 1974).

Clinicians also disagree about the time of discharge for patients who are undergoing weight restoration as inpatients. Crisp (1980) has long advocated that the weight restoration should match the population mean weight for height at the onset of illness, to allow both the patient and the family to reexperience the existential issues that precipitated the psychological regression. Others have aimed at restoration of the patient to either an age-appropriate weight (Casper, 1982) or a low-average weight (Garfinkel & Garner, 1982).

Weight Maintenance in Bulimia Nervosa

Programs at major centers no longer recommend diets of 1200 calories or less for patients involved in treatment for bulimia nervosa (even those who are overweight). Treatment protocols for bulimia nervosa usually advocate sufficient food intake to provide balanced daily nutrition to maintain weight and to prevent hunger. Disagreement occurs about the weight that should be maintained. Programs may (a) advocate no target weight but specify the caloric intake, (b) require a minimal weight of 90% of the ideal population norm, (c) require caloric intake to maintain current weight, or (d) require an individualized weight based on family history and estimation of set-point weight (Garner, Rockert, Olmstead, Johnson, & Coscina, 1985).

Relapse Prevention

Both anorexia nervosa and bulimia nervosa have fluctuating courses in response to environmental stresses. Relapse occurs within a year in about

50% of patients treated in hospitals for anorexia nervosa (Hsu, 1980). While these data covered studies from 1954 to 1978, the 50% relapse rate has not been appreciably reduced since then, indicating the need to develop techniques to strengthen therapist–patient bonds and to improve continuity of care during the transition between inpatient and outpatient care. More emphasis has been placed on relapse prevention for bulimia nervosa, and this concern is being partially addressed through exposure to high-risk foods and situations.

The Chronic Patient

The short history of bulimia nervosa has precluded collection of data about the chronic patient; however, many patients with anorexia nervosa have been followed for more than a decade. In general, a longer duration of illness consistently predicts poor outcome (Dally, 1969). Consequently, alternative treatment approaches may need to be considered for patients with multiple hospitalizations. Crisp (1980) has cautioned that coercive treatments may precipitate depression and suicide in chronic patients. Perhaps chronic patients should be admitted when their weight is dangerously low, but they should not be required to attain a target weight (Hsu, 1986). Hsu and Lieberman (1982) described a paradoxical approach in which they suggested to the chronic patient that it might actually be better to keep the anorexia nervosa after so many years of illness.

The Therapist

The treatment of both anorexia nervosa and bulimia nervosa require therapists who have extensive knowledge of the illness. The issue of whether therapists are more effective if they have experienced eating disorders has not been resolved. However, it appears that in lieu of actual experience, extensive knowledge of the eating disorder is equally well accepted by patients. In the case of anorexia nervosa, the patient must develop a high degree of trust in a therapist's expertise, because it is exceedingly difficult for the patient to accept the need for weight restoration. Weight restoration is highly frightening for the anorexic patient, and this fear can only be abated by her or his trust that the therapist is competent and will care for the patient adequately. With weight gain, the anorexic patient perceives total loss of control over eating, and further weight restoration awakens fears of having a mature body and menses. The therapist must also be very empathetic and able to bridge the lack of affect and affective expression in patients with anorexia nervosa.

In the case of bulimia nervosa, patients are wary of coming into therapy with therapists who are not highly well-informed about eating disorders. Knowledge about eating disorders is also essential for completing the educational process that must occur as a part of normalizing eating behavior. Also, the gender of the therapist may be an important issue that has not been sufficiently studied. While female therapists are often used in the treatment of females with anorexia nervosa, they offer both advantages and disadvantages. Female therapists may have difficulty because of (a) the female anorexic patient's conflict with her mother, (b) her natural competition with women, and (c) the career–home conflicts of anorexic patients. Advantages for female therapists are (a) the identification that occurs with the female anorexic patient; (b) the openness that anorexics can thereby generate, as opposed to their reluctance to be open with males; and (c) the ability of the patient with anorexia nervosa to pick up assertiveness from her female therapist, which she would not be able to do with a male therapist (Frankenberg, 1984).

Lacey (1984) has found no difference in outcome for patients with bulimia nervosa who were treated by two female therapists as opposed to those treated by a male and a female therapist working together. The patients, however, preferred two female therapists, considering them to be far more relevant and helpful to their needs. In either case, cotherapists may be preferable to a single therapist. Unfortunately, cost constraints may prevent the use of cotherapists in group therapy for eating disorders. However, only one study of group therapy that we know of is using one single group therapist rather than using two cotherapists (Mitchell, Pyle, Eckert, Hatsukami, Zimmerman, & Pomeroy, 1987a).

Iatrogenesis

In our treatment of eating disorders, we must ensure that the clinician does nothing to worsen the patient's condition. Garner (1985a) pointed out a number of iatrogenic factors that may worsen the clinical condition of eating disordered patients, such as (a) failure to attend to food and weight issues in psychotherapy, (b) unrealistic target weights in treatment, (c) behavior modification without attention to psychological issues, (d) classical psychoanalysis, (e) use of tube feeding, (f) abstinence models, (g) well-intentioned prevention campaigns featuring prominent people who have eating disorders, and (h) self-help and support groups with actively bulimic members.

TREATMENT STRATEGIES

Consistent with the shorter chronology of documented diagnosis of bulimia nervosa, the treatment literature related to the psychotherapy of anorexia nervosa is more extensive but includes fewer controlled psychotherapy studies than that for bulimia nervosa. Almost all researchers have emphasized the importance of psychotherapy for anorexia nervosa, although Russell (1970) advocates a basic nursing-support approach, with emphasis by the physician on honesty, empathy, and support. Bruch (1973, 1982, 1985) wrote extensively on the theory and practice of psychotherapy for anorexia nervosa, emphasizing fact-finding and careful attention to the patient's feelings, sensations, and ideas. More recently, the application of cognitive treatment approaches (Garner & Bemis, 1982) has provided a second viable treatment technique. Family therapy for anorexia nervosa has become very popular, but it is clearly more feasible for younger patients still living at their parents' home (Minuchin, Rosman, & Baker, 1978; Russell, Szmukler, Dare, & Eisler, 1987). Early reports of successful psychotherapy for bulimia nervosa stressed individual cognitive-behavioral therapy (Fairburn, 1981) and group approaches (Boskind-Lodahl & White, 1978; Johnson, Connors, & Stuckey, 1983). Currently, there is increasing support for the application of behavioral techniques, such as developing alterna-tives to binge-eating and using exposure and response prevention techniques (Rosen & Leitenberg, 1982) as important components of any psychotherapy for bulimia nervosa. It is impossible to discuss the psychotherapies of anorexia nervosa and bulimia nervosa without referring to their behavioral components. The multimodal approach developed for the psychotherapy of eating disorders usually includes behavioral techniques for weight restoration and maintenance, for controlling bulimic behaviors, or for relapse prevention. Specific treatment techniques for eating disorders involving behavioral therapy are covered in Chapter 20. Treatment techniques specific to males with eating disorders have not been developed or studied.

Even though controlled treatment studies are lacking, there are many areas of common agreement regarding the treatment of eating disorders in general and for anorexia nervosa in particular. Most researchers emphasize the multidimensional, heterogeneous nature of eating disorders. Consequently, comprehensive treatment may appropriately include family, individual, and group therapy, at times using behavioral, cognitive, and psychodynamic principals. All major programs emphasize normalizing food intake through structured eating, meal plans, or food diaries. In addition, the phasing or sequencing of treatment approaches for both anorexia nervosa (Garner, Garfinkel, & Irving, 1986) and bulimia nervosa (Fairburn, 1985; Pyle & Mitchell, 1985) has received increasing attention.

A number of treatment concepts for anorexia nervosa have endured the test of time: (a) a focus on food and nutrition; (b) the normalization of weight; (c) the importance of the therapeutic relationship and engaging the patient to deal with self-concept deficit; (d) the importance of the recognition of affect and the expression of affect; (e) the clarification of family interactional patterns and the improvement of family communication; (f) the confrontation of developmental issues around separation and autonomy, sexual fears, and identity formation; (g) the understanding of physical and psychological consequences of the illness, including the effects of starvation with its associated behavior, emotions, and thoughts; and (h) confrontation of the patients' internal conflict about their own illness (Garner & Garfinkel, 1985).

Individual Cognitive and Cognitive-Behavioral Therapies

The cognitive-behavioral approach to the treatment of both anorexia nervosa and bulimia nervosa is based on the premise that the central features of these disorders are irrational dysfunctional beliefs and values concerning body shape and weight. Individual cognitive-behavioral therapy was first recommended for bulimia nervosa (Fairburn, 1981) and shortly after for anorexia nervosa (Garner & Bemis, 1982). It has remained a primary treatment for bulimia nervosa, but it is still less frequently reported than psychodynamic therapy for the treatment of anorexia nervosa.

Fairburn's open study (1981) used individual therapy that included self-monitoring, goal-setting, problem-solving, and cognitive-restructuring techniques for an average duration of 7 months. The first stage consisted of eight appointments in 4 weeks, with an emphasis on establishing some degree of control over the habitual daily bulimic behavior, using behavioral techniques (which included self-monitoring, a prescribed pattern of regular eating, and stimulus–control measures similar to those used in behavioral treatment for obesity). Patients were also given education about body-weight regulation, dieting, and the adverse effects of vomiting and laxative abuse for weight control. The second stage, of approximately eight appointments in 8 weeks, included training in (a) strategies designed to reduce the tendency to diet, (b) problem-solving techniques, and (c) cognitive-restructuring procedures to modify isolated environmental cues that trigger binge–purging behavior. In the final stage, lasting 6 weeks, with three appointments, the emphasis was on maintenance of progress and relapse prevention. Fairburn was one of the first to recommend introduction of forbidden foods into the diets of patients with bulimia nervosa as part of the later stages of treatment. Fairburn's posttreatment results found that 9 of 11 subjects reported fewer than one binge–purge episode per month; his follow-up results at 1 year revealed that 5 out of the 6 patients contacted were having binge–purge episodes no more frequently than once every 2–3

months. These encouraging results influenced many clinicians to embrace these techniques.

Fairburn, Kirk, O'Connor, and Cooper (1986) later compared this approach with short-term focal psychotherapy (STP), which was also associated with impressive treatment outcome. STP was modeled after Rosen's (1979) brief psychotherapy, adapted on the basis of Bruch's (1973) writings on anorexia nervosa and Stunkard's (1980) psychotherapeutic approach to overweight people who binge-eat. This approach necessitates that eating problems be conceptualized as a maladaptive solution for other underlying difficulties. Attention is paid to the events and feelings that provoke episodes of overeating. A fact-finding, noninterpretive style is emphasized, to help patients develop confidence in their own opinions, feelings, and needs. Surprisingly, the STP, designed to be the treatment control, was remarkably effective, with the exception of elimination of self-induced vomiting, which was continuing at the rate of three times monthly at follow-up. Other advantages noted for cognitive-behavioral therapy were its positive effect on the patients' overall clinical state, general psychopathology, social adjustment, and their own assessment of outcome.

Freeman, Barry, Dunkeld-Turnbull, and Henderson (1988) compared weekly individual cognitive-behavioral therapy, following Beck, Rush, Shaw, and Emery's model (1979), with individual behavioral therapy, with supportive group therapy, and with a waiting-list control. Individual cognitive-behavioral treatment techniques included the identification and recording of automatic thoughts through self-monitoring and the restructuring of those thoughts, dealing initially with maladaptive cognitions relating to eating and weight, and then progressing to general psychological issues including depression, self-esteem, and assertiveness. Only minimal attempts were used to alter the abnormal behavior. Two therapists conducted all three treatments alternating in both kinds of individual therapy and acting as cotherapists for groups. Of the 92 original subjects, 65 completed treatment. All three treatment groups improved significantly in the frequency of bulimic behavior, with those in group therapy decreasing their binge-eating behavior from 6.3 to 0.8 episodes weekly. Those in individual cognitive-behavioral therapy decreased from 6.2 to 1.3

episodes weekly, and those in individual behavioral therapy decreased from 4.6 to 0.60 episodes weekly. Patients in behavioral therapy had a significantly greater decrease in the eating attitude scores, in irritability, in depression, and in anxiety than did those in group posttreatment. The efficacy of individual cognitive-behavioral therapy was more evident during follow-up when binge–purging frequencies were further reduced and when this group was significantly superior to the group therapy subjects, with regard to irritability, depression, and anxiety. There were no significant differences, however, between the two individual therapies. In this study, all three therapies were effective, with cognitive-behavioral and group therapies having higher dropout rates.

Ordman and Kirschenbaum (1985) had less positive results with individual cognitive-behavioral therapy and exposure and response prevention when compared with a brief-intervention waiting-list control. Only 20% of the 10 subjects in the study were in remission after treatment, and 30% were unchanged. The treatment group, however, did notice less discomfort with food and a shorter duration of the urge to vomit, which resulted in greater food consumption than in the control group.

The main proponents of individual cognitive-behavioral therapy for anorexia nervosa have been Garner and Bemis (1982, 1985). Their techniques were derived from the Beck, et al. (1979) cognitive-behavioral treatment of depression. This approach involves a commitment to clear specification of treatment methods and an objective assessment of change in target behaviors. Modifications to conventional cognitive therapy are adopted in the treatment of anorexia nervosa. Specific areas that should be pursued are (a) idiosyncratic beliefs related to food and weight, (b) the interaction of physical and psychological aspects of the disorder, (c) the patient's desire to retain certain focal symptoms, and (d) the prominence of fundamental self-concept deficit related to self-esteem and trust of internal state. Cooper and Fairburn (1984) have adapted their individual approach for treating bulimia nervosa to patients with anorexia nervosa but reported only preliminary results with five patients.

In summary, current studies would suggest that individual cognitive-behavioral therapy is an effective treatment for bulimia nervosa and that other individual therapies also may be effective treatments in the hands of able clinicians. Publication of controlled studies on the effectiveness of cognitive-behavioral therapy in the treatment of anorexia nervosa will be awaited with interest.

Individual Psychodynamic Psychotherapy

Psychodynamic psychotherapy continues to be the major psychotherapeutic modality for the treatment of patients with anorexia nervosa. Bruch (1973, 1978, 1982, 1985) has defined the phenomenology of anorexia nervosa, in which self-starvation represents the struggle for autonomy, competence, control, and self-respect. She has proposed a fact-finding psychotherapy aimed at correcting specific conceptual defects and distortions that evolved out of faulty developmental experiences. Therapy is aimed at helping the patient discover her or his "genuine self" by encouraging and confirming authentic expressions of her or his thoughts and feelings. Rather than exploring the symbolic significance of symptoms, experiences are reevaluated in order to understand how conceptual disturbances, largely derived from previous relationships, have interfered with the development of autonomy and self-confidence. Bruch (1985) cautions that during psychotherapy, the low weight must be corrected without disturbing the tenuous sense of autonomy that remains for the patient. At the same time, Bruch advocates clarifying family interactions to ally the entire family with the treatment effort.

Bruch believes that therapy should be initiated by identifying the symptom as one related to decreased self-worth and self-value, to point out the effects of starvation, and to indicate that the therapy is for the benefit of the patient, not his or her parents. Patients are encouraged to reduce their posture of "helpless passivity, hateful submissiveness, and indiscriminant negativism." Ongoing therapy centers on repeated review regarding both the patient's need to be good and to please others and the identification and reinforcement of a new personality based on internal needs rather than environmental expectations. The patient is also encouraged to identify developmental delays, and to confront (with the therapist) family mechanisms that encourage those delays. Patients also are helped to reduce their expectations for superperformance and curb their grandiose aspirations. Finally, the therapist works with patients to reduce their isolation from peers and family.

The second major force in the development of psychodynamic psychotherapy for anorexia nervosa has been Crisp (1980). Crisp emphasizes the phobic avoidance of weight and the fears of sexual maturity manifested by patients with anorexia nervosa. This developmental model assumes that anorexia nervosa represents an attempt to cope with the fears and conflicts associated with psychobiological maturity. The dieting and consequent starvation, then, become the mechanisms for the patient's regression to a prepubertal state. Such a model requires that weight restoration be continued to the point where developmental concerns arrested by the weight loss again surface. Individual therapy may then be directed toward developing more adult strategies for coping.

Goodsitt (1985) has borrowed from the self-theory of Kohut (1971) to develop a psychoanalytically oriented psychotherapy similar to that of Bruch. Casper's (1982) emphasis on self-esteem deficits addresses similar issues. Garner (1985b) has underscored the common themes present in individual therapy of anorexia nervosa. These include (a) the struggle for autonomy, independence, and individuality; (b) the inability of patient and family to handle adolescence and to break childhood bonds; and (c) the need for control, mastery, and competence in which the patient selects being thin as an area of mastery. Other elements of individual therapy include concerns about body image, emotional expressiveness, assertiveness, social skills, perfectionism, and depression. In addition, Garner (1985b) notes contraindications to individual psychodynamic psychotherapy, including severe starvation and metabolic abnormalities, severe depression or decompensation, poor motivation for change or failure to develop a trusting relationship, severely limited intellectual capacity or complete lack of psychological awareness, family relationships that sabotage therapeutic goals, or a preadolescent onset of the disorder.

In summary, psychodynamic psychotherapy has been recommended as a primary treatment for anorexia nervosa but has not been adequately described or demonstrated as an effective treatment for bulimia nervosa. No controlled studies have evaluated the efficacy of individual psychodynamic psychotherapy for either condition.

Group Psychotherapy

Bulimia Nervosa

Group psychotherapy potentially offers a cost-effective approach for large numbers of young men and women who are seeking treatment for bulimia nervosa. In fact, an initial cognitive behavioral group approach has been recommended as a cost-effective approach to treat less severe cases (Brotman, Alonso, & Herzog, 1985). On the other hand, group psychotherapy for anorexia nervosa, which is discussed later in this section, has limited advantages, except as an adjunctive treatment.

Several attributes of group psychotherapy offer specific benefits for the treatment of bulimia nervosa. Group treatment may provide sufficient structure and support (a) to permit interruption of the chronic habitual nature of the behavior; (b) to promote reduction of the social isolation and loneliness that accompany bulimia nervosa; (c) to increase greatly the number of people offering insight and support regarding the behavior; and (d) to permit group members to increase their own self-esteem by assisting other group members (Pyle & Mitchell, 1985). Because research on the effectiveness of group psychotherapy for bulimia is still in its infancy, issues relating to treatment definition, such as the general approach to be used, the treatment format, the optimal expectations for change, the type and number of therapists, and the criteria for selecting cases have not been systematically investigated. Often, group treatments reported in the literature have included all three conventional approaches: psychodynamic, cognitive-behavioral, and behavioral, which makes evaluation of treatment efficacy difficult.

Studies conducted in the 1980s, including most of the controlled studies on group therapy, have incorporated techniques developed in the context of individual therapy, such as the individual cognitive-behavioral approach of Fairburn (1981) and the exposure and response prevention (ERP) of

Rosen and Leitenberg (1982). Seven different group formats have been used to test cognitive-behavioral therapies as part of four controlled studies and one uncontrolled study. These studies have included (a) cognitive restructuring (as a control for other experimental groups) (Wilson, Rossiter, Kleifeld, & Lindholm, 1986; Yate & Sambrailo, 1984); (b) cognitive-behavioral and behavioral principles (Kirkley, Schneider, Agras, & Bachman, 1985; Lee & Rush, 1986; Schneider & Agras, 1985); (c) cognitive restructuring and ERP (Wilson et al., 1986); and (d) cognitive-behavioral therapy, behavioral techniques, and ERP (Yates & Sambrailo, 1984). In cognitive-behavioral groups, goal setting is almost always used to establish individual treatment goals. The number of patients per group were six to eight at the start of therapy, with roughly one fourth dropping out of the group by the end of treatment. The number of sessions ranged from 6 to 16. The intensity was as high as twice weekly for 6 weeks. The length of the groups was 1 1/2 hours, and they were most often conducted by two female therapists.

Results of early psychodynamic groups, all open studies, were reported by several authors (Dixon & Kiecolt-Glaser, 1984; Roy-Byrne, Lee-Benner, & Yager, 1984; Stevens & Salisbury, 1984). While there have been several recent studies of psychodynamic groups, only Frommer, Ames, Gibson, and Davis (1987) gave specific information on binge–purging frequency. Psychodynamic groups have included 5–10 members, with the number of sessions and the structure of the groups variable. Frommer et al. (1987) had a wide range of group members (2–9), with an average of 5 for their 19 groups. They did not compare outcome with group size, although this may be an important issue. Most studies described groups that were time limited, with 12–16 sessions. All sessions were 1 1/2 hours. All the groups were run by two female therapists. Dixon and Kiecolt-Glaser (1984) note that the groups ran more smoothly if negativism was *not* reinforced (i.e., patients were not allowed to talk at length about the difficulty of changing their bulimic behavior).

Two authors have reported on psychoeducational groups (Connors, Johnson, & Stuckey, 1984; Wolchik, Weiss, & Katzman, 1986). These groups usually have an educational or teaching component as part of the group therapy and are highly structured and time limited. The number of patients in the psychoeducational groups varies from 5 to 10. They are conducted in 7–12 sessions over 7–9 weeks, and they vary in length from 1 1/2 to 2 hours.

The University of Minnesota Program for Group Treatment of Bulimia Nervosa. The eating disorders program at the University of Minnesota has used intensive outpatient group treatment as its main treatment technique for bulimia nervosa (Mitchell et al., 1985b). The behavioral and cognitive-behavioral format consists of three phases: (1) psychoeducational, (2) interruption of bulimic behavior, and (3) behavior stabilization. The expectation is that all members of the group will stop the behavior on the first night of the second phase of the group program. The group is closed, with six to eight members; structured; and 10 weeks in duration, consisting of 22 sessions, decreasing in length from 3 hours to 1 1/2 hours nightly and in frequency from daily to weekly, with socialization outside of the group encouraged. There is emphasis on self-monitoring, weight maintenance, healthy eating, meal planning and introduction of feared foods, cognitive restructuring, cue restraint, alternative behaviors, response delay, assertiveness, and problem solving (Mitchell et al., 1985b). The major thrust of the treatment is to provide sufficient support so that all patients may rapidly interrupt their bulimic behaviors and stabilize their eating behaviors. Group integrity and patient independence are enhanced by rotation of treatment staff after the initial four sessions.

Since 1980, the feedback from many of more than 700 patients treated as part of open-outcome studies, and the introduction of treatment principles suggested by research literature, have contributed to major changes in the program. The treatment protocol evolved from the Overeaters Anonymous (OA) and behavioral structure used for the first six groups to a phased program with increasing emphasis on cognitive-behavioral principles. There have also been major changes in expectations for refraining from bulimic behavior. In the original model, patients were referred to other therapeutic modalities after a specific number of binge–purging episodes. A gradual shift was made to referring patients out of the program only if they failed to reduce their bulimic behavior. At present, they are referred to other treatments only if they endorse that they are unmotivated to change or they request an alternate treatment.

Another major change has been the introduction of the first phase—a psychoeducational component—to the program. Patients in early groups found it difficult to interrupt bulimic behavior on the first night without some preparation for eating three adequate meals a day. As a result of this problem, a 2-week initial phase was introduced, consisting of four 2-hour group meetings, which were designed to improve motivation, to help patients review the pros and cons of binge-eating, to educate them about bulimia and its treatment with cognitive-behavioral techniques, and to institute meal planning (the last item requiring a majority of the group time).

Expectations about the introduction of feared foods have also changed. In the earlier programs, patients were told to avoid binge foods until they had completed the treatment program and their eating behavior had stabilized for a period of months. Over time, however, feared foods have been introduced earlier in the group therapy, and patients now frequently begin eating feared foods before the interruption phase of the program begins. In Phase 2 (the interruption phase), the format of lectures, therapeutic meals, and group therapy have remained unchanged. Exposure both to high-risk situations and to response prevention has been a valued addition to the group therapy program during the third (stabilization) phase. Relaxation training was viewed negatively by patients and was dropped after feedback from participants in early groups. Data are currently being assessed from a controlled study with 200 subjects, comparing the efficacy of the current model with an antidepressant therapy (Mitchell, Pyle, Eckert, Hatsukami, Zimmerman, & Pomeroy, 1987a).

The Role Of Cognitive and Behavioral Techniques in Group Psychotherapy of Bulimia Nervosa. Cognitive therapy and behavioral principles are extensively used in group psycho-therapy. Self-monitoring was used almost without exception, with some studies monitoring both eating behavior and feelings (Connors et al., 1984; Kirkley et al., 1985). Cognitive restructuring was reported for almost all the group therapies. Cue restriction or alternative behaviors were used by a majority of the cognitive-behavioral programs, the psychoeducational programs, and the intensive group program at the University of Minnesota. The ERP was reported by three groups with some of the better treatment outcomes (Mitchell et al., 1985b; Wilson et al., 1986; Yates & Sambrailo, 1984). Assertiveness was stressed in six group treatment designs. Relaxation therapy received major emphasis in cognitive-behavioral groups, particularly in the cognitive-behavioral group therapy offered by Schneider and Agras (1985). Along with cognitive restructuring, it was felt to be a very valuable technique by the participants in the study by Lee and Rush (1986), although some group therapy patients have reported that relaxation therapy was not of value (Connors et al., 1984).

Group Psychotherapy for Adolescents with Bulimia Nervosa. Stuber and Strober (1987) have noted that evaluation of group psychotherapy for adolescents with bulimia nervosa is still in its infancy, and that there has been insufficient attention paid to this important group of patients. The authors noted that adolescents do not accept the behavioral and psychoeducational techniques used for adult bulimics. They believe that group psychotherapy may better fit an adjunctive role for adolescents (a) to reduce the secrecy and the isolation that surround the illness, (b) to reduce the rigidly fixed and irrational ideas concerning body weight or fasting, (c) to help patients develop alternative strategies to cope with stress and intrapsychic conflict, (d) to clarify and resolve psychically painful emotional states, and (e) to serve as a catalyst for movement in individual or family therapies.

Group Therapy for Anorexia Nervosa

Group therapy for anorexia nervosa is frequently a part of the therapeutic milieu of major inpatient programs. In order to participate in group therapy, the patient must not be at a stage of extreme starvation (Hall, 1985; Hedblom, Hubbard, & Anderson, 1982). In addition, the patient must have moved beyond the stage of denial and must have a mutually positive relationship with the therapist. Contrary to group therapy for other conditions, group therapy for anorexia nervosa is seen in the context of a variety of other forms of treatment in a specialized program, in both inpatient and outpatient psychotherapy, and it is seen as a mechanism to improve interpersonal relationships (Hall, 1985; Polivy, 1981). Group therapy for anorexia has received little attention in the literature. This may be related to the difficulty of involving patients with anorexia nervosa in group therapy (Hall, 1985). Anorexic patients have been described as withdrawn, anxious, rigid, egocentric, preoccupied with body weight and food, and less able to identify and express feelings. All of the aforementioned characteristics lend themselves poorly to group psychotherapy. In addition, the capacity of patients with anorexia nervosa to intellectualize tends to make them less accessible to therapists (Hall, 1985).

Family Therapy

Family therapy is viewed as an important component in the treatment of anorexia nervosa, mainly because of the influential writings of two groups of therapists: Minuchin and his colleagues (1978) at the Philadelphia Child Guidance Clinic, and Selvini-Palazzoli (1978) and co-workers in Milan. Both have based their treatment of anorexia nervosa on theoretical models that they have devised to explain the genesis of that illness. The structural family therapists (Minuchin and associates) seek to alter dysfunctional transactional patterns within the family system, by using active and straightforward directives around the symptom, as opposed to insight. The strategic therapists, with Selvini-Palazzoli most often associated with family treatment of anorexia nervosa, are also symptom oriented, but they attempt to uncover the hidden family gain, which they see as necessary to disrupt the maladaptive cycle. Both may use seemingly illogical and paradoxical interventions. Both of these therapeutic schools view family therapy as the primary treatment for anorexia nervosa. The work of both schools was exciting to therapists, and Minuchin's posttreatment and follow-up results (with a reported 86% recovery) created great interest. Minuchin, however, treated young inpatients with a short duration of illness coming from intact families—all characteristics associated with positive treatment outcome. However, Anderson (1985) pointed out that the enmeshed family described by Minuchin comprises only part of the families of patients with anorexia nervosa, limiting the applicability of the approach to a wider range of patients. In addition, many families of anorexic patients are unable to tolerate the anxiety and confrontation of these family approaches, and they discontinue therapy.

By the end of the 1970s, there was a clear tendency to develop an eclectic and integrated treatment for most eating disorders, which led to the current trend of eclecticism and integration of family therapy into a multidimensional treatment program (Garfinkel & Garner, 1982). This approach led to the abandonment of orthodox adherence to one particular school of family therapy. Instead, more family therapists started to combine concepts and strategies derived from different models. The writings of Vandereycken (Vandereycken & Meerman, 1984) are typical of the current generation of family therapists for anorexia nervosa. He advocates family therapy as a component to be integrated within a multidimensional approach that is guided by a constructive and positive attitude toward the family and is based on a pragmatic but flexible scientist–practitioner spirit (Vandereycken, 1987).

Although anorexia nervosa as an illness lends itself to the objective evaluation of the efficacy of psychological treatment, only one controlled trial with systematic follow-up has been reported for the family therapy of anorexia nervosa and bulimia nervosa. Russell et al. (1987) have completed a controlled evaluation of family therapy for anorexia nervosa and bulimia nervosa in a trial with 80 patients (57 with anorexia nervosa and 23 with bulimia nervosa). Patients were randomly assigned to family therapy or individual supportive therapy, and after 1 year of treatment, they were reassessed, using body weight, menstrual function, and ratings on the Morgan and Russell scales. The positive results of Minuchin et al. (1978) with young anorexics with short-term illness were confirmed by this study, which demonstrated that young (under age 19 years) anorexics with brief duration of illness (under 4 years) responded to the family therapy at a higher rate (60% good results) than they did to individual supportive therapy (10% good results). However, family therapy was not superior to individual therapy for bulimia nervosa.

Family therapy has been used less frequently for patients with bulimia nervosa because of the large number of these patients who are separated from their families. Schwartz, Barrett, and Saba (1985) reported encouraging results from an open unreplicated family therapy study of 30 bulimic patients and their families, who were seen for an average of 33 sessions over 9 months, with a range of 2 to 90 sessions. The primary interventions were structural family therapy and symptom-focused directives. Prior to treatment, all 30 patients were bingeing and purging more than 5 times ε week. After treatment, 66% had less than one episode per month, 10% had weekly episodes or less, and 14% were unchanged. Improvement was maintained at follow-up, which occurred an average of 16 months after the termination of treatment.

Other Therapies

Lacey (1983) described a treatment for bulimia nervosa which combined individual and group techniques to achieve excellent results in a controlled study that involved the use of behavioral and cognitive techniques, as well as psychodynamic psychotherapy. There were 30 subjects in the study, which used a waiting-list control for 15 subjects. Subjects contracted in advance to attend all sessions, to maintain current weight, and to eat a prescribed diet, which included 3 meals a day at set times. They attended weekly sessions involving 1/2 hour of individual therapy and 1 1/2 hours of group therapy weekly for 10 weeks. At the end of treatment, 80% were totally remitted and an additional 4 (or 93% of subjects total) were totally binge–purge free within 4 weeks after treatment. Results have been maintained over long-term follow-up (Lacey, 1986).

Hypnotherapy has been reported as an effective technique for the treatment of anorexia nervosa (Baker & Nash, 1987; Gross, 1984). However, the small number of patients that accept hypnosis (10%) (Gross, 1984) and the difficulty of direct hypnotic suggestion (Pettinati, Horne, & Staats, 1985) have often limited use to indirect approaches in a relatively small percentage of patients. Only isolated case studies have been reported for bulimia nervosa (Holgate, 1984), even though patients with bulimia nervosa may be more easily hypnotized (Pettinati et al., 1985).

Model Treatment Programs for Eating Disorders

Treatment for Anorexia Nervosa

Comprehensive multimodal treatment programs that provide continuity between inpatient and outpatient care and that place strong emphasis on psychotherapy have been the rule of thumb for anorexia nervosa. Three such model programs were described at the 1984 International Conference on Eating Disorders in Wales (Crisp, Norton, Jurczak, Bowyer, & Dunean, 1985; Garfinkel, 1985; Vandereycken, 1985). Crisp et al. (1985) described a program that provided bed rest on 3,000 calories daily, until the patient arrived at a target weight, defined as the population mean weight at the age of onset of the disorder. Patients were allowed to bathe 2 times weekly, to make phone calls twice weekly, and to participate in art therapy, individual psychotherapy, and weekend community groups. At the fifth week, family and/ or marital therapy was initiated, along with weekday community meetings, relaxation therapy, small group participation, and individual assessments. Patients were given options for meal selection on weekends. During the 6 weeks after they had reached their target weight, there was a gradual increase in the time that patients were up and around the ward, in combination with increasing off-ward privileges. There was also increased involvement in food preparation and more flexibility in diet. Weight loss immediately postdischarge remained a problem in the program, which was somewhat less rigid than earlier comprehensive programs. Nonetheless, two thirds of the patients were of normal body weight at long-term follow-up.

Garfinkel (1985) described the program at

Toronto, which was greatly influenced by the concepts of Bruch, and which was designed to provide behavioral reinforcement of weight gain. Garfinkel notes that a number of patients with anorexia nervosa can be treated with outpatient therapy in a well-organized program and that both inpatient and outpatient treatment require individual, family, and group psychotherapy. Medication for depression is commonly administered. A day center was started to help the transition to community living, and a number of self-help facilities were developed to provide additional support after discharge.

Vandereycken (1985) reported that his comprehensive program was continually modified on the basis of research results and patient feedback. The program had been developing between 1974 and 1980 from a strict medical weight restoration model to a behavioral contract system that provided gradually increasing freedom as the patient approached discharge weight. The patients were confined to their rooms, weighed daily, and given a fixed diet, although they could have visitors on weekends. When they reached 33% of their target weight gain (the difference between their weight at admission and their target weight), they ate their evening meals in the dining room, were weighed 3 times weekly, had a fixed maximum amount of food, were given freedom of movement within the hospital, and were allowed daily visits until they reached 67% of their target weight gain. From this time until they reached their total target weight, they ate all meals in the dining room, were weighed weekly, had a free choice of the food they ate, were allowed to leave the hospital, and spent weekends at home. Other additions to the program since 1980 include family therapy and both administrative and therapeutic group therapy sessions daily. Participants in this program gained an average of 0.7 to 3.0 kg/week. If they failed to gain the prescribed amount of weight, they were placed in an exception program, which placed a much higher emphasis on contingency management.

While these three programs all have satisfactory results, they require many months of hospitalization. This may be difficult for clinicians in the United States, who are faced with very restrictive standards for reimbursement. Innovative research designs will be required to test comprehensive inpatient–partial-hospitalization–outpatient programs for anorexia nervosa that will permit discharge while the weight gain phase is still continuing. At this time, there are no studies to indicate that such early discharge is compatible with positive treatment outcome.

Treatment for Bulimia Nervosa

The development of comprehensive treatment programs for bulimia nervosa is in its infancy. At this time, there is little indication that inpatient treatment is needed for bulimia nervosa in a well-organized treatment setting, with good medical evaluation and follow-up, and with ready availability of emergency medical and laboratory facilities. Two ways to reduce pretreatment dropouts may be (1) preparatory groups that help individuals to analyze their eating disordered behavior and to make rational decisions about entry into treatment, and (2) drop-in groups that provide support until a specific treatment modality recommended for the patient becomes available. Meal-planning clinics conducted by knowledgeable dietitians and/or therapists and specifically designed for individuals with anorexia nervosa and bulimia nervosa are an important precursor to behavior change. It is likely that a partial hospitalization program, operating evenings and weekends to cover peak binge–purging times for bulimic patients, could be the most effective treatment. This option is being more seriously considered, as some insurance companies are no longer paying for inpatient care for bulimia nervosa. In the absence of partial hospitalization, programs that would provide more direct outpatient support early in treatment to promote interruption of the habitual daily binge–purging behavior and subsequently to permit identification of environmental cues that may trigger the behavior would seem to be indicated. The latter treatment goal could be accomplished by either individual (Fairburn, 1981) or group approaches (Mitchell et al., 1985), which would provide cognitive restructuring and ERP as sequential treatments after reduction of high-frequency bulimic behaviors. Such programs could be offered concurrently with psychotherapy for other issues.

Programs for both anorexia nervosa and bulimia nervosa may provide adjunctive group support for spouses and families of women and men with eating disorders (Leichner, Harper, & Johnston, 1985). Their purpose is to provide information about the particular eating disorder the family member is experiencing, to enlist family support for treatment, and to reduce feelings of anger and frustration that occur in parents and family members of eating disordered individuals. More extensive family therapy may be needed for adult bulimia nervosa patients who continue to live at their parents' home so that the patient and the family may work toward a constructive separation that will provide the independence that is often associated with positive outcome.

Marital therapy may also be important in the treatment of individuals with eating disorders, as the marriage relationship may change dramatically when eating behavior becomes normalized and codependency is exposed. Local support groups and self-help groups contribute to a comprehensive support network, provided that a majority of their members are in remission. It is likely that women with eating disorders may also benefit from groups focusing on feminist issues and sociocultural pressures. Assertiveness training, relaxation training, and training in stress management and problem solving may also be valuable supports in relapse prevention. Combination treatment with antidepressants and psychosocial treatment may be required for many patients. More than one adequate trial of antidepressant therapy may be required before the right medication is found (i.e., desipramine, fluoxetine, or tranylcypromine).

Summary

Specialized centers for eating disorder treatment may provide optimal therapy; however, individuals clinicians who wish to treat their patients with eating disorders may be effective if: (a) they have adequate knowledge regarding the dietary, physical, sociocultural, and therapeutic aspects of treating eating disorders; (b) they are willing to be responsible for the normalization of eating behavior; (c) they know proper techniques for engaging the patient in therapy; (d) they have access to the indicated ancillary treatments, including adequate medical monitoring; (e) they are willing to have multiple appointments each week to provide support if needed; and (f) they use a noninterpretive fact-finding approach in partnership with their patient, to understand and change undesirable behavior.

CASE ILLUSTRATION

Mary L. is a 23-year-old, single female who came for eating disorder evaluation, was self-referred, and was requesting bulimia nervosa treatment. She related a history of bulimia nervosa for 5 years following a diagnosed episode of anorexia nervosa 6 years prior to evaluation. During her bout of anorexia nervosa, she lost weight until she weighed 85 pounds. At evaluation, she weighed 124 pounds and was 64 inches tall. She binge-ate three to four times weekly at evaluation, down from a high of three to four times daily. She reported one 6-month period of remission. She controls her weight by inducing vomiting each time she binge-eats. She goes on 24-hour fasts once or twice monthly. Her binges at time of evaluation occurred after eating a complete meal. The binges included ingestion of two handfuls of candy or a large number of crackers. While much smaller than her earlier binges, they were associated with a feeling of loss of control. Symptoms include "puffy" cheeks, but she denied ever having callouses on her knuckles from inducing vomiting. At evaluation, she was also exercising to control weight and to maintain physical fitness, although she rigidly controls the duration so that she "won't tend to overdo it."

She was first treated 5 years prior to evaluation with cognitive-behavioral therapy for 3 months. She also received 3 months of behavioral therapy, including extensive assertiveness training 4 years prior to the evaluation. She was treated 1 year prior to evaluation in group therapy for bulimia nervosa by her health maintenance organization, and she was also seen by a counselor at the university she was attending 1 year prior to and on the year of the evaluation. While she believed that all these treatments were helpful to her, she stated that she had been unable to eliminate the bulimic behaviors. She related her 6-month abstinence from bulimic behavior to going away to school and becoming more independent. Not surprisingly, she felt that her relapse was due to conflict with her mother over money and the discontinuation of her eating disorder group at the university, along with other stresses.

Psychiatric history was unremarkable, but medical history revealed a diagnosis of hiatal hernia 1 ½ years prior to evaluation. In recent months, she reported developing more cavities in her teeth and was told by her dentist that she had erosion of her teeth. Evaluation of chemical use indicated a social drinking pattern once or twice a month without intoxication, the consumption of four to five cans of diet cola daily, and eight cups of coffee daily, along with caffeine to study for finals. Family history revealed that there were no eating disorders in her family, although her mother tended to watch her own weight. Mary L. related that she had an uncle who was depressed and was on medication for depression and may or may not have been hospitalized. There was a strong family loading for alcoholism. A brother had a driving-while-intoxicated arrest and chemical dependency treatment; a sister also had problems with alcohol. A maternal grandmother and grandfather were "untreated" alcoholics, and a paternal grandfather was treated for alcoholism and recovered. At the time of evaluation, she was a senior at a state university, studying psychology and working parttime as a waitress, although she reported no disordered eating behavior either during or after work. She had four or five good friends, all of whom knew about her eating disorder. She was not dating at the time of evaluation because she did not like herself in her present state. She expressed motivation for treatment. On mental status examination, mood and affect were appropriate to interview content, and there was no evidence of anxiety, symptoms of major depression, or thought disorder.

Mary L. was referred to an intensive outpatient group therapy program for bulimia nervosa, where she reduced her binge–purging behavior almost 50% during the meal planning and psychoeducational phase of treatment. She stopped the behavior altogether during the second (intensive) phase, and she remained free of bulimic behavior until the 10th and final week of treatment, when she had two episodes of binge–purging behavior on a weekend. Because of this, she entered a maintenance support group for a period of 4 months and noted a slightly increasing frequency of binge–purging behavior that was maintained at a twice weekly rate. By the end of the 4 months maintenance treatment, she reported symptoms of intermittent sadness, irritability, and dysphoria. Following the initiation of antidepressant treatment with 20 mg of fluoxetine, there was an improvement in mood. In addition, she

found it much easier to refrain from binge–purging behaviors, and after 3 months of improved mood and remission of bulimic symptoms, the antidepressant was successfully discontinued. On 1-year follow-up, it was noted that she had experienced two episodes of binge– purging behavior following a disappointment over an unsuccessful job interview. In general, she was quite happy with her life-style and her eating habits, although she had reduced the number of meals she ate from three to two daily.

ALTERNATIVE TREATMENT OPTIONS

Assessing Alternative Treatments

Despite the fact that psychotherapy makes good pragmatic sense in treatment of anorexia nervosa, the long-term effectiveness of the alternative psychotherapy techniques remains to be evaluated, in part because of the small population in treatment. More research should be directed toward prevention of relapse, in addition to comparison of inpatient, outpatient, and partial hospitalization programs to restore and maintain weight. The role of specific elements of the multimodal treatments that are now favored should be evaluated, including comparison of the effects of medications and specific psychotherapeutic techniques, social skills training, family therapy, and work with restructuring irrational thoughts about food and body image.

More controlled studies have been and are being published regarding a number of alternative treatments for bulimia nervosa, but treatment protocols in the published literature often lack specific description, and studies usually do not evaluate whether the described treatment has been delivered. In addition, outcome studies use inconsistent criteria that are often poorly defined and biased by failure to control for the effects of separate treatments. An additional problem with outcome measures for bulimia nervosa is the necessity to rely on patient self-reports, in the absence of clear outcome criteria available for anorexia nervosa, such as weight gain and return of menses. Factors other than the treatment being evaluated must also be considered (i.e., subjects' motivation, treatment system, skill of therapists) for those studies reporting excellent results from all treatments being compared. Treatments that have been replicated in controlled studies at different centers are the most likely to have value for the clinician.

When one looks at the description of the sample, one should expect to see subjects who average 8 to 12 episodes of binge–purging behavior weekly with approximately a 5- to 6-year duration of illness, of whom 80–90% use self-induced vomiting as their primary method of weight control. One must question the outcome of studies that describe much lower baseline rates of bulimic behavior in their subjects or those studies that use a selected population, such as university students, as symptomatic volunteers.

Dropouts should be considered in any evaluation of treatment results, because retention of potential subjects in treatment is a legitimate measure of the effectiveness of that treatment. The dropout rate for patients in treatment for bulimia nervosa is high. Merrill, Mines, and Starkey (1987) reviewed six therapy groups and noted that 20 of the 53 subjects (38%) dropped out before the 20th week of treatment. Unstructured therapies that use a psychodynamic format report dropout rates as high as 53–69% (Dixon & Kiecolt-Glaser, 1984; Roy-Byrne et al., 1984). The dropout rate seems to be lower as amount of the structure increases, with cognitive-restructuring groups losing 25–30% of subjects, psychoeducational and cognitive-behavioral groups with heavy behavioral emphasis about 20%, and cognitive-restructuring plus ERP losing from 10 to 20% of their subjects. The intensive outpatient group program at the University of Minnesota, a highly structured program, notes a 13% rate of dropout prior to completion of treatment (Mitchell, Pyle, Hatsukami, Goff, Glotter, & Harper, 1989). Using a nondirective group therapy approach as a control, Kirkley et al. (1985) reported a 36% dropout rate, five times higher than that of cognitive-behavioral therapy experimental groups. In a controlled study, Freeman et al. (1988) found a 34% dropout rate for supportive group therapy, 32% for individual cognitive-behavioral therapy, and 17% for individual behavioral therapy. In contrast, Lacey's (1983) study combining individual and group psychotherapy had no dropouts in their 30 subjects, and Fariburn et al. (1986) had fewer than 10% of their patients drop out from both the therapies evaluated. Overall, existing data would suggest that group therapy alone has the highest dropout rate of the treatment modalities.

Most open studies and some controlled studies do not account for outside therapy during treatment and during the follow-up period. Roy-Byrne et al. (1984) reported that all but one of their original group members and all the group completers were in simultaneous individual psychotherapy, and that three of the eight subjects were on antidepressants. In a staggered baseline study, Connors et al. (1984) noted that 25% of their subjects were also in individual psychotherapy. Stevens and Salisbury (1984) noted that all of their group subjects remained in therapy at the time of follow-up, as did most of Abraham, Mira, and Llewelyn-Jones's (1984) subjects in individual psychotherapy. This problem is not limited to psychotherapy studies, however. Pope, Hudson, Jonas, and Yurgelon-Todd (1985), in studying the treatment of bulimia with imipramine, noted that almost all of their subjects required continued medication during the follow-up period. Unfortunately, treatments that are continued during the follow-up or that are coincident with or followed by another treatment are difficult to evaluate.

Outcome Measures

The rates of binge–purging behavior are excellent outcome measures for the treatment of bulimia nervosa, although the required use of self-report measures has been criticized. In defining binge-eating, the quantity of the eating binge has been suggested as an important factor (Katzman, Wolchick, & Braver, 1984). However, most researchers feel that the element of loss of control is key to defining binge-eating (a position reinforced by the DSM-III-R classification of bulimia nervosa). Patients may tend to overreport binge-eating on follow-up, calling an extra piece of bread or a slightly large meal a "binge" (Abraham et al., 1984). Mitchell, Davis, Goff, and Pyle (1986) have used the highest frequencies reported for any given month during the follow-up as a more conservative measure, which takes into account the fluctuating nature of bulimic symptoms and the possibility that study participants may attempt to reduce bulimic behaviors immediately prior to follow-up.

The reliability of a study that requires the use of

self-report measures may always be questioned. Obviously, reports from relatives or friends are also highly unreliable, considering the secretive nature of bulimia nervosa. While it is true that literature may be cited to support that bulimics underreport to please their interviewers or overreport because of their need for perfection, the time of reporting may be the most important factor (Pyle & Mitchell, 1986). In outcome studies, patients with bulimia nervosa may tend to underreport the binge–purging behavior to please their therapists, especially in face-to-face interviews. Reliance on self-report data has highlighted the urgency to develop other outcome measures. To date, biological markers such as serum amylase level and serum electrolytes to evaluate binge–purging behavior may include a high percentage of false negatives (Mitchell, Hatsukami, Pyle, Eckert, & Boutacoff, 1987b).

The rapidly fluctuating frequency of binge–purging behavior, mood, and general level of functioning of patients with bulimia nervosa in response to changes (e.g., moving, starting a new relationship, or experiencing a minor loss) leave outcome measures that emphasize statistically significant differences in the Eating Disorders Inventory (EDI) scores or in binge–purging behavior open to criticism. One of the important outcome measures is the percentage of reduction of bulimic behavior. Although percentage of reduction is a valid measure of the overall effectiveness of the treatment, relying only on percentage of reduction is unwise because symptoms of bulimia nervosa tend to be influenced by major life changes and stresses. Some investigators feel that total remission or only sporadic episodes of bulimic behavior are much better indicators of successful outcome than percentage of reduction. Nonetheless, a 75% reduction in binge–purging frequency is an indication of a successful treatment on the basis of current literature. If a treatment does not produce at least an average of 50% reduction, it may be considered ineffective. A 50% remission rate at both posttreatment and follow-up should be expected from successful treatments.

Both treatment success and avoidance of relapse may relate to a number of other measures, such as preoccupation with body image, weight, and other attitudes about nutrition that may be measured through such instruments as the EDI

(Garner & Olmstead, 1984). Psychological factors, including (a) depression, anxiety, and global improvement; (b) overall social adjustment; and (c) self-esteem, assertiveness, and self-control, may eventually be associated with the outcome of treatment.

Outcome Studies of Alternative Treatments

A number of studies report excellent reduction of bulimic behaviors. Group therapy studies using cognitive-behavioral and behavioral therapy (Kirkley et al., 1985; Schneider & Agras, 1985) have demonstrated a 91–95% reduction of bulimic behaviors that has been maintained at 89% at follow-up (Schneider & Agras, 1985). Freeman et al. (1988) reported that binge-eating behavior was reduced 87% for individual behavioral therapy and for group therapy and 79% for individual cognitive-behavioral therapy after treatments. Incomplete follow-up results indicated 100% reduction for group therapy, 95% for individual cognitive-behavioral therapy, and 80% for individual behavioral therapy (Freeman et al., 1988). Lacey (1983) noted a 95% reduction for a combination of individual therapy and group therapy for bulimia nervosa. The University of Minnesota intensive outpatient group program has reported a 95% posttreatment reduction in a controlled study (Mitchell, Pyle, Eckert Hatsukami, Zimmerman, & Pomeroy, 1988). Other controlled studies that have shown a 75–90% reduction in binge–purging frequency (equal to that of most drug studies) include individual cognitive-behavioral therapy with ERP (with a 79% reduction) (Ordman & Kirschenbaum, 1985) and both individual cognitive-behavioral therapy and STP (with 87% and 82% reductions in binge–purging behavior, respectively) (Fairburn et al., 1986). Studies that demonstrate less than a 50% reduction include waiting-list controls (a 35% reduction to a 12% increase) (Freeman et al., 1988; Lee & Rush, 1986) and a study of 19 psychodynamic therapy groups using a minimal amount of cognitive-behavioral therapy (showing a 12.2% reduction) (Frommer et al., 1987).

Several treatments report a high percentage of patients who engage in bulimic behaviors at a monthly rate or less, either after treatment or at follow-up. Two were English studies. Fairburn's

(1981) initial open study revealed an 82% rate of remission at posttreatment and 55% at follow-up (based on the original sample), while Lacey's (1983) study of individual and group therapy revealed an 80% posttreatment remission rate and a 93% remission rate on long-term follow-up. Freeman et al. (1988) report a 77% combined remission posttreatment for three treatments (individual behavioral therapy, individual cognitive-behavioral therapy, and group therapy). Mitchell et al. (1989) noted a 66% remission rate at 2- to 5-year follow-up of 100 subjects who started intensive outpatient group therapy. However, they also found that only 19% of patients in the 2- to 5-year follow-up had gone through the entire follow-up period with no episodes of bulimic behavior. In addition, one third of the subjects in remission at follow-up had relapsed and required one or more episodes of treatment.

Other positive results with group therapy include those of Schneider and Agras (1985), who reported a 54% remission rate posttreatment, and 38% at follow-up, and Wilson et al. (1986), who noted a 56% remission at both posttreatment and follow-up. In a controlled study, Fairburn et al. (1986) noted a 25% remission rate at posttreatment and 50% at follow-up for individual cognitive-behavioral therapy and a 33% remission at posttreatment and 50% at follow-up for STP. Huon and Brown (1985) noted a 40% remission rate at short-term follow-up and 68% at long-term follow-up with supportive group therapy.

Before we endorse more expensive psychotherapy treatments for bulimia nervosa, the efficacy reported for minimal intervention treatments must be further evaluated through replication. Huon (1985) has reported a 77% remission rate by administering self-help literature and providing contact with a recovering bulimic, and 57% remission rates by providing either a combination of literature and contact with an active bulimic or the literature alone. There were no remissions in a comparison control group. The recovery rates of other people with no treatment should also be evaluated. Stanton, Rebert, and Zinn (1986) determined that 42% of individuals with bulimia nervosa who were able to stop the behavior for 3 months did so with no formal treatment through emphasis on helping relationships, self-liberation, and counterconditioning. We may find that with

eating disorders, as others have found with the treatment of chemical dependency, a certain percentage of patients will go into remission, regardless of the treatment they receive.

In summary, outcome studies are lacking that compare alternative psychosocial therapies for anorexia nervosa. For bulimia nervosa, it appears that several types of individual therapies may show promise in addition to group therapies that are structured, closed, and time-limited, and that incorporate cognitive-behavioral and behavioral components. Work should be done to demonstrate that results from controlled studies are significantly better than those that demonstrate good outcome with only minimal intervention. When dropouts are considered, outcome from psychosocial treatments compares favorably with antidepressant treatment which may involve unpleasant side effects and risk for relapse when pharmacotherapy is discontinued.

REFERENCES

Abraham, S. F., Mira, M., & Llewellyn-Jones, D. (1984). Bulimia: A study of outcome. *International Journal of Eating Disorders, 3*, 175–180.

American Psychiatric Association (1987). *Diagnostic and statistical manual of mental disorders* (3rd ed., rev.; DSM-III-R). Washington, DC: Author.

Anderson, A. E. (1985). *Practical comprehensive treatment of anorexia nervosa and bulimia* (pp 138–139). Baltimore: Johns Hopkins University Press.

Baker, E. L., & Nash, M. R. (1987). Applications of hypnosis in the treatment of anorexia nervosa. *American Journal of Clinical Hypnosis, 29*, 185–193.

Beck, A. T., Rush, A. J., Shaw, B. F., & Emery, G. (1979). *Cognitive therapy of depression: A treatment manual.* New York: Guilford.

Bemis, K. M. (1985). "Abstinence" and "non-abstinence" models for treatment of bulimia. *International Journal of Eating Disorders, 4*, 407–437.

Boskind-Lodahl, M., & White, W. C. (1978). The definition and treatment of bulimarexia in college women—A pilot study. *Journal of the American College Health Association, 2*, 84–87.

Brotman, A. W., Alonso, A., & Herzog, D. B. (1985). Group therapy for bulimics: Clinical experience and practical recommendations. *Group, 9*, 15–23.

Brotman, A. W., Stern, T. A., & Herzog, D. B. (1984).

Emotional reactions of house officers to patients with anorexia nervosa, diabetes and obesity. *International Journal of Eating Disorders, 3*, 71–77.

Bruch, H. (1973). *Eating disorders: Obesity, anorexia nervosa and the person within.* New York: Basic Books.

Bruch, H. (1974). Perils of behavior modification in treatment of anorexia nervosa. *Journal of the American Medical Association, 230*, 1419–1422.

Bruch, H. (1978). *The golden cage.* Cambridge: Harvard University Press.

Bruch, H. (1982). Anorexia nervosa: Therapy and theory. *American Journal of Psychiatry, 139*, 1531–1538.

Bruch, H. (1985). Four decades of eating disorders. In D. M. Garner & P. E. Garfinkel (Eds.), *Handbook of psychotherapy for anorexia nervosa and bulimia.* New York: Guilford.

Cantwell, D. P., Sturzenberger, S., Borroughs, J., Salkin, B., & Green, J. K. (1977). Anorexia nervosa—An affective disorder? *Archives of General Psychiatry, 34*, 1084–1093.

Casper, R. C. (1982). Treatment principles in anorexia nervosa. *Psychiatry, 10*, 431–454.

Connors, M. E., Johnson, C. L., & Stuckey, M. R. (1984). Treatment of bulimia with brief psychoeducational group therapy. *American Journal of Psychiatry, 141*, 1512–1516.

Cooper, P. J., & Fairburn, C. G. (1984). Cognitive behavior therapy for anorexia nervosa: Some preliminary findings. *Journal of Psychosomatic Research, 28*, 493–499.

Crisp, A. H. (1980). *Anorexia nervosa—Let me be.* London: Academic Press.

Crisp, A. H., Norton, K. R. S., Jurczak, S., Bowyer, C., & Dunean, S. (1985). A treatment approach to anorexia nervosa—25 years on. *Journal of Psychiatric Research, 19*, 393–404.

Crisp, A., Palmer, R., & Kalucy, R. (1976). How common is anorexia nervosa? A prevalence study. *British Journal of Psychiatry, 218*, 549–554.

Dally, P. J. (1969). *Anorexia nervosa.* London: Heinemann.

Dixon, K. N., & Kiecolt-Glaser, J. (1984). Group therapy for bulimia. *Hillside Journal of Clinical Psychiatry, 2*, 156–170.

Fairburn, C. G. (1981). A cognitive-behavioral approach to the management of bulimia. *Psychological Medicine, 141*, 631–633.

Fairburn, C. G. (1983). Bulimia: Its epidemiology and management. In A. J. Stunkard & E. Stellar (Eds.), *Eating and its disorders.* New York: Raven Press.

Fairburn, C. G. (1985). Cognitive-behavioral treatment for bulimia. In D. M. Garner & P. E. Garfinkel (Eds.), *Handbook of psychotherapy for anorexia nervosa and bulimia.* New York: Guilford.

Fairburn, C. G., Kirk, J., O'Connor, M., & Cooper, P. J. (1986). A comparison of two psychological treatments for bulimia nervosa. *Behavioral Research and Therapy, 24*, 629–643.

Frankenburg, F. R. (1984). Female therapists in the management of anorexia nervosa. *International Journal of Eating Disorders, 3*, 25–33.

Freeman, C. P. L., Barry, F., Dunkeld-Turnbull, J., & Henderson, A. (1988). Controlled trial of psychotherapy for bulimia nervosa. *British Medical Journal, 296*, 521–525.

Frommer, M. S., Ames, J. R., Gibson, J. W., & Davis, W. N. (1987). Patterns of symptom change in short term group treatment of bulimia. *International Journal of Eating Disorders, 6*, 469–476.

Garfinkel, P. E. (1985). The treatment of anorexia nervosa. *Journal of Psychiatric Research, 19*, 405–411.

Garfinkel, P. E., & Garner, D. M. (1982). *Anorexia nervosa: A multidimensional perspective.* New York: Brunner/Mazel.

Garner, D. M. (1985a). Iatrogenesis in anorexia nervosa and bulimia nervosa. *International Journal of Eating Disorders, 4*, 701–726.

Garner, D. M. (1985b). Individual psychotherapy for anorexia nervosa. *Journal of Psychiatric Research, 19*, 423–433.

Garner, D. M., & Bemis, K. M. (1982). A cognitive-behavioral approach to anorexia nervosa. *Cognitive Therapy and Research, 6*, 1–27.

Garner, D. M., & Bemis, K. M. (1985). Cognitive therapy for anorexia nervosa. In D. M. Garner & P. E. Garfinkel (Eds.), *Handbook for psychotherapy of anorexia nervosa and bulimia.* New York: Guilford.

Garner, D., & Garfinkel, P. (1980). Socio-cultural factors in the development of anorexia nervosa. *Psychological Medicine, 10*, 647–656.

Garner, D. M., & Garfinkel, P. E. (1985). Introduction. In D. M. Garner & P. E. Garfinkel (Eds.), *Handbook for psychotherapy of anorexia nervosa and bulimia.* New York: Guilford.

Garner, D. M., Garfinkel, P. E., & Irving, M. T. (1986). Integration and sequences of treatment approaches for eating disorders. *Psychotherapy and Psychosomatics, 46*, 246–251.

Garner, D. M., Garfinkel, P. E., & O'Shaughnessy, M. (1985). The validity of the distinction between bulimia with and without anorexia nervosa. *American Journal of Psychiatry, 142*, 581–587.

Garner, D. M., Olmstead, M. P., Davis, R. B., Rockert, W., Goldbloom, D. S., & Eagle, M. (1988, May 9). Bulimia symptoms: Affect, state and trait measures. Paper presented at the 141st annual meeting of the American Psychiatric Association, Montreal, Canada.

Garner, D., Garfinkel, P., Schwartz, D., & Thompson, A. (1980). Cultural expectation of thinness in women. *Psychological Reports, 47*, 483–491.

Garner, D. M., & Olmstead, M. P. (1984). *Manual for the Eating Disorders Inventory.* Odessa, Fl: Psychological Assessment Resources.

Garner, D. M., Rockert, W., Olmsted, M. P., Johnson, C., & Coscina, D. V. (1985). Psychoeducational principles in the treatment of bulimia and bulimia nervosa. In D. M. Garner & P. E. Garfinkel (Eds.), *Handbook for psychotherapy of anorexia nervosa and bulimia.* New York: Guilford.

Goodsitt, A. (1985). Self-psychology and the treatment of anorexia nervosa. In D. M. Garner & P. E. Garfinkel (Eds.), *Handbook for psychotherapy of anorexia nervosa and bulimia.* New York: Guilford.

Gross, M. (1984). Hypnosis in the therapy of anorexia nervosa. *American Journal of Clinical Hypnosis, 26*, 175–181.

Hall, A. (1985). Group psychotherapy for anorexia. In D. M. Garner & P. E. Garfinkel (Eds.), *Handbook for psychotherapy of anorexia nervosa and bulimia.* New York: Guilford.

Halmi, K. A., Falk, J. R., & Schwartz, E. (1981). Binge-eating and vomiting: A survey of a college population. *Psychological Medicine, 11*, 697–706.

Hatsukami, D., Owen, P., Pyle, R., & Mitchell, J. E. (1982). Similarities and differences on the MMPI between women with bulimia and women with alcohol or drug abuse problems. *Addictive Behaviors, 7*, 435–439.

Hawkins, R. C., & Clement, P. F. (1982). Development and construct validation of a self-report measure of binge-eating tendencies. *Addictive Behaviors, 5*, 219–226.

Hedblom, J. E., Hubbard, F. A., & Anderson, A. E. (1982). Anorexia nervosa: Multidisciplinary treatment program for patient and family. *Social Work in Health Care, 7*, 67–83.

Herzog, D. B., & Copeland, P. M. (1985). Eating disorders. *New England Journal of Medicine, 313*, 295–303.

Holgate, R. A. (1984). Hypnosis in the treatment of

bulimia nervosa: A case study. *Australian Journal of Clinical and Experimental Hypnosis, 12*, 105–112.

Hsu, L. K. G. (1980). Outcome of anorexia nervosa—A review of the literature (1954–1978). *Archives of General Psychiatry, 37*, 1041–1046.

Hsu, L. K. G. (1986). The treatment of anorexia nervosa. *American Journal of Psychiatry, 143*, 573–581.

Hsu, L. K. G., Crisp, A. H., & Harding, B. (1979). Outcome of anorexia. *Lancet, 1*, 61–65.

Hsu, L. K. G., & Lieberman, S. (1982). Paradoxical intention in the treatment of chronic anorexia nervosa. *American Journal of Psychiatry, 139*, 650–653.

Hudson, J. I., Laffer, P. S., & Pope, H. G., Jr. (1982). Bulimia related to affective disorder by family history and response to the dexamethasone suppression test. *American Journal of Psychiatry, 137*, 695–693.

Hudson, J. E., Pope, H. G., Jonas, J. M., & Yurgelun-Todd, D. (1983). Family history study of anorexia nervosa and bulimia. *British Journal of Psychiatry, 142*, 133–138.

Huon, C. F. (1985). An initial evaluation of a self-help program for bulimia. *International Journal of Eating Disorders, 4*, 573–578.

Huon, C. F., & Brown, L. B. (1985). Evaluation of a group treatment for bulimia. *Journal of Psychiatric Research, 19*, 429–483.

Johnson, C., & Connors, M. E. (1987). *The etiology and treatment of bulimia nervosa: A biopsychosocial perspective.* New York: Basic Books.

Johnson, C., Connors, M. E., & Stuckey, M. (1983). Short-term group treatment of bulimia: A preliminary report. *International Journal of Eating Disorders, 2*, 199–208.

Johnson, C., & Larson, R. (1982). Bulimia: An analysis of moods and behavior. *Psychosomatic Medicine, 44*, 341–351.

Jones, D., Fox, M., Babigan, H., & Hutton, H. (1980). Epidemiology of anorexia nervosa in Monroe County, New York: 1960–1976. *Psychosomatic Medicine, 42*, 551–558.

Katzman, M. A., Wolchick, S. A., & Braver, S. L. (1984). The prevalence of frequent binge-eating and bulimia in a non-clinical college sample. *International Journal of Eating Disorders, 3*, 53–61.

Kirkley, B. G., Schneider, J. A., Agras, W. S., & Bachman, J. A. (1985). Comparison of two group treatments for bulimia. *Journal of Consulting and Clinical Psychology, 53*, 43–48.

Kohut, H. (1971). *The analysis of the self.* New York: International Universities Press.

Lacey, J. H. (1983). Bulimia nervosa, binge-eating, and psychogenic vomiting: A controlled treatment study and long-term outcome. *British Medical Journal, 286*, 1609–1613.

Lacey, J. H. (1984). Moderation of bulimia. *Journal of Psychosomatic Research, 28*, 397–492.

Lacey, J. H. (1986). An integrated behavioural and psychodynamic approach to the treatment of bulimia. *British Review of Bulimia and Anorexia Nervosa, 1*, 19–26.

Lee, N. F., & Rush, A. J. (1986). Cognitive-behavioral group therapy for bulimia. *International Journal of Eating Disorders, 5*, 599–615.

Leichner, P. P., Harper, D. W., & Johnston, D. M. (1985). Adjunctive group support for spouses of women with anorexia nervosa and/or bulimia. *International Journal of Eating Disorders, 4*, 227–235.

Levin, A. P., & Hyler, S. E. (1986). DSM-III personality diagnosis in bulimia. *Comprehensive Psychiatry, 27*, 47–53.

Merrill, C. A., Mines, R. A., & Starkey, R. (1987). The premature dropout in group treatment. *International Journal of Eating Disorders, 6*, 293–300.

Minuchin, S., Rosman, B. L., & Baker, L. (1978). *Psychosomatic families: Anorexia nervosa in context*. Cambridge: Harvard University Press.

Mitchell, J. E. (1983). Medical complications of anorexia nervosa and bulimia. *Psychiatric Medicine, 1*, 229–256.

Mitchell, J. E., Davis, L., Goff, G., & Pyle, R. L. (1986). A follow-up study of patients with bulimia. *International Journal of Eating Disorders, 5*, 441–450.

Mitchell, J., Hatsukami, D., Eckert, E., & Pyle, R. L. (1985a). Characteristics of 275 patients with bulimia. *American Journal of Psychiatry, 142*, 482–485.

Mitchell, J. E., Hatsukami, D., Goff, G., Pyle, R. L., Eckert, E. D., & Davis, L. E. (1985b). Intensive outpatient group treatment for bulimia. In D. M. Garner & P. E. Garfinkel (Eds.), *Handbook for psychotherapy of anorexia nervosa and bulimia*. New York: Guilford.

Mitchell, J. E., Hatsukami, D., Pyle, R. L., Eckert, E. D., & Boutacoff, L. I. (1987b). Metabolic acidosis as a marker for laxative abuse in patients with bulimia. *International Journal of Eating Disorders, 6*, 557–560.

Mitchell, J. E., Pyle, R. L., Eckert, E. D., Hatsukami, D., Zimmerman, R., & Pomeroy, C. (1987a). Antidepressants vs. grop psychotherapy in the treatment of bulimia. *Psychopharmacology Bulletin, 23*, 41–44.

Mitchell, J. E., Pyle, R. L., Eckert, E. D., Hatsukami, D., Zimmerman, R., & Pomeroy, C. (1988). Preliminary report: A treatment comparison study for bulimia nervosa. In O. Ploog & M. Pirke (Eds.), *The psychobiology of bulimia nervosa*. Berlin: Springer-Verlag.

Mitchell, J. E., Pyle, R. L., Hatsukami, D., Goff, G., Glotter, D., & Harper, J. (1989). A two to five year follow-up study of patients treated for bulimia nervosa. *International Journal of Eating Disorders, 8*, 157–166.

Ordman, A. M., & Kirschenbaum, D. S. (1985). Cognitive-behavioral therapy for bulimia: An initial outcome study. *Journal of Consulting and Clinical Psychology, 53*, 305–313.

Pettinati, H. M., Horne, R. L., & Staats, J. M. (1985). Hypnotizability in patients with anorexia nervosa and bulimia. *Archives of General Psychiatry, 42*, 1014–1016.

Polivy, J. (1981). Group therapy for anorexia nervosa. *Journal of Psychiatric Research, 3*, 279–283.

Pope, H. J., Jr., Hudson, J. I., Jonas, J. M., & Yurgelon-Todd, D. (1985). Treatment of bulimia with antidepressants: A research update. In W. H. Kaye & H. E. Gwirtsman (Eds.), *The treatment of normal weight bulimia*. Washington, DC: American Psychiatric Press.

Pyle, R. L. (1986). The epidemiology of eating disorders. *Pediatrician, 126*, 102–109.

Pyle, R., Halvorson, P., Neuman, P., & Mitchell, J. E. (1986). The increasing prevalence of bulimia in freshman college students. *International Journal of Eating Disorders, 5*, 631–748.

Pyle, R. L., & Mitchell, J. E. (1985). Psychotherapy of bulimia: The role of groups. In W. T. Kaye & H. E. Gwirtsman (Eds.), *The treatment of normal weight bulimia*. Washington, DC: American Psychiatric Press.

Pyle, R. L., & Mitchell, J. E. (1986). The prevalence of bulimia in selected samples. *Adolescent Psychiatry, 13*, 241–252.

Pyle, R. L., Mitchell, J. E., & Eckert, E. D. (1981). Bulimia: A report of 34 cases. *Journal of Clinical Psychiatry, 42*, 60–64.

Pyle, R. L., Mitchell, J. E., Eckert, E. D., Halvorson, P. A., Neuman, P. A., & Goff, G. M. (1983). The incidence of bulimia in freshman college students. *International Journal of Eating Disorders, 2*, 75–85.

Rodin, J., Silberstein, L. R., & Striegel-Moore, R. H. (1983). Women and weight: A normative discontent. In T. B. Sonderegger (Ed.), *Nebraska sympo-*

sium on motivation: Vol. 32, Psychology and gender (pp. 267–307).

Rosen, B. (1979). A method of structured brief psychotherapy. *British Journal of Medical Psychology, 52*, 157–162.

Rosen, J. C., & Leitenberg, H. (1982). Bulimia nervosa: Treatment with exposure and response preventions. *Behavior Therapy, 13*, 117–124.

Roy-Byrne, P., Lee-Benner, K., & Yager, J. (1984). Group therapy for bulimia: A year's experience. *International Journal of Eating Disorders, 3*, 97–116.

Russell, G. F. M. (1970). Anorexia nervosa—Its identity as an illness and its treatment. In J. H. Price (Ed.), *Psychological medicine* (Vol. 2). London: Butterworths.

Russell, G. F. M., Szmukler, G. I., Dare, C., & Eisler, I. (1987). An evaluation of family therapy in anorexia nervosa and bulimia nervosa. *Archives of General Psychiatry, 44*, 1047–1056.

Schneider, J. A., & Agras, W. S. (1985). A cognitive behavioral group treatment of bulimia. *British Journal of Psychiatry, 146*, 66–69.

Schwartz, R. C., Barrett, M. J., & Saba, G. (1985). Family therapy for anorexia nervosa and bulimia nervosa. In D. M. Garner & P. E. Garfinkel (Eds.), *Handbook for psychotherapy of anorexia nervosa and bulimia*. New York: Guilford.

Selvini-Palazzoli, M. (1978). *Self-starvation*. New York: Aronson.

Stanton, A. L., Rebert, W. M., & Zinn, L. M. (1986). Self-change in bulimia: A preliminary study. *International Journal of Eating Disorders, 5*, 917–924.

Stevens, E. V., & Salisbury, J. D. (1984). Group therapy for bulimic adults. *American Journal of Orthopsychiatry, 54*, 156–161.

Strober, M. (1984). Stressful life events associated with bulimia and anorexia nervosa: Empirical findings and theoretical speculations. *International Journal of Eating Disorders, 3*, 1–16.

Strober, M., Salkin, B., Burroughs, J., & Morrell, W. (1982). Validity of the bulimia–restrictor distinction in anorexia nervosa. *Journal of Nervous and Mental Disease, 170*, 345–351.

Stuber, M., & Strober, M. (1987). Group therapy in the treatment of adolescents with bulimia: Some preliminary observations. *International Journal of Eating Disorders, 6*, 125–131.

Stunkard, A. J. (1980). *Obesity*. Philadelphia: Saunders.

Theander, S. (1970). Anorexia nervosa: A psychiatric investigation of 94 female patients. *Acta Psychiatrica Scandinavica, Supplementum, 214*, 1–94.

Vandereycken, W. (1985). Inpatient treatment of anorexia nervosa: Some research guide changes. *Journal of Psychiatric Research, 19*, 413–422.

Vandereycken, W. (1987). The constructive family approach to eating disorders: Critical remarks on the use of family therapy in anorexia nervosa and bulimia. *International Journal of Eating Disorders, 6*, 455–467.

Vandereycken, W., & Meerman, M. (1984). *Anorexia nervosa: A clinicians guide to treatment*. Berlin: de Gruyter.

Wardle, J. (1980). Dietary restraint and binge-eating. *Behavioral Analysis and Modification, 4*, 201–209.

Weiss, S. R., & Ebert, M. H. (1983). Psychological and behavioral characteristics of normal-weight bulimics and normal weight controls. *Psychosomatic Medicine, 45*, 293–303.

Wilson, G. T., Rossiter, E., Kleifeld, E. I., & Lindholm, L. (1986). Cognitive-behavioral treatment of bulimia nervosa: A controlled evaluation. *Behaviour Research and Therapy, 24*, 277–288.

Wolchik, S. A., Weiss, L., & Katzman, M. A. (1986). An empirically validated, short term psychoeducational group treatment program for bulimia. *International Journal of Eating Disorders, 5*, 21–34.

Yates, A. J., & Sambrailo, F. (1984). Bulimia nervosa: A descriptive and therapeutic study. *Behaviour Research and Therapy, 22*, 503–517.

CHAPTER 20

Behavior Therapy

JUNE CHIODO

CONCEPTUALIZATION OF THE DISORDER

If there has been any equivocal professional consensus in the area of eating disorders since the late 1960s, it has been the recognition of and appreciation for the multifaceted nature of the clinical syndromes of anorexia nervosa and bulimia nervosa. Understanding eating disorders requires that researchers and clinicians wear biological, psychological, and social–cultural specialty hats; yet professional acumen dictates that the hats are often worn simultaneously. The interaction among the biological, psychological, and social areas in the development and maintenance of eating disorders is so close that it may not even be possible to untangle them (Bruch, 1985).

The diagnostic core features of anorexia nervosa are outlined in the *Diagnostic and Statistical Manual for Mental Disorders* (3rd ed.—revised) (DSM-III-R: American Psychiatric Association, 1987). To warrant a clinical diagnosis, the patient must refuse to maintain her (or his) weight above the minimum deemed appropriate for age and height, which allows for normal biological or hormonal functioning; the absence of three menstrual cycles indicates this hormonal dysregulation. Despite the low weight, the patient expresses an intense fear of gaining weight or becoming fat, and her or his perception of body weight, size, or shape is disturbed.

The incidence of anorexia nervosa, once considered fairly rare, is believed to have increased since the late 1960s (Jones, Fox, Babigian, & Hutton, 1980) and affects approximately 1% of the population (Crisp, Palmer, & Kalucy, 1976). Adolescent and young adult females account for approximately 90% of clinical cases (Bemis, 1978; Halmi, 1974). Some (Hay & Leonard, 1979) suggest that anorexia may be more common in males than the current statistics would indicate. However, it may be difficult to know because males could be reluctant to seek help or to admit to a stereotypically female disorder (Herzog, Norman, Gordon, & Pepose, 1984).

Clinical diagnosis for bulimia nervosa requires three core features: (1) binge-eating episodes perceived to be outside of the individual's voluntary control, which occur at least twice a week for a minimum of 3 months; (2) drastic weight-control methods, including self-induced vomiting, ingestion of laxatives or diuretics, strict dieting, fasting, and/or vigorous exercise; and (3) a persistent overconcern regarding her or his physical shape and weight.

Studies of the incidence of bulimia have yielded disparate results. Early reports that estimated binge eating among 66–86% females and 50–67% males (Hawkins & Clement, 1980) fueled the fear that there was an epidemic of eating disorders on the college campuses. The media and others failed to distinguish between binge eating and clinically significant behavior; closer examination of the Hawkins and Clement data, using more stringent criteria specific to the syndrome of bulimia, allowed a conservative estimate of 2% (Hart & Ollendick, 1985). Other studies using more stringent criteria, particularly the cooccurrence of binge-eating and vomiting, support the conservative prevalence estimate to be approximately 5%, and substantially lower among males (Halmi, Falk, & Schwartz, 1981; Johnson, Lewis, Love, Lewis, & Stuckey, 1984; Pyle, Halvorson, Neuman, & Mitchell, 1986).

Professionals and public alike refer to the well-publicized study by Garner and Garfinkel and their associates (Garner, Garfinkel, Schwartz, & Thompson, 1980) that documented subtle, yet apparent societal and media sanction from the late 1950s through the 1970s among women for an increasingly androgynous body shape. The 1960s rewarded thinness, a cultural ideal whose meritorious value was communicated subtly and overtly through peer groups, family constellations, and the media. Sensitivity among adolescent girls approaching puberty and experiencing concomitant changes in body fat composition is a long-standing concern, although feelings and attitudes toward bodily changes may be intensified during this time (Crisp, 1984). Surveys of high school students, particularly females, taken during this time mirrored the societal trend. A significant number of students reported dissatisfaction with their weight (Dwyer, Feldman, Seltzer, & Mayer, 1969; Huenemann, Shapiro, Hampton, & Mitchell, 1966). Although the cultural ideal of a thin body shape prevailed, the weight of the average person in our society increased during this time; females between the ages of 17 and 24 gained weight at a rate of approximately 0.3 lbs per year (Society of Actuaries and Association of Life Insurance Medical Directors of America, 1979).

The correlative association between greater cultural–interpersonal pressures for thinness and reported incidence of eating disorders proposed by authors in early writings (Bruch, 1973, 1978; Garner & Garfinkel, 1978, 1980; Ryle, 1939; Selvini Palazzoli, 1974) provides a starting point for current conceptual research. What is it about the psychological and biological constituency of vulnerable individuals who develop and maintain eating disorders, when a far greater number do not but yet are exposed to the same cultural environment that espouses peremptory body shape and weight messages?

Dieting, Feeling Fat, and the Onset of Eating Disorders

The age of onset for anorexia nervosa is bimodal, at ages 14 1/2 and 18 years (Halmi, Casper, Eckert, Goldberg, & Davis, 1979); and for bulimia occurs during late adolescence (17–19 years) (Agras & Kirkley, 1986; Fairburn & Cooper, 1982). Onset of eating disorders is marked by a period of self-initiated dieting (Casper, 1983; Fairburn & Cooper, 1984). In recounting their premorbid history, patients typically recall "feeling fat" during adolescence and that this feeling generally coincided with significant life events, such as disruptions in home or school life and remarks by friends or relatives concerning their weight or changing body shape (Davis, 1986; Strober, 1984). In order to restore control and a degree of autonomy in an otherwise unsettling environment, the patient initiates dieting.

Much has been written about self-imposed dietary restrictions with the ardent desire to achieve thinness as an adaptive problem-solving strategy; these behaviors maintain the patient's feelings of self-control, self-efficacy, and self-esteem or self-worth (Bruch, 1973; Garfinkel & Garner, 1982; Johnson, Connors, & Tobin, 1987; Slade, 1982; Vandereycken & Meermann, 1984). Various antecedents may trigger dieting, such as (a) confrontation (for whatever specific reasons) with an environment perceived as stressful; (b) emotions or variable mood states perceived as vague and difficult to control; and/or (c) situations perceived as failure experiences.

The notion of "feeling fat" may have etiological significance, for it could be reflected in a self-schemata that, when developed, assumes a critical position (Striegel-Moore, McAvay, & Rodin, 1986). Women who report "feeling fat," regardless of weight status, tend to be highly perfectionistic and set exceptionally high standards of excellence for themselves, both in their physical appearance and in other areas of their life. Feelings about their body are affected significantly by weight-related stimuli, as one would expect. However, satisfaction with their body is also affected in non-weight-related situations when they perceive failure. It is difficult, therefore, for these women to escape preoccupation with their body, eating, and dieting.

Dieting, Binge-Eating, and Weight-Control Strategies

Although approximately one third of the patients who self-impose strict dietary restriction experience conspicuous weight loss and subsequently warrant the clinical diagnosis of anorexia nervosa, the majority do not (Fairburn & Cooper, 1984). For them, rigid dietary control soon deteriorates and episodic binge eating ensues (Agras & Kirkley, 1986).

Four explanatory areas of research, though not necessarily mutually exclusive, currently account for the episodic occurrence of binge eating. The first explanation proposes a link between dietary restraint and binge eating. On a cognitive level, the patient believes that even a small ingestion of "forbidden food" is an infraction of dietary control, and the patient perceives this momentary lapse as catastrophic and as evidence of personal weakness. Her or his dysfunctional cognitive style, which is to view events in dichotomous terms (i.e., dieting vs. bingeing), subsequently leads to a total loss of control around food (Fairburn & Cooper, 1984; Garfinkel & Garner, 1982). Disinhibition of dietary restraint may be exacerbated among individuals who show basal or acute hyperinsulinemia (for review, see Rodin, 1985).

The second explanation posits that the patient's affective instability or negative mood states disinhibit dietary restraint and trigger binge-eating episodes (Abraham & Beaumont, 1982; Cooper & Bowskill, 1986; Davis, Freeman, & Solyom, 1985; Johnson & Larson, 1982; Johnson et al., 1987; Polivy & Herman, 1985). Anxiety and depression are the most common mood states (Andersen, 1987a). Some patients are genetically vulnerable to major affective disorders, which are thus etiologically linked through biology to binge eating (Hudson, Pope, Jonas, Yurgelun-Todd, 1983; Walsh, Roose, Glassman, Gladis, & Sadik, 1985). A coexisting affective disorder or a transient, negative mood state may also contribute to disinhibition of dietary restraint.

The third area of research argues that some patients may selectively crave carbohydrates because dietary restriction depletes the level of the neurotransmitter serotonin in the brain (Fernstrom & Wurtman, 1971). The amino acid precursor of serotonin, tryptophan, is unaffected by insulin; hence, the ingestion of carbohydrate-rich–protein-poor foods increases the ratio of tryptophan to the other large amino acids, which then allows for its transport to the brain. In a similar line, Kaye and Gwirtsman (1985) implicate both serotonin and norepinephrine neurotransmitters as the common

pathway for the development of bulimia; these neurotransmitters are involved in affect in neuroendocrine regulation, and in appetite and weight regulation.

Finally, the fourth area of research views dietary restraint and bingeing as secondary to vomiting, based on the anxiety model of bulimia (Rosen & Leitenberg, 1982). Vomiting becomes so effective in reducing anxiety and alleviating any guilt, that the patient may soon find it difficult to resist the urge to binge eat; consequently, the frequency of binge–purge episodes increases.

Social and Communication Skills

Difficulties in interpersonal relationships have been addressed by authors across orientations (Bruch, 1973; Crisp, 1967; Garfinkel & Garner, 1982; Slade, 1982). Eating-disordered patients report impaired social adjustment in the areas of job or school performance, social relationships, social and leisure activities, family environment, and marital relationships (Johnson & Berndt, 1983; Leon, Carroll, Chernyk, & Finn, 1985; Norman & Herzog, 1984).

An individual behavioral analysis may indicate that social skill deficits and anxiety (e.g., fear of negative evaluation, criticism, and social rejection) can serve to predispose the individual to developing weight- and food-related symptomatology (Chiodo, 1987; Fremouw & Heyneman, 1985). As Andersen (1985) states, "deficits in social skills become profound, and [anorexic] patients may be years behind their peers socially" (p. 49). Bulimics are characterized as nonassertive, socially isolated, and inhibited in their expression of anger, disappointment, and frustration, yet counterdependent and rebellious (Loro, 1984). Patients have particular difficulty in expressing anger for fear of losing all control or having to experience various interpersonal consequences, such as disappointment, rejection, and retaliation (Johnson et al., 1987).

Biological Predisposing and Maintaining Factors

Biological factors are intricately linked to the development and maintenance of eating disorders, as discussed in several excellent reviews (Garfinkel & Kaplan, 1985; Kaplan & Woodside,

1987). It is important, both for conceptual understanding and for treatment planning, to be able to distinguish cognitive and behavioral symptomatology, which are core features of the syndromes from those related to the starvation process and bingeing–purging behaviors. As Kaplan and Woodside indicate, the five systems believed to be pathogenetic include the hypothalamic–pituitary axis, central nervous system amines, central nervous system peptides, carbohydrate metabolism, and gastrointestinal hormones. Weight and food preoccupation and food related-behaviors, such as collecting and reading recipes, cooking, binge eating, wearing multiple layers of clothing to induce sweating, compulsive exercising, and becoming more socially isolated are attributable to the body's physiological responses to the starvation process.

DIAGNOSTIC ISSUES AND PROBLEMS

The refined selection of diagnostic criteria outlined in the DSM-III-R (American Psychiatric Association, 1987) is an improvement over its predecessor, the DSM-III (American Psychiatric Association, 1980). The relationship between anorexia nervosa and bulimia nervosa, however, remains the major unresolved issue (Fairburn, 1987). The DSM-III-R diagnoses are not mutually exclusive; hence, a patient could receive both diagnoses concurrently.

It was once thought that the DSM-III-R would allow for two diagnostic subtypes of anorexia nervosa: restrictive and bulimic. *Restrictive anorexics* achieve their marked weight loss by abstaining from any significant intake of food and do not binge eat; *bulimic anorexics*, on the other hand, maintain their low weight by extensive purging following episodic binge episodes. Approximately 48% of anorexics are bulimic, and they differ in terms of premorbid adjustment, course of development, and prognosis (Casper, Eckert, Halmi, Goldberg, & Davis, 1980; Garfinkel, Moldofsky, & Garner, 1980). Normal-weight bulimics and bulimic anorexics are more similar on pathological measures than are restrictive and bulimic anorexics considered together (Garner, Garfinkel, & O'Shaughnessy, 1985). Based on the number of psychopathological, treatment, and prognostic factors, Fairburn and Garner (1986)

argue that the diagnosis of bulimia nervosa should be made irrespective of weight if the three core features are present, thus overriding a diagnosis of anorexia nervosa. The diagnostic category of anorexia nervosa would be limited, therefore, to restrictors.

The most notable improvement in the DSM-III-R is that the core features for bulimia better denote a clinical syndrome; the change is reflected also by revised diagnostic label of *bulimia nervosa*. Not only does the DSM-III-R include the symptom of binge eating, but it also requires associated pathology, such as drastic weight control methods and a persistent overconcern with body shape and weight.

This change should help to distinguish between bulimia and obese binge eaters. Among obese persons who seek treatment, from 23% (Gormally, Black, Daston, & Rardin, 1982) to nearly 29% (Loro & Orleans, 1981) report frequent binge eating. Drastic weight-control behaviors (e.g., self-induced vomiting) and extreme concerns with body weight and shape are not common. Obese binge eaters who also meet the DSM-III criteria for bulimia, however, share cognitive, affective, and behavioral characteristics with normal-weight bulimics (Marcus, Wing, & Hopkins, 1988). Compared to obese nonbingers, they report significantly stricter standards for dieting compliance, greater dietary restraint, more depressive symptomatology, maladaptive cognitions, and dysphoria.

One ambiguity in the DSM-III-R criteria is how to operationalize "persistent overconcern with body shape and weight." Fairburn (1987) believes that while a number of indicators represent such overconcern (e.g., pursuit of weight loss, pursuit of thinness, fear of fatness, sensitivity to weight gain), a more sensitive operational definition might be obtained by determining the extent of importance that the person places on weight or shape. An undue importance, evidenced by the person's practice of evaluating him- or herself based on weight and shape, may be the central psychopathological feature.

Eating and Atypical Eating Disorders

Less than 10% of patients who present themselves at an eating disorders clinic may not meet the DSM-III criteria for either anorexia nervosa or bulimia nervosa (Mitchell, Pyle, Hatsukami, & Eckert, 1986). These patients could be divided into three groups: (1) persons who vomit or abuse laxatives for weight control, but who do not binge eat; (2) patients with anorexic tendencies or behavior but whose low weight does not warrant a clinical diagnosis; and (3) a heterogeneous group, whose low weight resulted from vomiting but who also may meet the criteria for conversion disorder.

Eating Disorders and Differential Psychiatric Diagnoses

Eating disorders are viewed by a number of researchers to be a variant of a major affective disorder (Herzog, 1984). This position is based on findings that eating-disordered patients (a) show more current and previous symptoms of affective illness and major depressive disorder, (b) have greater familial incidence and more genetic markers of affective disorders, (c) share neuroendocrine abnormalities similar to those observed in affective probands, and (d) respond to antidepressant medication.

Symptoms of weight loss and amenorrhea can occur in a number of psychiatric illnesses: conversion disorders, schizophrenia, and depression. The essential distinguishing features is that anorexic patients are overconcerned about the meaning and value of their weight loss, as expressed in disturbed body image cognitions and behaviors (Garfinkel & Kaplan, 1986).

Eating Disorders and Athletes

Some self-obligatory runners who show extreme weight loss, preoccupation with diet, and concern with body fat composition may resemble anorexics on personality and behavioral measures (Yates, Leehey, & Shisslak, 1983), but they do not evidence the characteristic psychopathology (Blumenthal, O'Toole, & Chang, 1984).

TREATMENT STRATEGIES

It goes without saying that choosing specific behavioral interventions is done so judiciously following a comprehensive, tripartite assessment (Hersen & Bellack, 1981) and that the therapist–patient relationship is extremely important (Bel-

lack & Hersen, 1985; Turkat & Brantley, 1981). The importance of a therapeutic alliance with eating-disordered patients is emphasized in a number of writings (e.g., Garner & Bemis, 1985; Johnson et al., 1987). Despite advances by behavior therapists working as scientists–practitioners in the area of eating disorders, some colleagues continue to hold steadfast the belief that, "Behavior modification relies on external reward systems; manipulation of a patient's behavior may heighten the sense of ineffectiveness and lack of control" (Position paper by the American College of Physicians, 1987, p. 30).

For the emaciated patient, the primary therapeutic task is to address the starvation-related symptomatology by establishing a nonnegotiable weight goal set above the patient's menstrual threshold (Frisch & McArthur, 1974); failure to do so only perpetuates the illness (Garner & Bemis, 1985). For nonemaciated patients, the immediate therapeutic goals are to normalize eating patterns by relaxing dietary restraint and minimizing the number and severity of binge-eating episodes, to eliminate unhealthy weight-control behaviors, and to improve overall social and interpersonal functioning. Long-term goals are designed for the patient to use the cognitive and behavioral skills within her or his repertoire, thereby enabling her or him to respond to a changing, stressful environment without relapse.

Very few conclusions can be drawn at this time regarding the comparative effectiveness of behavioral strategies, as the remainder of this section shows. There simply are not enough controlled studies that (a) carefully define the patient population, (b) operationalize treatment procedures, (c) randomize patients to treatment groups, (d) isolate specific treatment components, (e) give equal value to each treatment intervention, and (f) use eating-specific and global assessment dependent measures at posttreatment and long-term follow-up periods. This section reviews the various behavioral strategies and discusses overall treatment issues.

Operant Conditioning

As early as 1874, Gull described the practice of separating anorexics from their families and then allowing their return home to be contingent on weight gain. However, it was not until the mid-

1960s, when behavior therapy emerged in its own right as a discipline, through the work of Bachrach and colleagues (Bachrach, Erwin, & Mohr, 1965), that a series of empirical studies of operant conditioning for anorexia nervosa was launched. The essence of an operant conditioning paradigm is that material or social reinforcers (e.g., radio, books, hospital privileges, telephone conversations) are removed from the patient and then delivered contingently upon weight gain or some operationally defined food behavior, such as number of bites eaten or calories ingested (Agras & Werne, 1977; Van Buskirk, 1977). It has been utilized almost exclusively as an intervention to facilitate weight gain in the hospitalized, emaciated anorexic.

Operant conditioning is no more effective in promoting weight gain than are other therapeutic interventions; further, its short-term effectiveness does not persist once the patient leaves the hospital and resumes functioning in her or his natural environment (Bemis, 1987; Hsu, 1980). Worrisome also are the reports that the very nature of operationally defined food behaviors and weight-contingent contracts can become a vehicle for greater manipulative behaviors and a source of additional conflict between patient and staff (Schlemmer & Barnett, 1977; Vandereycken & Pierloot, 1983).

In an extensive review of the area, Bemis (1987) concludes that the ways in which operant conditioning procedures can be incorporated to facilitate clinically meaningful and permanent change has yet to be accomplished. If there is to be a therapeutic role for operant conditioning, then behavior therapists need to return to the conceptual drawing board and examine how the very formulation that unites the stimuli and contingencies that are instrumental in the expression of anorexic behavior can be adapted for clinical practice. At present, the lack of operant conditioning interventions that are based on the complex, functional relationships of the anorexic symptomatology and a reliance on weight as a sole criterion for outcome are serious shortcomings in the behavioral literature (Bemis, 1987; Chiodo, 1985).

Cognitive Restructuring

The bases for cognitive restructuring (also known as cognitive-behavior therapy) are Beck's theory and treatment for depression (Beck, Rush, Shaw, & Emery, 1979) and Ellis's (1962) rational-emotive therapy. At the heart of the eating-disordered patient's distortions in cognitive reasoning is an internalized, *overvalued* belief system with the equation that "being thin is equivalent to being attractive, which is equivalent to being happy." Extensive descriptions and clinical examples of the characteristic dysfunctional style are available elsewhere (cf. Fairburn, 1986; Garner & Bemis, 1982; Fairburn, Cooper, & Cooper, 1986; Garner, Garfinkel, & Bemis, 1982).

The rigid belief system brings order to the patient's chaotic environment; it is a means by which she or he can process experiences, integrate information, and evaluate personal performance and self-worth (Fairburn, 1981; Fairburn et al., 1986; Garner & Bemis, 1982). The faulty belief system expresses itself not only through the cognitive response channel via self-statements and automatic thoughts, but also through the behavioral channel in numerous pathological overt behaviors. For example, the belief that "weight gain means being out of control" may prompt the patient to diet and to weigh him or herself frequently for reassurance of being in control.

Proponents of cognitive restructuring argue that the overvalued ideas must be approached directly because they are of primary importance in the maintenance of dysfunctional cognitions and behaviors (Fairburn et al., 1986; Garner et al., 1982). Cognitive restructuring is conducted within a psychoeducational format that relies on a prospective, empirical, hypothesis-testing approach. The goal is for the patient to understand the relationship between beliefs, cognitions, and behaviors, thereby allowing the patient to evaluate and change her or his own behaviors. In order to do so, the beliefs that govern covert and overt behavior must first be identified. The therapist can help the patient to examine the dysfunctional cognitions and self-statements by a variety of procedures (e.g., decentering, decatastrophisizing, and reattribution techniques), including behavioral exercises and homework assignments that allow the patient to test the validity of personal beliefs within her or his own environment (for a full description, see Garner & Bemis, 1982).

In the most controlled study to date, Fairburn and associates (Fairburn, Kirk, O'Connor, & Cooper, 1986) report that patients participating in cognitive restructuring, as compared to a short-term focal psychotherapy, show significantly more improvements on measures of global clinical state, general psychopathology, social adjustment, and self-report outcome.

Exposure plus Response Prevention

Exposure plus response prevention (ERP) is most readily identified in the behavioral literature as a therapeutic intervention for obsessive–compulsive disorders. That is, when patients refrain from carrying out their ritualistic behaviors despite an intense urge to do so, they do not experience any of their feared disastrous consequences (see Foa & Steketee, 1979). Rosen and Leitenberg's (1982) anxiety model of bulimia similarly argues that prevention of the vomiting response allows the patient to experience reductions in anxiety and guilt, thereby facilitating normalization of eating patterns.

The ERP procedures are described thoroughly in Rosen and Leitenberg (1985). Each treatment session incorporates both the exposure and the response prevention components. By eating particular types or amounts of food until a strong urge to vomit is experienced, patients are exposed in the therapy session to their feared consequences of gaining weight. Once this occurs, the therapist can direct and maintain the patient's focus on whatever anxiety-provoking thoughts and sensations have been elicited. Because this is a time that is affectively charged, the therapist has direct access to identification and restructuring of the patient's misconceptions and irrational beliefs.

In order to allow for within-session habituation of anxiety and the weakening of the urge-to-vomit sensation, treatment sessions, at least initially, may require a 2-hour time block. Patients are instructed that treatment is most beneficial if vomiting does not occur for at least 2 1/2 hours. Once the patient demonstrates improvement within the therapy session, the patient is instructed to practice eating either certain foods or at certain times during the day that she or he would normally avoid, in order to promote generalization of treatment effects to the natural environment.

Rosen and Leitenberg (1987) compared a waiting-list control group to two treatment groups (in which the emphasis on formal ERP varied) and a third treatment group of cognitive restructuring.

Compared to the control group, all three treatment groups showed significant improvements to specific and general psychopathology, such as eating attitudes, depression, and self-esteem. However, the investigators were unable to replicate results obtained in studies of cognitive restructuring, leading Wilson and Smith (1987) to conclude that "it [the results] raises the ever-present question of actual comparability of specific treatment protocols" (p. 13). Wilson and Smith (1987) also warn that therapists usually encounter resistance to these procedures, a "clinical reality [that] will likely influence the ultimate acceptability of this treatment" (p. 13).

Self-Monitoring, Stimulus Control, and Eating Behaviors

A number of researchers (Fairburn, 1985; Garner, 1986; Halmi, 1985; Johnson et al., 1987) have borrowed from the obesity literature and adapted self-monitoring and stimulus-control strategies to help eating-disordered patients learn to regulate their eating behaviors and decrease dietary restraint.

Enlisting the help of the eating-disordered patient to record any number of parameters, such as food, mood states, or hunger and satiety ratings can be met with resistance (perhaps for reasons of control or shame at the quantity of food consumed during a binge episode). It is suggested that presentation of requests for self-monitoring should be communicated in a manner that conveys that data gathering is a collaborative, joint venture (Johnson et al., 1987). Self-monitoring data allow the patient and therapist to develop hypotheses regarding a functional analysis of the relationships among food cravings, hunger, mood states, and environmental stimuli.

Stimulus-control or behavioral strategies may include meal planning and food preparation, learning appropriate portion sizes, spacing meals throughout the day, limiting eating to one room in the house, practicing leaving food on the plate, placing utensils down between bites, and grocery shopping (Fairburn, 1985; Johnson et al., 1987). Patients are also taught both to identify emotional or situational triggers to binge-eating episodes and to develop a list of alternative behaviors that can substitute for binge eating. Also, they can try cognitive strategies to help distract themselves from thinking about food or practicing strategies to delay the initiation of binge-eating behaviors (Fairburn, 1985; Loro, 1984; Orleans & Barnett, 1984).

Anorexics need to alter their ritualistic eating habits, such as playing with or mixing food on their plates, cutting it into tiny pieces, and eating at inappropriate rates (Andersen, 1987b). Videotaped feedback may aid the patient to identify personal ritualistic eating behaviors (Andersen, 1987b), as may the therapist's modeling and shaping of appropriate mealtime behaviors.

Social Skills Training

A relatively large body of literature supports the notion that an individual's premorbid level of social competence is related to prognosis and later adjustment among psychiatric patients (Hersen & Bellack, 1976; Zigler & Phillips, 1961). *Social competence* refers to a wide range of cognitive processes and behavioral skills that are shaped by the individual's personal characteristics, the person's interactions with others, and the nature of antecedent and consequent environmental stimuli (Spence, 1987).

Excellent reviews of social skills training are available elsewhere (see Bellack & Hersen, 1979). The components of social competence are enumerated here only to highlight the complexity of interpersonal functioning relevant to eating-disordered patients. As Spence (1987) has summarized, social competence is partially the product of several factors: (1) individual personal characteristics, including (a) physical appearance and grooming habits; (b) demographic consideration such as age, gender, and social class; and (c) prior learning experiences; (2) affect control, or the ability to express emotional states without undue anxiety, fear, anger, or avoidance responses; (3) the nature and extent of maladaptive cognitions, particularly as to how those influence self-appraisal and self-concept; and (4) overt motor skills determined by the person's self-perception, social problem-solving abilities, and self-monitoring. Social competence is also influenced by environmental contingencies and sociocultural values that may reinforce maladaptive behavioral patterns. Different behaviors are required in different situations, and the patient needs to be able to analyze what is

expected and how behavior is judged. The patient's social network systems, such as family or peers, can serve to facilitate or hinder competent behavior.

Social skills and assertiveness training are recommended, under one guise or another, in numerous writings. Although Bruch (1978) adhered to a psychodynamic framework, she recommended that the "therapeutic focus must be on the patient's failure in self-expression, on the defective tools and concepts for organizing and expressing needs, and on the bewilderment in dealing with others" (p. 143). Andersen (1987b) recommended that anorexics receive social skills training throughout treatment, and that patients should be encouraged "to participate in social events, and to learn social skills for forming and maintaining friendships" (p. 94).

As Pillay and Crisp (1981) found, hospitalized anorexics who participated in social skills training both are less likely to terminate treatment and report a more rapid abatement in their levels of anxiety, depression, and fear of negative evaluation. Using modeling and role playing, nursing staff focused on increasing the anorexic's verbal skills to enhance spontaneity and ability to engage in non-weight-related general discussions (e.g., joining a conversation with familiar and unfamiliar persons).

Greater management and expression of emotions, needs, and feelings may help to weaken the functional association among interpersonal conflict, mood states, and binge eating. Patients may learn that covert articulation and overt expression of affect, feelings, and wishes may alleviate powerful urges to binge eat and may help facilitate satisfying social relationships and work relationships.

Behavioral Treatment Strategies: An Overview

As noted in the beginning of this section, it is difficult to draw firm conclusions regarding any sort of comparative treatment efficacy. There are only a handful of controlled studies, and these have been well reviewed recently by distinguished researchers in special area reviews in 1987 for both *Behavior Modification* (Andersen, 1987b; Bemis, 1987; Garner, Fairburn, & Davis, 1987; Rosen,

1987) and *Annals of Behavioral Medicine* (Wilson & Smith, 1987). This section does not detail the methodological shortcomings described in these reviews. Rather, the remainder of this section concerns itself with several treatment outcome issues and then addresses the more general question of how to interpret studies when the principal investigator and treatment team share the same conceptual model and value the same therapeutic strategies.

Standardization of Treatment

One of the difficulties in comparing results is that the nature of the implementation of, and the adherence to treatment protocol vary in the clinical setting. An exception, though, and a model for well-designed treatment studies, is provided by Fairburn and colleagues (Fairburn et al., 1986). These investigators not only employed a treatment manual detailing administration of cognitive-behavior therapy, but also audiotaped therapy sessions so that adherence to protocol could be assessed by independent raters.

Identification of Active Treatment Ingredients

It is difficult to distinguish between the active ingredients of cognitive-behavior therapy or ERP. As part of ERP, "the therapist also concurrently identifies and corrects various distorted or erroneous beliefs" (Rosen, 1987, p. 469). Although Rosen (1987) argues that formal ERP is superior to cognitive restructuring, the nature of the studies do not yet permit such determination.

Perhaps the important issue, though, is not which treatment is superior, but rather, for which patients are which procedures most effective, and why? Answering this question may allow clinicians to refine treatment and to enhance conceptual understanding of the disorders.

Principal Investigator-Therapist Nonequivalency

The few, seminal studies to date on cognitive restructuring were conducted by Garner and Fairburn, and the ERP studies have been conducted by Rosen, Leitenberg, and Wilson. Each group of researchers strongly supports either the cognitive-behavioral model or the anxiety model. However, as already noted, the research studies to date do not reflect the clear superiority of one approach over the other.

Case Illustration

Sandra, a 36-year-old married mother of two, presented herself at an eating-disorders clinic at a teaching hospital, stating that she had been referred by the local support group because she had appeared "too stressed out" at the meeting the previous evening. She appeared anxious and agitated; her high-pitched speech and motor behaviors were rapid. The eating-disorders program was explained by outlining the team approach. The primary treatment team consisted of a clinical psychologist (the author of this chapter), an internal medicine physician, and a nutritionist. The other specialists, a psychiatrist and a gastroenterologist, serve in a consulting role; residents, medical students, and graduate-level psychology students may be involved in any case. All patients are evaluated individually by members of the treatment team in the morning and then meet again the same afternoon, to review findings and treatment recommendations. Although the patient initially seemed enthusiastic about the program, she did not follow up until 3 months later by phone.

During the telephone conversation, she appeared more anxious and agitated than when first seen. She expressed feelings of being overwhelmed, that she "just can't do any more"; she was extremely fearful that she would gain weight because her bingeing was uncontrollable. She explained that during the 3-month interval, she and her family closed the sale of their house and moved to another part of town. As the rest of her family (husband, 9-year-old son, and 14-year-old daughter) were too busy to assist her to any appreciable degree, she undertook the bulk of the work. In addition, she was employed as an administrative assistant, and her boss required that she assume a greater workload (personnel had been cut) and asked her to work overtime four evenings a week.

She appeared for the initial evaluation, and the option of inpatient hospitalization was considered. The rationale for time-limited inpatient treatment was fourfold: (1) to provide immediate relief from an extremely stressful family and work environment; (2) to provide some interruption of the daily, multiple binge-purge episodes; (3) to allow for complete psychological assessment; and (4) to initiate individual and family treatment so that the patient would be able to make the transition from the safe hospital environment to her own home environment.

The first several days of hospitalization are used for the gathering of assessment data. During this time, the patient was subdued and talked little to nursing and medical staff. Meals were ordered 1 day in advance, and she was allowed to choose freely. Caloric and nutrient intake were assessed and monitored; the patient consumed largely protein-rich foods (e.g., fish, chicken, turkey), some fruit and vegetables, and little fat and carbohydrate; calories averaged 800–900 per day.

The patient's history revealed that she is the eldest of four children (two sisters and one brother). When the patient was 15 years old, her mother delivered the youngest child and delegated virtually all child care responsibilities to the patient. The patient suspects that the mother suffered from depression, and the father was preoccupied with his own work. The patient recalled that she socialized very little during this time; she cared for her siblings, including one of her younger sisters, whom she envied. She described this sister as outgoing, independent, thin, happy-go-lucky, and involved in extracurricular school activities. The patient remembers being captivated by televised beauty pageants, always comparing her height and weight to that of contestants. Although the patient was not overweight, she felt that she was. Despite her height (5'9"), she sought a weight no greater than "118 pounds." She believed that if she weighed more than this, she would be "fat and made fun of." The patient's other sister apparently was overweight, and she often listened sympathetically to this sister's stories of being teased and humiliated.

Following high school graduation, Sandra enlisted in the Air Force. She wanted to study nursing and "see the world." To her disappointment, she became stationed in a small, southwest city. She became attracted to a male fellow officer, whom she described as "wild, carefree, and fun." Although they quickly became engaged, the patient began to doubt her initial decision to marry him. Her mother, however, had planned to visit in the near future and pressed her over the telephone to get married. When the patient relayed this discussion to her boyfriend, he suggested that they marry quickly before her mother arrived. Feeling pressured from both mother and boyfriend and unable to express her own opposition to the idea, the patient consented.

Shortly after the wedding, she became preg-

nant and left the Air Force and all hopes for any sort of independence. The couple settled close to his family, and she assumed a lifestyle that she resented; she remained isolated at home and "hated" him for being a "mama's boy." After the birth of her second child, she embarked fervently upon dieting to lose the weight accumulated during pregnancy, and she occupied her time by reading diet books. When she "couldn't stand the diet any longer," she would eat "anything" until she was ready to recommit herself to a new diet.

As part of an ongoing research project, the patient consumed three test lunches that varied in nutrient composition (carbohydrate and protein, but equated for calories and fat). On one test day, she was required to refrain from eating lunch. Mood and behavior responses were monitored. The most notable result was that bingeing occurred after both the no-lunch and the carbohydrate-rich-protein-poor lunch conditions.

Before any formal treatment is initiated, the case conceptualization is discussed with the patient. As Sandra's history was presented, her limited opportunities for acquisition of social skills was emphasized. She also learned to infer that weight was important; she envied her thin sister and the thin pageant contestants, and she sympathized with the pain that her other, overweight sister experienced. Her distorted styles of reasoning were presented, using examples that she had provided during the history gathering. The relationship of familial history of affective disorders, obesity, and eating disorders was reviewed. Further, the relationship of dieting-bingeing and mood/behavioral antecedents and consequences was discussed in detail. The patient's own assessment data were reviewed and presented as evidence to support the need to reduce dietary restraint. Finally, the patient's feelings of anger and resentment throughout her history were traced. The association between her deficient skills to assert or express her feelings and binge eating was explored further.

In the program, patients are encouraged to comment during the conceptual presentation. They may clarify, question, validate, or provide further information. When the presentation is completed, the patient is then asked "now what do we do?" as a means of enlisting cooperation for treatment planning. By this time, the patient is versed in behavioral terminology and can discuss the need for developing skills, reducing anxiety, expressing feelings, and reducing avoidance behaviors. In essence, then, the conceptual presentation and discussion is viewed as the first treatment intervention. It conveys the message that therapy is a mutual endeavor, and it sets the stage for multicomponent interventions, including homework assignments. The patient understands that there is "no quick and easy solution" and that long-term therapy is necessary for addressing relapse prevention.

Sandra's specific treatment plan consisted of individual therapy, cognitive restructuring, social skills and assertiveness training, and stimulus-control strategies. Family therapy sessions were conducted, and several sessions attended by both spouses addressed the marital relationship. While the issue of divorce was addressed, both Sandra and her husband decided to work at improving their communication skills rather than consider divorce at this time. Sandra met with the nutritionist to learn to avoid counting calories, but to plan meals based on choices from the basic food groups.

At times, change was met with resistance, and she resorted to indirect and sometimes manipulative behaviors. She was confronted with her behavioral strategies, and they were examined with the task of trying to identify triggers for these behaviors. During her 3-week hospitalization stay, Sandra "practiced" her social skills with staff. The nursing staff also had to be taught to provide her with corrective feedback.

Sandra remained in outpatient therapy for the following 11 months. During this time, she became better able to identify the stimulus conditions that triggered her urges to binge eat. Once able to identify and articulate the specific mood states and environmental settings that served as binge-eating triggers, she learned to implement cognitive and behavioral changes to cope with such urges. A significant portion of individual therapy addressed the issue of self-esteem and self-worth. As Sandra's social skills improved, she began to derive a better sense of interpersonal effectiveness. Consequently, she relied less on her weight as the source of social acceptance. One indication of Sandra's improved social and psychological functioning was that by the end of this time, she decided to return to school to complete the remaining four semesters for her bachelor's degree. Further changes were evident by Sandra's relationship with her adolescent daughter. She was pleased that she was able to help her daughter develop a healthy sense of self-esteem and not to rely exclusively on weight and physical appearance for her view of herself.

ALTERNATIVE TREATMENT OPTIONS

As emphasized throughout this chapter, the etiology and course of eating disorders are multidimensional; it is difficult, if not impossible, for the clinician to limit his or her perspective to the psychological realm of the individual patient. For these reasons, the alternative treatment options described here should not really be viewed as alternatives to behavioral treatment. Rather, they can be incorporated as adjuncts within a behavioral framework, as shown in the preceding case illustration, when the assessment and formulation warrant doing so.

Family Therapy

As Sargent (1983) explains, the family is the primary social system of the child. A healthy family can bond together, share goals, change when necessary, establish itself as an entity, and at the same time allow its individual members free access to the external world. When a child develops an illness or unremitting physical symptoms (e.g., diabetes), healthy families can manage the problem and the child with little difficulty. Unhealthy families, however, are unable to manage the illness, and the child's symptoms serve to perpetuate family instability.

Strober and Humphrey (1987) reviewed studies that looked at eating-disordered patients and their families and concluded that familial characteristics contribute to the etiology and course of the disorders. How members relate to and interact with each other may be characterized by enmeshment, poor conflict resolution, emotional overinvolvement or detachment, and a lack of affection and empathy. For bulimic patients particularly, there are familial tendencies toward alcholism, obesity, and affective instability; these families are unable to meet each other's emotional needs and there is general familywide dissension.

Therapy, then involves all members of the patient's family (Minuchin, Rosman, & Baker, 1978). And even if the parents have separated or divorced prior to the start of therapy, then they and other important members are required to participate (Sargent, 1986). If the patient is young, either chronologically or developmentally, then parents are expected to assume responsiblity for the patient's symptoms. By contrast, if the daughter or son is older, the parents are encouraged to assume a collaborative and supportive role (Sargent, 1986).

The goal of family therapists is to contravene the interactional patterns that maintain the patient's symptomatology; a full discussion of therapeutic interventions designed to achieve these goals are detailed by Schwartz, Barrett, and Saba (1985).

Family members may in some way even undermine treatment, as suggested by Szmukler and colleagues (Szmukler, Eisler, Russell, & Dare, 1985). Parents of patients who terminated treatment prematurely were more highly critical of their daughters than were parents whose daughters and sons completed treatment. The number of critical comments was also associated with the type of therapy (individual vs. family therapy) and with dropout. Dropout was greater among patients in the family group whose mothers expressed more critical comments; the link between dropout and fathers who expressed greater critical comments was greater among patients in the individual therapy group.

There is a clear role for the component of family therapy in a multidimensional treatment program. The data by Szmukler et al. (1985) raise questions regarding the family's interaction pattern; these questions can be answered with a behavioral assessment of the familial environment. Behavioral observations of family interactions in the clinic (or, if luxury permits, direct home observations) can help to identify the aspects of the familial environment that maintain eating-disorder symptomatology. If the eliciting and controlling stimuli can be altered by family members, then change may be possible.

Often, however, the therapist does not have access to other family members. A number of bulimic patients are college students who have moved away from their parents' home. Some parents of adult patients may simply not wish to "be bothered" with therapy sessions. Whether or not parents consent to be involved, it is unquestionably therapeutic for the patient to learn how to deal with parents who do not wish to change. The ability to handle such difficult situations, of course, necessitates sophisticated social skills.

Psychopharmacology

The integration of behavior therapy and psychopharmacology "can only be conceptualized as natural and needed" (Bellack & Hersen, 1985, p. 15). Because drug therapy is discussed in the next chapter, herein, I only highlight the compatibility between the two interventions.

The primary treatment for eating disorders is the uniform intake of calorically adequate, nutritionally balanced foods and reduction of the patient's persistent overconcern for body shape, size, and weight. Drugs can complement behavior therapy as a method (a) to facilitate refeeding by reducing anxiety or postprandial symptoms, (b) to rectify electrolyte imbalances, (c) to ameliorate depressive symptomatology, and (d) to reduce bulimic behaviors (Kaplan & Woodside, 1987).

Herzog and Brotman (1987), best known for their work on the use of tricyclic antidepressants and eating disorders, echo the perspective that "medication has a *place* in the management of specific symptoms in these often treatment-resistant disorders (p. 54).

REFERENCES

Abraham, S. F., & Beumont, P. J. V. (1982). How patients describe bulimia or binge eating. *Psychological Medicine, 12*, 625–635.

Agras, W. S., & Kirkley, B. G. (1986). Bulimia: Theories of etiology. In K. D. Brownell & J. P. Foreyt (Eds.), *Handbook of eating disorders* (pp. 367–378). New York: Basic Books.

Agras, W. S., & Werne, J. (1977). Behavior modification in anorexia nervosa. In R. A. Vigersky (Ed.), *Anorexia nervosa* (pp. 291–304). New York: Raven Press.

American College of Physicians (1987). Eating disorders: Anorexia nervosa and bulimia (position paper) by the Health and Public Policy Committee, *Nutrition Today, 22*, 29–33.

American Psychiatric Association (1980). *Diagnostic and statistical manual for mental disorders* (3rd ed.). Washington, DC: Author.

American Psychiatric Association (1987). *Diagnostic and statistical manual for mental disorders* (3rd ed., rev.). Washington, DC: Author.

Andersen, A. E. (1985). *Practical comprehensive treatment of anorexia nervosa and bulimia*. Baltimore, MD: The Johns Hopkins University Press.

Andersen, A. E. (1987a). Uses and potential misuses of antianxiety agents in the treatment of anorexia nervosa and bulimia nervosa. In P. E. Garfinkel & D. M. Garner (Eds.), *The role of drug treatments for eating disorders* (pp. 59–73). New York: Brunner/Mazel.

Andersen, A. E. (1987b). Contrast and comparison of behavioral, cognitive-behavioral, and comprehensive treatment methods for anorexia nervosa and bulimia nervosa. *Behavior Modification, 11*, 522–543.

Bachrach, A. J., Erwin, W. J., & Mohr, J. P. (1965). The control of eating behavior in an anorexic by operant conditioning techniques. In L. P. Ullman & L. Krasner (Eds.), *Case studies in behavior modification* (pp. 153–163). New York: Holt, Rinehart, and Winston.

Beck, A. T., Rush, A. J., Shaw, B. F., & Emery, G. (1979). *Cognitive therapy of depression: A treatment manual.* New York: Guilford.

Bellack, A. S., & Hersen, M. (Eds.). (1979). *Research and practice in social skills training.* New York: Plenum.

Bellack, A. S., & Hersen, M. (1985). General considerations. In M. Hersen & A. S. Bellack (Eds.), *Handbook of clinical behavior therapy with adults* (pp. 3–22). New York: Plenum.

Bemis, K. (1978). Current approaches to the etiology and treatment of anorexia nervosa. *Psychological Bulletin, 85.*, 593–617.

Bemis, K. (1987). The present status of operant conditioning for treatment of anorexia nervosa. *Behavior Modification, 11*, 432–463.

Blumenthal, J. A., O'Toole, L. C., & Chang, J. L. (1984). Is running an analogue of analogue of anorexia nervosa? An empirical study of obligatory running and anorexia nervosa. *Journal of the American Medical Association, 252*, 520–523.

Bruch, H. (1973). *Eating disorders.* New York: Basic Books.

Bruch, H. (1978). *The golden cage.* Cambridge, MA: Harvard University Press.

Bruch, H. (1985). Four decades of eating disorders. In D. M. Garner & P. E. Garfinkel (Eds.), *Handbook of psychotherapy for anorexia nervosa and bulimia* (pp. 7–18). New York: Guilford.

Casper, R. C. (1983). On the emergence of bulimia nervosa as a syndrome. *International Journal of Eating Disorders, 2*, 3–16.

Casper, R. C., Eckert, E. D., Halmi, K. A., Goldberg, S. C., & Davis, J. M. (1980). Bulimia: Its incidence and clinical importance in patients with anorexia nervosa. *Archives of General Psychiatry, 37*, 1030–1034.

Chiodo, J. (1985). The assessment of anorexia nervosa and bulimia. In M. Hersen, R. M. Eisler, & P. M. Miller (Eds.), *Progress in behavior modification* (pp. 255–292). New York: Academic.

Chiodo, J. (1987). Bulimia: An individual behavioral analysis. *Journal of Behavior Therapy and Experimental Psychiatry, 18*, 41–49.

Cooper, P. J., & Bowskill, R. (1986). Dysphoric mood and overeating. *British Journal of Clinical Psychology, 25*, 155–156.

Crisp, A. H. (1984). The possible significance of some behavioral correlates of weight and carbohydrate intake. *Journal of Psychosomatic Research, 11*, 117–121.

Crisp, A. H. (1984). The psychopathology of anorexia nervosa: Getting the "heat" out of the system. In A. J. Strunkard & E. Stellar (Ed.), *Eating and its disorders* (pp. 209–234). New York: Raven Press.

Crisp, A. H., Palmer, R. L., & Kalucy, R. S. (1976). How common is anorexia nervosa: A prevalence study. *British Journal of Psychiatry, 218*, 549–554.

Davis, R. (1986). Assessing the eating disorders. *The Clinical Psychologist, 39*, 33–36.

Davis, R., Freeman, R., & Solyom, L. (1985). Mood and food: An analysis of bulimic episodes. *Journal of Psychiatric Research, 19*, 331–335.

Dwyer, J. T., Feldman, J. J., Seltzer, C. C., & Mayer, J. (1969). Body image in adolescents: Attitudes toward weight and perception of appearance. *American Journal of Clinical Nutrition, 20*, 1045–1056.

Ellis, A. (1962). *Reason and emotion in psychotherapy.* New York: Lyle Stuart.

Fairburn, C. G. (1981). A cognitive behavioral approach to the treatment of bulimia. *Psychological Medicine, 11*, 707–711.

Fairburn, C. G. (1985). Cognitive-behavioral treatment for bulimia. In D. M. Garner & P. E. Garfinkel (Eds.), *Handbook of psychotherapy for anorexia nervosa and bulimia* (pp. 160–182). New York: Guilford.

Fairburn, C. G. (1987). The definition of bulimia nervosa: Guidelines for clinicians and research workers. *Annals of Behavioral Medicine, 4*, 3–7.

Fairburn, C. G., & Cooper, P. J. (1982). Self-induced vomiting and bulimia nervosa: An undetected problem. *British Medical Journal, 284*, 1153–1155.

Fairburn, C. G., & Cooper, P. J. (1984). The clinical features of bulimia nervosa. *British Journal of Psychiatry, 284*, 1153–1155.

Fairburn, C. G., Cooper, Z., & Cooper, P. J. (1986). The

clinical features and maintenance of bulimia nervosa. In K. D. Brownell & J. P. Foreyt (Eds.), *Handbook of eating disorders* (pp. 389–404). New York: Basic Books.

Fairburn, C. G., & Garner, D. M. (1986). The diagnosis of bulimia nervosa. *International Journal of Eating Disorders, 5,* 403–419.

Fairburn, C. G., Kirk, J., O'Connor, M., & Cooper, P. J. (1986). A comparison of two psychological treatments for bulimia nervosa. *Behaviour Research and Therapy, 24,* 629–644.

Fernstrom, J. D., & Wurtman, F. J. (1971). Brain serotonin content: Increase following ingestion of carbohydrate diet. *Science, 174,* 1023–1025.

Foa, E. B., & Steketee, G. A. (1979). Obsessive–compulsives: Conceptual issues and treatment interventions. In M. Hersen, R. M. Eisler, & P. M. Miller (Eds.), *Progress in behavior modification* (pp. 1–53). New York: Academic.

Fremouw, W. J., & Heyneman, N. E. (1985). Cognitive styles and bulimia. *The Behavior Therapist, 6,* 143–144.

Frisch, R. E., & McArthur, J. W. (1974). Menstrual cycles: Fatness as a determinant of minimum weight necessary for their maintenance or onset. *Science, 185,* 949–951.

Garfinkel, P. E., & Garner, D. M. (1982). *Anorexia nervosa—A Multidimensional perspective.* New York: Brunner/Mazel.

Garfinkel, P. E., & Kaplan, A. S. (1985). Starvation based perpetuating mechanisms in anorexia nervosa and bulimia. *International Journal of Eating Disorders, 4,* 651–665.

Garfinkel, P. E., & Kaplan, A. S. (1986). Anorexia nervosa: Diagnostic conceptualizations. In K. D. Brownell & J. P. Foreyt (Eds.), *Handbook of eating disorders* (pp. 266–282). New York: Basic Books.

Garfinkel, P. E., Moldofsky, H., & Garner, D. M. (1980). The heterogeneity of anorexia nervosa. *Archives of General Psychiatry, 37,* 1036–1040.

Garner, D. M. (1986). Cognitive therapy for anorexia nervosa. In K. D. Brownell & J. P. Foreyt (Eds.), *Handbook of eating disorders* (pp. 301–327). New York: Basic Books.

Garner, D. M., & Bemis, K. M. (1982). A cognitive-behavioral approach to anorexia nervosa. *Cognitive Therapy and Research, 6,* 123–150.

Garner, D. M., & Bemis, K. M. (1985). Cognitive therapy for anorexia nervosa. In D. M. Garner & P. E. Garfinkel (Eds.), *Handbook of psychotherapy for anorexia nervosa and bulimia* (pp. 107–146). New York: Guilford.

Garner, D. M., Fairburn, C. G., & Davis, R. (1987). Cognitive-behavioral treatment of bulimia nervosa—A critical appraisal. *Behavior Modification, 11,* 398–431.

Garner, D. M., & Garfinkel, P. E. (1978). Socio-cultural factors in the development of anorexia nervosa. *Lancet, 2,* 674.

Garner, D. M., & Garfinkel, P. E. (1980). Socio-cultural factors in the development of anorexia nervosa. *Psychological Medicine, 10,* 647–656.

Garner, D. M., Garfinkel, P. E., & Bemis, K. (1982). A multidimensional psychotherapy for anorexia nervosa. *International Journal of Eating Disorders, 1,* 3–46.

Garner, D. M., Garfinkel, P. E., & O'Shaughnessy, M. (1985). The validity of the distinction between bulimia with and without anorexia nervosa. *American Journal of Psychiatry, 142,* 581–587.

Garner, D. M., Garfinkel, P. E., Schwartz, D., & Thompson, M. (1980). Cultural expectation of thinness in women. *Psychological Reports, 47,* 483–491.

Gormally, J., Black, S., Daston, S., & Rardin, D. (1982). The assessment of binge eating severity among obese persons. *Addictive Behavior, 7,* 47–55.

Gull, W. W. (1874). Anorexia nervosa (apepsia hysterica, anorexia hysterica). *Transactions of the Clinical Society of London, 7,* 22–28.

Halmi, K. A. (1974). Anorexia nervosa: Demographic and clinical features in 94 cases. *Psychosomatic Medicine, 36,* 18–25.

Halmi, K. A. (1985). Behavioral management for anorexia nervosa. In D. M. Garner & P. E. Garfinkel (Eds.), *Handbook of psychotherapy for anorexia nervosa and bulimia* (pp. 147–159). New York: Guilford.

Halmi, K. A., Casper, R. C., Eckert, E. D., Goldberg, S. C., & Davis, J. M. (1979). Unique features associated with age of onset of anorexia nervosa. *Psychiatry Research, 1,* 209–215.

Halmi, K. A., Falk, J. R., & Schwartz, E. (1981). Binge eating and vomiting: A survey of a college population. *Psychological Medicine, 11,* 697–706.

Hart, K. J., & Ollendick, T. H. (1985). Prevalence of bulimia in working and university women. *American Journal of Psychiatry, 142,* 851–854.

Hawkins, R. C., III, & Clement, P. F. (1980). Development and construct validation of a self-report measure of binge eating tendencies. *Addictive Behaviors, 5,* 219–226.

Hay, G., & Leonard, J. C. (1979). Anorexia nervosa in males. *Lancet, 2,* 574–575.

Hersen, M., & Bellack, A. S. (1976). Social skills training for chronic psychiatric patients: Rationale, research findings, and future directions. *Comprehensive Psychiatry, 18*, 559–580.

Hersen, M., & Bellack, A. S. (Eds.). (1981). *Behavioral assessment: A practical handbook*. New York: Pergamon.

Herzog, D. B., (1984). Are anorexic and bulimic patients depressed? *American Journal of Psychiatry, 141*, 1594–1597.

Herzog, D. B., & Brotman, A. W. (1987). Use of tricyclic antidepressants in anorexia nervosa and bulimia nervosa. In P. E. Garfinkel & D. M. Garner (Eds.), *The role of drug treatments for eating disorders* (pp. 36–58). New York: Brunner/Mazel.

Herzog, D. B., Norman, D. K., Gordon, C., & Pepose, M. (1984). Sexual conflict and eating disorders in 27 males. *American Journal of Psychiatry, 141*, 989–990.

Hsu, L. K. G. (1980). Outcome of anorexia nervosa: A review of the literature (1954 to 1978). *Archives of General Psychiatry, 37*, 1041–1046.

Hudson, J. I., Pope, H. G., Jonas, J. M., & Yurgelun-Todd, D. (1983). Phenomenologic relationship of eating disorders to major affective disorder. *Psychiatry Research, 9*, 345–354.

Huenemann, R. L., Shapiro, L. R., Hampton, M. D., & Mitchell, B. W. (1966). A longitudinal study of gross body composition and body conformation and their association with food and activity in a teenage population. *American Journal of Clinical Nutrition, 18*, 325–338.

Johnson, C., & Berndt, D. J. (1983). Preliminary investigation of bulimia and life adjustment. *American Journal of Psychiatry, 140*, 6.

Johnson, C., Connors, M. E. , & Tobin, D. L. (1987). Symptom management of bulimia. *Journal of Consulting and Clinical Psychology, 55*, 668–676.

Johnson, C., & Larson, R. (1982). Bulimia: An analysis of moods and behavior. *Psychosomatic Medicine, 44*, 341–351.

Johnson, C., Lewis, C., Love, S., Lewis, L., & Stuckey, M. (1984). Incidence and correlates of bulimic behavior in a female high school population. *Journal of Youth and Adolescence, 13*, 15–26.

Jones, D. J., Fox, M. M., Babigian, H. M., & Hutton, H. E. (1980). The epidemiology of anorexia nervosa in Monroe County, New York: 1960–1976. *Psychosomatic Medicine, 42*, 551–558.

Kaplan, A. S., & Woodside, D. B. (1987). Biological aspects of anorexia nervosa and bulimia nervosa. *Journal of Consulting and Clinical Psychology, 55*, 645–653.

Kaye, W. H., & Gwirtsman, H. E. (1985). Mood changes and patterns of food consumption during bingeing and purging: Are there underlying neurobiologic relationships? In W. H. Kaye & H. E. Gwirtsman (Eds.), *A comprehensive approach to the treatment of normal weight bulimia* (pp. 19–36). Washington, DC: American Psychiatric Press.

Leon, G. R., Carroll, K., Chernyk, B., & Finn, S. (1985). Binge eating and associated habit patterns within college student and identified bulimic populations. *International Journal of Eating Disorders, 4*, 43–57.

Loro, A. D., Jr. (1984). Binge eating: A cognitive-behavioral treatment approach. In R. C. Hawkins, W. J. Fremouw, & P. F. Clement (Eds.). *The binge–purge syndrome: Diagnosis, treatment, and research* (pp. 183–210). New York: Springer.

Loro, A. D., Jr., & Orleans, C. S. (1981). Binge eating in obesity: Preliminary findings and guidelines for behavioral analysis and treatment. *Addictive Behaviors, 6*, 155–166.

Marcus, M. D., Wing, R. R., & Hopkins, J. (1988). Obese binge eaters: Affect, cognitions, and response to behavioral weight control. *Journal of Consulting and Clinical Psychology, 56*, 433–439.

Minuchin, S., Rosman, B., & Baker, L. (1978). *Psychosomatic families: Anorexia nervosa in context*. Cambridge, MA: Harvard University Press.

Mitchell, J. E., Pyle, R. L., Hatsukami, D., & Eckert, E. D. (1986). What are atypical eating disorders? *Psychosomatics, 27*, 21–28.

Norman, D. K., & Herzog, D. B. (1984). Persistent social maladjustment in bulimia: A one-year follow-up. *American Journal of Psychiatry, 141*, 444–446.

Orleans, C. T., & Barnett, L. R. (1984). Bulimarexia: Guidelines for behavioral assessment and treatment. In R. C. Hawkins, W. Fremouw, and P. F. Clement (Eds.). *The binge–purge syndrome: Diagnosis, treatment, and research* (pp. 144–182). New York: Springer.

Pillay, M., & Crisp, A. H. (1981). The impact of social skills training within an established in-patient treatment program for anorexia nervosa. *British Journal of Psychiatry, 139*, 533–539.

Polivy, J., & Herman, C. P. (1985). Dieting and bingeing. *American Psychologist, 40*, 193–201.

Pyle, R. L., Halvorson, P. A., Neuman, P. A., & Mitchell, J. E. (1986). The increasing prevalence of bulimia in freshman college students. *International Journal of Eating Disorders, 5*, 631–647.

Rodin, J. (1985). Insulin levels, hunger, and food intake:

An example of feedback loops in weight regulation. *Health Psychology, 4,* 1–24.

Rosen, J. C. (1987). A review of behavioral treatments for bulimia nervosa. *Behavior Modification, 11,* 464–486.

Rosen, J. C., & Leitenberg, H. (1982). Bulimia nervosa: Treatment with exposure and response prevention. *Behavior Therapy, 8,* 385–392.

Rosen, J. C., & Leitenberg, H. (1985). Exposure plus response prevention treatment of bulimia. In D. M. Garner & P. E. Garfinkel (Eds.), *Handbook of psychotherapy for anorexia nervosa and bulimia* (pp. 193–209). New York: Guilford.

Rosen, J. C., & Leitenberg, H. (1987). The anxiety model of bulimia nervosa and treatment with exposure plus response prevention. In K. Pirke, D. Ploog, & W. Vandereycken (Eds.), *Psychobiology of bulimia nervosa.* Heidelberg: Springer–Verlag.

Ryle, J. A. (1939). Discussion on anorexia nervosa. *Proceedings of the Royal Society of Medicine, 32,* 735–739.

Sargent, J. (1983). The sick child: Family complications. *Developmental and Behavioral Pediatrics, 4,* 50–56.

Sargent, J. (1986). Family therapy for eating disorders. *The Clinical Psychologist,* 43–45.

Schlemmer, J. K., & Barnett, P. A. (1977). Management of manipulative behavior of anorexia nervosa patients. *Journal of Psychiatric Nursing, 15,* 35–41.

Schwartz, R. C., Barrett, & Saba, G. (1985). Family therapy for bulimia. In D. M. Garner & P. E. Garfinkel (Eds.), *Handbook of psychotherapy for anorexia nervosa and bulimia* (pp. 280–307). New York: Guilford.

Selvini Palazzoli, M. P. (1974). *Anorexia nervosa.* London: Chaucer.

Slade, P. (1982). Towards a functional analysis of anorexia nervosa and bulimia nervosa. *British Journal of Clinical Psychology, 21,* 53–61.

Society of Actuaries and Association of Life Insurance Medical Directors of America. (1979). *Build and blood pressure study.* Chicago, IL: Author.

Spence, S. H. (1987). Social behavior in adults: Inves-

tigation. In S. Lindsay & G. Powell (Eds.), *A handbook of clinical adult psychology* (pp. 213–239). Brookfield, VT: Gower.

Striegel-Moore, R., McAvay, G., & Rodin, J. (1986). Psychological and behavioral correlates of feeling fat in women. *International Journal of Eating Disorders, 5,* 935–947.

Strober, M. (1984). Stressful life events associated with bulimia in anorexia nervosa. *International Journal of Eating Disorders, 3,* 3–16.

Strober, M., & Humphrey, L. L. (1987). Familial contributions to the etiology and course of anorexia nervosa and bulimia. *Journal of Consulting and Clinical Psychology, 55,* 654–659.

Szmukler, G. I., Eisler, I., Russell, G. F. M., & Dare, C. (1985). Anorexia nervosa, parental "expressed emotion" and dropping out of treatment. *British Journal of Psychiatry, 147,* 265–271.

Turkat, I. D., & Brantley, P. B. (1981). On the therapeutic relationship in behavior therapy. *The Behavior Therapist, 4,* 16–17.

Van Buskirk, S. S. (1977). A two-phase perspective on the treatment of anorexia nervosa. *Psychological Bulletin, 84,* 529–538.

Vandereycken, W., & Meermann, R. (1984). *Anorexia nervosa—A clinician's guide to treatment.* New York: de Gruyter.

Vandereycken, W., & Pierloot, R. (1983). Drop-out during in-patient treatment of anorexia nervosa: A clinical study of 133 patients. *British Journal of Medical Psychology, 56,* 145–156.

Walsh, B. T., Roose, S. P., Glassman, A. H., Gladis, M., & Sadik, C. (1985). Bulimia and depression. *Psychosomatic Medicine, 47,* 123–131.

Wilson, G. T., & Smith, D. (1987). Cognitive-behavioral treatment of bulimia nervosa. *Annals of Behavioral Medicine, 9,* 12–17.

Yates, A., Leehey, K., & Shisslak, C. M. (1983). Running—An analogue of anorexia? *New England Journal of Medicine, 308,* 251–255.

Zigler, E., & Phillips, L. (1961). Social competence and outcome in psychiatric disorder. *Journal of Abnormal and Social Psychology, 63,* 264–271.

CHAPTER 21

Pharmacotherapy

THEODORE WELTZIN, HARRY GWIRTSMAN, DAVID C. JIMERSON, AND WALTER KAYE

CONCEPTUALIZATION OF THE DISORDERS

The eating disorders, anorexia and bulimia nervosa, are generally recognized as abnormal eating behaviors associated with cognitive misconceptions of body image, disturbances of mood, and a wide variety of hormonal and metabolic abnormalities. The diagnosis and treatment of eating disorders has come under the purview of psychiatric practice since the late 1950s. Currently, many psychiatric investigators conceptualize these disorders as being due to a combination of cultural–social, psychological, and biological factors (Garfinkel & Garner, 1982; Ploog & Pirke, 1987).

Treatment of eating disorders tends to employ behavioral, psychotherapeutic, or pharmacological approaches. The purpose of this chapter is to review the evidence for the efficacy of the available drug treatments for anorexia and bulimia nervosa. It should be noted that beneficial effects of medication are indirect evidence that disturbances of neurotransmitters exist and are corrected by medication. In fact, recent studies have focused on identifying neurochemical abnormalities that may predispose a person to develop an eating disorder or may perpetuate an already existing one. Therefore, prior to discussing specific pharmacological agents, it is worthwhile to review the question of neurotransmitter disturbances in the eating disorders.

Patients with eating disorders characteristically have disturbances of appetite, neuroendo-crine function, and mood. There are several reasons to believe that these disturbances are related to alterations in brain neurotransmitters. First, brain neurotransmitters modulate feeding behavior, mood, and hormonal secretion. Second, the fact that medication may benefit some of these patients implies that there must be psychobiological disturbances that medications correct. It should be emphasized that multiple factors contribute to the etiology of eating disorders. This chapter provides only a limited discussion of several neurotransmitters that may be involved in such illnesses and not a comprehensive overview of the psychopathology of the eating disorders.

Two methods have been used to study the relationship of abnormal eating behavior and neurochemical alterations in eating disordered patients. The most commonly used method is to measure neuroendocrine function. In general, hormonal disturbances in eating disordered patients (Newman & Halmi, 1988) are thought to reflect disturbances in either the hypothalamus or higher areas of the brain. Thus, hormonal disturbances in the eating disorders appear to reflect alterations in brain neurotransmitters that modulate hormonal function.

The possibility of neurotransmitter disturbances in patients with anorexia nervosa has been argued since the late 1970s. Mawson (1974) hypothesized that central catecholamine pathways might be involved in anorexia nervosa. Barry and Klawans (1976) suggested that increased activity of dopamine might theoretically account for much of the pathophysiology of this disorder, while

Redmond, Swann, and Heninger (1976) suggested that excessive norepinephrine activity might be contributory. Recently, Morley and Blundell (1988) have updated this argument by implicating that many neuropeptides that contribute to feeding behavior may also play a role in these illnesses.

In the interest of brevity, this chapter does not provide a comprehensive discussion of potential neurotransmitter abnormalities in these disorders; instead, we focus on two neurotransmitters, norepinephrine (NE) and serotonin (5-HT), for several reasons. First, each has a well-established role in the modulation of feeding, mood, and neuroendocrine function (Morley & Blundell, 1988). Second, disturbances in both of these systems have been found in the eating disorders. Third, many medications that have some effectiveness in the eating disorders act, in part, on these systems. Any success of psychotropic medication may be due to correcting a defect in these neurotransmitter systems.

It is important to emphasize that abnormalities in hormonal function and neurotransmitters may be secondary to malnutrition or weight loss and not the cause of aberrant behavior. Studying eating disordered patients after they have achieved nutritional stability may be one way of circumventing such problems and of identifying possible trait disturbances. Despite methodological limitations, many studies have been carried out, and, in fact, they offer some insight into pathophysiological processes in the eating disorders. This chapter reviews such studies to date and discusses their implications.

Norepinephrine (NE)

Theoretically, an intrinsic noradrenergic disturbance could contribute to the expression of the symptom complex in the eating disorders. Considerable animal and human data implicate noradrenergic pathways in the modulation of appetite. For example, treatments that increase intrasynaptic NE or that directly activate alpha-2 adrenoceptors tend to increase food consumption (Leibowitz & Shor-Posner, 1986). Also, NE dysfunctions could contribute to depression (Van Praag, 1980; Zis & Goodwin, 1982), to anxiety (Charney, Heninger, & Breier, 1984; Redmond & Huang,

1979), and to gonadotropin dysfunction (Loftstrom, 1977; McCann, 1970; Sawyer et al., 1974).

Alternatively, altered noradrenergic function might not be trait-related, but could be a consequence of some factor that affects noradrenergic activity. For example, disturbed NE function could be secondary to nutritional status. Considerable data in animals and humans suggest that feeding and weight gain increase sympathetic nervous system (SNS) activity (Landsberg & Young, 1978), while food restriction and weight loss produce the opposite effect. The effects of feeding on central nervous system (CNS) NE function are less clear. Some studies suggest that food reduction decreases NE (Pirke & Spyra, 1982), while others find that feeding reduces NE activity (McCaleb, Myers, Singer, & Willis, 1979). Noradrenergic function is also affected by other variables (Potter, Muscettola, & Goodwin, 1983), such as stress, physical activity, sodium balance, and hormonal status.

In an attempt to resolve these methodological problems, many investigators have studied anorexics both when underweight and after refeeding. Most studies have found reduced concentrations of 2-methoxy-4-hydroxy-phenylethylene glycol (MHPG) or VMA in 24-hour urines in underweight anorexics, with increased metabolite concentrations after refeeding and weight gain. In contrast, plasma NE values have been inconsistently changed after weight gain, and cerebrospinal fluid (CSF) NE and MHPG have been reported to be normal in the underweight state (Kaye, Gwirtsman, Jimerson, George, Karoum, & Ebert, 1987). The few studies of noradrenergic receptor function suggest that these receptors change in relation to nutritional status. For example, underweight anorexics have increased alpha-2 receptor sensitivity with a downregulation after weight gain. In one study, an upregulation of beta receptor activity after weight gain was found.

Perhaps the most interesting question is whether NE activity normalizes after recovery. Kaye, Jimerson, Lake, and Ebert (1985) reported reduced CSF and plasma NE measures in long-term weight-restored anorexics. Pirke, Pahl, Schweiger, and Warnhoff (1985) reported that these patients had elevated plasma ketones, suggesting that, despite normal weight, some of these patients were still dieting or starving at the time of study.

In summary, most investigators have postulated that starvation is the most important factor accounting for reduced SNS activity in underweight anorexics. However, other psychobiological alterations (such as stress, arousal, increased physical activity, depressive or anxiety disorder, macronutrient consumption, cortisol or thyroid function, fluid volume or electrolyte balance) may also be contributory. Because diet and many other factors alter noradrenergic function, it is uncertain whether reduced NE measures in long-term, weight-recovered anorexics are state related or trait related.

Normal-weight bulimics have been found (Buckholtz, George, Davies, Jimerson, & Potter, 1988; George, Kaye, Goldstein, Jimerson, 1988; Kaye et al., 1986; Pirke et al., 1985) to have reduced plasma NE levels and increased beta-adrenergic receptor responsiveness in the periphery and reduced CSF NE when abstinent from bingeing and vomiting. Such findings suggest that bulimic patients have persistent defects in noradrenergic function when abstinent. It is not known whether these defects reflect a trait-related noradrenergic disturbance that may contribute to alterations in feeding behavior, mood, and menstrual regulation, or if they are secondary to some factor related to abstinence from bingeing and vomiting. In either event, bulimia is a disorder with a high rate of recidivism. Antidepressant medications, which act in part on NE systems, have been shown to reduce bingeing behavior, independent of their effects on mood (see next section). Collectively, these data raise the intriguing possibility that antidepressants work in this illness by stabilizing NE function.

Serotonin

Treatments that increase intrasynaptic serotonin or that directly activate serotonin receptors tend to reduce food consumption (Leibowitz & Shor-Posner, 1986; Wurtman & Wurtman, 1979) and are thought to decrease carbohydrate selection and spare protein intake. Conversely, interventions that diminish serotonergic neurotransmissions or serotonin receptor activation reportedly increase food consumption and promote weight gain.

These data are consistent with the possibility that bingeing behavior is related to hyperserotonergic function. Moreover, serotonergic disturbances could contribute both to dysphoric mood (Coppen & Wood, 1982; Murphy, Campell, & Costa, 1978) and to neuroendocrine disturbances (see review by Smythe, 1977).

The question of a serotonin dysfunction is particularly relevant for normal-weight bulimia because antidepressant medications, which act in part on brain serotonin, have been found to be effective in reducing frequency of bingeing and in improving mood (see next paragraphs). In addition, several investigators have generated data supporting the possibility of a serotonergic disturbance in this illness. We reported (Kaye, Ebert, Gwirtsman, & Weiss, 1984a) that after weight recovery, nonbulimic anorexics have higher concentrations of CSF 5-hydroxyindoleacetic acid (5-HIAA) (after probenecid) than do bulimic anorexics.

The CNS serotonergic functional activity can be assessed in humans by the administration of a pharmacological agent that increases brain serotonin neurotransmission or that acts on a serotonin receptor. Brewerton, George, and Jimerson (1986a); and Brewerton et al., (1986b) have used such tools to study normal-weight bulimics. One probe uses the intravenous infusion of the 5-HT precursor L-tryptophan (100 mg/Kg), which is thought to increase serotonin neurotransmission. Another probe uses the oral administration of the 5-HT postsynaptic receptor agonist m-chlorophenylpiperazine (m-CPP) (0.5 mg/kg given orally [p.o.]) to bulimics). Both studies have demonstrated a blunted prolactin response, which may positively correlate with CNS serotonergic activity and may support the possibility that bulimics have hyposerotonergic activity. Brewerton, Mueller, George, Murphy, and Jimerson (1986c) have also reported an increase of migraine headaches in bulimics after the administration of m-CPP, as compared to controls. These results are of particular interest because of the 5-HT alterations that have been reported in migraine patients (Eadie & Tyrer, 1985).

If bulimic patients have a reduction of serotonin activity, then it is possible that bingeing and vomiting, by changing plasma amino acids, may enhance brain serotonin. This in turn may increase satiety and/or improve mood. This hypothesis is based on data showing that the intake of dietary carbohydrates increases the uptake of tryptophan (TRP)—the precursor of serotonin into the brain by increasing the *plasma TRP ratio* (the ratio of the plasma TRP concentration to the summed concentrations of other amino acids that compete with TRP for brain uptake) (Fernstrom & Wurtman, 1971, 1972). Our group (Kaye, Gwirtsman, Brewerton, & George, 1988a) reported that an increase in the TRP ratio during bingeing and vomiting was associated with satiety (i.e., cessation of bingeing and vomiting), but not with change in mood. This study supports the possibility that an increase in the TRP ratio may be associated with the termination of bingeing and vomiting.

In terms of anorexia nervosa, some (Gillberg, 1983; Kaye, Gwirtsman, George, Jimerson & Ebert, 1988b), but not all studies (Gerner et al., 1984) have found that weight loss and/or malnutrition in anorexia nervosa is associated with a significant reduction in CNS serotonergic metabolism that is reversed by refeeding and/or weight restoration. The influence of caloric restriction on serotonin is supported by a report that dieting can also alter serotonin function in healthy females (Goodwin, Fairburn, & Cowen, 1987). Interestingly, we have recently found (unpublished data) that anorexia nervosa patients after long-term weight recovery have greater than normal measures of the major serotonin metabolite (5-HIAA) in CSF. This finding implies that after nutritional restoration, anorexic patients have increased serotonin activity. Theoretically, this is consistent with several traits that anorexics display, such as increased satiety and obsessional behavior.

DIAGNOSTIC ISSUES AND PROBLEMS

Bulimia Nervosa

Bulimia is defined as the rapid ingestion of large amounts of food. The eating is usually inconspicuous and is terminated by sleep, social interruption, abdominal pain, or self-induced purging. Bulimic subjects purge themselves through vomiting, laxatives, or diuretics. The food consumed is often highly caloric. Periods of binge-eating are often interspersed with periods of fasting and dieting, and weight fluctuations are commonly seen. Bulimic individuals are aware that they have an abnormal eating pattern and yet are unable to alter it voluntarily. Associated features include depressed mood and self-deprecating thoughts (Johnson & Larson, 1982).

Bulimia can occur in underweight, normal weight, or overweight individuals, including patients with anorexia nervosa or obesity. We use the term *normal-weight bulimia* or *bulimic disorder* to describe nonanorexic patients with the preceding symptoms of binge-eating. Bulimic disorder is considerably more common than anorexia nervosa, with surveys placing the prevalence of the disorder in college populations at 4–13% (Johnson, Stuckey, Lewis, & Schwartz, 1982), with a distribution of 87% females and 13% males (Halmi, Falk, & Schwartz, 1981). The typical duration of the illness is reported to be at least 5 years (Fairburn & Cooper, 1982).

Two major points of controversy in the diagnosis and treatment of eating-disordered patients are (1) the relationship of eating disorders to affective disorder, substance abuse, and severe character pathology, and (2) the effect of these factors on diagnostic reliability and prognosis for eating disorders. Several recent lines of evidence point to a link between bulimia and affective disorder. Phenomenologically, bulimic patients display symptoms that often are similar in quality and severity to those of depressives (Fairburn & Cooper, 1982; Johnson & Larson, 1982). Bipolar (depressive and manic) mood characteristics can be observed (Kaplan, Garfinkel, Darby, & Garner, 1983). Family history studies consistently report a high incidence of first-degree relatives of bulimics with affective disorder (Gwirtsman, Roy-Byrne, Yager, & Gerner, 1983; Hudson, Pope, Jonas, Yurgelun-Todd, & Frankenburg, 1987). Also, neuroendocrine abnormalities of eating-disordered patients are similar to those observed in patients with major affective disorder (Gwirtsman et al., 1983).

Recent investigation has also suggested a link between bulimic behavior and alcoholism. Bulimic behavior has clinical qualities similar to addictive behavior (Hatsukami, Owen, Pyle, & Mitchell, 1982), and a number of investigators have reported an increased incidence of substance abuse both in eating-disordered subjects (Bulik, 1987; Mitchell, Hatsukami, Eckert, & Pyle, 1985) and in their first-degree relatives (Bulik, 1987; Hudson et al., 1987; Rivinus et al., 1984).

The incidence of eating disorders in a group of inpatients with borderline character disorder diagnosis has been reported by one group to be 31% (Piran et al., 1988). In one group of 14 patients referred for treatment, Brotman, Herzog, and Hamburg (1988) found 6 to have borderline diagnosis. They speculated that this subgroup can be expected to have a poorer outcome at follow-up. Other authors have reported up to 25% of eating disordered patients meet criteria for borderline personality disorder. Using different diagnostic instruments, Pope, Frankenburg, Hudson, Jonas, and Yurgelun-Todd (1987) found an incidence of 2% of patients whom they say met the criteria for a diagnosis of borderline character disorder. The overlap of diagnostic criteria, poor reliability of character diagnosis, and findings that suggest outcome is not related to borderline character traits are but a few of the problems with regard to this issue.

Anorexia Nervosa

Anorexia nervosa is defined as an eating disorder characterized by refusal to maintain body weight over a minimal normal weight; a fear of weight gain or becoming fat even though underweight; a disturbance in the way one's body size, shape, or weight is experienced; and amenorrhea, defined as the loss of three consecutive menses (DSM-III-R; American Psychiatric Association 1987). This disorder occurs in 1 of 250 females during adolescence, and the male:female ratio is approximately 1:20. The etiology of the illness is unknown, but predisposing factors have been thought to include psychodynamic, social, learning, family, and biological factors. Some evidence suggests success in treating anorexia nervosa with psychotherapy, family therapy, behavior modification, and drug treatments; however, over the long term, most patients do poorly despite treatment. Perhaps overly optimistic claims of success may be due to inadequate follow-up of the patient after treatment (Vandereycken & Pierloot, 1983) or to inadequate

assessment of placebo response rates (Hsu, 1980; Schwartz & Thompson, 1981).

TREATMENT STRATEGIES

Normal-Weight Bulimia

Despite its prevalence, the study of bulimic syndromes has only recently conformed to rigorous scientific methodology. For this reason, conclusions regarding strategies for pharmacological treatments remain tentative. In addition, preliminary studies suggest that group psychotherapy, usually taking a cognitive-behavioral approach, are moderately successful in reducing bulimic behavior (Bloskind-Lodahl & White, 1978; Lacey, 1983). Fortunately, research on bulimic disorder is rapidly evolving, and more definite conclusions concerning the efficacy of both pharmacotherapy and talk therapies should be forthcoming during the 1990s.

Tricyclic Antidepressants

As mentioned, several lines of evidence point to a link between bulimia and affective disorders. This has prompted a number of trials of conventional antidepressants with bulimic subjects (see Table 21.1). It is important to emphasize that it is not clear whether antidepressant medications are effective because they have a selective antibulimic action or because they have a nonspecific antidepressant effect. Our own clinical experience indicates that patients with bulimia and without signs and symptoms of severe depression still appear to respond well to antidepressants.

Most double-blind, placebo-controlled trials of tricyclic antidepressants, when used at adequate dosages, demonstrate that active drug is significantly better than placebo in reducing bingeing and vomiting behavior (see Table 21.1). Additionally, all studies that report a significant drug-related reduction in frequency of bingeing also reported an improvement in affective symptoms. Some groups found a correlation between change in binge frequency and mood improvement, while other investigators did not. Also, one of these studies (Pope, Hudson, Jonas, & Yurgelun-Todd, 1983) showed that the treated patients were less

TABLE 21.1.   Double-Blind, Placebo-Controlled Medication Trials in Bulimic Subjects[a]

Investigator	N	Medication	Length (weeks)	Drug vs. placebo[b]
Pope et al., 1983	22	Imipramine 200 mg q.d.	6	D > P
Agras, Dorian, Kirkley, Arnow, & Bachman, 1987	22	Imipramine 200 mg q.d.	16	D > P
Hughes, Wells, Cunningham & Ilstrup, 1986	22	Desipramine 200 mg q.d.	6	D > P
Mitchell & Groat, 1984	22	Amitriptyline 150 mg q.d.	8	D = P[d]
Walsh et al., 1988	50	Phenelzine 60–90 mg	8	D > P
Kennedy et al., 1986	18	Isocarboxazid 60 mg	6	D > P
Pope et al., 1988	40	Trazodone (dosage not provided)	6	D > P
Freeman, Morris, Cheshire, Casper, & Davis, 1988	40	Fluoxetine 60–80 mg	6	D > P
Sabine et al., 1983	50	Mianserin 60 mg	8	?D = P
Kaplan et al., 198	12	Carbamazepine (6–20 mcg/ml)	20	D = P
Wermuth et al., 1977	20	Diphenylhydantoin (10–20 mcg/ml)		D > P

[a]All studies were placebo controlled and double-blind. The studies with diphenylhydantoin and carbamazepine were crossover design; the others employed a parallel design. Note that q.d. refers to "four times daily"; otherwise, daily dosage should be inferred.
[b]HRS = Hamilton Rating Scale for Depression; BDI = Beck Depression Inventory; ZSRDS = Zung Self-Rated Depression Scale.

preoccupied by thoughts of food. It is worth mentioning that open trials of tricyclic antidepressants have been reported (Brotman, Herzog, & Woods, 1984; Hudson, Pope, & Jones, 1984), and, in general, the findings are similar to the controlled trials.

Monoamine Oxidase Inhibitors (MAOIs)

A number of studies have looked at the efficacy of MAOIs in bulimia (Kennedy, Piran, & Garfinkel, 1986; Walsh, Stewart, Roose, Gladis, & Glassman, 1984; Walsh et al., 1988); all reported improvement in bulimic symptoms similar to that with tricyclic antidepressants. Walsh et al. (1988) noted a high incidence of side effects that led to noncompliance in the phenelzine group and resulted in subjects stopping the medication even if

they had benefited from it. A similar trial also noted significant side effects in 40% of those on active drug (Kennedy et al., 1986). In an open trial, Roy-Byrne, Gwirtsman, Edelstein, Yager, and Gerner (1983) reported that only one of eight patients responded favorably to tranylcypromine at dosages of 30 mg or more. All authors recommend careful clinical evaluation of each patient with whom MAOI therapy is initiated, as many bulimic subjects exhibit impulsive behavior patterns and might have great difficulty with adherence to the low-tyramine diet necessary for these treatments.

Other Antidepressants

Trazodone has been studied in individual cases, in open trials, and most recently in a double-blind,

Reduction binge Frequency	Depression reduction[b]	Follow-up
4 of 9 > 75% 4 of 9 > 50% 1—NC	D > P HRS—50% reduction	1–8 months 18 of 22 significant decrease, including 6 abstinent
Mean—72% reduction on drug	D > P BDI—51% reduction	—

Mean—90% reduction
15 of 22 —100%
	ZSRDS—10 point reduction
	  (depressed subjects excluded from
	  study)	

Mean—63% reduction	D > P HRS—63% reduction	—
64% reduction 8 of 23—100%	D > P HRS—38% (depressed subjects)[c] HRS—13% (nondepressed subjects)[c]	40% of subjects reported significant side effects
Mean—40% reduction	D > P —	Poor compliance due to side effects
—	—	—
—	—	—
	?D > P	—
	—	—
6 of 19–75% 2 of 19–50% 6 of 19–20–40% 5 of 19–no change	—	18 months 2 of 6 binge free

— indicates that no data were provided for this category.
[c]Not statistically significant.
[d]Both placebo- and drug-treated group improved.
[e]D = active drug treatment; P = placebo; NC = no change.

placebo-controlled trial (Pope, Keck, McElroy, & Hudson, 1988). In this trial, trazodone was found to significantly improve bulimic symptoms compared to controls, and it was well tolerated by the subjects. Other studies have shown only moderate benefit (Hudson et al., 1984), and in one trial of three patients, symptoms were worsened when using trazodone (Wold, 1983).

Lithium, used primarily in bipolar affective disorder, has also been used in treatment-resistant depression and impulsive disorders. Both a case report of lithium being effective in treating an anorexic patient with bulimic symptoms (Stein, Hartshorn, Jones, & Steinberg, 1982) and a double-blind, placebo-controlled trial in anorexic subjects with bulimic symptoms (Gross et al., 1981) have suggested that lithium may be of

benefit in bulimia. In a trial with 14 normal-weight bulimic subjects, by 75–100% lithium carbonate was found to reduce bulimic behavior in 12 of the subjects (Hsu, 1984).

Fluoxetine, a new antidepressant with potent serotonin reuptake blockade, has also been tested in eating-disordered patients. Ferguson (1986) reported significant weight loss in obese fluoxetine-treated patients as compared to controls. He also reported a response to fluoxetine by a severely anorexic patient with bulimic symptoms (Ferguson, 1987). Freeman, Morris, Cheshire, Casper, and Davis (1988) reported a double-blind, placebo-controlled study in which fluoxetine-treated patients decreased their bulimic behavior.

Mianserin, another antidepressant, produced no symptomatic improvement in a British study

(Sabine, Yonace, Farrington, Barratt, & Wakeling, 1983); however, blood levels of the drug were not monitored, and the effectiveness of higher doses of mianserin remains undetermined.

Anticonvulsant Drugs

Electroencephalographic (EEG) abnormalities, principally those of diffuse slowing, but also of paroxysmal slow waves, 14 + 6 per-second spike and wave complexes, and paroxysmal dysrhythmias, have been found in a high percentage of bulimic subjects (35–72%) (Crisp, Fenton, & Scotton, 1968; Rau & Green, 1975; Rau, Struve, & Green, 1979; Wermuth, Davis, Hollister, & Stunkard, 1977), regardless of whether they were underweight at the time of the EEG.

In light of these findings, Wermuth et al. (1977) conducted a crossover trial in which 6 of 19 patients treated with diphenylhydantoin showed marked improvement (defined as 75% reduction in binge frequency) over placebo. There was neither a correlation between improvement and EEG abnormalities nor a change in weight or binge intensity in the unimproved group. Follow-up at 18 months revealed that 2 of the 6 improved patients were completely cured, 2 had stopped the drug and resumed binge-eating, and 2 had resumed binge-eating while on the drug. In general, diphenylhydantoin is thought to be only a weak antibulimic agent. Carbamazepine, another anticonvulsant, has been examined in a very preliminary controlled crossover trial of 6 cases (Kaplan et al., 1983). Only 1 patient with bipolar affective disorder experienced dramatic antidepressant and antibulimic relief from this agent. No follow-up data were provided.

Stimulant Medication

Ong, Checkley, and Russell (1983) achieved complete, albeit temporary, abolition of bulimic symptoms using an intravenous injection of methylphenidate (0.2 mg/Kg). Their drug-treated subjects reported less subjective hunger and consumed fewer calories during the 120 minutes following the infusion than individuals receiving the placebo. Patients developed feelings of euphoria and hyperalertness, however, following the infusion. The authors regarded this trial as a pharmacological dissection of the symptoms associated with bulimia, but they did not advocate the use of

analeptics or appetite suppressants in the treatment of this disorder. Fenfluramine, a nonaddictive stimulant, has also been found to reduce the amount of food eaten in bulimic subjects, a finding similar to that in normals (Robinson, Checkley, & Russell, 1985).

Opioid Antagonists

Recently, there has been interest in the role that endogenous opioids play in eating behavior. Opiates stimulate feeding and opiate antagonists attenuate feeding in both animal and human studies. Mitchell, Laine, Morley, and Levine (1986) reported that intravenous (IV) naloxone, when given before a binge, decreased the amount of food ingested in four of five subjects studied. Jonas and Gold (1986) reported naltrexone taken orally decreased bulimic symptoms.

Summary

The aforementioned studies and those in Table 21.1 suggest that tricyclic antidepressants and MAOIs, which are effective in affective disorders, panic disorder, and obsessive–compulsive disorder, are also effective in normal-weight bulimia. The efficacy of newer antidepressants, such as fluoxetine, appears similar to standard antidepressants, and lithium may be effective, but further controlled trials are needed.

The issue of whether antidepressant medications are effective because of a selective antibulimic action or merely because of a nonspecific antidepressant effect is unresolved. Both the critical examination of the published data and our own clinical experience indicate that patients with bulimia who do not have severe depression appear to respond well to antidepressants. Additionally, one group (Walsh et al., 1988) reported patients with an additional diagnosis of depression had a worse response to antidepressants, and phenelzine's effect was not related to depressive symptomatology.

Anticonvulsant and stimulant medication do not appear to be effective at this point and should be further studied to determine their utility, if any.

Anorexia Nervosa

A wide variety of psychoactive medications are reported beneficial in the treatment of anorexia nervosa. Most of these medications were assessed in uncontrolled trials. Often, these medications were given in association with other therapies so that it is unclear whether it was the medication or the other therapy that resulted in improvement. Furthermore, the criteria for improvement has often been weight gain, not a normalization of thinking or a reduction in their fears of being fat.

Short-term weight gain can often be achieved when treating anorexics, particularly in inpatient settings. It is another matter, however, to get anorexic patients to maintain weight in the long term. To our knowledge, all trials have been short term and usually associated with a weight-gaining program that assessed the effect of medication on the rate of weight gain. No follow-up studies have been done to determine whether any medications produce permanent beneficial effects.

Uncontrolled studies have shown efficacy of chlorpromazine (Crisp, Fenton, & Scotton, 1968; Hafner, Crisp, & McNeilly, 1976; Hall, 1975), L-dopa (Johanson & Knorr, 1977), phenoxybenzamine (Redmond et al., 1976), diphenylhydantoin (Green & Rau, 1974, 1977), amitriptyline (Beiberman et al., 1985; Moore, 1977; Needlemen & Waber, 1977); stimulants (Wulliemier, Rossel, & Sinclair, 1975), and naloxone (Moore, Mills, & Forster, 1981). None of these observations has been confirmed under double-blind, controlled conditions.

To dismiss these medications, however, because they have not been subjected to rigorous study leaves open the possibility of overlooking useful therapeutic agents. The clinician must rely on the psychopharmacological principles of balancing risks and benefits. If the patient has had multiple treatment failures or is severely incapacitated by dysphoric mood or obsessional thoughts, the use of novel treatment strategies should be considered.

Double-Blind Trials

The number of double-blind medication trials in anorexia nervosa is very limited (Table 21.2). These studies, for the most part, were performed on inpatients in an attempt to find an agent that might accelerate restoration of weight. Some studies also determined whether the medication influenced mood or anorexic attitudes. In contrast to claims from open trials, results from double-blind trials do not find a "magic bullet" drug that provides a significant remission of the anorexic symptom complex. Double-blind studies report limited success in treatment of specific problems, such as improving (a) the rate of weight gain during refeeding, (b) disturbed attitudes toward food and body image, (c) depression, or (d) gastrointestinal discomfort.

Two neuroleptics, pimozide (Vandereycken & Pierlott, 1982) and sulpiride (Vandereycken, 1984), have been investigated in anorexia because neuroleptics have been considered the drugs of choice (Dally & Sargent, 1960), and brain dopamine pathways may be disturbed (Barry & Klawans, 1976). Both drugs had limited success in accelerating weight gain or altering anorexic attitudes for some patients for part of the study, but overall drug effect was marginal. These studies do not support the use of pimozide or sulpiride in the routine treatment of anorexia nervosa. Whether other neuroleptics are useful remains unknown.

Recent literature describes a high incidence of mood disorders in anorexics (Cantwell, Sturzenberger, Burroughs, Salhin, & Green, 1977) and their families (Hudson et al., 1987). Several antidepressants have been investigated, including amitriptyline (Bieberman et al., 1985; Moore, 1977; Needleman & Waber, 1977), clomipramine (Lacey & Crisp, 1980), and lithium (Gross et al., 1981). None of these medications appears to improve mood significantly compared with the effects of placebos. Some partial effects were noted for weight gain, improved attitude, and weight maintenance following discharge, but these benefits were relatively minor. Thus, the advantages of using antidepressants in anorexics remains unknown but worthy of further study. Although antidepressants do not appear to be indicated as a routine part of weight restoration programs, they should be tried when an affective disorder is present.

Initial reports on cyproheptadine, a drug that is thought to act on the serotonergic and histaminergic systems (Stone, Wenger, Ludden, Stavorski, & Ross, 1961), indicated that it may have beneficial effects on weight gain, mood, and attitude in some patients (Goldberg, Halmi, Eckert, Casper, & Davis, 1979; Halmi, Eckert, & Falk, 1982). Reanalysis of cyproheptadine data in comparison to trials of amitriptyline or placebo found cyprohep-

TABLE 21.2. Controlled Medication Trials for Patients with Anorexia Nervosa[a]

Investigator	Number of patients	Medication and dosage	Time (weeks)	Weight gain[b]	Drug vs. Placebo Anorexic attitude[b]	Mood[b]	Comment
Moldofsky, Jeuniewic, & Garfinkel, 1977	5	Metoclopramide 30 mg	2	—	—	—	Decreased dyspepsia in 2 of 5 patients
Vigersky & Loriaux, 1977	24	Cyproheptadine 12 mg	8	NS	—	—	Outpatient study
Goldberg et al., 1979	105	Cyproheptadine 32 mg	7	D > P subgroup	Some improvement	Less hostile	Greater weight gain in more ill patients; drug improved eating and body image attitude
Halmi et al., 1986	72	Cyproheptadine 32 mg vs. amitriptyline 160 mg	Target weight	D > P NS	— —	D > P NS	Cyproheptadine better than placebo and amitriptyline in restructures; amitriptyline possibly better in bulimics
Bieberman et al., 1985	25	Amitriptyline 175 mg	5	NS	NS	NS	
Lacey and Crisp, 1980	16	Clomipramine 50 mg	10	NS	Appetite improved	NS	Drug group had increased appetite early
Gross et al., 1981	16	Lithium blood levels 1.0 meq/L	4	D > P	NS	NS	Drug group gained more weight last half of trial
Vandereycken & Peirloot, 1982	18	Pimozide 6 mg	6	NS	Slight improvement	—	D > P (p = .067) for weight gain; drug improved treatment attitude
Gross et al., 1983	11	THC 30 mg vs. diazepam 15 mg	4	NS	NS	NS	Severe dysphoria in 3 of 11 on THC
Vandereycken, 1984	18	Sulpiride 400 mg	6	NS	NS	NS	

[a]All studies were placebo-controlled, double-blind. The studies using metoclopramide, pimozide, tetrahydrocannobinol, (THC), and sulpiride employed a crossover design. The others employed a parallel design.

[b]Improvement in comparison with control group. NS = not significant; NT = not tested; D = active drug treatment; P = placebo; — = data not available.

tadine to improve weight gain significantly in restrictor anorexics, while amitriptyline was more effective in improving mood in anorexics with bulimic behavior (Halmi, Eckert, LaDu, & Cohen, 1986). This is intriguing because we reported that bulimic anorexics have reduced central serotonin compared to restrictor anorexics (Kaye et al., 1984a). These data suggest that subgroups of anorexics may respond differently to medication and may present new opportunities for selective drug treatment. Cyproheptadine appears to be modestly helpful in the restrictor subgroup of anorexics. It appears that tricyclic antidepressants should be used in the bulimic anorexics when medication is needed.

Two drugs, tetrahydrocannabinol (THC) and clonidine, were tested because of anecdotal reports of appetite stimulation. THC was not useful and, in fact, may have been detrimental, as it increased dysphoria in some patients (Gross et al., 1983). Clonidine was also found to have no therapeutic effect on increasing weight restoration, when compared to placebo (Casper, Schlemmer, & Javaid, 1987), even with doses that effected hemodynamic parameters.

CASE ILLUSTRATION

Lori is a 23-year-old single, white woman employed as a sales clerk for a retail store. Her weight at evaluation was 117 pounds, with a high weight in the past of 160 pounds and a low weight of 110 pounds. Her height was 5'4". She recounted always having had a "problem" with weight. At age 13 years, she went on a restrictive diet for 3 weeks and lost 10 pounds, but subsequently she gained all of the weight back.

Lori read about purging techniques (for example, vomiting, laxatives) in popular magazines, but her first personal experience with vomiting occurred at age 18 years. Following a large Mexican meal, she developed an upset stomach and subsequently vomited. Vomiting alleviated her feeling of fullness, decreased her dread of putting on weight, and introduced her to a practice that would allow her to eat as much as she wanted without gaining weight.

At first, the practice of purging was uncomfortable, but within several months, it became a way of life. Food became her "friend," a way to quell anger and reduce depression and anxiety. Prior to binge-eating, she felt lonely, empty, and

depressed, and her thoughts of failure shifted to food. Ambivalence about binge-eating produced a heightened state of anxiety. The decision to binge decreased her anxiety. During the binge, she escaped from her world of immediate cares to a dulled, inner-directed state. As the binge progressed, she experienced feelings of fullness, fatness, and loss of control. Tension built and then fell precipitously following the purge. What originally had been a "friend" became, over time, an uncontrollable habit. Consuming a loaf of bread, a half gallon of ice cream, a plate of spaghetti, and a bowl of cereal several times a day was expensive, time-consuming, and isolating, and it often took priority over socializing with friends or going to work. In addition, she had difficulty controlling her alcohol intake, and she reported frequent periods of drunkenness.

Lori had a very troubled childhood. On the surface, her parents were successful and respected in the community. However, her mother was an alcoholic who had frequent episodes of depression and was often unavailable emotionally for the patient. Her father's behavior was unpredictable, ranging from extreme passivity to displays of frightening rage. The patient was frequently in the middle of family disputes and felt responsible for maintaining peace between her parents. Her parents had high expectations of Lori and never seemed satisfied with her accomplishments.

On mental status examination, Lori was attractive, extroverted, and friendly. She described chronic feelings of depression accompanied by intermittent periods of disrupted sleep, crying spells, and suicidal thoughts. Her affect was bright and appeared incongruent with her stated depressed mood. She spoke of guilt and shame concerning the binge-eating and vomiting. She had difficulty verbalizing emotion and would often state that everything was "fine." Physical examination and pertinent laboratory data revealed no physical cause for her vomiting.

Lori reported that at the age of 21 years, she first decided that she wanted to stop bingeing and vomiting. She would typically be able to abstain, with great effort, for a couple of days, but when even a minor stressor would arise, she would resume her binge–purge behavior at the same rate or worse than before. She also began lying to friends and family about her eating and began stealing food and borrowing regularly from friends and family to buy food. Over the next few years, this pattern of trying to stop and being unsuccessful led her to becoming quite depressed; after a period of heavy bingeing and feeling suicidal, she confided to a friend about her problem and was seen by an emergency room psychiatrist. She was referred to a private therapist, whom she saw weekly and initially was able to decrease her bingeing.

When unable to stop bingeing, she began feeling guilty and lied to the therapist, telling the therapist she had stopped, in order not to disappoint her. As a result of her increasing guilt and frustration, she eventually was unable to continue with this therapist and left that treatment precipitously. She tried other treatments, which included an overeaters' support group, and a behavioral day treatment program, both of which she felt had helped her to stop her bingeing initially. In all situations, this was only with a great deal of effort, which she could keep going for up to a couple of weeks at a time, but she always resumed bingeing and would subsequently feel guilty and stop the treatment.

On initial evaluation at our program, in addition to a routine psychiatric and physical examination, she was asked to keep a diary to evaluate the number of binges weekly and also a Hamilton Rating Scale for Depression (HRSD) to assess the extent of depression. She was bingeing 1–3 times a day and had an HRSD score of 23. Several parallel therapeutic approaches were employed. She was entered into a structured cognitive-behavioral program that focused on methods to control binge-eating and to learn better methods of solving problems. She was started on desipramine, 50 mg/day, which was increased to 150 mg/day over the next 2 weeks. She reported feeling generally hopeful and was bingeing less, but only with a lot of effort. A tricyclic antidepressant (TCA) level was obtained, which was 98 ng/ml, and her dose was increased up to 250 mg/day, which gave her a level of 198 ng/ml. Over the next 2 weeks, she decreased her binge frequency to 1–2 binges a week, and she felt more hopeful that she could have more control over her eating. She also felt less depressed, as her HRSD score decreased to less than 10. At this point, she was able to recognize certain stressors that precipitated the urge to binge and was referred to a psychotherapist.

At 1-year follow-up, Lori was bingeing one to two times a month and felt less depressed and more in control of her life. A trial termination of the desipramine led to an increase in bingeing, which she could not tolerate. The desipramine

was reinstituted, with good results. Her weight at 1 year was 122 pounds. She felt this was too high, but she tolerated her mild discomfort, as she was afraid she would binge more frequently if she tried to lose weight.

ALTERNATIVE TREATMENT OPTIONS

Bulimia Nervosa

Studies of Treatment Options

Currently, there have been 12 controlled studies on pharamacological treatment of bulimic symptoms. All were double-blind, and the two anticonvulsant studies included crossover designs. Patient selection was careful in general and had usually excluded medical illness and other psychiatric illness, including major affective disorder, although the latter often could not be adequately excluded.

Several problems are shared by almost all of the studies. All studies, except that by Wermuth et al. (1977), failed to provide adequate long-term follow-up data. In an uncontrolled treatment trial (Pope, Hudson, Jonas, & Yurgelun-Todd, 1985), good results were found for both binge frequency and mood in 18 of 20 subjects. However, as this was an uncontrolled setting, these results are promising but only preliminary. Reference to the literature on psychological treatment of bulimia and our own clinical experience reveal that there is at least a 20–30% recidivism rate one year following the completion of a treatment program.

Another weakness found in all the aforementioned studies is the use of self-report of bulimic behavior as solid (veridical) outcome data. Clinically, these patients often lie or distort their behavior in order to please persons in authority while engaging in surreptitious eating and purging. Until independent outcome measures can be developed that do not rely on self-report, the entire treatment literature must be regarded as overly optimistic.

Inasmuch as bulimia is a heterogeneous disorder and may have several etiologies, improved diagnostic instruments may make it possible to match pharmacological treatment more closely to distinct classes of patients. For example, antidepressants should be of greater benefit to patients with associated depression. However, even in nondepressed subjects, these agents are as effective in reducing bingeing as in depressed subjects. Clearly, the relationship between antidepressants' antibulimic effects and their mood-elevating effects, as well as the correlation between mood changes and decreased binge frequency, needs further investigation.

The issue as to why those subjects who have EEG abnormalities do not necessarily respond better to anticonvulsants, as compared to those with normal EEGs, also needs to be clarified.

Finally, the effect of medications in treatment settings that employ a variety of nonpharmacological approaches should be assessed. Recently, two investigators studied the interaction between pharmacotherapy and psychotherapy (Anderson & Lindgren, 1984; Sommer & Ravaris, 1984), and both reported that the addition of antidepressants was helpful. Other reports, however, have suggested no benefit from the addition of antidepressants (Mitchell, personal communication).

Despite the shortcomings of the current state of the art, the preliminary results with antidepressants and, to a less extent, with anticonvulsants are quite encouraging, and research in this area should move rapidly.

Treatment Approaches

At present, it appears that antidepressant pharmacotherapy is effective in bulimic patients. Two points should be emphasized. First, bulimic patients need not be depressed to be candidates for trial of an antidepressant. Second, only a minority of patients completely cease bingeing and purging when placed on antidepressants. Many patients have a reduction in the frequency of bingeing and purging, but they still continue to engage in this behavior.

Patients should be started first on a TCA, such as desipramine or imipramine, tailoring the side-effect profile of the specific antidepressant to the patient's clinical response. Dosage levels should be increased within the standard range used in the treatment of major affective disorder until either an effect is achieved or an adequate blood level has been maintained for several weeks. Because of the medical complications of the illness, laboratory assessments, including electrolyte and creatinine measures measurement, as well as a cardiogram

and cardiac rhythm strip, should be obtained prior to initiation of treatment.

MAOIs such as phenelzine and tranylcypromine may be employed. However, because of their frequent side effects and the need for a tyramine-free diet, they should be reserved for treatment-resistant cases. Moreover, it should be cautioned that very impulsive patients should be excluded or should have therapy initiated only in the hospital. Agents such as fluoxetine, trazodone, or lithium might be reserved for patients either who are nonresponsive or who develop unacceptable side effects on other agents. Using this scheme, the clinician might expect a good result in up to one third of patients.

Anorexia Nervosa

The period of weight maintenance after recovery of weight has not been a particular focus of drug treatment in anorexia nervosa. Only 50–70% of anorexics are able to maintain a relatively normal weight after restoration of weight. The more severely ill patients may be able to gain weight in an inpatient treatment unit, but they rapidly lose weight after discharge. There are few systematic studies to assess whether medications improve mood and attitude or stabilize weight in the long term. These severely ill patients are problematic candidates for drug studies because of medical complications and limited cooperation. They are, however, the group that probably has the majority of the morbidity and mortality associated with anorexia nervosa, and a more aggressive and innovative pharmacological approach is warranted in these chronically ill patients.

Much remains to be learned. In contrast to some other major psychiatric illnesses, current pharmacological treatment options have limited benefit in patients with anorexia nervosa. However, we suspect that this will soon change for several reasons. First, we are beginning to recognize distinctions among subgroups of anorexics (for example, bulimics versus restrictor, or good- versus bad-prognosis patients) and it appears that some groups respond differently to different medication, allowing the hope for more selective treatments with better results. Second, much progress has been made in understanding which neuroendocrine and neurotransmitter systems are disturbed in anorexia nervosa. Recent data suggest that there may be trait-related alterations in serotonin (Kaye et al., 1984a) and norepinephrine (Kaye, Ebert, Raleigh, & Lake, 1984b) pathways in anorexia nervosa, two systems implicated in regulation of appetite, weight, and mood. These research findings lead to cautious optimism that we are on the edge of a new era in understanding and treating this disease.

SUMMARY

Increased research focusing on the eating disorders has put the clinician on firmer ground when choosing appropriate psychopharmacological treatments. Recent studies of patients with bulimia demonstrate that treatment with antidepressant medications may substantially reduce symptoms of bingeing and vomiting. The efficacy of pharmacological approaches to anorexia nervosa is more uncertain, in part because of the limited availability of long-term follow-up studies.

REFERENCES

Agras, W. S., Dorian, B., Kirkley, B. G., Arnow, B., & Bachman, J. (1987). Imipramine in the treatment of bulimia: A double-blind controlled study. *International Journal of Eating Disorders, 6*, 29–38.

American Psychiatric Association (1987). Diagnostic and statistical manual (3rd ed., Rev.). Washington, DC.

Anderson, R. B., & Lindgren, C. A. (1984, April 7). *The use of monoamine oxidase inhibitors as an adjunct to psychoanalytic therapy in the treatment of anorexia nervosa and bulimia*. Presented at the First International Conference on Eating Disorders, New York.

Barry, V. C., & Klawans, H. L. (1976). On the role of dopamine in the pathophysiology of anorexia nervosa. *Journal of Neural Transmission, 38*, 107–122.

Bieberman, J., Herzog, D. B., Rivinus, T. M., Harper, G. P., Ferber, R. A., Rosenbaum, J. F., Harmatz, J. S., Tondorf, R., Orsulak, P. J., & Schildkraut, J. J. (1985). Amitriptyline in the treatment of anorexia nervosa: A double-blind, placebo-controlled study. *Journal of Clinical Psychopharmacology, 5*, 10–16.

Bloskind-Lodahl, M., & White, W. C. (1978). The definition and treatment of bulimarexia in college women—A pilot study. *Journal of the American College Health Association, 27*, 84–97.

Brewerton, T. D., Goerge, D. T., & Jimerson, D. C. (1986a, May). *Neuroendocrine response to L-tryptophan in bulimia*. Presented at the 139th Annual Meeting of the American Psychiatric Association, Washington, DC.

Brewerton, T. D., Mueller, E., George, D. T., Brandt, H., Lesem, M., Narang, P., Jimerson, D. C., & Murphy, D. L. (1986b). *Blunted prolactin response to the serotonin agonist M-chlorophenylpiperazine (m-CPP) in bulimia*. Presented at the Colloquium Internationale Neuro-Psychopharmacologicium, Puerto Rico, December.

Brewerton, T. D., Mueller, E. A., George, D. T., Murphy, D. L., & Jimerson, D. C. (1986c, May). *Serotonin, bulimia and migraine: Results with M-CPP [NR22]a*. Presented at the 139th Annual Meeting of the American Psychiatric Association, Washington, DC.

Brotman, A. W., Herzog, D. B., & Hamburg, P. (1988). Long-term course in 14 bulimic patients treated with psychotherapy. *Journal of Clinical Psychiatry, 49*, 157–160.

Brotman, A. W., Herzog, D. B., & Woods, S. W. (1984). Antidepressant treatment of bulimia: The relationship between bingeing and depressive symptomatology. *Journal of Clinical Psychiatry, 45*, 7–9.

Buckholtz, N. S., George, D. T., Davies, A. O., Jimerson, D. C., & Potter, W. Z. (1988). Lymphocyte beta adrenergic receptor modification in bulimia. *Archives of General Psychiatry, 45*, 479–482.

Bulik, C. M. (1987). Drug and alcohol abuse by bulimic women and their families. *American Journal of Psychiatry, 144*, 1604–1606.

Cantwell, D. P., Sturzenberger, S., Burroughs, J., Salkin, B., & Green, J. K. (1977). Anorexia nervosa: An affective disorder? *Archives of General Psychiatry, 34*, 1087–1093.

Casper, R. C., Schlemmer, R. F., & Javaid, J. I. (1987). A placebo-controlled, crossover study of oral clonidine in acute anorexia nervosa. *Psychiatry Research, 20*, 249–260.

Charney, D. S., Heninger, G. R., & Breier, A. (1984). Noradrenergic function in panic anxiety: Effects of yohimbine in healthy subjects and patients with agoraphobia and panic disorder. *Archives of General Psychiatry, 41*, 751–763.

Coppen, A., & Wood, K. (1982). 5-Hydroxytryptamine in the pathogenesis of affective disorders. In J. C. Schoolar, B. T. Ho, & E. Usdin, E. (Eds.), *Serotonin in biological psychiatry* (pp. 249–258). New York: Raven Press.

Crisp, A. H., Fenton, G. W., & Scotton, L. (1968). A controlled study of the EEG in anorexia nervosa. *British Journal of Psychiatry, 114,* 1149–1160.

Dally, P. J., & Sargent, W. (1960). A new treatment of anorexia nervosa. *British Medical Journal, 1,* 1770–1773.

Eadie, M. J., & Tyrer, J. H. (Eds.) (1985). *The biochemistry of migraine.* Lancaster: MTP Press.

Fairburn, C. G., & Cooper, P. J. (1982). Self-induced vomiting and bulimia nervosa: An undetected problem. *British Medical Journal, 284,* 1153–1155.

Ferguson, J. M. (1986). Fluoxetine-induced weight loss in overweight nondepressed subjects. *American Journal of Psychiatry, 143,* 1496.

Ferguson, J. M. (1987). Treatment of an anorexic nervosa patient with fluoxetine. *American Journal of Psychiatry, 144,* 1239.

Fernstrom, J. D., & Wurtman, R. J. (1971). Brain serotonin content: Increase following ingestion of carbohydrate diet. *Science, 174,* 1023–1025.

Fernstrom, J. D., & Wurtman, R. J. (1972). Brain serotonin content: Physiological regulation by plasma neutral amino acids. *Science, 178,* 414–416.

Freeman, C. P., Morris, J. E., Cheshire, K. E., Casper, R. C., & Davis, J. M. (1988, April 22). *A double-blind controlled trial of fluoxetine vs. placebo for bulimia nervosa.* Presented at the Second International Conference of Eating Disorders. New York.

Garfinkel, P. E., & Garner, D. M. (1982). *Anorexia nervosa: A multidimensional perspective.* New York: Brunner/Mazel.

George, D. T., Kaye, W. H., Goldstein, D. S., & Jimerson, D. C. (1988). *Comparison of cardiovascular and behavioral responses to isoproterenol in bulimic patients and healthy controls.* Manuscript submitted for publication.

Gerner, R. H., Cohen, D. J., Fairbanks, L., Anderson, G. M., Young, J. G., Scheinin, M., Linnoila, M., Shaywitz, B. A., & Hare, T. A. (1984). CSF neurochemistry of women with anorexia nervosa and normal women. *American Journal of Psychiatry, 141,* 1441–1444.

Gillberg, C. (1983). Low dopamine and serotonin levels in anorexia nervosa (letter). *American Journal of Psychiatry, 140,* 948–949.

Goldberg, S. C., Halmi, K. A., Eckert, E. D., Casper, R. C., & Davis, J. M. (1979). Cyproheptadine in anorexia nervosa. *British Journal of Psychiatry, 134,* 67–70.

Goodwin, G. M., Fairburn, C. G., & Cowen, P. J. (1987). Dieting changes serotonergic function in women,
not men: Implications for the aetiology of anorexia nervosa? *Psychological Medicine, 17,* 839–842.

Green, R. S., & Rau, J. H. (1974). Treatment of compulsive eating disturbances with anticonvulsant medication. *American Journal of Psychiatry, 131,* 428–432.

Green, R. S., & Rau, J. H. (1977). The use of diphenylhydantoin in compulsive eating disorders: Further studies. In R. A. Vigersky (Ed.), *Anorexia nervosa* (pp. 377–385). New York: Raven Press.

Gross, H. A., Ebert, M. H., Faden, V. B., Goldberg, S. C., Kaye, W. H., Caine, E. D., Hawks, R., & Zinberg, N. (1983). A double-blind trial of delta-9-tetrahydrocannabinol in primary anorexia nervosa. *Journal of Clinical Psychopharmacology, 3,* 165–171.

Gross, H. A., Ebert, M. H., Faden, V. B., Goldberg, S. C., Nee, L. E., & Kaye, W. H. (1981). A double-blind, controlled trial of lithium carbonate in primary anorexia nervosa. *Journal of Clinical Psychopharmacology, 1,* 376–381.

Gwirtsman, H. E., Roy-Byrne, P., Yager, J., & Gerner, R. H. (1983). Neuroendocrine abnormalities in bulimia. *American Journal of Psychiatry, 140,* 559–563.

Hafner, R. J., Crisp, A. H., & McNeilly, A. S. (1976). Prolactin and gonadotrophin activity in females with anorexia nervosa. *Postgraduate Medical Journal, 52,* 76–79.

Hall, A. (1975). Treatment of anorexia nervosa. *New Zealand Medical Journal, 82,* 10–13.

Halmi, K. A., Eckert, E., & Falk, J. R. (1982). Cyproheptadine for anorexia nervosa. *Lancet, 1,* 1357–1358.

Halmi, K. A., Eckert, E. D., LaDu, T. J., & Cohen, J. (1986). Anorexia nervosa: Treatment efficacy of cyproheptadine and amitriptyline. *Archives of General Psychiatry, 43,* 177–181.

Halmi, K. A., Falk, J. R., & Schwartz, E. (1981). Binge-eating and vomiting: A survey of a college population. *Psychological Medicine, 11,* 697–706.

Hatsukami, D., Owen, P., Pyle, R., & Mitchell, J. (1982). Similarities and differences on the MMPI between women with bulimia and women with alcohol and drug abuse problems. *Addictive Behaviors, 7,* 435–439.

Hsu, L. K. G. (1980) Outcome of anorexia nervosa: A review of the literature (1954–1978). *Archives of General Psychiatry, 37,* 1041–1046.

Hsu, L. K. G. (1984). Treatment of bulimia with lithium. *American Journal of Psychiatry, 141,* 1260–1262.

Hudson, J. I., Pope, H. G., & Jonas, J. M. (1984). Treatment of bulimia with antidepressants: Theoretical considerations and clinical findings. In A. J.

Stunkard & E. Stellar (Eds.), *Eating and its disorders* (pp. 259–273). New York: Raven Press.

Hudson, J. I., Pope H. G., Jonas, J. M., Yurgelun-Todd, D., & Frankenburg, F. R. (1987). A controlled family history study of bulimia. *Psychological Medicine, 17*, 883–890.

Hughes, P. L., Wells, L. A., Cunningham, C. J., & Ilstrupp, D. M. (1986). Treating bulimia with desipramine: A double-blind placebo-controlled study. *Archives of General Psychiatry, 43*, 182–186.

Johanson, A. J., & Knorr, N. J. (1977). L-Dopa as treatment for anorexia nervosa. In R. A. Vigersky (Ed.), *Anorexia nervosa* (pp. 363–372). New York: Raven Press.

Johnson, C., & Larson, R. (1982). Bulimia: An anlysis of moods and behavior. *Psychosomatic Medicine, 44*, 341–351.

Johnson, C., Stuckey, M. K., Lewis, L. D., & Schwartz, D. M. (1982). Bulimia: A descriptive study survey on 316 cases. *International Journal of Eating Disorders, 2*, 3–16.

Jonas, J. M., & Gold, M. S. (1986). Naltrexone reverses bulimic symptoms. *Lancet, 1*, 807.

Kaplan, A. S., Garfinkel, P. E., Darby, P. L., & Garner, D. M. (1983). Carbamezepine in the treatment of bulimia. *American Journal of Psychiatry, 140*, 1225–1226.

Kaye, W. H., Ebert, M. H., Gwirtsman, H. E., & Weiss, S. R. (1984a). Differences in brain serotonergic metabolism between nonbulimic and bulimic patients with anorexia nervosa. *American Journal of Psychiatry, 141*, 1598–1601.

Kaye, W. H., Ebert, M. H., Raleigh, M., & Lake, C. R. (1984b). Abnormalities in CNS monoamine metabolism in anorexia nervosa. *Archives of General Psychiatry, 41*, 350–355.

Kaye, W. H., Gwirtsman, H. E., Brewerton, T. D., & George, D. T. (1988a). Bingeing behavior and plasma amino acids: A possible involvement of brain serotonin in bulimia nervosa. *Psychiatry Research, 23*, 31–43.

Kaye, W. H., Gwirtsman, H. E., George, D. T., Jimerson, D. C., & Ebert, M. H. (1988b). CSF 5-HIAA concentrations in anorexia nervosa: Reduced values in underweight subjects normalize after weight gain. *Biological Psychiatry, 23*, 102–105.

Kaye, W. H., Gwirtsman, H. E., George, D. T., Jimerson, D. C., Ebert, M. H., & Lake, C. R. (1986, May). *Disturbances in noraderenergic systems in normal weight bulimia: Sympathetic activation with bingeing, reduced noradrenergic activity after a month of*

abstinence from bingeing. Presented at the 139th Annual Meeting of the American Psychiatric Assocation, Washington, DC.

Kaye, W. H., Gwirtsman, H. E., Jimerson, D. C., George, D. T., Karoum, F., & Ebert, M. H. (1987, June). *Catecholamine function in anorexia nervosa at low weight and after weight restoration.* Presented at the 6th International Catecholamine Symposium, Jerusalem, Israel.

Kaye, W. H., Jimerson, D. C., Lake, C. R., & Ebert, M. (1985). Altered norepinephrine metabolism following long-term weight recovery in patients with anorexia nervosa. *Psychiatry Reserach, 14*, 333–342.

Kennedy, S., Piran, N., & Garfinkel, P. E. (1986). Isocarboxazid in the treatment of bulimia. *American Journal of Psychiatry, 143*, 1495–1496.

Lacey, J. H. (1983). Bulimia nervosa, binge eating, and psychogenic vomiting: A controlled treatment study and long term outcome. *British Medical Journal, 286*, 1609–1613.

Lacey, J. H., & Crisp, A. H. (1980). Hunger, food intake, and weight: The impact of clomipramine on a refeeding anorexia nervosa population. *Postgraduate Medical Journal, 56*, 79–85.

Landsberg, L., & Young, J. B. (1978). Fasting, feeding, and the regulation of the sympathetic nervous system. *New England Journal of Medicine, 298*, 1295–1301.

Leibowitz, S. F., & Shor-Posner, G. (1986). Brain serotonin and eating behavior. *Appetite, 7*, 1–14.

Lofstrom, A. (1977). Catecholamine turnover alterations in discrete areas of the median eminence of the 4- and 5-day cyclic rat. *Brain Research, 120*, 113–131.

Mawson, A. R. (1974). Anorexia nervosa and the regulation of intake: A review. *Psychological Medicine, 4*, 289–308.

McCaleb, M. L., Myers, R. D., Singer, G., & Willis, G. (1979). Hypothalamic norepinephrine in the rat during feeding and push–pull perfusion with glucose, 2–DG, or insulin, *American Journal of Physiology, 236*, R312–R321.

McCann, S. M. (1970). Neurohormonal correlates of ovulation. *Federation Proceedings, 29*, 1888–1894.

Mitchell, J. E., & Groat, R., (1984). A placebo-controlled double-blind trial of amitriptyline in bulimia. *Journal of Clinical Psychopharmacology, 4*, 186–193.

Mitchell, J. E., Hatsukami, D., Eckert, E. D., & Pyle, R. L. (1985). Characteristics of 275 patients with bulimia. *American Journal of Psychiatry, 142*, 482–485.

Mitchell, J. E., Laine, D. E., Morley, J. E., & Levine, A. S. (1986). Naloxone but not CCK-8 may attenuate binge-eating behavior in patients with bulimia syndrome. *Biological Psychiatry, 21,* 1399–1406.

Moldofsky, H., Jeuniewic, N., & Garfinkel, P. J. (1977). Preliminary report of metoclopramide in anorexia nervosa. In R. A. Vigersky (Ed.), *Anorexia nervosa* (pp. 373–375). New York: Raven Press.

Moore, D. C. (1977). Amitriptyline therapy in anorexia nervosa. *American Journal of Psychiatry, 134,* 1303–1304.

Moore, R., Mills, I. H., & Forster, A. (1981). Naloxone in the treatment of anorexia nervosa: Effect on weight gain and lipolysis. *Journal of the Royal Society of Medicine, 74,* 129–131.

Morley, J. E., & Blundell, J. E. (1988). The neurobiological basis of eating disorders: Some formulations. *Biological Psychiatry, 23,* 53–78.

Murphy, D. L., Campell, I., & Costa, J. L. (1978). Current status of the indoleamine hypothesis of affective disorders. In M. A. Lipton, A. DiMascio, & K. F. Killam (Eds.), *Psychopharmacology: A generation of Progress* (pp. 1235–1247). New York: Raven Press.

Needleman, H. L., & Waber, D. (1977). The use of amitriptyline in anorexia nervosa. In R. A. Vigersky (Ed.), *Anorexia nervosa* (pp. 357–362). New York: Raven Press.

Newman, M. M., & Halmi, K. A. (1988). The endocrinology of anorexia nervosa and bulimia nervosa. *Endocrinology and Metabolism Clinics of North America. 17* (1), 195–212.

Ong, Y. L., Checkley, S. A., & Russell, G. F. M. (1983). Suppression of bulimic symptoms with methylamphetamine. *British Journal of Psychiatry, 143,* 288–293.

Piran, N., Ennis, J., Swinson, R., Garfinkel, P., Barnes, R., Brouilette, C., Whynot, C., & Antony, M. (1988, April 22). *The incidence of eating disorders in borderline and anxiety disorder patients—A controlled investigation of the association between eating disorders and borderline personality disorders.* Presented at the Second International Eating Disorder Conference, New York.

Pirke, K. M., & Spyra, B. (1982). Catecholamine turnover in the brain and the regulation of luteinizing hormone and corticosterone in starved male rats. *Acta Endocrinologica, 100,* 168–176.

Pirke, K. M., Pahl, J., Schweiger, U., & Warnhoff, M. (1985). Metabolic and endocrine indices of starvation in bulimia: A comparison with anorexia nervosa. *Psychiatry Research, 15,* 33–39.

Ploog, D. W., & Pirke, K. M. (1987). Psychobiology of anorexia nervosa. *Psychological Medicine, 17,* 843–859.

Pope, H. G., Frankenburg, F. R., Hudson, J. I., Jonas, J. M., & Yurgelun-Todd, D. (1987). Is bulimia associated with borderline personality disorder? A controlled study. *Journal of Clinical Psychiatry, 48,* 181–184.

Pope, H. G., Hudson, J. I., Jonas, J. M., & Yurgelun-Todd, D. (1983). Bulimia treated with imipramine: A placebo-controlled, double-blind study. *American Journal of Psychiatry, 140,* 554–558.

Pope, H. G., Hudson, J. I., Jonas, J. M., & Yurgelun-Todd, D. (1985). Antidepressant treatment of bulimia: A two-year follow-up study. *Journal of Clinical Psychopharmacology, 5,* 320–327.

Pope, H. G., Keck, P. E., McElroy, S. L., & Hudson, J. I. (1988, April 22). *Treatment of bulimia nervosa with trazodone: A placebo-controlled, double-blind study.* Presented at the Second International Eating Disorders Conference, New York.

Potter, W. Z., Muscettola, G., & Goodwin, F. K. (1983). Sources of variance in clinical studies of MHPG. In J. W. Maas (Ed.), *MHPG: Basic mechanisms and psychopathology* (pp. 145–165). New York: Academic.

Rau, J. H., & Green, R. S. (1975). Compulsive eating: A neuropsychologic approach to certain eating disorders. *Comprehensive Psychiatry, 16,* 223–231.

Rau, J. H., Struve, F. A., & Green, R. S. (1979). Electroencephalographic correlates of compulsive eating. *Clinical Electroencephalography, 10,* 180–189.

Redmond, D. E., & Huang, Y. H. (1979). Current concepts: II. New evidence for the locus coeruleus–norepinephrine connection with anxiety. *Life Sciences, 25,* 2149–2162.

Redmond, D. E., Swann, A., & Heninger, G. R. (1976). Phenoxybenzamine in anorexia nervosa. *Lancet, 2,* 397.

Rivinus, T. M., Bieberman, J., Herzog, D. B., Kemper, K., Harper, G. P., Harmatz, J. S., & Houseworth, S. (1984). Anorexia nervosa and affective disorder: A controlled family history study. *American Journal of Psychiatry, 141,* 1414–1418.

Robinson, P. H., Checkley, S. A., & Russell, G. F. M. (1985). Suppression of eating by fenfluramine with bulimia nervosa. *British Journal of Psychiatry, 146,* 169–176.

Roy-Byrne, P., Gwirtsman, H. E., Edelstein, C. K., Yager, J., & Gerner, R. H. (1983). Response to "The psychiatrist as mind sweeper": Eating disorders and antidepressants. *Journal of Clinical Psychopharmacology, 3,* 60–61.

Sabine, E. J., Yonace, A., Farrington, A. J., Barratt, K. H., & Wakeling, A. (1983). Bulimia nervosa: A placebo-controlled double-blind therapeutic trial of mianserin. *British Journal of Clinical Pharmacology, 15,* 195s–202s.

Sawyer, C. H., Hilliard, J., Kanematsu, S., Scaramuzzi, R., & Blake, C. A. (1974). Effects of intraventricular infusions of norepinephrine and dopamine on LH release and ovulation in the rabbit. *Neuroendocrinology, 15,* 328–337.

Schwartz, D. M., & Thompson, M. G. (1981). Do anorectics get well? Current research and future needs. *American Journal of Psychiatry, 138,* 319–323.

Smythe, G. A. (1977). The role of serotonin and dopamine in hypothalamic–pituitary function. *Clinical Endocrinology, 7,* 325–341.

Sommer, F., & Ravaris, C. L. (1984, April 7). *The treatment of eating disorders: Psychotherapy alone vs. psychotherapy combined with antidepressant pharmacotherapy.* Presented at the First International Conference on Eating Disorders. New York.

Stein, G. S., Hartshorn, J., Jones, J., & Steinberg, D. (1982). Lithium in a case of severe anorexia nervosa. *British Journal of Psychiatry, 140,* 526–528.

Stone, C. A., Wenger, H. C., Ludden, C. T., Stavorski, J. M., & Ross, C. A. (1961). Antiserotonin–antihistamine properties of cyproheptadine. *Journal of Pharmacology and Experimental Therapeutics, 131,* 73–81.

Vandereycken, W. (1984). Neuroleptics in the short-term treatment of anorexia nervosa: A double-blind, placebo-controlled study with sulpride. *British Journal of Psychiatry, 144,* 288–292.

Vandereycken, W., & Pierloot, R. (1982). Pimozide combined with behavior therapy in the short-term treatment of anorexia nervosa. *ACTA Psychiatrica Scandinavica, 66,* 445–450.

Vandereycken, W., & Pierloot, R. (1983). Long-term outcome in anorexia nervosa: The problem of patient selection and follow-up duration. *International Journal of Eating Disorders, 2,* 237–242.

Van Praag, H. M. (1980). Central monoamine metabolism in depressions: II. Catecholamines and related compounds. *Comprehensive Psychiatry, 21,* 44–54.

Vigersky, R. A., & Loriaux, D. L. (1977). The effect of cyproheptadine in anorexia nervosa: A double-blind trial. In R. A. Vigersky (Ed.), *Anorexia nervosa,* (pp. 349–356). New York: Raven Press.

Walsh, B. T., Gladis, M., Roose, S. P., Sterwart, J. W., Stetner, F., & Glassman, A. H. (1988). Phenelzine vs. placebo in 50 patients with bulimia. *Archives of General Psychiatry, 45,* 471–475.

Walsh, B. T., Stewart, J. W., Roose, S. P., Gladis, M., & Glassman, A. H. (1984). Treatment of bulimia with phenelzine: A double-blind, placebo-controlled study. *Archives of General Psychiatry, 41,* 1105–1109.

Wermuth, B. M., Davis, K. L., Hollister, L. E., & Stunkard, A. J. (1977). Phenytoin treatment of the binge-eating syndrome. *American Journal of Psychiatry, 134,* 1249–1253.

Wold, P. (1983). Trazodone in the treatment of bulimia. *Journal of Clinical Psychiatry, 44,* 275–276.

Wulliemier, F., Rossel, F., & Sinclair, K. (1975). La therapie comportementale de l'anorexia nerveuse. *Journal of Psychosomatic Research, 19,* 267–272.

Wurtman, J. J., & Wurtman, R. J. (1979). Drugs that enhance central serotonergic transmission diminish elective carbohydrate consumption by rats. *Life Sciences, 24,* 895–903.

Zis, A. P., & Goodwin, F. K. (1982). The amine hypothesis. In E. S. Paykel (Ed.), *Handbook of affective disorders* (pp. 175–190). New York: Guilford.

Editorial Commentary: Anorexia and Bulimia

In recent years, clinical research investigators have focused increased attention on the treatment of anorexia nervosa and bulimia nervosa—two eating disorders exhibited primarily in young women. In addition to the obvious nutritional and psychological aspects of anorexia and bulimia, each of the disorders has very serious dental and medical sequelae, ranging from deteriorated dentition, to hormonal imbalance, to death in anorexia nervosa. Indeed, in anorexia nervosa, the mortality rate at times has been reported to be as high as 20%.

Not only has there been keen scholarly interest in these two recalcitrant eating disorders, but there has been a parallel upsurge of articles in the public media as well, fueled by the death of a famous popular singer from the effects of anorexia and the confession of an equally famous actress that she had suffered from bulimia. As a consequence of such publicity, the demand for treatment has increased (exponentially), and many new treatment programs for eating-disordered persons have appeared on the therapeutic scene. Unfortunately, however, many such programs promise more than they can deliver, given both our current knowledge of the etiology and assessment of anorexia and bulimia and the psychotherapeutic, behavioral, and pharmacological approaches to their remediation and prevention.

We should note that the authors of the three chapters in this section are most modest in their descriptions of what is known about the eating disorders in general and about the efficacy of the extant treatment strategies. Indeed, the fierce and acrimonious competition of proponents of differing theoretical persuasions previously encountered in the eating disorders literature is remarkably absent. Doctrinaire positions *are not* held, and each investigator, representing the different schools of thought, is open to the empirical contributions of the other. Perhaps this tack is taken in light of the enormous psychological and biological complexities of anorexia and bulimia.

In considering the descriptions of anorexia and bulimia, Pyle and Chiodo appear to have similar conceptualizations, albeit their different theoretical perspectives. On the other hand, Weltzin, Gwirtsman, Jimerson, and Kaye focus more on the neurotransmitter disturbances in these eating disorders, with attention directed particularly to norepinephrine and serotonin. Although Weltzin et al. report studies showing abnormalities in hormonal function and neurotransmitters, they are acutely aware that such altered biological functioning may be more a consequence of the disordered eating pattern than an etiologically significant factor in the disorders. Irrespective of whether altered biological functioning is an effect or a cause, its study has important implications for pharmacotherapeutics aimed at reregulation.

In looking at anorexia and bulimia, Pyle, Chiodo, and Weltzin et al. present clear diagnostic delineations between the two disorders, with anorexia often requiring protracted inpatient care, given the high mortality rate. On the other hand, bulimics almost always can be managed on an outpatient basis.

With increased study, both from a diagnostic

and a treatment perspective, it has become clear that anorexia and bulimia are not unitary disorders, but that there are subclasses within each diagnostic entity that respond differentially to treatment. Indeed, in the case of anorexia, two distinct subgroups have been identified: (1) restrictive anorexics who abstain from eating but do not binge, and (2) bulimic anorexics who maintain a very low weight by purging after bingeing.

In spite of commonalities in treating anorexics and bulimics, there are some pronounced differences. Indeed, in the case of anorexia nervosa, the first order of business is to restore the patient's weight to as close to normal (according to population statistics) as possible. In a structured inpatient setting, nutritional strategies, behavioral methods, or in dire cases, forced tube feeding, all have proven to be effective. But weight restoration is only part of the battle. In anorexia nervosa, there are a multitude of concomitant issues, such as perceptions of personal control, family disruption, distorted body image, and affective symptoms. Moreover, relapse prevention is critical, given recidivism rates of 50% or more.

Given the control issues in anorexia, it is not surprising that Pyle underscores the importance of the therapeutic relationship and the sensitivity of the therapist. Treatments showing promise include group and familial approaches, including the one espoused by Minuchin. Most interesting in Pyle's chapter is his emphasis on individual cognitive and cognitive–behavioral therapies to contravene the anorexic's dysfunctional beliefs and erroneous notions concerning body image. Indeed, he is endorsing the use of behavioral strategies as part of the comprehensive assault on the anoretic's manifold psychopathology.

From the behavioral perspective, a number of treatments have been carried out for both anorexia and bulimia, including contingency management, cognitive restructuring, exposure plus response prevention, self-monitoring, and social skills training. Unfortunately, given the absence of comparative studies, the relative efficacy of these strategies is not known. The situation is similar at this time with respect to pharmacological intervention, especially for anorexia nervosa. Although a number of psychotropic drugs appear to be of benefit, they have been tested in isolation in uncontrolled trials (i.e., open trials), very often in combination with some sort of behavior therapy.

In bulimia, the treatment studies are better controlled and a bit more definitive, suggesting that tricyclic antidepressants and monoamine oxidase inhibitors have value in normal-weight bulimics. On the other hand, anticonvulsants and stimulants do not appear to be useful, given the available data.

With all of the treatments for anorexia and bulimia, whether administered individually or in combination, the issue of recidivism has proven to be a major problem. It is undoubtedly for this reason that clinical programs use the shotgun approach, in which a mélange of psychotherapy, cognitive-behavior therapy, group therapy, family therapy, and pharmacotherapy are directed toward clients. At this juncture, the field would benefit most from a careful delineation of which strategies or combinations work best for which subset of eating-disordered patients. Once again, the combined behavioral–pharmacological approach appears to be very much understudied.

PART 8

Borderline Personality Disorder

CHAPTER 22

Psychotherapy

WILLIAM S. POLLACK

CONCEPTUALIZATION OF THE DISORDER

For over half a century, clinicians have been bedeviled by the seemingly chaotic myriad of behaviors and symptoms manifested by patients who more recently have come to be diagnosed as suffering from borderline personality disorder. The current conceptualization of borderline personality disorder (BPD) and its psychotherapeutic treatment have arisen from a long and arduous history of clinical trial and error, empirical investigation, and the increasingly in-depth psychological immersion by psychotherapists into the feeling states of patients in severe distress.

As early as 1930, psychoanalytically oriented clinicians were beginning to draw attention to a group of patients who appeared to be neither neurotic nor psychotic, but who, rather, seemed to fall on a continuum between these two disorders (Glover, 1932; Orberndorf, 1930). Hoch and Polatin (1949) viewed such patients as suffering from "pseudoneurotic schizophrenia." Stern (1938), however, was the first to use the term *borderline* to describe those patients whose clinical presentation included disorders of narcissism, rigid personality, a sense of personal inferiority, hypersensitivity to insult, and a deeply rooted, almost unshakable sense of anxiety. He argued that this "*borderline*" syndrome constituted a distinct, clinical diagnostic entity. By the late 1940s and early 1950s, others had come to agree that borderline patients were indeed a distinct and distinguishable diagnostic group with definitive, even pathognomic clinical symptomalogy (Deutsch, 1942; Wolberg, 1952).

Utilizing the newer psychodynamic theories of *ego psychology*, Knight (1953) argued that borderline patients suffered from severely weakened ego functions manifested in the areas of secondary-process thinking, realistic planning, adaptation to the environment, maintenance of object relations, and internal defenses against primitive aggressive and sexual impulses. More importantly, Knight put forth the seminal idea that the primary source of the observed ego dysfunctions were underlying *developmental failures*. These included problems with what Knight called "constitutional" development, disturbed early object relations, early traumatic events, and severe precipitating stress. It is this central concept of a *developmental delay, dysfunction,* or *deficit*—expressed in the borderline's often severe problems with internal affective tolerance, problematic interpersonal behaviors, and so on—that unifies most modern concepts of borderline disorder and provides a cohesive theme for many of the successful psychotherapeutic treatment strategies.

The author wishes to acknowledge the invaluable editorial assistance of Drs. Arlene Frank, Marsha Padwa, and Robert Waldinger, in reviewing earlier drafts of this manuscript. The author also wishes to thank his colleagues in the Departments of Psychology and Psychiatry at McLean Hospital/Harvard Medical School. Especially, he would like to acknowledge the therapeutic clinical and nursing staffs on Codman House III—and the willingness of his patients to help him to learn, to teach, to give and to take, in a way that has, hopefully, become increasingly therapeutic and useful.

As a harbinger of modern clinical concerns, Knight stressed the difficulty in treating borderline patients in psychotherapy. He called attention to these patients' tendency to regress within the treatment setting itself, apparently becoming worse. Often, within an unmodified transference-oriented psychotherapy, such patients would express overt dependency and emit extreme rageful reactions directed at their therapists, sometimes in conjunction with suicidal threats and self-destructive actions. These behaviors would often frighten clinicians, who were made severely anxious by these indirect and confusing expressions of developmentally early needs for caring, holding, or soothing. In some cases, the greater the therapeutic zeal of the treaters, and the more inclusive the treatment setting, the more severe the regression! Indeed, hospitalization often led to even more regressed and primitive behaviors, which left the treatment staff feeling intensely helpless and angry (Adler, 1985). The evocation of such countertransference reactions has become a definable characteristic of patients with borderline psychopathology. Consequently, Knight argued for practical modifications of classic psychotherapeutic technique. He proposed that a central goal in the treatment of borderline patients should be the strengthening of the ego's control over the overwhelming internal impulses. This approach was popularized by Zetzel (1971).

It was not until the next decade that systematic empirical studies of borderline psychopathology were undertaken. Grinker, Werble, and Drye (1968), in one such study, postulated that what had been defined as the "borderline syndrome" was most reasonably a consequence of a developmental arrest in childhood, leading to later adult deficits of ego functioning. Their findings supported the hypothesis that this so-called borderline syndrome was not merely an affective *state*, but, rather, an enduring personality trait or *disorder*. They also identified statistically distinct subgroups of borderline patients, but they highlighted four characteristics that were shared by all of the patients: (1) anger as the main or only affect; (2) defects in affectional relationships; (3) deficient sense of self-identity; and (4) depressive loneliness.

Gunderson and colleagues (Carpenter, Gunderson, & Strauss, 1977; Gunderson, 1977, 1982, 1984; Gunderson & Kolb, 1978; Gunderson & Singer, 1975) showed empirical distinctions between borderline patients and those suffering from psychotic disorders, and they provided a basis for more reliable and valid diagnosis of borderline patients. Based on this research and clinical experience, Gunderson (1984) argued for a more narrow, empirically based definition of borderline personality disorder.

In contrast to Gunderson, Kernberg (1967, 1975) has argued for a broader definition of the disorder, which he terms *borderline personality organization* (BPO). While agreeing that borderline patients are neither fully neurotic nor fully psychotic, he maintains that there is a core set of unique characteristics that argue for a conceptually separate and diagnostically distinct disorder: (a) a diffuse and unstable sense of identity, and (b) a use of more developmentally primitive internal defensive operations, especially those of splitting and projective identification. He sees these two characteristics as occurring within a generally intact capacity for reality testing. Regression to primary-process thinking is only transient and present under severe psychological pressure; secondary-process thinking returns with appropriate support.

In brief, Kernberg conceptualizes the borderline disorder as a disturbance within the self, particularly in *self* and *object representations* (introjects). He views these inner mental representations as being pathologically intertwined in borderline patients. This is said to occur as a result of a developmental fixation at, or a regression to an early stage of internalized object relations in which conflicting images of self and other are not adequately differentiated or integrated, and the balance among positively and negatively tinged (libidinal and aggressive) affects is not achieved.

Kernberg traces the defects in the borderline patient's ego to a predominance of *pathological aggression* and aggressive drive derivatives, tied either to primary biological predisposition, or developmental reactions to a frustrating environment. Regardless of the ultimate cause, the effect is both an inability to integrate such aggressive wishes, and a need to control them—in order to maintain a reservoir of positive connection with significant others—both in the present real world and in the internal representational world. Such a search for balance leads, in turn, to the regressive and defensive utilization of *splitting*.

According to Kernberg, splitting is used to keep apart "good" and "bad" introjects so that the person can preserve the limited, available good memories of the self and important others. Kernberg thus feels that borderline patients are using an unconscious primitive psychological defense to avoid noticing their own extremely angry feelings toward their early objects—and thereby desperately clinging to a modicum of positive connection with those on whom they are emotionally and physically dependent.

As one might imagine, however, splitting leads to major deficits in self-definition, self-versus-other differentiation, self-cohesion, and self-esteem. Peace is bought at a heavy price! Kernberg argues that the mechanism of splitting sets in motion other primitive defense mechanisms of the ego (e.g., projective identification, denial, idealization), which, in turn, prevent further integration from occurring and give rise to the symptoms so characteristic of borderline patients (Kernberg, 1967, 1975). The amalgam of cognitive, emotional, and clinical dysfunctions that emerges is termed "nonspecific manifestations of ego weakness." They include primitive free-floating anxiety (with lack of anxiety tolerance), lack of impulse control, lack of sublimatory channels, and occasional breakthroughs of primary-process thinking—transient psychosis.

In summary, then, Kernberg conceptualizes BPD as an object relations disorder, with pathology of internalized object relations. This pathology is brought about primarily as a result of excessive aggressive drives in infancy and early childhood—and the need to keep them from contaminating a sense of love toward one's caregiver. Although Kernberg pays lip service to the developmental concepts of Mahler (1971) and the significance of the separation–individuation phase of development, he virtually ignores the real interpersonal and environmental contributions to the etiology of the disorder. His model is primarily a classic conflict–drive theory, in which *conflict* over the binding of an excessive amount of aggression and rage leads to ego or self deficits.

On the other end of the conceptual spectrum are Buie and Adler. They offer a view of BPD that relies heavily on the research of developmental psychology, cognitive structuralism, and psychoanalytic developmental psychology. They integrate the object relations work of Winnicott—his concepts of "good-enough mothering" and the "holding environment" (Winnicott, 1965; see also Modell, 1976)—and Kohut's concept of the *selfobject* (Kohut, 1977). Adler and Buie have identified a core existential state of frightening and painful *aloneness*, which they argue is the sine qua non of borderline psychopathology (Adler, 1985; Adler & Buie, 1979; Buie & Adler, 1982). They propose that such aloneness is the result of a *developmental deficit* in the capacity, during times of distress, to recall in memory a sustaining, holding, or soothing object—the *"holding selfobject."* Because the resulting aloneness panic cannot be assuaged by the self, the affected individual engages in the intrapsychic defenses, interpersonal distancing operations, and the self-destructive activities for which borderline patients are only too well known.

Buie and Adler, unlike Kernberg, attribute this "aloneness deficit" to real deficiencies in the parents' capacity to hold and soothe their child early in life. They maintain that by age 2, individuals who will later suffer from BPD have already undergone disruptions in their caregiving environment—a holding environment. This disruption both impedes their capacity to learn how to use a *transitional object* to soothe themselves at times of distress and interferes with the normal development of *evocative memory*, a capacity to remember the caregiving functions of parental figures in their absence and during times of distress. The inability to achieve a solid form of *evocative memory*, or to utilize it at times of severe distress, leaves these individuals at an immense disadvantage in soothing or calming themselves when, in adulthood, they are most upset or hurt.

In addition, Adler and Buie emphasize the fact that the rage and *hurt* that these patients often display when faced with separations further damage whatever already fragile capacity they have to evoke a positively tinged memory of a supporting object. Consequently, at times of separation, they are left even further bereft and enraged. Intolerable panic and aloneness take hold as their positive connection with a significant other is lost. The reactions to such overwhelming distress include the familiar attempts at either dependent clinging or rageful self-harm.

Variations in the conceptualization of BPD have naturally led to a series of diagnostic approaches, issues, and problems, whose resolution and integration are made all the more salient by the swelling ranks of patients suffering from the disorder.

DIAGNOSTIC ISSUES AND PROBLEMS

Prevalence

Accurate estimates of the prevalence of BPD are somewhat elusive, but there is growing evidence that it may be the most commonly occurring DSM-III personality disorder (Frances, Clarkin, Gilmore, Hurt, & Brown, 1984; Kass, Spitzer, & Williams, 1983; Koenigsberg, Kaplan, Gilmore, & Cooper, 1985). A 1985 report suggests that up to 4% of the general population may suffer from this disorder (Institute of Medicine, 1985). Kroll, using Gunderson's Diagnostic Interview for Borderlines (DIB) in a cross-cultural study (Kroll, Carey, Sines, & Roth, 1982), found a diagnostic prevalence of 15–20% of an inpatient psychiatric population. Although more empirical studies are needed, BPD certainly represents a significant proportion of individuals who seek or are in need of psychological treatment.

It is noteworthy that the disorder appears to be more prevalent among women than among men. The female-to-male ratio ranges from 2:1 to 4:1, depending on the samples used (Gunderson, 1984; Stiver, 1988). Kass and colleagues (1983) have raised the possibility of gender bias in the application of BPD diagnostic criteria. But they do believe that there are genuine gender differences in prevalence of BPD, and a recent study by Bardenstein and McGlashan (1988) highlights some of those differences. Pope and colleagues (1983), however, raise the possibility that the differences are more apparent than real and that similarly disturbed male and female patients are simply labeled differently—as "antisocial" and "borderline," respectively. The same often occurs in outpatient practices, where male and female patients with moderate to severe personality disorders tend to be diagnosed as "narcissistic" and "borderline," respectively.

Morbidity

Although Axis I psychiatric disorders—especially schizophrenia and affective illness—are usually seen by clinicians as more serious than the personality disorders on Axis II, such an impression may be both erroneous and dangerous (Gunderson & Pollack, 1985). In fact, the presence of personality disorders, especially BPD, may represent a serious risk of morbidity.

Even in samples of well-treated patients, the long-term risk of suicide and chronic dysfunction is relatively high. Several longitudinal empirical reports (Carpenter et al., 1977; Gunderson, Carpenter, & Strauss, 1975) have found surprising similarities in the course of borderline and schizophrenic patients. Both groups showed unremitting symptomatology, evidence of sustained recidivism, poor employment functioning, and difficulty in social relations. Pope, Jonas, Hudson, Cohen, and Gunderson (1983) also provided evidence of severe impairments in long-term psychosocial functioning in patients with BPD.

Recent studies have been more optimistic, but they continue to caution clear risk of morbidity. For example, McGlashan (1986) found evidence for positive treatment outcome when borderline patients were followed for several *decades*, into middle age. However, even those patients showed severe, albeit, intermittent symptomatic psychopathology and ongoing urges toward impulsive solutions to pain; and the sample had a completed suicide rate of 3%. Stone, Hurt, and Stone (1987), in another long-term outcome study, also found a basis for some cautious optimism concerning morbidity, given appropriate treatment. Again, however, this is within a context of ongoing severe dysfunction, as well as an overall suicide rate of approximately 9%—with close to 8% of completed suicides occurring before the age of 30.

In sum, available data suggest that if borderline patients can be provided optimal treatment early on, they can make reasonable adjustment and suicidal enactment can be controlled. However, the opposite also appears true: the younger the patient, the less well contained, and less appropriately geared the treatment to the illness, the greater the likelihood for severe dysfunction over time, as well as completed suicide. Such findings argue for careful diagnostic evaluation, and for early intervention with appropriate, well-tested treatment paradigms.

Clinical Presentation

Despite some remaining diagnostic ambiguities, a reasonable consensus has been achieved concerning the diagnostic entity of BPD—first in the DSM-III and now in the DSM-III-R (American Psychiatric Association, 1980, 1987), where BPD is characterized as a "pervasive pattern of instability of self-image, interpersonal relationships, and mood, beginning by early adulthood and present in a variety of contexts" (1987, p. 346). Also noted is the interface between DSM-III-R BPD and other personality disorders on Axis II, as well as with the affective line on Axis I–with substance abuse seen as a possible complication of the illness. For a patient to meet a distinct DMS-III-R diagnosis of BPD, at least *five* of *eight behaviorally manifest* problems must be present, must be characterological in nature, and must lead to functional impairment (vocational/social) and/or an ongoing sense of internal distress (see American Psychiatric Association, 1987, pp. 346–347).

While the DSM-III-R guidelines are useful, I believe that a more complete and accurate picture of the borderline patient is achieved by focusing the diagnostic evaluation on the major psychodynamic aspects of the disorder. These can be dichotomized along two axes: (1) problems in and within the *self*, and (2) problems manifested along the lines of the *self in interaction* with others.

Problems within the Self

1. Noncohesive Sense of Self and an Unstable Identity. A core characteristic of borderline patients, and one of the most striking aspects of their presentation is their developmental difficulty in establishing a cohesive self (Kohut, 1971, 1977) and a stable sense of personal identity. Although such disturbances run deep, they remain difficult to define objectively, especially because patients with other personality disorders (e.g., narcissistic personality), younger patients in late adolescence

or early adulthood, and normal adults in life transitions or crises may sometimes manifest similar disturbances.

Related to this, theorists and clinicians have identified specific disturbances within borderline patients that are related to a fear of *separation* from significant objects. The inability to tolerate feeling or being alone is seen by Adler and Buie (1979) and Adler (1985) as the pathognomonic central core of borderline psythopathology. Masterson (1971) noted a similar vulnerability of borderline patients to "abandonment depression," and Mahler (1971) noted severe separation anxiety. Consequently, such patients may often be socially overactive or compulsively involved with others in order to avoid being alone. These attempts at interpersonal involvement are often frantic and short-lived.

2. Cognitive Disturbances–Transient Psychotic Experiences. Under severe stress, borderline patients often experience episodes of severe dissociation, including, at times, derealization or depersonalization, manifestations of paranoid thinking, and a host of primitive and regressive defenses. Such episodes cannot, however, be considered definitive for the diagnosis of BPD, because many other patients may have such experiences at times. In borderline patients, these experiences are almost always ego dystonic. They are *not* accepted by the patient as a consensual way of seeing the world. They often are accompanied by massive anxiety; and they may be the impetus for such patients seeking treatment.

3. Impulsive Behaviors. Impulsivity may manifest itself diversely, but it is usually linked to the borderline's unstable and noncohesive sense of self. While compulsive gambling, shoplifting, or eating disturbances may occur, the most prevalent form of impulsive activity in borderline patients, especially in young adults, is the abuse of alcohol or other drugs. Sexual promiscuity or deviance, used in an equally addictive manner, is also quite common. Indeed, the severity and prevalence of these impulsive behaviors has fueled the ongoing debate over their etiology. Psychoanalytic clinicians tie them to the underlying unstable, noncohesive self and the need for self-soothing (see Adler & Buie, 1979), while biologically oriented researchers take them as evidence that BPD may be part of a biological affective spectrum of disease (Akiskal, 1981).

4. Labile and Uncomfortable Affect. A striking characteristic of borderline patients, evident in the transferences they form and the countertransferences they evoke in therapy, is the experience of ongoing uncomfortable affects, including anger and a painful sense of emptiness or abandonment. At times, they express their anger in outbursts of extreme rage; at other times, they do so with an ongoing sense of bitterness or with apparently excessive demands on their primary objects. In my opinion, the anger is often a response to either past or present experiences of real hurt, trauma, and disappointment. With empathic probing, therapists often discover a terrifying sense of depression, loneliness, and loss lying behind the rage. They also are apt to uncover a sense of badness that these patients may feel about themselves (Gunderson, 1984; Kernberg, 1967, 1975, 1984).

Problems of the Self in Interaction with Others

1. Unstable and Intense Interpersonal Relationships. No therapist experienced in working with borderline patients can mistake their characteristic pattern of rapidly idealizing and then devaluing those on whom they depend, and their subtle, often nonverbal means of gaining support from significant others, usually through impulsive actions rather than words.

Some (e.g., Pollack, 1986; Stiver, 1985) have questioned the language used to describe the borderline patient's problematic relationships. Words such as "manipulative" often are used in a critical and pejorative manner and reflect a misunderstanding of the patient's needs. Therapists should seek, instead, to understand how such patients' developmental difficulties and present anxieties cause them to crave and seek, over and over again, close, dependent relationships, only to defend against acknowledging any need for them by pushing significant others away at times of stress. Such actions may also be linked to *actual* past *traumatic* experiences, including abuse, incest, and other forms of exploitation suffered at the hands of those on whom patients depended in childhood. (See case illustration, later in this chapter.)

2. Self-destructive Activity. Borderline patients are likely to engage in self-destructive behavior (including suicidal enactment) in a frantic effort to get others to intervene with or respond to them. Grunebaum and Klerman (1967) have delineated a subgroup of patients for whom acts of self-harm are a dynamic expression of inner feelings. Again, some have termed such acts "manipulative," with no appreciation of their function— that is, to engage the response of those around them. However, such self-destructive activity should be neither countertransferentially denied nor minimized because, as noted previously, there is also a *serious risk of completed suicide!* Suicide attempts are often a cause of therapeutic failure, therapist anxiety, and hospitalization of patients with BPD.

In addition to suicidal enactment and gesturing, borderline patients often engage in a wide range of apparently self-mutilating behaviors (e.g., cutting of the body without attempt to suicide, painful mutilation of genitals). These behaviors may be understood as an expression of an attempt at self-soothing, as well as a possible repetition of an earlier trauma (Buie & Adler, 1982).

3. Functional Failures. Although not emphasized in the DSM-III-R, the inability of borderline patients to effectively apply their talents in order to achieve success in the world is an important diagnostic feature. Many such patients show a potential for high achievement that falls by the wayside, often due to the affective overloading of their cognitive skills.

Functional incapacity, especially in vocational and occupational domains, helps in the differential diagnosis of BPD. Patients who experience problems related to cohesion of the self and to affective stability, but who can indeed function well with minimal support and intervention, may well be suffering from depressive disorders with characterological aspects or from less severe characterological disturbances. They do not, however, usually meet the criteria for BPD.

The Borders of Borderline

Other Personality Disorders

The capacity to make clear, empirically based distinctions among all of the personality disorders is not yet completely achievable. Pope et al. (1983) found that while BPD could be distinguished from both affective illness and schizophrenia, it was not easily distinguishable from either histrionic or antisocial personality disorders. They therefore questioned whether these personality disorders are appropriately separate categories. I believe that clinicians can make differential diagnoses with practical, therapeutic meaning if certain distinctions are kept in mind.

Although borderline patients engage in acts that may be considered antisocial, they are much more likely to experience shame or remorse; and although they may need to justify such acts for the survival of the self, the behaviors are usually egodystonic. In addition, borderline patients are less likely than antisocial or schizoid patients to be aloof and detached from their needs for people close to them. Rather, they engage in intense, unstable relationships with uncomfortable affects.

The border between borderline and histrionic personality disorder is less clear and requires greater differentiation. I would argue that the key distinction is functional incapacity. Histrionic patients are likely to perform at a much higher functional level and also to present a more stable inner sense of self than those with BPD; and the former are less apt to show evidence of *repeated self-destructive activity*.

Although borderline and narcissistic patients have some common features and disabilities, their expression of the need for a primary object on whom to depend differs radically. Borderline patients are likely to be open in their needs for support, while narcissistic patients tend to deny their dependency needs. On the other hand, when attached in a sustaining relationship, narcissistic patients are usually able to perform their roles effectively and to maintain a stable sense of themselves. By contrast, patients with BPD are more likely to have storms of affect that last longer and are much more disorganizing. Even in a supportive therapeutic environment, BPD patients may show persistent and major deficiencies in role performance and social relationships.

Affective Illness and Other Axis I Disorders

It is now clear that patients with BPD do *not* share the diagnosis of schizophrenia, and that the latter must take precedence in any diagnostic characteri-

zation. Since the late 1970s, however, the debate has reemerged around the question of whether patients with BPD actually suffer from some form of affective illness. Akiskal (1981, 1983) argues most strongly for viewing BPD as *merely* part of an affective spectrum of disease. Other researchers have highlighted the *overlap* between BPD and affective illness, but they have argued for two *distinct*, diagnosable disorders—BPD *and* major affective illness (Kroll et al. 1981; McGlashan, 1983, 1986; Pope et al. 1983; Stone et al., 1987). In the interest of brevity, this chapter does not fully air the debate concerning the overlap between affective illness and BPD. Gunderson and Elliot (1985) have reviewed the relevant issues and raise several putative explanatory hypotheses.

For clinicians, however, it is important to recognize that patients with BPD may present prominent affective symptoms and may meet criteria for dysthymic disorder, for cyclothymia, or for a major depression. When patients with an uncomplicated acute or episodic unipolar depression recover from their particular episode of the disorder, their functioning intermorbidly will likely be more adaptive than that of depressed patients who continue to suffer from concurrent and severely disabling BPD.

Differential Diagnosis

Interface with Neurological Disturbance

Recently, there has been interest in the interface of BPD with seizure disorders, most noticeably atypical partial complex seizures (TLE). The advent of more sensitive brain scanning devices and more sophisticated analysis of electroencephalograph (EEG) activity (e.g., nuclear magnetic resonance imaging [MRI], positron emission tomography [PET] scans, and brain electrical activity mapping [BEAM] EEG) has allowed for evaluation of electromagnetic activity and structural abnormalities in the brains of patients with personality disorders (Cowdry & Gardner, 1988; Schatzberg, 1983). There is some evidence of seizure activity, subclinical seizures, or atypical neurological disturbance in patients with BPD.

In addition, the clinical trials of antiseizure medication (e.g., valproic acid and carbamazepine) in BPD raise questions about the overlap of these disorders. While some argue that BPD is a subvariant of neurological dysfunction, the possibility remains of two distinct interactive disorders manifest simultaneously in certain patients. For the practicing clinician, it is important to note that neurological evaluation and, at times, trials of "neurological" medication may be useful in establishing a diagnosis and in alleviating some of the severe symptomatology of patients with BPD. It is unlikely, however, that this treatment alone will be sufficient.

Semistructured Interviews

For the clinician who wants additional help in making the diagnosis of BPD—beyond that provided in DSM-III-R—there are now available a number of standardized, semistructured interviews. These include the Schedule for Interviewing Borderlines (SIB) (Baron, Asnis, & Gruen, 1981); the Borderline Personality Disorder Scale (BPD Scale) developed by Perry (1984); the Structural Interview for the DSM–III Personality (SIDP) (Pfohl, Stangl, & Zimmerman, 1983); the Personality Disorder Examination (PDE) (Loranger, Oldham, Russakoff, & Susman, 1984); and the Diagnostic Interview for Borderlines (DIB) (Gunderson & Kolb, 1978; Kolb & Gunderson, 1980). All have their strengths and weaknesses and have been reviewed elsewhere (Pollack, 1986).

Summary of Issues

While debate continues over conceptualization, categorization, and assessment of BPD, there has been growing clarity in the delineation of a distinct, circumscribed personality disorder that can be reliably and validly diagnosed. For patient and clinician alike, however, diagnosis has its greatest meaning in informing specific therapeutic strategies that may be successful in remediating the degree of severe human suffering that a diagnosis of BPD connotes.

PSYCHODYNAMIC TREATMENT STRATEGIES

Historically, it has been argued that the treatment of choice for BPD is a modified or specialized form of psychoanalytic psychotherapy. Other approaches have also been suggested, and within psychodynamic psychotherapy, a wide range of techniques have been advocated: Adler (1985), Gunderson (1984), Kernberg (1984), Pollack (1986), Waldinger and Gunderson (1987). Current controversies center around (a) how supportive or exploratory the process should be, (b) how empathic or confrontive the therapist should be, (c) how often the therapy should take place, and (d) what other adjunctive treatments should be used and under what conditions. It is beyond the scope of this chapter to address all of these controversies. Rather, I highlight the major issues in the psychodynamic therapeutic treatment of BPD, and briefly describe other pragmatic treatment approaches.

Although there is debate as to the conditions necessary for successful use of individual psychotherapy with BPD, the most consistent *contraindication* for any form of this treatment is an untrained or an emotionally unavailable psychotherapist. I strongly concur with Gunderson (1984) that a novice should not treat a BPD patient without intensive supervision and support. I also believe that psychotherapists who have not yet achieved substantial understanding of their own psychological functioning are apt to become confused by countertransference feelings. At the least, they will not be therapeutically available and useful to such patients. At most, they could easily do extreme harm.

Supportive Versus Exploratory– Intensive Psychotherapy

I have argued elsewhere that one of the *least* productive debates in the BPD treatment literature has been the argument over the merits of intensive, exploratory, insight-oriented psychotherapy versus supportive, nonintensive psychotherapy. It has been suggested that the BPD's fragile ego and self-structure require a more supportive approach, involving infrequent (usually once per week) meetings and an effort to support rather than to uncover defenses (Friedman, 1975; Grinker et al., 1968; Knight, 1953; Zetzel, 1971). The assumption is that the creation of a sustaining psychotherapeutic relationship will allow borderline patients to order their chaotic inner experiences and, consequently, to gain stability in their daily life functions. Given the concerns of regressive reactions to a more intensive psychotherapy, such an approach is believed to bolster the alliance and decrease the possibility of unmanageable transference enactments and self-destructive activity.

Kernberg et al. (1972) have argued against the supportive approach, feeling that it leads to iatrogenic toxic side effects. They maintain that borderline patients do equally well in an *expressive* approach and that the negative side effects encountered in this treatment are better handled by using short-term inpatient hospital stays, pro re nata (p.r.n.), rather than by "watering down" the psychotherapy itself.

However, the distinctions between so-called supportive and intensive psychotherapies are rarely so clear cut. Kernberg himself argues for the *supportive* aspects of the *intensity* of the treatment, and this point has been echoed by Wallerstein (1983). In fact, the so-called supportive treatments may do more than bolster defenses or decrease suicide risks. They may also bring about internal structural changes usually ascribed only to insight-oriented psychotherapy. And most would agree with Greenberg (1977) and Levine (1979) that the establishment of a "sustaining object relationship" within psychotherapy is necessary. Indeed, most recent approaches to intensive psychotherapy for the character neuroses highlight the importance of the "holding environment" (Adler, 1985; Modell, 1976).

Clinical and common sense both dictate that any set of psychotherapeutic interventions that do not help the patient either to stem the tide of chaotic, overwhelming internal feelings or to limit suicidal enactment will not be very therapeutic in the long run. I believe that effective psychotherapists will, of necessity, blend supportive and interpretive techniques to react flexibly to varying needs and levels of functioning of their particular borderline patients.

Two Approaches to BPD

Having said that, it is worth examining two major psychoanalytically oriented paradigms for the individual psychotherapy of BPD: (1) Kernberg's "object relations" approach, and (2) Buie and Adlers' therapeutic "holding environment" approach. It is then valuable to consider what I believe is a more developmentally oriented, multimodal, yet still psychodynamic approach to BPD.

Kernberg

There are major clinical implications of Kernberg's conceptualization of BPD as a *pathology* of *internalized object relations* brought about by the incapacity to tolerate primitive aggression: (a) It leads to the belief that in therapy, the borderline patient will experience "a premature activation in the transference of very early conflict-laden object relations" (Kernberg, 1982, p. 472). (b) These conflicts in turn will get played out in the transference as a "pathological condensation of pregenital and genital aims *under the overriding influence of pregenital aggression* (Kernberg, 1982, p. 472, italics mine). (c) The end result will be a deep sense of distrust and fear of the therapist, who is often viewed as a potent "attacker."

Consequently, Kernberg's approach emphasizes the need to *control* transference enactment. To this end, he recommends limiting the patient's enactment while interpreting the need for such limits from the perspective of the transference relationship itself. Kernberg recommends this be done in an intensive psychoanalytic therapy organized around: (a) interpretation, (b) the maintenance of neutrality, and (c) the analysis of transference.

For Kernberg (1975, 1984), *interpretation* is fundamental, while suggestion, manipulation, and most other forms of "active intervention" should be eschewed. The only exception to this rule would be setting limits on the patient's acting out negative (especially self-destructive) impulses. To accomplish this, the therapist may add external structuring of the patient's life and/or may intervene in the patient's social network. But even such interventions should eventually be interpreted and wither away.

Although Kernberg advocates *empathic* responsiveness to the patient's needs, he maintains that the patient must face and bear those aspects of his or her inner life, which may at first be walled off or unbearable. He believes this goal can only be achieved through *maintenance of clinical neutrality*.

The active *analysis of transference* is the third aspect of Kernberg's approach and the major vehicle of therapeutic change. It is through transference interpretation that developmentally arrested object relations are finally integrated, making it possible for the BPD patient to tolerate ambivalent feelings. To accomplish this, Kernberg suggests that (a) the predominantly negative transference of borderline patients should be systematically elaborated and interpreted, highlighting the here-and-now aspect of the aggressive constellations; (b) typical defenses such as splitting and projective identification should be interpreted as soon as they enter the transference; and (c) limits must be set in order both to stop any acting out of the transference and to maintain the neutrality of the therapist (Kernberg, 1984).

Kernberg sees positive aspects of the transference as needing less interpretation and as forming the basis of a therapeutic alliance. Still, "grossly exaggerated idealizations" should not be left unchallenged. It is just that the negative transference must be interpreted first if the patient is to develop the capacity to deal with "primitive conflicts around aggression and the intolerance of ambivalence" (Kernberg, 1984, p. 106). It is for this reason that Kernberg advocates interpreting any current defenses that distort reality, even if these are attempts at self-soothing. Although Kernberg is aware of the need for holding or containing borderline patients (Bion, 1967; Winnicott, 1960), he cautions therapists not to lose their neutrality and "gratify" rather than interpret the patient's needs.

Clinicians will recognize in Kernberg's approach an opportunity to squarely face a patient's aggression without being overtly critical. By maintaining neutrality, the clinician calms and supports the patient and orders the intense chaotic feelings expressed in the treatment. Herein lies Kernberg's therapeutic optimism and the hope needed to sustain a very difficult treatment. Others, however, have criticized this approach.

Searles (1979a & b) has raised questions about the "Olympian" nature of Kernberg's treatment. The requirement of strict neutrality may demand more than a psychotherapist can practically provide or than borderline patients can tolerate (Tolpin & Kohut, 1980). I also have argued that Kernberg's emphasis on *aggression* may leave patients feeling as though they *are* actually bad

because they always seem so angry. In addition, many clinicians view their patients' aggression not as primary but either as a secondary and legitimate response to early environmental trauma or hurt or as a defense against a deeper sense of loneliness or abandonment. Kernberg's approach might then be experienced as a collusion with the patient's harsh superego, so that the patient begins to feel responsible for harm that was actually perpetrated by others.

Kernberg's approach may also be somewhat impractical. Economic and geographic considerations often require that the therapist play several roles, including a supportive one, in the midst of ongoing psychotherapy. This is not to diminish the importance of Kernberg's admonition against becoming too involved in patients' real lives and thereby enacting transference fantasies. Rather, it highlights the fact that one must often *do more than interpret* in order to help borderline patients. This view is echoed by Adler and Buie.

Adler and Buie

Based on the salient concepts of intolerable *aloneness* and developmental dysfunctions in the areas of holding introjects and self-soothing capacities, Adler and Buie (Adler, 1985; Adler & Buie, 1979; Buie & Adler, 1982) have advocated a somewhat different psychotherapeutic approach. They maintain that in order to cure what they conceptualize as the primary sector of borderline psychopathology—an inability to sustain a holding or soothing memory of significant others at times of separation or distress—the therapist must provide, *actual, active, interpersonal (self-object) functions*.

They suggest that the therapist begin the treatment by *not* disturbing the development of the supporting idealizing transference so as to *gradually* allow the issue of aloneness to unfold. As the patient comes to see the therapist as relatively reliable and sustaining, the patient may simultaneously begin to shed some of his or her characteristic distancing techniques. Then, the patient will come to consciously experience, or to reexperience, a vulnerable sense of dependence, especially when the panic of separation becomes manifest. This is most likely to occur when there is an *interruption* in the therapy, for example a vacation or a weekend. At those times, the patient's early felt needs for self-object support will reemerge, sometimes abruptly in the form of rage toward the entire environment (and particularly the therapist) for not providing the desired amount of continuous soothing or holding. This may be accompanied by a loss of evocative memory and a completely negative image of the therapist. A central therapeutic task, therefore, becomes the creation of an environment in which the patient can take in and hold onto real memories of sustaining and soothing at times of aloneness. From this develops an *internal structure*, which patients will eventually use to soothe themselves.

To achieve this goal, Adler and Buie recommend that the therapist use clarification, interpretation, and the setting of limits to protect patients from destructive enactment of their abandonment fears and rage. The therapist also may have to extend him- or herself directly to forestall more pathological regression (e.g., by offering intermittent telephone calls between sessions, by negotiating extra appointments, or by using brief periods of hospitalization). Adler and Buie argue that these holding actions sustain the patient and allow for the recognition that the therapist can tolerate the patient's rage, hurt, and loneliness and yet continue to be helpful (Winnicott, 1965). Especially useful is their reliance on *transitional objects*, such as postcards, stationery, or something that is specially valued in the context of the therapeutic work—to help sustain patients during times of need and separation.

If patient and therapist are able to see their way through this initial "crunch," then the second phase of treatment ensues—that of "optimal disillusionment." Borrowing from the work of Kohut (1977), Adler and Buie argue that patients can be helped to notice the reality of the transference and their need to idealize the therapist, and then to gradually relinquish that idealized view. Each moment of seeing the therapist as he or she really is helps the patient to integrate the soothing qualities once imagined to exist *only* in an idealized other person.

In the third and final phase of the treatment, the therapist admires and supports the emerging autonomous capacities of the patient. Separation is valued as an important part of life, and, if all goes well, the patient eventually comes to treat him- or herself and the significant others in life with the same respect, admiration, understanding, and feeling once expected from the psychotherapist.

A major advantage of Adler and Buie's approach is the emphasis on empathic understanding of the existential pain of aloneness, which so many borderline patients manifest. Also important is their flexible support for an active *interactional*, approach to treatment, and their recognition of the *legitimacy* of the need for *phase-appropriate dependency*, upon others. By allowing for a much more mutually oriented therapeutic process, such an approach certainly helps avoid iatrogenic struggles over limits.

Critics say that therapists using this approach may confuse the real needs for support with inappropriate gratification of more libidinally or aggressively derived demands, so that instead of providing necessary holding, an addictive collusive and countertherapeutic enactment between therapist and patient may be created. I believe that this is unlikely when the therapist is experienced, empathic, and willing to seek appropriate supervision, or *consultation*. Another critique of this approach is that it allows the patient and the therapist to avoid facing and bearing the patient's aggression and rage. Adler and Buie, like Kernberg, see rage as being central, but unlike Kernberg, they see it as best understood as a response to loss of the supportive object. Their goal, then, is not to confront but to help patients understand and sympathize with their own anger, as part of an ongoing process of internalizing the soothing qualities of the empathic psychotherapist.

While both Kernberg and Adler and Buie have set the standard for the psychodynamic treatment of BPD, the contributions of others should not be discounted. These include the contributions of Winnicott (1953, 1965, 1975) and Modell (1963, 1976, 1984), as well as Kohut and colleagues (Kohut, 1971, 1977; Kohut & Wolf, 1978; Tolpin, 1971). Their views, when understood within a *developmental* context, may be integrated into a new, theoretically sound, and practically useful series of treatment strategies for the borderline patient. As I show in this chapter, such an *integrated empathic approach*, which I have developed and practiced, can help to bridge the gap between the so-called "confrontational" camp of Kernberg and the "holding" camp of Adler and Buie.

AN INTEGRATED DEVELOPMENTAL–PSYCHODYNAMIC PSYCHOTHERAPEUTIC APPROACH

In my view, the frequency of psychotherapy must be intensive enough, and its duration extensive enough, to allow the distrusting borderline patient to develop a sense of trust. Only then will BPD patients openly share their distress, tolerate an investigation of the origins of their pain, and be willing to explore in the here-and-now more creative and less distracting solutions to past dilemmas of hurt and pain. I believe this requires face-to-face psychotherapy sessions to occur from two to four times a week, at least through the early period of therapy.

Phases of Treatment

If all goes well, the treatment will likely unfold in three stages: (1) holding, (2) understanding, and (3) moving on.

(Flexible) Holding

The first phase centers around the provision of "good enough" "holding" (see Modell, 1984; Winnicott, 1965). The patient must be able to see that the therapist is a *reliable, reasonably present* object, who can be depended on to accept patients' manifest *and* latent feelings, to remember them, and to reflect them in the absence of the patient's own capacity to do so. This requires that the therapist be able to tolerate and bear a substantial level of the patient's painful affects—including both sadness and rage. The therapist also must recognize that most borderline patients have *not* experienced a significant positive holding in the past, and that this is a *new* interpersonal matrix— one that is both deeply wished for and suspiciously viewed. How can one expect that patients who have been hurt again and again by others, or who have been defeated by their own repetitive pushing away of others at times of need, will believe that this particular relationship will be different? The

answer, of course, is that no reasonable person could have such trust. Empathically accepting the patient's inability to trust provides one of the greatest tools for later modification of the patient's own suspiciousness—tolerance of ambivalence.

The earliest phase of the therapy is usually marked by confused behavioral expressions of such ambivalence. There is a general disparaging of the psychotherapy and the therapist. Although there may be periods of idealization, the more severely disturbed the patient, the less likely it is that such a "honeymoon" phase will last. Usually, it gives way to a terrifying sense, on the patient's part, of the therapist's inadequacies—well before any form of optimal disillusionment can occur— and to rage at the therapist. The therapist must be able to survive these rageful attacks while understanding them as emanating from a deep sense of fear. The therapist also must be able to feel and to communicate the patient's sense of loss and loneliness even during moments of extreme rage and disconnection.

During this period, one cannot overestimate the patient's sensitivity to therapist rebuffs, misunderstanding, and hurt. The therapist must remain acutely aware of this, must be flexible to detect any derailment of trust or empathy, must analyze it openly and nondefensively, and must maintain an *active empathic* stance vis-à-vis the patient during times of defensive emotional withdrawal.

I have used the term *flexible* holding because, at times, the holding requires a certain *letting go*. Patients may need to enact a certain amount of disconnection from the treatment, and the therapist must tolerate this. To what extent and in what ways depends on both the particular needs of the patient and the capacities of the therapist. In all cases, however, titration of the holding and letting go must be a mutually discussed, interactive process between patient and therapist. By *negotiating*, the therapist forestalls more severe and bizarre forms of idealization–devaluation and communicates that relationships can be discussed, understood in depth, and changed over time. Through flexible holding, the therapist also provides an opportunity for the patient to soothe the self *through the psychotherapy*, and to internalize a sense of the caring therapist.

It is in this phase that the challenge first emerges

of integrating both *confrontation* of the patient's aggression and *soothing* of the patient's self. Again, the therapist must be flexible and empathically attuned to the patient. Some patients may need to be given considerable latitude to experience and express their rage with quiet support from the therapist. Others may require an immediate active response and clarification—including, at times, the setting of limits. I believe it matters less whether one confronts the aggression than whether the aggression is understood like any other aspect of the patient—as something to be valued, explored, and mastered.

Often, borderline patients are much more frightened of their own rage than they let on. Indeed, they may be using the rage defensively to hide other feelings, especially sadness and aloneness. One must be open to exploring the rage in all its facets with the patient, recognizing that BPD patients are (a) almost always able to sense whether the therapist is comfortable with their aggression, and (b) exquisitely sensitive to the therapist's capacity to know when the anger might be getting out of control. In general, when one is able to achieve a *balance* between tolerating the patient's aggressive *feelings* and setting limits on aggressively motivated destructive *actions*, patients will feel increasingly secure and be able to share a whole range of difficult and painful feelings. This should ultimately lead to the patient's increased tolerance of those feelings—the internalization of the holding phase.

Some borderline patients go through this phase without much limit setting or reflection on their aggression. Others have a stormy early phase, requiring an approach that, to some extent, mirrors Kernberg's. What remains essential, however, is the use of limits within the context of the *therapist's own sense of human limitation*, which is shared genuinely with the patient, while eschewing educational moralism.

(Interpretive) Understanding

Given sufficient flexible holding and soothing of the self, patient and therapist can then turn to an exploration of the patient's particular developmental history and *hurt*. I emphasize the term *hurt* because I believe that borderline patients have usually experienced some trauma in their childhood—whether it be *actual abuse*, emotional coldness, tragic loss, or an overwhelming sense of affect again and again that is not tolerated or tolerable.

There is now growing evidence that the majority of patients with moderate to severe BPD have been the victims of *actual* childhood trauma and/or abuse. Informal review of inpatients at McLean Hospital reveals a significant number of female patients with a diagnosis of BPD who have suffered sexual or physical abuse; and this is substantiated by a controlled study by Bryer, Nelson, Miller, and Krol (1987).

Such data must alert the clinician to the very *real* childhood *hurts* or *traumas* experienced by BPD patients and their effect on later adult functioning. It would not be extreme to suggest that at least some significant subgroup of BPD patients are suffering from a variant of *posttraumatic stress* in a characterological crystallization. The clinician must remain empathically aware of this reality and not *retraumatize* the patient through benign neglect or misunderstanding.

Therefore, I also emphasize the *particular* developmental history of the patient because there is no prototype of a borderline history. If a therapist begins to feel that the specific transference, or the unfolding of past history in the present, is stereotyped, she or he is losing the empathic edge in understanding the patient. As the patient feels held and soothed, and as the patient in small doses attempts such self-functions in the absence of the therapist (or while the therapist looks on admiringly), the capacity for genetic reconstruction of the particular history is enhanced. Often, such a phase will be ushered in either by patients reporting their dreams or by patients' experiences in the therapy that remind them of past disappointments—most notably, disappointments about separation.

Without minimizing the importance of understanding here-and-now difficulties, I believe it is the *linking* of the patient's present sense of suspiciousness and hurt to the patient's *past* history that gives meaning to an otherwise obscurely disconnected sense of feelings and behaviors. It is, indeed, the remembering and understanding of the past, and the bringing of it into the present transference, that enables the patient both to make sense of an inner feeling of chaos and to integrate an inter-mittently dissociated sense of self into a real and cohesive whole.

At least initially, the patient must be helped to see that even the most defensive, maladaptive, and confusing maneuvers (including dissociative states, and rageful enactments) were meant, at one time, to protect and sustain the self. As patients can come to *empathize with their own self-needs*, they are less likely to need to stand at so far a distance from the self. Here, Kohut's suggestion of eschewing a maturity morality comes into play. Border-line patients are not necessarily primitive or immature; they are opening up and growing. The concept of the patient's "thwarted need to grow" makes a great deal of sense. It also requires an understanding that the therapist too, will be grow-ing in the treatment. One might say that the thera-peutic task is (a) to develop a *mutually shared* developmental *story* of the patient's experience, and (b) to connect and *integrate* this story into the experiences of the present in a way that sustains inner emotional growth and leads to outer behav-ioral change.

(Relative) Moving On

In my view, the final phase of the treatment con-sists of consolidating the gains of the self around cohesion and soothing, and the esteem-regulating mechanisms that facilitate self-value—to permit and foster the growth of an array of thriving, autonomous functions. It must be remembered, however, that all such growth, autonomy, and moving on is relative and occurs within a larger framework of *interdependent relationships*.

At one time, the hallmark of mental health was considered to be totally individuated functioning. The need for dependence on another object was considered not essential, or at best secondary. It is now recognized that individuals can gain greater flexibility for internalization and autonomous self-functioning without abandoning the need for mature dependency on others (Kohut, 1980). From this perspective, the pathway to mental health is achieved through what I have termed a *balance between autonomy and affiliation*. This includes the sobering recognition that we live in an *interdependent* world where relationships are required to sustain us emotionally, just (as Kohut

has pointed out) as oxygen is required to sustain us biologically. Such an approach to human develop-ment has practical meaning for the borderline patient (see Pollack & Grossman, 1985).

Moving on in psychotherapy, then, must in-clude the willing recognition—by both therapists and patients—that the patients are able to under-stand themselves, soothe themselves, and help themselves, but also that some form of ongoing *interdependence* on significant others, including the psychotherapist, may be necessary for the patients to maintain psychological equilibrium and growth. Even more significantly, moving on requires that the patient and therapist view such continuing interpersonal needs not as evidence of residual pathology, but rather as evidence of health and cure!

Some patients will achieve almost complete internalization of the functions of the psychother-apy and not require an ongoing relationship with the therapist at all. Other patients may require some ongoing contact with the therapist, even if only intermittently. One must be careful, and clear, that such ongoing contact in no way repre-sents therapeutic failure. This becomes more pos-sible if one moves away from a purely autonomy-oriented focus toward a balanced approach in which the ongoing affiliative needs of the patient, especially as expressed toward the therapist, are tolerated and understood.

Autonomy and Affiliation: Achieving Balance

Most paradigms for the treatment of character disorders stress either the importance of separation–individuation (Kernberg, 1984; Mahler, 1971) or of human interconnection (Adler, 1985; Adler & Buie, 1979; Kohut, 1977). However, this is growing evidence to suggest that it is the *balance* of *autonomy* and *affiliation* that is critical. I have argued elsewhere (Pollack, 1982, 1983a, 1983b; Pollack & Grossman, 1985) that healthy development requires the capacities to experience and sustain both an independent sense of oneself *(autonomy)* and an interconnected rela-tion with others *(affiliation)*. Not only young chil-dren but also couples in the transition to parent-hood and fathers engaged in ongoing parenting have been shown to benefit from the provision of a healthy balance of support for both autonomous and affiliative tendencies (Grossman, Pollack, & Golding, 1988; Grossman, Pollack, Golding, & Fedele, 1987).

I believe that the historical emphasis solely on autonomy as a measure of mental health may well reflect a masculine bias in psychology–psychiatry, and one with important clinical implications. We may, for example, become so preoccupied with the negative aspects of so-called dependency that we discount the normal, healthy needs to remain dependent on significant others or on our social network throughout the life cycle. Women's normal, healthy need for ongoing relational activity has long been recognized (see Stiver, 1985). Recent research on families in development indicates that such *affiliative* urges and actions are equally salient for men (Pollack, 1989). In the treatment of BPD, such dependency needs are paramount.

It is a central premise of the integrated treatment regime described herein that borderline patients are *not suffering* from overdependency as much as from the inability to recognize the *legitimacy* of their need to depend on others and to build an *interdependent* network of support. The therapeutic goal, then, is to help the patient to tolerate aloneness on the one hand, and to tolerate togetherness on the other.

Countertransference: The Therapist's Own Aggression and Love

A major component of intensive psychotherapy with BPD patients is the mobilization of the therapist's own hateful and loving countertransference. Whether this is an aspect of projective identification (see Kernberg, 1984) or simply a hurt and angry response to accusations either of being an inadequate self-object or of providing a deficient holding environment, the therapist must remain aware of his or her own hate or love (Madow & Pollack, 1986; Maltsberger & Buie, 1974).

Adler and Buie (1972) have highlighted the dangerous countertransference-generated misuse of confrontation with borderline patients. Most often, this involves clarifications or interpretations ostensibly aimed at making psychological change. In reality, these interventions may reflect the therapist's unconscious aggression and may be intended to convince patients that they have been bad and should desist from such behavior. The result may be an increase in patients' self-hate and an engendering of self-destructive behavior. One cannot underestimate the borderline patient's capacity to unconsciously experience the therapist's anger and act it out. In order to forestall such events, therapists must accept and bear their own experiences of hate toward the patient without enacting them and must, when needed, seek consultation. Therapists who are angry and *unaware* may confront a borderline patient who is in the midst of a *struggle to survive*, with disastrous results. Therapists may likewise confuse the need to rescue or love the patient with therapeutic holding. This, too, may lead to desperate attempts to separate through enactment. Thus, therapist self-awareness and collegial consultation are essential.

Self-Destructive Behaviors

As noted earlier, borderline patients often are at risk for suicide and suicidal gestures. Therapists must be able not only to tolerate suicidal *wishes* and *fantasies*, but also to intervene when *actual suicide* threatens. Some patients with BPD may deal with the intolerance of their strong affects through minor forms of self-harm (cutting, minor accidents, head banging, sexual self-harm, etc.). Others may have the need to soothe themselves for long periods of time, with fantasies about death. One should not, however, intervene prematurely because some self-destructive activity may represent the patient's best and only means of maintaining a psychological equilibrium. Yet one must also recognize that rage and hurt may reach a point where self-destruction appears to patients as their only way out—and may lead to dangerous life-threatening enactment.

Whatever the circumstances, the therapist must always take the patient's feelings, thoughts, and plans *seriously*. Gunderson (1984) has created a simple and practical taxonomy of two classes of self-destructive activity in borderline patients. The first occurs in the presence of an ongoing connection to the therapist. Here, patients may be asking the therapist through the action to, "Please change things for me, or help me differently."

Such gestures can usually be clarified during the therapeutic hours or defused by rapid crisis intervention aimed at providing a safe environment in which the problem can be discussed.

The other type of self-destructive activity, however, occurs following an experience of abandonment, loss, or severe derailment in the psychotherapy, resulting in growing aloneness panic. Patients may need to harm themselves in small ways either to gain a sense of numbness or to expel the bad feelings. However, the guilt and emptiness may escalate quickly, leading to frantic requests for help and rapid reversion to serious self-destructive behavior. Often, psychotherapists mistake such desperate discussions and behaviors as attempts to "manipulate" the therapist to gain more time and caring. Failure to respond quickly and directly may well lead to a *completed suicide*.

Under these conditions, the therapist must be available and active and be willing to provide the patient with added structure, including more sessions, phone calls, or, if necessary, hospitalization. The dangers of therapeutic passivity are especially great in early phases of treatment, before an alliance is established. At this time, therapists must be careful to inquire after missed appointments and must be willing to telephone the patient should there be any suspicion or concern. When patients discuss their suicidal wishes or plans, therapists should inquire *actively* about what they mean. This should help to differentiate a cry for help from a sense of despair that requires more active intervention.

Recognizing One's Own Limits: Hospitalization and Consultation

When the patient appears unable to use additional therapeutic support (e.g., phone calls, more frequent sessions), short-term hospitalization should be considered. *Hospitalization* does *not necessarily* mean a *failure* of *psychotherapy*. The therapist's inner experience of anxiety may serve as a clue to the level of distress that the patient cannot put into words. Should a therapist's anxiety become so extreme that he or she is always worried about the patient's safety, then therapy and patient alike are both in jeopardy. This and the proposed interventions must be discussed openly with the patient. When the therapist is seriously concerned about the patient's safety, it is better to act first to create a secure environment and then to discuss with the patient what has occurred. An attempt to maintain outpatient psychotherapy at all costs is likely to cost too much. There will be little use for setting limits or for a therapeutically neutral working approach if the patient is no longer alive!

If patients are aware that their therapists do not believe in hospitalization or will not use it, they may have an unconscious need to push limits to the brink in a dangerous way. Indications for short-term inpatient hospitalization are (a) the failure of active structural additions to outpatient psychotherapy to stem the tide of self-destructive enactment, (b) the therapist's level of anxiety concerning the patient's safety reaching a point where reasonable comfort is no longer possible, (c) the abuse of substances, including food, requiring control or detoxification; and/or (d) countertransference experiences becoming so intense that patient and therapist need a breather in a setting where other skilled clinicians can help (see Gunderson, 1984; Madow & Pollack, 1986).

A day treatment program is sometimes an excellent alternative to inpatient hospitalization. Not only are such programs cost-efficient and flexible, but also they may provide the proper balance between the holding and the separation and autonomy, with less chance of inducing regression (Pollack, 1983a). In either day treatment or full hospitalization, the psychotherapist should feel comfortable with the philosophy of the treating unit, and there should be mutual trust between therapist and milieu staff. There are, of course, times when psychotherapists feel that they have "had enough" and cannot continue. Candidly expressing this while the patient is in the hospital can be especially useful. Under these conditions, the hospital staff may be helpful in finding an alternative psychotherapeutic arrangement.

The place of long-term, intensive inpatient hospitalization in the treatment of BPD has been reviewed elsewhere (Frosch, 1983; Gunderson, 1984). Generally, it seems advisable to reserve such treatment for those patients who have shown an inability to sustain reasonable functioning in intensive outpatient psychotherapy even with occasional brief hospitalizations.

Whenever hospitalization is being considered, seeking *consultation* on an outpatient basis should be considered. Often, psychotherapists are wary of opening their treatments to colleagues, especially when this occurs under the somewhat angry or negative demands of dissatisfied patients. Therapists should remember that consultation, like hospitalization, is not an indication of therapeutic failure; if the consultation is discussed openly with the patient, as it should be, it may provide patients with a useful model for problem solving. I recommend that both the therapist and the patient talk to the consultant. As long as such a process is not misused, it has many potential benefits for the therapist and patient alike.

CASE ILLUSTRATION

Ms. B. began her psychotherapy during a severe personal crisis, and in a state of total disarray. Her marriage of many years was disintegrating (though she and her husband were not separated and had no immediate plans for doing so). Caring for her 3-year-old son seemed like an intolerable burden, and a series of relationships with previous psychotherapists and psychopharmacologists had left her feeling despondent, enraged, and suicidal. During the vacation of her treating psychotherapist, she took an overdose of her antidepressant medication, which had proven only moderately effective, and was hospitalized. After defeating the efforts of several senior psychopharmacologists to completely control her depression with medication—antidepressants, antipsychotics, anticonvulsants, and so on—she was referred for intensive psychotherapy. She began treatment with a senior psychoanalytic clinician, which ended quickly in a transference–countertransference impasse. The patient experienced quasi-psychotic episodes—visual images of "bloody faces"—while the therapist felt helpless and intermittently enraged with the patient.

Ms. B's new psychotherapy began during her hospitalization, starting out with meetings four times weekly. Eventually, the patient made a transition to an aftercare environment, and finally to her home, resuming her parenting activities.

From the start, Ms. B presented herself as an attractive, intelligent, and perceptive woman, who was alternatively either intensely demanding or hopeless, emotionally hyperactive or enraged. She would often cry easily, and then quickly become infuriated at what might appear to an outside observer as a very minor slight. But to the patient, the slights felt like a major provocation.

The therapy began with a very brief phase of idealization—a honeymoon, in which the clinician was seen as extremely intelligent and caring. This quickly gave way to expressions of severe hopelessness, intense demand for help, and intermittent rage. One day, the patient was describing a tragic experience from her childhood, in what appeared to be so disassociated and distorted a manner that the therapist was unable to feel the emotional connection necessary to experience the pain with her. He began to realize a rising sense of disconnection in himself, and consequent boredom and removal. The therapist interrupted the patient's then emotionally flat monologue and inquired as to whether she might have been feeling somewhat overwhelmed by and, therefore, removed from, the sense of distress that she was discussing.

The patient responded by immediately falling silent, grimacing, and remaining in what appeared to be an angry removed stance for several moments:

T: You've become quiet.

P: (silence) . . .

T: Can you try to share what you're thinking or feeling?

P: (silence continues, with an angry look)

T: (after a long silence) I can only guess, but it feels like something I said may have hurt your feelings.

P: You're damn right! You seem to question my honesty, like everybody does, you bastard! . . . You're no different, you're just like the rest. Do you believe me or don't you?!

T: When I interrupted, and made some clarification it seemed like I stopped believing you, started doubting you . . . that hurt your feelings and you became very hurt and then very angry with me. It's your experience that counts, it's not a question of whether you're right or wrong; this is what happened to you; this is how you feel, and you worry that I can't reflect that. But if you're hurt, and then you're angry, it's extremely important to talk about it here, to discuss it with me.

P: Like who the hell wants to talk to someone when you're hurt and you're angry with them!!

T: That's right, trust takes time. We can't expect this right away, of course. But I think it has to be our goal, together at least, to talk about the hurt, especially when it happens here in the therapy, and to look at the sadness before it becomes very confusing anger.

The next day, the patient reported a "bizarre" experience that unfortunately had become somewhat commonplace in her past—a "seizure." Having been thoroughly worked up neurologically, it had become clear that these "seizures" were actually disturbing experiences of anxiety and syncope. The patient felt vulnerable, unable to protect and soothe herself, and she sensed an attack from a potential protector. In addition, however, she expressed her conflicts about wanting to be looked at and seen, as well as needing to hide such a wish—one which she felt was humiliating, shameful, and "selfish."

Slowly, over a period of approximately 2 years, she and her therapist were able to discuss these experiences, first from the sense of self-acceptance rather than of "blaming herself," and next attempting to understand them within the context of her personal history. Within this context, as the therapist encouraged "remembering," during the hours, the patient's history of having been severely abused and abandoned repeatedly as a child emerged. Only after reviewing these feelings time and time again, day after day, month in and month out, was the patient able to begin to discuss the nature of the wishes that were reemerging in the context of the transference itself: to be held like a "baby" by the therapist, to be looked upon, to have her needs reflected, and to be special in a way that also frightened her, as it had "sexual" connotations.

To a large extent, the issues were taken up from the perspective of the inconsistencies of the past caretaking, and the need for holding and understanding in the present. The patient's conflicts about being seen, reflected, and hidden/protected were also addressed within the context of her difficulties of vocational dysfunction and her parental anxieties in her present capacity to cherish and care for her young son—whom she loved very much. As the therapist actively encouraged the patient to explore these issues in depth, three events emerged almost simultaneously in the treatment, and they continued over time.

First, the patient became intermittently anxious, as she attempted to take up lifelong wishes for educational accomplishment, which she had put aside. She would make small steps in the direction of graduate school and then become extremely anxious. Coupled with this anxiety were suicidal thoughts, wishes, and at times, plans. Often the sense of "guilt" of making change and the fear of "shame" from "abandonment" that occurred each time the patient moved forward had to be met by active therapeutic interpretation and clarification, as well as by additional structure and support. There were frequent late-night telephone calls, which were reviewed in the subsequent psychotherapy hours. Discussion of the use of rehospitalization on an acute basis ensued, but the patient was able to use planned intercession telephone contact as an alternative. She also began to seek out a network of friends (many of whom had experienced similar abuse in their families of origin) as a means for additional structure between the therapeutic sessions.

Second, the patient also began to realize that the nature of her marital attachment was dysfunctional. For the first time, she engaged in a lengthy, thoughtful, and deep review about why she had chosen her present mate and the nature of their ongoing difficulties. She accepted the therapist's direct suggestion to attempt couples therapy to address these difficulties, but it met with little success. Her conceptualization of her husband as a caring but out-of-touch man who was quite enraged with her appeared to be verified by the context of the interpersonal work. The patient, her husband, and the couples therapist all came to the same conclusion—that an amicable parting or divorce was probably the most appropriate course.

Now, in the third year of intensive therapy, as the patient began to achieve real life change, to tolerate greater internal anxiety, and to differentiate the here-and-now difficulties from the traumas of the past, a broader and more mature interest in the nature of the psychotherapy emerged. This, in turn, was reflected in a series of more coherent transference paradigms, which were open to interpretation and genetic reconstruction. The patient was able to see the therapist, alternatively, as both mother and father. This father was brutal and uncaring, but promised some hope for the future. This mother was only intermittently available, but at times promised love. The cycling between maternal and paternal transference, love and hate, abandonment and understanding, now was *interpretable* within the treatment.

For the majority of this phase in treatment, the

patient felt held and understood. Yet, there would be intermittent moments of therapeutic derailment in which the patient would become terribly enraged, and at times suicidal. However, over time, the patient felt that the therapist was able to work through these issues with her. Occasionally, she would make a late-night phone call to discuss her distress. But increasingly, she was able to hold onto her feelings until the next session. She came to feel that the therapist was "human," and this had both negative and positive effects. The patient and therapist were able to discuss her sense of hurt and ensuing rage, and the patient was able to feel generally that the therapist was attempting to understand her and was helping her to understand. As the patient remembered more of the hurt and pain of the past—particularly the pain of abandonment and attack—she sought to organize her present life in new ways.

She also sought additional psychopharmacology consultation to reduce her use of medication. She gravitated toward self-help groups and greater personal interaction with other people who, like herself, were struggling with pain from the past in an attempt to have a more proactive and positive view in the future. Significantly, she and her husband separated, and she began dating other men. She appeared ready to "move on."

In the fourth year of therapy, the patient now became aware of her wish to reduce the frequency of her sessions but to continue in an intensive treatment; after discussion, her therapist agreed. Ms. B. now became more alive and interested in the nature of "relationships." The treatment no longer focused on the patient alone or on her own history, but also on the nature of her interpersonal activity in the present. The patient craved "information," and demanded that the therapist give her advice. At times, these demands were reasonable. But at other times, they seemed to be an attempt to deal with the conflictual wish about closeness to the therapist, which was interpreted rather than enacted. The patient would sometimes become angry, but she usually felt that the therapist was attempting to understand.

Ms. B. came to see herself as having a "delayed adolescence." She felt very hurt and angry that she needed to go through the pain of relationships and the possibility of separation at such a "late date." However, with the capacity to review these feelings of disappointment and disillusionment in the therapy, the growth continued outside the therapy sessions. The patient continued to build a series of relationships with increasingly appropriate males.

Equally important, the patient began to negotiate close personal friendships with a number of women. At times, the patient became upset and felt she was too "selfish." Now the therapist clarified that the need to protect herself, rather than engaging in relationships, came from the early experience that she and the therapist had reviewed over and over again—that a balance between having her own needs and caring about herself, as well as being interested in others was both reasonable and healthy. This was mirrored, in turn, by her wish expressed in the therapy to be more assertive, to be more reasonably critical of the therapist and his own personal habits. The therapist responded to this with excitement, as it reflected an individuated sense within the work.

Again, as the patient felt more individuated and strong in these areas, her suicidality, guilt, shame, and anxiety reemerged. These were again interpreted in the context of the fear that if she became "her own person," she would lose the people around her, and "behind her." The therapist was direct in reassuring the patient that her wishes to be her own person would not destroy the nature of the support, and that as she moved on, her need to come to the therapy would be decided by her rather than by the therapist. This relaxed the patient, and she continued during the fifth treatment year to pursue her independent needs in the context of an interpersonal connection.

This case vignette is left unfinished for two reasons: First, the treatment itself is not perfect and not complete. Therefore, it comes closest to the actual work between clinicians and borderline patients engaged in intensive psychoanalytic psychotherapy. Second, it highlights the argument that I have made throughout the chapter: that the treatment need not lead to complete separation or achievement of absolute autonomy.

The patient presently is continuing in an intensive treatment, as she becomes increasingly involved in the world of relationships. It is expected that there will be stops and starts along that road, but that over the next year the patient will reduce the frequency of her therapy, to the extent that it will probably no longer be considered ongoing and intensive—but rather intermittent and supportive. As she explores the world of relationships and frees herself from the inhibiting pain of separation, she may use the therapy and the therapist from time to time when anxieties reemerge. When and how to decide that the treatment is complete, or that termination should or has taken place, will be a mutual task between patient and therapist.

Above all, this case illustrates how genuine therapeutic change can ensue within the context of mutual understanding, transference interpretation, and a sense of flexible holding. The patient's past was understood from within her own perspective, while the therapist facilitated a balance between connectedness and independence within the treatment—a balance that Ms. B. struggled to internalize and succeeded in making her own.

ALTERNATIVE TREATMENT OPTIONS

Recently, alternative approaches for the treatment of BPD have been suggested. These include family treatment, vocational rehabilitation, structured group therapy, scientifically prescribed psychopharmacological interventions, and psychotherapeutic approaches reframed from a cognitive and behavioral standpoint. Whether these treatments for BPD should be considered alternatives to psychoanalytic psychotherapy or adjunctive interventions depends on one's philosophical approach. It is my contention that an *integrated, multimodal* approach is most reasonable and most consistent with clinical and research data. For example, there is now evidence that vocational and psychopharmacological interventions enhance the psychotherapeutic course of BPD and that cognitive approaches diminish self-destructive activity (Linehan, 1987a, 1987b; McGlashan, 1986; Stone et al., 1987). However, a definitive, longitudinal, empirical study of differential therapeutics in BPD has yet to be done. Until all of the "votes are counted," an integrated, multimodal approach, based on the patient's individual needs and capacities, seems warranted.

Families

In discussing psychotherapeutic approaches to BPD, Gunderson (1984) notes that some families of borderline patients are overinvolved with the patient. They can be contained within the context of family therapy. There also are neglectful families who are unlikely to stick with treatment and may enact their rage in a harmful way in a family therapy. Decisions regarding treatment of family members must, of course, take into account the characteristics and capacities of the patient. This view is echoed by E. Shapiro, and his colleagues (Shapiro, Zinner, Shapiro, & Berkowitz, 1975; Shapiro, Shapiro, & Zinner, 1977), who advocate a family therapeutic approach for borderline adolescents or young adults. They use conjoint weekly family therapy in conjunction with individual psychodynamic psychotherapy for the identified patient and ongoing couples treatment for the parents. The conjoint family treatment is carried out in tandem by the individual therapist and by the couples' therapist. When the borderline patient is older and married or is engaged in a significant relationship, ongoing couples treatment may also be a useful adjunct to individual psychotherapy.

Cognitive-Behavioral Techniques

Levendusky and colleagues (Berglas & Levendusky, 1985; Levendusky, Berglas, Dooley, & Landau, 1983; Levendusky & Dooley, 1985) have developed a promising treatment regimen for borderline patients, which centers around a modification of cognitive-behavioral techniques and may be used in conjunction with psychodynamic psychotherapy. They use the concepts of the therapeutic contract, group feedback, and structured cognitive-behavioral planning in helping borderline patients both to take increased responsibility for their lives and to begin to cope with the anxiety that ensues when such patients attempt greater social interaction or higher levels of vocational functioning. Of particular interest is their adjunctive use of (a) assertiveness training to help patients who feel downtrodden but who behave overly aggressively to meet their needs; (b) mood monitoring to help patients understand their affective lability while connecting their mood states to external events; and (c) a form of group social skills training to support the patients' acquisition of new behaviors.

Linehan and her research–clinical team (Linehan, 1981, 1987a, 1987b) also have created a cognitive-behavioral treatment for BPD, specifically for patients who engage in *parasuicide*.

Their approach of dialectical behavior therapy (DBT) has begun to show excellent results, and a full description of this approach is included elsewhere in this volume (see Chapter 23).

Group Psychotherapy

Horwitz (1977, 1980) has summarized many of the advantages of group psychotherapy with borderline patients, including the following: (a) The intensity of transference and countertransference reactions can be positively diluted through use of multiple therapeutic objects in the group; (b) Peer members in the group can aid in reality testing, can support appropriate social interaction, and can help titrate the need for social and emotional distance; (c) Peer pressure may help patients who have difficulties with their anger to find more reasonable outlets than they might find in individual psychotherapy alone; and (d) the group can provide opportunities for multiple identifications and can enable members to focus on issues such as jealousy, competition, and narcissistic defenses in a way that can be quite powerful and therapeutic.

Clinical experience also indicates that borderline patients are more likely to accept confrontations and interpretations from other patients earlier in treatment than they would from an individual therapist. Negativism toward authority and feelings of being controlled are less likely to emerge among peers in the group.

Macaskill (1982) notes that the group therapist, or the group itself, achieves effect by functioning along the lines of Winnicott's "holding environment" and becoming the "good-enough mother." Macaskill also stresses the capacity to provide soothing interpretations while instilling hope as important ingredients in effective group psychotherapy for BPD. Whether the groups should be diagnostically heterogeneous, as suggested by Wong (1980), or homogeneous, as argued by Stone and Weissman (1984), remains an open question.

Vocational Rehabilitation: Improving Work Skills

Rehabilitation aimed at enhancing work skills represents one of the greatest untapped resources in the treatment of BPD. Borderline patients are often severely deficient in vocational functioning. We have had good results in combining individual psychodynamic psychotherapy with a psychologically oriented approach to vocational rehabilitation outlined by Anthony (1977). Success in the workplace often enhances self-esteem and self-cohesion, and, in turn, positively affects progress in therapy. Nonetheless, analytically oriented clinicians have been reluctant to make full use of such approaches—although there is some evidence that such attitudes are changing (Pollack & Dion, 1985, 1987).

Psychopharmacology

Many researchers and clinicians advocate various psychopharmacological interventions for BPD. Medications suggested include (a) low-dose antipsychotics, (b) heterocyclic and "new wave" antidepressants, (c) monoamine oxidase inhibitors, (d) lithium, and most recently, (e) pemoline or methylphenidate, and (f) carbamazepine or valproic acid. The choice of drug, of course, relates to the theoretical connection postulated between BPD and other more biologically linked illnesses. Cole and Sunderland (1982), Cowdry and Gardner (1988), Gunderson and Elliott (1985), Liebowitz (1983), Soloff et al. (1986), and Chapter 24 of this volume have described the current psychopharmacological treatment regimens for borderline patients.

Whatever the approach chosen, one should consider the possibility that patients with BPD may also suffer from other biologically based illnesses, and vice versa. For example, clinicians who are used to treating depression psychopharmacologically may overlook a co-morbid personality disorder that could interfere with progress. On the other hand, therapists who tend to eschew medication may miss an opportunity to aid borderline patients by relieving biologically based depressive symptomatology. Once again, the issue of *balance* remains supreme.

It is also important to consider the psychodynamics of prescribing. The nature of the *transitional object transference* both to medication and to the prescribing treater (see Adelman, 1985) must be understood and addressed. The use of medication in psychotherapy is bound to have repercussions both within and outside of the treatment environment. Clinicians must consider the *meaning* of giving pills to patients with a yearning for closeness, and a need for early parenting; they should, therefore, proceed with caution and flexibility.

The need for a strong alliance between patient and therapist, or between patient and prescribing physician, is extremely important in BPD. Without it, patients may either not use their medication or use it in an inappropriate or self-destructive manner. If the prescribing physician and the psychotherapist are two different people, it is important to maintain frequent contact to avoid any splitting of these two helpers. It may be necessary to prescribe medication that is *least likely to be lethal* and, at times, to limit the number of pills per prescription, especially for patients who have suicidal impulses and are involved in an intensive psychotherapy.

SUMMARY

The psychotherapy of BPD poses many challenges, but it offers significant rewards—for clinician and patient, alike. Modern empirical research has supported the hypothesis that longer-term dynamic treatment has positive results, but it also has raised unanswered questions as to etiology, adjunctive therapeutics, efficacy, and biological interface.

The conceptualization of BPD and the integrated treatment paradigm described and illustrated herein may offer more than a *developmentally informed empathic psychotherapy matrix* with clinical utility. At its deepest and broadest moments, it suggests the possibilities for personal repair of the *self*, a repair that in borderline patients strikes at the heart of questions of life and death, pain and joy. In this sense, the psychotherapy of BPD remains only too humanly cathected and too humanly imperfect.

REFERENCES

Adelman, S. (1985). Pills as transitional objects: A dynamic understanding of the use of medication in psychotherapy. *Psychiatry 48*, 246–263.

Adler, G. (1985). *Borderline psychopathology and its treatment*. New York: Aronson.

Adler, G., & Buie, D. (1972). The misuses of confrontation with borderline patients. *International Journal of Psychoanalytic Psychotherapy, 1*, 109–120.

Adler, G., & Buie, D. (1979). Aloneness and borderline psychopathology: The possible relevance of child development issues. *International Journal of Psychoanalysis, 60*, 83–96.

Akiskal, H. (1981). Sub-affective disorders, dysthymic, cyclothymic and bipolar II disorders in the borderline realm. *Psychiatric Clinics of North America, 4*, 25–46.

Akiskal, H. (1983). The relationship of personality to affective disorders. *Archives of General Psychiatry, 40*, 801–810.

American Psychiatric Association. (1980). *Diagnostic and statistical manual of mental disorders* (3rd ed.). Washington, DC: Author.

American Psychiatric Association. (1987). *Diagnostic and statistical manual of mental disorders* (3rd ed., rev.). *(DSM-III-R)*. Washington, DC: Author.

Andrulonis, P., Glueck, B., Stroebel, C., Vogel, N., Shapiro, A., & Aldridge, D. (1981). Organic brain dysfunction and the borderline syndrome. *Psychiatric Clinics of North America, 4*, 47–66.

Anthony, W. A. (1977). Psychological rehabilitation: A concept in need of a method. *American Psychologist, 32*, 658–662.

Bardenstein, K. K., & McGlashan, T. H. (1988). The natural history of a residentially treated borderline sample: Gender differences. *Journal of Personality Disorders, 2*(1), 69–83.

Baron, M., Asnis, L., & Gruen, R. (1981). The Schedule for Interviewing Borderlines (SIB): A diagnostic interview for schizotypal features. *Journal of Psychiatric Research, 4*, 213–228.

Barrash, I., Kroll, J., Carey, K., & Sines, L. (1983). Discriminating borderline disorder from other personality disorders: Cluster analysis of the Diagnostic Interview for Borderlines. *Archives of General Psychiatry, 40*, 1297–1302.

Bauer, S., Hunt, H., Gould, M., & Goldstein, E. (1980). Personality organization, structural diagnosis and the structural interview. *Psychiatry, 43*, 224–233.

Berglas, S., & Levendusky, P. G. (1985). The therapeutic contract program: An individual oriented psychological treatment community. *Psychotherapy, 22*, 36–45.

Bion, W. R. (1967). *Second thoughts: Selected papers on psychoanalysis*. New York: Basic Books.

Brandschaft, B., & Stolorow, R. (1984). The borderline concept: Pathological character or iatrogenic myth? In J. Lichtenberg, M. Bornstein, & D. Silver (Eds.), *Empathy* (Vol. 2, pp. 333–357). Hillside, NJ: Analytic Press.

Bryer, J. B., Nelson, B. A., Miller, J. B., & Krol, P. A. (1987). Childhood sexual and physical abuse as factors in adult psychiatric illness. *American Journal of Psychiatry, 144,* 1426–1430.

Buie, D., & Adler, G. (1982). The definitive treatment of the borderline personality. *International Journal of Psychoanalytic Psychotherapy, 9,* 51–87.

Carpenter, W., Gunderson, J., & Strauss, J. (1977). Considerations of the borderline syndrome: A longitudinal comparative study of borderline and schizophrenic patients. In P. Hartocollis (Ed.), *Borderline personality disorders: The concept, the syndrome, the patient* (pp. 231–253). New York: International Universities Press.

Cole, J., & Sunderland, P. (1982). The drug treatment of borderline patients. In L. Grinspoon (Ed.), *Psychiatry* (Vol. 1, pp. 456–470). Washington, DC: American Psychiatric Press.

Cornell, D., Silk, K., Ludolph, P., & Lohr, N. (1983). Test–retest reliability of the diagnostic interview for borderlines. *Archives of General Psychiatry, 40,* 1307–1310.

Cowdry, R., & Gardner, D. (1988). Pharmacotherapy of borderline personality disorder: Alprazolam, carbamazepine, trifluoperazine and tranylcypromine. *Archives of General Psychiatry, 45,* 111–119.

Deutsch, H. (1942). Some forms of emotional disturbances and their relationship to schizophrenia. *Psychoanalytic Quarterly, 11,* 301–321.

Frances, A., Clarkin, J., Gilmore, M., Hurt, S.W., & Brown, R. (1984). Reliability of criteria for borderline personality disorder: A comparison of DSM-III and DIB. *American Journal of Psychiatry, 141,* 1080–1083.

Friedman, H. (1969). Some problems of inpatient management with borderline patients. *American Journal of Psychiatry, 126,* 299–304.

Friedman, H. (1975). Psychotherapy of borderline patients: The influence of theory on technique. *American Journal of Psychiatry, 132,* 1048–1052.

Frosch, J. (1970). Psychoanalytic considerations of the psychotic character. *Journal of the American Psychoanalytic Association, 18,* 24–50.

Frosch, J. P. (1983). *Current perspectives in personality disorders.* Washington, DC: American Psychiatric Press.

Gilligan, C. (1982). *In a different voice.* Cambridge, MA: Harvard University Press.

Giovacchini, P. (1979). *Treatment of primitive mental states.* New York: Aronson.

Glover, E. (1932). A psycho-analytic approach to classification of mental disorders. *Journal of Mental Science, 78,* 819–842.

Greenberg, S. (1977). *The supportive approach to therapy.* Unpublished manuscript, McLean Hospital, Belmont, MA.

Grinker, R., Werble, B., & Drye, R. (1968). *The borderline syndrome: A behavioral study of ego functions.* New York: Basic Books.

Grossman, F. K. (1985). Autonomy and affiliation: Parents and children. *Conference paper series.* Washington, DC: National Institute of Child Health and Development.

Grossman, F. K., Pollack, W. S., Golding, E. (1988). Fathers and children: Predicting the quality and quantity of fathering. *Developmental Psychology, 24*(1), 82–91.

Grossman, F. K., Pollack, W. S., Golding, E. R., & Fedele, N. M. (1987). Affiliation and autonomy in the transition to parenthood. *Family Relations, 36,* 263–269.

Grunebaum, H., & Klerman, G. (1967). Wrist slashing. *American Journal of Psychiatry, 124,* 524–534.

Gunderson, J. (1977). Characteristics of borderlines. In P. Hartocollis (Ed.), *Borderline personality disorders: The concept, the syndrome, the patient* (pp. 173–192). New York: International Universities Press.

Gunderson, J. (1982). Empirical studies of the borderline diagnosis. In L. Grinspoon (Ed.), *Psychiatry* (Vol. 1, pp. 414–437). Washington, DC: American Psychiatric Press.

Gunderson, J. (1983a). Discussion of Chessick, R.: Problems in the intensive psychotherapy of the borderline patient. *Dynamic Psychotherapy, 1,* 33–34.

Gunderson, J. (1983b, December). *Interfaces between psychoanalytic and empirical studies of borderline personality disorder.* Unpublished paper presented at the annual meeting of the American Psychoanalytic Association, New York.

Gunderson, J. (1984). *Borderline personality disorder.* Washington, DC: American Psychiatric Press.

Gunderson, J., Carpenter, W., & Strauss, J. (1975). Borderline and schizophrenic patients: A comparative study. *American Journal of Psychiatry, 132,* 1257–1264.

Gunderson, J., & Elliott, G. (1985). The interface between borderline personality disorder and affective disorder. *American Journal of Psychiatry, 142,* 277–288.

Gunderson, J., & Englund, D. (1981). Characterizing the families of borderlines. *Psychiatric Clinics of North America, 4,* 159–168.

Gunderson, J., & Kolb, J. (1978). Discriminating features of borderline patients. *American Journal of Psychiatry, 135,* 792–796.

Gunderson, J., Kolb, J., & Austin, V. (1981). The Diagnostic Interview for Borderline Patients. *American Journal of Psychiatry, 138,* 896–903.

Gunderson, J., & Pollack, W. (1985). Conceptual risks of the Axis I–II division. In H. Klar & L. J. Siever (Eds.), *Biological response styles: Clinical implications.* Washington, DC: American Psychiatric Press.

Gunderson, J., & Singer, M. (1975). Defining borderline patients: An overview. *American Journal of Psychiatry, 134,* 9–14.

Hoch, P., & Polatin, P. (1949). Pseudoneurotic forms of schizophrenia. *Psychiatric Quarterly, 23,* 248–276.

Horwitz, L. (1977). Group psychotherapy of the borderline patient. In P. Hartocollis (Ed.), *Borderline personality disorders: The concept, the syndrome, the patient* (pp. 399–422). New York: International Universities Press.

Horwitz, L. (1980). Group psychotherapy for borderline and narcissistic patients. *Bulletin of the Menninger Clinic, 44,* 181–200.

Hurt, S. W., Hyler, S. E., Frances, A., Clarkin, J. F., & Brent, R. (1984). Assessing borderline personality disorder with self-report, clinical interview, or semistructured interview. *American Journal of Psychiatry, 141,* 1228–1231.

Hyler, S. E., Rieder, R., Spitzer, R. L., & Williams, J. B. W. (1978). *Personality Diagnostic Questionnaire (PDQ).* New York: New York State Psychiatric Institute.

Institute of Medicine. (1985). A report of the board on mental health and behavioral medicine: Research on mental illness and addictive disorders: Progress and prospects. *American Journal of Psychiatry, 142,* (Suppl., July).

Kass, F., Skodol, A. E., Charles, E., Spitzer, R. L., & Williams, J. B. W. (1985). Scaled ratings of DSM-III personality disorders. *American Journal of Psychiatry, 142,* 627–630.

Kass, F., Spitzer, R. L., & Williams, J. B. W. (1983). An empirical study of the issue of sex bias in the diagnostic criteria of DSM-III Axis II personality disorder. *American Psychologist, 38,* 799–801.

Kernberg, O. (1965). Countertransference. *Journal of the American Psychoanalytic Association, 13,* 38–56.

Kernberg, O. (1967). Borderline personality organization. *Journal of the American Psychoanalytic Association, 15,* 641–685.

Kernberg, O. (1971). Prognostic considerations regarding borderline personality organization. *Journal of the American Psychoanalytic Association, 19,* 595–615.

Kernberg, O. (1975). *Borderline conditions and pathological narcissism.* New York: Aronson.

Kernberg, O. (1976). *Object-relations theory and clinical psychoanalysis.* New York: Aronson.

Kernberg, O. (1977). The structural diagnosis of borderline personality organization. In P. Hartocollis (Ed.), *Borderline personality disorders: The concept, the syndrome, the patient* (pp. 87–121). New York: International Universities Press.

Kernberg, O. (1981). Structural interviewing. *Psychiatric Clinics of North America, 4,* 169–195.

Kernberg, O. (1982). Supportive psychotherapy with borderline conditions. In J. Cavenar & H. Brodie (Eds.), *Critical problems in psychiatry* (pp. 180–202). Philadelphia, PA: Lippincott.

Kernberg, O. (1984). *Severe personality disorders psychotherapeutic strategies.* New Haven: Yale University Press.

Kernberg, O., Burstein, E., Coyne, L., Appelbaum, A., Horwitz, L., & Voth, H. (1972). Final report of the Menninger Foundation's psychotherapy research project: Psychotherapy and psychoanalysis. *Bulletin of the Menninger Clinic, 34,* 1–2.

Kibel, H. (1980). The importance of a comprehensive clinical diagnosis for group psychotherapy of borderline and narcissistic patients. *International Journal of Group Psychotherapy, 30,* 427–440.

Klein, D. (1977). Psychopharmacological treatment and delineation of borderline disorders. In P. Hartocollis (Ed.), *Borderline personality disorders: The concept, the syndrome, the patient* (pp. 365–384). New York: International Universities Press.

Klein, M. (1946). Notes on some schizoid mechanisms. *International Journal of Psychoanalysis, 27,* 99–110.

Knight, R. (1953). Borderline states. *Bulletin of the Menninger Clinic, 17,* 1–12.

Koenigsberg, H., Kaplan, R. D., Gilmore, M. M., & Cooper, A. M. (1985). The relationship between syndrome and personality disorder in DSM III: Experience with 2,462 patients. *American Journal of Psychiatry, 142,* 207–212.

Koenigsberg, H., Kernberg, O., & Schomer, J. (1983). Diagnosing borderline conditions in an outpatient setting. *Archives of General Psychiatry, 40,* 49–53.

Kohut, H. (1971). *The analysis of the self.* New York: International Universities Press.

Kohut, H. (1977). *The restoration of the self.* New York: International Universities Press.

Kohut, H. (1980). From a letter. In A. Goldberg (Ed.), *Advances in self-psychology.* New York: International Universities Press.

Kohut, H., & Wolf, E. (1978). The disorders of the self and their treatment: An outline. *International Journal of Psychoanalysis, 59,* 413–425.

Kolb, J., & Gunderson, J. (1980). Diagnosing borderline patients within semi-structured interviews. *Archives of General Psychiatry, 37,* 37–41.

Kroll, J., Carey, K., Sines, L., & Roth, M. (1982). Are there borderlines in Britain? A cross-validation of U.S. findings. *Archives of General Psychiatry, 39,* 60–63.

Kroll, J., Sines, L., Martin, K., Lari, S., Pyle, R., & Zander, J. (1981). Borderline personality disorder: Construct validity of the concept. *Archives of General Psychiatry, 38,* 1021–1026.

Levendusky, P. G., Berglas, S., Dooley, C. P., & Landau, R. J. (1983). Therapeutic contract program: A preliminary report on a behavioral alternative to the token economy. *Behavior Research and Therapy, 21,* 137–142.

Levendusky, P. G., & Dooley, C. P. (1985). An inpatient model for the treatment of anorexia nervosa. In S. Emmett (Ed.), *Theory and treatment of anorexia nervosa and bulimia—Biomedical, sociocultural and psychological perspectives* (pp. 211–213). New York: Brunner/Mazel.

Levine, H. B. (1979). The sustaining object relationship. *The Annual of Psychoanalysis, 7,* 203–232.

Liebowitz, M. (1983). Psychopharmacological intervention in personality disorders. In J. Frosch (Ed.), *Current perspectives on personality disorders* (pp. 68–93). Washington, DC: American Psychiatric Press.

Linehan, M. M. (1981). A social behavioral analysis of suicide and parasuicides: Implications for clinical assessment and treatment. In H. Glazer & J. Clarkin (Eds.), *Depression: Behavioral and directive intervention strategies.* New York: Brunner/Mazel.

Linehan, M. M. (1987a). Dialectical behavior therapy in groups: Treating borderline personality disorder and suicidal behavior. In C. M. Brody (Ed.), *Women in groups.* New York: Springer.

Linehan, M. M. (1987b). Dialectical behavioral therapy: A cognitive behavioral approach to parasuicide. *Journal of Personality Disorder, 1*(4), 328–333.

Loranger, A. W., Oldham, J. M. Russakoff, L. M., & Susman, V. L. (1984). *Personality disorder examination: A structured interview for making DSM-III Axis II diagnoses (PDE).* White Plains, NY: The New York Hospital—Cornell Medical Center, Westchester Division.

Macaskill, N. (1982). Therapeutic factors in group therapy with borderline patients. *International Journal of Group Psychotherapy, 32,* 61–74.

Madow, M., & Pollack, W. S. (1986). *Countertransference and inpatient psychiatry.* Manuscript submitted for publication.

Mahler, M. (1971). A study of the separation–individuation process and its possible application to borderline phenomena in the psychoanalytic situation. *Psychoanalytic Study of the Child, 26,* 403–424.

Mahler, M. (1972). Rapprochement subphase of the separation–individuation process. *Psychoanalytic Quarterly, 41,* 487–506.

Mahler, M., & Kaplan, L. (1977). Developmental aspects in the assessment of narcissistic and so-called borderline personalities. In P. Hartocollis (Ed.), *Borderline personality disorders: The concept, the syndrome, the patient* (pp. 71–86). New York: International Universities Press.

Mahler, M., Pine, F., & Bergman, A. (1975). *The psychological birth of the human infant.* New York: Basic Books.

Maltsberger, J. T., & Buie, D. H. (1974). Countertransference hate in the treatment of suicidal patients. *Archives of General Psychiatry, 30,* 625–633.

Masterson, J. (1971). Treatment of the adolescent with borderline syndrome (a problem in separation–individuation). *Bulletin of the Menninger Clinic, 35,* 5–18.

Masterson, J. (1976). *Psychotherapy of the borderline adult.* New York: Brunner/Mazel.

McGlashan, T. (1983). The borderline syndrome, II. Is borderline a variant of schizophrenia or affective disorder? *Archives of General Psychiatry, 40,* 1319–1323.

McGlashan, T. (1983). The Chestnut Lodge follow-up study, II. Long-term outcome of schizophrenia and the affective disorders. *Archives of General Psychiatry, 41,* 586–601.

McGlashan, T. H. (1986). The Chestnut Lodge follow-up study: III. Long-term outcome of borderline personalities. *Archives of General Psychiatry, 43,* 20–30.

Meissner, W. (1978). Theoretical assumptions of concepts of the borderline personality. *Journal of American Psychoanalytic Association, 26,* 559–578.

Millon, T. (1981). *Disorders of personality, DSM III.* New York: Wiley

Modell, A. (1963). Primitive object relationships and the predisposition to schizophrenia. *International Journal of Psychoanalysis, 44,* 282–291.

Modell, A. (1976). The holding environment and the therapeutic action of psychoanalysis. *Journal of the American Psychoanalytic Association, 24,* 285–308.

Modell, A. (1984). *Psychoanalysis in a new context.* New York: International Universities Press.

Oberndorf, C. (1930). The psycho-analysis of borderline cases. *New York State Journal of Medicine, 30,* 648–651.

Oldham, J., Clarkin, J. F., Appelbaum, A., Carr, A., Kernberg, O., Lotterman, A., & Haas, G. (1984). *A self-report instrument for borderline personality organization.* White Plains, NY: The New York Hospital—Cornell Medical Center, Westchester Division.

Perry, J. (1984). *The borderline personality disorder scale: Reliability and validity.* Unpublished manuscript.

Perry, J., & Klerman, G. (1980). Clinical features of the borderline personality disorder. *American Journal of Psychiatry, 137,* 165–173.

Pfohl, B., Stangl, D., & Zimmerman, M. (1983). *Structured Interview for DSM-III Personality Disorder (SIDP).* Iowa City, IA: University of Iowa Medical School, Department of Psychiatry.

Pollack, W. S. (1982). *"I-ness and "we-ness: Parallel lines of development.* Unpublished manuscript, Boston University, Boston, MA.

Pollack, W. S. (1983a). *The day hospital as a therapeutic holding environment.* The 1982 Proceedings of the annual conference on Partial Hospitalization, Boston, MA.

Pollack, W. S. (1983b). Object-relations and self psychology: Researching children and their family systems. *The Psychologist–Psychoanalyst, 4,* 14.

Pollack, W. S. (1986). Borderline personality disorder: Definition, diagnosis, assessment and treatment considerations. In P. A. Keller & L. G. Ritt (Eds.), *Innovations in clinical practice* (Vol. 5, pp. 103–135). Sarasota, FL: Professional Resource Exchange.

Pollack, W. S. (1989). *Boys and men: Developmental ramifications of autonomy and affiliation.* Paper presented at the Mid-winter Meetings, American Psychological Association, Division of Psychotherapy, Orlando, Florida.

Pollack, W. S., & Dion, G. (1985). *Functional disability, severity of illness and DSM III diagnosis: The creation of a scale.* Unpublished manuscript, Harvard Medical School, Belmont, MA.

Pollack, W. S., & Dion, G. (1987). Beyond DSM-III Axis V: Creating an alternative multiaxial measure of psychosocial functioning—Measuring severity of illness in hospitalized psychiatric patients. In S. M. Mirin (Ed.), *Current research in private psychiatric hospitals.* Washington, DC: National Association of Private Psychiatric Hospitals.

Pollack, W. S., & Grossman, F. K. (1985). Parent–child interaction. In L. L'Abate (Ed.), *The handbook of family psychology and therapy* (pp. 586–622). Homewood, IL: Dorsey Press.

Pope, H., Jonas, J., Hudson, J., Cohen, B. M., & Gunderson, J. G. (1983). The validity of DSM-III borderline personality disorder. *Archives of General Psychiatry, 40,* 23–30.

Rinsley, D. (1982). *Borderline and other self disorders.* New York: Aronson.

Roth, B. (1980). Understanding the development of a homogeneous identity-impaired group through countertransference phenomena. *International Journal of Group Psychotherapy, 30,* 405–426.

Roth, B. (1982). Six types of borderline and narcissistic patients: An initial typology. *International Journal of Group Psychotherapy, 32,* 9–27.

Schatzberg, A. (1983). *Brain imaging in atypical depressions.* Paper presented at the McLean Hospital Symposim on Atypical Depressions, New York.

Searles, H. (1979a). *Countertransference and related subjects: Selected papers.* New York: International Universities Press.

Searles, H. (1979b). The countertransference with the borderline patient. In J. Leboit & A. Capponi (Eds.), *Advances in psychotherapy of the borderline patient* (pp. 347–403). New York: Aronson.

Sharpiro, E., Shapiro, R., & Zinner, J. (1977). The borderline ego and the working alliance: Indications for family and individual treatment in adolescence. *International Journal of Psychoanalysis, 58,* 77–87.

Shapiro, E., Zinner, J., Shapiro, R., & Berkowitz, D. (1975). The influence of family experience on borderline personality development. *International Review of Psychoanalysis, 2,* 399–411.

Siever, L., & Gunderson, J. (1983). The search for a

schizotypal personality: A review. *Comprehensive Psychiatry, 24,* 199–212.

Soloff, P. H., George, A., Natman, R. S., Schultz, P. M., Ulrich, R. F., & Perel, J. M. (1986). Progress in pharmacotherapy of borderline disorders. *Archives of General Psychiatry, 43,* 691–697.

Spitzer, R., & Endicott, J. (1979). Justification for separating schizotypal and borderline personality disorders. *Schizophrenia Bulletin, 5,* 95–104.

Spitzer, R., Endicott, J., & Gibbon, M. (1979). Crossing the border into borderline personality and borderline schizophrenia: The development of criteria. *Archives of General Psychiatry, 36,* 17–24.

Spitzer, R., Williams, J., & Skodol, A. (1980). DSM-III: The major achievements and an overview. *American Journal of Psychiatry, 137,* 151–164.

Stangl, D., Pfohl, B., Zimmerman, M., Bowers, W., & Corenthal, C. (1985). A structured interview for the *DSM-III* personality disorder. *Archives of General Psychiatry, 42,* 591–596.

Stern, A. (1938). Psychoanalytic investigation of and therapy in the borderline group of neuroses. *Psychoanalytic Quarterly, 7,* 467–489.

Stiver, I. (1985). The meanings of "dependency" in female male relationships. *Work in progress series, stone center.* Wellesley, MA: The Stone Center for Developmental Services and Studies at Wellesley College.

Stiver, I. (1988). Developmental psychopathology: Introducing a consultant in the treatment of borderline patients. *McLean Hospital Journal, 13, 89–113.*

Stone, M. (1980). *Borderline syndromes.* New York: McGraw-Hill.

Stone, M., & Weissman, R. (1984). Group therapy with borderline patients. In N. Slavinka-Holy (Ed.), *Contemporary perspectives in group psychotherapy.* London: Routledge & Kegan Paul.

Stone, M. H., Hurt, S. W., & Stone, D. K. (1987). The PI 500: Long-term follow-up of borderline inpatients meeting DSM-III criteria. I. Global outcome. *Journal of Personality Disorders, 1*(4), 291–298.

Stororow, R. D., & Lachman, F. M. (1980). *Psychoa-nalysis of developmental arrests: Theory and treatment.* New York: International Universities Press.

Tolpin, M. (1971). On the beginnings of a cohesive self: An application of the concept of transmuting internalization to the study of the transitional object and signal anxiety. *The Psychoanalytic Study of the Child, 26,* 316–354.

Tolpin, M., & Kohut, H. (1980). The disorders of the self: The psychopathology of the first years of life. In S. I. Greenspan & G. Pollack (Eds.), *The course of life* (Vol. 1, pp. 425–442). Adelphi, MD: National Institute of Mental Health.

Waldinger, R. J., & Gunderson, J. G. (1987). *Effective psychotherapy with borderline patients.* New York: Macmillan.

Wallerstein, R. (1983, October 29). *Psychoanalysis and psychotherapy: Relative roles reconsidered.* Paper presented at the Boston Psychoanalytic Society and Institute Symposium, Boston, MA.

Winnicott, D. (1953). Transitional objects and transitional phenomena. *International Journal of Psychoanalysis, 34,* 89–97.

Winnicott, D. (1960). The theory of the parent–infant relationships. *International Journal of Psychoanalysis, 41,* 585–595.

Winnicott, D. (1965). *The maturational process and the facilitating environment.* New York: International Universities Press.

Winnicott, D. (1975). Hate in the countertransference (1947, pp. 194–203), and the depressive position in normal emotional development (1954, pp. 262–277). In *Through Paediatrics to Psychoanalysis.* New York: Basic Books.

Wolberg, A. R. (1952). The "borderline" patient. *American Journal of Psychotherapy, 6,* 694–710.

Wong, J. (1980). Combined group and individual treatment of borderline and narcissistic patients: Heterogeneous vs. homogeneous groups. *International Journal of Group Psychotherapy, 30,* 389–404.

Zetzel, E. (1971). A developmental approach to the borderline patient. *American Journal of Psychiatry, 128,* 867–871.

CHAPTER 23

Behavior Therapy

MARSHA M. LINEHAN AND ELIZABETH J. WASSON

CONCEPTUALIZATION OF THE DISORDER

There have been only two experimental studies documenting the effectiveness of behavior therapy (or *any* psychotherapy) with borderline personality disorder (BPD): those of Linehan (1987a) and of Turner (1987). Although cognitive therapists are currently developing theories (Pretzer, in press; Young, 1983, 1987, 1988), to date only Linehan and Turner have published their behavioral approaches to the disorder.

Turner proposes that maladaptive schema learned early in life are responsible for rapid dysjunctive shifts in mental and emotional sets characteristic of borderline individuals. These shifts lead to a disturbance in the sense of temporal continuity, and to cognitive confusion, disorientation, and derealization whenever a feared stressor occurs. Among the behavioral sequelae to these difficulties are interpersonal problems, social anxiety, cognitive dysfunction, depression, and impulsive behavior.

Because Turner's theory is essentially a cognitive one, and this chapter is devoted to behavior therapy, we focus here on Linehan's dialectical behavioral theory of the development of BPD. The following is a summary of Linehan's (1987c) theoretical position. The roots of Linehan's theory lie in a dialectical perspective of biosocial (behavioral) theory, based on clinical observation of recurring behavior–environmental patterns among individuals diagnosed as having borderline personalities.

Philosophical Underpinnings

A dialectical world view has been applied to socioeconomic history (Marx & Engels, 1970), the development of science, (Kuhn, 1970), biological evolution (Levins & Lewontin, 1985), analyses of sexual relations (Firestone, 1970), and, more recently, development of thinking in adults (Basseches, 1984). Wells (1972, cited in Kegan, 1982) has documented a shift toward dialectical approaches in almost every social and natural science during the past 150 years. Dialectical analysis is crucial to understanding the developmental analysis of both the borderline condition and the treatment process espoused by Linehan (1984, 1987b, 1987c, 1987d).

A dialectical framework stresses the fundamental interrelatedness and wholeness of reality, and it is in direct contradiction to traditional Cartesian reductionism. As Levins and Lewontin (1985) describe, in the Cartesian world view, parts are seen as homogenous entities, existing separately from the whole they comprise. In contrast, a dialectical view sees the internal heterogeneity of elements at every level such that knowing the parts of the whole depends on what facets of the whole are being considered. Elements are nonreducible, and there is no à priori independent existence of parts, only parts as they relate to a particular whole. Wholes themselves are, in turn, not static but comprise internal opposing forces (*thesis* and *antithesis*) out of whose *synthesis* evolves a new set of opposing forces. Thus, parts and whole are in constant interaction and re-creation of each other. At the same time, the ever-changing nature of the whole influences and is influenced by the external world of which it is a part. Thus, the founding principles of a dialectical world view are the *nonreducible* nature of reality and the *interconnectedness* of all things, both of which lead to a *wholeness* continually in the process of *change*.

The behavioral, tripartite systems view of human functioning is compatible, with slight modification, with a dialectical approach. In the tripartite view, behavioral responses are partitioned into three general subsystems: (1) the overt–motor system, (2) the physiological–emotional system, and (3) the cognitive–verbal system (Staats, 1975). A systems orientation suggests that the relationships among the three systems are dynamic such that change in any one will produce systemwide changes (Schwartz, 1982). No one system is viewed as primary. In turn, equal significance is accorded to the reciprocal influence of the interactions between the person system and the social-environmental system. From a dialectical point of view, addressing any one system in isolation from the others is not meaningful. Similarly, the individual cannot be isolated from his or her environment. Less obvious, but equally true, the environment cannot be isolated from the individual.

A dialectical–systems approach influences conceptualization on all levels. For example, it is immediately obvious that a dialectical view favors a dimensional rather than a categorical classification system inasmuch as categories reduce or alienate nature from itself by creating a myriad of self-contained, independent parts. Dimensions are defined by their opposing poles. A dialectical approach, rather than identifying phenomena as static points on a dimensional continuum, emphasizes the continuous creation of the phenomena out of the tension exerted by the coexistence of the forces of the opposing poles.

For example, the overriding dialectic accounting for the genesis of the borderline syndrome may be the tension generated by the juxtaposition of emotion invalidating environments and biologically predisposed vulnerability to emotional extremes. On the level of particular borderline behaviors, such as interpersonal dependence, a dialectical perspective would suggest that independence without dependence is a myth. Often, the problem for borderline clients is not too much dependence, as is commonly supposed, but too much *fear* of dependence, with good reason of course. (From our perspective, the question certainly can be raised of whether the world would not perhaps be better off if we emphasized dependence more and independence less!)

Most important, a dialectical account of psychopathology may allow greater compassion. Dialectics, with its systemic overtones, is incompatible with the assignment of blame, certainly a relevant issue with a label as stigmatized among mental health professionals as "borderline" (for examples of the misuse of the diagnosis, see Reiser & Levenson, 1984).

Fundamental Behavioral–Environmental Patterns

The behavioral patterns for BPD can be organized along three dialectical poles arranged around a biosocial axis: (1) emotional vulnerability versus invalidation, (2) active passivity versus apparent competence, and (3) unrelenting crises versus inhibited grieving. Those patterns above the axis (emotional vulnerability, active passivity, unrelenting crises) are originally most heavily influenced by biological factors associated with emotion regulation. Those patterns below the axis (invalidation, apparent competence, inhibited grieving) are most heavily influenced by social responses to emotional expressiveness. An account of the empirical bases of these syndromes may be found in Linehan (1987c).

Vulnerability Versus Invalidation

The *emotional vulnerability syndrome* refers to the inability of many borderline individuals to regulate emotional responses. They are exquisitely sensitive to any kind of stimuli (but most especially to emotional stimuli), they respond intensely to even low-level stimuli, and they have difficulty regulating the return to an emotional baseline. They cope by vacillating between shutting down, avoiding, and blocking all incoming emotional stimuli—a pattern associated with sensory overload—and intensely overreacting, which leads to various dysfunctional escape behaviors, such as substance abuse and parasuicide.

Current research on temperament suggests that

high autonomic and emotional reactivity is often constitutional in origin (Derryberry & Rothbart, 1984; Strelau, Farley, & Gale, 1986; Thomas & Chess, 1986). Cowdry and his associates (cited in Turkington, 1986) report data suggesting that borderline clients may have a low threshold for activation of limbic structures, a brain system associated with emotion regulation. Other studies suggest the emotional experience of the parasuicidal individual is one of chronic aversive affect, including anger, hostility, irritability, depression, and social discomfort and anxiety (see Linehan, 1981 for a review). These findings are congruent with the DSM-III-R BPD criteria of emotional lability and problems with anger.

The *invalidation syndrome* refers to the tendency to invalidate affective experiences, to oversimplify the ease of solving life's problems, and to attach great value to the power of thinking positively in overcoming any problem. The environment thus created is similar to the "high expressed emotion" pattern found in families of both depressed and schizophrenic clients with high relapse rates (Leff & Vaughn, 1985). *High expressed emotion* refers to high criticism and overinvolvement. We add to those two aspects a nonrecognition of the individual's actual state, such as in nonempathetic parenting and, most especially, abusive behaviors.

Developmentally, the crucial aspect of the invalidating environment is that it results in inadequate training in emotion-regulation skills. Emotionally vulnerable individuals do not learn adequately to label or control emotional reactions or to trust their own emotional responses as reflections of valid interpretations of individual and situational events. They often learn that extreme emotional displays are necessary to provoke a helpful environmental response.

The emotional result of this state of affairs is that the child, and later the adult, does not develop emotional tolerance and stability. Because emotional consistency and predictability, across time and across similar situations, are prerequisites for the development of a sense of self, a stable sense of identity fails to develop. A stable sense of self, in addition to emotional control skills, is a necessary ingredient for stable interpersonal relationships. Deficits in these areas give rise to the interpersonal problems so characteristic of this population.

Active Passivity Versus Apparent Competence

Active passivity refers to the tendency to approach problems passively and helplessly rather than actively and competently. There is also a corresponding tendency under extreme distress to demand active problem solving by the environment. This problem-solving style is intimately related to the preceding vulnerability–invalidation dimension. For example, Bialowas (cited in Strelau et al., 1986) found a positive relationship between high autonomic reactivity and dependency in a social-influence situation. Research by Eliasz (1985) suggests that people with high autonomic reactivity, independent of other considerations, may prefer passive self-regulation styles.

Inability to protect oneself from extreme negative affect and the resulting hopelessness may account for the interpersonal dependency of borderline individuals. When psychic pain is extreme, reaching out to others for problem resolution turns to emotional clinging and demanding behaviors. Predictably, threats of loss or actual loss of significant people leads to intense emotional responses.

The *apparent competence syndrome* refers to the tendency of borderline individuals to appear deceptively competent. The deception lies in the fact that the real competence they have is not generalized across all relevant situations. At times, the borderline person's apparent control is at the cost of almost total inhibition of negative affective experiences and expression. Adopting the beliefs of their environment—that they are competent to succeed no matter what—they may experience intense guilt about the presumed lack of motivation when they fall short of their objectives. At other times, they experience extreme anger at other people for the other's lack of understanding and unrealistic expectations. Both experiences—intense guilt and intense anger—can lead to dysfunctional behaviors, including suicide and parasuicide, aimed at reducing the painful emotional states.

Unrelenting Crises Versus Inhibited Grieving

The individual's high reactivity, together with the chronicity of the stress, produces states of *unrelenting crises*. The individual can never return to an emotional baseline before the next blow hits. From Selye's (1956) point of view, the individual is constantly approaching the exhaustion stage of stress adaptation. It may be that constitutional factors exacerbate the individual's initial emotional response and rate of return to baseline after each stressor. The magnitude and number of subsequent stressors are then increased by the individual's responses to the initial stressor. An inability to tolerate or reduce short-term stress without resorting to dysfunctional escape behaviors brings about further stressors. Inadequate interpersonal skills, inadequate social support networks, and so on further prolong the stress and weaken the ability to develop needed capabilities.

The *inhibited grieving syndrome* refers to a pattern of recurring, significant trauma and loss, together with an inability to experience and integrate these events. Crises of any type always involve some form of loss, whether the loss is concrete (e.g., loss of a person through death, loss of money or job, loss of a relationship through divorce), psychological (e.g., loss of predictability and control due to sudden, unexpected environmental changes; loss of wanted, nurturing parents through recognition of their limitations), or perceptual (e.g., the loss of acceptance borderline individuals experience when they interpret another person's remarks as critical of them). The accumulation of such losses leads to *bereavement overload*, a term coined by Kastenbaum (1969). Grief inhibition is understandable. We can only stay with a painful process or experience if we are confident that it will end someday. It is common to hear these individuals say they feel that if they ever do start to cry, they will never stop.

Social-Behavioral Underpinnings

A detailed description of learning theories and how they might account for much of the BPD syndrome is complex and beyond the scope of this chapter. Dialectical behavior theory (DBT) is based on the application of radical behavior theory, principles of classical conditioning, and discrete emotions theory regarding the development of adult borderline behaviors. Several other assumptions are central to DBT: First, individuals need emotional validation, certainly developmentally, in order to learn emotional regulation. Second, emotional expressiveness is punished in invalidating environments. Third, part of the emotional vulnerability of individuals with borderline syndrome is biological predisposition for a

stronger grief or anger response to standard stimulus conditions than exists in others. Basic research to corroborate these assumptions has not yet been conducted. Thus, the logic of the biosocial (behavioral) formulation of BPD described so far is based on theoretical speculation rather than on firm empirical experimentation.

DIAGNOSTIC ISSUES AND PROBLEMS

As a diagnostic category, BPD is controversial, both for behavioral researchers and for those adhering to a mainstream medical model of science. The term *borderline* itself, with its lack of specific referents, adds to the confusion. Although originating in psychoanalytic theories of psychopathology, *borderline* has been used by psychoanalysts in divergent contexts.

Theoretical and Diagnostic Dilemmas

Construct of Personality

A major problem with BPD from a behavioral point of view is the construct of *personality*. How does one operationalize *personality*? At a minimum, the notion of a personality disorder requires one to assume that individual behavior patterns (including patterns of action, cognitive processes, and physiological–emotional responses) are reasonably consistent across both time and situations. This assumption, however, has long been questioned by behaviorists. Mischel's (1968) now-classic summary of the empirical data underlying the premise that behavior is a function of *person characteristics* (i.e., personality) concluded that much behavioral variation formerly attributed to personality is instead due to situational characteristics. With some additional limits, Mischel's conclusion has withstood the test of intensive critical scrutiny over the years.

Categorical Versus Behavioral Focus

From a behavioral perspective, a categorical classification system is a problematic match for BPD, both because by definition a categorical approach espouses a different scientific paradigm from behaviorism, and because even within the context of a categorical classification system, BPD is unable to satisfy that system's requirements for validity. A fundamental problem is that a categorical approach assumes the existence and significance of some underlying essence of "borderlineness" that is not immediately accessible to investigation. Moreover, independent verification of the existence of such a phenomenon, such as locating a borderline gene or a particular ratio of various neurotransmitters that adds up to "borderlineness," has not been achieved.

Further problems with validity are reflected in the plethora of studies that find overlaps between measures of BPD and many Axis I and Axis II disorders, notably, affective disorders (Akiskal, 1981; Andrulonis, Glueck, Stroebel, & Vogel, 1982; Davis & Akiskal, 1986; Soloff, 1981; Frances, Clarkin, Gilmore, Hurt & Brown, 1984; Loranger, Oldham, Russakoff, & Susman, 1984; Perry, 1985; Pope, Jonas, Hudson, Cohen, & Gunderson, 1983), substance abuse (Loranger et al., 1984; Frances, Clarkin, Gilmore, Hurt, & Brown, 1984; Andrulonis et al., 1982; Loranger & Tulis, 1985), and other personality disorders, most usually histrionic, schizotypal, dependent, narcissistic, and antisocial personality disorders (Clarkin, Widiger, Frances, Hurt, & Gilmore, 1983; Frances et al., 1984; Kroll et al., 1981; Pope et al., 1983). Briere (1984) has detailed the many behavioral patterns that persons diagnosed with BPD hold in common with victims of sexual abuse.

In the absence of knowing what core problem constitutes "borderlineness" it is unclear what characteristics are its direct expression. As Widiger and Frances (1987) point out, the criteria sets of DSM-III-R are at times used diagnostically, and at times, definitionally. At times, the criteria are viewed as indicators of some underlying pathology (diagnostically), and at other times, they are used as operational criteria of a disorder (definitionally). Worse, research is, in many cases, not yet sufficiently advanced to know which criteria *are* definitional and which (if any) diagnostic. Problems with validity and diagnosis are thus, for the DSM-III-R categorical classification system, inextricably intertwined.

From a behavioral point of view a final problem involves the treatment utility of a categorical system of classification. Taken at face value, the generally good interrater reliability of some measures of BPD might seem to support the notion that a pattern of behaviors exists that for simplicity's sake, may be labeled "borderline." However, as Clarkin et al. (1983) point out, reliability of DSM-III criteria does not guarantee homogenous groupings of behaviors across subjects. They observe that DSM-III-R calls for meeting five out of eight criteria to receive the diagnosis, making 56 different ways to qualify for BPD. High interrater reliability can be achieved for the diagnosis even when behavioral clusters are nonoverlapping across subjects. Heterogeneity of criteria clusters across subjects is also suggested by mixed findings on intermeasure agreement. Clearly, this presents a formidable problem for treatment when treatment is aimed at reducing behaviors associated with the diagnosis. Ideally, treatment would consist of a flexible series of strategies that could be used singly or in different combinations to accommodate the possibly unique constellation of behaviors engaged in by any one borderline client.

Behavioral Perspectives

Personality, from the behaviorist's perspective, may best be regarded as a set of behavioral capabilities (Wallace, 1966). Defining *personality* or *personality disorder* from this framework, therefore, consists of defining the relevant behavioral and associated stimulus content domains and choosing behaviors thought to be representative samples of the domains of interest. Content validity then becomes the issue. Are the behaviors identified by current measures of BPD representative samples of the behavioral domains constituting borderline behaviors? The first step in answering such a question involves the development of instruments that assess measurable behavioral criteria. Both the DSM-III-R criteria and the Gunderson Diagnostic Interview for Borderlines (DIB) fulfill this requirement and offer high enough measurement reliability to be usable in research. Then, the crucial question from a behavioral point of view is not whether there is any underlying deep organizing principle to the particular behaviors labeled "borderline," but whether these behaviors truly cooccur. Unfortunately, studies that might answer this question, studies of the intercorrelation of borderline criterion behaviors, have not yet been done.

Conditional probability studies shed some light on clusters of criterion borderline patterns that tend to co-occur. Clarkin et al. (1983) found that the two most frequent combinations of five response patterns in their sample were (1) impulsivity, unstable–intense relationships, intense/uncontrolled anger, affective instability, and chronic feelings of boredom or emptiness, and (2) a similar combination in which chronic boredom and emptiness were replaced by physically self-damaging acts. Unfortunately, clustering, and certainly the diagnostic power of different criterion behavioral patterns, are influenced by base rates. Base rates, in turn, are influenced by the type of treatment setting. Thus, whereas Clarkin et al. (1983) found unstable/intense relationships and chronic feelings of boredom and emptiness to be the most sensitive and specific indicators of BPD in an outpatient population, Widiger, Frances, Warner, and Bluhm (1986), using a far more dysfunctional inpatient population, found impulsivity and physically self-damaging acts to be the most efficient indicators of the diagnosis.

Advantages of a Dimensional Approach

The poorness-of-fit between a categorical classification system and BPD is evidenced by the absence of data supporting a fundamental, underlying organizational principle, the frequency of overlap with numerous other diagnoses, and, within the category, the heterogeneity of criteria clusters across subjects. In addition, Frances et al. (1984) point out that where the distribution of scores for a diagnosis is uniform, such as was the case with their sample's scores on the DIB, cutoffs are arbitrary. The boundaries of classically defined categories depend upon points of rarity. The absence of points of rarity to define categories suggests that alternative systems of classification should be considered. Rather than discrete or prototypical categories, continuums may provide the best fit to the data. Continuums are, in turn, best represented by dimensional rather than categorical approaches to classification.

From a behavioral point of view, there are several advantages to a dimensional system of classification and diagnosis. First, dimensions may provide a more accurate and flexible fit to the data, because (a) dimensions can take account of phenomena excluded from consideration by diagnostic categories, (b) dimensions depend on finer measurements than categorical data, which in turn means that phenomena must be more carefully operationalized, more tied to observables, and (c)

the fit between dimensions and the characteristics of the natural occurrence of the phenomenon in question may be closer. Second, as Cloninger (1987) points out, there is little evidence of bimodal or multimodal distributions in the observed variation of so-called normal personality traits, suggesting that cognitive and social styles vary along continuums. Third, a dimensional approach has clear advantages for treatment, where dimensions are defined by specific classes of behaviors, and therefore clearly specify the targets of treatment.

Last, a dimensional approach has advantages over a categorical approach for research and theory-building analogous to the advantages of a phenomena-over-diagnosis approach endorsed by Persons (1986). By allowing inclusion of more of the overt phenomena organized into smaller chunks, a dimensional approach enables the study of single phenomena in isolation, permits the theory-rich recognition of the continuity of clinical phenomena with normal phenomena. By allowing attention to detail, it will most likely improve diagnosis.

The behavioral treatments offered to date represent an interesting blend of categorical and dimensional approaches. The treatments are modular, focused on specific behavioral targets, and, thus, fit a dimensional perspective. However, inclusion criteria for clients in the research studies, theoretical underpinnings of the treatments, and strategies for applying the treatment modules are based largely on categorical assumptions. Some aspect of "borderlineness" (i.e., some characteristic setting these clients apart from other clients) is presumed to moderate the influence of specific treatments targeted to specific behavioral phenomena.

APPROACHES TO TREATMENT

Overview

A core component of both Linehan's and Turner's treatments is the notion that borderline individuals have several important behavioral deficits. Turner focuses on interpersonal skill and anxiety-management deficits. Linehan also targets interpersonal skills, but she expands anxiety management to encompass emotional control, and she adds a focus on developing distress-tolerance skills. Both offer group plus individual treatment.

Turner's treatment consists of four sequential phases: (1) pharmacotherapy stabilization, (2) flooding procedures to inoculate clients against cognitive and mood experiences associated with their worst symptoms, (3) covert rehearsal and in vivo practice of coping strategies, and (4) interpersonal problem-solving training.

Linehan offers four sequential group treatments: (1) core skills (observing, describing, spontaneously participating, being mindful, being nonjudgmental, and focusing on effectiveness); (2) interpersonal skills; (3) emotion-regulation skills; and (4) distress-tolerance skills. Although the individual therapist has the task of helping the client integrate the skills into daily life, the rudiments of the skills are taught in group sessions.

Treatment targets (goals) in Linehan's therapy are hierarchically arranged as follows: (1) suicidal behaviors (parasuicide, high-risk suicide ideation), (2) behaviors interfering with the conduct of therapy, (3) escape behaviors interfering with a reasonably high quality of life (e.g., substance abuse, poor work behaviors, criminal behaviors, poor judgment), (4) behavioral-skill acquisition (emotion regulation, interpersonal effectiveness, distress tolerance, self-management), (5) other goals the client wants to focus on. Attention is shifted from a later target to a target earlier on the list when problems in that area resurface. Thus, therapy is somewhat circular, in that target focal points revolve over time.

Linehan's therapy has three overriding characteristics: (1) a problem-solving focus, (2) an emphasis on dialectical processes, and (3) observation and management of the contingencies operating in the client–therapist relationship. The problem-solving focus requires that the therapist address both the problematic client behaviors (in and out of sessions) and the therapy situations in a systematic manner, including the conduct of a collaborative behavioral analysis, formulation of hypotheses about possible variables influencing the problem, generation of possible changes (behavioral solutions), and trial and evaluation of the solutions.

The overriding dialectic is the necessity of accepting clients just as they are, within a context of trying to teach them to change. The tension of clients' excessive alternations between high and low aspirations and expectations relative to their own capabilities offers a formidable challenge to therapists, requiring moment-to-moment changes in the use of supportive-acceptance versus confrontation-change strategies. The term *dialectical* also suggests both the necessity of dialectical thinking on the part of the therapist and the targeting of nondialectical, rigid, and dichotomous thinking on the part of the client.

Specific Treatment Strategies

Dialectical behavior therapy is defined by its philosophical underpinnings, by its target behaviors, (both described previously) and by its treatment strategies. There are eight basic strategy groups, which are combined to deal with specific problematic situations: (1) dialectical, (2) problem solving, (3) irreverent communication, (4) consultant, (5) validation, (6) capability enhancement, (7) relationship, and (8) contingency strategies.

Dialectical Strategies

The primary dialectic is that of change in the context of acceptance of reality as it is. The therapist facilitates change by highlighting the dialectical oppositions arising in sessions and in everyday life, and by fostering their successive reconciliation and resolution at increasingly functional levels. Rigid adherence to either pole of the dialectic increases tension between client and therapist, and it inhibits reconciliation and synthesis.

The dialectical focus involves two levels of therapeutic behavior. First, the therapist is alert to the dialectical balance occurring within the treatment relationship itself. Second, the therapist teaches and models dialectical thinking. (See Basseches, 1984, for a very useful discussion of the characteristics of dialectical thinking.) Strategies include extensive use of metaphor, myth and paradox, nonresolution of ambiguity, focus on reality as constant change, cognitive challenging and restructuring, and reinforcement for use of intuitive, nonrational knowledge bases.

Problem-Solving Strategies

Although it may seem obvious, problem solving requires first an acceptance of the existence of a problem. As noted earlier, therapeutic change can only occur within the context of acceptance of the existing situation. In the case of borderline clients, problem solving is enormously complicated by their frequent tendency to view themselves in a negative manner and their inability to regulate their consequent emotional distress. On the one pole, they often have difficulty correctly identifying problems in their environment, tending instead to view all problems as somehow self-generated. On the other pole, the view that all problems are self-generated is so painful that the client often responds by inhibiting the process of self-reflection. By acknowledging the problem, therapist and client have already begun engaging in the change pole of the dialectic.

Identification of the problem(s) causing distress is often not easy. The usual tactic is to teach the client to use dysfunctional responses, such as parasuicide, as signals of a problem that needs to be solved. The therapist and the patient then conduct a thorough behavioral analysis of these signal responses. The chain of events leading up to the dysfunctional responses is examined in minute detail, including the reciprocal interaction between the environment and the client's responses (cognitive, emotional, and overt-behavioral). Hypotheses about variables influencing or controlling the dysfunctional behaviors are generated and evaluated.

Next, alternative response chains (i.e., adaptive solutions), which could have been made, and which could be made in the future, are generated and analyzed, as well as the client's response capabilities. It often becomes clear that the individual does not have the requisite response capabilities (skills). The therapist then moves to the capability-enhancement strategies. Sometimes, problem-solving requires the help of other professionals in the community (e.g., to obtain hospitalization, medication, or financial assistance). The therapist then moves to the consultant strategies. At times, it may be that the client has the requisite capabilities but is inaccurate in predicting current environmental response contingencies. At other times, current contingencies that do operate favor dysfunctional over functional behaviors. The therapist then moves to the contingency strategies. Finally, issues in the therapist–client relationship may be the source of the problem. In this case, use of the relationship strategies is in order.

Irreverent-Communication Strategy

The irreverent communication strategy in DBT requires the therapist to take a matter-of-fact, somewhat irreverent attitude toward dysfunctional problem-solving attempts, including suicidal behaviors, therapy interfering behaviors, and other escape behaviors. These behaviors are accepted as normal consequences of individual learning histories and current operating factors in the individual's life. Used judiciously, irreverent communication facilitates problem solving and at the same time does not reinforce suicidal behavior.

Consultant Strategy

In DBT, the therapist role is that of consultant to the client, not to other treatment professionals interacting with the client. Thus, the therapist helps clients modify their own behavior in order for them to interact effectively with other community professionals. As a rule, the DBT therapist does not assist other professionals in planning or modifying their behavior to be effective with the client. When asked directly, other professionals are advised to follow normal procedures. Clients are taught interpersonal skills, not the other professionals.

There are two exceptions to this rule. First, direct intervention is used when substantial harm may come to the client from professionals who are unwilling to modify their treatment unless a high-power person intervenes. The mental health and judicial systems and public assistance programs are examples of systems where intervention is often needed. Second, DBT group and individual therapists are in constant contact. From the point of view of DBT, the well-known phenomenon of staff splitting is seen as a problem of the treatment professionals rather than a client problem. Treatment staff are encouraged to use their interpersonal skills to work out these problems as they arise.

Validation Strategies

The essence of the validation strategies is the active acceptance of the client by the therapist and the communication of this acceptance to the client. Validation is in sharp contrast to the irreverent communication strategy, where the client's emotional pain is met with a matter-of-fact manner.

Validation involves three sequential steps. First, the individual is helped to identify relevant response patterns. Second, the therapist communicates accurate emotional empathy; understanding of (but not necessarily agreement with) beliefs, expectations, or assumptions; and recognition of behavioral patterns. Third, the therapist communicates that these response patterns make perfect sense in the context of the current situation and the individual's life experiences to date—even though we often do not have access to the information needed to understand their causes. Validation strategies lead the therapist to search for the inherent validity and functionality of the clients' responses. This is in contrast to the usual cognitive and behavior therapies, in which a primary focus of treatment is to search for and replace dysfunctional behavioral processes. The therapist serves as the dialectically opposing pole to the invalidating environments often experienced by the client.

Capability-Enhancement Strategies

In contrast to the validation strategies representing the forces of acceptance within the dialectic, the focus here is on change. Using these strategies, the therapist acts as teacher, insisting at every point that the client actively engage in acquiring and practicing capabilities needed to cope with everyday life. The borderline individual's passive problem-solving style is challenged directly, forcefully, and repeatedly. Behavioral-skill acquisition techniques are used. These techniques are discussed at length in behavior therapy texts and in the *DBT Treatment Manual* (Linehan, 1984). In the interest of brevity, their description is not provided here.

Relationship Strategies

There are five specific relationship strategies: (1) relationship acceptance, (2) reciprocal vulnerability, (3) relationship enhancement, (4) relationship problem solving, and (5) relationship generalization. *Relationship acceptance* requires therapist acceptance of the current client–therapist relationship, including the stage of therapeutic progress or lack thereof, at each successive moment. Requisite characteristics are patience; high tolerance for frustration, criticism, and hostile affect; and an ability to maintain a nonjudgmental behav-

ioral stance. *Relationship enhancement* involves a direct attempt to create a strong, positive client–therapist relationship. Generally, this is the focus of the first few months of therapy with the borderline client. *Relationship problem solving* is called for when a source of client difficulty is the interaction with the therapist. Relationship problem solving in DBT is done in the context of the therapeutic relationship as a real relationship (Linehan, in press). Using the aforementioned problem-solving approach, the therapist models means of working out difficult interpersonal issues. This strategy is useful both to repair the client–therapist relationship and to improve—via generalization—the client's ability to interact successfully with others. Generalization from and to other relationships, however is not assumed. Instead, as in all behavior therapy, generalization of behavior is an active focus of assessment and treatment.

Contingency Strategies

Contingency clarification and "professor" strategies involve giving the client information about what can be reasonably expected from the therapist and about the process and requirements of therapy, as well as telling the client what factors are known to influence behavior in general, and describing to the client any theories and data that might cast light on a particular client's behavior patterns. The *contingency management strategy* requires, as far as possible, the arrangement of therapist responses to reinforce adaptive, nonsuicidal behaviors and to extinguish maladaptive and suicidal behaviors. Due to the life-threatening nature of suicidal behavior, the therapist necessarily walks a dialectical tightrope, so to speak, neither reinforcing suicidal responses excessively nor ignoring them in such a manner that the client escalates them to a life-threatening level. The DBT therapist takes some short-term risk to enhance long-term advantage.

Supervision Additional Factor

An additional factor that is important in conducting DBT is the theory on which the therapy is based and the supervision offered the therapists. Because an essential part of treatment is to keep the therapist working and liking the client, group supervision is used to keep therapists on track and to provide them with support. The emphasis on dialectical processes within the therapists' supervisory sessions is aimed at preventing staff splitting. A major task of DBT supervision is to help therapists continue to reach out to clients, even when such responses are extremely difficult and often punished by the client. We find the theory on which the therapy is based a major asset in this regard.

CASE ILLUSTRATION

Background

Jane S. is a white, divorced, single woman, with a seizure condition that is only partially controlled. She has a high school education and is gifted with her hands. An accomplished mechanic who "can fix anything," she also draws well and plays banjo and guitar.

Jane was referred at age 28 years to the senior author by a psychiatric inpatient unit that planned to commit her to the state hospital if the referral was not accepted. Although she voluntarily entered the inpatient unit because of suicidal ideation, once there, she had recommenced a characteristic form of parasuicide—strangulation. A different therapist, whom Jane had seen for 2 years, had just terminated her because Jane had taken a nearly lethal drug overdose. In addition, Jane had been fired from her job and evicted from her apartment.

Jane had been hospitalized at least 30 times since the age of 12 years. Among the diagnoses she had accrued were schizophrenia, latent type, with minimal cerebral dysfunction; major depressive episode; organic brain syndrome with seizure disorder; passive–aggressive personality with suicidal acting-out; and BPD with depressive symptoms. At the time of referral, she met criteria for BPD on DSM-III and on Gunderson's DIB. Over the years, therapists had tried having Jane on a variety of antidepressant and antipsychotic drugs, none of them having lasting effect. She was continuously on either phenytoin (Dilantin) or carbamazepine (Tegretol) for her seizure disorder, although the dosages were frequently changed due to side effects and problems in controlling the seizures. She had been in individual psychotherapy for 9 years, but the longest stretch with any one therapist was the previous 2 years.

Hospital and school records, and Jane's self-reports, strongly suggest invalidating environments at home and at school, environments in which real problems such as sibling rivalry and learning disabilities were left untreated and unsolved. Hospital records report that her mother had not wanted her pregnancy with Jane and had attempted to miscarry several times. After birth, Jane was sent to live with her grandparents for her first few months. She was then returned to her biological parents, who raised her and two sisters: one older, and one younger, both only a year apart from Jane in age. Jane reports memories of always "losing" in verbal confrontations with her sisters and at school. She has apparently never been able to articulate her emotions well, and she coped either by withdrawing to her room for days at a time or by resorting to physical aggression.

Jane's parasuicidal behavior began at age 9 years, when, during an argument with her sisters, she tried to jump out of a camper moving at highway speeds. At 12, the age Jane dates the beginning of her troubles, she took an overdose and slit her wrists. This was about a year after her father was convicted of embezzlement at his job as a mailman, and the family "went into seclusion," withdrawing from social activities. Jane began running away and would stay away 2–3 days at a time. Over the years, she had continued to cut, head-bang, and overdose. Jane remembers having always been referred to as the "different" one in the family.

Unfortunately, invalidation extended to Jane's school environment as well. Although Jane's hospital records report her as "average" to "superior" in intelligence, she was labeled as "mentally retarded" for most of her school years and was placed in special education classes from second grade on, until it was discovered she had dyslexia (age 18 years). When Jane asked for remedial training at age 18 to help her get a job, she was again put in a class with mentally retarded students! She quit and a year later was refused further help because she could *not* demonstrate an ability to keep a job if trained to get one. After keeping a job for 2 years but being fired due to her epilepsy, she was refused training because she had demonstrated that she *could* find and keep a job.

When treatment began, Jane was going to sleep with a belt wrapped around her neck, tightly enough to seriously constrict circulation. She reported that this was the only way she could stop her painful emotions. During the previous year, she had on six occasions stopped taking her anti-seizure medications. Typically, her failure to comply precipitated a series of seizures that would leave her in a deep sleep for 2–3 days at a time. In addition, there were numerous minor drug overdoses and one nearly lethal one.

Treatment

The first targets of treatment were reducing para-suicidal activity and forming a treatment alliance with the therapist. An important step in forming the alliance had already been taken by virtue of the therapist being the only person willing to accept her in therapy and thereby keep the state from involuntarily committing her once again. This acceptance into therapy was presented as a positive contingency for a strong verbal commitment on Jane's part to actively work at eliminating parasuicide from her coping repertoire. A dialectical frame had been created. By accepting her into treatment, the therapist communicated acceptance of Jane as she was, with compassion for her misery, and at the same time, the conditions for acceptance redefined their supportive alliance as one committed to inducing change.

Behavioral analysis and insight strategies were used in sessions to begin tracing the sequence of events that elicited Jane's suicidal urges and behaviors. On diary cards that she was asked to fill out daily, Jane reported a high frequency of suicidal images that would suddenly appear, as if out of the blue. For example, upon going to clean a plate glass window, Jane would suddenly see the window smashing inward, the thousand shards of glass lacerating and gouging her body. It became clear from the diaries that long hours alone in her apartment correlated highly with suicidal images, which in turn were frequently followed by parasuicide. In contrast, hours spent on manual work activities, such as gardening, construction work, and fixing cars were correlated with low daily "misery," suicidal ideation, and urges toward parasuicide.

Concurrently, it became apparent that Jane's major therapy-interfering behavior was withdrawal. She would wear mirrored sunglasses, sink down into her chair, lower her head slightly, and remain silent. Therapist questions or comments were followed by long latencies, and many were not responded to at all. (Jane reported that in previous therapies, she would often go entire sessions without speaking.)

Behavioral analysis revealed that withdrawal increased in sessions following family interactions that Jane interpreted as rejecting, following interactions with the therapist in which Jane believed that her therapist took other people's side rather than Jane's (a common occurrence in the group therapy), or following unsuccessful assertive attempts directed at institutional systems (e.g., welfare, her bank). Generally, 3 weeks or so of rather extreme in-session withdrawal was the norm. Withdrawal also followed attempts by the therapist to direct therapy discussions toward previous interpersonal losses and rejections, toward unsuccessful assertion directed toward the "system," or toward current feelings in the session. Such withdrawal could usually be reversed if the therapist redirected the discussion to more neutral topics.

The therapist hypothesized that the behavioral and verbal withdrawal was a way of avoiding and/or inhibiting intense emotional responses, especially anger. Jane reported that her silences during sessions were attempts to ward off what felt to her to be imminent, uncontrollable emotions. She felt that if she talked, she would lose control. Her fears of "loss of control" included fears of attacking others physically. Also, if she talked, she would experience an emotional intensity that she would then have to tolerate alone after she left the session. These expectations appeared grounded in many previous experiences in which those outcomes were the norm, not the exception. Subsequent close observation of Jane during silences in sessions revealed that during these periods, she tensed most of her cheek, jaw, and throat muscles, and she appeared to have difficulty breathing. At times, she got up, saying she had to leave; at other times, she requested that a window be opened so she could breathe.

These in-session behaviors corresponded to a between-session style of withdrawal from and avoidance of any situation that either did or might elicit negative affect. Between-session withdrawal included staying in her apartment, lying in bed or on the floor; not opening mail, picking up clothes, washing dishes, or bathing; and avoiding contact with her family. As with in-session withdrawal, these behaviors could last for up to 3 weeks and characteristically followed perceived family, "system," or therapist rejections.

Over the first 4 months, a characteristic train of events leading to parasuicide was established: (1) rejection or problem—(2) painful emotion—(3) suicide fantasies—(4) if still in emotional pain, psychological withdrawal—(5) if still in pain, overdose or strangulation. The suicidal images appeared linked with current anger-eliciting incidents or reminders of previous losses and were reframed as signals of anger and/or grief that had not yet been resolved.

A number of strategies were used to treat the parasuicide and the therapy-interfering behaviors. Problem-solving strategies consisted of ongoing behavioral analyses, insight into repetitive patterns, and generation of alternative behaviors to preclude suicidal ideation or to cope with intense emotions and parasuicide urges when they arose. Jane agreed on a goal of spending at least 6 hours outside of her apartment each day, and she kept track of the number of hours out and the nature of the activities undertaken on her diary cards. In addition, behaviors incompatible with parasuicide were generated, such as inducing other intense internal stimuli (e.g., by squeezing ice cubes, standing under a hot shower), listening to relaxation tapes, working on projects, calling friends (or the therapist), mentally reviewing reasons against parasuicide, or leaving her apartment. Further, the alternative of simply experiencing and observing painful emotions (i.e., inhibiting maladaptive and impulsive escape behaviors) had been a goal of therapy from the beginning. This alternative behavior was shaped primarily during group and individual sessions and during phone calls to the therapist.

Contingency strategies, primarily using the relationship with the therapist as the contingent outcome, proved to be a powerful approach to reducing parasuicidal behaviors, to increasing the amount of verbal discourse in sessions, and to decreasing some between-session withdrawal–avoidance behaviors. At first, this consisted of reminding Jane of her initial commitment to work on stopping parasuicide and eliciting a new commitment, which now also included a good faith effort to approach experiencing at least some of the unbearably painful feelings of anger and grief she worked so hard to escape.

Over time, Jane disclosed some of the searing losses she had endured. The only two people Jane ever felt loved her, her grandfather and an aide at the state mental hospital, had died. When she was married, a baby she desperately wanted had to be aborted due to medical complications. Not long after, she returned home from work to find a note from her husband of several months saying "goodbye" and his clothes and all the furniture gone. She called her parents and asked them to come get her. They refused, saying that because her father had to go to work the next day, there wasn't time.

Eight months into therapy, Jane's strangling behavior had receded. The focus of therapy became experiencing and expressing her feelings of grief over the sense of never belonging to a family. During this period, Jane disclosed to the therapist an activity that she had engaged in for years but had never revealed to anyone. It consisted of involved fantasy activity where she played the role of a reclusive, helpless, frightened damsel in distress, always rescued by a family member. Diary accounts indicated an average of 6–8 hours daily devoted to this fantasy activity. The reinforcing effects of this fantasy on helpless and passive behavior patterns was explained to Jane repeatedly, and reducing the hours devoted to this fantasy became a new target of treatment. Jane contended that, after parasuicide, this activity was her most effective mode of affect control. Thus, until other more effective methods could be taught, the only treatment was daily self-monitoring.

During the next few months, Jane began to express fears of getting too close to the therapist and thereby setting herself up for another interpersonal rejection and subsequent unendurable emotional experience. Phone calls and therapy sessions were marked by long silences. At the same time, her noncompliance with her antiseizure medications became more frequent. Dialectical strategies employed here involved simultaneous validation of Jane's emotional pain with exhortations to expose herself to the painful stimuli and affects she was inhibiting. (Attempts to arrange inpatient flooding sessions to control Jane's behaviors were rejected by inpatient staff afraid of not being able to control Jane's behaviors subsequent to flooding sessions.) Medication noncompliance was framed as another way of avoiding difficult topics and painful emotions because generally noncompliance resulted in several days of seizures, hospitalization, cessation of discussions of other problems, and so on. It was pointed out that with this continuous "quitting," and avoidance, Jane's problems never were confronted. This point was made over and over again throughout therapy, using stories, metaphor, and what Jane accurately referred to as "lectures" from the therapist. In addition, therapist contingencies were used; the therapist often remarked that she was getting tired of "pulling Jane back up when she kept jumping off the mountain" (the therapy metaphor here was mountain climbing).

Over time, the therapist shaped "therapy work" and nonavoidance by both threatening withdrawal of therapy if Jane did not "work" in therapy and providing praise, encouragement, and warmth when Jane reported problem confrontation between sessions or reduced within-session avoidance behaviors. A gradual reduction in emotional inhibition was shaped by combining validation of emotional pain—a reinforcing consequence for both the experience and expression of emotion—with continued emphasis on appropriate emotion-control strategies.

Although at 14 months into therapy, strangling briefly reappeared in response to a series of major life crises (including bankruptcy, probably incurable neurological problems with one hand, etc.), it again receded. Jane is continuing with therapy now. Recently, Jane threw out her belt and agreed to discontinue her strangling behaviors. Her ability to confront problem situations has increased, including the ability to confront her therapist when she feels criticized and her mother in minor incidents when she feels rejected. She also agreed to continue group treatment. These gains have been made despite new stresses: Her father has been accused of child molestation, and, because of her hand problem, she may be unable to continue many activities, such as mechanics, that have been not only sources of satisfaction, but also potential sources of future income. At three years into therapy, she has had no hospitalizations for over two years and no parasuicide for 18 months. She just revealed, for the first time, a history of six yeras of childhood incest by her father.

ALTERNATIVE TREATMENT OPTIONS

There are four alternative treatment options for working with individuals meeting criteria for BPD: pharmacotherapy, psychiatric inpatient treatment, cognitive-behavioral therapy, and long-term psychodynamic therapy. Theoretically, at least, each could be integrated with or added to the DBT treatment of the borderline patient.

Pharmacotherapy

The utility of pharmacotherapy for the treatment of borderline patients is discussed extensively in Chapter 24. However, we would like to note here that there are very few studies of pharmacotherapy with highly suicidal outpatient borderline clients. The recent study by Cowdry and Gardner (1988) is

an exception here. To our knowledge, there is no direct evidence that pharmacotherapy of any type substantially reduces risk in an outpatient population. In our view, the risk of overdose poses a lethal side effect, so to speak, that cannot be ignored. Thus, the general protocol is to eliminate lethal drugs, including antidepressants and oral neuroleptics, from the treatment regime, at least until suicidal behaviors are well under control. When potentially lethal medication is required (e.g., lithium in a client also meeting criteria for bipolar disorder), attempts are made to induce the patient to arrange for control of the lethal medication by a third party (consultant strategy). At times, a therapist might require such control or monitoring of blood levels to prevent medication hoarding.

In the first study of the efficacy of DBT, neither the DBT group nor the treatment-as-usual group reported decreases in negative affect following 1 year of treatment (Linehan, 1987a). This is in contrast to clear reductions in parasuicidal behavior among the DBT clients. In other words, DBT clients learned more adaptive ways to cope, although they did not feel they were experiencing less intense emotional pain. These findings suggest that the addition of pharmacotherapy to address depressed moods, at least during the second year if not earlier, might be very helpful to these patients.

Psychiatric Inpatient Treatment

There are no empirical data showing that hospitalizing suicidal borderline clients actually reduces suicide risk. Indeed, among 10 studies that randomly assigned serious psychiatric patients, including presumably suicidal borderline patients, to either inpatient or outpatient treatment, none showed a superiority for inpatient treatment (Kiesler, 1982). In light of these points, DBT rarely recommends psychiatric hospitalization as a response either to suicide risk or to actual parasuicidal behavior. Generally, hospitalization is only recommended when a therapist believes that he or she cannot provide or arrange for the minimum level of support believed absolutely essential to keep the client alive at the moment. Hospitalization is often viewed as a treatment strategy to benefit the therapist rather than the client—a worthy goal.

In contrast to reservations about the efficacy of hospitalization held by a DBT therapist, our experience is that suicidal borderline patients often insist that they need to be hospitalized. Our strategy here is to validate the inherent wisdom of clients in determining what is best for themselves while validating our own point of view. When we disagree about the wisdom of hospitalization, we instruct the client in how to go about getting into a hospital, but we refuse to get actively engaged in the process. Every attempt is made to reinforce clients for both accurately estimating their capacities to endure and cope out of a hospital, as well as for trusting their own wise judgment in making decisions about care. Interestingly, with this approach, DBT subjects in the aforementioned treatment outcome study did not differ from community treatment-as-usual subjects in the number of admissions to a psychiatric inpatient unit. While the average days per visit appeared lower among the DBT subjects, the overall number of admissions was too low to test this statistically.

Cognitive Therapy

The application of cognitive therapies to BPD is receiving increasing attention (Pretzer, in press; Young 1987, 1988). In general, these treatments are modified versions of Beck's (1976) cognitive therapy. Young's treatment is more substantially revised and focuses on changing long-standing maladaptive schemas hypothesized as etiologically significant in the BPD. Both Turner's behavioral treatment and DBT incorporate many cognitive-therapy strategies. Unfortunately, there are no empirical data on the efficacy of these strategies with the borderline client. In many ways, DBT grew out of initial unsuccessful attempts by Linehan to apply cognitive-restructuring therapies to borderline clients. Borderline clients are particularly sensitive to the emotionally invalidating message that can sometimes be incorporated unwittingly within a cognitive approach (i.e., if you just think straight, you will not have these problems; logical, rational thought is superior to intuitive thought).

Long-term Psychodynamic Therapy

In our view, behavior therapy, at least DBT, is a comprehensive treatment for BPD. The treatment strategies are not rigid, and they lend themselves to modification with the specific and changing needs of each client. However, the treatment has only been demonstrated to be efficacious with extremely dysfunctional clients. Although not documented, we have a strong suspicion that the clients in our research are much more dysfunctional than clients described in typical psychodynamic treatment. Thus, it is within the realm of possibilities that behavior therapy might be most effective with clients at the first, most dysfunctional stage of the disorder. Psychodynamic therapy, or behavior therapy that is more similar to psychodynamic therapy, might be more effective at later stages.

REFERENCES

Akiskal, H. S. (1981). Subaffective disorders: Dysthmic, cyclothymic and bipolar II disorders in the "borderline" realm. *Psychiatric Clinics of North America, 4*, 25–46.

Andrulonis, P. A., Glueck, B. C., Stroebel, C. F., & Vogel, N. G. (1982). Borderline personality subcategories. *Journal of Nervous and Mental Disease, 170*, 670–679.

Basseches, M. (1984). *Dialectical thinking and adult development*. Norwood, NJ: Ablex.

Beck, A. T. (1976). *Cognitive therapy and the emotional disorders*. New York: International Universities Press.

Briere, J. (1984). *The effects of childhood sexual abuse on later psychological functioning: Defining a post-sexual-abuse syndrome*. Paper presented at the Third National Conference on Sexual Victimization of Children, Children's Hospital National Medical Center, Washington, DC.

Clarkin, J. F., Widiger, T. A., Frances, A., Hurt, S. W., & Gilmore, M. (1983). Prototypic typology and the borderline personality disorder. *Journal of Abnormal Psychology, 92*, 263–275.

Cloninger, C. R. (1987). A systematic method for clinical description and classification of personality variants. *Archives of General Psychiatry, 44*, 573–588.

Cowdry, R. W., & Gardner, D. L. (1988). Pharmacotherapy of borderline personality disorder. *Archives of General Psychiatry, 45*, 111–119.

Davis, G. C., & Akiskal, H. S. (1986). Descriptive, biological and theoretical aspects of borderline personality disorder. *Hospital and Community Psychiatry, 37*, 685–692.

Derryberry, D., & Rothbart, M. (1984). Emotion, attention, and temperament. In C. Izard, J. Kagan, & R. Zajonc (Eds.), *Emotions, cognition & behavior* (pp. 132–166). Cambridge: Cambridge University Press.

Eliasz, A. (1985). Mechanisms of temperament: Basic functions. In J. Strelau, F. H. Farley, & A. Gale (Eds.), *The biological bases of personality and behavior: Theories, measurement techniques, and development* (pp. 45–49). Washington, DC: Hemisphere.

Firestone, S. (1970). *The dialectic of sex: The case for feminist revolution.* New York: Bantam.

Frances, A. (1987). A critical review of four DSM-III personality disorders: Borderline, avoidant, dependent and passive aggressive. In G. L. Tischler (Ed.), *Diagnosis and classification in psychiatry* (pp. 85–100). New York: Cambridge University Press.

Frances, A., Clarkin, J. F., Gilmore, M., Hurt, S. W., & Brown, R. (1984). Reliability of criteria for borderline personality disorder: A comparison of DSM-III and the diagnostic interview for borderline patients. *American Journal of Psychiatry, 141,* 1080–1084.

Kastenbaum, R. J. (1969). Death and bereavement in later life. In A. H. Kutscher (Ed.), *Death and bereavement* (pp. 28–54). Springfield, IL: Charles C. Thomas.

Kegan, R. (1982). *The evolving self: Problem and process in human development.* Cambridge: Harvard University Press.

Kiesler, C. A. (1982). Mental hospitals and alternative care: Noninstitutionalization as potential public policy for mental patients. *American Psychologist, 37,* 349–360.

Kroll, J., Sines, L., Martin, K., Lari, S., Pyle, R., & Zander, J. (1981). Borderline personality disorder. *Archives of General Psychiatry, 38,* 1021–1026.

Kuhn, T. S. (1970). *The structure of scientific revolutions* (2nd ed.). Chicago: University of Chicago Press.

Leff, J. P., & Vaughn, C. (1985). *Expressed emotion in families: Its significance for mental illness.* New York: Guilford.

Levins, R., & Lewontin, R. (1985). *The dialectical biologist.* Cambridge: Harvard University Press.

Linehan, M. M. (1981). A social-behavioral analysis of suicide and parasuicide: Implications for clinical assessment and treatment. In H. Glaezer & J. Clarkin (Eds.), *Depression: Behavioral and directive intervention strategies* (pp. 229–294). New York: Brunner/Mazel.

Linehan, M. M. (1984). *Dialectical behavior therapy for treatment of parasuicidal women: Treatment manual.* Unpublished manuscript, University of Washington, Seattle, WA.

Linehan, M. M. (1987a, November). Behavioral treatment of suicidal clients meeting criteria for borderline personality disorder. In A. T. Beck (Chair), *Cognitive and behavioral approaches to suicide.* Symposium conducted at the Association for Advancement of Behavior Therapy, Annual Convention, Boston, MA.

Linehan, M. M. (1987b). Dialectical behavior therapy: A cognitive behavioral approach to parasuicide. *Journal of Personality Disorder, 1,* 328–333.

Linehan, M. M. (1987c). Dialectical behavior therapy for borderline personality disorder: Theory and method. *Bulletin of the Menninger Clinic, 51,* 261–276.

Linehan, M. M. (1987d). Dialectical behavior therapy in groups: Treating borderline personality disorders and suicidal behavior. In C. M. Brody (Ed.), *Women's therapy groups: Paradigms of feminist treatment* (pp. 145–162). New York: Springer.

Linehan, M. M. (1988). Perspectives on the interpersonal relationship in behavior therapy. *Journal of Integrative & Eclectic Psychotherapy, 7,* 278–290.

Loranger, A. W., Oldham, J. M., Russakoff, L. M., & Susman, V. (1984). Structured interviews and borderline personality disorder. *Archives of General Psychiatry, 41,* 565–568.

Loranger, A. W., & Tulis, E. H. (1985). Family history of alcoholism in borderline personality disorder. *Archives of General Psychiatry, 42,* 153–157.

Marx, K., & Engels, F. (1970). *Selected works.* New York: International Publishers.

Mischel, W. (1968). *Personality and assessment.* New York: Wiley.

Perry, J. C. (1985). Depression in borderline personality disorder: Lifetime prevalence at interview and longitudinal course of symptoms. *American Journal of Psychiatry, 142,* 15–21.

Persons, J. B. (1986). The advantages of studying psychological phenomena rather than psychiatric diagnoses. *American Psychologist, 41,* 1252–1260.

Pope, H. G., Jonas, J. M., Hudson, J. I., Cohen, B. S., & Gunderson, J. G. (1983). The validity of DSM-III borderline personality disorder. *Archives of General Psychiatry, 40,* 23–30.

Pretzer, J. (in press). *Clinical applications of cognitive therapy.* New York: Plenum.

Reiser, D. E., & Levenson, H. (1984). Abuses of the borderline diagnosis: A clinical problem with teaching opportunities. *American Journal of Psychiatry, 141,* 1528–1532.

Schwartz, G. E. (1982). Integrating psychobiology and behavior therapy: A systems perspective. In G. T. Wilson & C. M. Franks (Eds.), *Contemporary behavior therapy: Conceptual and empirical foundations* (pp. 119–141). New York: Guilford.

Selye, H. (1956). *The stress of life.* New York: McGraw-Hill.

Soloff, P. H. (1981). Pharmacotherapy of borderline disorders. *Comprehensive Psychiatry, 22,* 535–543.

Staats, A. W. (1975). *Social behaviorism.* Homewood, IL: Dorsey.

Strelau, J., Farley, F. H., & Gale, A. (1986). *The biological bases of personality and behavior: Psychophysiology, performance, and applications.* Washington, DC: Hemisphere.

Thomas, A., & Chess, S. (1986). The New York longitudinal study: From infancy to early adult life. In R. Plomin & J. Dunn (Eds.), *The study of temperament: Changes, continuities and challenges* (pp. 39–52). Hillsdale, NJ: Erlbaum.

Turkington, C. (1986). Limbic response seen in borderline cases. *APA Monitor, 17,* 18.

Turner, R.M. (1987, November). *A bio-social learning approach to borderline personality disorder.* Paper presented at the Association for Advancement of Behavior Therapy, Annual Convention, Boston, MA.

Wallace, J. (1966). An abilities conception of personality: Some implications for personality measurement. *American Psychologist, 21,* 132–138.

Wells, H. K. (1972). Alienation and dialectical logic. *Kansas Journal of Sociology, 8,* 7–32.

Widiger, T. A., & Frances, A. (1987). Definitions and diagnoses: A brief response to Morey and McNamara. *Journal of Abnormal Psychology, 96,* 286–287.

Widiger, T. A., Frances, A., Warner, L., & Bluhm, C. (1986). Diagnostic criteria for the borderline and schizotypal personality disorder. *Journal of Abnormal Psychology, 95,* 43–51.

Young, J. (1983, August). *Borderline personality: Cognitive theory and treatment.* Paper presented at the American Psychological Association Annual Convention, Philadelphia, PA.

Young, J. (1987). *Schema-focused cognitive therapy for personality disorders.* Unpublished manuscript, Cognitive Therapy Center of New York.

Young, J. (1988, April). *Schema-focused cognitive therapy for personality disorders.* Paper presented at the Society for the Exploration of Psychotherapy Integration, Cambridge, MA.

CHAPTER 24

Pharmacotherapy

DANIEL J. BUYSSE, R. SWAMI NATHAN, AND PAUL H. SOLOFF

CONCEPTUALIZATION OF THE DISORDER

The effective conceptualization and successful pharmacological treatment of any psychiatric disorder depend on the validity and reliability of the disorder's diagnosis. *Validity* assesses how well a diagnosis identifies what it is supposed to identify, and to what extent it can be distinguished from other diagnoses (Kaplan & Sadock, 1988). *Reliability* measures the reproducibility of a diagnosis or measurement (a) between two independent raters (interrater reliability) or (b) between two independent evaluation times (test–retest reliability) (Kaplan & Sadock, 1988). The conceptualization of borderline personality disorder (BPD) from a psychopharmacological perspective is therefore based on the presence of signs or symptoms that can be detected accurately and reliably. Diagnoses based on observed affects, behaviors, cognitions, and verified history are more likely to demonstrate acceptable reliability and validity than diagnoses based on more inferential concepts, such as defense mechanisms or ego strength.

Robins and Guze (1970) outlined five phases in the systematic study of psychiatric illnesses, which facilitate valid classification: (1) clinical description, (2) discrimination from other disorders, (3) follow-up studies, (4) family studies, and (5) laboratory studies. The conceptualization of BPD from a psychopharmacological perspective can be approached by summarizing the major research findings from each of these areas.

Clinical Description

Current conceptualizations of BPD derive from three main sources: (1) psychoanalytic formulations; (2) empirical studies of the biological relatives of schizophrenics; and (3) descriptive studies of nonpsychotic, significantly impaired patients (Gunderson & Singer, 1975; Liebowitz, 1979; Rieder, 1979; Stone, 1977).

Early psychoanalytic formulations, such as "ambulatory" and "pseudoneurotic" schizophrenia, "as-if" patients, and "stable–unstable" borderlines emphasized (a) a variety of neurotic presenting symptoms, (b) poor social functioning, (c) primitive defensive styles, and (d) a tendency toward brief, psychotic decompensations under stress (Deutsch, 1942; Hoch & Polatin, 1949; Schmideberg, 1947; Zilboorg, 1941). Inherent in many of these conceptualizations is a supposed relationship to more classical schizophrenia. Knight (1953) coalesced many of these previous descriptions in his conceptualization of the borderline state. More recent psychoanalytic thinking, exemplified by the writings of Kernberg (1975), emphasizes disturbances in object relations, but it addresses other structural characteristics as well as descriptive and genetic–dynamic features (Perry & Klerman, 1978).

The second major historical source for current conceptualizations of BPD also proposes a relationship between BPD and schizophrenia. However, rather than being psychoanalytic in origin, this tradition is based on family studies of the relatives of schizophrenic patients. These studies are discussed later in this chapter.

Finally, the descriptive–empirical approach to the conceptualization of BPD is exemplified by the work of Grinker, Werble, and Drye (1968). These researchers identified four common characteristics among hospitalized, nonschizophrenic, borderline patients: (1) anger as the main affect; (2) defects in affectional relationships; (3) absence of consistent self-identity; and (4) pervasive depression. In addition, Grinker and colleagues identified four subtypes of patients: (1) the psychotic border; (2) the core borderline syndrome; (3) the adaptive, affectless, defended, "as-if" persons; and (4) the neurotic border.

Diagnoses of BPD based on any one of these three primary sources do not always overlap. Perry and Klerman (1978) compared four sets of diagnostic criteria, derived from the writings of Knight, Kernberg, Grinker et al., and Gunderson and Singer. They found that of 104 total criteria, only one criterion appeared in all four systems, and over half of the criteria appeared in only one system.

Subsequently, several groups developed diagnostic criteria for BPD patients, which incorporate elements from each of these disparate sources (Gunderson & Singer, 1975; Perry & Klerman, 1980; Sheehy, Goldsmith, & Charles, 1980; Spitzer, Endicott, & Gibbon, 1979a). The Gunderson and Singer criteria were eventually formalized in the Diagnostic Interview for Borderlines (DIB) (Kolb & Gunderson, 1980), and the Spitzer et al. criteria formed the basis for the DSM-III and DSM-III-R categories of schizotypal and borderline personality disorders (American Psychiatric Association, 1980, 1987). These systems are neither mutually exclusive nor independent, and several key similarities are worth noting. First, all of the systems rely on empirical signs and symptoms rather than inferential concepts. Second, each system assesses many different areas of the patient's social and psychological functioning. Third, each system emphasizes specific categories of affective, cognitive, and impulse dyscontrol in the setting of disturbed interpersonal functioning. Agreement among these diagnostic systems, while imperfect, is considerably improved over those compared by Perry and Klerman (Kolb & Gunderson, 1980; Kroll et al., 1981; McGlashan, 1983).

Discrimination from Other Disorders

Several related questions pertain to the discrimination of BPD from other disorders: (1) Can BPD be distinguished from the major psychiatric syndromes (i.e., Axis I disorders)? (2) Can BPD be distinguished from other personality disorders? and (3) To what extent does diagnostic overlap, or comorbidity, occur?

The foregoing diagnostic schemas reliably discriminate patients with BPD from those with other psychiatric syndromes. The sensitivity of BPD diagnoses ranges from 70 to 95%, and specificity ranges from 75 to 95%, in distinguishing BPD patients from those with schizophrenia, neuroses, personality disorders, and other disorders (Gunderson & Kolb, 1978; Kolb & Gunderson, 1980; Perry & Klerman, 1980; Sheehy et al., 1980; Soloff & Ulrich, 1981; Spitzer et al., 1979a).

Discrimination of BPD from other personality disorders has been more difficult, due in part to the lower reliability of Axis II diagnoses, relative to Axis I diagnoses (Mellsop, Varghese, Joshua, & Hicks, 1982; Spitzer, Forman, & Nee, 1979b). In one study, 85% of BPD patients met criteria for other personality disorders (Pope, Jonas, Hudson, Cohen, & Gunderson, 1983), but successful discrimination of BPD from other personality disorders has been reported by others (Barrash, Kroll, Carey, & Sines, 1983; Perry & Klerman, 1980).

Most of the current debate regarding BPD and other personality disorders centers on the distinction of BPD from schizotypal personality disorder (SPD). Spitzer and Endicott (1979) have argued that the two disorders, while often occurring in conjunction, repeatedly demonstrate different clusters of symptoms, and may have different genetic diatheses. A recent study of DSM-III personality disorder symptoms supports this view (Widiger, Trull, Hurt, Clarkin, & Frances, 1987). This study found an overlap of 55–60% in BPD and SPD diagnoses, but an overall correlation of only .08 between specific symptoms for the two disorders. On the other hand, if transient psychotic symptoms are included as a criterion for BPD, this diagnosis subsumes most of SPD diagnoses as well (Gunderson, Siever, & Spaulding, 1983). Proponents of this view suggest that, if SPD exists, it is typified by lack of affectivity, social isolation and dysfunction, and somatization.

The separation of BPD from other psychiatric disorders is further complicated by the issue of comorbidity. The prevalence of comorbid affective disorders in BPD patients has been estimated at 14 to 81%, with major unipolar depression representing the majority of codiagnoses (Akiskal, Yerevanian, Davis, King, & Lemmi, 1981; Carroll et al., 1981; Gunderson & Elliott, 1985; Kroll et al., 1981; McGlashan, 1983a). A recent chart review (i.e., review of patients' charts) by Fyer, Frances, Sullivan, Hunt, and Clarkin (1988) documented the presence of at least one other DSM-III diagnosis (exclusive of substance abuse disorders) in 49% of an inpatient sample; 31% of these comorbid diagnoses were affective disorders. Conversely, the incidence of BPD in patients with affective disorder is usually reported at 25 to 50% (Charney, Nelson, & Quinlan, 1981; Gunderson & Elliott, 1985; Kroll et al., 1981), although it has been noted that the clinical state of depression may influence a patient's perception of self, and presumably, the diagnosis of a personality disorder (Hirschfeld et al., 1983). Comorbid personality disorders in patients with depression are associated with earlier age of onset, less social support, increased frequency of suicide attempts, worse response to pharmacological treatments, and higher rates of depression spectrum diagnoses in relatives (Charney et al., 1981; Pfohl, Stangl, & Zimmerman, 1984).

Comorbidity of organic disorders may also occur in patients with BPD. Neurologic "soft signs" have been found more commonly in patients with emotionally unstable character disorder (EUCD) and BPD than in control subjects and other psychiatric patients (Gardner et al., 1987; Quitkin & Klein, 1969; Quitkin, Rifkin, & Klein, 1976). Approximately 6–27% of BPD patients have a history of neurological disorders, which range from minimal brain dysfunction to head trauma and epilepsy (Andrulonis et al., 1980; Andrulonis, Glueck, Stroebel, & Vogel, 1982; Fyer et al., 1988).

Follow-up Studies

The validity of BPD is further supported by knowledge of its longitudinal course, and specifically, whether the diagnosis is stable over time, or whether patients subsequently receive a different diagnosis.

Follow-up studies have shown that 44–67% of BPD patients retain their diagnoses during follow-up periods of several years, a rate slightly lower than that for schizophrenia (Carpenter & Gunderson, 1977; McGlashan, 1983b, 1986; Pope et al., 1983). Also, BPD patients have a high rate of other personality and affective disorders at follow-up (Akiskal, 1981; McGlashan, 1983b, 1986; Pope et al., 1983), but studies have not concurred regarding subsequent diagnoses of schizophrenia and psychotic disorders. Pope and colleagues report no patients with schizophrenia at follow-up, while McGlashan reports that 20% of BPD and 55% of SPD patients subsequently qualify for schizophrenia diagnoses.

The long-term course of illness in BPD patients has also been assessed, but once again, there is no clear consensus. Some studies have suggested basically favorable outcomes for patients with EUCD and BPD (McGlashan, 1983a, 1983b, 1986; Rifkin, Levitan, Galewski, & Klein, 1972a, 1972b; Tucker, Bauer, Wagner, Harlam, & Sher, 1987), while others have been considerably more pessimistic (Carpenter & Gunderson, 1977; Grinker et al., 1968; Gunderson, 1975; Pope et al., 1983; Werble, 1970). In general, social functioning appears to improve with longer duration of follow-up, but suicidal thoughts and substance abuse are persistent problems. Most studies report functional outcomes of patients intermediate between those with affective disorders and those with schizophrenia, but it is unclear whether comorbid depression improves (Pope et al., 1983) or worsens (McGlashan, 1983b, 1986) the outcome. The relatively poor social functioning of BPD patients at follow-up most likely reflects their impulsiveness and chaotic interpersonal relationships.

Family Studies

Family studies of BPD fall into two main groups: those based on adoption studies, and those based on family histories and family studies of BPD patients.

The Danish adoption studies (Kety, Rosenthal, Wender, & Schulsinger, 1971; Rosenthal, Wender, Kety, Welner, & Schulsinger, 1971; Wender, Kety, Schulsinger, & Welner, 1974) were performed before modern criteria for the diagnosis of BPD, but descriptions of the original subjects with diagnoses of "borderline schizophrenia," "inadequate personality," and "possible schizophrenia" allow extrapolation to current diagnoses of BPD and SPD. The original studies examined the psychiatric diagnoses in biological and adoptive relatives of psychiatrically ill probands, and they have been reviewed using modern diagnostic criteria (Kendler, Gruenberg, & Strauss, 1981; Siever & Gunderson, 1979).

Taken together, these adoption studies indicate an excess of BPD- and SPD-like diagnoses in the biological relatives of probands with chronic schizophrenia and BPD-like diagnoses. They do *not* indicate an excess of chronic schizophrenia in the biological relatives of probands with BPD-like diagnoses. In fact, the only diagnosis seen in excess among the relatives of BPD-like probands is BPD. Finally, the studies suggest that biological, rather than environmental, effects mediate the familial aggregation in diagnoses.

Twin studies, which examine concordance rates in monozygotic (MZ) versus dizygotic (DZ) twins, are another means of assessing biological and environmental effects. Sixty-nine pairs of twins, each having an identified twin with BPD, SPD, or both, were compared with an equal number of control twins (Torgersen, 1984). Using a probandwise concordance method, Torgersen found increased concordance in MZ versus DZ twins for SPD, but not BPD. Although this seems to indicate a stronger genetic factor in SPD than in BPD, caution is warranted due to the small number of BPD probands.

Family studies of BPD patients have focused on a wider range of psychiatric diagnoses in relatives. An increased incidence of affective illness and character disorders has been described in the families of patients with borderline syndrome, EUCD, and borderline personality, relative to patients with psychotic disorders (Akiskal, 1981; Grinker et al., 1968; Rifkin et al., 1972a, 1972b; Stone, 1977). These early studies were equivocal regarding an increased incidence of psychotic disorders in the families of BPD patients. Several recent family studies have used DSM-III or DIB

criteria to define BPD (Loranger, Oldham, & Tulis, 1982; Pope et al., 1983; Soloff & Millward, 1983; Tucker et al., 1987). A constellation of consistent findings emerges from these studies. First, the morbid risk for BPD is increased in the families of BPD patients, but not in the families of affective disorder and schizophrenic patients. Second, the risk of schizophrenia is increased only in the families of schizophrenic probands. Third, the incidence of affective disorders is increased in the families of both affective disorder and BPD probands. Finally, alcohol and drug abuse, as well as other personality disorders, are frequently seen in the families of BPD patients.

Laboratory Studies

Neuroendocrine Tests: Dexamethasone Suppression and Thyrotropin-Releasing Hormone (TRH) Stimulation.

Several investigators have described a 60–75% rate of cortisol nonsuppression in response to dexamethasone administration among BPD patients. (Baxter, Edell, Gerner, Fairbanks, & Gwirtsman, 1984; Beeber, Kline, Pies, Manring, 1984; Carroll et al., 1981; Sternbach, Fleming, Extein, Pottash, & Gold, 1983). Abnormal tests were most frequently noted only among those patients with concurrent diagnoses of major depression, melancholia, or schizoaffective disorder. In contrast to the preceding studies, Soloff, George, and Nathan (1982), Steiner, Martin, Wallace, and Goldman (1984) and Nathan, Soloff, George, Peters, and McCarthy (1986) have described much lower rates of dexamethasone nonsuppression in BPD patients, ranging from 16 to 29%. Furthermore, the Soloff and Nathan studies did not find an increased number of abnormal responses among patients with concurrent major depressions.

Fewer results have been reported for the TRH stimulation test. The thyroid stimulating hormone (TSH) response to TRH stimulation has been reported to be abnormal in 18–46% of BPD patients (Garbutt, Loosen, Tipermas, & Prange, 1983; Nathan et al., 1983; Sternbach et al., 1983). Once again, there is a suggestion that patients with concurrent affective diagnoses have higher rates of abnormal test results. Sternbach et al. (1983) found that 75% of their BPD patients had at least one neuroendocrine abnormality using the dexamethasone suppression test (DST) and TRH stimulation tests.

Pharmacological Challenge: Stimulant Infusion. Schulz and colleagues (1985, 1988) hypothesized that infusion of amphetamine might help to define BPD's biological similarity to schizophrenia and depression; a link to schizophrenia would be manifested by a psychotic response, whereas a link to depression would be suggested by a lessening of dysphoria. Approximately 50% of BPD patients evidenced a psychotic response, indicated by unusual thought content, distractibility, and excitement. These responses were more often seen in patients with concomitant SPD diagnoses. Further work by Lucas, Gardner, Wolkowitz, and Lowdry (1987) demonstrated a dysphoric response in two thirds of BPD patients during methylphenidate infusion; anger, agitation, and anxiety were prominent.

Electroencephalography (EEG). Both waking and sleep EEGs have been examined systematically in patients with BPD. Compared to patients with dysthymic or major depressive disorders, BPD patients have a higher percentage of marginal or definite abnormalities on routine EEG (38–46% versus 10–13%), but most abnormalities are diffuse and bilateral rather than focal (Cowdry, Pickar, & Davies, 1985–1986; Snyder & Pitts, 1984). Cornelius and colleagues (1986) found a higher incidence of dysrhythmias in BPD versus normal controls, but there was no difference in the incidence of abnormalities between BPD patients and those with other personality disorders. More importantly, severity of EEG abnormalities did not correlate with severity of clinical symptoms, suggesting that such abnormalities were a nonspecific finding.

Several groups have reported sleep EEG similarities between BPD and depressed patients (Akiskal, 1981; Akiskal et al., 1985; Bell, Lycahi, Jones, Kelwalg, & Sitaram, 1983; McNamara et al., 1984; Reynolds et al., 1985). Specifically, both groups have shorter rapid-eye-movement (REM) latencies, and increased REM activity, relative to healthy controls. Although sleep EEG abnormalities are associated with current or past diagnoses of affective disorders in BPD patients, there has been no clear relationship between sleep findings and severity of depression.

Other Laboratory Tests. A variety of other laboratory tests have been examined in BPD and SPD patients, including reaction time, backward masking performance, auditory event-related potentials (P300), and smooth-pursuit eye movements. These have been reviewed in detail elsewhere (Siever, 1985). Basically, all of these tests reveal both abnormal or delayed information processing in schizophrenic patients and similar types and degrees of dysfunction in BPD and SPD patients. There has been some suggestion of greater impairment in SPD than in BPD patients. These results are not thought to be a direct result of depressive or psychotic symptoms or medication effects (Kutcher et al., 1987). Finally, Snyder, Pitts, and Gustin (1983) reported on a small series of BPD patients studied with computerized axial tomography (CAT) scans. No abnormal studies were found in any of the 26 patients.

Conceptualization: Summary

BPD has emerged as a reliably diagnosed entity with a set of distinct symptoms, including affective lability, impulsive and self-destructive behavior, volatile interpersonal relationships, and poor social functioning. Several diagnostic schemes also include cognitive distortions as a hallmark. The validity of the disorder is supported by family studies. However, further studies are needed to address other validity issues, including comorbidity, longitudinal stability, and biological heterogeneity in BPD patients.

DIAGNOSTIC ISSUES AND PROBLEMS

Differential Diagnosis

Differential diagnosis in BPD is complicated by the range of possible symptoms, the probable presence of subgroups within BPD, and the comorbidity with other disorders. Thus, the major diagnostic issue in BPD is often a question of which border a particular borderline patient approaches (e.g., affective, psychotic, organic, antisocial, or neurotic).

As previously discussed, affective disorders are a very common source of comorbidity and differential diagnostic difficulty. Soloff (1981) reported that the only Hamilton Rating Scale differences between BPD patients and patients with major depression were the lesser severity of depressed mood and greater severity of paranoid symptoms in the BPD group. However, more marked differences were noted on other rating scales, and those differences indicated greater hostility, irritability, and suspiciousness in the BPD patients. In keeping with these findings, other authors also cite high rates of atypical bipolar, atypical depressive, cyclothymic, or dysthymic symptoms in patients with concomitant BPD or with a differential diagnosis of BPD (Akiskal, 1981; Klein, 1975).

Other Axis I disorders included in the differential diagnosis of BPD include anxiety disorders (panic disorder, generalized anxiety disorder); psychotic disorders (schizophreniform disorder, brief reactive psychosis); substance-induced mental disorders (drug intoxications and dependence); and other organic mental disorders (residual attention deficit disorder, organic personality disorder). In fact, an unusually wide set of presenting symptoms may be an early clue to a BPD diagnosis.

Differential diagnosis of other personality disorders is often even more difficult. Overlap with other "dramatic cluster" diagnoses (histrionic, narcissistic, and antisocial) and with SPD is particularly common. Indeed, Pope et al. (1983) found that 85% of their borderline sample also met criteria for another personality disorder diagnosis, and Mellsop et al. (1982) found that 54% of patients with personality disorders had more than one Axis II disorder.

Specific Problems in Diagnosis

Borderline patients present five specific problems in diagnosis because of the nature of their psychopathology: (1) alcohol and other drug abuse, (2) odd communication, (3) affective lability, (4) lack of objectivity, and (5) other aspects of personality dynamics.

Alcohol and Other Drug Abuse. This manifestation of the borderline patient's impulsiveness can hinder the assessment process because of intoxication or withdrawal. In addition, BPD patients are frequently receiving psychotropic medications at the time of the initial interview, leaving the clinician to wonder which symptoms are caused by the disorder, which ones are caused by drugs, and which ones are not observable because they are suppressed by drugs.

Odd Communication. The patient's style of communication may obscure the relevant details of the clinical picture, particularly among those borderline patients with schizotypal features. Some patients may express themselves in vague, metaphorical, and digressive terms, which may frustrate even highly structured interviews (Carroll et al., 1981; Klein, 1975).

Affective Lability. The interviewer may get an unrealistic cross-section of the patient's overall affective state, depending on when she or he interviews the patient. In addition, the patient may have difficulty cooperating with assessment during extreme affective shifts.

Lack of Objectivity. Cowdry (1987) and Soloff et al. (1986b) have commented on the disparity between the patient's subjective complaint and the patient's behavior while interacting with peers. Indeed, the contradiction between stated mood and observed affect is often evident even during an initial interview with the patient.

Other Aspects of Personality Dynamics. Patients with BPD are marked by their chaotic and primitive interpersonal relationships; the clinician–patient dyad is merely a special instance of this. As such, it is subject to the same distortions, manipulations, idealizations, and devaluations that characterize the borderline's other relationships. The clinician must be aware of how each interaction with the patient (including the diagnostic process) affects the patient's other significant relationships, such as those with family members, other staff members, and other treating clinicians.

Diagnostic Considerations: Some Suggested Procedures

Although the diagnosis of BPD can be confusing and difficult to establish, the following five techniques can facilitate the process: (1) extended assessment period, (2) drug-free observation period, (3) hospitalization, (4) structured diagnostic instruments, and (5) multiple informants.

Extended Assessment Period.   Because of the lability inherent in the diagnosis of BPD, assessment over a longer-than-usual period of time can be helpful. Unfortunately, patients usually present themselves at a time of crisis, demanding immediate solutions to their most pressing current problems. To the extent that the clinician can extend the assessment period and avoid the premature use of any psychopharmacological agent, he or she will improve the accuracy of diagnosis and the likely effectiveness of the treatment. On an outpatient basis, assessment over at least two or three sessions is warranted.

Drug-Free Observation Period.   Because the use of substances and medications can confuse the clinical presentation of BPD patients, a period of drug-free observation often helps to clarify the diagnostic issues. Symptoms may abate in a supportive hospital environment without medications, and indications for pharmacotherapy may be modified substantially.

Hospitalization.   The first two considerations are often impossible on an outpatient basis, due to the severity of symptoms or poor compliance. In such instances, hospitalization may help to secure an accurate diagnostic formulation. Hospitalization also affords the opportunity for direct behavioral observation with peers, which may provide information absent from, or discrepant with, the patient's self-report.

Structured Diagnostic Instruments.   Because of the variability of presenting symptoms in BPD patients, structured diagnostic instruments allow for more consistent diagnosis, even in clinical settings. Several such instruments are available, including the DIB (Kolb & Gunderson, 1980); the Schedule for Interviewing Borderlines (SIB; Baron, 1981); the Borderline Personality Disorder Scale (BPD Scale; Perry, 1982); the Structured Interview for Personality Disorders (SIDP; Strangl, Pfohl, Zimmerman, Bowers, & Corenthal, 1985); and the Diagnostic Interview for Personality Disorders (DIPD; Zanarini, Frankenburg,

Chauncey, & Gunderson, 1987). These and other scales have been reviewed in detail elsewhere (Merikangas & Weissman, 1986; Reich, 1986). Consideration should also be given to using several different diagnostic schemas in patients with possible borderline disorders. BPD patients will frequently meet diagnostic criteria for pharmacologically treatable disorders such as hysteroid dysphoria or atypical depression if these disorders are considered (Soloff, George, Nathan, Schulz, & Perel, 1987).

Multiple Informants.   Another method of combating the possible distortions of the BPD patient is to include other sources of information. The most common sources would include family, close friends, other treating clinicians, and past medical records. In addition to improving the quality of information relating to the patient, this technique diminishes the possibilities of splitting and projection by the patient.

TREATMENT STRATEGIES

General Issues

It can be safely stated that no treatment of choice exists for the entire group of BPD patients. Faced with the task of prescribing medications for a borderline patient, the clinician must therefore ask a series of further questions: Which psychopharmacological agent should be used? At what dose? For which specific symptoms? In which patient? At what point during the course of the disorder? Using which outcome measures? Judged by whom? And for what duration? The existing literature addresses some, but not all of these questions.

Review of the Literature

Over 50% of hospitalized patients with BPD receive some form of pharmacotherapy, and those who do receive medications show more evidence of improvement than those who do not (Soloff, 1981b). However, despite the frequent use of medications in these patients, relatively few systematic medication trials have been performed. We now review the relevant literature according to major medication classes.

Neuroleptics. Early studies by Klein (1967, 1968) and by Hedberg, Houck, and Blueck (1971) suggested the efficacy of neuroleptics in the treatment of borderline-type patients. Klein found chlorpromazine to be significantly superior to placebo and nonsignificantly superior to imipramine, in patients with EUCD. Both Klein and Hedberg described some positive effects of neuroleptics in pseudoneurotic schizophrenics as well, although these medications were generally less effective than were antidepressants. Klein, Gittelman, Quitkin, and Rifkin (1980) have also suggested that schizoid/schizotypal and hysteroid dysphoric patients may benefit from phenothiazines, the former in terms of referential thinking, and the latter in terms of anxiety and lability.

Two retrospective chart review studies and one case series examined the use of neuroleptics in BPD patients. Although patients receiving medications showed a stronger trend toward improvement than patients not on medications, Soloff (1981b) found no statistical superiority for any specific medication, including neuroleptics. Cole, Salomon, Gunderson, Sunderland, and Simmonds (1984) reported that five of five schizotypal BPD patients and five of eight depressed BPD patients improved with neuroleptic treatment. Brinkley, Beitman, and Friedel (1979) found that low-dose, high-potency neuroleptics improved self-control, depression, anxiety, formal thought disorder, and social functioning in a case series of five patients.

In a more recent double-blind trial, Leone (1982) compared the effects of loxapine and chlorpromazine in DIB-defined borderline outpatients. Consistent improvement was noted in both medication groups, beginning within 2 days, and continuing throughout the 6-week trial. A wide range of symptoms, including hostility, depression, tension, and anxiety, were improved. Loxapine was statistically superior to chlorpromazine on several measures. However, no placebo control condition was used, which is of particular concern given the brief drug-free interval prior to treatment, the rapid improvements reported, and the unspecified other treatments (e.g., psychotherapy) involved.

Serban and Siegel (1984) compared two other neuroleptics—haloperidol and thiothixene—in a group of 52 BPD and SPD outpatients. At 3 months, 84% of the patients demonstrated moderate to marked improvement in a variety of symptoms, including anxiety, depression, derealization, and paranoia. More interestingly, characterological symptoms, such as negative self-image, also showed improvement. No differences between BPD, SPD, or mixed-symptom patients were noted, but thiothixene appeared statistically superior to haloperidol. The optimistic results of this study are restrained by the presence of unspecified other treatments and the absence of a placebo control group.

Goldberg and colleagues (1986) improved on prior study designs by including a placebo control group in their double-blind outpatient study of thiothixene in borderlines. Following careful diagnosis and a 7-day drug-free observation period, they administered low-dose thiothixene (2–35 mg; mean = 8.7) or placebo for 12 weeks. The placebo response was robust, showing decreased ratings of anger–hostility, interpersonal sensitivity, BPD criteria, and schizotypal symptoms. However, thiothixene treatment resulted in further improvements in psychotic cluster symptoms, obsessive–compulsive symptoms, and phobic anxiety. The drug condition was superior to placebo for all patient groups, but it was less striking for the pure BPD group than for the SPD and mixed groups.

Soloff and colleagues completed a randomized, double-blind, placebo-controlled study comparing the efficacy of haloperidol and amitriptyline in borderline inpatients (Soloff, George, Nathan, Schulz, & Perel, 1986a; Soloff et al., 1986b; 1986c; 1987). A total of 90 patients were studied after meeting criteria for BPD, SPD, or both. Therapeutic blood levels were achieved for both haloperidol (mean dose = 7.24 mg) and amitriptyline, and weekly ratings were completed by patients and trained raters. Patients consistently reported greater improvements than observers, with improvements beginning during the drug washout period. Haloperidol was significantly superior to placebo across a range of symptoms, including depression, paranoia, impulsivity, hostility, and schizotypal symptoms. Haloperidol was also superior to amitriptyline on several scales of the Symptom Checklist-90 (SCL-90), and it was no different on measures of depression. Differential response to medications among the patient subgroups was not observed. The authors, noting this lack of specificity, concluded that haloperidol had a wide range of symptomatic efficacy. It was also noted that severity of initial symptoms correlated with degree of improvement; therefore, the utility of haloperidol in less symptomatic patients remains to be demonstrated conclusively.

The most recent double-blind trial including neuroleptics has been reported by Cowdry and Gardner (1988). This crossover-design study included trials of placebo, trifluoperazine (average dose: 7.8 mg/day), tranylcypromine, carbamazepine, and alprazolam (see the following). Only 5 of 10 patients completed the full 42-day neuroleptic trial, 2 discontinuing because of clinical deterioration, and 3 because of medical complications. Patients who completed the trial showed a trend toward improvement relative to placebo by physician's global ratings, but the difference was not statistically significant. In contrast, patient ratings for depression, anxiety, and rejection sensitivity were significantly improved compared to placebo trials. However, no patients responded to trifluoperazine better than to other active agents. The authors note that both the initial selection process and outcome measures may have emphasized affective symptoms relative to psychotic-like symptoms, thus possibly biasing their findings against neuroleptic response.

Two features of these studies deserve emphasis: the significant response to placebo, and the incidence of side effects. Both Goldberg and Soloff noted significant placebo response, particularly during the washout period. Whether similar results would be noted with the administration of no pill at all is uncertain. On the other hand, very little effect of placebo was noted by Cowdry and Gardner (1988).

The incidence of side effects with neuroleptics was also fairly high. Klein et al. (1980) suggested that many EUCD patients do not prefer to be on an "even keel," but other authors report more substantial side effects. Leone (1982) reported more than one side effect in 31% of his patients, whereas Serban and Siegel (1984) found adverse reactions in 80% of their 52 subjects; 10 of these dropped out of the study because of side effects, as did 7 of 24 of Goldberg's medication cohort. Steiner, Elizur, and Davidson (1979) reported 9 cases of behav-

ioral toxicity due to low-dose neuroleptics in BPD patients; symptoms included increased psychosis, anxiety, agitation, and aggression. Cowdry and Gardner (1988), while finding that patients had fewer side effects during the last week of a trifluoperazine trial than with any other medication class, also had to terminate 3 of 10 drug trials because of medical complications (orthostatic hypotension, akathisia). One additional concern with neuroleptics is the risk of tardive dyskinesia. There is currently no longitudinal data regarding the development or course of this disorder in neuroleptic-treated BPD patients.

In summary, low-dose neuroleptics appear to be effective for a wide range of symptoms in borderline patients, including schizotypal, impulsive, and depressive symptoms. The magnitude of the effect is modest, and side effects may occur frequently.

Tricyclic Antidepressants (TCAs). Klein's early work with pseudoneurotic schizophrenic and EUCD patients, described previously herein, included double-blind trials of imipramine (Klein, 1967, 1968). Surprisingly, patients diagnosed as pseudoneurotic schizophrenic did best on imipramine; the antidepressant was significantly better than placebo, with a trend toward superiority over chlorpromazine as well. Aono et al. (1981) described similar results with amoxapine in nine clinically diagnosed pseudoneurotic schizophrenic patients. At 4 weeks, five of seven patients had a moderate to marked effect, including decreased depression, depersonalization, blunted affect, and hypoactivity; no change was noted in conceptual disorganization or suspiciousness. In general, Klein's EUCD patients did no better on imipramine than on placebo. Moreover, Klein subsequently suggested that imipramine was contraindicated in patients with hysteroid dysphoria because it could cause confusion, somatic distress, depersonalization, and hypomania (Klein et al., 1980).

Soloff's chart review study (1981b) found no outcome differences in antidepressant- versus neuroleptic-treated groups of BPD patients, but the chart review of Cole et al. (1984) showed that six of seven BPD patients with depressive symptoms responded to antidepressant treatment.

Liebowitz et al. (1984, 1988) have extensive

experience with the use of TCAs in a large sample of patients with atypical depression. Although these patients do not have BPD per se, their symptoms of hysteroid dysphoria, anxiety, and interpersonal dysfunction suggest similarities with BPD patients. A double-blind, placebo-controlled study of imipramine (average dose: 265 mg/day) and phenelzine resulted in significant improvement in 50% (19 of 38) of patients who completed a 6-week trial of the TCA. While this response rate was significantly better than placebo, it was significantly worse than for phenelzine (see the following study results). Imipramine treatment affected global outcome measures and SCL-90 measures of depression and hostility. There were no significant improvements, relative to placebo, on Schedule for Affective Disorder and Schizophrenia—Change (SADS-C) supplemental ratings of borderline, histrionic, labile, hysteroid dysphoria, and atypical depression symptoms. Demographic and diagnostic features regarding subsets of atypical depression did not distinguish imipramine responders from phenelzine responders.

The aforementioned Soloff study (Soloff et al., 1986a, 1986b, 1986c, 1987) is the only one to evaluate TCA agents in a double-blind, placebo-controlled trial in patients with research diagnoses of BPD. Amitriptyline treatment (mean dose = 147.6 mg; combined metabolite blood level = 245 ng/dl at Day 35) resulted in significant decreases in a variety of depressive and interpersonal symptoms. However, only one item on the SCL-90 ("Additional Items") showed statistical superiority for amitriptyline relative to placebo. In addition, there was a trend (p < 0.1) for superiority of the antidepressant versus placebo on the Beck Depression Inventory (BDI). Amitriptyline resulted in less change than haloperidol on other SCL-90 scales, and it was statistically less effective by these outcome measures. Of note was the lack of interaction between concurrent major depression and amitriptyline response.

Of even greater concern than their lack of efficacy is the TCAs' association with behavioral toxicity. Klein (1968) reported that, while it resulted in greater affective stability in 44% of EUCD patients, imipramine led to an anger response in 22% of them. Furthermore, this response was seen only in imipramine-treated patients (not with chlorpromazine or placebo), and it was fairly specific to EUCD, occurring in only 2% of other imipramine-treated patients. Soloff et al. (1986a, 1986b, 1986c, 1987) reported a similar dichotomy of responses to amitriptyline in BPD patients. Those who responded favorably to the drug showed a decrease in impulsiveness, while nonresponders (54% of the amitriptyline-treated group) demonstrated increased impulsiveness, paranoia, and hostility, along with decreased measures of global function. Amitriptyline nonresponders had higher baseline measures of hostility and psychoticism than responders. The dyscontrol response occurred despite improvements in depression scores, and increases in dose led to further exacerbation of symptoms. These findings are further supported by a case report of increased self-destructive, psychotic, and anxiety symptoms in a BPD patient treated with trazodone (Perse & Greist, 1984).

In summary, TCAs seem to affect a much narrower spectrum of symptoms than neuroleptics in BPD patients. Modest improvements are confined to the depressive symptom complex. Furthermore, significant behavioral toxicity, in the form of dyscontrol, may occur in a substantial proportion of patients.

Monoamine Oxidase Inhibitors (MAOIs). Few studies have systematically examined the role of MAOIs in the treatment of borderline patients. Hedberg et al. (1971), in the aforementioned study, used 20–30 mg/day of tranylcypromine in an 8-week crossover-design study of pseudoneurotic schizophrenics. Surprisingly, 50% of these patients responded better to the MAOI than to a neuroleptic or an MAOI–neuroleptic combination, based on clinicians' global judgments. Specific improvements were noted in areas of socialization, anxiety, dissociative symptoms, and thought disorder.

Liebowitz and Klein (1979, 1981) have reported on the use of phenelzine in patients with hysteroid dysphoria; 14 of 16 of their patients met DSM-III criteria for BPD at some point during the study. They studied the effects of this medication (15–75 mg/day) in combination with intensive psychotherapy, with a random placebo crossover after 3 months of successful treatment. At the end of 3 months, improvement was seen in 11 of 16 patients. Crossover to placebo led to deterioration in 4 of 6 patients. Features responsive to phenelzine included chronic emptiness, discomfort with being alone, and impulsivity. Less responsive features included identity disturbance and affective lability. These findings highlight the possible responsiveness of deeply ingrained so-called characterological features to pharmacotherapy; however, the patients' concurrent treatment with psychotherapy must also be considered.

The studies of atypical depressives by Liebowitz et al. (1984, 1988) build on this earlier work. A total of 119 patients completed trials of placebo, imipramine, or phenelzine. Phenelzine had a response rate of 71% (24 of 34 patients), as measured by the Clinical Global Impression Improvement Scale. The MAOI was found to be superior to placebo and imipramine on a number of other outcome measures as well, including the Global Assessment Scale (GAS), the SADS-C scale, and the Hopkins Symptom Checklist (HSC). Patients with panic attacks, hysteroid dysphoria, or both conditions all responded more consistently to phenelzine than to imipramine. Finally, SADS-C supplemental ratings for borderline, labile, and atypical depression symptoms all showed superiority for phenelzine relative to placebo as well as to imipramine.

Cowdry and Gardner (1988), in the study cited previously, used tranylcypromine (average dose: 40 mg/day) as one of their five medication conditions. Of 12 patients, 10 completed at least 21 days of treatment, and the MAOI provided the best response (according to Cowdry & Gardner) for more patients than any of the other treatments. Physicians' ratings indicated significant improvements in a wide variety of symptoms, including depression, anger, rejection sensitivity, capacity for pleasure, impulsivity, and suicidality, as well as global symptom severity. Improvements noted by patients were more modest, applying mainly to depression, anxiety, and rejection sensitivity. The authors concluded that tranylcypromine had its primary effects on mood, with behavioral improvement, when it occurred, being a secondary effect.

The main concern about the use of MAOIs in borderline patients is the potential for serious side effects, including orthostatic hypotension and hypertensive crises. Because dietary noncompliance can lead to serious adverse effects, and because BPD patients are known to be impulsive and subject to repeated suicidal gestures, careful patient selection is indicated for MAOI therapy. Under the most optimistic circumstances, improvement in mood, self-image, and impulsivity during MAOI treatment would decrease the likelihood of self-destructive behavior. Cowdry and Gardner (1988) did not report any intentional overdoses in their small series of 12 patients. Further, only 1 of the 12 patients had to discontinue a tranylcypromine trial because of orthostatic hypotension.

Lithium Carbonate.   Rifkin, Quitkin, Carrillo, Blumberg, and Klein (1972c) employed typical therapeutic doses of lithium carbonate in a double-blind placebo crossover study of patients with EUCD. At the end of 6-week trials, 67% of patients demonstrated their greatest improvement on lithium, 19% did so on placebo, and 14% showed no drug–placebo difference. Those who improved on lithium showed less variation in mood during drug treatment and showed lower mean values of extreme moods. The authors concluded that variation in mood is the symptom most sensitive to lithium treatment in patients with EUCD.

Carbamazepine.   Carbamazepine was one of the treatment conditions in the multidrug study described previously (Cowdry & Gardner, 1988; Gardner & Cowdry, 1986b). Sixteen BPD patients were treated with carbamazepine in doses of 200–1200 mg/day (mean = 820), reaching blood levels of 8–12 µg/ml, for a 6-week trial. Although no significant subjective mood effects were seen, a modest but significant observer-rated effect was noted. More importantly, 10 of 11 patients who completed both placebo and carbamazepine trials showed significantly fewer episodes of behavioral dyscontrol during the medication condition, an effect that the authors describe as the acquisition of a "reflective delay." Although baseline EEG and neurological findings were not discussed, the authors suggested that some BPD patients may have an " overactivity of the limbic system," with kindling secondary to emotional trauma or subtle central nervous system (CNS) injury.

However, 3 of 17 patients in this same study

developed melancholia during treatment with carbamazepine (Gardner & Cowdry, 1986a). Each of these patients had a history of prior major depressions, but they did not have current symptoms at the start of the study. The depressions seen during treatment were clearly different than the patients' usual symptoms of chronic dysphoria, and they were also distinct from previous episodes of depression.

Alprazolam. The positive effects of alprazolam have been suggested by case reports of three patients with DSM-III BPD (Faltus, 1984). These patients had previously been treated with numerous psychotropic agents, including neuroleptics, TCAs, lithium, and benzodiazepenes. In doses of 0.5 mg three times daily (t.i.d.) to 1 mg four times daily (q.i.d.), patients showed clinical improvement in a variety of symptoms such as anxiety, paranoia, volatility, thought disorder, and somatic preoccupation. Patients were also better able to use the cognitive aspects of psychotherapy.

Cowdry and Gardner (1988) (and Gardner & Cowdry, 1985) found no statistically significant improvements in either physicians' or patients' ratings during double-blind treatment with alprazolam. However, as mentioned previously, 2 of 12 patients had their best (according to Cowdry & Gardner) medication response to this drug compared to the other medications previously noted.

Unfortunately, the only statistically significant change in BPD patients treated with alprazolam in this study was a worsening of suicidality and behavioral dyscontrol. Of 12 patients treated with alprazolam (1–6 mg/day; mean = 4.7), 7 (58.3%) showed serious episodes of dyscontrol, including suicide attempts and assaultive behavior. This contrasts with only 1 (8%) of placebo-treated patients. Interestingly, patients sometimes reported feeling less anxious and depressed prior to the dyscontrol episodes. The two patients who demonstrated their best medication response to alprazolam did not manifest behavioral dyscontrol; otherwise, however, the study did not yield any specific characteristics of those who were likely to show either improvement or increased impulsivity.

Miscellaneous. Stimulant medications, including methylphenidate and pemoline, have been used to treat patients with residual-type attention deficit disorder (ADD-R) (Wender, Reimherr, & Wood, 1981; Wender, Reimherr, Wood, & Ward, 1985; Wood, Reimherr, Wender, & Johnson, 1976). These patients share similar symptoms with BPD patients, including impulsivity, irritability, emotional lability, short temper, substance abuse, and chronic interpersonal difficulties. Approximately 50–60% of such patients respond to methylphenidate treatment with improvements in anxiety, irritability, anger, mood lability, and impulsivity. Surprisingly, adult ADD-R patients do not seem to abuse their stimulant medication. Pemoline has been less successful, especially among those patients with mild to moderate symptoms. One case study reported beneficial effects of methylphenidate in a patient with *both* ADD-R and BPD (Hooberman & Stern, 1984).

A variety of other medications and adjuncts have been examined in the treatment of patients with BPD, including clonazepam (Freinhar & Alvarez, 1985–1986), levodopa (Bonnet & Redford, 1982), and TRH (Garbutt & Loosen, 1984). While positive responses were reported in some patients with each treatment, these findings await replication. Finally, a preliminary study also suggested that fluoxetine, a specific serotonin reuptake blocker, may have preferential activity in depressed patients with chronic or atypical symptoms (Reimherr, Wood, Byerly, Brainard, & Grosser, 1984).

Psychopharmacological Treatment: A Suggested Approach

Using the available literature and clinical experience as guides, an empirical approach to the pharmacological treatment of borderline patients can be suggested. We can return to the list of previously posed questions as an outline.

Which psychopharmacological agent should be used? At what dose? For which specific symptoms? (See Table 24.1) An emerging body of literature indicates some specificity of action for different medications in BPD patients. Table 24.1 serves as a guideline for use of these medications, but it is not meant to be definitive. In actual practice, most patients undergo several medication trials, at a variety of dose ranges, before

Table 24.1. Psychopharmacological Agents in Borderline Personality Disorder

	Neuroleptics	TCAs
Target symptoms	1. Anger, hostility 2. Schizotypal experiences (paranoia, referential thinking, illusions) 3. Anxiety, phobias, obsessive thinking 4. Derealization, depersonalization 5. Impulsivity 6. Depression, suicidality 7. Global functioning	Endogenous or melancholic pattern of depression
Spectrum of action	Wide	Narrow
Choice of specific agents	1. High-potency drugs may be tolerated better than low-potency drugs 2. Low-potency drugs may be useful in the presence of overactivation and sleep disturbance	No data to support choice of any specific agent
Typical doses	Haloperidol 1–10 mg/day Thiothixene 2–20 mg/day Perphenazine 4–16 mg/day Chlorpromazine 50–150 mg/day	Imipramine 100–200 mg/day Amitriptyline 100–200 mg/day
Side effects	1. Extrapyramidal symptoms • Akinesia • Cogwheel rigidity 2. Akathisia 3. Anticholinergic symptoms (with low-potency drugs) • Dry mouth • Visual blurring • Constipation • Urinary retention • Impotence	1. Anticholinergic • Dry mouth • Visual blurring • Constipation • Urinary retention • Impotence 2. Orthostatic hypotension
Precautions & warnings	Potential for tardive dyskinesia unknown in BPD patients	1. May be lethal in overdose 2. May precipitate behavioral dyscontrol, with increased suicidality, assaultiveness, and psychoticism

finding the optimal treatment. Furthermore, even so-called optimal treatment may result in unpleasant side effects and the deliberate or impulsive misuse of medications. In general, polypharmacy should be avoided.

In which patient? (See Table 24.2) As an alternative to the medication-based approach outlined in Table 24.1, it may also be useful to examine specific patient profiles as a guide to pharmacotherapy. Previous attempts at defining subgroups of BPD patients have met with little success in predicting responses to pharmacotherapy. For instance, several studies have failed to demonstrate differential medication responses in patients with BPD, SPD, or mixed symptoms; similarly, the presence of a major depressive episode does not necessarily presage a favorable response to TCAs. Nevertheless, in the absence of more precise guidelines, clinical pharmacotherapy must be guided by the dominant symptom pattern of the patient.

One method of grouping BPD patients, outlined in Table 24.2, is to consider which of three symptom types dominates the clinical picture: (1) depression and affective disturbances, (2) impulse control disturbances, or (3) psychoticlike disturbances.

At what point during the course of the disorder?

MAOIs	Carbamazepine	Benzodiazepenes and related agents
1. Atypical depressive or hysteroid dysphoric symptoms • Reactive, labile mood • Hyperphagia/weight gain • Hypersomnolence • Leaden paralysis • Rejection-sensitivity 2. Impulsivity 3. Self-destructiveness, suicidality 4. Characetrological features	1. Impulsivity, behavioral dyscontrol 2. Anger 3. Suicidality 4. Anxiety	1. Anxiety, panic 2. Paranoia 3. Volatility 4. Depression
Wide	Medium	Narrow
Tranylcypromaine may be more activating than phenelzine		Alprazolam may have more serious withdrawal effects than traditional benzodiazepenes
Tranylcypromine 20–60 mg/day Phenelzine 30–75 mg/day	Carbamazepine 200–1200 mg/day	Alprazolam 1–6 mg/day Lorazepam 1–6 mg/day
1. Orthostatic hypotension 2. Weight gain, edema 3. Neuromuscular (cramping, myoclonus) 4. Insomnia, sedation 5. Sexual dysfunction (anorgasmia)	1. Sedation 2. Ataxia 3. GI upset 4. Visual blurring	1. Sedation 2. Rebound anxiety on withdrawal
1. May be lethal in overdose 2. Risk of hypertensive crisis due to tyramine food reaction	1. May cause lethal bone marrow suppression; complete blood count (CBC) must be monitored 2. May precipitate melancholic depression	1. May precipitate behavioral dyscontrol: impulsivity, suicidality, assaultiveness 2. Abuse potential

Patients may present chronic, but relatively stable, symptoms. If the patient is reliable and cooperative, and if her or his environment is supportive, evaluation and empirical drug trials can commence on an outpatient basis. However, it is more often the case that the patient presents acute symptoms and situational crisis. Under such circumstances, the institution of outpatient drug trials is fraught with difficulty and unlikely to be successful. A brief inpatient hospitalization is recommended, not only for accurate assessment, but also to rapidly evaluate acute medication effects and side effects.

BPD patients are often considered for pharmacological treatment only after a variety of other unsuccessful treatment attempts. An accurate treatment history is essential, and it must be supplemented with secondary sources whenever possible. If the patient is actively involved in concurrent treatment, frequent communication with other therapists is mandatory.

Using which outcome measures? Judged by whom? The patient and the clinician must both have reasonable goals at the beginning of treatment. Suppression of specific symptoms is a reasonable goal in most BPD patients. This may help to improve social adaptation, check regression, and assist the progress of a multimodal treatment.

TABLE 24.2. Pharmacotherapy for Subgroups of Patients with Borderline Personality Disorder

	Primarily depressed patients	Primarily impulsive patients	Primarily psychotic patients

Major symptoms	1. Chronic depression
	2. Demanding dramatic presentation
	3. Atypical symptoms
	  • Mood reactivity
	  • Rejection-sensitivity
	  • Hyperphagia
	  • Hypersomnia
	  • Leaden paralysis
		1. Repleated impulsive behaviors in the setting of interpersonal stress
		  • Overdose
		  • Suicide threats
		  • Self-mutilation
		  • Drug (e.g., alcohol) binges
		  • Sexual promiscuity
		  • Antisocial acts
		2. Depression (variable)
			Multiple, stress-related, psychoticlike symptoms
			  • Paranoia
			  • Referential thinking
			  • Depersonalization/derealization
			  • Illusions, brief hallucinations
			  • Odd experiences
			  • Mild formal thought disorder

Overlap with other diagnosis	1. Major depression 2. Atypical depression 3. Dysthymic disorder 4. Hysteroid dysphoria	1. Bipolar affective disorder 2. Cyclothymic disorder 3. Organic mental disorder (including posttraumatic, seizure-associated, ADD-R) 4. Antisocial personality disorder	1. Schizotypal personality disorder 2. Brief reactive psychosis 3. Atypical psychosis 4. Pseudoneurotic schizophrenia
Pharmacotherapy	1. MAOIs 2. Neuroleptics 3. TCAs	1. Neuroleptics 2. Carbamazepine 3. Lithium 4. MAOI	Neuroleptics
Comments	1. Characterologic symptoms may improve with treatment 2. MAOIs and TCAs pose significant risk of overdose	1. Choice of agent may be dictated by results of organic and psychiatric evaluation 2. MAOIs should be used only with great caution 3. TCAs and benzodiazepines are relatively contraindicated	1. Schizotypal features may predict poor response to TCAs 2. Psychoticlike symptoms are often dynamically meaningful and mood congruent 3. Supportive and brief hospitalization are often sufficient to control symptoms

On the other hand, elimination of symptoms, cure, or the substitution of pharmacotherapy for a complete treatment approach are not reasonable goals.

Systematic drug studies of BPD patients repeatedly demonstrate the modest magnitude of improvement associated with pharmacotherapy alone. Specific symptoms are most responsive to medications, although some studies indicate that nontarget symptoms and characterological traits may also respond to some degree. The patient should clearly understand the expected results and the side effects in order to prevent disillusionment. Furthermore, because studies have repeatedly shown that patients and observers differ in their evaluation of a drug's effectiveness, systematic measures of both self-reported and observer-rated changes should be used.

For what duration? Most reported drug studies have lasted between 6 weeks and 3 months, but no generally accepted guidelines exist regarding duration of clinical treatment with any medication. Although suppression of symptoms may eventually lead to more effective social learning and character change, such a hypothesis remains untested. In addition, some of the medications discussed may have important long-term side effects—such as the development of tardive dyskinesia with neuroleptics. Therefore, the duration of treatment must remain an empirical issue, to be evaluated by the clinician and the patient in each individual case, by balancing the type and degree of beneficial and adverse effects.

Case Illustrations

The following case histories illustrate some of the typical symptoms and social histories seen in BPD patients. The two women presented similar clinical findings, mainly in affective and impulse-control areas, but despite their similarities, they each responded well to different medications. Improvements were seen in a wide range of symptoms, demonstrating the importance of objective and subjective follow-up ratings. Finally, each case shows that medications may improve functioning, but they may not alter some basic maladaptive personality traits.

Case 1

Ms. J, a 24-year-old divorced white woman, presented herself to a psychiatric evaluation center with a chief complaint of "feeling out of control." She had a long history of "temper tantrums," fighting, and being unable to make or keep close friends or to carry through with her life plans. The evaluation was precipitated by an argument with her male roommate, during which she threatened him with a knife. Ms. J had additional symptoms of low mood and low self-esteem, decreased energy, social isolation with a concomitant feeling of not wanting to be alone, sleep difficulties, and increased eating. When alone, Ms. J noted feeling "depressed, dark, evil, and bad." Her history was remarkable for paranoid and self-destructive feelings, derealization episodes, multiple alcohol and other drug abuse.

Significant family history included a mother who had been alternately diagnosed with either borderline personality disorder or bipolar affective disorder. Social history revealed lifelong conflict with the stepmother who raised her, disciplinary problems in school, two failed marriages in which she was physically abused, two children who had lived episodically with Ms. J, and several attempts at higher education and at employment, neither of which she could complete. Medical and neurological evaluation were unremarkable. Mental status examination revealed a very fashionable young woman, whose heavy makeup and hairstyle bordered on the bizarre. Her mood was reported as depressed, but her affect showed an appropriate range. Ms. J's speech was digressive, vague, and dramatic. She felt suspicious that others were watching her. Initial diagnostic impression was dysthymic disorder, in conjunction with BPD. Because of her poor social supports and her subjective distress, the patient was admitted to a general psychiatric inpatient unit. There, Ms. J's presentation was marked by contrasts: Her behavior alternated between social isolation and overinvolvement with other patients; her appearance varied from disheveled to extremely stylish; and her mood went from hopelessly depressed to euthymic. Ms. J had persistent difficulties with the unit's rules, frequently both blaming staff members for her failure to attend necessary meetings and refusing to participate in many group and individual sessions.

The patient was evaluated for participation in a research study of pharmacotherapy in BPD. She received a score of 9 out 10 on the DIB, fulfilled all of the DSM-III criteria for BPD and four of the criteria for SPD, and she also met criteria for atypical depression and hysteroid dysphoria. She was started on phenelzine under double-blind conditions, reaching a dose of 60 mg per day by the end of Week 1, and 75 mg per day at Week 6; platelet MAOI was 89.6%. The first 5-week phase of the study, initiated during the inpatient hospitalization, did not lead to improvements on the Hamilton Depression Rating Scale (HDRS) or the Atypical Depression Inventory (ADI). However, the GAS, Schizotypal Symptoms Inventory (SSI), BDI and SCL-90 all showed substantial improvements. The patient and staff both felt that Ms. J's mood and behavior were more stable than at admission, and she was discharged after approximately 3 weeks.

Outpatient follow-up continued for approximately 6 weeks. When Ms. J attempted to lower her dose of phenelzine to 45 mg, she noted an increase in dissociation and paranoia, which resolved after the dose was raised back to 60 mg. Side effects included symptomatic orthostatic hypotension and anorgasmia. Nevertheless, Ms. J recognized improvements in areas such as mood, impulse control, and a more mature decision-making style. During this time, she lost custody of her daughter (due in part to her failure to obtain legal representation), but she did not react violently or impulsively, as she felt she might have done previously. The clinical impression of improvement was substantiated by a variety of rating scales, including the HDRS, SSI, and BDI. The GAS, which had a minimum value of 45 during the inpatient stay, rose to a maximum of 75, indicating a noticeable decrease in the overall severity of symptoms.

Unfortunately, Ms. J. did not continue to attend outpatient sessions on a regular basis; instead, she adopted a walk-in approach. She did not actively engage in the psychotherapy that was recommended and offered. Approximately 4 months after her initial presentation to the hospital, the patient was arrested on a variety of charges, including shoplifting and armed robbery. Her family requested that the therapist become involved in efforts to have her released from jail, which he did not do. After she was released on bail, Ms. J. failed to appear for any further scheduled appointments, and her case was closed.

Comment. This patient experienced a wide range of symptoms, but she was more affected by impulse control problems and affective disturbance than by psychoticlike experiences. The hospitalization was useful in revealing a variabil-

ity in her presentation, which the patient herself could not describe. Although MAOI treatment did not appear to affect objective measures of mood initially, the patient rated herself as improved; over time, objective ratings also reflected this improvement. A wide range of symptoms, including psychotic-like symptoms and impulsivity, were affected by treatment. However, the patient continued to externalize responsibility for her treatment and for her life, and her antisocial traits remained.

Case 2

Ms. V, a 27-year-old divorced woman, presented herself for evaluation at the Mood Disorders Clinic with a chief complaint, "Nothing goes right for me." She specifically complained of an inability to develop long-lasting relationships, as well as chronic feelings of low self-esteem, low mood and hopelessness, suicidal thoughts, poor memory and concentration, anhedonia and poor motivation, hypersomnia, and hyperphagia. Despite these symptoms, her mood was reactive to positive events. She also noted a pattern of impulsive behavior, usually consisting of overeating, but also including spending sprees to the point of bankruptcy, sexual promiscuity, and temper tantrums. She claimed to feel alone even when she was around people. Ms. V's history was also notable for frequent episodes of depersonalization and two previous suicide gestures. At the time of evaluation, she was drinking alcohol daily, but she did not abuse other substances. She did not have a history that suggested true mania.

Family history was positive for alcoholism in Ms. V's father, and a so-called nervous breakdown in her mother. She herself had been married twice, and she had been abused in both marriages; her one daughter was living with one of Ms. V's ex-husbands. She worked as a licensed practical nurse (L.P.N.) at an area hospital, and she derived a great deal of satisfaction from her work. Medical evaluation disclosed a history of three prior closed-head injuries, but a routine EEG was interpreted as normal.

An initial diagnosis of BPD was substantiated by a score of 9 out of 10 on the DIB. Ms. V entered a pharmacotherapy research protocol for BPD, and she was assigned to haloperidol treatment on a random, double-blind basis. Her dose was raised to 3 mg per day by the end of the third week, but she developed intolerable sedation, and the dose was lowered to 2 mg per day.

Because of akathisia and muscle cramps, she was prescribed 2 mg two times daily (b.i.d.) of biperiden. She received pharmacotherapy in combination with supportive psychotherapy for a total of 11 weeks.

Within 4 weeks, Ms. V noted an improvement in her symptoms of depression, and she felt that she could tolerate frustrations without resorting to impulsive behaviors. These improvements were reflected in various rating scales, such as the HDRS, which decreased from 22 to 10; the BDI, which went from 34 to 15; and the GAS, which increased from 45 to 65. Modest improvement was also noted on the SSI. Continuation of treatment led to continued improvement in all areas. The patient felt in better control emotionally, despite a variety of stressors: "Things are worse, but I'm better." She credited both psychotherapy and medications for the improvements. At 11 weeks, the BDI score was 0, HDRS was 3, and GAS was 80.

During this time, Ms. V contemplated a move back to her home state to be closer to her daughter. After 4 months of treatment, she failed to keep a scheduled appointment, and she subsequently announced her intention to stop medication and all other treatment. Another appointment was scheduled to discuss these issues, but the patient did not attend. Further attempts to contact the patient were unsuccessful, and she was discharged.

Comment. Like the first patient, Ms. V initially presented with mainly affective and impulse control symptoms. She clearly benefited from treatment, but the relative contributions of psychotherapy and pharmacotherapy are uncertain. As in the first case, a wide range of symptoms, from depressed mood to impulsivity and schizotypal symptoms, showed improvement. Side effects of medication were present even at low doses, but they were manageable with dose reductions and anticholinergic agents. Ms. V's sudden exit from treatment could not be easily explained in light of her positive response to treatment.

ALTERNATIVE TREATMENT OPTIONS

As currently conceptualized, pharmacotherapy for the borderline patient is seen as an adjunct, rather than an alternative, to other treatments.

Although some authors have cautioned that pharmacotherapy can be ineffective or even harmful in the treatment of borderline patients (Gunderson, 1986), medications are generally regarded to be helpful in the management of at least some cases. While the long-term efficacy of any intervention in the treatment of BPD remains to be empirically proven, it is generally assumed that pharmacotherapy is directed against the *state* symptoms, while psychotherapy addresses the patient's underlying *trait* vulnerability and maladaptive character.

Several precautions are warranted in the use of multimodel treatments. First, reasonable goals and expectations are warranted for both the therapist and the patient. Neither pharmacotherapy nor psychotherapy are magic cures. Drugs may have more rapid onset of action, but their scope is more limited; psychotherapy may take longer to effect change, but its scope is wider. Second, neither pharmacotherapy nor psychotherapy should be perceived as a second-line treatment. If a patient is engaged in one form of therapy and is referred for institution of a second, the patient should not be seen (by her- or himself or by the clinician) as a treatment failure. Often, a patient may get the impression that one form of treatment is superior and that, if another treatment is required, she or he is beyond the help of the original treatment. Third, the psychological impact of pharmacotherapy must always be considered. The clinician–patient relationship is subject to the same maladaptive interpersonal qualities that characterize the borderline patient's other relationships. As a result, medications can be used for purposes of manipulation, idealization, devaluation, and suicidal acting out—They may become transitional objects and agents for playing out the psychotherapeutic transference (Adelman, 1985). Furthermore, the borderline patient may imbue his or her medications with qualities they do not actually possess. The inability to wean a patient from her or his medications, or, conversely, the development of unbearable side effects, may be clues to this process.

Finally, but also in the context of interpersonal aspects of pharmacotherapy, adequate communication must be fostered between the patient and the clinician(s). This is a difficult enough task with a relatively healthy patient and one therapist. However, if the patient has a BPD, and if psychotherapy, family therapy, and pharmacotherapy are provided by different clinicians, the sources for miscommunication increase exponentially. Continued contact among all involved service providers, patients, and families, is mandatory.

REFERENCES

Adelman, S. A. (1985). Pills as transitional objects: A dynamic understanding of the use of medication in psychotherapy. *Psychiatry, 48*, 246–253.

Akiskal, H. S. (1981). Subaffective disorders: Dysthymic, cyclothymic and bipolar II disorders in the "borderline" realm. *Psychiatric Clinics of North America, 4*, 25–46.

Akiskal, H. S., Yerevanian, B. I., Davis, G. C., King, D., & Lemmi, H. (1985). The nosologic status of borderline personality: Clinical and polysomnographic study. *American Journal of Psychiatry, 142*, 192–198.

American Psychiatric Association (1980). *Diagnostic and statistical manual of mental disorders* (3rd ed.) (DSM-III). Washington, DC: Author.

American Psychiatric Association (1987). *Diagnostic and statistical manual of mental disorders* (3rd ed. rev.) (DSM-III-R), Washington, DC: Author.

Andrulonis, P. A., Glueck, B. C., Stroebel, C. F., Vogel, N. G., Shapiro, A. L., & Aldridge, D. M. (1980). Organic brain dysfunction and the borderline syndrome. *Psychiatric Clinics of North America, 4*, 49–66.

Andrulonis, P. A., Glueck, B. C., Stroebel, C. F., & Vogel, N. G. (1982). Borderline personality subcategories. *The Journal of Nervous and Mental Disease, 170*, 670–679.

Aono, T., Kaneko, M., Numata, Y., Takahashi, Y., Yamamoto, T., & Kumashiro, H. (1981). Effects of amoxapine, a new antidepressant, on pseudoneurotic schizophrenia. *Folia Psychiatrica et Neurologica Japonica, 35*, 115–121.

Baron, M. (1981). *Schedule for interviewing borderlines*. New York: New York State Psychiatric Institute.

Barrash, J., Kroll, J., Carey, K., & Sines, L. (1983). Discriminating borderline disorder from other personality disorders. *Archives of General Psychiatry, 40*, 1297–1302.

Baxter, L., Edell, W., Gerner, R., Fairbanks, L., & Gwirtsman, H. (1984). Dexamethasone suppression test and Axis I diagnoses of inpatients with DSM-III

borderline personality disorder. *Journal of Clinical Psychiatry, 45*, 150–153.

Beeber, A. R., Kline, M. D., Pies, R. W., & Manring, J. M., Jr. (1984). Dexamethasone suppression test in hospitalized depressed patients with borderline personality disorder. *Journal of Nervous and Mental Disease, 172*, 301–303.

Bell, J., Lycaki, H., Jones, D., Kelwala, S., & Sitaram, N. (1983). Effect of preexisting borderline personality disorder on clinical and EEG sleep correlates of depression. *Psychiatry Research, 9*, 115–123.

Bonnet, K. A., & Redford, H. R. (1982). Levodopa in borderline disorders. *Archives of General Psychiatry, 39*, 862.

Brinkley, J. R., Beitman, B. D., & Friedel, R. O. (1979). Low-dose neuroleptic regimens in the treatment of borderline patients. *Archives of General Psychiatry, 36*, 319–326.

Carpenter, W. T., & Gunderson, J. G. (1977). Five year follow-up comparison of borderline and schizophrenic patients. *Comprehensive Psychiatry, 18*, 567–571.

Carroll, B. J., Greden, J. F., Feinberg, M., Lohr, N., James, N. McI., Steiner, M., Haskett, R. F., Albala, A. A., DeVigne, J. P., & Tarika, J. (1981). Neuroendocrine evaluation of depression in borderline patients. *Psychiatric Clinics of North America, 4*, 89–99.

Charney, D. S., Nelson, J. C., & Quinlan, D. M. (1981). Personality traits and disorder in depression. *American Journal of Psychiatry, 138*, 1601–1604.

Cole, J. O., Salomon, M., Gunderson J., Sunderland, P., & Simmonds, P. (1984). Drug therapy in borderline patients. *Comprehensive Psychiatry, 25*, 249–254.

Cornelius, J. R., Brenner, R. P., Soloff, P. H., Schulz, S. C., & Tumuluru, R. V. (1986). EEG abnormalities in borderline personality disorder: Specific or nonspecific? *Biological Psychiatry, 21*, 977–980.

Cowdry, R. W. (1987). Psychopharmacology of borderline personality disorder: A review. *Journal of Clinical Psychiatry, 48*, 15–25.

Cowdry, R. W., & Gardner, D. L. (1988). Pharmacotherapy of borderline personality disorder. *Archives of General Psychiatry, 45*, 111–119.

Cowdry, R. W., Pickar, D., & Davies, R. (1985–1986). Symptoms and EEG findings in the borderline syndrome. *International Journal of Psychiatry in Medicine, 15*, 201–211.

Deutsch, H. (1942). Some forms of emotional disturbance and their relationship to schizophrenia. *Psychoanalytic Quarterly, 11*, 301–321.

Docherty, J. P., Fiester, S. J., & Shea, T. (1986). Syndrome diagnosis and personality disorder. In A. J. Frances & R. E. Hales (Eds.), *American Psychiatric Association annual review* (Vol. 5, pp. 315–335). Washington, DC: American Psychiatric Press.

Faltus, F. J. (1984). The positive effect of alprazolam in the treatment of three patients with borderline personality disorder. *American Journal of Psychiatry, 141,* 802–803.

Freinhar, J. P., & Alvarez, W. A. (1985–1986). Clonazepam: A novel therapeutic adjunct. *International Journal of Psychiatry in Medicine, 15,* 321–329.

Fyer, M. R., Frances, A. J., Sullivan, T., Hunt, S. W., & Clarkin, J. (1988). Comorbidity of borderline personality disorder. *Archives of General Psychiatry, 45,* 348–352.

Garbutt, J. C., & Loosen, P. T. (1984). A dramatic behavioral response to thyrotropin-releasing hormone following low-dose neuroleptics. *Psychoneuroendocrinology, 9,* 311–314.

Garbutt, J. C., Loosen, P. T., Tipermas, A., & Prange, A. J., Jr. (1983). The TRH test in patients with borderline personality disorder. *Psychiatry Research, 9,* 107–113.

Gardner, D. L., & Cowdry, R. W. (1985). Alprazolam-induced dyscontrol in borderline personality disorder. *American Journal of Psychiatry, 142,* 98–100.

Gardner, D. L., & Cowdry, R. W. (1986a). Development of melancholia during carbamazepine treatment in borderline personality disorder. *Journal of Clinical Psychopharmacology, 6,* 236–239.

Gardner, D. L., & Cowdry, R. W. (1986b). Positive effects of carbamazepine on behavioral dyscontrol in borderline personality disorder. *American Journal of Psychiatry, 143,* 519–522.

Goldberg, S. C., Schulz, S. C., Schulz, P. M., Resnick, R. J., Hamer, R. M., & Friedel, R. O. (1986). Borderline and schizotypal personality disorders treated with low-dose thiothizene vs. placebo. *Archives of General Psychiatry, 43,* 680–686.

Grinker, R. R., Werble, B., & Drye, R. (1968). *The borderline syndrome: A behavioral study of ego functions.* New York: Basic Books.

Gunderson, J. G. (1986). Pharmacotherapy for patients with borderline personality disorder. *Archives of General Psychiatry, 43,* 698–700.

Gunderson, J. G., Carpenter, W. T., & Strauss, J. S. (1975). Borderline and schizophrenic patients: A comparative study. *American Journal of Psychiatry, 132,* 1257–1264.

Gunderson, J. G., & Elliott, G. R. (1985). The interface between borderline personality disorder and affective disorder. *American Journal of Psychiatry, 142,* 277–288.

Gunderson, J. G., & Kolb, J. E. (1978). Discriminating features of borderline patients. *American Journal of Psychiatry, 135,* 792–796.

Gunderson, J. G., Siever, L. J., & Spaulding, E. (1983). The search for a schizotype. *Archives of General Psychiatry, 40,* 15–22.

Gunderson, J. G., & Singer, M. T. (1975). Defining borderline patients: An overview. *American Journal of Psychiatry, 132,* 1–10.

Hedberg, D. L., Houck, J. H., & Blueck, B. C. (1971). Tranylcypromine–trifluoperazine combination in the treatment of schizophrenia. *American Journal of Psychiatry, 127,* 61–66.

Hirschfeld, R. M. A., Klerman, G. L., Clayton, P. M., Keller, M. G., McDonald-Scott, P., & Larkin, B. H. (1983). Assessing personality: Effects of the depressive state on trait measurement. *American Journal of Psychiatry, 140,* 695–699.

Hooberman, D., & Stern, T. A. (1984). Treatment of attention deficit and borderline personality disorders with psychostimulants: Case report. *Journal of Clinical Psychiatry, 45,* 441–442.

Houch, P. H., & Polatin, P. (1949). Pseudoneurotic forms of schizophrenia. *Psychiatric Quarterly, 23,* 248–276.

Kaplan, H. I., & Sadock, B. J. (1988). *Synopsis of psychiatry: Behavioral sciences, clinical psychiatry.*

Kendler, K. S., Gruenberg, A. M., & Strauss, J. S. (1981). An independent analysis of the Copenhagen sample of the Danish adoption study of schizophrenia. *Archives of General Psychiatry, 38,* 982–984.

Kernberg, O. F. (1975). *Borderline conditions and pathological narcissism.* New York: Aronson.

Kety, S. S., Rosenthal, D., Wender, P. H., & Schulsinger, F. (1971). Mental illness in the biological and adoptive families of adopted schizophrenics. *American Journal of Psychiatry, 128,* 302–306.

Klein, D. F. (1967). Importance of psychiatric diagnosis in prediction of clinical drug effects. *Archives of General Psychiatry, 16,* 118–126.

Klein, D. F. (1968). Psychiatric diagnosis and a typology of clinical drug effects. *Psychopharmacologia (Berl.), 13,* 359–386.

Klein, D. F. (1975). Psychopharmacology and the borderline patient. In J. E. Mack (Ed.), *Borderline states in psychiatry* (pp. 75–92). New York: Grune and Stratton.

Klein, D. F., Gittelman, R., Quitkin, F., & Rifkin, A. (1980). *Diagnosis and drug treatment of psychiatric disorders: Adults and children* (2nd ed.). Baltimore: Williams & Wilkins.

Knight, R. (1953). Borderline states. *Bulletin of the Menninger Clinic, 17*, 1–12.

Koenigsberg, H. W., Kernberg, O. F., & Schomer, J. (1983). Diagnosing borderline conditions in an outpatient setting. *Archives of General Psychiatry, 40*, 49–53.

Kolb, J. E., & Gunderson, J. G. (1980). Diagnosing borderline patients with a semi-structured interview. *Archives of General Psychiatry, 37*, 37–41.

Kroll, J., Sines, L., Martin, K., Lari, S., Pyle, R., & Zander, J. (1981). Borderline personality disorder. *Archives of General Psychiatry, 38*, 1021–1026.

Leone, N. F. (1982). Response of borderline patients to loxapine and chlorpromazine. *Journal of Clinical Psychiatry, 43*, 148–150.

Liebowitz, M. R. (1979). Is borderline a distinct entity? *Schizophrenia Bulletin, 5*, 23–38.

Liebowitz, M. R., & Klein, D. F. (1979). Hysteroid dysphoria. *Psychiatric Clinics of North America, 2*, 555–575.

Liebowitz, M. R., & Klein, D. F. (1981). Interrelationship of hysteroid dysphoria and borderline personality disorder. *Psychiatric Clinics of North America, 4*, 67–87.

Liebowitz, M. R., Quitkin, F. M., Stewart, J. W., McGrath, P. J., Harrison, W. M., Markowitz, J. S., Rabkin, J. G., Tricamo, E., Goetz, D. M., & Klein, D. F. (1988). Antidepressant specificity in atypical depression. *Archives of General Psychiatry, 45*, 129–137.

Liebowitz, M. R., Quitkin, F. M., Stewart, J. W., McGrath, P. J., Harrison, W., Rabkin, J., Tricamo, E., Markowitz, J. S., & Klein, D. F. (1984). Phenelzine versus imipramine in atypical depression: A preliminary report. *Archives of General Psychiatry, 41*, 669–677.

Loranger, A. W., Oldham, J. M., & Tulis, E. H. (1982). Familial transmission of DSM-III borderline personality disorder. *Archives of General Psychiatry, 39*, 795–799.

Lucas, P. B., Gardner, D. L., Wolkowitz, O. M., & Cowdry, R. W. (1987). Dysphoria associated with methylphenidate infusion in borderline personality disorder. *American Journal of Psychiatry, 144*, 1577–1579.

McGlashan, T. H. (1983a). The borderline syndrome: I. Testing three diagnostic systems. *Archives of General Psychiatry, 40*, 1311–1318.

McGlashan, T. H. (1983b). The borderline syndrome: II. Is it a variant of schizophrenia or affective disorder? *Archives of General Psychiatry, 40*, 1319–1323.

McNamara, E., Reynolds, C. F., III, Soloff, P. H., Mathias, R., Rossi, A., Spiker, D., Coble, P. A., & Kupfer, D. J. (1984). EEG sleep evaluation of depression in borderline patients. *American Journal of Psychiatry, 141*, 182–186.

Mellsop, G., Varghese, F., Joshua, S., & Hicks, A. (1982). The reliability of Axis II of DSM-III. *American Journal of Psychiatry, 139*, 1360–1361.

Merikangas, K. R., & Weissman, M. M. (1986). Epidemiology of DSM-III Axis II personality disorders. In A. J. Frances & R. E. Hales (Eds.), *American Psychiatric Association Annual Review* (Vol. 5, pp. 240–257). Washington, DC: American Psychiatric Press.

Nathan, R. S., Soloff, P. H., George, A., Peters, J. L., & McCarthy, T. (1986). DST and TRH tests in borderline personality disorder. *Proceeding of the 4th World Congress of Biological Psychiatry*, (pp. 563–563). Elsevier Press.

Perry, J. C. (1982). *The borderline personality disorder scale (BPD-Scale)*. Cambridge, MA: Cambridge Hospital.

Perry, J. C., & Klerman, G. L. (1978). The borderline patient. *Archives of General Psychiatry, 35*, 141–150.

Perry, J. C., & Klerman, G. L. (1980). Clinical features of the borderline personality disorder. *American Journal of Psychiatry, 137*, 165–173.

Perse, T., & Greist, J. H. (1984). Self-destructive behavior in a patient taking trazodone. *American Journal of Psychiatry, 141*, 1646–1647.

Pfohl, B., Stangl, D., & Zimmerman, M. (1984). The implications of DSM-III personality disorders for patients with major depression. *Journal of Affective Disorders, 7*, 309–318.

Pope, H. G., Jr., Jonas, J. M., Hudson, J. I., Cohen, B. M., & Gunderson, J. G. (1983). The validity of DSM-III borderline personality disorder. *Archives of General Psychiatry, 40*, 23–30.

Quitkin, F., & Klein, D. F. (1969). Two behavioral syndromes in young adults related to possible minimal brain dysfunction. *Journal of Psychiatric Research, 7*, 131–142.

Quitkin, F., Rifkin, A., & Klein, D. F. (1976). Neurologic soft signs in schizophrenia and character disorders. *Archives of General Psychiatry, 33*, 845–853.

Reimherr, F. W., Wood, D. R., Byerly, B., Brainard, J., & Grosser, B. I. (1984). Characteristics of responders to fluoxetine. *Psychopharmacology Bulletin, 20*, 70–72.

Reynolds, C. F., Soloff, P. H., Kupfer, D. J., Taska, L. S., Restifo, K., Coble, P. A., & McNamara, M. E. (1985). Depression in borderline patients: A prospective EEG sleep study. *Psychiatry Research, 14*, 1–15.

Rieder, R. O. (1979). Borderline schizophrenia: Evidence of its validity. *Schizophrenia Bulletin, 5*, 39–46.

Rifkin, R., Levitan, S. J., Galewski, J., & Klein, D. F. (1972a). Emotionally unstable character disorder—A follow-up study: I. Description of patients and outcome. *Biological Psychiatry, 4*, 65–79.

Rifkin, A., Levitan, S. J., Galewski, J., & Klein, D. F. (1972b). Emotionally unstable character disorder—A follow-up study: II. Prediction of outcome. *Biological Psychiatry, 4*, 81–89.

Rifkin, A., Quitkin, F., Carrillo, C., Blumberg, A. G., &Klein, D. F. (1972c). Lithium carbonate in emotionally unstable character disorder. *Archives of General Psychiatry, 27*, 519–523.

Robins, E., & Guze, S. B. (1970). Establishment of diagnostic validity in psychiatric illness: Its application to schizophrenia. *American Journal Psychiatry, 126*, 107–111.

Rosenthal, D., Wender, P. H., Kety, S. S., Welner, J., & Schulsinger, F. (1971). The adopted-away offspring of schizophrenics. *American Journal of Psychiatry, 128*, 307–311.

Schulz, S. C., Cornelius, J., Schulz, P., & Soloff, P. H. (1988). The amphetamine challenge test in patients with borderline disorder. *American Journal of Psychiatry, 145*, 809–814.

Schulz, S. C., Schulz, P. M., Dommisse, C., Hamer, R. M., Blackard, W. G., Narasimhachari, N., & Friedel, R. O. (1985). Amphetamine response in borderline patients. *Psychiatry Research, 15*, 97–108.

Serban, G., & Siegel, S. (1984). Response of borderline and schizotypal patients to small doses of thiothixene and haloperidol. *American Journal of Psychiatry, 141*, 1455–1458.

Sheehy, M., Goldsmith, L., & Charles, E. (1980). A comparative study of borderline patients in a psychiatric outpatient clinic. *American Journal of Psychiatry, 137*, 1374–1379.

Siever, L. J. (1985). Biological markers in schizotypal personality disorder. *Schizophrenia Bulletin, 11*, 564–575.

Siever, L. J., & Gunderson, J. G. (1979). Genetic determinants of borderline conditions. *Schizophrenia Bulletin, 5*, 59–86.

Snyder, S., & Pitts, W. M. (1984). Electroencephalography of DSM-III borderline personality disorder. *Acta Psychiatrica Scandinavica, 69*, 129–134.

Snyder, S., Pitts, W. M., & Gustin, Q. (1983). CT scans of patients with borderline personality disorder. *American Journal of Psychiatry, 140*, 272.

Soloff, P. H. (1981a). Affect, impulse and psychosis in borderline disorder: A validation study. *Comprehensive Psychiatry, 22*, 337–350.

Soloff, P. H. (1981b). Pharmacotherapy of borderline disorders. *Comprehensive Psychiatry, 22*, 535–543.

Soloff, P. H. (1987). A pharmacologic approach to the borderline patient. *Psychiatric Annals, 17*, 201–205.

Soloff, P. H., George, A. W., & Nathan, R. S. (1982). The dexamethasone suppression test in borderline personality disorders. *American Journal of Psychiatry, 139*, 1621–1623.

Soloff, P. H., George, A., Nathan, R. S., Schulz, P. M., & Perel, J. M. (1986c). Paradoxical effects of amitriptyline on borderline patients. *American Journal of Psychiatry, 143*, 1603–1605.

Soloff, P. H., George, A., Nathan, R. S., Schulz, P. M., & Perel, J. M. (1987). Behavioral dyscontrol in borderline patients treated with amitriptyline. *Psychopharmacology Bulletin, 23*, 177–181.

Soloff, P. H., George, A., Nathan, S., Schulz, P. M., Ulrich, R. F., & Perel, J. M. (1986b). Amitriptyline and haloperidol in unstable and schizotypal borderline disorders. *Psychopharmacology Bulletin, 22*, 177–182.

Soloff, P. H., George, A., Nathan, R. S., Schulz, P. M., Ulrich, R. F., & Perel, J. M. (1986c). Progress in pharmacotherapy of borderline disorders. *Archives of General Psychiatry, 43*, 691–697.

Soloff, P. H., & Millward, J. W. (1983). Psychiatric disorders in the families of borderline patients. *Archives of General Psychiatry, 40*, 37–44.

Soloff, P. H., & Ulrich, R. F. (1981). Diagnostic interview for borderline patients. *Archives of General Psychiatry, 38*, 686–692.

Spitzer, R. L., & Endicott, J. (1979). Justification for separating schizotypal and borderline personality disorders. *Schizophrenia Bulletin, 5*, 95–104.

Spitzer, R. L., Endicott, J., & Gibbon, M. (1979a).

Crossing the border into borderline personality and borderline schizophrenia. *Archives of General Psychiatry, 36*, 17–24.

Spitzer, R. L., Forman, J. B. W., & Nee, J. (1979b). DSM-III field trials: I. Initial interrater diagnostic reliability. *American Journal of Psychiatry* 136:815–817.

Steiner, M., Elizur, A., & Davidson, S. (1979). Neuroleptic-induced paradoxical behavioral toxicity in young borderline schizophrenics. *Confinia Psychiatry, 22*, 226–233.

Steiner, M., Martin, S., Wallace, J. E., & Goldman, S. (1984). Distinguishing subtypes within the borderline domain: A combined psychoneuroendocrine approach. *Biological Psychiatry, 19*, 907–911.

Sternbach, H. A., Fleming, J., Extein, I., Pottash, A. L. C., & Gold, M. S. (1983). The dexamethasone suppression and thyrotropin-releasing hormone tests in depressed borderline patients. *Psychoneuroendocrinology, 8*, 459–462.

Stone, M. H. (1977). The borderline syndrome: Evolution of the term, genetic aspects, and prognosis. *American Journal of Psychotherapy*, 345–365.

Strangl, D., Pfohl, B., Zimmerman, M., Bowers, W., & Corenthal, C. (1985). A structured interview for the DSM-III personality disorders: A preliminary report. *Archives of General Psychiatry, 42*, 591–596.

Torgersen, S. (1984). Genetic and nosological aspects of schizotypal and borderline personality disorders: A twin study. *Archives of General Psychiatry, 41*, 546–554.

Tucker, L., Bauer, S. F., Wagner, S., Harlam, D., & Sher, I. (1987). Long-term hospital treatment of borderline patients: A descriptive outcome study. *American Journal of Psychiatry, 144*, 1443–1448.

Wender, P. H., Rosenthal, D., Kety, S. S., Schulsinger, F., & Welner, J. (1974). Crossfostering. *Archives of General Psychiatry, 30*, 121–128.

Wender, P. H., Reimherr, F. W., & Wood, D. R. (1981). Attention deficit disorder ("minimal brain dysfunction") in adults. *Archives of General Psychiatry, 38*, 449–456.

Wender, P. H., Reimherr, F. W., Wood, D., & Ward, M. (1985). A controlled study of methylphenidate in the treatment of attention deficit disorder, residual type, in adults. *American Journal of Psychiatry, 142*, 547–552.

Werble, B. (1970). Second follow-up study of borderline patients. *Archives of General Psychiatry, 23*, 3–7.

Widiger, T. A., Trull, T. J., Hurt, S. W., Clarkin, J., & Frances, A. (1987). A multidimensional scaling of the DSM-III personality disorders. *Archives of General Psychiatry, 44*, 557–563.

Wood, D. R., Reimherr, F. W., Wender, P. H., & Johnson, G. E. (1976). Diagnosis and treatment of minimal brain dysfunction in adults. *Archives of General Psychiatry, 33*, 1453–1460.

Zanarini, M. C., Frankenburg, F. R., Chauncey, D. L., & Gunderson, J. G. (1987). The diagnostic interview for personality disorders: Interrater and test–retest reliability. *Comprehensive Psychiatry, 28*, 467–480.

Zilboorg, G. (1941). Ambulatory schizophrenia. *Psychiatry, 4*, 149.

Editorial Commentary: Borderline Personality Disorder

Although the behavioral patterns that characterize borderline personality disorder have been known for many years and have received a fair number of labels (e.g., "pseudoneurotic schizophrenia"), it is only in the last decade or so that there has been any semblance of scientific study of this diagnostic entity. Contributing to more reliable diagnostic appraisals have been the criteria posted in DSM-III and DSM-III-R and the several semi-structured interview schedules that have emerged to study this most complicated phenomenon. However, even with improvements in the operational criteria to make the diagnosis, Linehan and Wasson, in their chapter, alert the reader to the fact that research indicates that there is much overlap between borderline personality disorder and other personality disorders and atypical affective disorders. Also, within the diagnosis of borderline personality disorder itself, various patients will not always evince the identical cluster of symptoms. Therefore, given the heterogeneity of the disorder, its complexity, its numerous behavioral manifestations, its biological components, its pervasiveness and chronicity, and its resistiveness to treatment, it should not be surprising that there are no standard treatments that can be implemented, as in the case for the better defined affective disturbances.

In the three chapters comprising this section by Pollack (Chapter 22), Linehan and Wasson (Chapter 23), Buysee, Nathan, and Soloff (Chapter 24), distinctive perspectives on etiology and treatment are apparent. However, despite the differences, there is clear recognition of the disorder's extraor-dinary complexity and the resulting requirement of a multimodal approach to treatment. Indeed, in the absence of long-term controlled outcome studies that examine the differential efficacy of the psychoanalytic, behavioral, and pharmacological approaches, Pollack argues for "an integrated multimodal approach based on the patient's individual needs and capacities." Similarly, Linehan and Wasson acknowledge that the four alternative treatment strategies (i.e., pharmacotherapy, inpatient hospitalization, cognitive therapy, and long-term psychodynamic therapy) could theoretically be integrated with dialectical behavior therapy (DBT), the approach that they favor. And finally, Buysee et al., the proponents of the pharmacological treatment, argue that, "As currently conceptualized, pharmacotherapy for the borderline patient is seen as an adjunct, rather than an alternative, to other treatments."

In focusing on the distinctive approaches to borderline personality, Pollack, in the psychoanalytic mode, sees it as a regressive disorder marked by the patient's use of a primitive, albeit brittle, defensive structure. He dichotomizes problems along two dimensions: (1) the self, and (2) the self in interaction with others. Problems of the self include an unstable identity, cognitive disturbances (including psychotic experiences), impulsivity, and labile and uncomfortable affect. Self-problems in relation to others involve unstable and intense interpersonal relationships, self-destructive activity, functional failures, and functional incapacity. Pollack suggests that the therapeutic relationship is central to long-term treatment, and his approach is devoted to a "personal repair of the self," with ensuing therapy following three stages: "flexible holding," "understanding," and "moving on."

Linehan and Wasson follow a modified behavioral approach to borderline personality disorder, referred to as "DBT." Although this approach tends to provide an elegant description of the particular behaviors subsumed under the diagnostic label, it does not provide too much understanding in terms of etiology. Behavioral targets in the Linehan and Wasson strategy include suicidal behaviors, other behaviors that interfere with implementation of treatment, and the patient's escape behaviors (such as substance abuse, poor work behavior, poor judgment), and they recommend behavioral skill acquisition and additional goals identified by the patient. In dealing with the aforementioned problems, core skills, emotion-regulation skills, and distress-tolerance skills are taught to the patient. In so doing, the therapist must be exquisitely sensitive to the vicissitudes of the patient–therapist relationship, as is apparent in Pollack's approach to treatment. However, by contrast, the behavioral therapist is a bit more directive, at times functions in the role of teacher, but does not make the so-called transference issue (both positive and negative) *the* focal point of the treatment. However, in the case presented by Linehan and Wasson, some of the struggles encountered between the patient and therapist are nicely documented.

Bearing in mind that the pharmacological aspects of treating the borderline patient are not conceptualized as being central, Buysee et al. consider the biological approach, including use of laboratory tests (to help refine the diagnosis of concurrent disorders) and medication to counteract certain symptomatic behaviors. Buysee et al. point out that it is difficult to diagnose borderline patients, given their alcohol and other drug abuse, their odd communication, their affective lability,

their lack of objectivity, and their chaotic interpersonal relationships. For these reasons, they recommend an extended assessment period, involving drug-free observation, hospitalization, use of structured diagnostic instruments, and availability of multiple informants. Laboratory evaluations used in the process include neuroendocrine tests (e.g., dexamethasone suppression test), stimulant infusion, and electroencephalography. The research data with respect to these tests for borderline patients generally show that an abnormal response is obtained when there is a concurrent affective disorder.

As for treatment, several drugs have been evaluated, including: neuroleptics, tricyclic antidepressants, monoamine oxidase inhibitors (MAOIs), lithium, carbamazepine, and alprazolam: some in open trials, others in double-blind drug–placebo studies, and still others on a comparative basis. Overall, although tricyclic antidepressants have positive effects on depressive symptomatology, the neuroleptics appear to affect a wider spectrum of symptoms, including the affective ones. The MAOIs also seem to have some benefit, but concerns have been raised about negative side effects and their danger, considering the dietary restrictions required of such potentially impulsive patients. Lithium, on the other hand, yielded good results with respect to mood, but alprazolam tended to increase suicidality and behavioral dyscontrol.

Much more work remains to be done with this seemingly intractable disorder. Controlled studies with larger *N*s are first needed to determine the most effective psychotherapies, behavior therapies, and pharmacotherapies. This, then, should be followed by more comprehensive evaluations in which modalities are both contrasted and examined in additive fashion. In short, research at this time is still in its early stages, but a promising foundation has been laid.

PART 9

Alcoholism and Substance Abuse

CHAPTER 25

Psychotherapy

MARC GALANTER AND RICARDO CASTANEDA

CONCEPTUALIZATION OF THE DISORDERS

General Consideration

The development of effective preventive and therapeutic strategies for substance abuse disorders constitutes an important challenge for present-day society. The expected risk for alcoholism among the general population in the United States is 5% and lifelong prevalences for other drug dependencies have been estimated as 4% for cannabis, 2% for amphetamines, and 0.7% for opiates (American Psychiatric Association, 1987; Vischi et al. 1980). It is also believed that at least 6 million people in this country use some form of cocaine regularly (Resnick & Resnick, 1984).

Although males suffer from alcoholism five times more often than females (Goodwin, 1979), gender is not the only factor that affects the incidence of this disorder; cultural and ethnic contexts also determine wide differences in drinking practices (Castaneda & Galanter, 1988; Heath, Waddell, & Tapper, 1981; Kane, 1981). Contrasting drinking patterns among ethnic groups are associated with variations in the expression of alcoholism. Both inner-city American black (Fernandez-Pol, Bluestone, Missouri, Morales, & Mizruchi, 1986) and urban Puerto Rican (Castaneda & Galanter, in press) groups, for example, have been observed to display not only more severe drinking patterns, but also higher rates of cognitive impairment and more intense symptomatology during alcohol withdrawal than their urban white counterparts.

Risk Factors

There is no evidence to suggest the existence of a common personality organization among alcoholics or other drug abusers (Pattison, Sobell, & Sobell, 1977; Vaillant, 1983). Nonetheless, psychoanalysts have proposed a series of personality structures that predispose an individual to addictive behavior. In common, such personalities are said to have basic deficits in object relations (Balint, 1969) and self-concept (Kernberg, 1975) that determine reliance by the ego on compensatory mechanisms, such as denial and grandiosity. The alcoholic's frequent inability to satisfactorily manage his or her impulses and regulate emotions are seen, in this context, as consequences of a weak self or a deficient ego (Khantzian, 1982).

From a slightly different perspective, a large number of personality characteristics have, at some point or another, been identified as markers for alcoholism and other drug abuse. It seems, however, that because these clinical characteristics are as likely determinants of alcoholism and other drug abuse as they are the consequence of them, their value as diagnostic markers is questionable.

On the other hand, it has been definitely established that alcoholism and other drug abuse are familially transmitted (Cotton, 1979). Several studies of alcoholic groups have reported alcoholism rates of 50% among their fathers, 30% among their brothers, and 6% among their mothers (Goodwin, 1981). Among first- and second-degree male relatives of alcoholic males, the risk is 25% (Cotton, 1979).

Environmental factors such as home disruption, a disadvantaged urban upbringing, or a history of parental substance abuse and/or mental illness are not the only factors that have been found to explain such a familial transmission (Frances, Timm, & Bucky, 1980; Haarstrup & Thomsen, 1972; Helzer Robins, & Davis, 1976; Rosenberg, 1969). Twin, adoption, and family illness studies, and neuropsychiatric investigations as well, have demonstrated that genetic factors may also contribute to the familial transmission of alcoholism and other drug abuse. Frances et al. (1980), for example, reported a higher frequency of severe alcoholism, conduct disorders, sociopathy, and mental illness in general among the relatives of individuals with a strong family history of alcoholism than among those relatives of problem drinkers who had no such family history. Winokour (1979) also has studied the first-degree relatives of alcoholics. They have reported high prevalence of sociopathy and alcoholism among the males, and high rates of early onset depression among females.

Twin studies have added support to the notion of a genetic predisposition toward alcoholism, mainly by demonstrating that monozygotic twins generally have higher concordance rates for alcoholism than dizygotic twins (Kaij, 1960). Adoption studies by Goodwin, Schlusinger, Hemansen, Guze, & Winokour (1973) revealed that the incidence of alcoholism among the sons of alcoholic fathers was four times higher than that observed among a control group without such family history, irrespective of whether the subjects were raised by their own parents or by foster parents.

Evidence has recently accumulated to suggest the need to consider alcoholism as an expression of predisposing neurological deficits. Begleiter, Porjesz, Bihari, and Kissin (1984), for example, found a defect in the P3 component of the evoked brain potentials of a group of boys of alcoholic fathers that was similar to the defect observed in adult alcoholic males. Such a deficit, they propose, would determine specific decrements in memory processing. Multiple investigations on the biological sons of alcoholics have also reported an abnormally high incidence of attention-deficit hyperactivity disorder (Goodwin, Schlusinger, & Hemansen, 1975) and impairments of other neurop-

sychological functions, including memory, processing of language, regulation of emotions, and perceptual-motor functioning (Tartar, Hegedus, & Goldstein, 1984).

Abuse and Dependence

The multiplicity of substance abuse disorders, along with the frequent revisions of concepts and terminology used to describe them in the past 100 years, have hindered the development of an acceptable classification. At present, two concepts prevail in the substance abuse literature, "substance dependence" and "substance abuse," both of which initially appeared in the *Diagnostic and Statistical Manual of Mental Disorders* (3rd ed.) published in 1980.

Psychoactive Substance Dependence

At least some of the clinical features required to make this diagnosis must have persisted for at least 1 month or must have occurred repeatedly for a longer period of time. They include at least three of the following:

1. Alcohol or other drug often taken in larger amounts or over a longer period of time than the individual originally intended

2. Repeated and unsuccessful attempts to control substance use

3. Large investment of time spent (a) in activities necessary to get the substance, (b) in taking the substance, or (c) in recovering from its effects

4. Interference with work, school, or home obligations caused by frequent intoxication or withdrawal symptoms

5. Elimination or reduction of important social, occupational, or recreational activities because of substance use

6. Continued substance use despite the individual's knowledge of having a persistent or recurrent social, psychological, or physical problem that is either caused by or made worse by the use of the substance

7. The existence of *marked tolerance*: the need to increase by at least 50% the amount of the substance in order to achieve intoxi-

cation or a desired effect, or markedly diminished effect with continued use of the same amount

8. Characteristic withdrawal symptoms (a criterion that may not apply to cannabis, hallucinogens, or phencyclidine [PCP])

9. Substance often taken in order to relieve or prevent the occurrence of withdrawal symptoms

Severity of dependence is differentiated as follows:

Mild.   When there are only few, if any, symptoms in excess of those required to make the diagnosis, and there is only mild disruption of relationships with others or impairment in occupational or social functioning

Severe.   When there are many symptoms in excess of those required to make the diagnosis of dependence, and such symptoms markedly interfere with occupational functioning or with usual social activities or relationship

Moderate.   When the number of symptoms or the degree of functional impairment is intermediate between "mild" and "severe."

In Partial Remission.   If, during the previous 6 months, only some use of the substance has occurred, or no symptoms of dependence have been observed despite some substance use.

Psychoactive Substance Abuse

This diagnosis can be made only if the person has never met the criteria for dependence for this substance, and if the symptoms of the disturbance has persisted for at least 1 month, or they have occurred repeatedly over a longer period of time. At least one of the following clinical criteria is required:

1. Continued use despite the individual's knowledge of having a persistent or recurrent social, occupational, psychological, or physical problem that is either caused by or exacerbated by the use of the substance

2. Recurrent use in situations in which use represents a physical hazard, such as driving while intoxicated.

The DSM-III diagnostic categories of dependence and abuse are applicable to the following substances: alcohol, amphetamine or similarly acting sympathomimetic agents, anxiolytics, cannabis, cocaine, hallucinogens, hypnotics, inhalants (glue), opiates, PCP or similarly acting arylcyclohexamines, and sedatives.

DIAGNOSTIC ISSUES AND PROBLEMS

It is too early to evaluate the reliability and validity of the new concepts of psychoactive substance dependence and abuse as set forth in DSM-III-R. One reassuring circumstance, however, is that at least for alcoholism, the Feighner et al. (1972) set of diagnostic criteria, from which the DSM-III categories of abuse and dependence originally developed, have proved highly reliable in repeated challenges (Spitzer, Endicott, & Robins, 1975). As Robins (1982) points out, it is remarkable that "the diagnosis of alcoholism by symptom self-report is repeatedly found to be one of the most valid and reliable of the psychiatric diagnoses."

Diagnostic Problems

Self-Report

Several circumstances contribute to the clinician's difficulties in making a correct substance abuse diagnosis. First, the information available to the diagnostician frequently derives from the patient's self-report. Although self-report of alcoholic behavior has been found to be a reliable tool in research settings (Sobell, 1979), the clinician should interpret it with caution. The individual engaged in some form of substance abuse will frequently misrepresent the amount, frequency, and consequences of his or her drug use, not only because of defensive denial, but also because of frequently impaired memory and perception of reality. A chronic drug-dependent individual may, in fact, be utterly unable to provide a good history. It is always advisable to interview other people, such as family members, friends, or work associates, in order to clarify the history. A spouse, for example, might voice complaints of abusive or intoxicated behavior. Work and social associates might reveal the true magnitude of the time spent in obtaining the substance and recovering from its effects.

Psychiatric Symptoms

An important diagnostic consideration for the clinician is the need to differentiate between primary and secondary psychiatric symptoms. On the one hand, several psychiatric conditions, such as mood, conduct, and personality disorders, may predispose affected individuals to developing substance abuse. At a minimum, their primary symptomatology is frequently exacerbated by drug use (Galanter, Castaneda, & Ferman, 1988). On the other hand, chronic substance abuse or dependence is generally associated with a large variety of symptoms. These include, for example, behavioral disturbances frequently related to the need to obtain money or illegal drugs, which may wrongly suggest antisocial or other personality disorders. Complicating matters, the association between sociopathy and drug abuse often has been documented to be the source of diagnostic confusion (Schuckitt, 1985).

Mood disorders, mostly depression, are also frequent complications of drug abuse. This was illustrated by MMPI studies, which found that while 60% of recently detoxified alcoholics were depressed (Keeler, Taylor, & Miller, 1979), no evidence of depression could be obtained in a group of abstinent alcoholics (Pettinati, Sugarman, & Maurer, 1982). A general consensus exists that in 90% of heavy drinkers with symptoms of both alcoholism and depression, the correct diagnosis is alcoholism and not primary affective illness (Galanter et al., 1988). The presence of such symptoms, however, warrants prompt consideration by the clinician, as suicidal behavior in this population is by no means uncommon. Among heroin-dependent individuals, for example, the suicide rate is 25%, and among alcoholics, suicide has been observed to occur in at least 15 of every 100 patients (Galanter & Castaneda, 1985). Psychotic symptoms, such as hallucinations, delusions, and other disorders of thought, affect the behavior. Such psychotic symptoms can also cloud the diagnostic picture of the abuse of or dependence on hallucinogens, cocaine, amphetamines, marijuana, PCP, and inhaled substances, as well as withdrawal episodes from alcohol and other depressants. Simultaneous use of alcohol and other drugs by schizophrenic individuals can, in addition, obscure the expression of primary psychotic symptoms.

In addition to the occurrence of psychotic symptoms, associated features of drug abuse are anxiety, irritability, mood lability, and impairment of social and occupational functioning, all of which should be considered in the appropriate context of the existing addictive disorder, in order to prevent premature diagnoses and treatments. Final diagnosis should be postponed in the presence of any of these disturbances for at least 2 weeks because secondary symptoms are likely to recede after a period of recovery (Galanter, Castaneda, & Ferman, 1988).

A multitude of medical problems also contribute to diagnostic confusion. Alcoholism, for example, can result in permanent dementia; hallucinogen use can lead to protracted delusional states, and drugs such as marijuana, phencyclidine (PCP), and hallucinogens can induce motivational and cognitive deficits. Neuropsychological assessments in these circumstances are clearly indicated.

Polysubstance Dependence

Another frequent source of diagnostic confusion results from the simultaneous or sequential abuse of multiple substances. In much of the same way as depressed or anxious patients may develop a secondary addiction in their efforts to self-medicate their symptoms, primary drug abusers may also become dependent on another substance that counteracts distressing feelings and drug reactions. Characteristic among stimulant-dependent individuals, for example, is the consumption of sedatives and/or alcohol, to ameliorate the anxiety associated with withdrawal states and chronic dependence.

Polydrug abuse is not uncommon and in certain age and cultural subgroups may, indeed, be the rule more often than the exception. The frequently incongruous and even bizarre constellations of symptoms characteristic of this condition should not deter the clinician from trying to diagnose all the existing drug abuse disorders.

Treatment Strategies

We now consider a pragmatic psychotherapeutic approach to the alcohol-dependent patient. The origins of this approach lie in both network therapy, as developed by Speck (1967) and others, and in more widely used family therapy techniques.

This approach can be useful in addressing a broad range of addicted patients. These patients are characterized by the following clinical hallmarks of addictive illness relevant to this treatment model. First when they initiate consumption of their addictive agent, be it alcohol, cocaine, opiates, or depressant drugs, they frequently cannot limit that consumption to a reasonable and predictable level; this phenomenon has been termed *loss of control* by clinicians who treat alcohol- or other drug-dependent persons. Second, they have consistently demonstrated relapse to the agent of abuse; that is, they have attempted to stop using the drug for varying periods of time but have returned to it despite a specific intent to avoid it (Vaillant, 1981).

This treatment approach is not necessary for those abusers who can, in fact, learn to set limits on their alcohol or drug use; their abuse may be treated as a behavioral symptom in a traditional psychotherapeutic fashion. It is also not directed to those patients for whom the addictive pattern is most unmanageable, such as long-term intravenous opiate addicts, and others with unusual destabilizing circumstances, such as homelessness, severe character pathology, or psychosis. These patients may need special supportive care, such as drug substitution (e.g., methadone maintenance), inpatient detoxification, or long-term residential treatment.

In reviewing this material, the reader should focus on those aspects of the treatment outlined here that are at variance with her or his usual therapeutic approach. Whereas it is essential to rely on acquired clinical judgment and experience, it is equally important with the substance abuser to be prepared to depart from the usual mode of psychotherapeutic treatment. For example, activity rather than passivity is essential when a problem of drug exposure is suggested; the concept of therapist and patient enclosed in an inviolable envelope must be modified; immediate circumstances that may expose the patient to drug use

must take precedence over issues of long-term understanding and insight. These principles are applicable within the technique outlined here. Other approaches, too, such as the use of couples group therapy and other techniques discussed by Gallant, Rich, Bey, and Terranova (1970) may incorporate most of these principles.

The Initial Encounters

The patient should be asked to bring his or her spouse or a close friend to the first session. Drug-dependent patients often do not like certain things they hear when they first come for treatment and may deny or rationalize even if they have voluntarily sought help. Because of their denial of the problem, a significant other is essential both to history taking and to implementing a viable treatment plan. A close relation can often cut through the denial in the way that an unfamiliar therapist cannot and can therefore be invaluable in setting a standard of realism in dealing with the addiction.

Some patients make it clear that they wish to come to the initial session on their own. This is often associated with their desire to preserve the option of continued substance abuse and is born out of the fear that an alliance will be established independent of them to prevent this. Although a delay may be tolerated for a session or two, there should be no ambiguity at the outset that effective treatment can only be undertaken on the basis of a therapeutic alliance around the drug issue. This includes the support of significant others, and it is expected that a network of close friends and/or relations will be brought in within a session or two at the most.

Not only are the patients sometimes reluctant to establish a network, but their relatives may also be resistant. For example, it may be necessary to develop a strategy for engaging a resistant spouse to enter a cooperative role:

CASE 1

A 40-year-old lawyer came for treatment of his drinking problem primarily because his marriage was doing poorly. He secured his wife's agreement to come to the initial session and hoped that the therapy would serve as a bridge for improving their failing relationship. She was actually reluctant to establish closer ties to him and told me that she preferred not to be involved in the treatment. She came a half-hour late for the second conjoint session, citing heavy rains along the route from their home in an outlying suburb. She was in an angry mood, announcing that she could not come again, as she had to tend to their four children and organize their after-school activities. Rather than retreating from his position, the therapist expressed considerable regret that she was being compromised by the plan and stated his own appreciation that she had gone so far out of her way to help out. He pointed out to her how valuable she was to the plan (never noting in fact she was being much less than positive to date) and that he needed her to support his own imperfect ability to help her husband achieve sobriety, underlying the serious limitations of the individual therapist who alone treats the alcoholic. He agreed to her skipping a session the next week, giving acknowledgment to a relatively unimportant conflicting appointment, in exchange for her agreement to come the week thereafter. After a month, it became clearer to her that it was in her interest—on a pragmatic level—to participate.

Therapists are used to thinking that they are right and expecting (or at least hoping for) a good measure of respect for their views. This example is given to underline the strategic importance of generating whatever understanding may be necessary to achieve a viable relationship with a network member, even at the risk of feeling rejected. This may also take a good measure of cajoling and even manipulation at the outset of treatment.

The weight of clinical experience supports the view that abstinence is the most practical goal to propose to the addicted person for her or his rehabilitation (Gitlow & Peyser, 1980; Zimberg, 1982). For abstinence to be expected, however, the therapist should assure the provision of necessary social supports for the patient. Let us consider how a long-term support network is initiated for this purpose, beginning with availability of the therapist, significant others, and self-help group.

In the first place, the therapist should be available for consultation on the phone and should indicate to patients that she or he wants to be called if problems arise. This makes the therapist's commitment clear and sets the tone for a team effort. It begins to undercut one reason for relapse; the patient's sense that they will be on their own if they are unable to manage the situation. The astute therapist, though, will assure patients that he or she does not spend excessive time at the telephone or in emergency sessions, and therefore the patient will develop a support network that can handle the majority of day-to-day problems. This will generally leave the therapist only to respond to occasional questions of interpreting the terms of the understanding between her- or himself, patients, and support network members. If there is question about the ability of a given patient and network to manage the period between the initial sessions, the first few scheduled sessions may be arranged at intervals of only 1 to 3 days. In any case, frequent appointments should be scheduled at the outset of a pharmacological detoxification (as with benzodiazepines for alcoholism), so that the patient need never manage more than a few days medication at a time.

What is most essential, though, is that the network be forged into a working group to provide necessary support for the patient between the initial sessions. As discussed in the next section, membership ranges from one to several persons who are close to the patient. Larger networks have been used by Speck (1967) in treating schizophrenic patients. Contacts among network members at this stage typically include telephone calls (usually at the patient's initiative), dinner arrangements, and social encounters, and they should be preplanned to a fair extent during the joint session. These encounters are most often undertaken at the time when alcohol or other drug use is likely to occur. In planning together, however, it should be made clear to network members that relatively little unusual effort will be required for the long-term, that after the patient is stabilized, their participation will come to little more than attendance at infrequent meetings with the patient and therapist. This requires a major time commitment from the network members to the patient initially, but eventually, the reduction in commitment relieves both the network members and those patients who do not want to be placed in a dependent position.

Techniques in Social and Family Network Therapy

Introducing Alcoholic Anonymous and Disulfiram.   Use of self-help modalities is desirable whenever possible. For the alcoholic, certainly, participation in Alcoholics Anonymous

(AA) as described by Zimberg (1977), is strongly encouraged. Groups such as Narcotics Anonymous (NA), Pills Anonymous (PA), and Cocaine Anonymous (CA–in some communities) are modeled after AA, and they play a similarly useful role. One approach is to tell the patient that he or she is expected to attend at least two AA meetings in a week, in order to become familiar with the program. If, after a month, the patient is quite reluctant to continue and other aspects of the treatment are going well, nonparticipation may have to be accepted. This acceptance, as illustrated later herein, may sometimes be used as one bargaining "chip" in the game of securing compliance with other aspects of the treatment.

For the alcoholic, disulfiram (Antabuse) may be a useful tool in assuring abstinence, but it becomes much more valuable when carefully integrated into work with the patient and network. For example, it is a good idea to use the initial telephone contact to engage the patient's agreement to be abstinent from alcohol for the day immediately prior to the first session. The therapist then has the option of prescribing or administering disulfiram at that time. For a patient who is in earnest about seeking assistance for alcoholism, this is often not difficult, if some time is spent on the phone making plans to avoid a drinking context during that period. If it is not feasible to undertake this on the phone, it may be addressed in the first session. Such planning with the patient will almost always involve organizing time with significant others and, therefore, serves as a basis for developing the patient's support network. Disulfiram is typically initiated with a dose of 500 mg, and then 250 mg. It is taken every morning, when the urge to drink is generally lowest.

Anticipating the Recurrence of Drug Use. Most individual therapists, as described by Hayman (1956), and family therapists, such as Steinglass (1976), see the alcoholic or other drug abuser as a patient with poor prognosis. This is largely because, in the context of traditional psychotherapy, there are no behavioral controls to prevent the recurrence of drug use, and resources are not available for behavioral intervention if a recurrence takes place—which it usually does. A system of impediments to the emergence of relapse, which rests heavily on the actual or symbolic role of the network, must therefore be established. The therapist must have assistance in addressing any minor episode of drug use so that this ever-present problem does not lead to an unmanageable relapse or an unsuccessful termination of therapy.

Preventing Relapse. How can the support network be used to deal with recurrences of drug use when, in fact, the patient's prior association with these same persons did not prevent her or him from using alcohol or other drugs? In answering this question, it is necessary to clarify what the therapist must do to construct an effective support network. The following examples illustrate how this may be done. In Case 2, a specific format was defined with the network to monitor a patient's compliance with a disulfiram regimen:

CASE 2

A 33-year-old female public relations executive had moved to New York from a remote city 3 years before coming to treatment. She had no long-standing close relationships in the city, a circumstance not uncommon for a single alcoholic in a setting removed from her origins. She presented a 10-year history of heavy drinking that had increased in severity since her arrival, no doubt associated with her social isolation. Although she consumed a bottle of wine each night and additional hard liquor, she was able to get to work regularly. Six months before the outset of treatment, she had attended AA meetings for 2 weeks and had been abstinent during that time. She had then relapsed, though, and she became disillusioned with the possibility of maintaining abstinence. At the outset of treatment, it was necessary to reassure her that her prior relapse was in large part a function (a) of not having established sufficient outside supports (including a more sound relationship with AA), and (b) of having seen herself as having failed after only one slip. The therapist realized, though, that there was a basis for concern as to whether she should do any better now, if the same formula was reinstituted in the absence of sufficient reliable supports, which she did not seem to have. Together, therapist and patient came on the idea of bringing in an old friend whom she saw occasionally, and whom she felt she could trust. They made the following arrangement with her friend. The patient came to sessions twice a week. She would see her friend once each weekend. On each of these thrice-weekly occasions, she would be observed taking disulfiram, so that even if she missed a daily does in between, it would not be possible for her to resume drinking on a regular basis undetected. The interpersonal support inherent in this arrangement, bolstered by conjoint meetings with her and her friend, also allowed her to return to AA with a sense of confidence in her ability to maintain abstinence.

The ensuing example illustrates how an ongoing network may be used to abort an emerging relapse. A high index of suspicion for signs of trouble was important, as was a clear understanding with the network members that they would be mobilized when necessary. Also illustrated, however, is the serious vulnerability of the network whose members may deny or rationalize because of their own drug use.

CASE 3

A 34-year-old cameraman became addicted to cocaine and used it heavily on a daily basis. He acquired a considerable amount of capital by extensively dealing (i.e., selling) of the drug, primarily among friends and acquaintances, to support his habit. After a point, though, his wife moved out of the house and took their baby, saying she could no longer tolerate his heavy drug use. Ironically, she had been using cocaine herself, but to a lesser extent. The couple reunited in the context of a therapy predicated on the patient's abstinence (and secondarily, on hers, too). It was supported by a network consisting of his wife, the patient's brother, and a good friend.

The issue of relapse arose in an interesting context, one that illustrates how the subtleties of attitude among network members influence the patient's attitudes. Each network member had a contributing role. The wife, seeing her husband's boredom and disillusionment at the contraction of his successful but illicit drug sales career, suggested that he might be able to sell cocaine, although not use it himself. His friend had previously experienced difficulties with cocaine and had stopped on his own, but he still used it occasionally. The brother, a staunch advocate of abstinence from all drugs (and all other human frailties, for that matter), was feared by the patient as unable

to empathize with his problems, although the patient did feel considerable affection toward him. No network members provided a suitable model for comfortable abstinence, given these circumstances.

Difficulties gradually emerged when the patient had been in treatment for 6 months, with only one occasion of use of a small amount. The therapist was away on vacation for a month and returned to find that he had again taken cocaine on two occasions. On a third occasion, he had brought some over to the home of his friend from the network and was fortunately persuaded to return it to the supplier. Although he had not taken the drug on this third occasion, it seemed essential to seize on the circumstances to reverse his orientation toward intermittent use. The therapist therefore summoned the network for weekly meetings, three in all, during which the risks inherent in the patient's occasional use of drugs were examined in a nonjudgmental way. The group affirmed what had seemingly been clear, but had not been fully adopted, the need for total abstinence in order to avoid the vulnerability to serious relapse. In this situation, it became necessary to explore the ambivalence of the wife and the friend. The brother's rigidity was also addressed, to underline that a judgmental attitude was not constructive in this situation.

The Network for Treatment Monitoring.   The administration of disulfiram under observation is a treatment option that is easily adapted to work with social networks. A patient who has taken disulfiram cannot drink; a patient who agrees to be observed by a responsible party while taking disulfiram will not miss his or her dose without the observer's knowing. This may take a measure of persuasion and, above all, the therapist's commitment that such an approach can be reasonable and helpful. Case 4 shows one example of how this can take place.

CASE 4

Ted is a 55-year-old musician who, like many colleagues in his field, has had a successful career in the context of alcohol addition. He is a man whose discomfort with dependency and compliance leads him to disregard some of the most routine of social norms; he drives without a license, for example. Although he acknowledges no responsibility or concern for those who hold authority over him, he is solicitous and responsible toward those who rely on him. It is because of this that he decided to take action about his drinking when his wife was soon to deliver their first child, even though he had paid little attention to her concern previously. The two had a tacit understanding that they would not place "demands" on each other.

The patient presented himself saying that he wanted to have disulfiram prescribed and made it implicitly clear that he was not too interested in a great deal of professional advice. The therapist was concerned, though, because the therapist had little faith that the patient would continue taking disulfiram for a day longer than he wanted to, and that he might not want to for very long. Because compliance based on trust was hardly this patient's style, it seemed necessary to corral him into an arrangement whereby he would agree to be monitored for at least the initial months of abstinence.

The network began with his wife alone. The therapist had pressed him to attend AA meetings and to bring his college-age daughter from a previous marriage into the network. It seemed feasible to stage a negotiation in which the therapist would concede some points to him so that he could save face; he might then agree to having his wife observe him taking disulfiram. The therapist also conceded that the daughter's involvement should be a matter for his own decision, thereby making it clear that there was room for his own decision making in defining the therapeutic contract.

The therapist then said that the odds for his maintaining stable abstinence were significantly decreased if he did not go to AA meetings (it was clear to the therapist that he never would, anyway). The therapist told him, though, that the therapist could not, in good conscience, treat him if he neither went to AA nor participated in the observed disulfiram regimen. The odds of the treatment having a meaningful impact under such circumstances were not very good. The therapist was earnest, and this seemed to be a fair test of his commitment to treatment, anyway.

The patient agreed to comply to observation by his wife for a year, but he did not agree to long-term AA attendance. He continued with this disulfiram regimen with good reliability, as agreed, thus allowing him to get through his most vulnerable period. He then, subsequently, took the disulfiram on an ad hoc basis, while remaining abstinent and continuing in therapy.

Some patients are more easily convinced to attend AA meetings than the musician in this case. Others, although no more interested than the patient just described, may be more compliant. Therefore, the therapist must use this compliance, mobilizing the support network as appropriate, in order to continue pressure for the patient's involvement with AA for a reasonable trial. It may take a considerable period of time, but ultimately, a patient may experience something of a conversion, wherein he adopts the group ethos and expresses a deep commitment to abstinence, a measure of commitment rarely observed in patients who experience psychotherapy without AA. When this occurs, the therapist may assume a more passive role in monitoring the patient's abstinence and in keeping an eye on the patient's ongoing involvement in AA.

Technical Considerations

Defining the Network's Membership.   Establishing a network is a task that requires the active collaboration of patient and therapist. The two, aided by those parties who initially join the network, must search for the right balance of members. This process is not without problems, and the therapist must think in a strategic fashion. The following case illustrates this.

CASE 5

A 25-year-old male graduate student had been abusing cocaine since high school, in part drawing on funds from his affluent family, who lived in a remote city. At two points in the process of establishing his support network, the reactions of his live-in girlfriend (who worked with the therapist from the outset) were particularly important. Both he and she agreed to bring in his 19-year-old sister, a freshman at a nearby college. He then mentioned a "friend" of his, apparently a woman whom he found attractive, even though there was no history of an overt romantic involvement. The therapist sensed that his girlfriend did not like the idea, although she offered no rationale for excluding this potential rival. The idea of having to rely for assistance solely on a younger sister and two women who might see each other as competitors was unappealing. The therapist therefore suggested dropping the idea of including the "friend." The network then fell to evaluating the patient's uncle, whom he preferred to exclude, but whom his girlfriend thought appropriate. It later turned out (as the therapist had expected) that the uncle was in many ways a potentially disapproving representative of the parental generation. In this case, the therapist encouraged the patient to accept the uncle as a network member in order to round out the range of relationships within the group, and the therapist spelled out the rationale for this. In matter of fact, the uncle turned out to be caring and supportive, particularly after he was helped to understand the nature of the addictive process.

The therapist must carefully promote the choice of appropriate network members, just as the platoon leader selects those who will accompany her or him in combat. The network is crucial in determining the balance of the therapy.

Defining the Network's Task.   As conceived here, the therapist's relationship to the network is like that of a team leader rather than that of a family therapist. The network is established to implement a straightforward task: that of aiding the therapist to sustain the patient's abstinence. It must be directed with the same clarity of purpose that an organizational task force is directed to build more cars, to open a branch office, or to revise its management procedures. Competing and alternative goals must be suppressed or at least prevented from interfering with the primary task.

Unlike those involved in traditional family therapy, network members are not led to expect symptom relief or self-realization. This prevents the development of competing goals for the network's meetings. It also assures the members protection from having their own motives scrutinized and thereby supports their continuing involvement without the threat of an assault on their psychological defenses. Because network members have—kindly—volunteered to participate, their motives must not be impugned. Their constructive behavior should be commended. It is useful to acknowledge appreciation for the contribution they are making to the therapy. There is always a counterproductive tendency on their part to minimize the value of their contribution.

The network must, therefore, be structured as an effective working group with good morale. This is not always easy; as the following case shows:

CASE 6

A 45-year-old single woman served as an executive in a large family-held business—except when her alcohol problem led her into protracted binges. Her father, brother, and sister were prepared to banish her from the business, but they decided first to seek consultation. Because they had initiated the contract, they were included in the initial network and indeed were very helpful in stabilizing the patient. Unfortunately, however, the father was a domineering figure who intruded into all aspects of the business and often evoked angry outbursts from his children. The children typically reacted with petulance, which provoked him in return. The situation came to a head when both of the patient's siblings angrily petitioned the therapist to exclude the father from the network 2 months into the treatment. This presented a problem because the father's control over the business made his involvement important in securing the patient's compliance. The patient's relapse was still a real possibility. This potentially coercive role, however, was an issue that the group could not easily handle.

The therapist decided to support the father's membership in the group, indicating the constructive role he had played in getting the therapy started. It seemed necessary to support the earnestness of his concern for his daughter, rather than the children's dismay at their father's character pathology directly. The hubbub did, in fact, quiet down with time. The children became less provocative themselves, as the group responded to the therapist's pleas for civil behavior.

The Frequency of Network Sessions.   At the outset of therapy, it is important to see the patient with the group on a weekly basis for at least the first month. Unstable circumstances demand more frequent contacts with the network. Sessions can be tapered off to biweekly and then monthly intervals after a time.

In order to sustain the continuing commitment of the group (particularly that between the therapist and the network members), network sessions should be held every 3 months or so for the duration of the individual therapy. Once the patient has stabilized, the meetings tend less to address day-to-day issues. They may begin with a recounting by the patient of the drug situation. Reflections on the patient's progress and goals, or sometimes on the relations among the network members, may then be discussed. In any case, it is essential that an agreement be made that network members contact the therapist if they are concerned about the patient's possible use of alcohol or other drugs, and that the therapist contact the network members if she or he becomes concerned about a potential relapse.

Confidentiality.   Use of the network raises the issues of confidentiality and the nature of the therapist's commitment to the patient. The overriding commitment of the therapist to the patient is that the therapist support the patient in maintaining the drug-free state. Open communication on matters regarding alcohol and other drugs should be maintained among the network, the patient, and the therapist. The therapist must set the proper tone of mutual trust and understanding so that the patient's right to privacy is not otherwise compromised. It is also made explicit that absolute confidentiality applies to all other (nondrug-related) communications between therapist and patient and that network members should not expect to communicate with the therapist about any matter that does not directly relate to alcohol or other drug problems.

Intrusive Measures.   Certain circumstances may necessitate further incursions on the patient's autonomy in order to assure compliance with treatment. This is particularly true when the patient has begun treatment reluctantly, as with overt pressure from family or employer, or when the possibility of relapse will have grave consequences. Optional measures may include financial constraints, spousal separation, and urine monitoring. These, of course, can only be undertaken with the patient's agreement, based on the fact that greater or more immediate loss is being averted. Such steps may also provide greater certitude against relapse to all concerned, including an uneasy therapist and family.

CASE 7

A 35-year-old man had used heroin intranasally for 2 years and then intravenously for 8 months;

he had previously used other drugs. He was stealing money from the family business in which he worked. The patient underwent ambulatory detoxification, but he relapsed to heroin use and finally underwent a hospitalization that lasted 5 weeks. He was then referred to the therapist on discharge from the hospital and was to continue with meetings of Narcotics Anonymous. His network consisted of his mother and his wife and the following family members involved in the family business: his father, his younger sister and brother, and his uncle. His family was very concerned about allowing him to get involved again in the business. He therefore agreed to do two things so that he might be included with less concern on everyone's part: (1) The patient agreed to have his urine spot-checked on a regular basis, and (2) he and the therapist, along with the network, discussed his financial circumstances in the firm, clarifying what consequences might result should he return to active addiction. An informal but explicit agreement was reached in this matter, thereby helping the patient understand the constraints under which he was operating and leaving the family more comfortable about his return to work. Because this agreement was undertaken with the network, it became a part of the treatment plan.

Adapting Individual Therapy to the Network Treatment.   As noted, network sessions are scheduled on at least a weekly basis at the outset of treatment. This is likely to compromise the number of individual contacts. Indeed, if sessions are held once a week, the patient may not be seen individually for a period of time. This may be perceived as a deprivation by the patient unless the individual therapy is presented as an opportunity for further growth predicated on achieving stable abstinence assured through work with the network.

When individual therapy does begin, the traditional objectives of therapy must be ordered to accommodate the goals of the substance abuse treatment. For insight-oriented therapy, clarification of unconscious motivations is a primary objective; for supportive therapy, the bolstering of established constructive defenses is primary. In the therapeutic context that we are describing, however, the following objectives are given precedence:

1. Exposure to the Substance and to Relevant Cues. The therapy first must address the patient's exposure to substances of abuse, or exposure to cues that might precipitate alcohol or other drug use, as described by Galanter (1983). Both patient and therapist should be sensitive to this matter and should explore these situations as they arise.

2. Stable and Appropriate Social Context. The therapy should support a stable social context in an appropriate social environment— one conducive to abstinence with minimal disruption of life circumstances. Considerations of minor disruptions in place of residence, friends, or job need not be a primary issue for the patient with character disorder or neurosis, but they cannot go untended here. For a considerable period of time, the substance abuser is highly vulnerable to exacerbations of the addictive illness and must be viewed with considerable caution and in some respects, as one treats the recently compensated psychotic.

3. Individual Priorities Related to Psychological Conflict. After attending to the first two priorities, psychological conflicts that the patient must resolve, relative to her or his own growth, are considered. As the therapy continues, these come to assume a more prominent role. In the earlier phases, they are likely to directly reflect issues associated with previous drug use. Later, however, the tenor of treatment will come to resemble increasingly the traditional psychotherapeutic context. At this point, the therapist is in the admirable position of working with a patient who, while exercising insight into his or her problems, is also motivated by the realization of a new and previously untapped potential.

ALTERNATIVE TREATMENT OPTIONS

Treatment Settings Other Than the Clinician's Office

Inpatient Detoxification

Inpatient detoxification units allow for the removal of the patient from her or his habitual environment into a drug-free setting. This inter-vention not only interrupts drug use but also helps prevent the progression of the withdrawal process.

Once admitted, the patient can be thoroughly evaluated, regarding not only psychiatric status, but also medical and cognitive conditions. Proper diagnosis and treatment of psychiatric and medical complications can be extremely difficult to complete on an unstable ambulatory patient.

Inpatient settings constitute the ideal forum for the initial assessment of the patient's social and family support networks. Frequently, initial family interventions are only accomplished in the safe room of an inpatient detoxification unit.

Inpatient Rehabilitation

Very often, when immediate reinstatement to the community of the recently detoxified individual is not clinically advisable, the clinician may suggest referral to a drug rehabilitation facility. These settings provide such patients with a temporary residence until an appropriate living arrangement can be finally worked out, and they constitute an adequate environment for long-term treatment planning.

The typical rehabilitation unit is a residential community of recovering drug users whose experiences and feelings are shared in a new substance-free context. The average patient stays are about 28 days, and the programs generally adhere to a treatment model that incorporates addiction counselors as their primary therapists and, in the case of alcoholism rehabilitation centers, a strong AA orientation. Characteristically, attempts are made to recruit family members and employers into the process of restructuring the patient's social network. The treatment per se is delivered in the context of small groups, but often, appreciable changes are attributed to the application of systems therapy and crisis interventions (Stuckey & Harrison, 1982).

Therapeutic Communities

Protracted maladaptive behaviors and severe disaffiliation from the community are both adequate indications for patient referral to therapeutic communities for the treatment of drug abuse. These treatment settings provide inmates with a fairly structured environment and a life-style that generally is organized around a specific treatment philosophy and schedule of recovery. Most therapeutic communities follow a three-phase treatment program that aims at reshaping the individual patient under the influence of daily enforcement of specific behaviors and values strongly spoused by the commune. Initially, most of these programs have residents both participate in various forms of structured therapies and advance in some kind of job–privilege hierarchy. Eventually, each resident undergoes a period of transition back into the home community, following psychological and frequently vocational rehabilitation.

It has been suggested that there is a positive association between time spent in a therapeutic community and posttreatment outcome (De Leon, 1984; Holland, 1983; Stuckey & Harrison, 1982). Attrition rates, however, have traditionally been very high, up to 50% in fact, during the initial months of treatment.

Multimodality Outpatient Clinics

Most alcoholics in professional treatment in the United States attend multimodality outpatient clinics. For those alcoholics with associated nonacute medical or psychiatric disorders in particular, such a treatment setting represents an appropriate choice. Usually, this kind of clinic offers a variety of treatment modalities that include individual and group therapies, and recreational and vocational rehabilitation. Given their frequent association with medical institutions, these clinics can often assess and treat mild medical complications, and they serve as a referring source for the patient to those services and resources available in the community, such as vocational rehabilitation programs, medical facilities, and AA, NA, or CA.

Those patients capable of benefiting from these programs need to meet some minimal degree of stability regarding their social and medical statuses. The more socially intact and the more motivated and healthy the patient is, the more likely he or she will be to achieve and maintain abstinence from alcohol or other drugs.

Other Treatment Modalities

Family Therapies

Contrary to a widely held belief, alcoholics and other drug abusers are far more often found in the context of intact family situations than on Skid Row. Only a minority of alcoholics and other drug abusers live in social isolation and homelessness (World Health Organization, 1977). We already reviewed the evidence supporting the association between hereditary–environmental factors and alcoholism and other drug dependence. Substance abuse runs in families. Additionally, family interactions are intimately intertwined with substance abuse behavior and represent an important area of clinical study, as they are valuable from both diagnostic and treatment perspectives.

Systems Family Therapy

Reflecting this view, systems family therapists have proposed a model for both classifying and treating families with substance-abusing members (Steinglass, Weinec, & Mendelson, 1971). A key concept in the formulation of their topological scheme and methodology of treatment is that of the "alcoholic system." According to this model, families are classified according to the degree to which family patterns of interaction are structured around the behavior of the alcoholic member, from "a family with an alcoholic member" (when the behavioral patterns are only minimally organized around alcoholic behavior) to "an alcoholic family" (whose interactions are maximally dependent on the alcoholic member). Treatment success is measured according to not only the quality of abstinence achieved by the identified patient, but also the magnitude of improvement in the level of functioning of the family system or unit.

Strategic and Structural Family Therapies

Stanton and Todd (1982) have proposed a family model of addiction and treatment based on their extensive experience in applying a strategic–structural therapy approach to families with a heroin-dependent member. They see drug addiction as part of a cyclical process involving the parents (or parent surrogates) and the addict in an interdependent system. Addicted behavior serves an important protective function and helps to maintain the homeostatic balance of the family system. Central to this model is their contention that drug addiction also serves in a number of ways to resolve the dilemma of whether the addict can become an independent adult. The addict, in fact, maintains close contact with his or her family of origin, and the addicted behavior attempts to ameliorate serious parental problems and generally reflects family conflicts.

This therapy approach requires a different perspective of the addiction process and of the people and systems involved in it. Treatment strategies focus on the consequences of interactional behavior and specific acts, rather than on the content of family verbalizations. The goals of treatment are (1) total abstinence by the addicted member of both illegal and legal drugs (such as methadone); (2) a productive use of time by the addict, through gainful employment or through stable school or vocational training; (3) stable and autonomous living conditions by the addicted member.

Therapy is concerned mostly in correcting the repetitive interactional patterns that maintain drug use. The thrust of treatment is to alter their behavioral sequences, usually by taking advantage of spontaneous or induced crises in the family.

Large Self-help Groups for Substance Abusers

By far, the most notable example of self-help groups for substance abusers is AA. Derivative groups such as CA and NA are organized along the basic AA model that includes a fellowship of men and women who share their individual experiences with alcohol or other drugs and who derive support from each other in the context of large group gatherings.

The organization is premised on a list of beliefs known as the "twelve steps" as their basic philosophy of recovery, to be accepted and strictly followed by all members. The cohesiveness generated by self-disclosure, the adherence to a shared belief system, and a strong sense of mutual affiliation achieved in these twelve-step programs have proved indisputably efficacious in inducing and maintaining long-term abstinence. In this respect, Emerick, Lassen, and Edwards (1977) have noted that AA has been more effective as an enforcer of abstinence among its members than traditional psychotherapies, which, on the other hand, have proved more successful at effecting reduction and control of drinking behavior. Multiple internal surveys of AA members, for instance, have yielded the following statistics: More than half of the new members who remain in the fellowship for at least 3 months maintain abstinence for a conse-

quent year. Then, his or her chances of remaining sober for another year are an average of 86%.

This self-help movement originated in the 1930s as a social response to the lack of available professional treatment for alcoholics. It is now a worldwide organization with close to one million members in the United States and Canada alone (Castaneda & Galanter, 1987). AA, CA, and NA are by now widely regarded by professional treatment centers as a vital adjunct to the treatment of alcohol and other drug abuse. As AA itself has observed, more than 30% of its members credit a rehabilitation center or some form of professional counseling for their initial referral to AA.

The demonstrated success of the model of recovery promulgated by these self-help groups, and the identification through a series of controlled studies of mechanisms of psychological influence in contemporary charismatic religious sects (Galanter, 1984), have inspired the institution (in otherwise traditional treatment settings) of groups that attempt to capture in their design and overall organization the basic traits that characterize such large self-help groups and religious sects. Controlled studies have demonstrated that these peer-led therapy groups can yield improved cost-effectiveness and clinical outcome when compared to the traditional small treatment groups currently employed by most alcoholism treatment facilities (Galanter, Castaneda, & Salamon, 1987).

REFERENCES

American Psychiatric Association (1980). *Diagnostic and statistical manual of mental disorders*, (3rd ed.). Washington, DC: Author.

American Psychiatric Association (1987). *Diagnostic and statistical manual of mental disorders*. (3rd ed., rev.). Washington, DC: Author.

Balint, M. (1969). *The basic fault*. London: Tavistock.

Begleiter, H., Porjesz, B., Bihari, B. & Kissin, B. (1984). Event-related brain potentials in boys at risk for alcoholism. *Science, 225;*, 1493–1496.

Castaneda, R. & Galanter, M. (1988). Ethnic differences in drinking practices and cognitive impairment among detoxifying alcoholics. *Journal of Studies on Alcohol, 49 (4)*, 335–339.

Castaneda, R. & Galanter, M. (1987). A review of treatment modalities for alcoholism and their outcome. *American Journal of Social Psychiatry, 7 (4)*, 237–244.

Cotton, N. S. (1979). The familial incidence of alcoholism. *Journal of Studies on Alcohol, 40*, 89–115.

De Leon, G. (1984). The therapeutic community: Study of effectiveness. *National Institute of Drug Abuse Treatment Monograph Series*, Rockville, MD: National Institute of Drug Abuse Treatment.

Emerick, C., Lasse, D. L., & Edwards, M. T. (1977). Nonprofessional peers as therapeutic agents. In A. M. Razin, & A. S. Gurman, (Eds.), *Effective psychotherapy: A handbook of research*. New York: Pergamon.

Feighner, J., Robins, E., Guze, S., Woodruff, R., Winokour, G., & Munoz, R. (1972). Diagnostic criteria for use in psychiatric research. *Archives of General Psychiatry, 26*, 57–63.

Fernandez-Pol, B., Bluestone, H., Missouri, C., Morales, G., & Mizruchi, M. S. (1986). Drinking patterns of inner-city black Americans and Puerto Ricans. *Journal of Studies on Alcohol, 47*(2), 156–160.

Frances, R. J., Timm, S., & Bucky, S. (1980). Studies of familial and nonfamilial alcoholism. *Archives of General Psychiatry, 37*, 564–566.

Galanter, M. (1983). Cognitive labelling: Adapting psychotherapy to the treatment of alcohol abuse. *Journal of Psychiatric Treatment and Evaluation, 5*, 551–556.

Galanter, M. (1984). Self-help large group therapy for alcoholism: A controlled study. *Alcoholism: Clinical and Experimental Research, 8*(1), 16–23.

Galanter, M., & Castaneda, R. (1985). Self-destructive behavior in the substance abuser. *Psychiatric Clinics of North America, 8*(2), 251–261.

Galanter, M., Castaneda, R., & Salamon, I. (1987). Institutional self-help therapy for alcoholism: Clinical outcome. *Alcoholism: Clinical and Experimental Research, 11*(5), 1–6.

Galanter, R., Castaneda, R., & Ferman, J. (1988). Substance abuse among general psychiatric patients: A review of the "dual diagnosis" problem. *American Journal of Drug and Alcohol Abuse, 14 (2)*, 211–235.

Gallant, D. M., Rich, A., Bey, E., & Terranova, L. (1970). Group psychotherapy with married couples: A successful technique in New Orleans Alcoholism Clinic patients. *Journal of Louisiana State Medical Society, 122*, 41–44.

Gitlow, S. E., & Peyser, H. S. (Eds.). (1980). *Alcoholism: A practical treatment guide*. New York: Grune & Stratton.

Goodwin, D. W. (1979). Alcoholism and heredity. *Archives of General Psychiatry, 36*, 57–61.

Goodwin, D. W. (1981). *Alcoholism: The facts*. New York: Oxford University Press.

Goodwin, D. W., Schlusinger, F., & Hemansen, L. (1975). Alcoholism and the hyperactive child syndrome. *Journal of Mental and Nervous Disease, 150*, 349–353.

Goodwin, D. W., Schlusinger, F., Hemansen, L., Guze, S. B., & Winokour, G. (1973). Alcohol problems in adoptees raised apart from alcoholic biological parents. *Archives of General Psychiatry, 28*, 238–243.

Haarstrup, S., & Thomsen, K. (1972). The social backgrounds of young addicts as elicited in interviews with their parents. *Acta Psychiatrica Scandinavica, 48*, 146–173.

Hayman, M. (1956). Current attitudes to alcoholism of psychiatrists in Southern California. *American Journal of Psychiatry, 112*, 484–493.

Heath, D. B., Waddell, J. D., & Topper, M. T. (Eds.). (1981). Cultural factors in alcohol research and treatment of drinking problems. *The Journal of Studies on Alcohol Supplement, 9*, 217–240.

Helzer, J. E., Robins, I. N., & Davis, D. H. (1976). Antecedents of narcotic use and addiction: A study of 898 Vietnam veterans. *Drug and Alcohol Dependence, 3*, 183–190.

Holland, S. (1983). Evaluating community-based treatment programs: A model for strengthening inferences about effectiveness. *International Journal of Therapeutic Communities, 4*, 285–306.

Kaij, L. (1960). *Alcoholism in twins*. Stockholm: Almqvist & Wiksell.

Kane, P. (1981). *Inner-city alcoholism and ecological analysis, a cross-cultural study*. New York: Human Resources Press.

Keeler, M. H., Taylor, C. I., & Miller, W. C. (1979). Are all recently detoxified alcoholics depressed? *American Journal of Psychiatry, 136*, 586–588.

Kernberg, O. (1975). *Borderline conditions and pathological narcissism*. New York: Aronson.

Khantzian, E. S. (1982). Psychopathology, psychodynamics, and alcoholism. In E. Kaufman & E. M. Pattison (Eds.), *Encyclopedic handbook of alcoholism*, New York: Gardner Press.

Kohut, H. (1971). *The analysis of the self*. New York: International Universities Press.

Pattison, E. M., Sobell, M. B., & Sobell, I. C. (1977). *Emerging concepts of alcohol dependence*. New York: Springer.

Pettinati, H. M., Sugarman, A. A., & Maurer, H. S. (1982). Four year MMPI changes in abstinent and drinking alcoholics. *Alcoholism: Clinical and Experimental Research 6*, 487–494.

Resnick, R. B., & Resnick, E. (1984). Cocaine abuse and its treatment. *Psychiatric Clinics of North America, 7*(4), 713–728.

Robins, I. N. (1982). The diagnosis of alcoholism after DSM-III. In E. Kaufman & E. M. Pattison (Eds.), *Encyclopedic handbook of alcoholism* (pp. (40–55). New York: Gardner Press.

Rosenberg, C. M. (1969). Young drug addicts: Background and personality. *Journal of Nervous and Mental Disease, 148*, 65–73.

Schuckitt, M. A. (1985). The clinical implications of primary diagnostic groups among alcoholics. *Archives of General Psychiatry, 42*, 1043–1049.

Sobell, I. C. (1979). Reliability of alcohol abusers' self-reports of drinking behavior. *Behaviour Research and Therapy, 17*, 157–160.

Speck, R. (1967). Psychotherapy of the social network of a schizophrenic family. *Family Process, 6*, 208.

Spitzer, R., Endicott, J., & Robins, E. (1975). Clinical criteria for psychiatric diagnosis and DSM-III. *American Journal of Psychiatry, 132*(11), 1187–1192.

Stanton, D. & Todd, T. (1982). *The family therapy of drug and addiction.* New York: Guilford.

Steinglass, P., Weiner, S., & Mendelson, J. H. (1971). A systems approach to alcoholism: A model and its clinical applications. *Archives of General Psychiatry, 24*, 401–408.

Stuckey, R. F., & Harrison, J. S. (1982). The alcoholism rehabilitation center. In E. Kaufman & E. M. Pattison (Eds.), *Encyclopedic handbook of alcoholism* (pp. 865–873). New York: Gardner Press.

Tarter, R. E., Hegedus, A. M., & Goldstein, G. (1984). Adolescent sons of alcoholics: Neuropsychological and personality characteristics. *Alcoholism, Clinical and Experimental Research, 8*, 216–222.

Vaillant, G. E. (1981). Dangers of psychotherapy in the treatment of alcoholism. In M. H. Bean & N. E. Zimberg (Eds.), *Dynamic approaches to the understanding and treatment of alcoholism.* New York: Free Press.

Vaillant, G. E. (1983). *The natural history of alcoholism.* Cambridge, MA: Harvard University Press.

Vischi, T. R., Jones, K. R., Shank, E. L., & Lima, I. H. (1980). *The alcohol, drug abuse and mental health national data book.* Washington, DC: Department of Health and Human Services.

Winokour, G. (1979). Alcoholism and depression in the same family. In D. W. Goodwin & C. K. Erickson (Eds.), *Alcoholism and affective disorders.* New York: Medical & Scientific Books.

World Health Organization. (1977). *Manual of international statistical classification of diseases, injuries and causes of death (ICD-9).* Geneva: Author.

Zimberg, S. (1977). Alcoholics anonymous and the treatment and prevention of alcoholism. *Alcoholism: Clinical and Experimental Research, 1*, 91–102.

Zimberg, S. (1982). *The clinical management of alcoholism.* New York: Brunner/Mazel.

CHAPTER 26

Behavior Therapy

LINDA C. SOBELL, ANTHONY TONEATTO, AND MARK B. SOBELL

CONCEPTUALIZATION OF THE DISORDERS

This chapter focuses on the use and abuse of licit and illicit psychoactive drugs. The most recent (third edition, revised) version of the *Diagnostic and Statistical Manual* (DSM-III-R; American Psychiatric Association, 1987) includes 10 classes of psychoactive substances: alcohol; amphetamine or similarly acting sympathomimetics; cannabis; cocaine; hallucinogens; inhalants; nicotine; opioids; phencyclidine (PCP) or similarly acting arylcyclohexylamines; and sedatives, hypnotics, or anxiolytics.[1] Nicotine abuse, often not addressed in chapters on alcohol and other drug abuse (e.g., Callahan, Dahlkoetter, & Price, 1980; Sobell, Sobell, Ersner-Hershfield, & Nirenberg, 1982), is included in this chapter for two reasons. First, it has been accorded increasing attention and recognition as an addictive drug (e.g., U.S. Dept. of Health and Human Services [U.S. DHHS], 1988). Second, some researchers, acknowledging the high co-occurrence of tobacco, alcohol, and other drug use, have suggested important scientific and therapeutic benefits from the study of individuals who simultaneously use nicotine and

other substances (Bobo, Gilchrist, Schilling, Noach, & Schinke, 1987; Burling & Ziff, 1988; Grabowski, 1986; Kozlowski, Skinner, Kent, & Pope, 1989; Sobell, Sobell, Kozlowski, & Toneatto, in press).

The cardinal feature of psychoactive substance use disorders is continued use of the substance despite the likelihood of negative consequences for the user. While many explanations have been developed to account for compulsive drug use, no current theory adequately explains this phenomenon (for example, *negative reinforcement explanations* suggest that consumption of the drug (a) helps avoid or escape aversive events, (b) assists coping with stress, (c) reduces response-impairing anxiety, or (d) avoids withdrawal symptoms; *positive reinforcement explanations* include central nervous system [CNS] reward effects and peer acceptance; for a discussion of these approaches, see Baker, 1988; Blane & Leonard, 1987; Chaudron & Wilkinson, 1988). The task of explaining compulsive drug use becomes further complicated when one considers that single or simple drug use patterns are becoming less common (reviewed in Sobell, Sobell, & Nirenberg, 1988). In this regard, it has been asserted that "it is

The views expressed in this chapter are those of the authors and do not necessarily reflect those of the Addiction Research Foundation. The authors wish to thank Dr. Lynn Kozlowski for his valuable comments on an earlier version of this manuscript, Ms. Joanne Jackson for her patience in typing multiple drafts, and Ms. Gloria Leo for her careful proofreading.

[1]Caffeine abuse is not discussed in this chapter because adverse consequences and the development of pharmacological tolerance are uncommon (Griffiths & Woodson, 1988), although caffeine abuse is listed as a psychoactive substance abuse disorder in the latest version of the *Diagnostic and Statistical Manual of Mental Disorders* (3rd ed., rev., American Psychaitric Association, 1987).

very probable that regular use of a variety of psychoactive substances is the norm among regular users of any identified psychoactive drug" (Wilkinson, Leigh, Cordingley, Martin, & Lei, 1987, p. 280). Multiple psychoactive drug problems have become so pervasive that a polydrug abuse category was included in the DSM-III-R (Rounsaville, Kosten, Williams, & Spitzer, 1987).

For those involved in treatment and research with substance abusers, it is important to be aware of the commonalities and differences among the various psychoactive drug classes. In the following section, differences and commonalities among the various drug classes are discussed with respect to (a) dependence, liability, and tolerance, (b) natural history of substance abuse, (c) treatment goals, and (d) concurrent versus sequential treatment of multiple drug abuse.

Dependence Liability and Tolerance

The concept of a drug dependence syndrome as a key feature of psychoactive substance use (Edwards, Arif, & Hodgson, 1981) grew out of formulations initially developed for alcohol dependence (Edwards, Gross, Keller, & Moser, 1976; Edwards, Gross, Keller, Moser, & Room, 1977) and has been included in the World Health Organization's classification of alcohol and other drug problems. Dependence describes a pattern of compulsive drug seeking that comes to dominate one's activities and a syndrome of cognitive, behavioral, and physiological symptoms that occurs in the dependent individual upon cessation of drug taking (American Psychiatric Association, 1987; Davidson, 1987; Edwards et al., 1981). The core symptoms need not occur with the same frequency or intensity within or between drug classes, nor do all symptoms need to be present on any given occasion for dependence to be present (Edwards et al., 1981; Henningfield, 1984; U.S. DHHS, 1988). For example, for some drug classes, physiological withdrawal symptoms or use of the drug to alleviate withdrawal is either not evident (e.g., hallucinogens, PCP, cannabis, inhalants) or is less salient (e.g., amphetamine or similarly acting sympathomimetic drugs, cocaine). The severity of dependence symptoms has been conceptualized as lying along a continuum (see American Psychiatric Association, 1987; Edwards et al., 1977;

Maddux & Desmond, 1986; Pattison, Sobell, & Sobell, 1977) ranging from mild (i.e., often one or more psychosocial consequences, but not major withdrawal symptoms; e.g., episodic cocaine users or problem drinkers) to severe (i.e., major physiological withdrawal symptoms, pervasive drug seeking; e.g., daily opiate users or alcohol abusers experiencing delirium tremens).

Another salient feature of substance use disorders related to dependence is *acquired* (chronic) tolerance, where, with repeated use, an increasing dose of the substance is required to achieve the same desired effect(s) or intoxication. *Tolerance* can also be defined as a decrease in the pharmacological effects from the same amount of drug over repeated uses. In effect, the acquisition of a high level of tolerance enables a person to consume higher doses of drug, which, in turn, increase the likelihood that withdrawal symptoms will appear when drug use ceases. The time-course and magnitude of the development of tolerance varies considerably across drug classes. For example, substantial tolerance to nicotine can develop relatively quickly (e.g., within a year, an individual may be smoking > 20 cigarettes/day), whereas substantial tolerance to large doses of alcohol may take several years to develop.

Natural History of Substance Abuse

Natural history refers to the development and course of a disorder. Issues considered in this section include prevalence rates, genetic vulnerability, progressivity of the disorder, relapse rates, and natural recovery.

Prevalence

The rates of *illicit* psychoactive substance abuse in the adult population range from relatively rare for PCP to 4% of the adult population for cannabis (American Psychiatric Association, 1987). For *licit* drugs, the rates range from 7–15% for alcoholic abuse (American Psychiatric Association, 1987; Cahalan, 1970; Fillmore, 1988a; National Institute on Alcohol Abuse and Alcoholism [NIAAA], 1987) and to 30–40% for cigarette smoking (Ferrence, 1988; Harris, 1983; Remington, Forman, Gentry, Marks, Hogelin, & Trowbridge, 1985). Collectively, substance abuse prevalence rates indicate that with the exception of nicotine, most psychoactive substance abuse does not involve a sizable percentage of the adult population.

Genetic Vulnerability

A genetic basis for or vulnerability to drug dependence has frequently been suggested. With respect to alcohol abuse, several recent reviews have been extremely critical of the design, conduct, and interpretation of genetic studies (Finn & Pihl, 1987; Lester, 1988; Murray, Clifford, Gurling, Topham, Clow, & Bernadt, 1983; Peele, 1986; Searles, 1988). Despite some convincing statistical evidence that alcoholism may cluster in families for males with an alcoholic father, only a small proportion of those with alcohol problems are accounted for by such means, and even the vast majority of males with alcoholic fathers do not themselves become alcoholic (see Sigvardsson, Cloninger, & Bohman, 1985). For drugs other than alcohol, the genetic evidence is inconsistent (e.g., nicotine: Mangan & Golding, 1984; McClearn, 1983; U.S. DHHS, 1988; opiates: Maddux & Desmond, 1986).

Progressivity

While substance abuse problems can be scaled along a severity continuum, this does not mean that mild substance abuse necessarily predicts the development of severe dependence. For alcohol, considerable research suggests that only a minority of persons with alcohol problems at one time will have an equal or more serious problem if drinking continues (reviewed in Sobell & Sobell, 1987a; Taylor & Helzer, 1983). In fact, alcohol abusers tend to fluctuate between periods of heavy drinking and periods of abstinence or of lighter drinking without problems (Cahalan, 1970; Fillmore, 1988a). Although evidence for the progressivity of other drug problems has been less intensely studied, fluctuating patterns of drug use have been observed in a 20-year study of 10 opiate addicts (Maddux & Desmond, 1986).

Evidence for progressivity is strongest for nicotine, where individuals who smoke only a few cigarettes are very likely to progress toward heavier nicotine use (Krasnegor & Renault, 1979; Russell, 1976; Salber & Abeline, 1967). Persistent nicotine self-administration following an initial exposure has also been demonstrated in both animal and clinical laboratory studies (Grabowski, 1986).

Relapse Rates

Substance abuse is an extremely recalcitrant clinical disorder characterized both by very high relapse rates within 6 months following treatment (reviewed in Hunt, Barnett, & Branch, 1971; Sobell et al., 1988; Tims & Leukefeld, 1986) and by a lack of enduring, reliable treatments (Miller & Hester, 1986; Murray & Lawrence, 1984; Platt, 1986; Riley, Sobell, Leo, Sobell, & Klajner, 1987). The magnitude of the problem was captured by Rounsaville (1986), who asserted that "*relapse* (defined as resumption of substance abuse following a period of abstinence) is the rule and not the exception in substance abusers entering or completing treatment" (p. 172). This conclusion, however, is not new. Sixty years ago, a similar conclusion was reached.

> Evidence we have from most of the witnesses forbids any sanguine estimate as to the proportion of permanent cures which may be looked for from any method of treatment, however thorough. Relapse, sooner or later appears to be the rule, and permanent cure the exception. With two exceptions, the most optimistic observations did not claim a higher percentage of lasting cures from 15 to 20 percent. (Ministry of Health, cited in Terry & Pellens, 1928)

Natural Recovery

Surprisingly, the vast majority of individuals with substance abuse problems do not come to the attention of researchers or clinicians. In fact, compared to formal treatment, self-change or natural recoveries account for a high percentage of recoveries, especially for alcohol and nicotine (reviewed in DiClemente & Prochaska, 1982; Fillmore, 1988b; Stall & Biernacki, 1986; U.S. DHHS, 1988). Further, substance abusers who recover without formal intervention tend to exhibit milder problem severity or dependence, compared to those who enter treatment programs. Because present knowledge of substance abuse is largely based on treated populations, and because this represents only a small portion of all those who have substance abuse problems, our understanding of the disorder may be highly circumscribed or incomplete (Carmody, Brischetto, Pierce, Matarazzo, & Connor, 1986; Ockene, 1984; Roizen, 1977; Room, 1977).

Goals of Treatment

Traditionally, most substance abuse treatment programs strongly promote an abstinence goal for all clients (Riley et al., 1987; Rounsaville, 1986; Sobell & Sobell, 1987a; U.S. DHHS, 1986). In some instances, the rationale for an abstinence goal stems from the illicit nature of the drugs (e.g., opiates, cocaine) or their dependency potential (e.g., nicotine). However, when a drug is legally available, when it does not produce impairment or dysfunction when used in moderation, and if there are no serious organic complications caused by previous drug use, reduction of consumption to a nonproblem level can be an alternative goal to abstinence.

The strongest empirical support for the viability of a reduced consumption goal comes from the alcohol field (Heather & Robertson, 1983; Sobell & Sobell, 1987a).[2] First, many studies have demonstrated that problem drinkers and some chronic alcoholics have successfully reduced their alcohol consumption to a nonproblem level (Heather & Robertson, 1983; Pattison et al., 1977). Second, studies testing the efficacy of reduced drinking versus abstinence treatments have yielded generally equivalent long-term outcomes. Third, moderation outcomes occur with some frequency in abstinence-oriented treatments, especially for persons whose drinking problems are not severe (Heather & Robertson, 1983; Miller & Hester, 1986; Riley et al., 1987). Fourth, longitudinal studies indicate that many persons evaluated as having significant alcohol problems at one time will be drinking in moderation and without problems at a later time (Fillmore, 1988a).

With respect to cigarettes, while a reduction in the number smoked might seem a reasonable goal,

sustained limited use of cigarettes is uncommon (< 10% of smokers consume ≤ 10 cigarettes per day: Russell, 1976; U.S. DHHS, 1988). Furthermore, even minimal levels of cigarette smoking have been deemed hazardous to health (U.S. DHHS, 1986). An additional problem for reduced smoking approaches is that individuals who smoke very few cigarettes per day can adjust their puff and inhalation rates to still obtain significant nicotine and tar levels (i.e., nicotine dose and tar exposure is not necessarily a direct function of the number of cigarettes smoked: Benowitz, Hall, Herning, Jacob, Jones, & Osman, 1983; Kozlowski, 1981).

For some psychoactive drugs, a pharmacological intervention may be a helpful adjunct when the goal is abstinence. Maintenance on an agonist drug, such as methadone, can have several advantages. On a short-term basis, it can help stabilize other aspects of an abuser's life (e.g., methadone maintenance can help heroin addicts establish stable vocational functioning). Cigarette smokers who switch to nicotine gum (Nicorette®) can reduce the risk of developing lung disease caused by tar inhaled by smoking (Kozlowski, 1984), and others in the smoker's environment will not be exposed to sidestream smoke. Drug substitutes may not always lead to complete abstinence from drugs. In this regard, it has been suggested that opioid addicts may require methadone maintenance indefinitely (Dole & Nyswander, 1967). Also, long-term use of nicotine gum may be necessary for severely dependent cigarette smokers.

Multiple Drug Abuse: Concurrent or Sequential Treatment?

Individuals attempting simultaneously to cease use of multiple drugs will likely encounter difficulties beyond those expected when stopping one drug. In this regard, two issues emerge. First, some studies have shown increased excessive drinking to accompany periods of cessation from opioid use (Green, Jaffe, Carlisi, & Zaks, 1978), underscoring the importance of considering an individual's

---

[2]Over the years, the issue of reduced consumption goals for alcohol abusers has been highly controversial (Marlatt, 1983; Sobell & Sobell, 1984). This controversy, however, can be viewed as symptomatic of deeper problems involving conflicting conceptualizations of alcohol problems (see Sobell & Sobell, 1987a). For a detailed discussion of conceptual issues regarding goals in the treatment of alcohol problems, readers are referred to a special issue of the journal *Drugs & Society* (Sobell & Sobell, 1987b).

overall pattern of substance use in the formulation of treatment plans. Second, there is an extremely high rate of co-occurrence of cigarette smoking and the abuse of other psychoactive substances (e.g., 80–95% of alcohol and other drug abusers are heavy smokers; Bobo et al., 1987; Burling & Ziff, 1988; Istvan & Matarazzo, 1984; Kozlowski, Jelinek, & Pope, 1986; Taylor & Taylor, 1984; U.S. DHHS, 1987). Because nicotine addiction is highly prevalent among alcohol and other drug abusers, it is surprising that, until recently, nicotine was not only relatively ignored as a drug with serious dependence liabilities (Gritz, 1986), but was also considered diagnostically insignificant (U.S. DHHS, 1988). In fact, in the DSM-II (American Psychiatric Association, 1968) nicotine was not listed as a drug of abuse, and while it has been included in subsequent versions of the DSM(American Psychiatric Association, 1980, 1987), treatment for nicotine dependence has rarely been recognized as a reimbursable clinical disorder by insurance companies in the United States (Slade, 1987).

Despite the synergistic health hazards attributed to smoking and excessive drinking (Klatsky, Friedman, & Siegelaub, 1981; U.S. DHHS, 1982), the feasibility of stopping the use of two or more substances concurrently has been relatively unexplored (Battjes, 1988; Burling & Ziff, 1988). Whether multiple drug problems should be treated concurrently or sequentially is presently unresolved (Bobo & Gilchrist, 1983; Kozlowski et al., 1986, 1989). While it has been argued that attempting concurrent cessation of alcohol and tobacco use might be countertherapeutic due to an increased risk of relapse (Bobo & Gilchrist, 1983), it is similarly conceivable that continued use of one of these substances while trying to stop the other might also precipitate a relapse (e.g., if the act of smoking presented a stimulus complex previously associated with drinking). However, until research is forthcoming, treatment of individuals who wish to stop or reduce two or more substances must be based on a case-by-case analysis.

DIAGNOSTIC ISSUES AND PROBLEMS

Diagnostic formulations have clinical utility beyond the customary insurance and clinical recording requirements. They provide a common language with a standard set of definitions for researchers and clinicians. For alcohol abusers, diagnostic formulations can play an important role with respect to treatment goal decisions (i.e., severity of dependence should be taken into account when considering reduced drinking as a goal: see Sobell & Sobell, 1987a) and intensity of treatment (i.e., for clients with low dependence on alcohol and few psychosocial consequences, the treatment of choice may be a minimal or self-guided treatment: Annis, 1986; Heather & Robertson, 1983). For opiate addicts, diagnostic classifications play a similarly important role in treatment choice, as it is now suggested that methadone should only be prescribed for addicts who are unable to otherwise stop using opioids (Peachey, 1986).

Because abuse of multiple substances is becoming increasingly prevalent, multiple drug use should be assessed. A multiple substance abuse diagnosis not only calls attention to the possibility of pharmacological *synergism* (i.e., multiplicative effect of similarly acting drugs taken concurrently) and *cross-tolerance* (i.e., decreased effect of a drug due to a previous heavy use of pharmacologically similar drugs), but also has treatment implications (i.e., treatment of multiple drug users will not always parallel that for individuals who use one drug; see Kaufman, 1982).

Another diagnostic issue that has been frequently reported relates to the confluence of drug dependence and psychiatric problems (noted in Meyer & Kranzler, 1988). Affective and conduct disorders are the two most common psychiatric problems associated with substance abuse (Grande, Wolf, Schubert, Patterson, & Brocco, 1984; Meyer & Kranzler, 1988; Rounsaville, Weissman, Crits-Christoph, Wilber, & Kleber, 1982b; Solomon, 1983). Because several studies have shown that substance abusers with depressive (Rounsaville, Tierney, Crits-Christoph, Weissman, & Kleber, 1982a; Rounsaville et al., 1982b) or serious psychiatric symptoms (McLellan, Woody, Luborsky, O'Brien, & Druley, 1983; Meyer & Kranzler, 1988) have poorer treatment outcomes than substance abusers without these problems, it has been suggested that such patients should receive additional counseling. Finally, in addition to evaluating whether other psychiatric disorders are present, it is important to determine whether substance abuse is the primary or the secondary disorder.

TREATMENT STRATEGIES

Overview

The next section of this chapter reviews behavioral treatment studies of alcohol, tobacco, and other drug problems published over a relatively recent 5-year period (1984–1988). This review focuses on issues and trends relevant to practicing clinicians and clinical researchers. Consequently, this review is not an exhaustive survey of the treatment outcome literature. For a thorough presentation of treatment outcome findings, readers are referred to several other recent reviews (Callahan, Long, Pecsok, & Simone, 1987; Callahan & Pecsok, 1988; Glasgow & Lichtenstein, 1987; Miller & Hester, 1986; Riley et al., 1987; Schwartz, Lauderdale, Montgomery, Burch, & Gallant, 1987; Stitzer, Bigelow, & McCaul, 1983).

Studies satisfying the following criteria are included in the review: (1) to avoid overlap with existing reviews, studies had to be published from 1984 through 1988; (2) with some exceptions (noted when they occur), studies must have both employed an adult clinical population and used random assignment to groups; (3) outcome data relevant to substance use must have been reported for at least a 12-month follow-up period for alcohol and nicotine abusers, and a minimum of 6 months for other drug abusers (the shorter follow-up period for studies involving illicit drug abuse reflects the generally poorer quality of research in this area); (4) no case studies have been included, and (5) for alcohol studies, subjects had to have a primary diagnosis of alcohol abuse or dependence. Interventions that did not satisfy these criteria, but that were innovative and noteworthy, are included and so noted.

Studies in this review are organized into three sections reflecting the three major substances of abuse: (1) alcohol, (2) nicotine, and (3) other psychoactive drugs (the section on nicotine actually follows the section on other psychoactive substances). These distinctions reflect the fairly distinct methodologies that characterize treatment research with each substance, the differing levels of conceptual sophistication employed to explain the use of each substance, and the specific treatment and theoretical issues that are relevant to the three major substance groups.

Behavioral Treatment of Alcohol Abuse

Introduction

Recently, more sophisticated behavioral treatments have been developed for alcohol abuse. Several factors have contributed to this change: (a) the limited efficacy of traditional behavioral treatments (e.g., relaxation training, aversion conditioning, covert conditioning, social skills training, assertiveness training, contingency contracting; Childress, McClellan, & O'Brien, 1985; Wilson, 1987), (b) increasingly complex behavioral conceptualizations of alcohol abuse (Marlatt & Gordon, 1985; Sobell & Sobell, 1987a), and (c) the growing influence of cognitive factors in behavior therapy (Bandura, 1986; Beck, 1976; Marlatt & Gordon, 1985). Recent interventions have also encouraged greater client involvement in treatment (e.g., self-management approaches).

As is evident, the present review reflects the changing focus of behavioral treatments. The central features of these second-generation treatments blend old approaches with new, and they include (a) *self-management approaches* (e.g., self-monitoring of drinking, self-selection of goals, bibliotherapy), (b) *functional analysis of drinking* (i.e., identifying antecedents and consequences of high- and low-risk drinking situations), (c) *cognitive restructuring*, (d) *development of coping strategies to deal with high-risk drinking situations*, and (e) *provision of marital or family therapy* (when indicated).

Behavioral Self-Management (BSM)

Using a BSM treatment approach, Sanchez-Craig, Annis, Bornet, and MacDonald (1984) provided five to six sessions of cognitive-behavioral therapy to 70 problem drinkers who were randomly assigned to either an abstinence or a controlled-drinking goal. Significant improvements in drinking were obtained at posttreatment, with no differences between those advised to abstain versus those advised to moderate their drinking. Therapeutic gains were generally maintained over a 2-year follow-up, and over this same period, there were no changes in the proportion of subjects in the various outcome categories. Regardless of subjects' goal assignments at treatment, 70% moderated their drinking over the follow-up, compared with 5% who abstained. Because heavier drinking subjects were more likely to succeed if they moderated their drinking than if they abstained, the authors suggested that the conventional wisdom that abstinence should be required of heavier drinkers is unfounded (Sanchez-Craig & Lei, 1986).

Foy, Nunn, and Rychtarik (1984) added cognitive-behavioral treatment to the alcohol education and drinking management training that chronic hospitalized alcoholics routinely received. A second group received training in controlled drinking skills as well. Both treatments successfully reduced the number of abusive drinking days as compared to pretreatment. While the controlled-drinking-training subjects reported fewer abstinent days and more days of abusive drinking at the 6-month follow-up than those who did not receive such training, these differences disappeared by 12 months. At a 5- to 6-year follow-up, there were no significant group differences in drinking, with 18% of all subjects drinking moderately and 20% abstinent (Rychtarik, Foy, Scott, Lokey, & Prue, 1987).

Fink, Longabaugh, McCrady, Stout, Beattie, Ruggieri-Authelet, and McNeil (1985) reported a 2-year follow-up of 95 alcoholics (91% of initial sample) who had been treated in an abstinence-oriented program with either partial hospitalization or a complete inpatient hospitalization. They found that 23% were continuously abstinent, 40% showed continuous moderate drinking, and 37% were uncontrolled drinkers. The abstinent and moderate-drinking groups did not differ on any nondrinking dependent variable. Those receiving partial hospitalization were more likely to be abstinent than those who received inpatient treatment.

Elal-Lawrence, Slade, and Dewey (1986, 1987) permitted 139 problem drinkers to choose among (a) 6 weeks of inpatient treatment, (b) twice weekly outpatient treatment, or (c) once-a-week day-treatment program. Inpatients and day-program clients and those others without medical contraindications against drinking were also trained in controlled drinking. Over a 1-year follow-up, 45 subjects successfully abstained, 50 controlled their drinking, and 44 relapsed. Treatment and posttreatment variables predicting abstinence included desiring abstinence, attending AA, and receiving more residential care; controlled drinking was predicted by exposure to training in controlled drinking and receiving inpatient treatment only. These results provide support for the hypothesis that better treatment outcome is obtained when treatment is consistent with subjects' goal preferences. No evidence was found for a relationship between a controlled-drinking outcome and initial severity of the alcohol problem.

Skutle and Berg (1987) randomly assigned 48 problem drinkers recruited through newspaper advertisements to one of the following: (a) self-control-oriented bibliotherapy, (b) therapist-assisted self-control therapy, (c) coping-skills treatment, or (d) combined coping-skills treatment and self-control therapy. While all groups significantly decreased their alcohol consumption between intake and follow-up, no group differences were found. At 1-year follow-up, 7% of all subjects reported themselves as abstinent, and 24% reported drinking moderately with no heavy drinking episodes.

Robertson, Heather, Dzialdowski, Crawford, and Winton (1986) randomly assigned 37 problem drinkers to either nine sessions of cognitive-behavioral treatment or three to four sessions of assessment and advice. While the more intensively treated group reported less drinking at follow-up (mean interval = 15.5 months), this difference could be attributed to the heavy drinking of three subjects in the minimally treated group. Of the subjects located for follow-up, 50% (7 of 14) of the intensively treated group were moderating their drinking, compared to 42% (8 of 19) of the minimally treated group.

Duckert and Johnsen (1987) assigned 135 problem drinkers to one of two groups: cognitive-behavioral therapy only, or the same treatment supplemented with disulfiram. By the 21-month follow-up, the disulfiram treatment group reported greater reductions in daily alcohol consumption than the cognitive-behavioral-treatment- only group. This difference was attributed to the subjects' use of disulfiram. While 34% of the cognitive-behavioral therapy subjects initially chose abstinence as a treatment goal, only 10% successfully achieved their goal. The low rates of self-reported drinking, however, suggest that reduced drinking was common.

In a study of media-recruited problem drinkers ($N = 127$), Alden (1988) compared the efficacy of behavioral self-control treatment, drug counseling, and a waiting-list control group. Both treatment groups significantly decreased their drinking, had lower peak blood-alcohol levels, and reported more posttreatment abstinent and controlled-drinking days than the control group. The two treatment groups did not differ on any of these variables.

Booth, Dale, and Ansari (1984) treated 37 alcoholics with behavioral self-control therapy as part of a broader inpatient treatment program. Clients were allowed to choose their treatment goal in the final week of the 6-week program unless there were medical contraindications to drinking, in which case they were advised to be abstinent. Of the 32% who chose moderation, 42% were considered successful (abstinent or ≤ 4 ounces of alcohol consumed on any day) over a 1-year follow-up. The success rate for those *choosing* (i.e., self-chosen) abstinence was 27%; clients who chose moderation tended to be younger than abstinent clients and used aftercare sessions much less. Of those who were prescribed abstinence, only 20% were successful in achieving either abstinence or reduced drinking at follow-up. Drinking goal choice was associated with drinking outcome; 33% of those choosing moderation were drinking moderately at follow-up compared to only 4% of those who chose or were prescribed abstinence. Similarly, 20% of those choosing or prescribed abstinence were abstinent, compared to 8% of those choosing moderation.

Heather, Whitton, and Robertson (1986) gave either a behaviorally oriented self-help manual or an alcohol education manual to persons who responded to a newspaper advertisement. Of the 785 respondents, 31.5% (247) returned assessment questionnaires or agreed to a telephone interview. Of these, 44.9% (110 of 247) were contacted at the 1-year follow-up; no significant group differences in the amount of alcohol consumed in the previous week were noted (Heather, Robertson, MacPherson, Allsop, & Fulton, 1987). However, when subjects who had received additional treatment for alcohol abuse were excluded from this analysis, the self-help intervention did produce a significant decrease in consumption compared to the educa-

tion manual group. Addressing the issue of the relationship between dependency and treatment outcome, Heather et al. (1986) found that subjects classified as "heavy consumers–high dependence" reduced their drinking to levels below those who were classified as "low consumers–mild-to-no dependence." These findings contradict arguments that subjects with more serious alcohol problems cannot benefit from a self-help manual emphasizing moderation.

Orford and Keddie (1986a) permitted 46 subjects to choose either an abstinence or a controlled-drinking treatment goal. Subjects with no preference were randomly assigned to one of the two goals. Fifty percent in the abstinence group and 52% in the moderation group were considered treatment successes. Also, for those who expressed a goal preference, treatment consistent with the expressed goal preference yielded greater overall success (68% versus 31%). If the treatment goal was consistent with that indicated by an index of severity of alcohol dependence, the success rate was 47%, whereas if the treatment provided was inconsistent with dependence severity, the success rate was 58%. This suggests that successful treatment outcome is unrelated to whether the treatment received is congruent with treatment suggested by a dependency index. Drinking goal choice was also found to be unrelated to severity of dependence. Orford and Keddie concluded that treatment outcome was maximized when treatment paralleled subjects' goal choice rather than their degree of alcohol dependency.

Graber and Miller (1988) randomly assigned 24 problem drinkers recruited through media advertisements to six sessions of behavioral self-control therapy with either an abstinence or a reduced-drinking goal. There was a significant reduction in alcohol consumption between the start and the end of treatment but no significant group differences. These gains were maintained 3.5 years later. Similar percentages of subjects in both groups attained abstinence (16.5%), while only 8.5% of moderation-goal subjects successfully reduced their drinking compared to 16.5% of abstinence-goal subjects.

Sannibale (1988) randomly assigned 96 male problem drinkers who had been referred to a community treatment agency (74% were referred by the courts or by their employers) to one of the following conditions: (a) an abstinence-oriented, didactic, confrontational treatment, (b) a BSM treatment (where abstinence or controlled-drinking goals were permitted), or (c) a minimal treatment control group in which clients were simply encouraged to stop drinking. Of the 80 subjects (83%) contacted at 1-year follow-up, 40 had improved (7 were abstinent, 33 were drinking without problems). There were no group differences in outcome.

Other Treatments

The majority of alcohol behavioral treatment studies published since 1984 have used BSM strategies. Consequently, few studies have employed interventions that were common in the years before 1984. One exception to this trend involved 60 volunteers who participated in aversion therapy at a private alcohol inpatient program (Cannon, Baker, Gino, & Nathan, 1986). The subjects received five sessions pairing the smell and taste of alcohol with an emetic and up to six aftercare booster sessions. At a 1-year follow-up, 45% of the subjects were abstinent.

Ewing (1984) randomly assigned 31 inpatient alcohol abusers to an aversive conditioning or a control-conditioning group. Shock intensity was set by the client to be subjectively painful. Clients in the control condition received trials with imaginal shock (i.e., no actual shock). On the basis of clinical judgments of improved drinking behavior, no group differences in success rates were observed at the 13- to 40-month follow-up.

Eriksen, Björnstad, and Götestam (1986) investigated ($N = 24$) the efficacy of adding 8 weeks of group social skills training to an abstinence-oriented inpatient treatment ($n = 12$). A control group ($n = 12$) discussed attitudes toward alcohol, the effects of alcohol, reasons for drinking, and consequences of drinking. At a 1-year follow-up, none of the 23 subjects found reported abstinence. The skills training group did, however, report significantly fewer drinking days (mean = 79 days) than the control group (mean = 244 days) and were abstinent for a significantly longer period of time following treatment (52 days versus 8 days for the control group).

Issues in the Behavioral Treatment of Alcohol Abuse

The BSM techniques appear to reduce problem drinking. However, although it is clear that these techniques are effective, it is not clear that these strategies are superior to other behavioral or non-behavioral treatments. This finding is consistent with the conclusion reached earlier by Carey and Maisto (1985), who, in their review of behavioral self-control therapy, concluded that "no technique or combination of techniques is superior to any other in ameliorating alcohol problems. Self-control training appears to result in improvement that is at least comparable to the interventions against which it has been evaluated" (p.242). In the present review, interpersonal therapy, treatment for anxiety or depression, and drug counseling were found to benefit problem drinkers to the same degree as BSM. In some cases, treatments compared to a BSM intervention were superior (e.g., disulfiram-supplemented behavioral treatment was superior to the same treatment without disulfiram: Duckert & Johnsen, 1987).

As noted earlier, several behavioral techniques are grouped under the label BSM. Because there is no empirical basis for combining different BSM components, identifying effective elements is necessary to produce a more efficient and potent treatment. Moreover, the efficacy of the nonbehavioral treatments suggests that the effectiveness of BSM strategies may not lie in the specific treatment components (e.g., problem solving, cognitive restructuring, functional analysis), but rather in the activation of therapeutic change processes common to any intervention.

Goal Choice

Permitting alcohol abusers to choose their drinking goal (unless contraindicated) has become an increasingly common feature of behavioral interventions. This trend has been the result of several converging factors: (1) the recognition that many alcohol abusers end up moderating their drinking (as opposed to abstaining), regardless of whether they are encouraged to do so; (2) the lack of definitive evidence demonstrating that the severity of dependence is related to type of successful outcome (i.e., abstinence versus moderation); (3)

the acknowledgment that goal self-selection may serve as an important motivational factor contributing to treatment success; and (4) the unacceptability of long-term abstinence as a goal for many low-dependence younger clients.

Studies in this review that permitted subjects to choose their own drinking goal reported that substantial proportions of the samples chose reduced drinking. Furthermore, a sizable proportion of clients treated in abstinence-oriented treatments also were found to be drinking moderately at outcome. Thus, it is clear that many subjects attempt to moderate their drinking despite the advice they receive in treatment. Also, a moderate drinking goal does not predict poorer outcomes at posttreatment or at follow-up. Variables predicting choice of, or success at, moderate drinking include younger age, lighter drinking, and less exposure to an abstinence orientation. Goal choice also appears to be unrelated to severity of alcohol dependence (Elal-Lawrence et al., 1987; Eriksen et al., 1986; Orford & Keddie, 1986b; Sanchez-Craig & Lei, 1986). Finally, studies reviewed in this section provide support for the persuasion hypothesis, which suggests that successful outcomes are more likely if goals are congruent with clients' preferences (Orford & Keddie, 1986a).

Treatment Length

Early reviews of the treatment literature suggest that successful outcomes of alcohol abuse treatment are not a function of treatment length (Armor, Polich, & Stambul, 1978; Edwards et al., 1977; Emrick, 1974, 1975). Studies reviewed earlier in this section, as well as nonbehavioral studies relevant to this issue, continue to provide support for this view.

Chick, Ritson, Connaughton, Stewart, and Chick (1988) provided either 5 minutes of *simple advice* (urging the individual to stop drinking), 30 to 60 minutes of *amplified advice* (simple advice expanded to increase the subjects' motivation), or *extended treatment* (amplified advice plus the option of further treatment). Of the 58 subjects offered extended care, 56 attended at least one outpatient session and 32 attended at least 10 sessions; 28 of the 56 also attempted to moderate their drinking. At the 2-year follow-up, 39% of the advice-only groups and 58% of the extended-care

subjects reported no alcohol-related problems for the month preceding the follow-up. This difference in outcome was only marginally significant. A comparison of the two advice-only groups revealed no differences, although the trend favored greater improvement in the amplified group on several drinking variables.

Chapman and Huygens (1988) evaluated the efficacy of a 6-week inpatient program, a 6-week outpatient program, or a "single confrontational interview" with 113 alcoholics. A control group ($n = 40$) consisted of those who dropped out of any of these treatments and who, consequently, may have received some treatment. In the confrontational interview (lasting 1–2 hours, with a relative, friend, or spouse present), subjects were told that they possessed the personal resources to abstain from alcohol and should do so. No significant group differences were found on any of the drinking variables.

Zweben, Pearlman, and Li (1988) randomly assigned 218 couples, in which one partner had an alcohol abuse problem, to either a single advice session or eight sessions of conjoint marital counseling (communication–interactional approach). Only 116 couples (53%) completed both treatment and the 18-month follow-up. There were no significant group differences on any drinking outcome measure throughout follow-up or in the proportion of subjects falling into various outcome categories based on number of heavy drinking days. Of the entire sample, 59% were classified as greatly improved, with 10% reporting abstinence.

Orford and Keddie (1986a) compared intensive and brief forms of abstinence-oriented and moderation-oriented treatment and found 40% of the intensively treated group and 31% of the briefly treated group to be abstinent or drinking moderately at a 1-year follow-up. If the outcome criteria are liberalized to include those who have a fluctuating outcome but with long periods of abstinence or reduced drinking, then both treatment lengths produced a 56% success rate.

Fink et al. (1985) compared extended hospitalization with partial hospitalization and found no enduring difference in the two treatments over a 2-year period. While the groups did not differ in outcome, partial hospitalization was less costly.

Powell, Penick, Read, and Ludwig (1985) randomly assigned 174 male alcoholics to one of three outpatient treatments following inpatient treatment: (1) untreated medical maintenance (15-minute monthly medical examinations), (2) active support (approximately 100 hours), or (3) medication only (disulfiram and chlordiazepoxide). Intensity of treatment was not related to improvement on any dependent measure over a 12-month follow-up.

Robertson et al. (1986) found that nine sessions of cognitive-behavioral treatment reduced alcohol consumption and increased the number of abstinent days in the month prior to follow-up to a significantly greater degree than did an intervention consisting of three to four sessions of assessment and advice. Follow-up was for a mean interval of 15.5 months.

Skutle and Berg (1987) examined four different behavioral self-control interventions, one of which was limited to two sessions of bibliotherapy. The outcome of the bibliotherapy group did not differ from any of the more lengthy treatments at any of the follow-ups.

Antti-Poika, Karaharju, Roine, and Salaspuro (1988) treated injured male workers admitted to hospital and who were heavy drinkers (Michigan Alcoholism Screening Test score > 6). Subjects who received between one and three sessions of advice to remain abstinent or to moderate their drinking reduced their reported alcohol consumption by 50% at 6 months, compared to a control group (no counseling received) that increased their alcohol consumption.

Wallace, Cutler, and Haines (1988) recruited 909 heavy-drinking subjects from 47 group medical practices and randomly assigned them to two conditions: at least two sessions of physician-administered advice to reduce drinking, or a no-advice control group. Wallace et al. (1988) concluded that "intervention by general practitioners resulted in an appreciable reduction both in quantity of alcohol consumed and in the proportion of patients drinking excessively" (p. 667). It was estimated that if all general practitioners administered a similar brief treatment to their heavy-drinking patients, 15% of these patients would reduce their alcohol consumption to nonproblem levels.

Overall, this review parallels earlier reviews in concluding that briefer treatments are as effective as, or superior to, longer treatments in modifying drinking behavior. This, in turn, suggests that the source of therapeutic efficacy is not the amount or duration of treatment.

Behavioral Treatment of Other Drug Abuse

This section reviews research on behavioral treatments for abuse of substances other than alcohol or nicotine. Previous reviews of other drug abuse treatment research have concluded that advances in behavioral assessment and treatment of drug abuse lag behind developments in the alcohol field (e.g., Sobell et al., 1982, 1988). Treatments based on classical conditioning, such as extinction, continue to be common, but they have been found to have limited efficacy. For example, Childress, McLellan, and O'Brien (1986) exposed six abstinent opiate abusers who exhibited intense craving and withdrawal to 20 hours of drug-relevant stimuli. They found that both craving and withdrawal responses were almost completely eliminated following extinction treatment. Unfortunately, no follow-up data were provided. Childress, Ehrman, McLellan, and O'Brien (1987) replicated these results in a group of cocaine addicts; however, the benefits failed to generalize beyond the extinction program, as two thirds of the subjects relapsed within 2 months after treatment.

Operant conditioning-based interventions, usually contingency management, have also been used to treat illicit drug use. These strategies reward (illicit) drug-free status and/or punish nonprescribed drug use. As with extinction procedures, evidence for their efficacy is limited. In one such study, Crowley (1984) used aversive consequences to treat 17 substance-abusing professionals. Subjects agreed that their professional association would be informed, and their licenses surrendered, if drug use occurred during the contract period. Over half (53%) were drug free for the first 12 months of the contract and only 2 of the 17 lost their licenses during the contract period. There was no comparison treatment, however.

Dolan, Black, Penk, Robinowitz, and DeFord (1985) made aversive consequences contingent on illicit drug use by 21 methadone maintenance outpatients considered to be failures of previous treatments. The contract required subjects to undergo methadone detoxification and to wait at least 30 days before resuming methadone maintenance if they did not cease illicit drug use during a 30-day period. While 52% of the subjects eliminated illicit drug use during the 30-day contract (compared to 27% precontract), these gains deteriorated over a 2-month follow-up.

Over 9 weeks, McCaul, Stitzer, Bigelow, and Liebson (1984) gradually reduced daily methadone doses to 0 in 20 opiate addicts. During this period, subjects were randomly assigned to an experimental group ($10 and one take-home methadone dose for a negative urine sample) or a control group ($5 for a urine specimen). While the rate of illicit drug use was less in the experimental group, all subjects relapsed to their street drug upon stopping methadone.

Differential reinforcement for illicit drug use was also employed by Stitzer, Bickel, Bigelow, and Liebson (1986). They reinforced negative urine samples by increasing the dose of methadone and punished positive urines by decreasing the methadone dose. Although the incidence of negative urine tests increased, there were no reliable group differences. However, because 40% of the punished group dropped out of the study, compared to none of the reinforced group, the authors suggested that avoidance of illicit drugs should always be rewarded. Similar findings were reported by Iguchi, Stitzer, Bigelow, and Liebson (1987).

McCarthy and Borders (1985) randomly assigned subjects to either a structured treatment (i.e., methadone detoxification contingent on 4 consecutive months of drug use during the year) or an unstructured group (i.e., no contingency). At 12 months, 75% of the structured group were drug free compared to 25% of the unstructured group.

Magura, Casriel, Goldsmith, Strug, and Lipton (1988) used take-home methadone doses to reinforce drug-free urine samples by 32 polydrug-abusing (primarily cocaine) methadone patients. Weekly urine tests failed to show any change from the precontract to the contract phase. The authors concluded that the privilege of taking home methadone was not a potent reinforcer.

Rather than manipulating contingencies regarding illicit drug use, Schwartz et al. (1987) provided either immediate (within 3 days) or delayed (1 to 3 weeks) urinalysis feedback for 120 methadone maintenance patients. No effect was obtained for either group or any dependent measure.

In an earlier review, it was concluded that "contingency management methods have achieved only modest success with drug abusers . . . [and] have been found to have some value in terms of behavior management during treatment, but their efficacy in contributing to successful treatment outcome is unknown" (Sobell et al., 1982, p. 519). This conclusion remains unchanged for studies in the present review.

While extinction and contingency management approaches are reported relatively frequently in the drug abuse treatment literature, only a few studies of cognitive-behavioral interventions have been reported. In one of these studies, McLellan, Childress, Ehrman, and O'Brien (1986) randomly assigned 56 opiate addicts receiving methadone to one of three treatments: (1) cognitive-behavioral therapy and relaxation, (2) cognitive-behavioral therapy and relaxation supplemented with extinction sessions, or (3) drug counseling. At a 6-month follow-up, both cognitive-behavioral therapy groups were improved on multiple measures of functioning, while the drug counseling group showed little improvement. The authors concluded that the extinction procedures did not improve functioning beyond that attributed to cognitive-behavioral therapy alone. Also, because not all of the extinction stimuli (e.g., needles) were equally effective in eliciting conditioned responses, McLellan et al. (1986) concluded that extinction procedures should use idiosyncratically conditioned stimuli for each subject.

Woody, McLellan, Luborsky, and O'Brien (1985, 1987) found that 6 months of short-term psychoanalytic psychotherapy or cognitive-behavioral therapy for opiate addicts led to improvement on several dependent measures (including illicit drug use). Both formal treatments produced outcomes superior to a drug-counseling group that showed very little improvement.

Sanchez-Craig, Cappell, Busto, and Kay (1987) provided 42 long-term benzodiazepine users with four to five sessions of cognitive-behavioral therapy. Half the subjects were tapered off their drug, using study-supplied diazepam (gradual withdrawal), while half were tapered with a placebo (abrupt withdrawal). The placebo group reported more withdrawal symptoms and were more likely to supplement the supplied medications, but there were no group differences in success rates at 1-year posttreatment.

Higgitt, Golombok, Fonagy, and Lader (1987) investigated the efficacy of group cognitive therapy in withdrawing chronic benzodiazepine users. A control group received the same therapy by phone. To minimize the intensity of withdrawal distress, reduction of drug intake was determined by the severity of symptoms experienced by subjects. Cognitive therapy helped subjects cope with cognitive and behavioral manifestations of withdrawal. At posttreatment, 8 of 10 experimental subjects and 3 of 6 control subjects had significantly reduced benzodiazepine intake, which was maintained throughout the 1-year follow-up.

Roffman, Stephens, Simpson, and Whitaker (1988) randomly assigned 110 cannabis-dependent subjects to a group relapse prevention treatment (i.e., emphasized acquisition of effective means to cope with relapse to smoking marijuana) or a social support treatment (i.e., emphasized obtaining social support to overcome drug dependence). Subjects were recruited through advertisements and blocked according to gender. While 30% of the sample achieved abstinence (75% had expressed the desire to do so at assessment) at a 1-month follow-up, there were no group differences.

The generally uninspiring outcomes for drug abuse treatment reflect several obstacles to the development of effective intervention strategies. A stated goal of behavioral treatment of drug abuse is to develop and/or strengthen nondrug reinforcers in order to decrease the value of pharmacological reinforcement (e.g., Stitzer, Grabowski, & Henningfield, 1984). Yet, none of the studies reviewed used such alternative reinforcers. Most reinforcements have tended to be drug-related (e.g., increase in dose, take home drug privileges). Even more striking is the absence of nonpharmacological negative reinforcers (e.g., relaxation procedures) to help drug abusers cope effectively with the unpleasant affective states commonly antecedent to drug use.

While identification and manipulation of major reinforcements controlling drug abuse has been a central aim of many behavioral drug treatment approaches, their control by the therapist has hindered the development of coping skills by the client. It is critical that the client learn to control the exteroceptive and interoceptive cues associated with drug-seeking behavior. This has been a central feature of the BSM or self-control studies developed with alcohol abusers.

Relative to the literature on alcohol abuse, the quality of the behavioral treatment research on other drug abuse remains poor: controlled studies are still exceptions; attrition rates during treatment are high; little use is made of self-report of drug use by clients and/or collaterals; and follow-ups are rare and usually brief. The few cognitive-behavioral interventions reported to date tend to be methodologically superior (e.g., longer follow-up, better controlled) to extinction and contingency-management studies.

Behavioral Treatment of Nicotine Dependence

The studies in this section have been organized to reflect three major issues in the treatment of nicotine dependence: (1) the efficacy of behavioral treatments, (2) relapse prevention, and (3) the efficacy of pharmacological adjuncts to behavioral interventions.

Efficacy of Behavioral Treatment

Aversion treatments have been used in an attempt to eliminate smoking by creating aversive conditioned responses to cigarette smoke. *Rapid smoking* is a commonly employed strategy, which requires the inhalation of smoke every few seconds until continued smoking becomes too aversive. This technique has been found to yield good outcomes, especially when used as part of a multimodal treatment package (e.g., Hall, Sachs, & Hall, 1979; Hall, Rugg, Tunstall, & Jones, 1984a; Raw & Russell, 1980). Recently, less aversive treatment procedures (e.g., *rapid puffing*—rapid smoking but no inhalation; *focused smoking*—smoking for long periods of time but at a normal rate; *smokeholding*—retaining smoke in the mouth and throat for several minutes without inhaling) have been developed, which yield outcomes similar to rapid smoking (Schwartz, 1987). Generally, these new aversion treatments are also more effective when administered as part of a multicomponent behavioral treatment (U.S. DHHS,1988).

In one of these studies, Hall, Sachs, Hall, and Benowitz (1984) treated 18 media-recruited smokers who had cardiopulmonary disease with 8 sessions of medically supervised rapid smoking. At 1- and 2-year follow-ups, half of the subjects were still abstinent, compared to none in a waiting list control group ($n = 28$). Biochemical measures corroborated subjects' self-reports. The authors concluded that rapid smoking was a fairly successful treatment for smokers with mild to moderate cardiopulmonary disease. In another study evaluating rapid smoking (Hill, 1988), 60 subjects were first treated for 3 consecutive days with a behavioral cessation program and then received one session of relapse training: (a) in vivo relapse (rapid smoking of one cigarette), (b) imaginal relapse, or (c) abstinence training (i.e., any smoking discouraged). While 93% of the subjects were abstinent after the rapid smoking training, abstinent rates for the three groups were not significantly different (range: 11-40%) at 1-year posttreatment.

Lando and McGovern (1985) assigned 130 media-recruited subjects to one of four groups, the first three of which received seven maintenance sessions following smoking cessation treatment consisting of unstructured problem solving to maintain treatment gains: (1) oversmoking, (2) *nicotine fading* (which progressively reduces either the number of cigarettes smoked or the intake of nicotine through brand switching), (3) nicotine fading and smokeholding, or (4) a control group that received nicotine fading but no maintenance sessions. At a 1-year follow-up, there were no significant differences in abstinent rates among groups (range: 14-44%), leading the authors to conclude that an intensive maintenance treatment did not help avoid relapse to smoking.

Programs using BSM for nicotine dependence generally teach smokers (a) to identify and modify cues that predict smoking, (b) to rearrange environmental and social contingencies to support smoking cessation, and (c) to enhance cognitive and other behavioral coping skills in smoking situations. The BSM treatment programs provide for considerable client involvement in treatment and, thus, promote attributions of change to the client rather than to the therapist. Common BSM techniques in smoking programs include nicotine fading, stimulus control, functional analysis of smoking situations, contingency management, and self-monitoring. Nicotine fading has become increasingly popular as an alternative to aversive treatments. In summarizing the literature on nicotine fading, Schwartz (1987) concluded that success rates are comparable to other unimodal behavioral treatments such as aversive smoking.

Mothersill, McDowell, and Rosser (1988) assigned 333 subjects recruited from physicians' offices to one of four treatments: 15 minutes of medical advice by a physician, eight sessions of health education, a cigarette self-monitoring control group, and eight group sessions of nonaversive cognitive-behavioral treatment. The cognitive and health education group had the best posttreatment abstinence rates (40% and 35%, respectively). However, by 1-year posttreatment, the abstinence rates diminished for both groups (17% each). The physician-advice and self-monitoring groups changed little from the end of treatment (14% each at follow-up). There were no significant differences between any groups at either assessment point.

Etringer, Gregory, and Lando (1984) crossed satiation and nicotine fading with standard behavioral treatment and enriched group cohesiveness training. Subjects ($N = 72$) for the most part (i.e., friends and family members were still treated in the same group) were randomly assigned to one of the four conditions. While all groups had high posttreatment abstinence rates (range: 81-95%), at 1-year follow-up these rates dropped to 6-45%. The only significant group differences in abstinence occurred between the standard satiation treatment (12%) and the remaining groups (range: 37-64%), but only at 3 and 6 months posttreatment.

Nicki, Remington, and MacDonald (1984) assigned 49 media-recruited subjects to six weekly sessions of either nicotine fading/self-monitoring (NF/SM), NF/SM plus self-talk (covert speech to support abstinence), NF/SM plus self-efficacy training (coping with progressively more difficult smoking situations), or NF/SM plus self-talk and self-efficacy training. An attention control group ($n = 9$) was contacted initially and again at 12 months. There were no differences among the four experimental groups in the number of cigarettes smoked per week over the follow-up period, although there was a significant reduction from baseline for all four treated groups. All treatment groups had superior outcomes to the control group. Self-efficacy training added to NF/SM produced significantly greater abstinence (45%) compared to the NF/SM only group (13%).

Singh and Leung (1988) employed cigarette fading, self-monitoring, and contingency contracting with seven subjects who were permitted to reduce cigarette consumption at their own rate until they could achieve abstinence corroborated by collaterals for 3 consecutive days. Six of the seven subjects completed treatment, and five were abstinent at an 18-month follow-up. Despite the very small sample size, the authors concluded that allowing subjects to self-manage their own reduction in cigarette consumption may be a potentially effective smoking treatment.

Byrne and White (1987) assigned 274 media-recruited subjects to one of four treatments: self-directed BSM, six weekly group sessions of therapist-assisted BSM, six consecutive daily sessions of therapist-assisted BSM supplemented with covert sensitization, or four sessions of hypnotherapy. Complete baseline and follow-up data were available for only 131 subjects. While the number of cigarettes smoked decreased significantly by the end of treatment, there were no reliable group differences. At a 12-month follow-up, 31% of the sample was abstinent. Byrne and White (1987) concluded that more intense behavioral treatments were not superior to self-directed behavioral treatment or a nonbehavioral treatment.

Glasgow, Klesges, Klesges, Vasey, and Gunnarson (1985) assigned 48 subjects to one of three controlled smoking treatments: controlled smoking with relapse prevention, controlled smoking plus weekly carbon monoxide feedback, or a delayed waiting list control who received the controlled smoking program 5 weeks later. Abstinent rates at posttreatment and at a 2-½ year follow-up revealed significant reductions in smoking between the two treated groups and the waiting list control.

Despite impressive posttreatment abstinence

rates, none of the behavioral treatments reviewed maintained these gains over the follow-up periods. Behavioral treatments for nicotine dependence have not been shown to be superior to nonbehavioral interventions, but both forms of treatment are superior to nontreated control groups.

Maintenance of Treatment Effects: Relapse Prevention

The fact that it is estimated that 70–80% of people who attempt to quit smoking will resume regular smoking within 1 year (Stitzer & Gross, 1988) points to the need to develop treatments that will result in long-term posttreatment abstinence rates.

McIntyre-Kingsolver, Lichtenstein, and Mermelstein (1986) and Mermelstein, Cohen, Lichtenstein, Baer, and Kamarck (1986) investigated the efficacy of supplementing a BSM smoking cessation treatment with spouse training (reinforcement, problem-solving). Media-recruited subjects ($N = 64$) were seen weekly for six, 2-hour sessions. No significant differences in abstinence rates were found between subjects who received spouse training and those who did not (61% of all subjects were abstinent at posttreatment; 34% were abstinent after 12 months). McIntyre-Kingsolver et al. (1986) suggested that the lack of differences may have been due to the presence of *dual-role spouses* (who not only were expected to be supportive of the subjects' smoking cessation, but were also trying to quit smoking themselves). Subjects with this type of spouse tended to relapse more frequently (but not significantly more frequently) than those who had single-role spouses. At 12 months, not having a smoker in the home predicted abstinence, while having more smoking friends predicted relapse.

Brandon, Zelman, and Baker (1987) attempted to delay relapse to smoking by supplementing smoking cessation treatment with maintenance sessions. Subjects ($N = 57$) first received six group sessions of smoking cessation (control condition) and then received either no maintenance sessions or maintenance sessions (at 2, 4, 8, and 12 weeks posttreatment) consisting of either counseling only (coping with high risk situations) or counseling plus rapid puffing. There were no differences in abstinence rates between the two maintenance conditions 1-year posttreatment. While both maintenance groups had higher abstinence rates than the smoking cessation only group throughout follow-up, only the difference at 12 weeks posttreatment was significant (coinciding with the maintenance sessions). Following the termination of the maintenance sessions, the differences in abstinence rates for the smoking cessation only and the maintenance session groups were not statistically significant. The authors concluded that maintenance sessions appear to effectively retard the relapse process, but only during the maintenance period.

Scott, Prue, Denier, and King (1986) provided 19 nurses with a self-help manual that included instructions for fading nicotine use, followed by 3 weeks of BSM training. Daily therapist contact during the 3-week treatment and for 3 months afterward supplemented the manual. A waiting list control group of 10 nurses was also included. At a 1-year follow-up, 13% of the treated subjects were completely abstinent, compared to none in the waiting list group. The highest relapse rate occurred between 3 and 6 months postcessation, coinciding with the reduction in therapist contact from daily to unannounced weekly and monthly meetings.

Davis and Glaros (1986) assigned subjects to either a smoking cessation group treatment (e.g., self-monitoring, nicotine fading, contingency management, stimulus control), the cessation treatment plus relapse prevention, or an enhanced group, which received the cessation treatment and discussed additional problem situations. While there were significant reductions in smoking rate and carbon monoxide levels at the end of treatment for all groups, there were no group differences throughout a 12-month follow-up on any variable. The authors concluded that relapse prevention failed to improve long-term maintenance.

S. M. Hall et al. (1984b) crossed levels of aversive smoking (6 seconds versus 30 seconds) with either a relapse prevention group or a free-form smoking discussion group. Subjects (N =135) were recruited primarily through the media and from physicians. There were no significant differences in abstinence rates between the two aversive-smoking conditions. While the relapse prevention treatment yielded higher abstinence rates throughout much of the 12-month follow-up, this difference was only significant at the sixth

week. Relapse skills training appeared more effective for lighter smokers (< 20 cigarettes/day) at pretreatment. "Abstinent subjects in both groups were more likely to report skill use" (p. 381).

Davis, Faust, and Ordentlich (1984) compared the effectiveness of adding a maintenance component to self-help smoking cessation approaches. Participants (N = 1,237) were recruited from local lung associations. Subjects were assigned to one of four groups: American Lung Association (ALA) quit smoking pamphlets, the ALA pamphlets and a maintenance manual (discussing coping with urge-triggering situations), a behavioral smoking cessation manual, or the cessation manual plus the maintenance manual. The initial smoking cessation rates were quite low; the best outcome (25%) occurred for the ALA leaflets plus maintenance group. By 12 months, the highest abstinence rates were found in the two maintenance manual groups (18% each).

Russell, Epstein, Johnston, Block, and Blair (1988) conceptualized *exercise* as (a) a potential regulator of nicotine withdrawal-associated mood, (b) a means to control weight, (c) an activity incompatible with smoking, and (d) a pharmacological reinforcer (i.e., endorphin release). Their subjects (N = 42 women) received 4 consecutive days of a behavioral smoking cessation treatment and were expected to quit following their first meeting. After this, they were assigned to either nine weekly exercise classes, nine information meetings (e.g., relaxation, stress, exercise, dieting), or an attention control group that met briefly with the therapist to report withdrawal symptoms, and to have their weight and expired carbon monoxide measured. While initial cessation rates were not reported, there were no group differences over 18 months of follow-up. Thus, there appears to be no evidence for the efficacy of physical activity as a relapse prevention strategy.

Brown, Lichtenstein, McIntyre, and Harrington-Kostur (1984) assigned 46 subjects to seven weekly sessions of either nicotine fading with relapse prevention, nicotine fading with group discussion, or relapse prevention alone. Only 52% of the sample were not smoking at the end of treatment, and 12-month abstinent rates ranged from 0 to 19%.

To date, the results of relapse prevention treatments for nicotine dependence have not been very encouraging. Long-term outcome does not appear to be affected by the inclusion of spouse support, analysis of high-risk situations, posttreatment therapeutic contact, or physical activity. Several factors may contribute to the relative ineffectiveness of relapse prevention (e.g., few studies have evaluated whether the skills taught are actually learned; these treatments may be overly complex for clients).

Psychopharmacological Adjuncts to Behavioral Treatments

The development of nicotine agonists such as Nicorette® have led to investigation of the efficacy of combining psychopharmacological and behavioral treatments for nicotine dependence. There is evidence that nicotine replacements are effective in attenuating withdrawal discomfort and enhancing abstinence rates in smokers receiving combined drug and behavioral treatment (U.S. DHHS, 1988). Studies since 1984 continue to provide evidence for the efficacy of combining these treatments. Lando and McGovern (1985) investigated the effectiveness of supplementing nicotine gum with a behavioral self-help manual designed to augment the subjects' behavioral and cognitive coping mechanisms. A control group received a manual that provided information about smoking. Subjects ($N = 34$) were recruited from general practitioners who prescribed the nicotine gum. While the use of nicotine gum was strongly associated with abstinence at follow-up periods up to 6 months, it was unrelated to abstinence thereafter. Only 21% used the gum for the entire study year. One week after commencing nicotine gum use, the behavioral pamphlet and control manual groups reported 42% and 45% abstinence rates, respectively; at 1 year, these rates dropped to 19% and 22%, respectively.

Hjalmarson (1984) treated 206 smokers with a "deconditioning" behavioral intervention and either 2 mg nicotine gum or a gum placebo. Posttreatment abstinence rates were 77% and 52% for the nicotine and placebo gum groups, respectively; 1-year posttreatment rates declined to 29% and 18%, respectively. The group differences were significant. At 3 months posttreatment, 50% of the nicotine gum group were still using the gum, compared to 5% of the placebo gum group. The author concluded that supplementing psycho-

logical treatments for smoking cessation with nicotine gum improved abstinence rates for at least 1 year postcessation. These findings were later replicated in a larger sample ($N = 2,404$; Hjalmarson, 1985).

Hall and Killen (1985) treated 120 smokers with (a) four sessions of nicotine gum, (monitoring of gum use, discussion of plans to quit), (b) eight sessions of aversive smoking/relapse prevention, or (c) the two treatments combined. The combined condition yielded significantly higher abstinence rates following treatment (95% for combined versus 81% for gum only and 78% for the behavioral treatment) and at 1 year posttreatment (44%, 37%, and 28%, respectively).

Hall, Tunstall, Rugg, Jones, and Benowitz (1985) randomly assigned 20 media-recruited subjects to intensive behavioral treatment with nicotine gum, low intensity behavioral treatment with gum, or intensive behavioral treatment alone. The highest abstinence rates (95%) were observed in the high intensity/gum treatment group at 3 weeks posttreatment. However, this rate dropped to 77% by 12 months following treatment. Significant group differences in abstinence rates, which favored the high intensity/gum treatment at 6 months posttreatment, disappeared at 12 months. A similar study by Hall, Tunstall, Ginsberg, Benowitz, and Jones (1987) used 139 media-recruited subjects and found that those who received nicotine gum reported abstinence rates of 44% at 12 months posttreatment compared to 21% in the placebo gum condition. The two behavioral treatment intensity groups did not differ in outcome.

In a study reported by Wilson, Taylor, Gilbert, Best, Lindsay, Wilms, and Singer (1988), physicians were asked to provide the names of patients who smoked "at least one cigarette per day on most days" (p. 1571) and wanted to quit smoking. Interested patients were assigned to one of three conditions: (1) a usual-care group whose participants received the usual care from their physicians, but did not receive any additional intervention, (2) a gum-only group whose participants were offered nicotine gum, and (3) a gum-plus-counseling group whose participants received up to six sessions supporting their decision to quit. The gum-plus-counseling treatment produced significantly higher abstinence rates at 3 months but not at 12 months posttreatment. Despite the low abstinence rate (17%) in the gum-plus-counseling group over the 1-year follow-up, Wilson et al. (1988) concluded that if the intervention was administered by physicians nationwide, a considerable number of individuals would cease smoking.

In summary, while behavioral interventions for nicotine dependence are superior to minimal or no treatment controls, long-term abstinence rates are disappointing. The most promising smoking cessation treatments seem to be those that combine behavioral interventions with a pharmacological adjunct.

CASE ILLUSTRATION

It was intended that each chapter in this book should contain a case illustration reflecting state-of-the-art treatment. This chapter does not contain a case illustration for two reasons. First, while a review of all major psychoactive drugs of abuse (alcohol, nicotine, and other drugs) has some major advantages, a typical case is impossible to present, as interventions for the various drug problems discussed in this chapter are extremely diverse. Second, as noted previously, for some substances (e.g., cocaine), there is no definitive treatment, and for other drugs, the treatment of choice is a function of problem severity. For example, low alcohol dependence would suggest a minimal, short-term intervention with reduced drinking as a possible goal, whereas high dependence on alcohol might require more intensive treatment and no consideration of reduced drinking. Consequently, because a case illustration could neither adequately reflect the current treatments for the major drug classes or differences within a drug class, it was decided that in its stead, critical treatment issues and recommendations would be addressed in some detail for the different substances throughout the chapter.

ALTERNATIVE TREATMENT OPTIONS

Treatment for substance abuse has generally been of two types: pharmacological and nonpharmacological. Typically, the nonpharmacological interventions include family/marital therapy, individual/group psychotherapy, and behavior therapy

(Brown, 1984; Glasgow & Lichtenstein, 1987; Grabowski, Stitzer, & Henningfield, 1984; Hall, 1983; Miller & Hester, 1986). Pharmacotherapies fall into one of three categories[3]: (1) *Deterrent drugs* (e.g., anti-alcohol drugs for alcohol abuse) result in adverse side effects when the drug of abuse is ingested; except for the alcohol sensitizing drugs, there are no reported clinical tests of deterrent drugs for other psychoactive substances. (2) *Replacement or substitution drugs* (e.g., methadone for opiate dependence; nicotine for cigarettes) are generally safer, more manageable, and less addicting than the identified drug of abuse; replacement drugs lessen, but do not eliminate, withdrawal symptoms by providing some form of pharmacological substitution. (3) *Blockage or antagonist drugs* (e.g., naltrexone for opiate dependence; mecamylamine for nicotine dependence; serotonin reuptake inhibitors—zimelidine, citalopram, fluoxetine—for attenuating alcohol intake) are hypothesized to pharmacologically either block (through receptors that mediate reinforcing and toxic effects of the drug) the positive reinforcing effects of the abused substance or suppress the cravings for the drugs; the mechanism by which antagonist drugs work is not yet fully understood.

Pros and Cons

In reviewing the literature on alternative treatment options for substance abuse and comparing them with behavioral interventions, two conclusions repeatedly surfaced. The first is that *regardless of the substance abused, nondrug and drug treatments with demonstrated enduring effectiveness do not exist.* The following statements support this conclusion:

- "Despite the fact that many different responses exist within and between different substances, there is one common theme which emerges in treatment outcome evaluation: there is little evidence which demonstrates the effectiveness of one treatment over another" (Allsop & Saunders, 1986, p. 202).

---

[3]For purposes of this chapter, pharmacotherapy does not include drugs used to treat withdrawal symptoms.

- "There is no scientific evidence supporting the efficacy of any of the alcohol-sensitizing drugs" (Naranjo, 1988, p. 96).
- "Clinically, we are nowhere near a clear answer concerning the effectiveness of various psychosocial interventions in methadone treatment" (Hall, 1983, p. 616).
- "In sum, there appears reason to question the effectiveness of traditional treatment forms with nonopiate clients, although a definitive judgment is not possible at this time" (Brown, 1984, p. 297).
- "There is no definitive knowledge available for cocaine abuse treatment" (Kleber & Gawin, 1987, p. 132).
- "Preliminary data on pharmcologic treatments [for cocaine] are beginning to appear, and pharmacologic adjuncts may show promise in the future" (Kleber & Gawin, 1984, p. 22).
- "The discouraging message of the immense group of alcoholism treatment outcome studies is that there does not seem to be strong evidence for the effectiveness of any treatment type(s), but even more discouraging is that, among the studies that have demonstrated treatment effects, there is little evidence that such effects are maintained for any appreciable time" (Maisto & Carey, 1987, p. 174).
- "In the past 20 years, over 25,000 articles on smoking have been written, and a myriad of treatment approaches have been tried. Nevertheless, the large majority of smokers who attempt to quit have little long-term success, regardless of how they try to stop" (Colletti, Payne, & Rizzo, 1987, p. 243).
- "Treatments for alcohol problems with demonstrated enduring effectiveness do not exist, regardless of treatment orientations or treatment goals" (Riley et al., 1987, p. 107).
- "At this time, no *one* theory of relapse or model of maintenance training appears superior to others" (Glasgow & Lichtenstein, 1987, p. 297; emphasis in original).

- "The usefulness of all the current drugs, however, appears limited, and the ideal drug for use in treating alcoholism awaits discovery" (Sinclair, 1987, p. 1213).

Although optimal treatments for substance abuse presently do not exist, it would be unfair to conclude that no progress has been made over the past several decades. In most studies, some proportion of substance abusers do improve. Still, marked differences in efficacy between treatment approaches have not been convincingly demonstrated.

The second striking finding that emerged from a comparison of behavioral and nonbehavioral interventions is that *combined treatment elements, especially pharmacological and behavioral interventions, show considerable promise in the treatment of substance abuse.* Support for this conclusion is reflected in the following statements:

- "Currently, however, it appears no more likely that any single treatment will arise as a definitive treatment for all cocaine abusers than has occurred for opiate abusers. More likely, pharmacological approaches will become important adjuncts to psychological and life-style changing therapies" (Kleber & Gawin, 1987, p. 133).
- Several investigators (Glasgow & Lichtenstein, 1987; Grabowski et al., 1984; U.S. DHHS, 1988) agree with Shiffman (1986) that "the best current treatments for smoking combine pharmacotherapy and behavioral interventions" (p.203).
- "Nationwide process data from naltrexone clinics at that time showed that the clients receiving this combination of behavioral therapy and naltrexone stayed in treatment significantly longer than clients in any other naltrexone clinic in the country" (Callahan et al., 1987; p. 291).
- In a clinical trial evaluating the contribution that psychotherapy might offer to opiate addicts receiving methadone maintenance, it was concluded that psychotherapy would not have been possible without methadone to stabilize the patients (Woody et al., 1987).

- In a recent review of serotonin reuptake inhibitors (i.e., drugs that have been shown to consistently attenuate ethanol consumption with low dependence problem drinkers), it was asserted that "On average, the magnitude of response to these drugs is relatively modest, but the drugs were not offered in conjunction with other psychosocial interventions which would maximize the effect" (Naranjo & Sellers, 1988; p. 111).

Summary

Studies evaluating pharmacotherapy in combination with psychological interventions appear promising in the treatment of substance abuse. Recognition of the potential of new pharmacological agents as adjuncts to psychological interventions has begun (e.g., Callahan et al., 1987; Meyer & Kranzler, 1988; Naranjo & Sellers, 1988; U.S. DHHS, 1988). Interestingly, the fact that combined biological and environmental interventions may be more effective than either modality alone parallels the emerging recognition that both biological and environmental variables appear to contribute to the development of substance abuse problems (Callahan et al., 1987; Colletti et al., 1987; Shiffman, 1986; Sigvardsson et al., 1985; Sobell & Sobell, 1987a).

The results of the studies reviewed in this chapter suggest that we should not view drug and nondrug treatments as competitive, but rather as collaborative ventures. One important area that could possibly benefit from such collaboration is the development of treatments aimed at long-term maintenance of cessation of substance abuse problems. In this regard, one possibility is to pair a pharmacological intervention designed to attenuate or eliminate substance abuse with a behavioral intervention that instills effective methods of dealing with potential and real relapse situations.

REFERENCES

Alden, L. (1988). Behavioral self-management controlled drinking strategies in a context of secondary prevention. *Journal of Consulting and Clinical Psychology, 56,* 280–286.

Allsop, S. J., & Saunders, W. M. (1986). Commonalities in the addictive behaviors. In G. Edwards (Ed.), *Current issues in clinical psychology* (Vol. 4, pp. 197–209). New York: Plenum.

American Psychiatric Association. (1968). *Diagnostic and statistical manual of mental disorders* (2nd ed.). Washington, DC: Author.

American Psychiatric Association. (1980). *Diagnostic and statistical manual of mental disorders* (3rd ed.). Washington, DC, Author.

American Psychiatric Association. (1987). *Diagnostic and statistical manual of mental disorders* (3rd ed., rev.). Washington, DC: Author.

Annis, H. M. (1986). Is inpatient rehabilitation of the alcoholic cost effective? Con position. *Advances in Alcohol and Substance Abuse, 5,*175–190.

Antti-Poika, I., Karaharju, E., Roine, R., & Salaspuro, M. (1988). Intervention of heavy drinking—A prospective and controlled study of 438 consecutive injured male patients. *Alcohol & Alcoholism, 23,* 115–121.

Armor, D. M., Polich, J. M., & Stambul, H. B. (1978). *Alcoholism and treatment.* New York: Wiley.

Baker, T. B. (Ed.). (1988). Models of addiction [Special issue]. *Journal of Abnormal Psychology, 97* (2).

Bandura, A. (1986). *Social foundations of thought and action: A social cognitive theory.* Englewood Cliffs, NJ: Prentice-Hall.

Battjes, R. J. (1988). Smoking as an issue in alcohol and drug abuse treatment. *Addictive Behaviors, 13,* 225–230.

Beck, A. T. (1976). *Cognitive therapy and the emotional disorders.* New York: International Universities Press.

Benowitz, N. L., Hall, S. M., Herning, R. I., Jacob, P., III, Jones, R. T., & Osman, A. L. (1983). Smokers of low-yield cigarettes do not consume less nicotine. *New England Journal of Medicine, 309,* 134–142.

Blane, H. T., & Leonard, K. E. (Eds.) (1987). *Psychological theories of drinking and alcoholism.* New York: Guilford.

Bobo, J. K., & Gilchrist, L. D. (1983). Urging the alcoholic client to quit smoking cigarettes. *Addictive Behaviors, 8,* 297–305.

Bobo, J. K., Gilchrist, L. D., Schilling, R. F., Noach, B., & Schinke, S. P. (1987). Cigarette smoking cessation attempts by recovering alcoholics. *Addictive Behaviors, 12,* 209–215.

Booth, P., G., Dale, B., & Ansari, J. (1984). Problem drinkers' goal choice and treatment outcome: A preliminary study. *Addictive Behaviors, 9,*357–364.

Brandon, Y. H., Zelman, D. C., & Baker, T. B. (1987). Effects of maintenance sessions on smoking relapse: Delaying the inevitable? *Journal of Consulting and Clinical Psychology, 55,* 780–782.

Brown, B. S. (1984). Treatment of nonopiate dependency. In R. G. Smart, H. D. Cappell, F. B. Glaser, Y. Israel, H. Kalant, W. Schmidt, & E. M. Sellers (Eds.), *Research advances in alcohol and drug problems* (Vol. 8, pp. 291–308). New York: Plenum.

Brown, R. A., Lichtenstein, E., McIntyre, K. O., & Harrington–Kostur, J. (1984). Effects of nicotine fading and relapse prevention on smoking cessation. *Journal of Consulting and Clinical Psychology, 52,* 307–308.

Burling, T. A., & Ziff, D. C. (1988). Tobacco smoking: A comparison between alcohol and drug inpatients. *Addictive Behaviors, 13,* 185–190.

Byrne, D. G., & White, H. M. (1987). The efficacy of community-based smoking cessation strategies: A long term follow-up study. *International Journal of the Addictions, 22,* 791–801.

Cahalan, D. (1970). *Problem drinkers: A national survey.* San Francisco: Jossey-Bass.

Callahan, E. J., Dahlkoetter, J., & Price, K. (1980). Drug abuse. In R. G. Daitzman (Ed.), *Clinical behavior therapy and behavior modification* (pp. 175–248). New York: Garland Press.

Callahan, E. J., Long, M. A., Pecsok, E. H., & Simone, S. (1987). Opiate addiction. In T. D. Nirenberg & S. A. Maisto (Eds.), *Development in the assessment and treatment of addictive behaviors* (pp. 277–302). Norwood, NJ: Ablex.

Callahan, E. J., & Pecsok, E. H. (1988). Heroin addiction. In D. M. Donovan & G. A. Marlatt (Eds.), *Assessment of addictive behaviors* (pp. 340–420). New York: Guilford.

Cannon, D. S., Baker, T. B., Gino, A., & Nathan, P. E. (1986). Alcohol-aversion therapy: Relation between strength of aversion and abstinence. *Journal of Consulting and Clinical Psychology, 54,* 825–830.

Carey, K. B., & Maisto, S. A. (1985). A review of the use of self-control techniques in the treatment of alcohol abuse. *Cognitive Therapy and Research, 9,* 235–251.

Carmody, T. P., Brischetto, C. S., Pierce, D. K., Matarazzo, J., & Connor, W. E. (1986). A prospective five-year follow-up of smokers who quit on their own. *Health Education Research: Theory and Practice, 1,* 101–109.

Chapman, P. L. H., & Huygens, I. (1988). An evaluation of three treatment programmes for alcoholism: An experimental study with 6- and 18-month follow-ups. *British Journal of Addiction, 83,* 67–81.

Chaudron, C. D., & Wilkinson, D. A. (Eds.). (1988). *Theories on alcoholism.* Toronto: Addiction Research Foundation.

Chick, J., Ritson, B., Connaughton, J., Stewart, A., & Chick, J. (1988). Advice versus extended treatment for alcoholism: A controlled study. *British Journal of Addiction, 83,* 159–170.

Childress, A., Ehrman, R., McLellan, A. T., & O'Brien, C. P. (1987). Conditioned craving and arousal in cocaine addiction: A preliminary report. In L. S. Harris (Ed.), *Problems of drug dependence* (Research Monograph No. 81, pp. 74–80). Rockville, MD: National Institute on Drug Abuse.

Childress, A. R., McLellan, A. T., & O'Brien, C. P. (1985). Behavioral therapies for substance abuse. *International Journal of the Addictions, 20,* 947–969.

Childress, A. R., McLellan, A. T., & O'Brien, C. P. (1986). Abstinent opiate abusers exhibit conditioned craving, conditioned withdrawal and reductions in both through extinction. *British Journal of Addiction, 81,* 655–660.

Colletti, G., Payne, T. J., & Rizzo, A. A. (1987). Treatment of cigarette smoking. In T. D. Nirenberg & S. A. Maisto (Eds.), *Development in the assessment and treatment of addictive behaviors* (pp. 243–276). Norwood, NJ: Ablex.

Crowley, T. J. (1984). Contingency contracting treatment of drug-abusing physicians, nurses, and dentists. In J. Grabowski, M. L. Stitzer, & J. E. Henningfield (Eds.), *Behavioral intervention techniques in drug abuse treatment* (NIDA Research Monograph 46, pp. 68–83). Rockville, MD: National Institute on Drug Abuse.

Davidson, R. (1987). Assessment of the alcohol dependence syndrome: A review of self-report screening questionnaires. *British Psychological Society, 26,* 243–255.

Davis, A. L., Faust, R., & Ordentlich, M. (1984). Self-help smoking cessation and maintenance programs: A comparative study with 12-month follow-up by the American Lung Association. *American Journal of Public Health, 74,* 1212–1217.

Davis, J. R., & Glaros, A. G. (1986). Relapse prevention and smoking cessation. *Addictive Behaviors, 11,* 105–114.

DiClemente, C., & Prochaska, J. (1982). Self-change and therapy change of smoking behavior: A comparison of processes of change and cessation and maintenance. *Addictive Behaviors, 7,* 133–142.

Dolan, M. P., Black, J. L., Penk, W. E., Robinowitz, R., & DeFord, H. A. (1985). Contracting for treatment termination to reduce illicit drug use among methadone maintenance treatment failures. *Journal of Consulting and Clinical Psychology, 53*, 549–551.

Dole, V. P., & Nyswander, M. E. (1967). Heroin addiction: A metabolic disease. *Archives of Internal Medicine, 120*, 19–24.

Duckert, F., & Johnsen, J. (1987). Behavioral use of disulfiram in the treatment of problem drinking. *International Journal of the Addictions, 22*, 445–454.

Edwards, G., Arif, A., & Hodgson, R. (1981). Nomenclature and classification of drug- and alcohol-related problems: A WHO memorandum. *Bulletin of the World Health Organization, 59*, 225–242.

Edwards, G., Gross, M. M., Keller, M., & Moser, J. (Eds.). (1976). Alcohol-related problems in the disability perspective. *Journal of Studies on Alcohol, 37*, 1360–1382.

Edwards, G., Gross, M., Keller, M., Moser, J., & Room, R. (Eds.). (1977). *Alcohol-related Disabilities* (WHO Offset Publication No. 32). Geneva: World Health Organization.

Elal-Lawrence, G., Slade, P. D., & Dewey, M. E. (1986). Predictors of outcome type in treated problem drinkers. *Journal of Studies on Alcohol, 47*, 41–47.

Elal-Lawrence, G., Slade, P. D., & Dewey, M. E. (1987). Treatment and follow-up variables discriminating abstainers, controlled drinkers, and relapsers. *Journal of Studies on Alcohol, 48*, 39–46.

Emrick, C. D. (1974). A review of psychologically oriented treatment of alcoholism: I. The use and interrelationships of outcome criteria and drinking behavior following treatment. *Quarterly Journal of Studies on Alcohol, 35*, 523–549.

Emrick, C. D. (1975). A review of psychologically oriented treatment of alcoholism: II. The relative effectiveness of different treatment approaches and the effectiveness of treatment versus no treatment. *Quarterly Journal of Studies on Alcohol, 36*, 88–108.

Eriksen, L., Björnstad, S., & Götestam, K. G. (1986). Social skills training in groups for alcoholics: One-year treatment outcome for groups and individuals. *Addictive Behaviors, 11*, 309–329.

Etringer, B. D., Gregory, V. R., & Lando, H. A. (1984). Influence of group cohesion on the behavioral treatment of smoking. *Journal of Consulting and Clinical Psychology, 52*, 1080–1086.

Ewing, J. A. (1984). Electric aversion and individualized imagery therapy in alcoholism: A controlled experiment. *Alcohol, 1*, 101–104.

Ferrence, R. G. (1988). Sex differences in cigarette smoking in Canada, 1900–1978: A reconstructed cohort study. *Canadian Journal of Public Health, 79*, 160–165.

Fillmore, K. M., (1988a). *Alcohol use across the life course: A critical review of 70 years of international longitudinal research.* Toronto, Ontario: Addiction Research Foundation.

Fillmore, K. M. (1988b, February). *Spontaneous remission of alcohol problems.* Presented at the National Conference on Evaluating Recovery Outcomes, San Diego, CA.

Fink, E. B., Longabaugh, R., McCrady, B. M., Stout, R. L., Beattie, M., Ruggieri-Authelet, A., & McNeil, D. (1985). Effectiveness of alcoholism treatment in partial versus inpatient settings: Twenty-four month outcomes. *Addictive Behaviors, 10*, 235–248.

Finn, P. R., & Pihl, R. O. (1987). Men at risk for alcoholism: The effect of alcohol on cardiovascular response to unavoidable shock. *Journal of Abnormal Psychology, 96*, 230–236.

Foy, D. W., Nunn, L. B., & Rychtarik, R. G. (1984). Broad-spectrum behavioral treatment for chronic alcoholics: Effects on training in controlled drinking skills. *Journal of Consulting and Clinical Psychology, 52*, 218–230.

Glasgow, R. E., Klesges, R. C., Klesges, L. M., Vasey, M. W., & Gunnarson, D. F. (1985). Long-term effects of a controlled smoking program: A 2.5 year follow-up. *Behavior Therapy, 16*, 303–307.

Glasgow, R. E., & Lichtenstein, E. (1987). Long-term effects of behavioral smoking cessation intervention. *Behavior Therapy, 18*, 297–324.

Graber, R. A., & Miller, W. R. (1988). Abstinence or controlled drinking goals for problem drinkers: A randomized clinical trial. *Psychology of Addictive Behaviors, 2*, 20–33.

Grabowski, J. (1986). Acquisition, maintenance, cessation, and reacquisition: An overview and behavioral perspective of relapse to tobacco use. In F. M. Tims & C. G. Leukefeld (Eds.), *Relapse and recovery in drug abuse* (Research Monograph No. 72, pp. 36–48). Rockville, MD: National Institute on Drug Abuse.

Grabowski, J., Stitzer, M. L., & Henningfield, J. E. (1984). Therapeutic application of behavioral techniques: An overview. In J. Grabowski, M. L. Stitzer, & J. E. Henningfield (Eds.), *Behavioral intervention techniques in drug abuse treatment* (Research Monograph No. 46, pp. 1–7). Rockville, MD: National Institute on Drug Abuse.

Grande, T. P., Wolf, A. W., Schubert, D. S. P., Patterson, M. B., & Brocco, K. (1984). Association among alcoholism, drug abuse, and antisocial personality: A review of literature. *Psychological Reports, 55,* 455–474.

Green, J., Jaffe, J. H., Carlisi, J. A., & Zaks, A. (1978). Alcohol use in the opiate use cycle of the heroin addict. *International Journal of the Addictions, 13,* 1021–1033.

Griffiths, R. R., & Woodson, P. P. (1988). Caffeine physical dependence: A review of human and laboratory animal studies. *Psychopharmacology, 94,* 437–451.

Gritz, E. R. (1986). Overview: Smoking behavior and tobacco dependence. In J. K. Ockene (Ed.), *The pharmacologic treatment of tobacco dependence: Proceedings of the World Congress* (November, 1985, pp. 12–18). Cambridge, MA: Institute for the Study of Smoking Behavior and Policy.

Hall, R. G., Sachs, D. P. L., & Hall, S. M. (1979). Medical risk and therapeutic effectiveness of rapid smoking. *Behavior Therapy, 10,* 249–259.

Hall, R. G., Sachs, D. P. L., Hall, S. M., & Benowitz, N. L. (1984a). Two-year efficacy and safety of rapid smoking therapy in patients with cardiac and pulmonary disease. *Journal of Consulting and Clinical Psychology, 52,* 574–581.

Hall, S. M. (1983). Methadone treatment: A review of the research findings. In J. R. Cooper, F. Altman, B. S. Brown, & D. Czechowicz (Eds.), *Research on the treatment of narcotic addiction: State of the art.* (Treatment Research Monograph Series, pp. 575–632). Rockville, MD: National Institute on Drug Abuse.

Hall, S. M., & Killen, J. D. (1985). Psychological and pharmacological approaches to smoking relapse prevention. In J. Grabowski & S. M. Hall (Eds.), *Pharmacological adjuncts in smoking cessation* (Research Monograph No. 53, pp. 131–143). Rockville, MD: National Institute on Drug Abuse.

Hall, S. M., Rugg, D., Tunstall, C., & Jones, R. T. (1984b). Preventing relapse to cigarette smoking by behavioral skill training. *Journal of Consulting and Clinical Psychology, 52,* 372–382.

Hall, S. M., Tunstall, C. D., Ginsberg, D., Benowitz, N. L., & Jones, R. T. (1987). Nicotine gum and behavioral treatment: A placebo controlled trial *Journal of Consulting and Clinical Psychology, 55,* 603–605.

Hall, S. M., Tunstall, C. D., Rugg, D., Jones, R. T., & Benowitz, N. L. (1985). Nicotine gum and behavioral treatment in smoking cessation. *Journal of Consulting and Clinical Psychology, 53,* 256–258.

Harris, J. E. (1983). Cigarette smoking among successive birth cohorts of men and women in the United States during 1900–1980. *Journal of the National Cancer Institute, 71,* 473–479.

Heather, N., & Robertson, I. (1983). *Controlled drinking* (2nd ed.). New York: Methuen

Heather, N., Robertson, I., MacPherson, B., Allsop, S., & Fulton, A. (1987). Effectiveness of a controlled drinking self-help manual: One-year follow-up results. *British Journal of Clinical Psychology, 26,* 279–287.

Heather, N., Whitton, B., & Robertson, I. (1986). Evaluation of a self-help manual for media-recruited problem drinkers: Six month follow-up results. *British Journal of Clinical Psychology, 25,* 19–34.

Henningfield, J. E. (1984). Behavioral pharmacology of cigarette smoking. In T. Thompson, P. B. Dews, & J. E. Barrett (Eds.), *Advances in behavioral pharmacology* (Vol. 4, pp. 131–210). Orlando: Academic Press.

Higgitt, A., Golombok, S., Fonagy, P., & Lader, M. (1987). Group treatment of benzodiazepine dependence. *British Journal of Addiction, 82,* 517–532.

Hill, R. D. (1988). Prescribing aversive relapse to enhance nonsmoking treatment gains: A pilot study. *Behavior Therapy, 19,* 35–43.

Hjalmarson, A. I. M. (1984). Effect of nicotine chewing gum in smoking cessation. *Journal of the American Medical Association, 252,* 2835–2838.

Hjalmarson, A. I. M. (1985). Effects of nicotine chewing gum on smoking cessation in routine clinical use. *British Journal of Addiction, 80,* 321–324.

Hunt, W. A., Barnett, L. W., & Branch, L. G. (1971). Relapse rates in addiction programs. *Journal of Clinical Psychology, 27,* 455–456.

Iguchi, M., Stitzer, M., Bigelow, G., & Liebson, I. (1987). Contingency management with a polydrug-abuse methadone maintenance population: Take-home and dose incentives. In L. S. Harris (Ed.), *Problems of drug dependence* (Research Monograph No. 81, p. 298) Rockville, MD: National Institute on Drug Abuse.

Istvan, J., & Matarazzo, J. D. (1984). Tobacco, alcohol and caffeine use: A review of their interrelationships. *Psychological Bulletin, 95,* 301–326.

Kaufman, E. (1982). The relationship of alcoholism and alcohol abuse to the abuse of other drugs. *American Journal of Drug and Alcohol Abuse, 9,* 1–17.

Klatsky, A. L., Friedman, G. D., & Siegelaub, A. B. (1981). Alcohol and mortality: A ten-year Kaiser-Permanente experience. *Annals of Internal Medicine, 95,* 139–145.

Kleber, H. D., & Gawin, F. H. (1984). The spectrum of cocaine abuse and its treatment. *Journal of Clinical Psychiatry, 45*, 18–23.

Kleber, H. D., & Gawin, F. H. (1987). Pharmacological treatments of cocaine abuse. In A. W. Washton & M. S. Gold (Eds.), *Cocaine: A clinician's handbook* (pp. 118–134). New York: Guilford.

Kozlowski, L. T. (1981). Tar and nicotine delivery of cigarettes: What a difference a puff makes. *Journal of the American Medical Association, 245*, 158–159.

Kozlowski, L. T. (1984). Pharmacological approaches to smoking modification. In J. D. Matarazzo, S. M. Weiss, J. A. Herd, N. E. Miller, & S. M. Weiss (Eds.), *Behavioral health: A handbook of health enhancement and disease prevention* (pp. 713–728). New York: Wiley.

Kozlowski, L. T., Jelinek, L. C., & Pope, M. A. (1986). Cigarette smoking among alcohol abusers: Continuing and neglected problem. *Canadian Journal of Public Health, 77*, 205–207.

Kozlowski, L. T., Skinner, W., Kent, C., & Pope, M. (1989). Prospects for smoking treatment in individuals seeking treatment for alcohol and other drug problems. *Addictive Behaviors, 14*, 273–279.

Krasnegor, N. A., & Renault, P. F. (1979). *Technical review on cigarette smoking as an addiction* (Final Report). Rockville, MD: National Institute on Drug Abuse.

Lando, H. A., & Mcgovern, P. G. (1985). Nicotine fading as a nonaversive alternative in a broad-spectrum treatment for eliminating smoking. *Addictive Behaviors, 10*, 153–161.

Lester, D. (1988). Genetic theory: An assessment of the heritability of alcoholism. In C. D. Chaudron & D. A. Wilkinson (Eds.), *Theories on alcoholism* (pp. 1–28). Toronto: Addiction Research Foundation.

Maddux, J. F., & Desmond, D. P. (1986). Relapse and recovery in substance abuse careers. In F. M. Tims & C. G. Leukefeld (Eds.), *Relapse and recovery in drug abuse* (Research Monograph No. 72, pp. 49–71). Rockville, MD: National Institute on Drug Abuse.

Magura, S., Casriel, C., Goldsmith, D. S., Strug, D.L., & Lipton, D. S. (1988). Contingency contracting with polydrug-abusing methadone patients. *Addictive Behaviors, 13*, 113–118.

Maisto, S. A., & Carey, K. B. (1987). Treatment of alcohol abuse. In T. D. Nirenberg & S. A. Maisto (Eds.), *Development in the assessment and treatment of addictive behaviors* (pp. 173–211). Norwood, NJ: Ablex.

Mangan, G. L., & Golding, J. F. (1984). *The psy-chopharmacology of smoking*. New York: Cambridge University Press.

Marlatt, G. A. (1983). The controlled drinking controversy: A commentary. *American Psychologist, 38*, 1097–1110.

Marlatt, G. A., & Gordon, J. R. (Eds.), (1985). *Relapse prevention*. New York: Guilford.

McCarthy, J. J., & Borders, O. T. (1985). Limit setting on drug abuse in methadone maintenance patients. *American Journal of Psychiatry, 142*, 1419–1423.

McCaul, M. E., Stitzer, M. L., Bigelow, G. E., & Liebson, I. A. (1984). Contingency management interventions: Effects on treatment outcome during methadone detoxification. *Journal of Applied Behavior Analysis, 17*, 35–43.

McClearn, G. E. (1983). Commonalities in substance abuse: A genetic perspective. In P. K. Levison, D. R. Gerstein, & D. R. Maloff (Eds.), *Commonalities in substance abuse and habitual behavior* (pp. 323–341). Lexington, MA: Lexington Books.

McIntyre-Kingsolver, K., Lichtenstein, E., & Mermelstein, R. J. (1986). Spouse training in a multicomponent smoking-cessation program. *Behavior Therapy, 17*, 67–74.

McLellan, A. T., Childress, A. R., Ehrman, R., & O'Brien, C. P. (1986). Extinguishing conditioned responses during opiate dependence treatment: Turning laboratory findings into clinical procedures. *Journal of Substance Abuse Treatment, 3*, 33–40.

McLellan, A. T., Woody, G., Luborsky, L., O'Brien, C., & Druley, K. (1983). Increased effectiveness of substance abuse treatment: A prospective study of patient–treatment "matching." *Journal of Nervous and Mental Disease, 171*, 597–605.

Mermelstein, R., Cohen, S., Lichtenstein, E., Baer, J. S., & Kamarck, T. (1986). Social support and smoking cessation and maintenance. *Journal of Consulting and Clinical Psychology, 54*, 447–453.

Meyer, R. E., & Kranzler, H. R. (1988). Alcoholism: Clinical implications of recent research. *Journal of Clinical Psychiatry, 49*, 8–12.

Miller, W. R., & Hester, R. K. (1986). The effectiveness of alcoholism treatment: What research reveals. In W. R. Miller & N. Heather (Eds.), *Treating addictive behaviors: Processes of change.* (pp. 121–174). New York: Plenum.

Motherskill, K. J., McDowell, I., & Rosser, W. (1988). Subject characteristics and long term post-programming smoking cessation. *Addictive Behaviors, 13*, 29–36.

Murray, A. L., & Lawrence, P. S. (1984). Sequelae to

smoking cessation. A review. *Clinical Psychology Review, 4,* 143–157.

Murray, R. M., Clifford, C., Gurling, H. M. D., Topham, A., Clow, A., & Bernadt, M. (1983). Current genetic and biological approaches to alcoholism. *Psychiatric Developments, 2,* 179–192.

Naranjo, C. A. (1988). Current trends in the pharamcological treatment of alcohol-related problems. *Australian Drug and Alcohol Review, 7,* 93–98.

Naranjo, C. A., & Sellers, E. M. (1988). Serotonin uptake inhibitors attenuate ethanol intake in humans. *Australian Drug and Alcohol Review, 7,* 109–112.

National Institute on Alcohol Abuse and Alcoholism. (1987). *Sixth Special Report to the U.S. Congress on Alcohol and Health from the Secretary of Health and Human Services,* January 1987. (DHEW Publication No. ADM 87–1519). Washington, DC: U.S. Government Printing Office.

Nicki, R. M., Remington, R. E., & MacDonald, G. A. (1984). Self-efficacy, nicotine-fading/self-monitoring and cigarette-smoking behavior. *Behavior Research and Therapy, 22,* 477–485.

Ockene, J. K. (1984). Toward a smoke free society (Editorial). *American Journal of Public Health, 74,* 1198–1200.

Orford, J., & Keddie, A. (1986a). Abstinence or controlled drinking in clinical practice: A test of the dependence and persuasion hypotheses. *British Journal of Addiction, 81,* 495–504.

Orford, J., & Keddie, A. (1986b). Abstinence or controlled drinking in clinical practice: Indications at initial assessment. *Addictive Behaviors, 11,* 71–86.

Pattison, E. M., Sobell, M. B., & Sobell, L. C. (Authors/Eds.). (1977). *Emerging concepts of alcohol dependence.* New York: Springer.

Peachey, J. E. (1986). The role of drugs in the treatment of opioid addicts. *Medical Journal of Australia, 145,* 395–399.

Peele, S. (1986). The implications and limitations of genetic models of alcoholism and other addictions. *Journal of Studies on Alcohol, 47,* 63–73.

Platt, J. J. (1986). *Heroin addiction: Theory, research, and treatment.* Florida: Krieger.

Powell, B. J., Penick, E. C., Read, M. S. W., & Ludwig, M. D. (1985). Comparison of three outpatient treatment interventions: A twelve-month follow-up of men alcoholics. *Journal of Studies on Alcohol, 46,* 309–312.

Raw, M., & Russell, M. A. H. (1980). Rapid smoking, cue exposure and support in the modification of smoking. *Behaviour Research and Therapy, 18,* 363–372.

Remington, P. L., Forman, M. R., Gentry, E. M., Marks, J. S., Hogelin, G. C., & Trowbridge, F. L. (1985). Current smoking trends in the United States: The 1981–1983 behavioral risk factor surveys. *Journal of the American Medical Association, 253,* 2975–2978.

Riley, D. M., Sobell, L. C., Leo, G. I., Sobell, M. B., & Klajner, F. (1987). Behavioral treatment of alcohol problems: A review and a comparison of behavioral and nonbehavioral studies. In M. Cox (Ed.), *Treatment and prevention of alcohol problems: A resource manual* (pp. 73–115). New York: Academic.

Robertson, I., Heather, N., Dzialdowski, A., Crawford, J., & Winton, M. (1986). A comparison of minimal versus intensive controlled drinking treatment interventions for problem drinkers. *British Journal of Clinical Psychology, 25,* 185–194.

Roffman, R. A., Stephens, R. S., Simpson, E. E., & Whitaker, D. L. (1988). Treatment of marijuana dependence. *Journal of Psychoactive Drugs, 20,* 129–137.

Roizen, R. (1977). *Barriers to alcoholism treatment.* Berkeley, CA: Alcohol Research Group.

Room, R. (1977). Measurement and distribution of drinking patterns and problems in general populations. In G. Edwards, M. M. Gross, M. Keller, J. Moser, & R. Room (Eds.), *Alcohol-related disabilities* (pp. 61–87). Geneva: World Health Organization.

Rounsaville, B. J. (1986). Clinical implications of relapse research. In F. M. Tims & C. G. Leukefeld (Eds.), *Relapse and recovery in drug abuse* (Research Monograph No. 72, pp. 172–184). Rockville, MD: National Institute on Drug Abuse.

Rounsaville, B. J., Kosten, T. R., Williams, J. B. W., & Spitzer, R. L. (1987). A field trial of DSM-III-R psychoactive substance dependence disorders. *American Journal of Psychiatry, 144,* 351–355.

Rounsaville, B. J., Tierney, T., Crits-Christoph, K., Weissman, M. M., & Kleber, H. D. (1982a). Predictors of outcome in treatment of opiate addicts: Evidence for the multidimensional nature of addicts' problems. *Comprehensive Psychiatry, 23,* 462–478.

Rounsaville, B. J., Weissman, M. M., Crits-Christoph, K., Wilber, C., & Kleber, H. D. (1982b). Diagnosis and symptoms of depression in opiate addicts. *Archives of General Psychiatry, 39,* 151–156.

Russell, M. A. H. (1976). Tobacco smoking and nicotine dependence. In R. J. Gibbons, Y. Israel, H. Kalant, R. E. Popham, W. Schmidt, & R. Smart (Eds.), *Research advances in alcohol and drug problems* (pp. 1–46). New York: Wiley.

Russell, P. O., Epstein, L. H., Johnston, J. J., Block, D. R., & Blair, E. (1988). The effects of physical activity as maintenance for smoking cessation. *Addictive Behaviors, 13,* 215–218.

Rychtarik, R. G., Foy, D. W., Scott, T., Lokey, L., & Prue, D. M. (1987). Five–six-year follow-up of broad spectrum behavioral treatment for alcoholism: Effects of training controlled drinking skills. *Journal of Consulting and Clinical Psychology, 55,* 106–108.

Salber, E. J., & Abeline, T. (1967). Smoking behavior of Newton school children: Five year follow-up. *Pediatrics, 40* (Part 1), 363–372.

Sanchez-Craig, M., Annis, H. M., Bornet, A. R., & MacDonald, K. R. (1984). Random assignment to abstinence and controlled drinking: Evaluation of a cognitive-behavioral program for problem drinkers. *Journal of Consulting and Clinical Psychology, 52,* 390–403.

Sanchez-Craig, M., Cappell, H., Busto, U., & Kay, G. (1987). Cognitive-behavioral treatment for benzodiazepine dependence: A comparison of gradual versus abrupt cessation of drug intake. *British Journal of Addiction, 82,* 1317–1327.

Sanchez-Craig, M., & Lei, H. (1986). Disadvantages to imposing the goal of abstinence on problem drinkers: An empirical study. *British Journal of Addiction, 81,* 505–512.

Sannibale, C. (1988). The differential effect of a set of brief interventions on the functioning of a group of "early-stage" problem drinkers. *Australian Drug and Alcohol Review, 7,* 147–155.

Schwartz, B., Lauderdale, R. M., Montgomery, M. L., Burch, E. A., & Gallant, D. M. (1987). Immediate versus delayed feedback on urinalyses reports for methadone maintenance patients. *Addictive Behaviors, 12,* 293–295.

Schwartz, J. L. (1987). *Review and evaluation of smoking cessation methods: The United States and Canada, 1978–1985.* NIH Publication No. 87-2940). Washington, DC: U.S. Government Printing Office.

Scott, R. R., Prue, D. M., Denier, C. A., & King, A. C. (1986). Worksite smoking intervention with nursing professionals: Long-term outcome and relapse assessment. *Journal of Consulting and Clinical Psychology, 54,* 809–813.

Searles, J. S. (1988). The role of genetics in the pathogenesis of alcoholism. *Journal of Abnormal Psychology, 97,* 153–167.

Shiffman, S. (1986). Overview: Integrating pharmacologic and behavioral approaches to smoking cessation. In J. K. Ockene (Ed.), *The pharmacologic treatment of tobacco dependence: Proceedings of the World Congress* (November, 1985, pp. 196–204). Cambridge, MA: Institute for the Study of Smoking Behavior and Policy.

Sigvardsson, S., Cloninger, C. R., & Bohman, M. (1985). Prevention and treatment of alcohol abuse: Uses and limitations of the high risk paradigm. *Social Biology, 32,* 185–194.

Sinclair, J. D. (1987). The feasibility of effective psychopharmacological treatments for alcoholism. *British Journal of Addiction, 82,* 1213–1223.

Singh, N. N., & Leung, J. (1988). Smoking cessation through cigarette-fading, self-recording, and contracting: Treatment, maintenance and long-term follow-up. *Addictive Behaviors, 13,* 101–105.

Skutle, A., & Berg, G. (1987). Training in controlled drinking for early-stage problem drinkers. *British Journal of Addiction, 82,* 493–501.

Slade, J. (1987). Tobacco dependence as a recognized medical condition by tobacco company's health insurer. *Medical Information, 2.10* (TPLR), 5.121.

Sobell, L. C., Sobell, M. B., Kozlowski, L., & Toneatto, T. (in press). Alcohol or tobacco research versus alcohol and tobacco research. *British Journal of Addiction.*

Sobell, L. C., Sobell, M. B., & Nirenberg, T. D. (1988). Behavioral assessment and treatment planning with alcohol abusers: A review with an emphasis on clinical application. *Clinical Psychology Review, 8,* 19–54.

Sobell, M. B., & Sobell, L. C. (1984). The aftermath of heresy: A response to Pendery et al.'s (1982) critique of "Individualized behavior therapy for alcoholics." *Behaviour Research and Therapy, 22,* 413–440.

Sobell, M. B., & Sobell, L. C. (1987a). Conceptual issues regarding goals in the treatment of alcohol problems. *Drugs and Society, 1,* 1–37.

Sobell, M. B., & Sobell, L. C. (Eds.). (1987b). *Moderation as a goal or outcome of treatment for alcohol problems: A dialogue.* New York: Haworth.

Sobell, M. B., Sobell, L. C., Ersner-Hershfield, S., & Nirenberg, T. (1982). Alcohol and drug problems. In A. S. Bellack, M. Hersen, & A. E. Kazdin (Eds.), *International handbook of behavior modification and therapy* (pp. 501–553). New York: Plenum.

Solomon, J. (1983). Psychiatric characteristics of alcoholics. In B. Kissin & H. Begleiter (Eds.), *The pathogenesis of alcoholism: Vol. 6. Psychosocial factors* (pp. 67–112). New York: Plenum.

Stall, R., & Biernacki, P. (1986). Spontaneous remission from the problematic use of substances: An inductive model derived from a comparative analysis of the alcohol, opiate, tobacco, and food/obesity literatures. *International Journal of the Addictions, 21*, 1–23.

Stitzer, M. L., Bickel, W. K., Bigelow, G. E., & Liebson, I. A. (1986). Effect of methadone dose contingencies on urinalysis test results of polydrug-abusing methadone-maintenance patients. *Drug and Alcohol Dependence, 18*, 341–348.

Stitzer, M. L., Bigelow, G. E., & McCaul, M. E. (1983). Behavioral approaches to drug abuse. In M. Hersen, R. M. Eisler, & P. M. Miller (Eds.), *Progress in behavior modification* (Vol. 14, pp. 49–124). New York: Academic.

Stitzer, M. L., Grabowski, J., & Henningfield, J. E. (1984). Behavioral intervention techniques in drug abuse treatment: Summary of discussion. In J. Grabowski, M. L. Stitzer, & J. E. Henningfield (Eds.), *Behavioral intervention techniques in drug abuse treatment* (Research Monograph No. 46, pp. 147–156). Rockville, MD: National Institute on Drug Abuse.

Stitzer, M. L., & Gross, J. (1988). Smoking relapse: The role of pharmacological and behavioral factors. In O. F. Pomerleau & C. S. Pomerleau (Eds.), *Nicotine replacement: A critical evaluation* (pp. 163–184). New York: Liss.

Taylor, I. J., & Taylor, B. J. (Eds.). (1984). Double diagnosis: Double dilemma. The polyaddictions: Alcoholism, substance abuse, smoking, gambling. *Journal of Clinical Psychiatry, 45*, (Suppl. 12, Section 2).

Taylor, J. R., & Helzer, J. E. (1983). The natural history of alcoholism. In B. Kissin & H. Begleiter (Eds.), *The biology of alcoholism: Vol. 6. The pathogenesis of alcoholism: Psychosocial factors* (pp. 17–65). New York: Plenum.

Terry, C. E., & Pellens, M. (1928). *The opium problem.* New York: Bureau of Social Hygiene.

Tims, F. M., & Leukefeld, C. G. (Eds.). (1986). *Relapse and recovery in drug abuse* (Research Monograph No. 72, pp. 49–71). Rockville, MD: National Institute on Drug Abuse.

U.S. Department of Health and Human Services. (1982). *The health consequences of smoking: Cancer. A report of the Surgeon General* (DHHS Publi-

cation No. PHS 82-50179). Washington, DC: U.S. Government Printing Office.

U.S. Department of Health and Human Services. (1986). *The health consequences of using smokeless tobacco. A report of the advisory committee to the Surgeon General* (NIH Publication No. 86-2874). Washington, DC: U.S. Government Printing Office.

U.S. Department of Health and Human Services (1987). *Drug abuse and drug abuse research. The Second Triennial Report to Congress from the Secretary* (DHHS Publication No. ADM 87-1486). Washington, DC: U.S. Government Printing Office.

U.S. Department of Health and Human Services. (1988). *The health consequences of smoking: Nicotine addiction. A report of the Surgeon General* (DHHS Publication No. DHHS 88-8406). Washington, DC: U.S. Government Printing Office.

Wallace, P., Cutler, S., & Haines, A. (1988). Randomized controlled trial of general practitioner intervention in patients with excessive alcohol consumption. *British Medical Journal, 297*, 663–668.

Wilkinson, D. A., Leigh, G. M., Cordingley, J., Martin, G. W., & Lei, H. (1987). Dimensions of multiple drug use and a typology of drug users. *British Journal of Addiction, 82*, 259–273.

Wilson, D. M., Taylor, D. W., Gilbert, R., Best, J. A., Lindsay, E. A., Wilms, D. G., & Singer, J. (1988). A randomized trial of a family intervention for smoking cessation. *Journal of the American Medical Association, 260*, 1570–1574.

Wilson, G. T. (1987). Chemical aversion conditioning as a treatment for alcoholism: A reanalysis. *Behaviour Research and Therapy, 25*, 503–516.

Woody, G. E., McLellan, A. T., Luborsky, L., & O'Brien, C. P. (1985). Sociopathy and psychotherapy outcome. *Archives of General Psychiatry, 42*, 1081–1086.

Woody, G. E., McLellan, A. T., Luborsky, L. S. & O'Brien, C. P. (1987). Twelve-month follow-up of psychotherapy for opiate dependence. *American Journal of Psychiatry, 144*, 590–596.

Zweben, A., Pearlman, S., & Li, S. (1988). A comparison of brief advice and conjoint therapy in the treatment of alcohol abuse: The results of the marital systems study. *British Journal of Addiction, 83*, 899–916.

CHAPTER 27

Pharmacotherapy

HOWARD B. MOSS

CONCEPTUALIZATION OF THE DISORDER

With a few notable exceptions, the clinical psychopharmacological treatment of substance abuse disorders remains an underdeveloped area. However, advances in research may potentially yield a new pharmacological armamentarium with which to treat abusers of alcohol and other drugs. Basic scientists, psychopharmacologists, and clinicians are now constantly challenged by the rapidly changing trends in drugs of abuse. In recent years, the illicit market has introduced more potent and dangerous forms of existing drugs of abuse, and new "designer drugs" (i.e., chemically redesigned psychoactive substances) have been developed. The novel pharmacological properties of these compounds have stimulated researchers to investigate these substances with respect to biological mechanisms of drug action, the phenomenon of drug reinforcement, the psychobiology of addiction, and the clinical syndromes associated with their abuse.

According to the National Institute of Mental Health (NIMH) Epidemiologic Catchment Area program, alcoholism remains the most common psychiatric disorder among men (Robins, Helzer, Weissman, Orvaschel, Gruenberg, Burke, Regier, 1984). The costs of alcoholism to the alcoholics, to their families, and to society are enormous. Alcohol-related morbidity includes increased rates of liver disease, diseases of the central nervous system (CNS), gastrointestinal disease, cardiac and vascular diseases, endocrine disease, nutritional deficiencies, poisoning, cancers, metabolic derangements, fetal damage, and injuries from motor

vehicle and other accidents (U. S. Department of Health and Human Services, 1987). Social and familial consequences of alcohol abuse include criminality, broken families, reduced productivity on the job, lost employment, and property loss or damage. The economic costs to society of alcohol abuse are estimated to be over $89 billion/year. In comparison, other drug abuse is estimated to cost society nearly $50 billion/year (Harwood, Napolitano, Kristiansen, & Collins, 1984), and produces similar social consequences.

Research has yielded a new understanding of the mechanisms of the action of alcohol, and it is beginning to shed light on potential genetic mechanisms associated with the development of alcoholism. In addition, research has provided rational pharmacological treatment approaches addressing the withdrawal syndrome, alcohol craving, and the acquisition of abstinence.

Despite these technological advances in pharmacology, it is apparent from clinical experience that these new pharmacotherapies are useful primarily as adjuncts to psychosocial interventions. Thus, it is doubtful that successful treatment can neglect the social, cultural, and psychological factors leading to substance abuse while attending only to the biological and pharmacological domains.

BASIC PHARMACOLOGICAL CONCEPTS RELEVANT TO SUBSTANCE ABUSE

Central to the pharmacological approach to substance abuse treatments are the concepts of intoxication, tolerance, dependence, and the intrinsic reinforcing properties of drugs.

Intoxication

Intoxication refers primarily to the complex alterations of the normal functioning of the CNS produced by the pharmacological characteristics of a drug. This process includes disturbances in arousal, sensation, cognition, mood, and motor function. Each psychoactive drug produces its own pattern of perturbation of these brain processes, which depend on the specific nature of the drug's actions. For example, alcohol produces incoordination, memory deficits, attentional deficits, sedation, impairment in judgment, euphoria or dysphoria, and decrements in performance on a variety of tasks. The extent to which an individual displays the CNS effects of a drug depends on a variety of factors, including dose; route of administration; time of day; and individual constitutional factors such as gender and body habitus, liver functioning, phenotype of drug-metabolizing enzymes, rate of gastric emptying, renal functioning, and prior exposure to the drug. The effects of prior exposure to the drug or to a similarly acting compound are aspects of the concept of *tolerance*.

Tolerance

Tolerance refers to the changes that occur in an individual as a result of repeated exposure to alcohol or other drug (or another closely related compound) such that an increased amount of the drug is required to produce the same effect, or less effect is produced by the same dose of drug. (Kalant, LeBlanc, & Gibbins, 1971). The mechanisms of tolerance are generally described as either dispositional or functional. *Metabolic* or *dispositional tolerance* refers to changes in drug absorption, distribution, biotransformation, and excretion that lead to a reduction in the intensity and duration of exposure of an organ (e.g., the brain) to the drug. *Functional tolerance* refers to the changes in the target organ that render it less sensitive to the drug. Recently, the role of conditioned learning in the development of functional tolerance has stimulated much controversy. Tabakoff and colleagues (Tabakoff, Melchior, & Hoffman, 1984) have suggested further dividing the concept of functional tolerance into "environ-

ment-dependent" and "environment-independent" tolerance, with respect to forms of tolerance in which learning plays a major or a minor role.

Dependence

Dependence is a concept in flux. Previously, *dependence* was defined as "a state of discomfort produced by withdrawal of a drug from a subject who has been chronically or repeatedly exposed to it, and is alleviated by renewed administration of that drug or another with similar pharmacological actions." However, the *Diagnostic and Statistical Manual of Mental Disorders*, (3rd ed., rev., DSM-III-R, American Psychiatric Association, 1987) has significantly broadened the definition of *dependence* to "a syndrome of clinically significant behaviors, cognitions, and other symptoms that indicate loss of control of substance use and continued use of the substance despite adverse consequences." Thus, the new psychiatric nosology of DSM-III-R significantly downplays the importance of specific physiological and psychological aspects of a drug withdrawal syndrome in favor of a definition that emphasizes the compulsive aspects of use.

Drugs as Reinforcers

Animal studies carried out in the mid-1950s first suggested that drugs might be self-administered for their intrinsic reinforcing effects (Nichols, Headless, & Coppock, 1956). Since that time, the application of behavioral pharmacological techniques have revealed that the inherent reinforcing properties of some drugs do contribute to drug-seeking behavior in humans. Highly reinforcing drugs of abuse such as cocaine (Fischman & Schuster, 1982), nicotine (Henningfield & Griffiths, 1980), morphine (Wikler, 1952), alcohol (Mendelson & Mello, 1966), heroin (Mello & Mendelson, 1980), and marijuana (Mello & Mendelson, 1978) produce high rates of self-administration in laboratory settings. These effects may occur independent of the pharmacological phenomena of dependence and withdrawal. It is unclear, however, how much one can generalize from the human operant laboratory to a naturalistic setting. Further, most of these studies have been conducted with drug abusers as subjects. There may be specific characteristics about such preselected individuals that make them especially sensitive to the reinforcing properties of these drugs.

DIAGNOSTIC ISSUES AND PROBLEMS

The conceptualization of diagnostic constructs for psychoactive substance abuse disorders has evolved since Jellinek's time into various operationalized schemes. However, the construct validity of these taxonomic systems has frequently been without empirical verification. For example, it has been reported that three contemporary diagnostic criteria for alcoholism, specifically the Research Diagnostic Criteria (RDC), the Feigner Criteria, and the DSM-III (American Psychiatric Association 1980) criteria appear not to be concordant for classifying alcoholic individuals (Leonard, Bromet, Parkinson, & Day, 1984). Similarly, DSM-III criteria for alcohol abuse correlate poorly with self-reported drinking pattern, quantity, and consequences of alcohol consumption (Tarter, Arria, Moss, Edwards, & Van Thiel, 1987). The most recent nosological constructs are the revised criteria now accepted by the American Psychiatric Association (1987) in its DSM-III-R. Under this taxonomy, psychoactive substance abuse disorders are dichotomized into two categories: (1) psychoactive substance abuse; and (2) psychoactive substance dependence.

Under the previous system (DSM-III), a concerted effort was made to differentiate between substance "abuse" and "dependence." *Abuse* was diagnosed when the patient manifested a pathological pattern of use, as well as psychosocial impairment in functioning. *Dependence* was diagnosed by the presence of the same features plus the presence of tolerance or withdrawal as an indicator of physical dependence. This scheme implies that dependence is a more severe disorder, which may not necessarily be the case. An individual may, for example be physically dependent on tobacco, yet not suffer psychosocial consequences. In an effort to avoid some of these problematic inconsistencies of DSM-III (Rounsaville, Spitzer, & Williams, 1986), the abuse diagnosis has been deemphasized, while the dependence diagnosis is now underscored.

The sine que non for either of these diagnoses is the presence of a maladaptive compulsive pattern of use that would be viewed as undesirable across most cultural boundaries. However, physiological signs and symptoms as indicators of dependence have been downplayed. The new diagnostic criteria for psychoactive substance dependence in DSM-III-R provides a list of nine criteria, three of which must be met for the diagnosis to be made. Unfortunately, this framework yields 79,210 potential subtypes of alcohol dependence (Tarter et al., 1987), which may be excessively broad for heuristic or therapeutic differentiation. Another drawback of this method is that the clinician treating a patient with a psychoactive substance dependence diagnosis may not be alerted to the possibility of an impending withdrawal syndrome because physical signs are no longer an inherent criterion. Therefore, this system may be less useful in allowing the generation of an appropriate differential treatment plan, particularly if medical management of a withdrawal syndrome is indicated.

TREATMENT STRATEGIES

In general, three specific strategies have been applied to the pharmacological approach to chemical dependency: (1) attenuation of withdrawal symptoms, (2) alteration of the drug's stimulus properties in order to reduce drug-seeking behaviors, and (3) reduction of the craving for the abused substance. The first is the attenuation of withdrawal symptoms. In the past, compulsive alcohol-seeking and other drug-seeking behavior was thought to be motivated by the desire to avoid the unpleasant symptoms of the specific withdrawal syndromes. However, it is now known both that not all abusable drugs produce a withdrawal syndrome upon cessation of use and that some abusable drugs cause a withdrawal state that is clinically insignificant. Thus, the focus of pharmacological control of withdrawal states is directed toward reduction of the morbidity and mortality associated with acute abstinence, as well as toward making patients more comfortable so that they may competently participate in psychosocial therapies. In particular, the most severe form of alcohol withdrawal, delirium tremens, was associated with a 15% mortality rate earlier in this century (Thompson, Johnson, & Maddrey, 1975).

Advances in pharmacotherapy in the form of rational use of benzodiazepines have significantly reduced this death rate.

The second strategy for the pharmacotherapy of substance abuse problems involves alteration of the stimulus properties of the drug such that it no longer promotes drug-seeking behavior. This may take the form of either the *reduction of reinforcement* from alcohol or other drugs (i.e., "antagonist drugs") or the *development of aversion* to them (i.e., "deterrent drugs"). Examples of reinforcement-reduction techniques include naltrexone (Trexan) therapy and high-dose methadone maintenance for opiate abuse. An example of an aversive approach that is widely used clinically is disulfiram (Antabuse) treatment for alcoholism.

The third strategy involves using medications to reduce craving for the abused substance. *Craving* is a theoretical construct that represents the internal drive state propelling drug-seeking or other alcohol-seeking behavior (Rankin, Hodgson, & Stockwell, 1979). Although heightened during the withdrawal syndrome, craving appears to persist beyond the expression of physical withdrawal symptoms into the postwithdrawal interval. The existence of a subacute, protracted abstinence syndrome, extending weeks after the signs of the physical withdrawal syndrome have abated, has been noted by clinicians in opiate and alcohol addicts, but it is yet without careful empirical investigation (Meyer, 1986). Neuroadaptive changes may still be taking place beyond the classical withdrawal period. For example, the sleep disturbances of newly abstinent alcoholics may not normalize for 9–21 months (Williams & Rundell, 1981). Nonsuppression on the dexamethasone suppression test may persist for more than 3 weeks after classical physical alcohol withdrawal (Khan, Ciraulo, Nelson, Becker, Nies, & Jaffe, 1984). During this postwithdrawal interval, craving appears to be at its peak.

Two approaches have been taken to the reduction of craving. Drug substitution has been a frequently used means of modifying or eliminating craving and drug-seeking behavior. Methadone maintenance for heroin addiction is a classic example. Substitution of nicotine-containing gum for cigarettes (Hughes, Hatsukami, Pickens, Krahn, Malin, & Luknic, 1984) is another example. Chronic benzodiazepine treatment of alcoholics was suggested by Kissin (1975). Unfortunately, this approach involves first the re-addiction of the patient to another drug (though it is considered a socially acceptable choice) and then the gradual reduction of that drug's dosage. This may have short-term benefits, such as retention of the patient in treatment or reduced involvement in criminal activities, but ultimately, the patient still needs to undergo withdrawal of the drug and some degree of drug craving.

Correction of underlying physiological disturbances produced by chronic presence of a drug in the body is another approach. Recently, the attenuation of cocaine craving has been reported with bromocriptine (Parlodel), a dopamine agonist (Dackis & Gold, 1985), and with desipramine, a tricyclic antidepressant (Kleber & Gawin, 1986). The rationale for each approach is the reversal of cocaine-induced pathophysiology in the central dopaminergic and noradrenergic systems, respectively. Bromocriptine has also been reported by one researcher to be efficacious in the treatment of alcohol craving (Borg, 1983), however further experience with bromocriptine in alcoholics is obviously needed.

Pharmacological Treatment of the Withdrawal Syndrome

Withdrawal syndromes are generally treated either with drug substitutions that (a) possess cross-tolerance with the abused substance and possess a favorable pharmacokinetic profile or (b) with drugs that indirectly suppress physiological symptoms of the withdrawal syndrome through their separate actions on the autonomic nervous system (ANS) or on central neurotransmission.

Opiate Withdrawal

Opiate withdrawal is commonly managed in inpatients through the substitution method. The long-acting opiate methadone (half-life 15–22 hours) is substituted for heroin, morphine, or other opioids. Methadone is used because of its cross-tolerance with other opiates and its prolonged apparent half-life, and because it is well absorbed from the gastrointestinal tract (Jaffe & Martin, 1980). Typically, when withdrawal symptoms become apparent, a patient is given an initial oral dose of 15–20 mg of methadone. Doses are titrated against withdrawal symptoms during the first 24 hours up to a maximum of 80 mg. Once the patient is stabilized on an adequate amount of methadone to keep her or him symptom free for a 24-hour interval, gradual daily reduction may take place. Usually, a dose reduction of about 20% per day is well tolerated (Jaffe, 1980). Thus, the methadone substitution protocol may take anywhere from 10 days to 1 month for successful detoxification.

An important discovery in the treatment of the opiate withdrawal syndrome was the finding that clonidine, an alpha-2 adrenergic receptor agonist used clinically as an antihypertensive agent effectively reduces signs and symptoms of opiate withdrawal (Gold, Redmond, & Kleber, 1978). Typically, oral doses of 1–2 mg/day of clonidine are used to suppress the withdrawal symptoms of opiate addicts. Up to 10 days of clonidine treatment may be required, particularly if a longer-acting opiate is the drug of abuse or if clonidine is used for the purpose of methadone withdrawal (Charney, Sternberg, Kleber, Heninger, & Redmond, 1981). Clonidine, in combination with the long-term opiate antagonist, naltrexone, has been found to be effective for an even more rapid opiate detoxification regimen (Charney, Heninger, & Kleber, 1986). Detoxification from methadone can be successfully accomplished in 4–5 days using these two agents to simultaneously precipitate, and suppress the opiate withdrawal syndrome.

Alcohol Withdrawal

In the classic study by Isbell and associates (Isbell, Fraser, & Wikler, 1955), six volunteers maintained an excellent diet and consumed large amounts of alcohol for 48 days. Upon abrupt discontinuation of alcohol, these volunteers developed a broad spectrum of withdrawal symptoms, including seizures, hallucinations with a clear sensorium, and delirium tremens. Because a nutritional deficiency could be ruled out by the adequate dietary intake, the authors concluded that the withdrawal of alcohol alone was responsible for this syndrome. Since this report, a variety of pharmacological approaches have been applied to the treatment of the withdrawal syndrome. The two most successful treatments have involved (1) substitution with drugs that have some degree of

cross-tolerance with alcohol, yet have a different pharmacokinetic profile, and more recently, (2) treatment with those agents that decrease activity of the sympathetic nervous system (SNS). The safety and efficacy of benzodiazepine therapy in the treatment of the alcohol withdrawal syndrome is now well established. Clinical trials have demonstrated the superiority of benzodiazepine therapy over a variety of other pharmacological approaches, including antipsychotics (Kaim, Klett, & Rothchild, 1969), anticonvulsants (Sampliner & Iber, 1974), paraldehyde (Thompson, Johnson, & Maddrey, 1975), hydroxyzine (Runion & Fowler, 1978), and meprobamate (Wegner & Fink, 1965).

The first introduced benzodiazepine, chlordiazepoxide (Librium), has in recent years been the standard for treating the alcohol withdrawal syndrome. However, the appropriate dosing regimen for this drug is often problematic. The relatively slow rate of absorption following oral administration produces a delay of several hours for peak plasma concentrations. As a consequence of this delay, overtreatment with this pharmacological agent is not uncommon. Patients may therefore remain lethargic, ataxic, or confused for several days after the withdrawal state has resolved (Baskin & Easdale, 1982). A more rational approach involves the titration of a dose of a rapidly absorbed benzodiazepine against the presentation of clinical symptoms (e.g., the diazepam loading method of Sellers and associates, 1983). Diazepam is highly lipid-soluble, and oral administration results in peak plasma concentrations occurring in approximately 1 hour. Thus, the physician can administer a dose and readily observe for its impact on the alcohol withdrawal syndrome. As an additional benefit, the favorable pharmacokinetic profile of diazepam allows for the oral loading of the drug on the first day of treatment only. Because the half-life of diazepam is about 33 hours, and that of its active metabolite, desmethyldiazepam, is about 50 hours, therapeutic plasma concentrations will be present after only 1 day's loading for more than the 72 hours duration of a typical alcohol withdrawal syndrome. Briefly, the method protocol involves oral administration of 20 mg of diazepam every 2 hours until the patient is asymptomatic. After the first day, patients are then permitted to continue on diazepam and its active metabolite, with additional medication given only on an as-needed (p.r.n.) basis.

There is one limitation to this method. Patients with severely compromised liver function will not metabolize the drug, which readily causes an accumulation of the compound in the body. For patients with severe hepatic dysfunction, lorazepam may be a safer benzodiazepine. This drug does not depend on hepatic biotransformation for its excretion. Although the oral form of lorazepam has a similar delay in absorption as chlordiazepoxide, a rapidly absorbed sublingual preparation (Caille, Lacasse, Vezina, Porter, Shaar, & Dark, 1980) and a parenteral form (Spencer, 1980) may be very useful in the rational treatment of the alcohol withdrawal syndrome.

Recently, clonidine has been demonstrated to have efficacy in treatment of the alcohol withdrawal state (Wilkins, Jenkins, & Steiner, 1983). Clonidine stimulates the presynaptic alpha-adrenoceptors, which reduces noradrenergic transmission and thereby attenuates the activation of the SNS. In a comparative study of the relative efficacy of clonidine versus chlordiazepoxide, clonidine was found to be both more effective in reducing cardiovascular symptoms of withdrawal and as effective at improving cognitive capacity, reducing anxiety, and reducing subjective complaints of withdrawal (Baumgartner & Rowen, 1987). Although it lacks anticonvulsant properties, it also is without any intrinsic abuse potential. Thus, clonidine should be seriously considered as an alternative to benzodiazepines.

Cocaine Withdrawal

The recognition of a physical cocaine withdrawal syndrome or "crash" is a relatively recent phenomenon. The symptoms are generally opposite to those found with cocaine intoxication: Anergy, intense craving, hypersomnia, hyperphagia, decreased libido, irritability, psychomotor retardation, amotivation, and decreased attentional concentration are frequently exhibited symptoms of the withdrawal state (Dackis & Gold, 1985). The subjectively unpleasant cocaine crash is thought to act as a negative reinforcer, increasing drug-seeking behavior.

The catecholaminergic system is thought to be implicated both in the actions of cocaine and in the development of the withdrawal syndrome. Cocaine is a releaser of dopamine (Van Rossum & Hurkmans, 1964) and a potent inhibitor of the neuronal reuptake of dopamine and other catecholamines (Ross & Renyi, 1966). Chronic cocaine administration is associated with a depletion of catecholamines. Brain dopamine levels have been reported to fall after repeated administration of cocaine (Taylor & Ho, 1977). Chronic cocaine administration also results in a compensatory increase in the number of dopamine receptors in brain (Taylor, Ho, & Fagan, 1979) consistent with reduced dopaminergic transmission. A reduction in the urinary metabolite of central and peripheral norepinephrine has been reported in chronic cocaine abusers (Tennant, 1985). Increases in the number of beta adrenoceptors have also been reported with chronic cocaine administration (Banerjee, Sharmee, Kung-Cheung, Chanda, & Riggi, 1979). Therefore, the pathophysiology of this withdrawal condition has been hypothesized to result from a diminution of dopaminergic and/or noradrenergic neurotransmission produced by the chronic effects of cocaine.

Guided by these findings, two successful approaches to cocaine withdrawal have been reported. First, bromocriptine (a dopamine agonist) has been used successfully in low doses for the treatment of cocaine withdrawal (Dackis & Gold, 1985). Its use follows a physiological replacement strategy in which a dopamine agonist compensates for presynaptic depletion and downregulates postsynaptic receptors until natural physiological dopamine synthesis catches up with its losses.

Second, a similar observation is that tricyclic antidepressants such as desipramine and imipramine downregulate supersensitive beta adrenoceptors (Charney, Menkes, & Heninger, 1981) and dopamine receptors (Koide & Matshushita, 1981). This observation has led to successful clinical trials using these agents in the treatment of cocaine withdrawal (Kleber & Gawin, 1986). Tricyclic antidepressants appear efficacious independent of the presence of a depressive disorder in the substance abuser. The goal of this approach to treatment is not to deal with depression but to effect a pharmacological normalization of the catecholaminergic system.

Reinforcement Reduction or Aversion Development

Lithium Carbonate

Chronic lithium pretreatment has been reported to attenuate the euphoria and activation associated with a variety of stimulant compounds, including amphetamine (Flemembaum, 1974; Van Kammen & Murphy, 1975), cocaine (Cronson & Flamenbaum, 1978), and intravenous (IV) methylphenidate (Huey, Janowsky, Lewis, Abrams, Parker, & Clopton, 1981). Although these initial reports wer promising, later trials revealed less consistency in this effect (Angrist & Gershon, 1979). In an open trial of the comparative efficacy of lithium versus desipramine in the treatment of cocaine abuse, lithium was apparently not clinically effective (Gawin & Kleber, 1984). Therefore, routine use of lithium for stimulant abuse cannot be recommended.

Since the mid-1970s, there have been a number of reports in the literature both suggesting that lithium antagonizes some of the effects of alcohol intoxication and advocating its use in treatment of clinical alcoholism. Early reports from Kline and associates (Kline, Wren, Cooper, Varga, & Canal, 1974) and from Merry and associates (Merry, Reynolds, Bailey, & Coppen, 1976) suggested that lithium might be of benefit only in depressed alcoholics. However, studies on normal volunteers revealed that lithium reduced the subjective intoxication "high" from alcohol, and that lithium reduced alcohol-induced psychomotor performance deficits (Judd, Hubbard, & Huey, 1977; Linnoila, Saario, & Maki, 1974). Subsequently, a double-blind, placebo-controlled study of detoxified alcoholics receiving chronic lithium treatment demonstrated less intoxication, less of a desire to continue drinking, and less cognitive and psychomotor performance deficits when challenged with doses of alcohol (Judd & Huey, 1984). Then, in a double-blind, placebo-controlled clinical trial of lithium carbonate therapy for alcoholism initiated during inpatient treatment, Fawcett and associates (1987) found that subjects with a therapeutic lithium level demonstrated a better treatment outcome than the placebo group, and that these results were independent of the presence of affective symptoms. Thus, lithium therapy may be an extremely promising pharmacological approach to the treatment of alcoholism, possibly due to an alteration of the reinforcing aspects of alcohol intoxication.

The mechanism of action of lithium in attenuating reinforcement is unclear. Lithium affects dopaminergic, cholinergic, and noradrenergic neurotransmitter systems, which have been implicated in drug-related reward mechanisms. It also affects the serotonergic functioning, which may modulate the phenomena of functional tolerance.

Methadone and Naltrexone

Methadone maintenance as a method for treating opiate dependence was first started by Dole and Nyswander (1965). Part of the rationale for this approach was the development of cross-tolerance to heroin such that heroin addicts would not get high on illicit opiates. This blocking of the effects of street drugs (probably due to saturation of the opiate receptors, as well as to tolerance) also appeared to suppress drug-seeking activity and concurrent criminality. Thus, methadone maintenance was supposed to decrease the addict's criminal activity and to reduce both opiate and nonopiate drug use (McLellan, Luborsky, & O'Brien, 1982). However, the success of methadone maintenance in attenuating the reinforcing effects of heroin appears largely to be a dose-dependent phenomenon. Inadequate plasma levels of methadone (Tennant, 1987) or lower oral doses of methadone (Jaffe, 1987) may allow opiate-seeking behavior to persist. These authors suggest that both higher oral doses (> 80 mg/day) and concurrent measurement of plasma methadone levels with dose adjustment may benefit those in methadone who continue to engage in drug use and attendant criminality.

Naltrexone is an essentially pure opiate antagonist, which is orally effective, and structurally similar to oxymorphone. It appears to have little or no agonist activity. When patients are pretreated with naltrexone and then given doses of morphine, heroin, or other opiates, naltrexone significantly reduces or blocks the pharmacological effects of the opiates. Such blockade of opiate effects includes the subjective high from the opiate, as well as drug craving and the production of physical dependence. Thus, naltrexone pretreatment eliminates much of the intrinsically reinforcing properties of opiates.

Unfortunately, the clinical utility of this opiate-blocking drug appears to be limited. Poor patient compliance has plagued naltrexone programs. In one multicenter trial of naltrexone therapy, client retention in the program was reported to be as low as 6 weeks (Ginzburg, 1986). However, programs that combine pharmacotherapy with psychosocial support services do appear to have better naltrexone compliance, better retention rates, and superior treatment outcome (Resnick, Schuyten-Resnick, & Washton, 1980).

Disulfiram

Disulfiram (Antabuse) use was first initiated in Europe as a treatment for alcoholism in 1948 (Hald & Jacobsen, 1948). It was later introduced in the United States and it has since remained the only pharmaceutical available here that is specifically indicated for alcoholism therapy.

Disulfiram alters the intermediary metabolism of alcohol. Specifically, it inhibits the activity of the enzyme acetaldehyde dehydrogenase. Thus, when ethyl alcohol is ingested, blood acetaldehyde concentrations rise, resulting in an acetaldehyde reaction. This disulfiram-ethanol reaction (DER) consists of the rather unpleasant combination of vasodilation, sweating, intense throbbing in the head and neck, respiratory difficulties, nausea, vomiting, vertigo, chest pain, and hypotension. The hypotension may be severe and cause postural syncope. This reaction may last anywhere from 30 minutes to several hours.

The DER obviously reduces the reinforcing aspects of alcohol consumption. However, the clinical reality is that most alcoholics never drink while taking disulfiram. The knowledge of the possibility of having a DER is a sufficient deterrent to the consumption of alcohol. Thus, disulfiram may be viewed as an "active placebo."

The efficacy of disulfiram in the treatment of alcoholism is quite controversial. Fuller and Williford (1980) used life-table or actuarial methods to describe the outcome of three randomly assigned groups of alcoholic patients who were receiving counseling and medical care. The first group was given a daily therapeutic dose (250 mg) of disulfiram. The second group was told that they too would also be receiving disulfiram, but they were given the markedly subtherapeutic dose of 1 mg. The third group was told they would not be treated with the drug. The abstinence rates measured 1 year after discharge from the program indicated no difference between disulfiram therapeutic dose, and the 1 mg. subtherapeutic dose. Both of these groups, however, had superior outcome in comparison to the no-drug group. Thus, therapeutic doses of disulfiram may be no better than placebo. A similarly designed, large-scale, multicenter study was conducted by the Veterans Administration, which also looked at the effects of counseling in addition to disulfiram (Fuller et al., 1986). This time, there were no differences among the three groups in terms of abstinence. Thus, counseling alone appeared as effective as disulfiram or the low-dose active placebo. However, among the patients who relapsed, those receiving therapeutic doses of disulfiram had fewer drinking days than their counterparts in the subtherapeutic or counseling-only groups.

If disulfiram was a totally innocuous compound, there would be little controversy surrounding its use despite its placebolike status. However, the literature is riddled with suggestions that disulfiram may be responsible for a variety of adverse side effects. These include hepatotoxicity (Goyer & Major, 1979), carbon disulfide poisoning with polyneuropathy (Rainey, 1977), psychotic reactions (Bennet, McKeever, & Turk, 1951; Major et al., 1979), acute organic brain syndrome (Knee & Razani, 1974), and a worsening of preexisting schizophrenia (Heath, Nesselhof, Bishop, & Byers, 1965).

The majority of these adverse sequelae now appear to be dose-related because early dosing schedules exceeded the now-recommended 250–500 mg dose range. Two recent reports of disulfiram side effects at this lower dose did not implicate disulfiram in the production of either physical (Christensen, Ronsted, & Vaag, 1984) or psychiatric complications (Branchey, Davis, Lee, & Fuller, 1987). However, the former study was flawed by being only 6 weeks in duration, and the latter study carefully screened out subjects who had a history of organic mental disorder, schizophrenia, affective disorder, or a history of psychotropic drug abuse. Therefore, a longer duration of treatment, higher doses, and the use with patients who have preexisting psychiatric disorders could account for many of the earlier reports of problematic side effects. Until these issues are clarified, clinicians who believe in the clinical value of this compound should restrict their prescriptions to lower doses for a limited duration of treatment, and they should exercise restraint in the administration of disulfiram to those patients with preexisting hepatic, myocardial, neurological, or psychiatric illnesses.

Serotonin Reuptake Inhibitors

Several specific serotonin reuptake-inhibiting antidepressant drugs appear to have efficacy in the attenuation of alcohol consumption independent of their effects on depression. Zimelidine has been reported to reduce alcohol intake among non-depressed heavy drinkers (Naranjo, Sellers, Roach, Woodley, Sanchez-Craig, & Sykora, 1984). Unfortunately, the manufacturer has withdrawn this drug from clinical trials due to untoward side effects. However, other similarly acting agents, such as citalopram, fluoxetine, and fluvoxamine appear to have potential in reduction of alcohol consumption (Naranjo, Sellers, & Lawrin, 1985). The mechanism of action for these drugs is unclear; however, it has been suggested that they inhibit the neurobiological substrate for positive reinforcement that maintains alcohol-drinking behavior (Naranjo, Cappell, & Sellers, 1981).

Pharmacological Attenuation of Craving

Cocaine Craving

As previously noted, two approaches have been reported to have efficacy in the amelioration of cocaine craving in the postwithdrawal period. Dackis and Gold (1985) have noted dramatic improvement in cocaine craving with daily oral bromocriptine doses (0.625 mg three times daily—t.i.d.). They have hypothesized that bromocriptine treatment functionally reverses the depletion of dopamine produced by chronic cocaine administration, and that subjective craving is a response to this dopaminergic deficit.

Tennant and Rawson (1982) reported anecdotally that therapeutic doses of desipramine, a tricyclic antidepressant, facilitated cocaine withdrawal. Later, Gawin and Kleber (1984) reported that desipramine was efficacious in the reduction of craving for cocaine in the postwithdrawal interval in a group of psychotherapy-only treatment failures. They hypothesized that adrenergic beta receptor supersensitivity was the biological substrate for craving, and that tricyclics induce downregulation, thereby reducing craving (Kleber & Gawin, 1986).

Opiate Craving

Opiate craving has been successfully attenuated primarily by drug substitution. Methadone maintenance of opiate addiction still results in drug tolerance and dependence. Although a more prosocial drug thereby is used in this successful method for attenuation of craving and opiate-seeking behavior, methadone maintenance does not reduce the desire to use cocaine (Kosten, Rounsaville, & Kleber, 1987), nor does it totally relieve the psychological symptoms imposed by addiction. For example, reports suggest that anywhere from 20 to 30% of individuals on chronic methadone maintenance acquire a morbid fear or phobia of detoxification, which complicates subsequent successful methadone detoxification (Milby, Gurwitch, Wiebe, Ling, McLellan, & Woody, 1986).

Alcohol Craving

Kissin (1975) first argued for the use in alcoholics of chronic benzodiazepine therapy. He noted that because many patients are unable to deal with the symptoms of a protracted withdrawal syndrome, benzodiazepine therapy would reduce craving for alcohol and would retain patients in treatment. However, clinical experience diminished the enthusiasm for this approach. Benzodiazepines appear to have abuse potential in alcoholics. They clearly potentiate the effects of alcohol, and cross-addiction to benzodiazepines is not an uncommon occurrence.

Buspirone, a nonbenzodiazepine anxiolytic, has been suggested as an alternative therapy for alcoholics, based on its apparent lack of abuse potential and its lack of potentiation of the effects of alcohol (Meyer, 1986). However, few data exist concerning the effect of buspirone on alcohol craving.

Dopaminergic drugs may have some utility in the treatment of alcohol craving. Two dopamine agonists, bromocriptine (Borg, 1983) and apomorphine (Jensen, Christoffersen, & Noerregaard, 1977), have been reported to control withdrawal symptoms and reduce craving for alcohol for 2–26 weeks after detoxification. However, another report failed to find any benefit of apomorphine therapy on postintoxication symptoms (Wadstein, Ohlin, & Stenberg, 1978). Further controlled studies of these agents clearly should be done before routine clinical prescription can be recommended.

CASE REPORT

Mr. E is a 55-year-old divorced Caucasian male, who was admitted into an inpatient alcohol and other drug treatment program, upon the referral of his family physician. He had a 10-year history of heavy daily alcohol consumption. In the year prior to admission, he had been reprimanded and placed on probation at his work for having reduced productivity and for having alcohol on his breath. He also had gotten two motor vehicle citations in the preceding year for driving under the influence of alcohol. His divorce was prompted by incidents of verbal and physical abuse of his wife and children while he was intoxicated. Prior to admission, the patient still did not believe that he was an alcoholic.

Mr. E. was admitted to the inpatient unit mildly intoxicated, with a blood alcohol level of 90 mg/dl (per deciliter). His vital signs were initially within normal limits. His initial clinical withdrawal syndrome rating scale scores were low. He was given oral fluid and electrolyte replacements and made comfortable by the nursing staff. Approximately 5 hours later, Mr. E was found to have a rapid pulse, a slightly elevated temperature, and an elevated systolic blood pressure. He became tremulous, diaphoretic, and agitated. His clinical withdrawal score was moderately elevated. The decision was made to institute pharmacotherapy.

The patient was given an initial oral dose of 20 mg of diazepam. When clinical withdrawal ratings were performed 1 hour later, his severity of withdrawal score was slightly higher than the previous rating. He was then given another oral dose of 20 mg of diazepam and allowed to rest. One hour later, his clinical withdrawal score was unchanged from the previously elevated rating.

Another oral dose of 20 mg of diazepam was administered. One hour later, his withdrawal score, although still elevated, was lower than at the two previous ratings. The decision was made to withhold medication and to observe the patient for another hour. His next hourly withdrawal rating was even lower than the two previous ratings, but his vital signs were still abnormal. The clinical decision was made to give one last oral dose of diazepam. Two hours later, the patient had normal vital signs, and his clinical withdrawal rating scores were only slightly elevated. The patient appeared comfortable and in no acute distress. That night he got 5 hours of sleep. No additional medications were given to treat the alcohol withdrawal syndrome, and the patient remained stable.

Five days later, Mr. E. was actively participating in the psychotherapy program on the ward. He attended the psychoeducational programs, participated in the individual and group therapies, and was introduced to the fellowship of Alcoholics Anonymous (AA). Despite all these interventions, Mr. E. was concerned that he "wouldn't be able to stay away from the booze" after he was discharged. Therefore, the treatment team elected to suggest disulfiram therapy upon discharge, to give the patient the psychological crutch he needed to remain abstinent outside the hospital.

The patient met with the program physician, who explained to him what disulfiram was, what it did, and the details of the reaction he would have if he drank, and the physician warned him of the potential risks versus its benefits. After thinking this option over, the patient agreed to a 6-week trial of the drug as part of his aftercare plan. Mr. E. felt that taking disulfiram was "just the insurance I need to stay sober," and he consented to treatment. It was agreed that the treatment team would reevaluate his need for the drug at 6-week intervals.

Mr. E. was started on disulfiram 250 mg/day during his last week in the hospital, and this dose was continued after discharge. In addition to pharmacotherapy, the patient also attended twice weekly AA meetings, and returned for weekly aftercare therapy groups. Although the patient remained totally abstinent during his first 6 weeks outside of the hospital, and he never experienced a DER, he felt strongly that the drug helped his recovery. He requested another 6-week treatment interval with disulfiram as a crutch. The treatment team agreed. Mr. E. continued abstinence and actively participated in AA, as well as in aftercare therapy. At the next 6-week evaluation, however, the team felt that it was time to phase out the drug because his new behaviors seemed firmly established. Mr. E. was gradually tapered off disulfiram over about a week. Although he was somewhat anxious about how he would maintain sobriety without the drug, at the time of this writing, he has now totally abstained from alcohol for 14 months without reinitiation of pharmacotherapy.

ALTERNATIVE TREATMENT OPTIONS

The central controversy in the pharmacological management of substance abuse disorders may be whether to use pharmacotherapy at all. For example, several uncontrolled studies suggest that otherwise healthy patients in alcohol withdrawal can be safely treated without the use of psychoactive drugs (Shaw, Kolesar, Sellers, Kaplan, & Sandor, 1981; Whitfield, Thompson, Lamp, Spencer, Pfeifer, & Browning-Ferrando, 1978). Thus, pharmacotherapy is apparently not always mandatory.

In addition, frontline, nonphysician clinicians are frequently opposed to the use of psychoactive drugs for individuals with a preexisting psychoactive substance abuse disorder. In part, this perspective is due to the prominent influence of AA and Narcotics Anonymous (NA) as part of the treatment regimen of substance abusers. These self-help groups warn their members about the potential dangers of dependence on physician-prescribed or illicit psychoactive drugs as a substitute for the original addiction. In particular, AA warns alcoholics about the danger of becoming addicted to sedatives and hypnotics (Alcoholics Anonymous, 1984). In general, these highly influential self-help groups advocate that their members seek "nonchemical solutions for the aches and discomforts of everyday living."

Given the efficacy, proliferation, and well-deserved prestige of these self-help groups, the search for effective pharmacotherapeutic agents for alcohol and drug abuse disorders has generated limited interest among pharmaceutical concerns. For example, disulfiram, the only drug available in the United States that is indicated for the treatment of alcoholism, was first introduced in Europe in 1948, and later in the United States. No American pharmaceutical company has, until very recently, undertaken a research and development program to find other novel drug treatments for alcoholism.

Despite the lack of convincing empirical support for the notion that *all* psychoactive drugs are a danger to the alcoholic, the drug-free approach espoused by the substance abuse treatment community has reigned for nearly 40 years. However, research advances in the pharmacology of alcohol, cocaine, and other drugs of abuse, and recent investigations into the biological basis of heritable forms of substance abuse disorders, have renewed interest in potential psychopharmacological approaches to these conditions. Should new therapeutics be developed, the proof of the clinical safety and the efficacy of these compounds in substance abuse treatment is a burden that falls on the shoulders of researchers, pharmacologists, and clinicians. Dissemination of such new information to the substance abuse treatment community, including AA and NA, is an additional imperative.

REFERENCES

Alcoholics Anonymous. (1984). *The A. A. member—Medications and other drugs: A report from group of physicians in A. A.* New York: Alcoholics Anonymous World Services.

American Psychiatric Association (1980). *Diagnostic and statistical manual of mental disorders* (3rd ed.). Washington, DC: Author.

American Psychiatric Association (1987). *Diagnostic and statistical manual of mental disorders* (3rd ed., rev.). Washington, DC: Author.

Angrist, B., & Gershon, S. (1979). Variable attenuation of amphetamine effects by lithium. *American Journal of Psychiatry, 136,* 806–810.

Banerjee, S. P., Sharma, V. K., Kung-Cheung, L. S., Chanda, S. K., & Riggi, S. J. (1979). Cocaine and d-amphetamine induce changes in central beta-andrenoceptor sensitivty: Effects of acute and chronic drug treatment. *Brain Research, 175,* 119–130.

Baskin, S. I., & Easdale, A. (1982). Is chlordiazepoxide the rational choice among benzodiazepines? *Pharmacotherapy, 2,* 110–119.

Baumgartner, G. R., & Rowen, R. C. (1987). Clonidine vs. chlordiazepoxide in the management of acute alcohol withdrawal. *Archives of Internal Medicine, 147*, 1223–1226.

Bennet, A., McKeever, L., & Turk, H. (1951). Psychotic reactions during tetraethylthiuram disulfide (Antabuse) therapy. *Journal of the American Medical Association, 145*, 483.

Borg, V. (1983). Bromocriptine in the prevention of alcohol abuse. *Acta Psychiatrica Scandinavia, 68*, 100–110.

Branchey, L., Davis, W., Lee, K. K., & Fuller, R. K. (1987). Psychiatric complications in disulfiram treatment. *American Journal of Psychiatry, 144*, 1310–1312.

Caille, G., Lacasse, Y., Vezina, M., Porter, R., Shaar, S., & Darke, A. (1980). A novel route for benzodiazepine administration: A sublingual formulation of lorazepam. In L. Manzo (ed.), *Advances in neurotoxicity* (pp. 375–389). New York: Pergamon.

Charney, D. S., Heninger, G. R., & Kleber, H. D. (1986). The combined use of clonidine and naltrexone as a rapid, safe, and effective treatment of abrupt withdrawl from methadone. *American Journal of Psychiatry, 143*, 831–837.

Charney, D. S., Menkes, D. B., & Heninger, G. R. (1981). Receptor sensitivity and the mechanisms of action of antidepressant treatment. *Archives of General Psychiatry, 38*, 1160–1180.

Charney, D. S., Sternberg, D. E., Kleber, H. D., Heninger, G. R., & Redmond, D. E. (1981). The clinical use of clonidine in abrupt withdrawal from methadone. *Archives of General Psychiatry, 38*, 1273–1227.

Christensen, J. K., Ronsted, P., & Vaag, U. H. (1984). Side effects after disulfiram. *Acta Psychiatrica Scandinavia, 69*, 265–273.

Cronson, A. J., & Flamenbaum, A. (1978). Antagonism of cocaine highs by lithium. *American Journal of Psychiatry, 135*, 856–857.

Dackis, C. A., & Gold, M. S. (1985). Pharmacological approaches to cocaine addiction. *Journal of Substance Abuse Treatment, 2*, 139–145.

Dole, U. P., & Nyswander, M. (1965). A medical treatment for diacetylmorphine (heroin) addiction: A clinical trial with methadone hydrochloride. *Journal of the American Medical Association, 193*, 646–650.

Fawcett, J., Clark, D. C., Aagesen, C. A., Pisani, V. D., Tilkin, J. M., Sellers, D., McGuire, M., & Gibbons, R. D. (1987). A double-blind, placebo-controlled trial of lithium carbonate therapy for alcoholism. *Archives of General Psychiatry, 44*, 248–256.

Fischman, W. M. & Schuster, G. R. (1982). Cocaine self-administration in humans. *Federation Proceedings, 41*, 241–246.

Flemenbaum, A. (1974). Does lithium block the effects of amphetamine? *American Journal of Psychiatry, 131*, 7.

Fuller, R. K., Branchey, L., Brightwell, D. R., Derman, R. M., Emrick, C. D., Iber, F. L., James, K. E., & Lacoursiere, R. B. (1986). Disulfiram treatment of alcoholism: A Veterans Administration cooperative study. *Journal of the American Medical Association, 256*, 1449–1455.

Fuller, R. K., & Williford, W. O. (1980). Life-table analysis of abstinence in a study evaluating the efficacy of disulfiram. *Alcoholism: Clinical and Experimental Research, 4*, 298–301.

Gawin, F. H., & Kleber, H. D. (1984). Cocaine abuse treatment: An open pilot trial with lithium and desipramine. *Archives of General Psychiatry, 41*, 903–910.

Ginzburg, H. M. (1986). Naltrexone: Its clinical utility. In B. Stimmel (ed.), *Advances in alcohol & substance abuse* (pp. 83–101). New York: Haworth.

Gold, M. E., Redmond, D. C., & Kleber, H. D. (1978). Clonidine blocks acute opiate-withdrawal symptoms. *Lancet, 2*, 599–602.

Goyer, P. F. & Major, L. F. (1979). Hepatotoxicity in disulfiram-treated patients. *Journal of Studies on Alcohol, 40*, 133–137.

Hald, J., & Jacobsen, E. (1948). A drug sensitizing the organism to ethyl alcohol. *Lancet, 255*, 1001–1004.

Harwood, H. J., Napolitano, D. M., Kristiansen, P. L., & Collins, J. J. (1984). Economic costs to society of alcohol and drug abuse and mental illness. *Research Triangle Institute.*

Heath, R. G., Nesselhof, W., Bishop, M. P., & Byers, L. W. (1965). Behavioral and metabolic changes associated with administration of tetraethylthiuram disulfide (Antabuse). *Diseases of the Nervous System, 26*, 99–105.

Henningfield, J. E., & Griffiths, R. R. (1980). Effects of ventilated cigarette holders on cigarette smoking by humans. *Psychopharmacology, 68*, 115–119.

Huey, L., Janowsky, D., Lewis, J., Abrams, A., Parker, D., & Clopton, P. (1981). Effects of lithium carbonate on methylphenidate induced mood, behavior and cognitive processes. *Psychopharmacology, 73*, 161–164.

Hughes, J. R., Hatsukami, D. K., Pickens, R. W., Krahn, D., Malin, S., & Luknic, A. (1984). Effect of nicotine on the tobacco withdrawal syndrome. *Psychopharmacology* (Berlin), *83*, 82–87.

Isbell, H., Fraser, H. F., & Wikler, A. (1955). An experimental study of the etiology of "rum fits" and delirium tremens. *Quarterly Journal of Studies on Alcohol, 16*, 1–13.

Jaffe, J. H. (1980). Drug addiction and drug abuse. In A. G. Gilman, L. S. Goodman, & A. Gilman (Eds.), *The pharmacological basis of therapeutics* (pp. 535–584). New York: Macmillan.

Jaffe, J. H. (1987). Pharmacological agents in treatment of drug dependence. In H. Y. Meltzer (Ed.), *Psychopharmacology: The third generation of progress* (pp. 1605–1616). New York: Raven Press.

Jaffe, J. H., & Martin, W. R. (1980). Opioid analgesics and antagonists. In A. G. Gilman, L. S. Goodman, & A. Gilman (Eds.), *The pharmacological basis of therapeutics* (pp. 494–534). New York: Macmillan.

Jensen, S. B., Christoffersen, C. B., & Noerregaard, A. (1977). Apomorphine in outpatient treatment of alcohol intoxication and abstinence: A double-blind study. *British Journal of Addiction, 72*, 325–330.

Judd, L. L., Hubbard, R. B., & Huey, L. Y. (1977). Lithium carbonate and ethanol induced "highs" in normal subjects. *Archives of General Psychiatry, 34*, 463–467.

Judd, L. L., & Huey, L. Y. (1984). Lithium antagonizes ethanol intoxication in alcoholics. *American Journal of Psychiatry, 141*, 1517–1521.

Kaim, S. C., Klett, C. J., & Rothchild, B. (1969). Treatment of the acute alcohol withdrawal state: A comparison of four drugs. *American Journal of Psychiatry, 125*, 1640–1646.

Kalant, H., LeBlanc, A. E., & Gibbins, R. J. (1971). Tolerance to, and dependence on, some non-opiate psychotropic drugs. *Pharmacological Reviews, 23*, 135–191.

Khan, A., Ciraulo, D. A., Nelson, W. H., Becker, J. T., Nies, A., & Jaffe, J. H. (1984). Dexamethasone suppression test in recently detoxified alcoholics: Clinical implications. *Journal of Clinical Psychopharmacology, 4*, 94–97.

Kissin, B. (1975). The use of psychoactive drugs in the long-term treatment of chronic alcoholics. *Annals of the New York Academy of Sciences, 252*, 385–395.

Kleber, H., & Gawin, F. (1986). Psychopharmacological trials in cocaine abuse treatment. *American Journal of Drug and Alcohol Abuse, 12*, 235–246.

Kline, N. S., Wren, J. C., Cooper, T. B., Varga, E., & Canal, O. (1974). Evaluation of lithium therapy in chronic and periodic alcoholism. *American Journal of Medical Science, 268*, 15–22.

Knee, S. T., & Razani, J. (1974). Acute organic brain syndrome: A complication of disulfiram therapy. *American Journal of Psychiatry, 131*, 1281–1282.

Koide, T., & Matshushita, H. (1981). An enhanced sensitivity of muscarinic cholinergic receptors associated with dopaminergic receptor sub-sensitivity after chronic antidepressant treatment. *Life Sciences, 28*, 1139.

Kosten, T. R., Rounsaville, B. J., & Kleber, H. D. (1987). A 2.5 year follow-up of cocaine use among treated opioid addicts: Have our treatments helped? *Archives of General Psychiatry, 44*, 281–284.

Leonard, K. E., Bromet, E. J., Parkinson, D. K., & Day, N. (1984). Agreement among Feigner, RDC, and DSM-III criteria for alcoholism. *Addictive Behaviors, 9*, 319–322.

Linnoila, M., Saario, I., & Maki, M. (1974). Effect of treatment with diazepam or lithium and alcohol on psychomotor skills related to driving. *European Journal of Clinical Pharmacology, 7*, 337–342.

Major, L. F., Lerner, P., Ballenger, J. C., Brown, G. L., Goodwin, F. K., & Lovenberg, W. (1979). Dopamine-beta-hydroxylase in the cerebrospinal fluid: Relationship to disulfiram-induced psychosis. *Biological Psychiatry, 14*, 337–344.

McLellan, A. T., Luborsky, L., & O'Brien, C. P. (1982). Is substance abuse treatment effective? Five different perspectives. *Journal of the American Medical Association, 247*, 1423–1427.

Mello, N. K., & Mendelson, J. H. (1978). Behavioral pharmacology of human alcohol, heroin, and marijuana use. In J. Fishman (Ed.), *The bases of addiction*, (pp. 101–116). Berlin: Dahlem Konferenzen.

Mello, N. K., & Mendelson, J. H. (1980). Buprenorphine suppress heroin use by heroin addicts. *Science, 207*, 657–659.

Mendelson, J. H., & Mello, N. K. (1966). Experimental analysis of drinking behavior of chronic alcoholics. *Annals of the New York Academy of Science, 133*, 828.

Merry, J., Reynolds, C. M., Bailey, J., & Coppen, A. (1976). Prophylactic treatment of alcoholism by lithium carbonate: A controlled study. *Lancet, 2*, 481–482.

Meyer, R. E. (1986). Anxiolytics and the alcoholic parent. *Journal of Studies on Alcohol, 47*, 269–273.

Milby, J. B., Gurwitch, R. H., Wiebe, D. J., Ling, W., McLellan, A. T., & Woody, G. E. (1986). Prevalence and diagnostic reliability of methadone maintenance detoxification fear. *American Journal of Psychiatry, 143*, 739–743.

Naranjo, C. A., Cappel, H., & Sellers, E. M. (1981). Pharmacological control of alcohol consumption: Tactics for identification and testing of new drugs. *Addictive Behaviors, 6,* 261–269.

Naranjo, C. A., Sellers, E. M., & Lawrin, M. O. (1985). Moderation of ethanol intake by serotonin uptake inhibitors. In C. Shagass (Ed.), *Biological psychiatry 1985* (pp. 708–710). Amsterdam: Elsevier Science.

Naranjo, C. A., Sellers, E. M., Roach, C. A., Woodley, D. V., Sanchez-Craig, M., & Sykora, K. (1984). Zimelidine-induced variations in alcohol intake by nondepressed heavy drinkers. *Clinical Pharmacology and Therapeutics, 35,* 374–381.

Nichols, J. R., Headlee, C. P., & Coppock, H. W. (1956). Drug addiction: I. Addiction by escape training. *Journal of the American Pharmaceutical Association, 45,* 788–791.

Rainey, J. M. (1977). Disulfiram toxicity and carbon disulfide poisoning. *American Journal of Psychiatry, 134,* 371–378.

Rankin, H., Hodgson, R., & Stockwell, T. (1979). The concept of craving and its measurement. *Behaviour Research and Therapy, 17,* 389–396.

Resnick, R. B., Schuyten-Resnick, E., & Washton, A. M. (1980). Assessment of narcotic antagonists in the treatment of opioid dependence. *Annual Review of Pharmacology and Toxicology, 20,* 463–474.

Robins, L. N., Helzer, J. E., Weissman, M. M., Orvaschel, H., Gruenberg, E., Burke, J. D., & Regier, D. A. (1984). Lifetime prevalence of specific psychiatric disorders in three sites. *Archives of General Psychiatry, 41,* 949–958.

Ross, S. B., & Renyi, A. L. (1966). Uptake of some tritiated sympathomimetic amines by mouse brain cortex in vitro. *Acta Pharmacologica Toxicologica, 24,* 297–309.

Rounsaville, B. J., Spitzer, R. L., & Williams, J. B. W. (1986). Proposed changes in DSM-III substance abuse disorders: Descriptions and rationale. *American Journal of Psychiatry, 143,* 463–468.

Runion, H. I., & Fowler, A. (1978). A double-blind study of chlordiazepoxide and hydroxyzine HCl therapy in acute alcohol withdrawal. *Proceedings of the Western Pharmacologic Society, 21,* 303–309.

Sampliner, R., & Iber, F. L. (1974). Diphenylhydantoin control of alcohol withdrawal seizures. *Journal of the American Medical Association, 230,* 1430–1437.

Sellers, E. M., Naranjo, C. A., Harrison, B., Devenyi, P., Roach, C., & Sykora, K. (1983). Diazepam loading: Simplified treatment of alcohol withdrawal. *Clinical Pharmacology and Therapeutics, 34,* 822–826.

Shaw, J. M., Kolesar, G. S., Sellers, E. M., Kaplan, H. L., & Sandor, P. (1981). Development of optimal treatment tactics for alcohol withdrawal: I. Assessment and effectiveness of supportive care. *Journal of Clinical Psychopharmacology, 1,* 382–389.

Spencer, J. (1980). Use of injectable lorazepam in alcohol withdrawal. *Medical Journal of Australia, 2,* 211–212.

Tabakoff, B., Melchior, C. L., & Hoffman, P. (1984). Factors in ethanol tolerance. *Science, 224,* 523–524.

Tarter, R. E., Arria, A. M., Moss, H., Edwards, N. J., & Van Thiel, D. (1987). DSM-III criteria for alcohol abuse: Associations with alcohol consumption behavior. *Clinical and Experimental Research, 11,* 541–543.

Taylor, D., & Ho, B. T. (1977). Neurochemical effects of cocaine following acute and repeated injection. *Journal of Neuroscience Research, 3,* 95–101.

Taylor, D. L., Ho, B. T., & Fagan, J. D. (1979). Increased dopamine receptor binding in rat brain by repeated cocaine injections. *Communications in Psychopharmacology, 3,* 137–142.

Tennant, F. S. (1985). Effect of cocaine dependence on plasma phenylalanine and tyrosine levels and on urinary MHPG excretion. *American Journal of Psychiatry, 142,* 1200–1201.

Tennant, F. S. (1987). Inadequate plasma concentrations in some high-dose methadone maintenance patients. *American Journal of Psychiatry, 144,* 1349–1350.

Tennant, F. & Rawson, R. A. (1982). Cocaine and amphetamine dependence treated with desipramine. In *Problems of drug dependence.* Washington, DC: National Institute of Drug Abuse.

Thompson, W. L., Johnson, A. D., & Maddrey, W. L. (1975). Diazepam and paraldehyde for treatment of severe delirium tremens. *Annals of Internal Medicine, 82,* 175–180.

U.S. Department of Health and Human Services. (1987). Sixth Special Report to Congress on Alcohol and Health from the Secretary of Health and Human Services. Rockville, MD: Author.

Van Kammen, D. P., & Murphy, D. L. (1975). Attenuation of the euphoriant and activating effects of d- and 1-amphetamine by lithium carbonate treatment. *Psychopharmacologia* (Berlin) *44,* 215–224.

Van Rossum, J. M., & Hurkmans, J. A. (1964). Mechanism of action of psychomotor stimulant drugs: Significance of dopamine in locomotor stimulant action. *International Journal of Neuropharmacology, 3,* 227–236.

Wadstein, J., Ohlin, H., & Stenberg, P. (1978). Effects of apomorphine and apomorphine-L-Dopa carbidopa on alcohol postintoxication symptoms. *Drug and Alcohol Dependence, 3,* 281–287.

Wegner, M. E., & Fink, D. W. (1965). Chlordiazepoxide compared to meprobamate and promazine for the withdrawal symptoms of acute alcoholism. *Wisconsin Medical Journal, 64,* 436–440.

Whitfield, E. L., Thompson, G., Lamb, A., Spencer, U., Pfeifer, M., & Browning-Ferrando, M. (1978). Detoxification of 1,024 alcoholic patients without

psychoactive drugs. *Journal of American Medical Association, 293,* 1409–1410.

Wikler, A. (1952). A psychodynamic study of a patient during self-regulated readdiction to morphine. *Psychiatric Quarterly, 26,* 270–293.

Wilkins, A. J., Jenkins, W. J., & Steiner, J. A. (1983). Efficacy of clonidine in treatment of alcohol withdrawal state. *Psychopharmacology, 81,* 78–80.

Williams, H. L., & Rundell, O. H. (1981). Altered sleep physiology in chronic alcoholics: Reversal with abstinence. *Alcoholism: Clinical and Experimental Research, 5,* 318–325.

Editorial Commentary: Alcoholism and Substance Abuse

Of the disorders listed in DSM-III-R, few are as recalcitrant to treatment as alcoholism and other substance abuse. Although alcoholism and other substance abuse have been well-studied from numerous vantage points, and many psychotherapeutic and pharmacological interventions have been developed and tried, the long-term results are still quite disappointing. In general, the vast majority of patients treated for any sort of substance abuse eventually return to their favored substance, be it alcohol, nicotine, or illicit drugs.

The writers (Galanter & Castaneda; Sobell, Toneatto, & Sobell; Moss) of the chapters in this section are painfully aware of the resistant nature of the disorders they are treating, and they are most humble in the presentation of strategies that they pursue consistent with their theoretical bents. In each of the chapters, the importance of following a multimodal approach to treatment is fully acknowledged. Thus, the unitary deployment of psychotherapy, of behavior therapy, or of pharmacotherapy is discouraged. To the contrary, it is clear that many concurrent modalities must be carried out, including the use of an adjunctive network of individuals such as Alcoholics Anonymous (AA) with a family-oriented psychotherapy (Galanter & Castaneda), use of drugs in addition to behavioral self-management (BSM) techniques (Sobell et al.), or use of self-help groups in addition to other psychotherapies and a comprehensive pharmacological approach (Moss).

Difficulties encountered in treatment are identified in each of the chapters: First, alcoholism and other substance abuse represent approach behaviors that eventuate in short-term pleasurable responses that are mediated by the central nervous system (CNS). Indeed, the long-term negative medical and psychological sequelae of prolonged use are obfuscated by the immediate pleasure that alcoholics or other drug abusers receive from their favorite substance. Thus, motivating patients to consider the long-term effects of their abuse is a highly difficult therapeutic task. Second, for those who have become physiologically and/or psychologically dependent on the substance, the process of withdrawal can be painful and/or distressing. Third, in many instances, polydrug abuse is the norm, and the eradication of one addiction simply leads to the intensification of a concomitant addiction (e.g., switching from opiates to alcoholism). Moreover, alcoholics and other drug addicts tend to be heavy smokers as well. Fourth, in addition to the possible effects of genetic and familial influences for a given form of substance abuse (e.g., alcoholism), many individuals find it difficult to quit because of the negative impact of their particular peer group. Fifth, a most recent impediment to treatment is the use of newly developed ("designer") illicit drugs because very little is known about their chemical actions or possible antagonists. Sixth, in some instances, the substance abuse masks an underlying psychiatric condition (e.g., anxiety, affective disorder) that requires separate treatment. Seventh, conversely, prolonged use of psychoactive substances that affect the CNS may result in psychiatric and neurological symptoms that require medical management.

As pointed out by Moss in his chapter, the costs

of alcohol abuse and other drug abuse are staggering from both an economic and a societal perspective. In addition to costing our society over 150 billion dollars per year, alcohol and drug abuse are implicated in family dissolution, rape, child abuse, automobile accidents, burglary, theft, and other kinds of legal transgressions. But despite the tremendous problems of abuse (e.g., costliness to society, the difficulties in motivating the abuser to consider treatment, the medical sequelae of abuse, and the repeated recidivism of treated abusers), the authors of the three chapters do point out some encouraging trends in remediation. For example, Galanter and Castaneda note that peer-led therapy groups, such as AA, Cocaine Anonymous (CA), and Narcotics Anonymous (NA), "can yield improved cost-effectiveness and clinical outcome when compared to the traditional small treatment groups currently employed by most alcoholism treatment facilities." Indeed, internal surveys of AA members are most encouraging in that new members who remain for at least 3 months reportedly have more than a 50% chance of remaining abstinent for the following year. If abstinence is maintained in the first year, then the chances for abstinence are 86% the second year. Unfortunately, these figures have not been verified by independent research, and large-scale comparative analyses are still warranted in which the AA model would be pitted against an integrated behavioral-pharmacological approach with carefully matched sets of alcoholics.

In a positive vein, Sobell et al. document that BSM techniques (e.g., cognitive therapy) are effective in reducing problem drinking, whether the treatment administered was or was not consistent with the patient's goal of total abstinence or controlled drinking. However, such BSM techniques do not appear to be vastly superior to other behavioral strategies and nonbehavioral techniques, such as interpersonal therapy, a treatment usually offered to depressives and anxiety-disordered individuals. Regrettably, with respect to behavioral treatments of drug abuse, the results are *not* positive. There are very few controlled studies, the attrition rates are high, and follow-ups are brief or nonexistent. By contrast, in dealing with nicotine dependence, the behavioral treatment studies are much better controlled and more concerned with

relapse prevention and follow-up. Promising approaches include rapid smoking strategies and a variety of self-management techniques. But here too, the outcome data concerning relapse prevention are not terribly encouraging.

Moss, in his chapter on pharmacotherapy, details progress in the biological approach to alcoholism and other substance abuse. He argues that there are three specific targets in the pharmacological approach to chemical dependency: (1) alleviation of withdrawal symptoms, (2) either reduction of reinforcement or development of aversion to alcohol or other drugs, and (3) reduction of craving for the abused substance. Examples of the first category are the substitution of the long-acting opiate methadone for heroin, the use of chlordiazepoxide for alcohol withdrawal symptoms, and introduction of bromocriptine, a dopamine agonist for cocaine withdrawal. As for the second category, lithium carbonate has been administered to diminish the euphoria associated with stimulant compounds (e.g., amphetamines), whereas disulfiram (Antabuse) has been used to discourage chronic alcoholics from drinking. And finally, with respect to the third category, the administration of chronic benzodiazepine therapy has been recommended as a deterrent to craving for alcohol.

However, application of pharmacological strategies in the chemical dependency area is controversial, given that (1) the patient may not comply with the medical regimen, and (2) unpleasant side effects may develop in some instances. Furthermore, self-help groups, such as AA, are not reinforcing of the medical-model approach to treatment.

Moss makes it clear that the pharmacological approach should be used as adjunctive, which is consistent with the Sobell et al. point that some of the better successes with alcohol and nicotine dependence have involved a combined behavioral–pharmacological strategy. However, at this time, the two-pronged approach to treatment is understudied, both from the perspective of testing new pharmacological compounds and treating polydrug users. When contrasted to the work in the affective disorders or the anxiety disorders, the level of sophistication in the chemical dependency field lags far behind.

Indexes

Author Index

Aagesen, C. A., 512, 517
Abeline, T., 481, 504
Abraham, S. F., 348, 350, 357, 366
Abrams, A., 512, 517
Abrams, D. A., 29, 32
Adams, N. E., 26, 30
Adelman, S. A., 453, 454
Adler, A., 394, 395, 397, 398, 401, 402, 406, 407, 414, 415
Adler, R. H., 230, 238
Agras, W. S., 21, 28, 29, 30, 44, 45, 341, 342, 349, 350, 352, 354, 356, 357, 366, 376, 384, 360
Ahad, A., 273, 278, 281
Akiskal, H. S., 40, 45, 398, 399, 414, 458, 464, 268, 281, 424, 433, 438, 439, 440, 441, 454
Alabala, A. A., 438, 454
Alagna, S. W., 248, 254
Alcoholics Anonymous, 516
Alden, L., 486, 498
Aldridge, D. M., 438, 454
Allan, T., 233, 238
Allen, J. G., 12, 14
Allen, M. D., 43, 46
Allsop, S. J., 486, 498, 496, 501
Allsopp, L., 233, 236
Alonso, A., 340, 350
Al-Sadir, J., 233, 236
Alstrom, J. E., 215, 216
Alterman, I., 263, 264, 274, 281
Altesman, R. I., 43, 45, 230, 236
Altschuler, M., 278, 279
Alvarez, W. A., 317, 318, 325, 447, 455
American College of Physicians, 359, 366
American Psychiatric Association, 34, 45, 203,
216, 219, 236, 254, 384, 263, 279, 302, 303, 305, 313, 316, 324, 331, 332, 350, 375, 397, 414, 437, 454, 463, 476, 355, 358, 366, 479, 480, 483, 498, 507, 508, 516
Ames, J. R., 341, 351
Amick, A. E., 313, 314
Amies, P. L., 206, 207, 214, 216
Ananth, J., 259, 262, 263, 265, 270, 272, 273, 280
Anchin, J. C., 6, 13
Anderson, A. E., 343, 350, 352, 362, 366, 367, 357, 362
Anderson, G. M., 374, 385
Anderson, R. B., 383, 384
Anderson, S., 217
Anderson, W. H., 277, 282
Andrews, G., 279, 280
Andrews, J., 9, 13
Andrulonis, P. A., 424, 433, 438, 454
Angrist, B., 512, 516
Annesley, P. T., 277, 280
Annis, H. M., 483, 484, 498, 504
Ansari, J., 486, 498
Antelman, S. M., 317, 324
Anthony, J. C., 238, 255, 282
Anthony, J. D., 218
Anthony, W. A., 413, 414
Antony, M., 387
Antti-Poika, I., 489, 498
Aono, T., 444, 454
Appelbaum, A., 15
Appeltauer, L., 233, 238
Appleby, I. L., 217, 237
Arato, M., 277, 283
Arif, A., 480, 500

Kaser, H. E., 230, 238
Kass, F., 396, 416
Kastenbaum, R. J., 423, 434
Katz, D. L., 274, 283
Katzman, M. A., 341, 348, 354
Kaufman, E., 498, 501
Kay, G., 490, 504
Kaye, W. H., 357, 369, 371, 372, 373, 374, 381, 385, 386
Kazdin, A. E., 17, 29, 32
Keane, T. M., 303, 304, 307, 308, 309, 313, 314, 315, 316, 325
Keck, P. E., 274, 279, 282, 284, 377, 387
Keddie, 486, 488
Keegan, D., 222, 236
Keeler, M. H., 466, 477
Kegan, R., 420, 434
Keller, M. G., 455, 480, 500
Kellett, J., 215, 217
Killen, J. D., 495, 501
Kelly, D., 227, 237, 239
Kelwala, S., 440, 454
Kemper, K., 387
Kemph, J. P., 273, 280
Kendler, K. S., 439, 455
Kennedy, C. R., 209, 210, 214, 217
Kennedy, S., 376, 386
Kenny, K., 259, 265
Kent, C., 479, 502
Koepke, H. H., 321, 325
Kernberg, O. F., 7, 12, 14, 15, 394, 395, 398, 400–402, 406, 407, 416, 436, 437, 455, 456, 463, 477
Kerr, T. A., 273, 281
Kety, S. S., 438, 439, 455, 457, 458
Keys, D. J., 204, 215, 218, 225, 239
Khan, A., 509, 518
Khantzian, E. S., 463, 477
Kiecolt-Glaser, J., 341, 348, 351
King, A. C., 494, 504
King, D., 438, 454
Kitchner, I., 317, 320, 325
Kiesler, C. A., 432, 434
Kiesler, D. J., 6, 8, 11, 13, 15
Kilpatrick, D. G., 303, 304, 306, 308, 309, 312, 313, 314, 315
Kilts, C., 263, 264, 280, 281, 319, 324
Kim, S. W., 274, 282
Kinney, J., 217, 237

Kirk, J., 338, 351, 360, 368
Kirkley, B. G., 341, 342, 348, 349, 352, 356, 357, 366, 384, 376
Kirschenbaum, D. S., 339, 349, 353
Kissin, B., 464, 476, 514, 518
Kitts, C., 280
Klajner, F., 481, 503
Klatsky, A. L., 483, 501
Klawans, H. L., 371, 379, 384
Kleber, H. D., 483, 497, 502, 503, 509–512, 514, 517, 518
Kleifeld, E. I., 341, 354
Klein, D. F., 203, 217, 231, 237, 238, 438, 441, 443, 444, 445, 455, 446, 456, 457
Klein, D. K., 237
Klein, W. J., 324
Klerman, G., 398, 415
Klerman, G. L., 11, 15, 31, 436, 437, 455, 456
Klesges, R. C., 493, 500
Klesges, L. M., 493, 500
Klett, C. J., 510, 518
Kline, M. D., 439, 454
Kline, N., 227, 237
Kline, N. S., 512, 518
Klosko, J. S., 217
Knee, S. Y., 513, 518
Knesevich, J. W., 279, 282
Knight, R., 393, 400, 417, 436, 437, 456
Knight, R. P., 8, 15
Knorr, N. J., 379, 386
Kocan, D., 317, 324
Koenigsberg, H., 396, 417
Koenigsberg, H. W., 456
Koide, T., 511, 518
Kohrs, M. A., 231, 237
Kohut, H., 340, 352, 395, 397, 403, 406, 417, 419, 477
Kolb, J., 392, 400, 416, 417
Kolb, J. E., 437, 442, 455, 456
Kolb, L. C., 304, 314, 316, 320, 324, 325
Kolesar, G. S., 516, 519
Kopanda, R. T., 317, 325
Kosten, T. R., 320, 324, 325, 480, 503, 514, 518
Kotler, M., 325
Kovacs, M., 26, 32
Kozak, M. J., 248, 254, 257, 258, 259, 260, 264, 272, 280, 305, 308, 314
Kozlowski, L. T., 479, 482, 483, 502
Kraanen, J., 260, 264

Subject Index